Biopsychology

SECOND EDITION

John P. J. Pinel

University of British Columbia

ALLYN AND BACON

Boston   London   Toronto   Sydney   Tokyo   Singapore

To the memory of Donald Olding Hebb (1904–1985)
for his contributions to biopsychology

AND

To Maggie *and* Greg
for their love and support

Senior Editor: Laura Pearson
Editorial Assistant: Marnie Greenhut
Production Administrator: Elaine Ober
Editorial-Production Service: Deborah Schneck
Text Designer: Deborah Schneck
Cover Administrator: Linda Dickinson
Manufacturing Buyer: Megan Cochran

Copyright © 1993, 1990 by Allyn & Bacon
A Division of Simon & Schuster, Inc.
160 Gould Street
Needham Heights, MA 02194

Library of Congress Cataloging-in-Publication Data

Pinel, John P. J.
    Biopsychology / John P. J. Pinel. — 2nd ed.
        p.   cm.
    Includes bibliographical references and index.
    ISBN 0–205–13897–7
    1. Psychobiology.   I. Title.
    [DNLM: 1.   Behavior—physiology.   2.   Brain—physiology.
3. Psychophysiology.   WL   103   P651b]
QP360.P463   1992
152—dc20
DNLM/DLC
for Library of Congress   92–49418
                                                                                      CIP

Printed in the United States of America

10   9   8   7   6   5   4   3   96   95   94

CREDITS

Fig. 1.4 BETTMANN **Fig. 2.1** Photo by Donna Trahan; courtesy of the Laboratory of Comparative Behavioral Biology, New Iberia Research Center. **Fig. 2.4** © Phil A. Dotson, The National Audobon Society Collection/Photo Researchers, Inc. **Fig. 2.5** Animals Animals © Ben Osborne **Fig. 2.6** ©F.J. Hiersche/OKAPIA 1989, The National Audobon Society Collection/Photo Researchers, Inc. **Fig. 2.7** © Tom Myers, The National Audobon Society Collection/Photo Researchers, Inc. **Fig. 2.8** Top left: Animals Animals © Jim Tuten   Middle left: Animals Animals © Bates Littlehales   Bottom left: Animals Animals © John Chellman   Top right: Animals Animals © Jim Tuten.   Bottom right: Milton Feinberg/The Picture Cube. **Fig. 2.10** John Reader/Science Photo Library/Photo Researchers, Inc. **Fig. 2.17** © Lawrence Livermore Laboratory/Science Photo Library/Custom Medical Stock. **Fig. 2.20** © Porterfield-Chickering/Photo Researchers, Inc. **Fig. 2.23** Photograph courtesy of Arturo Alvarez-Buylla. **p.63** © Gary Larson/Courtesy Universal Syndicates. **Fig. 3.11** Courtesy of T. Chan-Ling, S. Tout, Z. Dreher, and J. Stone. **Fig. 3.28** © Custom Medical Stock. **Fig. 4.14** Courtesy of David Jacobowitz, NIMH, *Scientific American, June, 1974,* 230. **Fig. 5.4** Courtesy of Mallinkrodt Institute of Radiology, Washington University School of Medicine, St. Louis, Mo. **Fig. 7.6** Courtesy of Drs. Scott Mittman, David Copenhagen, and Maria Maglio. **Fig. 7.20** D.H. Hubel & T.N. Wiesel, *Scientific American,* Sept. 1979. **Fig. 7.24** © M.

Bruce/The Picture Cube. **Fig. 7.28** Photo by Denise Denton and Brad Howland; Brou, Sciascia, Linden and Lettvin, *Scientific American,* September 1986. **Fig. 8.15** © George Mars Cassidy/The Picture Cube. **Fig. 8.24** © OMIKRON/Photo Researchers, Inc. **Fig. 9.12** SECCHI-LECAQUE/ROUSSELA-UCLAF/CNRI/Science Photo Library/Custom Medical Stock **Fig. 9.22** © 1985 Martha Swope **Fig. 12.4** Animals Animals **pp.386–387** From *The Sleep Instinct* by R. Meddis, 1977, Routledge and Keegan Paul. **p.390–391** From *Some Must Watch While Some Must Sleep* by William E. Dement, published by Portable Stanford Books, Stanford Alumni Association, Stanford University. **p.399** From *Sleep and Wakefulness* by N. Kleitman. Reprinted by permission of Chicago University Press © 1963. **p.431** © Dratch/The Image Works **p.433** © D & I MacDonald/The Picture Cube **p.434** © M. Antman/The Image Works. **p.435** © Mark K. Walker/The Picture Cube. **p.437** © Andy Levin/Photo Researchers, Inc. **p.439** © Photo Researchers, Inc. **p.454** UPI/BETTMANN **Fig. 14.16** Courtesy of Stuart Zola-Morgan; S. M. Zola-Morgan, & L. R. Squire, *Science, 1990, 250,* 288–290. **Fig. 15.16** Courtesy of D. W. Tank, M. Sugimori, J. A. Connor, and R. R. Llinas; *Science, 242,* 773–777; copyright 1988 by the AAAS. **Fig. 15.23** Courtesy of G. Raisman; Raisman, Morris, & Zhow, *Progress in Brain Research, 71,* 1987, Elsevier Science Publishing. **p.610** © MacDonald/The Picture Cube.

Contents

Preface

This book is intended for use as a primary text in one- or two-semester undergraduate courses in biopsychology—variously titled *Biopsychology, Physiological Psychology, Brain and Behavior, Psychobiology, Behavioral Neuroscience*, or *Behavioral Neurobiology*. It is also intended for educated laypersons and professionals who are interested in a clear, engaging introduction to current biopsychological research.

My mood has changed in the three years since I wrote the preface to the first edition of *Biopsychology*. Three years ago I was worried that *Biopsychology* would not be widely read and that the years that I had spent writing it would prove to be a waste. In particular, I was concerned that instructors and students might react negatively to its unconventional style. Although the first edition of *Biopsychology* was intended for use as a textbook, there was much about it that was "untextbooklike." Rather than introducing biopsychology in the usual textbook fashion, it wove the principles of biopsychology together with clinical case studies, social issues, personal implications, and humorous anecdotes. It was a friendly mentor who spoke directly and personally to the reader and enthusiastically related recent advances in biopsychological research.

Now, as I begin to write the preface to this, the second edition of *Biopsychology*, my mood is more positive, thanks in large to the many letters of encouragement that I have received from students and other readers of the first edition. Spurred on by such letters, I am excited by the prospects of getting this edition into your hands. I have spent more than a year making *Biopsychology's* strong points stronger, responding to its shortcomings, and keeping it abreast of the exciting recent developments in biopsychological research. The success of the first edition notwithstanding, the second edition is better—substantially better. I hope that you enjoy it.

Features of the First Edition That Have Been Maintained in This Edition

The following are features of the first edition of *Biopsychology* that have been maintained and, in some cases, strengthened in this edition.

An emphasis on behavior   In many biopsychology textbooks, the coverage of neurophysiology, neurochemistry, and neuroanatomy subverts the coverage of behavioral research. This bias is most obvious in the obligatory chapter on research methods, where the various neuroanatomical, neurophysiological, and neurochemical research methods are typically described at great length while behavioral technology receives short shrift. In contrast, *Biopsychology* gives behavior top billing: It stresses that neuroscience is a team effort and that the unique contribution made by biopsychologists to this team is their behavioral expertise. Half of the research methods chapter (chapter 5) deals with methods for studying behavior; the other half deals with methods for studying the nervous system.

Extensive coverage of clinical and human research   *Biopsychology* provides more than the customary coverage of case studies of brain-damaged patients and of experiments of healthy human subjects. However, theory-driven experiments on laboratory species are the focus of most of the chapters. One of *Biopsychology's* dominant themes is that diversity is a major strength of biopsychological research: That major advances often result from the convergence of pure and applied research and of research involving human and nonhuman subjects.

A focus on the scientific method   Several of the themes that are woven through the chapters of *Biopsychology* focus on important, but frequently misunderstood, points about the scientific method. The following are four of them: (1) The scientific method is a means of answering questions that is applicable to daily life as it is to the laboratory. (2) The scientific method is fun—it is similar to the method that detectives use to solve unwitnessed crimes and that treasure hunters use to locate sunken galleons. (3) Widely accepted scientific theories are current best estimates rather than statements of absolute fact. (4) Even theories that ultimately prove to be wrong can contribute to the progress of science.

An emphasis on personal and social relevance   Several chapters—particularly those on eating, sleeping, sex, and drug abuse—carry strong personal and social messages. In these chapters, students are encouraged to consider the implications of biopsychological research for their lives outside the classroom. The food-for-thought questions at the end of these chapters are excellent topics for classroom discussion.

Wit and enthusiasm   An important element of biopsychology is missing from other biopsychology texts. In my experience, most biopsychology laboratories are places of enthusiasm and good humor, and I have tried to communicate these important elements of "biopsychological life" in my writing of *Biopsychology*.

Learning aids   *Biopsychology* has five specific features that are expressly designated to help students learn and remember the material:

- First are the lists of **key terms** and **definitions** that appear at the end of each chapter; these are designed to help students prepare for examinations.

- Second are the **study exercises** that punctuate the test. Rather than appearing at the end of each chapter, these exercises occur at key transition points, where students can benefit greatly by pausing to consolidate their understanding before proceeding to new material.

- Third are the **food-for-thought discussion questions** at the end of each chapter.

- Fourth are the many **demonstrations**, anecdotes, and metaphors that I have used to illustrate important principles.

- Fifth are the illustrations.

Color illustrations   *Biopsychology* features full color illustrations throughout. This greatly enhances its look and appeal, but there is far more to it than that. Being able to present photographs of color-coded brain scans and stained neural tissue at appropriate points in the text is necessary for the effective illustration of modern biopsychological research, and color greatly facilitates the interpretation of many drawings and graphs.

Illustrations that teach   The attractiveness of *Biopsychology's* illustrations belie their major strength: their pedagogy. Students can rely on each illustration to clarify the written text without introducing gratuitous details or nagging inconsistencies. The first edition of *Biopsychology* established a new standard of pedagogical illustration in biopsychology textbooks; there are more and better illustrations in this edition.

New Features of the Current Edition

The following are features of this edition of *Biopsychology* that were not in the first edition.

A broader definition of biopsychology   Biopsychology is more than the study of the neural mechanisms of behavior. This point is made more explicitly in this edition of *Biopsychology*. Comparative psychology has been included with physiological psychology, psychopharmacology, psychophysiology, and neuropsychology as a major division of biopsychology. *Comparative psychology* is defined as the division of biopsychology that focuses on the evolution, genetics, and adaptiveness of behavior.

Evolution, genetics, and development: learning to ask the right questions about the biology of behavior (Chapter 2)   Like most teachers, I am more concerned with improving the ways that students think than in having them memorize soon-to-be-forgotten details. Chapter 2, which is new to this edition, is expressly designed to achieve this goal. It is designed to teach students to stop thinking about the biology of behavior in terms of physiological-or-psychological and learned-or-innate dichotomies. It explains why these ways of thinking about biopsychological phenomena have become ingrained in our culture; it identifies their weaknesses; and it introduces more productive alternatives. Chapter 2 also introduces the fundamentals of evolution, genetics, and behavioral development.

Biopsychology of emotions and mental illness (Chapter 17)   Chapter 17 is the other new chapter in this edition. Its subject is the biopsychology of emotions. It begins with an historical introduction to biopsychological theories of emotion; then, as the chapter unfolds, the focus becomes increasingly clinical. The following are some of the topics that are covered in this new chapter: autonomic correlates of emotion, facial expression and emotion, brain damage and emotion, aggressive and defensive behavior, anxiety, stress, psychoneuroimmunology, schizophrenia, and affective disorders.

Topics that receive expanded coverage   In addition to the two new chapters, several topics receive expanded coverage in this edition of *Biopsychology*. They include the following: the spatial-frequency theory of vision, selective attention, sound localization, the effects of auditory cortex lesions, phantom limbs, peptides and eating, the kidneys, anorexia nervosa, hypothalamic mechanisms of copulatory behavior, the hypothalamus and sexual preference, lucid dreaming, suprachiasmatic nucleus transplantation, improving drug-related social and legal policies, the medial temporal cortex and amnesia, the hippocampus and cognitive maps, recovery from brain damage, and neural reorganization after brain damage.

New references   Biopsychology is one of the most rapidly progressing fields of science. This edition of *Biopsychology* has kept abreast of recent developments; it contains numerous references to articles that were published since the beginning of 1989.

How to Use the Text

A useful feature of *Biopsychology* from a course-design perspective is that each chapter is written so that it is as independent as possible from other chapters. Thus, it is feasible to omit chapters or to vary their sequence. Further flexibility in course design is provided by the appendices. The appendices summarize detailed information that is appropriate for some kinds of students and courses but not for others. For example, appendices illustrate the projections of the cranial nerves, the location of each hypothalamic nucleus, and the hormonal correlates of the human female menstrual cycle. By putting these details in appendices, each instructor can decide whether to assign them or not. There is a table in the Instructor's Manual that suggests sample syllabi for courses with different profiles.

Ancillary Materials That Are Available with Biopsychology

The ancillary materials available with *Biopsychology* differ in several ways from those that are available with comparable texts. The most obvious is that they have been prepared by the author of the text. New with this edition is the Allyn and Bacon biopsychology videotape and laserdisc—a biopsychology first.

Test bank   A large multiple-choice test bank is provided to the instructor of each class that uses *Biopsychology*. From the student's perspective, one of the most important parts of any textbook is the test bank—the clarity, difficulty, and focus of test questions have a substantial effect on the degree to which students are appropriately rewarded for their efforts.

The feedback that I received regarding the test bank for the first edition of *Biopsychology* was mixed. In general, users were pleased with the number, clarity, and accuracy of the questions, but some were displeased with the level of difficulty. There were not enough moderately easy items for some instructors' needs. The test bank for the second edition has more test items—over 2,000 in all—a good proportion of which are in the easy-to-moderate range. I have rated the difficulty of each item to further assist instructors with their test construction.

Instructor's manual   The instructor's manual for *Biopsychology* provides the instructor with a set of lecture notes that complement the test and a set of overhead transparency masters to accompany each lecture. There are notes for two one-hour lectures to accompany each chapter of the text, and there are two or three overhead masters to go along with each lecture. Each page of the instructor's manual is divided in two columns: a left column, which covers two-thirds of the page, and a right column, which covers one-third. The lecture notes are printed in the left column and the right column is left blank for each instructor to make individual insertions.

The instructor's manual can be used in two ways. Some instructors use it as a basis for preparing their own lectures—it can be obtained on computer disk from Allyn and Bacon for easy editing. Other instructors add their own touches in the right-hand columns and lecture directly from the manual.

Films for the humanities video and laserdisc   Instructors who adopt *Biopsychology* can now use a video to augment their lectures. Based on the *Films for the Humanities* series, this 60-minute video provides students with a 1-or-2-minute glimpses of key biopsychological phenomena. Sleep recording, growing axons, memory testing in monkeys, the formation of synapses, gender differences in brain structure, human amnesic patients, rewarding brain stimulation in rats, and brain-scan recording are a few of the offerings. The same material is also available in laserdisc format.

Study guide   Each chapter of the study guide includes three sections. Section I is composed of "jeopardy" study items—named after the popular television quiz show. The jeopardy study items are arranged in two columns: questions on the left and answers on the right. Sometimes there is nothing in the space to the right of a question, and the student's task is to write in the correct answer. Sometimes there is nothing in the space to the left of the answer, and the student's task is to write in the correct question. When the jeopardy study items are completed, the student has a list of questions and answers that summarize all of the main points in the chapter, and they are conveniently arranged for *bidirectional studying*.

Section II of each chapter is composed of essay study questions. Spaces are provided for the student to write outlines of the correct answers to each question. The essay study questions are designed to encourage students to consider general issues.

Section III of each chapter is a practice examination. It is recommended that students write the practice examination at least 24 hours before the scheduled time of their formal examination so that the results of the practice examination can be used to guide the last stages of their studying.

Book of readings   *Current Research in Biopsychology* (Pinel, 1991) is a selection of cutting-edge biopsychological research reports. Each article was selected on the basis of scientific criteria and on its ability to interest and motivate students. I have written introductions, glossaries, and study questions to help students get the most out of each article.

Acknowledgments

The preparation of the manuscript was a team effort. I did the writing and designed the illustrations, Lisa Kalynchuk did the library research and photocopying, and Maggie Edwards did everything else: editorial work, compilation of the reference list, preliminary artwork, and acquisition of photographs and permissions.

The Allyn and Bacon production team did a remarkable job of designing and producing this book. They shared my dream of a textbook that meets the highest standards of pedagogy but is still personal, attractive, and enjoyable. And, they did a splendid job of giving visual substance to this dream. Thank you Elain Ober, Deborah Schneck, Laura Pearson, Kathy Smith, Linda Dickinson, and Marnie Greenhut—the book is stunning from cover to cover.

The executives of Allyn and Bacon who guided this project also deserve acknowledgement. It is a pleasure to be associated with publishers who are willing to take chances in order to accomplish something special. Thank you John Isley, Susan Badger, John Gilman (who couldn't eat as many lobsters as Boris), and Bill Barke, my good friend who has supported me from the beginning.

Many colleagues contributed to this edition by providing me with encouragement and feedback. The following are those whose letters I managed to retrieve from my files:

B. Bulman-Fleming
University of Waterloo

Brian Bland
University of Calgary

Robin Bowers
College of Charleston

Peter Brunjes
University of Virginia

Steven Burns, M.D.
Huntington Beach

Peter Cain
University of Western Ontario

Michael Corcoran
University of Victoria

Immo Curio
University of Bonn

Lee Ellis
Minot State University

Julia Hannay
University of Houston

Cinidy Herzog
Frostburg State University

Bill Iacono
University of Minnesota

Gayle James
Lost Angeles Pierce College

Timothy Johnston
*University of North Carolina
at Greensboro*

Kenneth Kleinman
*Southern Illinois University
at Edwardsville*

Bryan Kolb
University of Lethbridge

Sheldon Lachman
Wayne State University

Michael Mana
University of Pittsburgh

Tom McCrystal
Capital University

Ronald Melzack
McGill University

George Michel
DePaul University

Ralph Mistlberger
Simon Fraser University

Ronald Mucha
University of Cologne

Dave Mumby
University of New Mexico

Jim Patton
Baylor University

Michael Peters
University of Guelph

Terry Pettijohn
Ohio State University

Martin Sarter
Ohio State University

Eliot Valenstein
University of Michigan

Lyn Raible
Kalamazoo College

Harold Siegel
Rutgers

Gundelina Velazco
De La Salle University

Neil Rowland
University of Florida

Cheryl Sisk
Michigan State University

Ian Whishaw
University of Lethbridge

Bob Sainsbury
University of Calgary

Jim Torcivia
California State University, Northridge

Steve Woods
University of Washington

I would also like to thank the following biopsychology instructors for providing Allyn and Bacon with reviews of my chapters. Although their identity was not revealed to me, their comments led to significant improvements in this edition.

Marie Banich
University of Illinois

Stanley Finger
Washington University

James Pierce
Purdue University—Calumet

Peter C. Brunjes
University of Virginia

Jon Kaas
Vanderbilt University

Martin Sarter
The Ohio State University

Leo Chalupa
University of California— Davis

Charles Kutscher
Syracuse University

Charles Weaver
Baylor University

Carl Erickson
Duke University

Lin Myers
California State University— Stanislaus

Finally, I would like to thank all of the students who sent me letters of friendship and encouragement after reading the first edition. Writing is a solitary enterprise; your letters have assured me that I am not alone.

To the Student

In the 1960s, I was, in the parlance of times, "turned on" by an undergraduate course in biopsychology. I could not imagine anything more interesting than a field of science dedicated to studying the relation between psychological functioning and the brain. My initial fascination has been nourished by twenty-five years as a student, teacher, and researcher of biopsychology. *Biopsychology* is my effort to share this fascination with you.

I have tried to make *Biopsychology* a different kind of textbook, a textbook that includes clear, concise, and well-organized explanations of the key points but is still interesting to read—a book from which you might suggest a suitable chapter to an interested friend or relative. To accomplish this goal, I thought a bit about what kind of textbook I would have liked when I was a student, and I decided immediately to avoid the stern formality and ponderousness of conventional textbook writing. What I wanted was a more relaxed and personal style. To accomplish this, I imagined that you and I were chatting as I wrote, and that I was telling you—usually over a glass of something—about the interesting things that go on in the field of biopsychology. Imagining these chats kept my writing from drifting back into conventional "textbookese," and it never let me forget who I was writing this book for. I hope that *Biopsychology* teaches you much, and I hope that reading it manages to generate in you the same personal feeling that writing it did in me. If you are so inclined, please write; I welcome your comments and suggestions. You can write to me at the Department of Psychology, University of British Columbia, Vancouver, B.C., Canada V6T 1Z4.

1

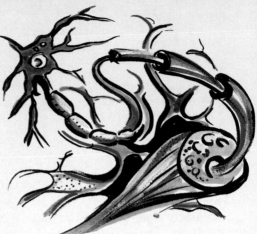

Biopsychology as a Neuroscience

The appearance of the human brain is far from impressive (see Figure 1.1). It is a squishy, wrinkled, walnut-shaped hunk of tissue weighing about 1.3 kilograms. It looks more like something that you might find washed up on a beach than like one of the wonders of the world—which it surely is. Despite its unprepossessing appearance, the human brain is an amazingly intricate network of neurons—**neurons** are cells that receive and transmit electrochemical signals. Contemplate for a moment the complexity of the brain's neural circuits. Consider the 100 billion neurons in complex array, the estimated 100 trillion connections between them, and the almost infinite number of paths that neural signals can follow through this morass.

FIGURE 1.1

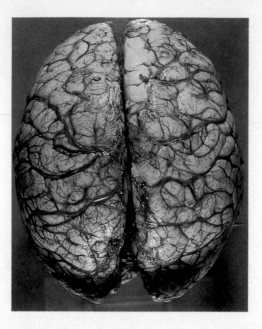

The complexity of the human brain is amazing, but it would be even more amazing if the human brain were not complex. An organ capable of creating a Mona Lisa, an artificial limb, and a supersonic aircraft; of traveling to the moon and to the depths of the sea; and of experiencing the wonders of an alpine sunset, a newborn infant, and a reverse slam dunk must be complex. Paradoxically, **neuroscience** (the study of the nervous system) may prove to be the brain's ultimate challenge: Does the brain have the capacity to understand something as complex as itself?

Neuroscience comprises several related disciplines. The primary purpose of this first chapter is to introduce you to one of them: biopsychology.

Before you proceed to the body of this chapter, I would like to introduce you to Jimmie G. Biopsychologists have learned much from the study of human brain damage—and you will too. But it is important that you do not grow insensitive to its personal tragedy. Jimmie G. introduces you to it.

[In 1975] Jimmie was a fine-looking man, with a curly bush of grey hair, a healthy and handsome forty-nine-year-old. He was cheerful, friendly, and warm.

'Hiya, Doc!' he said. 'Nice morning! Do I take this chair here?' . . . He spoke of the houses where his family had lived. . . . He spoke of school and school days, the friends he'd had, and his special fondness for mathematics and science . . . he was seventeen, had just graduated from high school when he was drafted in 1943. . . . He remembered the names of the various submarines on which he had served, their missions, where they were stationed, the names of his shipmates. . . . But there for some reason his reminiscences stopped. . . .

. . . I was very struck by the change of tense in his recollections as he passed from his school days to his days in the navy. He had been using the past tense, but now used the present . . .

A sudden, improbable suspicion seized me.

'What year is this, Mr. G.?' I asked, concealing my perplexity under a casual manner.

'Forty-five, man. What do you mean?' He went on, 'We've won the war, FDR's dead, Truman's at the helm. There are great times ahead.'

'And you, Jimmie, how old would you be?'. . .

'Why, I guess I'm nineteen, Doc. I'll be twenty next birthday.'

Looking at the grey-haired man before me, I had an impulse for which I have never forgiven myself . . .

'Here,' I said, and thrust a mirror toward him. 'Look in the mirror and tell me what you see.'. . .

He suddenly turned ashen and gripped the sides of the chair. 'Jesus Christ,' he whispered. 'Christ, what's going on? What's happened to me? Is this a nightmare? Am I crazy? Is this a joke?'—and he became frantic, panicked. . . .

. . . I stole away, taking the hateful mirror with me.

Two minutes later I re-entered the room. . . . 'Hiya, Doc!' he said. 'Nice morning! You want to talk to me—do I take this chair here?' There was no sign of recognition on his frank, open face.

'Haven't we met before, Mr. G?' I asked casually.

'No, I can't say we have. Quite a beard you got there. I wouldn't forget *you*, Doc!'. . .

. . . 'Where do you think you are?'

'I see these beds, and these patients everywhere. Looks like a sort of hospital to me. But hell, what would I be doing in a hospital—and with all these old people, years older than me. . . . Maybe I *work* here. . . . If I don't work here, I've been *put* here. Am I a patient, am I sick and don't know it, Doc? It's crazy, it's scary'. . . .

On intelligence testing he showed excellent ability. He was quick-witted, observant, and logical, and had no difficulty solving complex problems and puzzles—no difficulty, that is, if they could be done quickly. If much time was required, he forgot what he was doing. . . .

Homing in on his memory, I found an extreme and extraordinary loss of recent memory—so that whatever was said or shown to him was apt to be forgotten in a few seconds' time. Thus I laid out my watch, my tie, and my glasses on the desk, covered them, and asked him to remember these. Then, after a minute's chat, I asked him what I had put under the cover. He remembered none of them—or indeed that I had even asked him to remember. I repeated the test, this time getting him to write down the names of the three objects; again he forgot, and when I showed him the paper with his writing on it he was astounded . . .

'What is this?' I asked, showing him a photo in the magazine I was holding.

'It's the moon,' he replied.

'No, it's not,' I answered. 'It's a picture of the earth taken from the moon.'

'Doc, you're kidding! Someone would've had to get a camera up there! . . . how the hell would you do that?' . . .

He was becoming fatigued, and somewhat irritable and anxious, under the continuing pressure of anomaly and contradiction, and their fearful implications . . . And I myself was wrung with emotion—it was heartbreaking . . . to think of his life lost in limbo, dissolving.

He is, as it were . . . isolated in a single moment of being, with a moat . . . of forgetting all round him . . . He is a man without a past (or future), stuck in a constantly changing, meaningless moment. (pp. 22–28)[1]

Remember Jimmie G.; you will encounter him later.

1.1

What Is Biopsychology?

D. O. Hebb. (Photograph courtesy of McGill University.)

Biopsychology is the branch of neuroscience concerned with the biology of behavior—see Dewsbury (1991). Some refer to this field as "psychobiology" or "behavioral biology" or "behavioral neuroscience," but I prefer the term *biopsychology* because it denotes a biological approach to the study of psychology; the alternatives denote a psychological approach to the study of biology. Psychology commands center stage in this text. *Psychology* can be defined as the study of behavior, if the term *behavior* is used in its broadest sense to refer to all overt activities of the organism as well as the psychological processes that are presumed to underlie them (e.g., learning, memory, motivation, perception, and emotion).

The study of the biology of behavior has a long history, but biopsychology did not coalesce into a major neuroscientific discipline until this century. Although it is not possible to specify the exact date of biopsychology's birth, the publication of the *Organization of Behavior* in 1949 by D. O. Hebb played a key role in its emergence (see Milner & White, 1987). In his book, Hebb (see Figure 1.2) developed the first comprehensive theory of how complex psychological phenomena, such as perceptions, emotions, thoughts, and memories, might be produced by brain activity. Hebb's theory did much to discredit the then prevalent view that psychological functioning is too complex to have its roots in the physiology and chemistry of the brain. Hebb based his conclusions on experiments involving both humans and laboratory animals, on clinical case studies, and on logical arguments developed from his own insightful observations of daily life. This eclectic approach has become a hallmark of biopsychological inquiry.

In comparison to physics, chemistry, and biology, biopsychology is an infant—a raucous, healthy, rapidly growing infant, but nonetheless an infant. In this book, you will reap the benefits of biopsychology's youth. Because biopsychology does not have a long and complex history, you will have the luxury of moving directly to the excitement of current research.

[1]From *The Man Who Mistook His Wife for a Hat and Other Clinical Tales* (pp. 22–28) by Oliver Sacks. Copyright © 1970, 1981, 1983, 1984, 1985 by Oliver Sacks. Reprinted by permission of Summit Books, a division of Simon & Schuster, Inc.

1.2

What Is the Relation Between Biopsychology and the Other Disciplines of Neuroscience?

As its name implies, biopsychology is a synthesis of two general approaches to the study of neuroscience: biological and psychological. Biopsychologists are above all psychologists (persons dedicated to behavioral research); but they are psychologists who, like other neuroscientists, bring to their research a knowledge of the biology of their subjects. Accordingly, biopsychology's unique contribution to neuroscientific research is a knowledge of behavior and of the methods of behavioral research. You will appreciate the importance of this contribution if you consider that the ultimate purpose of the nervous system is to produce and control behavior.

Biopsychologists draw together knowledge from the other neuroscientific disciplines and apply it to the study of behavior. The integrative nature of biopsychology is reflected in the organization of this book. Although its focus is strictly biopsychological, there is not a single chapter in which information from other neuroscientific disciplines does not come into play. The following are some of the disciplines of neuroscience that are touched on in this book:

Biological psychiatry. Study of the biological bases of psychiatric disorders and their treatment through the manipulation of the brain (see Chapter 17).

Biopsychology. Study of the biological bases of behavior.

Developmental neurobiology. Study of how the nervous system changes as an organism matures and ages; **neurobiology** is a general term roughly equivalent to neuroscience (see Chapters 2 and 15).

Neuroanatomy. Study of the structure of the nervous system (see Chapter 3).

Neurochemistry. Study of the chemical bases of neural activity, particularly those that underlie the transmission of signals through and between neurons (see Chapters 4 and 17).

Neuroendocrinology. Study of the interactions of the nervous system with the endocrine glands and the hormones that they release (see Chapter 11).

Neuroethology. Study of the relation between the nervous system and behavior that occurs in the animal's natural environment (Camhi, 1984; Hoyle, 1984); in contrast, biopsychologists prefer to study behavior in controlled laboratory situations (see Chapter 2).

Neuropathology. Study of nervous system disorders (see Chapter 6).

Neuropharmacology. Study of the effects of drugs on the nervous system, particularly those influencing neural transmission (see Chapters 4, 13, and 17).

Neurophysiology. Study of the responses of the nervous system, particularly those involved in transmission of electrical signals through and between neurons (see Chapter 4).

Some scientists who are involved in research programs that require a synthesis of material from several disciplines of neuroscience coin terms to characterize their particular approach. They string together appropriate modifiers in sequence to create a label for what they do. The possibilities are limitless and at times almost humorous. What type of research do you think would interest a *developmental psychoneuroendocrinologist?*

Recently, I assessed biopsychology's contribution to neuroscience by recording the departmental affiliation of a random sample of neuroscientists selected from the membership directory of the **Society for Neuroscience.**

Table 1.1   Departmental Affiliations of Members of
the Society for Neuroscience

Departmental Affiliation	*Percentage of Sample*
Psychology	16.1
Physiology	14.3
Pharmacology	12.5
Biology	11.2
Anatomy	11.2
Neurology	6.7
Psychiatry	5.8
Neuroscience/Neurobiology	5.3
Neurosurgery	3.1
Pathology	3.1
Veterinary Medicine	1.8
Others	8.9
	100.0

The results are presented in Table 1.1. Clearly the contribution of biopsychology is substantial; about 16 percent of the members of the Society for Neuroscience listed psychology as their primary departmental affiliation. A published analysis of the graduate-student members of the Society for Neuroscience confirms this conclusion (Davis, Rosenzweig, Becker, & Sather, 1988)—see Figure 1.3.

FIGURE 1.3

The departmental affiliation of graduate-student members of the Society for Neuroscience. Only academic departments contributing over 5% of the graduate-student members are listed. (Adapted from Davis et al., 1988.)

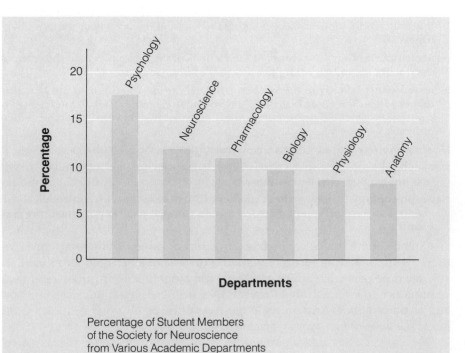

Percentage of Student Members
of the Society for Neuroscience
from Various Academic Departments

1.3

What Types of Research Characterize the Biopsychological Approach?

To characterize the diversity of biological research, this section discusses three major dimensions along which biopsychological research varies. Biopsychological research can involve either human or nonhuman subjects; it can take the form of either formal experiments or nonexperimental studies; and it can be either pure or applied.

Human and Nonhuman Subjects

Both human and nonhuman animals are the subject of biopsychological research. Of the nonhumans, rats are the most common subjects; however, mice, cats, dogs, and nonhuman primates are also widely used.

Humans have several advantages as experimental subjects: They can follow instructions, they can report their subjective experiences, and their cages are easier to clean. I am joking, of course, but the joke does serve to draw attention to one advantage that humans have over other species of experimental subjects: Humans are often cheaper. Because only the highest standards of animal care are acceptable, the cost of maintaining an animal laboratory can be prohibitive for all but the most well-funded researchers.

Of course, the greatest advantage that humans have as subjects in a field aimed at understanding the intricacies of human brain function is that they have human brains. In fact, you might wonder why biopsychologists study nonhuman subjects at all. How can the study of laboratory animals reveal anything about human brain function? The answer lies in the evolutionary continuity of the brain. The brains of all species are composed of neurons, and there are few gross structural differences among the brains of related species. For example, the brains of humans differ from the brains of other mammals primarily in their overall size and the extent of their cortical development. In other words, the differences between the brains of humans and those of related species are more quantitative than qualitative, and thus many of the principles of human brain function can be derived from the study of nonhumans (see Kolb & Whishaw, 1990).

Nonhuman animals have three advantages as subjects in biopsychological research. The first is that the brains and behavior of nonhuman subjects are more simple than those of human subjects. Hence, the study of nonhuman species is often more likely to reveal basic principles of brain-behavior interaction. The second is that insights frequently arise from a **comparative approach,** the comparison of different species. For example, comparing the behavior of species that do not have a cerebral cortex with the behavior of species that do can provide valuable clues about cortical function. The third is that it is possible to conduct research on laboratory animals that, for ethical reasons, is not possible on human subjects. This is not to say that the study of nonhuman animals is not governed by a rigid code of ethics—it is—but there are fewer ethical constraints on the study of laboratory species than on the study of humans. In my experience, most biopsychologists display considerable concern for their subjects whether they are of their own species or not; however, it is difficult to impartially weigh the potential benefits of one's own research with the distress that it might entail for one's subjects. Accordingly, the task of judging the acceptability of a given project is usually handled by an independent committee.

> . . . researchers cannot escape the logic that if the animals we observe are reasonable models of our own most intricate actions, then they must be respected as we would respect our own sensibilities. (Ulrich, 1991, p. 197)

Experiments and Nonexperiments

Biopsychological research involves both experiments and nonexperimental studies.

Experiments   The experiment is the method used by scientists to find out what causes what, and as such, it is almost single-handedly responsible for our modern way of life. It is paradoxical that a method capable of such complex feats is itself so simple. To conduct an experiment involving living subjects, the experimenter first designs two or more conditions under which the subjects will be tested. Usually a different group of subjects is tested under each condition **(between-subjects design),** but sometimes it is possible to test the same group of subjects under each condition **(within-subjects design).** The experimenter assigns the subjects to conditions, administers the treatments, and measures the outcome in such a way that there is only one relevant difference between the conditions that are being compared. This difference between the conditions is called the **independent variable.** The variable that is measured by the experimenter to assess the effect of the independent variable is called the **dependent variable.**

Why is it critical that there be no differences between conditions other than the independent variable? The reason is that when there is more than one difference, it is difficult to determine whether it was the independent variable or the unintended difference—called a **confounded variable**—that led to the observed effects on the dependent variable. If there is only one difference between experimental conditions, that difference must be responsible for any difference in the dependent variable; there is no other possibility. Although the experimental method seems simple—and it is, conceptually—eliminating all confounded variables can be quite difficult. Readers of research papers must be constantly on the alert for confounded variables that have gone unnoticed by the experimenters themselves.

An experiment by Lester and Gorzalka (1988) provides an interesting biopsychological illustration of the experimental method in action. The experiment was a demonstration of the so-called Coolidge effect in females. The **Coolidge effect** refers to the fact that once males become incapable of copulating with one sex partner, they often begin copulating with renewed vigor if a new sex partner becomes available. Before your imagination starts running wild, I should mention that the subjects in Lester and Gorzalka's experiment were hamsters, not students from the undergraduate subject pool.

Lester and Gorzalka argued that the lack of evidence of a Coolidge effect in female animals was not attributable to the fact that males and females are fundamentally different in this respect; they attributed the lack of evidence to the fact that it is more difficult to conduct well-controlled Coolidge-effect experiments in females. The confusion, according to Lester and Gorzalka,

FIGURE 1.4

President Calvin Coolidge. Many students think that the Coolidge effect is named after a biopsychologist named Coolidge. It was named after the following story about President Calvin Coolidge (Goldberg, 1990) — if the story isn't true, it should be. It seems that during a tour of a poultry farm, Mrs. Coolidge inquired of the farmer how his farm managed to produce so many eggs with such a small number of roosters. The farmer proudly explained that his roosters performed their duty dozens of times each day. "Perhaps you could point that out to Mr. Coolidge," replied the first lady in a pointedly loud voice.

The President, overhearing the remark, asked the farmer, "Does each rooster service the same hen each time?"

"No," replied the farmer, "there are many hens for each rooster."

"Perhaps you could point that out to Mrs. Coolidge," replied the President.

stemmed from the fact that the males of most mammalian species become sexually fatigued more readily than do the females. As a result, attempts to demonstrate the Coolidge effect in females are often confounded by the fatigue of the males. When, in the midst of copulation, a female is provided with a new sex partner, the increase in her sexual receptivity could be either a legitimate Coolidge effect or a reaction to the increased vigor of the new male. Because female mammals usually display little sexual fatigue, this confound is not a serious problem in demonstrations of the Coolidge effect in males.

Lester and Gorzalka devised a clever procedure to control for this confound. At the exact time that each subject was copulating with one male (the familiar male), the other male to be used in the test (the new male) was copulating with another female. Then, both males were given a rest while the female was copulating with a third male. Finally, the female subject was tested with either her original partner (the familiar male) or with the new male. The dependent variable was the amount of time that the female displayed **lordosis** (i.e., the arched-back, rump-up, tail-diverted posture of female rodent sexual receptivity) during each sex test. As illustrated in Figure 1.5, the females responded more vigorously to the new males than they did to the familiar males, despite the fact that both the new and familiar males were equally fatigued and both mounted the females with equal vigor. This experiment illustrates the importance of good experimental design and a theme that dominates Chapter 11 — that males and females are more similar than most people appreciate.

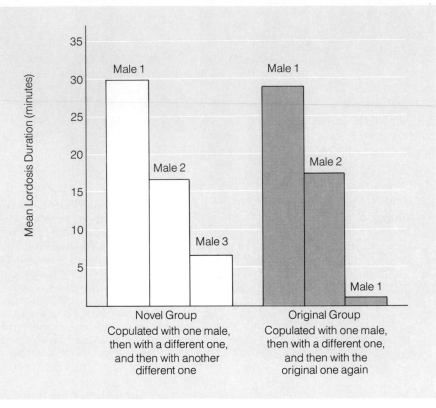

FIGURE 1.5

The experimental design and results of Lester and Gorzalka (1988). On the third test, the female hamsters were more sexually receptive to novel males than they were to the males with which they had copulated on the first test.

Quasiexperimental studies   It is not possible for biopsychologists to bring the experimental method to bear on all problems of interest to them. There are frequently physical or ethical impediments that make it impossible to assign subjects to particular conditions or to administer the conditions once the subjects have been assigned to them. For example, experiments on the causes of brain damage in human alcoholics are not feasible because it would not be ethical to assign a subject to a condition that involves years of alcohol consumption—some of you may be more concerned about the ethics of assigning subjects to a control condition that involves years of sobriety. In such prohibitive situations, biopsychologists conduct quasiexperimental studies. **Quasiexperimental studies** have the appearance of experiments, but they are not true experiments because potential confounded variables have not been controlled—for example, by the random assignment of subjects to conditions. When experimenters cannot create the conditions that they wish to study and assign subjects to them, they perform a quasiexperimental study on subjects who have, in a sense, assigned themselves to similar conditions in the real world.

For example, one team of researchers compared 100 detoxified, male alcoholics from an alcoholism treatment unit with 50 male nondrinkers obtained from various sources (Acker, Ron, Lishman, & Shaw, 1984). The alcoholics as a group performed more poorly on various tests of perceptual, motor, and cognitive ability, and their brain scans revealed extensive brain damage. Although this quasiexperimental study seems like an experiment in several respects, it is not. Because the subjects themselves decided which group they would be in—by drinking alcohol or not—the researchers had no means of ensuring that alcohol consumption was the only variable that distinguished between the two conditions. Can you think of other differences that could reasonably be expected to exist between a group of alcoholics and a group of abstainers—differences that could contribute to neuroanatomical or intellectual differences between them? There are several. For example, alcoholics as a group tend to be more poorly educated, more prone to accidental head injury, more likely to use other drugs, and more likely to have poor diets. Accordingly, quasiexperimental studies have revealed that alcoholics tend to have brain damage, but they have not proven why.

Have you forgotten Jimmie G.? He was the product of long-term alcohol consumption.

Case studies   **Case studies** are studies that focus on a single case or subject. A problem with case studies is their **generalizability,** the degree to which their results can be applied to other cases. Because humans differ markedly from one another in both their brain function and behavior, it is important to be skeptical of any theory based entirely on a few case studies.

Pure and Applied Research

Biopsychological research can be either pure or applied. Pure and applied research differ in a number of respects, but they can be distinguished less by their own attributes than by the motives of the individuals involved in their pursuit. **Pure research** is motivated primarily by the curiosity of the researcher—it is done solely for the purpose of acquiring knowledge. In contrast, **applied research** is intended to bring about some direct benefit to humankind.

Many scientists believe that pure research will ultimately prove to be of more practical benefit than applied research. Their view is that applications flow readily from an understanding of basic principles and that attempts to move directly to application without first gaining a basic understanding are shortsighted. Of course, it is not necessary for a research project to be completely pure or completely applied; many research programs have elements of both approaches.

One important difference between pure and applied research is that pure research is more vulnerable to the vagaries of political regulation because politicians and the voting public have difficulty understanding why research of no obvious practical benefit should be supported. If the decision were yours, would you be willing to grant hundreds of thousands of dollars to support the study of *motor neurons* of the squid; learning in recently hatched geese; the activity of single nerve cells in the visual systems of monkeys; the *hypothalamic hormones* of pigs and sheep; or the function of the *corpus callosum,* a large neural pathway that connects the left and right *cerebral hemispheres*? Which, if any, of these projects would you consider worthy of support? If it surprises you to learn that each of these seemingly esoteric projects was supported, you will be even more surprised to learn that each earned a Nobel Prize for its author. Table 1.2 lists the Nobel Prizes awarded for research involving the brain and behavior (Wilhelm, 1983).

Table 1.2 Nobel Prizes Awarded for Studies of the Nervous System and/or Behavior

Nobel Winner	Date	Accomplishment
Ivan Pavlov	1902	Research on the physiology of digestion
Camillio Golgi and Ramón Y Cajal	1906	Research on the structure of the nervous system
Charles Sherrington and Edgar Adrian	1932	Discoveries about the functions of neurons
Henry Dale and Otto Loewi	1936	Discoveries about the transmission of nerve impulses
Joseph Erlanger and Herbert Gasser	1944	Research on the functions of single nerve fibers
Walter Hess	1949	Research on the role of the brain in controlling behavior
Egas Moniz	1949	Development of prefrontal lobotomy for the treatment of psychosis
Georg Von Békésy	1961	Research on the auditory system
John Eccles, Alan Hodgkin, and Andrew Huxley	1963	Research on the ionic basis of neural transmission
Ragnor Granit, Haldan Hartline, and George Wald	1967	Research on the chemistry and physiology of the visual system
Bernard Katz, Ulf Von Euler, and Julius Axelrod	1970	Discoveries related to the mechanisms of synaptic transmission
Karl Von Frisch, Konrad Lorenz, and Nikolaas Tinbergen	1973	Studies of animal behavior
Roger Guillemin and Andrew Schally	1977	Discoveries related to hormone production by the brain
Herbert Simon	1979	Research on human cognition
Roger Sperry	1981	Research on the differences between the two cerebral hemispheres
David Hubel and Torsten Wiesel	1981	Research on information processing in the visual system
Rita Levi-Montalcini and Stanley Cohen	1986	Discovery and study of nerve and epidermal growth factors

1.4

What Are the Five Divisions of Biopsychology?

Biopsychology can be viewed as comprising five main divisions: (1) **physiological psychology,** (2) **psychopharmacology,** (3) **neuropsychology,** (4) **psychophysiology,** and (5) **comparative psychology.** All are characterized by an interest in the biology of behavior, but each involves a different approach to the topic. These five approaches are described here to illustrate biopsychology's diversity. For simplicity, they are presented as distinct approaches, but in reality they are not distinct. There is much overlap between them, and many biopsychologists regularly follow more than one approach in their research. In fact, they work best when used in combination.

Physiological Psychology

The research of physiological psychologists focuses on the manipulation of the nervous system through surgical, electrical, and chemical means in strictly controlled experimental settings (see Shuttlesworth, Neill, & Ellen, 1984). As a result, the subjects of physiological psychology research are almost always laboratory animals; the nature of the subject matter and the focus on formal experimentation precludes the use of human subjects in most instances. There is also a tradition of pure research in physiological psychology; the emphasis is usually on research that contributes to the development of theories of the neural control of behavior, rather than on research that is of immediate practical benefit.

Psychopharmacology

Psychopharmacology is similar to physiological psychology in most respects. In fact, many of the early psychopharmacologists were simply physiological psychologists who moved into drug research, and many of today's biopsychologists identify closely with both approaches. However, the study of the effects of drugs and behavior has expanded so rapidly in recent decades that psychopharmacology is regarded by many as an independent discipline. Psychopharmacologists study the effects of drugs on behavior and how these effects are mediated by changes in neural activity.

A substantial portion of psychopharmacological research is applied. Although drugs are frequently used by psychopharmacologists to study the basic principles of brain-behavior interaction, the purpose of many psychopharmacological experiments is to develop therapeutic drugs (see Chapter 17) or to reduce drug abuse (see Chapter 13). Psychopharmacologists study the effects of drugs on laboratory species—and on humans, if the ethics of the situation permits it (see McKim, 1986; Meltzer, 1987).

Neuropsychology

Neuropsychology is the study of the behavioral deficits produced in humans by brain damage. Obviously, such effects are not normally amenable to study by experimentation; human subjects cannot ethically be exposed to experimental treatments that endanger normal brain function. As a result, neuropsychology deals almost exclusively with case studies and quasiexperimental studies of patients with brain damage resulting from disease, accident, or neurosurgery. Because it is the outer layer of the cerebral hemispheres, the **neocortex,** that is most likely to be damaged by accident and is most accessible to surgery, the discipline has focused on this important part of the human brain.

Neuropsychology is the most applied of the biopsychological subdisciplines; the neuropsychological assessment of human patients, even when part of a program of pure research, is almost always done with an eye toward benefiting them in some way. Neuropsychological tests facilitate diagnosis and thus help the attending physician prescribe effective treatment. They can also be an important basis for patient care and counseling; Kolb and Whishaw (1990) described such an application.

Mr. R., a 21-year-old left-handed man, struck his head on the dashboard in a car accident 2 years prior to our seeing him. He was unconscious for a few minutes after the accident but other than a cut on the right side of his forehead and amnesia for the period just before and after the accident, Mr. R. appeared none the worse for his mishap. Prior to his accident Mr. R. was an honor student at a university, with plans to attend professional or graduate school. However, a year after the accident he had become a mediocre student who had particular trouble completing his term papers on time, and although he claimed to be studying harder than he had before the accident, his marks had fallen drastically in courses requiring memorization. He was referred for a neurological exam by his family physician, but it proved negative and an EEG and a CT scan failed to demonstrate any abnormality. He was referred to us for neuropsychological assessment, which revealed several interesting facts.

First, Mr. R. was one of about one-third of left-handers whose language functions are represented in the right rather than left hemisphere. This discovery was significant not only in interpreting his difficulties but also in the event that Mr. R. should ever require neurosurgery, since the surgeon would want to respect the speech zones of the neocortex. In addition, although Mr. R. had a superior IQ, his verbal memory and reading speed were only low-average, which is highly unusual for a person of his intelligence and education. These deficits indicated that his right temporal lobe may have been slightly damaged in the car accident, resulting in an impairment of his language skills. On the basis of our neuropsychological investigation we were able to recommend vocations to Mr. R. that did not require superior verbal memory skills, and he is currently studying architecture. (p. 128)[2]

Psychophysiology

Psychophysiologists study the relation between physiology and behavior by recording the physiological responses of human subjects (see Andreassi, 1989; Furedy, 1983). Because the subjects of psychophysiological research are human, the recording procedures employed by psychophysiologists are *noninvasive;* that is, the recordings are taken from the surface of the body. The usual measure of brain activity is the scalp **electroencephalogram (EEG).** Also commonly recorded in psychophysiological experiments are measures of muscle tension, eye movement, and **autonomic nervous system** (see Chapter 3) activity. Common measures of autonomic nervous system activity are heart rate, blood pressure, pupil dilation, and electrical conductance of the skin.

Most psychophysiological research focuses on understanding the physiology of psychological processes, such as attention, emotion, and information processing, but there have also been a number of interesting clinical applications of the psychophysiological method (see Iacono, 1985). For example, psychological experiments have indicated that schizophrenics (Iacono & Koenig, 1983) and their parents (Holzman, Solomon, Levin, & Waternaux, 1984) have difficulty tracking a moving object such as a pendulum—see Figure 1.6.

---

[2]From *Fundamentals of Human Neuropsychology,* 3rd Edition by Bryan Kolb and Ian Q. Whishaw. Copyright © 1980, 1985, 1990 W. H. Freeman and Company. Reprinted with permission.

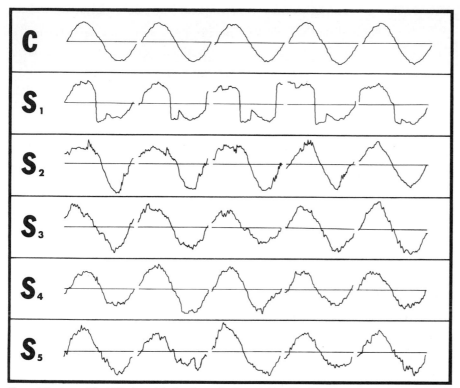

From "Features That Distinguish the Smooth-Pursuit Eye-Tracking
Performance of Schizophrenic, Affective-Disorder, and Normal Individuals" by
W. G. Iacono and W. G. R. Koenig, 1983, *Journal of Abnormal Psychology, 92,*
p. 39. Copyright 1983 by the American Psychological Association. Reprinted
by permission.

FIGURE 1.6

Visual tracking of a pendulum
by a normal control subject
(top) and five schizophrenics.

Comparative Psychology

Although most biopsychologists study the neural mechanisms of behavior,
there is more to biopsychology.

> . . . the "biology" in "psychobiology" should include the whole-animal ap-
> proaches of ethology, ecology, evolution . . . as well as the latest in physio-
> logical methods and thought. . . . The "compleat psychobiologist" should
> use whatever explanatory power can be found with modern physiological
> techniques, but never lose sight of the problems that got us going in the first
> place: the integrated behavior of whole, functioning, adapted organisms.
> (Dewsbury, 1991, p. 198)

The division of biopsychology that deals generally with the biology of behavior, rather than specifically with the neural mechanisms of behavior, is
called *comparative psychology.* Comparative psychologists compare the behavior of different species and focus on the genetics, evolution, and adaptive-·
ness of behavior. In contrast to *ethologists,* who conduct quasiexperimental
studies of animals behaving in their natural environments, comparative psychologists tend to focus on the experimental investigation of animal behavior
in controlled seminatural laboratory environments.

SELF TEST

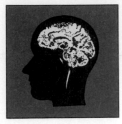

To make sure that you understand the distinctions among these five biopsychological approaches, fill in each of the following blanks. If you have difficulty, review the preceding section before continuing.

1. A biopsychologist who studies the memory deficits of human patients with brain damage would likely identify with the division of biopsychology termed _____.

2. Psychologists who study the physiological correlates of psychological processes by recording physiological signals from the surface of the human body are often referred to as _____.

3. The biopsychological research of _____ frequently involves the direct manipulation or recording of the neural activity of laboratory animals by various invasive surgical, electrical, and chemical means.

4. The division of biopsychology that focuses on the study of the effects of drugs on behavior is often referred to as _____.

5. _____ are biopsychologists who study the genetics, evolution, and adaptiveness of behavior by using the comparative method.

1.5

Converging Operations: How Do Biopsychologists Work Together?

Because none of the five biopsychological approaches to research is without its shortcomings, major biopsychological issues are rarely resolved by a single experiment or even by a series of experiments taking the same general approach. Progress is most rapid when different approaches are focused on a single problem in such a way that the strengths of one approach compensate for the weaknesses of others; this is called **converging operations.** Consider, for example, the relative strengths and weaknesses of neuropsychology and physiological psychology in the study of the psychological effects of damage to the human neocortex. The strength of the neuropsychological approach in this instance is that it deals directly with human patients; its weakness is that its focus on human patients precludes experiments. In contrast, physiological psychologists can bring the power of the experimental method and neuroscientific technology to bear on the question because their research involves nonhuman animals; the weakness here is that the relevance of research on laboratory animals to the neuropsychological deficits of human patients is always subject to question. Clearly these two approaches complement one

The answers to the preceding review questions are (1) neuropsychology, (2) psychophysiologists, (3) physiological psychologists, (4) psychopharmacology, and (5) comparative psychologists.

another well; together they can provide strong evidence for points of view that neither can defend individually.

To illustrate converging operations in action, let's return to the case of Jimmie G. The neuropsychological disorder from which Jimmie G. suffered was first described in the late 1800s by S. S. Korsakoff, a Russian physician, and it subsequently became known as **Korsakoff's syndrome.** The primary symptom of Korsakoff's syndrome is severe memory loss, which is made all the more heartbreaking—as you have seen in Jimmie G.'s case—by the fact that the patients are often otherwise reasonably capable. Because Korsakoff's syndrome commonly occurs in alcoholics, it was generally assumed to be a consequence of alcohol-produced brain damage. This conclusion proved to be a particularly good illustration of the inadvisability of basing causal conclusions on quasiexperimental research. It turned out that Korsakoff's syndrome is not solely the consequence of alcohol-produced brain damage; it is also caused by the *thiamin deficiency* (the vitamin B1 deficiency) that is commonly associated with chronic alcohol consumption—see Lishman (1990).

The first support for the thiamin-deficiency interpretation of Korsakoff's syndrome came from the discovery of the syndrome in malnourished patients who consumed little or no alcohol. Additional support came from experiments in which thiamin-deficient rats were compared with otherwise identical groups of control rats. Thiamin-deficient rats display memory deficits and patterns of brain damage that are similar to those observed in human alcoholics (Knoth & Mair, 1991; Mair, Knoth, Rabenchuk, & Langlais, 1991; Mair, Otto, Knoth, & Langlais, 1991). Alcoholics typically consume few vitamins because most of their caloric intake comes in the form of alcohol, and experiments on rats suggest that alcohol interferes with the metabolism of what little thiamin alcoholics do consume (Rindi, 1989). Alcohol has been shown to accelerate the development of brain damage in thiamin-deficient rats (Zimitat, Kril, Harper, & Nixon, 1990). The point of all this, if you have forgotten, is that progress in biopsychology typically comes from converging operations—in this case, from the convergence of neuropsychological case studies, quasiexperiments on human subjects, and controlled experiments on laboratory animals. The strength of biopsychology lies in its diversity.

So what has all this research done for Jimmie G. and others like him? Today, alcoholics are often counseled to stop drinking and are treated with massive doses of thiamin. The thiamin limits the development of further brain damage and sometimes leads to a slight improvement in the patient's condition (Tuck, Brew, Britton, & Loewy, 1984), but unfortunately, brain damage, once produced, is permanent. In some parts of the world, the fortification of alcoholic beverages with thiamin is currently being seriously considered (Wodak, Richmond, & Wilson, 1990).

1.6

Scientific Inference: How Do Biopsychologists Study the Unobservable?

The scientific method is a system of finding out things by careful observation, but many of the processes studied by scientists cannot be observed. Scientists routinely use their *empirical* (observational) methods to study processes, such as ice ages, gravity, evaporation, electricity, and nuclear fission, all of which for various reasons are not accessible to direct observation—their effects can be observed, but the processes themselves cannot. Biopsychology is no different from other sciences in this respect: One of its main goals is to characterize through observation the unobservable processes by which the nervous system controls behavior.

The method that biopsychologists and other scientists use to study the unobservable is called **scientific inference.** They carefully measure key events that they can observe, and use these measures as a basis for logically inferring the nature of events that they cannot observe. Like a detective carefully gathering clues from which to recreate an unwitnessed crime, a biopsychologist carefully gathers relevant measures of behavior and neural activity from which to infer the nature of the neural processes that regulate behavior. To illustrate scientific inference, I have selected a research project in which you can participate. By making a few simple observations of your own visual abilities under different conditions, you will be able to discover for yourself one of the basic principles by which the brain perceives motion.

How does your brain translate the movement of images on your retinas into perceptions of movement? One feature of the mechanism is immediately obvious. Hold your hand in front of your face, and then move its image across your retinas by moving your eyes, by moving your hand, or by moving both. You will notice that only those movements of the retinal image that are produced by the movement of your hand are translated into the perception of motion; movements of the retinal image that are produced by your own eye movements are not. Obviously, there must be a part of your brain that monitors the movement of your retinal image and subtracts from the total those movements of your retinal image that are produced by your own eye movements, leaving the remainder to be perceived as motion.

Let's try to characterize the nature of the information about your eye movement that is used by your brain in its perception of motion. Try the following. Shut one eye; then rotate your other eye slightly upward by gently pressing on your lower eyelid with your fingertip. What do you see? You see all of the objects in your visual field moving downward. Why? It seems that the brain mechanism that is responsible for the perception of motion does not consider eye movement per se. It considers only those eye movements that are actively produced by neural signals from the brain to the eye muscles, not those that are passively produced by external means. Thus when your eye was moved passively, your brain assumed that it had remained still and attributed the movement of your retinal image to the movement of objects in your visual field (see Figure 1.7).

It is possible to trick the visual system in the opposite way; instead of moving the eyes when no active signals have been sent to the eye muscles, the eyes can be held stationary despite the brain's attempts to move them. Because this experiment involves paralyzing the eye muscles, you cannot participate. Hammond, Merton, and Sutton (1956) injected d-*tubocurarine*, the paralytic substance with which some South American natives coat their blow darts, into the eye muscles of their subject—who was Merton himself. What do you think Merton saw when he tried to move his eyes? Merton saw the stationary visual world moving in the same direction as his attempted eye movements. If a visual object is focused on part of your retina and it stays focused there despite the fact that you have moved your eyes to the right, it too must have

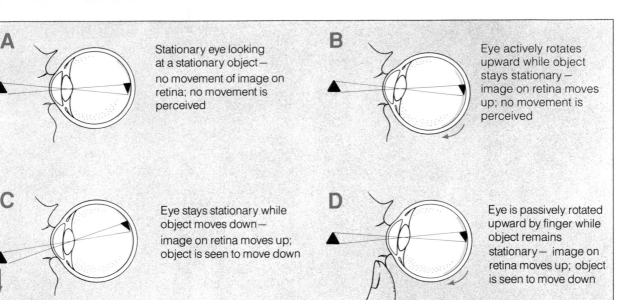

A Stationary eye looking at a stationary object— no movement of image on retina; no movement is perceived

B Eye actively rotates upward while object stays stationary— image on retina moves up; no movement is perceived

C Eye stays stationary while object moves down— image on retina moves up; object is seen to move down

D Eye is passively rotated upward by finger while object remains stationary— image on retina moves up; object is seen to move down

Therefore, the brain perceives movement by subtracting from the movement of the image on the retina any movement of the retinal image caused by active movement of the eyes.

FIGURE 1.7

The perception of motion under four different conditions.

moved to the right. Consequently, when Merton sent signals to his eye muscles to move his eyes to the right, his brain assumed that the movement had been carried out, and it perceived stationary objects as moving to the right. The point of this example is that biopsychologists can learn much about the activities of the brain without directly observing them—and so can you.

1.7

What Is Bad Science, and How Do You Spot It?

Scientists, like other people, make mistakes, and biopsychologists are no exception. In fact, two features of biopsychological inquiry make it particularly susceptible to error. The first is that biopsychological research has such a wide appeal that it tends to invite the participation of those who have had little or no first-hand experience with its complexities. The second is that it is often difficult to be objective when studying biopsychological issues. Whether we realize it or not, we all have many preconceptions about the brain and behavior ingrained in our thinking. You might wonder why a book about biopsychology would dwell, even momentarily, on errors in biopsychological research. There are two reasons. One is that an understanding of such errors provides important insights into what biopsychology is—the standards and methods of a discipline frequently grow out of its mistakes. The other is to encourage you to become good consumers of science. Individuals familiar with examples of scientific error are less likely to accept without question any statement credited to a scientist; they are more likely to have the basic skills necessary to evaluate for themselves the validity of various claims. In other words, one purpose of this final section of Chapter 1 is to improve your B.S. detection skills—B.S., of course, stands for bad science. The following are the descriptions of two examples of biopsychological analysis that are seriously flawed.

CASE 1

José Delgado demonstrated to a group of newspaper reporters a remarkable new procedure for controlling aggression. Delgado strode into a Spanish bull ring carrying only a red cape and a small radio transmitter. With the transmitter, he could activate a battery-powered stimulator that had previously been mounted on the horns of the other inhabitant of the ring. As the raging bull charged, Delgado calmly activated the stimulator and sent a weak train of electrical current from the stimulator through an electrode that had been implanted in the *caudate nucleus* of the bull's brain. The bull immediately veered from its charge. After a few such interrupted charges, the bull stood tamely as Delgado swaggered about the ring. According to Delgado, this demonstration marked a significant scientific breakthrough—the discovery of the caudate taming center and the fact that stimulation of this structure could eliminate aggressive behavior, even in bulls specially bred for their ferocity.

To those present at this carefully orchestrated event and to most of the millions who subsequently read about it, Delgado's conclusion was compelling. Surely if caudate stimulation could stop the charge of a raging bull, the caudate must be a taming center. It was even suggested that caudate stimulation through implanted electrodes might be an effective treatment for human psychopaths. What do you think?

Analysis of Case 1

The fact of the matter is that Delgado's demonstration provided little or no support for his conclusion. It should have been obvious to anyone who did not get caught up in the provocative nature of Delgado's media event that there are numerous ways in which brain stimulation can abort a bull's charge, most of which are more simple, and thus more probable, than the one suggested by Delgado. For example, the stimulation may have simply rendered the bull confused, dizzy, nauseous, sleepy, or temporarily blind rather than nonaggressive; or the stimulation could have been painful. Clearly, any observation that can be interpreted in so many different ways provides little support for any one interpretation. When there are several possible interpretations for a behavioral observation, the rule is to give precedence to the most simple one. This rule is called **Morgan's Canon.** The following comments of Valenstein (1973) provide a more reasoned view of Delgado's demonstration.

... actually there is no good reason for believing that the stimulation had any direct effect on the bull's aggressive tendencies. An examination of the film record makes it apparent that the charging bull was stopped because as long as the stimulation was on it was forced to turn around in the same direction continuously. After examining the film, any scientist with knowledge in this field could conclude only that the stimulation had been activating a neural pathway controlling movement. (p. 98)

. . . he [Delgado] seems to capitalize on every individual effect his electrodes happen to produce and presents little, if any, experimental evidence that his impression of the underlying cause is correct. (p. 103)

. . . his propensity for dramatic, albeit ambiguous, demonstrations has been a constant source of material for those whose purposes are served by exaggerating the omnipotence of brain stimulation. (p. 99)

CASE 2

In 1949, Dr. Egas Moniz was awarded the Nobel Prize in Physiology and Medicine for the development of **prefrontal lobotomy** (cutting connections between the *prefrontal lobes* and the rest of the brain) as a treatment for mental illness. Moniz's discovery was based on the report that Becky, a chimpanzee that frequently became upset when she made errors during the performance of a food-rewarded task, did not do so following a large, *bilateral* (both sides of the brain) lesion of her prefrontal cortex. After hearing about this isolated observation at a scientific meeting in the summer of 1935, Moniz persuaded neurosurgeon Almeida Lima to operate on a series of his (Moniz's) psychiatric patients. The first prefrontal lobotomy, performed in November of the same year, involved cutting out six large cores of prefrontal tissue with a device called a **leucotome** (see Figure 1.8).

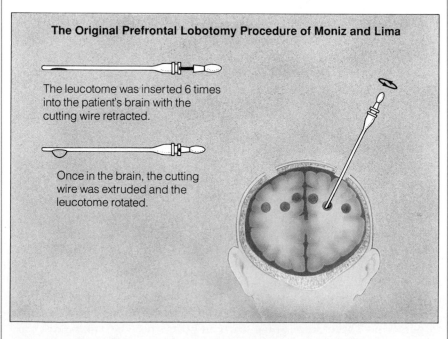

The Original Prefrontal Lobotomy Procedure of Moniz and Lima

The leucotome was inserted 6 times into the patient's brain with the cutting wire retracted.

Once in the brain, the cutting wire was extruded and the leucotome rotated.

FIGURE 1.8

The original prefrontal lobotomy procedure, which was developed by Moniz and Lima.

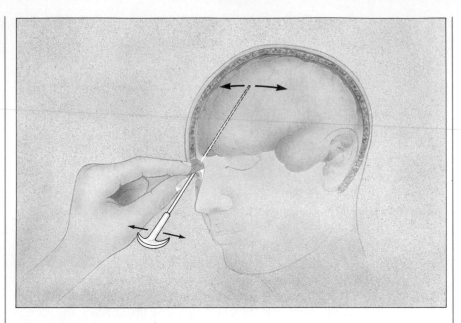

FIGURE 1.9

The transorbital procedure for performing prefrontal lobotomy.

Following Moniz's claims that prefrontal surgery was therapeutically successful and had no significant side effects, there was a rapid proliferation of various forms of prefrontal psychosurgery (see O'Callaghan & Carroll, 1982; Valenstein, 1980, 1986a). One such variation was **transorbital lobotomy,** which was popularized in the United States by Walter Freeman in the late 1940s. It involved inserting an icepick-like device under the eyelid, driving it through the *orbit* (the eye socket) with a few taps of a mallet, and pushing it into the frontal lobes, where it was waved back and forth to sever the connections between the prefrontal lobes and the rest of the brain (see Figure 1.9). This operation was frequently performed in the surgeon's office.

Analysis of Case 2

Incredible as it may seem, Moniz initiated his program of psychosurgery based on the observation of a single chimpanzee, thus displaying a complete lack of appreciation for the diversity of brain and behavior, both within and between species. No program of psychosurgery should ever be initiated without first assessing the effects of the surgery on a large sample of subjects from various nonhuman mammalian species.

A second major weakness in the scientific case for prefrontal psychosurgery was the failure of Moniz and others to carefully evaluate the consequences of the surgery in the first patients to undergo the operation. There were some early reports that the operation was therapeutically successful, but these were based, for the most part, on the general impressions of the very individuals who were least objective—the physicians who had prescribed the surgery. Patients were frequently judged as improved if they were more manageable, and little effort was made to evaluate more important aspects of psychological adjustment or to document the existence of adverse side effects.

Few lobotomies have been performed since the 1950s. The accumulation of reports that it was of no real therapeutic benefit and that it produced a wide range of undesirable side effects, such as amorality, lack of foresight, emotional unresponsiveness, epilepsy, and urinary incontinence, led to its eventual abandonment—but not before over 40,000 patients had been lobotomized in the United States alone. Some regard the fundamentals of scientific protocol

> as unduly strict: as unnecessary obstacles in the path of patients seeking treatment and therapists striving to provide it. However, the barely discarded practices of purging and blood-letting [and prefrontal lobotomy] should caution us against abandoning science for expediency. . . . Only by insisting on careful and controlled study . . . and only by observing the rules of science can the public be protected from inappropriate and bogus [scientific claims and clinical remedies] (Carroll, 1984, p. 109).

There is a particularly somber postscript to this story. Dr. Moniz was shot by one of his patients. The bullet became lodged in his spine and rendered him *paraplegic* (paralyzed below the waist).

Conclusion

The general purpose of this chapter was to introduce you to the field of biopsychology and to whet your appetite for more of it. You learned that biopsychology is the study of the biology of behavior, that it is one component of neuroscience, and that it in turn comprises five fundamentally different approaches: physiological psychology, psychopharmacology, neuropsychology, psychophysiology, and comparative psychology. Then, you were introduced to two important principles of biopsychological research: converging operations and scientific inference. Finally, you were provided with two examples of bad biopsychology, which illustrated the importance of adhering to the fundamental principles of scientific inquiry and of greeting claims of major scientific breakthroughs with a healthy degree of caution.

You are about to enter a world of amazing discoveries and intriguing ideas: the world of biopsychology. I hope that you enjoy it, and I hope that it challenges and stimulates you.

Food for Thought

1. In retrospect, the entire prefrontal lobotomy episode is shocking. How could physicians, who are intelligent, highly educated, and dedicated to helping their patients, participate in such a travesty? How could somebody win a Nobel Prize for developing a form of surgery that left over 40,000 mental cripples in the United States alone? Why did this happen? Could it happen today?

2. Chapter 1 tells you in general conceptual terms what biopsychology is. Another, and perhaps better, way of defining biopsychology is to describe what biopsychologists do. Ask your instructor what she or he did to become a biopsychologist and what she or he does each work day. I think that you will be surprised. Is she or he predominantly a physiological psychologist, psychopharmacologist, neuropsychologist, psychophysiologist, or comparative psychologist?

KEY TERMS

To help you study the material in this chapter, all of the key terms—those that have appeared in bold type—are listed and briefly defined here.

Applied research. Research that is intended to bring about some direct benefit to humankind.

Autonomic nervous system. The part of the peripheral nervous system that participates in the regulation of the internal environment.

Between-subjects design. An experimental design in which a different group of subjects is tested under each condition.

Biological psychiatry. Study of the biological bases of psychiatric disorders and their treatment through the manipulation of the brain.

Biopsychology. Study of the biology of behavior.

Case study. A study of a single case or subject.

Comparative approach. Studying biological processes by comparing different species.

Comparative psychology. The division of biopsychology that studies the evolution, genetics, and adaptiveness of behavior, often by using the comparative method.

Confounded variable. An additional, unintended difference between conditions in an experiment.

Converging operations. The use of several research approaches to solve a single problem.

Coolidge effect. When males incapable of continuing to copulate with one sex partner begin copulating with a new sex partner.

Dependent variable. The variable measured by the experimenter; the variable on which the independent variable acts.

Developmental neurobiology. Study of how the nervous system changes as an organism matures and ages.

Electroencephalogram (EEG). A measure of the general electrical activity of the brain, often recorded through the scalp.

Generalizability. The degree to which the results of a study can be applied to other individuals or situations.

Independent variable. The difference between experimental conditions that is arranged by the experimenter.

Korsakoff's syndrome. A neuropsychological disorder that is associated with chronic alcohol consumption; the primary symptom is a disturbance of memory.

Leucotome. Any one of the various surgical devices used for performing lobotomies—*leucotomy* is another word for lobotomy.

Lordosis. The arched-back, rump-up, tail-diverted posture of female rodent sexual receptivity.

Morgan's Canon. Of several possible interpretations for a behavioral result, the most simple should be given precedence.

Neocortex. The layer of neural tissue covering the cerebral hemispheres of humans and other mammals.

Neuroanatomy. The study of the structure of the nervous system.

Neurobiology. Neuroscience.

Neurochemistry. The study of the chemical bases of neural activity.

Neuroendocrinology. The study of the interaction of the nervous system with the endocrine system.

Neuroethology. The study of the relation between the nervous system and the behavior of animals in their natural environment.

Neurons. Cells of the nervous system that are specialized for receiving and transmitting electrochemical signals.

Neuropathology. The study of nervous system disorders.

Neuropharmacology. The study of the effects of drugs on the nervous system.

Neurophysiology. The study of the responses of the nervous system, particularly those involved in transmission of electrical signals through and between neurons.

Neuropsychology. The study of behavioral deficits produced in humans by brain damage.

Neuroscience. The scientific study of the nervous system; neurobiology.

Physiological psychology. Biopsychological research that focuses on the direct manipulation of the nervous system of animal subjects in controlled experimental settings.

Prefrontal lobotomy. Cutting the prefrontal lobes from the rest of the brain as a treatment for mental illness.

Psychopharmacology. The study of the effects of drugs on behavior.

Psychophysiology. The study of the relation between behavior and physiological signals recorded from the surface of the human body.

Pure research. Research motivated primarily by the curiosity of the researcher.

Quasiexperimental studies. Studies that have the appearance of experiments, but are not true experiments because potential confounded variables have not been controlled.

Scientific inference. The logical process by which observable events are used to infer the properties of unobservable events.

Society for Neuroscience. An international association of neuroscientists.

Transorbital lobotomy. A prefrontal lobotomy performed with an instrument inserted through the eye socket.

Within-subjects design. An experimental design in which the same subjects are tested in each condition.

ADDITIONAL READING

Each of the following books provides an excellent introduction to one of the five biopsychological subdisciplines:

Andreassi, J. L. (1989). *Psychophysiology: Human behavior and physiological response.* Hillsdale, New Jersey: Erlbaum.

Carlson, N. R. (1991). *Physiology of behavior* (4th ed.). Boston, Massachusetts: Allyn and Bacon.

Dewsbury, D. A. (1990). *Contemporary issues in comparative psychology.* Sunderland, Massachusetts: Sinauer.

Kolb, B., & Whishaw, I. Q. (1990). *Fundamentals of human neuropsychology* (3rd ed.). New York: Freeman.

McKim, W. A. (1986). *Drugs and behavior: An introduction to behavioral pharmacology.* Englewood Cliffs, New Jersey: Prentice-Hall.

This book provides an excellent overview of the topic of psychosurgery:

Valenstein, E. S. (1986). *Great and desperate cures: The rise and decline of psychosurgery and other radical treatments for mental illness.* New York: Basic Books.

The following article is a good discussion of what biopsychology is and how it is related to the other neurosciences:

Davis, H. P., Rosenzweig, M. R., Becker, L. A., & Sather, K. J. (1988). Biological psychology's relationships to psychology and neuroscience. *American Psychologist, 43,* 359–371.

This article argues convincingly that biopsychology is more than the study of the neural basis of behavior.

Dewsbury, D. A. (1991). "Psychobiology." *American Psychologist, 46,* 198–205.

2

Evolution, Genetics, and Development: Learning to Ask the Right Questions about the Biology of Behavior

We all tend to think about things in ways that have been ingrained in us by our **Zeitgeist** (pronounced ZYTE gyste), the general intellectual climate of our culture. That is why this is a particularly important chapter for you. You see, you are the intellectual product of a Zeitgeist that promotes ways of thinking about the biological bases of behavior that are inconsistent with the facts. The general purpose of this chapter is to help you bring your thinking about the biology of behavior in line with modern biopsychological science.

Most textbook chapters focus on answers. This chapter focuses on questions—the questions that people tend to ask about the biology of behavior. It tries to teach you to ask the right questions about the biology of behavior by describing why biopsychologists have abandoned traditional questions in favor of more insightful alternatives. Learning to ask the right questions is the first step toward getting the right answers.

Section 2.1 describes the evolution of two central biopsychological research questions. Its main point is that modern biopsychologists have come to think of behavior as the product of interactions among genes, experience, and the current situation. Section 2.2 deals with human evolution; Section 2.3, with behavioral genetics; and Section 2.4, with behavioral development.

2.1

Thinking about the Biology of Behavior: From Dichotomies to Relations and Interactions

We tend to ignore the subtleties, inconsistencies, and complexities of our existence and to think in terms of simple, mutually exclusive dichotomies: right-wrong, good-bad, attractive-unattractive, and so on. The allure of this way of thinking is its simplicity.

People's tendency to think about behavior in terms of dichotomies is illustrated by two questions that they commonly ask about it: (1) Is it physiological or is it psychological? (2) Is it inherited or is it learned? Both of these questions have proven to be misguided, yet they are among the most common questions asked in biopsychology classrooms. That is why I am dwelling on them here.

Is It Physiological or Is It Psychological?

The idea that human processes fall into one of two categories, physiological or psychological, grew out of a seventeeth-century conflict between science and the Roman church. For most of the history of Western civilization, the events of the universe were thought to occur at the whims of the gods, and truth was whatever was decreed to be true by those in authority. During the 1,000 or so years of the dark and middle ages (about 400 to 1400 A.D.), the Roman church was this authority. Then, in about 1400, things started to change. The famines, plagues, and marauding armies that had repeatedly swept Europe during the dark and middle ages subsided, and interest turned to art, commerce, and scholarship—this was the period of the *Renaissance* or rebirth (1400 to 1700). Some of the Renaissance scholars were not content to follow the dictates of the church and search for truth in the bible or in the writings of Greek philosophers. Instead, they started to study things directly by looking at them, recording what they saw, and drawing inferences from their observations. So it was that science was born.

The Renaissance was a difficult time for scientists. Because much of the rapidly accumulating scientific knowledge was at odds with church dogma, scientists risked excommunication, imprisonment, and even death. For example, in 1632 Galileo presented so much evidence in support of the *heliocentric* (sun-at-the-center) theory of the solar system that it made supporters of the church-sanctioned *geocentric* (earth-at-the-center) view look like simpletons. The Roman church was not amused. Galileo was arrested and imprisoned until his death 9 years later.

The conflict between science and the Roman church was resolved by the prominent French philosopher René Descartes (pronounced day CART). Descartes (1596–1650) proposed a philosophy that gave one part of the universe to science and the other part to the church. He argued that the universe is composed of two elements: (1) physical matter, which behaves according to the laws of nature and is thus a suitable object of scientific investigation, and (2) the human mind (soul or spirit), which lacks physical substance, controls human behavior, obeys no natural laws, and is thus the appropriate purview of the church. The human body, including the brain, was assumed to be entirely physical, and so were nonhuman animals.

Cartesian dualism, as Descartes's philosophy became known, was sanctioned by the Roman church, and so the idea that the human brain and the mind are separate entities became widely accepted. It has survived to this day, despite the intervening centuries of scientific progress. Most people now understand that some categories of human behavior have a physiological basis, but they still cling to the dualistic assumption that there is a category of human activity that transcends human physiology.

Is It Inherited or Is It Learned?

The tendency to think in terms of dichotomies extends to the way people think about the development of behavioral capacities. For centuries, scholars have debated whether humans and other animals inherit their behavioral capacities or whether they acquire them through learning. This issue is commonly referred to as the **nature-nurture issue.**

Most of the early North American experimental psychologists were totally committed to the nurture (i.e., learning) side of the nature-nurture issue. The degree of this commitment is illustrated by the oft-cited words of John B. Watson, the father of *behaviorism*.

> . . . we have no real evidence of the inheritance of [behavioral] traits. I would feel perfectly confident in the ultimately favorable outcome of careful upbringing of a healthy, well-formed baby born of a long line of crooks, murderers and thieves, and prostitutes. Who has any evidence to the contrary?
>   . . . Give me a dozen healthy infants, well-formed, and my own specified world to bring them up in and I'll guarantee to take any one at random and train him to become any type of specialist I might select—doctor, lawyer, artist, merchant-chief and, yes even beggar-man and thief. . . . (Watson, 1930, pp. 103–104)

At the same time that experimental psychology was taking root in North America, **ethology,** an approach to the study of behavior that emphasized the importance of inherited factors (i.e., nature) in behavioral development, was gaining momentum in Europe. Unlike the North American psychologists, who focused on the study of learned behaviors, the European ethologists focused on study of **instinctive behaviors,** behaviors that occur in all like members of a species even when there seems to have been no opportunity for them to have been learned. For example, Tinbergen and Perdeck (1950) studied the universal tendency of newly hatched herring-gull chicks to peck at the red dot on the bills of their parents—this causes the parents to regurgitate a yummy meal of half-digested fish. Because instinctive behaviors are not learned, the ethologists assumed that they are entirely innate. They were wrong, but then so were the early psychologists.

Problems with Thinking about the Biology of Behavior in Terms of Traditional Dichotomies

The physiological-or-psychological and nature-or-nurture questions are based on incorrect ways of thinking about the biology of behavior, and a new generation of questions is directing the current boom in biopsychological research. So, what is wrong with these old ways of thinking about the biology of behavior, and what are the new ways?

Physiological-or-psychological thinking runs into difficulty Not long after Descartes's mind-brain dualism was officially sanctioned by the Roman church, it started to come under public attack.

> In 1747, Julien Offroy de la Mettrie anonymously published a pamphlet that scandalized Europe. . . . La Mettrie fled to Berlin, where he was forced to live in exile for the rest of his life. His crime? He had argued that thought was produced by the brain—a dangerous assault, in the eyes of his contemporaries. . . . Not for the last time, the science of human mind had outgrown human imagination. (Corsi, 1991, cover)

Although many people still firmly believe that there is a purely psychological category of human activity that transcends human physiology, two kinds of evidence indicate otherwise. First, numerous studies have shown that even the most complex psychological processes (e.g., memory, emotion, or self-awareness) can be modified by damaging or stimulating the higher regions of the brain. Second, some nonhuman species have been found to possess abilities that were once assumed to be purely psychological and thus purely human (see Mellgren, 1983; Roitblat, Bever, & Terrace, 1984). The following two quotations illustrate these two kinds of evidence; both quotations deal with the study of self-awareness.

The first quotation describes Sacks's (1985) case of "the man who fell out of bed."[1] He was suffering from **asomatognosia,** a deficiency in the awareness of parts of one's own body. Asomatognosia typically involves the left side of the body and usually results from damage to the *right parietal lobe.* The

---

[1]From *The Man Who Mistook His Wife for a Hat and Other Clinical Tales* (pp. 53–55) by Oliver Sacks, 1985, New York: Summit Books. Copyright © 1970, 1981, 1983, 1984, 1985 by Oliver Sacks. Reprinted by permission of Summit Books, a division of Simon & Schuster, Inc.

second quotation describes Gallup's demonstrations of self-awareness in nonhuman primates (see Figure 2.1).[2]

> He had felt fine all day, and fallen asleep towards evening. When he woke up he felt fine too, until he moved in the bed. Then he found, as he put it 'someone's leg' in the bed—a *severed human leg,* a horrible thing! He was stunned, at first, with amazement and disgust. . . . [Then] he had a brainwave. . . . Obviously one of the nurses . . . had stolen into the Dissecting Room and nabbed a leg, and then slipped it under his bedclothes as a joke. . . . *When he threw it out of bed, he somehow came after it—and now it was attached to him.*
>
> 'Look at it!' he cried. . . . 'Have you ever seen such a creepy, horrible thing?' . . .
>
> 'Easy!' I said. 'Be calm! Take it easy!' . . .
>
> ' . . . why . . .' he asked irritably, belligerently.
>
> 'Because it's *your* leg,' I answered. 'Don't you know your own leg?' . . .
>
> . . . 'Ah Doc!' he said. 'You're fooling me! You're in cahoots with that nurse' . . .
>
> 'Listen,' I said. 'I don't think you're well. Please allow us to return you to bed. But I want to ask you one final question. If this—this thing—is *not* your left leg . . . then where is your own left leg?'
>
> Once more he became pale—so pale that I thought he was going to faint. 'I don't know,' he said. 'I have no idea. It's disappeared. It's gone. It's nowhere to be found' . . . (Sacks, 1985, 53–55)

FIGURE 2.1

The reactions of chimpanzees to their own images indicate that they are self-aware. In this photo the chimpanzee is reacting to the bright red, odorless dye that was painted on its eyebrow ridge while it was anesthesized.

[2]From *Toward a Comparative Psychology of Mind.*

An organism is self-aware to the extent that it can be shown capable of becoming the object of its own attention. . . . One way to assess an organism's capacity to become the object of its own attention is to confront it with a mirror.

. . . I gave a number of group-reared, preadolescent chimpanzees individual exposure to themselves in mirrors. . . . Invariably, their first reaction to the mirror was to respond as if they were seeing another chimpanzee. . . . After about two days, however. . . . they . . . started to use the mirror to groom and inspect parts of their bodies they had not seen before, and progressively began to experiment with the reflection by making faces, looking at themselves upside down, and assuming unusual postures while monitoring the results in the mirror. . . .

So in an attempt to provide a more convincing demonstration of self-recognition, I devised an unobtrusive and more rigorous test. . . . each chimpanzee was anesthetized. . . . I carefully painted the uppermost portion of an eyebrow ridge and the top half of the opposite ear with a bright red, odorless, alcohol soluble dye. . . .

Following recovery from anesthesia. . . . the mirror was then reintroduced as an explicit test of self-recognition. Upon seeing their painted faces in the mirror, all the chimpanzees showed repeated mark-directed responses, consisting of attempts to touch and inspect marked areas on their eyebrow and ear while watching the image. In addition, there was over a three-fold increase in viewing time. . . . Several chimpanzees also showed noteworthy attempts to visually examine and smell the fingers which had been used to touch these facial marks. I suspect that you would respond pretty much the same way, if upon awakening one morning you saw yourself in the mirror with red spots on your face. (Gallup, 1983, pp. 474–477)

Nature-or-nurture thinking runs into difficulty The history of nature-or-nurture thinking can be summed up by paraphrasing Mark Twain: "Reports of its death have been greatly exaggerated." Each time that it has been discredited, it has resurfaced in a slightly modified form. First, it was shown that genetics and learning are not the only factors that influence behavioral development—factors such as the fetal environment, nutrition, stress, and sensory stimulation are also influential. This led to a broadening of the concept of nurture to include a variety of experiential factors in addition to learning. In effect, it changed the nature-or-nurture dichotomy from "genetic factors or learning" to "genetic factors or experience." Next it was shown that behavior develops under the combined control of both nature and nurture (e.g., Hofer, 1981; Gottlieb, 1983; Johnston, 1987; Fentress & McLeod, 1986), not under the control of one or the other. Faced with this discovery, many people merely substituted one kind of nature-nurture thinking for another. They stopped asking, "Is it genetic or is it the result of experience?" and started asking, "How much of it is genetic and how much of it is the result of experience?"

Like earlier versions of the nature-nurture question, the how-much-of-it-is-genetic-and-how-much-of-it-is-the-result-of-experience version is fundamentally flawed. The problem is that it is based on the premise that genetic factors and experiential factors combine in an additive fashion—that a behavioral capacity, such as intelligence, is created through the combination of so many parts of genetics and so many parts of experience. Once you learn more about how genetic factors and experience interact, you will better appreciate the folly of this assumption, but for the time being, let me illustrate its weakness with a metaphor embedded in an anecdote.

Recently, one of my students told me that she had read that intelligence was one-third genetic and two-thirds experience, and she wondered whether this was true. She must have been puzzled when I began my response by describing an alpine experience. "I was lazily wandering up a summit ridge when I heard an unexpected sound. Ahead, with his back to me, was a young man sitting on the edge of a precipice, blowing into a peculiar musical instrument. I sat down behind him on a large sun-soaked rock, ate my lunch, and shared his experience with him. Then, I got up and wandered back down the ridge, leaving him undisturbed. I have frequently wondered about the musician, his music, and the powerful effect that it had on me. Then, I put the following question to my student: "If I wanted to get a better understanding of the music, would it be reasonable for me to begin by asking how much of it came from the musician and how much of it came from the instrument?"

"That would be dumb," she said. "The music comes from both; it makes no sense to ask how much comes from the musician and how much comes from the instrument. Somehow the music results from the interaction of the two, and you would have to ask about the interaction."

"That's exactly right," I said. "Now, do you see why . . . "

"Don't say any more," she interrupted. "I see what you're getting at. Intelligence is the product of the interaction of genes and experience, and it is dumb to try to find how much comes from genes and how much comes from experience."

"And the same is true of any other behavioral trait," I added.

Several months later the same student strode into my office, reached into her pack, and pulled out a familiar object. It was an instrument like the one that had intrigued me. "I believe that this is your mystery instrument," she said. "It's a Peruvian panpipe." She was right . . . again.

Asking the right questions about the biology of behavior   So far in this section, you have learned some of the reasons why people have tended to think about the biology of behavior in terms of dichotomies, and you have learned some of the reasons why this way of thinking is inappropriate. Now, let's look at the way of thinking about the biology of behavior that has been adopted by most of the women and men who are at the cutting edge of biopsychological science (see Kimble, 1989). This way of thinking is directing biopsychologists to key questions, and it is providing a strong theoretical infrastructure for the interpretation of their findings. It works for them, and it can work for you.

The way that modern biopsychologists think about biopsychological processes is illustrated in Figure 2.2. Like other powerful ideas, it is simple and logical. This 5-stage model boils down to the single premise that all behavior is the product of interactions among three factors: (1) an organism's genetic endowment, which is a product of its evolution, (2) its experience, and (3) its perception of the current situation. Please examine the model carefully and consider its implications; it sets the stage for the remainder of this book.

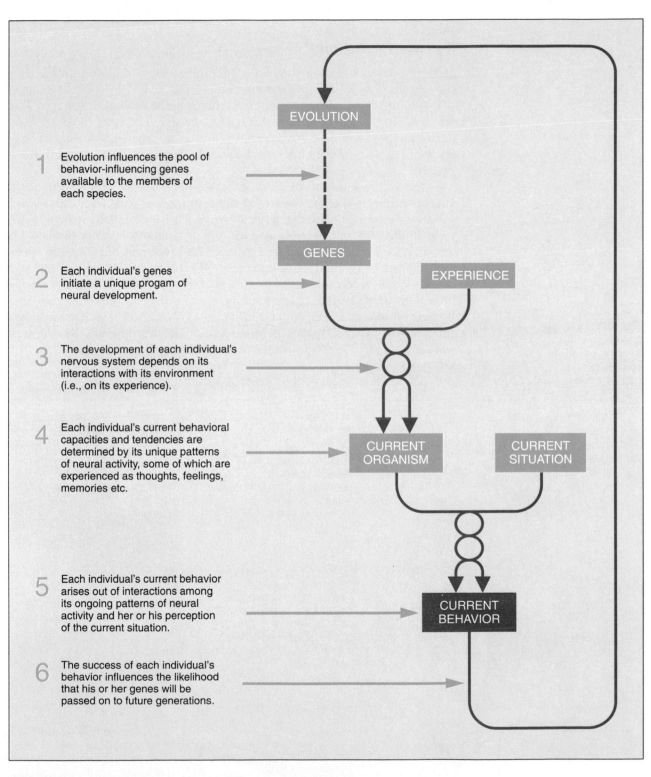

1 Evolution influences the pool of behavior-influencing genes available to the members of each species.

2 Each individual's genes initiate a unique progam of neural development.

3 The development of each individual's nervous system depends on its interactions with its environment (i.e., on its experience).

4 Each individual's current behavioral capacities and tendencies are determined by its unique patterns of neural activity, some of which are experienced as thoughts, feelings, memories etc.

5 Each individual's current behavior arises out of interactions among its ongoing patterns of neural activity and her or his perception of the current situation.

6 The success of each individual's behavior influences the likelihood that his or her genes will be passed on to future generations.

FIGURE 2.2

A schematic illustration of the way that most modern biopsychologists think about the biology of behavior.

2.2

Human Evolution

Modern biology began in 1859 with the publication of Charles Darwin's *On the Origins of Species.* In this monumental work, Darwin described his theory of evolution, the single most influential theory in the biological sciences. Darwin was not the first to suggest that species **evolve** (i.e., undergo gradual orderly change) from preexisting species, but he was the first to amass a large body of supporting evidence, and he was the first to suggest how evolution occurs.

Darwin presented three kinds of evidence to support his assertion that species evolve: (1) He documented the evolution of fossil records through progressively more recent geological layers. (2) He described striking structural similarities among living species (e.g., a human's hand, a bird's wing, and a cat's paw), which suggested that they had evolved from common ancestors. (3) And he pointed to the major changes that had been brought about in domestic plants and animals by programs of selective breeding. However, the most convincing evidence of evolution comes from direct observations of evolution in progress. For example, Grant (1991) recently observed evolution of the finches of the Galápagos Islands—a population studied by Darwin himself—after only a single season of drought. Figure 2.3 illustrates these four kinds of evidence.

FIGURE 2.3

Four kinds of evidence that support the theory that species evolve.

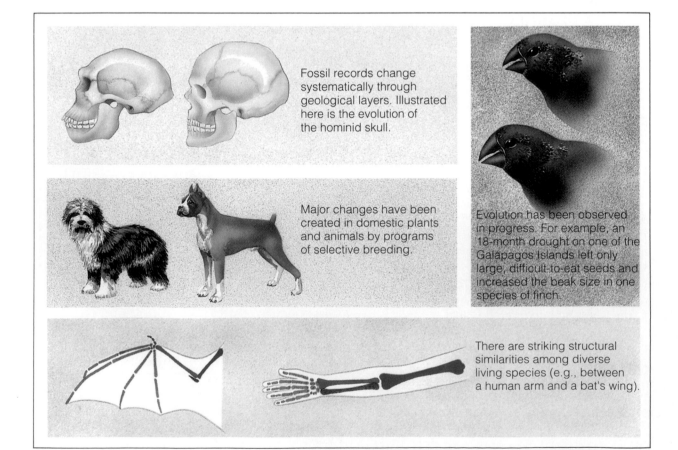

Fossil records change systematically through geological layers. Illustrated here is the evolution of the hominid skull.

Major changes have been created in domestic plants and animals by programs of selective breeding.

Evolution has been observed in progress. For example, an 18-month drought on one of the Galápagos Islands left only large, difficult-to-eat seeds and increased the beak size in one species of finch.

There are striking structural similarities among diverse living species (e.g., between a human arm and a bat's wing).

Darwin argued that evolution occurs through **natural selection.** He pointed out that the members of each species vary greatly in their structure, physiology, and behavior, and that those heritable traits that are associated with high rates of survival and reproduction are the most likely ones to be passed on to future generations. He argued that this process of natural selection, when repeated generation after generation, leads to the evolution of species that are better adapted to surviving and reproducing in their particular environmental niche. Darwin called this process *natural selection* to emphasize its similarity to the artificial selective breeding practices employed by breeders of domestic animals—just as race horse breeders create faster horses by selectively breeding the fastest of their existing stock, nature creates fitter animals by selectively breeding the fittest. **Fitness,** in the Darwinian sense, refers to the ability of an organism to survive and contribute large numbers of fertile offspring to the next generation.

The theory of evolution was at odds with the various dogmatic views of creation that were embedded in the nineteenth century Zeitgeist, and so it met with considerable initial resistance. Although traces of this resistance still exist, virtually none comes from people who understand the evidence.

> . . . evolution by natural selection meets no significant opposition within biological science. The principle of natural selection has a logical necessity to it; indeed, some have argued that it is a tautology rather than an empirical law . . . subsequent development of biology in major new areas like genetics and biochemistry has only reinforced Darwin's conclusion that the facts make a belief in the theory of evolution by natural selection "inescapable." (Daly & Wilson, 1983, p. 7)

Evolution and Behavior

Some behaviors play an obvious role in evolution—for example, the ability to find food, avoid predation, and defend one's young obviously increase an animal's ability to pass on its heritable characteristics to future generations. Other behaviors play a role that is less obvious but no less important; two examples are social dominance and courtship display.

Social dominance   The males of many social species establish a stable *hierarchy of social dominance* through a series of pair-wise encounters. In most species, these encounters involve a great deal of posturing and threatening, with very little physical damage. The dominant male wins encounters with all other males of the group; the number 2 male wins encounters with all males except the dominant male; and so on down the line. Once a hierarchy is established, hostilities diminish because lower ranking males learn to avoid or quickly submit to more dominant males.

Why is social dominance an important factor in evolution? The reason is that dominant males copulate more than nondominant males, and thus are more effective in passing on their characteristics to future generations. McCann (1981) studied the effect of social dominance on the rate of copulation in 10 bull elephant seals that cohabited the same breeding beach. As illustrated in Figure 2.4, these massive animals challenge one another by raising themselves to full height and pushing chest to chest. Usually the smaller of the two backs down; if it does not, a vicious neck-biting battle ensues. McCann

FIGURE 2.4

Two massive bull elephant seals challenge one another. The smaller, uninvolved elephant seals are females.

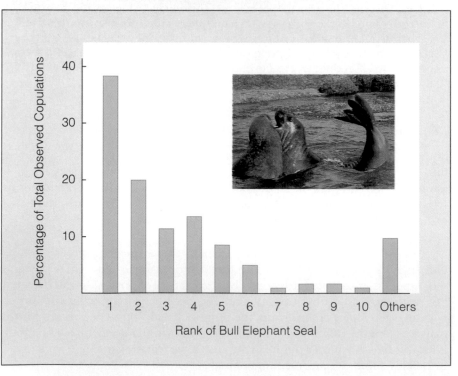

FIGURE 2.5

Dominant bull elephant seals copulate more frequently than those that are lower in the dominance hierarchy. (Adapted from McCann, 1981.)

found that the dominant male copulated 38 times during the study, whereas poor number 10 copulated only once—see Figure 2.5.

Courtship display   An intricate series of courtship displays precedes copulation in many species. The male approaches the female and signals his interest—the signal may be chemical, visual, auditory, or tactual. This signal may elicit a signal in the female, which may elicit another response in the

FIGURE 2.6
A courtship display of the male peacock.

male, and so on until copulation ensues. But copulation is unlikely to occur if one of the pair fails to react to the signals of the other.

Courtship displays are thought to promote the evolution of new species. Let me explain. A **species** is a group of organisms that is reproductively isolated from other organisms; the members of one species cannot produce fertile offspring by mating with members of other species. A new species begins to branch off from an existing species when some barrier discourages breeding between a subpopulation of the existing species and the remainder of the species. Once such a reproductive barrier forms, the subpopulation evolves independently of the remainder of the species until cross fertilization becomes impossible. The reproductive barrier may be geographic; for example, a few birds may fly together to an isolated island, where many generations of their offspring breed among themselves and evolve into a separate species. Alternatively—to get back to the main point of the paragraph—the reproductive barrier may be behavioral. A few members of a species may develop different courtship displays, and these may form a reproductive barrier between themselves and the rest of their **conspecifics** (i.e., members of the same species). Figure 2.6 illustrates a courtship display of the male peacock.

Human Evolution

By studying fossil records and comparing current species, we humans have looked back in time and pieced together the evolutionary history of our species. Human evolution, as it is currently understood, is summarized in this section.

FIGURE 2.7

Florida walking catfish travel on land by propelling themselves with their fins.

Evolution of vertebrates   Single-cell water-dwelling organisms first appeared on earth about 600 million years ago. About 150 million years later, the first **chordates** (KOR dates) evolved. Chordates are animals with dorsal nerve cords; they are 1 of the 20 or so large categories, or *phyla* (FY la) into which zoologists group animal species. The first chordates with spinal bones to protect their dorsal nerve cords evolved about 25 million years later. The spinal bones are called *vertebrae* (VERT eh bray), and the chordates that possess them are called **vertebrates.** The first vertebrates were primitive bony fishes. Today, there are seven classes of vertebrates: three classes of fishes, plus amphibians, reptiles, birds, and mammals.

Evolution of amphibians   About 410 million years ago, the first bony fishes ventured out of the water. Fishes that could survive on land for brief periods of time had two great advantages: They could escape from stagnant pools to nearby fresh water, and they could take advantage of terrestrial food sources. If you have difficulty with the concept of land-traveling fishes, you obviously do not live in Florida. *Florida walking catfish* routinely travel over land from pond to pond—see Figure 2.7.

The advantages of life on land were so great that natural selection transformed the fins and gills of bony fishes to legs and lungs, respectively—and so it was that the first **amphibians** evolved about 400 million years ago. Amphibians (e.g., frogs, toads, and salamanders) in their larval form must live in the water; only the adult amphibian can survive on land.

Evolution of reptiles   About 300 million years ago, reptiles (e.g., lizards, snakes, and turtles) evolved from amphibians. Reptiles were the first vertebrates to lay shell-covered eggs and to be covered by dry scales. Both these adaptations reduced the reliance of reptiles on watery habitats. A reptile does not have to spend the first stage of its life in the watery environment of a pond or lake; it spends the first stage of its life in the watery environment of a shell-covered egg. And once hatched, a reptile can live far from water because its dry scales eliminate water loss through its water-permeable skin.

Evolution of mammals   About 180 million years ago, during the height of the age of dinosaurs, an important set of changes began to evolve in one line of small reptiles. The females of this line fed their young with secretions from special glands called *mammary glands;* the members of this line are called **mammals** after these glands. Eventually mammals stopped laying eggs; instead, the females nurtured their young in the watery environment of their bodies until the young were mature enough to be born. The *duck-billed platypus* is the only remaining mammalian species that lays eggs.

Spending the first stage of life inside one's mother proved to have considerable survival value; it provided the long-term security and environmental stability necessary for complex programs of development to unfold. Today, there are 14 different orders of mammals. The one to which we belong is the order **primates.** We humans—in our usual humble way—named our order after the Latin *primus,* which means "first" or "foremost." There are five different groups of primates: prosimians, new-world monkeys, old-world monkeys, apes, and hominids. Humans (i.e., *Homo sapiens*) are the only surviving species of the hominid line. Examples of each of the five groups appear in Figure 2.8.

PROSIMIAN
A lemur

OLD-WORLD MONKEY
A Mandrill baboon

APE
A gorilla

HOMINID
A human

NEW-WORLD MONKEY
A Woolly monkey

FIGURE 2.8

Examples of the five different groups of primates.

The current *prosimians* (e.g., tree shrews and lemurs) resemble the first primates; they are small squirrel-like, insect-eating creatures with grasping feet, which are well-adapted to their *arboreal* (tree) existence. The *new-world monkeys* (e.g., squirrel monkeys and Woolly monkeys) currently inhabit the Americas. They are believed to have evolved from the prosimian line. Like the prosimians, they are arboreal, but their front paws are more hand-like, their brains are larger, their depth perception is better, and they are generally more humanoid in appearance. The *old-world monkeys* currently inhabit Africa and Asia; they have larger brains than new-world monkeys; and they live in more complex societies. Some old-world monkeys are primarily arboreal (e.g., macaques and langurs); others are primarily terrestrial (e.g., baboons and mandrills). Old-world monkeys have *opposable thumbs* and hardened skin pads on their buttocks, which are brilliantly colored in some species.

Apes (e.g., gibbons, orangutans, gorillas, chimpanzees) are thought to have evolved from a line of old-world monkeys. Unlike old-world monkeys, apes do not have tails, but they have retained other specializations that facilitate arboreal travel—for example, long arms and grasping hindfeet. Apes can walk upright for short distances, but they usually walk on all fours. Like old-world monkeys, apes have opposable thumbs that are not long enough to be of much use for precise manipulation (see Figure 2.9).

FIGURE 2.9

A comparison of the feet and hands of a human and an ape.

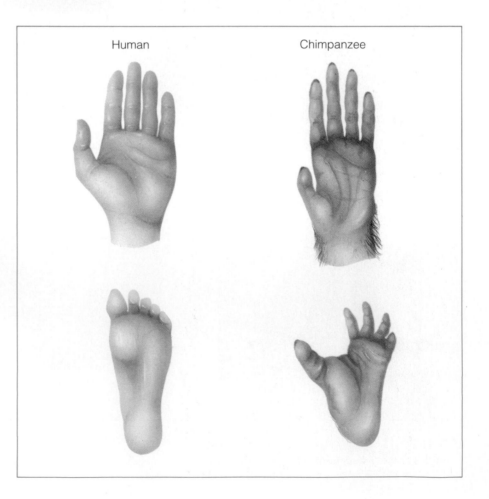

The birth of humankind   The *hominid* line is composed of two different genuses: the genus *Australopithecus* and the genus *Homo,* of which humans **(Homo sapiens)** are the only surviving species. The fossil and genetic evidence suggests that the Australopithecines evolved from a line of African apes about 5 million years ago (*australo* means *southern; pithecus* means *ape*). Three different species of Australopithecus are thought to have roamed the plains of Africa in small groups for about 3.5 million years before becoming extinct. Australopithecines were only about 1.3 meters (4 feet) tall, and they had small brains, but analysis of their pelvis and leg bones indicates that their walk was as upright as yours or mine. Any doubts about the upright gait of Australopithecines were erased by the discovery of the fossilized footprints pictured in Figure 2.10.

FIGURE 2.10

Australopithecine hominids strode across the African volcanic ash about 3.6 million years ago. They left a 70-meter trail that was discovered in 1978. There were two adults and a child, who walked in their footsteps.

The sudden appearance in the fossil record of a prehuman creature with a fully upright walk makes an important point about evolution. Darwin thought of evolution as a gradual, continuous process; however, the fossil record paints a different picture. The fossils of most species change little for millions of years; then, within a few thousand years, there is a significant transformation, presumably under pressure from some major change in the environment. Because major transformations occur relatively quickly, fossil records of intermediate stages are often difficult to find. Accordingly, the sudden appearance in the fossil records of the fully upright Australopithecines with no fossil evidence of an intermediate semistooped ancestor represents the rule rather than the exception. Like American football, evolution is characterized by brief periods of turmoil interspersed with long periods during which very little happens.

The first Homo species, **Homo erectus,** is thought to have evolved from a species of *Australopithecus* about 1.5 million years ago. It was so named because of the incorrect initial assumption that its predecessors were stooped. The most distinctive feature of the *Homo erectus* skull is its large brain cavity (about 850 cubic centimeters); it is far larger than that of Australopithecus (about 500 cc.), but far smaller than that of modern humans (about 1350 cc.). *Homo erectus* used tools and fire. It coexisted in Africa with *Australopithecus* for a few hundred thousand years, but *Australopithecus* gradually died out and *Homo erectus* spread into Asia—its remains have been found at Asian sites near Peking and on the Indonesian island of Java.

About 200,000 years ago, *Homo erectus* was gradually replaced in the fossil record by **Neanderthals.** Although Neanderthals were extremely short and stocky by modern human standards, the fact that their brain cavities were as large as those of modern humans has led many to conclude that they were the first true humans. Neanderthals were replaced in the fossil record by **Cro-Magnons** about 25,000 years ago, and with the ascent of Cro-Magnons came the first artistic artifacts (wall paintings and carvings). Ranching and farming were not established until 10,000 years ago, and writing did not appear until 3,000 years ago. Paradoxically, although the big three human attributes—big brain, upright walk, and free hands with a workable opposing thumb—have been with us for hundreds of thousands of years, most human accomplishments are of recent origin.

Figure 2.11 illustrates the main branches of vertebrate evolution. As you examine it, remember that only a small portion (less than 1%) of all species are still in existence; that evolution does not proceed in a straight line toward some optimal design (metaphorically, evolution is a bush, not a ladder, a scale, or even a tree); and that we humans have little reason to claim evolutionary supremacy—we are the one surviving species of a line (hominids) that has existed for only a blip of evolutionary time.

This is life's little joke. By imposing the model of the ladder on the reality of [evolutionary] bushes, we have guaranteed that our classic examples of evolutionary progress can only apply to unsuccessful lineages on the very brink of extermination—for we can linearize a bush only if it maintains but one surviving twig that we can falsely place at the summit of a ladder. [It is our own tenuousness as a species] that permits us to build a ladder reaching only to the heart of our own folly and hubris. (Gould, 1991, p. 181)

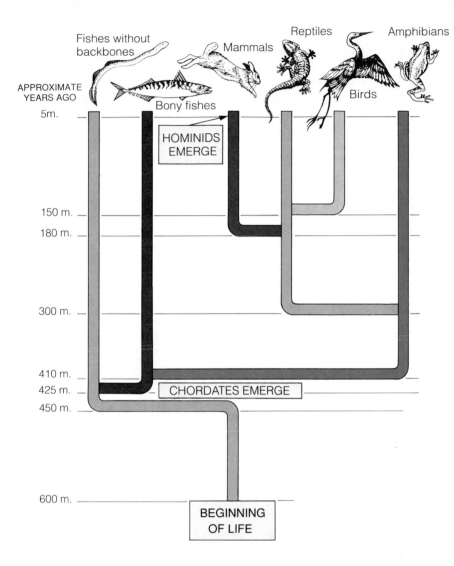

APPROXIMATE
YEARS AGO

Fishes without
backbones

Mammals

Reptiles

Amphibians

Bony fishes

Birds

5m.

HOMINIDS
EMERGE

150 m.

180 m.

300 m.

410 m.

425 m.

CHORDATES EMERGE

450 m.

600 m.

BEGINNING
OF LIFE

FIGURE 2.11
Vertebrate evolution.

Evolution of the Human Brain

Early research on the evolution of the human brain focused on size. This research was stimulated by the assumption that brain size and intellectual capacity are closely related. This assumption ran into two problems. First, it was shown that modern humans—whom modern humans believe to be the most intelligent of all creatures—do not have the biggest brains. At 1,350 grams, humans rank far behind whales and elephants, whose brains weigh between 5,000 and 8,000 grams (Harvey & Krebs, 1990). Second, the brains of deceased intellectuals (e.g., Einstein) were found to be no match for their gigantic intellects. Modern adult human brains vary greatly in size—between about 1,000 and 2,000 grams—but there is no clear relation between brain size and intelligence.

One obvious problem in relating brain size to intelligence is the fact that larger animals tend to have larger brains, presumably because larger bodies require more brain tissue to control and regulate them. Thus, the fact that large men tend to have larger brains than small men, that men tend to have larger brains than women, and that elephants have larger brains than humans does not suggest anything about the relative intelligence of these populations. This has led to the proposal that brain weight expressed as a percentage of total body weight might be a better measure of intellectual capacity. This measure allows humans (2.33%) to take their rightful place ahead of elephants (0.20%), but it also allows both humans and elephants to be surpassed by that intellectual giant of the animal kingdom, the shrew (3.33%).

> The physical structure of the brain must record intelligence in some way, but gross size and external shape are not likely to capture anything of value. I am, somehow, less interested in the weight, and convolutions of Einstein's brain than in the near certainty that people of equal talent have lived and died in cotton fields and sweat shops (Gould, 1980, p. 151).

A more reasonable approach to the study of brain evolution has been to compare the evolution of different brain regions. For example, it has been informative to consider the evolution of the **brain stem** separately from the evolution of the **cerebrum** (cerebral hemispheres). In general, the brain stem regulates reflex activities that are critical for survival (e.g., heart rate, respiration, blood glucose level), whereas the cerebrum is involved in more complex adaptive processes such as learning, perception, and motivation. Figure 2.12 is a schematic representation of the relative size of the brain stems and cerebrums of several species that are living ancestors of species from which humans evolved. This figure makes three important points about the evolution of the human brain. The first is that it has increased in size during evolution; the second is that most of the increase in size has occurred in the cerebrum;

Frog

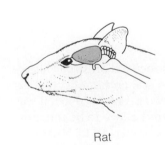

Rat

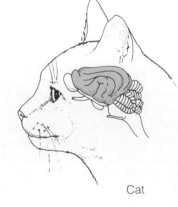

Cat

FIGURE 2.12

Schematic side views of the brains of a series of modern animals. They are in order of their evolutionary age, from the oldest (frog) to most recently evolved (human). Cerebrums are shown in peach color.

and the third is that there has been an increase in the number of **convolutions** (folds) on the cerebral surface, which has greatly increased the volume of **cerebral cortex,** the outermost layer of cerebral tissue.

More significant than the differences among the brains of various related species are their similarities. All brains are constructed of *neurons,* and the neural structures that compose the brains of one species can almost always be found in the brains of related species. For example, if one were to dissect the brains of a human, a monkey, a rat, and a mouse—common subjects of biopsychological research—one would find the same gross structures in each brain.

Conclusion

In this section, you have been confronted by two indisputable facts of life: (1) You and I and all other living animals are the cumulative products of 600 million years of adaptation; (2) We humans are related to all other animal species—in some cases, more closely than we like to admit. Pondering the implications of these truths can be humbling, but that is not why I introduced them here. I introduced them because of their pervasive influence on biopsychological research. Biopsychologists often study behavior and neural mechanisms by focusing on their adaptiveness and the environmental pressures that led to their evolution—this is called the **functional approach.** And biopsychologists often try to learn about the behaviors and neural mechanisms of one species, usually humans, by studying the behaviors and neural mechanisms of related species—this is called the **comparative approach.**

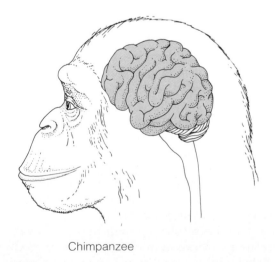

Chimpanzee

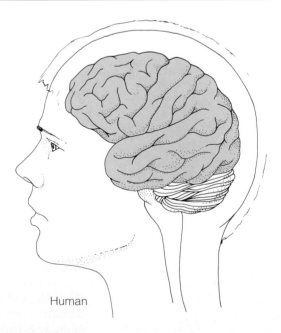

Human

2.3

Behavioral Genetics

Darwin did not understand two of the key facts on which his theory of evolution was based. He did not understand why conspecifics differ from one another, and he did not understand how anatomical, physiological, and behavioral characteristics are passed from parent to offspring. While Darwin puzzled over these questions, there was an unread manuscript in his files that contained the answers. It had been sent to him by an unknown Augustinian monk, Gregor Mendel. Unfortunately for Darwin (1809–1882) and for Mendel (1822–1884), the significance of Mendel's research was not recognized until the early part of this century, well after both of their deaths.

Mendelian Genetics

Mendel studied inheritance in pea plants. In designing his experiments, he made two wise decisions. He decided to study dichotomous traits, and he decided to begin his experiments by crossing the offspring of true-breeding lines. **Dichotomous traits** are traits that occur in one form or the other, never in combination—for example, seed color is a dichotomous pea plant trait; every pea plant has either brown seeds or white seeds. **True-breeding lines** are those in which interbred members always produce offspring with the same trait (e.g., brown seeds) generation after generation.

In one of his early experiments, Mendel studied the inheritance of seed color: brown or white. He began by cross breeding the offspring of a line of pea plants that had bred true for brown seeds with the offspring of a line of pea plants that had bred true for white seeds. The offspring of this cross all had brown seeds. Then Mendel bred these first-generation offspring with one another, and he found that about three quarters of the resulting second-generation offspring had brown seeds and about one-quarter had white seeds. Mendel repeated this experiment many times with various pairs of dichotomous pea plant traits, and each time the result was the same. One trait, which Mendel called the *dominant trait*, appeared in all of the first-generation offspring; the other trait, which he called the *recessive trait,* appeared in about one-quarter of the second generation offspring. Mendel would have obtained a similar result if he had conducted an experiment with true-breeding lines of brown-eyed (dominant) and blue-eyed (recessive) humans.

This finding challenged the central premise upon which all previous ideas about inheritance had rested: the premise that offspring inherit the traits of their parents. Somehow the recessive trait (e.g., white seeds) was passed on to one-quarter of the second-generation pea plants by first-generation pea plants that did not themselves possess it. An organism's observable traits are referred to as its *phenotype;* the traits that it can pass on to its offspring through its genetic material are referred to as its *genotype.*

Mendel devised a theory to explain his results. It comprised four ideas. First, Mendel proposed that there are two kinds of inherited factors for each dichotomous trait—for example, that a brown-seed factor and a white-seed factor control seed color. Today, we call these factors **genes.** Second, Mendel proposed that each organism possesses two genes for each of its dichotomous traits; for example, that each pea plant possesses either two brown-seed genes, two white-seed genes, or one of each. Organisms that possess two identical genes for a trait are said to be **homozygous** for that trait; those that possess two different genes for a trait are said to be **heterozygous** for that trait. Third, Mendel proposed that one of the two kinds of genes for each dichotomous trait dominates the other in heterozygous organisms—for example, pea plants with a brown-seed gene and a white-seed gene always have brown seeds because the brown-seed gene always dominates the white-seed gene. And fourth, Mendel proposed that each organism randomly inherits one of its "father's" two factors for each trait and one of its "mother's" two factors. Figure 2.13 illustrates how Mendel's theory accounts for the result of his experiment on the inheritance of seed color in pea plants.

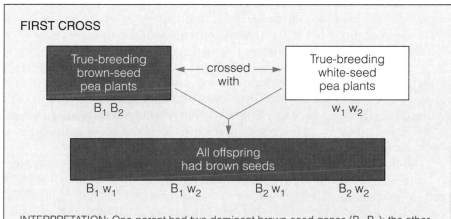

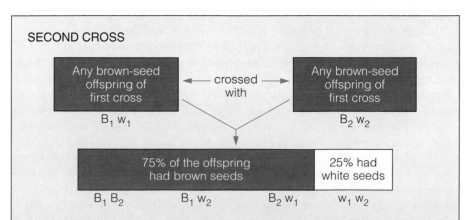

FIGURE 2.13

How Mendel's theory accounts for the results of his experiment on the inheritance of seed color in pea plants.

Chromosomes

It was not until 1903 that Sutton, an American geneticist, correctly inferred that genes are located on **chromosomes,** thread-like structures in the *nucleus* of each cell. Chromosomes occur in matched pairs, and each species has a characteristic number of pairs of chromosomes in each of its body cells—humans have 23 pairs. The two genes that control each trait are situated at the same location on both chromosomes of a particular pair.

The cell division that produces the **gametes** (egg cells or sperm cells) is called **meiosis** (MY oh sis). In meiosis, the chromosomes divide, and one chromosome of each pair goes to each of the two gametes that results from the division. As a result, each gamete has only half the usual number of chromosomes (23 in humans), and when a sperm cell and an egg cell combine during fertilization, a cell with the full complement of chromosomes is produced. All other cell division in the body occurs by **mitosis** (MY toe sis). Just prior to mitotic division, the number of chromosomes doubles so that when the division occurs, both daughter cells end up with the full complement of chromosomes. Figure 2.14 illustrates meiosis and mitosis.

Meiosis accounts for much of the genetic diversity within each species. In humans, for example, each meiotic division produces two gametes; each gamete contains one chromosome from each of the 23 pairs contained in each body cell. Because each of the 23 pairs is randomly sorted into the two gametes, each human can produce gametes with 2^{23} different combinations of chromosomes.

The first comprehensive study of **linkage** was published in 1915 by Morgan and his colleagues. They found that there are four different clusters of fruit fly genes. If the gene for one trait in a cluster was inherited by a fruit fly, that fruit fly had a higher probability (i.e., greater than 0.5) of inheriting genes for other traits in the same cluster. Because fruit flies have four pairs of chromosomes, Morgan and his colleagues concluded that linkage occurs between traits that are encoded on the same chromosome. They were correct; in every species in which linkage has been assessed, the number of clusters of linked traits has been found to equal the number of pairs of chromosomes.

The theory that genes on the same chromosome tend to be inherited together created a puzzle. If genes are passed down from generation to generation on chromosomes, why are the genes on the same chromosome not always inherited together? The linkage between pairs of genes on a single chromosome varies from almost complete (i.e., close to 1.0) to just above chance (i.e., just over 0.5). Morgan and his colleagues proposed that **crossing over** provided the solution to this puzzle. Figure 2.15 illustrates how crossing over works. During the first stage of meiosis, chromosomes that have the same general structure and encode the same traits line up in pairs. Then, they cross over one another at some random point, break apart at the point of contact, and exchange sections of chromosome. As a result, parents do not pass on intact chromosomal clusters of genes to their children—for example, each of your gametes contains chromosomes that are unique spliced-together combinations of chromosomes inherited from your mother and father.

The phenomenon of crossing over is important for two reasons. First, by ensuring that chromosomes are not passed intact from generation to generation, crossovers increase the diversity of the species—in a sense, crossing over shuffles the genetic deck before the chromosomes are randomly dealt out to

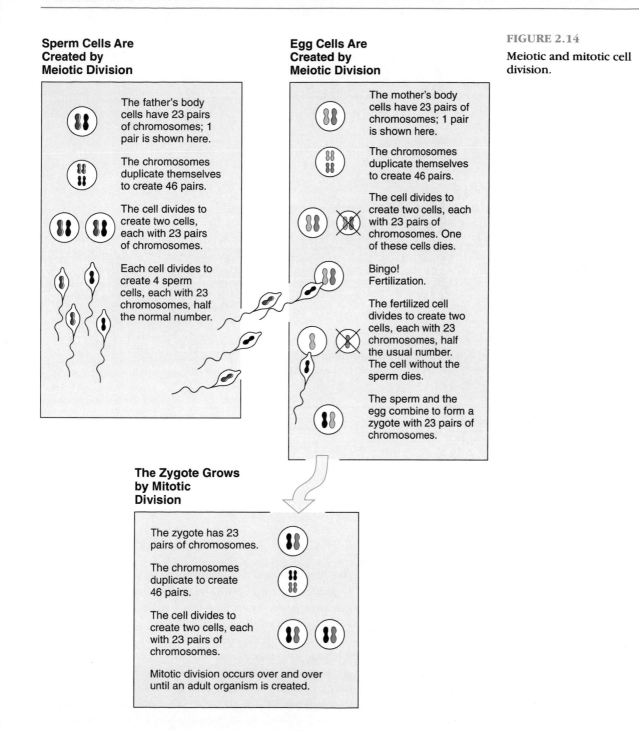

FIGURE 2.14

Meiotic and mitotic cell division.

Sperm Cells Are Created by Meiotic Division

The father's body cells have 23 pairs of chromosomes; 1 pair is shown here.

The chromosomes duplicate themselves to create 46 pairs.

The cell divides to create two cells, each with 23 pairs of chromosomes.

Each cell divides to create 4 sperm cells, each with 23 chromosomes, half the normal number.

Egg Cells Are Created by Meiotic Division

The mother's body cells have 23 pairs of chromosomes; 1 pair is shown here.

The chromosomes duplicate themselves to create 46 pairs.

The cell divides to create two cells, each with 23 pairs of chromosomes. One of these cells dies.

Bingo! Fertilization.

The fertilized cell divides to create two cells, each with 23 chromosomes, half the usual number. The cell without the sperm dies.

The sperm and the egg combine to form a zygote with 23 pairs of chromosomes.

The Zygote Grows by Mitotic Division

The zygote has 23 pairs of chromosomes.

The chromosomes duplicate to create 46 pairs.

The cell divides to create two cells, each with 23 pairs of chromosomes.

Mitotic division occurs over and over until an adult organism is created.

the next generation. Second, the study of crossovers has been one of the major means by which geneticists have been able to construct **gene maps** for many species. Because each crossover occurs at a random point along the length of a chromosome, geneticists have been able to determine the relative positions of the various genes along a chromosome by measuring the degree of linkage between them. The degree of linkage between two genes indicates

FIGURE 2.15
Crossing over.

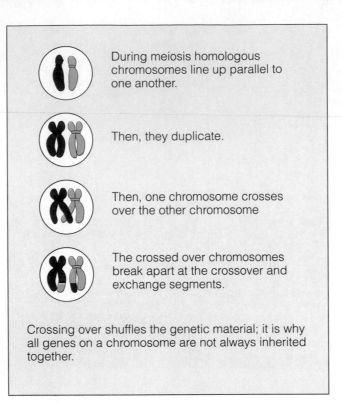

During meiosis homologous chromosomes line up parallel to one another.

Then, they duplicate.

Then, one chromosome crosses over the other chromosome

The crossed over chromosomes break apart at the crossover and exchange segments.

Crossing over shuffles the genetic material; it is why all genes on a chromosome are not always inherited together.

how close they are together on the chromosome; crossovers rarely occur between adjacent genes and frequently occur between genes at opposite ends of a chromosome. Detailed gene maps exist for several species, and rapid progress is currently being made in mapping human genes.

Mechanisms of Gene Action

Each chromosome is a double-stranded deoxyribonucleic acid (DNA) molecule. Each strand is a sequence of nucleotide bases that are attached to a chain of *phosphate* and *deoxyribose*. There are four nucleotide bases: *adenine, thymine, guanine,* and *cytosine.* It is the sequence of bases on each chromosome that constitutes the genetic code—just as the sequence of letters constitutes the code of our language.

The two strands that compose each chromosome are coiled around each other and bonded together by the attraction of adenine for thymine and guanine for cytosine. This specific bonding pattern has an important consequence. It means that the two strands that compose each chromosome are exact complements of one another. For example, the sequence adenine, guanine, thymine, cytosine, guanine on one strand is always attached to the complementary sequence thymine, cytosine; adenine, guanine, cytosine on the other. Figure 2.16 illustrates the structure of DNA. Figure 2.17 is a photomicrograph of a DNA molecule.

DNA is capable of self-duplication and translation. **Self-duplication** refers to the DNA molecule's ability to replicate (duplicate) itself. **Translation** refers to the DNA molecule's ability to translate its genetic information into

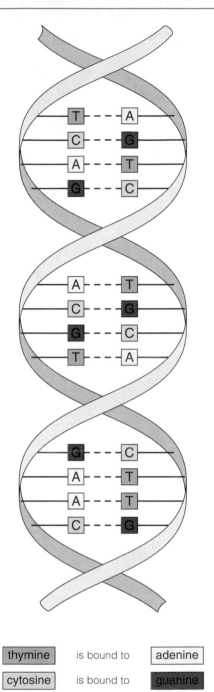

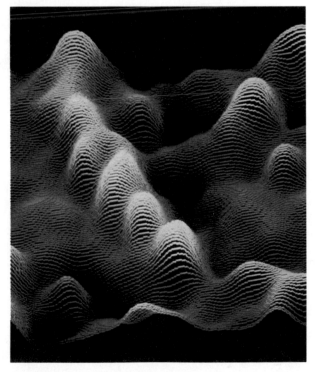

FIGURE 2.16

A schematic illustration of the structure of a DNA molecule. Notice its double-stranded coiled structure and the complementary binding of nucleotide bases, adenine to thymine and guanine to cytosine.

FIGURE 2.17

A photomicrograph of deoxyribonucleic acid (DNA). The line of peaks running down the left side represent the helices of one double-stranded molecule.

| thymine | is bound to | adenine |
| cytosine | is bound to | guanine |

proteins. Figure 2.18 illustrates how DNA duplicates itself during the process of mitotic cell division. The two strands of DNA separate; then the exposed nucleotide bases on each of the two strands attract complementary bases from the *cytoplasm* (inner fluid) of the cell until two double-stranded DNA molecules, both of which are identical to the original, have been created.

Chromosome duplication does not always go according to plan: There are errors. Sometimes these errors are gross errors—for example, in *Down's*

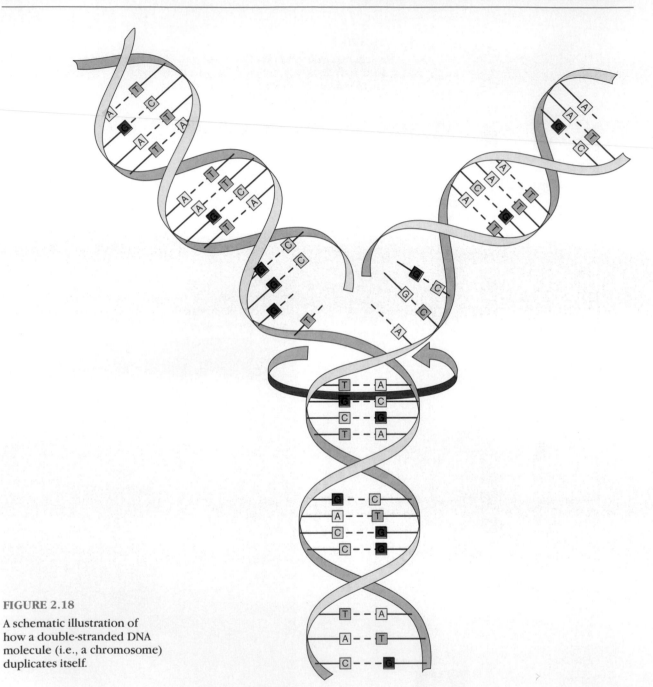

FIGURE 2.18

A schematic illustration of how a double-stranded DNA molecule (i.e., a chromosome) duplicates itself.

syndrome, which you will learn about in Chapter 6, there is an extra chromosome in each cell. But more commonly, errors in duplication take the form of **mutations,** accidental alterations in individual genes. In most cases, mutations disappear from the genetic pool within a few generations because the organisms that inherit them are less fit. Some scientists believe that in rare instances mutations increase fitness and in so doing contribute to the evolution of the species.

Figure 2.19 illustrates how a molecule of DNA translates its genetic information into proteins. **Proteins** are long chains of **amino acids**; they form the structure of cells and control their physiological activities. First, the double-stranded DNA molecule splits apart, and each strand serves as a *template* for the creation of a complementary strand of **ribonucleic acid** or RNA. RNA is

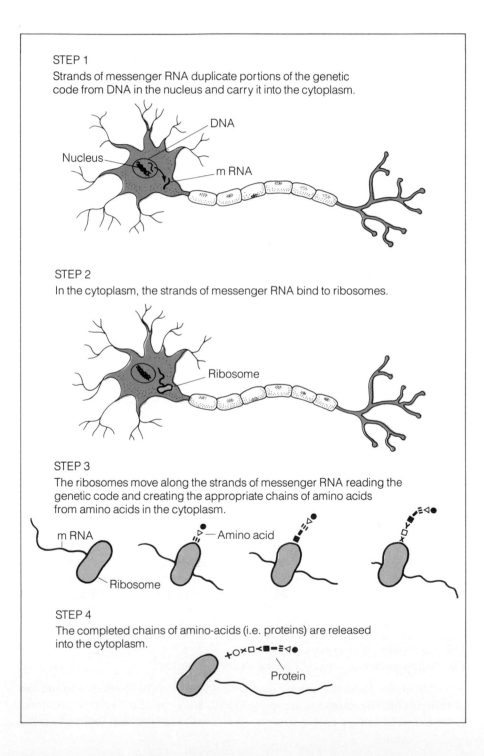

STEP 1

Strands of messenger RNA duplicate portions of the genetic code from DNA in the nucleus and carry it into the cytoplasm.

DNA

Nucleus

m RNA

STEP 2

In the cytoplasm, the strands of messenger RNA bind to ribosomes.

Ribosome

STEP 3

The ribosomes move along the strands of messenger RNA reading the genetic code and creating the appropriate chains of amino acids from amino acids in the cytoplasm.

m RNA

Amino acid

Ribosome

STEP 4

The completed chains of amino-acids (i.e. proteins) are released into the cytoplasm.

Protein

FIGURE 2.19

The translation of the genetic code into a neuronal protein by messenger RNA and ribosomes. The process is the same in all body cells.

similar to DNA except that it has *uracil* bases instead of thymine bases and a phosphate and ribose backbone instead of a phosphate and deoxyribose backbone. The resulting strand of RNA is called **messenger RNA** because it carries the genetic message from the nucleus into the cytoplasm of the cell. In the cytoplasm, one end of the strand of messenger RNA attaches to a structure called a **ribosome.** The ribosome then moves along the messenger RNA, reading the genetic code as it proceeds.

Each group of three consecutive bases along the messenger RNA is called a **codon.** Each codon instructs the ribosome to add a particular amino acid from the cytoplasm to the protein that it is constructing—there are 20 different kinds of amino acids in proteins. For example, the sequence guanine-guanine-adenine instructs the ribosome to add the amino acid glycine. The ribosome reads codon after codon and adds amino acid after amino acid until it reaches a codon that tells it that the protein is complete, whereupon the completed protein is released into the cytoplasm.

The section of a chromosome that contains the base sequences for the production of a single protein is called a **structural gene.** Next to each structural gene is an **operator gene,** which is a short segment of DNA that determines whether a strand of RNA will be transcribed from the adjacent structural gene. Operator genes are responsible for the fact that the cells of our body differ greatly from one another despite the fact that they all contain identical DNA. Under the influence of proteins in their environment, operator genes direct the protein synthesis in each cell and thus determine whether it will become a bone cell, a heart cell, or a neuron.

The Simple-Systems Approach

Mendel's research illustrates a theme that recurs throughout this text. This theme is that major advances in knowledge frequently result from the **simple-systems approach,** from the study of particularly simple examples of the phenomenon under investigation. What Mendel learned from the inheritance of dichotomous pea-plant traits he could not have learned from the inheritance of behavior in mammals.

Once fundamental principles have been revealed by the study of simple systems, it is often possible to apply them to complex systems. However, some early geneticists argued that Mendel's theory was not applicable to the inheritance of complex traits because complex traits are distributed normally (i.e., in a bell-shaped curve), not in the simple either-or manner of the traits studied by Mendel. They were wrong: Mendel's theory applies to the inheritance of all traits. The inheritance of complex traits is not different in principle from the inheritance of simple traits; it is just more complex. Complex traits, such as behavioral traits, are products of the interaction among the protein products of many genes (see Plomin, 1990a) and their intracellular and extracellular environments.

The Genetics of Human Behavior: The Minnesota Study of Twins Reared Apart

It is difficult to assess the contributions of genetics and experience to human development. The reason is that people who are genetically related also tend to be raised in similar environments. As a result, research has focused on the study of genetically related individuals who were separated in infancy by adoption. The most interesting and informative of these adoption studies have been the studies of identical twins reared apart. **Identical twins** (*monozygotic twins*) develop from the same zygote, which is why they are genetically identical; **fraternal twins** (*dizygotic twins*) develop from different zygotes, which is why they are no more likely to be similar than any pair of siblings. The most extensive of such studies is the Minnesota Study (Bouchard, Lykken, McGue, Segal, & Tellegen, 1990).

The Minnesota Study of Twins Reared Apart involved 56 pairs of identical twins who had been reared apart and 458 pairs of identical twins who had been reared together. Their ages ranged from 19 to 68 years. Each twin was brought to the University of Minnesota for approximately 50 hours of testing, which focused on the assessment of intelligence and personality. Would the identical twins reared apart prove to be similar because they were genetically identical, or would they prove to be different because they had been brought up in different family environments? As illustrated by Figure 2.20, they certainly looked similar, but what about their intellectual and personality traits?

The identical twins proved to be similar in both intelligence and personality, whether they were reared together or apart. The correlation between identical twins on the Wechsler Adult Intelligence Scale (see Chapter 5) was about .85 for those who had been reared together and about .70 for those who had been reared apart, and the average correlation between identical twins on various dimensions of personality was about .50 for both groups. These results are a particularly compelling demonstration of the important role played by genetic factors in the development of human intelligence and personality.

The results of the Minnesota study were widely disseminated by the popular press. Unfortunately, the meaning of the results was often distorted. Sometimes the misrepresentation of science by the popular press does not matter—or at least it does not matter much. This was not one of those times.

FIGURE 2.20
A pair of identical twins.

People's misbeliefs about the origins of human intelligence and personality are often translated into inappropriate and discriminatory social attitudes and practices. The following news story illustrates how the results of the Minnesota study were presented to the public.

Twins Prove Intelligence and Personality Inherited!

Bob and Bob don't know each other. But they were born on the same day, graduated with engineering degrees in the same year, and both married teachers named Brenda. They both wear wire-rimmed glasses, drive a red convertible, and smoke a pipe. Bob and Bob are 38-year-old identical twins who were separated by adoption shortly after birth. Dr. Thomas Bouchard and his colleagues recently brought Bob and Bob and 55 other pairs of genetically identical twins reared apart to the University of Minnesota. Each twin underwent 50 hours of intensive psychological testing.

Dr. Bouchard found that the pairs of twins were almost identical in their intelligence and personality, despite having been reared by different families. These findings are spearheading a psychological revolution. They show that intelligence and personality are mostly genetic rather than being the result of experience, as thought by most psychologists. The heritability estimates for IQ were found to be .70.

Nancy Baynes, chairperson of the school board, was phoned for comment. "We will discuss the implications of these findings at our next meeting," she said.

This story is misleading in four ways. You should have no difficulty spotting the first; it oozes nature-or-nurture thinking and all of the misconceptions associated with it. Second, by focusing on the similarities of Bob and Bob, it creates the impression that Bob and Bob and the other pairs of twins reared apart were virtually identical. They were not. It is easy to come up with a long list of similarities between any two people if one asks them enough questions and ignores the dissimilarities. Third, the story creates the impression that the results of the Minnesota study were revolutionary. On the contrary, the importance of the Minnesota study lies mainly in the fact that it constitutes a particularly thorough confirmation of the results of previous adoption studies (see Plomin, 1990b; Scarr & Kidd, 1983). And fourth, the story creates the false impression that the results of the Minnesota study make some general point about the relative contributions of genes and experience to the development of intelligence and personality. It does not, and neither does any other adoption study. Bouchard and his colleagues estimated the heritability of IQ to be .70, but they did not conclude that IQ is 70% genetic. A **heritability estimate** is an estimate of the proportion of the variability that occurred in a particular trait in a particular study that resulted from the genetic variation in that study. Its value depends on the amount of genetic and environmental variation in the study, and it cannot be applied to any other situation. For example, in the Minnesota study, there was relatively little environmental variation—all subjects were raised in industrialized countries (e.g., Britain, Canada, United States) by parents who could meet the strict standards required for adoption—and accordingly most of the variation in the subjects' IQs resulted from genetic variation. If the twins had been adopted by an assortment of European royalty, Borneo bushmen, Hungarian Gypsies, New York advertising executives, and Argentinian army officers, the resulting heritability estimates for IQ and personality would have been much lower. Bouchard et al. emphasize this point in their paper.

2.4

Behavioral Development: The Interaction of Genetic Factors and Experience

This chapter concludes with three examples of developmental research. Each makes the same point: that behavioral development is a product of the interaction of genetic factors and experience.

Selective Breeding of "Maze-Bright" and "Maze-Dull" Rats

You have already learned in this chapter that nature-or-nurture thinking dominated the study of behavior during the first half of this century, and that most psychologists of that era believed that behavior developed largely through learning. Tryon (1934) undermined this bias by showing that behavioral traits can be selectively bred.

Tryon focused his selective breeding experiment on the very behavior that had been the focus of early psychologists in their investigations of learning: the maze running of laboratory rats. Tryon began by training a large heterogeneous group of laboratory rats to run a complex maze; the rats received a food reward when they reached the goal box. Tryon then mated the females and males that least frequently entered incorrect alleys during training—he referred to these rats as "maze bright." And he bred the females and males that most frequently entered incorrect alleys during training—he referred to these rats as "maze dull." When the offspring of the maze-bright and maze-dull rats matured, their maze-learning performance was assessed. Then, the brightest of the maze-bright offspring were mated, and so were the dullest of the maze-dull offspring. This selective breeding procedure was continued for 21 generations, and the descendants of Tryon's original strains are available today to those interested in studying them. By the seventh generation, there was almost no overlap in the maze-learning performance of the two strains— with a few exceptions, the worst of the maze-bright strain made fewer errors than the best of the maze-dull strain—see Figure 2.21. To control for the possibility that good maze-running performance was somehow being passed from parent to offspring through learning, Tryon used a *cross-fostering control procedure.* However, the offspring of maze-bright rats made few errors even when they were reared by maze-dull rats, and the offspring of maze-dull rats made many errors even when they were reared by maze-bright rats.

Tryon assumed that learning a maze with few errors was an index of rat

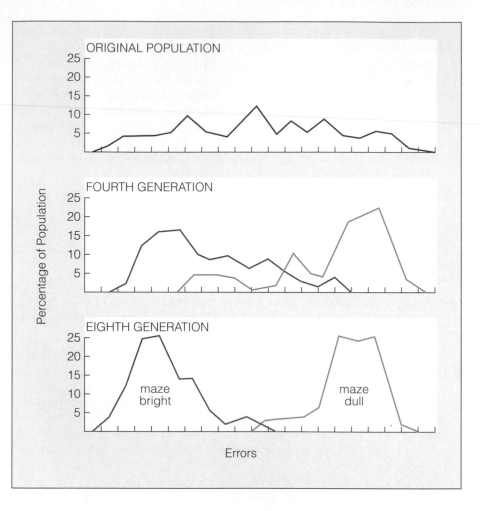

FIGURE 2.21

Through a program of selective breeding, Tryon created two behaviorally distinct strains, which he referred to as "maze bright" and "maze dull."

intelligence, and thus he concluded that he had selectively bred generally intelligent and generally dull strains. However, this is only one of several possible interpretations of his research; many factors other than general intelligence can influence maze-running performance. Perhaps Tryon's so-called maze-bright rats were not more intelligent; perhaps they could see better, were more hungry, were less curious about incorrect alleys, or less fearful of the experimental situation. This latter interpretation is the one that was supported by the experiments of Searle (1949). Searle compared Tryon's maze-bright and maze-dull rats on 30 different performance measures, and he found that the maze-bright rats were less emotional, but not generally superior in learning ability.

Since Tryon's seminal selective breeding experiments, many behavioral traits have been selectively bred: for example, open-field activity in mice (De-Fries, Gervais, & Thomas, 1978), susceptibility to alcohol-induced sleep in mice (McClearn, 1976), susceptibility to alcohol withdrawal seizures in mice (Crabbe, Kosubud, Young, Tam, & McSwigan, 1985), nest building in mice (Lynch, 1981), avoidance learning in rats (Brush, Froehlich, & Baron, 1979), open-field defecation in rats (Blizard, 1981), and mating in fruit flies. Today, most behavioral geneticists agree that any measurable behavioral trait that varies among members of a species can be selectively bred.

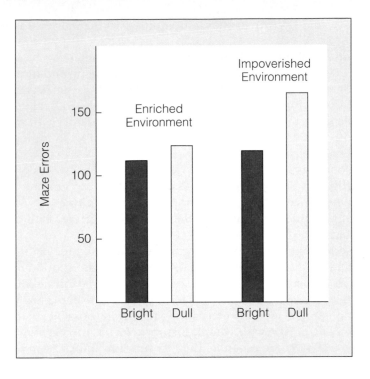

Maze-bright rats made fewer errors than maze-dull rats only if they had been reared in standard laboratory group cages.

Selective breeding studies have proven that genes influence the development of behavior: This in no way implies that experience does not. This point was clearly illustrated by Cooper and Zubek (1958) in a study of maze-bright and maze-dull strains. They reared maze-bright and maze-dull rats in one of two environments: (1) an impoverished environment (a barren wire-mesh group cage) or (2) an enriched environment (a wire-mesh group cage that contained tunnels, ramps, visual displays, and other objects designed to stimulate their interest). When they reached maturity, the maze-dull rats made more errors than the maze-bright rats only if they had been reared in the impoverished environment—see Figure 2.22. Apparently, enriched early environments can overcome the negative effects of disadvantaged genes.

Phenylketonuria: A Single-Gene Metabolic Disorder

In contrast to what you might expect, it is often easier to understand the genetics of a behavioral disorder than it is to understand the genetics of normal behavior. The reason is that many genes influence the development of a normal behavioral trait, but it takes only one abnormal gene to screw it up. A good example of this point is the neurological disorder, **phenylketonuria** or **PKU.**

PKU was discovered in 1934 when a Norwegian dentist, Asbjörn Fölling noticed a peculiar odor in the urine of his two mentally retarded children. He correctly assumed that the odor was related to their disorder, and he had their urine analyzed. High levels of **phenylpyruvic acid** were found in both samples. Spurred on by his discovery, Fölling identified other retarded children who had abnormally high levels of urinary phenylpyruvic acid, and he concluded that this subpopulation of retarded children were all suffering from the same disorder. The symptoms of PKU include vomiting, seizures, hyperactivity, and hyperirritability—in addition to mental retardation (see Nyhan, 1987).

The pattern of transmission of PKU through the family trees of afflicted individuals indicates that it is transmitted by a single gene mutation. About 1 in 100 people of European descent carry the PKU gene, but because it is recessive, PKU develops only in homozygous individuals (individuals who inherit a PKU gene from both their mother and their father). In the United States, about 1 in 15,000 white infants is born with PKU—the incidence is much lower among black infants.

The biochemistry of PKU turned out to be reasonably straightforward. PKU homozygotes lack **phenylalanine hydroxylase,** an enzyme that is required for the conversion of the amino acid *phenylalanine* to *tyrosine.* As a result, phenylalanine accumulates in the body and interferes with the normal development of the brain.

The blood of newborn infants is routinely screened for high phenylalanine levels in most modern hospitals. If the blood level is found to be high, the infant is immediately placed on a special phenylalanine-reduced diet, which reduces the amount of phenylalanine in the blood and usually prevents the development of mental retardation. It is now possible to determine whether or not a person with a family history of PKU is carrying the PKU gene (Woo et al., 1983); some potential carriers seek this information in order to make informed decisions about marriage and reproduction.

Like other behavioral traits, the behavioral symptoms of PKU result from an interaction between genetic and environmental factors: between the PKU gene and diet. And as is so often the case, the timing of this interaction is extremely important. The brains of human infants go through several major phases of development in the first few months after birth (see Chapter 15); experiences that occur during these phases often have lasting effects that they would not have if they occurred at some other time. For example, the special phenylalanine-reduced diet does not prevent the development of mental retardation in PKU homozygotes unless it is initiated within the first few weeks of life. Conversely, the restriction of phenylalanine in the diet can be permanently relaxed in late childhood with few adverse consequences. The period of development during which a particular experience must occur to have a major effect on development is referred to as its **sensitive period** (see Hinde, 1983).

Pregnant PKU monozygotes who have developed normally on a phenylalanine-reduced diet are usually not affected by high levels of phenylalanine, but their fetuses are. To protect their babies, they must go back on the phenylalanine-reduced diet prior to conception (see Nyhan, 1987).

Development of Birdsong

In the spring, the species-specific songs of male birds threaten conspecific male trespassers and attract potential mates. The male birds of some species can sing their species' songs even if they have never heard them before; the male birds of other species must learn to sing their songs from their conspecifics. The birds in this latter category—the song learners—are the focus of the present discussion. Much of the research on birdsong learning has involved three species: white-crowned sparrows, zebra finches, and canaries (see Figure 2.23).

FIGURE 2.23
Male canaries and zebra
finches are colorful and
common subjects of research
on birdsong development.
Illustration kindly provided
by *Trends in Neuroscience;*
original photograph by
Arturo Alvarez-Buylla.

Song development has been most thoroughly documented in the white-crowned sparrow (see Marler, 1970a; Marler, 1991; Petrinovich, 1988). Male white-crowned sparrows start singing when they are several months old, but their first twittering efforts, which are called **subsong,** bear only a vague resemblance to adult song. Then, over the ensuing 2 months, their subsong develops into adult song. Because each young white-crowned male learns the song of its white-crowned neighbors, regional dialects develop; the songs of white-crowned males living in one area are often slightly but distinctly different from the songs of white-crowned males living just a few miles away (Marler & Tamura, 1962).

In order to determine how white-crowned males learn to sing, Marler reared white-crowned males by themselves in sound-proof chambers and exposed them to various tape-recorded songs. He made two key observations (Marler, 1970b): (1) only those white-crowned males that were exposed to tape recordings of white-crown song between 10 and 50 days after hatching sang the normal white-crown song as adults, and (2) white-crowned males that were exposed to tape recordings of both white-crown song and the songs of other species between 10 and 50 days learned only the white-crown song. However, Petrinovich and his colleagues subsequently showed that Marler's technique of inducing song learning in white-crowned males was not ideal—they found that the song learning of white-crowned males could be improved either by increasing the number of times that they heard the tape-recorded songs or by exposing them to live singing birds. Under these more effective conditions, it was possible for white-crowned males to learn the songs of other species, even when they did not hear them until after they are 50 days old (see Petrinovich, 1988). Nevertheless, it is clear that portions of the male white-crowned sparrow brain are in some way specially prepared to learn the songs of their own species that they hear in the sensitive period between 10 and 50 days of age.

Figure 2.24 is a drawing of the neural circuit that is thought to control birdsong in zebra finches and canaries (Nordeen & Nordeen, 1990;

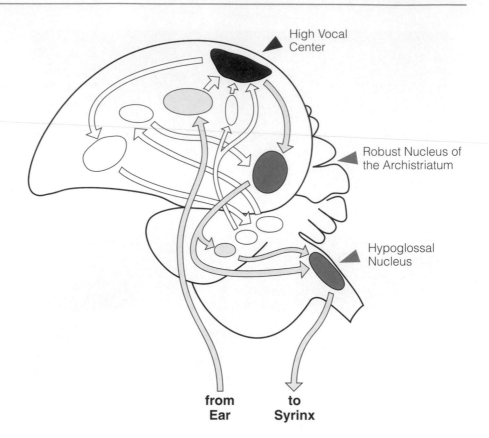

FIGURE 2.24

A schematic illustration of the neural circuit that is thought to control birdsong in zebra finches and canaries. Only the structures that are discussed in the text are labeled. (Adapted from Nottebohm, 1991.)

Nottebohm, 1991)—only the most thoroughly studied structures in this circuit are labeled. Auditory signals from the ear reach the *high vocal center* (HVC); signals from the high vocal center are transmitted to the *robust nucleus of the archistriatum* (RA); and signals from the robust nucleus of the archistriatum are transmitted to the *hypoglossal nucleus,* which contains the motor neurons that project to the vocal organ or **syrinx.**

In many species of songbirds, the syrinx is a double structure. Each half has a separate air supply—one from the left lung and one from the right—and each has its own muscles and innervation. The left syrinx is controlled by the left side of the brain, and the right syrinx is controlled by the right side of the brain. The songs of such birds are normally a blend of notes produced independently by the left and right sides of their brains; however, if one side of the brain is damaged, the other side can produce the entire song. Canaries are one of the species that can sing with either their left or right hemisphere. But interestingly, most canaries have a strong left-side preference; they produce far more notes with their left hemispheres (Nottebohm & Nottebohm, 1976). This observation is analogous to right-handedness in humans—the right hand, like the left syrinx, is controlled by circuits in the left hemisphere. The discovery of the left-hemisphere dominance of canary song was the first observation of a functional laterality in a nonhuman brain.

It seems reasonable to assume that the size of a neural structure bears some relation to the complexity of its function. Such a relation has been revealed by studies of the birdsong circuit. The high vocal center and the robust nucleus of the archistriatum are larger in males than in females, and they are larger in the males of species that sing many different songs than they are in the males of species that sing few songs (Canady, Kroodsma, & Nottebohm, 1984; Nottebohm, Kasparian, & Pandazis, 1981). Furthermore, they are twice as large during the breeding season as they are in the same males during other times of the year. This fluctuation in size is due to an annual cycle of neuron death and growth of new neurons (e.g., Paton, O'Loughlin, & Nottebohm, 1985; Alvarez-Buylla, Kirn, & Nottebohm, 1990). The sex hormone **testosterone** has been implicated in the death and growth of song-circuit neurons; testosterone levels are high during breeding season and low during other times of the year (see DeVoogd, 1991).

Conclusion

In this chapter, you were introduced to some of the fundamentals of human evolution, behavioral genetics, and behavioral development. But more importantly, you learned how to think productively about the biology of behavior. You learned that biopsychologists have rejected conventional physiological-or-psychological and nature-or-nurture dichotomies in favor of a more enlightened alternative. Now, they—and I hope you—view all behavior and the psychological processes that underlie it as products of patterns of neural activity, which are shaped by the interaction among genes, experience, and the current situation (see Figure 2.2).

After the first edition of this text was published, I received the following greeting card from a student in Southern California. She said that the card reminded her of me and that she was sure that I would find it amusing. I have included it here because it is consistent with the comparative thrust of this chapter and because I did find it amusing. I hope that you do too.

Food for Thought

1. Nature-or-nurture thinking about intelligence is sometimes used as an excuse for racial discrimination. How can the interactionist approach, which has been championed in this chapter, be used as a basis for arguing against discriminatory practices?

2. Imagine that you are a biopsychology instructor. One of your students asks you whether depression is physiological or psychological. What would you say?

KEY TERMS

To help you study the material in this chapter, all of the key terms—those that have appeared in bold type—are listed and briefly defined here.

Amino acids. The chemical elements from which proteins are synthesized.

Amphibians. Species that spend their larval phase in water and their adult phase on land.

Asomatognosia. A brain-damage-produced deficiency in awareness of one's own body.

Brain stem. The stem of the brain on which the cerebral hemispheres rest; it includes neural structures that regulate critical reflex activities such as heart rate and respiration.

Cartesian dualism. The philosophical position of Descartes; he argued that the universe is composed of two elements: physical matter and the human mind.

Cerebral cortex. The outermost layer of the cerebral hemispheres; most is neocortex.

Cerebrum. The portion of the brain that sits on the brain stem; the cerebral hemispheres.

Chordates. Animals with nerve chords.

Chromosomes. Thread-like structures of the cell nucleus; each chromosome is a DNA molecule.

Codon. A group of three consecutive nucleotide bases, which specifies the particular amino acid that is to be added to an amino acid chain during protein synthesis.

Comparative approach. Gaining insights into behavior and neural mechanisms (or other biological processes) by comparing species.

Conspecifics. Members of the same species.

Convolutions. Folds in the cerebral surface; convoluted brains have a greater area of cerebral cortex.

Cro-Magnons. They replaced Neanderthals as the earth's dominant hominid about 25,000 years ago; Cro-Magnons appear to have been the first animals to engage in artistic activity.

Crossing over. The exchange of sections between pairs of chromosomes; it occurs during the first stage of meiosis.

Deoxyribonucleic acid (DNA). Double-stranded, coiled molecules of genetic material.

Dichotomous traits. Traits that occur in one form or the other, never in combination.

Ethology. The study of the behavior of animals in their natural environment.

Evolve. To undergo gradual orderly change.

Fitness. The ability of an organism to survive and contribute its genes to the next generation.

Fraternal twins. Twins that develop from different zygotes and thus are no more likely to be similar than any pair of siblings; dizygotic twins.

Functional approach. The study of behavior and neural mechanisms by focusing on their adaptiveness and the environmental pressures that led to their evolution.

Gametes. Egg cells and sperm cells.

Gene. A unit of inheritance; the section of a chromosome that controls the synthesis of one protein.

Gene maps. Maps that indicate the relative positions of genes along a chromosome.

Heritability estimate. An estimate of the proportion of the variability that occurred in a particular trait in a particular study that resulted from the genetic variation in that study.

Heterozygous. When an organism possesses two different genes for a particular trait (e.g., one gene for blue eye color and one for brown eye color).

Homo erectus. The first Homo species, which was thought to have evolved from *Australopithecus* about 1.5 million years ago.

Homo sapiens. The human species.

Homozygous. When an organism possesses two identical genes for a particular trait (e.g., two genes for blue eye color).

Identical twins. Twins that develop from the same zygote and are thus genetically identical; monozygotic twins.

Instinctive behaviors. Behaviors that occur in all like members of a species, even when there has been no opportunity for them to have been learned.

Linkage. The tendency for traits that are encoded on the same chromosome to be inherited together.

Mammals. Animals that feed their young from mammary glands.

Meiosis. The process of cell division that produces cells with half the usual number of chromosomes (one of each pair); gametes are produced by meiosis.

Messenger RNA. A strand of RNA that carries a segment of the genetic code from the nucleus into the cytoplasm of the cell; messenger RNA molecules are transcribed from DNA.

Mitosis. Cell division that results in two daughter cells, each with the same number of chromosomes as the parent cell; with the exception of the gametes, all body cells are a product of mitotic division.

Mutations. Abnormal genes that are created by accidents of chromosome duplication.

Natural selection. Heritable traits that are associated with high rates of survival and reproduction are preferentially passed on to future generations.

Nature-nurture issue. Misguided debate about the relative contributions of nature (genes) and nurture (experience) to behavioral development.

Neanderthals. They became the dominant hominids about 200,000 years ago; they are considered to be the first true humans.

Nucleotide bases. DNA is composed of four nucleotide bases: adenine, thymine, guanine, and cytosine.

Operator gene. A short segment of DNA that determines whether or not a strand of RNA will be transcribed from the adjacent structural gene.

Phenylalanine hydroxylase. An enzyme required for the conversion of the amino acid phenylalanine to tyrosine; those who suffer from PKU lack this enzyme.

Phenylketonuria (PKU). A neurological disorder whose symptoms are vomiting, seizures, hyperactivity, hyperirritability, mental retardation, and high levels of phenylpyruvic acid in the urine.

Phenylpyruvic acid. A substance that is found in abnormally high concentrations in the urine of those suffering from phenylketonuria.

Primates. One of 14 different orders of mammals; there are five different groups of primates: prosimians, new-world monkeys, old-world monkeys, apes, and hominids.

Proteins. Long chains of amino acids.

Ribonucleic acid (RNA). A molecule that is similar to DNA except that it has a uracil base and a phosphate and ribose backbone.

Ribosome. A structure in the cytoplasm that manufactures proteins by reading the genetic code from strands of messenger RNA.

Self-duplication. Refers to the DNA molecule's ability to replicate (duplicate) itself.

Sensitive period. The period of development during which a particular experience must occur to have a major effect on development.

Simple-systems approach. An approach to research that involves the study of particularly simple examples of the phenomenon under investigation.

Species. A group of organisms that is reproductively isolated from other organisms; the members of one species cannot produce fertile offspring by mating with members of another.

Structural gene. A section of a chromosome that contains the base sequences for the production of a single protein.

Subsong. The first twittering songs of young birds; subsong bears only a vague resemblance to adult song.

Syrinx. The vocal organ of birds.

Testosterone. The sex hormone that has been implicated in the death and growth of song-circuit neurons.

Translation. Refers to the DNA molecule's ability to translate its genetic information into proteins.

True-breeding lines. Breeding lines in which interbred members always produce offspring with a particular trait, generation after generation.

Vertebrates. Those chordates that possess spinal bones.

Zeitgeist. The general intellectual climate of a culture.

ADDITIONAL READING

For those interested in evolution and its implications, the essays of Stephen J. Gould are enjoyable and informative—a tough combination to beat. The following is a recent collection:

Gould, S. J. (1991). *Bully for Brontosaurus.* New York: W. W. Norton.

The following text provides an excellent introduction to the field of human behavioral genetics:

Plomin, R. (1990b). *Nature and nurture: An introduction to human behavioral genetics.* Pacific Grove, California: Brooks/Cole.

The following articles straighten out some common misconceptions about the biology of behavior:

Dewsbury, D. A. (1989). Comparative psychology, ethology, and animal behavior. *Annual Review of Psychology, 40,* 581–602.

Johnston, T. D. (1987). The persistence of dichotomies in the study of behavioral development. *Developmental Review, 7,* 449–182.

Staddon, J. E. R., & Bueno, J. L. O. (1991). On models, be-

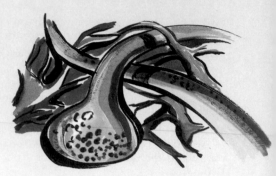

3

The Anatomy of the Nervous System

Understanding the neural bases of behavior is one of the primary objectives of biopsychology. Accordingly, biopsychologists must bring to their study of behavior a good working knowledge of neuroanatomy. You must do the same.

This chapter introduces you to the general structure of the human nervous system and to a few key neuroanatomical techniques.

General Layout of the Nervous System

The Major Divisions of the Nervous System

The nervous system has two major divisions: the **central nervous system (CNS)** and the **peripheral nervous system (PNS)**. The CNS is the portion of the nervous system that is located in the bony central core of the body (the skull and the spine); the PNS is the portion that is not. Figure 3.1 illustrates the human CNS and PNS.

The CNS is composed of two divisions: the brain and the spinal cord. The *brain* is the part of the CNS that is located in the skull; the *spinal cord* is the part that is located in the spine.

The PNS is also composed of two major divisions: the somatic nervous system and the autonomic nervous system. The **somatic nervous system** is the part of the PNS that interacts with the external environment. It is composed of **afferent nerves,** which carry sensory input from receptors in the skin, joints, eyes, ears, etc., to the CNS, and **efferent nerves,** which carry signals from the CNS to the skeletal muscles. The **autonomic nervous system (ANS)** is the part of the PNS that participates in the regulation of the internal environment. It is composed of afferent nerves, which carry signals from the organs of the body to the CNS, and efferent nerves, which carry signals from the CNS to the organs of the body. You will not get the terms *afferent* and *efferent* confused if you remember that many words that involve the idea of *going toward* something begin with an "a" (e.g., advance, approach, arrive) and that many words that involve the idea of *going away from* something begin with an "e" (e.g., exit, embark, escape).

The autonomic nervous system has two kinds of efferent nerves: sympathetic nerves and parasympathetic nerves. In general, the **sympathetic nerves** stimulate, organize, and mobilize energy resources to deal with threatening situations, whereas the **parasympathetic nerves** act to conserve energy. Most autonomic organs receive both sympathetic and parasympathetic input; and thus, their activities are controlled by the relative levels of sympathetic and parasympathetic activity. For example, heart rate is increased by signals from sympathetic nerves and decreased by signals from the parasympathetic nerves. The distribution of sympathetic and parasympathetic fibers is illustrated in Appendix I. (Ask your instructor whether or not you are responsible for material in the appendixes.)

Have you noticed that the nervous system is a system of twos? If you haven't, you will when you examine Figure 3.2.

Most of the nerves of the peripheral nervous system project from the spinal cord, but there are 12 exceptions: the 12 pairs of **cranial nerves,** which project from the brain. They are numbered in sequence from top to bottom. These include purely sensory (afferent) nerves such as the *olfactory nerves* (the first cranial nerves) and the *optic nerves* (the second cranial nerves), but most contain both sensory and motor fibers. The longest cranial nerve is the *vagus nerve* (the tenth cranial nerve), which contains motor and sensory fibers traveling to and from the gut. The 12 pairs of cranial nerves and their targets are illustrated in Appendix II; their functions are listed in Appendix III.

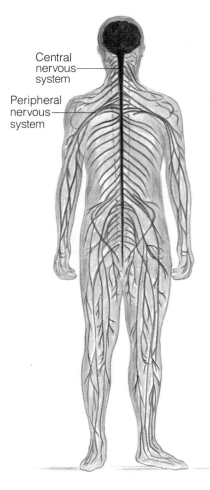

Central nervous system

Peripheral nervous system

FIGURE 3.1

The human central nervous system (CNS) and peripheral nervous system (PNS). The CNS is represented in red; the PNS in blue.

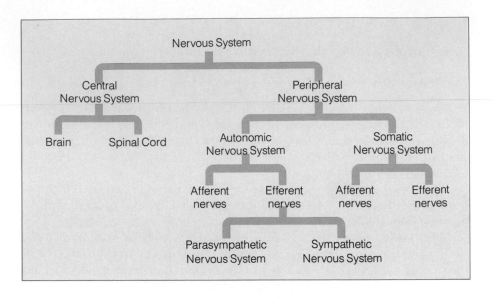

FIGURE 3.2

The major divisions of the nervous system.

The Meninges, the Ventricles, and the Cerebrospinal Fluid

The brain and spinal cord are the most protected organs in the body. They are encased in bone and swaddled in three protective membranes, the **meninges** (pronounced MEN in gees). The outer *menynx* (which, believe it or not, is the singular of meninges) is a tough membrane called the **dura mater** (tough mother). Immediately inside the dura mater is the spongy **arachnoid membrane.** Beneath the arachnoid membrane is a space called the **subarachnoid space,** which contains large blood vessels, and then comes the innermost menynx, the delicate **pia mater** (pious mother), which adheres to the surface of the CNS tissue itself.

Also protecting the central nervous system is the **cerebrospinal fluid (CSF),** which fills the subarachnoid space and the core of the spinal cord and brain. Running the length of the spinal cord is the small CSF-filled **central canal,** and in the core of the brain, there are four large CSF-filled internal chambers or **ventricles:** the two *lateral ventricles,* the *third ventricle,* and the *fourth ventricle.* The four cerebral ventricles, the central canal, and the *cerebral aqueduct,* which connects the third and fourth ventricles, are illustrated in Figure 3.3.

The cerebrospinal fluid provides the brain with considerable protection from mechanical injury. The important role played by the cerebrospinal fluid in supporting and cushioning the brain is all too apparent to patients who have had some of their cerebrospinal fluid drained away. They suffer raging headaches, and they experience stabbing pain if they jerk their heads.

Cerebrospinal fluid is continuously produced by networks of *capillaries* (small blood vessels), called **choroid plexuses,** which protrude into the ventricles from their pia mater lining (Spector & Johanson, 1989). The excess cerebrospinal fluid is continuously absorbed from the subarachnoid space into large blood-filled spaces or *sinuses,* which run through the dura mater and drain into the large *jugular veins* of the neck. Figure 3.4 illustrates the

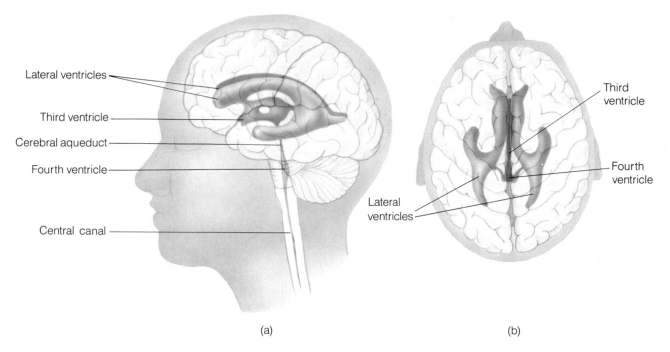

Lateral ventricles

Third ventricle

Cerebral aqueduct

Fourth ventricle

Central canal

Third ventricle

Fourth ventricle

Lateral ventricles

(a)

(b)

FIGURE 3.3

The cerebral ventricles as seen from the side and from above.

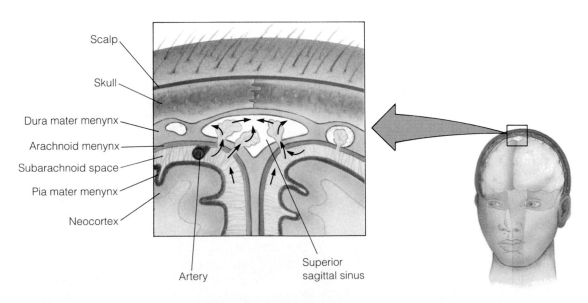

Scalp

Skull

Dura mater menynx

Arachnoid menynx

Subarachnoid space

Pia mater menynx

Neocortex

Artery

Superior sagittal sinus

FIGURE 3.4

The absorption of cerebrospinal fluid from the subarachnoid space into the superior sagittal sinus. Note the three meninges.

absorption of cerebrospinal fluid from the subarachnoid space into the large **superior sagittal sinus,** which runs in the dura mater along the top of the brain between the two hemispheres.

Occasionally the flow of cerebrospinal fluid from the lateral ventricles is blocked—usually by a tumor at one of the narrow channels, called **foramens,** that link the ventricles. The build-up of fluid in the ventricles causes the walls of the ventricles, and thus the entire brain, to expand, producing a condition called *hydrocephalus* (literally "water head"). Hydrocephalus is treated by draining the excess fluid from the ventricles and trying to remove the obstruction.

3.2

Neurons and Glia: The Building Blocks of the Nervous System

One of the most significant events in the study of the nervous system was the accidental discovery of the **Golgi stain** by Golgi (pronounced GOLE gee), an Italian physician, in the early 1870s. According to one of his laboratory assistants, Golgi was trying to stain the meninges by exposing a block of neural tissue first to potassium dichromate and then to silver nitrate, when he noticed an amazing thing. For some unknown reason, the *silver chromate* created by the chemical reaction between the potassium dichromate and the silver nitrate invaded a few neurons in each slice of tissue and stained each invaded neuron entirely black. This discovery made it possible to see the shape of individual neurons for the first time (see Figure 3.5)—stains that completely dye all of the neurons on a given slide reveal nothing of their structure because they are so tightly woven together. The accidental discovery of the Golgi stain ranks as one of the greatest blessings to befall neuroscience in its early years.

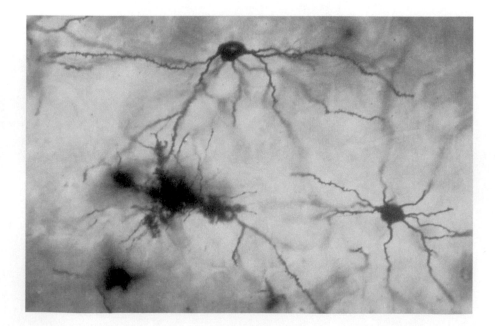

FIGURE 3.5

Neural tissue that has been stained by the Golgi method. Because only a few neurons take up the stain, their silhouettes are revealed in great detail. Usually only part of a neuron is captured in a single slice. (Courtesy of Steven Vincent, Kinsmen Laboratory of Neurological Research, University of British Columbia.)

Early in this century, Golgi-stain studies of primitive species provided insight into the evolution of the nervous system (Parker, 1919). In *sea anemones,* each neural circuit involves only a single neuron. There are neurons on each tentacle, and each neuron sends its fiber to a muscle fiber in the same tentacle. Thus, every time a tentacle is touched by a particle floating in the water, the tentacle contracts and brings the particle into contact with the mouth.

Certain simple jellyfish have a slightly more complex neural arrangement. Neural fibers that project from receptors do not terminate directly on muscle fibers; they terminate on an array of neurons, which in turn terminate on muscle fibers. The evolution of two-neuron circuits provided the potential for flexibility; the activation of a motor neuron could depend on the interaction among signals from various sensory neurons. Such two-stage nervous systems required, for the first time in evolutionary history, functional interactions among neurons. These interactions occur at **synapses,** where the terminals of one neuron release a neurotransmitter chemical that stimulates adjacent neurons.

The third advance in the evolution of the nervous system was identified in complex jellyfish and mollusks. In these creatures, there is a complex nerve net intervening between the sensory and motor neurons. The nervous systems of all "higher" organisms share with these complex jellyfish and mollusks the fact that their nervous systems comprise three basic kinds of neurons: *sensory neurons, motor neurons,* and *interneurons.* Figure 3.6 illustrates the evolution of the three-stage nervous system.

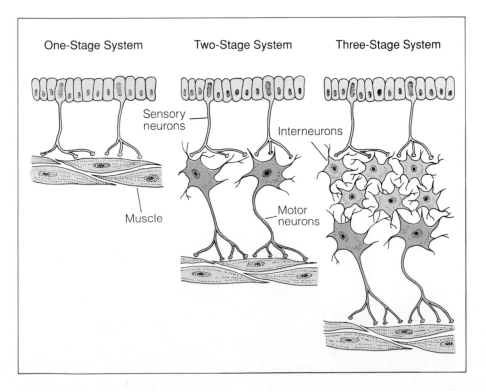

FIGURE 3.6

A schematic illustration of Parker's three stages of nervous system evolution: the one-stage circuit, the two-stage circuit, and the three-stage circuit.

The Structure of Neurons

The fact that the Golgi technique completely stains a few neurons on each slide black is both its strength and its weakness. Although it provides an excellent view of the silhouette of the few neurons that take up the stain, it provides no indication of the total number of neurons in an area or of the details of their inner structure. The first neural staining procedure to overcome these shortcomings was the **Nissl stain,** which was developed by Franz Nissl in the 1880s. The most common dye used in the Nissl method is *cresyl violet.* Cresyl violet and other Nissl dyes penetrate all cells on a slide and bind to structures in their **cell bodies** (metabolic centers). The structures to which Nissl stains bind are *ribosomes,* the structures that assemble amino acids into proteins under the direction of strands of *messenger RNA*—see Chapter 2. Ribosomes are present in all cells, but they are particularly dense in neuronal cell bodies. Presented in Figure 3.7 is a photograph of a slice of tissue cut from the *hippocampus* and stained with cresyl violet. Notice how only the neuron cell-body layers are densely stained.

Another neuroanatomical procedure that has provided a great deal of information about neuronal structure is **electron microscopy** (pronounced my CROSS cuh pee). Because of the nature of light, the limit of magnification in light microscopy is about 1500 times, which is not sufficient to reveal the fine anatomical details of neurons. Greater detail can be obtained by coating thin slices of neural tissue with an electron-absorbing substance that is taken up by different parts of neurons to different degrees. Then a beam of electrons is passed through the tissue onto a photographic film, and the result is an *electron micrograph,* which captures neuronal structure in exquisite detail (see Figure 4.13). Although the *scanning electron microscope* is not capable of as much magnification, it provides beautiful electron micrographs in three dimensions (see Figure 3.8).

With an arsenal of neuroanatomical techniques at their disposal (e.g., the Golgi stain, the Nissl stain, and electron microscopy), each providing a different view of neural tissue, neuroanatomists have been able to characterize the structure of neurons in great detail. The most important rule to remember

FIGURE 3.7

A Nissl-stained section (slice) of the hippocampus, a structure that plays an important role in learning and memory. Notice the well-defined cell-body layers. (Courtesy of Steven Vincent, Kinsmen Laboratory of Neurological Research, University of British Columbia.)

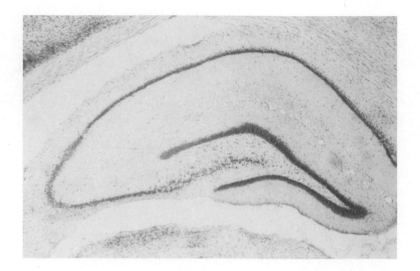

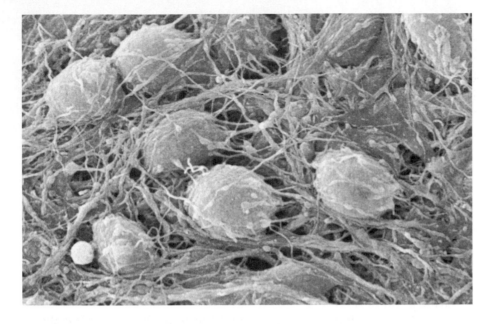

FIGURE 3.8

A scanning electron micrograph of a cluster of neuron cell bodies. Each cell body is studded with terminal buttons (Phototake/Scott).

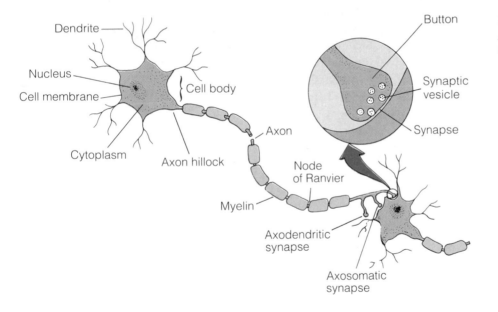

FIGURE 3.9

A schematic diagram of a multipolar neuron.

about the structure of neurons is that there are no rules: Neurons come in an incredible variety of shapes and sizes.

Many neurons are similar in major respects to the one illustrated schematically in Figure 3.9. Note the following structures:

Dendrites.   The short processes emanating from the cell body, which, along with the · cell body itself, receive most of the synaptic contacts from other neurons.

Nucleus.   The structure in the cell body that contains the genetic material.

Cell membrane.   The semipermeable membrane that encloses the neuron.

Cytoplasm.   The clear liquid of the neuron's interior.

Cell body.   The metabolic center of the neuron; also called the *soma*.

Axon hillock.   The cone-shaped region at the junction between the axon and the cell body.

Axon.   The long, narrow process that projects from the cell body.

Myelin.   The fatty insulation around many axons.

Nodes of Ranvier (pronounced rahn vee yay).   The *unmyelinated* gaps between sections of myelin.

Buttons.   The button-like endings of the axon branches; buttons release neurotransmitters into synapses.

Synaptic vesicles.   Tiny packets of neurotransmitter molecules; they tend to cluster in buttons next to the presynaptic membrane.

Synapses.   The gaps between adjacent neurons across which chemical signals are transmitted.

Axodendritic synapses.   Synapses between axons and dendrites.

Axosomatic synapses.   Synapses between axons and cell bodies (soma).

Figure 3.10 illustrates some of the diversity of neural structure. One simple way of classifying neurons is based on the number of processes emanating from their cell bodies. Most neurons have many processes extending from the cell body, and are thus classified as **multipolar neurons.** Neurons with one process extending from the cell body are **unipolar,** and those with two are **bipolar.**

Most of the nervous system structures that you will be introduced to later in this chapter are clusters of neural cell bodies. In the CNS these clusters of cell bodies are called **nuclei** (singular *nucleus*); in the PNS they are called **ganglia** (singular *ganglion*). Bundles of axons in the CNS are called **tracts;** those in the PNS are called **nerves.** Note that the word *nucleus* has two different meanings: a structure in the neuron cell body and a cluster of cell bodies in the CNS.

FIGURE 3.10

Unipolar neurons, bipolar neurons, multipolar neurons, and interneurons.

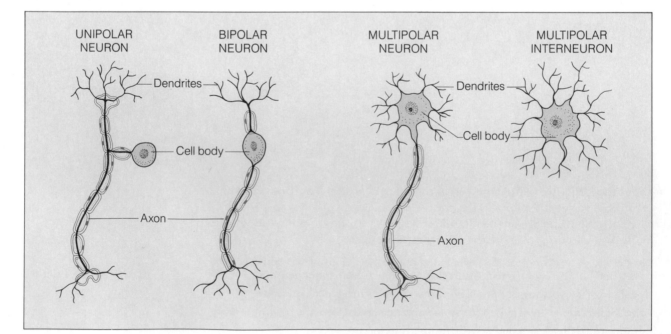

Glial Cells and Satellite Cells

Neurons are not the only cells in the nervous system. In the CNS, **glial cells,** or *neuroglia,* outnumber neurons 10 to 1. The term *neuroglia* literally means *nerve glue;* it alludes to the role of glial cells in providing a matrix that holds CNS neurons together. Glial cells also absorb dead cells and other neural debris. These functions are performed in the PNS by similar cells called **satellite cells.**

The largest glial cells are called **astroglia** or *astrocytes* (see Chan-Ling & Stone, 1991; Kimelberg & Norenberg, 1989) because they are star-shaped (from the Greek *astron,* meaning *star*). Because they envelop the blood vessels that course through the brain, astroglia are thought to play a role in the selective transfer of substances from blood to neurons. They are believed to be one of the mechanisms of the so-called **blood-brain barrier,** which keeps certain toxic substances in the blood from entering neurons (Goldstein & Betz, 1986)—see Figure 3.11.

Other glial cells, called **oligodendroglia** or *oligodendrocytes,* send out myelin-rich processes that wrap around the axons of many CNS neurons. The myelin sheaths formed by these processes increase the speed and efficiency of axonal conduction. A similar function is performed by **Schwann cells** (a class of satellite cells) in the PNS. The myelination of a PNS axon by a Schwann cell is illustrated in Figure 3.12. One of the main differences between Schwann cells and oligodendroglia is that only the former can guide axonal *regeneration* (regrowth) after damage. That is why there is normally little axonal regeneration in the mammalian CNS (see Chapter 15).

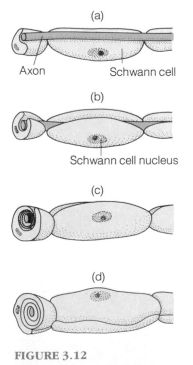

(a)

Axon   Schwann cell

(b)

Schwann cell nucleus

(c)

(d)

FIGURE 3.12

The myelination of a PNS axon. As they grow, Schwann cells wrap themselves around and around axons.

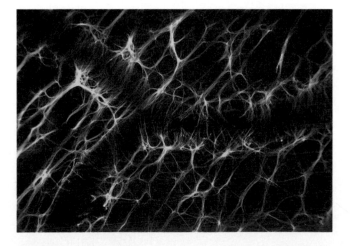

FIGURE 3.11

Astrocytes. Astrocytes form a supportive matrix for neurons and mediate the transfer of chemicals to neurons from the blood. Notice how astrocyte processes have an affinity for blood vessels, which are seen here as unstained channels through the astrocyte matrix.

3.3

Neuroanatomical Directions and Planes

Locations in the nervous system are usually described in relation to the orientation of the spinal cord. The system is straightforward for most *vertebrates*. As indicated in Figure 3.13, the nose end of such animals is referred to as the **anterior** end, and the tail end is referred to as the **posterior** end. These same coordinates are sometimes referred to as **rostral** (toward the beak) and **caudal** (toward the tail), respectively. The back is referred to as the **dorsal** surface, and the stomach is referred to as the **ventral** surface. **Medial** means toward the midline, and **lateral** means away from the midline.

We humans complicate this simple three-dimensional (anterior-posterior, ventral-dorsal, medial-lateral) system of neuroanatomical directions by insisting on walking around on our hind legs, thus changing the orientation of our brains in relation to our spines. You can save yourself some confusion if you remember that the system was adapted for use in primates in such a way that the terms used to describe the positions of various parts of the nervous system are the same in upright and nonupright animals. For example, notice in Figure 3.14 that the stomach and the bottom of the head are referred to as *ventral* in both humans and dogs, and that these labels do not change when an animal changes its posture. In primates, the terms **superior** and **inferior** are often used to refer to the top and bottom of the head, respectively.

In the next few pages, you will be seeing drawings of *sections* (slices) of the brain cut in one of three different planes: **horizontal, coronal (frontal),** or **sagittal.** These three planes are illustrated in Figure 3.15. A section cut down the center of the brain, between the two hemispheres, is called a *midsagittal section.* A section of tissue cut at a right angle to any long, narrow structure, such as the spinal cord or a nerve, is called a *cross section.*

FIGURE 3.13

Anatomical directions on a representative vertebrate.

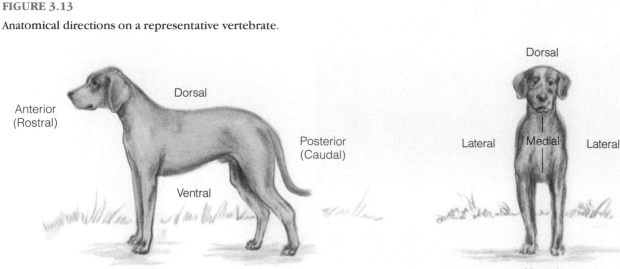

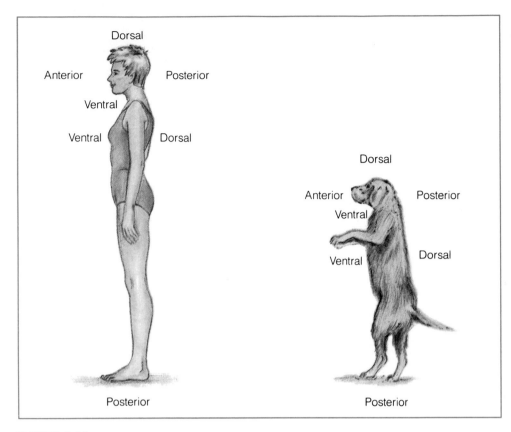

FIGURE 3.14

A comparison of neuroanatomical directions in humans and dogs.

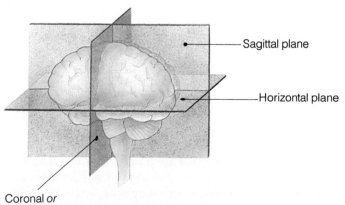

FIGURE 3.15

The orientation of horizontal, coronal (frontal), and sagittal sections in the human brain.

SELF TEST

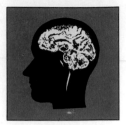

To test your comprehension of neuroanatomical directions, review the preceding section and fill in the following blanks:

1. The nose of a dog is _____ and _____ (or rostral) to the very top of its head.

2. The nose of a human is _____ (or inferior) and _____ to the very top of his or her head.

3. A slice taken in the _____ plane will expose both the tip of the nose and the throat.

4. A slice taken in either the _____ (or frontal) or the _____ plane will expose both eyes.

3.4

The Spinal Cord

In cross section, it is apparent that the spinal cord is composed of two different areas (see Figure 3.16): an inner H-shaped core of *gray matter* and a surrounding area of *white matter*. The gray matter is largely composed of cell bodies and unmyelinated interneurons, whereas the surrounding white matter is largely composed of ascending and descending myelinated axons. It is the myelin that gives the white matter its glossy white sheen. The four arms of the spinal gray matter are often referred to as the two **dorsal horns** and two **ventral horns.**

Pairs of *spinal nerves* pass between the vertebrae of the spine and enter the spinal cord—one from the left and one from the right—at 31 different levels of the spine. As shown in Figure 3.16, each of these 62 spinal nerves splits in two as it nears the cord, and its axons enter the cord via one of two roots: the *dorsal root* or the *ventral root.*

All dorsal root axons are sensory. Most are axons of sensory receptors in the skin, muscles, and joints. They are unipolar neurons with their cell bodies grouped together just outside the cord to form the *dorsal root ganglia;* their synaptic terminals are in the spinal cord gray matter (see Figure 3.17). In contrast, the neurons of the ventral root are multipolar neurons with their cell bodies in the ventral horns. Those that are part of the somatic nervous system project to skeletal muscles; those that belong to the ANS project to ganglia (groups of cell bodies in the PNS), where they synapse on neurons that project or to internal organs (heart, stomach, liver, etc.). See Appendix I.

The answers to the preceding review questions are: (1) ventral, anterior, (2) ventral, anterior; (3) midsagittal, and (4) coronal, horizontal.

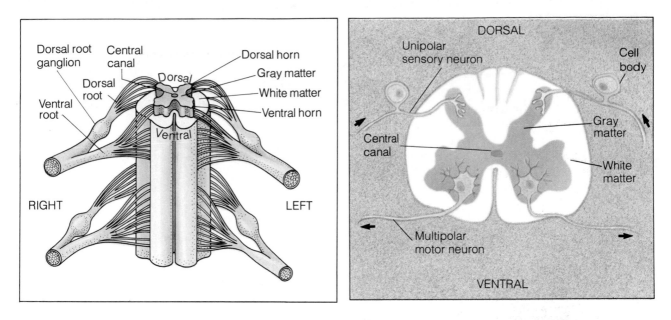

FIGURE 3.16

The peripheral nerves that are associated with two sections of the spinal cord.

FIGURE 3.17

A schematic cross section of the spinal cord.

3.5

The Five Major Divisions of the Brain

The vertebrate nervous system is considered to have five major divisions. In sequence from posterior to anterior, these are the *myelencephalon,* the *metencephalon,* the *mesencephalon,* the *diencephalon,* and the *telencephalon* (*encephalon* means *within the head*). These five divisions reflect the changes that the brain goes through during its embryological development. In the developing vertebrate embryo, the tissue that will eventually develop into the CNS is first recognizable as a fluid-filled tube (see Figure 3.18). The first indications of the developing brain are three swellings that occur at the anterior end of this tube. These are the antecedents of the *forebrain,* the *midbrain,* and the *hindbrain.*

In higher vertebrates, the forebrain undergoes extensive development. Large lateral outgrowths occur on the anterior end of the forebrain, and these eventually develop into the *cerebral hemispheres* or telencephalon. The posterior part of the forebrain, which does not develop into the cerebral hemispheres, is known as the diencephalon. There are also two divisions of the hindbrain. Swellings develop on the dorsal and ventral surface of the anterior portion of the hindbrain, and this portion is known as the metencephalon. The posterior portion of the hindbrain is the myelencephalon or *medulla.* The midbrain of an adult vertebrate is also known as the mesencephalon. The portion of the brain posterior to the telencephalon is often referred to as the **brain stem**—it is the stem from which the two cerebral hemispheres branch.

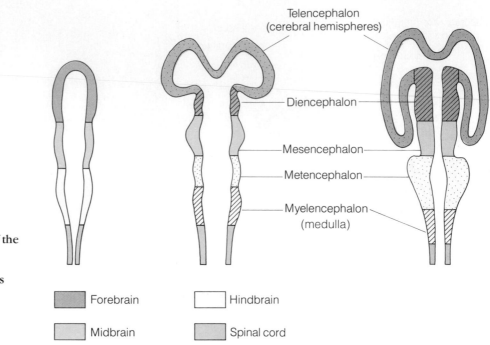

FIGURE 3.18

A schematic illustration of the early development of the mammalian brain (drawn from above). Compare this figure with Figure 3.19, which is color-coded according to the same scheme.

Telencephalon (cerebral hemispheres)

Diencephalon

Mesencephalon

Metencephalon

Myelencephalon (medulla)

Forebrain

Midbrain

Hindbrain

Spinal cord

3.6

The Major Structures of the Brain

The major structures of the brain, which are about to be described, are illustrated in the simplified schematic sagittal section of a generalized mammalian brain presented in Figure 3.19. Examine it carefully before you proceed.

Myelencephalon

Not surprisingly, the **myelencephalon** (medulla), the most posterior division of the brain, is composed almost entirely of tracts that carry signals between the rest of the brain and the body. In addition, it contains the nuclei of the cranial nerves that leave the brain at this level (see Appendix II).

An interesting part of the myelencephalon from a psychological perspective is the reticular formation. The **reticular formation** is a complex network of about 100 tiny nuclei that occupies the central core of the brain stem from the posterior boundary of the myelencephalon to the anterior boundary of the midbrain. Early neuroanatomists named it "the reticular formation" because of its net-like appearance—*reticulum* means *little net*. Sometimes the reticular formation is referred to as the *reticular activating system* (RAS) because parts of it seem to play a role in arousal; however, recent research suggests that the nuclei of the reticular formation are involved in a variety of specific, unrelated functions, including sleep, attention, movement, the maintenance of muscle tone, and various cardiac, circulatory, and respiratory reflexes. Accordingly, referring to this collection of nuclei as a "system" is misleading.

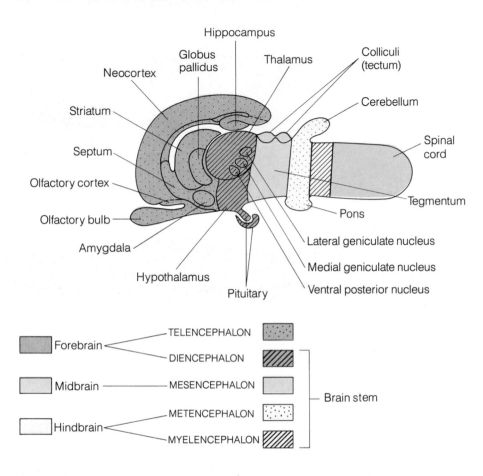

Forebrain {
  TELENCEPHALON
  DIENCEPHALON
}
Midbrain — MESENCEPHALON } Brain stem
Hindbrain {
  METENCEPHALON
  MYELENCEPHALON
}

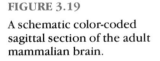

FIGURE 3.19

A schematic color-coded sagittal section of the adult mammalian brain.

Metencephalon

The **metencephalon,** like the myelencephalon, houses many ascending and descending tracts, the nuclei of cranial nerves, and part of the reticular formation. These structures create a bulge, called the **pons**, on the brain stem's ventral surface. The pons is one major division of the metencephalon; the other is the **cerebellum** (meaning *little brain*), the large convoluted structure on the brain stem's dorsal surface. The cerebellum is an important structure of the sensorimotor system (see Chapter 9).

Mesencephalon

The most obvious external feature of the **mesencephalon** or midbrain is the layer of tissue called the **tectum.** The word *tectum* means *roof,* and the tectum is the roof or dorsal surface of the midbrain. In mammals, the tectum forms two pairs of bumps or colliculi (little hills). The posterior pair have an auditory function and are called the **inferior colliculi;** the anterior pair have a visual function and are called the **superior colliculi.** In lower vertebrates, the tectum is composed of only a single pair of bumps, and it is referred to as the *optic tectum* because its function is entirely visual.

Figure 3.20 is a drawing of a cross section taken through the human midbrain. The entire area of the midbrain ventral to the tectum is referred to as

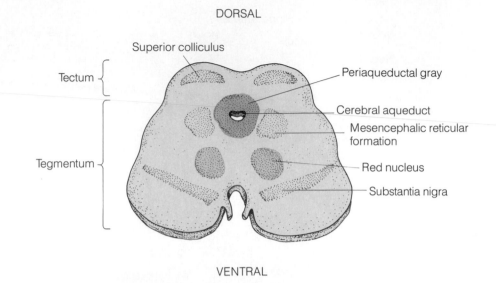

DORSAL

VENTRAL

FIGURE 3.20

A drawing of a cross section through the mammalian mesencephalon or midbrain.

the **tegmentum.** In addition to the reticular formation, cranial nerves, and tracts of passage, the tegmentum has three structures that are of particular interest to biopsychologists: the periaqueductal gray, the substantia nigra, and the red nucleus. The **periaqueductal gray** is the gray matter situated around the **cerebral aqueduct,** the duct connecting the third and fourth ventricles. The periaqueductal gray is of special interest because of its role in mediating the *analgesic* (pain-reducing) effects of opiate drugs (see Chapter 8). Both the **substantia nigra** and the **red nucleus** are important components of the sensorimotor system (see Chapter 9).

Diencephalon

The **diencephalon** is composed of two structures: the **thalamus** and the **hypothalamus.** The thalamus is a large two-lobed structure that is the top of the brain stem (see Figure 3.21). One lobe sits on each side of the third ventricle. The two lobes of the thalamus are joined by the **massa intermedia** which runs through the third ventricle. Surprisingly, many apparently normal people have been found to lack a massa intermedia.

The thalamus comprises many different pairs of nuclei, most of which project to the cortex. Some of the nuclei of the thalamus are sensory processing stations for specific sensory systems. They receive signals from sensory receptors, process them, and then transmit them to the appropriate areas of sensory cortex. For example, the **lateral geniculate nuclei,** the **medial geniculate nuclei,** and the **ventral posterior nuclei** are important processing stations in the visual, auditory, and somatosensory systems, respectively. Those thalamic nuclei that are not sensory processing stations project either specifically to particular areas of the cortex that do not have a sensory function, or they project diffusely to vast areas of cortex. The various thalamic nuclei are illustrated in Appendix IV.

Although the hypothalamus is a small structure (*hypo* means *less than*), only about one-tenth the size of the thalamus in humans, it plays an important role in the regulation of several motivated behaviors. In part, it exerts its ef-

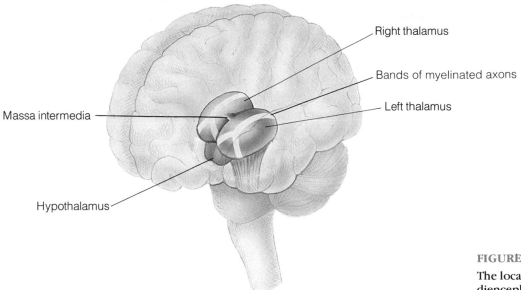

FIGURE 3.21
The location of the human diencephalon.

fects by regulating the release of hormones from the **pituitary gland** (see Chapter 11), which dangles from it on the ventral surface of the brain. The literal meaning of pituitary gland is *snot gland*. Because it was discovered in a somewhat gelatinous state behind the nose of an unembalmed cadaver, it was incorrectly assumed to be the main source of nasal mucus, and it was named accordingly.

On the inferior (ventral) surface of the brain (see Figure 3.22), just in front of the pituitary, is an X-shaped structure called the **optic chiasm.** The

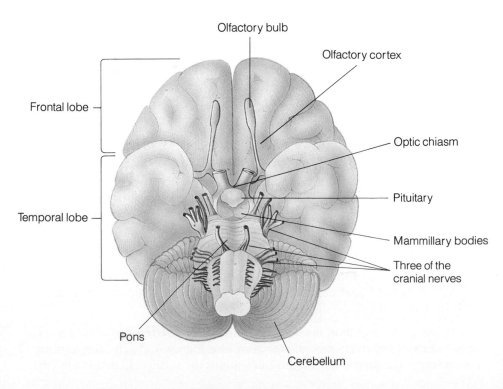

FIGURE 3.22
The inferior surface of the human brain.

optic chiasm is the point at which the *optic nerves* (the second cranial nerves) from each eye come together. The X-shape is created because some of the axons of the nerve **decussate** (cross over to the other side of the brain) at this point. The decussating fibers are said to be **contralateral** (projecting from one side of the body to the other), and the nondecussating fibers are said to be **ipsilateral** (staying on the same side of the body). The tiny pair of spherical structures just posterior to the pituitary are the **mammillary bodies,** two prominent nuclei of the hypothalamus. The mammillary bodies and the other nuclei of the hypothalamus are illustrated in Appendix V.

Telencephalon

The **telencephalon** is the largest division of the human brain, and it subserves its most complex functions. It initiates voluntary movement, interprets sensory input, and mediates various cognitive processes such as learning, speaking, and problem solving. Not surprisingly, it is the portion of the brain that is of most interest to many biopsychologists.

Cortex   The cerebral hemispheres are covered by a layer of tissue called the **cerebral cortex** (literally *cerebral bark*). In humans, the cortex is deeply furrowed. This furrowing has the effect of increasing the amount of cerebral cortex without increasing the overall volume of the brain—the surface area of the cerebral cortex is about 1.5 square feet. Not all mammals have furrowed cortices; for example, rats and some New World monkeys are *lissencephalic* (smooth-brained). Because the human brain is so highly convoluted, it is widely believed that the degree of cortical convolution is directly related to an animal's intellectual development; however, the degree of convolution appears to be related more to an animal's size. Every large mammal has a deeply convoluted cortex.

The large furrows in a convoluted cortex are called **fissures,** and the small ones are called **sulci** (singular *sulcus*). The ridges between fissures and sulci are called **gyri** (singular *gyrus*). The convolutions of the human brain and the degree to which they increase the area of cerebral cortex are illustrated in Figure 3.23. Notice that the cerebral hemispheres are almost completely separated by the **longitudinal fissure.** The hemispheres are joined by a few tracts called **commissures.** The largest is the **corpus callosum,** which is visible in Figure 3.23.

As indicated in Figure 3.24 the major landmarks on the surface of the human cortex are four deep fissures, the two **central fissures** and the two **lateral fissures,** and their adjacent gyri (gyruses). The **precentral gyri** serve a motor function, the **postcentral gyri** are **somatosensory** (i.e., receive input from sensory receptors of the skin, joints, and muscles), and the **superior temporal gyri** are largely auditory. These major fissures serve as a basis for dividing each hemisphere into four lobes: the **frontal lobe,** the **parietal** (pronounced pa RYE e tal) **lobe,** the **temporal lobe,** and the **occipital** (pronounced ok SIP i tal) **lobe.** The anterior, nonmotor cortex of the frontal lobe is called the **prefrontal cortex.** The function of occipital cortex is entirely visual (see Chapter 7).

About 90 percent of human cerebral cortex is **neocortex;** that is, it is six-layer cortex of relatively recent evolution (see Figure 3.25). By convention, the layers are numbered I through VI, starting at the surface. In mammals, two

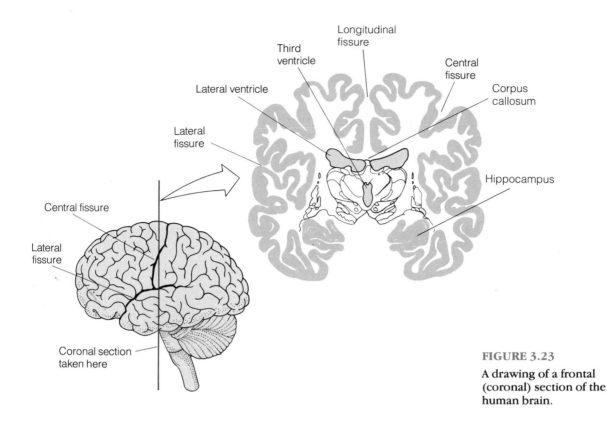

FIGURE 3.23

A drawing of a frontal (coronal) section of the human brain.

areas of cerebral cortex lack the six-layer structure characteristic of neocortex. One of these areas is the **olfactory cortex,** which is on the ventral surface of the frontal and temporal lobes, adjacent to the olfactory bulbs (see Figure 3.22). The olfactory cortex has three cell layers—two with cell bodies and one without. Almost all of the cerebral cortex of fish and most of the cerebral cortex of reptiles and birds is olfactory cortex. The other area of cerebral cortex in humans that is not neocortex is the hippocampus. The **hippocampus** is formed at the inferior, medial edge of the cortex as it folds back on itself in the medial temporal lobe—see Figure 3.23. This folding produces a shape that is somewhat reminiscent of a sea horse—*hippocampus* means *sea horse.* The hippocampus has only two cell layers, one with cell bodies and one without. Olfactory cortex and hippocampal cortex are often referred to as **paleocortex** (literally *old cortex*) because of their early evolutionary origins.

The cortex contains two kinds of neurons: **pyramidal cells** (multipolar neurons with pyramid-shaped cell bodies and long axons) and **stellate cells** (star-shaped interneurons). There are many kinds of stellate cells, including *granule cells, chandelier cells,* and *fusiform cells.* Layer I has few neurons; stellate cells are located in layers II through VI; and pyramidal cells are found primarily in layers II, III, and V.

The stellate cells of layer IV and the pyramidal cells of layer V serve opposite functions. Layer IV stellate cells receive sensory input to the neocortex; layer V pyramidal cells, the largest pyramidal cells of the neocortex, carry motor signals out of the neocortex to the brain stem and spinal cord. Accordingly, it is not surprising that regions of motor cortex are characterized by a

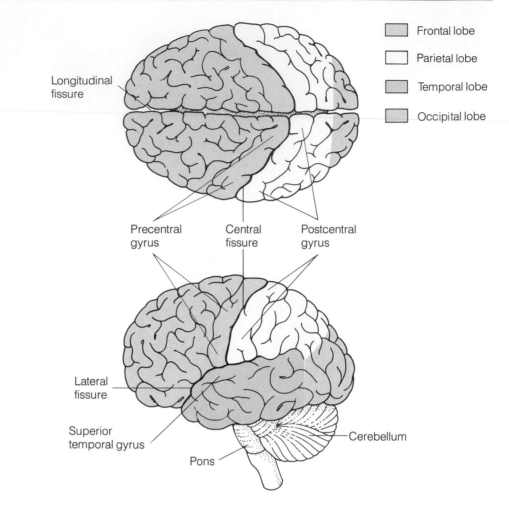

FIGURE 3.24

The lateral and dorsal surfaces of the human cerebral hemispheres.

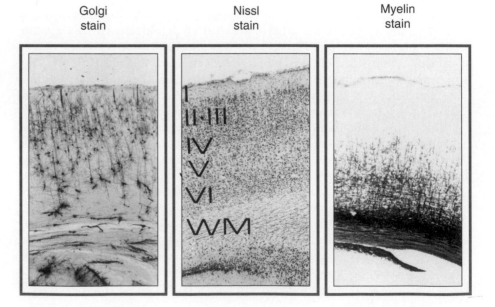

FIGURE 3.25

The neocortex. Adjacent slices of neocortex have been subjected to three different stains—Golgi (p. 70), Nissl (p. 72), and myelin (p. 90)—in order to illustrate its organization into six layers and underlying white matter (WM). The Golgi stain illustrates the shape of individual neurons, the Nissl stain illustrates the distribution of neural cell bodies, and the myelin stain illustrates the location of myelinated axons. (Supplied by Bryan Kolb, University of Lethbridge.)

particularly thick layer V, and regions of sensory cortex are characterized by a particularly thick layer IV. Interestingly, layer IV in the prefrontal cortex of primates, but not of other mammals, has a characteristic granular appearance because it is composed of particularly small, tightly packed stellate cells. Correlations between the anatomy and function of various regions of the neocortex are of major interest to biopsychologists—see Kolb and Tees (1990), Kolb and Whishaw (1990), and Bayer and Altman (1991).

The limbic system and the basal ganglia   Although much of the subcortical portion of the telencephalon is taken up by axons projecting to and from the neocortex, there are several large subcortical nuclear groups of importance. Most of them are considered to be part of either the *limbic system* or the *basal ganglia motor system.* Don't be misled by the word *system* in this context; it implies a level of certainty that is unwarranted. It is not entirely clear exactly what these hypothetical systems do, exactly which structures should be included in them, or even if it is appropriate to view them as unitary systems. Nevertheless, if not taken too literally, the concepts of a limbic system and a basal ganglia motor system provide a useful means of conceptualizing the organization of the subcortex.

The **limbic system** is a group of interconnected telencephalic and diencephalic structures that are believed to be involved in the regulation of motivated behaviors—including the four F's of motivation: fleeing, feeding, fighting, and sexual behavior. (This joke is as old as biopsychology itself, but it is a good one.) In addition to several structures about which you have already read (the hypothalamus, the mammillary bodies, the anterior nuclei of the thalamus, and the hippocampus), the amygdala, the cingulate cortex, the septum, and the fornix are commonly considered to be part of the limbic system. The **amygdala** (meaning "almond") is a large group of nuclei situated in the temporal lobe just anterior to the hippocampus, and the **septum** is situated on the midline just below the front of the corpus callosum and in front of the hypothalamus. The **cingulate cortex** is in a gyrus (the **cingulate gyrus**) that is hidden from external view in the longitudinal fissure just above the corpus callosum. The **fornix** (meaning "arch") is the major pathway of the system; it projects in an arc from the hippocampus along the edge of the third ventricle and then to the anterior nuclei of the thalamus, the septum, and the hypothalamus. The limbic system is illustrated in Figure 3.26.

The **basal ganglia** are illustrated in Figure 3.27. The basal ganglia include the **globus pallidus,** which sits just lateral to the thalamus in each hemisphere; the **putamen** (pronounced pew TAY men), which lies just lateral to the globus pallidus; the **caudate,** which is a long, curved structure that sweeps out of the anterior end of the putamen; and the *amygdala* (pronounced a MIG dah lah), which sits in the temporal lobe at the end of the caudate. The amygdala, you will recall, is also considered to be a component of the limbic system. The caudate and putamen together are known as the **striatum.**

The basal ganglia are thought to play a major role in the performance of voluntary motor responses. Of major interest is a pathway that projects to the striatum from the substantia nigra of the midbrain. *Parkinson's disease,* a disorder that is characterized by rigidity, tremors, and poverty of voluntary movement, is associated with the deterioration of this pathway (see Chapter 6).

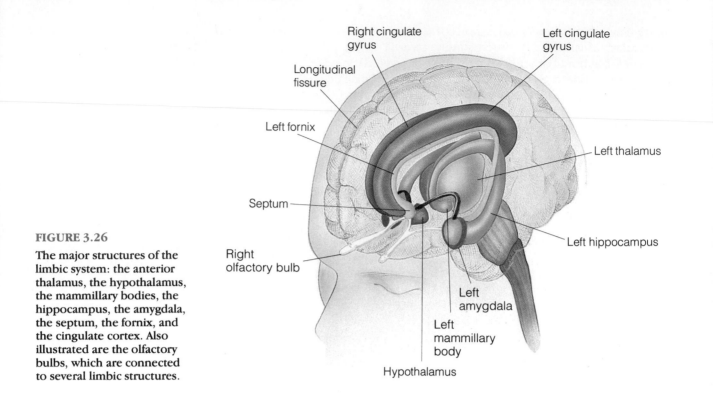

FIGURE 3.26

The major structures of the limbic system: the anterior thalamus, the hypothalamus, the mammillary bodies, the hippocampus, the amygdala, the septum, the fornix, and the cingulate cortex. Also illustrated are the olfactory bulbs, which are connected to several limbic structures.

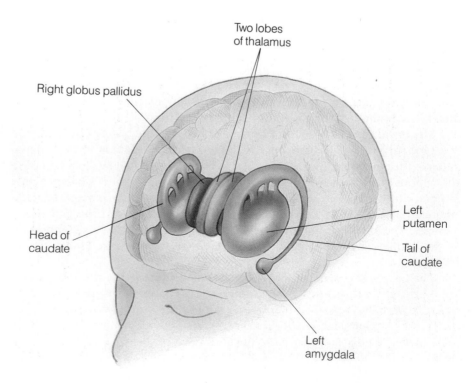

FIGURE 3.27

The basal ganglia: striatum (caudate plus putamen), globus pallidus, and amygdala.

Review of the Gross Anatomy of the Brain

If you have not previously studied the gross anatomy of the brain, your own brain is probably straining under the burden of new terms. It is time to pause and assess your progress. Test your knowledge of the brain by labeling the following (Figure 3.28) midsagittal section of the human brain. The correct answers are presented at the end of this chapter.

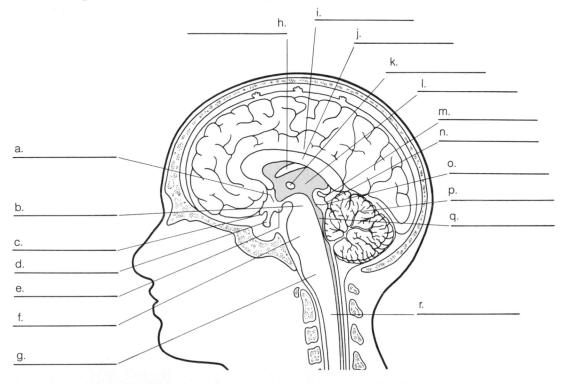

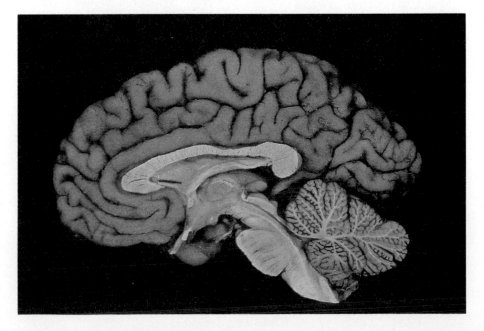

FIGURE 3.28

A midsagittal view of the human brain.

3.7

Neuroanatomical Tracing: Finding Out What Is Connected to What

Knowing how neural structures are connected to one another is important in understanding their function. This chapter concludes with a description of neuroanatomical techniques for tracing axons from one neural structure to another.

The first stain for studying axons was developed by Weigert in the 1880s. The **Weigert stain** selectively stains the sheaths of myelinated axons. Figure 3.29 is a Weigert-stained coronal section. Notice how the subcortical white matter is stained, while the cortex and various subcortical nuclear groups are not.

Although the Weigert stain is useful for visualizing myelinated areas of the CNS, it is not very useful for tracing axons for three reasons. First, it is of no use in tracking unmyelinated axons. Second, because the initial segment and terminal branches of myelinated axons are not myelinated, the Weigert stain cannot reveal exactly where a particular myelinated axon originates or where it terminates—the two most crucial pieces of information. And third, because the Weigert method stains all myelinated axons indiscriminately, once a my-

FIGURE 3.29

A Weigert-stained frontal section of the human brain. Notice that the white matter is stained black and the cortex and other nuclear groups are relatively unstained.

From *Fundamental Neuroanatomy* by Walle J. H. Nauta and Michael Feirtag. Copyright © 1986 W. H. Freeman and Company. Reprinted with permission.

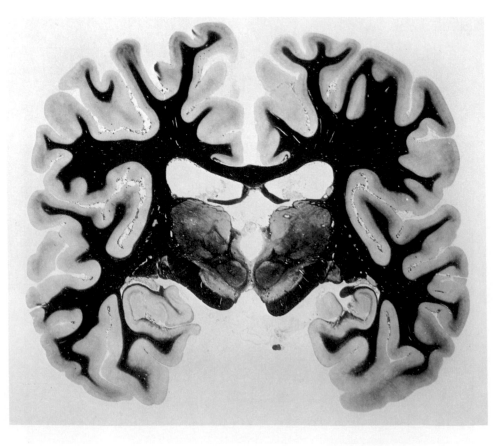

elinated axon (or group of axons) becomes intermingled with others, it is impossible to track it through a series of slices.

Modern neuroanatomical tracing techniques circumvent the problems with the Weigert method. These modern techniques are of two types: (1) *anterograde tracing methods* are used to determine where the axons that originate in a particular structure terminate; (2) *retrograde tracing methods* are used to determine where axons that terminate in a particular structure originate.

Anterograde Tracing

Many anterograde tracing studies employ a technique called **autoradiographic tracing.** This technique takes advantage of the fact that amino acids are absorbed from the extracellular medium by cell bodies, incorporated into proteins, and transported throughout the neuron. First, an amino acid is labeled with *tritium,* the radioactive isotope of hydrogen, and injected into the site whose anterograde projections are under investigation. Several days later, the brain is removed, hardened, and sliced; and the slices are coated with a photographic emulsion. Then the coated slides are stored in light-tight containers for several weeks. During this period, radioactive particles given off by the tritiated amino acid react with the photographic emulsion. The slides are then developed like a film to reveal the whereabouts of the tritiated amino acid at the time that the animal died. These locations of the tritiated amino acid mark the axons and buttons of the neurons whose cell bodies were at the site of injection.

Retrograde Tracing

A commonly used method of retrograde tracing is the **horseradish peroxidase (HRP)** technique. In the 1970s, it was discovered that horseradish peroxidase, an enzyme found in horseradish and various other plants, is readily taken up by the terminal buttons of axons and then transported back to their cell bodies at a rate of 200 to 300 millimeters per day. Accordingly, to discover the origins of the neural input to a site of interest, neuroscientists inject a minute quantity of horseradish peroxidase into it and wait for a day or two. Then, they slice the brain and expose the sections to a stain that dyes horseradish peroxidase. The location of the horseradish peroxidase marks the cell bodies of the neurons whose terminal buttons were at the site of the injection.

Conclusion

This chapter has introduced you to the neuron, to the general layout of the nervous system, to a basic vocabulary of neuroanatomical terms, and to a few neuroanatomical techniques.

Figure 3.30 concludes this chapter for reasons that too often get lost in the shuffle of neuroanatomical terms and technology. I have included it here to illustrate the beauty of the brain and the art of those who study its structure. I hope that you like it as much as I do.

FIGURE 3.30

Pyramidal cells. This slide was stained with a Golgi stain, and then it was counterstained with a Nissl stain. Characteristic of each pyramidal cell is its pyramid-shaped cell body, its *apical dendrite* (the major dendrite that extends vertically toward the cortical surface), and its *dendritic spines* (the bud-like synaptic sites on its dendrites). (Courtesy of Miles Herkenham, Unit of Functional Neuroanatomy, National Institute of Mental Health, Bethesda, MD.)

Food for Thought

1. Which of the following extreme positions do you think is closer to the truth? (a) The primary goal of all psychological research should be to relate psychological phenomena to the anatomy of neural circuits. (b) Psychologists should leave the study of neuroanatomy to neuroanatomists.

2. Perhaps the most famous and fortunate mistake in the history of biopsychology was made by Olds and Milner (see Chapter 12). They botched an electrode implantation operation on a rat, and the tip of the

stimulation electrode ended up in an unintended structure. When they subsequently tested the effects of electrical stimulation of this unknown structure, they made a fantastic discovery; the rat seemed to find the brain stimulation extremely pleasurable. In fact, the rat would press a lever for hours at an extremely high rate if every press produced a brief stimulation to its own brain through the electrode. If you had accidentally stumbled on this intracranial self-stimulation phenomenon, what neuroanatomical procedures would you have used to identify the stimulation site and the neural circuits involved in the pleasurable effects of the stimulation?

KEY TERMS

To help you study the material in this chapter, all of the key terms—those that have appeared in bold type—are either briefly defined here, or they appear in the table of key neuroanatomical terms that follows.

Afferent nerves. Nerves that carry signals toward the CNS.

Anterior. Toward the nose end of a vertebrate.

Arachnoid membrane. The menynx between the dura mater and the pia mater.

Astroglia. Large, star-shaped glial cells that play a role in the blood-brain barrier and form the supportive matrix for CNS neurons.

Autonomic nervous system (ANS). The portion of the PNS that participates in the regulation of the internal environment.

Autoradiographic tracing. An anterograde tracing technique in which a tritiated amino acid is injected into the site of interest.

Axodendritic synapses. Synapses between axons and dendrites.

Axon. The long, narrow process that leaves the cell body of many neurons.

Axon hillock. The cone-shaped region where the axon leaves the cell body.

Axosomatic synapses. Synapses between axons and cell bodies.

Bipolar neurons. Neurons with two processes extending from the cell body.

Blood-brain barrier. The mechanism that keeps certain toxic substances in the blood from penetrating the neural tissue.

Brain stem. The brain posterior to the telencephalon—the stem from which the two hemispheres branch.

Buttons. The bulbous endings of axon branches, which release neurotransmitters into synapses.

Caudal. Toward the tail end of a vertebrate.

Cell body (soma). The metabolic center of a neuron; the cell body contains the nucleus.

Cell membrane. The semipermeable membrane that encloses neurons and other cells.

Central canal. The small CSF-filled passage that runs the length of the spine.

Central nervous system (CNS). The portion of the nervous system within the skull and spine.

Cerebrospinal fluid (CSF). The protective colorless fluid that fills the subarachnoid space and the spaces in the core of the brain and spinal cord.

Choroid plexuses. The networks of capillaries that protrude into the ventricles and continuously produce CSF.

Commissures. Tracts joining the left and right cerebral hemispheres (e.g., the corpus callosum).

Contralateral. Projecting from one side of the body to the other.

Coronal section (frontal section). A slice of brain tissue cut in a plane that is parallel to the front of the brain.

Corpus callosum. The largest commissure.

Cranial nerves. The twelve pairs of nerves extending from the brain (e.g., optic nerves, olfactory nerves, and vagus nerves).

Cytoplasm. The clear, internal fluid of the cell.

Decussate. Cross over to the other side of the brain.

Dendrites. The short processes emanating from neuronal cell bodies.

Dorsal. Toward the back or toward the top of the brain.

Dorsal horns. The two dorsal arms of the spinal gray matter; where the dorsal roots enter.

Dura mater (tough mother). The outer menynx.

Efferent nerves. Nerves that carry signals away from the CNS.

Electron microscopy. A neuroanatomical procedure that is used to study the fine details of neural structure.

Fissures. The large furrows in the neocortex of humans and other animals with convoluted brains; sulci are small fissures.

Foramens. Narrow channels that link ventricles.

Ganglia (singular: ganglion). Clusters of neuronal cell bodies in the PNS.

Glial cells (neuroglia). The supportive cells of the CNS (e.g., astroglia and oligodendroglia).

Golgi stain. A neural stain that invades only a few of the cells in each slice of tissue.

Gyri (singular: gyrus). The ridges in the cerebral cortex between the sulci and the fissures.

Horizontal section. A slice of brain tissue cut in a plane that is parallel to the top of the brain.

Horseradish peroxidase (HRP). An enzyme that is readily taken up by the terminal buttons of axons and then transported back to their cell bodies.

Inferior. Toward the bottom of the primate brain.

Ipsilateral. On the same side of the body.

Lateral. Away from the midline.

Longitudinal fissure. The fissure that separates the two cerebral hemispheres.

Medial. Toward the midline.

Meninges (singular: menynx). The three protective membranes that swaddle the brain and spinal cord.

Multipolar neurons. Neurons that have more than two processes emanating from their cell bodies.

Myelin. A fatty insulation that is found around many axons.

Nerves. Large bundles of axons in the PNS.

Neurotransmitter. A chemical that is released into synapses from the buttons of active neurons and stimulates the neurons on the other side of the synapses.

Nissl stains. Neural stains that have an affinity for the RNA-rich structures of the neural cell bodies (e.g., *cresy violet*).

Nodes of Ranvier. The unmyelinated gaps between sections of myelin on myelinated axons.

Nucleus. The structure in the cell body that contains the DNA; or, a cluster of neuronal cell bodies in the CNS.

Oligodendroglia (oligodendrocytes). Glial cells that myelinate CNS axons.

Paleocortex (old cortex). The olfactory cortex and the hippocampus; cortex of early phylogenetic origin.

Parasympathetic nerves. Nerves of the ANS whose activity tends to conserve the body's energy resources.

Peripheral nervous system (PNS). The portion of the nervous system outside the skull and spine.

Pia mater (pious mother). The delicate, innermost menynx.

Posterior (caudal). Toward the tail end of a vertebrate, or toward the back of the head.

Prefrontal cortex. The anterior nonmotor cortex of the frontal lobe.

Pyramidal cells. Large cortical multipolar neurons with pyramid-shaped cell bodies.

Rostral (anterior). Toward the nose end of a vertebrate.

Sagittal section. A slice of brain tissue cut in a plane that is parallel to the side of the brain.

Satellite cells. Cells that provide a structural matrix for the neurons in the PNS.

Schwann cells. Satellite cells whose myelin-rich processes wrap around axons in the PNS.

Somatic nervous system. The portion of the PNS that interacts with the external environment.

Somatosensory. Referring to sensations from the body—for example from receptors in the skin, joints, and muscles.

Stellate cells. Star-shaped cortical interneurons; there are several varieties of stellate cells.

Subarachnoid space. The space beneath the arachnoid membrane, which contains the large blood vessels that are visible on the surface of the brain.

Sulci (singular: sulcus). Small fissures in the cerebral cortex.

Superior. Toward the top of the primate brain.

Superior sagittal sinus. A sinus that runs in the dura mater along the top of the brain between the two hemispheres.

Sympathetic nerves. Nerves of the ANS whose activity tends to mobilize energy resources and prepare the body for action

Synapses. The sites between adjacent neurons across which chemical signals are transmitted.

Synaptic vesicles. Tiny packets of neurotransmitter chemical, which are stored near the presynaptic membrane.

Tracts. Bundles of axons in the CNS.

Unipolar neurons. Neurons with one process emanating from the cell body.

Ventral. Toward the stomach surface of a vertebrate, or toward the bottom of the brain.

Ventral horns. The two ventral arms of spinal gray matter.

Ventricles. The four CSF-filled internal chambers of the brain; the two lateral ventricles, the third ventricle, and the fourth ventricle.

Weigert stain. Selectively stains the sheaths of myelinated axons.

KEY TERMS: NEUROANATOMICAL STRUCTURES

Telencephalon

cerebral cortex
- neocortex
- paleocortex
  - olfactory cortex
  - hippocampus

major fissures
- central fissure
- lateral fissure
- longitudinal fissure

major gyri
- precentral gyrus
- postcentral gyrus
- superior temporal gyrus
- cingulate gyrus

four lobes
- frontal lobe
- temporal lobe
- parietal lobe
- occipital lobe

limbic system
- amygdala
- hippocampus
- fornix
- septum
- cingulate cortex
- thalamus & hypothalamus

basal ganglia system
- globus pallidus
- striatum
  - putamen
  - caudate
- amygdala

Diencephalon

thalamus
- massa intermedia
- lateral geniculate nuclei
- medial geniculate nuclei
- ventral posterior nuclei

hypothalamus
- mammillary bodies

optic chiasm
pituitary gland

Mesencephalon

tectum
- superior colliculi
- inferior colliculi

tegmentum
- reticular formation
- cerebral aqueduct
- periaqueductal gray
- substantia nigra
- red nucleus

Metencephalon

reticular formation
pons
cerebellum

Myelencephalon

Like other divisions of the brain stem, it includes many tracts and several nuclei of cranial nerves.

reticular formation

ADDITIONAL READING

I recommend the following three books for those interested in learning more about neuroanatomy. The first is a wonderfully illustrated historical introduction to the brain; the second is a particularly clear neuroanatomy text; and the third is a classic collection of neuroanatomical illustrations.

Corsi, P. (1991). *The enchanted loom: Chapters in the history of neuroscience.* New York: Oxford.

Nauta, W. J. H., & Feirtag, M. (1986). *Fundamental neuroanatomy.* New York: Freeman.

Netter, F. H. (1962). *The CIBA collection of medical illustrations: Vol. 1, The nervous system.* New York: CIBA.

Answers to the Neuroanatomical Quiz on Page 89.

a. hypothalamus
b. tegmentum
c. optic chiasm
d. pituitary
e. mammillary body
f. pons
g. medulla (myelencephalon)
h. fornix
i. cingulate gyrus
j. corpus callosum
k. massa intermedia
l. third ventricle
m. superior colliculus
n. inferior colliculus
o. cerebral aqueduct
p. cerebellum
q. fourth ventricle
r. spinal cord

4

Neural Conduction and Synaptic Transmission

Chapter 3 introduced you to neural anatomy. This chapter introduces you to neural function—it is a chapter about how neurons work.

The nervous system's remarkable capacities result from the ability of neurons to conduct electrochemical signals and to transmit them across synapses. Neural conduction and synaptic transmission are the foci of this chapter. It begins with a description of how signals are generated in resting neurons; then, it follows the signals as they are conducted through neurons and transmitted across synapses to adjacent neurons.

4.1

The Neuron's Resting Membrane Potential

The key to neural function is the **membrane potential,** the difference in electrical charge that exists between the inside and the outside of a cell.

Recording the Membrane Potential

To record a neuron's membrane potential, it is necessary to position the tip of one electrode inside the neuron and the tip of another electrode outside the neuron in the extracellular fluid. Although the size and shape of the extracellular electrode are not critical, it is paramount that the tip of the intracellular electrode be fine enough to pierce the neural membrane without severely damaging it. The tips of intracellular **microelectrodes,** as they are called, are less than one thousandth of a millimeter in diameter—much too small to be seen by the naked eye.

To construct a microelectrode (see Figure 4.1), a fine glass tube is melted in the center and then pulled suddenly apart by an automated *microelectrode puller.* The infinitesimally small, but still hollow point at which the tube separates is the electrode tip. The tube is then filled with a concentrated salt solution through which neural signals can be recorded. The construction of the microelectrode is completed by inserting a wire into the solution through the larger end and sealing that end to fix the wire in place and to keep the solution from leaking out. The solution does not leak from the electrode tip because the opening is too small.

The intracellular and extracellular electrodes are connected by wires to an **oscilloscope,** a device that displays changes in the membrane potential over time as vertical displacements of a glowing spot as it sweeps across a fluorescent screen. Because the spot on an oscilloscope screen is produced by a beam of electrons, which has little inertia to overcome, an oscilloscope can accurately display even the most rapid changes in the membrane potential. Figure 4.2 is an illustration of how a membrane potential is recorded.

FIGURE 4.1

The construction of a microelectrode.

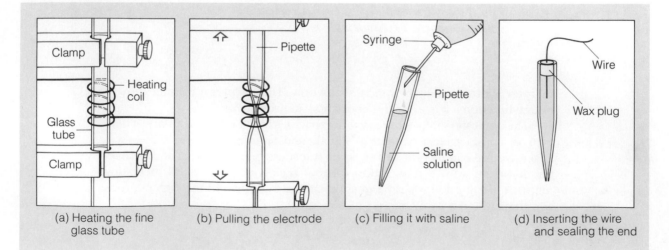

(a) Heating the fine glass tube

(b) Pulling the electrode

(c) Filling it with saline

(d) Inserting the wire and sealing the end

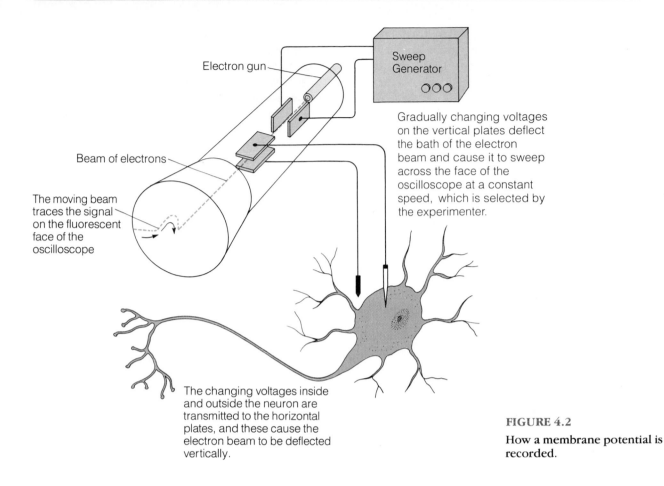

Electron gun

Sweep Generator

○○○

Gradually changing voltages on the vertical plates deflect the bath of the electron beam and cause it to sweep across the face of the oscilloscope at a constant speed, which is selected by the experimenter.

Beam of electrons

The moving beam traces the signal on the fluorescent face of the oscilloscope

The changing voltages inside and outside the neuron are transmitted to the horizontal plates, and these cause the electron beam to be deflected vertically.

FIGURE 4.2

How a membrane potential is recorded.

The Resting Membrane Potential

When both electrode tips are in the extracellular fluid, the voltage difference between them is zero. However, when the tip of the intracellular electrode is inserted into a neuron, a steady potential of about −70 millivolts (mV) is registered on the oscilloscope screen. This indicates that the potential inside the resting neuron is about 70 mV less than that outside the neuron. This steady membrane potential of about −70 mV is called the neuron's **resting potential.** In its resting state, with the −70 mV charge built up across its membrane, a neuron is said to be *polarized*.

The Ionic Basis of the Resting Potential

Why are resting neurons polarized? Like all salts in solution, the salts in neural tissue separate into positively and negatively charged particles called **ions.** The resting potential results from the fact that the ratio of negative to positive charges is greater inside the neuron than outside. Why this unequal distribution of charges occurs can be understood in terms of the interaction of four factors: two forces that act to distribute ions equally throughout the intracellular and extracellular fluids of the nervous system, and two features of the neural membrane that counteract these homogenizing influences.

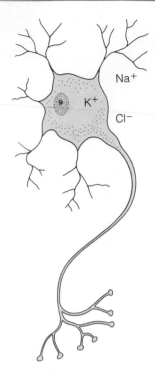

FIGURE 4.3

In its resting state, more Na⁺ and Cl⁻ ions are outside the resting neuron than inside, and more K⁺ ions are inside the neuron than outside. Not shown are the various negatively charged protein ions in the cytoplasm of the neuron.

The first of the two homogenizing forces is *random motion.* The ions in neural tissue are in constant random motion, and particles in random motion tend to become evenly distributed because they are more likely, for purely statistical reasons, to move down their *concentration gradients*—that is, they are more likely to move from areas of high concentration to areas of low concentration than vice versa. The second force that promotes the even distribution of ions is *electrostatic pressure.* Any accumulation of particular charges, positive or negative, in one area tends to be dispersed by the repulsion of like charges in the vicinity and the attraction of opposite charges concentrated elsewhere.

Despite the continuous homogenizing effects of random movement and electrostatic pressure, no single class of ions is distributed equally on the two sides of the neural membrane. Four kinds of ions contribute to the resting potential: sodium ions (Na⁺), potassium ions (K⁺), chloride ions (Cl⁻), and negatively charged protein ions. The concentration of both Na⁺ and Cl⁻ is greater outside a resting neuron than inside, whereas K⁺ ions are more concentrated on the inside. The negatively charged protein ions are synthesized inside the neuron and stay there. See Figure 4.3.

Two properties of the neural membrane are responsible for the unequal distribution of Na⁺, K⁺, Cl⁻, and protein ions in resting neurons. One of these properties is passive, that is, it does not involve the consumption of energy; whereas, the other is active, and does. The passive property of the neural membrane that contributes to the unequal disposition of ions is its differential permeability to Na⁺, K⁺, and Cl⁻, and protein ions. Both K⁺ and Cl⁻ ions readily diffuse through the neural membrane; Na⁺ ions diffuse through it with difficulty; and the negatively charged protein ions do not diffuse through it at all. Ions pass through the neural membrane at specialized pores called **ion channels;** each ion channel is specialized to some degree for the passage of particular ions.

In the 1950s, the classic experiments of Hodgkin and Huxley provided the first evidence that an energy-consuming process is involved in the maintenance of the resting potential. Hodgkin and Huxley began by wondering why the high extracellular concentrations of Na⁺ and Cl⁻ ions and the high intracellular concentration of K⁺ ions were not eliminated by the pressure for these ions to move down their concentration gradients through the membrane to the side of lesser concentration. Could the electrostatic pressure of −70 mV across the membrane be the counteracting force that maintained the unequal distribution of ions? To answer this question, Hodgkin and Huxley calculated for each of the three ions the electrostatic charge that would be required to offset the pressure for them to move down their concentration gradients. For Cl⁻ ions, this calculated value was −70 mV, the same as the actual resting potential. Hodgkin and Huxley thus concluded that when neurons are at rest, the unequal distribution of Cl⁻ ions across the neural membrane is maintained in equilibrium by the balance between the 70-mV force driving Cl⁻ ions down their concentration gradient into the neuron and the 70 mV of electrostatic pressure driving them out. The situation turned out to be different for the K⁺ ions. Hodgkin and Huxley calculated that −90 mV of electrostatic pressure would be required to keep intracellular K⁺ ions from moving down their concentration gradient and leaving the neuron, some 20 mV more than the resting potential. In the case of Na⁺ ions, the forces of both the concentration gradient and the electrostatic gradient were found to act in the same direction. In the resting neuron, the concentration of Na$^+$ ions outside the neuron creates 50 mV of pressure for Na$^+$ ions to move down their concentration gradient into the neuron, and this is added to the −70 mV of electrostatic pressure for them to move in the same direction.

According to Hodgkin and Huxley's measurements and calculations, Na$^+$ ions are continuously forced into resting neurons and K$^+$ ions are continuously forced out. Why then do the intracellular and extracellular concentrations of Na$^+$ and K$^+$ and the membrane potential remain constant in resting neurons? Hodgkin and Huxley concluded that there must be active mechanisms in the membrane to counteract the *influx* (in flow) of Na$^+$ ions by pumping them out as rapidly as they leak in, and to counteract the *efflux* (out flow) of K$^+$ ions by pumping them in as rapidly as they leak out. Figure 4.4 summarizes Hodgkin and Huxley's conclusions.

Hodgkin and Keynes (1955) confirmed the existence of an energy-consuming Na$^+$ pump in the neural membrane. They measured the transport of sodium ions out of a motor neuron by loading it with a radioactive isotope of sodium and measuring the accumulation of radioactivity in the extracellular fluid. Because the number of sodium ions that can passively diffuse from resting neurons against the concentration and electrostatic gradients is negligible, they concluded that the steady accumulation of radioactivity outside

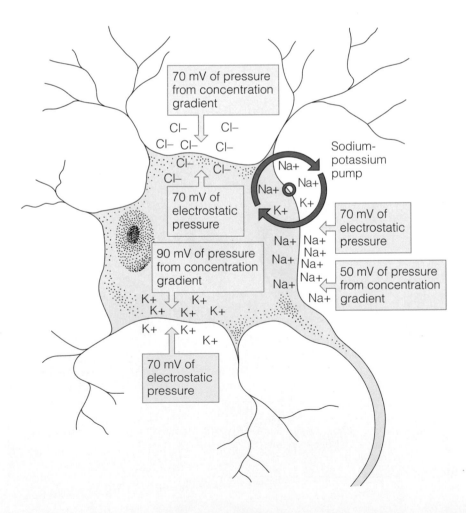

FIGURE 4.4

The passive and active forces that influence distribution of Na$^+$, K$^+$, and Cl$^-$ ions across the neural membrane. Passive forces from the electrostatic and concentration gradients continuously drive K$^+$ ions out of the resting neuron and Na$^+$ ions in; K$^+$ ions must be actively pumped in and Na$^+$ ions must be pumped out to maintain the resting equilibrium.

the neuron could result only from an active sodium-pumping action of the membrane. To provide evidence that this pumping process is energy consuming, Hodgkin and Keynes curtailed the use of energy by the neuron by bathing it in the metabolic poison, *dinitrophenol (DNP)*; this blocked the steady efflux of radioactive sodium. This experiment is illustrated in Figure 4.5.

FIGURE 4.5

Inhibition of the active transport of Na^+ ions out of the squid motor neuron by dinitrophenol (DNP).

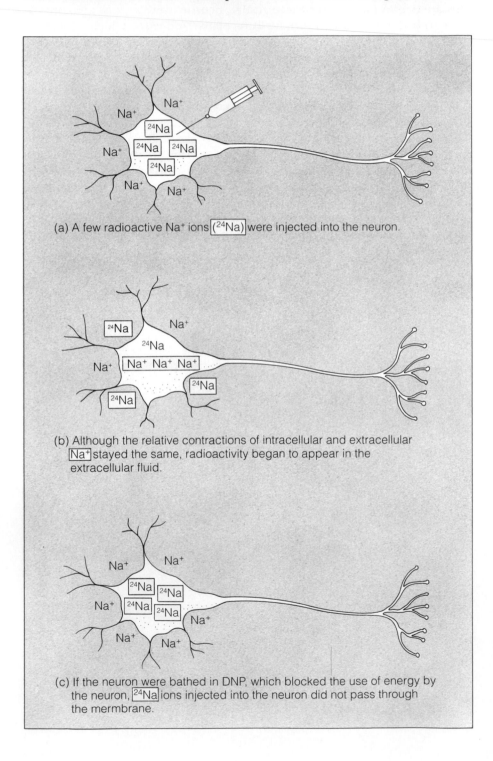

(a) A few radioactive Na^+ ions $\boxed{^{24}Na}$ were injected into the neuron.

(b) Although the relative contractions of intracellular and extracellular $\boxed{Na^+}$ stayed the same, radioactivity began to appear in the extracellular fluid.

(c) If the neuron were bathed in DNP, which blocked the use of energy by the neuron, $\boxed{^{24}Na}$ ions injected into the neuron did not pass through the mermbrane.

The active transport of Na^+ ions out of neurons and the active transport of K^+ ions into them are not independent processes. Active sodium and potassium transport seems to be carried out by a mechanism that exchanges Na^+ ions inside the neuron for K^+ ions outside—a mechanism commonly referred to as the **sodium-potassium pump.** Because sodium ions are normally transported out of the neuron at a rate that is 50 percent more than the rate at which potassium ions are transported in, it is assumed that under normal conditions sodium-potassium pumps exchange three Na^+ ions for every two K^+ ions.

Table 4.1 summarizes the major factors that are responsible for maintaining the differences between the intracellular and extracellular concentrations of Na^+, K^+, and Cl^- ions in resting neurons. These differences plus the negatively charged protein ions, which are trapped inside the neuron, are responsible for the resting membrane potential. Now that you understand these basic properties of the resting neuron, you are prepared to consider how neurons respond to input.

Table 4.1 The Factors Responsible for Maintaining the Differences in the Intracellular and Extracellular Concentrations of Na^+, K^+, and Cl^- Ions in Resting Neurons

Ion	*Summary of Factors Influencing the Location of Na^+, K^+, and Cl^- Ions*
Na^+	Na^+ ions are driven into the neuron by both the high concentration of Na^+ ions outside the neuron and the negative internal resting charge of -70 mV. However, the membrane is resistant to the passive diffusion of Na^+, and the sodium-potassium pump is thus able to maintain the high external concentration of Na^+ ions by pumping them out at the same slow rate as they leak in.
K^+	K^+ ions are driven out of the neuron by their high internal concentration, although this pressure is to a large degree offset by the internal negative charge. Despite the minimal pressure for the K^+ ions to leave the neuron, they do so at a substantial rate because the membrane offers little resistance to their passage. To maintain the high internal concentration of K^+ ions, they are pumped into neurons at the same rate as they diffuse out.
Cl^-	There is little resistance in the neural membrane to the passage of Cl^- ions. Thus, Cl^- ions are readily forced out of the neuron by the negative internal charge. As chloride ions begin to accumulate on the outside, there is increased pressure for them to move down their concentration gradient back into the neuron. When the point is reached where the electrostatic pressure for Cl^- ions to move out of the neuron is equal to the pressure for them to move back in, the distribution of Cl^- ions is held in equilibrium. This point of equilibrium occurs at -70 mV.
Protein Ions	Negatively charged protein ions are synthesized inside the neuron and are held there by the neural membrane.

4.2

The Generation and Conduction of Postsynaptic Potentials

When neurons fire, they usually release from their terminal buttons chemicals called **neurotransmitters,** which diffuse across the synaptic clefts and interact with specialized receptor molecules on the receptive membranes of the next neurons in the circuit. When neurotransmitter molecules bind to postsynaptic receptors, they have one of two effects, depending on the structure of both the neurotransmitter and the receptor in question. They may **depolarize** the receptive membrane (decrease the resting membrane potential, from −70 to −67 mV, for example) or they may **hyperpolarize** it (increase the resting membrane potential, from −70 to −72 mV, for example). The postsynaptic depolarizations are called **excitatory postsynaptic potentials (EPSPs)** because, as you will soon learn, they increase the likelihood that the neuron will fire. The postsynaptic hyperpolarizations are called **inhibitory postsynaptic potentials (IPSPs)** because they decrease the likelihood that the neuron will fire. Both EPSPs and IPSPs are **graded responses.** This means that the amplitudes of EPSPs and IPSPs are proportional to the intensity of the signals that elicit them—weak signals elicit small postsynaptic potentials; strong signals elicit large ones.

EPSPs and IPSPs travel passively from their sites of generation at synapses, usually on the dendrites or cell body, in much the same way that electrical signals travel through a cable. Accordingly, the transmission of postsynaptic potentials has two important characteristics. First, it is rapid—so rapid that it can be assumed to be instantaneous for most purposes. It is important not to confuse the duration of EPSPs and IPSPs with their rate of transmission; although the duration of EPSPs and IPSPs can vary considerably, they are all, whether brief or enduring, transmitted at great speed. Second, the transmission of EPSPs and IPSPs is *decremental.* EPSPs and IPSPs decrease in amplitude as they travel through the neuron, just as an electrical signal weakens as it travels through a long cable or as a sound grows fainter as it travels through air.

4.3

The Integration of Postsynaptic Potentials and the Generation of Action Potentials

The postsynaptic potentials created at a single synapse typically have little effect on the firing of the postsynaptic neuron. The receptive areas of most neurons are covered with thousands of synapses, and whether or not a neuron fires is determined by the net effect of their activity. More specifically, whether or not a neuron fires depends on the balance between the excitatory and inhibitory signals reaching its **axon hillock,** the conical structure at the junction between the cell body and the axon.

The graded EPSPs and IPSPs created by the action of neurotransmitters at particular receptive sites on the neural membrane are conducted instantly and decrementally to the axon hillock. If the sum of all of the depolarizations and hyperpolarizations reaching the axon hillock is sufficient to depolarize the membrane to a level referred to as its **threshold of excitation**—about −65 mV for many neurons—an **action potential (AP)** will be generated at the axon hillock. The action potential is a massive momentary (about 1 millisecond) reversal of the membrane potential from −70 to +50 mV. Unlike postsynaptic potentials, action potentials are not graded responses; their magnitude is not related in any way to the intensity of stimuli that elicit them. They are **all-or-none responses;** that is, they either occur full-blown, or they do not occur at all. See Figure 4.6 for an illustration of EPSPs, IPSPs, and APs.

In effect, each multipolar neuron adds together all the graded excitatory and inhibitory postsynaptic potentials reaching its axon hillock, and it "makes its decision" to fire or not to fire on the basis of their sum. Adding or combining a number of individual signals into one overall signal like this is called **integration.** Neurons integrate their postsynaptic potentials in two ways: over space and over time. Figure 4.7 illustrates the experimental procedure for demonstrating the three types of **spatial summation.** It illustrates: (1) how local EPSPs that are produced simultaneously on different parts of the receptive membrane sum to form a greater EPSP, (2) how simultaneous IPSPs sum to form a greater IPSP, and (3) how simultaneous EPSPs and IPSPs sum to cancel one another out.

Figure 4.8 illustrates the experimental procedure for demonstrating **temporal summation;** that is, how postsynaptic potentials produced in rapid succession at the same synapse sum to form a greater signal. The reason that stimulations of a neuron can summate over time is that the postsynaptic potentials that they produce outlast them. Thus, if a particular synapse is activated and then activated again before the original postsynaptic potential has dissipated, the effect of the second stimulus will be superimposed on the lingering postsynaptic potential produced by the first. Accordingly, it is possible

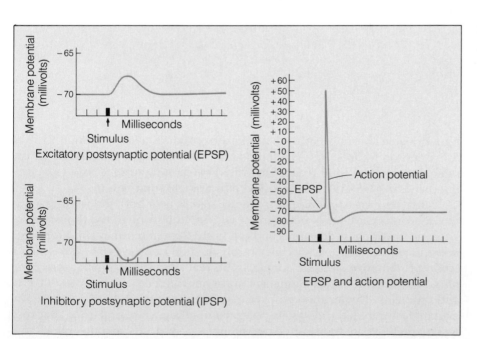

FIGURE 4.6

A record of the membrane potential of a neuron illustrating an EPSP, an IPSP, and an AP.

FIGURE 4.7
The three combinations of
spatial summation.

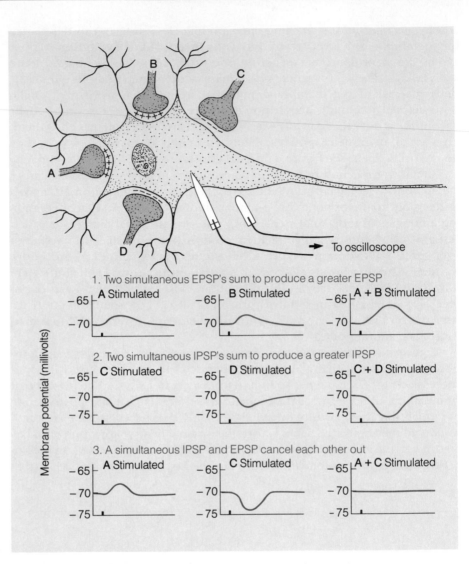

for a brief excitatory stimulus that does not produce a large enough EPSP to fire a neuron to do so if it is administered twice in rapid succession. In the same way, an inhibitory synapse activated twice in rapid succession can produce a greater IPSP than that produced by a single stimulation.

Most neurons continuously integrate signals over both time and space as the neuron is continually bombarded with stimuli through the thousands of synapses covering its dendrites and cell body. Remember that although schematic diagrams of neural circuitry rarely include neurons with more than a few representative synaptic contacts, the real situation is much more complex. For example, each mammalian motor neuron receives about 10,000 synaptic contacts. The location of a synapse on a receptive membrane is an important factor in determining its potential to influence neural firing. Because EPSPs and IPSPs are transmitted decrementally, synapses near the hillock trigger zone have the most influence on the firing of the neuron. This may explain

FIGURE 4.8

The two combinations of temporal summation.

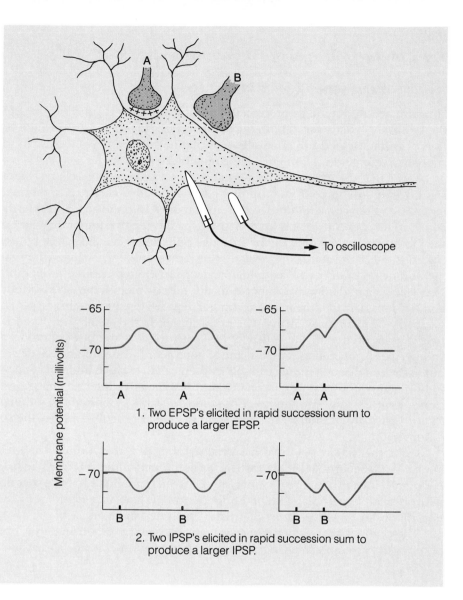

why synaptic contacts are often *segregated;* why axons from one part of the brain might all synapse on the cell body of the target neuron, whereas those from another part might favor dendritic target sites.

In some ways the firing of a neuron is like the firing of a gun. Both are all-or-none reactions triggered by graded responses. As a trigger is squeezed, it gradually moves back until it causes the gun to fire; as a neuron is stimulated, it becomes less polarized until the threshold of excitation is reached, and the neuron fires. And the firing of a gun and neural firing are both all-or-none events. Just as squeezing a trigger harder does not make the bullet travel faster or farther, stimulating a neuron more intensely does not increase the speed or amplitude of the resulting action potential.

4.4

The Conduction of Action Potentials

Ionic Basis of Action Potentials

How are action potentials produced, and how are they conducted through the neuron? The answer to both questions is basically the same: through action of **voltage-gated ion channels,** ion channels that open and close in response to changes in the voltage of the membrane potential.

Recall that the membrane potential of a neuron at rest is relatively constant despite the force from both the external positive charge and the high external sodium concentration for Na^+ ions to flow into the cell. The external concentration of Na^+ ions is held in check by the relative impermeability of the membrane to Na^+ ions and by an active pumping mechanism that pumps Na^+ ions out of the cell as they leak in. But things suddenly change when the membrane potential at the axon hillock drops to the threshold of excitation. The voltage-gated sodium channels in the hillock membrane open briefly, and Na^+ ions rush into the neuron, immediately driving the membrane potential from −70 to almost +50 mV. The rapid change in the membrane potential that is associated with the *influx* of Na^+ ions triggers the brief opening of voltage-gated potassium channels, and K^+ ions near the membrane are driven out of the cell through these channels by their relatively high internal concentration and by the positive internal charge. The positive internal charge also draws some Cl^- ions into the cell. Both the *efflux* of K^+ ions and the influx of Cl^- ions partially counteract the effects on the membrane potential of the sodium influx.

Once the action potential has reached its peak, the sodium channels close, and the neuron is repolarized by the continued efflux of K^+ ions. In fact, enough K^+ ions exit before the potassium channels are finally closed that the neuron is left hyperpolarized for a brief period of time—see Figure 4.6. The flow of ions during the action potential is illustrated in Figure 4.9.

The number of ions that flow through the membrane during an action potential is extremely small in relation to the total number inside and around

FIGURE 4.9

The flow of Na^+ and K^+ ions through an axonal membrane during an action potential.

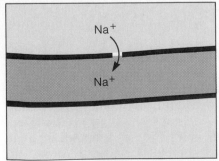

1. Sodium channels open and Na^+ ions rush into the neuron.

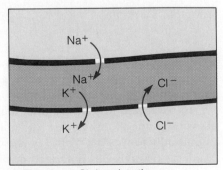

2. This draws Cl^- ions into the neuron and momentarily opens potassium channels to allow K^+ ions to flow out and briefly hyperpolarize the neuron.

the neuron. It involves only a few ions right next to the membrane. Therefore, an action potential has little effect on the relative concentrations of various ions inside and outside the neuron, and the membrane potential is rapidly re-established by the random movement of ions. The sodium-potassium pump plays only a minor role in the re-establishment of the resting potential. If the sodium-potassium pump is blocked by *dinitrophenol* (DNP), thousands of action potentials can occur before the extracellular concentrations of Na^+ ions and the intracellular concentrations of K^+ ions become so low that no more action potentials can be elicited.

Refractory Periods

There is a brief period of about 1 to 2 milliseconds after the initiation of an action potential during which it is impossible to elicit a second one. This period is called the **absolute refractory period.** The absolute refractory period is followed by the **relative refractory period,** a period during which it is possible to fire a neuron but only by applying higher than normal levels of stimulation. The end of the relative refractory period is the point at which the amount of stimulation necessary to fire a neuron returns to baseline.

The refractory period is responsible for two important characteristics of neural activity. First, it is responsible for the fact that action potentials normally travel along axons in only one direction. Because the portions of an axon over which an action potential has just traveled are left momentarily refractory, an action potential cannot reverse direction. Second, it is responsible for the fact that the rate of neural firing is related to the intensity of the stimulation. If a neuron is subjected to an extremely high level of continual stimulation, it fires and then fires again as soon as the absolute refractory period is over—a maximum of about 1,000 times per second. However, if the level of stimulation is of an intensity just sufficient to fire the neuron when it is at rest, the neuron does not fire again until both the absolute and relative refractory periods have run their course. And intermediate levels of stimulation produce intermediate rates of neural firing.

Conduction of Action Potentials

The conduction of action potentials along an axon differs from the conduction of EPSPs and IPSPs in two important ways. First, the conduction of action potentials along an axon is *nondecremental;* action potentials do not grow weaker as they travel along the axonal membrane. Second, action potentials are transmitted along the axonal membrane more slowly than postsynaptic potentials.

The reason for these two differences is that the conduction of EPSPs and IPSPs is passive, whereas the axonal conduction of action potentials is active. Once an action potential has been generated at the axon hillock, it travels passively along the axonal membrane to the adjacent voltage-gated sodium channels, which have yet to open. The arrival of the signal opens these channels, thus allowing Na^+ ions to rush into the neuron and generate a full-blown action potential on this portion of the membrane. This signal is then conducted passively to the next sodium channels, where another action potential is triggered. These events are repeated again and again until a full-blown action potential is triggered in the terminal buttons. Because the ion channels on the axonal membrane are so close together, it is usual to think of axonal transmission as a single wave of excitation spreading actively at a constant speed along the axon, rather than as a series of discrete events. The wave of excitation triggered by the generation of an action potential on the hillock membrane also spreads back through the cell body and dendrites of the neuron; however, because the sodium channels of the cell body and dendrites are not voltage-gated, the conduction of action potentials back through the cell body and dendrites is passive.

The following analogy may help you appreciate the major characteristics of axonal conduction. Consider a row of mouse traps on a wobbly shelf, each set and ready to be triggered. Each trap stores energy by holding back its striker against the pressure of the spring, in the same way that each sodium channel stores energy by holding back Na^+ ions, which are under pressure to move down their concentration and electrostatic gradients into the neuron. When the first trap in the row is triggered, the vibration is transmitted passively through the shelf, and the next trap is sprung—and so on down the line. The nondecremental nature of action potential transmission is readily apparent from this analogy; the trap at the end of the shelf strikes with no less intensity than did the first. This analogy also illustrates the refractory period; a trap cannot respond again until it has been reset, just as a section of axon cannot fire again until it has been repolarized. Furthermore, the row of traps can transmit in either direction, just like an axon. If stimulation of sufficient intensity is applied to the terminal end of an axon, an action potential will be generated that will travel along the axon back to the cell body. This is called **antidromic** conduction; axonal conduction in the natural direction, that is from cell body to terminal buttons, is called **orthodromic.**

Conduction in Myelinated Axons

In Chapter 3 you learned that the axons of many neurons are insulated from the extracellular fluid by segments of fatty tissue called *myelin.* In myelinated axons, ions can pass through the axonal membrane only at the gaps between the segments, the **nodes of Ranvier** (pronounced rahn vee yay). How then are action potentials transmitted in myelinated axons?

When an action potential is generated across the hillock membrane of a myelinated axon, the signal is conducted passively, that is instantly and decrementally, along the axon to the first node of Ranvier. Although the signal is somewhat diminished by the time is reaches the first node, it is still strong enough to open the voltage-gated sodium channels at the node and to generate another full-blown action potential. This action potential is conducted passively to the next node, where another full-blown action potential is elicited, and so on.

Myelination increases the speed of axonal conduction. Because conduction along the myelinated segments of the axon is passive, it occurs instantly, and the signal, in a sense, "jumps" down the axon from node to node. There is, of course, a slight delay at each node of Ranvier while the action potential is actively regenerated, but the conduction in myelinated axons is still much faster than in unmyelinated axons, in which passive conduction plays a less prominent role. The transmission of action potentials in myelinated axons is called **saltatory conduction,** from the Latin *saltare,* which means *to dance or jump.*

The Velocity of Axonal Conduction

At what speed are action potentials conducted along an axon? The answer to this question depends on two properties of the axon. Conduction is faster in large-diameter axons, and—as you have just learned—it is faster in those that are myelinated. Mammalian motor neurons are large and myelinated, and thus they can conduct at speeds of up to 100 meters per second (about 224 miles per hour). In contrast, small unmyelinated axons conduct action potentials at about 1 meter per second.

4.5

Synaptic Transmission: The Chemical Transmission of Signals from One Neuron to Another

You have already learned in this chapter how excitatory postsynaptic potentials are generated on the receptive membrane; how these graded potentials are conducted passively to the axon hillock; how the sum of these graded potentials triggers all-or-none action potentials; and how these all-or-none action potentials are actively conducted down the axon to the terminal buttons. In the remaining sections of this chapter, you will learn how signals are chemically transmitted from one neuron to another.

Structure of the Synapse

Figure 4.10 is a schematic representation of a synapse. In the cytoplasm of the terminal button, notice the **synaptic vesicles,** which are located near the *presynaptic membrane;* the **mitochondria,** which are important sources of energy; and the **cisternas,** which are neurotransmitter packaging plants similar to the *Golgi apparatus* of the cell body. Notice the web-like material that holds the *presynaptic membrane* and the *postsynaptic membrane* in close proximity.

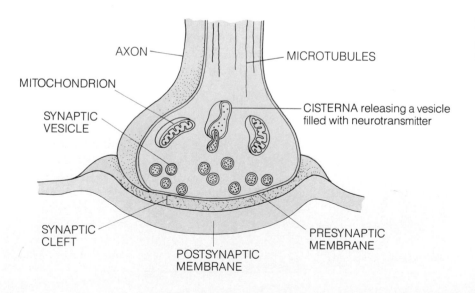

FIGURE 4.10

A schematic diagram of a synapse.

Mechanisms of Synaptic Transmission

Neural signals are transmitted from one neuron to another by chemical neurotransmitters. Neurotransmitter molecules are synthesized in the cytoplasm of the neuron, packaged in vesicles, and stored near presynaptic membranes, where they are ready for release. They are released in response to the arrival of action potentials at the terminal buttons. Once released by the neuron, neurotransmitter molecules induce signals in other neurons by binding to receptor molecules on their surface. Just how these steps in synaptic transmission are accomplished depends on the particular neurotransmitter under consideration. There are two fundamentally different systems of neurochemical transmission: one for *small-molecule neurotransmitters* and one for *large-molecule neurotransmitters* (see DeCamilli & Jahn, 1990; Matteoli & DeCamilli, 1991).

Small-molecule neurotransmitters   Small-molecule neurotransmitters are typically synthesized in the cytoplasm of the button and packaged in synaptic vesicles by the cisternas, which manufacture the vesicles from excess pieces of button membrane that break off into the cytoplasm (Miller & Heuser, 1984). Once filled with neurotransmitter, the vesicles are stored near areas of the presynaptic membrane that are particularly rich in *calcium channels* (Robitaille, Adler, & Charlton, 1990). When stimulated by action potentials, the calcium channels open and the Ca^{++} ions enter the button. The entry of the Ca^{++} ions causes the synaptic vesicles to fuse with the presynaptic membrane and empty their contents into the synaptic cleft. The process of neurotransmitter release, which is termed **exocytosis,** is illustrated schematically in Figure 4.11. Figure 4.12 is a photomicrograph of exocytosis in progress (Heuser, 1977)—see Knight, von Grafenstein, and Athayde (1989).

Once they are released, small-molecule neurotransmitters bind to receptor molecules on adjacent portions of the postsynaptic membrane. The binding of small-molecule neurotransmitters to their receptors influences postsynaptic neurons in one of two ways: it opens or closes **chemically gated ion channels** that are associated with the receptor, or it initiates a series of chemical reactions in the postsynaptic cell—molecules created in the cytoplasm by the binding of a neurotransmitter to a receptor molecule are called **second messengers.** In either case, the effects of small-molecule neurotransmitters on postsynaptic neurons are short-lived. Small-molecule neurotransmitters are quickly broken down by enzymes in the synaptic cleft, or they are quickly drawn back into the presynaptic button for recycling. Any second

FIGURE 4.11

A schematic representation of neurotransmitter release.

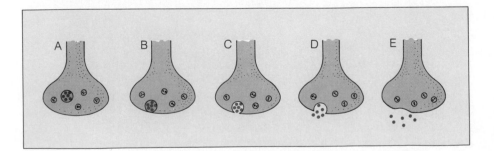

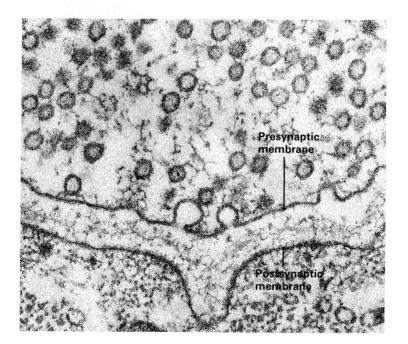

Presynaptic
membrane

Postsynaptic
membrane

FIGURE 4.12

A photomicrograph of a terminal button captured in the act of exocytosis. As you look at this photograph, exocytosis is occuring billions of times each second in your brain. Reproduced from Heuser, J. E., et al., the *Journal of Cell Biology*, 1979, *81*, 275–300 by copyright permission of The Rockefeller University Press.

messengers that have been created by small-molecule neurotransmitters are rapidly broken down by enzymes in the cytoplasm of the postsynaptic neurons.

Large-molecule neurotransmitters Large-molecule neurotransmitters are **peptides,** chains of amino acids that are fewer than 10 amino acids long (*polypeptides* are between 10 and 100 amino acids long, and *proteins* are more than 100 amino acids long). Peptides, like proteins, are synthesized in the cytoplasm of the cell body by ribosomes. Then, they are packaged in vesicles by the **Golgi apparatus** and transported to the buttons by long **microtubules** in the axonal cytoplasm at a rate of about 400 millimeters per day (Vallee & Bloom, 1991). The vesicles that contain large-molecule neurotransmitters are larger than those that contain small-molecule neurotransmitters; they have darker cores, and they do not congregate so closely to the presynaptic membrane (Thureson-Klein & Klein, 1990). Like the exocytosis of small-molecule neurotransmitters, the exocytosis of large-molecule neurotransmitters is controlled by Ca^{++} ions—but in a different way. Small-molecule neurotransmitters are released in a pulse each time that an action potential triggers a momentary increase in Ca^{++} ions next to the presynaptic membrane; large-molecule neurotransmitters are released gradually in response to a general increase in intracellular Ca^{++} ions, such as might occur during a general increase in the rate of neuron firing (DeCamilli & Jahn, 1990).

Large-molecule neurotransmitters tend to have widespread effects because they are often released into the extracellular fluid, the ventricles, or the bloodstream, rather than into synaptic clefts. Accordingly, they often bind to receptors at a considerable distance from their site of release. The binding of large-molecule neurotransmitters to receptors on neural membranes produces gradual long-lasting changes in the neurons via second-messenger systems (Schwartz, 1987).

The differences between small- and large-molecule neurotransmitter systems suggest that they serve different functions. Small-molecule neurotransmitters transmit brief excitatory and inhibitory messages to local postsynaptic receptors. In contrast, large-molecule neurotransmitters seem to function as **neuromodulators;** they are believed to increase or decrease the sensitivity of large populations of neurons to the local effects of small-molecule neurotransmitters. Neuromodulators are thought to influence behavior by regulating emotional and motivational tone.

4.6

The Neurotransmitters

There are three classes of neurotransmitters. Two are classes of small-molecule neurotransmitters, the *amino acid neurotransmitters* and the *monoamine neurotransmitters,* and one is a class of large-molecule neurotransmitters, the *peptide neurotransmitters.* In addition, there is acetylcholine, a small-molecule neurotransmitter that is in a class by itself. Professors who are late for lecture are also often in a class by themselves.

The Amino Acid Neurotransmitters

The neurotransmitters used in a vast majority of fast-acting, point-to-point synapses in the central nervous system are **amino acids,** the molecular building blocks of proteins. There are four that have proven to be neurotransmitters to the satisfaction of most experts: **glutamate, aspartate, glycine,** and **gamma-aminobutyric acid (GABA).** The first three are common in the proteins that we consume, whereas GABA is synthesized by a simple modification of the structure of glutamate. Glutamate is the most prevalent excitatory neurotransmitter in the mammalian CNS; GABA is the most prevalent inhibitory neurotransmitter. However, GABA has recently been shown to have excitatory effects at some synapses (Michelson & Wong, 1991).

The Monoamine Neurotransmitters

Monoamines are the second class of small-molecule neurotransmitters. Each is synthesized from a single amino acid—thus the name *monoamine.* Monoamine neurotransmitters are slightly larger than amino acid neurotransmitters, and their effects tend to be slightly more diffuse (see Iversen, 1987). The monoamines are present in small groups of neurons whose cell bodies are, for the most part, located in the brain stem. These neurons often have highly branched axons with many *varicosities* or swellings from which monoamine neurotransmitters are diffusely released into the extracellular fluid—see Figures 4.13 and 4.14.

There are four monoamine neurotransmitters: **norepinephrine, epinephrine, dopamine,** and **serotonin.** They are subdivided into two groups, **catecholamines** and **indolamines,** on the basis of their structure. Dopamine, norepinephrine, and epinephrine are catecholamines. Each is synthesized from the amino acid *tyrosine.* Tyrosine is converted to *L-DOPA,* which is

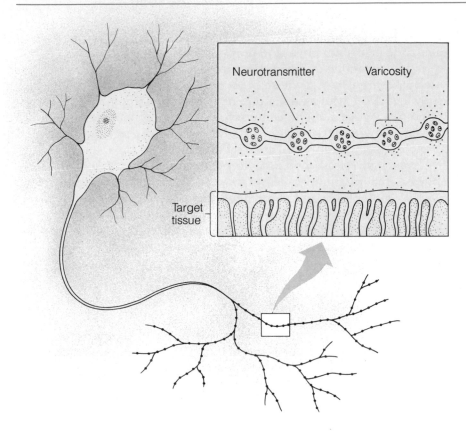

FIGURE 4.13

A schematic illustration of nondirected neurotransmitter release. The neurotransmitter is released from the varicosities and is widely dispersed to various target sites. Monoamines are typically released in this fashion.

FIGURE 4.14

Neural tissue exposed to formaldehyde vapor and viewed by a fluorescence microscope reveals a network of monoamine-containing neurons. Notice the string-of-beads appearance of the axons. Monoamine neurotransmitter is released diffusely from each varicosity (bead).

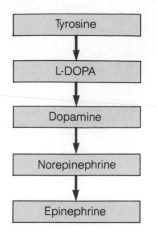

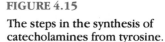

FIGURE 4.15

The steps in the synthesis of catecholamines from tyrosine.

in turn converted to dopamine. Neurons that release norepinephrine have an extra enzyme that is not present in dopaminergic neurons, and this enzyme converts the dopamine in them to norepinephrine. Similarly, neurons that release epinephrine have all the enzymes present in neurons that release norepinephrine, along with an extra one that converts norepinephrine to epinephrine (see Figure 4.15). In contrast to the other monoamines, serotonin (also called *5-hydroxytryptamine,* or *5-HT*) is synthesized from the amino acid *tryptophan* and is classified as an indolamine.

Neurons that release norepinephrine are called *noradrenergic;* those that release epinephrine are called *adrenergic.* There are two reasons for this. One is that epinephrine and norepinephrine used to be called *adrenaline* and *noradrenaline* respectively by some scientists, until a drug company registered *adrenaline* and *noradrenaline* as brand names. The other reason will become apparent to you if you try to say "norepinephrinergic."

Acetylcholine

Acetylcholine (Ach) is also a small-molecule neurotransmitter, but unlike the others, it is neither an amino acid nor a simple modification of one. It is created by adding an *acetyl group* to a *choline molecule.* Acetylcholine is the neurotransmitter at neuromuscular junctions, at most of the synapses in the autonomic nervous system (norepinephrine is the transmitter at the others), and at synapses throughout the CNS. It is deactivated in the synaptic cleft by being broken down in the synapse by the enzyme, **acetylcholinesterase;** all other small-molecule neurotransmitters are deactivated by reuptake into the terminal button.

Neuropeptides

Nine small-molecule neurotransmitters have been discussed so far: the four amino acids (glutamate, aspartate, glycine, and GABA), the four monoamines (dopamine, norepinephrine, epinephrine, and serotonin), and acetylcholine. These are the nine for which the evidence is largely complete—the nine that are accepted as bona fide neurotransmitters by even the most skeptical neuroscientists. The rapid accumulation of evidence that peptides also serve as neurotransmitters ranks as one of the major advances in neuroscience in the last decade. About 40 or so peptides currently qualify as putative neurotransmitters (Iversen, 1987), and the list is growing rapidly (see Appendix VI). A *putative neurotransmitter* is a suspected neurotransmitter, one for which the evidence is strong but not unequivocal.

Some neuropeptides have been known and studied for a long time as hormones, not as neurotransmitters. First, these peptides were shown to be released into the bloodstream by endocrine glands, and it was assumed that their role was restricted to the endocrine system. Then, one by one, each of the peptide hormones was shown to be present in neural tissue. Initially it was assumed that various neural structures simply served as the targets for hormones synthesized and released by endocrine glands, but it is now clear that some peptide hormones are synthesized and released by neurons as well as by endocrine glands.

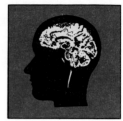

To review the neurotransmitters to which you have just been introduced, fill in the blanks in the following paragraph before proceeding.

Amino acids are the neurotransmitters in the vast majority of
(1) _____ -acting, _____ synapses.
Four amino acids have proven to be neurotransmitters to the satisfaction of
most experts: (2) _____ , (3) _____ ,
(4) _____ , and (5) _____ . In contrast to the amino acid neurotransmitters, the (6) _____
have slower, more diffuse effects, and they belong to one of two categories,
(7) _____ or indolamines. Belonging to the former
category are epinephrine, (8) _____ , and
(9) _____ ; and (10) _____ is the
only neurotransmitter belonging to the latter category. The neuropeptides,
which are short chains of (11) _____ , are the third major
class of neurotransmitters. Finally, there is (12) _____ ,
which is a neurotransmitter in a class by itself.

4.7

How Drugs Affect Synaptic Transmission

Drugs have two fundamentally different kinds of effects on synaptic transmission: they facilitate it, or they inhibit it. Drugs that facilitate the activity of the synapses of a particular neurotransmitter are said to be **agonists** of that neurotransmitter. Drugs that inhibit the activity of the synapses of a particular neurotransmitter are said to be its **antagonists.**

Figure 4.16 illustrates the seven basic mechanisms of neurotransmitter activity: (1) Neurotransmitter molecules are synthesized from chemical precursors in the cytoplasm under the influence of particular enzymes. (2) Then, they are stored in synaptic vesicles. (3) Any neurotransmitter that leaks from the vesicles is destroyed by enzymes. (4) When an action potential arrives at the synaptic button, the vesicles fuse with the presynaptic membrane, and the neurotransmitter molecules are released into the synaptic cleft. In the synaptic cleft, (5) the neurotransmitter molecules may bind to receptors in the presynaptic membrane of the neuron that just released them (**autoreceptors**) and in so doing inhibit subsequent neurotransmitter release; and (6) they may bind to receptors in the postsynaptic membrane and in so doing affect the activity of the postsynaptic neuron. (7) Finally, the action of the neurotransmitter is terminated either by mechanisms that draw the neurotransmitter back into the presynaptic neuron or by enzymes in the synaptic cleft that break it down.

The answers to the preceding questions are (1) fast, point-to-point, (2, 3, 4, 5) glutamate, glycine, aspartate, and GABA in any order, (6) monoamines, (7) catecholamines, (8, 9) dopamine and norepinephrine in either order, (10) serotonin, (11) amino acids, and (12) acetylcholine.

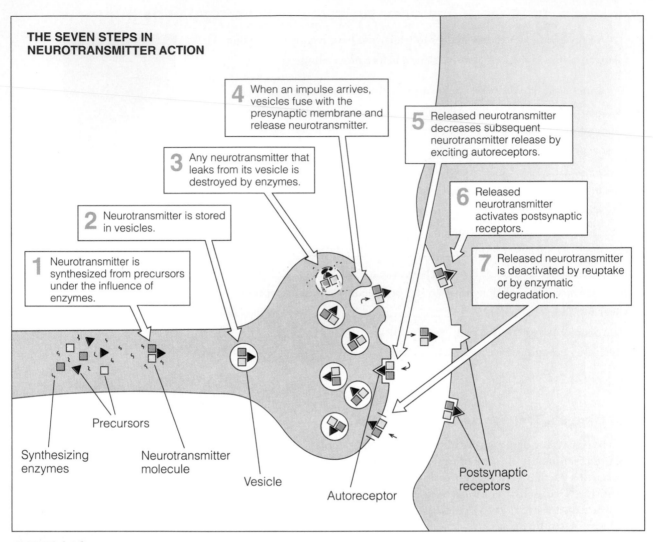

**THE SEVEN STEPS IN
NEUROTRANSMITTER ACTION**

4 When an impulse arrives, vesicles fuse with the presynaptic membrane and release neurotransmitter.

5 Released neurotransmitter decreases subsequent neurotransmitter release by exciting autoreceptors.

3 Any neurotransmitter that leaks from its vesicle is destroyed by enzymes.

6 Released neurotransmitter activates postsynaptic receptors.

2 Neurotransmitter is stored in vesicles.

1 Neurotransmitter is synthesized from precursors under the influence of enzymes.

7 Released neurotransmitter is deactivated by reuptake or by enzymatic degradation.

Precursors

Synthesizing
enzymes

Neurotransmitter
molecule

Vesicle

Autoreceptor

Postsynaptic
receptors

FIGURE 4.16

The seven steps in neurotransmitter action: (1) synthesis, (2) storage, (3) incidental destruction, (4) exocytosis (release), (5) inhibitory feedback via autoreceptors, (6) activation of postsynaptic receptors, and (7) deactivation.

Mechanisms of Agonistic Drug Effects

You have just learned from Figure 4.16 that there are seven basic steps in neurotransmitter action. Drugs have been shown to exert *agonistic* effects by interacting with six of them. These six proven mechanisms of agonistic drug effects are illustrated in Figure 4.17.

Mechanisms of Antagonistic Drug Effects

Drugs have been shown to exert *antagonistic* effects by interacting with five of the seven basic steps in neurotransmitter action. These five proven mechanisms of antagonistic drug effects are illustrated in Figure 4.18. A drug that exerts an antagonistic effect by binding to postsynaptic receptors and thereby blocking the access of the usual neurotransmitter is called a **false transmitter.**

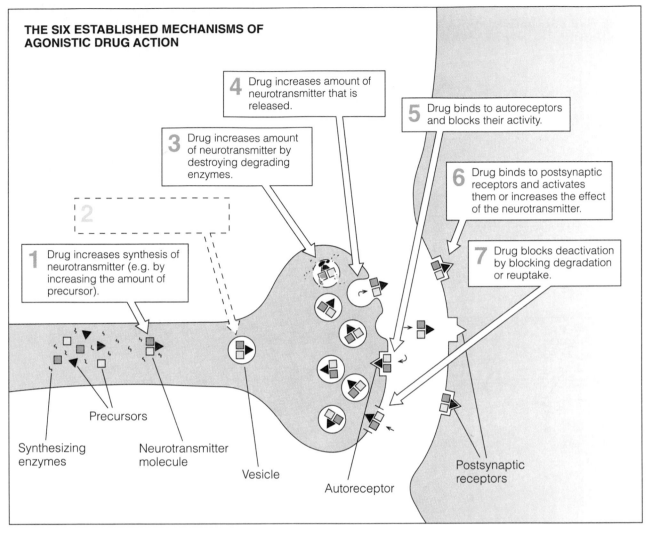

THE SIX ESTABLISHED MECHANISMS OF AGONISTIC DRUG ACTION

4 Drug increases amount of neurotransmitter that is released.

3 Drug increases amount of neurotransmitter by destroying degrading enzymes.

5 Drug binds to autoreceptors and blocks their activity.

6 Drug binds to postsynaptic receptors and activates them or increases the effect of the neurotransmitter.

2

1 Drug increases synthesis of neurotransmitter (e.g. by increasing the amount of precursor).

7 Drug blocks deactivation by blocking degradation or reuptake.

Precursors

Synthesizing enzymes

Neurotransmitter molecule

Vesicle

Autoreceptor

Postsynaptic receptors

FIGURE 4.17

The six proven mechanisms of agonistic drug action. Please compare with Figures 4.14 and 4.16.

Agonists and Antagonists: Some Examples

You will be introduced to many neurotransmitter agonists and antagonists in the remaining chapters. Here are four examples to clarify the concepts of *agonism* and *antagonism*. Morphine and benzodiazepines are agonists; atropine and *d*-tubocurarine are antagonists.

Morphine *Opium,* a resinous extract of the opium poppy, has long been used for both its euphoria-producing effects and its medicinal effects; it is effective in the treatment of pain, coughing, and diarrhea. The main active ingredient of opium is **morphine,** named after Morpheus, the Greek god of dreams. Morphine acts by stimulating receptors in the brain that are normally stimulated by a class of neuropeptides called *endorphins* (see Appendix VI) — in other words, morphine is an endorphin agonist. **Endorphin** is a general term that refers to any morphine-like substance that occurs naturally in the brain; it is a contraction of "endogenous morphine-like substance."

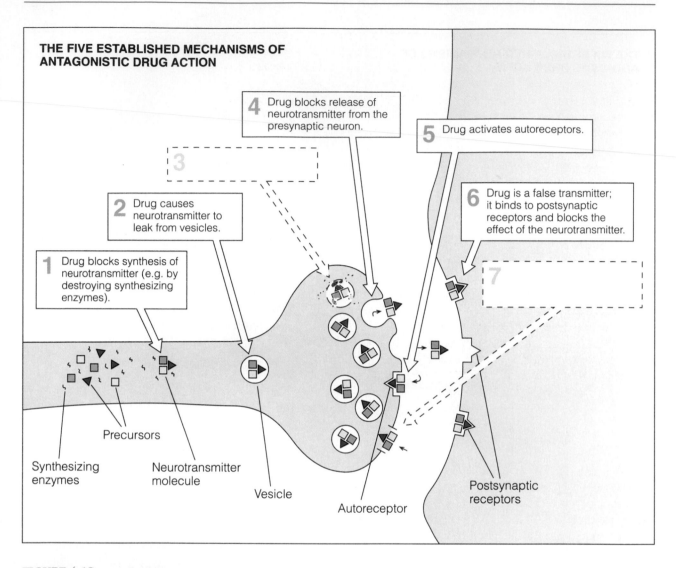

THE FIVE ESTABLISHED MECHANISMS OF ANTAGONISTIC DRUG ACTION

4 Drug blocks release of neurotransmitter from the presynaptic neuron.

5 Drug activates autoreceptors.

3

2 Drug causes neurotransmitter to leak from vesicles.

6 Drug is a false transmitter; it binds to postsynaptic receptors and blocks the effect of the neurotransmitter.

1 Drug blocks synthesis of neurotransmitter (e.g. by destroying synthesizing enzymes).

7

Precursors

Synthesizing enzymes

Neurotransmitter molecule

Vesicle

Autoreceptor

Postsynaptic receptors

FIGURE 4.18

The five proven mechanisms of antagonistic drug action. Please compare with Figures 4.14 and 4.15.

Benzodiazepines *Chlordiazepoxide* (marketed under the name *Librium*) and *diazepam* (marketed under the name *Valium*) belong to a class of drugs called **benzodiazepines**. Benzodiazepines have *anxiolytic* (anxiety-reducing), *sedative* (sleep-inducing), and anticonvulsant effects (see Sternbach, 1983). The benzodiazepines appear to exert their anxiolytic effects by serving as GABA agonists. Benzodiazepines bind to the GABA receptor, but they do not exert their agonistic effect by mimicking GABA's actions. Benzodiazepine molecules do not bind to the GABA receptor at the same site at which GABA molecules bind; they bind to another part of the GABA receptor molecule, and by so doing, they increase the binding of GABA molecules to the receptor and increase GABA's inhibitory effects. In view of the anxiolytic and anticonvulsant effects of benzodiazepines, it is not surprising that benzodiazepine binding sites are particularly dense in the *amygdala,* a structure known to play a role in emotion and in the propagation of temporal lobe seizures.

Atropine   Many of the drugs that are used in research and in medicine are extracts of plants that have long been used for medicinal and recreational purposes. For example, in the time of Hippocrates, the Greeks consumed extracts of the belladonna plant to treat stomach ailments and to make themselves more attractive. Greek women believed that its pupil-dilating effects enhanced their beauty; *belladonna* means *beautiful lady*. **Atropine** is the active ingredient of belladonna. It is a false transmitter; it exerts its antagonist effect by binding to a subtype of acetylcholine receptors, called *muscarinic receptors,* thereby blocking the effects of acetylcholine on them. The disruptive effect of high doses of atropine on memory was one of the earliest clues that Alzheimer's disease (see Chapter 6) might be associated with a disturbance of cholinergic activity.

d-*Tubocurarine*   South American Indians have long used *curare,* an extract of a certain class of woody vines, to kill their game—and occasionally their enemies. The active ingredient of curare is *d*-**tubocurarine.** Like atropine, *d*-tubocurarine is a false transmitter at cholinergic synapses, but it acts at a different subtype of acetylcholine receptors: *nicotinic receptors.* By binding to nicotinic receptors, *d*-tubocurarine paralyzes animals by blocking transmission at neuromuscular junctions, and this blockade eventually kills them by stopping respiration. Accordingly, when *d*-tubocurarine is used during surgery, the patient must be kept alive by a respirator.

4.8

The Diversity of Neural Conduction and Synaptic Transmission

Early research on the mechanisms of neural conduction and synaptic transmission focused almost exclusively on the study of one preparation: the **motor neuron** and its associated **neuromuscular junction** (the synapse-like cleft between motor neuron and muscle fiber). The main reasons for focusing on this preparation were its large size, its accessibility, and its simplicity (Kandel & Siegelbaum, 1985; Keynes, 1958). However, in the last two decades, spectacular technological advances have opened up CNS neurons and synapses to direct investigation. As a result, it is now apparent that neural conduction and synaptic transmission are much more diverse than was once believed. Although many CNS neurons and synapses function in much the same way as motor neurons and neuromuscular junctions, many do not. It is beyond the scope of this chapter to describe this diversity in detail; however, it would be misleading to leave the topic of neural conduction and synaptic transmission without providing you with some appreciation of its diverse nature. That is the purpose of the following paragraphs.

Not All Neurons Have Axons and Transmit Action Potentials!

The standard textbook neuron is a neuron with a long axon. This often creates the misconception that all neurons have axons. They do not. There are many neurons in the mammalian nervous system without axons—particularly in the complex CNS circuits that play important roles in activities such as learning, memory, motivation, and perception. Action potentials are the means by which neural messages are carried nondecrementally along axons, and thus action potentials do not occur in neurons without axons.

Not All Synapses Between Neurons Are Axodendritic or Axosomatic!

You have learned about *axodendritic synapses* (synapses between the axon terminals of the presynaptic neuron and the dendrites of the postsynaptic neuron) and *axosomatic synapses* (synapses between the axon terminals of the presynaptic neuron and the *soma* or cell body of the postsynaptic neuron). There are many other kinds of synapses. Axon terminal buttons often synapse on the axons of other neurons; axon shafts sometimes make direct synaptic contact with the dendrites or axons of other neurons; and some dendrites transmit signals across synapses to other dendrites or axons. It is also important to be aware that not all synapses are one-way streets. Some *dendrodentritic synapses* are **reciprocal synapses;** that is, they are capable of transmitting signals in either direction. Axodendritic synapses frequently occur on little specialized buds called **dendritic spines** (see Figure 3.30).

Axoaxonic synapses have been shown to mediate **presynaptic inhibition**—see Rudomin, 1990. Presynaptic and **postsynaptic inhibition** are compared in Figure 4.19. The major functional difference between the two is that postsynaptic inhibition reduces a neuron's responsiveness to all synaptic input, whereas presynaptic inhibition selectively reduces a neuron's responsiveness to only one channel of input.

Many Neurons Release More Than One Neurotransmitter!

Motor neurons release only one neurotransmitter, acetylcholine, and thus it was assumed that all neurons release only one neurotransmitter—this assumption is called **Dale's principle.** It does seem to be true that each neuron releases only one small-molecule neurotransmitter, but since the discovery of neuropeptides, there have been several well-documented reports of **coexistence,** the residence of two neurotransmitters in the same neuron. So far, all documented cases of coexistence involve a small-molecule neurotransmitter and a neuropeptide or more than one neuropeptide (see Jung & Scheller, 1991).

Not All Synapses Are Directed!

Neuromuscular junctions are **directed synapses,** synapses at which the presynaptic membrane and the receptive area of the postsynaptic cell are in close apposition. There are also many **nondirected synapses** in the nervous system; these are synapses at which the target receptors are some distance from the site of neurotransmitter release. As you have already learned, *monoaminergic neurons* commonly release their neurotransmitters into nondirected synapses—see Figures 4.13 and 4.14. The neurons of the *neuroendocrine system* are the most nondirected of all neurons; they release their neurotransmitters directly into the blood, and thus they can influence sites throughout the organism.

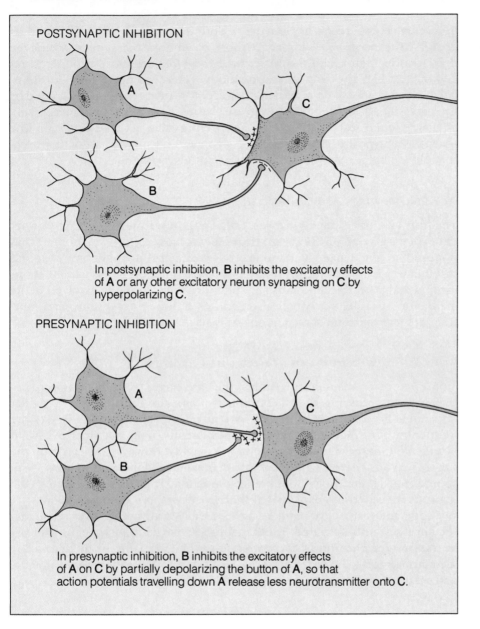

POSTSYNAPTIC INHIBITION

In postsynaptic inhibition, **B** inhibits the excitatory effects of **A** or any other excitatory neuron synapsing on **C** by hyperpolarizing **C**.

PRESYNAPTIC INHIBITION

In presynaptic inhibition, **B** inhibits the excitatory effects of **A** on **C** by partially depolarizing the button of **A**, so that action potentials travelling down **A** release less neurotransmitter onto **C**.

FIGURE 4.19

A schematic illustration of presynaptic and postsynaptic inhibition.

There Is More Than One Kind of Receptor for Each Neurotransmitter!

It was initially assumed that there is one kind of receptor for each neurotransmitter. However, it is now clear that each neurotransmitter binds to more than one class of receptors. The different classes of receptors that are acted on by a particular neurotransmitter are referred to as the *receptor subtypes* of that neurotransmitter. For example, you have already learned that there are two acetylcholine receptor subtypes, nicotinic receptors and muscarinic receptors. The *nicotinic receptors* are those cholinergic receptors to which the drug nicotine binds, and the *muscarinic receptors* are those cholinergic receptors to which the drug muscarine binds. The receptors of the neuromuscular junction are all nicotinic, and the receptors on the organs innervated by the parasympathetic nervous system are all muscarinic. Both cholinergic subtypes are found in the CNS. Psychoactive drugs that act specifically on one receptor subtype are, strictly speaking, agonists and antagonists of the receptor subtype, rather than of the neurotransmitter in general.

Not All Synapses Are Chemical!

The transmission at some synapses, called **gap junctions,** is electrical rather than chemical. Gap junctions are extremely narrow clefts—2 nanometers as opposed to the usual 30 nanometers—which are spanned by channels through which electrical current can flow. Transmission across gap junctions is rapid and inflexible, and thus gap junctions are frequently involved in the mediation of rapid, stereotypical responses of lower organisms. Gap junctions are rare in mammalian nervous systems.

Not All Neurons Remain at Rest Until Excited!

Motor neurons remain inactive unless they are excited, but this is not true of CNS neurons. Most fire almost continually. Some fire continually at a regular rate; some fire in bursts separated by regular intervals; and still others fire frequently, but irregularly. In the complex circuits of the mammalian CNS, it is difficult to determine the source of this activity; however, research on the simple nervous systems of invertebrates has suggested that many neurons fire spontaneously, that is, without being stimulated. The fact that so many CNS neurons are active may explain why inhibitory synapses are so prevalent.

Spontaneously active neurons have one major advantage over those that remain at rest until activated. Spontaneously active neurons have the capacity to transmit information in two ways: either by increasing or by decreasing their firing rates. The latter option is not open to neurons that do not fire unless stimulated.

Conclusion

The function of the nervous system, like the function of any circuit, depends on how signals are transmitted through it. Accordingly, an understanding of the basic principles of neural conduction and synaptic transmission is prerequisite to the study of the neural bases of behavior. This chapter has introduced you to these basic principles. They are summarized in Table 4.2.

Table 4.2 Summary of the Events Associated with the Transmission of Excitatory Signals Through a Multipolar Neuron and Across a Directed Chemical Synapse

Site	*Event*
Postsynaptic membranes on dendrites and cell body	When a neurotransmitter binds to its postsynaptic receptors, postsynaptic potentials are created either by the direct opening of chemically gated ion channels or by the synthesis of second messengers in the cytoplasm of the postsynaptic neuron.
Dendrites and cell body	Postsynaptic potentials are conducted instantly and decrementally to the axon hillock, which automatically sums or integrates them.
Axon hillock	If the integrated postsynaptic potential is an EPSP sufficient to drive the axon hillock membrane to its threshold of excitation, an all-or-none action potential is generated by the brief opening of voltage-gated sodium channels on the hillock membrane.
Axon	The action potential is nondecrementally transmitted down the axon. If the axon is myelinated, conduction is saltatory.
Terminal buttons	When an action potential arrives at a terminal button, it triggers an influx of Ca^{++} ions through voltage-gated calcium channels, and this in turn triggers the release of the neurotransmitter.
Postsynaptic membranes	The neurotransmitter moves across the synaptic cleft, where it binds to receptors in the postsynaptic membrane and generates postsynaptic potentials, thus beginning the next cycle of neural transmission.
Presynaptic button	The neurotransmitter is deactivated either by being broken down by enzymes or by being taken back into the cytoplasm of the button.

Food for Thought

1. Just as computers operate on binary (yes-no) signals, the all-or-none action potential is the basis of neural communication. The human brain is thus nothing more than a particularly complex computer. Discuss.

2. How have the findings described in this chapter changed your concept of brain function?

KEY TERMS

To help you study the material in this chapter, all of the key terms—those that have appeared in bold type—are either listed and briefly defined here or they appear in the table of neurotransmitters that follows.

Absolute refractory period. A brief period (1 to 2 milliseconds) after the initiation of an action potential during which it is impossible to elicit another action potential in the same neuron.

Acetylcholinesterase. The enzyme that breaks down acetylcholine.

Action potential (AP). The firing of a neuron; a massive momentary change in the membrane potential from -70 mV to $+50$ mV.

Agonists. Drugs that facilitate the transmission at the synapses of a particular neurotransmitter are called agonists of that neurotransmitter.

All-or-none responses. Responses that are not graded; responses, such as action potentials, that occur full blown or not at all.

Amino acids. The molecular building blocks of proteins and a class of neurotransmitters; amino acids are the neurotransmitters at the majority of fast-acting, point-to-point synapses in the central nervous system.

Antagonists. Drugs that inhibit transmission at the synapses of a particular neurotransmitter are called antagonists of that neurotransmitter.

Antidromic. An adjective that refers to signals traveling from axon terminals toward the cell body; such signals are elicited by electrical stimulation of the axon terminals.

Atropine. A false transmitter at muscarinic synapses.

Autoreceptors. Receptors, often on the presynaptic membrane, that are sensitive to a neuron's own neurotransmitter.

Axon hillock. The conical structure at the junction between the axon and cell body, where action potentials are normally generated.

Benzodiazepines. A class of drugs with anxiolytic properties.

Catecholamines. The subgroup of monoamines that are synthesized from tyrosine.

Chemically gated ion channels. Ion channels that are opened and closed by chemical changes.

Cisternas. Intracellular organelles that fill synaptic vesicles in terminal buttons with neurotransmitter.

Coexistence. The presence of two or more different neurotransmitters in the same neuron.

***d*-Tubocurarine.** The active ingredient of curare; a false transmitter at nicotinic synapses.

Dale's principle. The incorrect assumption that each neuron releases only a single neurotransmitter.

Dendritic spines. Specialized buds on dendrites at which axodendritic synapses often occur.

Depolarize. To decrease the membrane potential (e.g., from -70 mV to -60 mV).

Directed synapses. Synapses at which the site of neurotransmitter release and the receptor sites on the postsynaptic membrane are in close proximity.

Endorphin. A general term used to refer to any morphine-like substance that occurs naturally in the body.

Excitatory postsynaptic potentials (EPSPs). Graded postsynaptic depolarizations.

Exocytosis. The act of releasing the neurotransmitter.

False transmitter. A chemical that binds to a receptor and blocks the action of its neurotransmitter.

Gap junctions. Sites of electrical transmission between neurons.

Golgi apparatus. Structures in the cell bodies of neurons that manufacture synaptic vesicles and other membranes.

Graded response. A response whose magnitude is related to the magnitude of the stimulus.

Hyperpolarize. To increase the membrane potential (e.g., from -70 mV to -75 mV).

Inhibitory postsynaptic potentials (IPSPs). Postsynaptic hyperpolarizations, which decrease the likelihood that an action potential will be generated.

Integration. Adding or combining a number of signals into one overall signal.

Ion. A positively or negatively charged particle.

Ion channels. Pores in cellular membranes through which ions pass.

Membrane potential. The difference in electrical charge between the inside and the outside of a cell.

Microelectrodes. Intracellular recording electrodes.

Microtubules. Fine tubes in the cytoplasm that are responsible for intracellular transport of various materials.

Mitochondria. Structures in the cytoplasm of all cells that are responsible for the conversion of certain molecules into energy.

Motor neurons. Multipolar neurons with large axons that project to receptive sites on muscle fibers.

Neuromodulators. Neurotransmitters that increase or decrease the sensitivity of large populations of neurons to the effects of conventional point-to-point neurotransmitters; neuropeptides are thought to function as neuromodulators.

Neuromuscular junction. The synapse of a motor neuron on a muscle.

Neurotransmitters. Various chemicals that mediate the communication among neurons.

Nodes of Ranvier. The regular gaps in the axonal myelin.

Nondirected synapses. Synapses at which the site of neurotransmitter release and the target site are not close together.

Orthodromic. Axonal conduction from the cell body toward the terminal buttons.

Oscilloscope. A device that displays the changes in the membrane potential over time as vertical displacements of a glowing spot as it sweeps across a fluorescent screen.

Peptides. Short chains of amino acids, some of which function as neurotransmitters.

Postsynaptic inhibition. A form of inhibition that reduces a neuron's responsiveness to all excitatory synaptic inputs.

Presynaptic inhibition. A form of inhibition that selectively reduces a neuron's responsiveness to specific synaptic input; it is mediated by axoaxonal synapses.

Reciprocal synapses. Synapses capable of transmission in both directions.

Relative refractory period. A period after the absolute refractory period during which a higher than normal amount of stimulation is necessary to make a neuron fire.

Resting potential. The steady membrane potential of a neuron at rest, usually about –70 mV.

Saltatory conduction. Conduction of an action potential from node to node down a myelinated axon.

Second messengers. Molecules that are created in the cytoplasm of the postsynaptic cell in response to the activation of postsynaptic receptors; once created, second messengers influence the membrane potential of the postsynaptic cell.

Sodium-potassium pumps. Active transport mechanisms that pump Na^+ ions out of the cell and K^+ ions into the cell.

Spatial summation. The integration of signals that occur at the same time, but at different sites on the neuron.

Synaptic vesicles. Small spherical membranes that store neurotransmitter molecules and release them into the synaptic cleft.

Temporal summation. The integration of neural signals that occur at different times.

Threshold of excitation. The level of depolarization at the axon hillock necessary to generate an action potential, usually about –65 mV.

Voltage-gated ion channels. Ion channels that open and close in response to changes in the membrane potential.

KEY TERMS: The Nine Universally Recognized Neurotransmitters

aspartate
glycine
GABA
glutamate   } amino acids

dopamine
norepinephrine   } catecholamines
epinephrine
serotonin   } indolamine   } monoamines

acetylcholine

ADDITIONAL READING

For a systematic introduction to neural conduction and synaptic transmission that is much more detailed than that provided by this chapter, the following text is hard to beat.

Kandel, E. R., & Schwartz, J. H. (Eds.). (1991). *Principles of neural science* (second edition). New York: Elsevier.

Scientific American is one of the few scientific journals that can be purchased at your local newsstand. It specializes in making the research of the world's greatest scientists accessible to the educated public in beautifully illustrated, well-written articles. The following are several that are relevant to this chapter.

Dunant, Y., & Israël, M. (1985). The release of acetylcholine. *Scientific American, 252,* 58–66.

Gottlieb, D. I. (1988). GABAergic neurons. *Scientific American, 258,* 82–89.

Keynes, R. D. (1979). Ion channels in the nerve-cell membrane. *Scientific American, 240,* 126–135.

Llinás, R. R. (1982). Calcium in synaptic transmission. *Scientific American, 247,* 56–65.

Schwartz, J. H. (1980). The transport of substances in nerve cells. *Scientific American, 242,* 152–171.

Snyder, S. H. (1985). The molecular basis of communication between cells. *Scientific American, 253,* 132–141.

The following book is an excellent introduction to neurotransmitters, drugs, and the brain.

Snyder, S. H. (1986). *Drugs and the Brain.* New York: Scientific American Books.

5

What Biopsychologists Do: The Research Methods of Biopsychology

PART 1   Methods of Studying the Nervous System

5.1   *Methods of Visualizing Human Brain Damage*

5.2   *Recording Psychophysiological Activity from the Surface of the Human Body*

5.3   *Invasive Physiological and Pharmacological Research Methods*

PART 2   Behavioral Research Methods of Biopsychology

5.4   *Neuropsychological Testing*

5.5   *Biopsychological Paradigms of Animal Behavior*

Chapters 1 and 2 introduced you to the general interests, ideas, and approaches that characterize biopsychology. In Chapters 3 and 4, your introduction to biopsychology was temporarily curtailed while prerequisite background material in neuroanatomy and neurophysiology was presented. This chapter gets down to the nitty gritty; it describes the specific day-to-day activities of the biopsychology laboratory. It is intended to sharpen your understanding of biopsychology by describing how biopsychologists do their research.

The organization of this chapter reflects biopsychology's intrinsic duality. It has two major parts: one dealing with methods for studying the nervous system and the other dealing with methods for studying behavior.

PART 1: Methods of Studying the Nervous System

5.1

Methods of Visualizing Human Brain Damage

Neuropsychologists assess the behavioral deficits of brain-damaged patients. In order to relate these deficits to neural dysfunction, they must obtain information about the location, nature, and extent of the patients' brain damage. There are three potential sources of this information: neurosurgeons' reports, postmortem tissue samples, or pictures of the living brain. The following are techniques that are used to obtain pictures of the living brain.

Contrast X-rays

To take an X-ray photograph, an X-ray beam is passed through the test object. Each of the molecules through which it passes absorbs some of the radiation, and the unabsorbed portion of the beam leaving the test object is projected onto a photographic plate. Accordingly, X-ray photography is effective in characterizing internal structures that differ substantially from their surroundings in the degree to which they absorb X-rays—for example, a revolver in a suitcase full of clothes or a bone in flesh. That is why a standard X-ray photograph of the head can reveal the location of a skull fracture, but it is of little use in visualizing the various structures of the brain. By the time an X-ray beam passes through the numerous overlapping structures of the brain, which differ only slightly from one another in their ability to absorb X-rays, it carries little information about the shape of the individual structures through which it passed.

One way to increase the usefulness of X-ray technology in the study of brain pathology is to highlight parts of the brain with a substance that readily absorbs X-rays. The structures in which the *radio-opaque substance* accumulates stand out from other structures on X-ray photographs.

There are two such **contrast X-ray** techniques that have been widely used to study the brain. **Pneumoencephalography** involves temporarily replacing some of the cerebrospinal fluid with air. Because air is radio-opaque, the ventricles and fissures of the brain are clearly visible in the subsequent contrast X-ray, which is called a *pneumoencephalogram*. A local deformation of a ventricle or a fissure may indicate the location of a tumor, and a general increase in the size of ventricles or fissures is indicative of diffuse brain damage. **Angiography** is a procedure for visualizing the cerebral circulatory system by infusing a radio-opaque dye through a cerebral artery during X-ray photography (see Figure 5.1). *Angiograms* are most useful in identifying the location of vascular damage, but the displacement of blood vessels from their normal position can indicate the location of a tumor.

Computerized Axial Tomography

Computerized axial tomography (CAT) is a computer-assisted X-ray procedure for visualizing the brain in three dimensions. The procedure provides a series of X-ray photographs of horizontal sections of the living brain, which characterize its three-dimensional structure. During computerized axial tomography, the neurological patient lies with his or her head positioned in the center of a large cylinder as depicted in Figure 5.2. On one side of the cylinder is an X-ray tube that projects an X-ray beam through the head of the patient to an X-ray detector mounted on the other side. The X-ray tube and detector automatically rotate around the head of the subject at one level of the brain, taking a series of individual measurements as they rotate. These are combined by the computer to generate one section of the *CAT scan* (see Figure 5.3). Then, the X-ray tube and detector are moved along the axis of the patient's body to another level of the brain, and the process is repeated. Scans of eight or nine horizontal brain sections are usually obtained from each patient.

Magnetic Resonance Imaging

Despite the technological sophistication of computerized axial tomography, it is not the last word in techniques for providing three-dimensional images of the brain. **Magnetic resonance imaging (MRI)** has even higher powers of resolution (see Figure 5.4). MRI is not an adaptation of X-ray photography;

FIGURE 5.1

A cerebral angiogram of a healthy subject. (Courtesy of William Robertson, Department of Radiology, Vancouver General Hospital.)

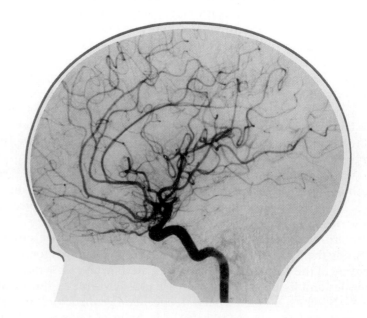

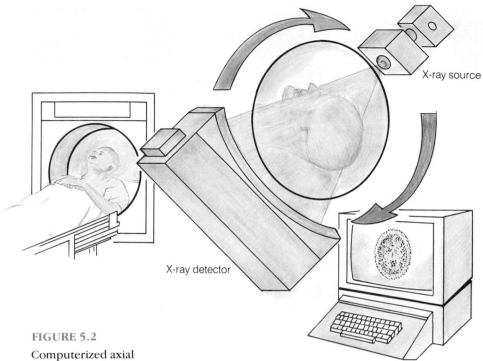

X-ray source

X-ray detector

FIGURE 5.2

Computerized axial
tomography.

FIGURE 5.3

A CAT scan section. Notice
the tumor in the occipital
lobe. (Courtesy of J. McA. Jones,
Good Samaritan Hospital and
Medical Center, Portland, Oregon.)

FIGURE 5.4

An MRI scan.

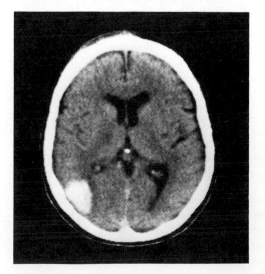

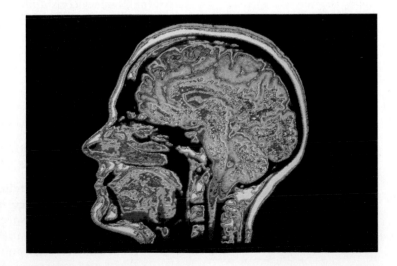

FIGURE 5.5

A color photograph of a PET scan. Areas of high activity are indicated by reds and yellows. From "Positron Tomography: Human Brain Function and Biochemistry" by Michael E. Phelps and John C. Mazziotta, May 17, 1985, *Science, 228* (9701), p 804, Copyright 1985 by the AAAS. Reprinted by permission. Courtesy of Drs. Michael E. Phelps and John Mazziotta, UCLA School of Medicine.

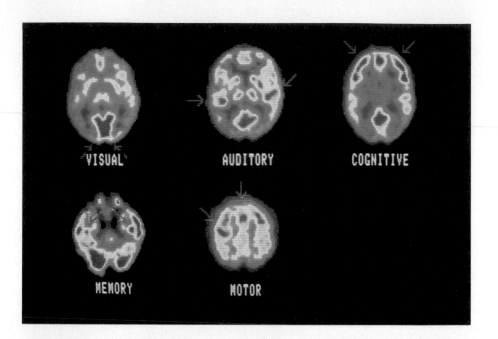

instead, the images are constructed from the measurement of waves that hydrogen atoms emit when they are activated by radio-frequency waves in a magnetic field. The clarity of MRI stems from the fact that the concentration of hydrogen atoms in different neural structures varies substantially—see Moonen, van Zijl, Frank, Le Bihan, and Becker (1990).

Positron Emission Tomography

Another technique for viewing the living human brain is **positron emission tomography (PET).** *PET scans* provide information about the metabolic activity of the brain. In the most common version of PET, the patient is injected with radioactive **2-deoxyglucose (2-DG).** Because of its similarity to glucose, the primary metabolic fuel of the brain, 2-deoxyglucose is taken up rapidly by active (i.e., energy-consuming) neurons. However, unlike glucose, 2-deoxyglucose cannot be metabolized, and it thus accumulates in active neurons until it can be gradually broken down and released. Thus, if PET is performed on a patient while he or she is engaged in an activity such as reading, the PET scan will indicate the areas of the brain most active during the activity (see Figure 5.5).

5.2

Recording Psychophysiological Activity from the Surface of the Human Body

Psychophysiologists record indices of physiological activity from the surface of the human body. In this section of the chapter, five of the most widely studied psychophysiological measures are introduced: one measure of brain activity (the scalp EEG), two measures of somatic nervous system activity (muscle tension and eye movement), and two measures of autonomic nervous system activity (skin conductance and cardiovascular activity).

Scalp Electroencephalography

The *electroencephalogram* (EEG) is a gross measure of the electrical activity of the brain; it is recorded by a device called an *electroencephalograph* or EEG machine. In experiments on human subjects, each channel of EEG activity is usually recorded between two large, disk-shaped electrodes, about half the size of a dime, that are taped to the scalp. There are two basic variations of **electroencephalography.** In *monopolar recording,* one electrode is placed at the target site and the other electrode is attached to the subject at a point of relative electrical silence—for example, an earlobe. In *bipolar recording,* the EEG signal is recorded between electrodes placed at two active sites.

The scalp EEG activity reflects the sum of electrical events throughout the head. These include action potentials and postsynaptic potentials (EPSPs and IPSPs) and electrical signals from skin, muscles, blood, and eyes. Thus, the utility of the scalp EEG clearly does not lie in its ability to provide an unclouded view of neural activity. Its value as a research and diagnostic tool rests on the fact that some recognizable EEG wave forms are associated with particular states of consciousness or particular types of cerebral pathology. For example, **alpha waves** are 8-to-12 per second, high-amplitude waves that are associated with relaxed wakefulness. A few examples of EEG wave forms and their psychological correlates are presented in Figure 5.6.

Because EEG signals decrease in amplitude as they spread from their source, a comparison of signals recorded from various sites can indicate their origin. Figure 5.7 illustrates a classic problem encountered by clinical electroencephalographers. How would you solve it?

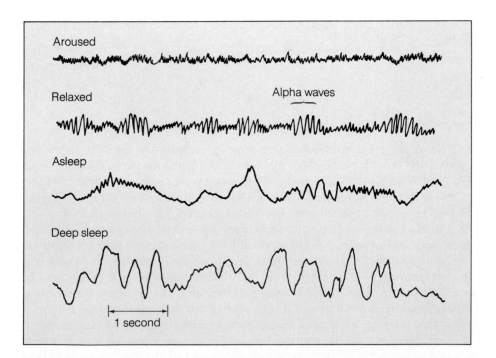

FIGURE 5.6

Some typical electroencephalograms and their psychological correlates.

DEMONSTRATION

You are serving as a research assistant in a psycho-physiology laboratory, and your task is to conduct a pilot study on several of your classmates. The first step of the experiment is to record two channels of bipolar EEG activity, and to do this you attach four electrodes—A, B, C, and D—to the scalp of one of your friends. You then set the dials on the EEG machine so that electrodes A and B are compared on the first channel of EEG activity, and electrodes C and D are compared on the second. You are alarmed to notice epileptic spikes in your friend's EEG. You notice that all of the epileptic spikes are being displayed on the first channel. This indicates that your friend has a focus of epileptic activity near A, near B, or near both. How can you determine which of these three possibilities is correct? When you solve this basic problem, you will have located your friend's epileptic focus and discovered on your own the electroencephalographic technique called **triangulation.**

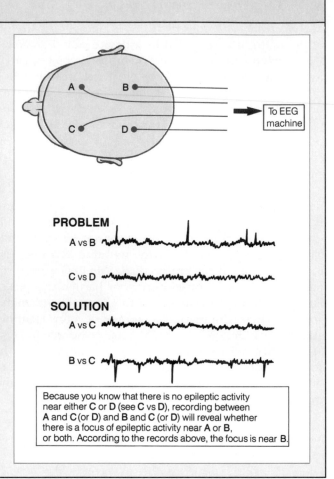

FIGURE 5.7

The triangulation problem.

Event-Related Potentials and Signal Averaging

In some cases, psychophysiologists are more interested in the EEG waves that accompany certain events than they are in the background EEG signal (e.g., Hillyard & Kutas, 1983). These accompanying waves are generally referred to as **event-related potentials (ERPs).** One commonly studied type of event-related potential is the **sensory evoked potential,** the change in the cortical EEG signal that is elicited by the momentary presentation of a sensory stimulus. As illustrated in Figure 5.8, the cortical EEG that follows a sensory stimulus has two components: the response to the stimulus (the signal) and the ongoing background EEG activity (the noise)—the *signal* is the part of any recording that is of interest; the *noise* is the part that isn't. The problem in recording sensory evoked potentials is that the noise of the background EEG is often so great that the sensory evoked potential is almost completely masked—measuring a sensory evoked potential can be like measuring a whisper at a rock concert. The method used to reduce the noise of the background EEG is called **signal averaging.** First, a subject's response to a stimulus, such as a click, is recorded many—let's say, 1,000—times. Then a computer identifies

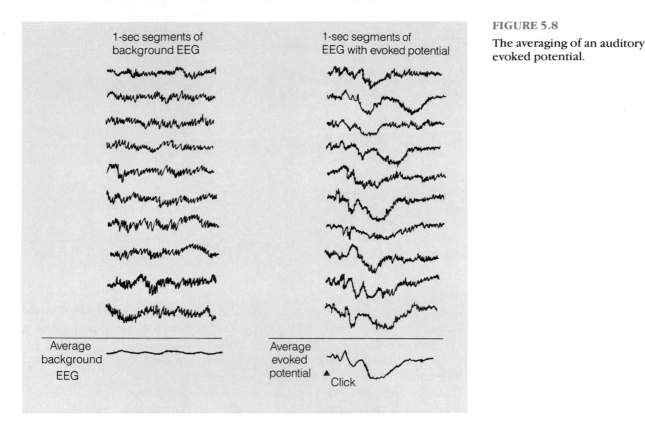

FIGURE 5.8
The averaging of an auditory evoked potential.

the millivolt value of each of the 1,000 traces at their starting points (i.e., at the click) and calculates the mean of these 1,000 scores. Next, it considers the value of each of the 1,000 traces 1 millisecond (msec) from their start, for example, and calculates the mean of these values. Then, it repeats this process at the 2-msec mark, the 3-msec mark, and so on. When these averages are plotted, the average response evoked by the click is apparent because the random background EEG is canceled out by the averaging. See Figure 5.8.

The analysis of *average evoked potentials* (AEPs) focuses on the various peaks or waves in the averaged signal. Each wave is characterized by its direction, positive or negative, and by its latency. For example, the **P300 wave** illustrated in Figure 5.9 is the positive wave that occurs about 300 msec after a momentary stimulus that has considerable meaning for the subject (Sutton, Teuting, Zubin, & John, 1967; Sutton & Ruchkin, 1984). In contrast, the small waves recorded in the first few milliseconds after a stimulus are not influenced by the meaning of the stimulus. These small waves are called **far-field potentials** because, although they are recorded from the scalp, they originate in the sensory nuclei of the brain stem (Jewett & Williston, 1971; Vaughan & Arezzo, 1988).

Electromyography

Skeletal muscles are each composed of millions of thread-like muscle fibers. Each muscle fiber contracts in an all-or-none fashion when activated by the motor neuron that innervates it. At any given time, a few fibers in each resting

FIGURE 5.9

An average auditory evoked potential. Notice the P300 wave. The P300 wave occurs only if the stimulus is meaningful; in this case the click signals the imminent delivery of a reward. By convention, positive EEG waves are always shown as downward deflections.

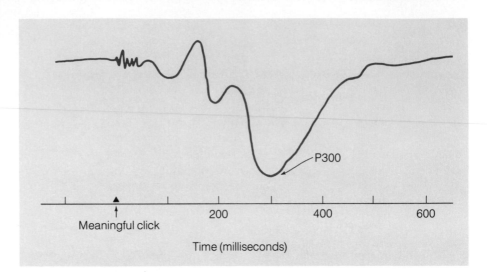

muscle are likely to be contracting, thus maintaining the overall tone of the muscle. Movement results when a large number of fibers contract at the same time. Under normal conditions, the impulses reaching a muscle are staggered so that the all-or-none responses of individual muscle fibers combine to produce fluid responses of the muscle as a whole.

Electromyography is a procedure for measuring the electrical discharge of muscles. The resulting record is called an *electromyogram* (EMG). EMG activity is usually recorded between two electrodes taped to the surface of the skin over the muscle of interest. An EMG record is presented in Figure 5.10. You will notice from this figure that the main correlate of an increase in muscle contraction is an increase in the amplitude of the EMG signal, which reflects the number of fibers contracting at any one time. Most psychophysiologists do not work with raw EMG signals; they convert them to a more workable form by a process called *signal integration*. The signal is fed into a computer that calculates the total amount of EMG spiking per unit of time—in consecutive 0.1-second intervals, for example. The total EMG activity per unit of time is then plotted, and the result is a smooth curve, the amplitude of which is a simple, continuous measure of level of muscle contraction over time (see Figure 5.10).

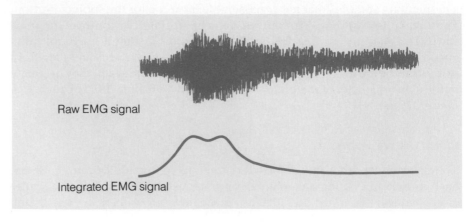

FIGURE 5.10

The relation between a raw EMG signal and its integrated version. The subject tensed the muscle beneath the electrodes, and then gradually relaxed it.

Eye Movement

The electrophysiological technique for recording eye movements is called **electrooculography,** and the resulting record is called an *electrooculogram* (EOG). Electrooculography is based on the fact that there is a steady potential difference between the front (positive) and back (negative) of the eyeball. Because of this steady potential, when the eye moves, a change in the electrical potential can be recorded between electrodes placed around the eye. It is usual to record EOG activity between two electrodes placed on each side of the eye to measure its horizontal movements, and between two electrodes placed above and below the eye to measure its vertical movements (see Figure 5.11).

Electrodermal Activity

Emotional thoughts and experiences are associated with increases in the ability of the skin to conduct electricity. The two most commonly employed indices of *electrodermal* activity are the **skin conductance level (SCL)** and the **skin conductance response (SCR).** The SCL is a measure of the background level of skin conductance that is associated with a particular situation, whereas the SCR is a measure of the transient changes in skin conductance that are associated with discrete experiences. The physiological bases of skin conductance changes are not fully understood, but there is considerable evidence implicating the sweat glands. Although the main function of sweat glands is to cool the body, they tend to become active in emotional situations—as you are almost certainly aware. Although sweat glands are distributed over most of the body surface, it is those of the hands, feet, armpits, and forehead that are particularly responsive to emotional stimuli. Few young lovers have escaped the dreaded duo: clammy hands and hircismus. (I recommend *Mrs. Byrnes Dictionary of Obscene, Obscure, and Preposterous Words* for those of you who collect unusual words such as *hircismus* which, by the way, means underarm odor.)

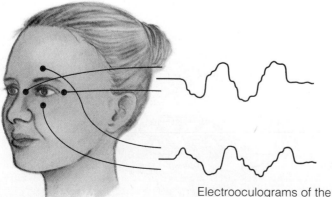

Electrooculograms of the
subject as she scanned
a circle

FIGURE 5.11

The typical placement of electrodes around the eye for electrooculography. The two electrooculogram traces were recorded when the subject scanned a circle. Notice that the two traces are out of phase.

Cardiovascular Activity

The presence in our language of terms such as "chicken-hearted," "heart-ache," "white with fear," and "blushing bride" indicates that modern psycho-physiologists were not the first to recognize the relation between *cardiovascular activity* and emotion. The cardiovascular system has two parts: the blood vessels and the heart. The blood vessels are pathways for the distribution of oxygen and nutrients to the tissues of the body, the removal of metabolic wastes, and the transmission of hormonal messages. The heart pumps the blood through the blood vessels.

The cardiovascular system responds to increased energy demands or emotional stimuli in two ways: by producing general increases in blood flow and by preferentially shunting blood into particular parts of the body. Blood can be distributed preferentially to particular tissues because the cardiovascular system, rather than being a single closed loop of vessels, is connected in parallel, as illustrated in Figure 5.12. The selective distribution of blood to various tissues is accomplished by the activity of *sphincter muscles* (any muscles whose contraction closes a bodily channel) in the walls of the *arterioles*. Constriction of particular arterioles reduces the blood flowing to areas of the body supplied by them, whereas dilation increases it.

Three different measures of cardiovascular activity are frequently employed in psychophysiological research: heart rate, arterial blood pressure, local blood volume.

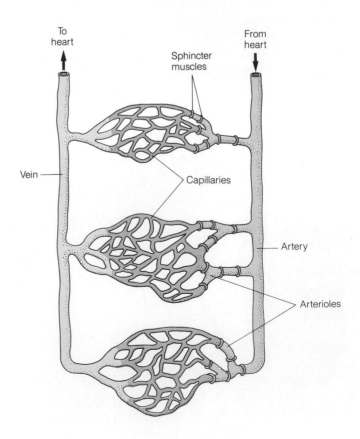

FIGURE 5.12

A schematic representation of the parallel organization of the circulatory system. Blood flow is directed by the arteriole sphincters.

Heart rate   The electrical signal that is associated with each heartbeat can be recorded through electrodes placed on the chest. The recording is called an **electrocardiogram** (abbreviated either **ECG,** for obvious reasons, or **EKG,** from the original German). The average resting heart rate of a healthy adult is about 70 beats per minute, but it increases abruptly at the sound or thought of a dental drill.

Blood pressure   Measuring arterial blood pressure involves two independent measurements: a measurement of the peak pressure during the periods of heart contraction, the *systoles,* and a measurement of the minimum pressure during the periods of relaxation, the *diastoles.* Blood pressure is usually expressed as a ratio of systolic over diastolic blood pressure in mmHg (millimeters of mercury). The normal resting blood pressure for an adult is about 130/70 mmHg. A blood pressure of more than 140/90 mmHg is viewed as a serious health hazard and is called **hypertension.**

I am sure that most of you have had your blood pressure measured with a *sphygmomanometer,* a crude device composed of a hollow cuff, a rubber bulb for inflating it, and a pressure gauge for measuring the pressure in the cuff (*sphygmos* is Greek for *pulse*). The methods used to measure blood pressure in modern psychophysiological research are fully automated (see Linden & Estrin, 1988).

Blood volume   Changes in the volume of blood in particular parts of the body are associated with psychological events. The best-known example of such a change is the engorgement of the genitals that is associated with sexual arousal in both males and females. **Plethysmography** refers to the various techniques for measuring changes in the volume of blood in a particular part of the body (from the Greek *plethysmos,* meaning *an enlargement*). One method of measuring these changes is to record the volume of the target tissue by wrapping a strain gauge around it. Although this method has utility in measuring blood flow in fingers, or in similarly shaped organs, the possibilities for employing it are somewhat restricted. Another plethysmographic method is to shine a light through the tissue under investigation and to measure the amount of the light that is absorbed by it—the more blood that there is in a structure, the more light will be absorbed.

5.3

Invasive Physiological and Pharmacological Research Methods

Efforts to study brain-behavior relations in human subjects are impeded by the necessity of adhering to lines of research that involve no direct interaction with the organ of interest: the brain. We turn now from a consideration of the *noninvasive* techniques employed in research on human subjects to a consideration of more direct procedures. This section introduces some of the physiological and pharmacological methods that are employed in biopsychological studies of laboratory animals.

Most techniques used in biopsychological research on laboratory animals fall into one of four categories: lesion methods, electrical stimulation methods, invasive recording methods, and psychopharmacological methods. Each of these four methods is discussed in this section of the chapter, but we will begin with a description of *stereotaxic surgery.*

Stereotaxic Surgery

The first step in many biopsychological experiments is the placement of an electrode or some other device at a specific target site in the brain. This is a relatively straightforward matter if the target site is on the surface of the brain, but in most cases, it is not. *Stereotaxic surgery* is the means by which experimental devices are precisely positioned in the brain. Two things are required in stereotaxic surgery: an atlas to provide directions to the target site and an instrument for getting there. The **stereotaxic atlas** is used to locate structures in much the same way that a geographic atlas is used to locate a geographic landmark. There is, however, one important difference; in contrast to the surface of the earth, which has only two dimensions, the brain has three. Accordingly, the brain is represented in a stereotaxic atlas by a series of individual maps, one per page, each representing the structure of a single, two-dimensional coronal brain slice. In stereotaxic atlases, all distances are given in millimeters from a designated reference point. In some rat atlases, the reference point is **bregma,** the point on the skull where two of the major *sutures* (seams) intersect. The **stereotaxic instrument** has two parts: a *head holder,* which firmly holds each subject's brain in the prescribed position and orientation, and an *electrode holder,* which holds the device to be inserted. The electrode holder can be moved in three dimensions: anterior-posterior, dorsal-ventral, or lateral-medial (front-back, up-down, or side to side, respectively) by a system of precision gears. The implantation of an electrode in the amygdala of a rat is illustrated in Figure 5.13.

Lesion Method

Those of you with an unrelenting drive to dismantle objects to see how they work will appreciate the lesion method. In the lesion method, a part of the brain is removed, damaged, or destroyed; then, the behavior of the subject is carefully assessed in an effort to determine the functions of the lesioned structure. Four lesion methods are discussed here: aspiration lesions, radio-frequency lesions, knife cuts, and cryogenic blockade.

Aspiration lesions   When a lesion is to be made in an area of cortical tissue that is accessible to the eyes and instruments of the surgeon, **aspiration** is frequently the method of choice. The cortical tissue is drawn off by suction created in a fine-tipped hand-held glass pipette. Because the underlying white matter is slightly more resistant to suction than the cortical tissue itself, a skilled surgeon can delicately peel off the layers of cortical tissue from the surface of the brain, leaving the underlying white matter and major blood vessels undamaged.

Radio-frequency lesions   Subcortical lesions are most frequently made by passing high-frequency (radio-frequency) current through the target tissue from the tip of a stereotaxically positioned electrode. It is the heat from the current that destroys the tissue. The size and shape of the lesion are deter-

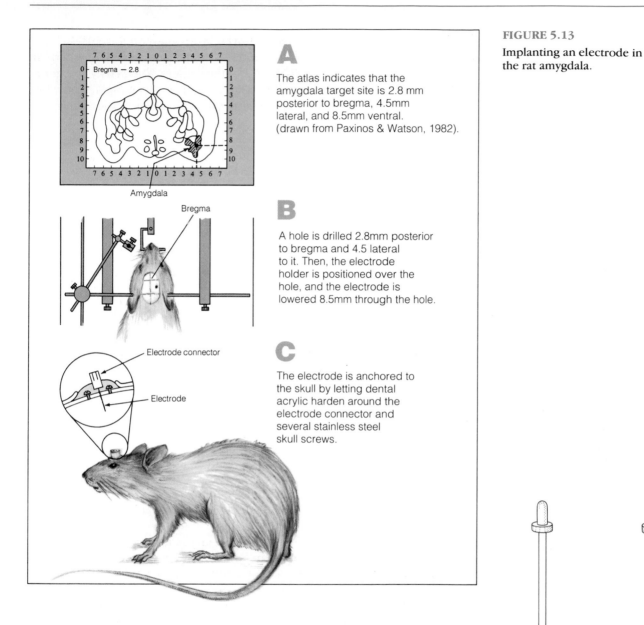

A

The atlas indicates that the amygdala target site is 2.8 mm posterior to bregma, 4.5mm lateral, and 8.5mm ventral. (drawn from Paxinos & Watson, 1982).

Bregma — 2.8

Amygdala

B

Bregma

A hole is drilled 2.8mm posterior to bregma and 4.5 lateral to it. Then, the electrode holder is positioned over the hole, and the electrode is lowered 8.5mm through the hole.

C

Electrode connector

Electrode

The electrode is anchored to the skull by letting dental acrylic harden around the electrode connector and several stainless steel skull screws.

FIGURE 5.13

Implanting an electrode in the rat amygdala.

mined by the duration and intensity of the current and the configuration of the electrode tip.

Knife cuts   Cutting or sectioning is used to eliminate conduction in a nerve or tract. A tiny, well-placed cut can unambiguously accomplish this task without producing extensive damage to surrounding tissue. How does one insert a knife into the brain to make a cut without severely damaging the overlying tissue? The method is depicted in Figure 5.14.

Cryogenic blockade   **Cryogenic blockade** is an attractive alternative to destructive lesions. When coolant is pumped through an implanted *cryoprobe*, such as the one depicted in Figure 5.15, neurons near the tip are cooled and stop firing. The temperature is maintained above the freezing level so that there is no structural damage. Then, when the tissue is allowed

Blade

The sectioning device is stereotaxically positioned in the brain.

Then, the blade is retracted to make the cut.

FIGURE 5.14

A device for performing subcortical "knife" cuts.

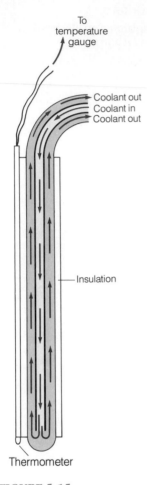

FIGURE 5.15
A cryoprobe.

to warm up, normal neural activity returns. A cryogenic blockade is functionally similar to a lesion in that it eliminates the contribution of a particular area of the brain to the ongoing behavior of the subject. This is why cryogenic blockades are sometimes referred to as functional or *reversible lesions*. Reversible lesions can also be produced with microinjections of local anesthetics into the brain.

Interpreting lesion effects   Before you leave this section on lesions, a word of caution is in order. Lesion effects are deceptively difficult to interpret. Because the structures of the brain are so small, so convoluted, and so tightly packed together, even a highly skilled surgeon cannot completely destroy a structure without producing significant damage to adjacent structures. There is, however, an unfortunate tendency to lose sight of this fact. For example, a lesion that leaves major portions of the amygdala intact and damages an assortment of neighboring structures, comes to be thought of simplistically as an *amygdala lesion*. Such an apparently harmless abstraction can be very misleading. If you believe that lesions referred to as amygdala lesions involve no other tissue, you will incorrectly attribute all of the behavioral effects of such lesions to amygdala damage; and conversely, if you believe that so-called amygdala lesions involve the entire amygdala, you will incorrectly conclude that the amygdala does not participate in behaviors uninfluenced by the lesion.

Electrical Stimulation

Clues about the function of a neural structure can be obtained by stimulating it with electrical current. It is usual to administer electrical stimulation to the nervous system across the two tips of a *bipolar electrode*—two insulated wires wound tightly together and cut at the end. Weak pulses of current produce an immediate increase in the firing of neurons near the tip of the electrode.

Electrical stimulation of the brain is an important biopsychological research tool because it often has behavioral effects. It can elicit a number of behavioral sequences, including eating, drinking, attacking, copulating, and sleeping. The particular behavioral response that is elicited depends upon the location of the electrode tip, the parameters of the current, and the test environment in which the stimulation is administered. Electrical stimulation of a particular brain structure usually has behavioral effects that are opposite to those produced by a lesion to the same structure. These effects are important clues to the structure's function.

Invasive Recording Methods

Intracellular unit recording   *Intracellular unit recording* was discussed at length in Chapter 4. It is the most informative method of studying the electrophysiological responses of individual neurons. Intracellular unit recording provides a moment by moment record of the graded fluctuations in one neuron's membrane potential. Most studies using this recording procedure are performed on chemically immobilized animals because it is next to impossible to keep the tip of a microelectrode positioned inside a neuron of a freely moving animal. See Figure 5.16.

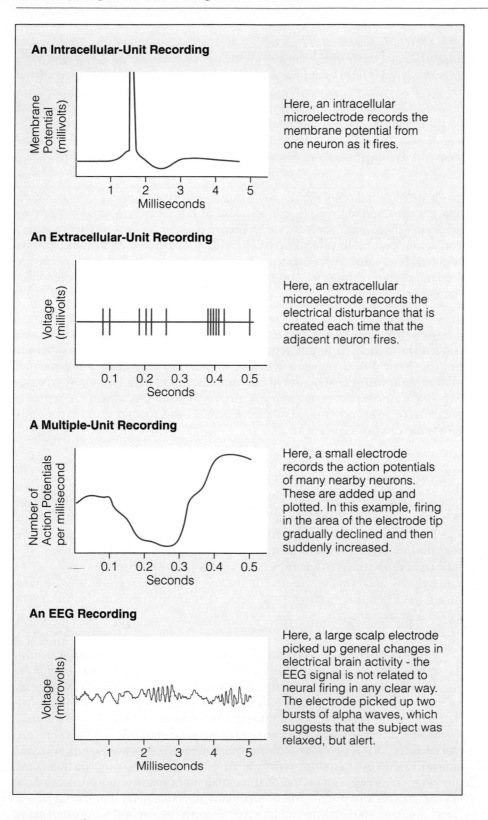

An Intracellular-Unit Recording

Here, an intracellular microelectrode records the membrane potential from one neuron as it fires.

An Extracellular-Unit Recording

Here, an extracellular microelectrode records the electrical disturbance that is created each time that the adjacent neuron fires.

A Multiple-Unit Recording

Here, a small electrode records the action potentials of many nearby neurons. These are added up and plotted. In this example, firing in the area of the electrode tip gradually declined and then suddenly increased.

An EEG Recording

Here, a large scalp electrode picked up general changes in electrical brain activity - the EEG signal is not related to neural firing in any clear way. The electrode picked up two bursts of alpha waves, which suggests that the subject was relaxed, but alert.

FIGURE 5.16

Four methods of recording the electrical activity of the nervous system.

Extracellular unit recording   It is possible to record the action potentials of a neuron through a microelectrode whose tip is positioned in the extracellular fluid next to it. Each time the neuron fires, a blip is recorded on the oscilloscope. Accordingly, *extracellular unit recording* provides a record of the firing of a neuron, but it provides no information about the neuron's membrane potential. It is difficult, but not impossible, to record extracellularly from a single neuron in a freely moving animal without the electrode tip shifting away from the neuron (e.g., Siegel, 1983). See Figure 5.16.

Multiple-unit recording   In *multiple-unit recording,* the electrode tip is larger than that of a microelectrode, and thus it picks up signals from many neurons—the larger the electrode, the more neurons contribute to the signal. The action potentials picked up by the electrode are fed into an integrating circuit, which adds them together. A multiple-unit record is a graph of the total number of recorded action potentials per unit of time (e.g., per second). See Figure 5.16.

Invasive EEG recording   In laboratory animals, EEG signals are recorded through large implanted electrodes rather than through scalp electrodes. Cortical EEG signals are frequently recorded through stainless steel skull screws, whereas subcortical EEG signals are typically recorded through stereotaxically implanted bipolar electrodes. Bipolar electrodes are typically constructed from two fine insulated wires twisted together and cut evenly across the tip. See Figure 5.16.

Psychopharmacological Methods

The major research strategy of psychopharmacology is to administer drugs that either increase or decrease the effects of particular neurotransmitters and to observe the behavioral consequences. You learned in the preceding chapter how *agonists* and *antagonists* affect neurotransmitter systems. Described here are the various routes of drug administration, several methods of using chemicals to make selective brain lesions, and three methods of measuring the chemical activity of the brain that are particularly useful in biopsychological research.

Routes of drug administration   In most psychopharmacological studies, drugs are administered peripherally by feeding them to the subject; by injecting them through a tube into the stomach (*intragastrically,* IG); or by injecting them hypodermically into the peritoneal cavity of the abdomen (*intraperitonally,* IP), into a large muscle (*intramuscularly,* IM), into the fatty tissue beneath the skin (*subcutaneously,* SC), or into a large surface vein (*intravenously,* IV). A problem with peripheral routes of administration is that many drugs do not readily pass through the blood-brain barrier. To overcome this problem, drugs can be injected in small amounts through a fine, hollow needle, called a **cannula,** which has been stereotaxically implanted in the brain. Such microinjections can be made directly into neural tissue, or if more widespread exposure of the brain to a drug is desired, larger volumes can be injected into the ventricles through an *intraventricular cannula.*

In some cases, researchers wish to study the effects of chronic drug exposure. This can be done by implanting drug pellets, which gradually enter general circulation over a period of days. Alternatively, the drug can be repeatedly injected through an implanted cannula from a tiny, preprogrammed, battery-operated infusion pump mounted on the skull of the subject (e.g., Blackshear, 1979).

Selective chemical lesions   The effects of surgical, electrolytic, and cryogenic lesions are frequently difficult to interpret because they affect all neurons in the target area. In some cases, it is possible to make more selective lesions by injecting toxic chemicals that have an affinity for certain components of the nervous system. There are many selective **neurotoxins.** For example, when *kainic acid* and *ibotenic acid* are administered by microinjection, they are preferentially taken up by cell bodies at the tip of the cannula and destroy those neurons, while leaving neurons with axons passing through the area largely unscathed. Another widely used selective neurotoxin is **6-hydroxydopamine (6-OHDA).** It is taken up only by those neurons that release the neurotransmitters *norepinephrine* or *dopamine,* and thus it leaves other neurons at the injection site undamaged.

Measuring the chemical activity of the brain   There are many procedures for measuring the chemical activity of the brain (see Westerink & Justice, 1991). The following are three that have proven to be particularly useful in biopsychological research. First is the *2-deoxyglucose (2-DG)* technique. An animal subject injected with radioactive 2-DG is placed in a test situation where it must engage in the activity of interest. Because 2-DG is similar in structure to glucose, the brain's main source of energy, neurons active during this test absorb it at a high rate, but they do not metabolize it. The subject is then killed, and its brain is removed and sliced. The slices are subjected to **autoradiography;** that is, they are coated with a photographic emulsion, stored in the dark for a few days, and then developed much like film. Areas of the brain that absorbed high levels of the radioactive 2-DG during the test appear as spots on the slides. See Figure 5.17.

The other two neurochemical procedures that I have chosen to introduce to you here are particularly useful in biopsychological research because they allow the researcher to measure cerebral neurochemical activity in behaving animals—most techniques require that animals be killed so that tissue samples can be extracted. One of these techniques, **cerebral dialysis** (see Robinson & Justice, 1991), involves passing a fine tube through the brain. The tube has a short semipermeable section that is positioned at the site of interest so that neurochemicals from the site diffuse into the tube and are carried by a solution flowing through the tube directly to an automated *chromatograph* (a device for measuring the chemical constituents of blood and other liquids and gases) for continuous, on-line analysis. The other technique is **in vivo voltammetry** (Blaha, Coury, Fibiger, & Phillips, 1990; Blaha & Jung, 1991), a procedure for inferring the changes in the extracellular concentration of specific chemicals at the tip of a carbon-based electrode from changes in the flow of current as the voltage across the electrode is gradually increased. The technique takes advantage of the fact that some chemicals are readily oxidized at characteristic current intensities, thus releasing a flow of electrons.

FIGURE 5.17

The accumulation of radioactivity in three frontal sections taken from the brain of a Richardson's ground squirrel. The subject was injected with radioactive 2-deoxyglucose, and then it viewed brightly illuminated black and white stripes for 45 minutes through its left eye while its right eye was covered. Because the ground-squirrel visual system is largely crossed, most of the radioactivity accumulated in the visual structures of the right hemisphere (the hemisphere on the right). (Courtesy of Rod Cooper, University of Calgary.)

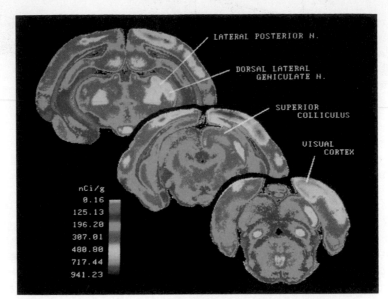

PART 2: The Behavioral Research Methods of Biopsychology

We turn now from the methods used by biopsychologists to study the nervous system to those that deal with the behavioral side of biopsychology. As you progress through this section of the chapter, it will become apparent that a fundamental difference between behavior and the nervous system is reflected in the nature of the methods that are used in their investigation. This difference is one of visibility. The nervous system and its activities are not ordinarily observable, whereas behavior is continuously on display in all its diversity and complexity. In essence, behavior is the overt expression of covert neural activity. Because of the inherent invisibility of neural activity, the primary objective of the methods used in its investigation is to render the unobservable observable. In contrast, the major objectives of behavioral research methods are to control, to simplify, and to objectify. A single set of such procedures developed for the investigation of a particular behavioral phenomenon is commonly referred to as a **behavioral paradigm.** Each behavioral paradigm normally comprises a method for producing the behavioral phenomenon under investigation and a method of objectively measuring it.

There is an unfortunate tendency to underestimate both the critical role that effective behavioral paradigms play in the progress of neuroscience and the ingenuity and effort required to develop them. Perhaps this is a consequence of behavior's visibility—we all seem to undervalue the familiar. Do not make this mistake! Remember that behavior is the ultimate manifestation of nervous system activity. In the final analysis, the purpose of all neural activity is the production of behavior. Measuring it is no simple matter (see Jacobs et al., 1988; Whishaw, Kolb, & Sutherland, 1983).

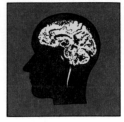

SELF TEST

The research methods of biopsychology illustrate a psychological disorder suffered by many scientists; I call it "unabbreviaphobia," the fear of leaving any term unabbreviated. As a means of reviewing the first half of this chapter, write out the following abbreviations in full.

1. CAT: _____

2. MRI: _____

3. PET: _____

4. 2-DG: _____

5. EEG: _____

6. ERP: _____

7. AEP: _____

8. EMG: _____

9. EOG: _____

10. SCL: _____

11. SCR: _____

12. ECG: _____

13. EKG: _____

14. IP: _____

15. IM: _____

16. IV: _____

17. SC: _____

18. 6-OHDA: _____

The answers to the preceding questions are: (1) computerized axial tomography, (2) magnetic resonance imaging, (3) positron emission tomography, (4) 2-deoxy-glucose, (5) electroencephalogram, (6) event-related potential, (7) average evoked potential, (8) electromyogram, (9) electrooculogram, (10) skin conductance level, (11) skin conductance response, (12) electrocardiogram, (13) electrocardiogram, (14) intraperitoneal, (15) intramuscular, (16) intravenous, (17) subcutaneous, and (18) 6-hydroxydopamine.

5.4

Neuropsychological Testing

A patient suspected of suffering from some sort of nervous system dysfunction is usually referred to a *neurologist*. However, neurological examinations typically focus on sensory and motor function, and thus they rarely reveal subtle changes in emotional, motivational, or intellectual function. This is the domain of the neuropsychologist.

Because of the diversity and complexity of psychological function, a thorough neuropsychological assessment typically requires several hours, spread over 2 or 3 days. As a result of the onerous nature of neuropsychological assessment, it is prescribed in only selected cases. Neuropsychological tests are normally administered: (1) to serve as a basis for diagnosis, particularly in cases in which brain imaging, EEG, and neurological testing have proven equivocal; (2) to serve as a basis for counseling and caring for neurological patients; or (3) to evaluate the effectiveness of treatment. This section introduces some of the tests that are commonly employed in the neuropsychological assessment of general intelligence, language lateralization, memory, language, and perceptual-motor function.

Tests of General Intelligence

Most neuropsychological assessments begin with a so-called intelligence test such as the **Wechsler Adult Intelligence Scale (WAIS).** The intelligence quotient (IQ) is a notoriously poor measure of brain damage; however, a skilled neuropsychologist can sometimes draw inferences about a patient's neuropsychological dysfunction from the pattern of deficits on the various subtests. For example, low scores on subtests of verbal ability tend to be associated with left hemisphere damage, whereas right hemisphere damage tends to reduce scores on performance subtests. The 11 subtests of the WAIS are illustrated in Table 5.1.

Tests of Language Lateralization

It is usual for one hemisphere to participate more than the other in language-related abilities. Two tests are commonly used to determine which hemisphere predominates: The **sodium amytal test** (Wada, 1949) and the **dichotic listening test** (Kimura, 1973). The sodium amytal test involves injecting sodium amytal, which is an anesthetic, into either the left or right *carotid arteries* of the neck. This temporarily blocks the function of the ipsilateral hemisphere, but leaves the contralateral hemisphere largely unaffected. While the brain is partially anesthetized, several tests of language function are quickly administered to the patient. Later, the entire process is repeated for the other side. When the injection is made on the side dominant for speech—the left for most people—the patient is completely mute for about 2 minutes. When the injection is on the nondominant side, there are typically just a few minor speech problems. Because the sodium amytal test is invasive, it can be administered only for medical reasons—usually to determine the dominant speech hemisphere prior to brain surgery.

In the standard version of the dichotic listening test, subjects wearing ste-

Table 5.1 The eleven subtests of the WAIS in chronological order. The Verbal Scale comprises the information, digit span, vocabulary, arithmetic, comprehension, and similarities subtests. The Performance Scale comprises the picture completion, picture arrangement, block design, object assembly, and digit symbol subtests (Wechsler, 1981).

Information Twenty-nine questions of general information are read to the subject; for example, "Who was the president of the United States during the Civil War?"

Picture Completion The subject must identify the important part missing from 20 drawings; for example, a door with no doorknob.

Digit Span Three digits are read to the subject at 1-second intervals and the subject is asked to repeat them in the same order. Two trials are given at three digits, four digits, five digits, and so on until the subject fails both trials at one level.

Picture Arrangement Ten sets of cartoon drawings are presented to the subject, and the subject is asked to arrange each set so that they tell a sensible story.

Vocabulary The subject is asked to define a list of 35 words ranging in difficulty from "bed" to "tirade."

Block Design The subject is presented with blocks that are red on two sides, white on two sides, and half red and half white on the other two. The subject is shown pictures of nine patterns and is asked to duplicate them by arranging the blocks.

Arithmetic The subject is presented with 14 arithmetic questions and must answer them without the benefit of pencil and paper.

Object Assembly The subject is asked to put together the pieces of four jigsaw-like puzzles to form familiar objects.

Comprehension The subject is asked 16 questions that test the ability to understand general principles; for example, "Why should people pay taxes?"

Digit Symbol The subject is presented with a key that matches each of a series of symbols with a different digit. On the lower part of the page is a series of digits, and the subject is given 90 seconds to write the correct symbol next to as many digits as possible.

Similarities The subject is presented with a pair of items and is asked to explain how the items in each pair are similar.

reo headphones hear three spoken digits presented in sequence to one ear, and at the same time three different digits are presented to the other ear. After a brief delay, the subjects are asked to report as many of the six digits as they can. Kimura found that the superior ear on the dichotic listening test was normally the ear contralateral to the dominant hemisphere for speech, as determined independently by the sodium amytal test—the right ear for most people.

Tests of Memory

Brain damage can have extremely specific effects on different aspects of memory. Thus, a variety of tests are needed to properly assess the memorial deficits of neurological patients. A battery of tests called the *Wechsler Memory Scale* is widely employed to assess memory dysfunction. It includes a brief survey of orientation in space and time and of awareness of current public information (Where are you? What day is it? Who is the mayor?), a test of the ability to read and to recall logical stories; a **digit-span test** (see Table 5.1); and a test of the memory for both related (motor-car) and unrelated (wagon-shampoo) paired associates. In the **paired-associate test,** pairs of words are read to the patient, and the patient's memory for the pairs is subsequently tested by assessing his or her ability to respond to the first word of each pair with the appropriate second word. Unfortunately, because of its predominantly verbal character, the Wechsler Memory Scale is inadequate for assessing memory for nonverbal material or for assessing the memorial abilities of patients with serious language-related deficits.

Tests of Language

Language is one of the most complex human abilities. Consequently, it is usual to administer a brief screening test of language abilities and to follow it up with a more extensive testing if deficits are revealed by the initial screening. One screening test for language-related problems is the **token test,** which is surprisingly effective in view of its simplicity. Twenty tokens of two different shapes (squares or circles), two different sizes (large or small), and five different colors (white, black, yellow, green, and red) are placed on a table in front of the subject. The task of the patient is to touch the tokens as instructed. The test begins with simple instructions, such as "touch a red square," being read by the examiner, and progresses to more difficult instructions, such as "touch the small, round circle and then the large, green square." Finally, the subject is asked to read the instructions aloud and follow them.

Tests of Perceptual-Motor Function

Most patients who are referred for neuropsychological testing will have already had their basic sensory-motor abilities evaluated by a neurologist. The neurologist will have assessed the ability of patients to detect the presence of simple stimuli and their ability to control each major voluntary muscle of the body. In addition, basic aspects of sensory-motor coordination will have been evaluated by checking the status of various reflexes, such as the pupillary and patellar (knee-jerk) reflexes, and various reflexively regulated voluntary behaviors, such as walking and balancing. However, in some instances, the sensory-motor problems of a neurological patient are too subtle to be revealed by conventional neurological tests.

One commonly used neuropsychological test of complex visuospatial ability is the *block-design subtest* of the WAIS (see Table 5.1). The **Rey-Osterrieth Complex Figure Test** is another. In the Rey-Osterrieth Complex Figure Test, the subject is asked to copy the Rey-Osterrieth Figure onto a sheet of paper with a pencil; this task is no problem for normal subjects. The value of this test stems from the fact that people with right-hemisphere damage often make different types of errors than those with left-hemisphere damage. Patients with right-hemisphere damage tend to copy all of the details, but they link them together inappropriately; those with damage to the left hemisphere tend to get the overall configuration correct, but they omit the details. Asking a subject to draw the figure from memory is a means of assessing nonverbal memory. Figure 5.18 illustrates the performance on the block-design test and the Rey-Osterrieth Complex Figure Test of a subject who suffered a stroke in the right hemisphere (Goodglass & Kaplan, 1979).

There is a group of perceptual-motor tests that assess the patient's ability to inhibit incorrect motor responses. The best known of such tests is the **Wis-**

BLOCK-DESIGN TEST

Test standard

Subject's response

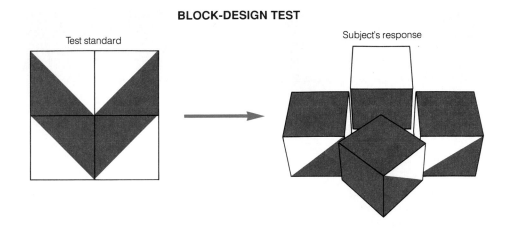

REY-OSTERRIETH COMPLEX FIGURE TEST

Test standard

Subject's response

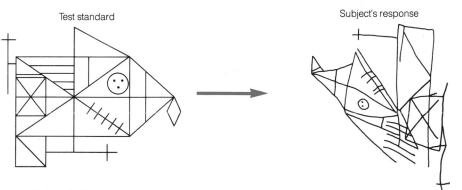

FIGURE 5.18

The performance of a patient with right-hemisphere damage on the Block-Design and Rey-Osterrieth Complex Figure Tests. In the usual version of these tests, the patient responds with the test standards in full view. Why don't you try the memory version of the Rey-Osterrieth Test? Study the figure, wait 1 minute, and then see how well you can draw it.

Test standards are from *Wechsler Adult Intelligence Scale.* Copyright © 1955 by The Psychological Corporation. Reproduced by permission. All rights reserved. Subject's responses are from "Assessment of Cognitive Functions in the Brain Injured Patient," by H. Goodglass and E. Kaplan in *Handbook of Behavioral Neurobiology,* Vol. 2 (p. 20) by M. Gazzaniga (Ed.), 1979, New York, Plenum Publishing Corporation. Copyright 1982 by Plenum Publishing Corporation. Reprinted with permission.

consin Card Sorting Test, which is illustrated in Figure 5.19. On each of the Wisconsin cards is from one to four identical symbols (either triangles, stars, circles, or crosses) of the same color (either red, green, yellow, or blue). The subject is confronted with four stimulus cards that differ from one another in form, color, and number. The task of the patient is to correctly sort cards from a deck into piles in front of the stimulus cards; however, he or she does not know whether to do this by sorting according to form, color, or number. The patient begins by guessing and is told after each card is sorted whether it was sorted correctly or incorrectly. At first, the task of the patient is to learn to sort

FIGURE 5.19

The Wisconsin Card Sorting Test. This woman is just starting the test; in front of which of the four piles should she place this card?

by color, but as soon as the patient makes several consecutive correct responses, the sorting principle is changed (to shape or number) without any indication other than the fact that responses based on color become incorrect. And once this new principle is learned, the sorting principle is changed again. Patients with *frontal-lobe damage* often continue to sort on the basis of color for 100 or more trials after this strategy becomes incorrect. The tendency to keep making previously appropriate responses when they become inappropriate is termed **perseveration.**

5.5

Biopsychological Paradigms of Animal Behavior

Illustrative examples of the behavioral paradigms that are used to study the biopsychology of laboratory species are provided here under three separate headings: (1) paradigms for the assessment of species-common behaviors, (2) traditional conditioning paradigms, and (3) seminatural animal learning paradigms. In each case, the focus is on methods used to study the behavior of the laboratory rat, the most common subject of biopsychological research.

Assessment of Species-Common Behaviors

Many of the behavioral paradigms that are used in biopsychological research are used to study species-common behaviors. **Species-common behaviors** are those that are displayed by virtually all members of a species, or at least by all those of the same age and sex. Commonly studied species-common behaviors include grooming, swimming, eating, drinking, copulating, fighting, and nest building. Described here are the open-field test, tests of aggressive and defensive behavior, and tests of sexual behavior.

Open-field test   The **open-field test** involves scoring the behavior of an animal in a large, barren chamber. It is usual to measure general activity with an automated activity recorder or by drawing lines on the floor of the chamber and counting the number of line-crossings during the test. It is also common in the open-field test to count the number of *boluses* of excrement that were dropped by an animal during the test. Low activity scores and high bolus counts are frequently used as indicators of fearfulness. Fearful rats are highly **thigmotaxic,** that is, they rarely venture away from the walls of the test chamber, and they rarely engage in such activities as rearing and grooming. Rats are often fearful when they are first placed in a strange open field, but this fearfulness declines with repeated exposure to the same open field.

Aggressive and defensive behavior   Typical patterns of aggressive and defensive behavior can be observed during combative encounters between the dominant male rat of an established colony and a smaller male intruder (see Blanchard & Blanchard, 1988). This is called the **colony-intruder paradigm.** The behaviors of the dominant male are considered to be aggressive, and those of the hapless intruder, defensive. The dominant male of the colony (i.e., the *alpha male*) moves sideways toward the intruder, with its hair bristling. When it nears the intruder, it tries to push it off balance, and it tries to deliver bites to the back and flanks. The defender tries to protect its back and flanks by rearing up on its hind legs and pushing the attacker away with its forepaws, or by rolling onto its back. Accordingly, piloerection, lateral display, and flank and back biting indicate conspecific aggression in the rat; whereas freezing, boxing, and rolling over indicate defensiveness.

Some tests of rat defensive behavior assess reactivity to the experimenter, rather than to another rat. The test developed by Albert (e.g., Albert, Petrovic, Jonik, & Walsh, 1991) is a good example of such a test. The rat is confronted in the test box by a sequence of test stimuli: a pencil held in front of its nose, a tap on the back with a pencil, a poke in the side with a pencil, a gloved hand in front of the nose, a gloved hand grasping its tail, and a hand around its abdomen. The response to each stimulus is rated on a scale from 0 (no response) to 3 (defensive attack). Rats with bilateral *septal lesions* are notoriously reactive to these stimuli.

Sexual behavior   Most attempts to study the physiological bases of rat sexual behavior have focused on the copulatory act itself. The male mounts the female from behind and clasps her hindquarters. If the female is receptive, she responds by assuming the **lordosis** posture; that is, she sticks her hindquarters in the air by bending her back in a U, and she deflects her tail to the side. During some mounts, the male inserts his penis into the female's vagina—this act is called **intromission.** After intromission, the male dismounts by jumping backwards. He then returns a few seconds later to mount and intromit once again. Following about 10 such cycles of mounting, intromitting, and dismounting, the male mounts, intromits, and **ejaculates,** that is, deposits his sperm (Dewsbury, 1967; McClintock, 1984). The number of mounts required to achieve intromission, the number of intromissions required to achieve ejaculation, and the interval between ejaculation and the reinitiation of mounting are three common measures of male sexual behavior. The intensity of the female's response is frequently scored in terms of the proportion of mounts that produce lordosis (i.e., her **lordosis quotient**) and how much her back bends during lordosis.

Mendelson and Gorzalka (1987) have developed a special test chamber for studying rat sexual behavior that has advantages over the conventional small cylindrical chambers. Because the *Mendelson box* is narrow (see Figure 5.20), it insures that all interactions between the rats will be observable from the most revealing angle (i.e., from the side), and because it contains a series of ledges, it permits the subjects to engage in approach and avoidance behaviors by moving vertically through the apparatus.

Traditional Conditioning Paradigms

Learning paradigms play a major role in biopsychological research. This is so for three reasons. The first is that learning is a phenomenon of primary interest to psychologists. The second reason is that learning paradigms provide a technology for producing and controlling animal behavior—because animals cannot follow instructions from the experimenter, it is often necessary to train them to behave in a fashion consistent with the goals of the experiment. The third reason is that it is possible to infer much about the sensory, motor, motivational, and cognitive state of an animal from its ability to learn various tasks and to perform various learned responses.

FIGURE 5.20

Rats in a Mendelson box. The male is pursuing the female with naughty intent. (Courtesy of Scott Mendelson and Boris Gorzalka.)

If you have taken a previous course in psychology, you will likely be familiar with the **Pavlovian** and **operant conditioning** paradigms. In the Pavlovian conditioning paradigm, the experimenter pairs an initially neutral stimulus called a *conditional stimulus* (e.g., a tone or a light) with an *unconditional stimulus* (e.g., meat powder), a stimulus that elicits a reflexive or *unconditional response* (e.g., salivation). As a result of these pairings, the conditional stimulus eventually acquires the capacity, when administered alone, to elicit a *conditional response* (e.g., salivation), a response that is usually similar to the unconditional response. In operant conditioning, the rate at which a particular voluntary response (such as a lever press) is emitted is increased or decreased by *reinforcing* it or *punishing* it, respectively.

One of the most widely used operant paradigms in biopsychology is the self-stimulation paradigm. In the **self-stimulation paradigm**, animals press a lever to administer reinforcing electrical stimulation to certain so-called "pleasure centers" in their own brains (e.g., Phillips & Fibiger, 1989; Stellar, 1990). A similar paradigm is the **drug self-administration paradigm** in which animals inject drugs into themselves through implanted cannulas by pressing a lever (e.g., Mello, Mendelson, Bree, & Lukas, 1989).

Although conventional Pavlovian and operant conditioning paradigms are still widely employed in physiological psychology and psychopharmacology, the discovery in the 1950s of *conditioned taste aversion* (e.g., Garcia & Koelling, 1966) stimulated the development of laboratory learning paradigms that mimick situations that an animal might encounter in its natural environment. The 50s was a time of sock hops, sodas at Al's, crewcuts, and drive-in movies. In the animal-behavior laboratory, it was a time of lever presses, key-pecks, and shuttles made in response to flashing lights, tones, and geometric patterns. Then, along came rock 'n roll, and along came the conditioned taste aversion paradigm. Things have not been the same since.

Seminatural Animal Learning Paradigms

Conditioned taste aversion   **Conditioned taste aversion** refers to the observation that many animals develop an aversion for tastes whose consumption has been followed by illness. In the standard conditioned taste aversion experiment, rats that receive an *emetic*—a nausea-inducing drug—after their first experience with a palatable solution, subsequently refuse to drink the solution. The ability of rats to readily learn the relation between a particular taste and subsequent illness unquestionably increases their chances of survival in their natural environment, where potentially edible substances are not routinely screened by government agencies. Rats and many other animals are *neophobic* (afraid of new things); thus, when they first encounter a new food, they consume it in only small quantities. If they subsequently become ill, they will not consume it again. Conditioned aversions also develop to familiar tastes, but these typically require more than a single trial to be learned.

Humans also develop conditioned taste aversions. Cancer patients have been reported to develop aversions to foods consumed before nausea-inducing chemotherapy (Bernstein & Webster, 1980). Also, many of you will be able to testify on the basis of personal experience about the effectiveness of conditioned taste aversions. I still have vivid memories of a batch of laboratory punch that I overzealously consumed after eating two pieces of blueberry pie . . . but that is another story—albeit a particularly colorful one.

Research on conditioned taste aversion challenged three principles of learning (see Revusky & Garcia, 1970) that had grown out of research on traditional operant and classical conditioning paradigms. First, it challenged the view that animal conditioning is always a gradual step-by-step process; enduring taste aversions can be established in only a single trial. Second, it showed that *temporal contiguity* is not essential for conditioning; rats acquire taste aversions even when they do not become ill until several hours after eating. Third, it challenged the *principle of equipotentiality,* the view that conditioning proceeds in basically the same manner regardless of the particular stimuli and responses under investigation. Rats appear to be particularly well prepared to learn associations between tastes and illness; it is only with difficulty that they learn relations between the color of food and nausea or between taste and footshock. The discovery of conditioned taste aversion encouraged the development of other seminatural laboratory paradigms that focused on forms of learning for which the subjects seemed specially prepared.

Radial arm maze   The **radial arm maze** taps the well-developed spatial abilities of rodents. The survival of rats in the wild depends on their ability to navigate quickly and accurately through their environment and to learn which locations in it are likely to contain food and water. This task is much more complex for a rodent than it is for us. Most of us obtain food from locations where the supply is continually replenished—we go to the market confident that we will find enough food to satisfy our needs. In contrast, the foraging rat must learn, and retain, a complex pattern of spatially coded details. It must not only learn where morsels of food are likely to be found, but it must also remember which of these sites it has recently stripped of their booty so as not to revisit them too soon. The radial arm maze was designed by Olton and Samuelson (1976) to study these spatial abilities. The radial arm maze (see Figure 5.21) is a central platform with an array of arms—usually eight or more—radiating from it. At the end of each arm is a food cup, which may or may not be baited, depending on the purpose of the experiment.

FIGURE 5.21
A radial arm maze.

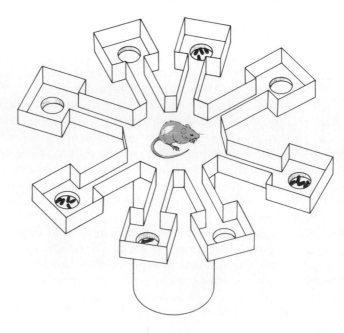

In one version of the radial-arm-maze paradigm, rats are placed each day in a radial arm maze that has all arms baited. After a few days of experience, rats rarely visit the same arm twice in the same day, even when control procedures make it impossible for them to recognize odors left during previous visits to an arm or to make their visits in a systematic sequence. Because the arms are identical, rats must orient themselves in the maze with reference to external room cues; thus their performance can be disrupted by rotating the maze or by changing the appearance of the room.

Morris water maze   Another seminatural learning paradigm that has been designed to study the spatial abilities of rats is the **Morris water maze** (Morris, 1981). The rats are placed in a circular, featureless pool of cool milky water, and they must swim until they discover the escape platform, which is invisible just beneath the surface of the water. The rats are allowed to rest on the platform before being returned to the water for another trial. Despite the fact that the starting point of the rats is varied from trial to trial, the rats learn after only a few trials to swim directly to the platform, presumably by using spatial cues from the room as a reference. Adaptations of this task have proven extremely useful for assessing the navigational skills of lesioned or drugged animals (Kolb, 1989; Sutherland & Dyck, 1984).

Conditioned defensive burying   Yet another seminatural learning paradigm that has proven useful in biopsychological research is the **conditioned defensive burying paradigm** (e.g., Pinel & Mana, 1989; Pinel & Treit, 1978). In the conditioned defensive burying paradigm, rats receive a single aversive stimulus (e.g., shock, airblast, or odor) from an object mounted on the wall of the chamber just above the floor, which is littered with bedding material. After a single trial, almost every rat learns that the test object is a threat and responds to it by spraying the bedding material at it with their head and forepaws (see Figure 5.22). Because many subjects completely

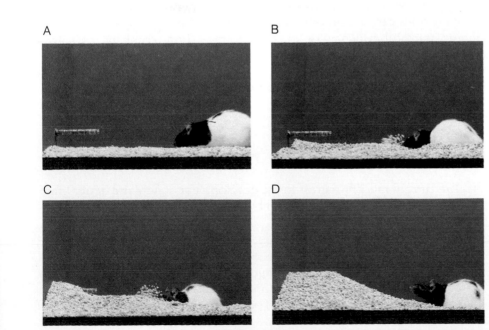

FIGURE 5.22

A rat burying a test object from which it has just received a single mild shock.

(Photograph by Jack Wong.)

cover the source of aversive stimulation during the test period, this response has been termed *conditioned defensive burying.* Treit has shown that anti-anxiety drugs reduce the amount of conditioned defensive burying and has used the paradigm to study the neurochemistry of anxiety (e.g., Treit, 1987). The burying response does not develop normally in rats that have been reared in cages with wire-mesh floors, rather than bedding-covered floors (Pinel, Jones, & Whishaw, 1992; Pinel, Symons, Christensen, & Tees, 1989).

Paradigms of avian memory   With the growing awareness of the remarkable abilities of animals to learn and remember things that are important for their survival in their natural environments, biopsychologists have shown an increasing interest in the memorial capacities of birds. For example, there has been considerable interest in the abilities of some species of birds to sing as adults songs that they heard for only a brief period during their infancy (Marler, 1991; Nottebohm, 1991); to follow specific migration routes after making only a single trip with adult birds (Baker, 1982); and to retrieve seeds from thousands of different cache sites (Shettleworth, 1983). Laboratory paradigms have been designed for the investigation of each of these phenomena.

Conclusion

This chapter has introduced you to the research methods of biopsychology: to its neural methods in Part 1 and to its behavioral methods in Part 2. Before leaving the chapter, it is important that you appreciate how these methods work together. Seldom, if ever, is an important biopsychological issue resolved by a single set of methods. The reason for this is that neither the methods used to manipulate the brain nor the methods used to assess the behavioral consequences of these manipulations are totally selective; there are no methods of manipulating the brain that change only a single aspect of brain function, and there are no methods of measuring behavior that do not reflect a variety of psychological processes. Thus, any experiment that uses a single set of methods can be interpreted in more than one way, and it cannot provide unequivocal evidence for any one interpretation. Problems are solved only when several methods are brought to bear on a single problem in such a way that all interpretations but one can be ruled out. This approach, as you learned in Chapter 1, is called **converging operations.**

Food for Thought

1. The current rate of progress in the development of new and better brain scanning devices will soon render behavioral tests of brain damage obsolete. Discuss.

2. You are taking a physiological psychology laboratory course, and your instructor gives you two rats: one rat with a lesion in an unknown structure and one normal rat. How would you test the rats to determine which has the lesion? How would your approach differ from what you might use to test a human patient suspected of having brain damage?

KEY TERMS

To help you study the material in this chapter, all of the key terms—those that have appeared in bold type—are listed and briefly defined here.

Alpha waves. Eight-to-twelve-per-second, high-amplitude cortical EEG waves, which frequently occur during relaxed wakefulness.

Angiography. A contrast X-ray technique that involves infusing a radio-opaque dye through a cerebral artery.

Aspiration. A lesion technique in which the tissue is drawn off by suction through the tip of a hand-held glass pipette.

Autoradiography. The radiation released from a radioactively labeled substance such as 2-DG is photographically developed so that regions of high uptake are visible on a brain slice.

Behavioral paradigm. A single set of procedures developed for the investigation of a particular behavioral phenomenon.

Bregma. A landmark on the surface of the skull commonly used as a reference point in stereotaxic surgery.

Cannula. A tube or hypodermic needle that is implanted in the body for the purpose of introducing or extracting substances; for example, an intraventricular cannula.

Cerebral dialysis. A method for recording moment-by-moment changes in brain chemistry in behaving animals; a fine tube with a short semipermeable section is passed through the brain and into an automated chromatograph for on-line analysis of neurochemicals diffusing through the semipermeable section.

Colony-intruder paradigm. A small male intruder rat is placed in an established colony in order to study the aggressive responses of the dominant male (the alpha male) and the defensive responses of the intruder.

Computerized axial tomography (CAT). A computer-assisted X-ray procedure for visualizing the brain in three dimensions.

Conditioned defensive burying. A paradigm in which the subject responds to an aversive stimulus by spraying material at it.

Conditioned taste aversion. The aversion developed by animals to tastes that have been followed by illness.

Contrast X-ray techniques. X-ray techniques that involve the injection of a radio-opaque substance.

Converging operations. Solving a scientific question by using several methods to rule out all interpretations but one.

Cryogenic blockade. Temporarily eliminating neural activity in a particular part of the brain by cooling it with a cryoprobe.

2-deoxyglucose (2-DG). A substance similar to glucose; it is taken up by active neurons and accumulates in them because, unlike glucose, it cannot be used by neurons as a source of energy.

Dichotic listening test. A test of speech lateralization in which patients hear different sequences of digits simultaneously presented to two ears.

Digit-span test. A classic test of verbal short-term memory.

Drug self-administration paradigm. An operant conditioning paradigm in which animals press a lever to administer reinforcing drugs to themselves.

Ejaculation. Ejection of sperm.

Electrocardiogram (ECG or EKG). A recording of the electrical activity of the heart.

Electroencephalography. Recording the gross electrical activity of the brain through large electrodes; in humans, EEG electrodes are usually taped to the surface of the scalp.

Electromyography. A procedure for measuring the electrical discharge of muscles.

Electrooculography. A technique for recording eye movements through electrodes placed around the eye.

Event-related potentials (ERPs). The EEG waves that regularly accompany certain psychological events.

Far-field potentials. EEG signals recorded in an attenuated form at a distance from their source.

6-hydroxydopamine (6-OHDA). A neurotoxin that selectively destroys those neurons that release norepinephrine or dopamine.

Hypertension. Chronically high blood pressure.

Intromission. Insertion of the penis into the vagina.

In vivo voltammetry. A procedure for inferring the changes in the extracellular concentration of specific chemicals at the tip of a carbon-based electrode from changes in the flow of current as the voltage across the electrode is gradually increased.

Lordosis. The female rat's arched-back posture of sexual receptivity.

Lordosis quotient. The proportion of mounts that produce lordosis.

Magnetic resonance imaging (MRI). A procedure in which high-resolution images of the structures of the living brain are constructed from the measurement of waves that hydrogen atoms emit when they are activated by radiofrequency waves in a magnetic field.

Morris water maze. A pool of milky water with a goal platform just beneath the surface.

Neurotoxins. Neural poisons; some neurotoxins (such as kainic acid, ibotenic acid, and 6-OHDA) are selective, that is, they destroy specific parts of the brain.

Open-field test. Scoring the behavior of a subject in a large, barren chamber.

Operant conditioning. The rate at which a particular voluntary response is emitted is increased or decreased by reinforcing it or punishing it, respectively.

P300 wave. The positive EEG wave that usually occurs about 300 milliseconds after a momentary stimulus that has meaning for the subject.

Paired-associate test. Pairs of words are read to the subject, and the subject's memory is subsequently tested by assessing his or her ability to respond to the first word of each pair with the appropriate second word.

Pavlovian conditioning. A paradigm in which the experimenter pairs an initially neutral stimulus (conditional stimulus) with a stimulus (unconditional stimulus) that elicits a reflexive response (unconditional response); after several pairings the neutral stimulus elicits a response (conditioned response).

Perseveration. The tendency to keep making previously appropriate responses after they have become inappropriate.

Plethysmography. Measuring changes in the volume of blood in a part of the body.

Pneumoencephalography. A contrast X-ray technique that involves temporarily replacing some of the cerebral spinal fluid with air.

Positron emission tomography (PET). A technique for visualizing the metabolic activity in the brain by measuring the accumulation of radioactive 2-deoxyglucose (2-DG).

Radial arm maze. A multiple-arm maze designed to test spatial ability in rats.

Rey-Osterrieth Complex Figure Test. A neuropsychological test of complex visuospatial ability.

Self-stimulation paradigm. A paradigm in which animals press a lever to administer reinforcing electrical stimulation to their own brains.

Sensory evoked potential. A change in the electrical activity of the brain that is elicited by the momentary presentation of a stimulus.

Signal averaging. A method used to reduce the noise of the background EEG when trying to measure event-related potentials.

Skin conductance level (SCL). A measure of the steady level of skin conductance associated with a particular situation.

Skin conductance response (SCR). A measure of the transient changes in skin conductance associated with brief experiences.

Sodium amytal test. A test involving the anesthetization of one hemisphere and then the other to determine which hemisphere plays the dominant role in language.

Species-common behaviors. Behaviors that are performed in the same manner by virtually all like members of a species.

Stereotaxic atlas. A series of two-dimensional maps that provide a three-dimensional representation of the brain.

Stereotaxic instrument. A device for performing stereotaxic surgery; it is composed of two parts, a head holder and an electrode holder.

Thigmotaxic. Tending to stay near the walls of an open field.

Token test. A test for aphasia that involves following verbal instructions to touch or move tokens of different colors and shapes.

Triangulation. A standard bipolar electroencephalographic technique for determining which of the two sites being compared on a channel of abnormal EEG is the source of abnormality observed in the channel; both suspect sites are individually compared with a site known to be normal.

Wechsler Adult Intelligence Scale (WAIS). A popular test of general intelligence.

Wisconsin Card Sorting Test. A neuropsychological test that evaluates a patient's ability to inhibit previously correct motor responses.

ADDITIONAL READING

The following are provocative discussions of two different behavioral testing strategies:

Jacobs, W. J., Blackburn, J. R., Buttrick, M., Harpur, T. J., Kennedy, D., Mana, M. J., MacDonald, M. A., McPherson, L. M., Paul, D., & Pfaus, J. G. (1988). Observations. *Psychobiology, 16,* 3–19.

Whishaw, I. Q., Kolb, B., & Sutherland, R. J. (1983). The analysis of behavior in the laboratory rat. In T. E. Robinson (Ed.), *Behavioral approaches to brain research.* New York: Oxford University Press.

An interesting, colorful, and simple introduction to modern brain imaging techniques is provided by:

Sochurek, H., & Miller, P. (1987). Medicine's new vision. *National Geographic, 171,* 2–41.

6

Human Brain
Damage and
Animal Models

Much of what we know about human brain function has been learned from the study of its dysfunction. The behavioral changes that are associated with particular patterns of brain damage provide important insights into the normal functions of the afflicted structures. This chapter is an introduction to the topic of human brain damage and its behavioral effects.

To make you more aware of the personal tragedy underlying the academic discourse that follows, this chapter begins with a look at the life of one neurological patient, sublieutenant L. Zasetsky. Zasetsky suffered a bullet wound to his left parietal and occipital lobes, and his life was irrevocably changed. In his book, *The Man With a Shattered World* (1972), the eminent Soviet neuropsychologist, A. R. Luria, has documented Zasetsky's struggle to regain his mental faculties. The following is Luria's paraphrased description of his first meeting with Zasetsky.

I first met Zasetsky 3 months after he had been wounded. I was struck by how young he looked. When I asked him how he was feeling, he shyly replied, "Okay." But my further questioning only confused him. He had difficulty understanding my questions, but even when he did, he had difficulty answering. Each question initiated a frantic struggle to come up with the right words.

"What town are you from?"
"At home . . . there's . . . I want to write . . . but just can't."
"Do you have any relatives?"
"There's . . . my mother . . . and also—what do you call them?"
"Try reading this," I suggested.
"What's this? . . . No, I don't know . . . don't understand . . . what is this?"

"All right, then," I said. "Try to write your name." He awkwardly picked up the pencil, by the wrong end at first. He was shocked to discover that he couldn't form a single letter. The truth was becoming apparent to him. Somehow he had become illiterate.

"Well, then, take a look at this picture and tell me what you see."
"Over here there's . . . he's . . . he's sitting. And this one here is . . . is . . . And there's this . . . I don't know! Certainly is something there, but . . . but what's it called?"

"Could you raise your right hand?"
"Right? Right? . . . Left? No, I don't know . . . What does right mean? . . . Or left? . . . No, I can't."

When I asked him to list the months of the year, he did it with ease and was reassured. But when I asked him what season comes before winter, he became confused again.

"Before winter? After winter? . . . Summer? . . . Or something! No, I can't get it."

In the years to come, Zasetsky's verbal abilities improved somewhat, and I learned more about his problems. He had great difficulty gauging the spatial relationships among objects; he could often not locate parts of his own body; he would often be unaware of the right side of things that he was looking at; and he had difficulty remembering recent events, although many of his memories of childhood returned.

His response to nature was as keen as ever; he enjoyed the singing of the birds and the beauty of the lake. And oh how he wanted to accomplish what was asked of him. Each failure renewed his sense of loss. What type of brain injury had damaged some of his faculties but left others intact? His grasp of his immediate world, his will, and his desire to accomplish and experience had all been spared—enough had been spared to enable him to experience the anguish of his every failure and shortcoming.

Remember Zasetsky and his struggle; you will encounter them again.

6.1

Causes of Brain Damage

This section of the chapter provides an introduction to six causes of brain damage: tumors, cerebrovascular disorders, closed-head injuries, infections of the brain, neurotoxins, and genetic factors.

Brain Tumors

A **tumor** or *neoplasm* (literally, *new growth*) is a mass of cells that grows independently of the rest of the body. About 20% of tumors found in the human brain are **meningiomas** (see Figure 6.1), tumors that grow between the *meninges* (the three membranes that cover the CNS). All meningiomas are **encapsulated tumors;** that is, they grow within their own membrane. As a result, they are particularly easy to identify on a CAT scan; they can influence the function of the brain only by the pressure they exert on surrounding tissue; and they are almost always **benign**—that is, they can be surgically removed with little risk of further tumor growth. Unfortunately, encapsulation is the exception, rather than the rule when it comes to brain tumors. With the exception of meningiomas, most brain tumors are infiltrating. **Infiltrating tumors** are those that grow diffusely through normal tissue, and as a result, they are usually **malignant;** it is difficult to remove them completely, and any cancerous tissue that remains after surgery continues to grow.

About 10% of all brain tumors do not originate in the brain. They grow from tumor fragments carried to the brain by the bloodstream from some other part of the body—the brain seems to be a particularly fertile ground for tumor growth. These are called **metastatic tumors**—*metastasis* is a general term that refers to the transmission of disease from one organ to another. Most metastatic brain tumors originate as cancers of the lungs. Obviously the chances of recovering from a cancer that has already attacked two or more separate sites is slim at best. Figure 6.2 illustrates the ravages of metastasis.

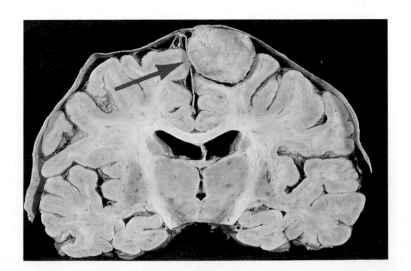

FIGURE 6.1

A meningioma. (Courtesy of Kenneth Berry, Head of Neuropathology, Vancouver General Hospital.)

Multiple metastatic brain tumors. The arrows indicate some of the areas of damage. (Courtesy of Kenneth Berry, Head of Neuropathology, Vancouver General Hospital.)

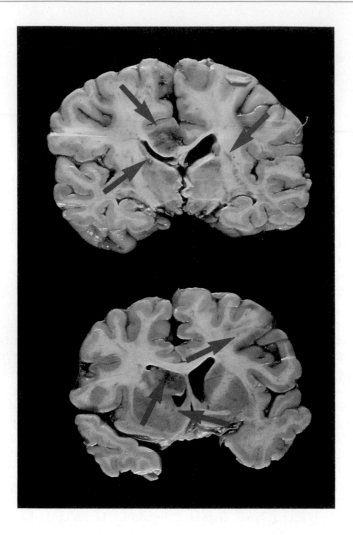

Infiltrating brain tumors are often untreatable, but there is reason for optimism. Tumor growth results from the dysfunction of mechanisms that regulate normal cell division and growth. It was recently discovered that normal cells contain *tumor suppressor genes,* which become dysfunctional during the growth of certain types of tumors. Efforts to understand and treat tumor growth (i.e., cancer) are currently focusing on these genes (see Sager, 1989).

Cerebrovascular Disorders

The term *stroke* refers to any severe, sudden attack. Because brain damage from disorders of the cerebral circulatory system frequently occurs with great suddenness and severity, stroke is commonly used as a synonym for *cerebrovascular disorder.* However, not all cerebrovascular disorders are characterized by sudden onset, and not all cerebral disorders of sudden onset are vascular in origin (see Zivin & Choi, 1991).

There are two main types of cerebrovascular disorders. One, termed *intracerebral hemorrhage* (bleeding), occurs when a cerebral blood vessel is ruptured and blood seeps into the surrounding neural tissue and damages it. Aneurysms are a common cause of intracerebral hemorrhage. An **aneurysm**

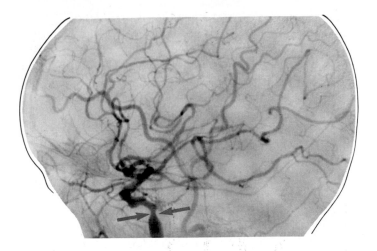

FIGURE 6.3

An angiogram that illustrates narrowing of the carotid artery, the main route of blood to the brain (see arrows). Compare this angiogram with the normal angiogram in Figure 5.1. (Courtesy of William D. Robertson, Department of Radiology, Vancouver General Hospital.)

is a pathological balloon-like dilation that forms in the wall of a blood vessel at a point where the elasticity of the vessel wall is defective. These are points of weakness in the cerebrovascular system, and they sometimes burst. Aneurysms can be **congenital**—that is, present at birth—or they can result from exposure to vascular poisons or infection. Individuals who have aneurysms should make every effort to avoid high blood pressure.

The second type of cerebrovascular disorder, termed **cerebral ischemia,** is a disruption of the blood supply to an area of the brain, which eliminates its supply of glucose and oxygen and kills it. An area of ischemic brain damage is called an **infarct.** There are three main causes of infarcts: thrombosis, embolism, and arteriosclerosis. In **thrombosis,** a plug called a *thrombus* is formed and blocks blood flow at the site of its formation. A thrombus may be composed of a blood clot, fat, oil, an air bubble, tumor cells, or any combination thereof. **Embolism** is similar except the plug, called an *embolus* in this case, is carried by the blood from a larger vessel, where it was formed, to a smaller one, where it becomes lodged—in essence, an embolus is just a thrombus that has taken a trip. In **arteriosclerosis,** the walls of blood vessels thicken, often as the result of fat deposits, and this produces narrowing of the vessels, which may eventually lead to complete blockage. The *angiogram* (see Chapter 5) in Figure 6.3 illustrates partial blockage of the carotid artery.

Closed-Head Injuries

It is not necessary for the skull to be penetrated for the brain to be seriously damaged. In fact, any blow to the head should be treated with extreme caution, particularly when confusion, sensory-motor disturbances, or loss of consciousness ensue. Brain injuries that are produced by blows that do not penetrate the skull are called *closed-head injuries*.

Contusions are closed-head injuries that involve damage to the cerebral circulatory system. Such damage produces internal hemorrhaging, which results in a **hematoma,** a localized collection of clotted blood in an organ or tissue—in other words, a bruise. It is paradoxical that the very hardness of the skull, which protects the brain from penetrating injuries, is frequently a major factor in the development of contusions. Many contusions occur when the brain slams against the inside of the skull. As illustrated in Figure 6.4, blood from such injuries can accumulate in the *subdural space,* the space between the dura mater and arachnoid membrane, and severely distort the surrounding neural tissue. It may surprise you to learn that contusions frequently occur on the side of the brain opposite the side struck by a blow. The reason for such so-called **contrecoup injuries** is that the blow causes the brain to strike the inside of the skull on the other side of the head.

When there is a disturbance of consciousness following a blow to the head and there is no evidence of a contusion or other structural damage, the diagnosis is **concussion.** It is commonly assumed that concussions entail a temporary disruption of normal cerebral function with no long-term damage. However, the punch-drunk syndrome suggests otherwise. The **punch-drunk syndrome** refers to the **dementia** (general intellectual deterioration) and cerebral scarring that is observed in boxers and other individuals who experience repeated concussions. If there were no damage associated with a single concussion, the effects of many concussions could not summate to produce severe damage. One of the most dangerous aspects of concussion is the complacency with which it is regarded—flippant references to it, such as "having one's bell rung," do little to communicate its hazards.

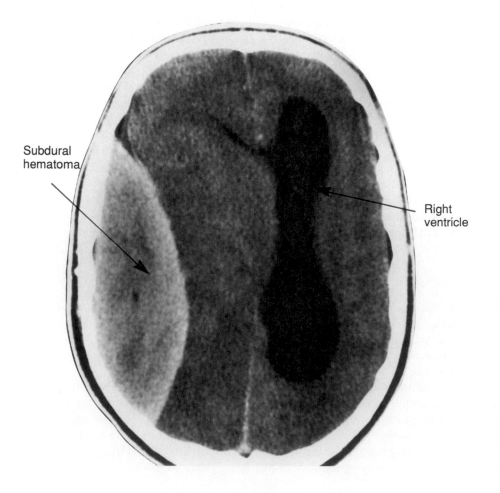

FIGURE 6.4

A CAT scan of a subdural hematoma. Notice that pressure from the hematoma has displaced the left lateral ventricle, which is not visible in the scan. (Courtesy of William D. Robertson, Department of Radiology, Vancouver General Hospital.)

Infections of the Brain

An invasion of the brain by microorganisms is referred to as a brain infection, and the inflammation associated with it is commonly referred to as **encephalitis.** Bacteria and viruses are two kinds of organisms that commonly invade the brain. Bacteria frequently attack and inflame the meninges, causing a disorder known as **meningitis,** and they can also cause the formation of pockets of pus in the brain called **brain abscesses.** *Syphilis* is the most well-known bacterial brain infection. Syphilis bacteria are passed from infected to non-infected individuals via contact with genital sores; the infecting bacteria then go into a dormant stage; and finally, several years later, they become virulent and attack many parts of the body, including the brain. The syndrome of insanity and dementia that results from a syphilitic infection is called **general paresis.**

Syphilis has a particularly interesting history (see Klawans, 1990). The first Europeans to visit America stripped the natives of their gold and left smallpox in return. But the deal was not totally one-sided; the booty carried back to Europe by the sailors of Columbus and the adventurers that followed included a cargo of syphilis bacteria. Until then, syphilis had been restricted to the Americas, but it was quickly distributed to the rest of the world. Penicillin and other antibiotics are no panacea for bacterial brain infections; they can eliminate the infection, but they cannot reverse brain damage that has already been produced.

There are two types of viral infections of the nervous system: **neurotropic** infections, which have a particular affinity for neural tissue, and **pantropic** infections, which attack neural tissue, but do not attack it preferentially. Rabies is a well-known example of a neurotropic viral infection, which is usually transmitted through the bite of a rabid animal. The fits of rage caused by the virus's effects on the brain increase the probability that rabid animals that normally attack by biting (e.g., dogs, cats, raccoons, bats, mice, etc.) will spread the disorder. Although the effects of the rabies virus on the brain are ultimately lethal, it does have one redeeming feature. The rabies virus does not usually attack the brain for at least a month after it has been contracted, thus allowing time for a preventive vaccination. The *mumps* and *herpes* viruses are common examples of pantropic viruses; they typically attack other tissues of the body, but they can spread into the brain with dire consequences.

Neurotoxins

The nervous system can be damaged by exposure to any one of a variety of toxic chemicals, which can enter general circulation from the gastrointestinal tract, from the lungs, or through the skin. For example, heavy metals such as mercury and lead can accumulate in the brain and permanently damage it, thus producing a **toxic psychosis** (chronic insanity produced by a neurotoxin). Have you ever wondered why Alice in Wonderland's Mad Hatter was a mad hatter and not a mad something else? In eighteenth- and nineteenth-century England, hatmakers were commonly driven mad by the mercury used in the preparation of the felt that they used to make hats. In a similar vein, the word "crackpot" originally referred to the toxic psychosis observed in people—primarily the British poor—who steeped their tea in cracked ceramic pots with lead cores.

Sometimes the very drugs used to treat neurological disorders prove to have toxic effects. Some of the antipsychotic drugs that were introduced in the early 1950s provide an example of distressing scope. By the late 1950s, literally millions of psychotic patients were being chronically maintained on these drugs. However, the initial enthusiasm for antipsychotic-drug therapy was tempered by the discovery that many of the patients developed a motor disorder termed **tardive dyskinesia (TD).** Its primary symptoms are involuntary smacking and sucking movements of the lips, thrusting and rolling of the tongue, lateral jaw movements, and puffing of the cheeks. Unfortunately, tardive dyskinesia is not responsive to treatment. Once it has developed, even lowering the dose of the offending drug does not help; in fact, it sometimes makes the symptoms worse. You will find out more about this unfortunate episode in Chapter 17, and you will learn how safer antipsychotic drugs have been developed.

Brain damage from the neurotoxic effects of recreational drugs is also a serious problem. You have already learned (in Chapter 1) how alcohol produces brain damage through a combination of its direct toxic effects and its effects on thiamin metabolism. Do you remember the case of Jimmie G.? You will learn more about the neurotoxic effects of recreational drugs in Chapter 13.

Some neurotoxins are *endogenous* (produced in the patient's own body) rather than *exogenous* (from outside the body). For example, the body can produce antibodies that attack its own myelin, thus producing multiple sclerosis, which you will read about in the next section. And in some cases, the brain's own neurotransmitters can function as neurotoxins; *excitatory amino acid neurotransmitters,* such as glutamate and aspartate, can damage neurons by overexciting them. Accordingly, any disorder that increases the release of excitatory amino acids (EAAs) can produce damage in postsynaptic neurons (see Choi & Rothman, 1990; Faden, Demediuk, Panter, & Vink, 1989; Taylor, 1991; Weiss, Hartley, Koh, & Choi, 1990).

Genetic Factors

Normal human cells have 23 pairs of chromosomes; however, sometimes accidents of cell division occur, and the fertilized egg ends up with an abnormal chromosome or with an abnormal number of normal chromosomes. Then, as the fertilized egg divides and redivides, these chromosomal anomalies are duplicated in every cell of the body. A common example of a disorder that is caused by such a genetic accident is **Down's syndrome,** which occurs in 0.15% of all live births. Down's syndrome is associated with an extra chromosome in pair 21. The consequences of the superfluous chromosome 21 are disastrous. In addition to the characteristic disfigurement—flattened skull and nose, folds of skin over the inner corners of the eyes, and short fingers (see Figure 6.5)—the Down's child is retarded and often dies before reaching adulthood. The probability of giving birth to a child with Down's syndrome increases with advancing maternal age.

Few neuropsychological diseases of genetic origin are the result of faulty chromosomal duplication. Most are caused by abnormal recessive genes that are passed from patient to offspring—in Chapter 2, you learned about one such disorder, *phenylketonuria* (PKU). Inherited neuropsychological disorders are rarely associated with faulty dominant genes because dominant

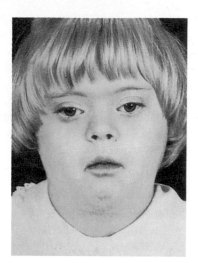 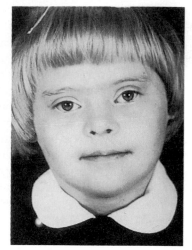

Before surgery   After surgery

FIGURE 6.5

A child with Down's syndrome before and after plastic surgery. The purpose of these photographs is not to promote cosmetic surgery; it is to challenge our culture's reaction to patients with Down's syndrome. The little girl on your left and the little girl on your right are the same; they deserve the same respect and consideration. (Courtesy of Kenneth E. Salyer, Director, International Craniofacial Institute.)

genes that disturb neuropsychological function tend to be eliminated from the gene pool—every individual who carries one is at a major survival and reproductive disadvantage. In contrast, individuals who inherit one abnormal recessive gene do not develop the disorder, and the gene is likely to be passed on to future generations—only individuals who inherit two of them are affected. However, there are two situations in which neurological disorders are associated with dominant genes. One is the case in which an abnormal dominant gene manifests itself only in rare environmental circumstances. The other is the case in which an abnormal dominant gene is not expressed until the individual is well past puberty—you will learn in the next section of this chapter that the gene for Huntington's disease is of this type.

Now is a good time, before you leave this subsection on genetic factors, for me to remind you of the key point of Chapter 2: that all behavioral capacities and tendencies arise out of an interaction between genes and experience. It is important for you to remember this as you read the next section because it is as true of neuropsychological disorders as it is of normal behavior.

6.2

Neuropsychological Diseases

The discussion of neuropsychological dysfunction continues. However, this section focuses on the neuropsychological diseases themselves, rather than on their causes.

It is not always easy to decide whether an individual has a neuropsychological disease. Is an individual who performs poorly on intelligence tests, sleeps longer than most, or displays aggressive behavior in inappropriate contexts suffering from a disorder of the brain, or does he or she simply represent the extreme of normal biological function? The problem of *differential diagnosis*—that is, the problem of deciding which particular neural disorder a patient has—is even more thorny. Each neuropsychological patient displays an array of complex behavioral symptoms that is unique—no two neuropsychological patients display exactly the same pattern of symptoms. Physicians and scientists search for clusters of neuropsychological symptoms that tend to occur together. When they identify a recurring cluster, they coin a term for it. This term and the cluster of symptoms that it represents come to be thought of as a neuropsychological disease. The assumption on which this approach is based is that all patients with a particular cluster of symptoms will prove to have the same underlying neural pathology that has been caused by the same factors. This assumption does not always turn out to be correct. As more is found out about the patients with a particular cluster of neuropsychological symptoms, it is usually necessary to redefine the disorder—perhaps by excluding some cases, including others, or dividing the disorder up into subtypes. The more that is known about the causes and neural bases of a neuropsychological disorder, the more accurately it can be diagnosed; and the more accurately that it can be diagnosed, the more readily its causes and neural bases can be identified.

Epilepsy, Parkinson's disease, Huntington's disease, multiple sclerosis, and Alzheimer's disease are the disorders that are discussed in this section of the chapter.

Epilepsy

The primary symptom of epilepsy is the epileptic seizure, but not all persons who suffer seizures are considered to have epilepsy. It is not uncommon for otherwise healthy persons to have a seizure during temporary illness or following exposure to a convulsive agent. The label *epilepsy* is applied to only those patients whose seizures appear to be generated by their own chronic brain dysfunction. About 1% of the population are diagnosed as epileptic at some point in their lives.

In view of the fact that epilepsy is characterized by epileptic seizures—or more accurately, by spontaneously recurring epileptic seizures—you might think that the task of diagnosing epilepsy would be an easy one. But you would be wrong. The task is made difficult by the diversity and complexity of epileptic seizures. You are probably familiar with those seizures that take the form of **convulsions** (motor seizures); these often involve tremors (*clonus*), rigidity (*tonus*), and loss of both balance and consciousness. But many seizures do not take this form; instead, they involve subtle changes of thought, mood, or behavior that are not easily distinguishable from normal ongoing activity. In such cases, the diagnosis of epilepsy rests heavily on electroencephalographic evidence.

The value of scalp electroencephalography in suspected cases of epilepsy stems from the fact that epileptic seizures are associated with bursts of high-amplitude EEG spikes, which are often apparent in the scalp EEG during an attack (see Figure 6.6), and from the fact that individual spikes often punctuate the scalp EEGs of epileptics between attacks. Although the observation of spontaneous epileptic discharges is incontrovertible evidence of epilepsy, the failure to observe them does not mean that the patient is not epileptic. It could mean that the patient is epileptic but did not happen to experience epileptic discharges during the test, or that epileptic discharges did occur during the test but were not recorded through the scalp electrodes.

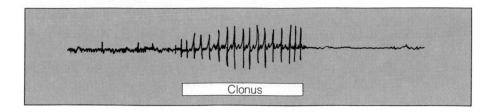

FIGURE 6.6
EEG activity before, during, and after a clonic convulsion.

Some epileptics experience peculiar psychological changes just before a convulsion. These changes, called **epileptic auras,** may take many different forms: for example, a bad smell, a specific thought, a vague feeling of familiarity, a hallucination, or a tightness of the chest. Epileptic auras are important for two reasons. First, the nature of the auras provides clues concerning the location of the epileptic focus. Second, because the epileptic auras that are experienced by a particular patient are often similar from attack to attack, they warn the patient of an impending convulsion. For most people, the warning of an impending convulsion is an advantage, but for some it can become an experience of great dread, as the normal parts of their brains struggle to keep in touch with reality.

Once an individual has been diagnosed as epileptic, it is usual to assign him or her to one of two general categories, partial or generalized epilepsy, and then to one of their respective subcategories. The various seizure types are so different from one another that there are many who believe that epilepsy is best viewed not as a single disease, but as a number of different, but related, diseases. Supporting this view is the fact that epilepsy has no single cause; almost any kind of brain disturbance can cause seizures.

Partial seizures　　A **partial seizure** is one that does not involve the entire brain. For reasons unknown, the epileptic neurons at a focus begin to discharge together in bursts, and it is this synchronous bursting of neurons (see Figure 6.7) that produces epileptic spiking in the EEG. This synchronous activity may stay restricted to the focus until the seizure is over, or it may spread to other, healthy, areas of the brain—but, in the case of partial seizures, not to the entire brain. The specific behavioral symptoms of a partial epileptic seizure depend on where the disruptive discharges begin and into what structures they spread. Because partial seizures do not involve the entire brain, they are not usually accompanied by a total loss of consciousness or equilibrium.

There are two major categories of partial seizures: simple and complex. **Simple partial seizures** are those partial seizures whose symptoms are primarily sensory and/or motor—they are sometimes called *Jacksonian seizures* after the famous nineteenth-century neurologist, Hughlings Jackson. As the epileptic discharges spread through the sensory or motor areas of the brain, the symptoms spread through the body. In contrast, **complex partial sei-**

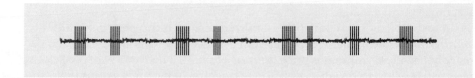

FIGURE 6.7
The bursting of an epileptic neuron (extracellular unit recording).

zures are usually restricted to the temporal lobes, and those who experience them are said to have *temporal lobe epilepsy.* Complex partial seizures typically begin with an aura, which may develop into a **psychomotor attack.** In psychomotor attacks, the patients engage in compulsive, repetitive, simple behaviors commonly referred to as *automatisms* (e.g., doing and undoing a button) or in more complex behaviors that appear almost normal. The diversity of psychomotor attacks is illustrated by the following four cases that were reported by Lennox (1960):

> A war veteran subject to many automatisms read in the newspaper about a man who had embraced a woman in a park, followed her into a women's toilet, and then boarded a bus. From the description given, he realized he was the man.

> One morning a doctor left home to answer an emergency call from the hospital and returned several hours later, a trifle confused, feeling as though he had experienced a bad dream. At the hospital he had performed a difficult . . . [operation] with his usual competence, but later had done and said things deemed inappropriate.

> A young man, a music teacher, when listening to a concert, walked down the aisle and onto the platform, circled the piano, jumped to the floor, did a hop, skip, and jump up the aisle, and regained his senses when part way home. He often found himself on a trolley [bus] far from his destination.

> A man in an attack went to his employer and said, "I have to have more money or [I] quit." Later, to his surprise, he found that his salary had been raised. (pp. 237–238)

Although patients appear to be conscious throughout their psychomotor attacks, they usually have little or no subsequent recollection of them. About half of all cases of epilepsy are of the complex partial variety—the temporal lobes are particularly susceptible to epileptic discharges.

Generalized seizures   **Generalized seizures** are those that involve the entire brain. Some generalized seizures begin as focal discharges that gradually spread through the entire brain. In other cases, the discharges seem to begin almost simultaneously in all parts of the brain. Such sudden-onset generalized seizures may result from diffuse pathology, or they may begin focally in a structure, such as the thalamus, that projects to many parts of the brain.

Like partial seizures, generalized seizures occur in many different forms. One is the **grand mal** (literally, *big trouble*) seizure. The primary symptoms of a grand mal seizure are loss of consciousness, loss of equilibrium, and a violent *tonic-clonic convulsion*—that is, a convulsion involving both tonus and clonus. Tongue biting, urinary *incontinence,* and *cyanosis* (turning blue from excessive extraction of oxygen from the blood during the convulsion) are common manifestations of grand mal convulsions. The shortage of oxygen in the blood (**hypoxia**) that accompanies a grand mal convulsion can itself cause brain damage.

A second major category of generalized seizure is the **petit mal** (literally, *small trouble*). Petit mal seizures are not associated with convulsions; the primary behavioral symptom is the *petit mal absence,* a disruption of consciousness that is associated with a cessation of ongoing behavior, a vacant look, and sometimes with fluttering eyelids. The EEG of a petit mal seizure is different

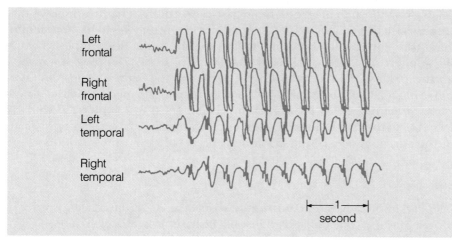

FIGURE 6.8
The bilaterally symmetrical
3-per-second spike-and-wave
EEG discharge of a petit mal
attack.

from that of other seizures; it is a bilaterally symmetrical **3-per-second spike-and-wave** (see Figure 6.8). Petit mal seizures are most common in children, and they frequently cease at puberty. They often go undiagnosed, and thus children with petit mal epilepsy are sometimes considered to be "daydreamers" by their parents and teachers and "space cadets" by their playmates.

Although there is no cure for epilepsy, in many cases, the frequency and severity of seizures can be reduced by anticonvulsant medication. Brain surgery is prescribed only in life-threatening situations.

Parkinson's Disease

Parkinson's disease or parkinsonism is a movement disorder that affects about 1% of the population, usually in adulthood. Its initial symptoms are mild—perhaps no more than a stiffness or tremor of the fingers—but they gradually increase in severity with advancing years. The most common symptoms of the full-blown disorder are: (1) a tremor that is pronounced during inactivity but is suppressed during both voluntary movement and sleep, (2) muscular rigidity, (3) continual involuntary shifts in posture (*cruel restlessness*), (4) slowness of movement (*bradykinesia*), and (5) a shuffling, wide-based gait with a forward-leaning posture that frequently leads to *festination,* the tendency to take faster and faster steps to keep from falling forward. There is usually no intellectual impairment. Like epilepsy, Parkinson's disease seems to have no single cause; brain infections, strokes, tumors, traumatic brain injury, and neurotoxins have all been implicated in specific cases. However, in the majority of cases, no cause is obvious, and there is no family history of the disorder (see Calne et al., 1987).

Parkinson's disease is associated with degeneration of the *substantia nigra,* the midbrain nucleus whose neurons project via the **nigrostriatal pathway** to the **striatum** of the basal ganglia (see Chapter 3). The neurotransmitter of substantia nigra neurons is *dopamine,* and there is almost a total lack of dopamine in the substantia nigras and striatums of long-term Parkinson's patients.

The symptoms of Parkinson's disease are alleviated in many patients by injections of **L-DOPA,** the chemical from which dopamine is synthesized in dopaminergic neurons. Dopamine itself is ineffective because it does not readily pass through the blood-brain barrier. Recently, it has been shown that **deprenyl,** a dopamine agonist, slows down the progressive development of Parkinson's disease if it is taken regularly as soon as the first symptoms of the disorder are observed (Parkinson Study Group, 1989). Deprenyl is a **mono-amine oxidase (MAO) inhibitor;** it increases the level of dopamine and other monoamines by inhibiting the activity of monoamine oxidase, an enzyme in the brain that breaks down monoamines. In Chapter 15, you will learn about the recent attempts to alleviate Parkinson's disease by transplanting healthy dopaminergic tissue into the brains of Parkinson's patients.

Huntington's Disease

Like Parkinson's disease, **Huntington's disease** is a progressive disorder of motor function; but unlike Parkinson's disease, it is relatively rare, it has a strong genetic basis, and it is always associated with severe dementia. The first motor symptoms take the form of increased fidgetiness, but they slowly grow worse until the behavior of the patient is characterized by the incessant involuntary performance of a variety of rapid, complex, jerky movements that involve entire limbs rather than individual muscles. Huntington's disease is sometimes called *Huntington's chorea* because the twisting, writhing, grimacing movements displayed by some Huntington's patients have a dance-like quality—*chorea* is from the Greek word for *dance,* as is "chorus line" and "choreography."

Huntington's disease is passed from generation to generation by a single dominant gene; thus, all of the individuals carrying the gene develop the disorder, as do about half their offspring. The Huntington's gene is readily passed from parent to child because the first symptoms of Huntington's disease do not appear until the parent is well past his or her peak reproductive years (at about 45 years of age). There is no cure; death occurs approximately 15 years after the appearance of the first symptoms. Autopsy reveals gross degeneration of the striatum and diffuse thinning of the cerebral cortex.

If one of your parents were to develop Huntington's disease, the chance would be 50/50 that you too would develop it. If you were in such a situation, would you want to know your fate? Medical geneticists have discovered the location of the lethal Huntington's gene (Wexler, Rose, & Housman, 1991). They have also developed a test that can tell relatives of Huntington's patients whether or not they too are carrying the gene (Gilliam, Gusella, & Lehrach, 1987; Martin, 1987). One advantage of the test is that it permits the relatives of Huntington's patients who have not inherited the gene to have children without the fear of passing on the disorder.

Much of the early research on Huntington's disease was aimed at tracing the family trees of those with the disorder. The first recorded cases of the disease were reported in 1630 in the town of Bures, England (Vessie, 1932). At that time, afflicted individuals were judged to be witches and executed. Many North American cases of Huntington's disease can be traced to two families who fled Bures. Once in North America, these poor unfortunates were dealt with more humanely—only one of them was hanged. In the last few decades, the prevalence of Huntington's disease has declined as the result of genetic counseling.

Shortly after the first edition of this textbook appeared in print, I received the following letter, which I have altered slightly to protect the identity of its author and his family. It speaks for itself.

```
                    Mr. Walter S. Miller
                    1500 N. Severn-Langdon Rd.
                    Manchester, Connecticut  22022
                    Z9/900-854

============================================================

                                      August 5, 1991


Dr. John P.J. Pinel
Department of Psychology
University of British Columbia
Vancouver, B.C.  Canada  V6T., 1Y7.

Dear Dr. Pinel:

        I am worried about my children and their future.
In fact, I am worried sick.  After reading your book I feel
that you are my friend and I have nowhere else to turn.

        My wife came down with Huntingdon's disease 7
years ago, and today she can't walk or take care of herself.
I have three young children.  Where can I take them to see
if they have inherited my wife's infected cells?  I am
presently incarcerated, which adds to my psychological pain.
I look to be released soon, and could take my wife and kids
just about any wheres to find help and get answers.

        Any kind of advice that you could give us would be
greatly appreciated by me and my family.  I wish to thank
you for any assistance that you can give.

        God Bless you and give you and yours His love and
peace!  I remain with warmest personal regards.


        Very truly yours,

        Walter S. Miller.

        Walter S. Miller

WSM:
```

THE UNIVERSITY OF BRITISH COLUMBIA

Department of Psychology
2136 West Mall
Vancouver, B.C. Canada V6T 1Z4

Tel: (604) 822-2755
Fax: (604) 822-6923

November 25, 1991

Mr. Walter S. Miller
1500 N. Severn-Langdon Road
Manchester, Connecticut 22022
U.S.A.

Dear Mr. Miller:

I was saddened to learn of your unhappy state of affairs. In requesting my advice, I hope that you understand that I am a scientist, not a physician. In any case, the following is my assessment.

If your wife does in fact have Huntington's disease and not some other neurological disorder, each of your children has a 50/50 chance of developing Huntington's disease in adulthood. I am sure that you are aware that there is currently no cure.

I advise you to seek the advice of a local neurologist, who can explain your options to you and provide you with the advice and support that you sorely need. You must decide whether or not to subject your children to the tests that are required to determine whether or not they are carrying the Huntington's gene. One option would be to wait for your children to reach legal age and then allow them to make the decision for themselves. Some people whose parents develop Huntington's disease decide to take the test; others decide not to. In either case, it is extremely important for them not to risk passing on the Huntington's gene to future generations.

I am sorry that I cannot provide you with a more optimistic assessment, but your children's situation is too serious for me to be less than totally frank. Again, please consult a neurologist as soon as possible.

Do not lose hope. There is a chance (1/8) that none of your children is carrying the Huntington's gene. I wish you, your wife, and your children good fortune.

Cordially,

John P.J. Pinel
Professor

Multiple Sclerosis

Multiple sclerosis (MS) typically begins in early adult life. It is a progressive disease of CNS myelin. First, there are microscopic areas of degeneration on axon myelin sheaths, but eventually there is a breakdown of both the myelin and the associated axons, along with the development of many areas of hard scar tissue—*sclerosis* literally means *hardening.* Figure 6.9 illustrates degeneration in the white matter of a patient with multiple sclerosis.

The diagnosis of multiple sclerosis is difficult because the nature of the disorder depends on the number, size, and position of the sclerotic lesions. Furthermore, in some cases, there are lengthy periods of remission (up to 2 years), during which the patient seems almost normal; these are but oases in the cruel progression of the disorder. Common symptoms of multiple sclerosis are urinary incontinence, visual disturbances, weakness, numbness, tremor, and **ataxia** (loss of motor coordination).

Epidemiological studies of multiple sclerosis have provided evidence of the environmental and genetic factors that influence its development (McDonald, 1984). **Epidemiology** is the study of the various factors, such as diet, geographic location, age, sex, and race, that influence the distribution of a disease in the general population. Evidence that environmental factors influence the development of multiple sclerosis comes from the finding that the incidence of multiple sclerosis is far greater in people who spent their childhood in a cool climate, even if they subsequently moved to a warm climate. Evidence of genetic involvement comes from the finding that multiple sclerosis is rare among certain groups, such as gypsies and orientals, even when they live in environments in which the incidence of the disease is high in other groups. Further evidence of a genetic factor in multiple sclerosis comes from comparisons of the concordance of the disease in *monozygotic* (about 36%) and *dizygotic* (about 12%) twins (e.g., Currier & Eldridge, 1982; McFarland, Greenstein, McFarlin, Eldridge, Xu, & Krebs, 1984).

A model of multiple sclerosis can be induced in laboratory animals by injecting them with myelin and a preparation that stimulates the body's immune reaction. Because the resulting disorder, which is termed **experimental allergic encephalomyelitis,** is similar in some respects to multiple sclerosis, it has led to the view that multiple sclerosis results from a faulty immune reaction that attacks the body's own myelin as if it were a foreign substance (see Allegretta, Nicklas, Sriram, & Albertini, 1990). Many researchers believe that this faulty autoimmune reaction is the result of a slow-acting infection that is contracted early in life.

FIGURE 6.9

Some of the areas of sclerosis (see arrows) in the white matter of a patient with MS. (Courtesy of Kenneth Berry, Head of Neuropathology, Vancouver General Hospital.)

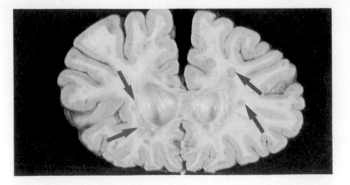

Alzheimer's Disease

Alzheimer's disease is the most common cause of *dementia* (Wurtman, 1985). It is estimated that one-third of all nursing-home beds in North America are filled by individuals suffering from this disorder. Alzheimer's disease is a disease of the aged. It sometimes appears in individuals as young as 40, but the likelihood of manifesting it becomes greater with advancing years. About 5% of the general population over the age of 65 suffer from Alzheimer's disease, and the proportion is 11% in those over 85. Alzheimer's disease is progressive. Early Alzheimer's disease is characterized by depression and a general decline in cognitive ability; the intermediate stages are marked by irritability, anxiety, and complete loss of speech; and in its advanced stages, the patient deteriorates to the point that even simple responses such as swallowing and bladder control are difficult. Alzheimer's disease is terminal.

Alzheimer's disease is characterized by neurons that contain tangles of *neurofibrils* (thread-like structures in the neural cytoplasm), by a loss of neurons, and by multiple *plaques* (clumps of degenerating neurons interspersed with abnormal protein that is collectively referred to as **amyloid**). Figure 6.10 is a section of the brain of a patient who died of Alzheimer's disease; the section has been treated with a stain that has an affinity for amyloid plaques. Alzheimer's disease appears to preferentially attack neurons in which *acetylcholine* is the neurotransmitter (Summers, Majovski, Marsh, Tachiki, & Kling, 1986).

Although the cause of Alzheimer's disease is still unknown, its association with Down's syndrome is an important clue. You may recall that Down's syndrome is the result of a genetic accident that creates an extra chromosome 21 in each cell—three rather than two. The fact that almost all Down's patients who survive to middle age develop Alzheimer's disease suggested that at least some cases of Alzheimer's disease may also be associated with chromosome 21. This has recently been proven to be the case. The gene mutation associated with a form of Alzheimer's disease that runs through families was found to be on chromosome 21 (Goate et al., 1991), as was the gene that controls

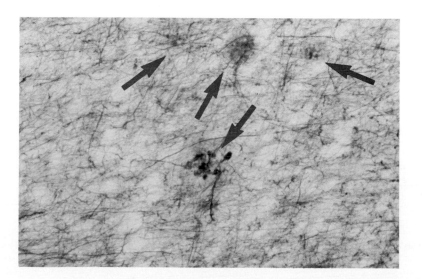

FIGURE 6.10

Amyloid placques (see arrows) in the brain of a patient with Alzheimer's disease. (Courtesy of Steven Vincent, Kinsmen Laboratory of Neurological Research, University of British Columbia.)

the production of amyloid proteins (see Esch et al., 1990; Levy et al., 1990; van Broeckhoven et al., 1990). However, it remains to be seen whether all cases of Alzheimer's disease are caused by a mutation to the same gene.

SELF TEST

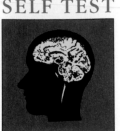

Before proceeding to the discussion of animal models of neuropsychological disorders, test your knowledge of the disorders by filling in the following blanks.

1. The two major categories of epileptic seizures are _____ and _____ seizures.

2. The disorder characterized by tremor at rest, bradykinesia, cruel restlessness, and festination is _____ .

3. _____ is passed from generaton to generation by a single dominant gene.

4. Parkinson's disease is associated with degeneration in the _____ dopamine pathway.

5. Experimental allergic encephalomyelitis is an animal model of _____ .

6. The most common cause of dementia is _____ .

7. _____ attacks are complex partial seizures that are similar in many respects to normal behavior.

8. Alzheimer's disease is associated with _____ syndrome.

6.3

Animal Models of Human Neuropsychological Diseases

The first two sections of this chapter focused on neuropsychological diseases and their causes, but they also provided some revealing glimpses into the various ways in which researchers have attempted to solve the various puzzles of neurological dysfunction. This section focuses on one of them: the experimental investigation of animal models. Because the laboratory experimen-

The answers to the preceding questions are (1) partial and generalized (or vice versa), (2) Parkinson's disease, (3) Huntington's disease, (4) nigrostriatal, (5) multiple sclerosis, (6) Alzheimer's disease, (7) Psychomotor, and (8) Down's.

tation necessary to identify the neuropathological basis of human neuropsychological disorders is seldom possible on the patients themselves,
animal models of the disorders play a particularly important role in their
investigation.

Three different types of animal models are used in medical research
(Kornetsky, 1977). There are **homologous animal models,** which are diseases in animals that duplicate the human disorder; the *etiology* (causes),
symptoms, and prognosis of the model resemble those of the human disorder
in every major respect. There are **isomorphic animal models,** which resemble the human disorder, but are artificially produced in the laboratory in a
way that does not reflect normal etiology. And finally, there are **predictive
animal models,** which do not resemble the human disorder in key respects,
but are of value in predicting some aspects of the disorder, such as its response to various drugs.

In a sense, the three types of animal models represent a hierarchy. A predictive model enables one to make certain predictions about the disorder that
it models. An isomorphic model permits predictions and the study of underlying mechanisms. And, a homologous model serves as a basis for studying all
aspects of a disorder, including its causes. Accordingly, to understand a
model's potential uses and limitations, it is important to recognize which type
of model it is. One difficulty in this respect is that we currently do not understand the mechanisms underlying most neuropsychological disorders well
enough to assess the degree to which they are faithfully mirrored by an animal
model. Another difficulty is that even the best animal models seem to model
only some aspects of a disorder. Consequently, animal models must be employed with caution. Studying an animal model is like exploring a section of
an unknown maze. One enters an unfamiliar section with little more than a
hope that its exploration will prove fruitful, and it is only after each of its arms
has been carefully explored that it is possible to know whether the decision to
enter the section was wise. In the same way, it is not possible to evaluate the
numerous animal models of neuropsychological dysfunction that are currently under investigation until each has been thoroughly explored. Surely,
only a few animal models will lead toward the goals of understanding and
prevention, but only time and effort can tell which ones these are.

Completing this chapter is a discussion of three animal models that are
currently the focus of intensive investigation.

The Kindling Model of Epilepsy

In 1969, Goddard, McIntyre, and Leech delivered one mild electrical stimulation per day to rats through implanted amygdalar electrodes. There was no
behavioral response to the first few stimulations, but soon each stimulation
began to elicit a convulsive response. The first convulsions were mild, involving only a slight tremor of the face. However, with each subsequent stimulation, the elicited convulsions became more generalized, until each convulsion involved the entire body. Each of these fully generalized kindled
convulsions was characterized in rats by the following progression of symptoms: facial tremor, rhythmic jaw movements, rhythmic head nodding, fore-
limb clonus, rearing up on the hind legs, and falling (e.g., Racine, 1972;
1978). This effect became known as the **kindling phenomenon.**

Although kindling is most frequently studied in rats subjected to repeated amygdalar stimulation, it is a remarkably general phenomenon. For example, kindling has been reported in mice (Leech & McIntyre, 1976), rabbits (Tanaka, 1972), cats (Adamec, 1990), dogs (Wauquier, Ashton, & Melis, 1979), and various primates (Wada, 1990a). Moreover, kindling can be produced by the repeated stimulation of many brain sites other than the amygdala, and it can be produced by the repeated application of initially subconvulsive doses of convulsive chemicals (Cain, 1986; Mori & Wada, 1990; Post, Weiss, Clark, Nakajima, & Pert, 1990).

There are many interesting features of kindling (see Racine & Burnham, 1984; Wada, 1990b), but two warrant emphasis. The first is that the neural changes underlying kindling are permanent. A subject that has been kindled and then left unstimulated for several months still responds to each low-intensity stimulation with a generalized convulsion (Goddard et al., 1969; Wada & Sato, 1974). The second is that kindling is produced by distributed, as opposed to massed, stimulations. If the intervals between successive stimulations are shorter than an hour or two, it usually requires many more stimulations to kindle a subject, and under normal circumstances, no kindling at all occurs at intervals of less than about 20 minutes (Racine, Burnham, Gartner, & Levitan, 1973).

Much of the interest in kindling stems from the fact that it models epilepsy in two ways. First, the convulsions elicited in kindled animals are similar in many respects to those observed in some types of human epilepsy. Second, the kindling phenomenon itself is comparable to the **epileptogenesis** (the development or genesis of epilepsy) that can follow a head injury—some individuals who at first appear to have escaped serious injury after a blow to the head begin to experience convulsions a few weeks later, and these convulsions sometimes begin to recur more and more frequently and with greater and greater intensity. Accordingly, many studies have been conducted in order to determine which drugs block the kindling of motor convulsions and which block the elicitation of convulsions in animals that have already been kindled (e.g., Pinel, Kim, & Mana, 1990). The study of Racine, Livingston, and Joaquin (1975) is a particularly good example of the latter approach. They found that an anticonvulsant commonly used in the treatment of human epileptics, *diphenylhydantoin* (Dilantin), blocked convulsions elicited in kindled rats by neocortical stimulation, but not those elicited by amygdalar stimulation. Conversely, another commonly used anticonvulsant, *diazepam* (Valium), blocked kindled convulsions elicited by amygdalar stimulation, but had no effect on neocortical kindled convulsions. These data suggest that the response of human epileptics to various anticonvulsant drugs may depend on the location of the epileptic focus.

It must be stressed that the kindling model as it is applied in most laboratories is not isomorphic. You will recall from earlier in this chapter that epilepsy is a disease in which epileptic attacks recur spontaneously; in contrast, kindled convulsions are elicited. However, a model that overcomes this shortcoming has been developed. If subjects are kindled for a very long time— about 300 stimulations in rats—a syndrome can be induced that is truly epileptic in the sense that the subjects begin to display spontaneous seizures and continue to display them even after the regimen of stimulation is curtailed (e.g., Pinel, 1981; Shouse et al., 1990; Wada, Sato, & Corcoran, 1974).

Amphetamine Model of Schizophrenia

Amphetamine abuse can lead to a syndrome called **amphetamine psychosis,** which is similar in many respects to schizophrenia—the abuse of other stimulant drugs (e.g., cocaine) can have a similar effect. The symptoms of amphetamine psychosis include compulsive pacing, stereotypic touching and picking of the face and extremities, repeated assembling and disassembling of objects, distortion of time and space, extreme reactivity, olfactory and tactile hallucinations, and paranoia. Fortunately, once individuals displaying amphetamine psychosis stop taking the drug, these symptoms dissipate in a day or two, but sometimes they do not dissipate completely. There are frequently residual delusions and mannerisms that persist long after amphetamine abuse has stopped, and a full-blown psychotic episode can sometimes be reinstated by a single dose of the drug after long periods of abstinence (Bell, 1973). Amphetamine and other stimulants have been found to exacerbate the schizophrenic symptoms of psychotic patients (Janosky, Huey, & Storms, 1977), and antischizophrenic drugs have been shown to counteract the symptoms of amphetamine psychosis (Angrist, Rotrosen, & Gershon, 1980).

Although the behavioral effects of amphetamine are not the same in each species, in mammals there is always a general increase in locomotor activity (pacing) and other repetitive, apparently functionless, behaviors (e.g., Haber, Barchas, & Barchas, 1981). Because these so-called *behavioral stereotypies* resemble behaviors that are commonly associated with amphetamine psychosis in humans, they have been widely used as an animal model of human schizophrenia. The following is a description of the amphetamine-induced open-field behavior of the rat.

> Doses that range from 0.3 to 1.5 mg/kg (*d*-amphetamine injected subcutaneously) produce an increase in forward locomotion. . . . This ambulation persists for approximately 40 to 90 minutes, depending on the dose, and is followed by a period of sleep. Administration of higher doses elicits a multiphasic response pattern that consists of early and late phases of ambulation, and an intermediate phase of focused stereotypy during which locomotion is absent. The focused stereotypy phase is characterized by sniffing, repetitive head and limb movements, and oral behaviors (e.g., licking, biting and/or gnawing) expressed over a small area of the cage floor. Although these behaviors are most prominent during the focused stereotypy phase, they may appear intermittently during other phases of the drug response. The time course of each phase is dose-dependent: with increasing doses, the initial locomotor phase decreases in duration as the animal spends progressively more time in focused stereotypy and in the last phase of locomotion. In fact, at doses of 5.0 to 10.0 mg/kg the total duration of the response may exceed 5 or 6 hours before the animal goes to sleep. (Rebec & Bashore, 1984, p. 154)

Because many of the drugs effective in the treatment of human schizophrenia attenuate the stereotypies induced in laboratory animals by amphetamine, the amphetamine model has been widely used to assess the efficacy of various antischizophrenic drugs and to study their mechanisms of action. However, Rebec and Bashore (1984) have argued that progress in this area of research has been impeded by the lack of precise behavioral assessment. Most investigators lump the complex behavioral changes observed during the

course of a test into one or two scores—for example, a single measure of locomotor activity and a single measure of stereotypy—but Rebec and Bashore
contend that a more selective behavioral approach is warranted. They have
offered the following lines of evidence in support of their contention: (1)
Some of the behavioral symptoms of amphetamine psychosis in humans
occur in individuals who chronically use amphetamine but do not become
psychotic. (2) Although amphetamine psychosis typically occurs only after
long-term amphetamine abuse, some of the behavioral effects of amphetamine in laboratory animals, such as the oral stereotypies (licking and biting),
actually decline with repeated exposure. (3) Some clinically effective antischizophrenic agents block some of the stereotypical behaviors elicited in
animals by amphetamine but leave others, such as the oral stereotypies,
unaffected (Costall & Naylor, 1977; Iversen & Koob, 1977). On the basis
of the preceding observations, Rebec and Bashore concluded that the
amphetamine-produced locomotion, but not oral stereotypy, models amphetamine psychosis, and they stressed the need for careful and independent
assessment of each of the behavioral aspects of the amphetamine model.

MPTP Model of Parkinson's Disease

Parkinson's disease . . . rarely occurs before the age of 50. It was somewhat
of a surprise then to see a group of young drug addicts at our hospital in
1982 who had developed symptoms of severe and what proved to be irre-
versible parkinsonism. The only link between these patients was the recent
use of a new 'synthetic heroin.' They exhibited virtually all of the typical
motor features of Parkinson's disease, including the classic triad of bradykinesia (slowness of movement), tremor and rigidity of their muscles. Even
the subtle features, such as seborrhea (oiliness of the skin) and micro-
graphia (small handwriting), that are typical of Parkinson's disease were
present. After tracking down samples of this substance, the offending agent
was tentatively identified as 1-methyl-4-phenyl-1,2,3,6-tetrahydropyridine
or **MPTP**. . . . After nearly two and a half years, there has been no sign of
remission, and most are becoming increasingly severe management problems. (Langston, 1985, p. 79)

Researchers immediately tried to turn the misfortune of these few to the
advantage of many by developing a much-needed animal model of
Parkinson's disease (Langston, 1986). It was quickly established that various
nonhuman primates responded to MPTP like humans (Burns, Chiueh,
Markey, Ebert, Jacobowitz, & Kopin, 1983; Langston, Forno, Robert, & Irwin,
1984), but attempts to develop a rodent model have been less successful. A
parkinsonian-like syndrome can be produced in some mice, but, unlike
Parkinson's disease and the MPTP syndrome in primates, it does not persist
for more than a few weeks (Duvoisin, Heikkila, Nicklas, & Hess, 1986).

The study of the brains of primates exposed to MPTP has revealed highly
selective damage to the substantia nigra. Although the brain damage in
Parkinson's patients is somewhat more diffuse, the MPTP data suggest that
cell loss in the substantia nigra is responsible for the motor symptoms of the
disease. Considering that the substantia nigra is the major source of the
brain's dopamine, it is not surprising that the level of this transmitter is
greatly reduced in both the MPTP model and in the naturally occurring disor-

der. Paradoxically, in some monkeys, MPTP produces a major depletion of dopamine without producing any gross motor symptoms (Taylor, Elsworth, Roth, Sladek, & Richmond, 1990).

Conclusion

This chapter began with the tragic case history of sublieutenant Zasetsky, the man with a shattered world. Then, it discussed the causes of brain damage, common neuropsychological disorders, and the study of animal models. The following tragic case history of a 30-year-old woman who was poisoned by MPTP (Ballard, Tetrud, & Langston, 1985) completes the circle.[1]

> During the first 4 days of July 1982, . . . [she] used 4½ grams of a "new synthetic heroin." The substance was injected IV [intravenously] three or four times daily and caused a burning sensation at the site of injection. . . .
>
> She had brief auditory hallucinations and visual distortions with larger doses. After 3 days of use, she felt "weak" and "slow," but used the drug for another day. Four days later, she was described by family as sitting quietly without moving all day, staring into space "like a zombie." She later said that she felt fully alert during this period and was aware of the environment, but had difficulty initiating speech and could move only with great effort. She also noted intermittent "shaking" of the left arm. Her family provided total care for her, including all dressing, feeding, and bathing.
>
> On July 21, 1982, she was admitted to our neurobehavioral unit. She had the appearance of a "wax doll," sitting immobile with head and arms held in flexion. General examination [revealed] . . . facial seborrhea [oiliness], . . . a breakdown of horizontal smooth [visual] pursuit, . . . infrequent blinking, continuous drooling, . . . and difficulty initiating speech. Tongue protrusion was slow, limited to about 1 cm. Voluntary movements were profoundly slowed. Left to herself, she remained motionless. . . . A resting tremor of 5 to 6 Hz in the right hand and foot disappeared on volitional movement. . . . She could not rise from a chair without assistance. Gait was shuffling, with small steps, loss of associated movement . . . and loss of postural reflexes. Sensation was normal. The remainder of the neurologic examination was normal, including mental status. . . .

> After 2 years of treatment, there has been no improvement in her parkinsonism, and she has suffered a variety of therapeutic complications. (pp. 949–951)

Before leaving this chapter, pause for a moment to contemplate the plight of this woman and of others who suffer from MPTP poisoning or from advanced parkinsonism. These are intelligent, sensitive, alert people—people just like you—who are trapped for the rest of their lives in a body that does not work.

---

[1]From "Permanent Human Parkinsonism Due to 1-methyl-4-phenyl-1,2,3,6-tetrahydropyridine (MPTP): Seven Cases" by P. A. Ballard, J. W. Tetrud, and J. W. Langston, 1985, *Neurology, 35,* 949–956. Reprinted by permission.

Food for Thought

1. An epileptic is brought to trial for assault. The lawyer argues that her client is not a criminal and that the assaults in question were psychomotor attacks. She points out that her client takes her medication faithfully, but that it does not help. The prosecution lawyer argues that the defendant has a long history of violent assault and must be locked up. What do you think that the judge should do?

2. Describe a bizarre incident you have observed that you think in retrospect might have been a psychomotor or petit mal attack.

3. The more that is known about a disorder, the easier it is to diagnose; and the more accurately that it can be diagnosed, the easier it is to find things out about it. Explain and discuss.

KEY TERMS

To help you study the material in this chapter, all of the key terms—those that have appeared in bold type—are listed and briefly defined here.

Alzheimer's disease. The major cause of dementia in old age; it is characterized by neurofibrillary tangles, neurodegeneration, and amyloid plaques.

Amphetamine psychosis. A psychotic state that is produced by amphetamine abuse; it is similar to schizophrenia.

Amyloid. A protein that is found in clumps of degenerating neurons in Alzheimer's patients.

Aneurysm. A balloon-like dilation that forms in the wall of a blood vessel at a point where the elasticity of the vessel wall is defective.

Arteriosclerosis. A condition in which the walls of blood vessels thicken and narrow.

Ataxia. Loss of motor coordination.

Benign. A tumor is benign if it can be removed without leaving vestiges of it that continue to grow in the body.

Brain abscess. Pocket of pus in the brain.

Cerebral ischemia. A damage-producing disruption of blood supply to an area of the brain.

Complex partial seizures. Seizures that are characterized by various complex psychological phenomena and are thought to result from temporal lobe discharges.

Concussion. When there is a disturbance of consciousness following a blow to the head with no cerebral bleeding or obvious structural damage.

Congenital. Present at birth.

Contrecoup injury. A contusion that occurs on the side of the brain opposite to the side of the blow.

Contusion. A closed-head injury that involves bleeding.

Convulsions. Motor seizures.

Dementia. General intellectual deterioration.

Deprenyl. A monoamine oxidase inhibitor that has been shown to retard the development of Parkinson's disease.

Down's syndrome. A disorder that is associated with the presence of an extra chromosome in pair 21, resulting in disfigurement and mental retardation.

Embolism. When a plug forms in a larger blood vessel and is carried to a smaller one where it blocks the passage of blood.

Encapsulated tumor. A tumor that grows within its own membrane.

Encephalitis. The inflammation associated with brain infection.

Epidemiology. The study of factors that influence the distribution of a disease in the general population.

Epileptic aura. A psychological symptom that precedes the onset of a convulsion.

Epileptogenesis. Development of epilepsy.

Experimental allergic encephalomyelitis. A model of multiple sclerosis that can be induced in laboratory animals by injecting them with myelin and a preparation that stimulates the body's immune system.

Generalized seizures. Seizures that involve the entire brain.

General paresis. The insanity and intellectual deterioration resulting from syphilitic infection.

Grand mal. A seizure whose symptoms are loss of consciousness, loss of equilibrium, and a violent tonic-clonic convulsion.

Hematoma. A bruise.

Homologous animal model. A disorder in animals that duplicates a human disorder in every respect.

Huntington's disease. A progressive disorder of motor and intellectual function that is produced in adulthood by a dominant gene.

Hypoxia. Shortage of oxygen in the blood.

Infarct. An area of ischemic brain damage.

Infiltrating tumor. A tumor that grows diffusely through surrounding tissue.

Isomorphic animal model. A disorder in animals that resembles a human disorder, but is artificially produced in the laboratory.

Kindling phenomenon. The progressive intensification of convulsions elicited by a series of distributed low-intensity stimulations—most commonly by daily electrical stimulations to the amygdala.

L-DOPA. The chemical precursor of dopamine; it is used in the treatment of Parkinson's disease.

Malignant. A tumor is malignant if it cannot be surgically removed without continued growth in the body.

Meningiomas. Tumors that grow between the meninges.

Meningitis. Inflammation of the meninges, which is usually caused by bacterial infection.

Metastatic tumors. Tumors that originate in one organ and spread to another.

Monoamine oxidase (MAO) inhibitor. A drug that increases the activity of monoamine neurotransmitters by inhibiting monoamine oxidase, an enzyme in neurons that breaks down monoamines.

MPTP. A neurotoxin that produces a disorder in primates that is similar to Parkinson's disease.

Multiple sclerosis (MS). A progressive disease of the CNS myelin.

Neurotropic. Viral infections that have a particular affinity for neural tissue.

Nigrostriatal pathway. The pathway along which axons from the substantia nigra project to the striatum.

Pantropic. Viral infections that can infect brain tissue, but have no preference for it.

Parkinson's disease. A movement disorder that is associated with degeneration of dopaminergic neurons in the nigrostriatal pathway.

Partial seizure. A seizure that does not involve the entire brain.

Petit mal. A generalized seizure that is characterized by a disturbance of consciousness and a 3-per-second spike-and-wave discharge.

Predictive animal model. A model that does not resemble the human disorder in key respects, but is of value in predicting some aspect of the disorder.

Psychomotor attack. An epileptic attack in which the patient engages in compulsive behaviors that, although inappropriate, have the appearance of normal behaviors.

Punch-drunk syndrome. The mental disturbances that result from repeated concussions.

Simple partial seizure. Partial seizures in which the symptoms are primarily sensory and/or motor.

Striatum. A structure of the basal ganglia, which is the terminal structure of the dopaminergic nigrostriatal pathway.

Tardive dyskinesia (TD). A motor disorder that results from chronic use of certain antipsychotic drugs.

3-per-second spike-and-wave. The characteristic EEG of the petit mal seizure.

Thrombosis. When a plug blocks blood flow at the site of its formation.

Toxic psychosis. Psychiatric disturbance that is caused by exposure to toxic chemicals.

Tumor (neoplasm). A mass of cells that grows independently of the rest of the body.

ADDITIONAL READING

I strongly recommend the following two books. Both are collections of entertaining, personal essays about neuropsychological patients.

Klawans, H. L. (1990). *Newton's madness: Further tales of clinical neurology.* New York: Harper Row.

Sacks, O. (1985). *The man who mistook his wife for a hat and other clinical tales.* New York: Summit Books.

7

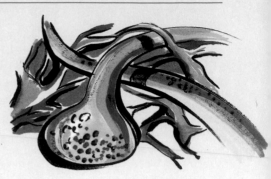

The Visual System: From Eye to Cortex

This chapter is about the visual system. Most people think that their visual systems have evolved to respond as accurately as possible to the patterns of light that enter their eyes. They, of course, recognize the obvious limitations in their visual system's accuracy, and they appreciate those curious instances, termed *visual illusions,* in which it is "tricked" into seeing things the way they aren't. But such shortcomings are generally regarded as minor imperfections in a system that responds quite faithfully to the external world. Despite its intuitive appeal, this way of thinking about the visual system is wrong. The visual system does not produce an accurate internal copy of the external world. It does much more. From the tiny, distorted, upside-down, two-dimensional retinal images projected upon the visual receptors lining the backs of our eyes, the visual system creates an accurate, richly detailed, three-dimensional perception, which is—and this is the really important part—in some respects even better than the external reality from which it was created.

Regardless of what you may have heard to the contrary, "What you see is not necessarily what you get." One of my primary goals in this chapter is to help you recognize and appreciate the inherent creativity of your own visual system.

This chapter is composed of five sections. The first three sections take you on a journey from the external visual world to the visual receptors of the retina, and from there over the major visual pathway to the primary visual cortex. The last two sections describe how the neurons of the visual system mediate the perception of two particularly important features of the visual world: edges and color.

You will learn in this chapter how understanding the visual system requires the integration of two types of research: (1) research that probes the visual system with sophisticated neuroanatomical, neurochemical, and neurophysiological techniques, and (2) research that focuses on the assessment of what we see. Both types of research receive substantial coverage, but it is the second that provides you with a unique educational opportunity: the opportunity to participate in the very research that you are studying. Throughout this chapter, you are encouraged to demonstrate visual phenomena to yourself by testing your own visual system. These demonstrations are designed to give you a taste of the excitement of scientific discovery and to illustrate the relevance of what you are learning in this chapter to life outside its pages.

Light Enters the Eye and Reaches the Retina

Everybody knows that cats, owls, and other nocturnal animals can see in the dark. Right? Wrong! Some animals have special adaptations that allow them to see under very dim illumination, but no animal can see in complete darkness. It is the light reflected into your eyes from the objects around you that is the basis for your ability to see them; if there is no light, there is no vision.

You may recall from high-school physics that light can be thought of in two different ways: as discrete particles of energy called *photons* traveling through space at about 300,000 kilometers (186,000 miles) per second, or as waves of energy. Both theories are useful; in some ways light behaves like a particle, and in others it behaves like a wave. Physicists have learned to live with this nagging inconsistency, and we must do the same.

Light is sometimes defined as waves of electromagnetic energy that are between 380 and 760 nanometers (billionths of a meter) in length (see Figure 7.1). There is nothing special about these wavelengths except that the human visual system responds to them. In fact, some animals can see wavelengths that we cannot. For example, rattlesnakes can see *infrared waves,* which are too long for humans to see; and as a result, they can see warm-blooded prey

FIGURE 7.1

The electromagnetic
spectrum and the colors that
are associated with the
portion of the spectrum that
is visible to humans.

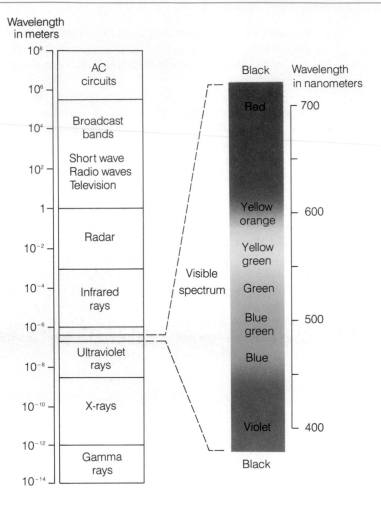

in what for us would be complete darkness (Newman & Hartline, 1982). Accordingly, if I were writing this book for rattlesnakes, I would be forced to suggest another, equally arbitrary, definition of light.

Wavelength and intensity are two properties of light that are of particular interest: wavelength because it plays an important role in the perception of color, and intensity because it plays a similarly important role in the perception of brightness. The terms *wavelength* and *color* tend to be used interchangeably in everyday speech, and so do *intensity* and *brightness*. For example, we commonly refer to an intense light with a wavelength of 700 nanometers as being a bright red light, when in fact it is our perception of the light, not the light itself, that is bright and red. I know that this distinction may seem trivial to you now, but I am confident that you will appreciate the importance of it by the end of the chapter.

Figure 7.2 is a drawing of a horizontal section taken through the middle of the right eye of a human. The amount of light reaching the retinas is regulated by the donut-shaped bands of contractile tissue, the *irises*, which give our eyes their characteristic blue or brown color. Light enters the eye through the *pupil*, the hole in the iris. The adjustment of pupil size in response to

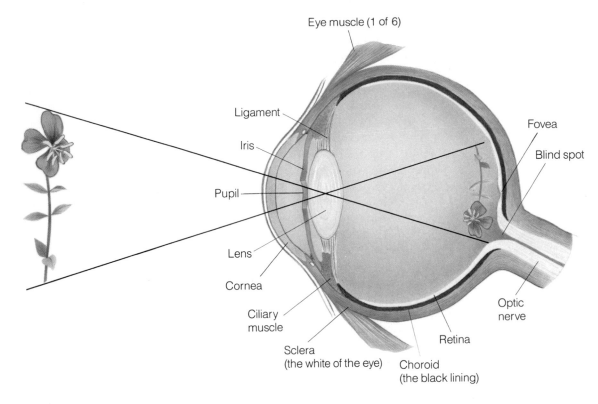

FIGURE 7.2

A drawing of a section (slice) cut from a human eye.

changes in illumination represents a compromise between **sensitivity** (the ability to detect the presence of dimly lit objects) and **acuity** (the ability to see the details of objects). When the level of illumination is high and sensitivity is thus not important, the visual system takes advantage of the situation by constricting the pupils. When the pupils are constricted, the image falling on each retina is sharper, and there is a greater *depth of focus;* that is, a greater range of depths can be simultaneously kept in focus on the retinas. However, when the level of illumination is too low to adequately activate the receptors, the pupils dilate to let in more light.

Behind each pupil is a *lens,* which focuses incoming light on the retina. When we direct our gaze at something near, the tension on the ligaments holding each lens in place is reduced by the contraction of the **ciliary muscles,** and the lens assumes its natural cylindrical shape. (Be alert here; the fact that the tension on the lens is reduced by muscle contraction is counterintuitive. See Figure 7.2.) This increases its ability to *refract* (bend) light and thus brings close objects into sharp focus. To focus on a distant object, the ciliary muscles relax and the lens is flattened. The process of adjusting the configuration of the lenses to bring images into focus on the retina is called **accommodation.**

No description of the eyes of vertebrates would be complete without a discussion of their most obvious feature, the fact that they come in pairs. One reason why vertebrates have two eyes, rather than say one or even three, is the fact that vertebrates have two sides: left and right. Consequently, by having one eye on each side, which is by far the most common arrangement, it is possible for vertebrates to see in almost every direction without moving their heads. Clearly this is an efficient arrangement. Why then do some animals, including humans, and many other mammals have their eyes mounted side by side on the fronts of their heads? This arrangement sacrifices the ability to see behind so that what is in front can be viewed through both eyes simultaneously—an arrangement that is an important basis for our visual system's ability to create three-dimensional perceptions (i.e., to see depth) from two-dimensional retinal images. Why do you think that the two-eyes-on-the-front arrangement has evolved in some species but not in others?

The movements of your eyes are coordinated so that each point in your visual world is projected to corresponding points on your two retinas. To accomplish this, your eyes must *converge* (turn slightly inward); convergence is greatest when you are inspecting things that are close. But the positions of the retinal images on your two eyes can never correspond exactly because your two eyes do not view the world from exactly the same position. Because **binocular disparity** (i.e., the difference in the position of images on the two retinas) is greater for close objects than for distant objects, your visual system can use the degree of binocular disparity to construct one three-dimensional perception from two two-dimensional retinal images (Julesz, 1986).

DEMONSTRATION

The demonstration of binocular disparity and convergence is the first of the demonstrations that punctuate this chapter. If you compare the views from each eye (by quickly closing one eye and then the other) of objects at various distances in front of you—for example, your finger held at different distances—you will notice that the disparity between the two views is greater for closer objects. Now try the mysterious demonstration of the cocktail sausage. Face the farthest wall (or some other distant object), and bring the tips of your two pointing fingers together at arm's length in front of you—with your nails away from you, unless you prefer sausages with fingernails. Now, with both eyes open, sight through the notch between your touching fingertips, but focus on the wall. Do you see the cocktail sausage between

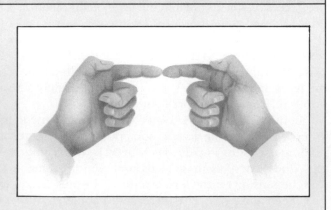

your fingertips? Where did it come from? To prove to yourself that the sausage is a product of binocularity, make it disappear by shutting one eye. Warning: Do not eat this sausage.

7.2

The Retina and the Translation of Light into Neural Signals

Figure 7.3 illustrates the cellular structure of the retina. There are five different layers of cells: **receptors, horizontal cells, bipolar cells, amacrine cells,** and **retinal ganglion cells.** Notice that the amacrine cells and horizontal cells appear to be specialized for *lateral communication* (i.e., for transmission across channels of sensory input). No more will be said about lateral communication here, but you will learn later in the chapter that it plays an extremely important role in vision.

Also notice in Figure 7.3 that the retina is inside-out in the sense that the light reaches the receptor layer only after passing through the other four layers. Then, once the receptors are activated, the neural message is transmitted back out through the retinal layers before reaching the retinal ganglion cells, whose axons project across the inside of the retina before exiting the eyeball. This "inside-out" arrangement is less than optimal for two reasons. One is that the incoming light is distorted by the retinal tissue through which it must pass before reaching the receptors; the other is that for the retinal ganglion cell axons to leave the eye, there must be a gap in the receptor layer. This receptorless area of the retina is called the **optic disk** or *blind spot.*

A cross section of the foveal portion of the retina is illustrated in Figure 7.4. The **fovea** is a tiny indentation about .33 millimeter in diameter. The thinning of the retinal ganglion cell layer at the fovea reduces the distortion of incoming light in the central part of the retina, which—as you will soon

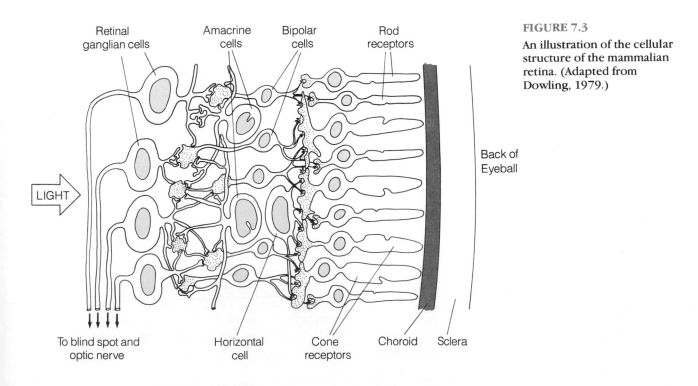

Retinal ganglian cells   Amacrine cells   Bipolar cells   Rod receptors

LIGHT

Back of Eyeball

To blind spot and optic nerve   Horizontal cell   Cone receptors   Choroid   Sclera

FIGURE 7.3

An illustration of the cellular structure of the mammalian retina. (Adapted from Dowling, 1979.)

FIGURE 7.4

An illustration of a cross
section of the human fovea.
(Adapted from Rushton,
1962.)

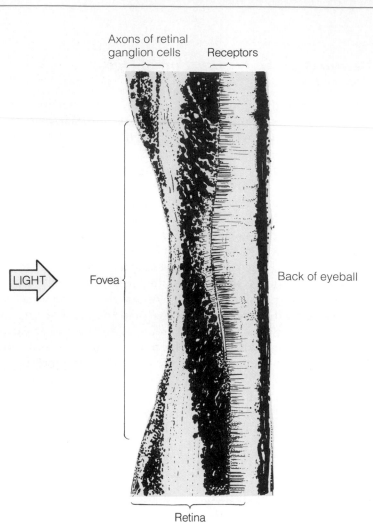

Axons of retinal
ganglion cells   Receptors

LIGHT

Fovea

Back of eyeball

Retina

learn—is the part of the retina that is specialized for high-acuity vision. The
gaps in the retinal images that result from each eye's blind spot require a
more creative solution. Because your visual receptor layers both have gaps in
them (i.e., the optic disks), you might expect that your visual images would
have gaps in them too. But they don't; somehow your visual system fills in the
gaps—as you will learn from the following demonstration.

<hr>

DEMONSTRATION

First, prove to yourself that you have a blind spot.
Close your left eye, and stare directly at the A in
Figure 7.5, trying as hard as you can not to shift
your gaze. While keeping the gaze of your right
eye fixed on the A, hold the book at different distances from you until the black dot to the right of
the A becomes focused on your blind spot and
disappears (about 20 centimeters or 8 inches).

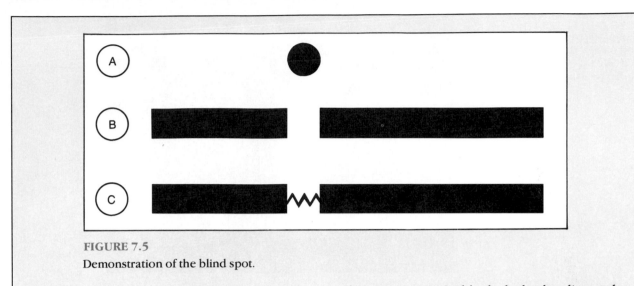

FIGURE 7.5
Demonstration of the blind spot.

Why then is there not a black hole in your perception of the world when you look at it with one eye? You will discover the answer by holding the book at the same distance and changing the focus of your gaze to B. Suddenly the broken line to the right of B becomes whole. Now switch your gaze to C. What do you see?

You have just experienced **completion.** The visual system uses information provided by the receptors around the blind spot to fill in the gaps in your retinal images. When the visual system detects a straight bar going into one side of the blind spot and another straight bar leaving the other side, it fills in the missing bit for you, and what you see is a continuous straight bar, regardless of what is actually there. The completion phenomenon is one of the most compelling demonstrations that the visual system does not just create a faithful copy of the external world; it creates perceptions of stimuli that are not even there.

Rod and Cone Vision

You undoubtedly noticed in Figure 7.3 that there are two different receptor types in the human retina, rod-shaped receptors called **rods** and cone-shaped receptors called **cones**—see Figure 7.6. The existence of two different receptor types puzzled researchers until 1866, when it was first noticed that species that are active only at night tend to have rod-only retinas, that species that are active only in the day tend to have cone-only retinas, and that species that are active during both day and night (e.g., humans) have both rods and cones. From these initial observations emerged the **duplexity theory** of vision: the theory that rods and cones are the receptors for two different kinds of visual systems, which are intertwined in many species (e.g., humans). The cone-driven system (i.e., the **photopic** system) takes advantage of good lighting to provide high-acuity (fine-detailed), colored perceptions of the world. In dim illumination, there is not enough light to reliably excite the cone system, and the more sensitive, rod-driven system (i.e., the **scotopic** system) takes over. However, the sensitivity of the scotopic system is not achieved without cost; scotopic vision lacks both the detail and color of photopic vision.

FIGURE 7.6

A photomicrograph of rods and cones. The cylindrical cells are the rods; the smaller, conical cells are the cones.

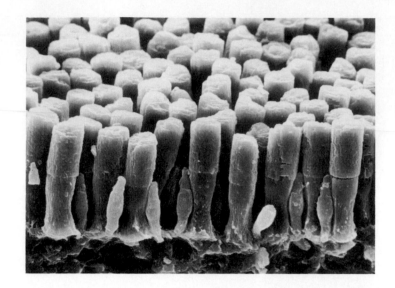

Strong support for the duplexity theory comes from case studies of human patients who lack either rods or cones. Individuals lacking functional rods suffer *night blindness;* they have normal vision under daylight conditions, but in dim light they become functionally blind. In contrast, individuals without functional cones display *day blindness;* their perception is normal under dim illumination, but they have great difficulty seeing in daylight, and what they do see lacks color and detail.

The differences between photopic (cone) and scotopic (rod) vision result in part from a difference in the way that the two systems are "wired." As illustrated schematically in Figure 7.7, there is a large difference between the two

FIGURE 7.7

A schematic representation of the convergence of rods and cones on retinal ganglion cells. There is a high degree of convergence in the rod system and a low degree of convergence in the cone system.

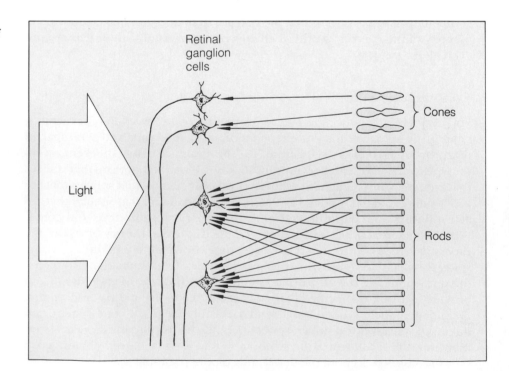

systems in *convergence.* The output of several hundred rods may ultimately converge on a single retinal ganglion cell, whereas it is not uncommon for a retinal ganglion cell to receive input from only a few cones. As a result, the effects of dim light simultaneously stimulating many rods can summate to influence the firing of a retinal ganglion cell onto which the output of the stimulated rods converges, whereas the effects of the same dim light applied to a sheet of cones cannot summate to the same degree, and the retinal ganglion cells may not respond to the light. However, the convergent scotopic system pays for its high degree of sensitivity with a low level of acuity. When a retinal ganglion cell that receives input from hundreds of rods changes its firing, the brain has no way of knowing which portion of the rods contributed to the change. Although a more intense light is required to change the firing of a retinal ganglion cell that receives signals from cones, when it does react there is less ambiguity about the location of the stimulus that triggered the reaction.

Rods and cones differ in their distribution on the retinas. As illustrated in Figure 7.8, there are no rods at all in the fovea, only cones. At the boundaries

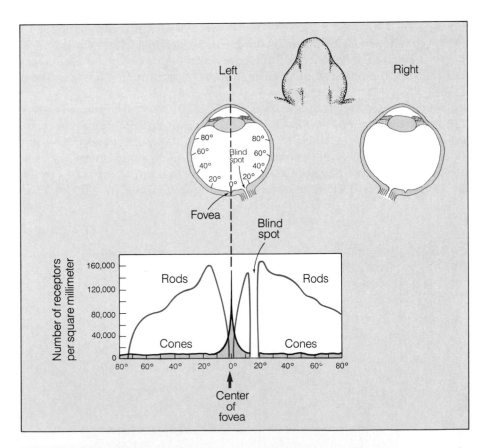

FIGURE 7.8

The distribution of rods and cones over the human retina. The figure illustrates the number of rods and cones per square millimeter in a horizontal slice cut through the fovea and blind spot of the left eye, as a function of distance from the center of the fovea. (Adapted from Lindsay & Norman, 1977.)

of the foveal indentation, the proportion of cones declines markedly, and there is an increase in the number of rods. The density of rods reaches a maximum at 20° from the center of the fovea. You may be puzzled by the fact that in the periphery of the retina, there are many more rods in the **nasal hemiretina** (the half of the retina next to the nose) than in the **temporal hemiretina** (the half next to the temples). The solution to this puzzle is as plain as the nose on your face. In fact, it is the nose on your face. Because your nose blocks the input of light onto the edges of your temporal hemiretinas, there is less need for receptors there.

Generally speaking, more intense lights appear brighter. However, wavelength also has a substantial effect on the perception of brightness. Because our visual systems are not equally sensitive to all wavelengths in the visible spectrum, lights of the same intensity, but of different wavelengths, can differ markedly in brightness. A graph of the relative brightness of lights of the same intensity presented at different wavelengths is called a *spectral sensitivity curve.* By far the most important thing to remember about spectral sensitivity curves is that humans and other animals with both rods and cones have two of them: a **photopic spectral sensitivity curve** and a **scotopic spectral sensitivity curve.** The photopic spectral sensitivity of humans is determined by having them judge the brightness of different wavelengths of light shone on the fovea. The scotopic sensitivity of subjects is determined by asking them to judge the relative brightness of different wavelengths of light shone on the periphery of the retina at an intensity too low to activate the few peripheral cones.

The scotopic and photopic spectral sensitivity curves of human subjects are plotted in Figure 7.9. Notice that under scotopic conditions, the visual system is maximally sensitive to wavelengths of about 500 nanometers, and thus a light of 560 nanometers would have to be much more intense than one at 500 nanometers to be seen as equally bright. In contrast, under photopic conditions, the visual system is maximally sensitive to wavelengths of about

FIGURE 7.9

Human photopic and scotopic spectral sensitivity curves. The peak of each curve has been arbitrarily set at 100%.

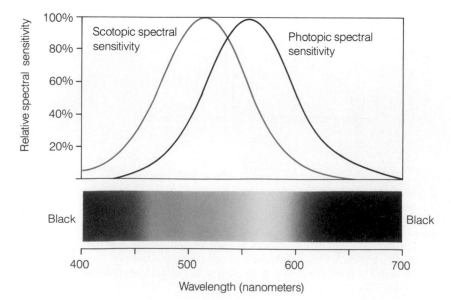

560 nanometers, and thus a light at 500 nanometers would have to be much more intense than one at 560 nanometers to be seen as equally bright.

Because of the difference in scotopic and photopic spectral sensitivity, an interesting visual effect can be observed during the transition from photopic to scotopic vision. In 1825, Purkinje described the following occurrence, which has become known as the **Purkinje effect** (pronounced pur KIN gee). One evening, just before dusk, Purkinje was walking in his garden, and he noticed how bright most of his yellow and red flowers appeared in relation to his blue ones. What amazed him was that just a few hours later the relative brightness of his flowers had somehow been reversed; the entire scene, when viewed at night, appeared only in shades of gray, but most of the blue flowers appeared as brighter grays than did the yellow and red ones. Can you explain this shift in relative brightness by referring to the photopic and scotopic spectral sensitivity curves in Figure 7.9?

Eye Movement

If cones are in fact responsible for mediating high-acuity, color vision under photopic conditions, how can they accomplish their task when most of them are crammed into the fovea? Look around you. What you see is not a few colored details at the center of a grayish scene. You see an expansive, richly detailed, lavishly colored visual world. How can such a perception be the product of a photopic system that, for the most part, is restricted to a few degrees in the center of your visual field? The following demonstration provides a clue.

DEMONSTRATION

Close your left eye, and with your right eye, stare at the fixation point in Figure 7.10, at a distance of 12 centimeters (4.75 inches). Be very careful that your gaze does not shift. What you will notice when your gaze is fixed is that it is difficult to see detail and color at 20° or more from the fixation point. Now look at the page without fixing your gaze, and notice the difference that eye movement makes.

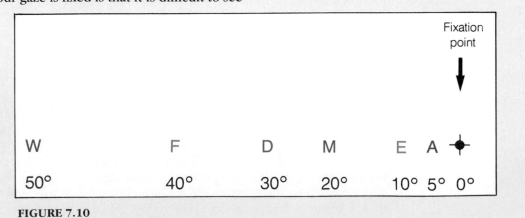

FIGURE 7.10
The retinal distribution of high-acuity color vision. (Adapted from Coren and Ward, 1989.)

What this demonstration shows us is that what we see is not determined just by what is projected on the retina at that instant (e.g., Cumming, 1978). Although we are not aware of it, the eye continually scans the visual field by making a series of brief fixations. About three fixations occur every second, and they are connected by very quick eye movements called **saccades** (Kowler, 1990; Whittaker & Cummings, 1990). The visual system *integrates* (adds together) the foveal images from the preceding few fixations to produce a wide-angled, high-acuity, richly colored perception. It is because of this *temporal integration* that the world does not vanish momentarily each time that you blink.

One way of demonstrating the critical role played by eye movement in vision is to study what happens to vision when all eye movement is stopped. However, because of the risks inherent in paralyzing the eye muscles, researchers have taken an alternative approach. Rather than stopping eye movement, they have stopped the primary consequence of eye movement, the movement of the retinal image across the retina. They have accomplished this by projecting test stimuli from a tiny projector mounted on a contact lens. Each time that the eye moves, the lens and the projector move with it, thus keeping the retinal image fixed on the same receptors, as if the eye had remained still. The effect on vision of stabilizing the retinal image is dramatic (e.g., Pritchard, 1961). After a few seconds of viewing, a simple **stabilized retinal image** disappears, leaving a featureless gray field. The movements of the eyes then increase, presumably in an attempt to bring the image back. However, such movements are futile in this situation because the stabilized retinal image simply moves with the eyes. In a few seconds, the stimulus pattern, or part of it, spontaneously reappears, only to disappear once again.

Why do stabilized images disappear? The answer lies in the fact that the neurons of the visual system respond to change rather than to steady input. Most neurons of the visual system respond vigorously when a stimulus is presented, moved, or terminated, but they respond only weakly to a continuous, unchanging stimulus. Apparently, one function of eye movements is to keep the retinal image moving back and forth across the receptors, thus ensuring that the receptors and the neurons to which they are connected receive a continually changing pattern of stimulation. When a retinal image is stabilized, parts of the visual system stop responding to the image, and it disappears.

Visual Transduction: The Translation of Light to Neural Signals

Transduction refers to the conversion of one form of energy to another; *visual transduction* refers to the conversion of light to neural signals by the visual receptors. The first major advance in the study of visual transduction came in 1876 when a red *pigment* (a pigment is any substance that absorbs light) was extracted from the predominantly rod retina of the frog. This pigment had a curious property. When **rhodopsin,** as the pigment became known, was exposed to continuous intense light, it was bleached (lost its color) and it lost its ability to absorb light, but when it was returned to the dark, it regained both its redness and its light-absorbing capacity.

It is now clear that the absorption and bleaching of rhodopsin by light is the first step in rod-mediated vision. Evidence for this view comes from demonstrations that the degree to which rhodopsin absorbs light in various situations predicts how humans see under the very same conditions. For example, it has been shown that the degree to which rhodopsin absorbs lights of different wavelengths is related to the ability of humans and other animals with rods to detect the presence of different wavelengths of light under scotopic conditions. Figure 7.11 illustrates the relation between the **absorption spectrum** of rhodopsin and the human scotopic spectral sensitivity curve. The goodness of the fit leaves little doubt that, in dim light, our sensitivity to various wavelengths is a direct consequence of rhodopsin's ability to absorb them.

Since the discovery that the bleaching action of light on rhodopsin is the basis of scotopic visual transduction, neurochemists have clarified the nature of the bleaching reaction (Applebury, 1991; Wald, 1968). Rhodopsin is a compound made up of two molecules: *retinal* and *opsin.* As illustrated in Figure 7.12, when rods are exposed to light, the thread-like opsin molecule is released from some of its points of contact with the retinal molecule and begins to straighten out. This chemical change induces a neural signal. If rods are exposed to intense light, the opsin and retinal separate completely, and the cells lose their capacity to absorb light and generate signals. When bleached rods are placed in the dark, the opsin and retinal assume their original configuration, and the rhodopsin regains its ability to absorb light and generate signals. Because retinal is synthesized from *vitamin A,* a diet lacking vitamin A can lead to night blindness.

The bleaching of rhodopsin is one of the fastest chemical reactions ever recorded (Schoenlein, Peteanu, Mathies, & Shank, 1991). It occurs in 200 *femtoseconds.* For the mathematically inclined, this is 200×10^{-15} second; for the rest of us, it is enough to remember that it is darn fast.

The bleaching of rhodopsin initiates a cascade of chemical events inside the rods (Pugh & Lamb, 1990; Uhl, Wagner, & Ryba, 1990; Yau & Baylor,

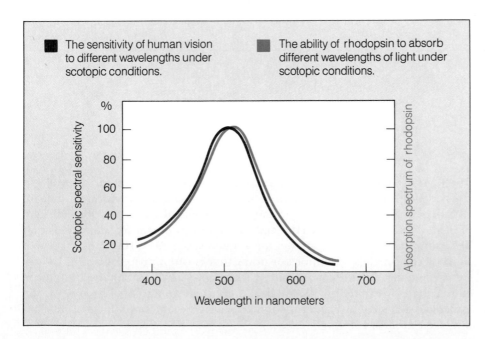

■ The sensitivity of human vision to different wavelengths under scotopic conditions.

■ The ability of rhodopsin to absorb different wavelengths of light under scotopic conditions.

FIGURE 7.11

The absorption spectrum of rhodopsin compared with the human scotopic spectral sensitivity curve.

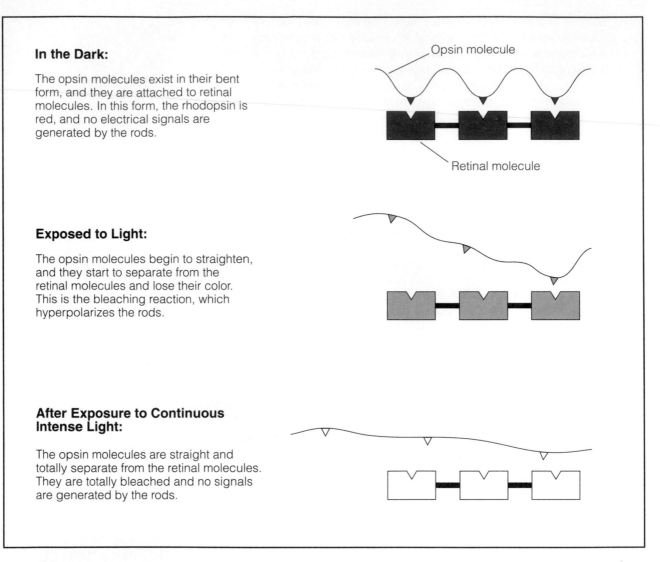

In the Dark:

The opsin molecules exist in their bent form, and they are attached to retinal molecules. In this form, the rhodopsin is red, and no electrical signals are generated by the rods.

Opsin molecule

Retinal molecule

Exposed to Light:

The opsin molecules begin to straighten, and they start to separate from the retinal molecules and lose their color. This is the bleaching reaction, which hyperpolarizes the rods.

After Exposure to Continuous Intense Light:

The opsin molecules are straight and totally separate from the retinal molecules. They are totally bleached and no signals are generated by the rods.

FIGURE 7.12

A schematic illustration of the response of the rhodopsin molecule to light.

1989). These chemical events stimulate the closure of sodium ion channels in the rod membranes (see O'Brien, 1982). The closing of the sodium ion channels, which are normally open in the dark, hyperpolarizes the rods (Schnapf & Baylor, 1987) and reduces the number of neurotransmitter molecules that are continually released from their terminals (Yau, 1991). The transduction of light by rods makes an important point that is often misunderstood by students: Signals are often transmitted through neural systems by inhibition, rather than by excitation. Although the cone photopigments have yet to be isolated, their structure and function appear to be similar to those of rhodopsin (see Nathans, 1989).

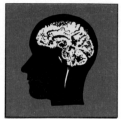

Before proceeding to the last two sections of the chapter, which describe how the visual system mediates the perception of edges and color, review what you have learned so far about the visual system by filling in the following blanks.

1. Neural signals are carried from the retina to the lateral geniculate nuclei by the axons of _____ cells.

2. The area of the retina that mediates high-acuity vision is the _____ .

3. Cones are the receptors of the _____ system.

4. The photopigment of rods is _____ .

5. The most important organizational principle of the retina-geniculate-striate system is that it is laid out _____ .

6. The retinal ganglion cells from the nasal hemiretinas decussate via the _____ .

7. Evidence that rhodopsin is the scotopic photopigment is provided by the fit between the _____ spectrum of rhodopsin and the scotopic spectral sensitivity curve.

8. The high degree of _____ characteristic of the scotopic system increases its sensitivity, but decreases its acuity.

9. The axons of retinal ganglion cells leave the eyeball at the optic disk or _____ .

7.3

From Retina to the Primary Visual Cortex

Many pathways in the brain carry visual information, but by far the largest and most thoroughly studied visual pathway is the **retina-geniculate-striate pathway,** which, as its name implies, conducts signals from the retina to the **striate cortex (primary visual cortex)** via the **lateral geniculate nuclei** of the thalamus. The organization of this retina-geniculate-striate pathway is illustrated in Figure 7.13. Examine it carefully.

The following are the correct answers to the preceding questions: (1) retinal ganglion, (2) fovea, (3) photopic, (4) rhodopsin, (5) retinotopically, (6) optic chiasm, (7) absorption, (8) convergence, and (9) blind spot.

FIGURE 7.13

The retina-geniculate-striate system: the neural projections from the retinas through the lateral geniculate nuclei to the left and right primary visual cortex (striate cortex). (Adapted from Netter, 1967.)

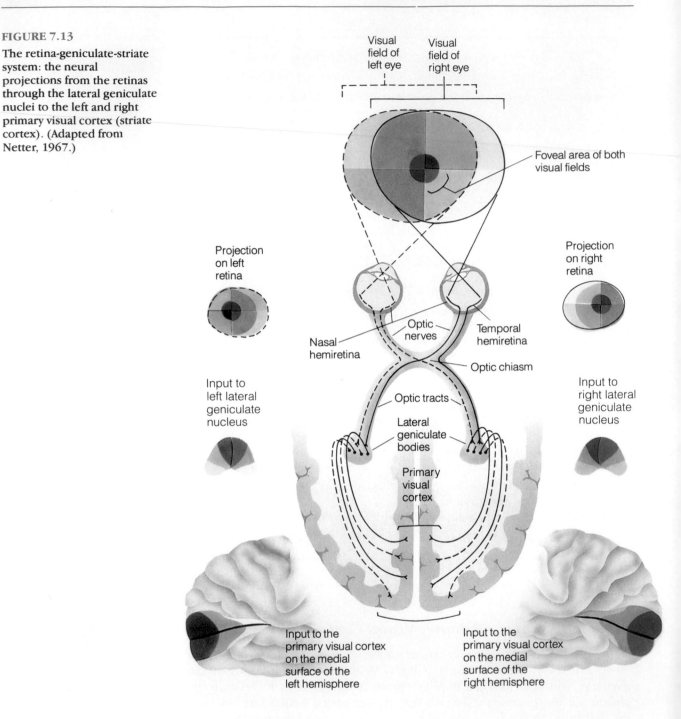

The main thing to notice from Figure 7.13 is that all signals from the left visual field reach the right striate cortex, either ipsilaterally via the *temporal hemiretina* of the right eye or contralaterally via the *nasal hemiretina* of the left eye—and that the opposite is true of all signals from the right visual field. Each lateral geniculate nucleus has six layers, and each layer receives input from all parts of only one retina. All of the lateral geniculate neurons that project to the primary visual cortex terminate in the lower part of cortical layer IV, thus producing a characteristic stripe or striation when viewed in cross section—hence, the name *striate cortex.*

The retina-geniculate-striate system is **retinotopic;** each level of the system is organized like a map of the retina. This means that two stimuli presented to adjacent areas of the retina excite adjacent neurons at all levels of the system. The retinotopic layout of striate cortex has a disproportionate representation of the fovea; although the fovea is only a small part of the retina, a relatively large proportion of primary visual cortex (about 25%) is dedicated to the analysis of its input. A dramatic demonstration of the retinotopic organization of the primary visual cortex was provided by Dobelle, Mladejovsky, and Girvin (1974). They implanted an array of electrodes in the primary visual cortices of patients who were blind because of damage to their eyes. If electrical current was administered simultaneously through an array of electrodes forming a shape, such as a cross, on the surface of a patient's cortex, the patient reported "seeing" a glowing image of that shape.

7.4

Seeing Edges

This section of the chapter is about "seeing edges." Seeing edges does not sound like a particularly important topic, but it is. Edges are the most informative features of any visual display because they define the extent and position of the various objects in it. Given the importance of perceiving visual edges and the unrelenting pressure of natural selection, it is not surprising that the visual systems of many species are particularly good at edge perception.

Before considering the visual mechanisms underlying edge perception, it is important to appreciate exactly what a visual edge is. In a sense, a visual edge is nothing; it is the place where two different areas of a visual image meet. Thus, the perception of an edge is really the perception of a *contrast* between two adjacent areas of the visual field. This section of the chapter reviews the perception of edges (i.e., the perception of contrast) between areas that differ from one another in brightness. Color contrast is discussed in the following section.

Lateral Inhibition and Contrast Enhancement

Carefully examine Figure 7.14. The graph just beneath the figure indicates what is there—a series of homogeneous stripes of different intensity. But this is not exactly what you see, is it? What you see is indicated in the bottom graph. Adjacent to each edge, the brighter stripe looks brighter than it really is and the darker stripe looks darker than it really is. The nonexistent stripes of brightness and darkness running adjacent to the edges are called *Mach bands;* they enhance the contrast at each edge and make each edge easier to see. It is important to appreciate that **contrast enhancement** is not something that occurs just in books. Although we are normally unaware of it, every edge that we look at is highlighted for us by the contrast-enhancing mechanisms of our nervous systems. Thus our perception of edges is better than the real thing.

FIGURE 7.14
Mach bands.

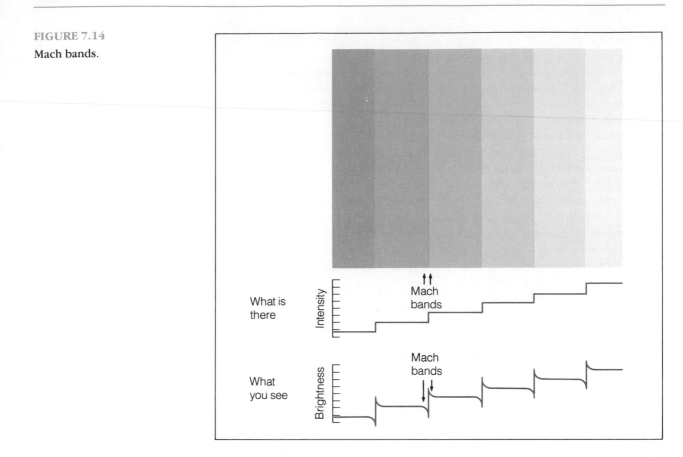

The Mach band demonstration is so compelling that you may be confused by it. You may think that the Mach bands have been created by the printers of the book, rather than by your own visual system. To prove to yourself that the Mach bands are a creation of your own visual system, conduct the following experiment. View each stripe individually by covering the adjacent ones with two pieces of paper, and you will see at once that each stripe is completely homogeneous. Now take the paper away and the Mach bands will suddenly reappear.

The classic studies of the physiological basis of contrast enhancement were conducted on the eyes of an unlikely subject: the *horseshoe crab* (e.g., Ratliff, 1972). The *lateral eyes* of the horseshoe crab are ideal for certain types of neurophysiological research. Unlike mammalian eyes, they are composed of very large receptors called **ommatidia,** each with its own large axon. The ommatidium axons of each lateral eye are interconnected by a lateral neural network called the **lateral plexus.** In order to understand the physiological basis of contrast enhancement in the horseshoe crab, you must know two things. The first is that if a single ommatidium is illuminated, it fires at a rate that is proportional to the intensity of the light striking it; more intense lights produce more firing. The second is that when a receptor fires, it inhibits its neighbors via the lateral plexus—this inhibition is called **lateral inhibition**

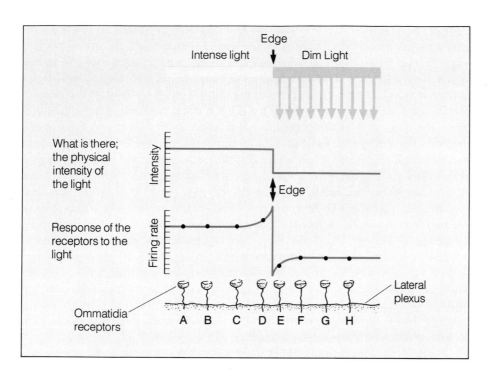

FIGURE 7.15
How lateral inhibition produces contrast enhancement.
(Adapted from Ratliff, 1972.)

because it spreads laterally across the array of receptors, or *mutual inhibition* because neighboring receptors inhibit one another. The amount of lateral inhibition produced by a receptor is greatest when it is most intensely illuminated, and it has its greatest effect on immediate neighbors.

The neural basis of contrast enhancement can be understood in terms of the firing rates of the receptors on each side of an edge, as indicated in Figure 7.15. Notice that the receptor adjacent to the edge on the more intense side (receptor D) fires more than the other intensely illuminated receptors (A,B,C), while the receptor adjacent to the edge on the less well-illuminated side (receptor E) fires less than the other receptors on that side (F,G,H). Lateral inhibition accounts for these differences. Receptors A, B, and C all fire at the same rate because they are all receiving the same high level of stimulation and the same high degree of lateral inhibition from all their highly stimulated neighbors. Receptor D fires more than A, B, and C because it receives as much stimulation as they do, but less inhibition because many of its neighbors are on the dimmer side of the edge. Now consider the receptors on the dimmer side. Receptors F, G, and H fire at the same rate because they are all being stimulated by the same low level of light and receiving the same low level of inhibition from their neighbors. However, receptor E fires even less because it is receiving the same excitation, but more inhibition because many of its immediate neighbors are on the other side of the border in the more intense light. Now that you understand the neural basis of contrast enhancement, take another look at Figure 7.14.

Receptive Fields of Visual Neurons

The Nobel-Prize-winning research of Hubel and Wiesel is the fitting climax to this discussion of edge perception; their methods have been adopted by a generation of sensory neurophysiologists. The subjects in Hubel and Wiesel's experiments are single neurons in the visual systems of cats and monkeys. First, the tip of a microelectrode is positioned near a single neuron in the visual area of interest. During testing, eye movements are blocked by *d-tubo-curarine* (see Chapter 4), and the images on a screen in front of the subject are focused sharply on the retina by the experimenter using an adjustable lens. The next step in the procedure is to identify the receptive field of the neuron. The **receptive field** of a visual neuron is the area of the visual field within which it is possible for a visual stimulus to influence the firing of that cell. Visual system neurons tend to be continually active, and thus effective stimuli are those that either increase or decrease the rate of firing. The final step in the method is to record the responses of the neuron to various stimuli within its receptive field in order to characterize the types of stimuli that most influence its activity. Then, the electrode is advanced slightly and the entire process of identifying and characterizing the receptive field properties is repeated for another neuron, and then for another, and another, and so on (see Kuffler, 1953). The general strategy involves beginning such studies near the input end of a sensory system and gradually working up through "higher" and "higher" levels of the system in an effort to understand the increasing complexity of the neural responses at each level.

Hubel and Wiesel (e.g., 1979) used their procedure to study the retina-geniculate-striate system of the monkey. Given the relatively simple circuitry of the pathway from the retina to the primary visual cortex, it is not surprising that many retinal ganglion cells, lateral geniculate neurons, and **lower-layer-IV neurons** (the striate cortex neurons that receive input from geniculate neurons) have similar receptive fields. Most of the receptive fields of the neurons at these three levels of the retina-geniculate-striate system are round. Because there is less convergence in foveal circuits, neurons with receptive fields in the foveal area have smaller receptive fields than do those with receptive fields in the periphery.

Most retinal ganglion cells, lateral geniculate cells, and primary visual cortex cells in the lower region of layer IV respond in two different ways to a spot of white light that briefly appears in their receptive field. Depending on where in the cell's receptive field the light appears, the cell displays either *on firing* or *off firing;* that is, it displays an increased rate of firing while the light is on, or it displays a reduced rate of firing while the light is on followed by a burst of firing when it is turned off.

The receptive fields of most retinal ganglion cells, lateral geniculate cells, and lower layer IV cells fall into one of the two categories, which are illustrated in Figure 7.16. **On-center cells** respond to lights shone in the central region of their fields with "on" firing and to lights shown in the periphery of their fields with inhibition, followed by "off" firing when the light is turned off. **Off-center cells** display the opposite pattern, with "off" firing in response to lights in the center of their receptive fields and with "on" firing to lights in the periphery. Cells with these on-center and off-center concentric receptive fields are termed **X-type cells** (Sherman, 1985), and they are by far the most prevalent type of neuron in the retina-geniculate-striate system.

X-type cells respond best to contrast. Figure 7.17 illustrates this point. The most effective way to influence the firing rate of an X-type cell is to maximize the contrast between the center and the periphery of its receptive field by illuminating the entire center or the surround, while leaving the other re-

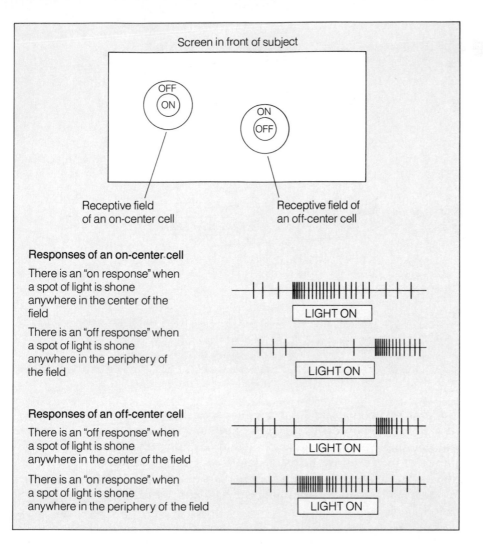

Screen in front of subject

OFF
ON

ON
OFF

Receptive field
of an on-center cell

Receptive field of
an off-center cell

Responses of an on-center cell

There is an "on response" when
a spot of light is shone
anywhere in the center of the
field

LIGHT ON

There is an "off response" when
a spot of light is shone
anywhere in the periphery of
the field

LIGHT ON

Responses of an off-center cell

There is an "off response" when
a spot of light is shone
anywhere in the center of the field

LIGHT ON

There is an "on response" when
a spot of light is shone
anywhere in the periphery of the field

LIGHT ON

FIGURE 7.16

The receptive fields of an
on-center cell and an
off-center cell.

gion completely unilluminated. Diffusely illuminating both regions of the receptive field has little effect. On the basis of this evidence, Hubel and Wiesel
suggested that the function of many neurons in the retina-geniculate-striate
system is to respond to the degree of brightness contrast between the two
areas of their receptive fields (see Livingstone & Hubel, 1988).

Except for the neurons in lower layer IV, the neurons of the striate cortex
have receptive field properties that are different from those of retinal ganglion cells and lateral geniculate cells. In the same way that X-type neurons
are most responsive to circular edges, straight edges are favored by neurons
of the striate cortex. The receptive fields of striate cortex neurons are complex and diverse and, as a result, extremely difficult to categorize. However, it
is usual to consider most of them as belonging to one of two different classes,
simple and complex, each with numerous subtypes (e.g., Gilbert, 1977;
Kuffler, Nicholls, & Martin, 1984).

Simple cells of the visual cortex have receptive fields like those of the
lower-layer-IV cells; they can be divided into two static, mutually antagonistic

FIGURE 7.17

The response of an on-center cell to contrast.

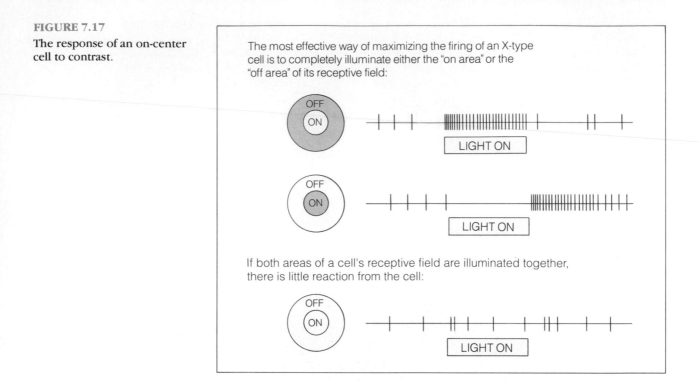

"on" and "off" regions, and they are unresponsive to diffuse light. The difference is that the borders between the "on" and "off" regions of the receptive fields of simple cortical cells are straight lines rather than circles. Several examples of the receptive fields of simple cells are presented in Figure 7.18. Notice that simple cells respond best to bars of light in a dark field, dark bars in a light field, or single edges between dark and light areas. Each simple cell

FIGURE 7.18

Examples of visual fields of simple cortical cells.

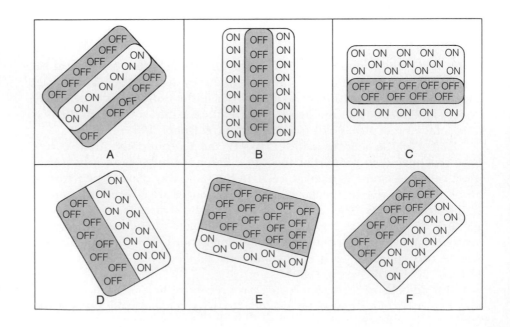

responds maximally only when its preferred straight-edge stimulus is in a particular position and in a particular orientation. For example, a 45° narrow bar of light that completely fills the "on" region of receptive field A in Figure 7.18 would produce robust "on" firing in that cell; if the bar of light were moved or rotated slightly, a weaker "on" response would be produced.

Complex cells are more numerous than simple cells. Like simple cells, complex cells respond best to straight-line stimuli in a specific orientation, and they are unresponsive to diffuse light. However, complex cortical cells differ from simple cortical cells in two important respects. The first is that it is not possible to divide the receptive fields of complex cells into static "on" and "off" regions. A complex cell responds to a particular straight-edge stimulus of a particular orientation regardless of its position within the receptive field of that cell. Thus, if a stimulus (e.g., a 45° bar of light) that produces "on" firing in a particular complex cell is swept across its receptive field, the cell will respond continuously to it as it moves across the field. Many complex cells display a direction preference; that is, they respond more robustly to the movement of a straight line across their receptive fields in a particular direction. How did Hubel and Wiesel discover the "preferences" of complex cortical cells?

> We were inserting the glass slide with its black spot into the slot of the ophthalmoscope when suddenly over the audiomonitor the cell went off like a machine gun. After some fussing and fiddling we found out what was happening. The response had nothing to do with the black dot. As the glass slide was inserted its edge was casting onto the retina a faint but sharp shadow, a straight dark line on a light background. That is what the cell wanted, and it wanted it, moreover, in just one narrow range of orientations.
>   This was unheard of. (Hubel, 1982, p. 517)

The second way that complex cortical cells differ from simple cortical cells is that many are **binocular.** Virtually all of the simple cortical cells and the neurons of the retina-geniculate-striate pathway are **monocular;** they respond to stimulation of either the right eye or the left eye, but not to both. In contrast, over half the complex cortical cells respond to stimulation of either eye. If the receptive field of a binocular complex cell is measured through one eye and then the other, the two receptive fields turn out to have almost exactly the same position in the visual field, as well as the same orientation and directional selectivity. In other words, what you learn about the cell by stimulating one eye is confirmed by stimulating the other. What is more, if the appropriate stimulation is applied through both eyes simultaneously, a binocular cell usually fires more robustly than if only one eye is stimulated.

Over 50% of the binocular cells in the striate cortex of the monkey display some degree of ocular dominance; that is, they respond more robustly to stimulation of one eye than they do to the same stimulation of the other. In addition, some binocular cells fire best when the preferred stimulus is presented to both eyes at the same time, but in slightly different positions on the two retinas (e.g., Bishop & Pettigrew, 1986). In other words, these cells respond to *retinal disparity*. Presumably, they play a role in the perception of depth (Ohzawa, DeAngelis, & Freeman, 1990).

On the basis of their data, Hubel and Wiesel advanced a *hierarchical model* of the monkey primary visual cortex. In this model, the complexity of the receptive fields of neurons at progressively higher levels of the visual system is attributable to the convergence of input from the preceding level. Specifically, they proposed that neurons with cell bodies in lower layer IV converge on simple cells and that simple cells in turn converge on complex cells.

The primary visual cortex is divided into functionally independent columns of cells. If you advance an electrode vertically through the layers of visual cortex, stopping to plot the receptive fields of many cells along the way, each cell in the column has a receptive field in the same general area of the visual field. The area of the visual field covered by all of the receptive fields of cells in a given column is called the **aggregate field** of that column. Furthermore, all of the cells along a vertical electrode track respond best to straight lines in the same orientation, and those that are monocular or that display ocular dominance are more responsive to stimulation of the same eye. If you advance an electrode horizontally through the tissue, each successive cell that is encountered has a receptive field in a slightly different location and is maximally responsive to straight lines of a slightly different orientation. And during a horizontal electrode pass, the tip passes alternately through areas of left-eye dominance and right-eye dominance. Figure 7.19 illustrates these findings.

Hubel and Wiesel proposed that the primary visual cortex is divided into functionally independent columns, each of which is responsible for analyzing the input from one area of the visual field. They further proposed that each functional cortical column is divided into two, with half being dominated by the right eye and half by the left eye. Input from the eyes has been found to enter lower layer IV independently in alternating patches. The best evidence of this alternating arrangement comes from a study (LeVay, Hubel, & Wiesel, 1975) in which a radioactive amino acid was injected into one eye in sufficient quantities to cross the synapses of the retina-geniculate-striate system and show up in lower layer IV of the primary visual cortex, and to a lesser degree in the layers just above and below it. The alternating patches of radioactivity and nonradioactivity in the autoradiograph in Figure 7.20 indicate alternating patches of input from the two eyes. These patches of input from the two eyes then project vertically to the other layers of the primary visual cortex so that all of those neurons above or below a particular patch that display ocular dominance "prefer" the same eye.

Hubel and Wiesel also proposed that each half of a functional cortical column with the same ocular dominance is subdivided into smaller columns, each with a preference for a particular straight-edge orientation. These subcolumns of orientation specificity were visualized in a study (Hubel, Wiesel, & Stryker, 1977) in which *radioactive 2-DG* was injected into monkeys that then spent 45 minutes viewing a pattern of vertical stripes moving back and forth. As you know from previous chapters, radioactive 2-DG is taken up by active neurons and accumulates in them, thus identifying the location of neurons that are particularly active during the test period. The autoradiograph in Figure 7.21 reveals the columns of cells in the primary visual cortex that were activated by exposure to the moving vertical stripes. Notice that the neurons in the lower portions of layer IV show no orientation specificity; remember, these are X-type cells, which do not respond preferentially to straight-line stimuli.

Figure 7.22 summarizes Hubel and Wiesel's theory of primary-visual-cortex organization.

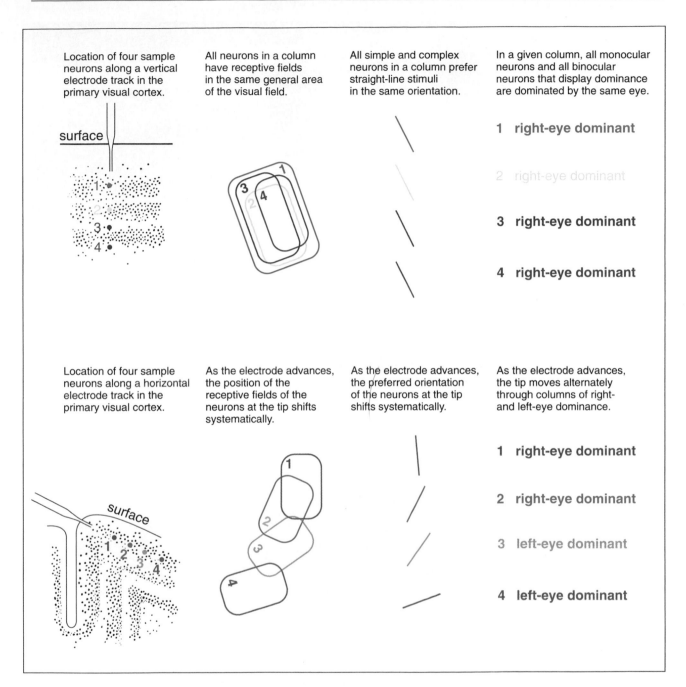

Location of four sample neurons along a vertical electrode track in the primary visual cortex.

All neurons in a column have receptive fields in the same general area of the visual field.

All simple and complex neurons in a column prefer straight-line stimuli in the same orientation.

In a given column, all monocular neurons and all binocular neurons that display dominance are dominated by the same eye.

1 **right-eye dominant**

2 right-eye dominant

3 **right-eye dominant**

4 **right-eye dominant**

Location of four sample neurons along a horizontal electrode track in the primary visual cortex.

As the electrode advances, the position of the receptive fields of the neurons at the tip shifts systematically.

As the electrode advances, the preferred orientation of the neurons at the tip shifts systematically.

As the electrode advances, the tip moves alternately through columns of right- and left-eye dominance.

1 **right-eye dominant**

2 **right-eye dominant**

3 left-eye dominant

4 **left-eye dominant**

FIGURE 7.19

The organization of the primary visual cortex; the receptive-field properties of cells encountered along typical vertical and horizontal electrode tracks in the primary visual cortex.

Spatial-Frequency Theory

Science does not stand still. Hubel and Wiesel barely had time to place their Nobel prizes on their mantel before an important qualification to their theory was proposed. DeValois, DeValois, and their colleagues (see DeValois & De-Valois, 1988) proposed that the visual cortex operates on a code of spatial frequency, not on a code of straight lines and edges as hypothesized by Hubel and Wiesel. In support of the **spatial-frequency theory** is the observation

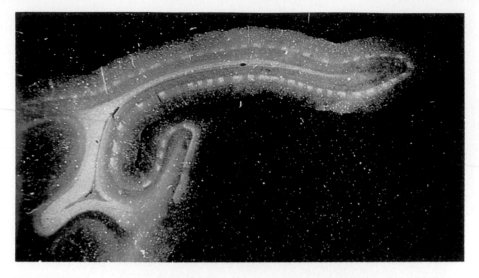

FIGURE 7.20

The alternating input into lower layer IV of the primary visual cortex from the left and right eyes. Radioactive amino acids that were injected into one eye were subsequently revealed on autoradiographs of the visual cortex as patches of radioactivity alternating with patches of nonradioactivity. (*Scientific American*, September 1979)

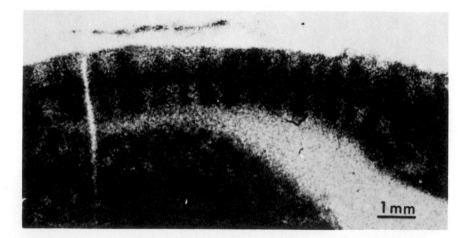

FIGURE 7.21

The columns of orientation specificity in the primary visual cortex of the monkey as revealed by 2-DG autoradiography.

From "Orientation Columns in Macaque Monkey Visual Cortex Demonstrated by the 2-Deoxyglucose Autoradiographic Technique" by D. H. Hubel, T. N. Wiesel, and M. P. Stryker. Reprinted by permission from *Nature*, Vol. 269, page 329. Copyright © 1997 by Macmillan Magazines Ltd.

A block of tissue such as this is assumed to analyze visual signals from one area of the visual field.

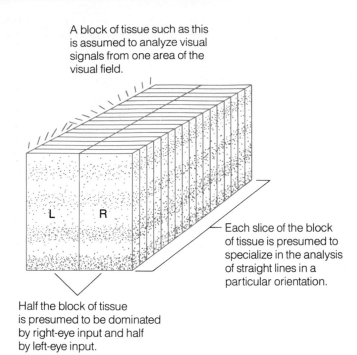

L R

Each slice of the block of tissue is presumed to specialize in the analysis of straight lines in a particular orientation.

Half the block of tissue is presumed to be dominated by right-eye input and half by left-eye input.

FIGURE 7.22

Hubel and Wiesel's model of the organization of functional columns in primary visual cortex.

that visual cortex neurons respond even more robustly to sine-wave gratings that are placed at specific angles in their receptive fields than they do to bars or edges. A **sine-wave grating** is a set of equally spaced, parallel, alternating light and dark stripes that is created by varying the light across the grating in a sine-wave pattern—see Figure 7.23. Sine-wave gratings differ from one another in frequency (the width of their stripes), amplitude (the magnitude of the difference in intensity between the dark and light stripes), and angle.

FIGURE 7.23

A sine-wave grating. (Adapted from DeValois and DeValois, 1988.)

Intensity of light across the gradient

The spatial-frequency theory is based on two physical principles. The first (see Figure 7.24) is that any visual stimulus can be represented by plotting the intensity of light along lines running through it. The second (see Figure 7.25) is that any curve, no matter how irregular, can be broken down into constituent sine waves by a mathematical procedure that is called **Fourier analysis.**

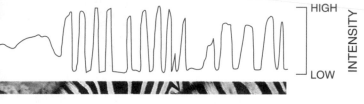

FIGURE 7.24

A visual stimulus can be represented by plotting the changes in the intensity of light along slices running through it. For example, plotted here are the changes in intensity along one slice of a scene that would interest any hungry lion.

FIGURE 7.25

Any wave can be broken down into component sine waves by Fourier analysis. For example, the complex wave at the top is composed of all of the sine waves drawn beneath it. See also Figure 8.10. (Adapted from DeValois and DeValois, 1988.)

The spatial-frequency theory of visual cortex function (see DeValois & De-Valois, 1988) is that each functional module of visual cortex performs a sort of Fourier analysis on the visual pattern in its receptive field; the neurons in each module are thought to respond selectively to various frequencies and orientations of sine-wave gratings. When all of the visual cortex neurons that are influenced by a particular scene respond together, a perception of the scene is created by the summation of its various constituent sine-wave gratings.

The primary support for the spatial-frequency theory is that primary-visual-cortex neurons are more responsive to sine-wave gratings than they are to straight lines. Most neurons in the primary visual cortex respond best when a sine-wave grating of a particular frequency is presented at a particular angle in a particular location of the visual field. However, straight-edge stimuli, which have been used in most studies of visual-cortex neurons, can readily be translated into component sine-wave gratings of the same orientation. Thus, the recent research on spatial-frequency detection by visual neurons extends and complements previous research rather than refuting it.

7.5

Seeing Color

Color is one of the most obvious qualities of human visual experience. So far in this chapter, we have limited our discussion of vision to the so-called **achromatic colors:** black, white, and gray. Black is experienced when there is an absence of light; the perception of white is produced by an intense mixture of a wide range of wavelengths in roughly equal proportion; and the perception of gray is produced by the same mixture at lower intensities. In this section, we deal with the perception of **chromatic colors**—colors such as blue, green, and yellow. The correct term for chromatic colors is *hues,* but in everyday language, they are referred to simply as colors; and for the sake of simplicity, I will do the same.

What is there about a visual stimulus that determines the color that we perceive? To a large degree the perception of an object's color depends on the wavelengths of light that it reflects into the eye. Figure 7.1 is an illustration of the colors that are associated with individual wavelengths; however, outside the laboratory one rarely encounters objects that reflect single wavelengths. Sunlight and most sources of artificial light contain complex mixtures of most visible wavelengths. Most objects absorb the different wavelengths of light that strike them to varying degrees and reflect the rest. It is the mixture of wavelengths that an object reflects that influences our perception of its color.

With the development and refinement of methods for studying the responses of individual receptors and neurons in the visual system, an impressive amount has been learned in the last two or three decades about how the visual system responds to different wavelengths. However, in some ways, it is even more impressive that the basic mechanisms of color vision were derived in the last century by individuals whose research technology was limited to their own ingenuity and observational skills. Through careful observation of the perceptual abilities of their subjects, these behavioral scientists were able to infer some of the major features of the physiological basis of color vision.

You have already encountered in this chapter many instances in which scientific gains have resulted from the convergence of behavioral, neurochemical, and neurophysiological research; however, the early advances in the study of the neural basis of color vision occurred long before it was possible to bring modern neurochemical and neurophysiological procedures to bear.

The **component theory** of color vision—often referred to as the *trichromatic theory*—was proposed by Young in 1802 and refined by Helmholtz in 1852. According to this theory, there are three different kinds of color receptors (cones), each with a different spectral sensitivity, and the color of a particular stimulus is presumed to be encoded by the ratio of activity in the three kinds of receptors. Young and Helmholtz derived their theory from the observation that any color of the visible spectrum can be matched by mixing together three different wavelengths of light in different proportions. This can be accomplished with any three wavelengths, provided that the color of any one of them cannot be matched by mixing the other two. The fact that three is normally the minimum number of different wavelengths necessary to match every color suggested that there were three types of receptors.

Another theory of color vision, the **opponent-process theory,** was proposed by Hering in 1878. He suggested that there are two different classes of cells in the visual system for encoding color, and another one for encoding brightness. Hering hypothesized that each of the three classes of cells encoded two complementary perceptions. One class of color-coding cells signaled red by changing its activity in one direction (e.g., hyperpolarization) and red's complementary color, green, by changing its activity in the other (e.g., hypopolarization). Another class of color-coding cells was hypothesized to signal blue and its complement, yellow, in the same opponent fashion; and a class of brightness-coding cells was hypothesized to similarly signal both black and white. **Complementary colors** are pairs of colors that produce white when combined (e.g., green light and red light).

Hering based his opponent-process theory of color vision on several behavioral observations. One was that the complementary colors blue and yellow, and red and green cannot exist together in the same color; there is no such thing as a yellowish blue or a greenish red. Another was that the afterimage produced by staring at red is green and vice versa, and the afterimage produced by staring at yellow is blue and vice versa.

A somewhat misguided debate raged for many years between supporters of the component (trichromatic) and opponent theories of color vision. I say "misguided" because it was fueled more by the adversarial predispositions of the scientists than by the incompatibility of the two theories. In fact, research subsequently proved that both color-coding mechanisms coexist in the same visual systems (see Hurlbert, 1991).

It was the development in the early 1960s of **microspectrophotometry,** a technique for measuring the absorption spectrum of the photopigment contained in a single cone, that allowed researchers (e.g., Dartnall, Bowmaker, & Mollon, 1983; MacNichol, 1964; Marks, Dobelle, & MacNichol, 1964; Wald, 1964) to confirm the conclusion that had been reached by Young over a century and a half before. They found that there are indeed three different kinds of cones in the retinas of vertebrates with good color vision, and they found that each of the three has a different photopigment with its own characteristic absorption spectrum. As illustrated in Figure 7.27, some cones are maximally sensitive to short wavelengths; some are maximally sensitive to medium

DEMONSTRATION

Have you ever noticed complementary after-images? You can see them by staring at the fixation point on the left of Figure 7.26 for 1 minute under intense illumination without moving your eyes and then quickly shifting your gaze to the fixation point on the right.

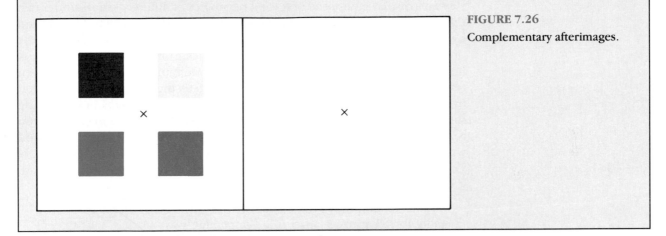

FIGURE 7.26
Complementary afterimages.

wavelengths; and a third class of cones is most sensitive to long wavelengths. The photopigments in these three classes of cones have not yet been isolated, but the genes that control their synthesis have been located (see Nathans, 1989).

Although the coding of color by cones seems to operate on a purely component basis, there is evidence of opponent processing at all subsequent levels of the retina-geniculate-striate system. The first neurophysiological evidence for opponent processing of color came from an electrophysiological study of retinal neurons in the carp, a fish with excellent color vision (Svaetichin, 1956). Neurons in the carp retina respond in one direction (hyperpolarization or depolarization) to red-appearing wavelengths and in the other direction to green-appearing wavelengths. And other retinal cells code blue-appearing and yellow-appearing wavelengths in the same fashion.

Although it is now well established that both component and opponent processing coexist in the visual systems of animals that are capable of perceiving color, neither can account for one of the most important characteristics of color vision: color constancy. **Color constancy** refers to the fact that the perceived color of an object is not a simple function of the wavelengths reflected by it. As I write this at 7:15 on a December morning, it is dark outside, and I am writing by the light of a tiny incandescent desk lamp. Later in the morning, when my students arrive, I turn on my nasty fluorescent office lights. And finally, later in the day as the sun shifts to my side of the building, I turn off my lights and work by natural light. The point of all this is that these different light sources differ substantially in the wavelengths that they contain. As a result, the wavelengths reflected by various objects in my office—my blue shirt, for example—change substantially during the course of the day. The important point is that although the wavelengths reflected by my shirt change markedly, its color does not. My shirt will be just as blue in midmorning and in late

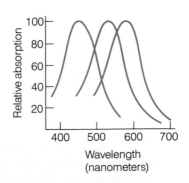

FIGURE 7.27
The absorption spectra of the three classes of cones.

afternoon as it is now. Oh, there may be subtle changes, but for the most part it remains blue. Color constancy is the tendency for an object to stay the same color despite major changes in the wavelengths of light that it reflects.

One of the best demonstrations of the capacity of an object's color to remain constant during major variations in the wavelengths of light reflected by it was devised by Land (1977), inventor of the Polaroid camera. Subjects viewed a display composed of several rectangles of different colors under two different conditions of background illumination. The wavelengths reflected by each part of the multicolored display were carefully measured, and the proportion of different wavelengths in the background illumination was adjusted prior to both viewings so that the wavelengths reflected by the green rectangle during the second viewing were exactly the same as those reflected by the white rectangle during the first. Amazingly, although the light entering the eye from the white rectangle during the first viewing and from the green rectangle during the second was identical, the white rectangle appeared white, and the green appeared green in both cases.

Although the phenomenon of color constancy is counterintuitive, its advantage is obvious.

Imagine the purpose of color as an aid to seeing. Color vision improves the ability to tell surfaces apart in a memorable way, so that nourishment, threats and so on can be learned and reliably recognized. Since color vision supports many more distinctions than monochromatic black-and-white vision, there is surely an advantage to seeing in color. Yet unreliable distinctions are useless. Indeed, they are a hindrance. . . . The ability to recognize things would be lessened if their color changed simply because of a change in the illumination. (Brou, Sciascia, Linden, & Lettvin, 1986, p. 87)

How does the visual system produce constant perceptions of an object's color despite wide variations in the wavelengths that it reflects? Although this question is far from being answered, it is clear that this remarkable ability lies in the perception of contrast between adjacent areas of a visual display. Somehow the visual system compares the wavelengths of lights reflected by adjacent areas of a visual display, and from this information it estimates and discounts variations in background illumination in the perception of an object's color. Support for this idea is provided by the computer-generated visual display of Brou, Sciascia, Linden, and Lettvin (1986)—see Figure 7.28. Please take the time to participate in the following demonstration; it is truly amazing.

DEMONSTRATION

Figure 7.28 demonstrates how color constancy can break down when we look at displays that lack sharply defined areas of contrast. Examine it. It may surprise you to learn that the four differently colored hexagons (six-sided figures) are all emitting exactly the same wavelengths. Although you may have difficulty believing this, you can prove that it is so by eliminating the effect of the adjacent context. Cut four holes in a piece of paper so that the four hexagons, but not the rest of the figure, will be visible through it. Place the sheet of paper over the figure, and compare the four hexagons. Now do you believe me?

This same figure can be used to make another point about color vision. Stare at a point in the center of the figure without moving your eyes,

FIGURE 7.28

The computer-generated display of Brou, Sciascia,
Linden, and Lettvin (1986). (Courtesy of Jerome Y. Lettvin;
photo by Denice Denton and Brad Howland)

and in just a few seconds you will see the hexagons disappear. Eye movements play an important role in the comparison of the wavelengths reflected by different parts of the visual field and
thus in the perception of color. When there are no
sharply defined areas of contrast, this fact becomes more apparent.

If the perception of color depends on the analysis of contrast between
adjacent areas of the visual field, there should be neurons somewhere in the
visual system that are responsive to color contrast. And there are. For example, the so-called **dual-opponent color cells** in the monkey visual cortex respond with vigorous "on" firing when the center of their circular receptive
field is illuminated with one wavelength, such as green, and the surround is
simultaneously illuminated with another wavelength, such as red. And the
same cells display vigorous "off" responding when the pattern of illumination
is reversed; for example, red in the center and green in the surround. In essence, dual-opponent color cells respond to the contrast between the wavelengths reflected by adjacent areas of their receptive field.

FIGURE 7.29

Hubel and Wiesel's model of cortical organization with the position of the peg-like columns that contain dual-opponent color cells. (Adapted from Livingstone & Hubel, 1984.)

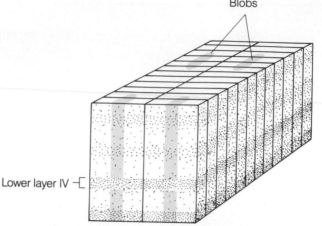

Livingstone and Hubel (1984) have found that these dual-opponent color cells are distributed in the primary visual cortex in peg-like columns that penetrate the layers of the primary visual cortex (one exception is the lower regions of layer IV), as illustrated schematically in Figure 7.29. The neurons in these peg-like columns have particularly high concentrations of **cytochrome oxidase;** thus, their distribution in the primary visual cortex can be visualized by staining slices of tissue with stains that have an affinity for this enzyme. When a section of striate tissue is cut parallel to the cortical layers and stained in this way, the pegs are seen as "blobs" of stain scattered over the cortex (unless the section is from lower layer IV). To the relief of instructors and students alike, the term **blobs** has become the accepted scientific label for *peg-like, cytochrome-oxidase-rich, dual-opponent color columns.*

Conclusion

This chapter began by describing the passage of light into the eye to the receptor layer of the retina. Then it followed the transmission of neural signals from the retinal receptors to the primary visual cortex via the retina-geniculate-striate system. It concluded by discussing those aspects of retina-geniculate-striate system structure and function that influence the perception of edges and color. There were two general themes. The first theme was that vision is a creative process, and numerous examples of the visual system's capacity for creativity were provided: the completion effect, contrast enhancement, and color constancy, to name a few. The second theme was that progress in neuroscience is greatest when a variety of research approaches are brought to bear on the same questions. This theme of converging operations pervades much of this book, but there is no other area of research in the neurosciences in which the convergence of neuroanatomical, neurochemical, neurophysiological, and behavioral research has led to so many important insights.

In this chapter, there were opportunities for you to demonstrate to yourself important principles of visual function. I hope that you took advantage of them, and I hope they had the intended effect of demonstrating to you the amazing abilities of your own visual system and the relevance of what you learned in this chapter to your everyday life.

Food for Thought

1. In vision, as in photography, one frequently has to sacrifice sharpness (acuity) to increase sensitivity. Discuss.

2. Why is it so important to distinguish between intensity and brightness and between wavelength and color?

3. If you mix equal proportions of red and green light, you get white light, or something close to white depending on the exact wavelengths of red and green. However, if you mix equal portions of red and green paint, you get an approximation of black paint. Explain this paradox.

KEY TERMS

To help you study the material in this chapter, all of the key terms—those that have appeared in bold type—are listed and defined here.

Absorption spectrum.   A graph of the ability of a substance to absorb light of different wavelengths.

Accommodation.   Focusing images on the retinas by adjusting the configuration of the lenses.

Achromatic colors.   Black, white, and gray.

Acuity.   Ability to see detail.

Aggregate field.   The area encompassing all of the receptive fields of all of the neurons in a given column of visual cortex.

Amacrine cells.   A layer of retinal cells whose function is lateral communication.

Binocular.   Integrating input from both eyes.

Binocular disparity.   The difference between the retinal image of the same object on the two retinas.

Bipolar cell layer.   The middle layer of the retina.

Blobs.   Cytochrome-oxidase-rich, dual-opponent color columns.

Chromatic colors.   The hues; colors such as blue, green, and yellow.

Ciliary muscles.   The eye muscles that control the lenses.

Color constancy.   The tendency of an object to appear the same color even when the wavelengths that it reflects change.

Complementary colors.   Pairs of colors that produce white when combined in equal measure; every color has a complementary color.

Completion.   Using information obtained from receptors around a blind spot to create a perception of the missing portion of the retinal image; the visual system does this automatically.

Complex cells.   Cells in the visual cortex that respond optimally to straight-edge stimuli in a certain orientation in any part of their receptive field.

Component theory (trichromatic theory).   The theory that the relative amount of activity produced in three different classes of cones by a light determines its perceived color.

Cones.   The visual receptors that mediate high-acuity color vision in good lighting.

Contrast enhancement.   The enhancement of the perception of edges; it is thought to be mediated by lateral inhibition.

Cytochrome oxidase.   An enzyme present in particularly high concentrations in the dual-opponent color cells of the visual cortex.

Dual-opponent color cells.   Neurons that respond to the differences in the wavelengths of light stimulating adjacent areas of their receptive field.

Duplexity theory.   The theory that rods and cones are the receptors for two different systems: one for scotopic conditions (rods) and one for photopic conditions (cones).

Fourier analysis.   A mathematical procedure for breaking down a complex wave form (e.g., an EEG signal) into component sine waves of various frequency.

Fovea.   The central indentation of the retina.

Horizontal cells.   A layer of cells in the retina whose function is lateral communication.

Lateral geniculate nucleus.   The six-layered thalamic structure that receives input from the retina and transmits its output to the primary visual cortex.

Lateral inhibition.   Inhibition of adjacent neurons or receptors in a topographic array.

Lateral plexus.   The lateral neural network that interconnects the visual receptors of the horseshoe crab.

Lower-layer-IV neurons.   The striate cortex neurons that receive signals from lateral geniculate neurons.

Microspectrophotometry.   A technique that has been used to measure the absorption spectrum of the photopigment contained in a single visual receptor.

Monocular.   Processing input from one eye only.

Nasal hemiretina.   The half of each retina next to the nose.

Off-center cells. Cells that respond to lights shone in the center of their receptive fields with "off firing" and to lights shone in the periphery of their fields with "on firing."

Ommatidia. The visual receptors of the horseshoe crab.

On-center cells. Cells that respond to lights shone in the center of their receptive fields with "on firing" and to lights shone in the periphery of their fields with "off firing."

Opponent-process theory. The theory that a receptor or neuron signals one color when it responds in one way (e.g., by increasing its firing rate) and signals its complementary color when it responds in the opposite way (e.g., by decreasing its firing rate).

Optic disk (blind spot). The area on the retina where the axons of retinal ganglion cells penetrate the retina and leave the eye.

Photopic spectral sensitivity curve. The graph of the sensitivity of cone-mediated vision to different wavelengths of light.

Photopic vision. Cone-mediated vision.

Primary visual cortex. The area of the cortex that receives direct input from the lateral geniculate nuclei.

Purkinje effect. In intense light, red and yellow wavelengths look brighter than blue or green wavelengths of equal intensity; in dim light, blue and green wavelengths look brighter than red and yellow wavelengths of equal intensity.

Receptive field. The receptive field of a visual neuron is the area of the visual field within which it is possible for the appropriate visual stimulus to influence the firing of the neuron.

Receptors. Cells that are specialized to receive chemical, mechanical, or radiant signals from the environment.

Retina-geniculate-striate pathway. The large visual pathway from the retina to the primary visual cortex (striate cortex) via the lateral geniculate nuclei of the thalamus.

Retinal ganglion cells. The layer of cells in the retina whose axons leave the eyeball.

Retinotopic. The neural inputs of the system are organized in such a way that they map the retina.

Rhodopsin. The photopigment of rods.

Rods. The visual receptors that mediate achromatic, low-acuity vision under dim light.

Saccades. The rapid movements of the eyes between fixations.

Scotopic vision. Rod-mediated vision.

Scotopic spectral sensitivity curve. The graph of the sensitivity of rod-mediated vision to different wavelengths of light.

Sensitivity. The ability to detect the presence of weak stimuli; more sensitive eyes can detect the presence of weaker lights.

Simple cells. Cells in the visual cortex that respond maximally to straight-edge stimuli in a certain position and orientation.

Sine-wave grating. An array of equally spaced, parallel, alternating dark and light stripes that is created by varying the light across the grating in a sine-wave pattern.

Spatial-frequency theory. The theory that the visual cortex encodes visual patterns in terms of their component sine-wave gratings.

Stabilized retinal image. A retinal image that does not shift across the retina when the eye moves; this can be accomplished by projecting images from a contact-lens-mounted microprojector.

Striate cortex. Primary visual cortex.

Temporal hemiretina. The half of each retina next to the temple.

Transduction. A general term referring to the conversion of one type of energy to another; rods and cones transduce certain wavelengths of radiant energy into neural signals.

X-type cells. Cells with concentric on and off receptive fields.

ADDITIONAL READING

The best introductory readings for those interested in the biopsychology of perception are *Scientific American* articles. Their large color illustrations are without rival. The following six articles provide excellent coverage of topics discussed in this chapter.

Brou, P., Sciascia, T. R., Linden, L., & Lettvin, J. Y. (1986). The colors of things. *Scientific American, 255,* 84–91.

Hubel, D. H., & Wiesel, T. N. (1979). Brain mechanisms of vision. *Scientific American, 241,* 150–162.

Land, E. H. (1977). The retinex theory of color vision. *Scientific American, 237,* 108–128.

Nathans, J. (1989). The genes for color vision. *Scientific American, 260,* 42–49.

Ratliff, F. (1972). Contour and contrast. *Scientific American, 226,* 90–101.

Schnapf, J. L., & Baylor, D. A. (1987). How photoreceptor cells respond to light. *Scientific American, 256,* 40–47.

For those interested in learning more about the spatial-frequency theory of vision, which I could discuss only briefly in this chapter, I recommend the following book. It is a classic.

DeValois, R. L., & DeValois, K. K. (1988). *Spatial vision.* New York: Oxford University Press.

8

Mechanisms of Perception

There are two chapters in this text whose primary focus is sensory. You have just finished the first, Chapter 7, and this is the second. Chapter 7 is a tough act to follow because it showcases the highly successful single-unit approach to the study of vision. It describes how the analysis of individual receptors and neurons in the retina-geniculate-striate system, the major neural pathway between the eye and the cortex, has provided major insights into the neural basis of mammalian vision. To be sure, the single-unit approach has been used to good advantage in the study of other sensory systems and in the study of other parts of the visual system, but the retina-geniculate-striate system has been its most successful arena. No other system in the mammalian brain is as well understood.

This chapter is more general than its predecessor. Rather than focusing on one part of one sensory system, it discusses all five **exteroceptive sensory systems** (the five sensory systems that interpret stimuli from outside the body): vision, touch, hearing, smell, and taste.

8.1

Introductory Concepts

Sensation and Perception

Psychologists frequently find it useful to divide the general process of perceiving into two distinct phases: one called "sensation" and the other called "perception." They use the word **sensation** to refer to the process of detecting the presence of simple stimuli and the word **perception** to refer to the higher-order process of integrating, recognizing, and interpreting complex patterns of sensations. The need for this distinction is most apparent in neuropsychological patients who experience severe perceptual deficits in the absence of sensory dysfunction. Dr. P.,[1] the man who mistook his wife for a hat (Sacks, 1985), is such a patient.

> Dr. P. was a musician of distinction, well-known for many years as a singer . . . and as a teacher. . . . It was obvious within a few seconds of meeting him that there was no trace of dementia [intellectual deterioration] . . . He was a man of great cultivation and charm who talked well and fluently, with imagination and humour. . . .
> "What seems to be the matter?" I asked him at length.
> "Nothing that I know of," he replied with a smile, "but people seem to think that there's something wrong with my eyes."
> "But *you* don't recognise any visual problems?"
> "No, not directly, but I occasionally make mistakes." . . .
> . . . It was while examining his reflexes . . . that the first bizarre experience occurred. I had taken off his left shoe and scratched the sole of his foot with a key—a frivolous-seeming but essential test of a reflex—and then, excusing myself to screw my ophthalmoscope together, left him to put on the shoe himself. To my surprise, a minute later, he had not done this.
> "Can I help?" I asked.
> "Help what? Help whom?" . . .
> "Your shoe," I repeated. "Perhaps you'd put it on."
> He continued to look downwards, though not at the shoe, with an intense but misplaced concentration. Finally his gaze settled on his foot.
> "That is my shoe, yes?" Did I mis-hear? Did he mis-see?
> "My eyes," he explained, and put his hand to his foot. "This is my shoe, no?"
> "No, it is not. That is your foot. *There* is your shoe."
> Was he joking? Was he mad? Was he blind? If this was one of his 'strange mistakes', it was the strangest mistake I had ever come across.
> I helped him on with his shoe (his foot), to avoid further complication. . . . I resumed my examination. His visual acuity was good: he had no difficulty seeing a pin on the floor. . . .
> He saw all right, but what did he see? . . .
> "What is this?" I asked, holding up a glove.
> "May I examine it?" he asked, taking it from me . . .
> "A continuous surface," he announced at last, "infolded on itself. It appears to have"—he hesitated—"five outpouchings, if this is the word."

[1] From *The Man Who Mistook His Wife for a Hat and Other Clinical Tales* (pp. 7–13) by Oliver Sacks, 1985, New York: Summit Books. Copyright © 1970, 1981, 1983, 1984, 1985 by Oliver Sacks. Reprinted by permission of Summit Books, a division of Simon & Schuster, Inc.

"Yes," I said cautiously. "You have given me a description. Now tell me what it is."

"A container of some sort?"

"Yes," I said, "and what would it contain?"

"It would contain its contents!" said Dr. P., with a laugh. "There are many possibilities. It could be a change purse, for example, for coins of five sizes. It could . . . "

. . . "Does it not look familiar? Do you think it might contain, might fit, a part of the body?"

No light of recognition dawned on his face. . . .

I must have looked aghast, but he seemed to think he had done rather well. There was a hint of a smile on his face. He also appeared to have decided the examination was over and started to look around for his hat. He reached out his hand and took hold of his wife's head, tried to lift it off, to put it on. He had apparently mistaken his wife for a hat! His wife looked as if she was used to such things.

Dr. P.'s case illustrates in a most compelling fashion how human brain damage can disrupt specific perceptual abilities while leaving associated capacities of sensation relatively undisturbed.

The Traditional Model of Sensory System Organization

The five exteroceptive sensory systems are thought to be similarly organized. According to the traditional model (see Merzenich & Kaas, 1980), a major pathway from each receptor organ leads to the thalamus, the collection of nuclei that sits on top of the brain stem (see Chapter 3). Each thalamic sensory relay nucleus receives input from one sensory system and relays most of its output to a circumscribed area of the neocortex, the **primary sensory cortex** for that sensory system. Much of the output of each area of primary sensory cortex is in turn transmitted to adjacent cortical areas, the **secondary sensory cortex** for that system. The ultimate destinations of sensory input, according to the traditional model, are the ill-defined and poorly understood areas of cortical tissue that are referred to collectively as association cortex. **Association cortex** is assumed to relate the activities of the various sensory systems, to translate sensory input into programs for motor output, and to mediate complex cognitive activities such as thinking and remembering. Figure 8.1 is a schematic diagram of this traditional model.

The Hierarchical Organization of Sensory Systems

A *hierarchy* is a system whose members can be assigned to specific levels or ranks with respect to one another. In this chapter, you have already encountered two ways in which sensory systems are hierarchically organized. First, you learned how neuropsychologists have found it useful to regard various aspects of sensory function as falling into one of two categories, sensation or perception, which differ in their level of complexity. And then you learned how the traditional model of sensory system organization involves a flow of information from receptors into progressively higher and more complex areas of the brain. Implicit in both of these hierarchical schemes is the idea that the

FIGURE 8.1

The traditional model of sensory system organization. Only three sensory systems are illustrated.

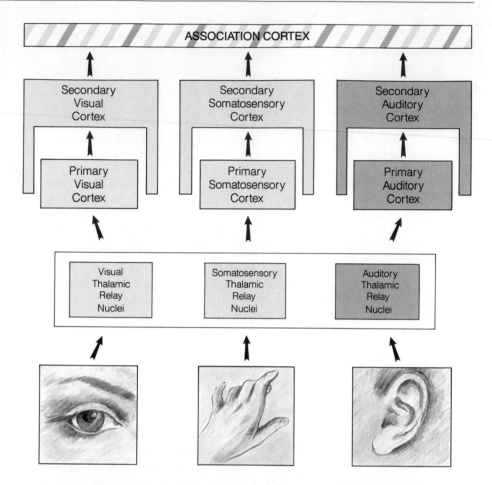

two hierarchies are closely related. It is widely held that structures at progressively "higher" levels of a sensory system play a role that is less and less sensory and more and more perceptual. The idea is that each level of the system analyzes the input from the preceding level, and in so doing, adds to the complexity of the analysis. Although it is not possible to specify a clear dividing line between sensation and perception, many adhere to the convention that sensation is subcortical and perception is cortical.

8.2

Cortical Mechanisms of Vision

The analysis of the visual system in Chapter 7 ended at the level of the primary visual (striate) cortex, but the primary visual cortex is not the ultimate destination of visual information. It is the port of entry of visual information into the complex analytic circuitry of the cortex (see Kaas & Garraghty, 1991). Chapter 7 has delivered you to the threshold of the cortex; Chapter 8 leads you across that threshold.

Neurological patients with suspected damage to the visual cortex are frequently given a test called **perimetry.** The patient's head is held motionless on a chin rest as she or he stares with one eye at a fixation point on a screen. A small dot of light is then flashed on various parts of the screen, and the patient presses a button to record when the dot is in view. Then, the entire process is repeated for the other eye. The result is a map of the visual field of each eye, which indicates any area of blindness. You may recall from Chapter 7 that we all have a blind spot in each eye.

Damage to the primary visual cortex in one hemisphere produces a **scotoma** (i.e., an area of blindness) in the contralateral visual field (see Figure 7.13). A scotoma that was produced by a bullet wound to the left primary visual cortex is illustrated in Figure 8.2. Notice that the area at the center of the field of vision has been spared. This is a common occurrence with visual-cortex damage. It is called **macular sparing**—the macula is the central part of the retina (including the fovea) that has a yellowish pigment.

Blindsight: Seeing Without Seeing

Patients who have lost all of their primary visual cortex report being totally blind—which is not surprising. It is surprising, however, that some of these *cortically blind* patients can perform visually guided tasks, such as grabbing

FIGURE 8.2

The perimetric maps of a subject with a bullet wound to the left primary visual cortex. The areas of blindness are indicated in blue. (Adapted from Teuber, Battersby, & Bender, 1960.)

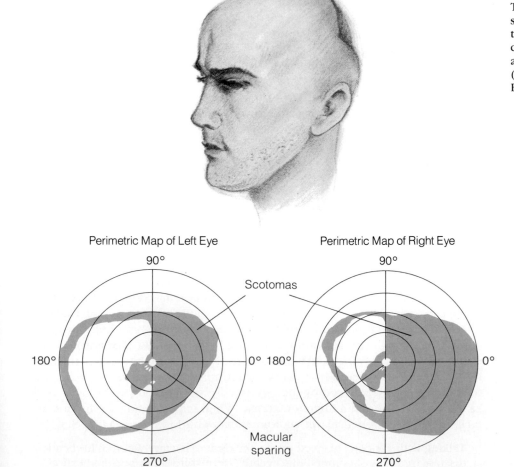

a moving object or indicating its direction of movement, all the while claiming to see nothing. It is this ability of cortically blind subjects to perform visually mediated tasks without conscious awareness that is known as **blindsight** (see Carey, Goodale, & Sprowl, 1990; Corbetta, Marzi, Tassinari, & Aglioti, 1990; Cowey & Stoerig, 1991). If blindsight confuses you, imagine how it confuses people who experience it. Consider, for example, the reactions to blindsight of D.B., a patient who was blind in his left visual field following surgical removal of his right occipital lobe (Weiskrantz, Warrington, Sanders, & Marshall 1974).

> Even though the patient had no awareness of "seeing" in his blind [left] field, evidence was obtained that (a) he could reach for visual stimuli [in his left field] with considerable accuracy; (b) could differentiate the orientation of a vertical line from a horizontal or diagonal line; (c) could differentiate the letters "X" and "O". These tasks could be performed accurately only if the stimuli were larger than a critical size. (p. 726)
>
> Needless to say, he was questioned repeatedly about his vision in his left half-field, and his most common response was that he saw nothing at all. . . . When he was shown his results he expressed surprise and insisted several times that he thought he was just "guessing." When he was shown a video film of his reaching and judging orientation of lines, he was openly astonished. (p. 721)

In view of the fact that visual information is conducted over several pathways, it is not surprising that some visual capacities could survive destruction of the primary visual cortex. In this respect, most interest has been directed at a pathway that goes from each retina to the *superior colliculi* of the midbrain, then to the *pulvinar nuclei* of the thalamus, and from there directly to areas of the secondary visual cortex, thus bypassing the primary visual cortex. One theory is that the retina-geniculate-striate system mediates pattern and color vision, whereas the **collicular-pulvinar pathway** plays a role in the detection and localization of objects in space (Rafal, Smith, Krantz, Cohen, & Brennan, 1990; Schneider, 1969). However, this theory has not stood up well to experimental tests (Goodale, 1983; Mlinar & Goodale, 1984).

Completion of Scotomas

Many patients with extensive scotomas are unaware of their deficits. One of the factors that contributes to this lack of awareness of scotomas is the phenomenon of **completion** (see Chapter 7). When patients with scotomas look at a complex figure, part of which lies in their scotoma, they often report seeing a complete figure. In some cases, this completion may depend on residual visual capacities in the scotoma; however, completion also occurs in cases in which this explanation can be ruled out. For example, some **hemianopsic** patients (patients with a scotoma covering half their field of vision) see an entire face when they focus on a person's nose, even when the side of the face in the scotoma is covered by a blank card. Consider the interesting example of completion experienced by the esteemed physiological psychologist Karl Lashley (1941) during a migraine attack. When experiencing a migraine attack, Lashley developed a large scotoma next to his fovea (see Figure 8.3).

> Talking with a friend I glanced just to the right of his face wherein his head disappeared. His shoulders and necktie were still visible but the vertical

Lashley's Scotoma   What Lashley saw.

FIGURE 8.3
The completion of a
migraine-produced scotoma
as described by Karl Lashley.

stripes on the wallpaper behind him seemed to extend down to the necktie. It was impossible to see this as a blank area when projected on the striped wallpaper of uniformly patterned surface although any intervening object failed to be seen.

Secondary and Association Cortex of the Visual System

Virtually all of the occipital lobe and large portions of the temporal and parietal lobe are involved in human vision—see Figure 8.4. There are two large areas that are considered to be *secondary visual cortex* for two reasons: because they receive major projections from the primary visual cortex and from several other structures lower in the visual hierarchy (e.g., from the thalamus), and because they seem to be involved in a "higher" level of visual analysis than is the primary visual cortex. These two areas of secondary visual cortex are the **prestriate cortex** (also called the *peristriate cortex*), the band of tissue in the occipital lobe that almost totally surrounds the primary visual cortex, and the **inferotemporal cortex,** the cortex of the inferior temporal lobe. In contrast, the **posterior parietal cortex** is considered to be *association cortex* because, in addition to its input from primary and secondary visual cortices, it receives major input from auditory cortex and somatosensory cortex.

It has been hypothesized that information flows out of primary visual cortex along two major pathways (Ungerleider & Mishkin, 1982). One leads to inferotemporal cortex via prestriate cortex and is crucial for object recognition; the other leads to posterior parietal cortex via prestriate cortex and is crucial for the perception of movement and spatial location—see Desimone and Ungerleider (1989). Most of the support for this theory has come from studies of the visual abilities of monkeys with posterior parietal and inferotemporal lesions. For example, Pohl (1973) found that posterior parietal lesions in monkeys produced a severe deficit on a test of visuospatial ability, but did not disrupt their ability to recognize objects, whereas lesions of the inferotemporal cortex had the opposite pattern of effects. Because the symptoms of parietal dysfunction include misreaching in the dark and difficulties

FIGURE 8.4

The visual areas of human
neocotex.

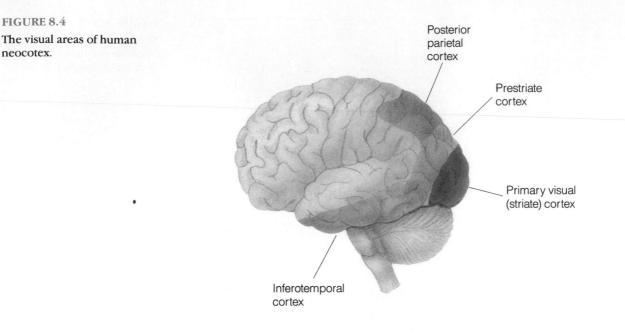

in localizing both tactile and auditory stimuli (e.g., Ridley & Ettlinger, 1975), it seems that the posterior parietal cortex plays a role in the location of objects in space irrespective of the sensory modality through which they are perceived. Baizer, Ungerleider, and Desimone (1991) injected different fluorescent dyes into the inferotemporal and posterior parietal cortices of monkeys. These dyes were absorbed by buttons in the area and transported back to the cell bodies, thus revealing the location of neurons whose axons project into inferotemporal and posterior parietal cortex. Neurons in areas of prestriate cortex known to be responsive to visual form and color were found to project into inferotemporal cortex; neurons in areas of prestriate cortex known to be responsive to spatial location and movement were found to project into posterior parietal cortex.

Single-unit recording studies in monkeys indicate that inferotemporal, prestriate, and posterior parietal areas are each composed of several discrete areas, each of which is a complete map of the retina. Each area is composed of neurons that are preferentially sensitive to a particular aspect of the visual world (see Schiller, 1986). In monkeys, there are at least 20 such areas, each of which receives either direct or indirect input from primary visual cortex. Each independent area is thought to perform a different analysis of the visual image, and visual perception is believed to be a product of their combined activity (Desimone & Ungerleider, 1989).

Zeki and his colleagues (1991) recently provided evidence of multiple areas of specialization in human visual cortex. They injected a radioactive marker into the blood of human subjects, and then they used *positron emission tomography* (PET) to reveal those areas of visual cortex that became active while the subjects viewed colored or moving visual displays—more blood flows into active areas of the brain. When a stationary uncolored stimulus was viewed, certain areas of the striate and prestriate cortex became active. When the uncolored stimulus was presented in color, activity increased in an area of

An area of human prestriate cortex that was activated by viewing colored, but not gray, images.

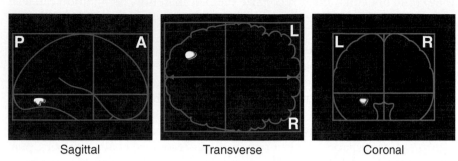

Sagittal　　　　　Transverse　　　　　Coronal

An area of human prestriate cortex that was activated by viewing moving, but not stationary, images.

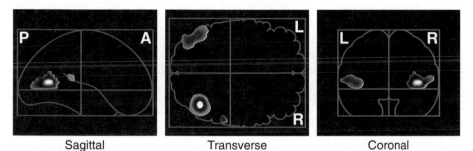

Sagittal　　　　　Transverse　　　　　Coronal

FIGURE 8.5

An area of human visual cortex that responds selectively to color and one that responds selectively to motion. (Adapted from Zeki et al., 1991.)

prestriate cortex that is part of the inferotemporal pathway. When the uncolored stimulus was presented in motion, activity increased in an area of prestriate cortex that is part of the posterior parietal pathway—see Figure 8.5.

Prosopagnosia

Agnosia is a failure of recognition (from the Greek *gnosis* meaning *to know*) that is not attributable to sensory, verbal, or intellectual impairment. Most cases of agnosia are specific to a particular sensory system; the patient cannot recognize material when it is presented in one sensory modality, but can when it is presented in another. **Visual agnosia** is commonly classified according to the specific category of visual material that cannot be recognized: *prosopagnosia, object agnosia,* and *color agnosia* refer to difficulty in recognizing faces, objects, and colors, respectively.

Prosopagnosia, like other forms of agnosia, is extremely rare, but it has generated considerable interest because of its theoretical implications (see Damasio, Tranel, & Damasio, 1990). Patients with prosopagnosia have difficulty telling one human face from another; in severe cases they cannot recognize their own face in a mirror. However, they almost never have difficulty recognizing faces as faces or in identifying individual components of a face (e.g., noses, eyes, ears). Tranel and Damasio (1985) reported the cases of two prosopagnosics who reliably displayed large electrodermal *skin conductance* *responses* (see Chapter 5) to pictures of familiar faces, despite the fact that they could not consciously recognize them. Apparently, recognition can take place in prosopagnosics at a level of the nervous system that does not involve conscious awareness.

It is believed by some that prosopagnosia results from damage to an area of visual cortex that is specifically dedicated to the recognition of faces. The main evidence for this view is that patients who have difficulty recognizing faces have little difficulty recognizing other test objects (e.g., a chair, a pencil, or a door). Stop reading for a moment and give this line of evidence some thought. It is seriously flawed. Because prosopagnosics have no difficulty recognizing faces as faces, the fact that they can recognize chairs as chairs, pencils as pencils, and doors as doors is not relevant. The critical question is whether or not they can recognize which chair, which pencil, and which door. Two clinical cases have a bearing on this point: in one case, a farmer lost his ability to recognize particular cows when he became prosopagnosic; in the other, a bird watcher lost his ability to distinguish between species of birds when he became prosopagnosic. These two cases demonstrate that the perceptual difficulties of at least some prosopagnosics are not restricted to faces; their problem appears to be one of distinguishing visually similar members of complex classes of visual stimuli (Damasio, 1990; Damasio, Damasio, & Van Hoesen, 1982).

In a few cases, it has been possible to subject the brains of deceased prosopagnosics to histological scrutiny (e.g., Damasio, 1985; Meadows, 1974). In most cases, bilateral damage to the inferior prestriate area and the adjoining portions of the inferotemporal cortex has been found. Consistent with this observation is the discovery of neurons in the inferotemporal cortex of monkeys (Hasselmo, Rolls, Baylis, & Nalwa, 1989; Rolls, 1985) and sheep (Kendrick & Baldwin, 1987) that respond selectively to faces. Figure 8.6 summarizes the responses that were recorded from such a neuron in the inferotemporal cortex of a monkey before, during, and after the presentation of various stimuli (Gross, Desimone, Albright, & Schwarz, 1985).

FIGURE 8.6

The firing rate of a monkey inferotemporal neuron before, during, and after the presentation of monkey faces at different angles. The profile view (100°) was most effective in increasing the firing rate of this cell. (Adapted from Gross et al., 1985.)

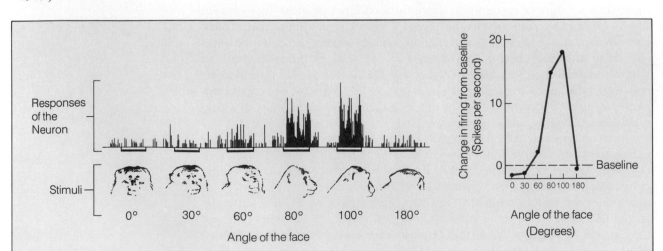

Perception of Subjective Contours

Do you recall the theme of the preceding chapter: that our visual perceptions are often better than physical reality? Figure 8.7 illustrates this point (see Spillman & Werner, 1990). It illustrates that we often see visual contours where none exist. Nonexistent visual contours that are seen are called **subjective contours.**

Some theories of perception regard subjective contours as products of cognition. They assume that subjects try to make sense of ambiguous stimuli by considering various possibilities and settling on the most simple. However, the perception of subjective contours is more automatic than this. Prestriate neurons, which are relatively low in the visual-system hierarchy, respond to subjective contours (Peterhans & von der Heydt, 1991)—see Figure 8.8. Neurons lower in the visual-system hierarchy do not.

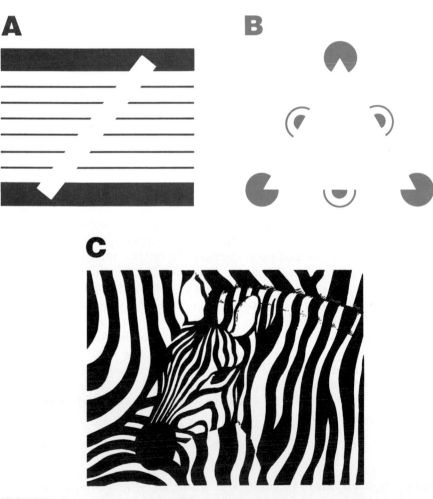

FIGURE 8.7

Subjective contours. The white bar in A and the white triangle in B do not physically exist. The ability of your visual system to see contours that do not exist help you "see" boundaries between objects of similar brightness, color, and pattern; see C.

FIGURE 8.8

Neurons of the monkey prestriate cortex, but not those of the striate cortex, respond to subjective contours of a particular orientation. (Adapted from Peterhans & von der Heydt, 1991.)

A prestriate cell fires in response to a 45° stimulus line moving across its receptive field.

The same cell fires in response to a 45° subjective contour moving across its field in the same direction.

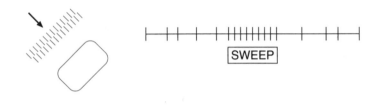

8.3

Audition

The next time that you enter a concert hall, take note of the complex feats performed by your auditory system. Notice its amazing ability to perceive dozens of different sounds at the same time—the musicians tuning their instruments, the chatter of the audience, the rustle of clothes, the clatter of seats—and its even more amazing ability to keep all of these channels of sound separate. Notice too that after the music has driven all other sounds from your conscious experience, the whisper of your name by a friend immediately gains access to your consciousness. Somehow your auditory system can block from consciousness all stimuli except those of a particular kind, while unconsciously monitoring the blocked-out sounds just in case something comes up that requires attention. This adaptive capacity of your auditory system is referred to as the **cocktail-party phenomenon** after your ability to "focus in on" specific conversations at a cocktail party, while unconsciously monitoring other conversations for a piece of interesting gossip.

Sound

Sounds are vibrations of the molecules in the air. Humans hear only those molecular vibrations between about 20 and 20,000 Hz (*Hertz* or cycles per second). These vibrations travel through the air at about 1,238 kilometers (743 miles) per hour—the so-called sound barrier. Figure 8.9 illustrates the relation between the physical dimensions of sound and our perceptions of them. The perceived *loudness, pitch,* and *timbre* of a sound are related to the

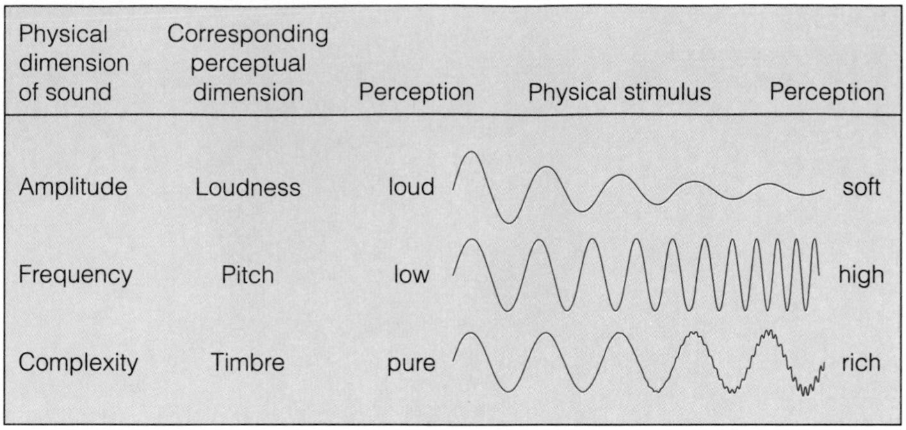

Physical dimension of sound	Corresponding perceptual dimension	Perception	Physical stimulus	Perception
Amplitude	Loudness	loud		soft
Frequency	Pitch	low		high
Complexity	Timbre	pure		rich

FIGURE 8.9

The relation between the physical and perceptual dimensions of sound.

amplitude, frequency, and *complexity* of the vibrations, respectively. Most research is done with pure tones—that is, with sine wave stimuli—but in real life, each sound is a combination of many different sine waves, and it is the particular combination of waves that gives each sound its characteristic quality or **timbre.** Figure 8.10 illustrates the characteristic complex waveform of sounds produced by a clarinet and how such a complex sound is the sum of a variety of different sine waves.

The Ear

Figure 8.11 illustrates how sounds make their way through the *outer, middle,* and *inner ear* and ultimately activate receptors. Sound waves travel down the *auditory canal* and cause the **tympanic membrane** (eardrum) to vibrate. These vibrations are then transferred to the three **ossicles** (small bones) of the middle ear: the *malleus* (the hammer), the *incus* (the anvil), and the *stapes* (the stirrup). The vibrations of the stapes trigger vibrations of a membrane, called the **oval window,** which in turn transfers vibrations to the fluid of the **cochlea** (from *kokhlos,* meaning *land snail*). The cochlea is a long,

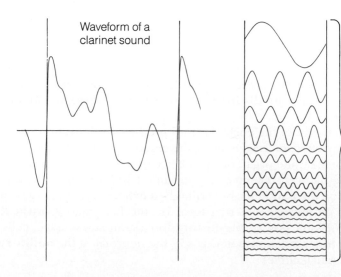

Waveform of a clarinet sound

When added together, these sine waves produce the clarinet sound plotted on the left.

FIGURE 8.10

A complex sound wave that was produced by a clarinet, and its component sine waves. (Adapted from Stereo Review, 1977.)

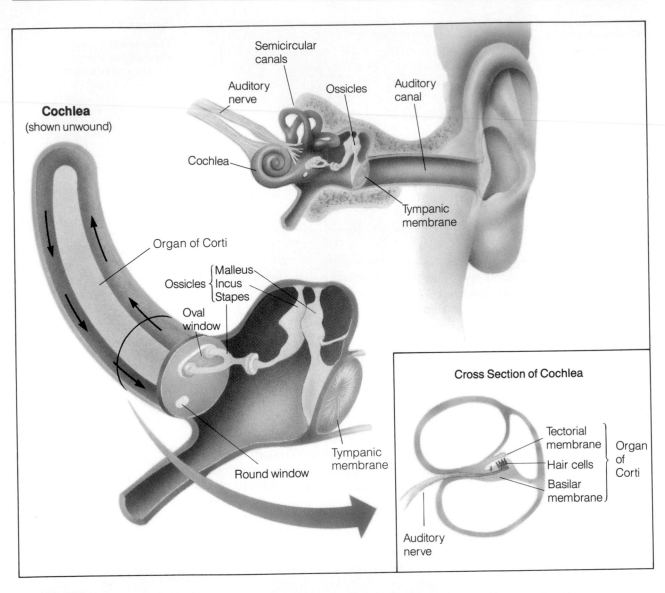

FIGURE 8.11
Anatomy of the ear.

coiled tube with a membranous structure running down its center almost to its tip. This internal membrane contains the auditory receptor organ, the **organ of Corti.** The vibrations of the oval window produce pressure changes in the cochlear fluid, which are dissipated by an elastic cochlear membrane, the **round window.**

Each pressure change in the cochlear fluid produces a deflection of the organ of Corti. Each deflection travels along the organ of Corti as a wave. As is illustrated in Figure 8.11, the organ of Corti is composed of a **basilar membrane** in which the hair-cell receptors are mounted and a **tectorial membrane,** which rests on the **hair cells.** Accordingly, a deflection of the organ of Corti at any point produces a shearing force on the hair cells (Corwin & Warchol, 1991) at the same point. This shearing force stimulates the hair cells, and in so doing, it triggers action potentials in the neurons of the **auditory nerve** (the eighth cranial nerve).

Also illustrated in Figure 8.11 are the **semicircular canals,** which are the receptive organs of the vestibular system. The **vestibular system** carries information about the direction and intensity of head movements, and it helps us maintain our balance through its output to the motor system. The vestibular system is an **interoceptive sensory system,** in contrast to the **exteroceptive sensory systems,** which are the focus of this chapter.

The most important principle of cochlear function is that different frequencies produce maximal stimulation of hair cells at different points along the basilar membrane; higher frequencies produce greater activation closer to the windows. Thus, sounds of different frequency activate different hair cells, and the signals thus created are carried out of the ear and into the brain by different neurons. Most other structures of the auditory system are organized according to this principle. In the same way that the organization of the visual system is **retinotopic,** the auditory system is **tonotopic;** the neurons composing most auditory structures are arrayed on the basis of the frequencies to which they are particularly responsive.

From the Ear to the Primary Auditory Cortex

There is no single major auditory pathway to the cortex comparable to the retina-geniculate-striate pathway of the visual system. Instead, there is a complex network of auditory pathways—Figure 8.12 illustrates some of them. Notice that signals from each ear are transmitted to both the ipsilateral and contralateral auditory cortex over several different routes. The axons of the *auditory nerve* synapse in the ipsilateral *cochlear nuclei,* from which many projections lead to the *superior olivary nuclei* (the superior olives) at the same level. The axons of the olivary neurons project via the *lateral lemniscus* tract to the *inferior colliculi,* where they synapse on neurons that project to the *medial geniculate nuclei* of the thalamus, which in turn project to the auditory cortex.

In humans, much of the primary auditory cortex and the adjacent areas of secondary auditory cortex are in the depths of the *lateral fissure* (see Figure 8.13)—the "armpit" of the brain. Although the auditory cortex is generally thought of as a temporal-lobe structure, the various areas of secondary auditory cortex—each a separate tonotopic map—extend into the parietal cortex. Cats are widely used to study the auditory cortex because most of their auditory cortex is readily accessible on the surface of the temporal lobes. Caution must be exercised in drawing inferences about the auditory cortex of humans, a species with highly developed language abilities, from the study of a species without these abilities (see Dooling & Hulse, 1989). In most humans, language abilities are controlled primarily from the left hemisphere, and much of the left auditory cortex appears to be specialized for speech analysis. Chapter 16 focuses on this important topic.

Tonotopic Organization of the Primary Auditory Cortex

The theory that the auditory cortex is tonotopically organized is an old one. In 1960, Woolsey wrote an influential review of research on the topic. He concluded, as others had done before him, that the anterior portions of the primary auditory cortex responded to high-frequency tones and that more

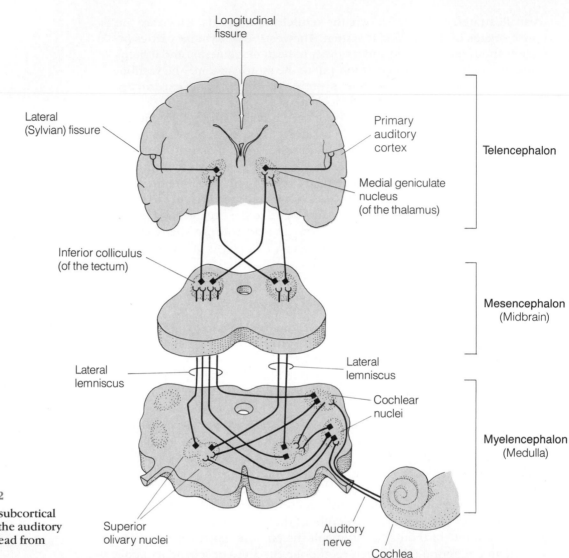

FIGURE 8.12

Some of the subcortical pathways of the auditory system that lead from one ear.

posterior portions responded to progressively lower frequencies. And he proposed that areas of secondary auditory cortex were organized in a similar way. Soon there were several attempts to test this theory by recording the responses of single neurons in auditory cortex of cats to pure tones. Although these unit-recording experiments generally confirmed the anterior-to-posterior high-to-low-frequency organization that had been suggested by previous studies, they did not support the idea that the organization is strictly tonotopic. In various subjects, the neurons in a particular area of auditory cortex (as defined by surrounding sulci) responded to a wide range of frequencies.

In 1975, Merzenich, Knight, and Roth explained the inconsistency of the existing unit-recording data. Using improved procedures, Merzenich and his colleagues were able to record from many more neurons in each cat than had previously been possible. Consequently, they were able to develop tonotopic

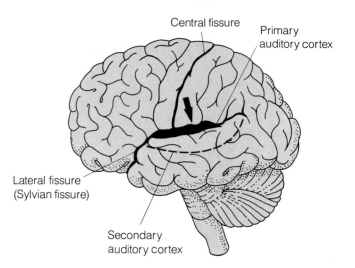

FIGURE 8.13

Location of auditory cortex in the human brain. The arrow indicates that most of the auditory cortex is hidden in the depths of the Sylvian fissure.

maps for individual cats, rather than combining data from different subjects into a single map, as previous investigators had done. This approach enabled them to make two important observations. First, they found that the primary auditory cortex of each cat was strictly tonotopic (see Figure 8.14), with each cell in a given column of cortex responding best to the same frequencies. Second, they found that the exact position of the primary auditory cortex in relation to the surrounding sulci varied considerably from cat to cat. Thus, if one combined all of the data recorded from different subjects to produce a map of the average tonotopic layout, what one obtained was a "fuzzy picture" of the strictly organized tonotopic maps of individual subjects. I hope that you do not forget this lesson. Remember that although the cortices of the members of the same species operate according to the same principles, there are differences among individual members that can obscure these principles when data from different subjects are averaged.

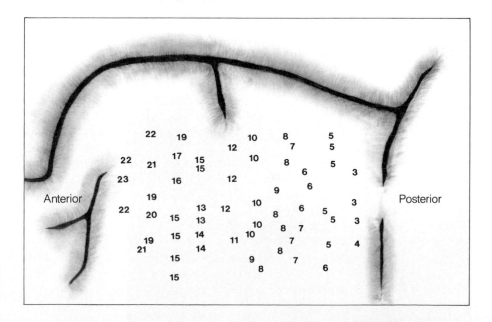

FIGURE 8.14

The tonotopic organization of an area of cat primary auditory cortex. Each number illustrates the frequency in *kilohertz* (thousands of cycles per second) to which the neurons at that site were most responsive. Notice the systematic anterior-to-posterior high-to-low-frequency gradient. (Adapted from Merzenich et al., 1974.)

Sound Localization

Localization of sounds in space is mediated by both the lateral and medial superior olives, but in different ways. When a sound originates to our left, it reaches the left ear first, and it is louder at the left ear than at the right ear. Some neurons in the *medial superior olives* are sensitive to slight differences in the time of arrival of signals from the two ears. In contrast, some neurons in the *lateral superior olives* are sensitive to slight differences in the amplitude of sounds from the two ears (see Heffner & Masterton, 1990). In the mammal, the medial and lateral superior olives project to the *superior colliculus.* Those layers of the superior colliculus that receive auditory input from the superior olives are laid out according to a map of auditory space (see King & Moore, 1991)—an exception to the usual tonotopic organization. Because you localize sound on the basis of differences in the intensity and timing of sounds at the two ears, it is impossible to tell whether a sharp sound exactly equidistant from your two ears is in front of you, behind you, or above you.

The comparative approach has led many researchers who are interested in sound localization to study the *barn owl.* You see, the barn owl can locate sounds in space better than any other animal whose hearing has been tested. The barn owl is a nocturnal hunter, and it must be able to locate field mice solely by the rustling sounds that they make in the dark.

The most striking anatomical feature of the barn owl is its facial ruff (see Figure 8.15), which is an effective reflector of high-frequency sounds and which accounts, in part, for its remarkable sound-localizing ability. Barn owls locate sounds in the horizontal dimension by comparing the loudness of sounds at the two ears. The ability to locate sounds in the vertical dimension

FIGURE 8.15

A barn owl. Its facial ruff is an important component of an auditory system that allows it to catch mice and other small prey in total darkness.

is not important for most land-dwelling animals, but it is critical for barn owls because they hunt from the air. The facial ruff is the key to the ability of barn owls to locate sounds in the vertical dimension. The barn owl's right ear is more sensitive to sounds above the horizontal plane because the ruff on the right is directed slightly upward; the left ear is more sensitive to sounds below the horizontal plane because the ruff on the left is directed slightly downward. This vertical difference is greater for higher frequencies because the ruff reflects higher frequencies more effectively. Accordingly, in order to locate sounds in the vertical dimension, the barn owl's auditory system must compare the intensities detected at each ear for each frequency. Barn owls cannot locate single-frequency sounds in vertical space, and they cannot locate complex sounds in vertical space if their ruffs have been shaved off (Knudsen, 1981).

Effects of Damage to Auditory Cortex

Because the human auditory cortex is ensconced in the lateral fissure, it is not frequently damaged. When it is, the damage to it is often incomplete, and there is inevitably damage to surrounding tissue. That is why efforts to understand the effects of auditory cortex damage have relied heavily on comparative research (see Berkley & Stebbins, 1990; Phillips, 1989).

You might think that complete bilateral lesions of the auditory cortex would inevitably produce deafness. Remarkably, complete bilateral lesions of primary auditory cortex produce few, if any, permanent deficits in the ability of many laboratory species to detect the presence of pure tones (e.g., Kavanagh & Kelly, 1988). Even bilateral cortical lesions that include both primary and secondary auditory cortex produce little permanent hearing loss in most species. There is, however, one well-documented exception; monkeys experience a profound hearing loss following bilateral lesions of primary and secondary auditory cortex (Heffner & Heffner, 1990). The same is likely true of humans.

The ability to localize brief sounds is disrupted by auditory cortex lesions in most mammals—rats are the one proven exception (Kelly, 1980). For example, Heffner and Heffner (1988) found that monkeys with bilateral auditory cortex lesions could not discriminate between two sounds at different locations in the same *hemifield* (left or right), but they could discriminate between a left sound and a right sound. Kavanagh and Kelly (1987) found that ferrets with unilateral auditory cortex lesions could not locate sounds in the contralateral hemifield. There is some evidence that humans with large auditory cortex lesions that extend into the parietal lobe have similar difficulties, particularly when the lesions are on the right side (de Renzi, 1982).

Word deafness   In humans, the most interesting consequence of bilateral auditory cortex damage is word deafness. **Word deafness** is a difficulty in the perception of speech that occurs in the absence of deficits in the ability to detect individual sounds. Word deafness is often the final stage of recovery from a more global disorder. For example, following bilateral damage to the auditory cortex, a patient may be temporarily deaf; then, in the ensuing weeks, her or his ability to detect individual sounds may recover, leaving permanent word deafness. Word deaf patients describe speech sounds as "buzzes" or "static" or "noise" (Phillips, 1989).

Heffner and Heffner (1989) observed a syndrome in monkeys that bears a striking similarity to human word deafness. Following bilateral auditory cortex lesions, monkeys had great difficulty detecting sounds, but this ability recovered substantially over the ensuing weeks. However, monkeys with bilateral lesions never regained their ability to discriminate among various conspecific vocalizations. Unilateral left-hemisphere lesions of the auditory cortex produced transient deficits in the discrimination of conspecific sounds; unilateral right-hemisphere lesions did not.

The results of several studies of word-deaf patients indicate that their perceptual deficits are not restricted to linguistic sounds (e.g., Auerbach, Allard, Naeser, Alexander, & Albert, 1982; Yaqub, Gascon, Al-Nosha, & Whitaker, 1988). Word-deaf patients had considerable difficulty identifying brief sounds of all kinds, and they had difficulty judging the temporal order of sounds that were presented in rapid succession. Thus, it seems that word deafness is the most obvious and debilitating manifestation of a more global auditory temporal-processing disorder.

8.4

Somatosensation: Touch and Pain

Somatosensation is a general term that refers to sensations of the body. Although it is common to think of the somatosensory system as a single system, it is most appropriately viewed as three separate, but interacting, systems: (1) an *exteroceptive system,* which senses external stimuli that are applied to the skin; (2) a *proprioceptive system,* which monitors information about the position of the body that comes from receptors in the muscles, joints, and organs of balance; and (3) an *interoceptive system,* which provides general information about conditions within the body (e.g., temperature, blood pressure). This discussion deals almost exclusively with the exteroceptive (touch) system. Just as the touch system is only one component of the somatosensory trio, it too comprises three somewhat distinct systems (cf. Dykes, 1983): systems for perceiving *mechanical stimuli* (touch), *thermal stimuli* (hot and cold), and *nociceptive stimuli* (pain).

Cutaneous Receptors and Peripheral Pathways

There is considerable disagreement concerning the number, nature, and function of receptors in the skin. One view is that there are six kinds of receptors in the skin (see Figure 8.16). **Glabrous** or hairless skin, such as that on the palms of your hands, is thought to contain four kinds of receptors. Two of these are rapidly adapting and thus respond only briefly to changes in tactile stimulation: the **Pacinian corpuscle,** the largest and most deeply positioned cutaneous receptor, and the **Meissner corpuscle,** which is located just beneath the outermost layer of skin (the *epidermis*). In contrast, the **Merkel receptor** and the **Ruffini corpuscle** respond continuously to long, unchanging tactile stimuli. Like glabrous skin, hairy skin has Pacinian corpuscles, Ruffini corpuscles, and Merkel receptors, but instead of the rapidly adapting Meissner corpuscles, it has rapidly adapting **hair receptors** near the base of each hair.

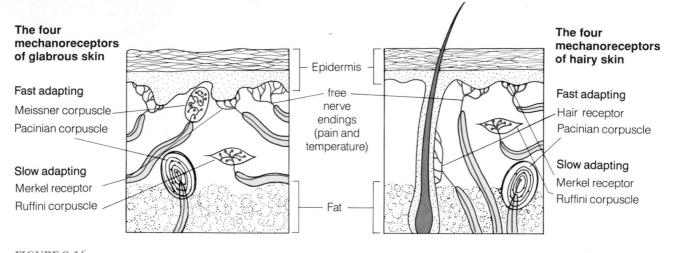

FIGURE 8.16

The six major cutaneous receptors.

To appreciate the functional significance of the fast and slowly adapting cutaneous receptors, consider what happens in response to a long-lasting skin indentation of constant pressure. Such a stimulus initially evokes a burst of firing in all receptors, which evokes a sensation of being touched; however, after a few hundred milliseconds, only the slowly adapting receptors remain active, and the quality of the sensation changes markedly (Martin, 1985). In fact, we are usually unaware of constant mechanical stimuli. Think for a moment about the pressure on your ankles from your socks or the feel of your wrist watch; clearly this information was being continuously sensed, but until I drew your attention to it, it did not enter your consciousness. Notice how little we can tell about objects from unchanging tactile input. Accordingly, when we try to identify objects by touch, we manipulate them in our hands so that the pattern of stimulation continually changes. The identification of objects by touch is termed **stereognosis.**

The perception of both pain and temperature changes appears to be mediated by **free nerve endings**—the sixth and last cutaneous receptor, if you have been counting—although parts of the body that have only free-nerve-ending receptors (e.g., the cornea and the outer ear) are also sensitive to touch. They are called *free nerve endings* because they have no specialized structures associated with the receptive portion of their membranes. Some cutaneous neurons with free nerve endings appear to signal temperature changes at low levels of activity and pain at higher levels; others are sensitive to either painful stimuli or temperature, but not both. Furthermore, different populations of temperature receptors seem responsible for signaling warming as opposed to cooling (Sinclair, 1981). A discomforting study by Bazett, McGlone, Williams, and Lufkin (1932) suggests that warm-sensitive and cold-sensitive free nerve endings are located in different layers of cutaneous tissue. Carlson provides a particularly colorful description of this study.

> The investigators lifted the prepuce (foreskin) of uncircumcised males with dull fishhooks. They applied thermal stimuli on one side of the folded skin and recorded the rate at which the temperature changes were transmitted through the skin by placing small temperature sensors on the opposite side. They then correlated these observations with verbal reports of warmth and

coolness. The investigators concluded that cold receptors were close to the skin and that warmth receptors were located deeper in the tissue. (This experiment shows the extremities to which scientists will go to obtain information—pun intended.) (p. 221)

The neural fibers that carry information from the somatosensory receptors gather together in peripheral nerves and then enter the spinal cord via the dorsal roots. The area of the body that is innervated by the two dorsal roots of a given segment of the spinal cord is called its **dermatome.** Figure 8.17 is a dermatomal map of the human body. Because there is considerable overlap between adjacent dermatomes, destruction of a single dorsal root typically produces little somatosensory loss.

FIGURE 8.17

Dermatomes of the human spinal segments. S, L, T, and C refer respectively to the *sacral, lumbar, thoracic,* and *cervical* regions of the spinal cord. V1, V2, and V3 stand for the three branches of the trigeminal nerve (cranial nerve V).

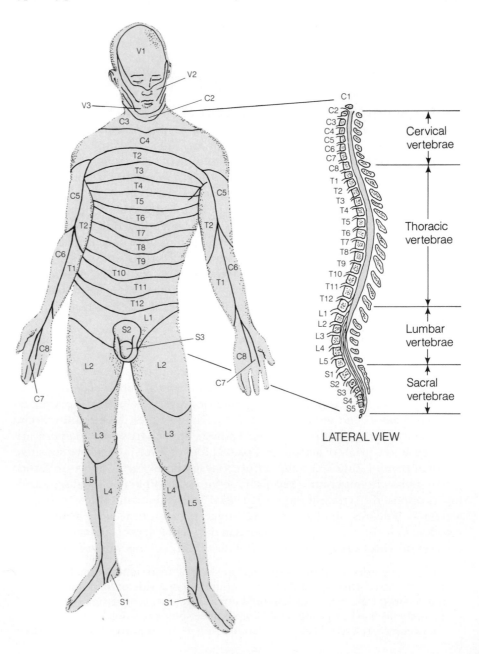

The Two Major Ascending Somatosensory Pathways

Somatosensory information ascends in the human CNS over two major pathways: the dorsal-column medial-lemniscus system and the anterolateral system. For the most part, the **dorsal-column medial-lemniscus system** carries information to the cortex about touch and proprioception. As illustrated in Figure 8.18, the sensory neurons of the dorsal-column medial-lemniscus

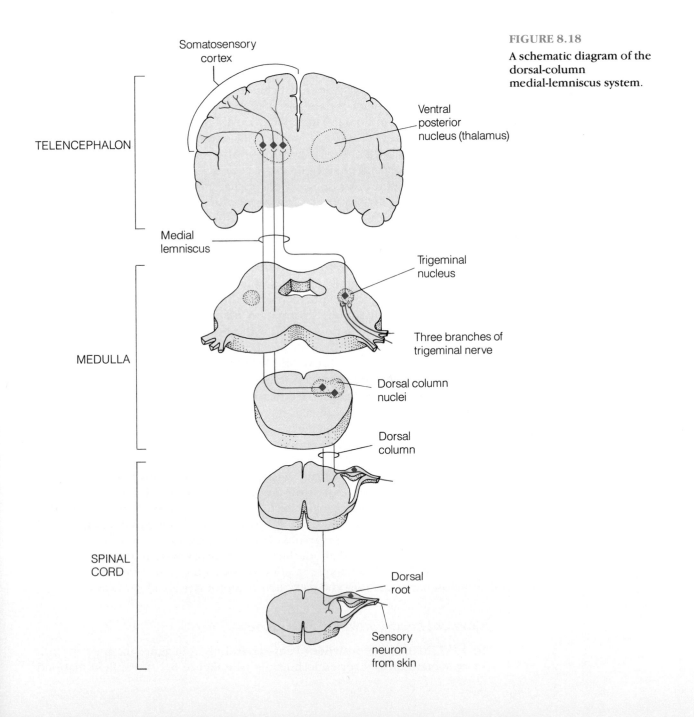

FIGURE 8.18

A schematic diagram of the dorsal-column medial-lemniscus system.

system are very long. They course from receptors in the skin through the periphery and then into the spinal cord via a dorsal root. Then, they ascend ipsilaterally in the **dorsal columns.** Finally, they synapse on neurons of the **dorsal column nuclei** of the lower brain stem (medulla). The axons of these second-order neurons *decussate* (cross over to the other side of the brain) and ascend in the **medial lemniscus** to the contralateral *ventral posterior nucleus* of the thalamus. The ventral posterior nuclei also receive input via the branches of the **trigeminal nerve** that carry somatosensory information from the contralateral areas of the face. The neurons of the ventral posterior nucleus project to the *primary somatosensory cortex* (SI), the *secondary somatosensory cortex* (SII), and the posterior parietal cortex. Neuroscience trivia collectors will almost certainly want to add to their collection the fact that the dorsal column neurons that originate in the toes are the longest neurons in the human body.

The **anterolateral system,** which is illustrated in Figure 8.19, carries information about touch, but its primary function seems to be to carry information about pain and temperature. Most dorsal root neurons of the anterolateral system synapse almost as soon as they enter the spinal cord, in the gray matter of the dorsal horns. The axons of most of the second-order neurons decussate and ascend to the brain in the contralateral anterolateral portion of the spinal cord; however, some ascend ipsilaterally. The anterolateral system comprises three different tracts: the **spinothalamic tract,** which projects to the *ventral posterior nuclei* of the thalamus (as does the dorsal-column medial-lemniscus system); the **spinoreticular tract,** which projects to the *reticular formation* (and then to the *parafascicular* and *intralaminar nuclei* of the thalamus); and the **spinotectal tract,** which projects to the *tectum* (the colliculi of the midbrain). Branches of the trigeminal nerve carry pain and temperature information from the skin of the face to the same thalamic sites. The pain and temperature information that reaches the thalamus is then widely distributed to various parts of the brain, including SI, SII, and the posterior parietal cortex.

An attempt by Mark, Ervin, and Yakolev (1962) to alleviate the chronic pain of patients in the advanced stages of cancer suggests that the different anterolateral pathways subserve different types of pain. Lesions to the ventral posterior nuclei, which receive input from both the spinothalamic tract and the dorsal-column medial-lemniscus system, produced some loss of cutaneous sensitivity to touch, to temperature change, and to sharp pain, but they had no effect on deep, chronic pain. In contrast, lesions of the parafascicular and intralaminar nuclei, which receive input via the spinoreticular tract, reduced chronic pain without disrupting cutaneous sensitivity.

A word of caution is in order here. You may have missed the "for the most parts," the "are thought tos," and the "seems tos" that are liberally sprinkled through the preceding paragraphs. They are there for an important reason: The more that is learned about the somatosensory system, the clearer it becomes that there is no simple relation between the perception of particular somatosensory qualities and particular receptor types and pathways.

Cortical Localization of Somatosensation

In 1937, neurosurgeon Wilder Penfield and his colleagues mapped the primary somatosensory cortex in humans (see Figure 8.20). Penfield mapped

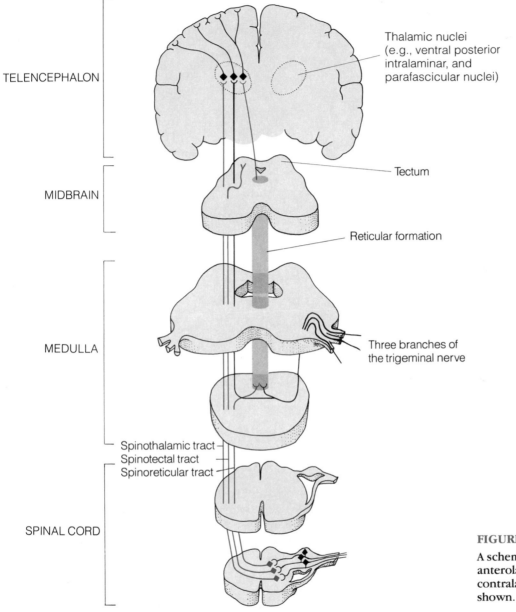

TELENCEPHALON

Thalamic nuclei
(e.g., ventral posterior
intralaminar, and
parafascicular nuclei)

MIDBRAIN

Tectum

Reticular formation

MEDULLA

Three branches of
the trigeminal nerve

Spinothalamic tract
Spinotectal tract
Spinoreticular tract

SPINAL CORD

FIGURE 8.19

A schematic diagram of the
anterolateral system. Only
contralateral pathways are
shown.

the cortices of conscious patients prior to neurosurgery by applying electrical
stimulation to the cortical surface. When stimulation was applied to the
postcentral gyrus, the patients reported somatosensory sensations in various
parts of their bodies. When Penfield mapped the relation between the sites of
stimulation and the parts of the body in which the sensation was felt, he confirmed that the human primary somatosensory cortex is **somatotopically** organized (i.e., organized according to a map of the body surface). Figure 8.20
is a schematic representation of a coronal section through the postcentral
gyrus. It illustrates the somatotopic map, or **somatosensory homunculus**
(*homunculus* means *little man*) as it has been termed. Evidence of a second

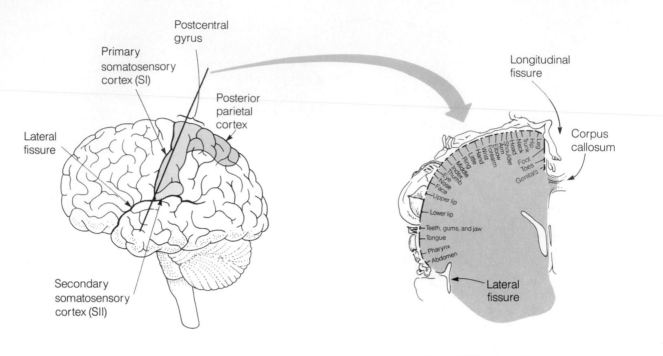

**Lateral View of
Left Hemisphere**

**Coronal Section Taken
Through the Left Hemisphere
at the Indicated Plane**

FIGURE 8.20

The location of human primary (SI) and secondary (SII) somatosensory cortex, and an illustration of the primary somatosensory homunculus.

somatotopically organized area, SII, which is just below SI and extends into the lateral (Sylvian) fissure, was obtained in a similar manner. SII receives much of its input from SI (Pons, Garraghty, Friedman, & Mishkin, 1987). In contrast to SI, whose input is largely contralateral, SII receives substantial input from both sides of the body.

You will notice from Figure 8.20 that the somatosensory homunculus is distorted. The greatest proportion of somatosensory cortex is dedicated to receiving input from the parts of the body that are capable of the finest tactual discriminations (e.g., hands, lips, and tongue).

Kaas, Nelson, Sur, and Merzenich (1981) found that in monkeys, the strip of primary somatosensory cortex is not one strip at all, but rather four parallel strips, each with a similar, but separate, somatotopic organization. Apparently Penfield and his colleagues had not noticed that SI comprised four independent, parallel strips because they had used electrodes incapable of fine resolution. Kaas and his colleagues found that most of the neurons in a particular strip of somatosensory cortex are sensitive to the same kind of somatosensory input (e.g., deep pressure or cutaneous touch). Like the primary visual and auditory cortices, somatosensory cortex is characterized by columnar organization; each neuron in a particular column responds to the same stimuli and has a receptive field on the same part of the body.

Effects of Somatosensory Cortex Damage in Humans

Corkin, Milner, and Rasmussen (1970) assessed the somatosensory abilities of patients both before and after unilateral parietal excision (removal) for the relief of epilepsy. Patients with lesions involving SI displayed some loss in their ability to detect light touch, to judge the position of joints, to identify the exact location of touches, and to identify objects by touch (stereognosis). All of these deficits were minor unless they involved a hand, and most involved only the side of the body contralateral to the excision. Bilateral somatosensory dysfunction following a unilateral parietal cortex lesion is a sign of SII damage.

Somatosensory Agnosias

When a patient cannot recognize objects by touch, but has neither intellectual nor sensory impairments, the diagnosis is **astereognosia.** A related disorder is **asomatognosia,** the failure to recognize parts of one's own body. Asomatognosia is almost always indicative of right-hemisphere damage.

It was time to see Aunt Betty—she wasn't really my aunt, but I grew up thinking that she was. She was my mother's best friend. She had had a stroke in her right hemisphere.

As we walked to her room, one of the medical students described the case. "Left hemiplegia (left-side paralysis)," I was told.

Aunt Betty was lying on her back with her head and eyes turned to the right. "Betty," I called out. Not Aunt Betty, but Betty. I was 37; I'd dropped the "Aunt" long ago—at least 2 years earlier.

I approached her bed from the left, but Aunt Betty did not turn her head or even her eyes to look towards me.

"Hal," she called out. "Where are you?"

I turned her head gently toward me. We talked. It was clear that she had no speech problems, no memory loss, and no confusion. She was as bright as ever. But her eyes still looked to the right as if the left side of her world did not exist.

I picked up her right hand and held it in front of her eyes. "What's this?" I asked.

"My hand, of course," she said with an intonation that suggested what she thought of my question.

"Well then what's this," I said, as I held up her limp left hand where she could see it.

"A hand."

"Whose hand?"

"Your hand, I guess," she replied. She seemed genuinely puzzled. I carefully placed her hand on the bed.

"Why have you come to this hospital?" I asked.

"To see you," she replied hesitantly. I could tell that she didn't really know the answer.

"Is there anything wrong with you?"

"No."

"How about your left hand and leg?"

"They're fine," she said. "How are yours?"

"They're fine too," I replied. There was nothing else to do. Aunt Betty was in trouble.[2]

As in the case of Aunt Betty, asomatognosia is often accompanied by **anosognosia,** the denial of one's own neurological symptoms, and **contralateral neglect,** the tendency not to respond to stimuli that are contralateral to a right-hemisphere injury. You will learn more about contralateral neglect in the next chapter.

The Paradoxes of Pain

Pain is a unique sensory experience in the sense that it seems to lack clear cortical representation. No area of the cortex has yet been discovered that results in pain when stimulated, that responds selectively to painful stimuli (but see Talbot, Marrett, Evans, Meyer, Bushnell, & Duncan, 1991), or that abolishes pain when lesioned (see Sweet, 1982). *Prefrontal lobotomy* (see Chapter 1) has been shown to reduce the emotional impact of pain, but it does not alter pain thresholds.

The value of pain is not fully appreciated by most people. To appreciate the positive aspects of pain, consider a case of someone born with the inability to perceive it.

> The best documented of all cases of congenital insensitivity to pain is Miss C., a young Canadian girl who was a student at McGill University in Montreal. . . . The young lady was highly intelligent and seemed normal in every way except that she had never felt pain. As a child, she had bitten off the tip of her tongue while chewing food, and had suffered third-degree burns after kneeling on a radiator to look out of the window. . . . She felt no pain when parts of her body were subjected to strong electric shock, to hot water at temperatures that usually produce reports of burning pain, or to a prolonged ice-bath. Equally astonishing was the fact that she showed no changes in blood pressure, heart rate, or respiration when these stimuli were presented. Furthermore, she could not remember ever sneezing or coughing, the gag reflex could be elicited only with great difficulty, and corneal reflexes (to protect the eyes) were absent. A variety of other stimuli, such as inserting a stick up through the nostrils, pinching tendons, or injections of histamine under the skin—which are normally considered as forms of torture—also failed to produce pain.
>
> Miss C. had severe medical problems. She exhibited pathological changes in her knees, hip, and spine, and underwent several orthopaedic operations. The surgeon attributed these changes to the lack of protection to joints usually given by pain sensation. She apparently failed to shift her weight when standing, to turn over in her sleep, or to avoid certain postures, which normally prevent inflammation of joints. . . .
>
> . . . Miss C. died at the age of twenty-nine of massive infections . . . [exacerbated by] extensive skin and bone trauma.[3]

[2](Paraphrased from *Newton's Madness: Further Tales of Clinical Neurology* by Harold L. Klawans, 1990)

[3]From *The Challenge of Pain* (pp. 16–17) by Ronald Melzack and Patrick D. Wall, 1982, London: Penguin Books Ltd. Copyright © Ronald Melzack and Patrick D. Wall, 1982.

Patients such as Miss C. demonstrate one paradox of pain: that pain, which seems so bad, is in fact indispensable for survival. There is a second paradox of pain: that pain, which is the most intense of all sensory experiences, can be effectively suppressed by cognitive and emotional factors. For example, men participating in religious ceremonies swing from ropes attached to giant meat hooks in their backs without any evidence of pain (Kosambi, 1967); massive wounds suffered by soldiers in battle are often associated with little pain (Beecher, 1959); and people injured in life-threatening situations frequently feel no pain until the threat is over.

Melzack and Wall (1965) proposed a theory of the neural basis of pain that could account for the ability of cognitive and emotional factors to block the perception of pain. They proposed that signals descending from the brain can activate neural gating circuits in the spinal cord to block incoming pain signals. This **gate-control theory,** as it became known, was for many years a thorn in the side of researchers who preferred to equate pain with tissue damage and to ignore the powerful analgesic effects of cognitive and emotional factors.

Mechanisms of Descending Pain Control

The first important step toward the identification of the neural basis of descending pain control was taken by Reynolds (1969). He found that electrical stimulation of several areas of the brain, particularly those in the area of gray matter just around the *cerebral aqueduct* (the duct between the third and fourth ventricles), had analgesic (pain-reducing) effects. Reynolds was able to perform abdominal surgery on rats with no analgesia other than that provided by electrical stimulation of the **periaqueductal gray (PAG)** area. Mayer and Liebeskind (1974) subsequently showed that PAG stimulation can reduce sensitivity to a variety of painful stimuli without diminishing sensitivity to other somatosensory input, that the analgesia produced by stimulating any one site in the PAG affects only part of the body, and that the analgesia produced by PAG stimulation can outlast the stimulation by many minutes (see Oliveras & Besson, 1988; Thorn, Applegate, & Johnson, 1989).

The second important step toward the identification of the descending pain-control system resulted from the study of the analgesic effects of morphine and other opiates (see Chapter 12). Great excitement was created by the discovery that there are specialized receptor sites for opiates on neurons in many parts of the brain, including the PAG. This discovery suggested that such substances occur naturally in the body: Why else would there be receptors for them? The possibility that there were internally manufactured (*endogenous*) opiates caught the imagination of many investigators, and in the ensuing years, several different endogenous opiates—generally referred to as **endorphins**—were isolated (e.g., Hughs, Smith, Kosterlitz, Fothergill, Morgan, & Morris, 1975). This suggested that the analgesic effects of pharmaceutical opiates, such as morphine, are mediated by a neural system that is normally activated by the body's own opiates.

In their classic reviews, Basbaum and Fields (1978) and Fields and Basbaum (1984) argued that analgesia is mediated by a descending circuit that involves opiate-sensitive neurons in the PAG. They proposed that the input from the PAG excites serotonergic neurons of the *raphé nuclei* (a collection of serotonergic nuclei that is situated in the core of the medulla),

FIGURE 8.21
Basbaum and Field's model
of the descending analgesia
circuit.

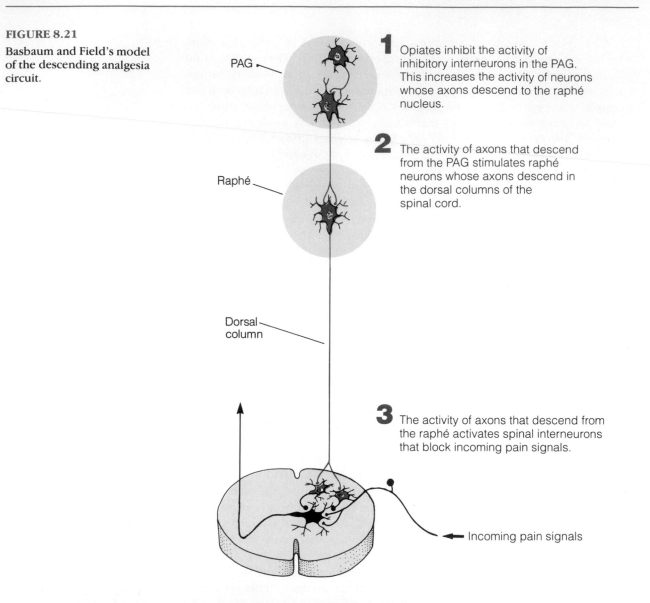

PAG

1 Opiates inhibit the activity of
inhibitory interneurons in the PAG.
This increases the activity of neurons
whose axons descend to the raphé
nucleus.

2 The activity of axons that descend
from the PAG stimulates raphé
neurons whose axons descend in
the dorsal columns of the
spinal cord.

Raphé

Dorsal
column

3 The activity of axons that descend from
the raphé activates spinal interneurons
that block incoming pain signals.

◄— Incoming pain signals

which in turn project down the dorsal columns of the spinal cord and excite
opiate-sensitive interneurons that block incoming pain signals in the dorsal
horn. This PAG-raphé-dorsal-column analgesia circuit is summarized in Figure 8.21. Evidence for it has come from a variety of sources. For example,
microinjection of opiate antagonists, such as *naloxone* or *naltrexone,* into
the PAG has been found to block the analgesia produced by *systemic injection* (injection into the general circulatory system) of morphine (Yeung &
Rudy, 1978), and activation of the raphé nucleus with electrical stimulation
has been shown to inhibit pain neurons in the dorsal horn of the spinal cord
(Oliveras, Besson, Guilbaud, & Liebeskind, 1974). Moreover, the analgesic
effects of morphine and PAG stimulation have been attenuated by lesioning
the fibers that descend from the raphé, by lesioning the raphé itself, or by
depleting the raphé neurons of their *serotonin* transmitter (e.g., Basbaum,
Clanton, & Fields, 1976). The fact that blockage of the PAG-raphé-dorsal-col-

umn circuit does not block all analgesia (see Terman, Shavit, Lewis, Cannon, & Liebeskind, 1984) suggests that other circuits must be capable of mediating the effects of analgesic agents.

Phantom Limbs

Almost every amputee who has lost an arm or leg continues to feel the presence of the amputated limb—the perception of an amputated limb is referred to as a **phantom limb** (Melzack, 1990). At first, the limb feels quite normal, and an amputee may try to pick up something with a phantom hand or take a step with a phantom leg. However, as time passes the phantom limb begins to change. For example, it may become separated from the body. The reality of the phantom limb is often enhanced by wearing a *prosthesis* (an artificial body part). Amputees in whom a phantom leg has begun to telescope into the stump report that it emerges to fill an artificial leg each time the leg is strapped on.

About 50% of amputees experience chronic severe pain in their phantom limbs (see Jensen & Rasmussen, 1989). Some patients report that their phantom toes or fingers are cramped or contorted or that fingernails are biting into phantom flesh. There is currently no explanation why some amputees develop severe phantom limb pain and others do not, and various pharmacological and surgical treatments have proven only marginally effective in treating it. One patient experienced cramping pain from a phantom limb that was awkwardly wrapped around the back of his head, and he gained relief by thinking about shifting it to a more comfortable position.

8.5

The Chemical Senses: Smell and Taste

Olfaction (smell) and *gustation* (taste) are referred to as the chemical senses because their function is to monitor the chemical content of the external environment. It is the responses of the olfactory system to molecules released into the air that determine a substance's odor; airborne molecules are detected when they are drawn by inhalation over the receptors of the *olfactory epithelia,* two tiny patches of mucous membrane in the recesses of the nasal passages. A substance's taste depends on the response of the gustatory system to those molecules in the mouth that excite the taste receptors of the tongue and oral cavity.

When we are eating, taste and smell act in concert (McBurney, 1986; Oakley, 1986). Molecules of food excite both taste and smell receptors and produce an integrated sensory impression termed **flavor.** Although most people understand that olfaction contributes to a food's flavor, few appreciate just how great this contribution is. When you weigh the relative contributions of taste and smell to flavor, you will always give olfaction its due recognition if you remember that people with no sense of smell have difficulty distinguishing the flavors of apples and onions.

Taste and smell have the dubious distinction of being the least understood of the exterosensory systems (see Freeman, 1991; Scott & Giza, 1990). One reason for this lack of knowledge is that chemical stimuli are inherently more difficult to control and administer than nonchemical stimuli, such as lights, tones, and touches. Another is that loss of the ability to taste or smell does not pose serious problems for individuals living in societies such as ours in which potential foods are screened by governmental agencies. Nevertheless, the chemical senses are of considerable interest to many. One interesting feature of the chemical senses is their phylogenetic primitiveness. Even the most simple unicellular animals have receptors that are designed to sense the presence of chemicals in the external environment. In mammals, this primitiveness is reflected by the rich connections that both the gustatory and olfactory systems make with the *paleocortex* (see Chapter 3).

Interest in the chemical senses has been stimulated by the major role that they play in the social lives of many species. The members of many species release **pheromones,** chemicals that affect the behavior of their conspecifics. The study of pheromones has led to many remarkable findings—at least they are remarkable to humans, who rely primarily on visual, auditory, and somatosensory signals to guide their social behavior. For example, Murphy and Schneider (1970) showed that the sexual and aggressive behavior of the golden hamster is entirely under the control of olfactory cues. Unfamiliar male hamsters that were placed in an established colony were attacked and killed by the resident males; in contrast, unfamiliar ovulating (sexually receptive) females were pursued, mounted, and impregnated. Remarkably, if the resident males were first rendered *anosmic* (unable to smell), these aggressive and sexual responses did not occur. Murphy and Schneider confirmed the olfactory basis of hamster aggressive and sexual behavior in a particularly devious fashion. They swabbed a male intruder with the vaginal secretions of an ovulating female hamster before placing it in a cage with resident male hamsters. The change of fragrance converted the intruder from an object of hamster assassination to an object of hamster lust.

The chemical senses participate in some interesting forms of learning. Animals that suffer from gastrointestinal upset after consuming a particular food develop a lasting aversion to its flavor (*conditioned taste aversion;* Chapter 5). Conversely, it has been shown that rats develop preferences for flavors that they encounter in their mother's milk (Galef & Sherry, 1973) or on the breath of conspecifics (Galef, 1989). As adults, male rats nursed by lemon-scented mothers copulate more effectively with females that smell of lemons (Fillion & Blass, 1986)—a phenomenon that has been aptly referred to as the *I-want-a-girl-just-like-the-girl-who-married-dear-old-dad phenomenon* (Diamond, 1986).

The idea that humans, like many other species, release odors that can elicit sexual advances from members of the opposite sex, has received considerable attention because of its financial and recreational potential. There have been several suggestive findings. For example: (1) The olfactory sensitivity of women is greatest when they are ovulating (e.g., Doty, Snyder, Huggins, & Lowry, 1981). (2) The menstrual cycles of women living together tend to become synchronized (McClintock, 1971). (3) Humans—particularly women—can judge the sex of an individual on the basis of breath (Doty, Green, Ram, & Yankell, 1982) or underarm odor (Schleidt, Hold, & Attili, 1981). And (4) men can judge the stage of a woman's menstrual cycle on the basis of her vaginal odor (Doty, Ford, Preti, & Huggins, 1975). However, there is still no convincing evidence that any of these human odors serve as sex attractants (Doty, 1986); to put it mildly, the body odors that were employed in the aforementioned studies were not attractive to many subjects.

The Olfactory System

It is not yet known what features of a molecule give it its characteristic odor. Because we can discriminate between thousands of different odors, researchers have reasonably assumed that olfaction, like color vision (see Chapter 7), is organized according to *component principles;* that is, that there are a few primary receptor types and that the perception of various odors is produced by different ratios of activity in the different types. Amoore and his colleagues made an ambitious attempt to develop such a theory (e.g., Amoore, Johnston, & Rubin, 1964). They studied over 600 odiferous substances and concluded that their perception could be explained by the combinations of activity in seven different types of receptors, each sensitive to molecules of a particular overall size, shape, or charge. Unfortunately, there have been so many exceptions to this theory that its specifics have been largely abandoned. However, its major premise, that the olfactory system works on component principles, continues to be a rallying point for many researchers in the field.

The olfactory receptors are in the upper part of the nose, embedded in a layer of mucus-covered tissue called the **olfactory mucosa.** They have their own axons, which pass through a porous portion of the skull (the **cribriform plate**) and enter the **olfactory bulbs** (the first cranial nerves). In the olfactory bulbs, they synapse on neurons that project diffusely via the *lateral olfactory tract* to the *olfactory paleocortex* in the medial temporal lobes. From the olfactory paleocortex, one major pathway leads to the **medial dorsal nucleus** of the thalamus and then to the *olfactory neocortex* on the inferior surface at the very front of the frontal lobes; another projects diffusely to various structures of the limbic system. The thalamic-neocortical projection is thought to mediate the conscious perception of odors; the limbic projection is thought to mediate the emotional response to odors. Figure 8.22 is a schematic repre-

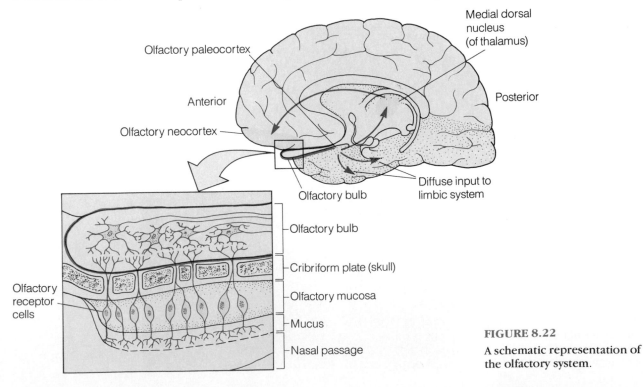

FIGURE 8.22

A schematic representation of the olfactory system.

sentation of the olfactory system (see Scott, 1986). Notice that the olfactory system is the only system that projects to the cortex (the paleocortex) before projecting to the thalamus.

The olfactory receptors have a lifespan of only about 35 days. When they die, either from natural causes or from physical damage, they are replaced by new receptors whose axons grow out to the appropriate layer of the olfactory bulb and establish functional synaptic connections.

The Gustatory System

The taste receptors are found on the tongue and parts of the oral cavity. Taste receptors typically occur in clusters of 50 or so called **taste buds.** On the tongue, taste buds are often located around small protuberances called *papillae.* The relation between taste receptors, taste buds, and papillae (singular: *papilla*) is illustrated in Figure 8.23. The distribution of taste buds on the

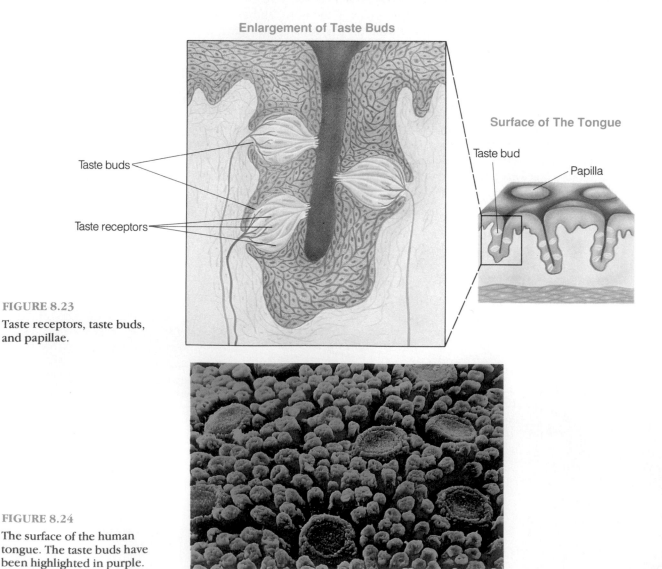

FIGURE 8.23

Taste receptors, taste buds, and papillae.

FIGURE 8.24

The surface of the human tongue. The taste buds have been highlighted in purple.

surface of the human tongue is illustrated in Figure 8.24. Unlike olfactory receptors, taste receptors do not have their own axons; each neuron that carries impulses away from a taste bud receives input from many receptors. Taste receptors survive for only 10 days and are replaced by new cells.

It is commonly believed that all tastes can be produced by a combination of four primary tastes: *sweet, sour, salty,* and *bitter.* However, this assumption has been repeatedly challenged. For example, there are many tastes that cannot be described in terms of the four primaries (e.g., Schiffman & Erickson, 1980); there is no evidence that taste buds or individual taste receptors come in four varieties; and most neurons of the gustatory system respond to all four primaries (Yamamoto et al., 1985), although they may have a clear preference. Some areas of the tongue are more sensitive to some tastes than to others. The front of the tongue is particularly sensitive to salty and sweet, the sides to sour, and the back to bitter.

Signals generated in taste receptors stimulate adjacent second-order neurons. The major pathways over which signals in these second-order neurons are transmitted to the cortex are illustrated in Figure 8.25. Gustatory afferents

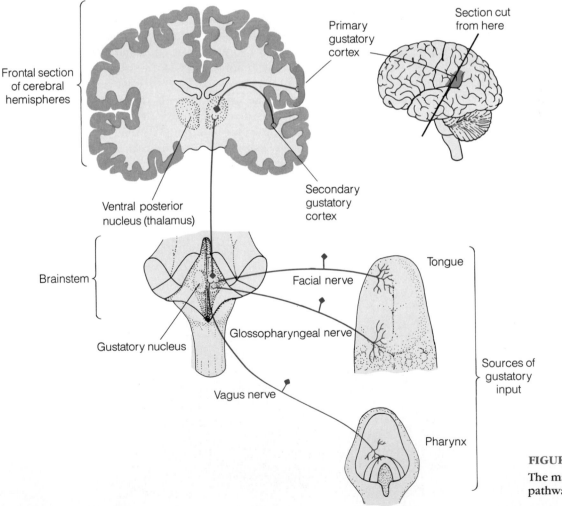

FIGURE 8.25

The major gustatory pathways.

leave the mouth as part of the *facial* (VII), *glossopharyngeal* (IX), and *vagus* (X) cranial nerves, which carry information from the front of the tongue, back of the tongue, and back of the oral cavity, respectively. These fibers all terminate in the **solitary nucleus** of the medulla, where they synapse on neurons that project to a portion of the **ventral posterior nucleus** of the thalamus (a different portion than that which serves as a relay nucleus for oral stimulation in the somatosensory system). The axons of the ventral posterior nucleus project to the *primary gustatory cortex,* which is near the face area of the somatosensory homunculus, and to the *secondary gustatory cortex,* which is hidden from view in the lateral fissure. The gustatory system, like the olfactory system, also projects to various parts of the *limbic system.* The projections to the hypothalamus are thought to play a role in regulating hunger. Unlike the projections of other sensory systems, the projections of the gustatory system are primarily ipsilateral (see Figure 8.25).

Brain Damage and the Chemical Senses

The inability to smell is called **anosmia;** the inability to taste is called **ageusia.** The most common neurological cause of anosmia is a blow to the head that causes a displacement of the brain within the skull and shears the olfactory nerves as they pass through the holes in the cribriform plate—see Figure 8.26. Approximately 6% of patients hospitalized for traumatic head injuries are found to have olfactory deficits of some sort (e.g., Zusho, 1983). In contrast, ageusia is extremely rare, presumably because sensory signals from the mouth are carried over three separate pathways. However, ageusia for the anterior two-thirds of the tongue on one side is commonly observed after damage to the ear on the same side of the body. This is because the **chorda tympani,** the branch of the cranial facial nerve (VII) that carries gustatory information from the anterior two-thirds of the tongue, passes through the mid-

FIGURE 8.26

Shearing of the olfactory nerves by a blow to the head. (Adapted from Costanzo and Becker, 1986.)

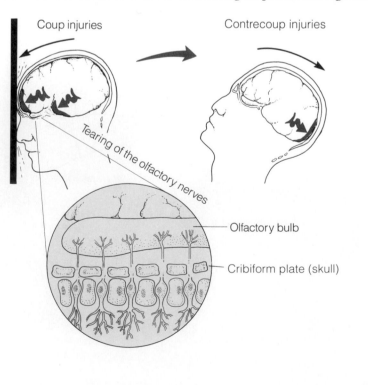

dle ear. One noteworthy feature of ageusia and anosmia is that they tend to occur together. This suggests that there is some, as yet unidentified, area in the brain where taste and smell interact. Because only those patients who complain to their physicians about faulty smell and taste are likely to have these abilities tested—and then only crudely—the number of neurological patients suffering olfactory and gustatory deficits is undoubtedly much higher than current figures suggest (Costanzo & Becker, 1986).

SELF TEST

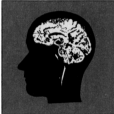

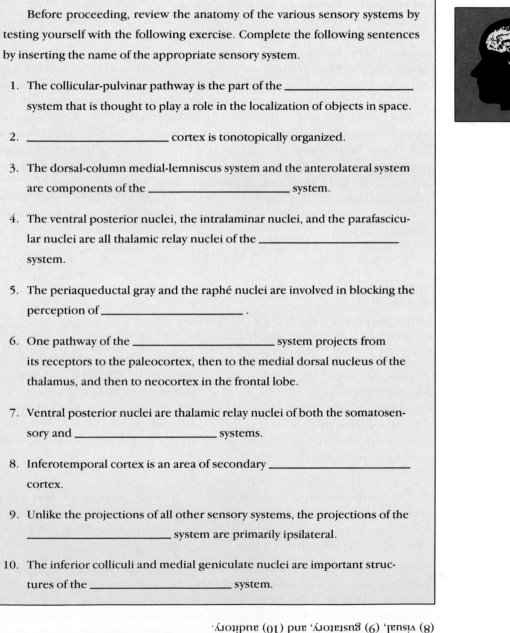

Before proceeding, review the anatomy of the various sensory systems by testing yourself with the following exercise. Complete the following sentences by inserting the name of the appropriate sensory system.

1. The collicular-pulvinar pathway is the part of the _____ system that is thought to play a role in the localization of objects in space.

2. _____ cortex is tonotopically organized.

3. The dorsal-column medial-lemniscus system and the anterolateral system are components of the _____ system.

4. The ventral posterior nuclei, the intralaminar nuclei, and the parafascicular nuclei are all thalamic relay nuclei of the _____ system.

5. The periaqueductal gray and the raphé nuclei are involved in blocking the perception of _____ .

6. One pathway of the _____ system projects from its receptors to the paleocortex, then to the medial dorsal nucleus of the thalamus, and then to neocortex in the frontal lobe.

7. Ventral posterior nuclei are thalamic relay nuclei of both the somatosensory and _____ systems.

8. Inferotemporal cortex is an area of secondary _____ cortex.

9. Unlike the projections of all other sensory systems, the projections of the _____ system are primarily ipsilateral.

10. The inferior colliculi and medial geniculate nuclei are important structures of the _____ system.

The following are the correct answers to the preceding questions: (1) visual, (2) auditory, (3) somatosensory, (4) somatosensory, (5) pain, (6) olfactory, (7) gustatory, (8) visual, (9) gustatory, and (10) auditory.

8.6

Selective Attention

Psychologists have long been intrigued by the phenomenon of **selective attention,** the ability of some animals to focus on only a small subset of the stimuli that are being received by their sensory organs—the subset that is relevant to their current goals (see Näätänen, 1990). Selective attention improves the perception of those stimuli that are its focus. You do not perceive the pressure of your socks on your ankles until you attend to it, and you do not necessarily hear one voice in a crowd until you focus on it.

Experiments have shown that selective attention is associated with an increase in the reactivity of neurons in the area of secondary sensory cortex that is associated with the stimuli to which the subject is attending. For example, Moran and Desimone (1985) trained monkeys to attend to stimuli presented at one location of their visual field and to ignore stimuli presented at another. When both locations were in the receptive field of a *prestriate cortex* or *inferotemporal cortex* neuron, the neuronal response to stimuli in the ignored location was substantially reduced. In a follow-up study, Spitzer, Desimone, and Moran (1988) increased the amount of attention that monkeys paid to test stimuli by increasing the difficulty of their discrimination task. Increasing attention was associated with an increase in the responsiveness and selectivity of prestriate neurons. Attention does not seem to influence the activity of neurons in primary sensory cortex (Corbetta, Miezen, Dobmeyer, Shulman, & Petersen, 1990).

8.7

Conclusion: General Principles of Sensory System Organization

Each sensory system is specialized to receive, encode, and interpret a different kind of sensory information. In chapters such as this, which compare several different sensory systems, these specializations inevitably come to be the focus of discussion. Nevertheless, it is important not to lose sight of the commonalities—the principles of sensory system organization that are common to more than one system. Seven such general principles emerged in this chapter. They summarize its main points:

1. *Sensory systems are hierarchical systems.* In each sensory system, there is a general flow of information from "lower" to "higher" structures; the functions of "higher" structures are more perceptual and less sensory than those of "lower" structures.

2. *Sensory systems are parallel systems.* The first models of sensory system function were **serial models;** that is, they were models in which information flowed between components by only one route. However, it is now clear that parallel models provide a more accurate representation of sensory function. **Parallel models** are those in which information can flow between components by various routes. See Figure 8.27.

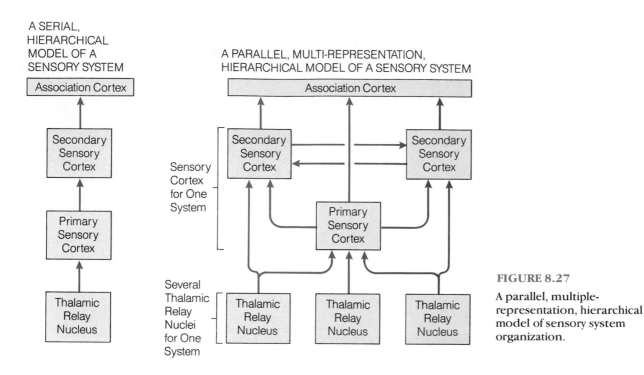

A SERIAL, HIERARCHICAL MODEL OF A SENSORY SYSTEM

A PARALLEL, MULTI-REPRESENTATION, HIERARCHICAL MODEL OF A SENSORY SYSTEM

FIGURE 8.27

A parallel, multiple-representation, hierarchical model of sensory system organization.

3. *All exteroceptive sensory systems project to the neocortex via the thalamus.* Although there are major differences among the five exteroceptive sensory systems in the routes by which their signals ascend through the various levels of the nervous system, in each of the five there is a major pathway from the thalamus to the neocortex. It is common for each sensory system to have more than one pair of thalamic relay nuclei (e.g., both the *pulvinar nuclei* and the *lateral geniculate nuclei* relay visual signals).

4. *Sensory cortex is organized in columns.* In all five exteroceptive sensory systems, the neurons in a given column of cortical tissue tend to be responsive to the same kinds of sensory input.

5. *The surface of the sensory cortex is systematically arrayed.* The cortex of the visual, auditory, and somatosensory systems are retinotopically, tonotopically, and somatotopically organized, respectively. The principles of gustatory and olfactory system organization have yet to be discovered. The advantage of such organization is that it facilitates interaction among adjacent channels (columns) of communication.

6. *There is multiple representation of each sensory system in the cortex.* As research on sensory cortex has progressed, more sensory areas have been discovered and areas that were once thought to be a single area have been found to comprise several separate cortical maps.

7. *The reactivity and selectivity of neurons in secondary sensory cortex is enhanced by selective attention.* There are mechanisms in the secondary sensory cortex of each system for increasing the sensitivity of neurons to the particular stimuli to which the subject is attending.

Figure 8.27 completes the chapter by comparing the traditional serial, hierarchical model, which began the chapter, with a parallel, multiple-representation, hierarchical model that better illustrates current thinking about sensory systems.

Food for Thought

1. Many amputees who suffer from phantom-limb pain receive little or no treatment for it—"after all, it's all in their heads." Discuss.

KEY TERMS

To help you study the material in this chapter, all of the key terms—those that have appeared in bold type—are listed and briefly defined here.

Ageusia.   The inability to taste.

Agnosia.   The inability to recognize sensory stimuli of a particular class; patients whose poor performance on recognition tests can be attributed to sensory, verbal, or intellectual deficits are excluded from this diagnosis.

Anosmia.   Inability to smell.

Anosognosia.   Denial of one's own neurological symptoms.

Anterolateral system.   The part of the somatosensory system that ascends in the anterolateral portion of spinal white matter; the anterolateral system transmits signals related to pain and temperature.

Asomatognosia.   The failure to recognize parts of one's own body.

Association cortex.   Areas of cortex that receive input from more than one sensory system.

Astereognosia.   The inability to recognize objects by touch.

Auditory nerve.   The eighth cranial nerve, which carries signals from the hair cells rooted in the basilar membrane.

Basilar membrane.   The part of the organ of Corti in which the hair cell receptors are embedded.

Blindsight.   The ability of cortically blind subjects to perform visually mediated tasks without conscious awareness of vision.

Chorda tympani.   The branch of the cranial facial nerve (VII) that carries gustatory information from the anterior two-thirds of the tongue.

Cochlea.   The long, coiled structure of the inner ear, which houses the organ of Corti and its auditory receptors.

Cocktail-party phenomenon.   Our ability to unconsciously monitor the contents of one conversation while consciously focusing on another.

Collicular-pulvinar pathway.   A visual pathway that is thought to play a role in detection and localization of objects in space.

Completion.   When a person with a scotoma views a figure that is partly in the scotoma, the visual system often "fills in" or completes the missing portion of the perception.

Contralateral neglect.   A disorder that is characterized by a tendency not to respond to parts of one's own body or external objects that are contralateral to a brain injury.

Cribriform plate.   The porous portion of the skull through which the axons of olfactory receptors pass to synapse in the olfactory bulbs.

Dermatome.   The area of the body that is innervated by the dorsal roots of a given segment of the spinal cord.

Dorsal column.   A column of somatosensory axons that ascend in the dorsal portion of the spinal cord white matter.

Dorsal-column medial-lemniscus system.   A major pathway by which information about touch and proprioception ascends from the spinal cord to the medulla.

Dorsal column nuclei.   Medullar nuclei on which ascending dorsal-column axons synapse.

Endorphins.   Endogenous (internally produced) opiates.

Exteroceptive sensory systems.   The five sensory systems that receive information about conditions outside the body (vision, touch, hearing, taste, and smell).

Flavor.   The combined impression of taste and smell.

Free nerve endings.   Anatomically unspecialized cutaneous receptors, which detect pain and skin temperature changes.

Gate-control theory.   The theory that neural signals that descend from the brain can activate neural gating circuits in the spinal cord to block incoming pain signals.

Glabrous skin.   Hairless skin.

Gustatory nucleus.   A medullar nucleus on which the gustatory afferent fibers terminate.

Hair cells. The receptors of the auditory system.

Hair receptors. Receptors at the base of hair roots, which respond to movements of the hair.

Hemianopsic. Patients with a scotoma that covers half their field of vision.

Inferotemporal cortex. The cortex of the inferior temporal lobe; an area of secondary visual cortex.

Interoceptive sensory system. A sensory system that receives information about conditions inside the body (e.g., the vestibular system).

Macular sparing. Damage to the visual cortex often spares the ability to see images received by the center of the macula (the central portion of the retina).

Medial dorsal nucleus. The nucleus of the thalamus to which the neurons in the olfactory bulb project.

Medial lemniscus. The somatosensory pathway between the dorsal column nuclei and the ventral posterior nucleus of the thalamus.

Meissner corpuscle. A touch receptor that is located just beneath the outermost layer of glabrous skin.

Merkel receptor. A touch receptor that responds continuously to long, unchanging tactile stimuli.

Olfactory bulbs. The first cranial nerves; they are the terminals for the axons of olfactory receptor cells, and their output goes primarily to the olfactory paleocortex.

Olfactory mucosa. The membrane that lines the upper nasal passages and contains the olfactory receptor cells.

Organ of Corti. The auditory receptor organ; it comprises the basilar membrane, the hair cells, and the tectorial membrane.

Ossicles. Small bones of the middle ear; the malleus, incus, and stapes.

Oval window. The cochlear membrane that transfers vibrations from the ossicles to the fluid of the cochlea.

Pacinian corpuscle. The largest and most deeply positioned cutaneous receptor.

Parallel model. A model in which information can flow from one component to another by several routes.

Perception. The higher order process of integrating, recognizing, and interpreting complex patterns of sensations.

Periaqueductal gray (PAG). The area around the cerebral aqueduct that contains opiate receptors; stimulation of the PAG produces analgesia.

Perimetry. The method used to map scotomas.

Phantom limb. The vivid perception by an amputee of her or his lost limb.

Pheromone. An odor that is released by an animal and affects the behavior of its conspecifics.

Posterior parietal cortex. An area of association cortex that receives input from the visual, auditory, and somatosensory systems.

Prestriate cortex. The area of secondary visual cortex that almost totally surrounds primary visual cortex.

Primary sensory cortex. The area of cortex in a sensory system that is the primary recipient of input from the thalamus.

Prosopagnosia. An inability to recognize faces that is not attributable to general sensory, verbal, or intellectual deficits.

Retinotopic. To be organized according to the spatial map of the retina.

Round window. The cochlear membrane through which the pressure created in the fluid of the cochlea dissipates.

Ruffini corpuscle. A touch receptor that responds continuously to long, unchanging tactile stimuli.

Scotoma. An area of blindness in the visual field.

Secondary sensory cortex. The areas of cortex in a sensory system that receive input from the primary sensory cortex of the same system, but not from any other sensory systems.

Selective attention. The ability to focus on a small subset of the multitude of stimuli that are being received at any one time.

Semicircular canals. The receptive organs of the vestibular system.

Sensation. The simple process of detecting the presence of stimuli.

Serial model. A model in which the flow of information between components can occur by only one route.

Solitary nucleus. The first relay nucleus of the gustatory system; it is located in the medulla.

Somatosensory homunculus. The somatotopic map that constitutes the primary somatosensory cortex.

Somatotopic. Organized according to a map of the surface of the body.

Spinoreticular tract. The tract of the anterolateral system that projects to the reticular formation.

Spinotectal tract. The tract of the anterolateral system that projects to the tectum.

Spinothalamic tract. The tract of the anterolateral system that projects to the ventral posterior nucleus of the thalamus.

Stereognosis. The identification of objects by touch.

Subjective contours. Nonexistent visual contours that are seen.

Taste buds. Clusters of taste receptors.

Tectorial membrane. The cochlear membrane that rests on the hair cells.

Timbre. The quality of a sound.

Tonotopic. Organized according to the frequency of sound; the cochlea and the auditory cortex are tonotopic structures.

Trigeminal nerve. The cranial nerve that carries somatosensory information from the face.

Tympanic membrane. The eardrum.

Ventral posterior nucleus. A thalamic relay nucleus in both the somatosensory and gustatory systems.

Vestibular system. The sensory system that detects changes in the direction and intensity of head movements, and contributes to the maintenance of balance via its output to the motor system.

Visual agnosia. A failure to recognize visual stimuli that is not attributable to sensory, verbal, or intellectual impairment.

Word deafness. A difficulty in the perception of speech that occurs in the absence of any difficulty in detecting individual sounds.

ADDITIONAL READING

The following articles describe the development of sensory prosthetics for the deaf or blind:

Brooks, P. L., Frost, B. J., Mason, J. L., & Gibson, D. M. (1986). Continuing evaluation of the Queen's University tactile vocoder. II: Identification of open set sentences and tracking narrative. *Journal of Rehabilitation Research and Development, 23,* 129–138.

Craig, J. C. (1977). Vibrotactile pattern perception: Extraordinary observers. *Science, 196,* 450–452.

Loeb, G. E. (1990). Cochlear prosthetics. *Annual Review of Neuroscience, 13,* 357–371.

More detailed coverage of many of the topics that were discussed in this chapter is provided by the following text:

Kandel, J. H., & Schwartz, J. H., second edition (1991). *Principles of neuroscience.* New York: Elsevier.

9

The Sensorimotor System

Yesterday, I was standing in a checkout line at the local market. I furtively scanned the headlines on the prominently displayed magazines—WOMAN GIVES BIRTH TO CAT; FLYING SAUCER LANDS IN CLEVELAND SHOPPING MALL; HOW TO LOSE 20 POUNDS IN 2 DAYS. Then, my mind began to wander, and I started to think about writing this chapter. That is when I began to watch Rhonda's movements and to wonder about the neural system that controlled them. Rhonda was the cashier—the best in the place.

I was struck by the complexity of even her most simple responses. As she deftly transferred a bag of tomatoes to the scale, there was a coordinated adjustment in almost every part of her body. In addition to her obvious finger, hand, arm, and shoulder movements, coordinated movements of her head and eyes tracked her hand to the tomatoes; and there were adjustments in the muscles of her feet, legs, trunk, and other arm, which kept her from lurching forward. The accuracy of these responses suggested that they were guided in part by the patterns of visual, somatosensory, and vestibular change that they produced—the term *sensorimotor* in the title of this chapter formally recognizes that communication between sensory and motor systems is essential for effective behavior (cf. Brooks, 1986; Goodale, 1983).

As my purchases flowed through her left hand, Rhonda registered the prices with her right hand and bantered with Rick, "the bagger." I was intrigued by how little of what Rhonda was doing appeared to be under conscious control. She seemed to make general decisions about which items to pick up and where to put them, but she never seemed to give any thought to the exact means by which these decisions were carried out. It did not concern her that every reaching response can be made in infinite combinations of finger, wrist, elbow, shoulder, and body adjustments. The higher parts of Rhonda's sensorimotor system—perhaps her cortex—seemed to issue conscious general commands to other parts of the system, which unconsciously produced the specific patterns of muscular responses needed to carry them out. The automaticity of her performance was a far cry from the slow, effortful responses that had characterized her first days at the market. Somehow experience had integrated her individual movements into smooth sequences, and it seemed to have transferred the movements' control from a mode that involved conscious effort to one that did not.

I was suddenly jarred from my contemplations by a voice. "Sir, excuse me, sir, that will be $18.65," Rhonda said, with just a hint of delight at catching me in mid-daydream. I hastily paid my bill, muttered "Thank-you," and scurried out of the market. As I write this, I am smiling both at my own embarrassment and at the thought that Rhonda has unknowingly introduced you to three principles of sensorimotor control that are themes of this chapter: (1) The sensorimotor system is hierarchically organized. (2) Motor output is guided by sensory input. (3) Practicing a response sequence changes the nature and the locus of its sensorimotor control.

This chapter is organized around the hierarchical model of the sensori-motor system that is depicted in Figure 9.1. Notice the close correspondence between the levels of the model and the sections of this chapter.

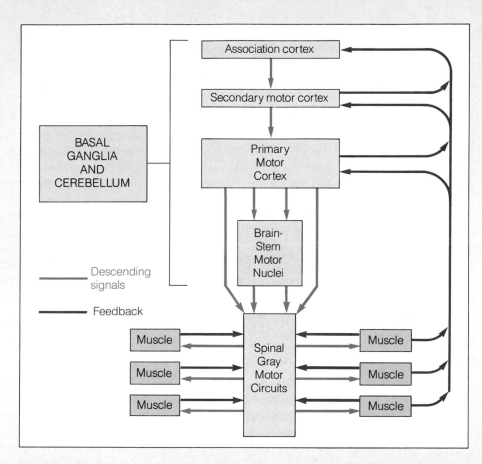

FIGURE 9.1
A hierarchical model of the sensorimotor system.

Three Principles of Sensorimotor Function

Before I describe the neural components of the model in Figure 9.1, let's consider in more detail the three principles that govern its operation—the three principles already introduced by Rhonda. Remarkably, these are the very same principles that govern the operation of a large, efficient company.

The Sensorimotor System Is Hierarchically Organized

The output of both the sensorimotor system and a large, efficient company is directed by commands that cascade down through the levels of a hierarchy—from the highest level, the association cortex or president, to the lowest level, the muscles or the workers. Like the orders that are issued from the office of a company president, the commands that emerge from the association cortex specify general goals rather than specific plans of action. Neither the association cortex nor the president routinely gets involved in the details. The association cortex or the president can exert direct control over the lower levels of their respective hierarchies if they so choose—the association cortex may inhibit an eye-blink reflex to enable the insertion of a contact lens and a president may personally make a delivery to an important customer—but such instances are the exception rather than the rule. The main advantage of this arrangement is that the higher levels of the hierarchy are left free to perform more complex functions.

Motor Output Is Guided by Sensory Input

Efficient companies continuously monitor the effectiveness of their own activities, and they use this information to fine-tune them. The sensorimotor system does the same. The eyes, the organs of balance, and the receptors in skin, muscles, and joints all monitor the progress of our responses; and they feed their information back into sensorimotor circuits. In most instances, this **sensory feedback** plays an important role in directing the continuation of the responses that produced it. The only responses that are not normally influenced by sensory feedback are brief, all-or-none, high-speed movements (i.e., *ballistic movements*), such as swatting a fly.

Behavior in the absence of just one kind of sensory feedback—the feedback that is carried by the somatosensory nerves of the arms—was studied in G. O., a former darts champion. G. O. had suffered from an infection that had selectively destroyed the somatosensory nerves of his arms (Rothwell, Traub, Day, Obeso, Thomas, & Marsden, 1982). G. O. had great difficulty performing intricate responses such as doing up his buttons or picking up coins, even under visual guidance. Other difficulties resulted from his inability to adjust his motor output in the light of unanticipated external disturbances; for example, he could not keep from spilling a cup of coffee if somebody brushed against him. However, G. O.'s greatest problem was his inability to maintain a constant level of muscle contraction.

> The result of this deficit was that even in the simplest of tasks requiring a constant motor output to the hand, G. O. would have to keep a visual check on his progress. For example, when carrying a suitcase, he would frequently glance at it to reassure himself that he had not dropped it some paces back.

However, even visual feedback was of little use to him in many tasks. These tended to be those requiring a constant force output such as grasping a pen whilst writing or holding a cup. Here, visual information was insufficient for him to be able to correct any errors that were developing in the output since, after a period, he had no indication of the pressure that he was exerting on an object; all he saw was either the pen or cup slipping from his grasp. (Rothwell et al., 1982, p. 539)

Many adjustments in motor output that occur in response to sensory feedback are controlled by the lower levels of the sensorimotor hierarchy. In the same way, large companies run more efficiently if the clerks do not have to check with the company president each time they encounter a minor problem.

Learning Changes the Nature and Locus of Sensorimotor Control

When a company is just starting up, each individual decision is made by the company president after careful consideration. However, as the company develops, many individual actions are coordinated into sequences of prescribed procedures that are routinely carried out by junior executives. Similar changes occur during sensorimotor learning. During the initial stages of motor learning, each individual response is performed under conscious control. For example, as a beginning skier goes into a turn, each movement—the pole plant, the shift in weight from the inside edge of the downhill ski to the outside edge of the uphill ski, and then the ankle roll that transfers the weight to the inside edge—is performed individually under conscious control. However, after several years of practice, these individual responses become organized into continuous integrated sequences of action that flow smoothly and are adjusted by sensory feedback without conscious regulation. If you think for a moment about the sensorimotor skills that you have acquired (e.g., typing, swimming, knitting, basketball playing, dancing, piano playing), you will appreciate that the organization of individual responses into continuous motor programs and the transfer of their control to lower levels of the nervous system characterizes most forms of sensorimotor learning.

9.2

Posterior Parietal Association Cortex

Before an effective, purposeful movement, such as picking up a cup, can be initiated, certain sensory information is required. For example, the nervous system must know the original positions of the parts of the body that are to be moved, and it must know the positions of any external objects with which the body is going to interact. The current thinking (e.g., Cheney, 1985; Ghez, 1985; Humphrey, 1979) is that the **posterior parietal cortex** plays an important part in the integration of such sensory information. You may recall from Chapter 8 that the posterior parietal cortex is classified as *association cortex* because it receives input from more than one sensory system.

Four lines of evidence suggest that the posterior parietal cortex plays an important role in integrating the sensory information that is necessary for initiating voluntary responses. First, as indicated in Figure 9.2, the posterior parietal cortex receives input from the three sensory systems that are involved in

FIGURE 9.2

The major neural input and output of the posterior parietal cortex of humans.

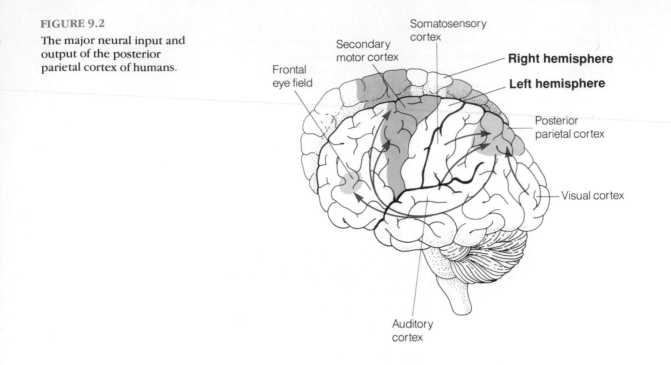

defining the spatial location of parts of the body and external objects: the somatosensory system, the visual system, and the auditory system. Second, much of the output of the posterior parietal cortex is transmitted to the motor cortex. Third, some posterior parietal cortex neurons discharge at high rates only when the subject is reaching for an object; others discharge at high rates only during the manual exploration of objects; and still others discharge at high rates just before and during eye movements that are directed toward objects that suddenly appear in the visual field (Bushnell, Goldberg, & Robinson, 1981; Goldberg & Bushnell, 1981; Motter & Mountcastle, 1981)—posterior parietal eye-movement neurons project to the **frontal eye fields,** which play a major role in the control of eye movement (see Figure 9.2). And fourth, *apraxia* and *contralateral neglect* are associated with posterior parietal damage.

Apraxia

Apraxia is a disorder of voluntary movement that is not attributable to a simple motor deficit (e.g., paralysis or weakness) or to deficits in comprehension or motivation (cf. Benton, 1985). Depicted in Figure 9.3 are two objective tests on which apraxic patients have extreme difficulty, the **Kimura Box Test** (Kimura, 1977) and the **Serial Arm Movements and Copying Test** (Kolb & Milner, 1981). Apraxic patients have difficulty making specific movements when they are requested to do so, but they can readily perform the same movements when they are not thinking about what they are doing.

Although apraxia is often caused by unilateral damage to the left posterior parietal lobe, its symptoms are bilateral. In contrast, lesions of the right posterior parietal lobe produce a bilateral disruption of constructional movements—that is, movements that are designed to assemble components of an

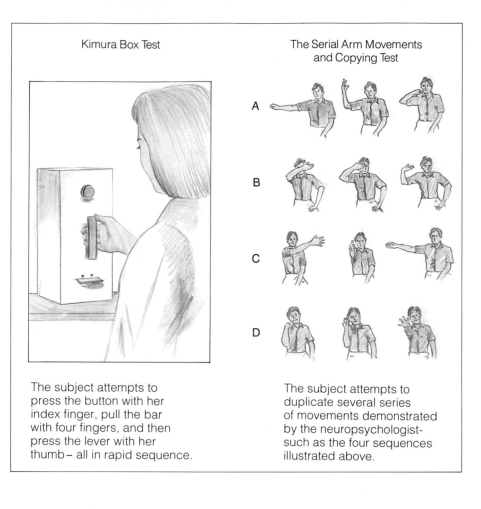

Kimura Box Test

The Serial Arm Movements and Copying Test

A

B

C

D

The subject attempts to press the button with her index finger, pull the bar with four fingers, and then press the lever with her thumb – all in rapid sequence.

The subject attempts to duplicate several series of movements demonstrated by the neuropsychologist- such as the four sequences illustrated above.

FIGURE 9.3

Two tests of apraxia: The Kimura Box Test and Serial Arm Movements and Copying Test. (Adapted from Kimura, 1977, and Kolb & Whishaw, 1990.)

object to form a whole. Patients with right posterior parietal lobe lesions have difficulty completing the *block design subtest* of the Wechsler Adult Intelligence Scale (WAIS), in which blocks with patterns on them must be assembled to form a particular overall design; and they also have difficulty doing jigsaw puzzles, such as those of the WAIS *object assembly* subtest (see Chapter 5). Patients who display deficits on such tests are said to have **constructional apraxia.** Figure 9.4 is a drawing from an old (1917) photograph of a brain-damaged war veteran who is failing a test of constructional apraxia.

Contralateral Neglect

Contralateral neglect is a disturbance of the patient's ability to respond to visual, auditory, and somatosensory stimuli on the side of the body contralateral to the side of a brain lesion (see Heilman, Watson, & Valenstein, 1985). Contralateral neglect is usually associated with large lesions of the right posterior parietal lobe (see Heilman & Watson, 1977). For example, Mrs. S. suffered from contralateral neglect after a massive stroke to the posterior portions of her right hemisphere. Like many other neuropsychological patients, she developed ways of dealing with her deficiency.

FIGURE 9.4
A drawing of a 1917
photograph of a patient with
constructional apraxia. This
war veteran is clearly having
difficulty duplicating the
stack of blocks on his left.
(Drawn from Poppelreuter,
1917.)

She has totally lost the idea of 'left', with regard to both the world and her own body. Sometimes she complains that her portions are too small, but this is because she only eats from the right half of the plate—it does not occur to her that it has a left half as well. Sometimes, she will put on lipstick, and make up the right half of her face, leaving the left half completely neglected: it is almost impossible to treat these things, because her attention cannot be drawn to them. . . .

. . . she has worked out strategies for dealing with her [problem]. She cannot look left, directly, she cannot turn left, so what she does is turn right—and right through a circle. Thus she requested, and was given, a rotating wheelchair. And now if she cannot find something which she knows should be there, she swivels to the right, through a circle, until it comes into view. . . . If her portions seem too small, she will swivel to the right, keeping her eyes to the right, until the previously missed half now comes into view; she will eat this, or rather half of this, and feel less hungry than before. But if she is still hungry, or if she thinks on the matter, and realises that she may have perceived only half of the missing half, she will make a second rotation till the remaining quarter comes into view.[1]

9.3

Secondary Motor Cortex

The posterior parietal association cortex is thought to contribute to the production of purposeful voluntary movement by defining the spatial coordinates that guide such behavior. However, something else is required before

[1]From *The Man Who Mistook His Wife for a Hat and Other Clinical Tales* (pp. 73–74) by Oliver Sacks, 1985, New York: Summit Books. Copyright © 1970, 1980, 1983, 1984, 1985 by Oliver Sacks. Reprinted by permission of Summit Books, a division of Simon & Schuster.

an effective movement can be initiated: a plan of action that specifies the sequence of movements that are required to accomplish the desired end. The development of this plan appears to be carried out by two areas of *secondary motor cortex*. These areas are the **supplementary motor area** (SMA) and the **premotor cortex.** Figure 9.5 illustrates the location of these two areas, along with the major sources of their input and the major targets of their output. They also project to the primary motor cortex of the contralateral hemisphere via the corpus callosum, and they are diffusely connected to adjacent areas of *prefrontal cortex.*

Supplementary Motor Area

The supplementary motor area was discovered by Penfield and his colleagues as they mapped the cortex of conscious neurosurgical patients by stimulating it (e.g., Penfield & Rasmussen, 1950). Stimulation of an area at the top of the frontal lobes just in front of the primary motor cortex elicited complex movements of the body, usually contralateral to the site of stimulation. Penfield called this area, which is largely hidden from view in the longitudinal fissure, the *supplementary motor area.* It is **somatotopically organized;** stimulation of particular areas of the supplementary motor area are associated with complex movements of particular parts of the body (Brinkman & Porter, 1983; Tanji & Kurata, 1983).

Support for the view that the supplementary motor area is involved in the planning of voluntary movements comes from the observation that single neurons in the supplementary motor areas typically become active several milliseconds before a response is performed. Furthermore, both monkeys and humans with supplementary motor area lesions have difficulty performing movements in proper sequence. For example, Brinkman (1984) found that monkeys with unilateral lesions of the supplementary motor area had difficulty picking up a peanut with their contralateral hand; all of the individual reaching and grasping movements of the contralateral arm, hand, and fingers were appropriate, but they were poorly coordinated with one another.

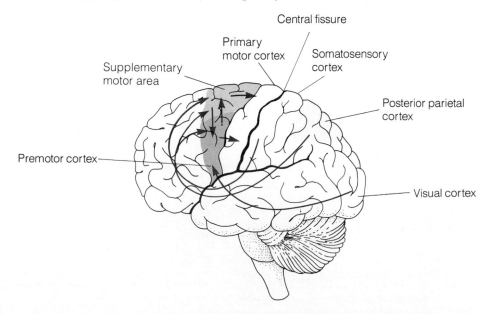

FIGURE 9.5

The location of the supplementary motor area and premotor cortex of the human brain. Major projections from both areas terminate in the primary motor cortex.

These same monkeys had particular difficulty coordinating the movements of their two hands, as illustrated in Figure 9.6.

The neuroanatomical connections of the supplementary motor area are consistent with the idea that it fulfills a complex integrative sensorimotor function. Its primary input comes from posterior parietal cortex and from sensory cortex, mainly somatosensory cortex. Its primary output goes to primary motor cortex. In addition, the supplementary motor area projects to several subcortical motor structures and receives feedback from them. Some of its connections are contralateral, but most are ipsilateral.

Premotor cortex

The premotor cortex lies anterior to the primary motor cortex and lateral to the supplementary motor area (see Figure 9.5). Its neuroanatomical organization suggests that its function is intimately related to that of the supplementary motor area. Like the supplementary motor area, the premotor cortex is somatotopically organized and projects bilaterally to the primary motor cortex and to a variety of subcortical motor structures. The premotor and supplementary motor areas are reciprocally innervated; that is, they each send neural projections to the other.

Although the supplementary motor area and premotor cortex are similarly connected to most structures, the sensory input to the premotor cortex is primarily visual—that to the supplementary motor area is primarily somatosensory. If a monkey is going to reach for an object that is placed in

FIGURE 9.6

Illustration of a deficit in bimanual coordination that is produced by a unilateral supplementary motor area lesion. (Adapted from Brinkman, 1984.)

A normal monkey gets a piece of food from a hole in a sheet of plastic.

Transparent plastic sheet

A monkey with a unilateral supplementary motor area lesion loses the food.

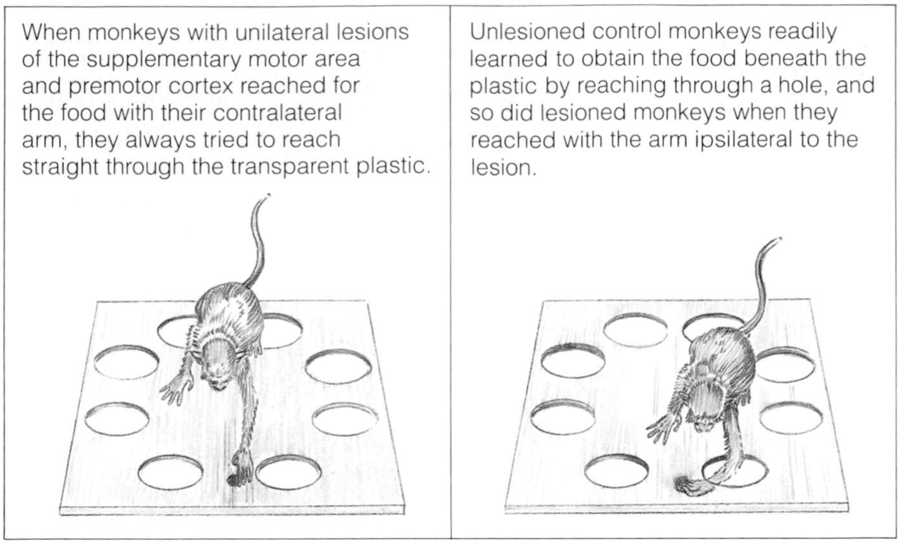

| When monkeys with unilateral lesions of the supplementary motor area and premotor cortex reached for the food with their contralateral arm, they always tried to reach straight through the transparent plastic. | Unlesioned control monkeys readily learned to obtain the food beneath the plastic by reaching through a hole, and so did lesioned monkeys when they reached with the arm ipsilateral to the lesion. |

FIGURE 9.7

Monkeys with unilateral lesions of both the supplementary motor area and premotor cortex could not perform this task with their contralateral arms. Instead of reaching through a hole in the plastic to obtain the food, they reached directly for the food and repeatedly banged their hands. (Adapted from Moll & Kuypers, 1977.)

front of it, some premotor neurons respond as soon as the object appears, whereas others respond just before the reaching movement is initiated (Brinkman & Porter, 1983; Weinrich & Wise, 1982). Such anticipatory activity provides strong support for the idea that the premotor cortex has a motor-programming function.

Humans and monkeys with premotor damage commonly display a *grasp reflex.* When the palm of the hand is touched, the hand closes with an exaggerated grasping movement. Presumably, there is a functional spinal grasp-reflex circuit in all of us, which would always be activated by palmar stimulation if it were not for the inhibitory effect of the premotor cortex. Lesions of the premotor cortex apparently remove this inhibition.

Unilateral lesions of both the supplementary motor area and premotor cortex had an interesting effect on the performance of a reaching task (Moll & Kuypers, 1977), which is consistent with their putative motor-programming function. This effect is illustrated in Figure 9.7.

9.4

Primary Motor Cortex

The **primary motor cortex,** which is located in the *precentral gyrus* of the frontal lobe (see Figure 9.8), is strategically placed in the sensorimotor hierarchy. It is the major point of convergence of cortical sensorimotor signals, and it is the major point of departure of sensorimotor signals from the cortex.

FIGURE 9.8

The motor homunculus: the somatotopic map of human primary motor cortex. Stimulation of sites in the primary motor cortex elicits movement in the indicated parts of the body. (Adapted from Penfield & Rasmussen, 1950.)

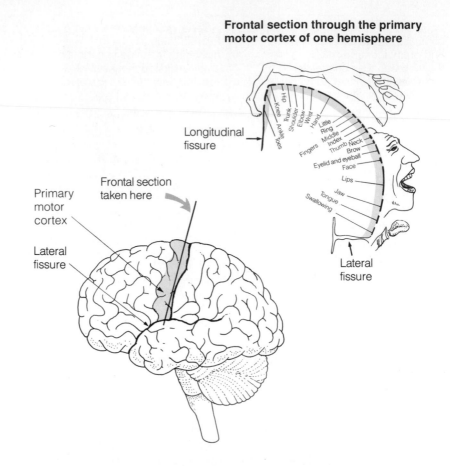

The Motor Homunculus

The somatotopic layout of the human motor cortex was first inferred in the mid-1800s. Hughlings Jackson, regarded by many as the father of neuroscience, observed that some epileptics had motor seizures that began in a certain part of the body and systematically spread through the body from its point of origin. Jackson correctly inferred that the progression of epileptic seizures through the body reflected a disturbance of neural activity that was spreading over a somatotopically organized motor area. Support for this hypothesis came in 1870; Fritsch and Hitzig found that electrical stimulation of different parts of the precentral gyrus of dogs produced contractions of different contralateral muscles. In 1937, Penfield and Boldrey reported a similar finding in human patients who were stimulated during neurosurgery. The somatotopic layout of the human primary motor cortex is commonly referred to as the **motor homunculus.** It is illustrated in Figure 9.8. Notice that most of the primary motor cortex is dedicated to the control of parts of the body, such as the hands and mouth, that are capable of intricate movements. More recent research has revealed that in monkeys—and thus presumably in humans—there are two different areas in the primary motor cortex of each hemisphere that control the contralateral hand (see Stick & Preston, 1983).

The primary motor cortex receives indirect somatosensory, visual, and auditory information via the posterior parietal cortex, the supplementary motor area, and the premotor cortex. In addition, it receives sensory input directly from the primary somatosensory cortex. Each site in the primary motor cortex controls the movements of a particular group of muscles, and each receives somatosensory feedback, via the somatosensory cortex, from receptors in these muscles and in the joints that they influence. But there is one notable exception to this general pattern of feedback. One of the hand areas in the primary motor cortex of each hemisphere receives input from receptors in the skin, rather than from receptors in the muscles and joints. Presumably this adaptation is the basis for the highly developed stereognosic abilities of your hands. Close your eyes, and explore an object with your hands. Notice how **stereognosis,** the process of identifying objects by touch, is based on a complex interplay between motor responses and the somatosensory stimulation produced by them.

Damage to the human primary motor cortex has less effect than you might expect, given that it is the major point of departure of motor fibers from the cortex. Damage to the primary motor cortex disrupts a patient's ability to move one body part independently of others (e.g., one finger independently of others; Schieber, 1990), it produces **astereognosia** (i.e., deficits in stereognosis), and it reduces the speed and force of a patient's movements. There are two reasons why primary-motor-cortex damage does not produce paralysis: one is that subcortical structures can initiate behavioral sequences; the other is that some cortical motor fibers bypass the primary motor cortex and descend directly into subcortical structures.

The Cortical Blood Flow Studies

Roland and his colleagues (e.g., Roland, Larsen, Lassen, & Skinhøj, 1980; Roland, Skinhøj, Lassen, & Larsen, 1980) measured changes in the flow of blood into different areas of the cortex of human patients as they participated in different sensorimotor activities. The rationale for their method is based on the finding that blood flow increases in those regions of the nervous system that are particularly active. To measure regional blood flow in the cortex of conscious human subjects, an inert, slightly radioactive chemical, *xenon 133,* was injected into the carotid artery, and then the accumulation of radioactivity in various parts of the ipsilateral cortex was measured with a bank of 254 *scintillation counters* that was placed next to the head. For each subject, regional cortical blood flow was first measured during a 45-second period of relaxation with eyes shut. Then, 20 minutes later, a second injection was administered, but this time the subject engaged in some activity during the 45-second test period. The output of each scintillation counter was fed into a computer that assessed the amount of change between the baseline resting condition and the test condition.

The major results of Roland et al.'s regional blood flow studies are summarized in Figure 9.9, which shows the patterns of regional blood flow that were associated with four different activities of the contralateral hand: (1) The first display shows the areas of increased blood flow that occurred in the left hemisphere during a prescribed sequence of finger movements of the right hand. There was increased blood flow in the supplementary motor area, in the hand area of the primary motor cortex, and to a lesser degree, in the primary somatosensory cortex and the frontal cortex. (2) The second display shows the increases in blood flow that occurred when the subjects remained

FIGURE 9.9

The sensorimotor regions of the cortex of the human left hemisphere that display increases in blood flow during various voluntary activities of the right hand. (Adapted from Roland et al., 1980.)

1. Areas activated by a series of finger movements of the right hand.

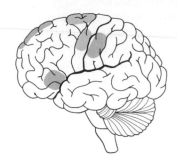

2. Areas activated by just thinking about performing a series of right-hand finger movements.

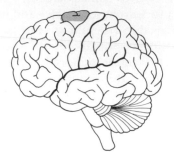

3. Areas activated by making a series of forceful flexions with one finger of the right hand.

4. Areas activated by the performance of a finger maze with the right hand.

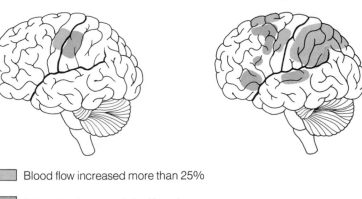

☐ Blood flow increased more than 25%

☐ Blood flow increased significantly, but less than 25%

motionless, but thought of performing the same sequence of right-hand finger movements. The increases were restricted to the supplementary motor area. (3) The third display illustrates the left-hemisphere changes that occurred during forceful repeated flexions of one finger of the right hand. There was an increase in blood flow of the hand areas of the primary motor and somatosensory areas. (4) The fourth display illustrates the blood flow changes that occurred during the performance of a *finger maze test*—the subjects moved their finger along a wire grid in response to verbal instructions from the experimenter (e.g., "move two spaces to the left, move one space forward, move three spaces back," and so on). Finger-maze performance was associated with activity increases in the supplementary, premotor, posterior parietal, primary motor, and somatosensory areas. There was also activation of the auditory cortex and the frontal eye fields.

Roland and his colleagues concluded that the primary motor and somatosensory areas can execute a series of simple repeated movements without the contribution of other cortical areas, that the supplementary motor area is responsible for developing and executing programs for controlling the sequencing of patterns of motor output, that the premotor cortex is involved in the learning of new motor programs or in the modification of existing ones, that the posterior parietal cortex provides sensory information to the supplementary motor and premotor areas, and that the supplementary motor and premotor areas exert most of their influence through the primary motor cortex. On this note, the chapter descends into the subcortical levels of the sensorimotor hierarchy.

9.5

Cerebellum and Basal Ganglia

The cerebellum and the basal ganglia are both important sensorimotor structures, but neither is part of the system of structures through which signals descend to the sensorimotor circuits of the spinal cord. Instead, both the cerebellum and the basal ganglia interact with different levels of the sensorimotor system, and in so doing they coordinate and modulate its activities.

Cerebellum

The complexity of the cerebellum is suggested by its structure. Although it constitutes only 10% of the mass of the brain, it contains more than half of its neurons. The cerebellum is thought to receive information about plans of action from the primary motor cortex, about descending motor signals from the brain stem motor nuclei, and about feedback from motor responses via the somatosensory and vestibular systems. By comparing these three sources of input, the cerebellum is thought to correct ongoing movements that deviate from their intended course, via its output to the brain stem motor nuclei. It is also presumed to modify central motor programs, and in so doing, to play a major role in learning (see Leiner, Leiner, & Dow 1989).

The consequences of diffuse cerebellar damage are devastating. The patient loses the ability to precisely control the direction, force, velocity, and amplitude of his or her movements, and to adapt patterns of motor output to changing conditions. He or she has difficulty maintaining steady postures (e.g., standing), and attempts to do so frequently lead to tremor. There are also severe disturbances in balance, gait, speech, and the control of eye movement.

Basal Ganglia

The basal ganglia are not as large as the cerebellum, nor do they contain as many neurons, but in one sense they are more complex. Unlike the cerebellum, which is organized systematically in lobes, columns, and layers, the basal ganglia are a maze of axons, dendrites, and cell bodies.

The connections of the basal ganglia suggest that, like the cerebellum, they perform a modulatory function. The basal ganglia are part of a loop that receives cortical input from various areas of the cortex and transmits it back to the cortex—largely the motor cortex—via the thalamus (see Goldman-Rakic & Selemon, 1990). They contribute no fibers to descending motor pathways.

One theory of basal ganglia function is that they play a particularly important role in the modulation of slow movements. This theory was initially inferred from the observation of patients with Parkinson's disease (see Chapter 6), a disorder that is associated with degeneration of dopamine terminals in the striatum (i.e., the caudate and putamen). Parkinson's disease is characterized by an extreme difficulty in initiating and coordinating slow, purposeful movements, such as walking, yet Parkinson's patients can perform simple, rapid responses at normal speed. A study in monkeys supports this theory, as well as the theory that the cerebellum plays a complementary role in modulation of fast movements (DeLong & Strick, 1974). Intact monkeys were trained to push a lever rapidly in response to one light and slowly in response to another. Basal ganglia neurons were more likely to be active during slow movements, and cerebellar neurons were more likely to be active during fast movements.

SELF TEST

Before continuing your descent into the sensorimotor circuits of the spinal cord, review the sensorimotor circuits of the cortex, cerebellum, and basal ganglia by completing the following statements.

1. Most of the direct sensory input received by the premotor area comes from the _____ system.

2. Direct sensory input to the supplementary motor area comes primarily from the _____ system.

3. The _____ cortex is the main point of departure of motor signals from the cortex.

4. Humans and monkeys with _____ cortex damage display a grasp reflex.

5. The foot area of the motor homunculus is in the _____ fissure.

6. Visual, auditory, and somatosensory input converges on the _____ cortex.

7. An area of the frontal cortex called the _____ plays a major role in the control of eye movement.

8. Contralateral neglect is often associated with large lesions of the right _____ lobe.

9. The secondary motor area that is largely hidden from view on the medial surface of each hemisphere is the _____ area.

10. According to the model presented in the preceding pages, the _____ cortex plays an important role in integrating the sensory information that is responsible for initiating voluntary responses.

11. The _____ are part of a loop that receives input from various cortical areas and transmits it back to the motor cortex via the thalamus.

12. Although the _____ constitutes only 10% of the mass of the brain, it contains more than half the neurons.

9.6

Descending Motor Pathways

Neural signals are conducted from the primary motor cortex to the motor neurons of the spinal cord over four different pathways. Two pathways descend in the *dorsolateral* portion of the spinal cord, and two descend in the *ventromedial* area of the spinal cord.

The Dorsolateral Corticospinal Tract and the Dorsolateral Corticorubrospinal Tract

One group of axons that descends from the primary motor cortex decussates in the *medullary pyramids* and then continues to descend in the contralateral dorsolateral spinal white matter. This group of axons constitutes the **dorsolateral corticospinal tract.** Most notable among its neurons are the **Betz cells,** which are extremely large neurons of the primary motor cortex. Their axons terminate in the lower regions of the spinal cord on motor neurons that project to the muscles of the leg. They are thought to be the means by which we exert rapid and powerful voluntary control over our legs—under most circumstances, our leg muscles are controlled by reflexive *central sensorimotor programs* of postural adjustment. Most axons of the dorsolateral corticospinal pathway synapse on small interneurons of the spinal gray matter, which synapse on the motor neurons of distal muscles of the wrist, hands, fingers, and toes. Primates and the few other mammals that are capable of moving their digits independently (e.g., hamsters and raccoons) have dorsolateral corticospinal tract neurons that synapse directly on digit motor neurons.

A second group of axons that descends from the primary motor cortex synapses in the *red nucleus* of the midbrain. The axons of the red nucleus cells then decussate and descend through the medulla, where some of them terminate in the nuclei of those cranial nerves that control the muscles of the face. The rest continue to descend in the dorsolateral portion of the spinal cord. This pathway is called the **dorsolateral corticorubrospinal tract—** *rubro* refers to the red nucleus. The axons of the dorsolateral corticorubrospinal tract synapse on interneurons that in turn synapse on motor neurons that project to the distal muscles of the arms and legs.

The two divisions of the dorsolateral motor pathway, the direct dorsolateral corticospinal tract and the indirect dorsolateral corticorubrospinal tract, are illustrated schematically in Figure 9.10.

The Ventromedial Corticospinal Tract and the Ventromedial Cortico-Brainstem-Spinal Tract

Just as there are two major divisions of the dorsolateral motor pathway, one direct (the corticospinal tract) and one indirect (the corticorubrospinal tract), there are two major divisions of the ventromedial motor pathway, one direct and one indirect. The direct ventromedial pathway is the **ventromedial corticospinal tract,** and the indirect one—as you might infer from its cumbersome, but descriptive name—is the **ventromedial cortico-brainstem-spinal tract.**

The long axons of the ventromedial corticospinal tract descend ipsilaterally from the primary motor cortex directly into the ventromedial areas of the spinal white matter. As each axon of the ventromedial corticospinal tract de-

FIGURE 9.10

The two divisions of the dorsolateral motor pathway: the dorsolateral corticospinal tract and the dorsolateral corticorubrospinal motor tract. The projections from only one hemisphere are shown.

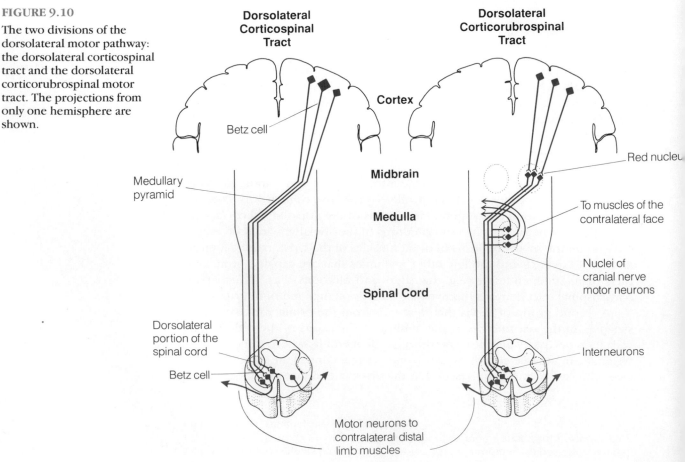

scends, it branches diffusely and innervates the interneuron circuits in several different spinal segments on both sides of the spinal gray matter.

The ventromedial cortico-brainstem-spinal tract comprises motor cortex axons that feed into a complex network of brain stem structures. The axons of some of the neurons in this complex brain stem motor network then descend bilaterally in the ventromedial portion of the spinal cord. Each side carries signals from both hemispheres, and each neuron synapses on the interneurons of several different spinal cord segments. What brain stem structures interact with the ventromedial cortico-brainstem-spinal tract? There are four major ones: (1) the **tectum,** which receives auditory and visual information about spatial location; (2) the **vestibular nucleus,** which receives information about balance from receptors in the semicircular canals of the inner ear; (3) the **reticular formation,** which, among other things, contains motor programs for complex species-common movements such as walking, swimming, and jumping; and (4) the motor nuclei of those cranial nerves that control the muscles of the face.

The two divisions of the descending ventromedial pathway, the direct ventromedial corticospinal tract and the indirect ventromedial cortico-brainstem-spinal tract, are illustrated in Figure 9.11.

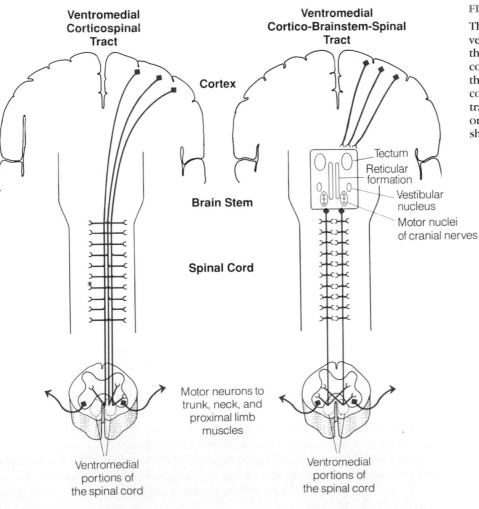

Ventromedial Corticospinal Tract

Ventromedial Cortico-Brainstem-Spinal Tract

Cortex

Tectum
Reticular formation
Vestibular nucleus
Motor nuclei of cranial nerves

Brain Stem

Spinal Cord

Motor neurons to trunk, neck, and proximal limb muscles

Ventromedial portions of the spinal cord

Ventromedial portions of the spinal cord

FIGURE 9.11

The two divisions of the ventromedial motor pathway: the ventromedial corticospinal tract and the ventromedial cortico-brainstem-spinal tract. The projections from only one hemisphere are shown.

The Two Dorsolateral Motor Pathways and the Two Ventromedial Pathways Compared

The descending dorsolateral and ventromedial pathways are similar in that each is composed of two major tracts, one whose axons descend directly to the spinal cord and another whose axons synapse in the brain stem on neurons that in turn descend to the spinal cord. However, the two dorsolateral tracts differ from the two ventromedial tracts in two major respects: (1) The two ventromedial tracts are much more diffuse; many of their axons innervate interneurons on both sides of the spinal gray matter and in several different segments, whereas the axons of the two dorsolateral tracts terminate in the contralateral half of one segment, sometimes directly on a motor neuron. (2) The motor neurons that are activated by the two ventromedial tracts project to proximal muscles of the trunk and limbs (e.g., shoulder muscles), whereas the motor neurons that are activated by the two dorsolateral tracts project to distal muscles (e.g., finger muscles).

Because all four of the descending sensorimotor tracts originate in the cortex, they are all presumed to mediate voluntary movement; however, major differences in their routes and destinations suggest that they have different functions. This difference was demonstrated in two experiments that were published by Lawrence and Kuypers in 1968. In their first experiment, Lawrence and Kuypers cut the left and right dorsolateral corticospinal tracts of their monkey subjects at the point at which they decussate (i.e., in the medullary pyramids). Following surgery, these monkeys could stand, walk, and climb quite normally; however, their ability to use their limbs for activities other than walking and climbing was impaired. For example, their reaching movements were weak and poorly directed, particularly in the first few days following the surgery. Although there was a substantial improvement in their reaching over the ensuing weeks, two other deficits remained unabated. First, they never regained the ability to move their fingers independently of one another; when they picked up pieces of food, they did so by using all of their fingers as a unit, as if they were glued together. And second, they never regained the ability to release objects from their grasp; as a result, once they picked up a piece of food, they often had to root for it in their hand like a pig rooting for truffles in the ground. In view of this latter problem, it is remarkable that they had no difficulty releasing their grasp on the bars of their cage when they were climbing. This point is important because it shows that the same response performed in different contexts can be controlled by different parts of the central nervous system.

In their second experiment, Lawrence and Kuypers (1968b) made additional transections in the monkeys whose dorsolateral corticospinal tracts had already been transected in their first experiment. The dorsolateral corticorubrospinal tract was transected in half these monkeys. They could stand, walk, and climb after this second transection, but when they were sitting, their arms hung limply by their sides (remember that monkeys normally use their arms for standing and walking). In those few instances in which the monkeys did use an arm for reaching, they used it like a rubber-handled rake—they threw it out from the shoulder and used it to draw small objects of interest back along the floor. The other half of the monkeys had both of their ventromedial tracts transected in the second experiment. In contrast to the first group, these subjects had severe postural abnormalities; they had great difficulty walking or sitting. If they did manage to sit or stand without clinging to the bars of their cages, the slightest disturbance, such as a loud noise, frequently made them fall. Although they had some use of their arms, the additional transection of the two ventromedial tracts eliminated their ability to control their shoulders. When they fed, they did so with elbow and whole-hand movements while their upper arms hung limply by their sides.

What do these classic experiments tell us about the roles of the various descending sensorimotor tracts in the control of movement? They suggest that the two ventromedial tracts are involved in the control of posture and whole-body movements (e.g., walking and climbing) and that they can exert control over the limb movements involved in such activities. In contrast, both dorsolateral tracts, the corticospinal tract and the corticorubrospinal tract, control the reaching movements of the limbs; this redundancy was presumably the basis for the good recovery of limb movement after the initial lesions of the corticospinal dorsolateral tract. However, only the corticospinal division of the dorsolateral system is capable of independent movements of the digits.

9.7

Sensorimotor Spinal Circuits

Muscles

Motor units are the smallest units of motor activity. Each motor unit comprises a single motor neuron and all of the individual skeletal muscle fibers that it innervates—see Figure 9.12. When the motor neuron fires, all the muscle fibers of its unit contract together. Motor units differ appreciably in the number of muscle fibers they contain; it is those with the fewest—those of the fingers and face—that permit the highest degree of selective motor control.

A skeletal muscle comprises hundreds of thousands of thread-like muscle fibers all bound together in a tough membrane and attached to a bone by a

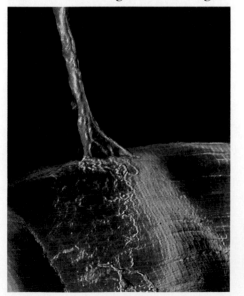

FIGURE 9.12

An electron micrograph of a motor neuron (pink) and a few of the muscle fibers that it innervates.

tendon. Acetylcholine, which is released by motor neurons at *neuromuscular junctions,* activates the **motor end-plate** target sites on each muscle fiber and causes the fiber to contract. All of the motor neurons that innervate the fibers of a single muscle are called its **motor pool.**

Although it is an oversimplification (see Gollinick & Hodgson, 1986), skeletal muscle fibers are often considered to be of two basic types: fast and slow. *Fast muscle fibers,* as you might guess, are those that contract and relax quickly. Although they are capable of generating great force, they fatigue quickly because they are poorly vascularized, which gives them a pale color. In contrast, *slow muscle fibers,* although slower and weaker, are capable of more sustained contraction because they are more richly vascularized and hence much redder. Muscles have different proportions of fast and slow fibers depending on their function.

Many skeletal muscles belong unambiguously to one of two categories. There are **flexors,** which act to bend or flex a joint, and there are **extensors,** which act to straighten or extend it. Figure 9.13 illustrates the *biceps* and *triceps,* the flexors and extensors, respectively, of the elbow joint (see Chapter 4). Any two muscles whose contraction produces the same movement, be it flexion or extension, are said to be **synergistic,** whereas those that act in opposition, like the biceps and triceps, are said to be **antagonistic.**

To understand how muscles work, it is important to realize that muscles have elastic, rather than inflexible cable-like properties. If you think of an increase in muscle tension as being analogous to an increase in the tension of an elastic joining two bones, you will appreciate that muscle contraction can be of two types. As illustrated in Figure 9.14, excitation of a muscle can increase the tension that it exerts on two bones without shortening and pulling them together; this is termed **isometric contraction.** Or it can shorten and pull them together; this is termed **dynamic contraction.** The tension in a

FIGURE 9.13

The biceps and triceps are the flexors and extensors, respectively, of the elbow joint.

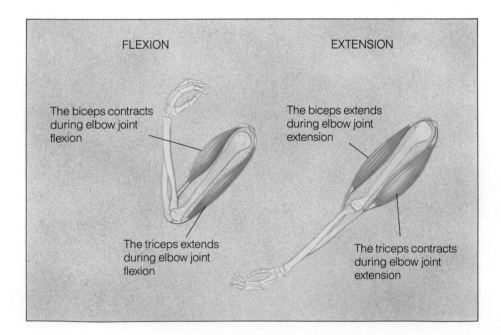

FLEXION

EXTENSION

The biceps contracts during elbow joint flexion

The triceps extends during elbow joint flexion

The biceps extends during elbow joint extension

The triceps contracts during elbow joint extension

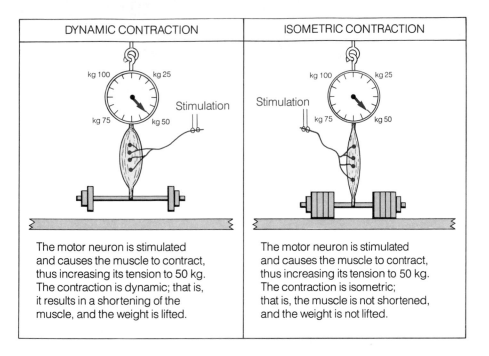

DYNAMIC CONTRACTION	ISOMETRIC CONTRACTION
The motor neuron is stimulated and causes the muscle to contract, thus increasing its tension to 50 kg. The contraction is dynamic; that is, it results in a shortening of the muscle, and the weight is lifted.	The motor neuron is stimulated and causes the muscle to contract, thus increasing its tension to 50 kg. The contraction is isometric; that is, the muscle is not shortened, and the weight is not lifted.

FIGURE 9.14
Isometric and dynamic muscular contraction.

muscle can be increased by increasing the number of neurons in its motor pool that are firing, by increasing the firing rates of those that are already firing, or by a combination of the two.

The Receptor Organs of Muscles

The activity of skeletal muscles is monitored by two kinds of receptors: Golgi tendon organs and muscle spindles. **Golgi tendon organs** are embedded in the tendons, which connect each skeletal muscle to bone, and **muscle spindles** are embedded in the muscle tissue itself. Because of their different locations, Golgi tendon organs and muscle spindles respond to different aspects of muscle contraction. As illustrated in Figure 9.15, Golgi tendon organs respond to increases in muscle tension (i.e., to the pull of the muscle on the tendon), but they are completely insensitive to changes in muscle length. In contrast, muscle spindles respond to changes in muscle length, but they do not respond to changes in muscle tension.

Under normal conditions, the function of Golgi tendon organs is to provide the CNS with information about muscle tension, but they also serve a protective function. When the contraction of a muscle is so extreme that there is a risk of damage, the Golgi tendon organs excite inhibitory interneurons in the spinal cord that cause the muscle to relax.

Figure 9.16 is a schematic diagram of the *muscle-spindle feedback circuit.* Examine it carefully. Notice that each muscle spindle has its own thread-like **intrafusal muscle,** which is innervated by its own **intrafusal motor neuron.** Why would a receptor have its own muscle and motor neuron? The reason becomes apparent when you consider what would happen to a muscle spindle without them. Figure 9.17A illustrates such a hypothetical muscle spindle. Without its intrafusal motor input, a muscle spindle would fall slack

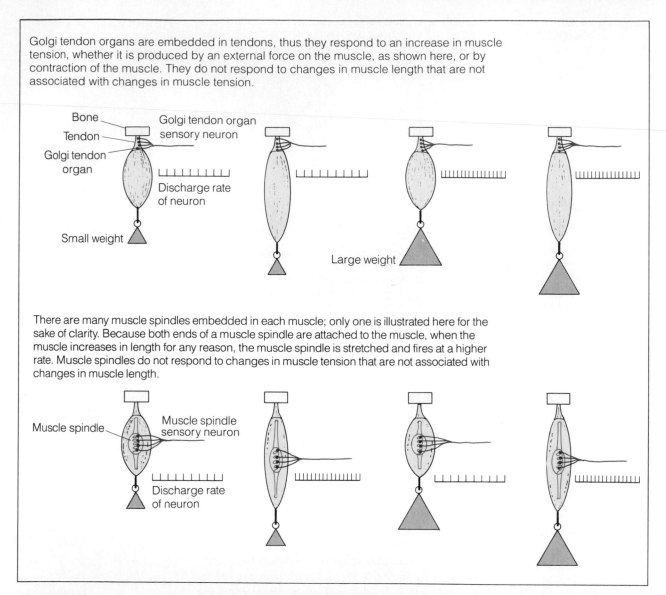

FIGURE 9.15

Golgi tendon organs and muscle spindle receptors. Each tendon has
many Golgi tendon organs, and each muscle has many muscle spindles.
One of each is schematically represented here to illustrate the following
point: Because Golgi tendon organs are hooked up in series with the
muscles and muscle spindles are hooked up in parallel with muscles,
Golgi tendon organs respond to muscle tension (muscle pull) and
muscle spindles respond to muscle length.

each time that the skeletal muscle (also called the **extrafusal muscle**) contracted. In this slack state, the muscle spindle could not do its job, which is to
respond to slight changes in extrafusal muscle length. As illustrated in Figure
9.17B, the intrafusal motor neuron solves this problem by shortening the intrafusal muscle each time that the extrafusal muscle becomes shorter, thus
keeping enough tension on the middle, stretch-sensitive portion of the muscle spindle so that it remains sensitive to slight changes in the length of the
extrafusal muscle.

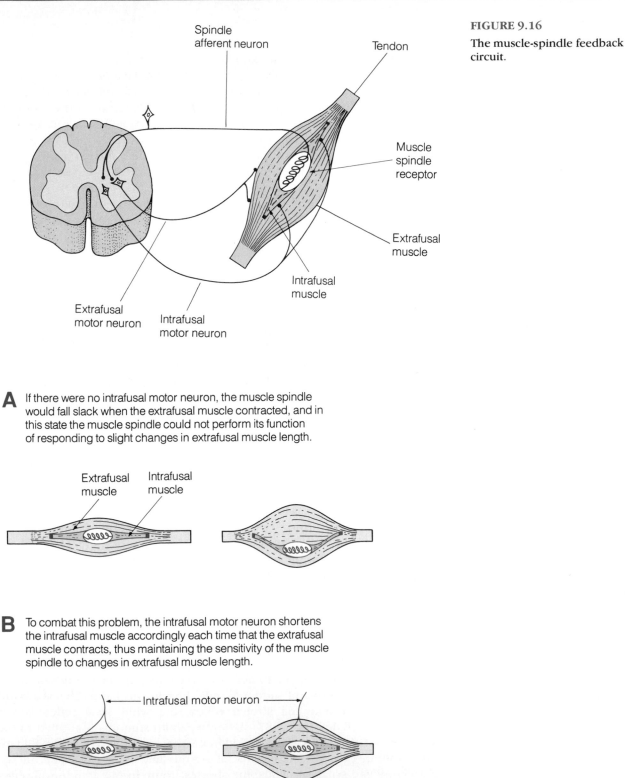

FIGURE 9.16

The muscle-spindle feedback circuit.

A If there were no intrafusal motor neuron, the muscle spindle would fall slack when the extrafusal muscle contracted, and in this state the muscle spindle could not perform its function of responding to slight changes in extrafusal muscle length.

B To combat this problem, the intrafusal motor neuron shortens the intrafusal muscle accordingly each time that the extrafusal muscle contracts, thus maintaining the sensitivity of the muscle spindle to changes in extrafusal muscle length.

FIGURE 9.17

The function of the intrafusal motor neuron. Represented in A is a hypothetical muscle spindle without an intrafusal motor neuron. In B, the intrafusal motor neuron adjusts the tension on the muscle spindle during changes in length of the extrafusal muscle so that it remains sensitive to slight changes in extrafusal muscle length.

The Stretch Reflex

When the word *reflex* is mentioned, the first thing that comes to many people's minds is an image of themselves sitting on the edge of their doctor's examination table having their knees rapped with a little rubber-headed hammer. The resulting leg extension is called the **patellar tendon reflex** (*patella* means *knee*). The patellar tendon reflex is a **stretch reflex,** a reflex that is elicited by a sudden external stretching force on a muscle.

When the doctor strikes the tendon of your knee, the extensor muscle running along your thigh is stretched. This initiates the chain of events that is depicted in Figure 9.18. The sudden stretch of the thigh muscle stretches its muscle-spindle stretch receptors, and this in turn initiates a volley of action potentials that is carried from the stretch receptors into the spinal cord via the *dorsal root* by **spindle afferent neurons.** This volley of action potentials excites motor neurons in the *ventral horn* of the spinal cord, which respond by sending action potentials back to the muscle whose stretch originally excited them. The arrival of these impulses back at the starting point results in a compensatory muscle contraction and a sudden leg extension.

The method by which the patellar tendon reflex is typically elicited in a doctor's office—that is, by a sharp blow to the tendon of a completely relaxed muscle—is designed to make the reflex readily observable. However, it does little to communicate the adaptive significance of the stretch reflex. In real life situations, the purpose of the stretch reflex is to keep external forces from altering the intended position of the body. When an external force, such as somebody brushing against your arm while you are holding a cup of coffee, causes an unanticipated extrafusal muscle stretch, the muscle-spindle feedback circuit produces an immediate compensatory contraction of the muscle that counteracts the force and keeps you from spilling the coffee—unless of course you are wearing your best clothes. The mechanism by which the stretch reflex maintains limb stability is illustrated in Figure 9.19. Examine Figures 9.18 and 9.19 carefully because the muscle-spindle feedback system illustrates two of the principles of sensorimotor system function that are the focus of this chapter: the important role played by sensory feedback in the regulation of motor output and the ability of lower circuits in the motor hierarchy to take care of "business details" without the involvement of higher levels.

The Withdrawal Reflex

I am sure that at one time or another, you have touched something painful—a hot pot, for example—and suddenly pulled back your hand. This is a **withdrawal reflex.** Unlike the stretch reflex, the withdrawal reflex is not *monosynaptic* (Eidelberg, 1987). When a painful stimulus is applied to the hand, the first responses are recorded in the motor neurons of the arm flexor muscles about 1.6 milliseconds later, about the time that it takes a neural signal to cross two synapses. Thus, the shortest route in the withdrawal-reflex circuit involves one interneuron. Other responses are recorded in the motor neurons of the arm flexor muscles after the initial volley; these responses are triggered by signals that have traveled over multisynaptic pathways—some involving the cortex (see Matthews, 1991). See Figure 9.20.

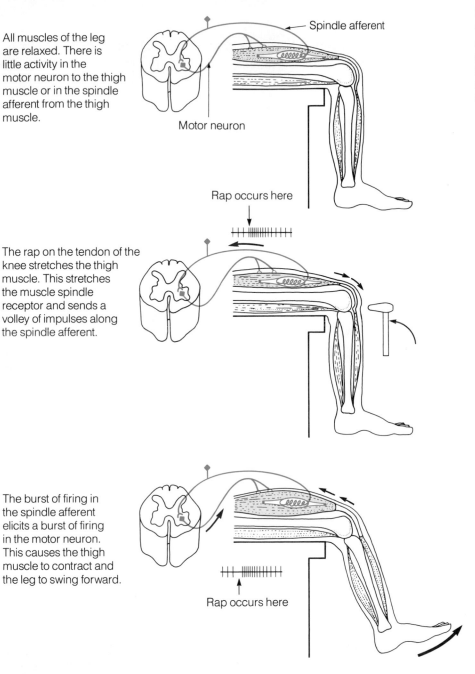

All muscles of the leg are relaxed. There is little activity in the motor neuron to the thigh muscle or in the spindle afferent from the thigh muscle.

Spindle afferent

Motor neuron

Rap occurs here

The rap on the tendon of the knee stretches the thigh muscle. This stretches the muscle spindle receptor and sends a volley of impulses along the spindle afferent.

The burst of firing in the spindle afferent elicits a burst of firing in the motor neuron. This causes the thigh muscle to contract and the leg to swing forward.

Rap occurs here

FIGURE 9.18

The elicitation of the stretch reflex. Only a single muscle spindle is depicted, but all of the muscle spindles in a muscle come into play during a stretch reflex.

Reciprocal Innervation

Reciprocal innervation is an important principle of spinal cord circuitry. It refers to the fact that antagonistic muscles are innervated in such a way that when one is contracted, the other relaxes to permit a smooth, unimpeded motor response. Figure 9.20 illustrates the role of reciprocal innervation in the withdrawal reflex. "Bad news" of a sudden painful event in the hand arrives in the dorsal horn of the spinal cord and has two effects: the signals excite both excitatory and inhibitory interneurons. The excitatory interneurons

FIGURE 9.19

The maintenance of limb
position by the
muscle-spindle feedback
system.

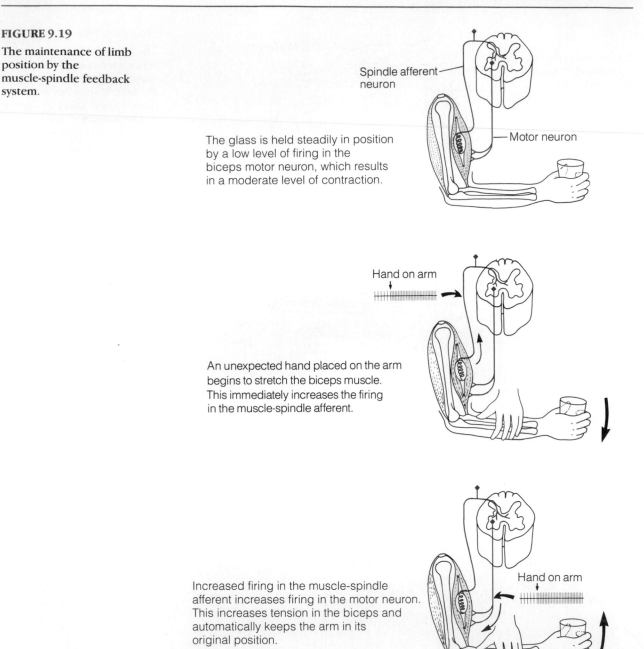

The glass is held steadily in position
by a low level of firing in the
biceps motor neuron, which results
in a moderate level of contraction.

An unexpected hand placed on the arm
begins to stretch the biceps muscle.
This immediately increases the firing
in the muscle-spindle afferent.

Increased firing in the muscle-spindle
afferent increases firing in the motor neuron.
This increases tension in the biceps and
automatically keeps the arm in its
original position.

excite the motor neurons of the elbow flexors; the inhibitory interneurons
inhibit the motor neurons of the elbow extensors. Thus, a single sensory
input produces a coordinated pattern of motor output; the activities of agonists and antagonists are automatically coordinated by the internal circuitry of
the spinal cord.

Movements are quickest when there is simultaneous excitation of all agonists and complete inhibition of all antagonists; however, this is not the way
that voluntary movement is normally produced. In practice, both agonists and

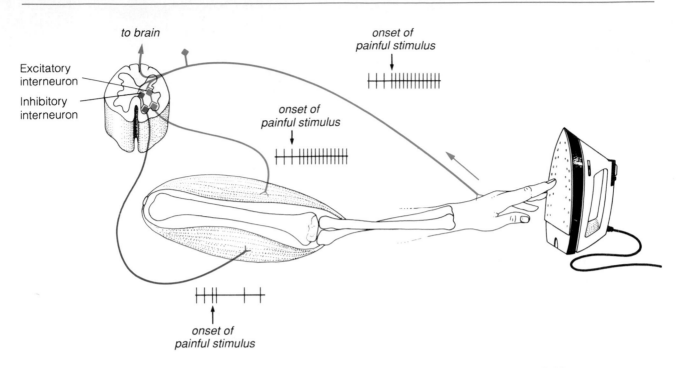

to brain

onset of
painful stimulus

Excitatory
interneuron

Inhibitory
interneuron

onset of
painful stimulus

onset of
painful stimulus

FIGURE 9.20

The reciprocal innervation of antagonistic muscles in the arm. During a withdrawal reflex, elbow flexors are excited, whereas extensors are inhibited.

antagonists are always contracted to some degree, and movements are produced by adjustment in the level of relative **cocontraction.** Movements that are produced by cocontraction are smooth, and they can be stopped with precision by a slight increase in the contraction of the antagonistic muscles. Moreover, cocontraction insulates us from the effects of unexpected external forces.

Recurrent Collateral Inhibition

Like most workers, muscle fibers and the motor neurons that innervate them need an occasional break, and there are inhibitory neurons in the spinal cord that make sure that they get it. Each motor neuron branches just before it leaves the spinal cord, and the branch synapses on a small inhibitory interneuron, which inhibits the very motor neuron from which it receives its input. The inhibition produced by these local feedback circuits is called **recurrent collateral inhibition,** and the small inhibitory interneurons that mediate recurrent collateral inhibition are called the *Renshaw cells.* As a consequence of recurrent collateral inhibition, each time that a motor neuron fires, it momentarily inhibits itself and shifts the responsibility for the contraction of a particular muscle to other members of the muscle's motor pool.

Figure 9.21 is a summary figure; it illustrates recurrent collateral inhibition and the other factors that directly influence the activity of motor neurons.

Walking and Running: A Complex Sensorimotor Reflex

Most reflexes are much more complex than withdrawal and stretch reflexes. Think for a moment about the complexity of the program of reflexes that is needed to control an activity such as walking. Such a program must integrate

FIGURE 9.21

A summary illustration of the signals that influence the activity of a motor neuron.

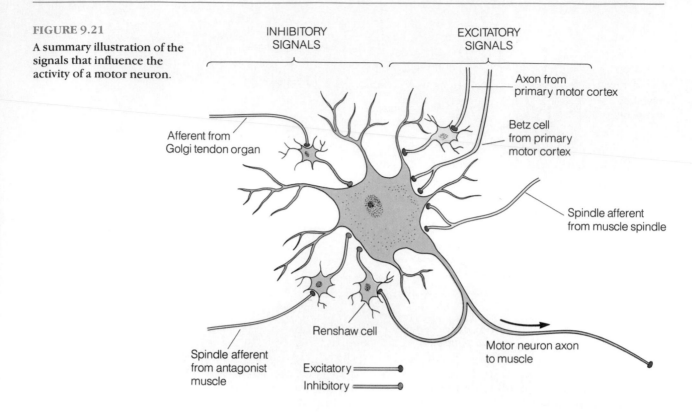

visual information from the eyes; somatosensory information from the feet, knees, hips, arms, etc.; and information about balance from the semicircular canals of the inner ears. And it must produce, on the basis of this information, an integrated series of movements that involves the muscles of the trunk, legs, feet, and upper arms. It must also be incredibly flexible; it must be able to adjust its output immediately to changes in the slope of the terrain, to instructions from the brain, or to external forces such as a bag of groceries. Nobody has yet managed to build a robot that can come close to duplicating these feats.

Grillner (1985) showed that walking is largely controlled by circuits in the spinal cord. Grillner's subjects were cats whose spinal cords had been separated from their brains by transection. He suspended the cats in a sling over a treadmill, and amazingly, when the treadmill was started so that the cats received sensory feedback like that which normally accompanies walking, they began to walk.

9.8

Central Sensorimotor Programs

Early in this chapter, it was pointed out that the sensorimotor system is like the hierarchy of a large, efficient company. Since then, you have learned how the executives, the supplementary motor area and premotor cortex, issue commands based on information supplied to them by the posterior parietal lobe. And you have learned how these commands are forwarded to the managing director, the primary motor cortex, for distribution over four main channels of communication, the two dorsolateral and the two ventromedial spinal motor pathways, to the metaphoric office managers of the sensorimotor hierarchy, the spinal sensorimotor circuits. Finally, you learned how spinal sensorimotor circuits direct the activities of the workers, that is, the muscles. The major role played by sensory feedback at each stage of the sensorimotor hierarchy has been emphasized throughout.

The theory on which this chapter is based is that the sensorimotor system is organized on the basis of a hierarchy of **central sensorimotor programs** (see Brooks, 1986; Georgopoulos, 1991). This theory is that the sensorimotor system does not produce behavior by controlling individual muscles—in fact, only a few muscles can be individually contracted (i.e., those of the fingers and face). Instead, the sensorimotor system is organized to produce functional patterns of coordinated muscle activity. The central-sensorimotor-program theory suggests that all but the highest levels of the sensorimotor system have certain patterns of activity programmed into them, and that complex movements are produced by activating the appropriate combinations of these programs. Accordingly, if your association cortex decides that you might like to look at a magazine, it activates high-level programs—perhaps in your motor cortex—that in turn activate lower-level programs—perhaps in your brain stem—for walking, bending over, picking up, and thumbing through. These programs in turn activate specific spinal programs that control the various elements of the sequences and cause your muscles to complete the objective. Once activated, each level of the sensorimotor system is capable of operating on the basis of current sensory feedback, without the direct control of higher levels. Thus, although the highest levels of your sensorimotor system retain the option of directly controlling your activities, most of the individual responses that you make are performed without direct cortical involvement, and you are barely aware of them. In much the same way, a company president who wishes to open a new branch office simply issues the command to one of her executives, and the executive responds in the usual fashion by issuing a series of commands to the appropriate people lower in the hierarchy, who in turn do the same. Each of the executives and workers of the company knows how to complete many different tasks and executes them in the light of current conditions when instructed to do so. Good companies have mechanisms for insuring that the programs of action at different levels of the hierarchy are well coordinated and effective, and so does the sensorimotor system; this is the task of the cerebellum and basal ganglia.

How do we get our central motor programs? The results of an important experiment by Fentress (1973) indicate that some fundamental central motor programs are not learned. Fentress showed that adult mice raised from birth without forelimbs still made the patterns of shoulder movements typical of grooming in their species, and that these were well-coordinated with normal tongue, head, and eye movements. For example, the mice blinked each time they made the shoulder movements that would have swept their forepaws across their eyes. Fentress's study also demonstrated the importance of sensory feedback in the operation of central sensorimotor programs. The forelimbless mice, deprived of normal tongue-forepaw contact during face grooming, would often interrupt ostensible grooming sequences to lick a cage mate or even the floor.

Theories of sensorimotor learning emphasize two kinds of processes that influence central motor programs (e.g., Annett, 1985; Johnson, 1984): **response chunking** and changing the level of control. According to the response-chunking hypothesis, practice combines the central control of individual response elements into individual programs that control long sequences (or chunks) of behavior. In a novice typist, each response necessary to type a word is individually triggered and controlled, whereas in a skilled typist, sequences of letters are activated as a unit, with a marked increase in speed and continuity. An important principle of chunking is that chunks can themselves be combined into higher-order chunks. For example, the responses needed to type the individual letters and digits of one's address may be chunked into longer sequences necessary to produce the individual words and numbers, and these chunks may in turn be combined so that the entire address is typed as a unit.

Shifting the level of control to lower levels of the sensorimotor system during training (see Seitz, Roland, Bohm, Greitz, & Stone-Elander, 1990) has two advantages. One is that it frees up the higher levels of the system to deal with more esoteric aspects of performance. For example, skilled pianists can concentrate on interpreting a piece of music because they do not have to consciously focus on pressing the right keys, and skilled secretaries can take dictation while performing other simple mental tasks (Hirst, Spelke, Reaves, Canarack, & Neisser, 1980). The other advantage is that it permits great speed because different circuits at the lower levels of the hierarchy can act simultaneously without interfering with one another. It is possible to type 120 words per minute only because the circuits responsible for activating each individual key press can become active before the preceding response has been completed (Grudin, 1983; Rummelhart & Norman, 1982). See Figure 9.22.

FIGURE 9.22

The learning of new central sensorimotor programs depends on response chunking and transferring control to lower levels of the sensorimotor hierarchy. As a result, these dancers can perform complex sequences of practiced body movements at an amazing rate while keeping the higher levels of their nervous system free to deal with the esoteric aspects of their performance.

Epilogue

Last evening I stopped off to pick up a few fresh vegetables and some fish for dinner, and I once again found myself waiting in Rhonda's line. It was the longest, but I am a creature of habit. This time I felt rather smug as I watched her. All of the reading and thinking that had gone into the preparation of this chapter had provided me with some new insights into what she was doing and how she was doing it. I wondered whether she appreciated her own finely tuned sensorimotor system as much as I did. Then I hatched my plot—a little test of Rhonda's muscle-spindle feedback system. How would Rhonda's finely tuned sensorimotor system react to a bag that looked heavy, but was in fact extremely light? Next time, I would get one of those paper bags at the mushroom counter, blow it up, drop one mushroom in it, and then fold up the top so that it looked completely full. I smiled at the thought. But I wasn't the only one smiling. My daydreaming ended abruptly and the smile melted from my face as I noticed Rhonda's extended hand and her amused grin. Will I never learn?

Food for Thought

1. Both sensorimotor systems and large businesses are complex systems trying to survive in a competitive milieu. It is no accident that they function in similar ways. Discuss.

2. We humans tend to view cortical mechanisms as preeminent, presumably because we are the species with the largest cortices. However, one might argue from several perspectives that the lower sensorimotor circuits are more important. Discuss.

KEY TERMS

To help you study the material in this chapter, all of the key terms—those that have appeared in bold type—are listed and briefly defined here.

Antagonistic muscles. Pairs of muscles that act in opposition.

Apraxia. A loss of the ability to perform voluntary movements; apraxic patients have difficulty performing responses on request that they readily perform when they are not thinking about it.

Astereognosia. A difficulty in recognizing objects by touch that is not attributable to a simple sensory deficit or to general intellectual impairment.

Betz cells. Large neurons of the primary motor cortex that synapse directly on spinal motor neurons, mainly in the lower spinal cord.

Central sensorimotor programs. Patterns of activity that are programmed into the sensorimotor system; complex movements are produced by activating the appropriate combinations of these programs.

Cocontraction. Under normal circumstances antagonistic muscles are both contracted to some degree.

Constructional apraxia. Inability to perform tests of construction (e.g., WAIS block designs subtest) in the absence of primary sensory deficits or general intellectual impairment.

Contralateral neglect. A disturbance of the patient's ability to respond to visual, auditory, and somatosensory stimuli on one side of the body, usually the left side of the body following damage to the right parietal lobe.

Dorsolateral corticorubrospinal tract. A descending motor tract that synapses in the red nucleus of the midbrain, decussates, and descends in the dorsolateral spinal white matter.

Dorsolateral corticospinal tract. A motor tract that leaves the primary motor cortex, descends to the medulla, decussates in the medullary pyramids, and then descends in the contralateral dorsolateral spinal white matter.

Dynamic contraction. A contraction of a muscle that causes the muscle to shorten.

Extensors. Muscles that act to straighten or extend a joint.

Extrafusal muscle. Skeletal muscle.

Flexors. Muscles that act to bend or flex a joint.

Frontal eye fields. The areas of the frontal cortex, located just in front of the motor cortex, that play a role in the control of eye movements.

Golgi tendon organs. Receptors that are embedded in tendons; they are sensitive to the amount of tension in the muscle to which their tendon is attached.

Intrafusal motor neuron. A motor neuron of an intrafusal muscle; its activity adjusts the tension on muscle spindles.

Intrafusal muscles. The thread-like muscles of the muscle spindle.

Isometric contraction. Contraction of a muscle that increases the force of its pull, but does not shorten it.

Kimura Box Test. An objective test of apraxia.

Motor end-plate. The receptive area on a muscle fiber at a neuromuscular junction.

Motor homunculus. The somatotopic map in the primary motor cortex.

Motor pool. All of the motor neurons that innervate a given muscle.

Motor units. All of the muscle fibers that are innervated by a single neuron.

Muscle spindles. Receptors that are embedded in muscle tissue; they are sensitive to muscle length.

Patellar tendon reflex. The stretch reflex that is elicited when the patellar tendon is struck.

Posterior parietal cortex. The cortex of the posterior parietal lobe, which is thought to receive and integrate the spatial information that guides voluntary behavior.

Premotor cortex. An area of secondary motor cortex which is lateral to the supplementary motor area.

Primary motor cortex. The cortex of the precentral gyrus, which is the major point of departure for signals descending from the cortex into lower levels of the sensorimotor system.

Recurrent collateral inhibition. The inhibition of a neuron that is produced by its own activity via a collateral branch of its axon and an inhibitory interneuron; in the spinal cord, the recurrent collateral inhibition of motor neurons is mediated by Renshaw cells.

Response chunking. Practice combines the central sensorimotor programs that control individual responses into programs that control sequences of responses (chunks of behavior).

Reticular formation. A complex network of nuclei in the core of the brain stem; among other things, it contains motor programs for complex species-common movements such as walking and swimming.

Sensory feedback. The sensory signals that are produced by a response and are used to guide the continuation of the response.

Serial Arm Movements and Copying Test. An objective test of apraxia.

Somatotopic. Organized according to a map of the surface of the body.

Spindle afferent neurons. Neurons that carry signals from muscle spindles into the spinal cord via the dorsal root.

Stereognosis. The process of identifying objects by touch.

Stretch reflex. A reflexive counteracting reaction to an unanticipated external stretching force on a muscle.

Supplementary motor area. The area of the secondary motor cortex that is within and adjacent to the longitudinal fissure.

Synergistic. Pairs of muscles that produce a movement in the same direction.

Tectum. The division of the midbrain that comprises the superior and inferior colliculi; it receives auditory and visual information about spatial location.

Ventromedial cortico-brainstem-spinal pathway. The indirect ventromedial motor pathway; descends bilaterally from the primary motor cortex to several interconnected brain stem motor structures, and then it descends in the ventromedial portions of the spinal cord.

Ventromedial corticospinal pathway. The direct ventromedial motor pathway; it descends ipsilaterally from the primary motor cortex directly into the ventromedial areas of the spinal white matter.

Vestibular nucleus. The brain stem nucleus that receives information about balance from the semicircular canals.

Withdrawal reflex. The reflexive withdrawal of a limb when it comes in contact with a painful stimulus.

ADDITIONAL READING

For those who are interested in a more detailed introduction to the sensorimotor system, I recommend relevant chapters from the following two books. The first covers the sensorimotor system from a neurophysiological perspective; the second from a neuropsychological perspective.

Kandel, E., & Schwartz, J. H. (1991). *Principles of neural science* (2nd ed.). New York: Elsevier.

Kolb, B., & Whishaw, I. Q. (1990). *Fundamentals of human neuropsychology* (3rd ed.). New York: Freeman.

10

The Biopsychology of Eating and Drinking

This chapter is about the biopsychology of ingestive behavior: the biopsychology of eating and drinking. It has the air of a detective novel. You are provided with the clues (i.e., the data) that have been gathered by scientist detectives, and you are implicitly challenged to come up with solutions before they are revealed to you. The following puzzle illustrates a major theme of the chapter: that unintentional, unrecognized assumptions frequently block the way to otherwise obvious solutions.

"It's been a tough day," Slade thought to himself as he held down the brim of his hat with one hand and clutched the collar of his trench coat with the other to protect himself from the biting wind. The star witness had skipped town, and now Boris was on the streets once again, armed and looking for him. Stella, the chief's secretary, had offered him her couch for a few days—just until things blew over.

As he turned the corner, Slade saw the lights come on in Stella's second-story apartment. Then Stella appeared at the window. Slade sensed immediately that something was wrong. Stella's face was taut and distorted, and the open window exposed her body and the flapping curtains to the full force of the gale. "Damn that Boris," he cursed to himself as he raced up the stairs.

He moved cautiously down the hall toward the sound of Stella's muffled sobs. He paused, drew his revolver, and burst into the apartment. Stella turned, and, with a look of terror on her face, she fainted into Slade's arms. Then Slade saw the problem; there on the floor by the window lay the body of Freddie the Finn. As Slade examined the body—Freddie's, not Stella's—he noticed the tell-tale signs: the pieces of broken glass scattered around the body, the water on the carpet, and the end table laying on its side beneath the window.

"One of the easiest cases I ever solved," Slade thought, as he attempted to rouse Stella, "a clear case of accidental death by asphyxiation."

Your challenge is to figure out the details of Freddie's death from these clues. The solution to this puzzle and its relation to the biopsychology of eating and drinking are explained later in this chapter.

After providing a brief description of digestion, this chapter traces the evolution of research on the biopsychology of eating from the first influential experiments, which were conducted in the early part of this century, to the present. The second half of the chapter deals with drinking. It emphasizes the similarities between the regulation of eating and the regulation of drinking, and between the approaches that biopsychologists have taken in their investigation.

10.1

Digestion

In order to appreciate the basics of digestion, it is useful to consider the body without its protuberances, that is, as a simple living tube with a hole at each end. In order to supply itself with water, energy, and other nutrients, the tube puts food and liquids into one of its holes—typically the one with teeth—and passes them down its internal canal so that they can be absorbed through the specialized membranes lining its inner surface. The leftovers are jettisoned

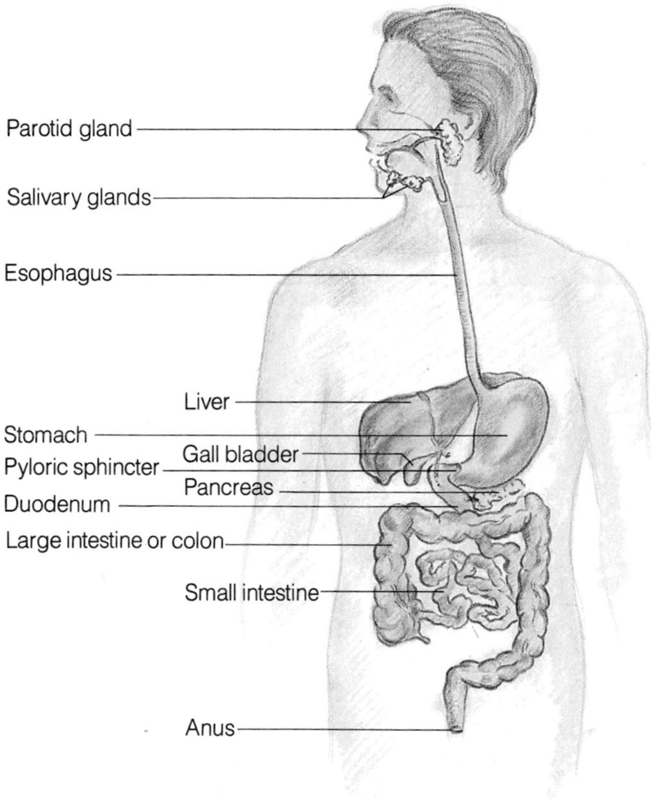

STEPS IN DIGESTION

1. Chewing breaks up food and mixes it with saliva.

2. Saliva lubricates food and begins its digestion.

3. Swallowing moves food and drink down the esophagus to the stomach.

4. The primary function of the stomach is to serve as a storage reservoir. The hydrochloric acid in the stomach breaks food down into small particles, and pepsin begins the process of breaking down protein molecules to amino acids.

5. The stomach gradually empties its contents through the pyloric sphincter into the duodenum, the upper portion of the intestine, where most of the absorption takes place.

6. Digestive enzymes in the duodenum, many of them from the gall bladder and pancreas, break down protein molecules to amino acids and starch and complex sugar molecules to simple sugars. Simple sugars and amino acids readily pass through the duodenum wall into the bloodstream and are carried to the liver.

7. Fats are emulsified (broken into droplets) by bile, which is manufactured in the liver and stored in the gall bladder until it is released into the duodenum. Emulsified fat cannot pass through the duodenum wall and is carried by small ducts in the duodenum wall into the lymphatic system.

8. The large intestine absorbs most of the remaining water and electolytes from the waste, and the remainder is ejected from the anus.

FIGURE 10.1

The gastrointestinal tract and the process of digestion.

from the other end. Although this is not a particularly appetizing description of eating and drinking, it does serve to illustrate the frequently misunderstood point that, strictly speaking, food and water have not been consumed until they have been absorbed from the **gastrointestinal tract. Digestion** is the gastrointestinal process of breaking down food and drink and absorbing them into the body. The gastrointestinal tract and the process of digestion are illustrated in Figure 10.1.

10.2

Early Studies of Eating: The Homeostatic Set-Point Model

The search for the physiological basis of eating initially focused on the stomach. The procedure developed by Cannon and Washburn in 1912 for studying stomach contractions is illustrated in Figure 10.2. It was a perfect collaboration; Cannon had the ideas, and Washburn had the ability to swallow a balloon. First, Washburn swallowed an empty balloon tied to the end of a thin tube. Then, Cannon pumped some air into the balloon and connected the end of the tube to a water-filled glass U-tube so that Washburn's stomach contractions produced an increase in the level of the water at the other end of the U-tube. Washburn reported a "pang" of hunger each time that a large stomach contraction was recorded.

Cannon and Washburn's results were soon confirmed by a case study of a patient with a tube implanted through his stomach wall just above the navel. The patient had accidentally swallowed some acid, which caused the walls of his *esophagus* to fuse shut. The tube was implanted to provide the patient with a means of feeding himself; it also provided a window through which the activities of his stomach could be observed (Carlson, 1912). When there was food in the patient's stomach, small rhythmic contractions, subsequently termed **peristaltic contractions,** mixed the food and moved it along the digestive tract. In contrast, when the stomach was empty, there were large contractions that were associated with the patient's reports of hunger. Recordings of these peristaltic and hunger-related stomach contractions are illustrated in Figure 10.3.

The theory that the stomach plays the major role in hunger and satiety was tempered by two early observations. First, cutting the neural connections between the gastrointestinal tract and the brain had little effect on the food intake of experimental animals or human patients. Second, humans whose stomachs had been surgically removed and their esophaguses "hooked up"

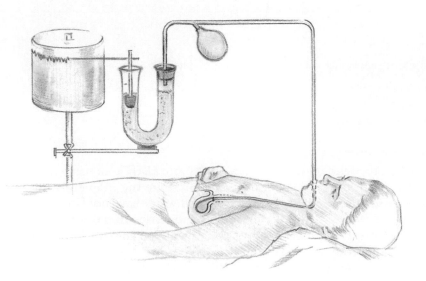

FIGURE 10.2

The system that was developed by Cannon and Washburn in 1912 for measuring stomach contractions.

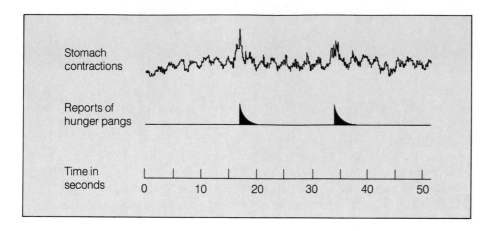

FIGURE 10.3
Peristaltic and hunger-related
stomach contractions.
(Adapted from Carlson,
1912.)

directly to their **duodenums** continued to report feelings of hunger and satiety, and they maintained their normal body weights by eating more meals of smaller size.

An influential early experiment was conducted by Adolph in 1947. He added nonnutritive roughage to the diet of rats to reduce its **nutritive density** (calories per unit of volume). When the nutritive density of the diet was reduced by less than 50%, the rats learned to increase their volume of intake just enough to maintain their caloric intake at its usual level. However, when the nutritive density was reduced by more than 50%, their increases in consumption were not sufficient to maintain their body weights. This experiment made three important points: (1) that rats somehow monitor their caloric intake, (2) that a decrease in caloric intake produces a compensatory increase in eating, and (3) that stomach distension inhibits the consumption of large volumes of food.

The idea that eating is regulated by some mechanism that is sensitive to the caloric value of food received further support from an early experiment of Epstein and Teitelbaum (1962). The procedure that they used is illustrated in Figure 10.4. A fine tube was fed through the rat's scalp, forward beneath the skin to its nose, and then back down its *pharynx* (i.e., its throat) into its stomach. This **nasopharyngeal gastric fistula** was connected to a liquid food pump so that each time the rat pressed a lever, a small amount of liquid diet was pumped into its stomach. This procedure is known as **intragastric feeding.** Remarkably, the rats in Epstein and Teitelbaum's experiment learned to self-administer approximately the same quantity of the diet each day, and when the nutritive density of the diet was reduced by diluting it with water, they responded by increasing their lever pressing just enough to maintain their usual level of caloric intake.

An interesting early case study, which will become relevant later in the chapter, focused on a man named Tom (Wolf & Wolff, 1947). At the age of nine, Tom tried to sneak a drink of what he thought was beer. It was in fact scalding hot clam chowder, which severely burnt his esophagus. This necessitated the implantation of a fistula through the wall of his stomach through which Tom fed himself. Tom found that food consumed in this fashion did not satisfy his hunger. Eventually, Tom solved this problem by chewing his

Nasopharyngeal Gastric Fistula

Intragastric Feeding

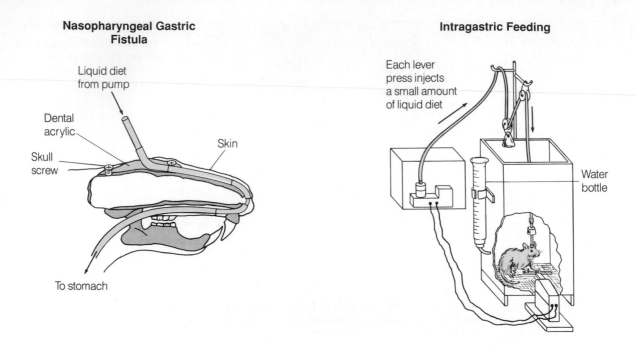

FIGURE 10.4

A nasopharyngeal fistula and how a rat delivers liquid food through it to its own stomach. (Adapted from Epstein & Teitelbaum, 1962.)

food and then spitting it down his tube. There was, however, one exception. After taking a taste or two of beer, he quickly poured the remainder directly into his stomach.

The Glucostatic Theory

The early research on eating had established that signals arising from the gut can influence hunger and satiety, but the fact that eating was not disrupted by severing the neural connections between the gut and the brain suggested that information about conditions in the gut must be communicated to the brain via the body's other route of internal communication: the circulatory system. It suggested that some component of food is absorbed from the gastrointestinal tract into the bloodstream and carried to the brain, where it produces satiety by providing feedback about the body's increasing energy supply. Which component of food provides this critical feedback? There were three obvious possibilities—the three sources of the energy that we derive from food: (1) **lipids** (fats), (2) **amino acids** (the breakdown products of proteins), and (3) **glucose,** a simple breakdown product of complex **carbohydrates** (starches and sugars).

The **glucostatic theory** of feeding was proposed by several individuals in the late 1940s and early 1950s. They proposed that the primary stimulus for hunger is a decrease in the level of blood glucose below its set point, and that the primary stimulus for satiety is an increase in the level of blood glucose above its set point. It made sense that the main purpose of eating should be to defend a blood-glucose set point because glucose is the body's, and in particular the brain's, primary fuel. The term *glucostat* was intended to emphasize the functional similarity between the hypothesized mechanism and a thermostat. Physiological systems, such as the hypothesized glucostatic system, that maintain **homeostasis** (the constancy of the body's internal environment) are called *homeostatic systems.*

Mayer's (1955) version of the glucostatic theory was particularly influential because it dealt with a serious problem that was associated with earlier versions of the theory. Mayer postulated that it was glucose utilization, rather than the blood-glucose level per se, that was regulated by feeding. Under normal circumstances this distinction is of little consequence because there is normally a high correlation between the level of blood glucose and the level of glucose utilization. The reason for postulating that glucose utilization, rather than the blood-glucose level, provides the critical signal for the regulation of food intake was that it could account for those few instances in which high blood-glucose levels are associated with **hyperphagia** (overeating). For example, Mayer argued that people with **diabetes mellitus** overeat despite very high levels of blood glucose because their *pancreases* do not produce sufficient quantities of the hormone **insulin,** which is needed for glucose to enter most cells of the body and to be utilized by them. Mayer suggested that glucose utilization is monitored by cells, termed **glucoreceptors,** that compare the levels of glucose entering the brain and the levels of glucose leaving it, and that this information is used to stimulate or inhibit feeding in order to maintain glucose utilization around a prescribed utilization set point.

The glucostatic theory received a major boost from the results of a brilliantly conceived series of experiments that appeared to identify the location in the brain of the critical glucoreceptors. Mayer and Marshall (e.g., Marshall, Barrnett, & Mayer, 1955; Mayer & Marshall, 1956) reasoned that they could determine the location of glucoreceptors in the brains of mice by injecting **gold thioglucose** into them. They assumed that the glucose in the compound would bind preferentially to the glucoreceptors, wherever they might be, and that the tissue in the area would be destroyed by the gold, which is a *neurotoxin* (nervous system poison). Remarkably, the mice that were injected with gold thioglucose began to eat huge quantities of food, and they became extremely obese. Subsequent histological examination of their brains revealed damage in the *ventromedial hypothalamus* (VMH)—see Figure 10.5. Mayer and Marshall concluded that the VMH is a satiety center.

The Lipostatic Theory

The **lipostatic theory** of eating also rose to prominence in the 1950s and 60s. It was based on the observation that the level of body fat (i.e., body lipids) is normally maintained at a relatively constant level. According to the lipostatic theory (e.g., Kennedy, 1953), every person has a set point for body fat, and deviations from this set point produce compensatory adjustments in the level of eating. The most frequently cited support for this theory is the failure of short-term diet programs to produce long-term reductions in weight; as soon as dieters stop "dieting," they regain the weight that they have just lost. In adults, changes in body weight reflect changes in the amount of body fat because the weight of other tissues normally remains relatively constant.

The lipostatic and glucostatic theories are complementary, not mutually exclusive. The glucostatic theory was thought to account for meal initiation and termination, whereas the lipostatic theory was thought to account for long-term regulation. Thus, the dominant view in the 1950s and 60s was that eating is regulated by the interaction between two set-point systems: a short-term glucostatic system and a long-term lipostatic system.

The Hypothalamic Feeding Centers

It had been known since the early 1800s that hypothalamic tumors can produce *hyperphagia* and *obesity* in human subjects. But it was not until the development of stereotaxic surgery (see Chapter 5) in the late 1930s that experimenters were able to assess the effects of damage to particular areas of the hypothalamus on the eating behavior of experimental animals. The ensuing research (see Stellar, 1954) seemed to suggest that eating-related signals are received and integrated by two different regions of the hypothalamus: a **ventromedial hypothalamus (VMH)** satiety center and a **lateral hypothalamus (LH)** feeding center (see Figure 10.5).

The VMH Satiety Center   In 1940, it was discovered that large bilateral lesions in the ventromedial region of the hypothalamus produce hyperphagia and extreme obesity in rats (Hetherington & Ranson, 1940). Although the *ventromedial nucleus* (VMN) was only one of several hypothalamic structures that were damaged by such lesions, it was generally assumed that the hyperphagia and obesity resulted from VMN damage. Figure 10.6 illustrates the weight gain and food intake of an adult rat with bilateral VMH lesions.

The VMH hyperphagia syndrome has two different phases. The first phase is the **dynamic phase,** which begins as soon as the subject regains consciousness after the operation. It is characterized by several weeks of grossly excessive eating and rapid weight gain. As the rat approaches its *asymptotic* (maximal) weight, consumption gradually declines to a level that is just sufficient to maintain a stable level of obesity. This period of stability is called the **static**

FIGURE 10.5

The location in the rat brain of the ventromedial hypothalamus and the lateral hypothalamus.

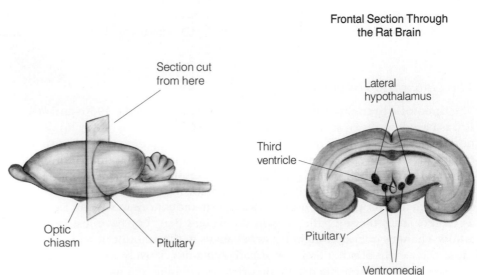

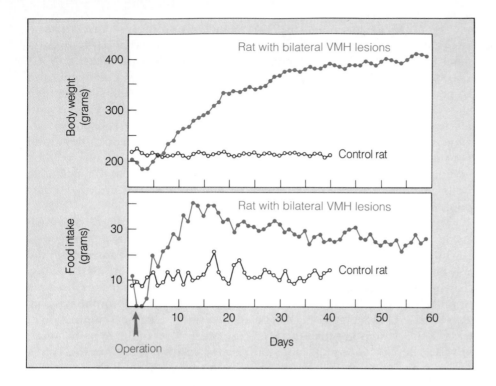

FIGURE 10.6

Postoperative hyperphagia
and obesity in a rat with
bilateral VMH lesions.
(Adapted from Teitelbaum,
1961.)

phase. The most important feature of the static phase is that the animal "defends" its new body weight. If a rat in the static phase is deprived of food until it has lost a substantial amount of weight, it will temporarily increase its intake until the lost weight is regained; if it is made to gain weight by forced feeding, it will temporarily reduce its intake until the excess is lost.

The phenomenon of VMH hyperphagia has been interpreted in terms of both glucostatic and lipostatic theories. The glucostatic interpretation of VMH hyperphagia is that VMH lesions produce hyperphagia by destroying glucoreceptors and thereby attenuating the satiety-producing effects of feeding (Brobeck, 1955; Miller, Bailey, & Stevenson, 1950). This interpretation is consistent with the observation that most of the increased food intake of rats with VMH lesions is attributable to the fact that they eat more per meal, rather than more meals (Teitelbaum & Campbell, 1958). The lipostatic interpretation of VMH hyperphagia is that VMH lesions somehow increase the set point for body fat (Hoebel & Teitelbaum, 1961). In support of this latter view, Keesey and Powley (1975) showed that VMH lesions produce less hyperphagia in rats made obese prior to the lesions.

Paradoxically, despite their prodigious levels of consumption, VMH-lesioned rats in some ways seem less hungry than unlesioned controls. Although VMH-lesioned rats eat much more than normal rats when palatable food is readily available, they are less willing to work for it (Teitelbaum, 1957) or to consume it if it is slightly unpalatable (Miller, Bailey, & Stevenson, 1950). Weingarten, Chang, and Jarvie (1983) have shown that the finickiness of VMH rats is a consequence of their obesity, not a primary effect of their lesion; VMH rats are no less likely to consume unpalatable food than are unlesioned rats of equivalent obesity.

The LH feeding center   In 1951, Anand and Brobeck reported that bilateral lesions to the lateral hypothalamus (LH) produced **aphagia** (a complete cessation of eating). Even rats that were first made hyperphagic by VMH lesions were rendered aphagic by the addition of LH lesions. Anand and Brobeck concluded that the lateral region of the hypothalamus is a feeding center. Teitelbaum and Epstein (1962) subsequently discovered two important features of *the LH syndrome.* First, they found that the aphagia was accompanied by **adipsia** (a complete cessation of drinking). Second, they found that the lesioned rats would partially recover if they were kept alive by tube feeding. After several days, the lesioned rats would begin to eat wet, palatable foods, such as chocolate chip cookies soaked in milk, and eventually they would eat dry food pellets if water were concurrently available.

Many studies have shown that electrical stimulation of the LH can elicit eating (e.g., Miller, 1957, 1960). However, to put this finding in perspective, it is important to keep two things in mind. The first is that eating is not the only behavior that can be elicited by electrical stimulation of the LH: drinking, gnawing, temperature changes, sexual activity, and many other responses can be reliably elicited by LH stimulation in the appropriate environmental contexts. The second is that eating can be elicited by the electrical stimulation of areas of the brain other than the LH—e.g., other parts of the hypothalamus, amygdala, hippocampus, thalamus, and frontal cortex (e.g., Robinson, 1964). Accordingly, the term "hunger center" is a misnomer both in the sense that the LH is not the only structure that is involved in the production of eating and in the sense that eating is not the only motivated behavior that is influenced by the LH.

Is stimulation-induced eating motivated by hunger? Do LH-stimulated subjects eat because they are hungry or because the current elicits eating responses in the absence of motivation to engage in them? The discovery that LH stimulation can cause satiated rats to run a maze or press a lever to obtain food (e.g., Coons, Levak, & Miller, 1965) suggested that the stimulation was indeed making them hungry rather than merely eliciting eating movements.

The Dual-Center Set-Point Model

The model in Figure 10.7 characterizes the explanation of eating that was offered by many textbooks in the 1950s and 60s. Although the contributions of factors other than blood glucose and body fat were briefly acknowledged, the basic system was thought to be a set-point negative-feedback circuit in which hypothalamic hunger (LH) and satiety (VMH) centers received signals about deviations from set points of blood glucose and body fat and produced the appropriate compensatory motivational changes. The impact of the dual-center set-point theory was extraordinary. When it was at the height of its influence, it was served up to wave after wave of students as if the evidence for it were unassailable. There was a sense that the major questions about the regulation of eating had been answered and that only the details remained to be resolved.

The two-decade reign of the dual-center set-point theory of eating was a period of transition. The dual-center set-point theory was both the culmination of the first 50 years of research on eating and the beginning of the modern era. The dual-center set-point theory integrated the relevant assumptions and theories of the first 50 years of research on the biopsychology of eating

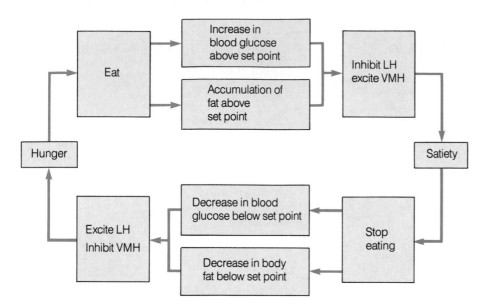

FIGURE 10.7

The dual-center set-point model of eating, which was presented as the physiological basis of eating by most texts in the 1950s and 60s, by many in the 1970s, and by a few in the 1980s and 90s.

into one theory, and that theory served as the primary target of attack for ensuing research. There is nothing special about the intellectual hammering that the theory took. All good theories are challenged, and their weaknesses, once exposed, contribute to the development of improved theories, which in their turn are challenged.

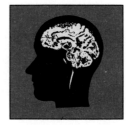

SELF TEST

Before entering the modern era of research on eating, complete the following exercise, which recapitulates the findings of the early years. And while you're at it, why don't you give the puzzle of Freddie the Finn one more try, if you haven't already solved it.

1. The primary function of the _____ is to serve as a storage reservoir for undigested food.

2. Most of the absorption of nutrients into the body takes place through the wall of the _____ or upper intestine.

3. Stomach contractions are correlated with reports of _____ .

4. Rats maintained in laboratory cages with access to only a single food increase their consumption of it when its _____ density is reduced.

5. Feeding by pressing a lever that causes a liquid diet to be pumped through a nasopharyngeal gastric fistula is called _____ feeding.

(Test continues on the following page.)

6. Arguably, the most important conclusion of the early era of research on eating was that eating is regulated by more than _____ , mechanism.

7. Mayer argued that people with diabetes mellitus overeat because their bodies are unable to _____ glucose.

8. Gold thioglucose injected into mice created large lesions in the general area of the ventromedial hypothalamus and rendered them _____ and obese.

9. Large bilateral lesions of the lateral hypothalamus made rats _____ and adipsic.

10. During the _____ phase, the weight of a rat with large bilateral VMH lesions remains relatively constant.

10.3

Reconsidering the Early Assumptions about the Biopsychology of Eating

The dual-center set-point theory of eating is seriously flawed. Nevertheless, it dominated the field in the 1950s and 60s, and even today it is presented in a few texts as the current theory of eating. I attribute its tremendous staying power to the assumptions on which it is based; they are so engrained in the way that we think about eating that it is difficult to think about eating in alternative ways. The most obstructive incorrect assumptions are those that we don't even realize that we are making.

Reference to obstructive assumptions brings us back to the case of Freddie the Finn. Earlier in the chapter, you left Freddie lying in a pool of water and broken glass on the floor of Stella's apartment, and you were warned about the hazards of unrecognized assumptions. If you didn't make the usual mistake of assuming that Freddie was a human from Finland, you likely had little difficulty figuring out that Freddie was Stella's pet fish whose bowl had been knocked to the floor by the wind blowing through her open window. However, if you did unwittingly wander into the logical trap that I set for you, the experience will have left you with a better appreciation of how easy it is to make an incorrect assumption without realizing that you have made any assumption at all, and of how difficult it can be to solve a problem once this has happened. You should now be better able to appreciate the accomplishments

The following are the answers to the preceding questions: (1) stomach, (2) duodenum, (3) hunger, (4) nutritive, (5) intragastric, (6) one, (7) use (or metabolize), (8) hyperphagic, (9) aphagic, and (10) static.

of modern biopsychologists who, with great insight, have recognized the obstructive assumptions of the 50s and 60s and conducted innovative studies to expose them.

So, what were the unrecognized assumptions that impeded early progress in the study of eating? Two were particularly problematic: (1) the assumption that eating is normally a product of internal energy deficits and (2) the assumption that the homeostasis of the body's energy resources implies set-point regulation of eating. These assumptions had two adverse effects on the early study of eating. First, they focused early research on the study of deprivation-induced eating to the exclusion of other important factors such as taste, social factors, and learning. Second, they colored the interpretation of experimental results. Early results were inevitably interpreted in terms of deviations from set points, and little attention was given to reasonable alternatives. If you find it difficult to extricate yourself from the seductive simplicity of the deprivation and set-point assumptions, think for a moment about your own eating behavior. The assumption that you eat only when your energy stores deviate from an energy set point is humbled by a piece of pecan pie with whipped cream served at the end of a large meal.

10.4

Current Research on the Biopsychology of Eating

The modern era of research on eating has been an era of revolution and progress. Obstructive assumptions have been identified, tested, and discarded; and new, more enlightening theories have been developed. This section describes some of the key attacks on dual-center set-point thinking, and some of the new directions in which the study of the biopsychology of eating is currently headed.

The Influence of Palatability on Eating

Imagine your favorite food. Perhaps it is a succulent morsel of lobster meat covered with melted garlic butter, a piece of chocolate cheesecake, or a plate of sizzling home-made french fries. Are you starting to feel a bit hungry? If the home-made french fries—my personal weakness—were sitting in front of you right now, wouldn't you reach out and have one, or maybe the whole plateful? Have you not on occasion felt discomfort after a large main course, only to proceed to "polish off" a substantial dessert? The usual answers to these questions lead unavoidably to the conclusion that an important factor in human eating is the anticipated pleasurable effect of eating the food. The anticipated pleasurable effect of eating a particular food at a particular time is referred to as that food's **incentive property** (Cabanac, 1990).

Nonhuman animals also consume food for its incentive properties. The overwhelming effects of palatability on the eating behavior of rats can be readily demonstrated by modifying the palatability of the standard rat lab chow without changing its nutritive value. The addition of a small amount of *saccharin,* which increases the sweetness of the chow without adding calories, produces a substantial increase in both consumption and body weight. The addition of bitter-tasting *quinine* has the opposite effects.

The Effects of Variety on Palatability: Sensory-Specific Satiety

There is an old country-and-western song in which the male singer tries to justify his infidelity by crooning metaphorically that when you eat steak every day, the occasional plate of beans can taste mighty fine. Although this creative attempt to placate his mate meets with little success, it does acknowledge the effect of variety on palatability. Even a commonly preferred taste, such as that of steak, becomes less palatable if it is continually experienced. Barbara and Edmund Rolls and their colleagues have studied this phenomenon and termed it **sensory-specific satiety.** In one study (Rolls, Rolls, Rowe, & Sweeney, 1981), human subjects were asked to rate the palatability of eight different foods, and then they ate a meal of one of them. After the meal, they were asked to rate the palatability of the eight foods once again, and it was found that their rating of the food that they had just eaten had declined substantially more than had their ratings of the other seven foods. Moreover, when the subjects were offered an unexpected second course, they consumed most of it unless it was the same as the first.

The phenomenon of sensory-specific satiety has two important consequences. First, it encourages the consumption of a varied diet. If there were no sensory-specific satiety, an animal would tend to eat its preferred food and nothing else, and the result could be life-threatening malnutrition. Second, sensory-specific satiety encourages animals that have access to a variety of foods to eat a lot; an animal that has eaten "its fill" of one food will often begin eating again if it is offered a different one. This encourages animals to take full advantage of times of abundance, which are all too rare in nature.

The effect of offering a laboratory rat a varied diet of highly palatable foods—commonly referred to as a **cafeteria diet**—is dramatic. For example, adult rats that were offered bread and chocolate in addition to their usual laboratory diet increased their intake of calories an average of 84%, and after 120 days they had increased their body weights an average of 49% (Rogers & Blundell, 1980). The spectacular effects of cafeteria diets on consumption and body weight clearly run counter to the idea that eating is rigidly controlled by internal energy deficits. If you consider for a moment that almost all of us in this society are exposed each day to cafeteria diets, you will better understand why obesity is such a common problem. Our eating system evolved under conditions in which food shortages were a major threat to our survival; it does not always function well under conditions of continuous, unlimited, varied access.

Rolls (1990) suggested that sensory-specific satiety has two kinds of effects. She believes that there are relatively brief effects that influence the selection of foods within a single meal and relatively long-lasting effects that influence the selection of foods from meal to meal. Some foods seem relatively immune to long-lasting sensory-specific satiety; foods such as rice, bread, potatoes, sweets, and green salads can be eaten almost every day with only a slight decline in their palatability (Rolls, 1986).

Re-examination of the Glucostatic Theory

Although the glucostatic theory of eating has been subjected to severe criticism (e.g., Friedman & Stricker, 1976; Russek, 1975, 1981), it still has supporters (e.g., Le Magnen, 1981). Two general arguments can be mounted against the notion that the initiation and termination of meals are controlled, respectively, by decreases and increases in blood glucose. The first is the evidence, which you have just seen, that taste exerts substantial control over eating. The second is that the metabolic processes of the body are geared to keep blood glucose levels and glucose utilization by the brain relatively constant, even during severe fluctuations in food intake and energy output. It does not seem likely that a signal that is itself maintained at a relatively constant level could bear the primary responsibility for the regulation of eating.

Figure 10.8 illustrates how the relative constancy of blood glucose levels is maintained during the three phases of energy metabolism that are associated with eating a meal (see Woods, Taborsky, & Porte, 1986): (1) the **cephalic phase,** which covers the brief period between the sight, odor, and taste of food and the beginning of its absorption into the bloodstream, (2) the **absorptive phase,** which covers the period of time during which the energy absorbed into the bloodstream from the meal is meeting all of the body's energy needs, and (3) the **fasting phase,** which covers the period from the completion of the absorptive phase to the preparation for the next meal.

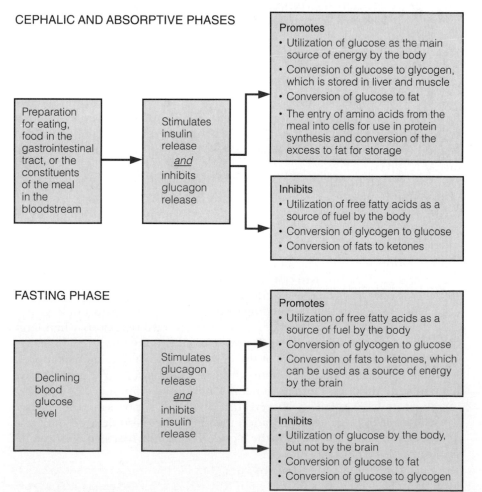

CEPHALIC AND ABSORPTIVE PHASES

Preparation for eating, food in the gastrointestinal tract, or the constituents of the meal in the bloodstream → Stimulates insulin release *and* inhibits glucagon release

Promotes
- Utilization of glucose as the main source of energy by the body
- Conversion of glucose to glycogen, which is stored in liver and muscle
- Conversion of glucose to fat
- The entry of amino acids from the meal into cells for use in protein synthesis and conversion of the excess to fat for storage

Inhibits
- Utilization of free fatty acids as a source of fuel by the body
- Conversion of glycogen to glucose
- Conversion of fats to ketones

FASTING PHASE

Declining blood glucose level → Stimulates glucagon release *and* inhibits insulin release

Promotes
- Utilization of free fatty acids as a source of fuel by the body
- Conversion of glycogen to glucose
- Conversion of fats to ketones, which can be used as a source of energy by the brain

Inhibits
- Utilization of glucose by the body, but not by the brain
- Conversion of glucose to fat
- Conversion of glucose to glycogen

FIGURE 10.8

The three phases of energy metabolism: cephalic, absorptive, and fasting phases.

Energy metabolism is primarily under the control of two pancreatic hormones: insulin and glucagon. **Insulin** is released from the *pancreas* during the cephalic and absorptive phases, and it promotes the utilization of glucose as a source of energy by the body and the conversion of glucose to glycogen and fat. **Glycogen,** which is stored in liver and muscle, and fat, which is stored beneath the skin, are the primary forms in which the body stores energy. Insulin thus keeps blood glucose levels from increasing markedly during the absorptive phase, when there are substantial amounts of glucose entering the blood from the meal. In contrast, **glucagon,** which is released from the pancreas during the fasting phase, keeps the blood levels of glucose from declining precipitously by promoting the conversion of glycogen to glucose. During the fasting phase, most cells cannot use glucose as a source of energy because glucose cannot enter them without insulin; instead they derive energy from **free fatty acids** that are released from fat. However, because glucose can enter the cells of the CNS in the absence of insulin, CNS cells continue to use glucose as their primary source of energy throughout the fasting phase.

The extent to which the body will go to maintain the relative constancy of blood glucose levels is demonstrated during starvation. At such times, the body attempts to keep blood glucose levels from falling by breaking down its own tissues and converting the released amino acids to glucose, a process called **gluconeogenesis.** During starvation, the brain derives a portion of its energy from **ketones,** a breakdown product of fat.

What evidence is there in favor of glucostatic theories of eating? Support comes from the observation (Le Magnen, 1981) that there is often a slight—less than 6%—decrease in the blood glucose levels of rats just before they start to eat a meal. This line of evidence has two weaknesses. One is that decreases in blood glucose levels do not always precede eating (Strubbe & Steffens, 1977). The other is that the decline in blood glucose before a meal may be a response elicited by the intention to start eating, not the other way around (de Castro, 1981; Friedman, 1981; Rowland, 1981a; Sclafani, 1981; Stricker, 1981).

Also offered in support of glucostatic theories of eating is the widely reported finding that insulin injections both reduce blood glucose levels and increase eating. The problem with this line of evidence is that insulin injections must reduce blood glucose levels by about 50% in order to initiate feeding (Rowland, 1981b), a level of reduction never seen under free-feeding conditions. Moreover, infusions of metabolic fuels other than glucose can block insulin-induced eating without attenuating the decline in blood glucose (Stricker, Rowland, Saller, & Friedman, 1977). Overall, the research on glucose deficits suggests that the feeding system is designed to prevent large glucose deficits, not to react to them; but on those rare occasions when large glucose deficits do occur, they are a powerful motivating force.

What about the other side of the coin: Do glucose injections suppress feeding? The results of experiments designed to answer this question have been mixed. Although there have been some positive findings, a number of investigators have failed to observe the predicted suppressive effects (see Geiselman, 1987). Campfield, Brandon, and Smith (1985) delayed the onset of meals by infusing glucose into the blood of rats at the first sign of a premeal decline in blood glucose.

Regulation of Body Fat: Regulatory Effect of Energy Expenditure

A serious shortcoming of the dual-center set-point theory is that it is based on the premise that the regulation of the body's energy resources occurs entirely at the intake end of the system (Keesey & Powley, 1986). We now know that the body responds to shortages and excesses of energy resources by regulating how efficiently it uses the energy at its disposal. This point is made by the progressively declining effectiveness of weight-loss programs (Garrow, 1974). Initially, low-calorie diets produce substantial weight loss, but the rate of weight loss diminishes with each successive week. Eventually an equilibrium is achieved, and little or no further weight loss occurs (see Figure 10.9). All dieters are familiar with this disappointing trend.

Why does the rate at which weight is lost on a fixed low-calorie diet decline? The answer lies in the fact that the efficiency with which the body uses its energy resources is inversely related to the level of body fat. As a dieter loses body fat, he or she starts to use his or her energy resources more efficiently, which counteracts further weight loss. Conversely, weight gain on high-calorie diets is counteracted by a progressive decrease in the efficiency of energy utilization.

The mechanism by which the body adjusts the efficiency of its energy utilization in response to its levels of body fat has been termed **diet-induced thermogenesis.** Fatter animals tend to waste more energy by generating excess heat. Rothwell and Stock (1979, 1982) created a group of obese rats by maintaining them on a cafeteria diet, and they found that the resting level of energy expenditure in these obese rats was 45% greater than in control rats. Moreover, the obese rats had more than twice the control level of **brown adipose tissue,** which is the main nonmuscular site of heat generation in the body (Trayhurn & James, 1981).

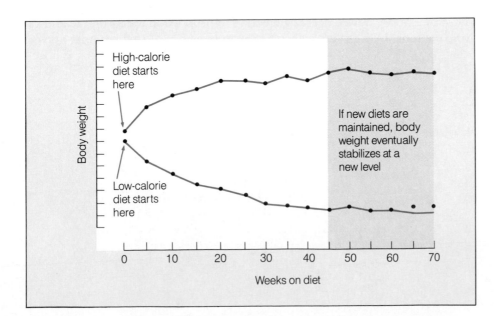

FIGURE 10.9

The diminishing effect on body weight of a low-calorie diet and a high-calorie diet.

Role of the Gastrointestinal Tract in Satiety

Interest in the role of the gastrointestinal tract in satiety declined in the 1950s and 1960s, when hypothalamic centers reigned supreme. However, recent studies of **sham eating** (see Figure 10.10) have provided evidence of a *gastrointestinal satiety mechanism*. In sham-eating experiments, the food that an animal eats has no postingestinal consequences; it passes immediately out of its body through an esophageal cannula. Evidence of a gastrointestinal satiety mechanism has come from experiments in which sham eating has been curtailed by injections of food into the gastrointestinal tract (Gibbs, Maddison, & Rolls, 1981; Liebling, Eisner, Gibbs, & Smith, 1975).

How does the presence of food in the gastrointestinal tract inhibit eating? At first it was hypothesized that gastrointestinal satiety is mediated by some constituent of the food, such as glucose, that is absorbed from the gastrointestinal tract and carried to the brain, or by some neural signal that is transmitted from the gastrointestinal tract to the brain via the *vagus*. However, these hypotheses were ruled out by experiments in which food in the gastrointestinal tract produced satiety even when absorption was prevented by blocking the passage of food from the stomach to the duodenum (Deutsch, Young, & Kalogeris, 1978; Kraly & Smith, 1978), or when transmission of neural signals from the gastrointestinal tract to the brain was blocked by *vagotomy* (cutting the vagus) (Kraly & Gibbs, 1980). By ruling out neural and nutrient transmission of satiety signals from the gastrointestinal tract to the brain, these sham-eating experiments lent support to the only remaining possibility. They suggested that the presence of food in the gastrointestinal tract leads to the release of some chemical in the blood that serves as a satiety signal. This hypothesis was confirmed by Koopmans.

As illustrated in Figure 10.11, Koopmans (1981) transplanted an extra stomach and length of intestine into several rats, and he joined the major arteries and veins of the implants to the recipients' own circulatory systems. Koopmans found that food injected into the transplanted stomachs and kept there by a noose device decreased eating in proportion to its volume and caloric content. Because the transplanted stomachs had no functional nerves,

FIGURE 10.10

Sham eating.

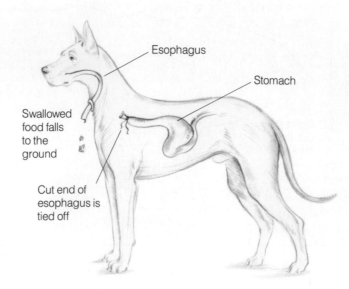

Esophagus

Stomach

Swallowed food falls to the ground

Cut end of esophagus is tied off

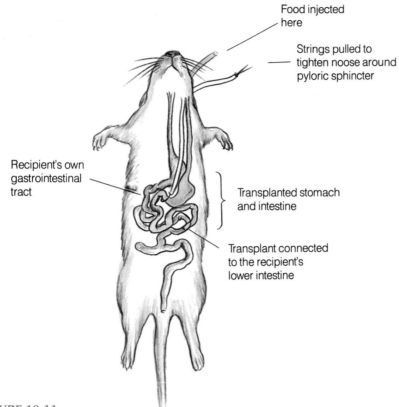

Food injected here

Strings pulled to tighten noose around pyloric sphincter

Recipient's own gastrointestinal tract

Transplanted stomach and intestine

Transplant connected to the recipient's lower intestine

FIGURE 10.11

Koopmans (1981) implanted an extra stomach and length of small intestine in each subject and connected its major blood vessels to those of the recipient. Food injected into the extra stomach and kept there by a noose around the pyloric sphincter decreased eating in proportion to its volume and caloric value.

the gastrointestinal satiety signal had to be reaching the brain through the blood. And because nutrients are not absorbed from the stomach, this blood-borne satiety signal could not have been a nutrient. It had to be some chemical or chemicals that were released from the gastrointestinal tract in response to the food. These gastrointestinal satiety chemicals proved to be *peptides,* short chains of amino acids.

The Regulation of Eating by Peptides

Ingested food triggers the release of peptides by interacting with receptors in the gastrointestinal tract. In 1973, Gibbs, Young, and Smith injected one of these peptides, **cholecystokinin (CCK),** into hungry rats and found that they ate smaller meals. This led to the hypothesis that circulating peptides provide the brain and other organs of digestion with information about the quantity and nature of food in the gastrointestinal tract, and that this information plays a role in satiety.

There is now considerable support for the hypothesis that peptides can function as satiety signals. Several gut peptides have been shown to bind to receptors in the brain, and close to a dozen different gut peptides have been reported to reduce food intake (e.g., *CCK, bombesin, glucagon,* and *somatostatin;* see Woods & Gibbs, 1989).

It is conceivable that at least part of the inhibitory effect of peptides on eating is indirect—mediated by their effects on peripheral organs (see Weller, Smith, & Gibbs, 1990). For example, McHugh and Moran (1985) have proposed that the inhibitory action of CCK on stomach emptying contributes to its satiety-producing effect. However, Dourish, Rycroft, and Iversen (1989) found that selective antagonists of central nervous system CCK receptors are 100 times more effective in increasing feeding than selective antagonists of peripheral CCK receptors (see Cooper & Dourish, 1990). Furthermore, Conover, Collins, and Weingarten (1989) found that CCK reduced food consumption even under conditions in which it did not retard gastric emptying.

Demonstrating that injections of a peptide can reduce eating is not enough to prove that it normally functions as a satiety signal. Two other criteria must be met: (1) the peptide must reduce eating at doses that do not make the subject ill, and (2) it must reduce eating at blood levels comparable to those that normally exist after a meal. There is evidence that CCK, insulin, and bombesin can meet these two additional criteria (see Woods & Gibbs, 1989), but other putative peptide satiety hormones have yet to be subjected to critical tests.

Woods and Porte and their colleagues have postulated that insulin plays a role in the regulation of feeding by providing the brain with information about *adiposity* (i.e., the amount of body fat). The fact that blood insulin levels are generally higher in fatter people supported this hypothesis; but how can widely fluctuating levels of blood insulin provide the brain with accurate information about relatively stable reserves of body fat (Panksepp, 1975)? A solution was suggested by Woods and Porte (1977). They found that insulin from general circulation penetrates the cerebrospinal fluid at a very slow rate, and thus, that the level of insulin in cerebrospinal fluid does not reflect the moment to moment fluctuations in the level of insulin in the blood. Accordingly, they suggested that it is the levels of insulin in cerebrospinal fluid that provide the brain with information about levels of fat in the body. In support of this hypothesis was the discovery of specific insulin binding sites in the hypothalamus and other parts of the brain (Baskin et al., 1983; Porte & Woods, 1981) and the observation that infusing insulin into the lateral ventricle of baboons for 2 to 3 weeks produced a dose-dependent decline of food intake and weight (Woods, Lotter, McKay, & Porte, 1979). At the highest dose, food intake was reduced by close to 75% without altering blood insulin or blood glucose levels (however, see Willing, Walls, & Koopmans, 1990; Hannah & Hansen, 1990).

Hypothalamic Regulation of Eating: A Re-evaluation

You have already learned that bilateral lesions of the ventromedial hypothalamus (VMH) produce both hyperphagia and obesity. The traditional interpretation of these effects is that the VMH is a satiety center, but today this view has few adherents; there is now strong evidence that the primary role of the hypothalamus is the regulation of energy metabolism, not the regulation of eating. Why then do VMH-lesioned animals overeat and become obese? The initial interpretation was that VMH-lesioned animals become obese because they overeat; however, recent evidence suggests that the converse is true. It suggests that their tendency to become obese causes them to overeat. Bilateral VMH lesions increase the body's tendency to produce fat (**lipogenesis**) and decrease its tendency to release fats into the bloodstream (**lipolysis**)— perhaps as the result of the increases in insulin release that occur following the lesion (e.g., Powley, Opsahl, Cox, & Weingarten, 1980). Because the calories of VMH-lesioned rats are converted to fat at such a high rate, the rats must keep eating to ensure that they have enough calories in their blood to meet their immediate energy requirements. The rats with VMH lesions are like misers who run to the bank each time they make a bit of money and deposit most of it in a savings account from which withdrawals cannot be made. The following observations have supported this interpretation: (1) Insulin levels in the blood are elevated after VMH lesions, even when the rats have not yet been allowed to overeat, and the degree of this **hyperinsulinemia** displayed by each rat is a good predictor of its subsequent weight gain (Hustvedt & Løvø, 1972). (2) Rats with VMH lesions accumulate more fat than do controls, even when they eat the same amount of food (Han, Feng, & Kuo, 1972; Slaunwhite, Goldman, & Bernardis, 1972). (3) During the day, when normal rats sleep and derive their energy from fat stores, VMH rats get some of their energy from gluconeogenesis, which is normally observed only in starving animals (Holm, Hustvedt, & Løvø, 1973). (4) Cutting the branch of the vagus nerve that transmits signals from the brain to the pancreas eliminates the hyperphagia and obesity produced by VMH lesions in rats (Sawchenko, Eng, Gold & Simson, 1977).

It had long been assumed that large bilateral VMH lesions produce obesity and hyperphagia through damage to the *ventromedial nuclei* (VMN), rather than to adjacent structures that are also damaged by the lesion. However, Gold and his colleagues (Gold, 1973; Gold, Jones, Sawchenko, & Kapatos, 1977) produced obesity and hyperphagia by cutting *ventral noradrenergic bundle* axons that travel past the VMN on their way to the **paraventricular nuclei.** Discrete electrolytic lesions of the paraventricular nuclei (Leibowitz, Hammer, & Chang, 1981) and *6-hydroxydopamine* lesions of the entire ventral noradrenergic bundle produced similar effects. Furthermore, microinjection of the putative satiety peptide hormone, CCK, into the paraventricular nuclei inhibited food intake (Faris & Olney, 1985), whereas microinjection of the putative hunger peptide **substance Y,** stimulated feeding (Gray & Morley, 1986). On the basis of these observations, it has been suggested that ventral noradrenergic bundle damage, rather than VMN damage, is responsible for the obesity and hyperphagia produced by bilateral VMH lesions (Gold, 1973). However, the fact that VMH lesions exacerbate the obesity and hyperphagia produced by total 6-hydroxydopamine lesions of the ventral noradrenergic bundle suggests that not all of the symptoms of VMH lesions are attributable to ventral noradrenergic bundle damage (Ahlskog, Randall, & Hoebel, 1975).

The role of the LH in feeding is still not well understood. One complication is that the behavioral effects of LH lesions are very general; large bilateral lesions of the LH produce general motor disturbances and a general lack of responsiveness to sensory input, of which food and drink are but two examples. A second complication is that the LH is a relatively large, complex, and ill-defined area with many nuclei and several major tracts coursing through it.

A third complication is that the aphagia associated with the LH syndrome differs markedly from subject to subject, perhaps as a result of different lesion placements; for example, some aphagic rats develop serious gastric ulcers, while others do not (Schallert, Whishaw, & Flannigan, 1977). A fourth complication is that although LH stimulation elicits eating in rats, it also increases their aversive taste reactions to the food (e.g., mouth gapes and tongue protrusions; Berridge & Valenstein, 1991).

Learning and Eating

The modern era of feeding research has been characterized by an increasing awareness of the major role played by learning in determining when we eat, what we eat, how much we eat, and even how the food that we eat is digested and metabolized. The conception of the feeding system has changed from that of an immutable system that maintains glucose and fat levels at predetermined set points, to that of a flexible system that operates within certain general guidelines, but is "fine-tuned" by experience. The following are some of the findings that have contributed to the evolution of this new concept.

Learning and the cephalic phase of digestion   The digestive and metabolic events that are elicited by food-predicting cues (e.g., the smell of food or the dinner bell) are referred to as *cephalic-phase responses* (e.g., salivation, insulin secretion, and various gastric secretions). Pavlov (1927) was the first to demonstrate that a cephalic-phase response can be conditioned. He showed that the sight or smell of milk elicits copious salivation in puppies that have been raised on a milk diet, but not in those that have been raised on solid foods. He also showed, in his classic experiments, that salivation is elicited by a tone that predicts the presentation of food. Detke, Brandon, Weingarten, Rodin, and Wagner (1989) found that the release of insulin in response to a food-predicting cue is greater in a context in which the subjects expect to eat.

Learning and meal initiation   Weingarten (1983, 1984) has shown that learning can influence the initiation of a meal. During the conditioning phase of one of his experiments, Weingarten presented a 4.5-minute buzzer-and-light conditional stimulus to rats before each of their meals. Each meal, which consisted of a small amount of a highly palatable liquid diet, was presented during the last half minute of the conditional stimulus. The rats received six such meals per day at irregular intervals, and at the midpoint between each meal, a pure tone was sounded. This conditioning procedure was continued for 11 consecutive days. Throughout the ensuing test phase of the experiment, the palatable liquid diet was continuously available in the rats' home cages. Despite the fact that the subjects were never deprived during the test phase, each time that the buzzer and light were presented, the rats started to eat—eating in response to the pure tone was rare. Weingarten's research suggests that we do not become hungry at meal times because we are experiencing an energy deficit—few of us in this society begin meals in need of energy. We become hungry because of the presence of external cues that have previously predicted a meal—conditional cues such as the time of day or the sight, smell, and taste of food. Hosts who serve *hors d'oeuvres* to their dinner guests understand this principle well.

Learning what to eat   There are many substances in the environment; some are edible and some are not. How do humans and other mammals know what to eat? Part of the answer is that they are born with preferences for tastes that are associated in nature with critical nutrients—tastes such as sweet, salty, and fatty. The other part of the answer is that animals have the ability to learn the relation between taste and postingestinal consequences. Animals readily learn to avoid tastes that are followed by illness (*conditioned taste aversion;* Chapter 5), and they also learn to prefer tastes that are followed by an infusion of nutrients (Arbour & Wilkie, 1988; Baker & Booth, 1989; Lucas & Sclafani, 1989; Sclafani, 1990).

Social influences also have a major impact on what animals eat (Rozin, 1988). For example, rats learn to prefer flavors that they experience in mother's milk (Galef & Sherry, 1973) and those that they smell on the breaths of other rats (Galef, 1989; Galef, Attenborough, & Whiskin, 1990).

In addition to energy, food supplies us with essential vitamins and minerals. How do animals select a diet that provides all of the vitamins and minerals that they need? To answer this question, researchers have studied how dietary deficiencies influence diet selection. Two patterns of results have emerged: one for sodium deficiency and the other for deficiencies in other essential vitamins and minerals. When an animal is deficient in sodium, it develops an immediate and compelling preference for the taste of sodium salt— it does not have to learn to eat foods rich in sodium (see Rowland, 1990b). In contrast, an animal that is deficient in some mineral other than sodium must learn to consume foods that are rich in the missing nutrient by experiencing their positive postingestinal effects. For example, rats maintained on a diet deficient in **thiamin** (vitamin B_1) develop an aversion to the taste of that diet and a preference for the taste of thiamin-rich diets (thiamin itself imparts no taste to food).

Why are dietary deficiencies so common in societies, such as ours, in which many healthy foods are readily available? One reason is that, in order to maximize profits, manufacturers sell foods with the tastes that we prefer, with most of the essential nutrients extracted from them; even rats prefer chocolate chip cookies to nutritionally complete rat chow. The second reason is illustrated by the classic study of Harris, Clay, Hargreaves, and Ward (1933). When thiamin-deficient rats were offered two new diets, one with thiamin and one without, within days almost all of them were eating the complete diet and avoiding the deficient one. However, when they were offered 10 new diets, only one of which contained the badly needed thiamin, few developed a preference for the complete diet. The number of different substances consumed each day by most people in industrialized societies is immense, and such variety makes it very difficult for our bodies to use their natural ability to learn which foods are beneficial and which are not.

Learning how much to eat   Experience also plays an important role in determining when meals are terminated (see Booth, 1985; Weingarten, 1990). Weingarten and Kulikovsky (1989) used the sham-feeding procedure to demonstrate the effect of learning on satiety (see Figure 10.12). First, they determined how much flavored sucrose solution was consumed by food-deprived rats during daily real-feeding tests. Then, during the sham-eating phase of the experiment, some rats sham ate the same solution, whereas others sham ate a similar solution with a different flavor. When the flavor stayed

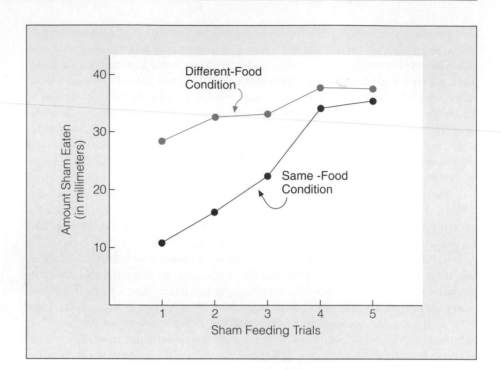

FIGURE 10.12

Change in the magnitude of sham feeding over repeated sham-feeding trials. The rats in one group sham ate the same diet that they had eaten before the sham-feeding phase; the rats in another group sham ate a diet different from the one that they had previously eaten. (Adapted from Weingarten, 1990.)

the same, the rats started out sham eating about the same amount as they had eaten during the real feeding; then, on ensuing days they sham ate more and more. When the flavor was different, they sham ate large quantities right from the start. Weingarten and Kulikovsky concluded that the amount that we eat at a meal is largely influenced by our previous experience of the postingestinal effects of the same foods.

10.5

Current Biopsychological Theories of Eating: Incentives and Settling Points

The modern era of research on the biopsychology of eating has led to a new generation of theories. Many of these new theories are based on two important ideas about eating: (1) that eating is controlled by the incentive properties of food, and, (2) that eating is one component of a settling-point system that maintains homeostasis.

Incentives and Eating

Several authors (e.g., Bolles, 1980; Booth, 1981; Collier, 1980, Rolls, 1981; Toates, 1981) have argued that humans and other animals are not driven to eat by internal energy deficits; they are drawn to eat by the anticipated pleasure-producing effects of food, that is, by the food's incentive properties. This new way of thinking about eating does not deny the importance of internal regulatory factors. In fact, it suggests how internal regulatory factors exert their effects. According to incentive theories, both internal and external factors influence eating in the same way, by changing the incentive value of available foods (see Cabanac, 1971). You have already learned in this chapter about a variety of factors that can change a food's incentive value. For example, the incentive value of a particular food is reduced if its consumption has been followed by gastrointestinal upset or if a large amount of that food has recently been consumed, and the incentive value of all foods is reduced by a full stomach. On the other side of the coin, experiencing the health-promoting effects of a food increases the incentive value of that particular food, and deprivation or expecting a meal tend to increase the incentive value of all palatable foods. If you have difficulty appreciating the degree to which the incentive value of a food can change, think about how you would feel about a turkey sandwich after a 3-day fast, and how you would feel about the same sandwich just after your last, gut-straining mouthful of a turkey dinner.

Since the proposal of incentive theories of eating, the interaction between the energy resources of the body and the incentive properties of food has become an important area of research (e.g., Bedard & Weingarten, 1989; Scott, 1990). For example, Booth (1981) asked subjects to rate the momentary pleasure produced by the flavor, the smell, the sight, or just the thought of various foods at different times after consuming a high-calorie, high-carbohydrate liquid diet. There was strong evidence of an immediate sensory-specific decrease in palatability; as soon as the drink was consumed, foods of the same or similar flavor were judged to be much less palatable. This was followed by a general decrease in the palatability of all substances about 30 minutes later. Thus, it appears that signals from taste receptors produce an immediate decline in the incentive value of similar tastes, and that some signal that is associated with the increased energy supply from a meal produces a general decrease in the incentive properties of all foods.

Incentive theories of eating receive strong support from Rolls and Rolls's (1982) discovery of neurons in the LH that respond to the incentive properties of food, rather than to food itself. When monkeys were repeatedly allowed to eat one palatable food, the response of the LH neurons to it declined, although their response to other palatable foods did not. Furthermore, neurons that responded to the sight of food would come to respond to a neutral stimulus that reliably predicted the presentation of food (see Figure 10.13). The repeated presentation of a palatable food (e.g., a banana) to a monkey without allowing the monkey to eat it eventually rendered that item incapable of producing its usual neural response (Mora, Rolls, & Burton, 1976).

The influential study of intragastric feeding by Teitelbaum and Epstein (1962), which was mentioned earlier in the chapter, seems to contradict the notion that internal states influence eating by changing the incentive value of food. Teitelbaum and Epstein reported that rats can maintain their usual body weight by pressing a lever to inject calorically appropriate amounts of food directly into their stomachs through a nasopharyngeal gastric fistula. Several authors have failed to replicate this finding; Holman (1968) showed why. He demonstrated that oral stimulation from the chilled liquid diet as it

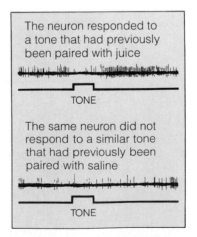

FIGURE 10.13

The response of a neuron in the vicinity of the lateral hypothalamus to the expectation of food. (Adapted from Rolls, Sanghera, & Roper-Hall, 1979.)

was pumped down the nasopharyngeal cannula was an unrecognized, but critical, factor in Teitelbaum and Epstein's results. Holman found that rats would not reliably lever press to inject solutions maintained at body temperature down nasopharyngeal cannulas and that they would not lever press to inject any solution directly through the stomach wall in the absence of concomitant oral stimulation. Holman concluded that intragastric injections do not reinforce lever pressing directly, but that they do so by influencing the incentive properties of the oral stimuli associated with them. Recall Tom, the beer-loving patient with the fused esophagus, who was satisfied by food poured into his stomach only if he tasted it first.

A recent article by Woods (1991) drives the final nail into the coffin of the assumption that internal energy deficits are the major motivating factor in food consumption. Woods makes three important points: first, that we eat to prevent energy deficits, not to correct them; second, that we are usually in homeostatic balance when we start to eat; and third, that the main short-term consequence of eating is the disruption of homeostasis. After a large meal, there is a substantial and potentially harmful elevation of glucose and insulin levels in the blood.

Settling Points and Eating

Since the beginning of the study of the physiological basis of eating early in this century, many researchers have been searching the nervous system for a certain kind of eating circuit: one that involves mechanisms that are sensitive to deviations from one or more hypothetical set points. Although such a model can account for the homeostasis (stability) of the body's energy resources, it has two major flaws. The first is that it is unnecessarily complex; homeostasis can be explained without having to postulate set points and deviation detectors. The second is that it cannot account for instances in which eating is clearly not homeostatic. Despite these serious flaws, set-point thinking has dominated the study of eating. In fact, until recently, alternatives to set-point theories have not been seriously considered because homeostasis and set-point mechanisms have been inseparable in many people's thinking. It has been implicitly assumed that the existence of homeostasis implies the existence of set-point mechanisms. It doesn't; there are other possibilities— once again, we encounter in this chapter the obstructive effect of an incorrect unrecognized assumption. Remember the lesson of Freddie the Finn.

Many investigators (e.g., Booth, Fuller, & Lewis, 1981) now believe that eating is not part of a system that is designed to defend a body-weight set point. They argue that body weight tends to drift around a natural **settling point,** the level at which the various factors that influence it achieve an equilibrium. The seductiveness of the set-point theory is attributable in no small part to the existence of a compelling set-point model: the thermostat. Figure 10.14 is a model that I like to use to explain the settling point theory. I call it the **leaky-barrel model.**

The leaky-barrel model is an analogy. (1) The amount of water entering the hose is analogous to the amount of food available to the subject; (2) the water pressure at the nozzle is analogous to the incentive value of the available food; (3) the amount of water entering the barrel is analogous to the amount of consumed energy; (4) the water level in the barrel is analogous to

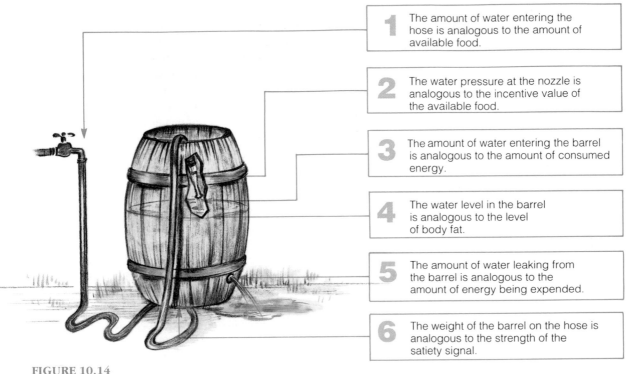

1 The amount of water entering the hose is analogous to the amount of available food.

2 The water pressure at the nozzle is analogous to the incentive value of the available food.

3 The amount of water entering the barrel is analogous to the amount of consumed energy.

4 The water level in the barrel is analogous to the level of body fat.

5 The amount of water leaking from the barrel is analogous to the amount of energy being expended.

6 The weight of the barrel on the hose is analogous to the strength of the satiety signal.

FIGURE 10.14

The leaky-barrel model: A settling-point model of eating and body-weight homeostasis.

the level of body fat; and (5) the amount of water leaking from the barrel is analogous to the amount of energy being expended; and (6) the weight of the barrel on the hose is analogous to the strength of the satiety signal.

The essence of the settling-point theory of eating and body weight is that the level of fat in the body, like the level of water in a leaky barrel, rather than being regulated around a predetermined set point, is regulated around a natural settling point, the point at which various factors that influence its level achieve an equilibrium. An equilibrium is always achieved because of negative feedback: Decreases in fat levels always produce reactions that increase them, and vice versa. Let's see how well the settling-point theory accounts for the three lines of evidence commonly offered in support of set-point models.

Finding 1: Total body fat—usually inferred from body weight—remains relatively constant in many adult animals. Therefore, it must be regulated around a set point. Rebuttal 1: Constant body weight does not require, or even imply, a set point. Consider the leaky-barrel model. As water from the tap begins to fill the barrel, the weight of the water in the barrel increases. This increases the amount of water leaking out of the barrel and decreases the amount of water entering the barrel by increasing the pressure of the barrel on the hose. Eventually this system settles into an equilibrium where the water level stays constant, but because this level is neither predetermined nor actively defended, it is more appropriately referred to as a *settling point* (Wirtshafter & Davis, 1977) than a set point. A neuron's resting potential is another well-known biological settling point (see Chapter 4).

Finding 2: If a subject's intake of food is reduced, metabolic changes occur that counteract the effects of the reduction, and weight loss is limited. The opposite occurs when the subject overeats. Therefore, there must be a set point for body fat that is actively defended. Rebuttal 2: The leaky-barrel model lacks a set point and yet responds in exactly the same way. When water intake is reduced, the water level in the barrel begins to drop, but the drop is counteracted by a decrease in leakage attributable to the falling water pressure in the barrel. Eventually, a new settling point is achieved, but the reduction in water level is not as great as one might expect because of the offsetting changes. The opposite happens when water inflow is increased.

Finding 3: After an individual has lost a substantial amount of weight, either by dieting, exercise, or even by **lipectomy,** the surgical removal of fat (Faust, Johnson, & Hirsch, 1977), there is a tendency for the original weight to be regained once the subject returns to his or her previous eating-and-energy-related lifestyle. Surely the fact that the lost weight is regained proves that there is an actively defended set point. Rebuttal 3: Again, these results can be accounted for without having to postulate the existence of a set point. Reducing the water level in the leaky-barrel model—whether by temporarily decreasing input (dieting), by temporarily increasing output (exercising), or by scooping out some of the water (lipectomy)—produces only a temporary drop in the settling point. When the original conditions are reinstated, the water level inexorably drifts back to the original settling point. The course of the typical weight-reduction diet is illustrated and interpreted in Figure 10.15.

FIGURE 10.15

The five stages of a typical (unsuccessful) weight-loss program.

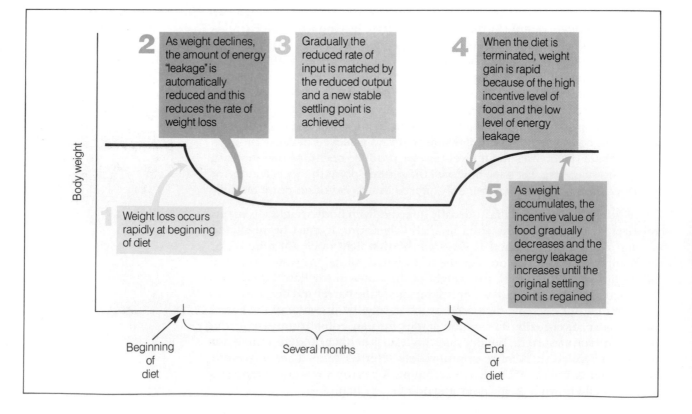

　　As you have just seen, the leaky-barrel model readily accounts for the homeostasis of body weight, and it does it without having to postulate the existence of a set-point mechanism for which there is no direct evidence. Unlike set-point theories, settling point theories can also account for those instances in which there are long-term changes in body weight. Any time there is a permanent change in any factor that influences the availability or incentive value of food or the output of energy, body weight will drift to a new settling point and stay there.

10.6

Drinking and the Regulation of Body Fluids

The remainder of the chapter focuses on the biopsychology of drinking. Many people think of eating (ingesting vitamins, minerals, and sources of energy) and drinking (ingesting water) as separate behaviors, but in practice they are not. Most of the food that we eat contains water, and most of the liquids that we drink are sources of energy, vitamins, and minerals.

　　Two themes will emerge from the discussion of drinking. One is that there are fundamental similarities between the regulation of drinking and the regulation of eating. The other is that the study of these two ingestive behaviors has evolved in parallel.

The Dry-Mouth Theory of Thirst

Just as early studies of eating focused on peripheral factors (i.e., the stomach), so too did early studies of drinking. Early studies of drinking focused on the motivating effects of a dry mouth. Dry mouth is one consequence of water deficiency, but the evidence suggests that it is not the primary factor in thirst. For example, producing chronic dry mouth by removing the *salivary glands* does not substantially increase water intake unless subjects are fed dry food or maintained in a very hot environment (e.g., Epstein, Spector, Samman, & Goldblum, 1964). Conversely, blocking the sensation of dry mouth with local anesthetics or neural transection does not decrease water intake (Grossman, 1967). The most convincing evidence against the dry-mouth theory of thirst comes from studies of **sham drinking.** In sham drinking experiments, the water that a subject drinks flows down its esophagus and then out of its body through a fistula before it can be absorbed. Despite their lack of a dry mouth, subjects with water deficit sham drink copiously (Maddison, Wood, Rolls, Rolls, & Gibbs, 1980).

Intracellular and Extracellular Fluid Compartments

Most research on drinking is based on the premise that drinking is motivated by a deficit in the body's water resources (i.e., by a deviation from various water-resource set points). Hypotheses about the specific deficit-related signals that produce *thirst* (the motivation to drink) have grown out of a consideration of the body's fluid resources and their regulation.

The body can be thought of as two separate fluid-filled compartments: an *intracellular compartment* and an *extracellular compartment*. As depicted in Figure 10.16, about two-thirds of the body's water is inside cells, and about one-third is outside. The water found in the extracellular compartment is found in the *interstitial fluid* (the fluid in which the cells are bathed), the blood, and the *cerebrospinal fluid* (CSF).

Normally the fluids in the intracellular and extracellular body-fluid compartments are **isotonic,** that is, of equal concentration. In other words, the proportion of the intracellular fluid that is composed of *solutes* (substances dissolved in a fluid) is normally the same as the proportion of the extracellular fluid that is composed of solutes. In this isotonic state there is no tendency for the water inside cells to be drawn out of cells, or for water in the interstitial fluid to be drawn into cells. However, if the fluid in one of the compartments is made more concentrated than the other (by adding solutes to it or by removing water from it), the more concentrated fluid draws water from the less concentrated fluid through the cell membranes until their isotonicity is reestablished. Conversely, if the concentration of the solution in one of the compartments is decreased (by adding water to it or by removing solutes from it), water is drawn from it into the other compartment. The pressure that draws water from less-concentrated (**hypotonic**) solutions through semipermeable membranes into more-concentrated (**hypertonic**) solutions is called **osmotic pressure** (see Figure 10.17).

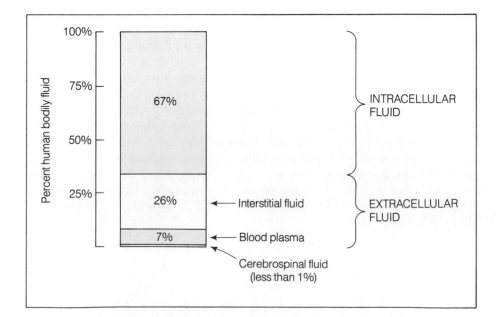

FIGURE 10.16

The proportion of fluid normally present in the fluid compartments of the human body.

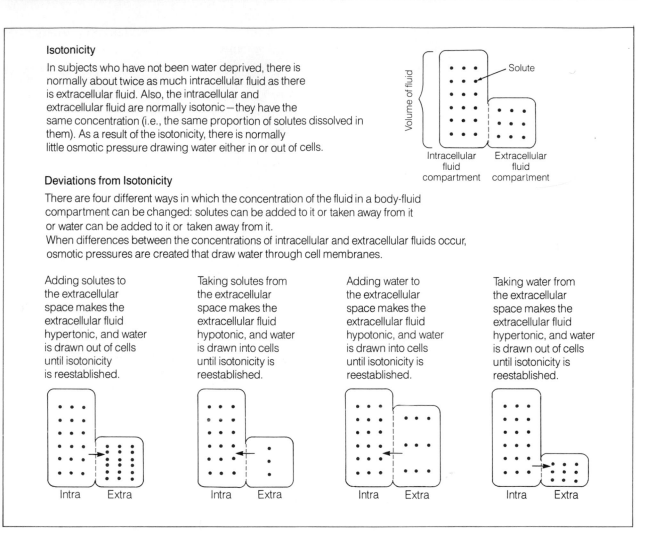

Isotonicity

In subjects who have not been water deprived, there is normally about twice as much intracellular fluid as there is extracellular fluid. Also, the intracellular and extracellular fluid are normally isotonic—they have the same concentration (i.e., the same proportion of solutes dissolved in them). As a result of the isotonicity, there is normally little osmotic pressure drawing water either in or out of cells.

Deviations from Isotonicity

There are four different ways in which the concentration of the fluid in a body-fluid compartment can be changed: solutes can be added to it or taken away from it or water can be added to it or taken away from it.
When differences between the concentrations of intracellular and extracellular fluids occur, osmotic pressures are created that draw water through cell membranes.

Adding solutes to the extracellular space makes the extracellular fluid hypertonic, and water is drawn out of cells until isotonicity is reestablished.

Taking solutes from the extracellular space makes the extracellular fluid hypotonic, and water is drawn into cells until isotonicity is reestablished.

Adding water to the extracellular space makes the extracellular fluid hypotonic, and water is drawn into cells until isotonicity is reestablished.

Taking water from the extracellular space makes the extracellular fluid hypertonic, and water is drawn out of cells until isotonicity is reestablished.

FIGURE 10.17
Illustration of isotonicity, hypertonicity, and hypotonicity.

The Kidneys: Regulation of Water and Sodium Levels

Sodium is the major solute in body fluids. Thus, the regulation of water and sodium levels is intimately related. The regulation of the body's water and sodium resources is reasonably straightforward. We normally consume far more water and sodium than we need, and the excess is drawn from the blood and excreted. This is the function of the *kidneys.* Blood enters the kidneys via the *renal arteries,* where various impurities and excess sodium and water are extracted. Blood leaves the kidneys via the *renal veins,* and urine leaves via the *ureters,* which channel it to the *bladder* for temporary storage—see Figure 10.18.

There are approximately one million independent functional units, which are called **nephrons,** in each human kidney (see Figure 10.19). Each

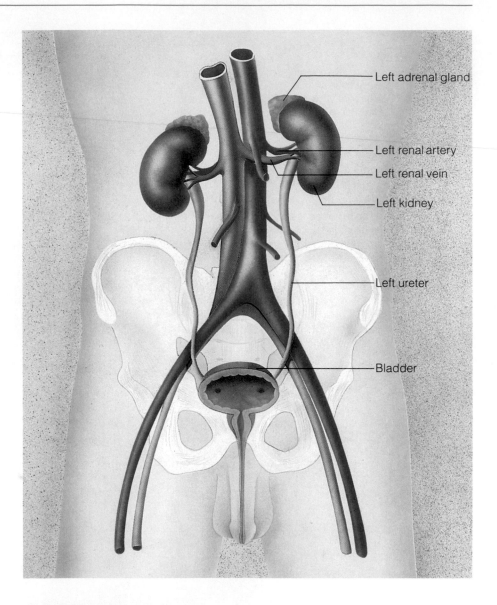

FIGURE 10.18

The kidneys. Blood enters through the renal arteries;
blood and urine exit through the renal veins and ureters, respectively.

nephron is a complex tangle of capillaries and tubules. Excess water and sodium pass from the capillaries to the tubules, to the ureters.

Urination is not the only mechanism of water loss. Significant quantities
of water are also lost by perspiration, by respiration, by defecation (in the
feces), and by evaporation through the skin. See Figure 10.20.

Regular water consumption is important for our survival because we humans lose water at a high rate and because we have a limited capacity to store
excess water. In this sense, drinking is different than eating. Most people can
live for weeks without eating, but nobody can survive more than a few days
without water.

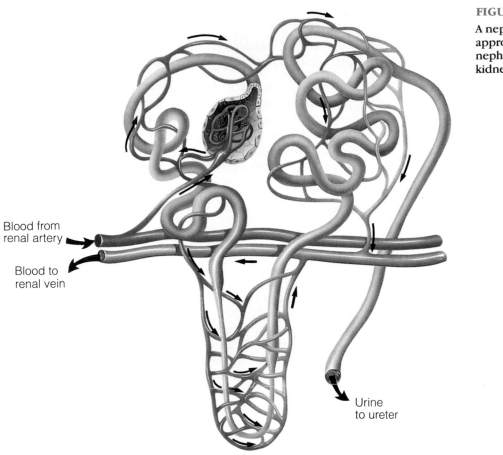

FIGURE 10.19
A nephron. There are approximately 1 million nephrons in each human kidney.

Blood from renal artery

Blood to renal vein

Urine to ureter

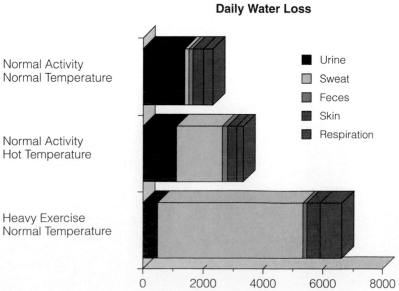

Daily Water Loss

Normal Activity Normal Temperature

Normal Activity Hot Temperature

Heavy Exercise Normal Temperature

■ Urine
□ Sweat
▨ Feces
▨ Skin
▨ Respiration

0   2000   4000   6000   8000

Milliliters of Water

FIGURE 10.20
Sources of water loss from the human body. (Adapted from Guyton, 1987.)

10.7

Deprivation-Induced Drinking:
Cellular Dehydration and Hypovolemia

When there are significant decreases in the body's water resources, the body reacts in two ways: steps are taken to conserve the body's declining water resources, and there are increases in thirst. There are two different physiological systems that mediate deprivation-induced drinking: one that is sensitive to reductions in intracellular fluid volume (**cellular dehydration**) and one that is sensitive to reductions in blood volume (**hypovolemia**).

Cellular Dehydration and Thirst

As the bartenders who supply free salted nuts well know, salt (sodium chloride) makes one thirsty. The thirst produced by salty food is caused by cellular dehydration. Because salt does not readily pass into cells, it accumulates in the extracellular fluid, making it hypertonic and drawing water from cells into the interstitial fluid. Salt consumption has little effect on blood volume. Cellular dehydration is usually induced in experimental animals, not by offering them salted nuts, but by injecting hypertonic solutions of salt or other solutes that do not readily pass through cell membranes (see Fitzsimons, 1972; Gilman, 1937). Cellular dehydration can also be produced by depriving subjects of water, but because water deprivation also reduces the volume of water in the extracellular compartment, researchers interested specifically in the role of cellular dehydration usually study drinking in response to the injection of hypertonic solutions.

   Osmoreceptors   Most of the research on cellular dehydration has been aimed at locating the cells in the body that are responsible for detecting it. The cells that detect cellular dehydration are called **osmoreceptors.**

FIGURE 10.21

Nondeprived dogs began to drink when hypertonic sodium chloride solutions were infused through the carotid arteries—the greater the concentration of the solution, the more they drank. (Adapted from Rolls & Rolls, 1982.)

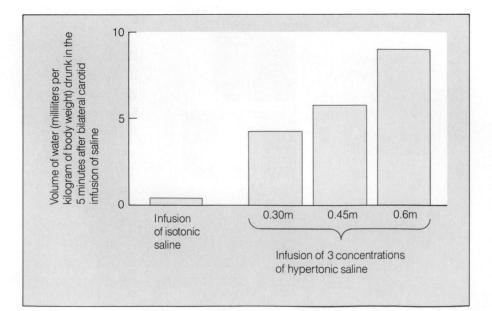

Evidence that osmoreceptors in the brain play a role in drinking comes from studies in which hypertonic solutions have been injected into the *carotid arteries* (arteries of the neck, which carry blood to the brain) of nondeprived animals. In one study, solutions of sodium chloride were bilaterally infused through the carotid arteries of nondeprived dogs at concentrations that increased cerebral osmolarity without having a significant effect on the osmolarity of the body as a whole (Wood, Rolls, & Ramsay, 1977). Figure 10.21 shows that the infusions increased the dogs' water consumption during a subsequent 5-minute test and that the amount of water that was consumed during the test was a function of the concentration of the infused solution.

Four lines of evidence suggest that osmoreceptors that encourage drinking are located in the *lateral hypothalamus* and the *lateral preoptic area* of the hypothalamus: First, minute quantities of slightly hypertonic saline injected bilaterally into various sites in the lateral preoptic area and lateral hypothalamus (see Figure 10.22) elicited drinking in rats (Blass & Epstein,

FIGURE 10.22

The lateral preoptic area and the lateral hypothalamus are sites into which microinjections of hypertonic solutions can elicit drinking in rats.

Lateral views of the rat brain illustrating the location of the lateral preoptic area and the lateral hypothalamus

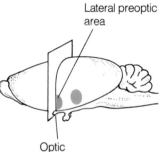

Lateral preoptic area

Optic chiasm

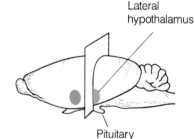

Lateral hypothalamus

Pituitary

Frontal section through the lateral preoptic area

Frontal section through the lateral hypothalamus

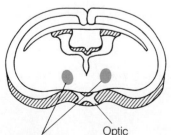

Lateral preoptic area

Optic chiasm

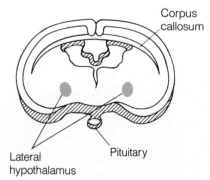

Corpus callosum

Lateral hypothalamus

Pituitary

1971; Peck & Blass, 1975) and rabbits (Peck & Novin, 1971). Second, control injections of hypertonic sucrose solutions into the same sites elicited drinking, whereas hypertonic urea injections did not. Sucrose, like sodium chloride, does not readily enter cells, and thus it draws water out of them, whereas urea readily enters cells, and thus it has no dehydrating effect. Third, drinking elicited by an injection of sodium chloride into the *peritoneum* (abdominal cavity) was suppressed by the bilateral infusion of small amounts of water directly into sites in the lateral preoptic area (Blass & Epstein, 1971). And fourth, the firing of neurons in the lateral hypothalamus and lateral preoptic area increased in proportion to the hypertonicity of solutions of sodium chloride or sucrose that were injected into the carotid artery (Malmo & Malmo, 1979; see Figure 10.23).

In addition to increasing water consumption, hypothalamic osmoreceptors also control the release of **antidiuretic hormone (ADH),** also known as *vasopressin,* from the posterior pituitary. Antidiuretic hormone is a peptide that conserves bodily fluids by decreasing the volume of urine produced by the kidneys. The hypothalamic osmoreceptors that control ADH release do not appear to be the same ones that control drinking. Intracerebral injections of hypertonic solutions that induce drinking do not always induce ADH release, and vice versa. Other osmoreceptors that regulate ADH release are distributed throughout the stomach, the **hepatic-portal system** (the branch of the circulatory system that carries water and other nutrients from the duodenum to the liver), and other parts of the gut. Whether or not these gut osmoreceptors also play a role in the regulation of drinking has not yet been clearly established.

Hypovolemia and Thirst

In addition to producing cellular dehydration, water deprivation produces hypovolemia, a reduction in blood volume. Hypovolemia, like cellular dehydration, is an important stimulus for thirst. It is selectively induced in experimental animals in one of two ways. One method is to withdraw blood from

FIGURE 10.23

The increases in the integrated multiple unit activity of rat lateral preoptic area neurons in response to hypertonic sucrose or sodium chloride injections into the carotid artery. (Adapted from Malmo & Malmo, 1979.)

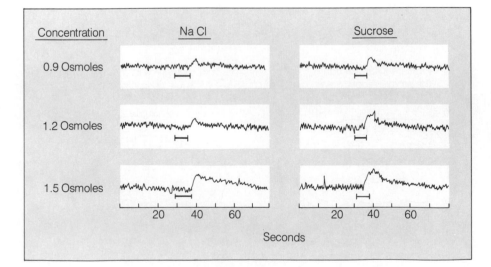

the subjects; the other is to inject a colloid substance into the peritoneal cavity. **Colloids** are glue-like substances with molecules much too large to pass through cell membranes. Thus, colloids that are injected into the peritoneum stay there, and like sponges, they draw blood plasma out of the circulatory system by osmotic pressure. Neither bleeding nor colloid injections change the osmolarity of the extracellular fluid; they reduce blood volume without producing cellular dehydration.

Hypovolemia is detected by **baroreceptors** (blood pressure receptors) in the wall of the heart and by **blood-flow receptors** in the kidneys, and the activity of these two kinds of receptors initiates a series of compensatory reactions. The decreased firing of the baroreceptors in the heart triggers the release of ADH from the posterior pituitary, which in turn increases water conservation by causing the kidneys to reabsorb more water from the urine. Both the ADH and the increased activity of the blood-flow receptors in the kidneys cause the kidneys to release **renin.** Renin causes the formation of the peptide hormone **angiotensin II,** and the angiotensin II in turn produces a compensatory increase in blood pressure by constricting the peripheral blood vessels and triggering the release of aldosterone from the adrenal cortices. **Aldosterone** causes the kidneys to reabsorb much of the sodium that would otherwise have been lost in the urine. Because sodium accounts for 95% of the osmolarity of blood plasma, the maintenance of high levels of sodium in the blood is critical for the prevention of further decreases in blood volume; the higher the concentration of the blood, the more water it will retain. These physiological reactions to hypovolemia are summarized in Figure 10.24.

In addition to increasing the conservation of bodily fluids, a reduction in blood volume induces drinking (Fitzsimons, 1961). The search for the mechanisms that mediate this **hypovolemic drinking,** as it has been termed, has focused directly on the baroreceptors in the heart and the blood-flow receptors in the kidneys. Evidence suggests that both play a role. For example, Fitzsimons (1972) implicated the renal blood-flow receptors by showing that partially tying off the renal arteries of rats to reduce renal blood flow causes them to drink. And Stricker (1973) implicated the cardiac baroreceptors in hypovolemic drinking by showing that injections of colloid into the peritoneal cavity of **nephrectomized** rats (i.e., rats whose kidneys have been removed) caused them to drink. This implicated the cardiac baroreceptors because hypovolemic drinking in kidneyless rats cannot possibly be mediated by receptors in the kidneys. See Figure 10.25.

Angiotensin II and hypovolemic drinking   The discovery that the intraperitoneal injection of kidney extracts causes rats to drink suggested that the kidneys produce a **dipsogen,** a substance that induces drinking. This dipsogen proved to be the peptide, angiotensin II. In many species, infusion of angiotensin II increases drinking without influencing other motivated behaviors (e.g., Fitzsimons & Simons, 1969).

Much of the research on the dipsogenic effect of angiotensin II has been directed at discovering its site of action in the brain. Two early clues focused attention on the **subfornical organ (SFO),** a midline structure on the dorsal surface of the third ventricle, just between the openings from the two lateral ventricles (see Figure 10.26). The first clue was that the subfornical organ is one of only a small number of sites in the brain that are not protected by the

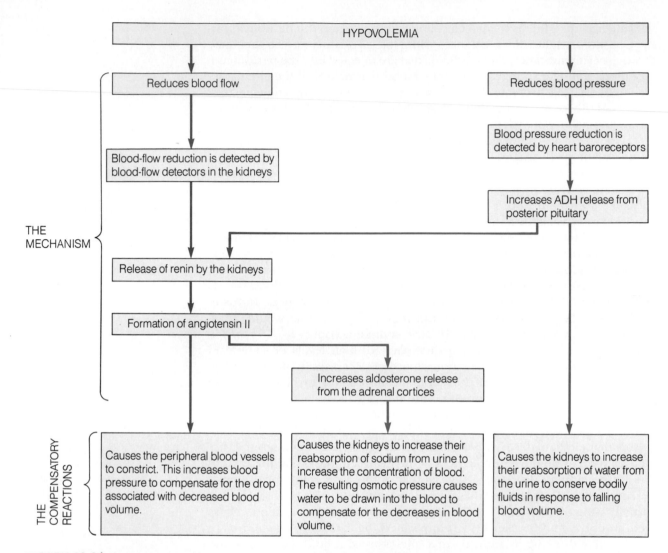

FIGURE 10.24

A summary of the compensatory physiological reactions to hypovolemia.

blood-brain barrier (see Chapter 3). The second clue was that intraventricular infusions of angiotensin II proved to be particularly effective in inducing drinking. The following four findings subsequently confirmed the hypothesis that the subfornical organ is the site of the angiotensin II receptors that mediate hypovolemic drinking: (1) Microinjections of angiotensin II into the subfornical organ reliably elicit drinking (e.g., Simpson, Epstein, & Camardo, 1978). (2) **Saralasin,** a blocker of angiotensin II receptors, blocks the dipsogenic action of intraventricular injections of angiotensin II (Fitzsimons, Epstein, & Johnson, 1978). (3) Destruction of the subfornical organ abolishes the drinking induced by intravenous injection of angiotensin II (Simpson et al., 1978). (4) Neurons in the subfornical organ display dose-dependent increases in firing in response to microinjections of angiotensin II (Phillips & Felix, 1976).

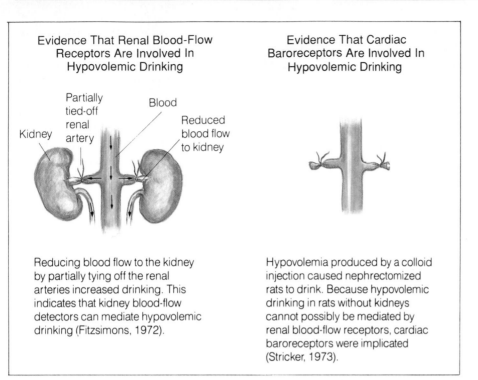

Evidence That Renal Blood-Flow Receptors Are Involved In Hypovolemic Drinking

Reducing blood flow to the kidney by partially tying off the renal arteries increased drinking. This indicates that kidney blood-flow detectors can mediate hypovolemic drinking (Fitzsimons, 1972).

Evidence That Cardiac Baroreceptors Are Involved In Hypovolemic Drinking

Hypovolemia produced by a colloid injection caused nephrectomized rats to drink. Because hypovolemic drinking in rats without kidneys cannot possibly be mediated by renal blood-flow receptors, cardiac baroreceptors were implicated (Stricker, 1973).

FIGURE 10.25

Evidence that both cardiac baroreceptors and kidney blood-flow detectors mediate hypovolemic drinking.

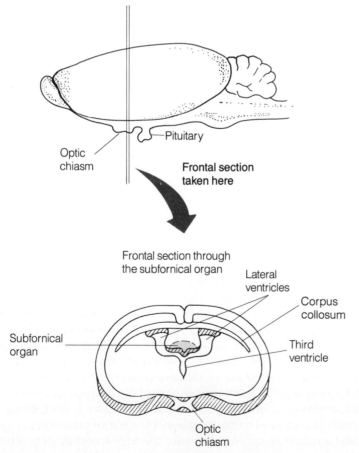

FIGURE 10.26

The location of the subfornical organ in the rat. It is on the midline dorsal surface of the third ventricle between the openings to the two lateral ventricles.

The kidney is not the body's only source of angiotensin II; it is also synthesized by the brain. The finding that lesions of the subfornical organ permanently block the ability of blood-borne angiotensin II to promote drinking suggests that the subfornical organ is the primary mediator of the dipsogenic effect of any angiotensin II that is released by the kidney into general circulation. However, the fact that lesions of the subfornical organ do not permanently block drinking induced by intraventricular injection of angiotensin II (e.g., Buggy, Fisher, Hoffman, Johnson, & Phillips, 1975) suggests that brain-produced angiotensin II or its metabolites can activate receptors in the brain that are normally insulated from general circulation by the blood-brain barrier (Epstein, 1987).

The subfornical synapses that mediate drinking in the rat appear to be cholinergic. Injections into the subfornical organ of **carbachol** (an acetylcholine-like drug) elicit drinking in rats (Simpson & Routtenberg, 1974)—as do carbachol injections into a variety of other medial diencephalic and limbic structures (e.g., Swanson & Sharpe, 1973). Moreover, systemic or intraventricular injections of *atropine,* a muscarinic acetylcholine antagonist, reduce deprivation-induced drinking in rats (e.g., Block & Fisher, 1970). However, interest in cholinergic thirst circuits has waned since it became apparent that carbachol does not elicit robust drinking responses in laboratory species other than the rat (see Grossman, 1990).

Drinking Produced by Naturally Occurring Water Deficits

As you have just learned in the preceding two subsections, the dipsogenic effects of intracellular and extracellular dehydration are often studied independently of one another. However, because water deprivation simultaneously reduces the water in both the intracellular and extracellular fluid compartments, the key to understanding the drinking that results from naturally occurring water shortages lies in understanding the interaction of the deficits in the two compartments. Rolls and her colleagues (e.g., Ramsay, Rolls, & Wood, 1977; Rolls, Wood, & Rolls, 1980) have studied the relative effects that intracellular and extracellular fluid deficits after overnight water deprivation have on drinking. They injected their water-deprived subjects (rats, dogs, and monkeys) with either water or isotonic saline. The water, because it was hypotonic, was quickly taken up by the dehydrated cells; thus it eliminated the intracellular deficit without substantially influencing the extracellular deficit. Conversely, the saline, because it was isotonic, was not taken up by cells to any significant degree; thus it eliminated the extracellular deficit without substantially influencing the intracellular deficit. The elimination of the intracellular deficit reduced the drinking of the water-deprived subjects by about 75%, and the elimination of the extracellular deficit reduced drinking by about 15% (Rolls & Rolls, 1982). Where do the systems that detect intracellular and extracellular water deficits converge to produce thirst and drinking? Because large bilateral lesions of the lateral hypothalamus eliminate drinking in response to both cellular dehydration and hypovolemia, "these tissues remain the favored candidates for the zone of convergence of thirst afferents and for their transformation into the urge to drink" (Epstein, 1982, p. 197; see Grossman, 1990).

Spontaneous Drinking: Drinking in the Absence of Water Deficits

Like the study of eating, the study of drinking has until recently focused almost exclusively on deficit-induced consumption. Water deficits are powerful motivators, and understanding how their motivating effects are mediated is important; however it is also important not to lose sight of the fact that most drinking—like most eating—occurs in the absence of deficits (see Rowland, 1990a&b). Drinking in the absence of fluid deficits is called **spontaneous drinking.**

The fact that drinking regularly occurs in the absence of water deficits suggests that drinking is motivated by the *positive incentive properties* of potential beverages; it suggests that the motivation to drink comes from the anticipated pleasurable effects of the drinking. We tend to prefer drinks that have a pleasurable flavor (e.g., fruit juice, soda, milk) or a pleasurable pharmacologic effect (e.g., beer, coffee, tea)—or, better yet, both. According to the positive-incentive theory of drinking, water deprivation increases the positive incentive value of virtually all salt-free beverages—after 24 hours of water deprivation, human subjects report that water itself has a pleasant taste (Rolls, Wood, Rolls, Lind, Lind, & Ledingham, 1980).

Flavor

The effects of flavor on drinking can be demonstrated by simply adding a bit of saccharin to the water of nondeprived rats. Their water intake skyrockets (Rolls, Wood, & Stevens, 1978). Conversely, there is a substantial decrease in fluid consumption if the palatability of a rat's water supply is reduced by adding a small amount of quinine to it. When rats were maintained for 60 days with quinine-adulterated water as their only source of fluid, their fluid intake decreased substantially, but there were no signs of ill health (Nicolaidis & Rowland, 1975). Like humans, rats with unlimited access to water or other palatable fluids drink far more than they need.

Food

Water is required for the digestion and metabolism of food. Consequently, drinking often occurs in association with eating. Rats, for example, drink about 70% of their total water intake during meals; they drink little when they are food deprived. Eating-related drinking is greater when the food is dry and when it is protein-rich—proteins draw large amounts of water out of the body into the digestive tract.

The release of insulin that is associated with food consumption may be a factor in eating-related drinking. Insulin injections have been shown to increase drinking in both rats (Novin, 1964) and humans (Brime et al., 1991).

Learning

Animals normally drink to prevent water deficits, not just to correct them. They generally drink more water than they need, and they learn to increase their drinking in anticipation of water deficits. Human joggers learn to drink before starting out on a hot day, and rats learn to drink in response to an odor that has been repeatedly paired with a subcutaneous injection of formalin, which induces temporary hypovolemia (Weisinger, 1975). A similar point was made in a study by Fitzsimons and Le Magnen (1969). They studied the increased water consumption of rats forced to shift to a high-protein diet. Initially, the increased drinking occurred long after the protein meal was consumed, presumably in response to the hypovolemia that it created. But eventually copious drinking occurred with, rather than after, each meal. Apparently, the rats learned to adjust their water intake to prevent the protein-produced dehydration.

10.9

Drinking and Satiety

What terminates a bout of drinking? Set-point theories suggest that it is a return to internal water-resource set points. There are three problems with this idea. The first is that the elimination of water deficits could not possibly be responsible for terminating drinking that is initiated in the absence of water deficits. The second is that even when drinking is triggered by water deprivation, it usually stops before the water has been absorbed into the body from the gastrointestinal tract. The third is that the amount that we drink is not rigorously regulated. In one study (Dicker & Nunn, 1957), rats were maintained on a daily water ration that was only about 60% of the amount that they consumed when they could drink as much as they wanted to drink; urine excretion was reduced, and the rats remained healthy.

Various sham-drinking preparations have been used to study the contribution of oral factors to satiety. In their first postdeprivation bout of sham drinking, most animals sham drink an amount that is proportional to the length of the preceding period of water deprivation; longer periods of water deprivation produced more sham drinking (see Blass & Hall, 1976), despite the fact that the water exits the gastrointestinal tract through a fistula before it can be absorbed (see Figure 10.27). This relation could be a product of previous learning, or it could reflect the fact that longer periods of water deprivation produce greater increases in the incentive value of water.

FIGURE 10.27

During their first postdeprivation bout of sham drinking, animals with open esophageal, gastric, or duodenal fistulas sham drink an amount that is proportional to the duration of the preceding period of water deprivation.

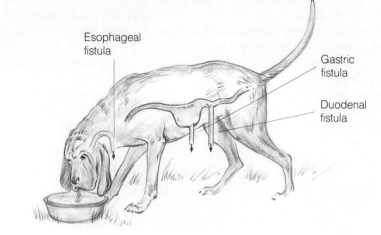

To what degree do injections of water into the stomach or bloodstream reduce the duration of postdeprivation drinking bouts? In rats, infusions of water directly into the stomach or into the bloodstream reduced deprivation-induced drinking by only 30% of the amount injected (e.g., Rowland & Nicolaidis, 1976). Remarkably, even total replenishment of an animal's water resources has only a modest (about 30%) inhibitory effect on deprivation-induced drinking. These findings are troublesome for any theory of satiety that is based on the premise that bouts of drinking are terminated by a return to internal fluid set points.

Drinking and Sensory-Specific Satiety

Sensory-specific satiety has a major effect on drinking—as it does on eating. This has been demonstrated in two ways. The first is by showing that animals display less preference for a beverage when it is continuously available than they do for the same beverage when it is only periodically available. For example, Figure 10.28 illustrates a phenomenon known as the **saccharin elation**

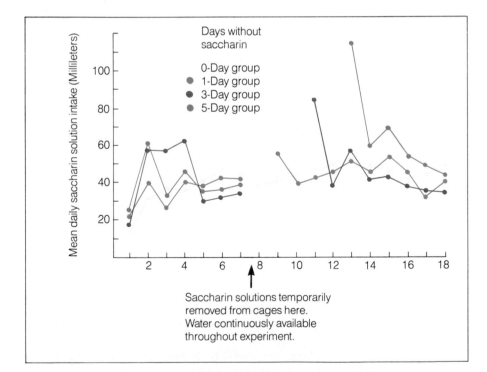

FIGURE 10.28

The saccharin elation effect. Four groups of rats had continuous access to water and a saccharin solution for 8 days. The saccharin solution was withdrawn for 0, 1, 3, or 5 days, but the rats continued to have free access to water. Longer periods of saccharin withdrawal produced greater increases in saccharin drinking. (Adapted from Pinel & Rovner, 1977.)

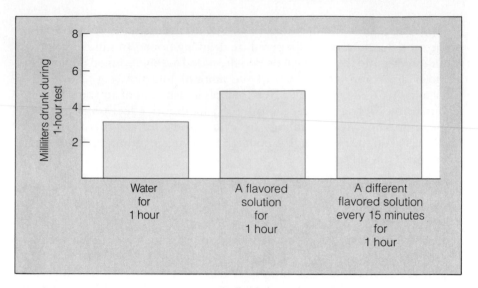

FIGURE 10.29

The effects of variety on the fluid intake of nondeprived rats during a 60-minute test. The rats in one group had access to water for the 60 minutes; the rats in another group had access to flavored water; and the rats in the third group were presented with water of a different flavor every 15 minutes. (Adapted from Rolls, Wood, & Rolls, 1980.)

effect; rats living with continuous access to water and a saccharin solution consume large amounts of the saccharin solution, but they consume even more of it after the saccharin solution has been withdrawn for several days (e.g., Pinel & Rovner, 1977). A similar elation effect has been demonstrated with weak solutions of quinine and of alcohol (Pinel & Huang, 1976; Sinclair, 1972).

The second way that the effect of sensory-specific satiety on drinking has been demonstrated is by showing that animals drink more when they have access to a variety of beverages. For example, Rolls and Wood (cited in Rolls, Wood, & Rolls, 1980) offered nondeprived rats access to water for 1 hour, to water with an artificial flavor added to it for 1 hour, or to water with a different artificial flavor added to it every 15 minutes during the hour. As illustrated in Figure 10.29, the addition of one flavor to the water increased intake by 88%, whereas the availability of four sequential flavors increased intake by 182%.

Grossly excessive drinking is referred to as *polydipsia.* One method of inducing polydipsia, as you have just seen, is to provide subjects with a variety of palatable beverages. Another is to present a small pellet of food every minute or so to subjects who have continuous access to water (Falk, 1964). In the intervals, they drink huge volumes of water. For example, rats drink about 10 times more than they would if the food were given all at once during the test. This excessive drinking is called **schedule-induced polydipsia.**

Conclusion: A Biopsychological Perspective of Anorexia Nervosa

You likely entered this chapter the same way that biopsychologists entered the 1970s, assuming that eating and drinking are motivated by deviations from internal energy and water set points. In this chapter, you have accompanied contemporary biopsychologists as they have shed their early assumptions about the regulation of eating and drinking and developed an entirely new theoretical perspective—one that is more consistent with the results of controlled laboratory experiments and with the realities of everyday experience. Biopsychologists—and, I hope, you—now understand that the regulation of eating and drinking is much more flexible and adaptive than they had first assumed: (1) We are not driven to eat and drink by internal deficits; we are drawn to eat and drink by the anticipated pleasurable effects of eating and drinking (i.e., by the incentive properties of available food and drink). (2) Our bodies' energy and water resources are not regulated at static set points; they are maintained around flexible settling points (i.e., the points at which the various factors that influence energy and water balance are in equilibrium). (3) The regulation of our bodies' energy and water resources does not depend solely on eating and drinking; when palatable foods and drinks are abundant, excessive consumption is largely counteracted by a decrease in the efficiency of resource utilization (e.g., by diet-induced thermogenesis or by excessive urination). (4) The neural systems that control eating and drinking act to correct deficits, but this is not their usual function; their usual function is to prevent deficits. We prevent energy and water deficits in two ways: by habitually consuming more than we require and by learning. We learn to anticipate deficits, and we learn to prefer tastes that have been associated with health-promoting effects.

Anorexia Nervosa

Everybody has heard of **anorexia nervosa;** it is one of the most prevalent ingestive disorders in our society. Anorectics have a pathological fear of obesity. As a result, they eat little and suffer from health-threatening weight loss. They often have an unrealistic image of their own bodies; they perceive their bodies as fat despite their emaciated appearance.

About 50% of anorectic patients periodically lose control and engage in *binges* of eating. These binges are almost always followed by some kind of purging—for example, by "megadoses" of laxatives or by self-induced vomiting. People who are not anorectic but display recurring cycles of fasting, binging, and purging are said to suffer from **bulimia nervosa.**

Anorexia nervosa is most common in young, white middle- and upper-class females. The incidence among North American students of both sexes is about 2.5% (see Schlundt & Johnson, 1990); however, in a study of dancers who were attending an exclusive ballet school, the incidence was found to be 9% (Szmukler, Eisler, Gillies, & Hayward, 1985).

Many people find it difficult to appreciate the tragedy of anorexia; anorectics seem strangely out of place in a society in which overconsumption and obesity are a major health problem. People who are struggling to eat less often have little sympathy for those who seem to be refusing to eat. But it is difficult to be untouched by anorexia when you stare it in the face.

She began by telling me how much she had been enjoying the course and how sorry she was to be dropping out of university. She was articulate and personable, and her grades were first class. Her problem was anorexia; she weighed only 82 pounds, and she was about to be hospitalized.

"But don't you want to eat?" I asked naively. "Don't you see that your plan to go to medical school will go up in smoke if you don't eat?"

"Of course I want to eat. I know that I am terribly thin—my friends tell me that I am. Believe me, I know that this is wrecking my life. I try to eat, but I just can't force myself. In a strange way, I am pleased with my thinness."

She was upset, and I was embarrassed by my insensitivity. "It's too bad you're dropping out of the course before we cover the chapter on eating," I said, groping for safer ground.

"Oh, I've read it already," she responded. "It's the first chapter that I looked at. It had quite an effect on me; a lot of things started to make more sense. The bit about positive incentives and learning was really good. I think that my problem began when food started to lose its incentive value for me—in my mind, I kind of associated food with being fat and all the boy-friend problems that I was having. This made it easy to diet, but every once in a while I would get so hungry that I would lose control and eat all of the things that I shouldn't. I would eat so much that I would feel ill. So I would put my finger down my throat and make myself throw up. This made me feel a bit better, and it kept me from gaining weight, but I think that it taught my body to associate my favorite foods with illness—kind of a conditioned taste aversion. Now, food has no incentive value for me whatsoever. What do you think of my theory?"

Her insightfulness impressed me; it made me feel all the more sorry that she was going to discontinue her studies.

After a lengthy chat, she got up to leave, and I walked her to the door of my office. I wished her luck, and made her promise to come back for a visit. The image of her emaciated body walking down the hallway from my office has stayed with me.

This chapter began on an unconventional note, and it ended on another. It began with the mystery of Freddie the Finn, and it ended with a personal encounter with anorexia nervosa. In between, you learned how modern research on the biopsychology of eating and drinking has exposed the incorrect implicit assumptions of the 1950s and 60s and has led to the development of promising new theories.

Food for Thought

1. Set-point theories suggest that attempts at permanent weight loss are a waste of time. What do settling-point theories suggest?

2. Most of the dietary problems that people in our society face occur because the conditions under which we live are different from those in which our species evolved. Discuss.

3. There are many parallels between the regulation of eating and drinking. Describe four of them.

KEY TERMS

To help you study the material in this chapter, all of the key terms—those that have appeared in bold type—are listed and briefly defined here.

Absorptive phase. The metabolic phase during which the body is operating on the energy from a recently consumed meal and is storing the excess as body fat and glycogen.

Adipsia. Complete cessation of drinking.

Aldosterone. The hormone that is released from the adrenal cortices in response to angiotensin II; aldosterone causes the kidneys to reabsorb much of the sodium that would otherwise be lost in the urine.

Amino acids. The breakdown products of protein.

Angiotensin II. A peptide hormone that is synthesized in the blood in response to renin release; it produces a compensatory increase in blood pressure by constricting the peripheral blood vessels, by triggering the release of aldosterone from the adrenal cortices, and by stimulating thirst.

Anorexia nervosa. An eating disorder that is characterized by a pathological fear of obesity that results in health-threatening weight loss.

Antidiuretic hormone (ADH). A hormone released from the posterior pituitary that encourages the conservation of bodily fluids by decreasing the volume of urine produced by the kidneys.

Aphagia. Complete cessation of eating.

Baroreceptors. Blood pressure receptors.

Blood-flow receptors. Receptors that monitor the volume of blood flowing through the kidneys.

Brown adipose tissue. The main nonmuscular site of heat generation in the body.

Bulimia nervosa. An eating disorder that is characterized by recurring cycles of fasting, binging, and purging.

Cafeteria diet. A diet offered to experimental animals that is composed of a wide variety of palatable foods.

Carbachol. An acetylcholine agonist that elicits drinking when injected into the subfornical organ of rats.

Carbohydrates. Sugars and starches.

Cellular dehydration. Reduction in intracellular fluid volume.

Cephalic phase. The metabolic phase during which the body prepares for food that is about to be absorbed; it is initiated by the presence of food in the gastrointestinal tract, or by the sight or smell of palatable food.

Cholecystokinin (CCK). A peptide that is released by the gastrointestinal tract and is thought to signal satiety.

Colloids. Glue-like substances with molecules too large to pass through cell membranes.

Diabetes mellitus. A disorder in which the pancreas does not produce sufficient insulin, thus preventing blood glucose from entering cells of the body.

Diet-induced thermogenesis. The increased heat production of obese subjects.

Digestion. The process by which food is broken down and absorbed through the lining of the gastrointestinal tract.

Dipsogen. A substance that induces drinking.

Duodenum. The upper portion of the intestine through which most of the glucose and amino acids are absorbed into the bloodstream.

Dynamic phase. The first phase of the hyperphagia syndrome induced by VMH lesions, which is characterized by grossly excessive eating and weight gain.

Fasting phase. The metabolic phase that begins when energy from the preceding meal is no longer sufficient to meet the needs of the body; during this phase, energy is extracted from fat and glycogen stores.

Free fatty acids. Released from fat, they are the main source of the body's energy during the fasting phase.

Gastrointestinal tract. The channel through which food and drink pass through the core of the body; its major components are the stomach and the intestines.

Glucagon. A pancreatic hormone that promotes the conversion of glycogen to glucose and the utilization of fat by the body.

Gluconeogenesis. The process by which glucose is synthesized from the breakdown products of the body's own tissue; this normally occurs only during starvation.

Glucoreceptors. Cells that are thought to detect glucose levels in the body.

Glucose. A simple sugar, which is the breakdown product of more complex sugars and starches (carbohydrates); the body's, and in particular the brain's, main source of energy.

Glucostatic theory. The theory that blood glucose level or blood glucose utilization is the main regulatory factor in controlling daily food intake.

Glycogen. One of the forms in which energy is stored in the body, primarily in the liver.

Gold thioglucose. A neurotoxin, which is thought to bind to glucoreceptors.

Hepatic-portal system. The branch of the cardiovascular system that carries water and other nutrients absorbed from the duodenum to the liver.

Homeostasis. The stability of an organism's internal environment.

Hyperinsulinemia. A condition in which too much insulin is released into the blood.

Hyperphagia. Overeating.

Hypertonic. More concentrated than some reference solution.

Hypotonic. Less concentrated than some reference solution.

Hypovolemia. Decreased blood volume.

Hypovolemic drinking. Drinking induced by decreased blood volume.

Incentive properties. The incentive properties of a food are the pleasurable effects anticipated from eating it.

Insulin. A pancreatic hormone that facilitates the entry of glucose into cells and the conversion of glucose to fat and glycogen.

Intragastric feeding. When an animal feeds itself by pressing a lever that causes food to be pumped directly into its stomach.

Isotonic. Two solutions are said to be isotonic if they contain the same concentration of solutes.

Ketones. The breakdown products of fat, which can be used as a source of energy for the brain when glucose is in short supply.

Lateral hypothalamus (LH). An area of the hypothalamus once thought to be the feeding center.

Leaky-barrel model. A settling-point model of body-fat regulation; an alternative to traditional set-point models.

Lipectomy. The surgical removal of body fat.

Lipids. Fats.

Lipogenesis. The production of body fat.

Lipolysis. The breakdown of body fat.

Lipostatic theory. The theory that eating is controlled by deviations from a hypothetical body-fat set point.

Nasopharyngeal gastric fistula. A tube that runs under the scalp down a nostril and into the stomach and allows food to be pumped directly into the stomach.

Nephrectomized. Organisms from which the kidneys have been removed.

Nephrons. The independent functional units of the kidney; each nephron is a complex tangle of capillaries and tubules.

Nutritive density. Calories per unit volume of food.

Osmoreceptors. Receptors sensitive to dehydration.

Osmotic pressure. The pressure that draws water from a hypotonic solution to a hypertonic solution.

Paraventricular nuclei. Hypothalamic nuclei; it is now thought that the hyperphagia and obesity caused by large VMH lesions result from damage to the paraventricular nuclei or other connections.

Peristaltic contractions. Small rhythmic contractions that move food along the digestive tract.

Renin. A hormone that is released from the kidneys in response to increasing ADH levels or decreasing signals from cardiac baroreceptors; renin stimulates the synthesis of the peptide hormone angiotensin II.

Saccharin elation effect. Nondeprived animals that normally have continuous access to a saccharin solution prefer it to water even more than usual following a period during which it was not available.

Saralasin. A blocker of angiotensin II receptors.

Schedule-induced polydipsia. An animal receiving a pellet of food every minute or so consumes huge volumes of water between pellets.

Sensory-specific satiety. When a particular food is consumed, more satiety is produced for foods of the same taste than for other foods.

Settling point. The point at which various factors that influence the level of some regulated function achieve an equilibrium.

Sham drinking. Drinking that occurs in animals with esophageal, gastric, or duodenal fistulas; the water drunk by such an animal flows out through its fistula.

Sham eating. The animal chews and swallows food, which leaves the body through an esophageal fistula.

Spontaneous drinking. Drinking in the absence of fluid deficits.

Static phase. The second phase of the VMH hyperphagia syndrome during which the animal regulates its body weight at a greatly elevated level.

Subfornical organ (SFO). The midline structure on the dorsal surface of the third ventricle that is thought to be the site of the angiotensin II receptors that mediate the dipsogenic effects of angiotensin II.

Substance Y. A putative hunger peptide hormone.

Thiamin. Vitamin B_1.

Ventromedial hypothalamus (VMH). The area of the hypothalamus that was once thought to be the satiety center.

ADDITIONAL READING

The following books provide excellent coverage of current research on eating and drinking.

Capaldi, E. D., & Powley, T. L. (1990). *Taste, experience, and feeding.* Washington, D.C.: American Psychological Association.

Grossman, S. P. (1990). *Thirst and sodium appetite: Physiological basis.* New York: Academic Press.

Schneider, L. H., Cooper, S. J., & Halmi, K. A. (1989). *The psychology of human eating disorders: Preclinical and clinical perspectives.* New York: New York Academy of Sciences.

Schlundt, D. G., & Johnson, W. G. (1990). *Eating disorders: Assessment and treatment.* Boston: Allyn and Bacon.

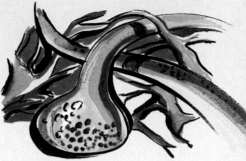

11

Hormones and Sex

This chapter is about hormones and sex, a topic that fascinates most people. Perhaps it is because we hold our own sexuality in such high esteem that we are intrigued by the fact that it is influenced by the secretions of a pair of glands that some regard as unfit topics of conversation. Perhaps it is because we each think of our gender as fundamental and immutable that we are fascinated by the fact that it can be altered with a snip or two and a few hormone injections. Perhaps what fascinates us is the idea that our sex lives might be enhanced by the application of a few hormones. For whatever reason, the topic of hormones and sex is always a hit. Some remarkable things await you in this chapter; let's go directly to them.

Hormones influence sex in two ways: (1) by influencing the development from conception to sexual maturity of the anatomical, physiological, and behavioral characteristics that distinguish one as female or male, and (2) by activating the reproduction-related behavior of sexually mature adults. The *developmental* and *activational* effects of sex hormones are dealt with in the second and third sections of this chapter; the first section prepares you for these topics by introducing the neuroendocrine system. The fourth section discusses the role of the hypothalamus in sexual behavior and sexual preference.

The Men-Are-Men-and-Women-Are-Women Attitude

Almost everybody brings to the topic of hormones and sex a piece of excess baggage, the men-are-men-and-women-are-women attitude—or "mamawawa." The men-are-men-and-women-are-women attitude is seductive; it seems so right that we are continually drawn to it without considering alternative views. Unfortunately, it is a seductive idea of the worst kind: a fundamentally flawed seductive idea. The men-are-men-and-women-are-women attitude is the tendency to think about "femaleness" and "maleness" as discrete, mutually exclusive, complementary categories. In thinking about hormones and sex, this general attitude leads one to assume that females have female sex hormones that give them female bodies and make them do female things, and that males have male sex hormones that give them male bodies and make them do male things. Despite the fact that this men-are-men-and-women-are-women approach to hormones and sex is totally wrong, its simplicity, symmetry, and comfortable social implications continually draw us to it. That is why this chapter grapples with it throughout.

11.1

The Neuroendocrine System

This section introduces the general principles of neuroendocrine function by focusing on the small subset of glands and hormones that are directly involved in sexual development and behavior. It begins with a few basic facts about hormones, glands, and reproduction; then it describes a line of research that is the parent of many of our current theories of neuroendocrine function.

Glands and Hormones

There are two types of glands: exocrine glands and endocrine glands. **Exocrine glands** (e.g., sweat glands) release their chemicals into ducts, which carry them to their targets, mostly on the inner and outer surfaces of the body. **Endocrine glands** (ductless glands) release their chemicals, which are called **hormones,** directly into the circulatory system. Once released by an endocrine gland, a hormone travels through the circulatory system until it reaches the targets on which it normally exerts its effect (e.g., the skin, other endocrine glands, and sites in the nervous system).

The endocrine glands are illustrated in Figure 11.1. By convention, only those organs whose primary function is the release of hormones are referred to as endocrine glands. However, other organs (e.g., the stomach, liver, and intestine) also release hormones into general circulation (see Chapter 10), and they are thus, strictly speaking, also part of the endocrine system.

Neurohormones are hormones that interact with the nervous system. They are like neurotransmitters in the sense that they are chemicals that influence neural activity; however, because neurohormones are released into general circulation rather than into synapses, they typically exert their effects more slowly, for a longer duration, and at greater distances from their site of release. Moreover, because there are receptors for each neurohormone in several different parts of the nervous system, the effects of neurohormones

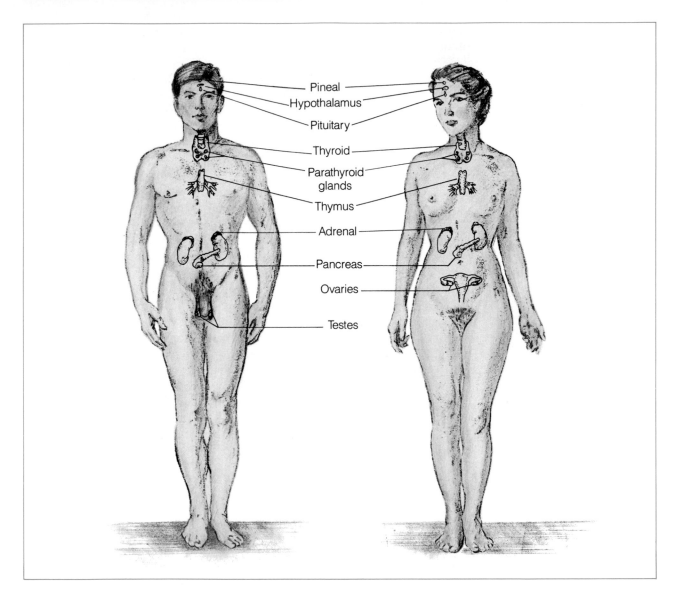

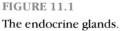

FIGURE 11.1
The endocrine glands.

are characteristically widespread. Although it is important to appreciate these distinctions, it is also important to realize that the same chemicals can function as both neurohormones and neurotransmitters; some neurohormones are synthesized and released by cerebral neurons, as well as by endocrine glands.

The Gonads

Central to any discussion of hormones and sex are the **gonads:** the male **testes** (pronounced TEST eez) and the female **ovaries** (see Figure 11.1). The primary function of the testes and ovaries is the production of *sperm cells* and *ova,* respectively. After **copulation** (sexual intercourse), a single sperm cell may combine with an *ovum* to form a cell called a **zygote,** which contains all of the information that is necessary for the growth of a complete adult organism.

With the exception of ova and sperm cells, each cell of the human body has 23 pairs of chromosomes. In contrast, the ova and sperm cells contain only half that number, one member of each of the 23 pairs. Thus, when a sperm cell fertilizes an ovum, the resulting zygote ends up with the full complement of 23 pairs of chromosomes, one of each pair from the father and one of each pair from the mother.

Of particular interest in the context of this chapter is the pair of chromosomes called the **sex chromosomes,** so named because they contain the genetic programs that direct sexual development. The cells of females have two large x-shaped sex chromosomes, called *X chromosomes.* In males, one sex chromosome is an X chromosome, and the other is a small x-shaped chromosome called a *Y chromosome.* (There must be a good reason for calling a small x-shaped chromosome a Y chromosome, but I don't know what it is.) Consequently, the sex chromosome of every ovum is an X chromosome, whereas half the sperm cells have X chromosomes, and half have Y chromosomes. Your gender and all its social, economic, and personal ramifications was determined by which of your father's sperm cells won the dash to your mother's ovum. If a sperm cell with an X sex chromosome won, you are a female; if one with a Y sex chromosome won, you are a male.

Writing this section reminded me of my grade 7 basketball team, "The Nads." The name puzzled our teacher because it was not at all like the names that are usually favored by pubescent boys—names like the "Avengers," the "Marauders," and the "Vikings." Her puzzlement ended abruptly at our first game as our fans began to chant their support. You guessed it; "Go Nads, Go! Go Nads, Go!" My 14-year-old spotted-faced teammates and I considered this to be humor of the most mature and sophisticated sort. The teacher didn't.

The Gonadal Hormones

The gonads do more than create sperm and egg cells; they also produce and release hormones. Most people are surprised to learn that the testes and ovaries release the very same hormones. The two main classes of gonadal hormones are **androgens** and **estrogens; testosterone** is the most common androgen, and **estradiol** is the most common estrogen. The fact that ovaries release more estrogens than they do androgens and that testes release more androgens than they do estrogens has led to the common, but misleading, practice of referring to androgens as "the male sex *hormones*" and to estrogens as "the female sex *hormones.*" This practice should be avoided because of its men-are-men-and-women-are-women implication that androgens produce maleness and that estrogens produce femaleness—they don't. The ovaries and testes also release a class of hormones called **progestins.** The most common progestin is **progesterone,** which in females prepares the uterus and the breasts for pregnancy. Its function in males is unclear.

Sex Hormones of the Adrenal Cortex

Because the primary function of the **adrenal cortex** (the outer covering of the adrenal gland; see Figure 11.1) is the regulation of salt and glucose levels in the blood, the adrenal cortices are not generally thought of as sex glands. However, each adrenal cortex produces all of the hormones that are produced by the ovaries and testes. Most of these adrenal sex hormones are released in only small amounts, and their role in sexual development and behavior is not well understood.

The Hormones of the Pituitary

The pituitary gland is frequently referred to as the *master gland* because many of its hormones are tropic hormones. *Tropic hormones* are those whose primary function is to influence the release of hormones from other glands; *tropic* is an adjective that describes things that stimulate or change other things. For example, the **gonadotropins** are a group of pituitary tropic hormones that travel from the pituitary through the circulatory system to the gonads, where they stimulate the release of gonadal hormones.

The pituitary gland is really two glands, the **posterior pituitary** and the **anterior pituitary,** which fuse during the course of embryological development. The posterior pituitary develops from a small outgrowth of hypothalamic tissue that eventually comes to dangle from the *hypothalamus* on the end of the **pituitary stalk** (see Figure 11.2). In contrast, the anterior pituitary begins as part of the same embryonic tissue that eventually develops into the roof of the mouth; during the course of development, it pinches off and migrates up to assume its position next to the posterior pituitary. It is the anterior pituitary that releases tropic hormones, and thus, it is the anterior pituitary in particular, rather than the pituitary in general, that qualifies as the master gland.

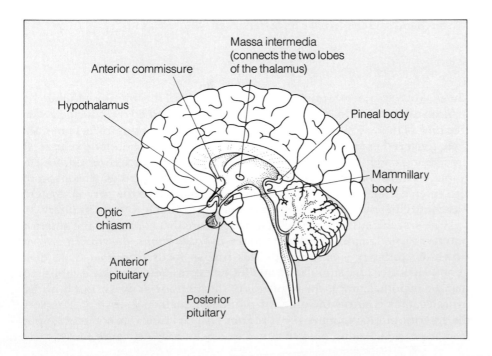

FIGURE 11.2

A midline view of the anterior and posterior pituitary and surrounding structures.

Female Gonadal Hormone Levels Are Cyclic; Male Gonadal Hormone Levels Are Steady

The major difference between the endocrine function of men and women is that in women the levels of gonadal and gonadotropic hormones go through a cycle that repeats itself every 28 days or so (see Appendix VII). It is these more-or-less regular hormone fluctuations that control the female **menstrual cycle.** In contrast, human males are, from a neuroendocrine perspective, rather dull creatures; the levels of their gonadal and gonadotropic hormones change little from day to day. An interest in this fundamental difference between females and males was the original stimulus for a particularly fruitful line of experiments. By the 1950s, the study of sex hormones had ascended from the loins to the pituitary, and then in the 1950s interest in the mechanisms of sex-hormone cyclicity directed the attention of researchers on upward to the brain. The ensuing study of the brain's regulation of sex-hormone cyclicity left in its wake many of our current ideas about hormonal function, two Nobel Prizes, and a general inclination for scientists to "think neuroendocrine" in situations in which "thinking endocrine" had previously been the norm. This influential line of research is the focus of the remainder of this first section of the chapter.

Because the anterior pituitary is the conductor of the endocrine orchestra, many early scientists assumed that an inherent difference between the male and female pituitary was the basis for the difference in their patterns of gonadotropic and gonadal hormone release. However, this hypothesis was discounted by a series of clever transplant studies (Harris & Jacobsohn, 1952). In these studies, a cycling pituitary removed from a mature female rat became a steady-state pituitary when transplanted at a suitable site in a male, and a steady-state pituitary removed from a mature male began to cycle once transplanted in a female. What these studies established was that anterior pituitaries are not inherently female (cyclical) or male (steady state); their patterns of hormone release are controlled by some other part of the body. The master gland seemed to have its own master. Where was it?

Neural Control of the Pituitary

The nervous system was implicated in the control of the anterior pituitary by behavioral research on birds and other animals that breed only during a specific time of the year. It was found that the seasonal variations in the light-dark cycle triggered many of the breeding-related changes in hormone release. If the lighting conditions under which the animals lived were reversed, for example, by transporting them across the equator, their breeding seasons were also reversed (Marshall, 1937). Somehow visual input to the nervous system was controlling the release of tropic hormones from the anterior pituitary.

The search for the particular neural structure that controlled the anterior pituitary turned, naturally enough, to the *hypothalamus,* the structure from which the pituitary is suspended. This shift in focus paid immediate dividends. Hypothalamic stimulation and lesion experiments quickly established that the hypothalamus is the regulator of the anterior pituitary. But how the hypothalamus controls the anterior pituitary remained a mystery. You see, the anterior pituitary, unlike the posterior pituitary, receives no neural input from the hypothalamus, or from any other structure—see Figure 11.3.

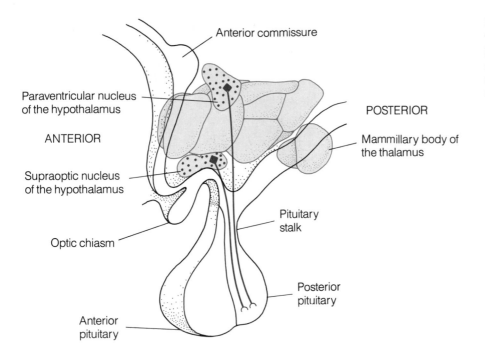

Anterior commissure

Paraventricular nucleus
of the hypothalamus

ANTERIOR

POSTERIOR

Mammillary body of
the thalamus

Supraoptic nucleus
of the hypothalamus

Pituitary
stalk

Optic chiasm

Posterior
pituitary

Anterior
pituitary

FIGURE 11.3
The neural connections
between the hypothalamus
and the pituitary. The
anterior pituitary has no
neural connections.

Control of the Anterior and Posterior Pituitary by the Hypothalamus

There are two different mechanisms by which the hypothalamus controls the pituitary: one for the posterior pituitary and one for the anterior pituitary. The two major hormones of the posterior pituitary, **vasopressin** and **oxytocin,** are manufactured in the cell bodies of neurons in the **paraventricular nuclei** and **supraoptic nuclei** of the hypothalamus (see Figure 11.4). They are then transported down the axons of these neurons to their terminals in the posterior pituitary and are stored there until the arrival of action potentials causes them to be released into the bloodstream—neurons that release hormones into general circulation are called **neurosecretory cells.** Oxytocin stimulates contractions of the uterus during labor and the ejection of milk during suckling. Vasopressin (also called *antidiuretic hormone*) facilitates the reabsorption of water by the kidneys.

The means by which the hypothalamus controls the release of hormones from the neuron-free anterior pituitary was more difficult to explain. Harris (1955) suggested that the release of hormones from the anterior pituitary was itself regulated by hormones released from the hypothalamus. Two findings provided early support for this hypothesis. One was the discovery of a vascular network, the **hypothalamopituitary portal system,** that seemed well suited to the task of carrying hormones from the hypothalamus to the anterior pituitary. As illustrated in Figure 11.4, a network of hypothalamic capillaries feeds a bundle of portal veins that carries blood down the pituitary stalk into another network of capillaries in the anterior pituitary; *portal* is a general term that refers to any vein that connects one capillary network with another. The other was the discovery that cutting the portal veins of the pituitary stalk disrupts the release of anterior pituitary hormones until the damaged veins regenerate (Harris, 1955).

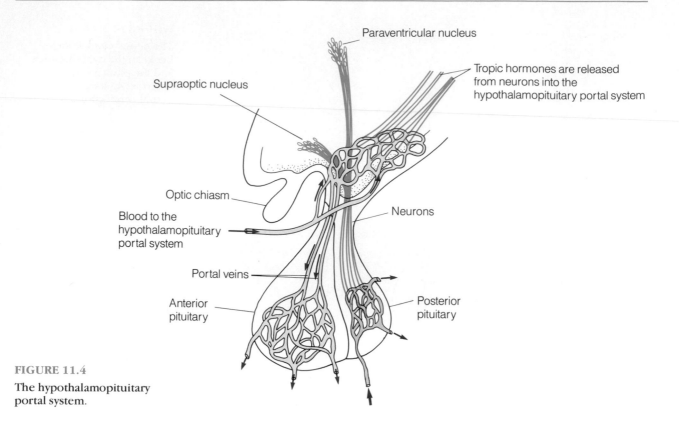

Paraventricular nucleus

Tropic hormones are released
from neurons into the
hypothalamopituitary portal system

Supraoptic nucleus

Optic chiasm

Neurons

Blood to the
hypothalamopituitary
portal system

Portal veins

Anterior
pituitary

Posterior
pituitary

FIGURE 11.4
The hypothalamopituitary
portal system.

The Isolation and Synthesis of Hypothalamic Hormones

It was suggested that each anterior pituitary hormone might be controlled by its own hypothalamic hormone. The putative (hypothesized) hypothalamic hormones that were thought to exert their influence by stimulating the release of an anterior pituitary hormone were referred to as **releasing factors;** those thought to exert control by inhibiting the release of an anterior pituitary hormone were referred to as **inhibitory factors.** Efforts to isolate these putative hypothalamic releasing and inhibitory factors led to a major breakthrough in 1969. Guilleman and his colleagues isolated **thyrotropin-releasing hormone** from the hypothalami of sheep, and Schally and his colleagues isolated the same hormone from the hypothalami of pigs. Thyrotropin-releasing hormone triggers the release of **thyrotropin** from the anterior pituitary, which in turn stimulates the release of hormones from the *thyroid gland*. It is difficult to appreciate the effort that went into the initial isolation of thyrotropin-releasing hormone. Releasing and inhibiting factors exist in such small quantities that a mountain of hypothalamic tissue is required to extract even minute quantities. For example, Schally (1978) reported that the work of his group required over one million pig hypothalami. And where did Schally get such a quantity of pig hypothalami? From Oscar Mayer & Company—where else?

Why would two research teams dedicate over a decade of their lives to accumulate a pitifully small quantity of thyrotropin-releasing hormone? The reason was that it enabled both Guilleman and Schally to determine thyrotropin-releasing hormone's chemical composition and then to develop methods of synthesizing larger quantities of it for research and clinical use. For their efforts, Guilleman and Schally were awarded Nobel Prizes in 1977.

You may have noticed a change in terminology during the preceding discussion: from "releasing factors" to **releasing hormones.** This shift reflects the usual practice of referring to a hormone as a "factor" or "substance" until it has been isolated and its chemical structure identified.

Gonadotropin-Releasing Hormone

Within the context of hormones-and-sex research, Schally and Guilleman's isolation of thyrotropin-releasing hormone, a nonsex hormone, was important because it confirmed that hypothalamic releasing hormones control the release of hormones from the anterior pituitary and thus provided the major impetus for the isolation and synthesis of **gonadotropin-releasing hormone** by Schally and his group in 1970. Gonadotropin-releasing hormone stimulates the release of both of the anterior pituitary's gonadotropins, **follicle stimulating hormone (FSH)** and **luteinizing hormone (LH)** (Schally, Kastin, & Arimura, 1971).

Feedback in the Neuroendocrine System

The hypothalamus controls the pituitary, and the pituitary in turn controls other endocrine glands, but neuroendocrine regulation is not a one-way street. Hormones often feed back on the very structures that triggered their release: the pituitary, the hypothalamus, and other sites in the brain (see McEwen, Davis, Parsons, & Pfaff, 1979). Most of this feedback is negative. The function of **negative feedback** is the maintenance of stability; high gonadal hormone levels in the blood often have effects on the hypothalamus and pituitary that decrease gonadal activity, and low levels often have effects that increase gonadal activity. Although negative feedback is the rule in the neuroendocrine system, **positive feedback** can also occur; occasionally, increases in the level of a circulating hormone produce further increases and decreases produce further decreases. For example, just before **ovulation** (the release of a mature ovum from the package of cells, or **follicle,** in which it develops), injection of a small dose of estradiol produces an increase, rather than the usual decrease, in the release of estradiol from the ovary, by stimulating the release of gonadotropin-releasing hormone from the hypothalamus and by increasing the sensitivity of the anterior pituitary to the gonadotropin-releasing hormone that reaches it. It has been suggested that a shift from the usual negative feedback mode to a positive feedback mode may be the key factor in producing the surge in the levels of progesterone and estradiol in the blood of females that is responsible for triggering ovulation (see Appendix VII for details of the hormone fluctuations that occur during the *menstrual cycles* of human females). A similar mechanism has been proposed to account for the surge of gonadal hormones that occurs in both males and females during puberty.

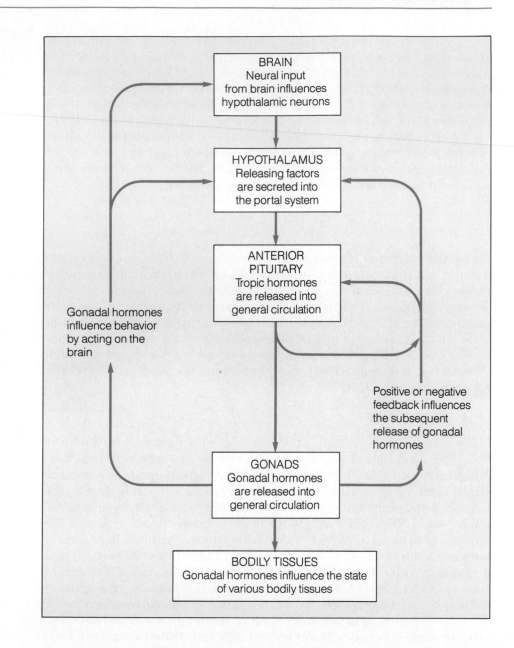

FIGURE 11.5

A summary model of the regulation of gonadal hormones.

Pulsatile Hormone Release

Many hormones tend to be released in pulses (Karsch, 1987); they are discharged several times per day in large surges, which typically last no more than a few minutes. Hormone levels in the blood are regulated by changes in the frequency and duration of the hormone pulses (Reame, Sauder, Kelch, & Marshall, 1984). One consequence of **pulsatile hormone release** is that there are often large minute-to-minute fluctuations in the levels of circulating hormones (e.g., Koolhaas, Schuurman, & Wiepkema, 1980). Accordingly, when the pattern of human male gonadal hormone release is referred to as steady, it means that there are no major systematic changes in circulating gonadal hormone levels from day to day, not that the levels never vary.

A Summary Model of Gonadal Endocrine Regulation

Pictured in Figure 11.5 (on the facing page) is a summary model of the regulation of gonadal hormones. According to this model, the brain controls the release of gonadotropin-releasing hormone from the hypothalamus into the hypothalamopituitary portal system, which carries it to the anterior pituitary. In the anterior pituitary, the gonadotropin-releasing hormone stimulates the release of gonadotropins, which are carried by the circulatory system to the gonads. In response to the gonadotropins, the gonads release androgens, estrogens, and progestins, which feed back onto the pituitary and hypothalamus to regulate subsequent gonadal hormone release. Armed with this general perspective of neuroendocrine function, you are ready to consider how gonadal hormones direct sexual development (Section 11.2) and activate sexual behavior (Section 11.3), and how the hypothalamus influences sexual behavior and preference (Section 11.4).

11.2

Hormones and Sexual Development

You have undoubtedly noticed that humans are *dimorphic,* that they come in two standard models: female and male. This section describes how hormones control the development of those physical characteristics that identify us as male or female. The last part of this section is special because it focuses on three cases of exceptional sexual development. These three cases are extraordinarily interesting, but there is another reason for focusing on them. It is expressed by the widely misunderstood proverb, "the exception proves the rule." Most people think that this proverb means that the exception "proves" the rule in the sense that it establishes its truth, but this is clearly wrong—the truth of a rule is challenged, not confirmed, by exceptions to it. The word *proof* comes from the Latin *probare,* which means *to test*—as in "proving ground" or "printers proof"—and this is the sense in which it is used in the proverb (Gould, 1980). Accordingly, this seemingly nonsensical proverb actually capsulizes an important principle of scientific inquiry: It makes the point that the explanation of exceptional cases is a challenge for any theory. Thus, the explanation of the three exceptional cases that cap off this section is a major test for the theory of normal sexual development that evolves in the preceding parts of the section.

Sexual differentiation in mammals begins at fertilization with the production of two kinds of zygotes: one with an XX (female) pair of sex chromosomes and one with an XY (male) pair. It is the genetic information on these sex chromosomes that normally determines whether development will occur along female or male lines. But be cautious here; do not fall into the seductive embrace of the men-are-men-and-women-are-women assumption. Do not begin by assuming that there are two parallel genetic programs for sexual development: one for female development and another for male development. As you are about to learn, sexual development unfolds according to an entirely different principle, one that many males—particularly those who still stubbornly adhere to notions of male pre-eminence—find unsettling. This principle is that we are all genetically programmed to develop female bodies; genetic males develop male bodies only because their female program of development is overruled.

Fetal Hormones and the Development of the Reproductive Organs

Gonads Figure 11.6 illustrates the structure of the gonads as they appear 6 weeks after fertilization. Notice that at this stage of development, each fetus, regardless of its genetic sex, has the same pair of structures, called *primordial gonads—primordial* means *existing at the beginning.* Each primordial gonad has an internal core or *medulla,* which has the potential to develop into a testis, and each has an outer covering or *cortex,* which has the potential to develop into an ovary.

Six weeks after conception, the Y chromosome of the male triggers the synthesis of **H-Y antigen,** and this hormone causes the medulla of each primordial gonad to grow and to develop into a testis. There is no female coun-

FIGURE 11.6

The development of a testis and an ovary from the medulla and cortex, respectively, of the primordial structure that is present 6 weeks after conception.

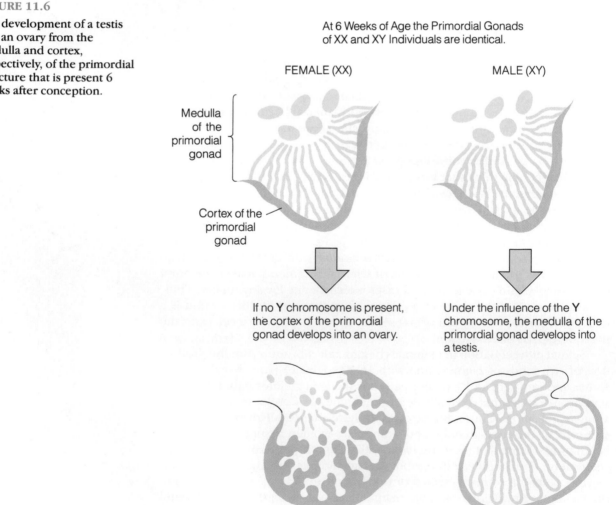

At 6 Weeks of Age the Primordial Gonads of XX and XY Individuals are identical.

FEMALE (XX)   MALE (XY)

Medulla of the primordial gonad

Cortex of the primordial gonad

If no **Y** chromosome is present, the cortex of the primordial gonad develops into an ovary.

Under the influence of the **Y** chromosome, the medulla of the primordial gonad develops into a testis.

terpart of H-Y antigen (Haseltine & Ohno, 1981); in the absence of H-Y anti-gen, the cortical cells of the primordial gonads automatically develop into ovaries (Jost, 1972). Accordingly, if H-Y antigen is injected into a genetic female fetus 6 weeks after conception, the result is a genetic female with testes; or if drugs that block the effects of H-Y antigen are injected at the appropriate time into a male fetus, the result is a genetic male with ovaries. Such "mixed-gender" cases expose in a dramatic fashion the weakness of "mamawawa" thinking (Crews, 1988).

Internal reproductive ducts   Six weeks after fertilization, both males and females have two complete sets of reproductive ducts. They have a male **Wolffian system,** which has the capacity to develop into the male reproductive ducts (e.g., the *seminal vesicles,* which hold the fluid in which sperm cells are ejaculated, and the *vas deferens,* through which the sperm cells travel to the seminal vesicles). And they have a female **Müllerian system,** which has the capacity to develop into the female ducts (e.g., the *uterus,* the upper part of the *vagina,* and the *fallopian tubes,* through which ova travel from the ovaries to the uterus, where they can be fertilized). In the third month of male fetal development, the testes secrete testosterone and **Müllerian-inhibiting substance.** The testosterone stimulates the development of the Wolffian system (see Figure 11.7), and the Müllerian-inhibiting substance causes the Müllerian system to degenerate and the testes to descend into the **scrotum,** the sac that holds the testes outside the body cavity (Wilson, George, & Griffin, 1981). Because it is testosterone that triggers Wolffian development—not the sex chromosomes—genetic females who are injected with testosterone during the appropriate fetal period develop male reproductive ducts along with their female ones (Jost, 1972).

The differentiation of the internal ducts of the female reproductive system (see Figure 11.7) is not under the control of ovarian hormones; the ovaries are almost completely inactive during fetal development. The development of the Müllerian system occurs in any fetus that is not exposed to testosterone during the critical fetal period. Accordingly, normal female fetuses, ovariectomized female fetuses, and orchidectomized male fetuses all develop female reproductive ducts (Jost, 1972). **Ovariectomy** refers specifically to the removal of the ovaries, and **orchidectomy** refers specifically to the removal of the testes (*orchis* is Greek for *testicle*). **Gonadectomy** and **castration** both refer generally to removal of gonads, either ovaries or testes.

External reproductive organs   There is a basic difference between the differentiation of the external reproductive organs and the differentiation of the internal reproductive organs (i.e., the gonads and reproductive ducts). As you have just read, every normal fetus develops separate precursors for the male (medulla) and female (cortex) gonads and for the male (Wolffian system) and female (Müllerian system) reproductive ducts; then only one set, male or female, develops. In contrast, the male and female external **genitals** (reproductive organs) develop from the same precursor. This *bipotential precursor* and its subsequent differentiation are illustrated in Figure 11.8.

In the second month of pregnancy, the bipotential precursor of the external reproductive organs consists of four parts: the glans, the urethral folds, the lateral bodies, and the labioscrotal swellings. Then it begins to differentiate. The *glans* grows into the head of the *penis* in the male or the **clitoris** in

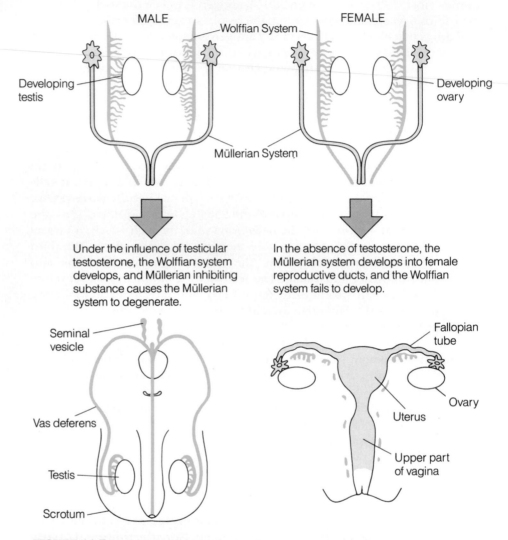

At 6 weeks, all human fetuses have the antecedents of both male (Wolffian) and female (Müllerian) reproductive ducts.

MALE   FEMALE

Wolffian System

Developing testis

Developing ovary

Müllerian System

Under the influence of testicular testosterone, the Wolffian system develops, and Müllerian inhibiting substance causes the Müllerian system to degenerate.

In the absence of testosterone, the Müllerian system develops into female reproductive ducts, and the Wolffian system fails to develop.

Seminal vesicle

Vas deferens

Testis

Scrotum

Fallopian tube

Ovary

Uterus

Upper part of vagina

FIGURE 11.7

The development of the internal ducts of the male and female reproductive systems.

the female; the *urethral folds* fuse in the male or enlarge to become the *labia minora* in the female; the *lateral bodies* form the shaft of the penis in the male or the hood of the clitoris in the female; and the *labioscrotal swellings* form the *scrotum* in the male or the *labia majora* in the female.

Like the development of the internal reproductive ducts, the development of the external genitals is controlled by the presence or absence of testosterone. If testosterone is present at the appropriate stage of fetal development, male external genitals develop from the bipotential precursor; if testosterone is not present, the development of the external genitals proceeds along female lines.

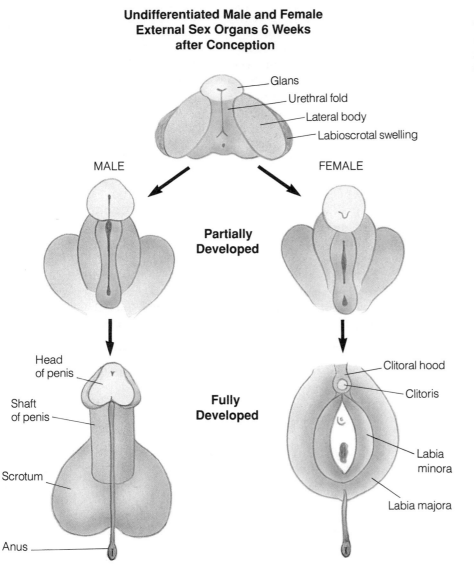

**Undifferentiated Male and Female
External Sex Organs 6 Weeks
after Conception**

Glans
Urethral fold
Lateral body
Labioscrotal swelling

MALE   FEMALE

**Partially
Developed**

Head
of penis

Shaft
of penis

Scrotum

Anus

**Fully
Developed**

Clitoral hood
Clitoris

Labia
minora

Labia majora

FIGURE 11.8
The development of male
and female external
reproductive organs from the
same bipotential precursor.

Perinatal Hormones and the Differentiation of the Brain

There are differences between the brains of women and men. Because experiments on human sexual differentiation are unethical, efforts to identify the factors that lead to gender differences in brain structure and function have focused on the study of other species. Rats are useful subjects for the study of hormones and brain development because they are born just 22 days after conception. At 22 days of age, the period during which hormones can influence their genital development is largely over, but the period during which hormones can influence their brain development is just beginning. Accordingly, it is possible to study the effects of hormones on brain development, unconfounded by changes on genital development, by manipulating the hormone levels of *neonatal* (newborn) rats.

Most of the early experiments on the development of sex differences in the brain focused on the factors that control the development of the cyclic and steady patterns of gonadotropin release in females and males, respectively. The seminal experiments were conducted by Pfeiffer in 1936. In his experiments, some neonatal rats (males and females) were gonadectomized and some were not, and some received gonad transplants (ovaries or testes) and some did not. Remarkably, Pfeiffer found that gonadectomizing neonatal rats of either genetic sex caused them to develop into adults with the female cyclic pattern of gonadotropin release. In contrast, transplantation of testes into gonadectomized or intact male or female neonatal rats caused them to develop into adults with the steady male pattern of gonadotropin release. Transplantation of ovaries had no effect on the pattern of hormone release. Pfeiffer concluded that the female cyclic pattern of gonadotropin release develops unless the preprogrammed female cyclicity is overridden by testosterone during perinatal development (see Harris & Levine, 1965).

Pfeiffer incorrectly concluded that the presence or absence of testicular hormones in neonatal rats influenced the development of the pituitary because he was not aware of what we know today: that the release of gonadotropins from the anterior pituitary is controlled by the hypothalamus. Once this was discovered, it became apparent that Pfeiffer's experiments had provided the first evidence of the role of neonatal androgens in the sexual differentiation of the brain (i.e., of the hypothalamus). Other differences between female and male brains has been shown to be under similar hormonal control: The presence of perinatal testosterone leads to the development of male brain characteristics; its absence leads to the development of female brain characteristics (see Gorski, 1985).

Aromatization and brain differentiation   All gonadal and adrenal sex hormones are **steroid** compounds. This means that they are all derived from *cholesterol,* a fatty organic compound. Because the steroid hormones have similar structures, they are readily converted from one to the other. For example, the addition of a simple benzene ring to a testosterone molecule changes it to estradiol—this process is called **aromatization.** There is good evidence that aromatization is a critical step in the masculinization of the brain by testosterone in some species. According to this theory, perinatal testosterone does not directly masculinize the brain; the brain is masculinized by estradiol that is aromatized from perinatal testosterone. Although the idea that estradiol—the alleged female hormone—masculinizes the brain is counterintuitive, there is strong evidence for it in several species. In the rat, for example, (1) the enzyme that is necessary for aromatization of testosterone is present in neonates (Selmanoff, Brodkin, Weiner, & Siiteri, 1977); (2) neonatal injections of estradiol masculinize the brain (Gorski, 1971); (3) **dihydrotestosterone,** an androgen that cannot be converted to estrogen, has no masculinizing effect on the brain (Whalen & Rezek, 1974); and (4) agents that block the aromatization of testosterone (McEwen, Lieberburg, Chaptal, & Krey, 1977) or block estrogen receptors (Booth, 1977) interfere with the masculinizing effects of testosterone on the brain.

How do genetic females keep from being masculinized by their mother's estradiol, which circulates through the fetal blood supply (Ojeda, Kalra, & McCann, 1975)? In the rat, alpha fetoprotein is the answer. **Alpha fetopro-**

tein is present in the blood of rats during the perinatal period (Plapinger, McEwen, & Clemens, 1973), and it deactivates circulating estradiol by binding to it. Then how does estradiol masculinize the brain of the male fetus in the presence of the deactivating effects of alpha fetoprotein? Because testosterone is immune to alpha fetoprotein, it can travel unaffected from the testes to the brain, where it enters cells and is converted there to estradiol. The estradiol is not broken down in the brain because alpha fetoprotein does not readily penetrate the blood-brain barrier. In primates, female fetuses are protected from the masculinizing effects of their mother's estrogens by a *placental barrier*. Unfortunately, this placental barrier is not so effective against synthetic estrogens (e.g., *diethylstilbestrol*). As a result, the female offspring of mothers who have been exposed to synthetic estrogens while pregnant may display a variety of male characteristics (see McEwen, 1983).

Perinatal Hormones and Behavioral Development

In view of the fact that perinatal hormones influence the development of the brain, it should come as no surprise that they also influence the development of behavior. Most of the research on hormones and behavioral development has focused on the role of perinatal hormones in the development of sexually dimorphic copulatory behaviors in laboratory animals (Feder, 1981, 1984).

Phoenix, Goy, Gerall, and Young (1959) were among the first to systematically demonstrate that the perinatal injection of testosterone can both **masculinize** and **defeminize** a genetic female's adult copulatory behavior. First, they injected pregnant guinea pigs with testosterone. Then, when the litters were born, they ovariectomized the female offspring. Finally, when these ovariectomized female guinea pigs reached maturity, they injected them with testosterone and assessed their copulatory behavior. Phoenix and his colleagues found that the females that had been exposed to perinatal testosterone displayed much more male-like mounting behavior in response to testosterone injections in adulthood than did adult females that had not been exposed to perinatal testosterone. And when as adults they were injected with progesterone and estradiol and mounted by males, they displayed less **lordosis,** the intromission-facilitating arched-back posture of female receptivity. Grady, Phoenix, and Young (1965) performed the complementary study on male rats and found that the lack of early exposure of male rats to testosterone had both **feminizing** and **demasculinizing** effects on their copulatory behavior as adults. Male cats castrated shortly after birth failed to display the normal male copulatory pattern of mounting, **intromission** (penis insertion), and **ejaculation** (ejecting sperm) when they were treated with testosterone and given access to a sexually receptive female; and when they were injected with estrogen and progesterone as adults, they exhibited more lordosis than did uncastrated controls. The aromatization of perinatal testosterone to estradiol seems to be important for both the defeminization and the masculinization of rodent copulatory behavior (Goy & McEwen, 1980; Shapiro, Levine, & Adler, 1980).

Most of the research on hormones and behavioral development has focused on the copulatory act itself. As a result, we know relatively little about the role of hormones in the development of the complex search and **proceptive behaviors** (i.e., solicitation behaviors) that precede copulation, or in the development of other gender-related behaviors that are not directly related to reproduction. The following are some of the reported effects of perinatal testosterone on development of noncopulatory behaviors: it disrupts the proceptive hopping, darting, and ear wiggling of receptive female rats (Fadem & Barfield, 1981); it increases the aggressiveness of female mice (Edwards, 1969); it disrupts the maternal behavior of female rats (Ichikawa & Fujii, 1982); and it increases rough social play in female monkeys (Goy, 1970) and rats (Meaney & Stewart, 1981).

In thinking about hormones and behavior, it is important to remember that feminizing and demasculinizing effects do not always go together; nor do defeminizing and masculinizing effects. Hormone treatments can enhance or disrupt female behavior without affecting male behavior, and vice versa.

Puberty: Hormones and the Development of Secondary Sex Characteristics

During childhood, levels of circulating gonadal hormones are low, reproductive organs are immature, and males and females differ little in general appearance. This period of developmental quiescence ends abruptly with the onset of puberty. **Puberty** is the transitional period between childhood and adulthood during which fertility is achieved, the adolescent growth spurt occurs, and the secondary sex characteristics develop. **Secondary sex characteristics** are those features other than the reproductive organs that distinguish sexually mature men and women. The bodily changes that occur during puberty are illustrated in Figure 11.9—you are undoubtedly familiar with at least half of them.

Puberty is associated with an increase in the release of hormones by the anterior pituitary. The increase in the release of **growth hormone,** which is the only anterior pituitary hormone that does not have an endocrine gland as its primary target, acts directly on bone and muscle tissue to produce the pubertal growth spurt. Increases in gonadotropic and **adrenocorticotropic hormone** release cause the gonads and adrenal cortex to increase their release of gonadal and adrenal hormones, which in turn initiate the maturation of the genitals and the development of secondary sex characteristics.

The general principle guiding normal pubertal sexual maturation is a simple one. In pubertal males, androgen levels are higher than estrogen levels, and masculinization is the result; in pubertal females, estrogen predominates, and the result is feminization. Individuals castrated prior to puberty do not become sexually mature unless they receive *replacement injections* of androgen or estrogen. But even here, in its only sphere of relevance, the men-are-men-and-women-are-women approach to hormones and sex stumbles badly. You see, **androstenedione,** an androgen that is released primarily by the adrenal cortices, is normally responsible for the growth of pubic and **axillary hair** (underarm hair) in females. It is hard to take seriously the practice of referring to androgens as "male hormones" when one of them is responsible for the development of the female pattern of pubic hair growth. The female pattern is an inverted pyramid; the male pattern is a pyramid—see Figure 11.9.

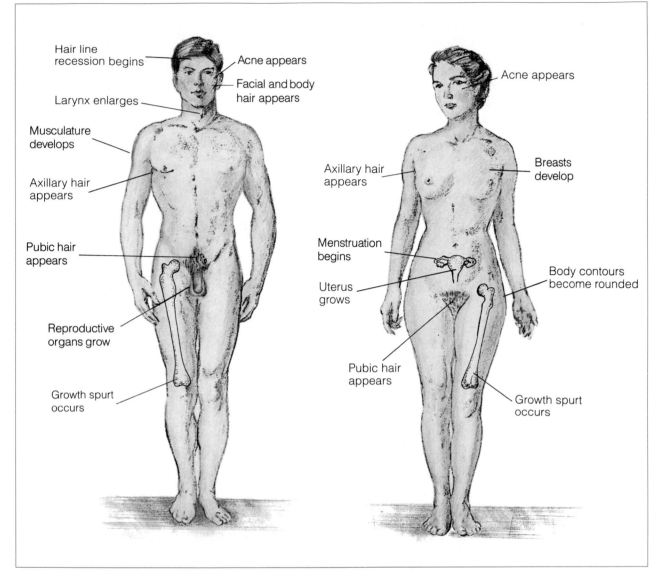

FIGURE 11.9

The changes that occur in males and females during puberty.

Do you remember how old you were when you started to go through puberty? In most North American and European countries, puberty begins at about 11 years of age for girls and 12 for boys. I am sure that you would have been unhappy if you had not started puberty until you were 15 or 16, but this was the norm in North America and Europe just a century and a half ago. Presumably, this 4-year acceleration of puberty has resulted from an improvement in dietary, medical, and socioeconomic conditions.

SELF TEST

Before proceeding to a consideration of three cases of abnormal human sexual development, review the basics of normal development by completing the following exercise.

1. Six weeks after conception, the Y chromosome of the human male triggers the production of _____ .

2. In the absence of H-Y antigen, the cortical cells of the primordial gonads develop into _____ .

3. In the third month of male fetal development, the testes secrete testosterone and _____ substance.

4. The hormonal factor that triggers the development of the human Müllerian system is the lack of _____ around the third month of fetal development.

5. The scrotum and the _____ develop from the same bipotential precursor.

6. The female pattern of cyclic _____ release from the anterior pituitary develops in adulthood unless androgens are present in the body during the perinatal period.

7. The sexually dimorphic nuclei of the _____ area are larger in male rats and humans than in female rats and humans.

8. It has been hypothesized that perinatal testosterone must first be changed to estrogen before it can masculinize the male rat brain. This is called the _____ hypothesis.

9. _____ is normally responsible for pubic and axillary hair growth in human females during puberty.

The answers to the preceding questions are the following: (1) H-Y antigen, (2) ovaries, (3) Müllerian inhibiting, (4) androgen (or testosterone), (5) labia majora, (6) gonadotropin, (7) preoptic, (8) aromatization, and (9) androstenedione.

Three Cases of Exceptional Human Sexual Development

So far in Section 11.2, you have learned "the rules" according to which hormones influence sexual development. Now, three exceptions are offered to "prove (i.e., to test) these rules."

CASE 1

The Case of Anne S.

Anne S., an attractive 26-year-old female, sought treatment for two sex-related disorders: lack of menstruation and pain during sexual intercourse (Jones & Park, 1971). She sought help because she and her husband of 4 years had been trying without success to have children, and she correctly surmised that her lack of a menstrual cycle was part of the problem. A physical examination revealed that Anne was a healthy young woman. Her only readily apparent peculiarity was the sparseness and fineness of her pubic and axillary hair. Examination of the external genitals revealed no abnormalities; however, there were some problems with her internal genitals. Her vagina was only 4 centimeters long, and her uterus was grossly underdeveloped.

At the start of this chapter, I said that you would encounter some amazing things, and the diagnosis of Anne's case certainly qualifies as one of them. Anne's doctors concluded that she was a man. No, this is not a misprint; they concluded that Anne, the attractive young housewife, was in fact Anne, the happily married man. Three lines of evidence supported this diagnosis. First, analysis of some cells scraped from the inside of Anne's mouth revealed that they were of the male XY type. Second, a tiny incision in Anne's abdomen, which enabled Anne's physicians to look inside, revealed a pair of internalized testes, but no ovaries. Finally, hormone tests revealed that Anne's hormone levels were those of a male.

Anne suffers from **androgenic insensitivity syndrome;** all of her symptoms stem from the fact that her body lacks the ability to respond to androgens. During development, Anne's testes released normal amounts of androgens for a male, but her body could not respond to them, and her development thus proceeded as if no androgens had been released. Her external genitals, her brain, and her behavior developed along preprogrammed female lines, without the effects of androgens to override the female program, and her testes did not descend from her body cavity. Furthermore, Anne did not develop normal internal female reproductive ducts because, like other genetic males, her testes released Müllerian inhibiting substance—that is why her vagina was short and her uterus undeveloped. At puberty, Anne's testes released enough estrogens to feminize her body in the absence of the counteracting effects of androgens; however, adrenal androstenedione was not able to stimulate the growth of pubic and axillary hair.

Money and Ehrhardt (1972) studied the psychosexual development of 10 androgen insensitive patients and concluded that the placidity of their childhood play, their goals, their fantasies, their sexual behavior, and their maternal tendencies—several had adopted children—all "conformed to the idealized stereotype of what constitutes femininity in our culture" (p. 112). Apparently, without the masculinizing effects of androgens, infants who look like females and are raised as females come to think and act like females—even when they are genetic males.

An interesting issue of medical ethics is raised by the androgenic insensitivity syndrome. Many people believe that physicians should always disclose all relevant findings to their patients. If you were Anne's physician, would you tell her that she is a man? Would you tell her husband? Anne's vagina was surgically enlarged, she was counseled to consider adoption, and, as far as I know, she is still happily married and unaware of her genetic sex.

CASE 2

The Adrenogenital Syndrome

The **adrenogenital syndrome** is characterized by a deficit in the release of the hormone *cortisol* from the adrenal cortices, which results in adrenal hyperactivity and the excessive release of adrenal androgens. This has little effect on the development of males, other than accelerating the onset of their puberty, but it has major effects on the development of genetic females. Females who suffer from the adrenogenital syndrome are usually born with an enlarged clitoris and partially fused labia, as illustrated in Figure 11.10. Their internal ducts are usually normal because the adrenal androgens are released too late to stimulate the development of the Wolffian system. If identified at birth, the abnormalities of the external genitals are surgically corrected, and cortisol is ad-

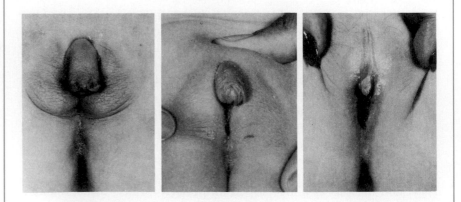

FIGURE 11.10

Genetic female babies with the adrenogenital syndrome display varying degrees of clitoral enlargement and labial fusion. The case on the right has been surgically treated. Courtesy John Money, Ph.D. First published in: JH Med. Journal 122: 160–167, 1968.

ministered to reduce the levels of circulating adrenal androgens. These early-treated cases frequently begin to menstruate later than normal, but otherwise they grow up to be physically normal, and they thus provide an excellent opportunity to study the effects of fetal androgen exposure on psychosexual development.

Cortisone-treated adrenogenital teenage girls typically display a high degree of "tomboyishness" and little interest in maternity (e.g., Ehrhardt, Epstein, & Money, 1968). They prefer boys' clothes, play mainly with boys, show little interest in handling babies, and tend to daydream about future careers rather than motherhood. It is important not to lose sight of the fact that many teenage girls in this culture display similar characteristics—and why not? Accordingly, the behavior of treated adrenogenital females, although perhaps tending toward the masculine, is well within the range that is considered normal by the current standards of our culture.

The most interesting questions about the development of females with adrenogenital syndrome concern the development of their romantic and sexual preferences. They seem to lag behind normal females in dating and marriage—perhaps because of the delayed onset of their menstrual cycle—but in other respects their sexual interests appear normal. Most are heterosexual, although one study has reported a slight tendency toward bisexuality (Ehrhardt & Meyer-Bahlburg, 1981).

Prior to the development of cortisone therapy in 1950, genetic females with adrenogenital syndrome were left untreated. Some were raised as boys and some were raised as girls, but the direction of their pubertal development was unpredictable. In some cases, adrenal androgens predominated and masculinized their bodies; in others ovarian estrogens predominated and feminized their bodies. Thus, some who were raised as girls were transformed at puberty into men, and others who were raised as boys were transformed into women. The emotional impact of these transformations was traumatic.

One such case (Money & Ehrhardt, 1972) was referred for treatment at the age of 12. At birth, her external genitals were somewhat ambiguous, but she was raised as a female without incident until puberty. At puberty, her sudden masculinization was the subject of great distress, both for her and her parents. Treatment involved surgical enlargement of her vagina, removal of her large clitoris, and the initiation of cortisone therapy, which suppressed androgen release and allowed her ovarian estrogens to feminize her body. She became an attractive young woman. Narrow hips and mildly short stature remained unchanged, as the *epiphyses* [the ends of bones, where bone growth takes place] of the bones had already fused under the influence of precocious masculinization. These two signs alone remained as reminders of the past, except for a small amount of coarse facial hair, requiring removal by electrolysis. The voice was husky, but so used as to be not mistaken as masculine. . . . The capacity for orgasm was not lost. The proof came fifteen years later, upon establishment of a sexual relationship and marriage. (p. 157) Not all cases of adrenogenital syndrome that were left untreated until puberty were resolved so satisfactorily.

CASE 3

Sex Reassignment of a Twin with Ablatio Penis

One of the most famous cases in the literature on sexual development is that of a male identical twin whose penis was accidentally destroyed during circumcision at the age of 7 months. Because there was no satisfactory way of surgically replacing the lost penis, a widely respected expert in such matters, John Money, recommended that the boy be castrated, that an artificial vagina be created, that the boy be raised as a girl, and that estrogen be administered at puberty to feminize the body. After a great deal of consideration and anguish, the parents followed Money's advice.

Money's (1975) report of this case of **ablatio penis** has been influential. It has been seen by some as the ultimate test of the *nature-nurture controversy* (see Chapter 2) with respect to the development of sexual identity and behavior. It seemed to pit the masculinizing effects of male genes and male hormones against the effects of being reared as a female. And the availability of a genetically identical control subject, the twin brother, made the case all the more interesting. According to Money, the outcome of this case comes down strongly on the side of the *social-learning theory* of sexual identity. Money reported in 1975, when the patient was 12, that "she" had developed as a normal female, thus confirming his prediction that being raised as a girl would override the masculinizing effects of male genes and early androgens. Because it is such an interesting case, Money's description of it has been featured in many textbooks of psychology, medicine, sociology, and women's studies, as well as in many television, magazine, and newspaper stories, each time carrying with it the message that the sexual identity and sexual behavior of men and women is largely a matter of upbringing.

In 1980, a British news team that was preparing a report on the case discovered that several psychiatrists had examined the patient in 1976, when she was 13, and had reached a conclusion that conflicted with Money's. Their conclusion was that the patient was having significant psychological problems, including considerable ambivalence toward the female role. She refused to draw pictures of females, she aspired to occupations that are commonly regarded as masculine (e.g., auto mechanic), and her masculine gait was the object of scorn from classmates, who referred to her as "cave woman." Clearly, things were not as cut-and-dried as Money's 1975 report had made them out to be.

It is scientifically regrettable that so much of a theoretical and philosophical superstructure has been built on the supposed results of a single, uncontrolled and unconfirmed case. It is further regrettable that we here in the United States had to depend for a clinical follow-up by a British investigative journalist team for a case originally and so prominently reported in the American literature. The issues raised by this case are too important to be settled by the media. For scientific and medical reasons, a full updated scientific report on both twins is called for and hopefully will be forthcoming from the team presently associated with this case. . . . It is further hoped that this particular case will be resolved to the best interest of the particular twin and family involved. The twin should be allowed to truly express any desired sexual identity with familial, social, and medical support. (Diamond, 1982, pp. 184–185)

Does current theory pass the test of these three exceptions? I think so. Current theories of hormones and sexual development greatly increase the understanding of each of these three cases, and they provide an effective basis for prescribing treatment. Because each of the three patients is male in some respects and female in others, each is a challenge to the men-are-men-and-women-are-women assumption.

11.3

The Effects of Gonadal Hormones on Adults

Once an individual reaches sexual maturity, gonadal hormones begin to play a role in activating reproductive behavior. These activational effects are the focus of this section. It has three parts. The first deals with the role of hormones in activating the reproduction-related behavior of men. The second deals with the role of hormones in activating the reproduction-related behavior of women. And the third deals with the current epidemic of anabolic steroid use.

Male Reproduction-Related Behavior and Testosterone

The important role played by gonadal hormones in the activation of male sexual behavior is clearly demonstrated by the asexualizing effects of orchidectomy. Bremer (1959) reviewed the cases of 157 orchidectomized Norwegians. Many had committed sex-related offenses and had agreed to castration to reduce the length of their prison term. Two important generalizations can be drawn from Bremer's study. The first is that orchidectomy leads to a reduction in sexual interest and behavior; the second is that the rate and degree of the loss is variable. According to Bremer, about half the cases became completely asexual within a few weeks of the operation; others quickly lost their ability to achieve an erection, but continued to experience some sexual interest and pleasure; and a few continued to copulate successfully, although somewhat less enthusiastically, for the duration of the study. There were also bodily changes: a reduction of hair on the trunk, extremities, and face; the deposition of fat on the hips and chest; a softening of the skin; and a reduction in strength. Of the 102 sex offenders in the study, only 3 were reconvicted of sex offenses. Accordingly, Bremer recommended castration as an effective treatment of last resort for male sex offenders.

Why do some men remain sexually active for months after orchidectomy, despite the fact that testicular hormones are cleared from their bodies within days? It has been suggested that adrenal androgens may play some role in the maintenance of sexual activity in some castrated men, but there is no evidence for this suggestion (Davidson, Kwan, & Greenleaf, 1982). Alternatively, it has been suggested that *endorphins* may play a role in maintaining the sexual interest of castrated men; Miller and Baum (1987) showed that *naloxone,* an opiate antagonist, further reduced the sexual motivation and behavior of castrated male rats.

Orchidectomy, in one fell swoop—or, to put it more precisely, in two fell swoops—removes a pair of glands that release many hormones. Because testosterone is the major testicular hormone, the major symptoms of orchidectomy have been generally attributed to the loss of testosterone, rather than to the loss of some other testicular hormone or to some nonhormonal consequence of the surgery. The therapeutic effects of testosterone **replacement injections** have confirmed this assumption.

The very first case report of the effects of testosterone replacement therapy was that of a 38-year-old World War I veteran, who was castrated in 1918 at the age of 19 by a shell fragment that removed his testes but left his penis undamaged.

> His body was soft; it was as if he had almost no muscles at all; his hips had grown wider and his shoulders seemed narrower than when he was a soldier. He had very little drive. . . .
>
> Just the same this veteran had married, in 1924, and you'd wonder why, because the doctors had told him he would surely be **impotent** [unable to get an erection]. . . . He confessed that he made some attempts at sexual intercourse "for his wife's satisfaction" but he confessed that he had been unable to satisfy her at all. . . .
>
> Dr. Foss began injecting it [testosterone] into the feeble muscles of the castrated man in good stiff doses [I assume that no pun was intended]. . . .
>
> After the fifth injection, erections were rapid and prolonged. . . . But that wasn't all. During twelve weeks of treatment he had gained eighteen pounds, and all his clothes had become too small. Originally, he wore fourteen-and-a-half inch collars. Now fifteen-and-a-half were too tight. . . . testosterone had resurrected a broken man to a manhood he had lost forever. (de Kruif, 1945, pp. 97–100)

Since this first clinical trial, testosterone has breathed sexuality into the lives of many men. It initiates puberty in men who have failed to develop because of childhood testicular dysfunction, and it returns the sexuality of men who have lost it to postpubertal testicular problems. Testosterone does not, however, eliminate the *sterility* (inability to reproduce) of males who lack functional testes.

The fact that testosterone is necessary for male sexual behavior has led to two assumptions: (1) that the level of a man's sexuality is a function of the amount of testosterone that he has in his blood, and (2) that a man's sex drive can be increased by increasing his testosterone levels. Both assumptions are incorrect. Sex drive and testosterone levels are uncorrelated in healthy men, and testosterone injections do not increase their sex drive. It seems that each male has far more testosterone than is required to activate the neural circuits that produce his sexual behavior, and that having more than the minimum is of no advantage in this respect (Sherwin, 1988). An experiment by Grunt and Young (1952) clearly illustrates this point. First, Grunt and Young rated the sexual behavior of each of the male guinea pigs in their experiment. Then, on the basis of the ratings, Grunt and Young divided the male guinea pigs into three experimental groups: low, medium, and high sex drive. Following castration, the sexual behavior of all of the guinea pigs fell to negligible levels within a few weeks (see Figure 11.11), but it recovered after the initiation of a series of testosterone replacement injections. The important point is that although each subject received the same, very large replacement injections of testosterone, the injections simply returned each to its previous level of copulatory activity. With respect to the effects of testosterone on sexual behavior, more is not necessarily better.

Dihydrotestosterone, a nonaromatizable androgen, has failed to reactivate the copulatory behavior of castrated male rats in several studies (see MacLusky & Naftolin, 1981). This suggests that in male rats the activational effects of testosterone on sexual behavior may be produced by estradiol that has been aromatized from the testosterone. However, dihydrotestosterone has proven effective in activating sexual behavior in orchidectomized primates (e.g., Davidson, Kwan, & Greenleaf, 1982).

Gonadal Hormones and Female Reproduction-Related Behavior

Sexually mature female rats and guinea pigs display 4-day cycles of gonadal hormone release. There is a gradual increase in the secretion of estrogen by the developing follicle in the 2 days prior to ovulation, followed by a sudden surge in progesterone as the egg is released. These sequential surges of estrogen and progesterone initiate **estrus,** a period of 12 to 18 hours during which

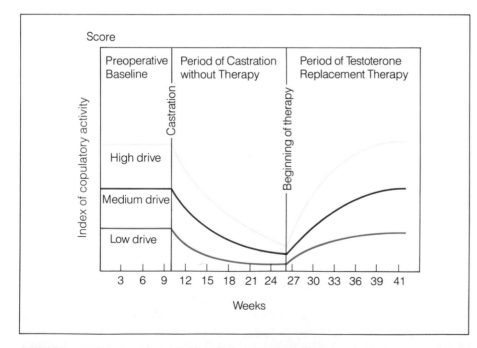

FIGURE 11.11

The sexual behavior of male rats with low, medium, and high sex drive is disrupted by castration and returned to its original level by very large replacement injections of testosterone. (Adapted from Grunt & Young, 1952.)

the female is: (1) *fertile,* (2) *receptive* (likely to assume the *lordosis* posture when mounted), (3) *proceptive* (likely to engage in behaviors that serve to attract the male), and (4) *sexually attractive* (smelling of chemicals that attract males). The close relation between the cycle of hormone release and the **estrous cycle** (i.e., the cycle of sexual receptivity) in female rats and guinea pigs and in many other mammalian species suggests that female sexual behavior in these species is under hormonal control. The effects of ovariectomy and subsequent replacement injections confirm this conclusion. Unlike the gradual and unpredictable decline in male sexual behavior that occurs after orchidectomy, ovariectomy produces a rapid decline of both proceptive and receptive behaviors. Ovariectomized rats and guinea pigs can be brought into a state of estrus by an injection of estrogen, followed a day and a half later by an injection of progesterone.

Women are not at all like female rats and guinea pigs when it comes to the hormonal control of their sexual behavior. The sexual motivation and behavior of women are not associated with their menstrual cycles (see Sanders & Bancroft, 1982), and ovariectomy has surprisingly little effect (e.g., Martin, Roberts, & Clayton, 1980). Ovariectomy does decrease the vaginal lubrication of women, which can interfere with intercourse if a commercial lubricant is not used, but there is typically little or no associated decline in their sexual motivation (Dennerstein & Burrows, 1982) or in the feminine appearance of their bodies. Estrogen replacement therapy replenishes the vaginal lubrication.

There is evidence that the sex drive of women is under the control of androgens, not estrogens (see Sherwin, 1988). According to this theory, enough androgen is released from the human adrenal glands to maintain the sexual motivation of women after their ovaries have been removed. Support for this androgen theory of human female sexuality has come from three sources. (1) Experiments in nonhuman female primates: Replacement injections of testosterone, but not estradiol, increased the proceptivity of ovariectomized and adrenalectomized rhesus monkeys (see Everitt & Herbert, 1972; Everitt, Herbert, & Hamer, 1971). (2) Correlational studies in healthy women: Various measures of sexual motivation were correlated with testosterone levels, but not estradiol levels (see Bancroft, Sanders, Davidson, & Warner, 1983; Morris, Udry, Khan-Dawood, & Dawood, 1987). (3) Clinical studies of women following *hysterectomy* (surgical removal of the internal reproductive organs): Replacement injections of testosterone, but not estradiol, increased their sexual motivation (see Sherwin, 1985; Sherwin, Gelfand, & Brender, 1985).

Anabolic Steroids and Athletes

Steroids are hormones that are synthesized from *cholesterol;* all gonadal hormones are steroids. **Anabolic steroids** are steroids, such as testosterone, that have *anabolic,* or growth-promoting, effects. Testosterone itself is not very useful as an anabolic drug because it is broken down soon after injection and because it has undesirable side effects. Chemists have managed to synthesize a number of potent anabolic steroids that are long-acting, but they have not managed to synthesize one that does not have side effects. We are currently in the midst of an epidemic of anabolic steroid abuse. Many athletes and body builders are self-administering appallingly large doses to increase their muscularity and strength.

Do anabolic steroids really increase the muscularity and the strength of the athletes that use them? Initially, the athletes said "yes," and the scientists said "no." The athletes were right. The early scientific studies, although well designed, involved doses of steroids much smaller than those that were being used by most athletes—in part, because of the concern of the experimenters for the welfare of their subjects. On the basis of these early studies, it was concluded that anabolic steroids do not improve athletic performance. However, more recent studies, in which larger doses of anabolic steroids have been administered for longer periods of time, have proven their efficacy (see Haupt & Rovere, 1984). In fact, many athletes believe that it is impossible to compete successfully at the highest levels of their sports without an anabolic-steroid boost. It is difficult indeed to ignore the testimonials of steroid users such as the gentleman pictured in Figure 11.12.

> The most popular story of the 1976 Montreal Olympics involved the success of East German women swimmers. When asked why so many of their women had deep voices, an East German coach replied, "We have come here to swim, not sing." (*New York Times,* quoted in Goldman, 1984, p. 19)

It is the sex-related side effects of anabolic steroids that are of primary relevance here. It has proven extremely difficult to document these side effects because most athletes who use anabolic steroids will not admit it for fear of being banned from competition. Nevertheless, there is general agreement (Goldman, 1984; Haupt & Rovere, 1984; Wilson & Griffin, 1980) that athletes who take high doses of anabolic steroids risk the following sex-related side effects. In men, the negative feedback from high levels of anabolic steroids reduces gonadotropin release; this leads to a reduction in testicular activity

FIGURE 11.12

An athlete who has used anabolic steroids to augment his training program. Carl Iwasaki/*Sports Illustrated.*

which can result in *testicular atrophy* (wasting away of the testes) and sterility. *Gynecomastia* (i.e., breast growth in men) can occur, presumably as the result of the aromatization of anabolic steroids to estrogens. In women, anabolic steroids can produce *amenorrhea* (cessation of menstruation), sterility, *hirsutism* (the excessive growth of body hair), growth of the clitoris, development of a masculine body shape, baldness, and deepening and coarsening of the voice.

Both men and women who use anabolic steroids can suffer muscle spasms, muscle pains, blood in the urine, acne, general swelling from the retention of water, bleeding of the tongue, nausea, vomiting, and a variety of psychotic behaviors, including fits of depression and anger (Pope & Katz, 1987). Oral anabolic steroids produce cancerous liver tumors.

The side effects of anabolic steroid abuse make two important points about hormones and sex. The first is that testosterone-like substances do not produce increases in the sexual motivation and behavior of people with testosterone levels in the normal range. The second is that the effects of hormones on the structure of the human body are not restricted to critical prenatal and pubertal periods. Although there are periods in one's life when hormones (or other agents or experiences) have a particularly great effect on development, they can also influence development outside these periods when administered in high enough doses.

11.4

The Hypothalamus and Sexual Behavior

Many parts of the brain are involved in mammalian sexual behavior. However, the discovery that gonadotropin release is controlled by the hypothalamus focused the study of the neural bases of sexual behavior on this structure. This section, the final section of the chapter, introduces this research.

Structural Differences Between the Male Hypothalamus and the Female Hypothalamus

You have already learned that the male hypothalamus and the female hypothalamus are functionally different in their control of anterior pituitary hormones (steady vs. cyclic release, respectively). In the 1970s, structural differences between male and female hypothalami were discovered in rats (Raisman & Field, 1971). Most notably, Gorski, Gordon, Shryne, and Southam (1978) discovered a nucleus in the **medial preoptic area** of the rat hypothalamus that was several times larger in males. They called this nucleus the **sexually dimorphic nucleus.** See Figure 11.13.

At birth, the sexually dimorphic nuclei of male and female rats are the same size. In the first few days after birth, the male sexually dimorphic nuclei grow at a high rate, and the female sexually dimorphic nuclei do not. The growth of the male sexually dimorphic nuclei is triggered by estradiol, which has been aromatized from testosterone (see McEwen, 1987). Accordingly, castrating day-old, but not 4-day-old, male rats significantly reduces the size of their sexually dimorphic nuclei as adults, whereas injecting neonatal (newborn) female rats with testosterone significantly increases the size of theirs—see Figure 11.14 (Gorski, 1980). The size of a male rat's sexually dimorphic

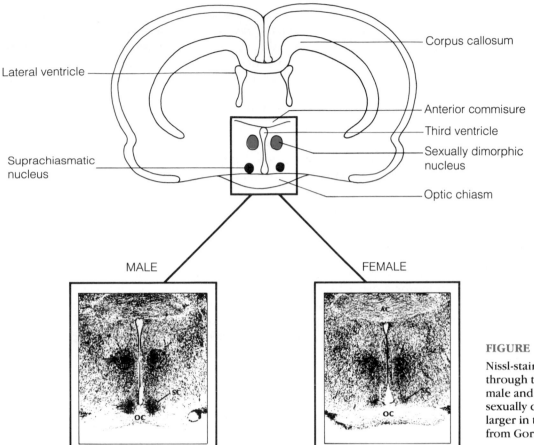

FIGURE 11.13

Nissl-stained coronal sections through the preoptic area of male and female rats. The sexually dimorphic nuclei are larger in the male. (Adapted from Gorski et al., 1978).

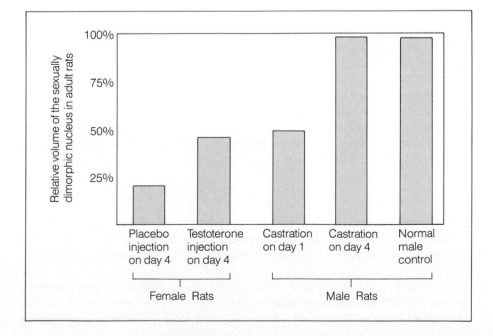

FIGURE 11.14

The effects of neonatal testosterone exposure on the size of the sexually dimorphic nuclei in male and female rats. (Adapted from Gorski, 1980.)

nuclei is correlated with its level of sexual activity (Anderson, Fleming, Rhees, & Kinghorn, 1986). Although the overall size of the sexually dimorphic nuclei diminishes only slightly in male rats that are castrated in adulthood, specific areas of the nucleus do degenerate (Block & Gorski, 1988).

Since the discovery of the sexually dimorphic nuclei in rats, other structural differences between male brains and female brains have been identified in other species (see Witelson, 1991)—for example, you learned in Chapter 2 that some of the nuclei that are involved in birdsong are larger in male birds than in female birds. In humans, there are nuclei in the preoptic (Swaab & Fliers, 1985) and anterior (Allen, Hines, Shryne, & Gorski, 1989) regions of the hypothalamus that are substantially larger in men than women. The gender difference in the human preoptic area is not apparent in children who are less than 2 years old (Hofman & Swaab, 1989).

The Hypothalamus and Male Sexual Behavior

The medial preoptic area of the hypothalamus plays a key role in male sexual behavior. Destruction of the medial preoptic area abolishes sexual behavior in the males of many species, and selective destruction of the sexually dimorphic nuclei has been shown to reduce the sexual behavior of male rats (De Jonge et al., 1989; Turkenburg et al., 1988). In contrast, medial-preoptic-area lesions have no effect on female sexual behavior, but they do eliminate the mounting behavior that is occasionally observed in female rats (Singer, 1968). Accordingly, bilateral medial-preoptic lesions appear to abolish male copulatory behavior in both sexes. On the other side of the coin, electrical stimulation of the medial-preoptic area elicits copulatory behavior in male rats (Malsbury, 1971), and copulatory behavior can be reinstated in castrated male rats by medial-preoptic implants of testosterone (Davidson, 1980).

It is not clear why males with medial-preoptic lesions stop copulating. Animals with medial-preoptic-area lesions vigorously approach and investigate receptive females, and they make clumsy attempts to mount them (e.g., Malsbury & Pfaff, 1974; Powers, Newman, & Bergondy, 1987). They seem to want to copulate, but for some unknown reason, they can't. Everitt and Stacey (1987) studied the effects of medial-preoptic-area lesions on male rats that had been trained to press a lever for access to receptive females, which dropped into their test chambers through a trap door in the ceiling. Following medial-preoptic-area lesions, the male rats continued to press the lever at a high rate to receive their "reinforcements from the sky," but they never managed to copulate with them. In contrast, orchidectomized males stopped pressing the lever. Apparently, orchidectomy abolishes the sexual motivation of male rats, but medial-preoptic lesions do not.

The Hypothalamus and Female Sexual Behavior

The *ventromedial hypothalamus* (VMH) contains circuits that are critical for female sexual behavior. Electrical stimulation of the VMH facilitates the sexual behavior of female rats, and VMH lesions reduce it (see Pfaff & Modianos, 1985).

The ability of injections of estradiol and progesterone to bring ovariectomized females into estrus is mediated by their action on neurons in the ventromedial nucleus. Rubin and Barfield (1983) induced estrus in ovariectomized rats by injecting first estradiol and then progesterone into the VMH. Blaustein, King, Toft, and Turcotte (1988) showed that the priming injection of estradiol produces a massive increase in progesterone receptors in the hypothalamus; it is this increase that presumably allows a subsequent progesterone injection to initiate estrus.

The induction of estrus by estradiol and progesterone appears to be mediated by the action of VMH neurons on the *midbrain central gray*. There are many neurons in the ventromedial nucleus whose axons project to the midbrain central gray, and many of these contain the neuropeptide, *substance P*. Support for the hypothesis that these neurons mediate the hormonal induction of estrus comes from the finding that substance P injections into the midbrain central gray of ovariectomized rats facilitates lordosis (Dornan, Malsbury, & Penney, 1987).

Hormones, the Hypothalamus, and Sexual Preference

So far, this chapter has avoided the issue of sexual preference. As you know, some people are **heterosexuals** (they prefer sex partners of the opposite gender), some are **homosexuals** (they prefer sex partners of the same gender), and some are **bisexuals** (they are sexually attracted to members of both sexes). A discussion of recent research on sexual preference is a fitting conclusion to this chapter because it ties together its hormone, hypothalamus, exception-proves-the-rule, and anti-mamawawa themes.

Many people mistakenly assume that sexual preference has something to do with current hormone levels. It doesn't. Heterosexuals and homosexuals do not differ in their levels of circulating hormones. Castration reduces the sexual behavior of both heterosexuals and homosexuals, but it does not redirect it, and replacement injections simply reactivate the preferences that existed prior to castration.

Efforts to determine whether or not perinatal hormone manipulations can influence the development of sexual preference have focused on nonhuman species for ethical reasons. A consistent pattern of findings has emerged from this research (see Ellis & Ames, 1987). In rats, hamsters, ferrets, pigs, zebra finches, and dogs, perinatal castration of males or testosterone treatment of females has been shown to induce same-sex preferences (see Adkins-Regan, 1988; Baum, Erskine, Kornberg, & Weaver, 1990). On one hand, prudence should be exercised in applying the results of these experiments on laboratory species to the development of sexual preferences in humans. It would be a mistake to ignore the profound cognitive and emotional components of human sexuality, which have no counterpart in laboratory animals; in general, the sexual behavior of humans and other primates is more influenced by experience than is the sexual behavior of other mammals (e.g., Goy, 1978). On the other hand, it would also be a mistake to think that a pattern of results that runs so consistently through so many mammalian species has no relevance to humans.

Do perinatal hormone levels influence the sexual preferences of adult humans? Because the effects of hormones on the development of sexual preferences are not ethically accessible to experimental investigation in humans, the evidence on this point is cloudy—but there are some indications that the answer is "yes." The strongest support for this view comes from the *quasi-experimental study* (see Chapter 1) of Ehrhardt et al. (1985). They interviewed adult women whose mothers had been exposed to *diethylstilbestrol* (a synthetic estrogen) during pregnancy. The subjects' responses indicated that they were significantly more sexually attracted to women than was a group of matched control subjects. Ehrhardt and her colleagues concluded that perinatal estrogen exposure does encourage homosexuality and bisexuality in women, but that its effect is relatively weak—the sexual behavior of all but 1 of the 30 subjects was primarily heterosexual.

Does sexual preference have a genetic basis? A recent study by Bailey and Pillard (1991) suggests that it does. They identified a group of male homosexuals who had twin brothers; 52% of the monozygotic twin brothers and 22% of the dizygotic twin brothers were homosexual.

A Difference in the Brains of Homosexuals and Heterosexuals?

LeVay (1991) recently published the results of a postmortem study that may prove to be a major breakthrough in the study of human sexual preference. He compared the neuroanatomy of three groups of subjects: heterosexual men, homosexual men, and women, who were assumed to be heterosexual. Reports of gender differences in the anterior and preoptic areas of the hypothalamus of various species, including humans, focused LeVay's research on these areas. LeVay confirmed a previous report (Allen, Hines, Shryne, & Gorski, 1989) that the *third interstitial nucleus of the anterior hypothalamus* (INAH 3) is more than twice as large in heterosexual men than in women. In addition, he found that it is more than twice as large in heterosexual men than in homosexual men—see Figure 11.15.

LeVay's report created a kerfuffle in the popular media, largely for the wrong reasons. To put LeVay's finding in proper perspective, you should ask yourself two questions about it. First, "Is it reliable?" You should remain a bit skeptical about any finding until it has been replicated, preferably by a different group of investigators; this is particularly true in an emotion-charged area of research such as the study of homosexuality. Perhaps by the time that you read this, attempts to replicate LeVay's finding will have been reported. Second, "What does it mean?" LeVay's finding does not prove, as implied in many newspaper articles, that homosexuality results from a small INAH 3. Like all correlations, LeVay's observation is subject to a variety of causal interpretations (see Chapter 1). Being a homosexual may cause small INAH 3s, rather than vice versa, or some unrecognized third factor may have been responsible for the correlation. LeVay considered one such possibility and ruled it out: the possibility that AIDS was responsible for the correlation. Many of the homosexual brains in LeVay's study came from men who had died of AIDS, which is why LeVay was able to obtain such a large sample of male homosexual brains and why he did not include female homosexuals in his study. However, even when LeVay considered only those subjects who had died of other causes, the correlation between sexual preference and the size of the INAH 3 was still present.

Despite the fact that LeVay's study has proven nothing about the neural mechanisms of homosexuality or its causes, it is potentially of great importance. By locating a readily identifiable difference in the brains of male heterosexuals and homosexuals, in a part of the brain that is important for both

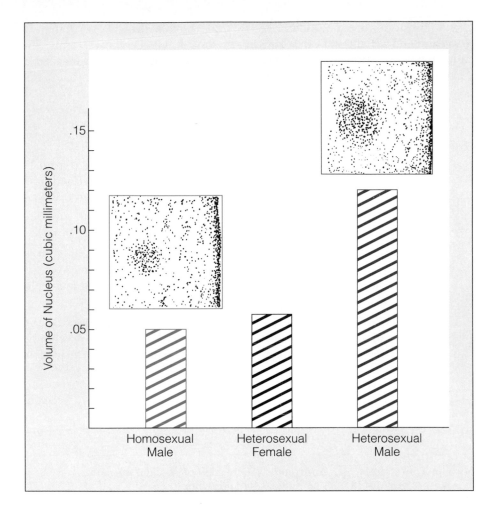

FIGURE 11.15

LeVay (1991) found that the third interstitial nucleus of the anterior hypothalamus (INAH 3) is larger in heterosexual males than in females and homosexual males. (Drawings based on the histological material of LeVay, 1991.)

hormonal regulation and sexual behavior, LeVay has provided a focus for the next generation of research on human sexual preference.

Conclusion

The primary purpose of this chapter was to describe the role of hormones in sexual development and behavior. But there were also two important sub-themes: (1) that exceptional cases play a particularly important role in testing scientific theory and (2) that the men-are-men-and-women-are-women attitude is a misleading perspective from which to consider sexual matters. If you now appreciate why exceptional cases have been so important in the study of hormones and sex, you have learned a fundamental principle that has relevance to all fields of scientific inquiry. If you now are better able to resist the seductive appeal of the men-are-men-and-women-are-women attitude, you are leaving this chapter a more tolerant and understanding person than when you began it. I hope that you now have an abiding appreciation of the fact that maleness and femaleness are slight, multidimensional, and at times ambiguous variations of one another.

Some stories are too good not to be told; the following is one of them. I just can't end a chapter about sex without telling it. It is about my Granny. She was puzzled by "this oral sex thing" that she had read about in a magazine. "Good heavens," she exclaimed. "Whatever do they talk about?"

Food for Thought

1. Over the last century and half, the onset of puberty has changed from 15 or 16 to 11 or 12, but there has been no corresponding acceleration in psychological and intellectual development. Precocious puberty is like a loaded gun in the hand of a child. Discuss.

2. Do you think that sex-change operations should be permitted? Why?

3. What should be done about the current epidemic of anabolic steroid abuse? Would you make the same recommendation if a safe anabolic steroid were developed? If a drug were developed that would dramatically improve your memory, would you take it?

4. Discuss LeVay's report of a difference in the brains of heterosexual and homosexual men. Discuss with respect to the physiological-or-psychological and the learned-or-innate dichotomies, which were criticized in Chapter 2.

KEY TERMS

To help you study the material in this chapter, all of the key terms—those that have appeared in bold type—are listed and briefly defined here.

Ablatio penis.   Accidental destruction of the penis.

Adrenal cortex.   The outer layer of an adrenal gland; the adrenal cortices release gonadal hormones and hormones that regulate the salt and glucose levels of the blood.

Adrenocorticotropic hormone.   The anterior pituitary hormone that causes the adrenal cortex to release its hormones.

Adrenogenital syndrome.   A disorder characterized by a decrease in the release of the hormone cortisol from the adrenal cortices, which results in the production of high levels of adrenal androgens and masculinizes the bodies of genetic females.

Alpha fetoprotein.   A protein present in the blood of neonatal rats that deactivates circulating estradiol by binding to it.

Anabolic steroids.   A group of steroid drugs that are derived from the testosterone molecule and that have powerful anabolic or growth-promoting effects.

Androgenic insensitivity syndrome.   A developmental disorder of genetic males; their insensitivity to androgens causes them to develop female bodies.

Androgens.   One class of gonadal hormones; testosterone is the major androgen.

Androstenedione.   The adrenal androgen that triggers the growth of pubic and axillary hair in pubertal human females.

Anterior pituitary.   The part of the pituitary gland that releases tropic hormones.

Aromatization.   The chemical process by which testosterone is converted to estradiol.

Axillary hair.   Underarm hair.

Bisexual.   Individuals who are sexually attracted to members of both sexes.

Castration.   The surgical removal of the gonads (testes or ovaries).

Clitoris.   The female analogue of the head of the male penis.

Copulation.   Sexual intercourse.

Defeminizing.   Suppressing or disrupting female characteristics.

Demasculinizing.   Suppressing or disrupting male characteristics.

Dihydrotestosterone.   An androgen that cannot be converted to estrogen (i.e., that cannot be aromatized).

Ejaculation. Ejection of sperm.

Endocrine glands. The glands that release hormones into the general circulation of the body.

Estradiol. The most prevalent estrogen.

Estrogens. A major class of gonadal hormones; estradiol is the major estrogen.

Estrous cycle. A cycle of sexual receptivity and non-receptivity displayed by many female mammals; female rats and guinea pigs have estrous cycles of about 4 days; human females do not have estrous cycles.

Estrus. The portion of the estrous cycle characterized by fertility and sexual receptivity; "estrus" is a noun and "estrous" is an adjective.

Exocrine glands. The glands that secrete chemicals into ducts.

Feminizing. Enhancing or producing female characteristics.

Follicle. The package of cells within which each ovum begins its development in the ovary.

Follicle stimulating hormone (FSH). The gonadotropic hormone that stimulates development of ovarian follicles.

Genitals. The reproductive organs.

Gonadectomy. The surgical removal of the gonads (testes or ovaries).

Gonadotropin-releasing hormone. The hypothalamic releasing hormone that controls the release of the two gonadotropic hormones.

Gonadotropins. The two pituitary tropic hormones (i.e., follicle stimulating hormone and luteinizing hormone) that stimulate the release of gonadal hormones.

Gonads. The testes and ovaries.

Growth hormone. An anterior pituitary hormone that acts directly on bone and muscle tissue to produce the pubertal growth spurt.

H-Y antigen. The protein that stimulates the cells of the medullary portion of the primordial gonads to proliferate and develop into testes.

Heterosexual. An individual who is sexually attracted to members of the opposite bodily sex.

Homosexual. An individual who is sexually attracted to members of the same bodily sex.

Hormones. Chemicals released by the endocrine system into general circulation.

Hypothalamopituitary portal system. A vascular network that carries hormones from the hypothalamus to the anterior pituitary.

Impotent. Males unable to achieve a penile erection.

Inhibitory factors. Hypothalamic hormones thought to regulate anterior pituitary hormones by inhibiting their release.

Intromission. Insertion of the penis into the vagina.

Lordosis. The intromission-facilitating, arched-back, tail-to-the-side posture of female rodent receptivity.

Luteinizing hormone (LH). One of the gonadotropic hormones; one of its functions is to cause the developing ovum to be released from its follicle.

Masculinizing. Enhancing or producing male characteristics.

Medial preoptic area. An area of the hypothalamus that plays a key role in the control of male sexual behavior; the sexually dimorphic nuclei are in this area.

Menstrual cycle. The hormone-regulated cycle in women of follicle growth, egg release, uterus lining build-up, and menstruation.

Müllerian-inhibiting substance. The substance released during male development that causes the precursors of the female reproductive ducts to degenerate.

Müllerian system. The embryonic precursors of the female reproductive ducts.

Negative feedback. A signal from the change of a measure in one direction that results in a compensatory change in the other direction; for example, an increase in the release of gonadal hormones often reduces their subsequent release.

Neurohormones. Hormones that interact with the nervous system.

Neurosecretory cells. Neurons specialized for the release of hormones into general circulation.

Orchidectomy. The removal of the testes.

Ovariectomy. The removal of the ovaries.

Ovaries. The female gonads.

Ovulation. The release of the ovum from the follicle in which it develops; ovulation signals the beginning of the fertile period of the menstrual cycle.

Oxytocin. One of the two major hormones released by the posterior pituitary; in females, it stimulates contractions of the uterus and the ejection of milk during suckling.

Paraventricular nucleus. One nucleus of the hypothalamus in which the hormones of the posterior pituitary are synthesized.

Pituitary stalk. The structure connecting the hypothalamus and the pituitary.

Positive feedback. A signal from the change of a measure in one direction that causes a further change in the same direction.

Posterior pituitary. The part of the pituitary gland that contains the terminals of hypothalamic neurons.

Proceptive behaviors. Behaviors that serve to attract the sexual advances of the other sex.

Progesterone. A progestin that prepares the uterus and breasts for pregnancy.

Progestins. A class of gonadal hormones; progesterone is the major progestin.

Puberty. The transitional period between childhood and adulthood during which fertility is achieved, the adolescent growth spurt occurs, and the secondary sex characteristics develop.

Pulsatile hormone release. Virtually all hormones are released from endocrine glands in large pulses or surges, which typically occur several times a day and last for several minutes each.

Releasing factors. Suspected (putative) releasing hormones; releasing hormones are called releasing factors until they have been isolated from hypothalamic tissue.

Releasing hormones. Chemicals synthesized in the hypothalamus that stimulate the release of hormones from the anterior pituitary.

Replacement injection. The injection of a hormone whose natural release has been curtailed by the removal of the gland that normally releases it.

Scrotum. The sac that holds the male testes.

Secondary sex characteristics. Structural features, other than the reproductive organs, that distinguish men from women.

Sex chromosomes. The pair of chromosomes (XX or XY) that contains the genetic information that directs sexual development.

Sexually dimorphic nuclei. A pair of nuclei in the preoptic area that are larger in males than in females.

Steroid. A class of hormones that are derived from cholesterol; all gonadal and adrenal hormones are steroids.

Supraoptic nucleus. A nucleus of the hypothalamus in which the hormones of the posterior pituitary are synthesized.

Testes. Male gonads.

Testosterone. The most common androgen.

Thyrotropin. An anterior pituitary hormone that stimulates the release of hormones from the thyroid gland.

Thyrotropin-releasing hormone. A hypothalamic hormone that stimulates the release of thyrotropin from the anterior pituitary; the first releasing hormone to be isolated.

Vasopressin. One of the two major hormones of the posterior pituitary; it facilitates reabsorption of water by the kidneys.

Wolffian system. The embryonic male reproductive duct system.

Zygote. The cell formed from the fusion of a sperm cell and an ovum; it contains all the information necessary for the growth of a complete adult organism.

ADDITIONAL READING

The following book, although somewhat dated, contains lavishly illustrated, introductory articles on many areas of neuroendocrine research, each written by an expert in her or his field:

Krieger, D. T., & Hughes, J. C. (1980). *Neuroendocrinology*. Sunderland, Massachusetts: Sinauer.

The following article is a review of clinical cases of abnormal sexual development and what they tell us about the factors that influence the development of sexual identity and preference.

Money, J. (1987). Sin, sickness, or status? Homosexual gender identity and psychoneuroendocrinology. *American Psychologist, 42,* 384–399.

12

Sleep, Dreaming, and Circadian Rhythms

Most of us have a fondness for eating, drinking, and sex, the three highly esteemed motivated behaviors discussed in Chapters 10 and 11. But the amount of time that is devoted to these three behaviors by even the most amorous gourmands pales in comparison to the amount of time that he or she spends sleeping—most of us will sleep for well over 175,000 hours in our lifetimes. This extraordinary commitment of time implies that sleep fulfills a critical biological function. But what is it? And what about dreaming; why do we spend so much time dreaming? And why do we tend to get sleepy at about the same time every day? Answers to these questions await you in this chapter.

Almost every time that I give a lecture about sleep, somebody asks, "How much sleep do we need?" and each time, I provide the same unsatisfying answer. I explain that there are two fundamentally different answers to this question, but that neither has emerged a clear winner. One answer stresses the presumed health-promoting and recuperative powers of sleep and suggests that people need as much sleep as they can comfortably get. The other answer is that many of us sleep more than we need to and are consequently sleeping part of our lives away. Just think how your life could change if you slept 5 hours per night instead of 8. You would have an extra 21 waking hours each week, a mind-boggling 10,952 hours each decade.

As I prepared to write this chapter, I began to think of some of the personal implications of the idea that we get more sleep than we need. That is when I decided to do something a bit unconventional. While I write this chapter, I am going to be your subject in a sleep-reduction experiment. I am going to try to get no more than 5 hours of sleep per night—11:00 P.M. to 4:00 A.M.—until this chapter is written. As I begin, I am excited by the prospect of having more time to write, but a little worried that this extra time might be obtained at a personal cost that is too dear.

It is the next day now—4:50 Saturday morning to be exact—and I am just beginning to write. There was a party last night, and I didn't make it to bed by 11:00, but considering that I slept for only 3 hours and 35 minutes, I feel quite good. I wonder what I will feel like later in the day? In any case, I will report my experiences to you at the end of the chapter.

The following case study challenges several common beliefs about sleep. Ponder its implications before proceeding into the body of the chapter.

> Miss M . . . is a busy lady who finds her ration of twenty-three hours of wakefulness still insufficient for her needs. Even though she is now retired she is still busy in the community, helping sick friends whenever requested. She is an active painter and has recently finished a biography of William Morris, the British writer and designer. Although she becomes tired physically, when she needs to sit down to rest her legs, she does not ever report feeling sleepy. During the night she sits on her bed . . . reading, writing, crocheting or painting. At about 2:00 A.M. she falls asleep without any preceding drowsiness often while still holding a book in her hands. When she wakes about an hour later, she feels as wide awake as ever. It would be wrong to say that she woke refreshed because she did not complain of tiredness in the first place.
>
> To test her claim we invited her along to the laboratory. She came willingly but on the first evening we hit our first snag. She announced that she did not sleep at all if she had interesting things to do, and by her reckoning a visit to a university sleep laboratory counted as very interesting. Moreover, for the first time in years, she had someone to talk to for the whole of the night. So we talked.
>
> In the morning we broke into shifts so that some could sleep while at least one person stayed with her and entertained her during the next day. The second night was a repeat performance of the first night. . . . Things had

not gone according to plan. So far we were very impressed by her cheerful response to two nights of sleep deprivation, but we had very little by way of hard data to show others.

In the end we prevailed upon her to allow us to apply EEG electrodes and to leave her sitting comfortably on the bed in the bedroom. She had promised that she would co-operate by not resisting sleep although she claimed not to be especially tired. . . . At approximately 1:30 A.M., the EEG record showed the first signs of sleep even though . . . she was still sitting with the book in her hands. . . .

The only substantial difference between her sleep and what we might have expected from any other seventy-year-old lady was that it was of short duration. . . . [After 99 minutes], she had no further interest in sleep and asked to be allowed to leave the bedroom so that she could join our company again. (Meddis, 1977, pp. 42–44)

The Physiological and Behavioral Correlates of Sleep

The Three Standard Psychophysiological Measures of Sleep

It was first observed in the 1930s that there are major changes in the human EEG during the course of a night's sleep (Loomis, Harvey, & Hobart, 1936). Although the EEG waves that accompany sleep are generally large and slow, there are periods throughout the night that are dominated by low-voltage, fast waves that are similar to those of waking subjects. In 1953, Aserinsky and Kleitman discovered that *rapid eye movements* (REMs) occur under the closed eyelids of sleeping subjects during these periods of low-voltage, fast EEG activity. And in 1962, Berger and Oswald discovered that there is also a loss of electromyographic activity in the neck muscles during these same sleep periods. Subsequently, the **electroencephalogram (EEG),** the **electrooculogram (EOG),** and the neck **electromyogram (EMG)** became the three standard psychophysiological bases for defining stages of sleep (Rechtschaffen & Kales, 1968). Figure 12.1 depicts how EEG, EOG, and EMG activity are recorded during a sleep experiment. If being a subject in a sleep experiment looks like an easy way to earn a little extra cash, it is.

A subject's first night in the sleep laboratory is often fitful. That is why it is the usual practice to have a subject sleep several nights in the laboratory before beginning to study his or her sleep patterns. The disturbance of sleep observed during the first night in a sleep laboratory is called the **first-night phenomenon.** It is well known to markers of introductory psychology examinations because of the creative definitions of it that are offered by students who forget that it is a sleep-related, rather than a sex-related, phenomenon.

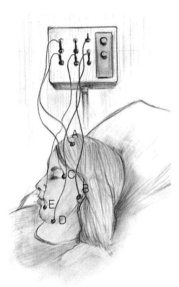

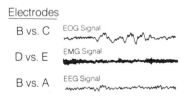

FIGURE 12.1

A subject participating in a sleep experiment.

The Five Stages of Sleep EEG

The EEG of a subject during a typical night's sleep is commonly divided into four separate classes: stage 1, stage 2, stage 3, and stage 4. Examples of these four stages of sleep EEG are presented in Figure 12.2. After a subject shuts her or his eyes and prepares to go to sleep, **alpha waves** (8 to 12 Hz; i.e., 8 to 12 cycles per second) begin to punctuate the low-amplitude, high-frequency EEG of active wakefulness. Then, as the subject falls asleep, there is a sudden transition to a period of stage 1 sleep EEG. Stage 1 sleep EEG is a low-amplitude high-frequency signal that is similar to, but slower than, that of active wakefulness. Then, as the subject continues to sleep, there is a progressive increase in the amplitude of the EEG waves and a slowing of their frequency, which is customarily divided into three stages: 2, 3, and 4. The primary distinguishing feature of stage 2 sleep EEG, in addition to the fact that it has a slightly higher amplitude and lower frequency than stage 1, is the fact that it is punctuated by two characteristic wave forms: **K complexes,** which are composed of a single large negative wave (upward deflection) followed by a single large positive wave (downward deflection), and **sleep spindles,** which are 1-to-2-second waxing and waning bursts of 12-to-14-Hz waves. Stage 3 sleep EEG is defined by the occasional presence of **delta waves,** the largest and slowest EEG waves, with a frequency of 1 to 2 Hz. The defining feature of stage 4 sleep EEG is the predominance of delta waves.

After spending some time in stage 4, sleeping subjects retreat back through the stages of sleep EEG to stage 1. However, when they return to

FIGURE 12.2

Waking EEG, presleep EEG, and the four stages of sleep EEG. Each trace is 30 seconds long.

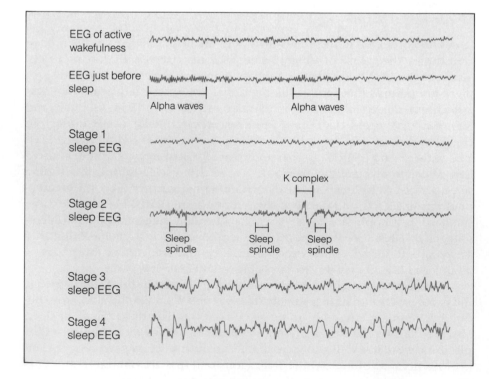

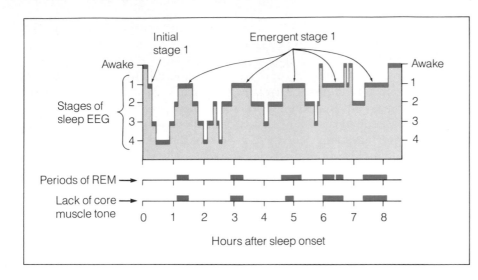

FIGURE 12.3

The stages of EEG during a typical night's sleep and their relation to periods of REM and lack of tone in core muscles.

stage 1, things are not at all the same as they were the first time through. The first period of stage 1 EEG during a night's sleep (**initial stage 1 EEG**) is not marked by any noteworthy electromyographic or electro-oculographic change, whereas subsequent periods of stage 1 sleep EEG (**emergent stage 1 EEG**) are accompanied by REMs and by a loss of tone in the muscles of the body core.

After the first cycle of sleep EEG—from initial stage 1 to stage 4 and back to emergent stage 1—the rest of the night is spent like a pendulum, going back and forth through the stages. Figure 12.3 illustrates the cycles of a typical night's sleep and the close relation between emergent stage 1 sleep, REMs, and the lack of tone in the core muscles. Notice that each cycle tends to be about 90 minutes long and that as the night progresses, more and more time is spent in emergent stage 1 sleep, and less and less time is spent in the other stages, particularly in stage 4. Notice also that there are brief periods during the night when the subject is awake; these periods of wakefulness are usually not remembered in the morning.

Let's pause here to get some sleep-stage terms straight. Emergent stage 1 sleep is often called **paradoxical sleep** because the EEG and autonomic activities that are associated with it are similar to those of wakefulness, and stages 3 and 4 are sometimes lumped together and called **delta sleep** after the delta waves that characterize them. The term **deep sleep** is commonly used, but I am going to refrain from using it here because of its ambiguity. Some researchers refer to stage 4 sleep as deep sleep because stage 4 sleep is characterized by the largest and slowest EEG waves; other researchers refer to emergent stage 1 sleep as deep sleep because during emergent stage 1 sleep the muscles are most relaxed and it is most difficult to awaken experimental animals. (Note that although it has proven most difficult to awaken laboratory animals from emergent stage 1 sleep, the results of comparable studies in humans have been mixed; see Cohen, 1979.) In this chapter, I will adopt the common practice of referring to that stage of sleep that is characterized by rapid eye movements, loss of core muscle tone, and low-amplitude high-frequency EEG as **REM sleep,** and I will use the term **slow-wave sleep (SWS)** to refer to stages 2, 3, and 4 together.

REMs, loss of core muscle tone, and low-amplitude high-frequency EEG are not the only physiological correlates of human REM sleep. Cerebral activity (e.g., oxygen consumption, blood flow, and neural firing in many structures) increases to near-waking levels, and there is a general increase in autonomic nervous system activity (e.g., in blood pressure, pulse, and respiration). The muscles of the extremities occasionally twitch, and there is always some degree of penile or clitoral erection.

12.2

REM Sleep and Dreaming

Kleitman's laboratory was an exciting place in 1953. Kleitman and his colleagues were driven by the fascinating implication of their discovery of REM sleep. With the exception of the loss of muscle tone in the core muscles, all of the other measures suggested that REM sleep episodes were emotion-charged. Could REM sleep be the physiological correlate of dreaming? Could REM sleep provide researchers with a window into the subjective inner world of dreams? They began by waking a few subjects in the middle of REM episodes and asking them if they had been dreaming. The results were remarkable.

> The vivid recall that could be elicited in the middle of the night when a subject was awakened while his eyes were moving rapidly was nothing short of miraculous. It [seemed to open] . . . an exciting new world to the subjects whose only previous dream memories had been the vague morning-after recall. Now, instead of perhaps some fleeting glimpse into the dream world each night, the subjects could be tuned into the middle of as many as ten or twelve dreams every night. (Dement, 1978, p. 37)

The results of a controlled comparison between REM and nonREM (NREM) awakenings were published in 1957 (Dement & Kleitman): 80% of the awakenings from REM sleep, but only 7% of the awakenings from NREM sleep, led to dream recall. The phenomenon of dreaming, which for centuries had been the subject of wild speculation, was finally rendered accessible to scientific investigation. The following anecdote related by Dement communicates some of the excitement felt by those involved in the discovery.

> I decided to be a subject primarily out of envy; having listened with amazement and awe as many subjects recounted their dreams, I wished to enjoy the experience myself. . . . On the first night I felt like an actor preparing for a performance as I sat in front of the mirror donning my "makeup" of electrodes. I will never forget this "opening night.". . .
> A hastily trained medical student . . . was monitoring the EEG and supervising my arousals. I went to sleep prepared for an exciting night and woke up with a certain urgency. . . . I searched my mind . . . I could remember nothing. . . . So I went back to sleep and was suddenly aware of being wrenched from the void once again. This time I could remember nothing except a very, very vague feeling of a name or a person. Disappointed but sleepy, I dozed off again.

The next time I was jolted awake—still unable to recall anything—I began to worry. Why didn't I remember a dream? I had expected to dazzle the medical student with my brilliant recall! After a fourth and fifth awakening with exactly the same results, I was really upset. What in the world was wrong? I began to doubt the whole REM-dreaming hypothesis. . . .

The experience had left me exhausted and extremely puzzled, and I was anxious to look at the polygraphic record of my miserable night. Upon examining the record I discovered, to my utter delight and relief, that the medical student had been mistakenly arousing me in NREM. Not once had I awakened during a REM period.

The next night, with additional instruction . . . the medical student hit the REM periods right on the button, and vivid recall flooded my mind with each awakening. (Dement, 1978, pp. 38–39)

Testing Common Beliefs about Dreaming

The high correlation between REM sleep and dream recall provided an opportunity to test some common beliefs about dreaming. The following are five such beliefs that have been subjected to empirical tests.

1. Many people believe that external stimuli can become incorporated into their dreams. Dement and Wolpert (1958) sprayed water on sleeping subjects after they had been in REM sleep for a few minutes, and a few seconds after the spray, each subject was awakened. In 14 of 33 cases, the water was incorporated into the dream report. The following narrative was reported by a subject who had been dreaming that he was acting in a play.

I was walking behind the leading lady when she suddenly collapsed and water was dripping on her. I ran over to her and water was dripping on my back and head. The roof was leaking. . . . I looked up and there was a hole in the roof. I dragged her over to the side of the stage and began pulling the curtains. Then I woke up. (Dement & Wolpert, 1958, p. 550)

2. Some people believe that dreams last only an instant, but research suggests that dreams run on "real time." In one study (Dement & Kleitman, 1957), subjects were awakened 5 or 15 minutes after the beginning of a REM episode and asked to decide on the basis of the duration of the events in their dreams whether they had been dreaming for 5 or 15 minutes. They were correct in 92 of 111 cases.

3. Some people claim that they do not dream. However, they have just as much REM sleep as "normal dreamers." Moreover, they report dreams if they are awakened during REM episodes (Goodenough, Shapiro, Holden, & Steinschriber, 1959), although they do so less frequently than do normal dreamers.

4. Penile erections are commonly assumed to be indicative of dreams with sexual content. However, penile erections are no more complete during dreams with frank sexual content than during those without it (Karacan, Goodenough, Shapiro, & Starker, 1966). Even babies have REM-related penile erections.

5. Most people believe that sleep talking and sleep walking (**somnambulism**) occur during dreams. This is not so; sleep talking and somnambulism occur least frequently during dreaming, when core muscles tend to be totally relaxed. They occur most frequently during stage 4 sleep.

The Interpretation of Dreams

The Freudian theory of dreams has been widely disseminated to the general public through movies, television, and literature as if it were fact. As a result, many people view dreams as symbolic representations of repressed sexual conflict. However, although the Freudian theory of dreams has been the basis for many an interesting story, there is no convincing evidence for it.

Hobson (1989) recently proposed a more parsimonious theory of sleep, which he calls the **activation-synthesis hypothesis.** This theory proposes that dream content reflects the random activity of cerebral circuits during REM sleep and the brain's inherent tendency to make sense of and give form to these ambiguous signals. According to this view, dreams are deeply personal. Each person's dreams reflect the particular information, capacities, and tendencies that are stored within his or her brain. They are not symbolic representations of repressed thoughts, nor do they focus exclusively on sexual conflict.

Lucid Dreams

The reality of dreams is usually quite distinct from the reality of consciousness. There are, however, dreams, which are called **lucid dreams,** where this distinction becomes blurred. These are dreams in which the dreamer is aware at the time that she or he is dreaming and can influence the course of the dream. The experience of a lucid dream is something like being awake in a dream (see Blackmore, 1991). The existence of lucid dreams was proven by experiments in which sleeping subjects signaled to the experimenter from their dreams that they were aware that they were dreaming—for example, by moving their eyes back and forth eight times (Hearne, 1978; LaBerge, 1985).

In various surveys, about 50% of respondents report having had at least one lucid dream (e.g., Gackenbach & LaBerge, 1988). However, because the concept of lucid dreaming is a difficult one to grasp, these figures are likely overestimates. Because many people find lucid dreaming to be a positive experience, several techniques have been devised for training people to have them. One such technique involves signaling to the sleeping subject each time that he or she is dreaming; a mild shock is administered to the wrist at the start of each REM period (Hearne, 1990).

People who regularly have lucid dreams have recently been used to study dreaming—it is like having a conscious person right in a dream, who can relay information about it out into the conscious world. For example, in one study, the subject was instructed to draw large triangles with his right arm as soon as he "got into" a dream and to signal to the experimenter with eye movements just before he drew each one. EMG activity that was consistent with triangle drawing was recorded from the right forearm each time that the eye-movement signal was received (Schatzman, Worsley, & Fenwick, 1988). In another study, a woman who could create various positive sexual encounters in her lucid dreams was shown to experience real physiological orgasms (LaBerge, Greenleaf, & Kedzierski, 1983) during each dream encounter.

12.3

Why Do We Sleep?

Recuperative and Circadian Theories

We humans have a tendency toward self-aggrandizement; we tend to think that most of what we do has a special, higher-order function. For example, it has been suggested that human sleep helps reprogram our complex computer-like brains, or that it permits some kind of emotional release to maintain our mental health. This is why many people are surprised to learn that virtually all mammals and birds sleep and that their sleep is much like ours; it is characterized by high-amplitude, low-frequency EEG waves punctuated by periods of low-amplitude, high-frequency activity. Even fish, reptiles, amphibians, and insects go through periods of inactivity and unresponsiveness that are similar to mammalian sleep.

The fact that sleep is so common in the animal kingdom suggests that it serves a critical function, but there is no consensus on what this critical function is. There are two general theoretical approaches to the function of sleep: *recuperation theories* and *circadian theories.* The essence of the recuperation theories is that being awake disrupts the *homeostasis* of the body in some way and that sleep is required to restore it. In contrast, the circadian theories argue that sleep is not a response to internal imbalance. According to the circadian theories, a neural mechanism has evolved to encourage animals to sleep during those times of the day when they do not usually engage in activities necessary for their survival. For example, prehistoric humans in their natural environment likely had enough time to get their eating, drinking, and reproducing out of the way during the daytime, and their strong motivation to sleep at night may have evolved to conserve their energy resources and to make them less susceptible to mishap (e.g., predation) in the dark. The circadian theory views sleep as an instinct somewhat akin to the instinct to engage in sexual activity. In essence, recuperation theories view sleep as a nightly repairman who fixes damage produced by wakefulness, while the circadian theories regard sleep as a strict parent who demands inactivity because it keeps us out of trouble. Choosing between the recuperation and circadian approaches to sleep is the logical first step in the search for the physiological basis of sleep. Is the sleep system run by a biological clock that produces compelling urges to sleep at certain times of the day to conserve energy and protect us from mishap or is it a homeostatic system whose function is to correct some adverse consequence of staying awake?

Table 12.1 illustrates the average number of hours per day that various mammalian species spend sleeping. Explaining the large between-species differences in daily sleep time is one of the central challenges that must be met by any successful theory of sleep. Why do cats tend to sleep 14 hours a day, and horses sleep only 2?

Circadian theories have done a better job than the recuperative theories of explaining the substantial between-species differences in sleep times. Recuperative theories predict that species that expend more energy should sleep longer, but there is no apparent correlation between a species' sleep time and its level of activity, its body size, or its body temperature. The fact that giant sloths sleep 20 hours per day is a strong argument against the theory that sleep is a compensatory reaction to energy expenditure. In contrast,

Table 12.1   The Number of Hours of Sleep per Day Averaged by Various Mammalian Species.

Hours of Sleep per Day	Mammalian Species
20	giant sloth
19	opossum, brown bat
18	giant armadillo
17	owl monkey, nine-banded armadillo
16	Arctic ground squirrel
15	tree shrew
14	cat, golden hamster
13	mouse, rat, gray wolf, ground squirrel
12	Arctic fox, chinchilla, gorilla, raccoon
11	mountain beaver
10	jaguar, vervet monkey, hedgehog
9	rhesus monkey, chimpanzee, baboon, red fox
8	human, rabbit, guinea pig, pig
6	gray seal, gray hyrax, Brazilian tapir
5	tree hyrax, rock hyrax
3	cow, goat, elephant, donkey, sheep
2	roe deer, horse

the circadian theory correctly predicts that the daily sleep time of each species is related to how vulnerable it is while it is asleep and how much time that it must spend each day to feed itself and to take care of its other survival requirements. For example, zebras sleep only 2 or 3 hours a day; they must graze almost continuously to get enough to eat, and when they are asleep they are extremely vulnerable to predatory attack. In contrast, African lions often sleep more or less continuously for 2 or 3 days after they have gorged themselves on a kill. The photograph in Figure 12.4 says it all.

FIGURE 12.4

After gorging themselves on a kill, African lions sleep almost continuously for 2 or 3 days. And where do they sleep? Anywhere they want.

The next two sections of this chapter deal with two topics—circadian sleep cycles and sleep deprivation—that have a bearing on the question of whether sleep is fundamentally circadian or recuperative.

12.4

Circadian Sleep Cycles

The world in which we live cycles from light to dark and back again once every 24 hours, and most surface-dwelling species have adapted to this regular change in their environment by developing a variety of so-called **circadian rhythms** (see Rusak & Bina, 1990; Takahashi, 1991)—*circadian* means lasting about 1 day. For example, most species display a regular circadian sleep-wake cycle. Humans take advantage of the light of day to take care of their biological needs, and then they sleep for much of the night, whereas **nocturnal animals,** such as rats, sleep for much of the day and stay awake at night. Although the so-called sleep-wake cycle is the most obvious circadian rhythm, "it is virtually impossible to find a physiological, biochemical, or behavioral process in animals which does not display some measure of circadian rhythmicity" (Groos, 1983, p. 19). Each day our bodies adjust themselves in a variety of ways to meet the demands of the two environments in which we live: light and dark.

Our circadian cycles are kept on their once-every-24-hours schedule by regular daily cues in the environment. The most important of these cues for the regulation of mammalian circadian rhythms is the daily cycle of light and dark—environmental cues that can entrain circadian rhythms are called **zeitgebers** (pronounced "ZITE gay bers"), a German word that means *time givers*. In controlled laboratory environments, it is possible to lengthen or shorten circadian cycles by adjusting the duration of the light-dark cycle; for example, when exposed to alternating 10-hour periods of light and 10-hour periods of dark, subjects' circadian cycles conform to a 20-hour day.

Free-Running Circadian Sleep-Wake Cycles

In a world without 24-hour cycles of light and dark, other regular cues in the environment can entrain circadian cycles. For example, the circadian sleep-wake cycles of hamsters living in continuous darkness or in continuous light can be entrained by regular daily bouts of social interaction (Mrosovsky, 1988), hoarding (Rusak, Mistlberger, Losier, & Jones, 1988), eating (Jilge, 1991; Mistlberger, 1990), or exercise (Mistlberger, 1991). Hamsters display particularly clear circadian sleep-wake cycles and are the favorite subjects of circadian-cycle researchers.

What happens to circadian rhythms in an environment that is devoid of *zeitgebers*? Remarkably, under conditions in which there are absolutely no temporal cues, humans and other animals maintain all of their circadian rhythms. Circadian rhythms in constant environments are said to be **free-running,** and their duration is called the **free-running period.** Free-running periods vary in length from subject to subject, they are of relatively constant

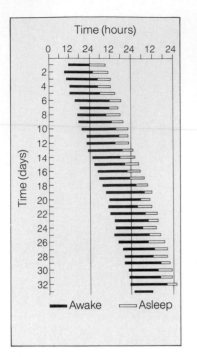

FIGURE 12.5

A typical free-running
25.3-hour circadian
sleep-wake cycle. Each day
the subject went to sleep
approximately 12.3 hours
later than he had the day
before. (Adapted from Wever,
1979, p. 30.)

duration within a given subject, and they are usually longer than 24 hours—about 25 hours in most humans. It seems that we all have an internal *biological clock* that habitually runs a little slow unless it is *entrained* by time-related cues in the environment. Perhaps the most remarkable characteristic of free-running circadian cycles is that they do not have to be learned. Even rats that are born and raised in an unchanging laboratory environment (i.e., in continuous light or in continuous darkness) display regular free-running sleep-wake cycles of about 25 hours (Richter, 1971).

A typical free-running circadian sleep-wake cycle is illustrated in Figure 12.5 (Wever, 1979). Notice its regularity. Without any external cue, this man fell asleep approximately every 25.3 hours for an entire month. The fact that such regularity was maintained despite day-to-day variations in physical and mental activity provides strong support for the dominance of circadian factors over recuperative factors in the regulation of sleep. Figure 12.6 provides an extreme illustration of this point; a full 24 hours of sleep deprivation on day 24 had little effect on the subsequent free-running circadian sleep-wake cycle of this rat.

The correlation between the length of a period of wakefulness and the length of the following period of sleep is negative, even when the cycle is free running. This means that on those occasions when a subject stays awake longer than usual, the following sleep tends to be shorter than usual (Wever, 1979). We appear to be programmed to have sleep-wake cycles of approximately 24 hours; hence, the longer that one stays awake during a particular cycle, the less time there is for sleep. In contrast, the recuperative theory of sleep incorrectly predicts that longer periods of wakefulness will be followed by longer periods of sleep.

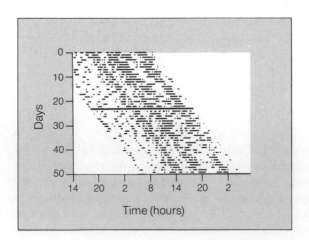

FIGURE 12.6

The effect of 24 hours of sleep deprivation on the free-running activity-rest circadian rhythm of a rat. Black bars indicate periods of activity; thus, long blank spaces are generally indicative of sleep. On day 24, the rat was totally deprived of sleep, yet the timing of its 25.3-hour free-running circadian rest-activity cycle was unaffected. (Adapted from Borbély, 1982.)

Many animals display a circadian cycle of body-temperature that is related to their circadian sleep-wake cycle; they tend to sleep during the falling phase of their circadian body-temperature cycle and awaken during its rising phase. However, when subjects are housed in constant laboratory environments, their sleep-wake and body-temperature cycles sometimes break away from one another. This phenomenon is called **internal desynchronization.** For example, in one case the free-running sleep-wake and body-temperature periods of a human subject were both 25.7 hours. Then, for some unknown reason, there was an increase in the free-running period of the sleep-wake cycle to 33.4 hours and a decrease in the free-running period of body temperature to 25.1 hours. The potential for the simultaneous existence of two different free-running periods suggests that there may be more than one circadian timing mechanism.

Jet Lag and Shift Work

Modern industrialized societies are faced with two different disruptions of circadian rhythmicity. One is **jet lag,** a case in which the zeitgebers that control the phases of various circadian rhythms are accelerated during eastern flights (*phase advances*) or decelerated during western flights (*phase delays*). The other is *shift work,* a case in which the zeitgebers stay the same, but workers are forced to adjust their natural sleep-wake cycles in order to meet the demands of changing work schedules. Both of these circadian changes produce disturbances in the duration and patterning of sleep, reports of fatigue and general malaise, and deficits on a variety of objective tests of physical and cognitive function. These disturbances can last for many days; for example, it typically takes about 10 days to completely adjust to a Tokyo-to-Boston flight—a phase advance of 10.5 hours.

What can be done to reduce the disruptive effects of shift work and jet lag? Companies that employ shift workers have had great success in improving the productivity and job satisfaction of their shift workers by scheduling phase delays rather than phase advances; whenever possible, shift workers are transferred from their current schedule to one that begins later in the day (see Coleman, 1986). It is much more difficult to go to sleep 4 hours earlier and get up 4 hours earlier (a phase advance) than it is to go to sleep 4 hours later and get up 4 hours later (a phase delay).

Two approaches have been proposed for the reduction of jet lag. One is the common-sense approach of gradually shifting one's sleep-wake cycle in the days prior to the flight (see Hobson 1989). The other is administering treatments after the flight that promote the required shift in the circadian rhythm. For example, exposure to intense light early in the morning has been shown to promote phase advances (Czeisler et al., 1989); Daan and Lewy (1984) used this method to accelerate the adaptation of a subject to the 9-hour phase advance that resulted after a flight from the United States to Europe. The results of a study in hamsters (Mrosovsky & Salmon, 1987) suggests that a good workout early in the morning of the first day after an eastern flight might promote adaptation to the resulting phase advance; hamsters that engaged in one 3-hour bout of wheel running 8 hours before their usual period of activity adapted quickly to an 8-hour advance in the light-dark cycle (see Figure 12.7).

FIGURE 12.7

A period of exercise (shown in red) accelerates adaptation to an 8-hour phase advance in the circadian light-dark cycle. (Adapted from Mrosovsky & Salmon, 1987.)

Rats were active each day during the 10-hour dark phase of their light-dark cycle. Then, the cycle was advanced by 8 hours. The rat circadian cycle of sleep and activity gradually adapted to the phase advance over the ensuing 8 or 9 days.

◀ 8-hour
phase advance

Rats that ran in a running wheel on the day of the phase advance, 7 hours prior to their normal activity time (shown in red), adapted to the phase advance in 1 or 2 days.

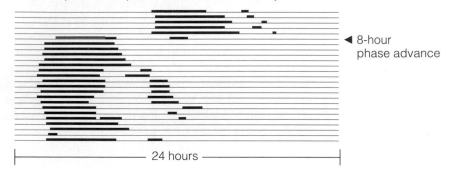

◀ 8-hour
phase advance

|———————————— 24 hours ————————————|

12.5

Effects of Sleep Deprivation

Recuperation and circadian theories of sleep make different predictions about the effects of sleep deprivation. Because the recuperation theory is based on the premise that sleep is a response to the accumulation of some debilitating effect of wakefulness, it predicts (1) that long periods of wakefulness will produce physiological and behavioral disturbances, (2) that these disturbances will grow steadily worse as the sleep deprivation continues, and (3) that after a period of deprivation has ended, much of the missed sleep will be regained. In contrast, the circadian theory predicts (1) that there will be no debilitating effects of sleep deprivation other than those that can be attributed to an increase in the tendency to fall asleep, (2) that the increase in the desire to sleep that is produced by sleep deprivation will be greatest during the phases of the circadian cycle when the subjects normally sleep, and (3) that there will be little or no compensation for the loss of sleep once the period of deprivation has ended. Think about these predictions for a moment. On which side do you think the scientific evidence falls? You may be surprised to learn that the bulk of the evidence from sleep-deprivation studies confirms the predictions of the circadian theory. For example, consider Kleitman's

(1963) description of one of the earliest sleep-deprivation studies, which he conducted in 1922, and Dement's (1978) widely publicized case study of Randy Gardner.

Kleitman's Classic Sleep-Deprivation Study

While there were differences in the many subjective experiences of the sleep-evading persons, there were several features common to most. . . . during the first night the subject did not feel very tired or sleepy. He could read or study or do laboratory work, without much attention from the watcher, but usually felt an attack of drowsiness between 3 A.M. and 6 A.M. . . . Next morning the subject felt well, except for a slight malaise which always appeared on sitting down and resting for any length of time. However, if he occupied himself with his ordinary daily tasks, he was likely to forget having spent a sleepless night. During the second night . . . reading or study was next to impossible because sitting quietly was conducive to even greater sleepiness. As during the first night, there came a 2–3 hour period in the early hours of the morning when the desire for sleep was almost overpowering. . . . Later in the morning the sleepiness diminished once more, and the subject could perform routine laboratory work, as usual. It was not safe for him to sit down, however, without danger of falling asleep, particularly if he attended lectures. . . .

The third night resembled the second, and the fourth day was like the third. . . . At the end of that time the individual was as sleepy as he was likely to be. Those who continued to stay awake experienced the wavelike increase and decrease in sleepiness with the greatest drowsiness at about the same time every night. (Kleitman, 1963, pp. 220–221)

The Case of Randy Gardner

As part of a 1965 science fair project, Randy Gardner and two classmates, who were entrusted with keeping him awake, planned to break the then world-record of 260 hours of consecutive wakefulness. Dement read about the project in the newspaper, and seeing an opportunity to collect some important data, joined the team, much to the comfort of Randy's worried parents. Randy proved to be a friendly and cooperative subject, although he did complain vigorously when his team would not permit him to close his eyes for more than a few seconds at a time. However, in no sense could Randy's behavior be considered abnormal or disturbed. Near the end of his vigil, Randy held a press conference attended by reporters and television crews from all over the United States, and he conducted himself impeccably. When asked how he had managed to stay awake for 11 days, he replied politely, "It's just mind over matter." Randy went to sleep exactly 264 hours and 12 minutes after his alarm clock had awakened him 11 days before. And how long did he sleep? Only 14 hours the first night, and thereafter he returned to his usual 8-hour schedule. Although it may seem amazing that Randy did not have to sleep longer to "catch up" on his lost sleep, the lack of substantial recovery sleep is typical of such cases.

Mrs. Maureen Weston has supplanted Randy Gardner in the Guinness Book of World Records. During a rocking-chair marathon in 1977, Mrs. Weston kept rocking for 449 hours (18 days, 17 hours)—an impressive bit of "rocking around the clock." By the way, my own modest program of sleep-reduction is now in its tenth day.

Many studies have been conducted for the purpose of documenting the debilitating physiological effects of long-term wakefulness that are predicted by the recuperation theory of sleep. In view of the variety of physiological, motor, and cognitive tests that have been employed in these studies, their results have been remarkably consistent. Karadžić (1973), after reviewing the studies of the physiological effects of sleep deprivation (including studies of heart rate, respiration rate, blood pressure, skin conductance, body temperature, body weight, EMG, EEG, and evoked responses), reached the following conclusion: "There is little evidence that sleep deprivation, for periods even exceeding 200 hours, produces any marked physiological alterations" (p. 173), a conclusion echoed by Horne (1982) and Martin (1986).

One might expect that the complex cognitive abilities of human subjects might be particularly sensitive to disruption by sleep deprivation; however, this has not been found to be the case. For example, subjects deprived of sleep for one night displayed no deficits whatsoever on a battery of abstract reasoning, spatial relations, logical reasoning, and comprehension tests that were written under demanding time constraints (Percival, Horne, & Tilley, 1983). Paradoxically, it is the boringly easy tests of mental ability—particularly those requiring long periods of continuous attentiveness—that are most likely to be disrupted by sleep deprivation (Meddis, 1977; Webb, 1968; Wilkinson, 1965). This has led to the hypothesis that many of the behavioral deficits that are associated with sleep deprivation result from the subject's inability to stay awake. After 2 or 3 days of sleep deprivation, it becomes very difficult to keep subjects from having microsleeps during the performance of sedentary boring tasks. **Microsleeps** are brief periods (usually 2 or 3 seconds long) of sleep EEG during which the eyelids droop and the subjects become less responsive to external stimuli, even though they remain sitting or even standing.

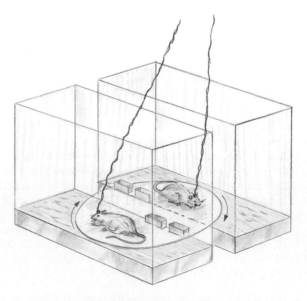

FIGURE 12.8

The carousel apparatus, which is used to deprive one rat of sleep while its yoked control is exposed to the same number and pattern of disk rotations. The disk on which both rats rest rotates every time the experimental rat has a sleep EEG. (Adapted from Rechtschaffen, Gilliland, Bergmann, & Winter, 1983.)

Studies using a **carousel apparatus** (see Figure 12.8) to deprive rats of sleep suggest that sleep deprivation may not be as inconsequential as the research on human subjects suggests. Two rats, an experimental rat and its *yoked control,* are placed in separate chambers of the apparatus. Each time that the EEG activity of the experimental rat indicates that it is sleeping, the disk, which serves as the floor of half of both chambers, starts to slowly rotate and the sleeping experimental rat gets shoved off the disk into a shallow pool of water. The yoked control is exposed to exactly the same pattern of disk rotations, but if it is not sleeping, it can easily avoid getting dunked by walking in the direction opposite to the direction of disk rotation. In one study using the carousel apparatus (Rechtschaffen, Gilliland, Bergmann, & Winter, 1983), the experimental rats died after several days, while the yoked control animals stayed reasonably healthy. The fact that human subjects have been sleep deprived for similar periods of time without dire consequences argues for caution in interpreting this finding. It may be that repeatedly being plunged into water while sleeping kills the experimental rats not because it keeps them from sleeping, but because it is extremely stressful and physically damaging. This interpretation is consistent with the pathological symptoms that were revealed in the experimental rats by postmortem examination: swollen adrenal glands, collapsed lungs, fluid in the lungs, gastric ulcers, internal bleeding, skin lesions, scrotal damage, swollen limbs, and enlarged bladders.

Selective Sleep Deprivation

Researchers have attempted to determine the specific functions of the different stages of sleep by conducting studies in which subjects can sleep as much as they like, but they are prevented from having a particular stage of sleep. The overwhelming majority of these *selective sleep-deprivation studies* have been studies of REM-sleep deprivation, stimulated by a general fascination with dreaming and by the many provocative theories concerning its function. These theories fall into three general categories (Webb, 1973): (1) those that hypothesize that REM sleep is necessary for the maintenance of an individual's mental health, (2) those that hypothesize that REM sleep is necessary for the maintenance of normal levels of motivation, and (3) those that hypothesize that REM sleep is necessary for the processing of memories. Accordingly, the purpose of most REM-deprivation studies has been to document the particular personality, motivational, or memorial disturbances that are predicted by the experimenter's pet theory.

REM-sleep deprivation has been shown to have two consistent effects (see Figure 12.9). First, with each successive night of REM-sleep deprivation, there is a greater tendency for subjects to initiate REM sequences. Thus, as REM-sleep deprivation proceeds, subjects have to be awakened more and more frequently to keep them from accumulating significant amounts of REM sleep. For example, during the first night of REM-sleep deprivation in one experiment (Webb & Agnew, 1967), the subjects had to be awakened 17 times to keep them from having extended periods of REM sleep, but during the seventh night of deprivation, they had to be awakened 67 times. Second, following REM-sleep deprivation, subjects have more than their usual amount of REM sleep for the first two or three nights (Brunner, Dijk, Tobler, & Borbély, 1990).

FIGURE 12.9

The two consistent effects of
REM-sleep deprivation.

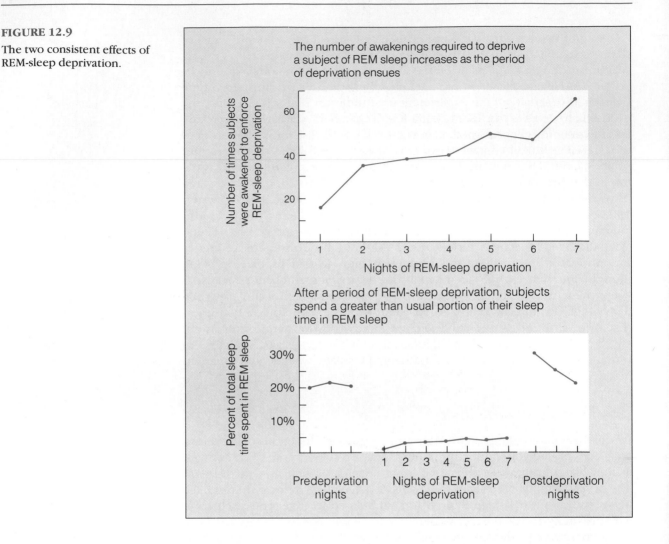

Early claims (Dement, 1960) that REM-sleep deprivation leads to personality, motivational, and memorial disturbances have not received strong support. The most convincing evidence that REM-sleep deprivation is not severely debilitating comes from the study of the effects of *tricyclic antidepressant drugs.* Because tricyclic antidepressants selectively block REM sleep, patients who regularly take large doses get little or no REM sleep for months at a time, and yet they experience no serious side effects that can be attributed to their REM-sleep loss.

Interim report   It is an appropriate point, here at the end of the section on sleep deprivation, for me to file a brief progress report. It has now been 2 weeks since I began my 5-hours-per-night sleep schedule. Generally, things are going well. My progress on this chapter has been faster than usual. I am not having any difficulty getting up on time or in getting my work done, but I am finding that it takes a major effort to stay awake in the evening. If I try to read the newspaper or watch a bit of television after 10:30, I experience attacks of microsleep. However, there are those around me who delight in making sure that these transgressions last no more than a few seconds.

12.6

Recuperation and Circadian Models Combined

If you began the chapter thinking of sleep as a recuperative process, as most people do, you were probably surprised to learn that sleep is closely regulated by circadian factors and that sleep deprivation appears to have relatively few adverse effects. However, it is important not to overreact to this evidence. Although recuperative factors may be somewhat less important in controlling sleep than you first thought, and circadian factors somewhat more important, it is not necessarily an all-or-none issue; recuperation and circadian models are not mutually exclusive. In fact, Borbély (1984) has proposed a model of sleep that integrates the effects of both circadian and sleep-deprivation factors. This two-process model is illustrated in Figure 12.10. The postulated circadian sleep-promoting factor is illustrated in the top trace of the figure. This factor is assumed to take the form of a sine wave with minimum at about 4:00

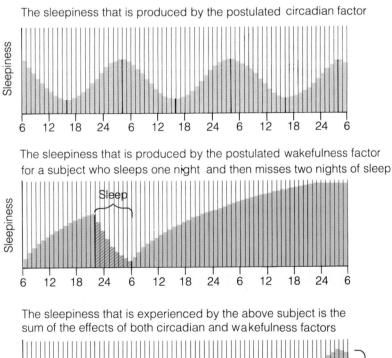

FIGURE 12.10

A model of how circadian factors and the duration of wakefulness interact to determine the propensity for sleep. (Adapted from Borbély, 1984.)

P.M. and a maximum at about 4:00 A.M. The postulated sleep-promoting effects of wakefulness are illustrated in the middle trace for a subject who slept on the first night between 11:00 P.M. and 6:00 A.M. and then missed the next two nights' sleep. The bottom trace illustrates how the effects of the circadian and wakefulness factors hypothetically combine to influence the subject's sleepiness.

If sleep is influenced by the duration of the preceding period of wakefulness, why has sleep deprivation had so little effect on subsequent sleep times in most studies? The answer seems to be that it is slow-wave sleep in particular, rather than sleep in general, that plays the major recuperative role following sleep deprivation. Several lines of evidence support this view: (1) Although subjects regain only a small proportion of their total lost sleep after a period of sleep deprivation, they regain most of their lost stage 4 sleep (e.g., Borbély, Baumann, Brandeis, Strauch, & Lehmann, 1981; Horne, 1976). (2) Subjects who have reduced their usual sleep time get less stage 1 and stage 2 sleep, but the amount of their stage 3 and 4 sleep remains the same as before (Mullaney, Johnson, Naitoh, Friedman, & Globus, 1977; Webb & Agnew, 1975). (3) Short sleepers normally get as much stage 3 and 4 sleep as long sleepers (e.g., Jones & Oswald, 1966; Webb & Agnew, 1970). (4) If subjects are asked to take an extra nap in the morning after a full night's sleep, it contains little stage 3 or 4 sleep, and it does not reduce the duration of the following night's sleep (e.g., Åkerstedt & Gillberg, 1981; Hume & Mills, 1977; Karacan, Williams, Finley, & Hursch, 1970). (5) After sleep deprivation, the slow-wave sleep EEG of both humans (Borbély, 1981; Borbély, Baumann, Brandeis, Strauch, & Lehmann, 1981) and rats (Mistlberger, Bergmann, & Rechtschaffen, 1987) is characterized by a higher proportion of slow waves.

SELF TEST

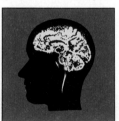

Before you proceed to the next section of the chapter, complete the following exercise to consolidate what you have learned so far.

1. The three most commonly studied psychophysiological correlates of sleep are EEG, EMG, and _____ .

2. _____ stage 1 EEG is accompanied by neither REM nor loss of muscle tone.

3. Stage 4 sleep EEG is distinguished by a predominance of _____ waves.

4. Environmental cues that can entrain circadian rhythms are called _____ or time givers.

5. In contrast to the prediction of the recuperative model of sleep, when a subject stays awake longer than usual, the following period of sleep tends to be _____ , even under free-running conditions.

6. The most convincing evidence that REM-sleep deprivation is not debilitating comes from the study of patients taking _____ .

7. After a lengthy period of sleep deprivation, a subject's first night of sleep is only slightly longer than usual, but it contains a much higher proportion of _____ waves.

8. _____ sleep in particular, rather than sleep in general, appears to play the major recuperative role.

The Physiological and Neurochemical Bases of Sleep

The first influential theory of the physiology of sleep was proposed by Bremer in 1936. He hypothesized that sleep is caused by a reduction of sensory input to the forebrain. To test his hypothesis, he severed the brain stems of cats between their *inferior colliculi* and *superior colliculi* in order to disconnect their forebrains from ascending sensory input (see Figure 12.11)—this surgical preparation is called a **cerveau isolé preparation** (pronounced "ser-voe ees-o-lay"; literally *isolated forebrain*). As you might well imagine, cerveau isolé preparations are not too useful for the study of behavior because the subjects are paralyzed below the level of the transection, but they can be used to assess neurophysiological responses of the forebrain in the absence of ascending influences. In support of his hypothesis, Bremer found that the cortical EEG of the isolated cat forebrains was indicative of almost continuous slow-wave sleep. Only when strong visual or olfactory stimuli were presented (the cerveau isolé has intact visual and olfactory input) could the continous high-amplitude, slow-wave activity be **desynchronized** (i.e., changed to low-amplitude, high-frequency activity), but this arousing effect barely outlasted the stimuli. Bremer's theory is classed as a *passive theory of sleep* because it postulated no mechanism of active sleep regulation; it viewed sleep as a passive consequence of a decline in sensory input.

The Reticular-Activating-System Theory of Sleep

Bremer's passive sensory theory of sleep regulation was gradually replaced by the theory that sleep is actively regulated by an arousal mechanism in the *reticular formation*—by a **reticular activating system.** Three findings contributed to the wide acceptance of this reticular-activating-system theory of sleep (see Figure 12.11). The first finding came from a study of the **encéphale isolé**

FIGURE 12.11

Evidence for the passive sensory theory of sleep and for the active reticular-activating-system theory.

Evidence for Bremer's 1937 Passive
Sensory Theory of Sleep

Level of cerveau
isolé transection

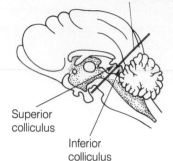

Superior
colliculus

Inferior
colliculus

Cats with a midcollicular transection (cerveau isole preparation) displayed a continuous sleep (slow-wave) EEG, Bremer concluded that sleep occurs when there is little sensory input to the forebrain.

Evidence for Moruzzi and Magoun's Active
Reticular-Activating-System Theory of Sleep

Lesions at the midcollicular level that damaged the reticular formation core, but left the sensory fibers intact, produced a continuous sleep (slow-wave) corticalEEG.

Electrical stimulation of reticular formation desynchronized the cortical EEG and awakened sleeping cats.

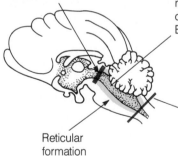

Reticular
formation

Cats with a transection of the caudal brain stem (encéphale isolé preparation) displayed normal sleep-wake cycles of cortical EEG. This suggested that a wakefulness-producing area was between the levels of the cerveau and encéphale isolé transections.

preparation (pronounced on-say-fell ees-o-lay), an experimental preparation in which the brain is disconnected from the rest of the nervous system by a transection of the caudal brain stem. Despite cutting most of the same sensory fibers as the cerveau isolé transection, the encéphale isolé transection did not disrupt the normal cycle of sleep EEG and wakefulness EEG (Bremer, 1937). This suggested that a mechanism for maintaining wakefulness was located somewhere in the brain stem between the two transections. The second finding was that partial transections at the cerveau isolé level disrupted normal sleep-wake cycles of cortical EEG only when they severed the reticular-activating-system core of the brain stem; when the partial transections were restricted to more lateral areas, which contain the ascending sensory tracts, they had little effect on the cortical EEG (Lindsley, Bowden, & Magoun, 1949). The third finding was that electrical stimulation of the reticular formation of sleeping cats awakened them and produced a lengthy period of EEG desynchronization (Moruzzi & Magoun, 1949). On the basis of these three early findings, Moruzzi and Magoun (1949) proposed that low levels of activity in the reticular formation produce sleep and that high levels produce wakefulness.

Three Important Discoveries about the Neural Basis of Sleep

The wave of research that was stimulated by the reticular-activating-system theory led to several discoveries. The following three are particularly important (see Steriade & Hobson, 1976).

Sleep is not a state of neural quiescence   Because the body is inactive during sleep, it had long been assumed that sleep is a state of general neural quiescence. Single unit recording studies have revealed that this is not the case. Many neurons in the brain are less active during slow-wave sleep than they are during relaxed wakefulness, but the reduction in their firing rate rarely exceeds 10%—a far cry from the total inactivity that was initially assumed. Moreover, during REM sleep, many neurons are even more active than they are during relaxed wakefulness.

There are sleep-promoting circuits in the brain   The reticular-activating-system theory of sleep suggested that sleep is a consequence of low levels of activity in circuits whose primary role is the maintenance of wakefulness. This view was altered by two observations: that the stimulation of certain brain sites can induce sleep and that discrete bilateral lesions can disrupt it. Both of these findings suggest that there are structures in the brain whose function is the promotion of sleep. One such sleep-promoting structure appears to be in the caudal brain stem (medulla). Anesthetizing (Magni, Moruzzi, Rossi, & Zanchetti, 1957) or cooling (Berlucchi, Maffei, Moruzzi, & Strata, 1964) the caudal brain stem causes sleeping cats to awaken immediately.

The various correlates of sleep are dissociable   Most neurophysiological theories of sleep have treated REM sleep and slow-wave sleep (SWS) as if each was a unitary entity. However, evidence has accumulated that the physiological changes that go together to define REM sleep sometimes break apart and go their separate ways—and the same is true of the changes that define SWS. For example, during REM-sleep deprivation, penile erections, which normally occur during REM sleep, begin to occur during SWS. And during total sleep deprivation, slow waves, which normally occur only during SWS, begin to occur during wakefulness. This suggests that REM sleep, SWS, and wakefulness are not each controlled by a single mechanism; each state seems to result from the interaction of a variety of mechanisms, which are capable under certain conditions of operating independently of one another.

The classic example of the dissociation between the behavioral and EEG indices of SWS is the study of Feldman and Waller (1962), who compared the effects of lesions to the cat midbrain reticular formation with those of lesions to the adjacent posterior hypothalamus. The hypothalamic lesions produced behavioral sleep that persisted even when the cats' desynchronized cortical EEG suggested that they were awake. In contrast, the midbrain reticular formation lesions produced a high-amplitude slow-wave cortical EEG that persisted even when the cats were fully alert (see Vanderwolf & Robinson, 1981).

The Structures of the Brain That Have Been Implicated in Sleep and Dreaming

Many areas of the brain have been implicated in sleep. The following are four of them: the raphé nuclei, the basal forebrain region, the REM sleep circuits in the caudal reticular formation, and the suprachiasmatic nuclei.

Raphé nuclei   Early evidence of a sleep-promoting area in the medulla focused attention on the **raphé** (pronounced "ra-fay") **nuclei,** a cluster of serotonin-producing nuclei that runs in a thin strip down the midline of the caudal reticular formation (see Figure 12.12). Lesions that destroy 80 to 90% of the raphé nuclei in cats produced complete insomnia for 3 or 4 days, which was followed by a partial recovery that never exceeded more than 2.5 hours of sleep per day, all of which was SWS (Jouvet & Renault, 1966). Cats normally sleep about 14.5 hours per day, which is one reason why they are favored as subjects in sleep experiments.

Supporting the theory that the raphé nuclei promote sleep was the observation that an injection of **parachlorophenylalanine (PCPA),** which temporarily blocked the synthesis of serotonin, produced temporary insomnia in cats (Mouret, Bobillier, & Jouvet, 1968). However, when PCPA was injected every day, both REM sleep and SWS eventually recovered to 80% of their normal levels, despite the fact that serotonin levels remained low (Dement, Mitler, & Henriksen, 1972). Further challenges to the raphé-nucleus-serotonin theory of sleep came from the discovery that serotonin injections do not induce sleep and the discovery that PCPA injections do not disrupt sleep in species other than cats (see Vanderwolf, 1988).

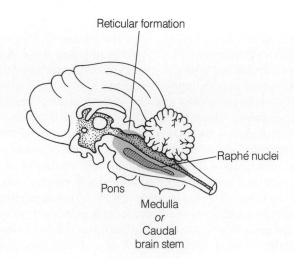

FIGURE 12.12

The location of the raphé nuclei.

Basal forebrain region   Although much of the research on the physiology of sleep has focused on the brain stem, there is some evidence that an area of the forebrain just in front of the hypothalamus is also involved. This ill-defined area, which includes the preoptic area, is generally referred to as the **basal forebrain region.** As can be seen in Figure 12.13, bilateral lesions of this area in cats produce a substantial reduction of daily sleep time that is maximal 2 weeks after the lesion and recovers somewhat thereafter (McGinty & Sterman, 1968). Electrical stimulation of the basal forebrain produces cortical EEG synchrony (Sterman & Clemente, 1962a), drowsiness, and sometimes sleep (Sterman & Clemente, 1962b).

Studies by Sterman and Clemente (1962a & b) are widely cited to support the theory that the basal forebrain region is involved in sleep; they reported that electrical stimulation of the area causes cats to fall asleep. However, their study was uncontrolled, and cats normally fall asleep almost immediately when placed in a barren test box. A subsequent controlled experiment (Lo-Piccolo, 1977) found no indication that basal forebrain stimulation promotes sleep in cats.

Caudal reticular formation REM-sleep circuits   REM sleep appears to be controlled from a variety of sites scattered throughout the caudal reticular formation, with each site being responsible for controlling one of the major indices of REM sleep (Siegel, 1983; Vertes, 1983). The approximate location of these putative regulatory centers is illustrated by Figure 12.14. The main challenge now facing those that study the physiological basis of REM

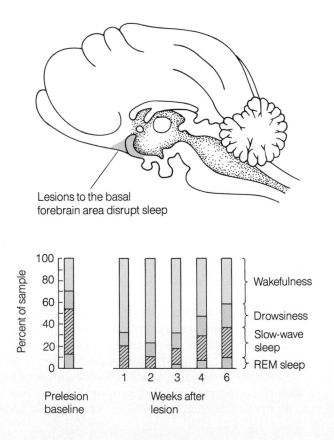

FIGURE 12.13

The effects of basal forebrain lesions on the sleep of cats. (Adapted from McGinty & Sterman, 1968.)

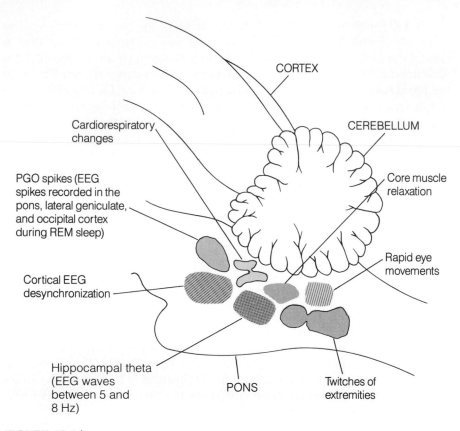

FIGURE 12.14

A schematic sagittal section taken about 3 millimeters from the midline of the brain stem of the cat. Illustrated are the areas that seem to control various indices of REM sleep. (Adapted from Vertes, 1983.)

sleep is to determine how and why the activity of these respective structures becomes coordinated during normal REM cycles.

Microinjections of cholinergic agonists into the pontine portion of the caudal reticular formation of sleeping cats elicit immediate and prolonged REM sleep (Qualtrochi, Mamelak, Madison, Macklis, & Hobson, 1989). It thus appears that REM onset is triggered by cholinergic neurons in the pontine reticular formation that activate the other areas of the caudal reticular formation that control the various indices of REM sleep. In sleeping human subjects, the intravenous infusion of cholinergic agonists and antagonists increases and decreases, respectively, the amount of REM sleep (Sitaram, Moore, & Gillin, 1978).

Two interesting cases of REM-sleep dysfunction have been reported in human subjects with brain-stem damage. In one, which presumably resulted from damage to the cholinergic pontine-reticular-formation REM-sleep generator, the patient had almost no REM sleep (Lavie, Pratt, Scharf, Peled, & Brown, 1984). In accordance with previous failures to identify negative consequences of REM-sleep deprivation, this patient did not appear to be adversely affected by his lack of REM sleep. After receiving his injury, he completed high school and law school and now has a thriving law practice. In the other case, which presumably resulted from damage to the portion of the caudal reticular formation that mediates the relaxation of core muscles during sleep, the patient appeared to act out his dreams.

> I was a halfback playing football, and after the quarterback received the ball from the center he lateraled it sideways to me and I'm supposed to go around end and cut back over tackle and—this is very vivid—as I cut back over tackle there is this big 280-pound tackle waiting, so I, according to football rules, was to give him my shoulder and bounce him out of the way . . . when I came to I was standing in front of our dresser and I had [gotten up out of bed and run and] knocked lamps, mirrors and everything off the dresser, hit my head against the wall and my knee against the dresser. (Schenck, Bundlie, Ettinger, and Mahowald, 1986)

Remarkably, a similar syndrome of acting out one's dreams seems to occur in cats following lesions of the caudal reticular formation.

> To a naive observer, the cat, which is standing, looks awake since it may attack unknown enemies, play with an absent mouse, or display flight behavior. There are orienting movements of the head or eyes toward imaginary stimuli, although the animal does not respond to visual or auditory stimuli. These extraordinary episodes . . . are a good argument that "dreaming" occurs during REM sleep in the cat. (Jouvet, 1972, pp. 236–237)

It must be an adventure to sleep in the same room with either humans or cats with this sleep disorder.

Neurons in two areas of the caudal reticular formation seem to play a role in inhibiting REM sleep: the *noradrenergic* neurons of the **locus coeruleus** (Lydic, McCarley, & Hobson, 1983) and the *serotonergic* neurons of the **dorsal raphé nuclei** (Trulson & Jacobs, 1979). Neurons in both areas are active during slow-wave sleep but are almost totally quiescent during REM sleep. This finding has contributed to the view (see Hobson, 1989) that the recurring cycle of REM sleep is controlled in the caudal reticular formation by a reciprocal interaction between excitatory cholinergic neurons and inhibitory noradrenergic and serotonergic neurons.

The suprachiasmatic nuclei: The circadian clock   The fact that circadian sleep-wake cycles persist in the absence of circadian signals from the environment suggests that the physiological systems that regulate sleep must be controlled by some internal timing mechanism. The first breakthrough in the search for the location of this **circadian clock** was Richter's 1967 discovery that large medial hypothalamic lesions disrupt circadian cycles of eating, drinking, and activity in rats. Next, in the early 1970s, the **suprachiasmatic nuclei (SCN)** were identified as the specific medial hypothalamic structures that controlled circadian cycles of adrenal hormone release (Moore & Eichler, 1972), drinking, and activity (Stephan & Zucker, 1972). By the late 1970s, the SCN had been shown to control all kinds of rhythms, including the sleep-wake cycle (Ibuka, Inouye, & Kawamura, 1977; Rusak, 1979; Rusak & Zucker, 1979).

Most of the early studies of the SCN were demonstrations that bilateral SCN lesions abolish various circadian cycles, even in the presence of a circadian light-dark cycle. SCN lesions do not reduce the amount of time that mammals spend sleeping (e.g., Coindet, Chouvet, & Mouret, 1975; Stephan & Nunez, 1977), but they do abolish its circadian periodicity. Under certain conditions, SCN lesions can abolish some circadian rhythms but not others (e.g., Boulos & Terman, 1980); this suggests that the SCN are not the only circadian timing mechanisms.

Further support for the conclusion that the SCN contain a circadian timing mechanism comes from the observation that the SCN display circadian cycles of electrical, metabolic, and biochemical activity (e.g., Moore, 1982), and that they do so even when they have been surgically isolated from the rest of the brain by circular knife cuts (Groos & Hendricks, 1982; Inouye & Kawamura, 1982). Figure 12.15 shows that the SCN of rats take up less radioactive 2-deoxyglucose during the night than they do during the day, when the rats normally sleep (Schwartz & Gainer,1977). Furthermore, electrical stimulation of the SCN has been shown to produce phase shifts in free-running rhythms (Rusak & Groos, 1982; Zatz & Herkenham, 1981).

How does the 24-hour light-dark cycle entrain the sleep-wake cycle and other circadian rhythms? To answer this question, researchers began at the obvious starting points—the eyes. They tried to identify and track the specific neurons that left the eyes and carried information about light and dark to the biological clock. The fact that cutting the *optic nerves* as they left the eyes of rats eliminated the ability of the light-dark cycle to influence circadian rhythms suggested that they were on the right track. However, when the **optic tracts** were cut at the point where they left the *optic chiasm,* the ability of the light-dark cycle to entrain circadian rhythms was not lost. As illustrated in Figure 12.16, these two findings together suggested that the critical axons were branching off from the optic nerve in the vicinity of the optic chiasm. This inference led to the discovery of two small tracts that leave the optic chiasm and project to the adjacent hypothalamus (Hendrickson, Wagoner, & Cowan, 1972; Moore & Lenn, 1972). And where in the hypothalamus do you

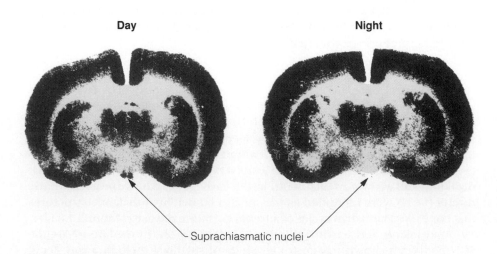

FIGURE 12.15

Autoradiographs illustrating the increased uptake of radioactive
2-deoxyglucose by the rat SCN during the day (from Schwartz & Gainer, 1977).
(Dr. William Schwartz, published in SCIENCE, Vol. 197, pages 1089–91,
September 9, 1977. Copyright 1977 by the AAAS.)

Transection of the optic nerves eliminated the ability of light-dark cycles to entrain circadian rhythms

Transection of the optic tracts did not eliminate the ability of light-dark cycles to entrain circadian rhythms

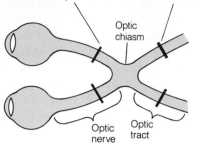

Optic chiasm

Optic nerve

Optic tract

This suggested that the visual neurons critical for entraining circadian rhythms branched off from the major visual pathways in the area of the optic chiasm and projected to the circuits responsible for controlling circadian rhythms. The retinohypothalamic tracts were subsequently found to terminate in the suprachiasmatic nuclei.

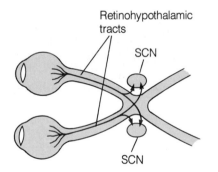

Retinohypothalamic tracts

SCN

SCN

FIGURE 12.16

The discovery of the retinohypothalamic tracts. Neurons from each retina project to both the ipsilateral and contralateral suprachiasmatic nuclei (SCN).

think that these two **retinohypothalamic tracts** terminate? If you guessed the SCN, you are correct. Although we now know how signals from visual zeitgebers influence the SCN, it is still not clear how the SCN control the sleep-producing circuits of the reticular formation (Groos, 1984).

Before we leave the topic of the SCN, I would like to tell you about two recent SCN experiments that I think are quite special. The first is an experiment by Ralph, Foster, Davis, and Menaker (1990). Ralph and his colleagues removed the SCN from the fetuses of a strain of mutant hamsters that had an abnormally short, 20-hour, free-running sleep-wake cycle. Then, they transplanted the SCN into normal adult hamsters whose sleep-wake cycles had been abolished by SCN lesions. These transplants restored free-running sleep-wake cycles in the recipients, but remarkably, they were about 20 hours long rather than the original 25 hours. Transplants in the other direction, that is from normal hamster fetuses to SCN-lesioned adult mutants, had the complementary effect; they restored free-running sleep-wake cycles that were about 25 hours long rather than the original 20 hours.

The second special SCN experiment that I want to tell you about was by Rusak, Robertson, Wisden, and Hunt (1990). They studied the mechanism by which 30 minutes of intense artificial light during the night can initiate a phase advance in the circadian sleep-wake cycles. Rusak and his colleagues exposed rats and hamsters to 30-minute periods of intense light at various points in their light-dark cycle; then they killed them and exposed their brain tissue to labeled *antibodies* with an affinity either for a protein called *Fos,* which has been shown to influence DNA transcription, or for the messenger RNA that is replicated from the so-called *c-fos* gene, which directs the synthesis of *Fos.* They found that exposure of rats or hamsters to 30-minute periods of light at points in the light-dark cycle at which they trigger phase advances (e.g., in the middle of the dark phase) caused SCN cells to increase both their transcription of *c-fos* messenger RNA and their production of the *Fos* protein. This suggests that the *Fos* protein is involved in the reprogramming of circadian cycles by the SCN in response to changes in the light-dark cycle.

Neural mechanisms of sleep: summary   Considerable progress has been made in our understanding of the neural mechanisms of sleep, particularly in two areas. We now understand that the circadian rhythmicity of sleep is controlled by the suprachiasmatic nuclei, and we understand that the cycles of REM sleep are controlled by interactions among circuits in the caudal reticular formation. However, our understanding of the circuits that cause us to fall asleep is less developed. The theory that sleep results from a general decrease in reticular activating system activity is out of step with the current knowledge of the intricacy and specificity of reticular formation circuits, and support for hypothetical basal forebrain and raphé sleep mechanisms has been inconsistent.

12.8

Hypnotic and Antihypnotic Drugs

Hypnotics

Barbiturates (e.g., pentobarbital, phenobarbital) and alcohol are powerful **hypnotic drugs** (sleep-promoting drugs); however, they are rarely prescribed for that purpose. Both barbiturates and alcohol produce a variety of adverse side effects—including daytime lethargy, tolerance, withdrawal, convulsions, and disturbed sleep patterns—and both are highly addictive.

Benzodiazepines (e.g., Valium and Librium) are prescribed for their hypnotic effects, although they are most frequently prescribed for the treatment of anxiety. Although benzodiazepines are safer than barbiturates, they are not without their adverse side effects. For example, they often result in daytime lethargy, and they are addictive. Furthermore, because insomnia is one of the after-effects of benzodiazepine exposure, benzodiazepines can exacerbate the very problem that they were intended to correct. It is disturbing that benzodiazepines and other hypnotic drugs are so widely prescribed by general practitioners, despite their hazards and despite the lack of evidence that they produce more than short-term improvements in sleep. There is clearly a need for research in this area.

Evidence that the raphé nuclei play a role in sleep suggested that serotonergic drugs might be effective hypnotics. Efforts to demonstrate the hypnotic effects of serotonergic drugs have focused on **5-hydroxy-tryptophan (5-HTP),** the precursor of serotonin, because 5-HTP, but not serotonin, readily passes through the blood-brain barrier. Injections of 5-HTP reverse the insomnia produced in cats (Pujol, Buguet, Froment, Jones, & Jouvet, 1971) and rats (Laguzzi & Adrien, 1980) by the serotonin antagonist, PCPA. However, they are of no therapeutic benefit in the treatment of sleep disorders (see Borbély, 1983).

Antihypnotics

Antihypnotic drugs (sleep-reducing drugs) increase the activity of the *catecholamine neurotransmitters* (Hartmann, 1978); both *stimulants* (e.g., cocaine and amphetamine) and *tricyclic antidepressants* increase the activity of catecholamines (norepinephrine, epinephrine, and dopamine) by increasing their release and/or by blocking their re-uptake from the synapse. From the perspective of the treatment of sleep disorders, the most important property of antihypnotic drugs is that they act preferentially on REM sleep. They can totally suppress REM sleep, even at doses that have little effect on total sleep time.

Using stimulant drugs to treat chronic excessive sleepiness is a risky proposition. Most are highly addictive, and they produce a variety of adverse side effects such as loss of appetite. Moreover, unless stimulants are taken at just the right doses and at just the right times, there is a danger that they will interfere excessively with normal sleep.

Endogenous Sleep Factors

In the last decade, there has been a revival of the idea that sleep is caused by the build-up of sleep-inducing chemicals in the body. Chemicals that have been hypothesized to function as sleep inducers are referred to as the **endogenous sleep factors.**

Delta sleep-inducing peptide (DSIP) is an endogenous sleep factor. The effects of DSIP were first demonstrated using a **parabiotic preparation,** a preparation in which two subjects share one physiological system. Monnier et al. (1975) connected the circulatory systems of two rabbits and found that when the thalamus of one was stimulated at a frequency that elicited cortical slow waves, both rabbits tended to fall asleep. This suggested that a sleep factor in the blood of the stimulated rabbit was affecting both rabbits. DSIP was subsequently isolated from the blood of stimulated rabbits, its structure characterized, and methods for synthesizing it developed.

Although DSIP has been shown to promote sleep in several experiments (e.g., Scherschlicht, 1983; Schneider-Helmert, 1985; Shoenenberger & Graf, 1985), its role in sleep induction is still not widely accepted (see Graf & Kastin, 1984), primarily for two reasons. One is that demonstrations of the sleep-promoting effects of DSIP have been unsystematic and inconsistent.

The other is that DSIP produces a variety of physiological effects (e.g., hyperthermia), which raises the possibility that sleep might be a secondary consequence of one of DSIP's other effects.

12.9

Sleep Disorders

Many sleep disorders fall into one of two complementary categories: (1) **insomnia**, disorders of initiating and maintaining sleep, and (2) **hypersomnia**, disorders of excessive sleep or sleepiness. In various surveys, approximately 30% of the respondents report significant sleep-related problems. However, it is important to recognize that complaints of insomnia and hypersomnia are often issued by people whose sleep appears quite normal in controlled sleep tests. For example, many people who complain of insomnia actually sleep a reasonable amount (e.g., 6 hours a night), but they believe that they should sleep more (e.g., 8 hours a night). As a result, they spend more time in bed than they should and have difficulty sleeping. Often, the anxiety associated with their inability to sleep makes it even more difficult for them to sleep. Such patients can often be helped by counseling them to go to bed only when they are very sleepy (see Anch, Browman, Mitler, & Walsh, 1988). Others with disturbed sleep face more substantive problems.

Insomnia

Many cases of insomnia are **iatrogenic** (physician created). Paradoxically, sleeping pills prescribed by well-intentioned physicians are a major cause of insomnia. At first, hypnotic drugs are effective in increasing sleep, but soon the patient is trapped into a rising spiral of drug use, as *tolerance* to the drug develops (see Chapter 13) and more and more drug is required to produce its original hypnotic effect. Soon the patient cannot stop taking the drug without running the risk of experiencing *withdrawal symptoms* (see Chapter 13), which unfortunately feature insomnia as the primary symptom. The following case study illustrates this problem.

> Mr. B. was studying for a civil service exam, the outcome of which would affect his entire future. He was terribly worried about the test and found it difficult to get to sleep at night. Feeling that the sleep loss was affecting his ability to study, he consulted his physician for the express purpose of getting "something to make me sleep." His doctor prescribed a moderate dose of barbiturate at bedtime, and Mr. B. found that this medication was very effective . . . for the first several nights. After about a week, he began having trouble sleeping again and decided to take two sleeping pills each night. Twice more the cycle was repeated, until on the night before the exam he was taking four times as many pills as his doctor had prescribed. The next night, with the pressure off, Mr. B. took no medication. He had tremendous difficulty falling asleep, and when he did, his sleep was terribly disrupted. . . . Mr. B. now decided that he had a serious case of insomnia, and returned to his sleeping pill habit. By the time he consulted our clinic several years later, he was taking approximately 1,000 mg sodium amytal every night, and his sleep was more disturbed than ever. . . . Patients may go on for years and years—from one sleeping pill to another—never realizing that their troubles are caused by the pills. (Dement, 1978, p. 80)

Sleep apnea is another common cause of insomnia. In sleep apnea, the patient temporarily stops breathing many times each night. Each time, the patient awakens, begins to breathe again, and drifts back to sleep. Sleep apnea usually leads to a sense of having slept poorly, and thus it is usually diagnosed as insomnia. However, some patients are totally unaware of their multiple awakenings and instead complain of excessive sleepiness during the day; such cases are diagnosed as *hypersomnia*. Sleep apnea syndromes are thought to be of two types: (1) those resulting from obstruction of the respiratory passages by muscle spasms or *atonia* (lack of muscle tone), and (2) those resulting from the failure of the central nervous system to stimulate respiration. Obstructive apnea is most common in overweight people; the prevalence of CNS apnea increases with age (see Mendelson, 1987).

Two other causes of insomnia are usually lumped together because they both involve the legs: nocturnal myoclonus and restless legs. **Nocturnal myoclonus** is a periodic twitching of the body during sleep, primarily a periodic twitching of the legs. Most patients suffering from this disorder are unaware of the nature of their problem, and they generally complain of poor sleep and day-time sleepiness. In contrast, people with **restless legs** are all too aware of their problem. They complain of a hard-to-describe tension or uneasiness in their legs that keeps them from falling asleep. Benzodiazepines are often prescribed in cases of nocturnal myoclonus and restless legs because of their hypnotic, *anxiolytic* (antianxiety), muscle relaxant, and anticonvulsant properties; however, they are rarely effective.

Many insomniacs get much more sleep than they think. In one large study, insomniacs claimed to take an average of 1 hour to fall asleep and to sleep an average of only 4.5 hours per night, but when they were tested in a sleep laboratory, they were found to have an average sleep latency of only 15 minutes and an average nightly sleep duration of 6.5 hours. It used to be common medical practice to assume that people who claimed to suffer from insomnia but slept more than 6.5 hours per night were neurotic. However, this practice stopped when some of those diagnosed as neurotic *pseudo-insomniacs* were subsequently found to be suffering from sleep apnea, nocturnal myoclonus, or other sleep-disturbing problems. Insomnia is not necessarily a problem of too little sleep; it is often a problem of too little undisturbed sleep.

Hypersomnia

Narcolepsy is a disorder of hypersomnia; it is characterized by repeated, brief (10-to-15-minute) daytime sleep attacks. Narcoleptics typically sleep only about an hour per day more than average; it is the inappropriateness of their sleep episodes that defines their condition. Most of us occasionally fall asleep on the beach, in front of the television, or in the most *soporific* (sleep-promoting) of all daytime sleep sites, the large, dimly lit lecture theater. But narcoleptics fall asleep in the middle of a conversation, while eating, while engaging in sexual activities, or even while scuba diving. Narcolepsy is treated with stimulants, taken in the morning.

Cataplexy is a disorder that is often associated with narcolepsy. Cataplexy is a sudden loss of muscle tone during wakefulness, which is sometimes triggered by an emotional event. In its mild form, it may simply require that the patient sit down for a few seconds until it passes. In its extreme form the patient drops to the ground as if shot and remains there for a minute or two, all the while remaining fully conscious. The fact that narcoleptics, unlike normal subjects, go directly into REM sleep when they fall asleep (Rechtschaffen, Wolpert, Dement, Mitchell, & Fisher, 1963) has led to the view that narcolepsy is a disorder in which REM-sleep phenomena encroach on wakefulness. According to this view, an attack of cataplexy occurs when the lack of core muscle tonus that normally occurs during REM sleep occurs during wakefulness. Cataplexy is treated with **tricyclic antidepressants** taken in the evening.

Have you ever experienced a period of paralysis or a vivid dreamlike state just as you are falling asleep or waking up? Many people have. These experiences are called **sleep paralysis** and **hypnogogic hallucinations,** respectively. Like cataplexy, both are thought to result from the encroachment of REM-sleep phenomena into wakefulness and both are common in cases of narcolepsy.

Research on the mechanisms of cataplexy and sleep paralysis has focused on the cells of the caudal reticular formation that control muscle relaxation during REM sleep: the cells of the **nucleus magnocellularis.** Recently, Siegel et al. (1991) recorded the activity of these neurons in dogs that experienced cataplectic attacks when they became excited. Of the cells of the caudal reticular formation that were active during REM sleep, only those of the nucleus magnocellularis were also active during cataplectic attacks. This confirms the hypothesis that cataplectic attacks result from the encroachment of REM-related atonia into wakefulness.

12.10

Conclusion: The Effects of Sleep Reduction

I began this chapter 4 weeks ago with both zeal and trepidation. I was fascinated by the idea that I could wring 2 or 3 extra hours of living out of each day by sleeping less, and I hoped that adhering to a sleep-reduction program while writing about sleep would create an enthusiasm for the subject that would color my writing and be passed on to you. On the other hand, I was more than a little concerned about the negative effect that losing 3 hours of sleep per night might have on me.

The research on sleep reduction suggests that my objective was reasonable. There have been only two systematic studies of long-term sleep reduction. In one (Webb & Agnew, 1974), a group of 16 subjects slept for only 5.5 hours per night for 60 days, with only one detectable deficit on an extensive battery of mood, medical, and performance tests, a slight deficit on a test of auditory vigilance. In the other (Friedman, Globus, Huntley, Mullaney, Naitoh, & Johnson, 1977; Mullaney, Johnson, Naitoh, Friedman, & Globus, 1977), 8 subjects reduced their nightly sleep by 30 minutes every 2 weeks until they reached 6.5 hours per night, then by 30 minutes every 3 weeks until they reached 5 hours, and then by 30 minutes every 4 weeks thereafter. After a subject indicated that he or she did not want to reduce his or her sleep further, he or she slept for 1 month at the shortest duration of nightly sleep that was achieved, then for 2 months at the shortest duration plus 30 minutes. Finally, each subject slept each night for 1 year for however long he or she preferred. The minimum duration of nightly sleep achieved during this experiment was 5.5 hours for two subjects, 5.0 hours for four subjects, and an impressive 4.5 hours for two subjects. In each of the subjects, a reduction in sleep time was associated with an increase in sleep efficiency: with a decrease in the amount of time that it took the subjects to fall asleep after going to bed, a decrease in the number of night-time awakenings, and an increase in the proportion of stage 4 sleep. After the subjects had reduced their sleep to 6 hours per night, they began to experience daytime sleepiness, and this became a problem as sleep time was further reduced. Nevertheless, there were no deficits on any of the mood, medical, or performance tests given to the subjects throughout the experiment. The most encouraging result was the observation that during the 1-year follow-up, all subjects slept less than they had previously—between 7 and 18 hours less each week—with no excessive sleepiness.

Rather than using the gradual step-wise reduction method of Friedman and his colleagues, I jumped into my 5-hours-per-night sleep schedule with both feet. This proved to be less difficult than you might think. I took advantage of a trip to the East Coast from my home on the West Coast to reset my circadian clock. When I was in the East, I got up at 7:00 A.M. each morning, which is 4:00 A.M. here on the West Coast, and I just kept on the same schedule when I got home. I decided to add my extra waking hours to the beginning of my day rather than to the end so that there would be no temptation for me to waste them—there are not too many distractions around this university at 5:00 A.M.

Figure 12.17 is a record of my sleep times for the 4-week period that it took me to write a first draft of this chapter. I didn't quite meet my goal of sleeping less than 5 hours every night, but I didn't miss by much—my overall mean was 5.05 hours per night. Notice that in the last week, there was a tendency for my circadian clock to run a bit slow; I began sleeping in until 4:30 A.M. and staying up until 11:30 P.M.

What were the positives and negatives of my experience? The main positive was the time to do things that it created—having an extra 21 hours per week was wonderful. Furthermore, because my daily routine was out of synchrony with everybody else's, I spent little time sitting in rush-hour traffic. The only negative of the experience was sleepiness. It was no problem during the day, when I was active. However, staying awake during the last hour before I went to bed—an hour during which I usually engaged in sedentary activities, such as reading—was at times a problem. This is when I became personally familiar with the phenomenon of microsleep, and it was then that I required some assistance in order to stay awake. Going to bed and falling asleep each night became a fleeting but satisfying experience.

I began this chapter with a question, "How much sleep do we need?" Then, I gave you my best professorial, it-could-be-this-it-could-be-that answer. However, that was a month ago. Now, after experiencing sleep reduction first hand, I am less inclined toward wishy-washiness on the topic of sleep. Two lines of evidence suggest that the answer to this question is about 5½ hours for most people. First, most committed subjects who are active during the day can reduce their sleep to about 5½ hours per night without great difficulty or adverse consequences. Second, the quality of a night's sleep declines precipitously after the first 5½ hours; there is little slow-wave sleep after this point (see Figure 12.3). Why then do most of us sleep 8 to 10 hours each

FIGURE 12.17

Sleep record of J.P.J.P. during a 4-week sleep-reduction program.

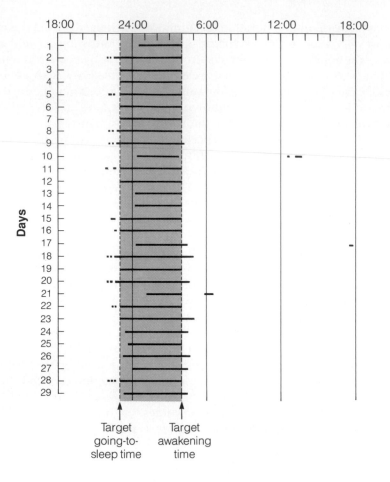

night? The reason may be that, as an incentive, sleep ranks up there with the big three consummatory behaviors of Chapters 10 and 11. When food, drink, and sex are freely available, most of us partake of more than is required for survival. It seems that the same is true of sleep.

Food for Thought

1. Do you think that your life could be improved by changing when or how long you sleep each day? In what ways? What negative effects do you think such changes might have on you?

2. Some people like to stay up late, some people like to get up early, others like to do both, and still others like to do neither. Design a sleep-reduction program that is tailored to your own biology and life style and that is consistent with the research literature on circadian cycles and sleep deprivation. Design a program that would produce the greatest benefits for you with the least discomfort.

3. How has reading about sleep research changed your views about sleep? Give three specific examples.

KEY TERMS

To help you study the material in this chapter, all of the key terms—those that have appeared in bold type—are listed and briefly defined here.

Activation-synthesis hypothesis. The theory that dream content reflects the random activity of cerebral circuits during REM sleep and the brain's inherent tendency to make sense of and give form to these ambiguous signals.

Alpha waves. 8-to-12 Hz rhythmic EEG waves; they commonly punctuate the EEG of human subjects just before they fall asleep.

Antihypnotic drugs. Sleep-reducing drugs.

Barbiturates. A class of hypnotic drugs (e.g., pentobarbital and phenobarbital); they are rarely used to treat insomnia because of their dangerous side effects.

Basal forebrain region. The area of the forebrain just in front of the hypothalamus.

Benzodiazepines. A class of anxiolytic drugs (e.g., Valium and Librium) that are often prescribed as sleeping pills.

Carousel apparatus. An apparatus used to study the effects of sleep deprivation in laboratory rats.

Cataplexy. A disorder characterized by sudden losses of muscle tone; it is often seen in cases of narcolepsy.

Cerveau isolé preparation. An experimental preparation in which the forebrain is disconnected from the rest of the brain by a midcollicular transection.

Circadian clock. An internal timing mechanism that is capable of maintaining daily cycles of physiological change, even when there are no temporal cues from the environment.

Circadian rhythms. Diurnal (daily) cycles of bodily function.

Deep sleep. Used by some researchers to refer to stage 4 sleep and by others to refer to REM sleep.

Delta sleep. That portion of sleep punctuated by delta waves; i.e., stages 3 and 4.

Delta sleep-inducing peptide (DSIP). A putative endogenous sleep factor.

Delta waves. The largest, slowest EEG waves.

Desynchronized EEG. Low-amplitude, high-frequency EEG.

Dorsal raphé nuclei. Nuclei in the dorsal portion of the cluster of raphé nuclei; some of the dorsal raphé nuclei are inactive during REM sleep and active during SWS.

Electroencephalogram (EEG). A gross measure of the electrical activity of the brain; commonly recorded from the scalp of human subjects.

Electromyogram (EMG). A measure of the electrical activity of muscles.

Electro-oculogram (EOG). A measure of eye movement.

Emergent stage 1 EEG. The first period of stage 1 EEG (low-voltage, fast activity) during a night's sleep is called initial stage 1; the subsequent periods of stage 1 EEG are called emergent stage 1.

Encéphale isolé preparation. An experimental preparation in which the brain is separated from the rest of the nervous system by a transection of the caudal brain stem.

Endogenous sleep factors. Sleep-inducing chemicals produced in the body.

First-night phenomenon. The sleep disturbances experienced during the first few nights that a subject sleeps in a laboratory.

Free-running period. The duration of one cycle of a free-running rhythm.

Free-running rhythms. Circadian rhythms that do not depend on environmental cues to keep them running on a regular schedule.

5-Hydroxytryptophan (5-HTP). The precursor of serotonin.

Hypersomnia. A disorder characterized by excessive sleep or sleepiness.

Hypnogogic hallucinations. Vivid dreamlike states that some people occasionally experience just as they are falling asleep; they are common in cases of narcolepsy.

Hypnotic drugs. Sleep-promoting drugs.

Iatrogenic disorder. A physician-created disorder.

Initial stage 1 EEG. The period of stage 1 EEG that occurs at the onset of sleep; unlike other periods of stage 1 EEG, it is not associated with dreaming.

Insomnia. A disorder of initiating and maintaining sleep.

Internal desynchronization. When the free-running circadian cycles of two different processes begin to cycle on different schedules.

Jet lag. When zeitgebers that control circadian rhythms are accelerated during eastern flights or decelerated during western flights.

K complexes. The large biphasic EEG waves that are characteristic of stage 2 sleep EEG.

Locus coeruleus. A noradrenergic nucleus of the caudal reticular formation that is inactive during REM sleep and active during SWS.

Lucid dreams. Dreams in which the dreamer is aware that she or he is dreaming and can influence the course of the dream.

Microsleeps. Brief periods of sleep EEG that are commonly observed in sleep-deprived subjects while they remain sitting or standing; the eyelids droop and there is a decrease in responsiveness to external stimuli.

Narcolepsy. A disorder of hypersomnia characterized by repeated, brief daytime sleep attacks.

Nocturnal myoclonus. Periodic sleep-disrupting twitching of the legs during sleep.

Nucleus magnocellularis. A nucleus of the caudal reticular formation; it promotes relaxation of the core muscles during REM sleep and during cataplectic attacks.

Parabiotic preparation. A physiological preparation in which two subjects share one physiological system.

Parachlorophenylalanine (PCPA). A chemical that blocks the synthesis of serotonin and produces insomnia.

Paradoxical sleep. Emergent stage 1 sleep; so called because the EEG signals and ANS changes associated with it are similar to those of wakefulness.

Raphé nuclei. A cluster of serotonin-producing nuclei running in a thin strip down the midline of the caudal reticular formation.

Rapid eye movement sleep (REM sleep). The stage of sleep characterized by rapid eye movements, loss of core muscle tone, and low-amplitude high-frequency EEG.

Restless legs. Insomnia caused by a tension or uneasiness in the legs that keeps people from falling asleep.

Reticular activating system. The reticular formation is commonly referred to as the reticular activating system because it contains circuits that maintain wakefulness.

Retinohypothalamic tracts. Tracts running from the retinas to the suprachiasmatic nuclei of the hypothalamus.

Sleep apnea. A condition in which sleep is repeatedly disturbed by momentary interruptions in breathing.

Sleep paralysis. A sleep disorder that is characterized by attacks of paralysis just as a person is falling asleep.

Sleep spindles. 1-to-2-second bursts of 12-to-15-Hz EEG waves characteristic of stage 2 sleep.

Slow-wave sleep (SWS). Sleep stages 2, 3, and 4.

Somnambulism. Sleep walking.

Suprachiasmatic nuclei (SCN). Nuclei of the hypothalamus that control the circadian cycles of various bodily functions.

Tricyclic antidepressants. Drugs that are commonly prescribed for the treatment of depression; because they suppress REM sleep, they are also prescribed for the treatment of REM-sleep-related disorders such as cataplexy.

Zeitgebers. Environmental cues, such as the light-dark cycle, that entrain circadian rhythms.

ADDITIONAL READING

There are several interesting introductions to the topic of sleep; the following four are my favorites:

Dement, W. C. (1978). *Some must watch while some must sleep.* New York: W. W. Norton.

Hartmann, E. L. (1973). *The functions of sleep.* Westford, MA: Murray Printing Company.

Hobson, J. A. (1989). *Sleep.* New York: Scientific American Library.

Meddis, R. (1977). *The sleep instinct.* London: Henley and Boston.

13

Drug Abuse and Reward Circuits in the Brain

13.1	*The Basic Principles of Drug Action*
13.2	*Five Commonly Abused Drugs*
13.3	*Biopsychological Theories of Addiction and Reward Circuits in the Brain*

Psychoactive drugs are drugs that influence subjective experience and behavior by acting on the nervous system. In the preceding chapters, you have repeatedly encountered psychoactive drugs functioning at their best, in the study of the nervous system and in the treatment of its disorders. This chapter focuses on the sinister side of psychoactive drugs: their abuse.

There are three main sections in this chapter. Section 13.1 introduces you to some basic pharmacological principles and concepts. Section 13.2 discusses five commonly abused drugs (tobacco, alcohol, marijuana, cocaine, and heroin), and Section 13.3 describes a circuit in the brain that is thought to be involved in drug addiction. A concluding case study of one remarkable addict, Sigmund Freud, ties the three sections together and provides closing food for thought.

While reading this chapter, it is important for you to keep from being misled by the legal and social status of the drugs under discussion. Most laws governing drug abuse in various parts of the world were enacted in the last century or in the early part of this one, long before there was any scientific research on the topic (see Musto, 1991). Many people do not appreciate this fact, and they equate drug legality with drug safety. This point was recently made to me in a particularly ironic fashion.

I was invited to address a convention of high school teachers on the topic of drug abuse. When I arrived at the convention center to give my talk, I was escorted to a special suite, where I was encouraged to join the executive committee in a round of drug taking—the drug was a special high-proof single-malt whiskey. Later, the irony of the situation had its full impact. As I stepped to the podium under the influence of a psychoactive drug (i.e., the whiskey), I looked out through the haze of cigarette smoke at an audience of educators, who had invited me to speak to them because they were concerned about the unhealthy impact of drugs on their students. The welcoming applause gradually gave way to the melodic tinkling of ice cubes in liquor glasses, and I began. They did not like what I had to say.

13.1

The Basic Principles of Drug Action

Drug Administration and Absorption

Psychoactive drugs are usually administered in one of four ways: by oral ingestion; by injection; by inhalation; or by absorption through the mucous membranes of the nose, mouth, or rectum. The route of administration influences the rate at which, and the degree to which, the drug reaches its sites of action.

Ingestion The oral route is the preferred route of administration for many drugs. Once they are swallowed, they dissolve in the fluids of the stomach and are carried by them to the intestine, where they are absorbed into the bloodstream. Those drugs that are not readily absorbed from the digestive tract or are broken down into inactive metabolites before they can be absorbed must be taken by some other route. The two main advantages of the oral route over other routes are its ease and relative safety. Its main disadvantage is its unpredictability; absorption from the digestive tract into the bloodstream can be greatly influenced by difficult-to-gauge factors such as the amount and type of food in the stomach. Drugs, such as alcohol, that readily pass through the stomach wall take effect soon after ingestion because they do not have to be carried to the intestine to be absorbed.

Injection Drug injection is common in medical practice because the effects of injected drugs are large, rapid, and predictable. Drug injections are typically made into the fatty tissue just beneath the skin [**subcutaneously (SC)**], into large muscles [**intramuscularly (IM)**], or directly into veins at points where they run just beneath the skin [**intravenously (IV)**]. Many addicts prefer the intravenous route because the bloodstream delivers the drug directly to the brain. However, the speed and directness of the intravenous route are mixed blessings; after an intravenous injection, there is little or no opportunity to counteract the effects of an overdose, an impurity, or an allergic reaction. Furthermore, many addicts develop scar tissue, infections, and collapsed veins at the few sites on their bodies where there are large accessible veins.

Inhalation   Some drugs can be absorbed into the bloodstream through the rich network of capillaries in the lungs. Many anesthetics are commonly administered by *inhalation,* as are tobacco and marijuana. The two main shortcomings of this route are that it is difficult to precisely regulate the dose of inhaled drugs, and many inhaled substances damage the lungs.

Absorption through mucous membranes   Some drugs can be administered through the mucous membranes of the nose, mouth, and rectum. Cocaine, for example, is commonly self-administered through the nasal membranes (i.e., snorted)—but not without damaging them.

Penetration of the Central Nervous System by Drugs

Once a drug enters the bloodstream, it readily enters the circulatory system of the central nervous system. Fortunately, a protective filter, the *blood-brain barrier,* makes it difficult for many potentially dangerous blood-borne chemicals to pass from the circulatory system of the CNS into the CNS per se (see Chapters 3 and 5).

Mechanisms of Drug Action

Psychoactive drugs influence the nervous system in many ways (see Koob & Bloom, 1988). Some, such as alcohol and many of the general anesthetics, act diffusely on neural membranes throughout the CNS. Others act in a less general way: by binding to particular synaptic receptors; by influencing the synthesis, transport, release, or deactivation of particular neurotransmitters; or by influencing the chain of chemical reactions elicited in postsynaptic neurons by the activation of their synaptic receptors (see Chapter 4). Although some drugs are much more selective in their actions than others, the lesson taught by decades of psychopharmacological research is that no psychoactive drug has effects that are entirely selective. At doses high enough to produce psychological changes, all psychoactive drugs influence CNS activity in more than one way.

Drug Metabolism and Elimination

The actions of most drugs are terminated when enzymes that are synthesized by the liver stimulate their conversion to nonactive forms, a process referred to as **drug metabolism.** In most cases, drug metabolism eliminates a drug's ability to pass through lipid membranes so that it can no longer penetrate the blood-brain barrier. Small amounts of some psychoactive drugs pass from the body in urine, sweat, feces, breath, and mother's milk before they can be metabolized.

Drug Tolerance

Drug tolerance is a state of decreased sensitivity to a drug that develops as a result of exposure to it. Drug tolerance can be demonstrated in two ways: by showing that a given dose of the drug has less effect than it had before exposure to it, or by showing that it takes more of the drug to produce the same effect. In essence, what this means is that tolerance is a shift in the *dose-response curve* (a graph of the magnitude of the effect of different doses of the drug) to the right (see Figure 13.1).

There are three important points to remember about the specificity of drug tolerance. The first is that exposure to one drug can produce tolerance to other drugs that act by the same mechanism. This is known as **cross tolerance.** The second is that tolerance often develops to some effects of a drug but not to others. Failure to understand this second point can have tragic consequences for people who think that because they have become tolerant to some effects of a drug (e.g., to the nauseating effects of alcohol or tobacco), they are tolerant to all of them. In fact, tolerance may develop to some effects of a drug while the sensitivity to other effects increases—increases in sensitivity are called **sensitization** (Robinson, 1991). The third is that drug tolerance is not a unitary phenomenon in the sense that there is a single basic mechanism underlying all examples of it. When a drug is administered at active doses, many kinds of adaptive changes can occur to reduce the effect of the drug. It is usual to refer to tolerance that results from a reduction in the amount of drug getting to its sites of action as **metabolic tolerance.** Drug tolerance resulting from a reduction in the reactivity of the target sites to the

FIGURE 13.1

Drug tolerance is a shift in the dose-response curve to the right as the result of exposure to the drug.

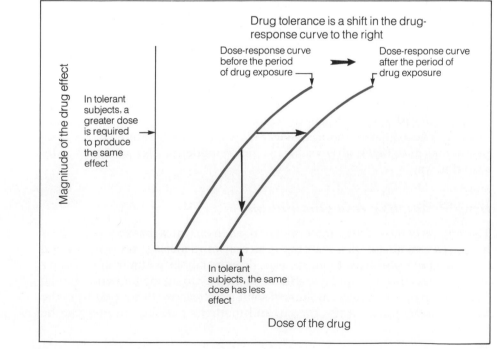

drug is called **functional tolerance.** Tolerance to psychoactive drugs is largely functional.

Several different kinds of neural adaptations have been shown to contribute to the development of functional tolerance to psychoactive drugs. For example, exposure to a drug can reduce the degree to which it subsequently binds to receptors on neural membranes; it can reduce the impact of the drug's binding on neural activity; and it can produce changes in the structure of neural membranes that diminish the drug's effect. These changes are often studied by neurochemists in experiments in which tissue cultures are exposed to measured concentrations of the drug in strictly controlled chemical environments. However, such *in vitro* studies (studies of tissue outside of living organs) fail to capture one of the most important features of drug tolerance: that drug tolerance is influenced by learning (see Poulos & Cappell, 1991).

Psychopharmacologists have taken two different approaches in their studies of learning and drug tolerance: (1) They have studied the effect on tolerance of what subjects do while they are exposed to the drug, and (2) they have studied the effect on tolerance of the environments in which the drug is administered. Those studies of drug tolerance that have focused on the behavior of subjects during drug exposure have often employed the **before-and-after design** (Chen, 1968). In before-and-after experiments, two groups of subjects receive the same series of drug injections and the same series of tests, but the subjects in one group receive the drug before each test, whereas those in the other group receive the drug after each test. At the end of the experiment, all subjects receive the same dose of the drug followed by a test so that the degree to which the drug disrupts test performance in the two groups can be compared. For example, in one experiment (Pinel, Mana, & Kim, 1989), two groups of rats received exactly the same regimen of alcohol injections, one injection every 2 days for the duration of the experiment. During the tolerance-development phase, the rats in one group received each alcohol injection 1 hour before a mild convulsive brain stimulation so that the anticonvulsant effect of the alcohol could be experienced on each trial. The rats in the other group received their injections 1 hour after each convulsive stimulation so that the anticonvulsant effect could not be repeatedly experienced. At the end of the experiment, all of the subjects received a test injection of alcohol, followed 1 hour later by a convulsive stimulation so that the amount of tolerance to the anticonvulsant effect of alcohol could be compared in the two groups. As illustrated in Figure 13.2, the rats that received alcohol on each trial before a convulsive stimulation became tolerant to alcohol's anticonvulsant effect, whereas those that received the same injections and stimulations, but in the reverse order, did not. This same pattern of findings has been reported in many other experiments involving different drugs and different drug effects (e.g., Demellweek & Goudie,1983; Mana, Kim, Pinel, & Jones, 1991; Poulos & Hinson, 1984; Traynor, Schlapfer, & Barondes, 1980; Wenger, Tiffany, Bombadier, Nicholls, & Woods, 1981)— perhaps the most provocative of these is an experiment in which tolerance to the disruptive effects of alcohol on male sexual behavior developed fully in male rats only if they were allowed to engage in sexual activity after each injection (Pinel, Pfaus, & Christensen, 1991). Together, these various effects— which are generally referred to as *contingent drug tolerance* (Carlton & Wolgin, 1971)—suggest that many forms of tolerance are adaptations to the

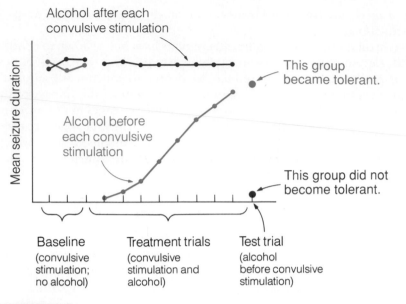

FIGURE 13.2

Tolerance to the anticonvulsant effect of alcohol depends on the repeated experience of the anticonvulsant effect. The rats that received alcohol (1.5 g/kg) on each trial before a convulsive stimulation became tolerant to its anticonvulsant effect; those that received the same injections after a convulsive stimulation on each trial did not become tolerant. (Adapted from Pinel, Mana, & Kim, 1989.)

repeated experience of the drug effect (e.g., the anticonvulsant effect of alcohol), rather than to exposure to the drug per se. The major strength of this **drug-effect theory of tolerance** is that it explains how tolerance can develop to one effect of a drug, while at the very same time in the same subject not develop to other effects of a drug (see Pinel, Kim, & Mana, 1990; Poulos & Cappell, 1991).

The other line of research to demonstrate the major effect of learning on drug tolerance has focused on the environment in which the drug effects are experienced. For example, in one study (Crowell, Hinson, & Siegel, 1981), two groups of rats received 20 alcohol and 20 saline injections in an alternating sequence, one injection every other day. The only difference between the two groups was that the rats in one group received all 20 alcohol injections in a distinctive test room and the 20 saline injections in their colony room, while the rats in the other group received the alcohol in the colony room and the saline in the distinctive test room. Then, the tolerance of all rats to the **hypothermic** (temperature-reducing) effects of alcohol was assessed in both environments. As illustrated in Figure 13.3, tolerance was observed only when the rats were injected in the environment that had previously been paired with alcohol administration. This *situational specificity of drug tolerance* has been demonstrated in many other experiments involving a variety of drugs (e.g., Lê, Poulos, & Cappell, 1979; Mansfield & Cunningham, 1980; Siegel, 1978).

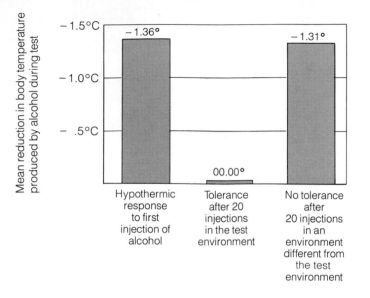

FIGURE 13.3

The situational specificity of tolerance to the hypothermic effects of alcohol. (Adapted from Crowell et al., 1981.)

The numerous demonstrations of the situational specificity of drug tolerance led Siegel and his colleagues to propose that addicts may be particularly susceptible to the lethal effects of a drug *overdose* when the drug is administered in a new context. Their hypothesis is that addicts become tolerant when they repeatedly self-administer their drug in the same environments, and as a result, they begin taking larger and larger doses to counteract the diminution of drug effects. Then, when the addict administers her or his usual massive dose in an unusual situation, tolerance effects are not present to counteract the effects of the drug, and there is a greater risk of death from overdose. In support of this hypothesis, Siegel, Hinson, Krank, and McCully (1982) found that 96% of a group of heroin-tolerant rats died following a high dose of heroin administered in a novel environment, but only 64% died following the same dose administered in their usual injection environment. Heroin kills by suppressing respiration.

Of the several noteworthy theories that have been proposed to account for the situational specificity of drug tolerance (see Baker & Tiffany, 1985; Eikelboom & Stewart, 1982; Paletta & Wagner, 1986), Siegel's theory has been the most influential. Siegel views each incidence of drug administration as a Pavlovian conditioning trial (see Chapter 5) in which various environmental stimuli that regularly predict the administration of the drug (e.g., pubs, washrooms, needles, other addicts) are conditional stimuli, and the drug effects are unconditional stimuli. The central assumption of the theory is that conditional stimuli that predict drug administration come to elicit conditional responses opposite to the unconditional effects of the drug. Siegel has termed these hypothetical opposing conditional responses **conditioned compensatory responses.** The theory is that as the stimuli that repeatedly predict the effects of a drug come to elicit greater and greater conditioned compensatory responses, they increasingly counteract the unconditional effects of the drug and produce situationally specific tolerance. A schematic illustration of Siegel's conditioned compensatory response theory is presented in Figure 13.4.

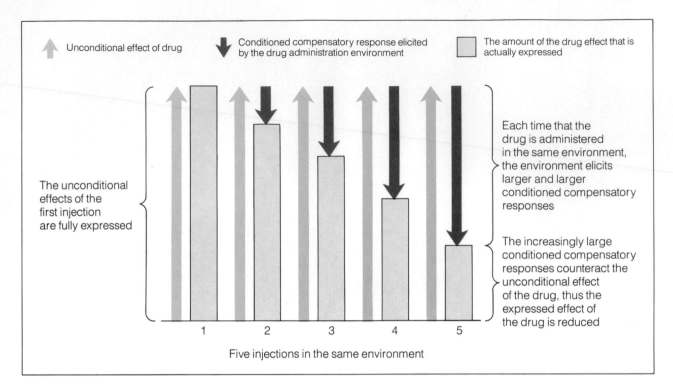

FIGURE 13.4

A schematic illustration of the conditioned compensatory response interpretation of the situational specificity of drug tolerance.

Drug Withdrawal and Physical Dependence

After substantial amounts of a drug have been in the body for a long time (e.g., several days), its sudden elimination can trigger an illness called a **withdrawal syndrome.** The nature and severity of the withdrawal symptoms depend on the particular drug in question, on the duration and degree of the preceding drug exposure, and on the speed with which the drug is eliminated from the body. Withdrawal symptoms are generally assumed to be produced by some of the same functional changes that underlie drug tolerance. It is assumed that the presence of the drug produces compensatory changes in the nervous system that offset the drug effects and produce tolerance. Then, when the drug is eliminated from the body, these compensatory changes, without the drug to offset them, manifest themselves as withdrawal symptoms. As a result, withdrawal effects are usually opposite to the initial effects of the drug; for example, the withdrawal of anticonvulsants often triggers convulsions, and, as you learned in Chapter 12, the withdrawal of sleeping pills often produces insomnia. Individuals who suffer withdrawal reactions when they stop taking a drug are said to be **physically dependent** on that drug.

Addiction, Physical Dependence, and Psychological Dependence

Not all drug users are addicts. **Addicts** are those drug users who continue to use a drug despite the drug's adverse effects on their health and social life, and despite their repeated efforts to stop. The greatest source of misconception about drug addiction comes from the tendency of some experts and most lay people to equate it with physical dependence. The addict is seen as a person who is helplessly trapped on a merry-go-round of drug taking, withdrawal symptoms, and further drug taking to combat the withdrawal symptoms. Although appealing in its simplicity, this conception of drug addiction is wrong. Addicts sometimes take drugs to alleviate their withdrawal symptoms, but this is usually not the primary motivating factor in their addiction. If it were, addicts could be easily cured by hospitalizing them for a few days, until their withdrawal symptoms have subsided. This treatment approach has proven to be totally ineffective; most addicts quickly renew their drug taking even after months of enforced abstinence. This is an important issue; we will return to it later in this chapter.

When physical dependence was believed to be the major cause of addiction, the term *psychological dependence* was coined to refer to exceptions to this general rule. **Psychological dependence** referred to compulsive drug taking in the absence of physical dependence. However, now that it is clear that physical dependence is not the major motivating factor in addiction, there is little need for a special category of psychological dependence.

Five Commonly Abused Drugs

This section is about five commonly abused drugs: tobacco, alcohol, marijuana, cocaine, and heroin.

Tobacco

Next to *caffeine,* tobacco is the most widely used psychoactive drug in our society. When a cigarette is smoked, **nicotine,** the major psychoactive ingredient of tobacco, and numerous other chemicals, including *carbon monoxide,* are absorbed through the lungs. Because considerable tolerance develops to some of the immediate adverse effects of tobacco, the effects of smoking a cigarette on nonsmokers and smokers can be quite different. Nonsmokers often respond to a few puffs of a cigarette with various combinations of nausea, vomiting, coughing, sweating, abdominal cramps, dizziness, flushing, and diarrhea. In contrast, smokers report that they are more relaxed, more alert, and less hungry after a cigarette.

There is no question that heavy smokers are drug addicts in every sense of the word (Jones, 1987). The compulsive drug craving, which is the major defining feature of addiction, is readily apparent in any heavy smoker who has run out of cigarettes or who is forced by circumstance to refrain from smoking for several hours. Furthermore, heavy smokers who stop smoking experience a variety of withdrawal effects such as depression, anxiety, restlessness, irritability, constipation, and difficulties in sleeping and concentrating. Only about 20% of all attempts to stop smoking are successful for 2 years or more (Schelling, 1992).

The consequences of long-term tobacco use are alarming. **Smokers' syndrome** is characterized by chest pain, labored breathing, wheezing, coughing, and a heightened susceptibility to infections of the respiratory tract. Chronic smokers are highly susceptible to a variety of potentially lethal lung disorders including pneumonia, *bronchitis* (chronic inflammation of the bronchioles of the lungs), *emphysema* (loss of elasticity of the lung from chronic irritation), and lung cancer. Although the increased risk of lung cancer receives the greatest publicity, smoking also increases the risk of cancer of the larynx (voice box), mouth, esophagus, kidneys, pancreas, bladder, and stomach. Smokers also run a great risk of developing a variety of cardiovascular diseases, which may culminate in heart attack or stroke. According to the American Surgeon General, about 400,000 Americans die each year from smoking-related disorders (Schelling, 1992).

Sufferers from **Buerger's disease** provide a shocking illustration of the addictive power of nicotine. Buerger's disease is a condition in which the blood vessels, especially those supplying the legs, are constricted whenever nicotine enters the bloodstream.

> If a patient with this condition continues to smoke, gangrene may eventually set in. First a few toes may have to be amputated, then the foot at the ankle, then the leg at the knee, and ultimately at the hip. Somewhere along this gruesome progression gangrene may also attack the other leg. Patients are strongly advised that if they will only stop smoking, it is virtually certain that the otherwise inexorable march of gangrene up the legs will be curbed. Yet surgeons report that it is not at all uncommon to find a patient with Buerger's disease vigorously puffing away in his hospital bed following a second or third amputation operation. (Brecher, 1972, pp. 215–216)

The adverse effects of tobacco smoke are unfortunately not restricted to those who smoke. There is now strong evidence that individuals who live or work with smokers are more likely to develop heart disease and cancer than those who don't. Even the unborn are vulnerable; smoking during pregnancy increases the likelihood of miscarriage, stillbirth, and early death of the child. The levels of nicotine in the blood of breast-fed infants are frequently as great as those in the blood of the mother.

Alcohol

Ethyl alcohol is a psychoactive drug, which readily invades all parts of the body because of its solubility and small molecular size. Most of its psychological effects are attributable to the fact that it depresses neural firing, and thus it is classified as a **depressant.** However, at low doses, it acts like a mild *stimulant;* it produces a general feeling of well-being and it facilitates social interaction.

At moderate doses, the drinker experiences various degrees of cognitive, perceptual, verbal, and motor impairment, as well as a loss of control that can lead to a variety of socially unacceptable actions. High doses result in unconsciousness, and if blood levels reach 0.5%, there is a risk of death from respiratory depression. The tell-tale red flush of alcohol intoxication is produced by the dilation of blood vessels in the skin; this increases the amount of heat that is lost from the blood to the air and leads to a decrease in body temperature. Alcohol is a **diuretic;** that is, it increases the production of urine by the kidney.

Alcohol, like many addictive drugs, produces both tolerance and physical dependence. The livers of heavy drinkers metabolize alcohol more quickly than do the livers of nondrinkers, but this increase in metabolic efficiency contributes only slightly to overall alcohol tolerance—most alcohol tolerance

is functional. Alcohol withdrawal often produces a mild syndrome of headache, nausea, vomiting, and tremulousness, which is euphemistically referred to as a *hangover* (Pinel & Mucha, 1980); however, in its severe form, the alcohol withdrawal syndrome is life-threatening.

A full-blown alcohol withdrawal syndrome comprises three phases. The first phase begins about 5 or 6 hours after the cessation of a long bout of heavy drinking and is characterized by severe tremors, agitation, headache, nausea, vomiting, abdominal cramps, profuse sweating, and sometimes hallucinations. The defining feature of the second phase, which typically occurs between 15 and 30 hours after cessation of drinking, is convulsive activity. The third phase, which usually begins a day or two after the cessation of drinking and lasts for 3 or 4 days, is called **delirium tremens** (the DTs). The DTs are characterized by disturbing hallucinations, bizarre delusions, agitation, confusion, *hyperthermia* (high temperature), and *tachycardia* (rapid heartbeat). The convulsions and the DTs produced by alcohol withdrawal can be lethal.

Alcohol attacks almost every tissue in the body. Chronic alcohol consumption produces extensive brain damage and an associated disorder known as **Korsakoff's syndrome** (see Chapter 14), which is characterized by severe memory loss, sensory and motor dysfunction, and severe *dementia* (intellectual deterioration). It also causes extensive scarring or **cirrhosis** of the liver, which is the major cause of death among heavy alcohol users. It erodes the muscles of the heart and thus increases the risk of heart attack. It irritates the lining of the digestive tract, and in so doing increases the risk of oral and liver cancer, stomach ulcers, *pancreatitis* (inflammation of the pancreas), and *gastritis* (inflammation of the stomach). And not to be forgotten is the carnage that it produces on our highways.

Like nicotine, alcohol readily penetrates the placental membrane and affects the fetus. The result is that the offspring of mothers who consume substantial quantities of alcohol during their pregnancy frequently suffer from a disorder known as **fetal alcohol syndrome (FAS)** (see Mattson, Barron, & Riley, 1988). The FAS child suffers from some or all of the following symptoms: mental retardation, poor coordination, poor muscle tone, low birth weight, retarded growth, and various physical deformities. In rats, a single day of alcohol exposure during the brain growth spurt can significantly reduce adult brain weight (Goodlett, Marcussen, & West, 1990).

Marijuana

Marijuana is the name commonly given to the dried leaves and flowers of the common hemp plant (**Cannabis sativa**). The usual mode of consumption is to smoke these leaves in a *joint* (a cigarette of marijuana) or pipe, but it is also effective when ingested orally if first baked into an oil-rich substrate, such as a chocolate brownie, to promote absorption from the gastrointestinal tract. The psychoactive effects of marijuana are largely attributable to a constituent called delta-9-tetrahydrocannabinol (**delta-9-THC**); however, marijuana contains over 80 *cannabinoids* (chemicals of the same chemical class as delta-9-THC), which may also be psychoactive (see Kephalas, Kiburis, Michael, Miras, & Papadakis, 1976). Most of the cannabinoids are found in a sticky resin covering the leaves and flowers of the plant, which can be extracted and dried to form a dark cork-like material called **hashish.** The hashish can be further processed into an extremely potent product called *hash oil.*

Written records of marijuana use go back 6,000 years in China, where its stem was used to make rope, its seeds were used as a grain, and its leaves and flowers were used for their psychoactive and medicinal effects. One story of ancient cannabis use, whose misrepresentation has had a major impact on modern attitudes toward the drug, involved a Muslim sect headed by one Hashishin-i-Sabbah, a fanatic who tried to purge the Muslim religion of false prophets by having his followers assassinate them. Hashishin reportedly rewarded his successful assassins with a psychoactive drug, which was likely opium (Grinspoon, 1977), but the story spread that it was hashish. Both the words "assassin" and "hashish" were derived from his name.

Cannabis cultivation spread from the Middle East into Western Europe; however, in Europe, it was grown primarily for the manufacture of rope, and its psychoactive properties were largely forgotten. During the period of European imperialism, rope was in high demand for sailing vessels. In 1611 the American colonies responded to this demand by growing cannabis as a cash crop—George Washington was one of the more notable cannabis growers.

The practice of smoking the leaves of the cannabis plant and the word "marijuana" itself seem to have been introduced to the southern United States in the early part of this century by Mexican immigrants, and its use gradually became popular among certain subgroups, such as the poor in city ghettos and jazz musicians. In 1926, an article appeared in a New Orleans newspaper exposing the "menace of marijuana," and soon similar stories were appearing in newspapers all over the United States under titles such as "the evil weed," "the killer drug," and "marijuana madness." The population was told that marijuana turned normal people into violent, drug-crazed criminals who rapidly become addicted to heroin. The old story of Hashishin was revived in a revised form, which had Hashishin giving hashish to his followers, not as a reward for a job well done, but to transform them into killers. The result was the enactment of many laws against the drug. In many states, marijuana was legally classified as a **narcotic** (a legal term generally used to refer to opiates) and punishment was dealt out accordingly. (The structure of marijuana and its physiological and behavioral effects bear no resemblance to those of the other narcotics; thus, legally classifying marijuana as a narcotic was like passing a law that red is green.)

The popularization of marijuana smoking among the middle and upper classes in the 1960s stimulated a massive program of research that has lasted

a quarter of a century, yet there is still considerable confusion about marijuana among the general population. One of the difficulties in characterizing the effects of marijuana is that they are subtle, difficult to measure, and greatly influenced by the social situation.

> At low, usual "social" doses, the intoxicated individual may experience an increased sense of well-being: initial restlessness and hilarity followed by a dreamy, carefree state of relaxation; alteration of sensory perceptions including expansion of space and time; and a more vivid sense of touch, sight, smell, taste, and sound; a feeling of hunger, especially a craving for sweets; and subtle changes in thought formation and expression. To an unknowing observer, an individual in this state of consciousness would not appear noticeably different. (National Commission on Marijuana and Drug Abuse, 1972, p. 68)

At unusually high oral doses equivalent to several rapidly smoked joints, the preceding symptoms are intensified and other symptoms may appear. Short-term memory is likely to be impaired, and the ability to carry out tasks involving multiple steps to reach a specific goal declines. Speech often becomes slightly slurred, and meaningful conversation becomes difficult. A sense of unreality, emotional intensification, sensory distortion, slight motor impairment, and general silliness are also common. However, even after very high doses, an unexpected knock at the door can often bring about the return of a reasonable semblance of normal behavior. In the light of such effects, the earlier claims that marijuana would trigger a wave of violent crimes in the youth of America seem absurd. It is difficult to imagine how anybody could believe that the red-eyed, gluttonous, sleepy, giggling products of common social doses of marijuana would be more likely to commit violent criminal acts. In fact, marijuana actually curbs aggressive behavior (Tinklenberg, 1974). There is one effect of marijuana that warrants special mention because of its serious consequences. Marijuana-intoxicated drivers can stop as quickly as normal drivers, but they are not always so quick to notice the things for which they should stop (Moskowitz, Hulbert, & McGlothin, 1976).

What are the hazards of long-term marijuana use? The main risk appears to be lung damage. Those who regularly smoke marijuana tend to have deficits in respiratory function (e.g., Tilles, Goldenheim, Johnson, Mendelson, Mello, & Hales, 1986), and they are more likely to develop a chronic cough, bronchitis, and asthma (Abramson, 1974). Some authors list four other adverse effects of regular marijuana use; however, in each case, the evidence is either indirect, inconsistent, or incomplete (see Mendelson, 1987). First, there have been reports that chronic marijuana smoking lowers the plasma *testosterone* levels of males (e.g., Kolodny, Masters, Kolodner, & Toro, 1974), but the reported reductions have been too slight to influence sexual behavior, and several studies have failed to confirm them. Second, there has been some suggestion that marijuana can adversely influence the *immune system,* but it has yet to be demonstrated that marijuana smokers are generally more susceptible to infection than are comparable marijuana nonsmokers. Third, because *tachycardia* (rapid heart rate) is one of the most reliable effects of marijuana, there has been some concern that chronic marijuana consumption might cause cardiovascular problems, but again there is no direct evidence for this hypothesis. Fourth, many people have hypothesized that the relaxation produced by marijuana could reach pathological proportions and produce what is generally referred to as **amotivational syndrome.** The evidence that marijuana use causes a significant amotivational syndrome is far from strong (see Mendelson, Kuehnle, Greenberg, & Mello, 1976)—no significant difference was found between the grade point averages of marijuana smokers and nonsmokers in a study of 2,000 college students (Brill & Christie, 1974). Nevertheless, it seems unlikely that heavy users would not experience some decline in productivity.

The addiction potential of marijuana is low. Most people who use marijuana do so only occasionally, and most who use it as youths curtail their use in their 30s and 40s. Tolerance can develop to marijuana during periods of sustained use (Babor, Mendelson, Greenberg, & Kuehnle, 1975), and withdrawal symptoms (e.g., nausea, diarrhea, sweating, chills, tremor, restlessness, sleep disturbance) can occur, but only in contrived laboratory situations in which massive oral doses are regularly administered.

Some of the effects of marijuana have been shown to be of clinical benefit (see Cohen & Stillman, 1976). The most notable example is marijuana's ability to block the nausea of cancer patients undergoing chemotherapy—*Nabilone,* a synthetic cannabis analogue, is now sometimes prescribed with chemotherapy (Lemberger & Rowe, 1975). Marijuana has also been shown to block seizures (Corcoran, McCaughran, & Wada, 1973), to dilate the bronchioles of asthmatics, and to decrease the severity of *glaucoma* (i.e., a disorder characterized by an increase in the pressure of the fluid inside the eye), but it is not normally prescribed for these purposes.

Delta-9-THC exerts its psychological effects by binding to receptors that are particularly dense in the basal ganglia, hippocampus, cerebellum, and neocortex (Howlett et al., 1990). Because delta-9-THC does not occur naturally in the body, these receptors must normally perform some other function; however, what this function is remains a mystery. The recent cloning of the gene for the delta-9-THC receptor (Matsuda et al., 1990) should greatly facilitate its investigation.

Cocaine

Cocaine is prepared from the leaf of the coca bush, which is found primarily in Peru and Bolivia. A crude extract called *coca paste* is usually made directly from the leaves; then **cocaine hydrochloride,** the nefarious odorless white powder, is extracted from the paste. Cocaine hydrochloride is sometimes converted by abusers to its free-base form and smoked in a pipe. **Crack** is an impure free-base product that is widely used because it is relatively inexpensive.

Cocaine hydrochloride is an effective local anesthetic, and it was once widely prescribed as such until it was supplanted by synthetic analogues such as *procaine* and *lidocaine.* It is not, however, cocaine's anesthetic actions that are of interest to its users. People eat, smoke, snort, or inject cocaine in its various forms in order to experience its psychological effects. Users report being swept by a wave of well-being; they feel self-confident, alert, energetic, friendly, outgoing, fidgety, and talkative; and they have less desire for food and sleep. These effects are similar to those produced by **amphetamine,** another widely abused stimulant. **Stimulant drugs** are those such as caffeine, nicotine, amphetamine, and cocaine, whose primary effect is to increase neural activity. Coca-Cola is a commercial stimulant preparation consumed by many people around the world. Today, its stimulant action is attributable to caffeine, but when it was first introduced, "the pause that refreshes" packed a real wallop in the form of small amounts of cocaine.

Like alcohol, cocaine is frequently consumed in *binges* (see Gawin, 1991). Cocaine addicts tend to go on so-called **cocaine sprees,** in which extremely high levels of intake are maintained for periods of a day or two. During a cocaine spree, users become increasingly tolerant to the euphoria-producing effects of cocaine. Accordingly, larger and larger doses are often administered to maintain the initial level of euphoria. The spree usually ends when the cocaine is gone or when it begins to have serious toxic effects. During these binges, extremely high blood levels of cocaine are achieved, and

sleeplessness, tremors, nausea, and psychotic behavior often occur. The syndrome of psychotic behavior observed during cocaine sprees is called **cocaine psychosis.** It is similar to, and has often been mistakenly diagnosed as, *schizophrenia.* Although cocaine is extremely addictive, there are typically no obvious withdrawal effects after abrupt termination of a cocaine spree other than a general feeling of lethargy and depression. During cocaine sprees, there is a risk of seizures, loss of consciousness, and death from respiratory arrest or stroke. Although tolerance develops to most effects of cocaine, repeated cocaine exposure makes subjects even more sensitive to its convulsive effects (Stripling & Ellinwood, 1976)—this is an example of sensitization. Fatalities from cocaine overdose are most likely following IV injection; cocaine snorting damages the nasal membranes; and cocaine smoking damages the lungs.

The Opiates: Heroin and Morphine

Opium, the sap that exudes from the seeds of the opium poppy, has several psychoactive ingredients, most notably **morphine** and its weaker relative, **codeine.** These drugs, their stronger and more notorious relative **heroin,** and other drugs that have similar structures or effects are commonly referred to as the **opiates.** The opiates have a Jekyll-and-Hyde problem of major proportions. On their Dr. Jekyll side, opiates are unmatched as **analgesics** (painkillers), and they are also extremely effective in the treatment of cough and diarrhea. But unfortunately, the kindly Dr. Jekyll always brings with him the evil Mr. Hyde, the risk of addiction.

Archeological evidence suggests that the practice of eating opium became popular in the Middle East sometime before 4,000 B.C., and then it spread throughout Africa, Europe, and Asia (see Berridge & Edwards, 1981; Latimer & Goldberg, 1981). Three historic events fanned the flame of opiate addiction. First, in 1644, the Emperor of China banned tobacco smoking, and many Chinese tobacco smokers tried smoking opium and liked it. Because smoking opium has a greater effect on the brain than does eating it, many people became addicted to opium as the practice of opium smoking slowly spread to other countries. Second, morphine, the most potent constituent of opium, was isolated from opium in 1803, and in the 1830s it became available commercially. Third, the hypodermic needle was invented in 1856, and soon injured soldiers (e.g., those of the American Civil War) were introduced to morphine through a needle; during this era morphine addiction was known as *soldiers' disease.*

Most people are surprised to learn that until the late 1800s, opium was legally available and consumed in great quantity in many parts of the world, including Europe and North America. For example, in 1870, opiates were available in cakes, candies, and wines, as well as in a variety of over-the-counter medicinal offerings. Opium potions such as *laudanum* (a very popular mixture of opium and alcohol), *Godfrey's Cordial,* and *Dalby's Carminative* were very popular. (The word *carminative* should win first prize for making a sow's ear at least sound like a silk purse—a carminative is a drug that expels gas from the digestive tract, thus reducing stomach cramps and flatulence. *Flatulence* is the obvious pick for second prize.) There were even over-the-counter opium potions just for baby: potions such as *Mrs. Winslow's*

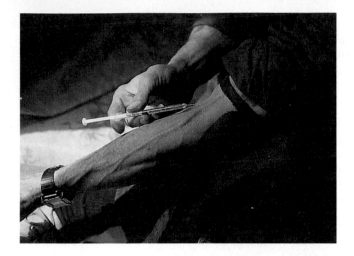

Soothing Syrup and the aptly labeled *Street's Infant Quietness* were popular in many households. Although pure morphine could not be purchased without a prescription during the late 1800s, it was so frequently prescribed by physicians for so many different maladies that morphine addiction was very common among those who could afford doctors.

The **Harrison Narcotics Act,** passed in 1914, made it illegal to sell or use opium, morphine, or cocaine in the United States. However, the Act did not include heroin. Heroin had been synthesized in 1870 by adding two acetyl groups to the morphine molecule, which greatly increased its ability to penetrate the blood-brain barrier. In 1898, heroin was marketed by the Bayer Drug Company; it was freely available without prescription and was widely advertised as a super aspirin. Tests showed that heroin was a more potent analgesic than morphine and that it was less likely to induce nausea and vomiting. Moreover, the Bayer Company, on the basis of flimsy evidence, claimed that heroin was not addictive; this is why it was not covered by the Harrison Narcotics Act. The consequence of this omission was that opiate addicts in the United States, forbidden by law to use opium or morphine, turned to the readily available and much more potent heroin, and the flames of addiction were further fanned. In 1924, the U.S. Congress made it illegal for anybody to possess, sell, or use heroin. Unfortunately, the laws enacted to stamp out opiate addiction in the United States have been far from successful: an estimated 2,000,000 Americans currently use heroin, and organized crime flourishes on the proceeds.

The effect of opiates most valued by opiate addicts is the *rush* that follows intravenous injection. The *heroin rush* is a wave of intense, abdominal, orgasmic pleasure that evolves into a state of serene, drowsy euphoria. Many opiate users, drawn by these pleasurable effects, begin to use the drug more and more frequently. Then, once they reach a point where they keep themselves drugged much of the time, tolerance and physical dependence develop and contribute to the problem. Opiate tolerance encourages addicts to progress to higher doses, to more potent drugs (e.g., heroin), and to more direct routes of administration (e.g., IV injection); and physical dependence adds to the already high motivation to take the drug.

The direct health hazards of opiate addiction are surprisingly minor. The main risks are constipation, pupil constriction, menstrual irregularity, and reduced libido (sex drive). Many opiate addicts have taken large, prescribed doses of pure heroin or morphine for years with no serious ill effects. In fact, opiate addiction is more prevalent among doctors, nurses, and dentists than among other professionals (e.g., Brewster, 1986).

> An individual tolerant to and dependent upon an opiate who is socially or financially capable of obtaining an adequate supply of good quality drug, sterile syringes and needles, and other paraphernalia may maintain his or her proper social and occupational functions, remain in fairly good health, and suffer little serious incapacitation as a result of the dependence (Julien, 1981, p. 117).

> One such individual was Dr. William Steward Halsted, one of the founders of Johns Hopkins Medical School and one of the most brilliant surgeons of his day . . . known as "the father of modern surgery." And yet, during his career he was addicted to morphine, a fact that he was able to keep secret from all but his closest friends. In fact, the only time his habit caused him any trouble was when he was attempting to reduce his dosage . . . (McKim, 1986, p. 197).

The classic heroin withdrawal syndrome usually begins 6 to 12 hours after the last dose of heroin. The first withdrawal sign is typically an increase in restlessness; the addict begins to pace and fidget. Watering eyes, running nose, yawning, and sweating are also common during the early stages of heroin withdrawal. Then the addict often falls into a fitful sleep called the *yen*, which typically lasts for several hours. After the sleep is over, the original symptoms may be joined in extreme cases by chills, shivering, profuse sweating, goose-flesh, nausea, vomiting, diarrhea, cramps, pains, dilated pupils, tremor, and muscle spasms. The goose-flesh skin and leg spasms of the opiate withdrawal syndrome are the basis for the expressions "going cold turkey" and "kicking the habit." The symptoms are typically most severe in the second or third days after the last injection, and by the seventh day they have all but disappeared. The symptoms of opiate withdrawal are not trivial, but their severity has been widely exaggerated. Opiate withdrawal is about as serious as a bad case of the flu—a far cry from the convulsions, delirium, and risk of death associated with alcohol withdrawal.

> Opiate withdrawal is probably one of the most misunderstood aspects of drug use. This is largely because of the image of withdrawal that has been portrayed in the movies and popular literature for many years. . . . Few addicts . . . take enough drug to cause the . . . severe withdrawal symptoms that are shown in the movies. Even in its most severe form, however, opiate withdrawal is not as dangerous or terrifying as withdrawal from **barbiturates** or alcohol. (McKim, 1986, p. 199)

Because opiates create relatively few direct health problems for those addicts with an affordable source of pure drug, the main risks of opiate addiction are indirect. They are risks that arise out of the battle between the relentless addictive power of opiates and the attempts of governments to eradicate them by making them illegal. The opiate addicts who cannot give up their habits—treatment programs report success rates of only 10%—are caught in the middle. Because most opiate addicts must purchase their morphine and heroin from illicit dealers at greatly inflated prices, those who are not wealthy become trapped in a life of poverty and petty crime. They are poor, they are undernourished, they receive poor medical care, they are often driven to prostitution, and they run great risk of contracting AIDS and other infections from unsterile needles. Moreover, they never know for sure what they are injecting: some street drugs are poorly processed, and virtually all have been *cut* (stretched by adding some similar-appearing substance to it) to some unknown degree. The exact number of heroin-related deaths is impossible to determine, but their number is substantial, and it is likely to increase in the next few years as the number of drug-related cases of AIDS goes up. What makes these deaths particularly tragic is that many of them seem to be caused by the very laws that were designed to prevent them.

Comparison of the Hazards of Tobacco, Alcohol, Marijuana, Cocaine, and Heroin

One way of comparing the adverse effects of tobacco, alcohol, marijuana, cocaine, and heroin is to compare the prevalence of their use in society as a whole. In terms of this criterion (see Figure 13.5), it is clear that tobacco and alcohol have a far greater impact than do marijuana, cocaine, and heroin. But what about the individual drug user? Who is taking greater risks with his or her health: the cigarette smoker, the alcohol drinker, the marijuana smoker, the cocaine user, or the heroin user? You now have the information to answer this question. I have included the following tables to help you in your analysis. First, list all of the demonstrated major health hazards of each of the five drugs—be sure to focus on direct hazards of the drug, not on indirect hazards created by its legal and social status. Then, on the basis of your five lists, rank the five drugs in terms of their overall health risks. Would you have ranked the drugs in the same way before you read this chapter?

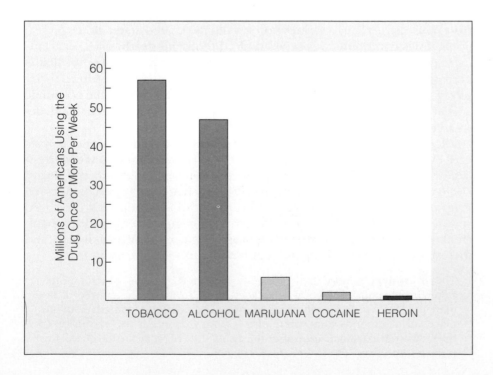

FIGURE 13.5

Prevalence of drug use in the United States. Figures are based on a survey of people 12 years of age and over who live in households. (Adapted from Goldstein and Kalant, 1990.)

SELF TEST

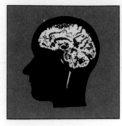

List the major direct health hazards of the following five drugs. Omit indirect hazards that result from the drugs' legal or social status.

Tobacco	Alcohol	Marijuana	Cocaine	Heroin
1. _____	1. _____	1. _____	1. _____	1. _____
2. _____	2. _____	2. _____	2. _____	2. _____
3. _____	3. _____	3. _____	3. _____	3. _____
4. _____	4. _____	4. _____	4. _____	4. _____
5. _____	5. _____	5. _____	5. _____	5. _____
6. _____	6. _____	6. _____	6. _____	6. _____

On the basis of comparisons among your five lists, rate the five drugs in terms of the overall dangerousness of their direct health hazards.

Most Hazardous   1. _____

                        2. _____

                        3. _____

                        4. _____

Least Hazardous   5. _____

The Drug Dilemmas: Striking the Right Balance

Drug abuse is currently a serious problem. In the United States alone, recreational drugs contribute to several hundred thousand deaths each year. Furthermore, the public must bear the brunt of the crime and violence that is perpetrated by addicts, who are often forced to steal and prostitute themselves to fuel their expensive habits; the public must also bear the economic burdens of increased medical care, increased law enforcement, and decreased productivity.

Recently, several eminent psychopharmacologists and political scientists have evaluated the American approach to drug control in the light of current data; they all recommended sweeping changes—see Goldstein and Kalant (1990), Jarvik (1990), and Nadelman (1989). Each of these experts concluded that the current American system of drug control is both poorly conceived and ineffective. The following quotes provide glimpses of their disenchantment with a system that treats addiction as a crime, rather than a disease, and tries to combat it by reducing the supply and punishing the users.

> The investment of more than 70% of the federal [U.S.] drug control money into supply reduction seems misplaced. . . . Curtailing the supply of demanded drugs has been compared to squeezing a balloon: constrict it in one place and it expands somewhere else. . . . An example is the expansion of the California marijuana crop after the availability of Mexican marijuana was reduced (Jarvik, p. 339).

> The greatest beneficiaries of the drug laws are . . . drug traffickers. More than half of all organized crime revenues are believed to derive from the illicit drug business. (Nadelman, p. 941).

> Drug treatment programs remain notoriously underfunded, turning away tens of thousands of addicts seeking help even as increasing billions of dollars are spent to arrest, prosecute, and imprison illegal drug . . . users. (Nadelman, p. 942).

The experts differ with the American public about what to do about the drug problem. The experts say (1) that there is no way of stopping the supply—every major drug bust merely increases the street prices of drugs and encourages more illicit suppliers to enter the market; (2) that it makes little sense to persecute and punish the sick and the weak; and (3) that it is hypocritical to take Draconian measures against some drugs while allowing others that are more dangerous to be openly advertised. Recent surveys suggest that the American public, frustrated with the drug problem and not understanding the issues, want even more money to be spent on the approach that is currently proving so ineffective.

The following are some of the recommendations that have been made by the experts: (1) The only way of reducing recreational drug use is by reducing the demand; some of the billions that are currently being spent on arresting and supporting drug users in crowded jails would be better spent on education, research, and social programs. (2) More emphasis should be placed on caring for addicts rather than persecuting them. (3) Unlike the current laws, the laws that govern drug use should be enforceable and they should be tailored to the hazards of each drug. (4) Judges should be given greater discretion in sentencing; for example, the current 5-year minimum sentence for anybody caught sharing a small amount of heroin or cocaine with a friend is unduly harsh. (5) All cigarette and alcohol advertising should be curtailed. (6) The possession of small amounts of marijuana for personal use has been legalized in some parts of the country; the effects of this legalization should be carefully monitored. If it does not lead to a significant increase in use, other states should follow suit to allow the legal system to focus on more serious problems. (7) Experimental clinics should be established in which addicts, as a first step in their treatment, are provided with small daily doses of their drug. The potential advantages of such programs are many: they would encourage addicts to enter treatment; they would bring addicts in contact with health care professionals who are experienced in dealing with the health problems of addicts (e.g., AIDS and malnutrition); they would allow some addicts who have not been able to shake their habits to live reasonably normal, productive lives; and they would reduce the amount of drug-related crime. (8) And finally, lessons should be learned from countries such as England and Holland that have successfully taken approaches to drug control that are more in tune with the preceding recommendations.

One does not normally find a discussion of legal and social policy in a biopsychology textbook. Please excuse my digression, but I believe that the drug problem is a serious one and that biopsychologists have important things to say about it. They have a responsibility to bring the relevant research literature to the attention of policy makers and the educated public. I hope that I have interested you enough to pursue the issue further—the articles of Goldstein and Kalant (1990), Jarvik (1990), and Nadelman (1989) are a good place to start.

13.3

Biopsychological Theories of Addiction and Reward Circuits in the Brain

So far in this chapter, you have been introduced to some basic psychopharma-cological concepts (Section 13.1); to five commonly abused drugs (Section 13.2); and to some of the social, legal, and political implications of biopsychological research on drug abuse (Section 13.2). This, the third and final section of the chapter, focuses on a theory of addiction that links it to activity in a particular circuit in the brain: the *mesotelencephalic dopamine pathway*.

Physical-Dependence Theories of Addiction

Early attempts to explain the phenomenon of drug addiction attributed it to physical dependence. According to the **physical-dependence theory of addiction**, physical dependence traps addicts in a vicious circle of drug taking and withdrawal symptoms. The idea was that drug users whose intake had reached a level sufficient to induce physical dependence were driven by their withdrawal symptoms to self-administer the drug each time they attempted to curtail their intake.

Early drug-addiction treatment programs were based on the physical-dependence theory of addiction. They attempted to break the vicious circle of drug taking by gradually withdrawing drugs from addicts in a hospital environment—gradual withdrawal produces less severe withdrawal symptoms than does sudden withdrawal. Unfortunately, once discharged, almost all of the **detoxified addicts** (addicts who have none of the drug to which they are addicted in their body and are no longer experiencing withdrawal symptoms) returned to their former drug-taking habits. The failure of this approach to treatment is not surprising for two reasons. First, some highly addictive drugs, such as cocaine, do not produce severe withdrawal distress (see Gawin, 1991). Second, the pattern of drug taking routinely displayed by many addicts involves an alternating cycle of binges and detoxification (Mello & Mendelson, 1972). There are a variety of reasons for this pattern of drug use; for example, some addicts adopt it because weekend binges are compatible with their work schedule, others adopt it because they do not have enough money to use drugs continuously, and still others have it forced on them because their binges often land them in jail. In some ways, the most pitiful of the addicted intermittent drug users are those who keep trying to quit, but each time are drawn back to drug use. The point is that whether detoxification is by choice or necessity, it does not stop an addict from renewing her or his drug-taking habit.

Modern physical-dependence theories of drug addiction attempt to account for the fact that addicts frequently relapse after lengthy drug-free periods by postulating that withdrawal symptoms can be conditioned (e.g., Ludwig & Wikler, 1974; O'Brien, Ternes, Grabowski, & Ehrman, 1981; Wikler, 1980). According to this theory, when addicts who have remained drug-free for a considerable period of time return to a situation in which they have previously experienced the drug, conditioned withdrawal effects opposite to the effects of the drug (Siegel's hypothesized conditioned compensatory responses) are elicited. These conditioned withdrawal effects are presumed to result in a powerful craving for the drug to counteract them. Although there is good evidence that conditioned withdrawal effects can occur in some situations (see Siegel, 1983), the theory that *relapse* is motivated by an attempt to counteract them encounters two major problems (see Eikelboom & Stewart, 1982; Zelman, Tiffany, & Baker, 1985). One is that many of the effects elicited by environments that have previously been associated with drug administration are similar to those of the drug rather than being antagonistic to them (Stewart & Eikelboom, 1987). The second is that experimental animals and addicts often display a preference for drug-predictive cues, even when no drug is forthcoming (e.g., Bozarth & Wise, 1981; Mucha, Van der Kooy, O'Shaughnessy, & Bucenieks, 1982; White, Sklar, & Amit, 1977). For example, some detoxified heroin addicts called *needle freaks* derive pleasure from sticking an empty needle into themselves (Levine, 1974; O'Brien, Chaddock, Woody, & Greenstein, 1974). It seems unlikely that relapse could be motivated by an attempt to suppress conditioned drug effects that are either similar to the effects of the drug, pleasurable, or both.

Positive-Incentive Theories of Addiction

The failure of physical-dependence theories to fully account for the major aspects of addiction has lent support to the theory that the primary reason that most addicts take drugs is not to escape or avoid the unpleasant consequences of withdrawal or conditioned withdrawal, but rather to obtain the drugs' pleasurable effects. This **positive-incentive theory of addiction** acknowledges that addicts may sometimes self-administer drugs to suppress withdrawal symptoms or to escape from other unpleasant aspects of their existence, but they hold that the primary factor in most cases of addiction is the craving for the positive-incentive (pleasure-producing) properties of the drugs (McAuliffe et al., 1986; Stewart, de Wit, & Eikelboom, 1984). Strong anecdotal support for this view comes from the addicts themselves:

> I'm just trying to get high as much as possible. I would have to spend $25 a day on heroin to avoid withdrawal, but I actually use about $50 worth. If I could get more money, I would spend it all on drugs. All I want is to get loaded. I just really like shooting dope. I don't have any use for sex; I'd rather shoot dope. I like to shoot dope better than anything else in the world. I have to steal something every day to get my dope.

Notice that the evolution of theories of addiction from physical-dependence to positive-incentive theories reflects the general trend in the study of motivation. You have already learned in the preceding chapters that eating, drinking, sexual behavior, and sleeping appear to be motivated by the anticipation of pleasure rather than deviations from homeostasis.

Some of the pleasurable effects of drugs may not be direct. Most drugs of addiction have been reported to have **disinhibitory effects;** they release from inhibition behaviors that are usually not performed because of inhibitory factors that normally suppress them (Pfaus & Pinel, 1989). All you have to do is go to your local "singles bar" to see the ability of alcohol to release various forms of courtship behavior from inhibition. If engaging in such normally inhibited behaviors is pleasurable, it could very well be an indirect, but important, motivating factor in some cases of drug addiction, particularly during the early phases. As far as I know, no psychopharmacologists have tested this theory.

The Intracranial-Self-Stimulation Phenomenon

Attempts to understand the neural basis of addiction have focused on the study of **intracranial self-stimulation (ICS),** a phenomenon that was discovered by Olds and Milner in 1954. Olds and Milner found that rats will repeatedly press a lever to administer brief bursts of electrical stimulation to specific sites in their own brains. They argued that the brain sites that animals will self-stimulate are those that normally mediate the pleasurable effects of rewarding stimuli—stimuli such as food, water, sex, and addictive drugs. Since Olds and Milner's important discovery, many species other than rats have been shown to engage in self-stimulation behavior—for example, fish (Boyd & Gardner, 1962) and humans (Bishop, Elder, & Heath, 1963).

The discovery of intracranial self-stimulation provided researchers with a technique for studying the neural basis of pleasure, and with increasing acceptance of the idea that pleasure is the primary motivating factor in drug addiction, the study of intracranial self-stimulation began to have a major impact on ideas about the neural basis of addiction. Many researchers now believe that the neural circuits that mediate intracranial self-stimulation are the very ones that mediate the rewarding effects of addictive drugs. Accordingly, this chapter digresses for a few pages to describe the fundamentals of intracranial self-stimulation before linking them to the topic of drug addiction.

Early studies of intracranial self-stimulation were based on the assumption that it is a unitary phenomenon; that is, they were based on the assumption that the fundamental properties of intracranial self-stimulation are the same regardless of the site of stimulation. Most early studies of intracranial self-stimulation involved septal or lateral hypothalamic stimulation because the rates of self-stimulation from these sites are spectacularly high—rats typically press a lever thousands of times per hour for stimulation of these sites, stopping only after they have become exhausted. Illustrated in Figure 13.6 is a rat lever pressing for electrical brain stimulation.

Early studies of intracranial self-stimulation suggested that lever pressing for brain stimulation was fundamentally different from lever pressing for natural reinforcers such as food or water. Two puzzling observations contributed to this view. First, despite their extremely high response rates, many rats stopped pressing the self-stimulation lever almost immediately when the current-delivery mechanism was shut off. This finding was puzzling because high rates of operant responding are generally assumed to indicate that the reinforcer is particularly pleasurable, whereas rapid rates of *extinction* are usually assumed to indicate that it is not. Would you stop pressing a lever that had been delivering $100 bills the first few times that a press did not produce one? Second, experienced self-stimulators often did not recommence lever pressing when they were returned to the apparatus after being briefly removed from it. In such cases, the rats had to be **primed** by a few free stimulations to get them going again—the experimenter simply pressed the lever a couple of times, and the hesitant rat immediately began to self-stimulate at a high rate once again.

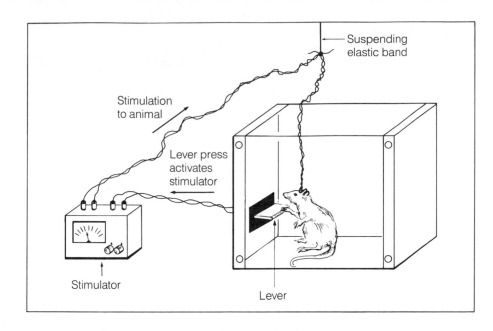

FIGURE 13.6
A rat pressing a lever for
rewarding brain stimulation.

These differences between lever pressing for rewarding lateral hypothalamic or septal stimulation and lever pressing for food or water seemed to
discredit Olds and Milner's original theory that intracranial self-stimulation
involves the activation of natural reward circuits in the brain. Accordingly,
many of the investigators who studied self-stimulation in the 1950s and 60s
viewed it as some kind of artifact—albeit a particularly interesting one. However, since then, the pendulum of opinion has swung back to its original position, and the current consensus seems to be that the circuits mediating intracranial self-stimulation phenomena are reward circuits.

The return to the reward-circuit view of intracranial self-stimulation was
based on four kinds of evidence. First, brain stimulation through electrodes
that mediate self-stimulation often elicits natural motivated behaviors such as
eating, drinking, maternal behavior, and copulation in the presence of the
appropriate goal objects. This evidence led Glickman and Schiff (1967) to
suggest that the activation of circuits that produce species-typical motivated
behaviors is the physiological basis of reward. Second, increasing levels of
natural motivation (for example, by food or water deprivation, by hormone
injections, or by the presence of prey objects) often increases self-stimulation
rates (e.g., Caggiula, 1970). Third, lever pressing for stimulation at some
brain sites (other than the lateral hypothalamus and septum on which the
early studies focused) is often quite similar to lever pressing for natural rewards (i.e., acquisition is slow, response rates are low, extinction is slow, and
priming is not necessary). And fourth, it became clear that subtle differences
between the situations in which rewarding brain stimulation and natural rewards were usually studied contributed to the impression that their rewarding effects are qualitatively different. For example, comparisons between
lever pressing for food and lever pressing for brain stimulation are usually
confounded by the fact that subjects pressing for brain stimulation are nondeprived and by the fact that the lever press delivers the reward directly and

immediately. In contrast, in studies of lever pressing for natural rewards, subjects are often deprived and they press a lever for a food pellet or drop of water that they then must approach and consume to experience rewarding effects. In a clever experiment, Panksepp and Trowill (1967) eliminated these confounds and found that some of the major differences between lever pressing for food and lever pressing for brain stimulation disappeared. When non-deprived rats lever pressed to inject a small quantity of chocolate milk directly into their mouths through an intraoral tube, they behaved remarkably like self-stimulating rats; they quickly learned to lever press, they pressed at high rates, they extinguished quickly, and some even had to be primed.

The Medial Forebrain Bundle and Intracranial Self-Stimulation

A theory that resulted from the early research on intracranial self-stimulation was that the rewarding effects of brain stimulation are mediated by a single neural system: the **medial forebrain bundle (MFB)** (Olds & Olds, 1963). The medial forebrain bundle is a large, complex bundle of fibers that courses directly through the lateral hypothalamus and innervates the septum, as well as a variety of other structures that support intracranial self-stimulation. It includes both ascending and descending axons, as well as numerous interneurons. Three lines of evidence argued against the notion that activation of the medial forebrain bundle is the critical event underlying the reinforcing effects of brain stimulation. First, animals were found to lever press for stimulation to a variety of brain structures (see Figure 13.7) that have no direct connection to the medial forebrain bundle. Second, extensive lesions of the medial forebrain bundle were found to have little effect on septal self-stimulation (Valenstein & Campbell, 1966). And third, 2-deoxyglucose studies (see Chapter 5) indicated that although rewarding brain stimulation to the medial forebrain bundle activates the bundle (Gallistel, Gomita, Yadin, & Campbell, 1985), rewarding brain stimulation applied to other sites does not (e.g., medial prefrontal cortex; Yadin, Guarini, & Gallistel, 1983). Notice that these three lines of evidence do not prove that the medial forebrain bundle does not mediate the rewarding effects of stimulation to some brain sites; they simply prove that the medial forebrain bundle does not mediate all intracranial self-stimulation. In fact, one component of the medial forebrain bundle, the mesotelencephalic dopamine system, has been strongly implicated in intracranial self-stimulation at several sites, and as you are about to learn, it has been also implicated in drug addiction.

The Mesotelencephalic Dopamine System

The **mesotelencephalic dopamine system** refers to the ascending projections of dopamine-releasing neurons from the mesencephalon (midbrain) into various regions of the telencephalon (see Chapter 3). It courses through the lateral hypothalamus as part of the medial forebrain bundle. As indicated in Figure 13.8, the neurons that compose the mesotelencephalic dopamine system have their cell bodies in two different midbrain nuclei, the **substantia nigra** and the more medial **ventral tegmental area,** and their axons project to a variety of telencephalic sites, including specific regions of prefrontal

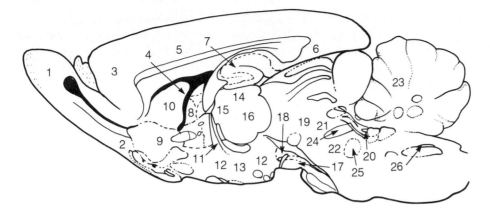

FIGURE 13.7

The major intracranial self-stimulation sites in the rat brain. (Adapted from Phillips & Fibiger, 1989.)

TELENCEPHALON
1. Olfactory Bulb
2. Prepyriform Cortex
3. Prefrontal Cortex
4. Subfornical organ
5. Cingulate Cortex
6. Entorhinal Cortex
7. Hippocampus
8. Septum
9. Nucleus Accumbens
10. Striatum

DIENCEPHALON
11. Fornix
12. Lateral Hypothalamus
13. Ventromedial Hypothalamus
14. Mediodorsal Nucleus of Thalamus
15. Nucleus Paratenialis of Thalamus
16. Central Nucleus of Thalamus

MESENCEPHALON
17. Substantia Nigra
18. Ventral Tegmental Area
19. Periaqueductal Grey
20. Mesencephalic Nucleus of Trigeminal Nerve
21. Dorsal Raphé
22. Median Raphé

METENCEPHALON
23. Cerebellum
24. Superior Cerebellar Peduncle
25. Motor Nucleus of Trigeminal Nerve

MYELENCEPHALON
26. Nucleus Tractus Solitarius

STRUCTURES NOT SHOWN
Globus Pallidus
Amygdala
Habenula

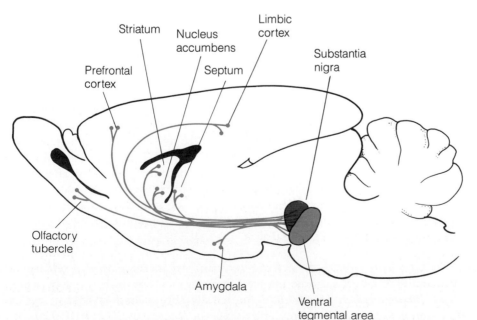

FIGURE 13.8

The mesotelencephalic dopamine system.

neocortex and limbic cortex, the nucleus accumbens (a nucleus adjacent to the septum), the olfactory tubercle, the amygdala, the septum, and the striatum. It was originally thought that all of the dopamine neurons in the substantia nigra project to the striatum and that all of those arising in the ventral tegmental area project to limbic and cortical structures. However, recent research has revealed a considerable intermingling of these projections, and the original distinction between the so-called *nigrostriatal pathway* and the *mesocortical limbic pathway* has become blurred (Björkland & Lindvall, 1986). Because the role of the mesotelencephalic dopamine system in intracranial self-stimulation and drug self-administration is the focus of the following two subsections, you might find it useful to review Figure 13.8 before proceeding.

The Mesotelencephalic Dopamine System and Intracranial Self-Stimulation

Although it is generally acknowledged that animals stimulate their brains for a variety of rewarding effects and that these different effects are likely mediated by different neural systems, some researchers believe that the mesotelencephalic dopamine system plays a particularly important role in the rewarding effects of the brain stimulation (e.g., Bozarth, 1987; Phillips & Fibiger, 1989; Porrino, 1987; Wise & Rompre, 1989). Four kinds of experiments have supported this view: (1) mapping experiments, (2) dopamine-turnover experiments, (3) 2-deoxyglucose experiments, and (4) unilateral brain lesion experiments.

Mapping experiments   After Routtenberg and Malsbury (1969) established that rats will lever press for mesencephalic stimulation, Crow (1972) carefully mapped the area and found that the positive mesencephalic self-stimulation sites were in the substantia nigra or ventral tegmental area. Subsequently, Corbett and Wise (1980) conducted a study in which movable electrodes were used to identify positive and negative intracranial self-stimulation sites along the track of each electrode. Then, the brains were sectioned along the electrode track and subjected to **fluorescence histochemistry** (exposing neural tissue to formaldehyde vapor and viewing it through a fluorescence microscope reveals monoamine-containing neurons; see Figure 4.14) to identify the precise location of dopamine-containing cell bodies. Corbett and Wise found that the current thresholds for self-stimulation were lower and response rates were higher in the areas of the substantia nigra and ventral tegmental area in which the dopaminergic neurons were most dense. The research of Shizgal and his colleagues (e.g., Bielajew & Schizgal, 1986; Shizgal & Murray, 1989) suggests that the mesotelencephalic dopamine system may also mediate the rewarding effects of stimulation to sites other than the substantia nigra and ventral tegmental area. They showed, for example, that rewarding stimulation of the lateral hypothalamus activates nondopaminergic neurons that project to the ventral tegmental area.

Dopamine-metabolism experiments   An increase in the release of dopamine in an area can be inferred from an increase in the ratio between *3, 4 dihydroxyphenylacetic acid* (mercifully abbreviated **DOPAC**), one of dopamine's major metabolites, and dopamine. Increases in the DOPAC/dopamine ratio in various terminals of the mesotelencephalic dopamine system have been reported after bouts of ventral tegmental area (Fibiger, LePiane, Jakubovic, & Phillips, 1987) or lateral hypothalamic (Garrigues & Cazala, 1983) self-stimulation. These increases in dopamine release were seen only at dopamine terminals ipsilateral to the stimulation site, thus indicating that they were not attributable to the general increase in motor activity that occurs during intracranial self-stimulation.

2-deoxyglucose experiments Porrino and her colleagues (Porrino, 1987; Porrino, Esposito, Seeger, Crane, Pert, & Sokoloff, 1984) have used the *2-deoxyglucose technique* (see Chapter 5) to study the patterns of increased neural activity that are associated with self-stimulation of the ventral tegmental area and the substantia nigra. There were some differences in the patterns of activity that were associated with self-stimulation at the two sites, but in both cases high levels of 2-deoxyglucose accumulated in the prefrontal cortex, nucleus accumbens, septum, and mediodorsal thalamus, thus suggesting that activity in these terminals of the mesotelencephalic dopamine system mediates the rewarding effects of mesencephalic stimulation.

Lesion experiments Convincing evidence that the mesotelencephalic dopamine system can mediate brain-stimulation reward comes from studies in which the system has been destroyed unilaterally by injections of *6-hydroxydopamine* (6-OHDA; see Chapter 5). For example, Fibiger, LePiane, Jakubovic, and Phillips (1987) showed that 6-OHDA lesions ipsilateral to a stimulation electrode in the ventral tegmental area reduced self-stimulation, whereas contralateral lesions did not. The fact that contralateral lesions produced no deficit suggests that general motor deficits produced by the lesions did not contribute to the decline in self-stimulation rate.

The Mesotelencephalic Dopamine System and the Rewarding Effects of Addictive Drugs

Evidence that the mesotelencephalic dopamine system mediates the rewarding effects of intracranial stimulation led to the hypothesis that it also mediates the rewarding effects of addictive drugs (see Koob & Bloom, 1988) — which brings us back to the main point of this section. Many of the experiments that have tested this hypothesis have employed the **drug self-administration paradigm** (see Yokel, 1987), which was developed to approximate human drug addiction. In drug self-administration experiments, laboratory rats or primates can press a lever to inject drugs into themselves through implanted cannulas. They readily learn to press a lever to inject the drugs to which humans become addicted, and once they have learned to self-administer an addictive drug, their drug-taking behavior often mimics the drug taking of human addicts. For those researchers interested in the neural basis of addiction, drug self-administration studies in which the lever press injects minute quantities of the drug directly into particular brain sites have proven particularly enlightening (see Bozarth, 1987; Koob, Vaccarino, Amalric, & Bloom, 1987); however, the neural substrates of only opiate and stimulant (i.e., amphetamine and cocaine) self-administration have been extensively investigated in this fashion (Wise, 1987).

Neural substrates of opiate reward   To determine whether the rein-forcing properties of opiates are mediated by their action on central or on peripheral opiate receptors, Koob, Pettit, Ettenberg, and Bloom (1984) ad-ministered one of two opiate antagonists (see Chapter 4) to rats that were self-administering intravenous injections of heroin. One opiate antagonist was **naloxone,** which readily penetrates the blood-brain barrier and enters the CNS; the other was a derivative of naloxone, which does not. They found that the injections of the naloxone at low doses produced a temporary in-crease in the self-administration of heroin, whereas injections of the deriva-tive had no effect. This suggests that the reinforcing effects of opiates are mediated by their effects within the CNS. (At first glance, the finding that an opiate antagonist increases opiate self-administration might seem counterin-tuitive. The idea is that because naloxone counteracts the effects of heroin, the rats self-administer more to produce the same degree of reinforcement—just as addicts take larger doses of weaker drugs.)

Three lines of evidence suggest that the rewarding effects of opiates are mediated by the mesotelencephalic dopamine system. First, rats have been shown to lever press for microinjections of opiates into either the ventral teg-mental area (e.g., Phillips & LePiane, 1980) or the nucleus accumbens (e.g., Goeders, Lane, & Smith, 1984)—Bozarth and Wise (1982) showed that rats that self-administer morphine to the ventral tegmental area are not physically dependent, thus supporting the positive-incentive theory of addiction. Sec-ond, microinjections of opiate antagonists into the ventral tegmental area and nucleus accumbens have been shown to increase the intravenous self-administration of opiates (Britt & Wise, 1983; Vaccarino, Pettit, Bloom, & Koob, 1985). And third, dopamine antagonists (Phillips, Spyraki, & Fibiger, 1982) or electrolytic lesions to the nucleus accumbens (Kelsey, Carlezon, & Falls, 1989) have been shown to prevent the development of opiate-induced preferences in the **conditioned place-preference paradigm.** Normally, if opiates are administered to rats in a distinctive chamber of a two- or three-chamber test apparatus, they prefer to stay in the opiate-paired compartment during a subsequent test, during which no drugs are administered. The main advantage of the condition place-preference paradigm is that the subjects are tested in the absence of drugs, which means that a measure of the incentive value of a drug can be obtained that is unconfounded by other effects that the drugs might have on behavior (see Carr, Fibiger, & Phillips, 1989; Van der Kooy, 1987).

Neural substrates of stimulant reward   Both cocaine and amphet-amine increase transmission at both dopaminergic and noradrenergic syn-apses, cocaine by blocking reuptake of dopamine and norepinephrine from synapses and amphetamine by both blocking their reuptake and increasing their release. Current evidence suggests that the rewarding effects of cocaine and amphetamine are attributable specifically to their dopaminergic effects (see Wise & Bozarth, 1987). Dopamine antagonists, but not norepinephrine antagonists, have been shown to block the rewarding effects of intravenous stimulants (e.g., Goeders, Dworkin, & Smith, 1986; Risner & Jones, 1980) in rats and their euphoria-producing effects in humans (Gunne, Änggård, & Jönsson, 1972).

The involvement of the mesotelencephalic dopamine system in stimulant-produced reward has been established in three ways (see Kuhar, Ritz, & Boja,

1991): (1) by demonstrations that dopamine-depleting lesions of either the ventral tegmental area (Roberts & Koob, 1982) or the nucleus accumbens (Roberts, Corcoran, & Fibiger, 1977; Roberts, Koob, Klonoff, & Fibiger, 1980)—but not of the other terminal structures of the mesotelencephalic dopamine system (Roberts & Zito, 1987)—disrupt intravenous self-administration of amphetamine; (2) by studies showing that rats will lever press for microinjections of amphetamine directly into the nucleus accumbens (Hoebel, Monaco, Hernandez, Aulisi, Stanley, & Lenard, 1983); and (3) by a PET scan study in human subjects that found that the time course of cocaine-induced euphoria parallels the binding of the cocaine at dopamine synapses in the striatum (Fowler et al., 1989).

Conclusion

In Section 13.1, you were introduced to basic pharmacological concepts and phenomena; recent psychopharmacological studies of the situational specificity and response contingency of drug tolerance were highlighted. Section 13.2 discussed five commonly abused drugs: tobacco, alcohol, marijuana, cocaine, and heroin; current scientific knowledge about these five drugs was presented within a historical and legal context, and the gaps that exist between common belief, legal status, and scientific findings were emphasized. Finally, Section 13.3 argued that the pleasure-producing effects of drugs, rather than their ability to suppress withdrawal symptoms, is the primary factor in addiction. Recent studies of rewarding brain stimulation and drug self-administration suggest that the mesotelencephalic dopamine system mediates the pleasure-producing effects of some addictive drugs.

To illustrate in a more personal way some of the things that you have learned about addiction, this chapter concludes with a series of quotes that describe the interactions of one drug addict with two drugs of abuse: cocaine and tobacco. The addict was Sigmund Freud, a man of very special significance to psychology. Freud's battles with these two drugs have sobering implications. The following excerpts are from a report written in 1972 by Edward Brecher.

> The chief ingredient in coca leaves, the alkaloid cocaine, was isolated in pure form in 1844. Little use was made of it in Europe, however, until 1883, when a German army physician . . . issued it to Bavarian soldiers during their autumn maneuvers. . . .
>
> Among those who read [the] . . . account with fascination was a poverty-stricken twenty-eight-year-old Viennese neurologist, Dr. Sigmund Freud. . . . "I have been reading about cocaine, the essential ingredient of coca leaves, which some Indian tribes chew to enable them to resist privations and hardships," Freud wrote his fiancée, Martha Bernays, on April 21, 1884. "I am procuring some myself and will try it. . . . "
>
> In addition to taking cocaine himself, Freud offered some to his friend and associate, Dr. Ernst von Fleischl-Marxow, who was suffering from an exceedingly painful disease of the nervous system, and who was addicted to morphine. . . .
>
> Freud even sent some of this precious cocaine to Martha. . . . "he pressed it on his friends and colleagues, both for themselves and their patients; he gave it to his sisters. In short, looked at from the vantage point of

present knowledge, he was rapidly becoming a public menace." (pp. 272–273)

Freud's famous essay "Song of Praise" to cocaine was published in July 1884. In this article, Freud wrote in such glowing terms about his own personal experiences with cocaine that he created a wave of interest in the drug. But within a year, there was a critical reaction to Freud's premature advocacy.

In July 1885, a German authority on morphine addiction named Erlenmeyer launched the first of a series of attacks on cocaine as an addicting drug. In January 1886 Freud's friend Obersteiner, who had first favored cocaine, reported that it produced severe mental disturbances [later called cocaine psychosis]. . . . Other attacks soon followed; and Freud was subjected to "grave reproaches." Freud continued to praise cocaine as late as July 1887. . . . But soon thereafter he discontinued all use of it both personally and professionally. Despite the fact that he had been taking cocaine periodically over a three-year span, he appears to have had no difficulty in stopping. (p. 274)

Some 9 years later in 1894, when Freud was 38, his physician and close friend ordered him to stop smoking because it was causing a heart arrhythmia. Freud was a heavy smoker; he smoked approximately 20 cigars per day.

Freud did stop for a time . . . but his subsequent depression and other withdrawal symptoms proved unbearable. . . .

Within seven weeks, Freud was smoking again.

On a later occasion, Freud stopped smoking for fourteen very long months. . . .

More than fifteen years later, at the age of fifty-five, Freud was still smoking twenty cigars a day—and still struggling against his addiction. [In a letter written at the time, he commented on the sudden intolerance of his heart for tobacco.]

Four years later he wrote . . . that his passion for smoking hindered his analytic studies. Yet he kept on smoking.

In February 1923, at the age of sixty-seven, Freud noted sores on his right palate and jaw that failed to heal. They were cancers. An operation was performed—the first of thirty-three operations for cancer of the jaw and oral cavity which he endured during the sixteen remaining years of his life. "I am still out of work and cannot swallow," he wrote shortly after his first operation. "Smoking is accused as the etiology [i.e., cause] of this tissue rebellion." Yet he continued to smoke.

In addition to his series of cancers . . . Freud now suffered attacks of "tobacco angina" [i.e., heart pains] whenever he smoked. . . . Yet he continued to smoke.

At seventy-three, Freud was ordered to retire to a sanitarium for his heart condition. He made an immediate recovery [because he stopped smoking] . . . for twenty-three days. Then he started smoking one cigar a day. Then two. Then three or four. . . .

In 1936, at the age of seventy-nine . . . Freud had more heart trouble. . . . His jaw had by then been entirely removed and an artificial jaw substituted; he was in almost constant pain; often he could not speak and sometimes he could not chew or swallow. Yet at the age of eighty-one, Freud was still smoking what . . . , his close friend at this period, calls, "an endless series of cigars."

Freud died of cancer in 1939. . . . (pp. 214–215)

Food for Thought

1. There are many misconceptions about drug abuse. Describe three. What do you think are the reasons for these misconceptions?

2. A man who had been a heroin user for many years was found dead of an overdose at a holiday resort. He appeared to have been in good health, and no foul play was suspected. What factors might have led to his death?

3. If you had an opportunity to redraft the current legislation related to drug abuse in the light of what you have learned in this chapter, what changes would you make? Why?

KEY TERMS

To help you study the material in this chapter, all of the key terms—those that have appeared in bold type—are listed and briefly defined here.

Addicts. Those drug users who continue to use a drug despite the adverse effects of the drug on their health and life, and despite their repeated efforts to stop using it.

Amotivational syndrome. Chronic lack of motivation produced by drug use; marijuana is thought by some people to produce amotivational syndrome.

Amphetamine. A stimulant drug that blocks the reuptake of dopamine and norepinephrine and increases their release.

Analgesic. Pain-killing.

Barbiturates. A class of depressant drugs; the barbiturate withdrawal syndrome is similar to the alcohol withdrawal syndrome.

Before-and-after design. An experimental design used to demonstrate contingent drug tolerance; the experimental group receives the drug before each of a series of behavioral tests, while the control group receives the drug after each test.

Buerger's disease. A nicotine-produced disease in which blood flow to the legs is restricted; it ultimately results in gangrene, which requires amputation.

Cannabis sativa. The common hemp plant; the source of marijuana.

Cirrhosis. Scarring; cirrhosis of the liver is caused by alcohol.

Cocaine hydrochloride. A strong stimulant and analgesic that is extracted from coca paste.

Cocaine psychosis. Psychotic behavior observed during a cocaine spree; it is similar in many respects to schizophrenia.

Cocaine sprees. Binges of cocaine use.

Codeine. A weak psychoactive ingredient in opium.

Conditioned compensatory responses. Responses elicited by stimuli that are regularly associated with drug taking; they are opposite to the effects of the drug, and they are thought to contribute to tolerance development.

Conditioned-place-preference paradigm. A test that assesses an animal's preference for environments in which it has previously experienced drug effects.

Crack. The free-base form of cocaine.

Cross tolerance. When exposure to one drug creates tolerance to another drug.

Delirium tremens (DTs). A phase of the alcohol withdrawal syndrome characterized by hallucinations, delusions, and extremely agitated behavior.

Delta-9-THC. The main psychoactive ingredient of marijuana.

Depressants. A class of drugs that depress neural activity and behavior (e.g., alcohol and barbiturates).

Detoxified addicts. Addicts who have none of the drug to which they are addicted in their body and who are no longer experiencing withdrawal symptoms.

Disinhibitory effects. The release from inhibition of behaviors that are normally suppressed.

Diuretic. A drug that increases the production of urine.

DOPAC. A major metabolite of dopamine.

Drug-effect theory of tolerance. The theory that an animal must experience the effect of the drug to become tolerant to that effect.

Drug metabolism. The conversion of a drug from its active form to a nonactive form.

Drug self-administration paradigm. Laboratory animals repeatedly press a lever to inject an addictive drug into themselves.

Drug tolerance. A state of decreased susceptibility to a drug that develops as a result of exposure to the drug; a shift in the dose-response curve to the right.

Ethyl alcohol. The alcohol that is commonly consumed by humans.

Fetal alcohol syndrome (FAS). A syndrome produced by prenatal exposure to alcohol; characterized by mental retardation, low birth weight, and a variety of other physical abnormalities.

Fluorescence histochemistry. Exposing neural tissue to formaldehyde vapor and viewing it through a fluorescence microscope reveals monoamine-containing neurons.

Functional tolerance. Tolerance resulting from a reduction in the reactivity of the nervous system to the drug.

Harrison Narcotics Act. Passed in 1914, this Act made it illegal to sell or use opium, morphine, or cocaine in the U.S.A.

Hashish. The processed resin of Cannabis.

Heroin. A powerful semisynthetic opiate.

Hypothermic. Temperature-reducing.

Intracranial self-stimulation (ICS). An animal repeatedly presses a bar to receive electrical stimulation to certain sites in its brain.

Intramuscularly (IM). Injected into muscle.

Intravenously (IV). Injected into a vein.

Korsakoff's syndrome. The severe memory loss and dementia that is commonly associated with alcohol addiction.

Medial forebrain bundle (MFB). A neural pathway that courses through the lateral hypothalamus and innervates the septum and other forebrain structures; it was once thought to mediate the effects of all rewarding brain stimulation.

Mesotelencephalic dopamine system. The ascending projections of dopamine-releasing neurons from the substantia nigra and ventral tegmental area of the mesencephalon (midbrain) into various regions of the telencephalon.

Metabolic tolerance. Tolerance that results from a reduction in the amount of drug getting to its sites of action.

Morphine. The major active ingredient in opium.

Naloxone. An opiate antagonist that readily penetrates the blood-brain barrier.

Narcotic. A legal classification of certain drugs, mostly opiates.

Nicotine. The major psychoactive ingredient of tobacco.

Opiates. Morphine, codeine, heroin, and other chemicals with similar structures or effects.

Opium. The sap that exudes from the opium poppy; it contains many psychoactive ingredients, including morphine and codeine.

Physical-dependence theory of addiction. The theory that the main factor motivating drug addicts to take drugs is the prevention or termination of withdrawal symptoms.

Physically dependent. Individuals who suffer from withdrawal symptoms when they stop taking a drug are said to be physically dependent on that drug.

Positive-incentive theory of addiction. The theory that the primary factor in most cases of addiction is a craving for the pleasure-producing effects of drugs.

Priming. Inducing a rat to resume self-stimulation by providing it with a few "free" stimulations.

Psychoactive drugs. Drugs that influence subjective experience and behavior by acting on the nervous system.

Psychological dependence. Compulsive drug-taking that occurs in the absence of physical dependence.

Sensitization. An increase in the sensitivity to a drug effect that develops as the result of exposure to the drug; the opposite of drug tolerance.

Smoker's syndrome. The chest pain, labored breathing, wheezing, coughing, and heightened susceptibility to infections of the respiratory tract commonly observed in smokers.

Stimulant drugs. Drugs that increase neural and behavioral activity; for example, caffeine, nicotine, amphetamine, and cocaine.

Subcutaneously (SC). Injected under the skin.

Substantia nigra. A midbrain nucleus that includes the cell bodies of some of the neurons in the mesotelencephalic dopamine system.

Ventral tegmental area. A midbrain nucleus that includes the cell bodies of some of the neurons in the mesotelencephalic dopamine system.

Withdrawal syndrome. The illness brought on by the elimination from the body of a drug to which the subject has become physically dependent.

ADDITIONAL READING

There are a number of paperbacks that provide interesting introductions to the topic of drug abuse. The following two are my favorites:

Julien, R. M. (1981). *A primer of drug action*. San Francisco: Freeman.

McKim, W. A. (1986). *Drugs and behavior*. Englewood Cliffs, New Jersey: Prentice-Hall.

The following three articles are essential reading for anybody who is interested in the development of more effective approaches to the drug problem.

Goldstein, A., & Kalant, H. (1990). Drug policy: Striking the right balance. *Science, 249,* 1513–1519.

Jarvik, M. E. (1990). The drug dilemma: Manipulating the demand. *Science, 250,* 387–392.

Nadelmann, E. A. (1989). Drug prohibition in the United States: Costs, consequences, and alternatives. *Science, 245,* 939–947.

14

Memory and Amnesia

Ironically, the person who has contributed more than any other to our understanding of the neuropsychology of memory is not a neuropsychologist. In fact, although he has collaborated on dozens of studies of memory, he has no formal research training and not a single degree to his name. He is H.M., a man who in 1953 at the age of 27 had the medial portions of his temporal lobes removed for the treatment of a severe case of epilepsy. Just as the Rosetta Stone has provided archaeologists with important clues to the meaning of Egyptian hieroglyphics, H.M.'s postsurgical memory deficits have been instrumental in the achievement of our current understanding of the neuropsychological bases of memory.

Much of the first section of this chapter (Section 14.1) deals with H.M. It deals with the impact of his memory problems on his everyday life, the results of the 40-year program of testing that has followed his operation, and the implications of this testing for current theories of memory. Subsequent sections of the chapter describe the amnesias associated with Korsakoff's syndrome (Section 14.2), with Alzheimer's disease (Section 14.3), and with nonpenetrating brain injuries (Section 14.4). Section 14.5 focuses on the use of animal models to study the neural bases of amnesia, and Section 14.6 discusses the theoretical issues that are the focus of current memory research. The chapter ends with the ironic case of R.M., a biopsychologist who suffered a severe blow to his head and had an opportunity to study his own amnesia firsthand.

14.1

The Amnesic Effects of Bilateral Medial-Temporal Lobectomy and the Unfortunate Case of H.M.

Early Theories of Memory Storage

In the mid-1950s, when the first reports of H.M.'s case began to appear, the study of the neural bases of memory was dominated by two ideas. First, the field of memory research was reeling from Lashley's fruitless search for the location of the **engram**, the change in the brain responsible for storing a memory. Lashley, the most influential physiological psychologist of the day, had spent 35 years training rats, cats, and monkeys to perform complex learning tasks and then cutting, destroying, or removing specific parts of their brains in a vain attempt to erase the memory of their training. For example, in one series of studies, rats received lesions of various sizes to different parts of the cerebral cortex after they had learned a maze task. Ten days later, their retention of the task was assessed. Lashley found that only very large cortical lesions disrupted retention and, more importantly, that the particular site of the lesion was of little consequence; cortical lesions of equal size produced similar effects regardless of their location. On the basis of these findings, Lashley concluded that memories for complex tasks are stored diffusely throughout the neocortex (the **principle of mass action**) and that all parts of the neocortex play an equal role in their storage (the **principle of equipotentiality**). Although Lashley conceded that certain areas of the neocortex may play a more important role than other areas in the storage of certain memories—for example, the visual cortex may play a more important role in the storage of memories of visual stimuli—he argued that memories were stored diffusely and equally throughout these functional areas. The impact of Lashley's work was to discourage theories of memory that assigned specific memorial abilities to specific parts of the brain.

The second idea about the physiological bases of memory that became prevalent in the mid–1950s is the theory that there are two different memory storage mechanisms: a *short-term* system and a *long-term* system. According to this theory, which is still influential, each memory is held in short-term storage while the physiological changes necessary for long-term storage are taking place. For example, in order to remember a new phone number, we hold it in short-term storage by actively thinking about it until its presence in short-term storage produces the physiological changes that underlie its long-term storage. The hypothetical transfer of a memory from short-term to long-term storage is called **consolidation.** According to the most influential consolidation theory (Hebb, 1949), the memory for a particular event is stored in the short-term mode by *reverberating neural activity* (neural activity that goes around and around in closed-loop circuits). This reverberatory activity is believed to produce structural changes in the synapses of that circuit that facilitate the later occurrence of the same pattern of activity. It is this structural synaptic facilitation that is the putative basis of long-term storage (see Figure 14.1). The major prediction of this theory is that experiences that are not held in short-term storage for a sufficient period of time by conscious consideration will not become integrated into the store of long-term memories. The

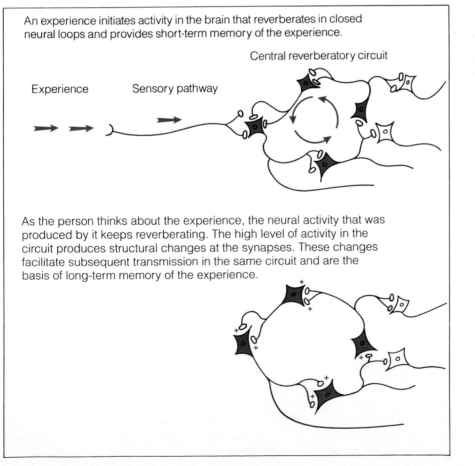

An experience initiates activity in the brain that reverberates in closed neural loops and provides short-term memory of the experience.

Central reverberatory circuit

Experience   Sensory pathway

As the person thinks about the experience, the neural activity that was produced by it keeps reverberating. The high level of activity in the circuit produces structural changes at the synapses. These changes facilitate subsequent transmission in the same circuit and are the basis of long-term memory of the experience.

FIGURE 14.1

An illustration of Hebb's 1949 theory of how short-term memories are consolidated into long-term memories.

classic example of this prediction is the loss of recall that is experienced by people when they are distracted just after they have looked up a new phone number.

Bilateral Medial-Temporal Lobectomy

During the 11 years preceding his surgery, H.M. suffered an average of one generalized convulsion each week and many partial convulsions each day, despite massive doses of anticonvulsant medication. Electroencephalography suggested that H.M.'s convulsions arose from foci in the medial portions of both his left and right temporal lobes. Because the removal of one medial-temporal lobe had proven to be an effective treatment for patients with a unilateral temporal lobe focus (see Van Buren, Ajmone-Marsan, Mutsuga, & Sadowski, 1975), the decision was made to perform a **bilateral medial-temporal lobectomy** on H.M. This operation (see Figure 14.2) had been performed on only a few previous occasions; it has never been performed again. By the way, the term **lobectomy** refers to an operation in which a large part of one lobe of the brain is removed; the term **lobotomy** refers to an operation in which a large part of one lobe is separated from the rest of the brain by a cut, but is not removed.

In one sense, H.M.'s bilateral medial-temporal lobectomy was an unqualified success. The incidence of his generalized convulsions was reduced from one per week to one every 2 or 3 years, and minor attacks occurred only once or twice a day, despite a substantial reduction in the level of his anticonvulsant medication. Furthermore, H.M. entered surgery a reasonably well-balanced, stable individual with normal perceptual abilities and superior intelligence, and he left it in the same condition.

FIGURE 14.2

The portions of the medial-temporal lobes that were removed from the brain of H.M. (Adapted from Scoville & Milner, 1957.)

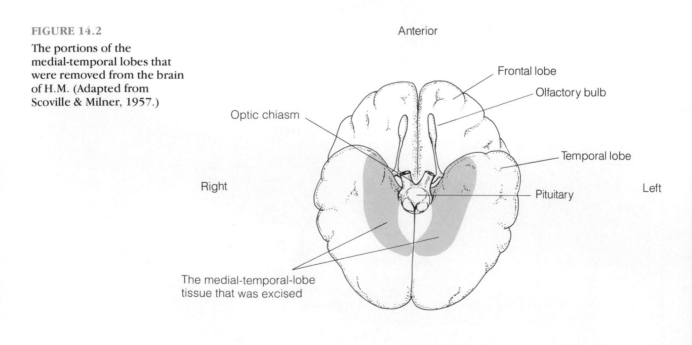

H.M.'s memory defect is not accompanied by any general intellectual loss. In 1953, shortly before his operation, he obtained an intelligence quotient of 104 on Form I of the Wechsler-Bellevue Intelligence Scale; the verbal quotient was 101 and the performance quotient 106. When tested again in 1955, two years after the operation, he achieved a full-scale quotient of 112, with a verbal quotient of 107 and a performance quotient of 114. This postoperative improvement may well have been due to a reduction in the frequency of his minor attacks, which preoperatively had been observed to occur as often as 12 times during a single two-hour testing session. Seven years later, in 1962, he showed further improvement; when tested with Form II of the Wechsler Intelligence Scale, his full-scale I.Q. was 118, the verbal and performance quotients being 109 and 125, respectively. (Milner, Corkin, & Teuber, 1968, pp. 218–219)

H.M.'s Postsurgical Memory Deficits

In assessing the amnesic effects of brain surgery, it is usual to administer two kinds of tests: tests of the patient's ability to remember things learned before the surgery and test of the patient's ability to remember things learned after the surgery. Deficits on the former tests lead to a diagnosis of **retrograde** (backward-acting) **amnesia;** those on the latter tests lead to a diagnosis of **anterograde** (forward-acting) **amnesia.** Like his intellectual abilities, H.M.'s memory for events predating his surgery remains largely intact. He has a mild retrograde amnesia for those events that occurred in the 2 years before his surgery; his memory for more remote events (e.g., the events of his childhood) is normal. In contrast, H.M. suffers from a devastating anterograde amnesia; he cannot form new long-term memories. His ability to hold items in short-term storage is well within the normal range—he has a **digit span** (see Chapter 5) of 6 digits (Wickelgren, 1968); however, once he stops thinking about something that has just happened to him, it is lost forever from his memory. In effect, H.M. became suspended in time on that day in 1953 when he regained his health, but lost his future. Consider the following descriptions of H.M.'s personal life.

> As far as we can tell, this man has retained little if anything of events subsequent to the operation, although his I.Q. rating is actually slightly higher than before. Ten months before I examined him, his family had moved from their old house to a new one a few blocks away on the same street. He still had not learned the new address (though remembering the old one perfectly), nor could he be trusted to find his way home alone. He did not know where objects in constant use were kept, and his mother stated that he would read the same magazines over and over again without finding their contents familiar. . . . forgetting occurred the instant the patient's focus of attention shifted . . . (Milner, 1965, pp. 104–105)

> During three of the nights at the Clinical Research Center, the patient rang for the night nurse, asking her, with many apologies, if she would tell him where he was and how he came to be there. He clearly realized that he was in a hospital but seemed unable to reconstruct any of the events of the previous day. On another occasion he remarked "Every day is alone in itself, whatever enjoyment I've had, and whatever sorrow I've had." Our own impression is that many events fade for him long before the day is over. He often volunteers stereotyped descriptions of his own state, by saying that it is "like waking from a dream." His experience seems to be that of a person

who is just becoming aware of his surroundings without fully comprehending the situation, because he does not remember what went before. . . .

He still fails to recognize people who are close neighbours or family friends but who got to know him only after the operation. When questioned, he tries to use accent as a clue to a person's place of origin and weather as a clue to the time of year. Although he gives his date of birth unhesitatingly and accurately, he always underestimates his own age and can only make wild guesses as to the date. . . . [Having aged since his surgery, he does not recognize a current photograph of himself.]

After his father's death, H.M. was given protected employment in a state rehabilitation centre, where he spends week-days participating in rather monotonous work, programmed for severely retarded patients. A typical task is the mounting of cigarette-lighters on cardboard frames for display. It is characteristic that he cannot give us any description of his place of work, the nature of his job, or the route along which he is driven each day, to and from the centre. (Milner, Corkin, & Teuber, 1968, pp. 216–217)

H.M. has lived in a nursing home for many years. He spends much of each day doing crossword puzzles; his progress on a crossword puzzle is never lost because it is written down.

The Formal Assessment of H.M.'s Anterograde Amnesia

This subsection describes H.M.'s performance on six standardized neuropsychological tests of memory. His performance on the first three tests illustrates his anterograde memory deficit; his performance on the last three tests illustrates an aspect of his anterograde memory that has survived.

Digit span +1 test   H.M. was asked to repeat 5 digits that were read to him at 1-second intervals. He repeated the sequence correctly. On the next trial the same 5 digits were presented in the same sequence with 1 new digit added to the end. The same 6-digit sequence was presented several times until he got it right, and then another digit was added to the end of it, and so on. After 25 trials of this **digit span +1 test,** H.M. had not managed to repeat the 8-digit sequence. Normal subjects can expand their digit spans to about 15 digits after 25 digit-span +1 trials (Drachman & Arbit, 1966).

Block-tapping memory-span test   Milner (1971) demonstrated that H.M.'s anterograde amnesia was not restricted to verbal material by assessing his performance on a nonverbal analogue of the digit-span test, the **block-tapping memory-span test.** An array of nine blocks was spread out on a board in front of H.M., and he was asked to watch the neuropsychologist touch a sequence of them and then to repeat the same sequence of touches. H.M.'s block-tapping span was normal, but, unlike normal subjects, he could not learn to touch a sequence of one greater than his immediate block-tapping span even when the same sequence was repeated 12 times. Amnesia for information in every sensory modality is termed **global amnesia;** H.M. has global amnesia.

Verbal and nonverbal matching-to-sample tests   On each trial of a **matching-to-sample test,** a sample item is presented to the subject. Then after a delay, an array of test items is presented from which the subject must select the one that matches (i.e., is the same as) the sample. Sidman, Stoddard, and Mohr (1968) tested H.M. with verbal and nonverbal forms of this test (see Figure 14.3). When the stimuli were verbal (i.e., sequences of three consonants), H.M. had no difficulty even at the longest, 40-second delay. In contrast, when the stimuli were nonverbal (i.e., different shapes of ellipses), H.M. could not perform at delays of more than 5 seconds. A control group of school children made almost no errors on either the verbal or the nonverbal versions of the test. Sidman and his colleagues then concluded that the verbal

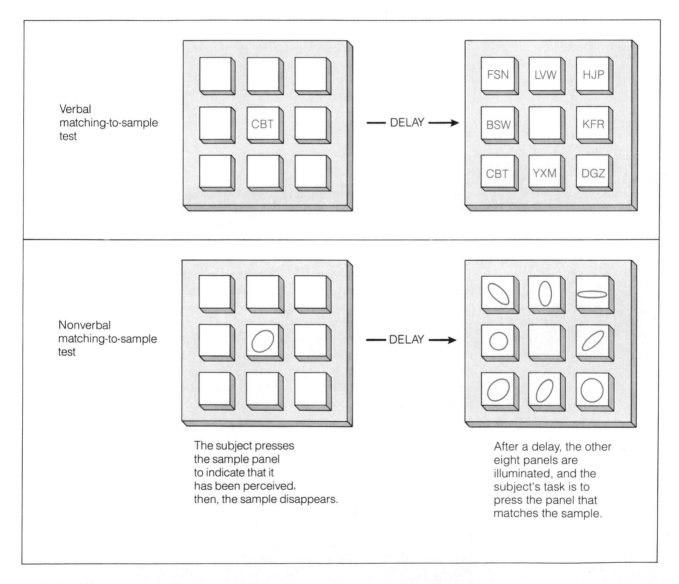

The subject presses the sample panel to indicate that it has been perceived, then, the sample disappears.

After a delay, the other eight panels are illuminated, and the subject's task is to press the panel that matches the sample.

FIGURE 14.3

The verbal and nonverbal matching-to-sample tests given to H.M. by Sidman, Stoddard, and Mohr (1968). H.M. performed without error on the verbal form of the test up to the longest, 40-second, retention interval, but he could not perform the nonverbal form at intervals of greater than 5 seconds.

FIGURE 14.4

The mirror-drawing test.

matching-to-sample performance of H.M. was superior to his performance on the nonverbal version of the test because letters, but not ellipses, can be actively rehearsed—we have no words for different ellipses that would allow us to rehearse them.

Mirror-drawing test   The first indication that H.M.'s anterograde amnesia did not apply equally to all long-term memories came from the results of a **mirror-drawing test** (Milner, 1965). H.M.'s task was to draw a line within the boundaries of a star-shaped target by watching his hand in a mirror (see Figure 14.4). H.M. was asked to trace the star 10 times on each of 3 consecutive days, and the number of times that he went outside the boundaries on each trial was recorded. As can be seen in Figure 14.5, H.M.'s performance improved over the 3 days, thus indicating good retention of the task. However, each day, he insisted that he had never seen the task before.

FIGURE 14.5

Retention of the mirror-drawing task by H.M. (Adapted from Milner, 1965.)

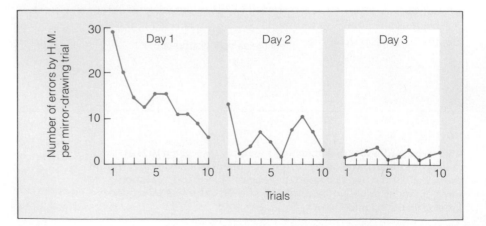

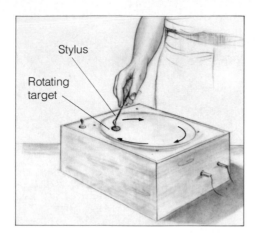

FIGURE 14.6

The rotary-pursuit task. The subject tries to keep the stylus in contact with the rotating target. Time on target is automatically timed.

Rotary-pursuit test   In the **rotary-pursuit test,** the subject tries to keep the tip of a stylus in contact with a target that is rotating on a revolving turntable (see Figure 14.6). Corkin (1968) found that H.M.'s performance of the rotary-pursuit task improved significantly over nine daily practice sessions, despite the fact that each day he claimed that he had never seen the pursuit rotor before. He retained his improved performance over a 7-day retention interval.

Incomplete-pictures test   The **incomplete-pictures test** (Gollin, 1960) employs 5 sets of 20 fragmented drawings. Each set contains drawings of the same objects, but they differ in their degree of sketchiness. As illustrated in Figure 14.7, set 1 contains the most fragmented drawings, and set 5 the complete drawings. The subject is first shown all 20 of the most sketchy cards (i.e., set 1) and asked to identify them. Then the unrecognized items in set 2 are presented in a different order. If necessary, the presentation is repeated with the unidentified items in sets 3, 4, and finally 5 until all 20 items have been identified. Figure 14.8 illustrates the initial performance of H.M. on this test and his performance on the same test 1 hour later. H.M. displayed substantial savings even though he did not recall previously performing the task (Milner, Corkin, & Teuber, 1968).

Other Cases of Bilateral Medial-Temporal Lobectomy

It is risky to base theories on a single case. However, there is evidence that H.M.'s case is not idiosyncratic. For example, Milner (1965) reported three cases in which the surgical removal of one medial temporal lobe produced memory deficits similar to H.M.'s. Because unilateral medial-temporal lobectomy normally produces only slight deficits, Milner suggested that these three patients may have had preexisting damage to the contralateral medial-temporal

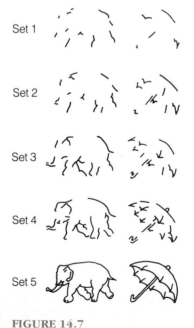

FIGURE 14.7

The five sets of two of the drawings from the incomplete-pictures test. (Adapted from Gollin, 1960.)

FIGURE 14.8

H.M.'s initial performance on the incomplete-pictures test and his savings on the same test administered 1 hour later. (Adapted from Milner, Corkin, & Teuber, 1968.)

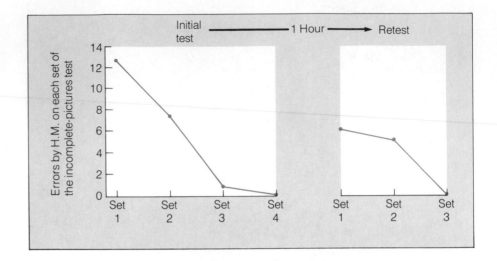

lobe. One of them died of unrelated causes 15 years after surgery, and the discovery of extensive hippocampal atrophy contralateral to his surgical lesion confirmed Milner's hypothesis.

The Influence of H.M.'s Case on the Search for the Neural Basis of Memory

I began this chapter by asserting that H.M. has contributed more than any other person to our current understanding of the neuropsychology of memory. The following are six important ideas about memory that are a legacy of his case:

1. H.M.'s case was the first to implicate the medial temporal lobes in memory. It spawned a massive research effort aimed at clarifying the memorial functions of the hippocampus, amygdala, and other medial-temporal-lobe structures.

2. H.M.'s case challenged the view that memory functions are diffusely and equivalently distributed throughout the brain. Clearly, the medial temporal lobes play an important role in memory that is not shared by other parts of the brain. In making this point, H.M.'s case renewed efforts to relate particular brain structures to particular memorial processes.

3. H.M.'s case supported the view that there are distinct modes of storage for short-term and long-term memory. The fact that bilateral medial-temporal lobectomy abolishes the ability to form certain kinds of long-term memories without significantly disrupting performance on tests of short-term memory is strong evidence for this dual-system hypothesis.

4. H.M.'s case showed that an amnesic subject might claim no recollection of a previous experience, while at the same time demonstrating memory

for it by improved performance—recall H.M.'s savings without conscious recollection on the mirror-drawing test, the incomplete-pictures test, and the rotary-pursuit test. Tests on which memories are expressed by conscious declaration have been labeled tests of **explicit memory** (i.e., recall and recognition tests); tests on which memories are expressed by improved test performance have been termed tests of **implicit memory** (see Graf & Schacter, 1985, 1987).

5. H.M.'s case suggested that the medial temporal lobes play a role in memory consolidation. H.M.'s capacity to store short-term memories has remained intact, as has his capacity to store most long-term memories that were formed before his operation. His problem is that he cannot transfer short-term explicit memories to long-term storage.

6. The 2-year time span covered by H.M.'s mild retrograde amnesia challenged the notions of memory consolidation that were popular in the 1950s and 60s. According to Hebb's consolidation theory, memories are transferred from short-term to long-term storage in a few seconds or perhaps minutes, after which they are as resistant to disruption as they are going to get. The fact that H.M.'s memory for events that occurred in the 2 years prior to his surgery was more susceptible to disruption than his memory for more remote events suggests that the resistance of memories to disruption continues to increase for years after acquisition.

The Case of R.B.: The Hippocampus and Medial-Temporal-Lobe Amnesia?

Bilateral medial-temporal lobectomy damages several major structures: most notably, the hippocampus, the amygdala, the medial temporal cortex, and the temporal stem. The **temporal stem** is a tract that runs just above the hippocampus; axons of temporal cortex neurons funnel through the temporal stem on their way to other parts of the brain. In their original report of H.M.'s case, Scoville and Milner (1957) concluded that the amnesic effects of bilateral medial-temporal lobectomy are attributable to hippocampal damage. Although they provided little evidence for this conclusion, it was widely accepted.

The recent case of R.B. lends support to the view that the amnesic effects of bilateral medial-temporal lobectomy result from hippocampal damage (Zola-Morgan, Squire, & Amaral, 1986). At the age of 52, R.B.'s brain was damaged during cardiac-bypass surgery; there was an equipment malfunction that interrupted the flow of blood to R.B.'s brain. The resulting **ischemia** (a damage-producing interruption of blood supply) left R.B. amnesic.

Although R.B.'s amnesia was not as severe as H.M.'s, it was comparable in many respects. R.B. died in 1983 of a heart attack, and a detailed postmortem examination of his brain was carried out with the permission of his family. The only obvious brain damage was to one area (the **CA1 subfield**) of one layer (the **pyramidal cell layer**) of the left and right hippocampi—see the photograph of R.B.'s hippocampus in Figure 14.9. R.B.'s case suggests that hippocampal damage by itself can produce amnesia. However, this issue is far from settled, as you will learn later in the chapter.

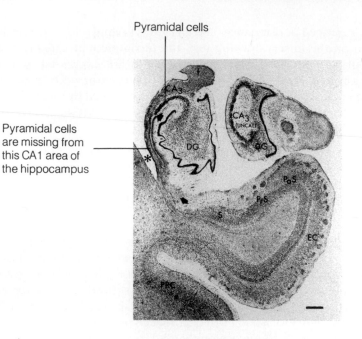

Pyramidal cells

Pyramidal cells
are missing from
this CA1 area of
the hippocampus

FIGURE 14.9

This Nissl-stained cross section through the hippocampus of R.B. reveals
selective damage to the pyramidal cell layer of the CA1 subfield. The
CA1 region of R.B.'s pyramidal cell layer is the only region of the layer
that lacks cell bodies. CA stands for *cornu ammonis,* which is another
name for hippocampus. (From Zola-Morgan et al., 1986; photograph
supplied by Stuart Zola-Morgan.)

14.2

The Amnesia of Korsakoff's Syndrome

Although the study of H.M., R.B., and the few other amnesic patients with
bilateral medial-temporal-lobe damage has been extremely informative, patients with Korsakoff's syndrome have served as subjects in the vast majority
of studies of human amnesia. **Korsakoff's syndrome,** as you have learned in
previous chapters, is a disease that is common in individuals who chronically
consume alcohol. In its advanced stages, it is characterized by a variety of sensory and motor problems, extreme confusion, striking personality changes,
and a risk of death from liver, gastrointestinal, or heart disorders. Postmortem
neuroanatomical examination typically reveals extensive peripheral nerve
damage, lesions to the medial *diencephalon* (the thalamus and hypothalamus), and diffuse damage to a variety of other brain structures, most notably
the neocortex and cerebellum.

Korsakoff patients typically suffer from retrograde and anterograde amnesia. Unlike patients with bilateral medial-temporal-lobe damage, Korsakoff
patients have difficulty recalling events that occurred many years prior to
their hospitalization. For example, in a study conducted in the early 1970s
(Marslen-Wilson & Teuber, 1975), Korsakoff patients proved to be worse than
H.M. at recognizing the faces of individuals who had been famous in the
1930s and 1940s.

In general, the memory of Korsakoff patients for recent events is disrupted more than their memory for remote events. One possible interpretation of this finding is that the brain damage associated with Korsakoff's syndrome produces a long gradient of retrograde amnesia. However, because Korsakoff's syndrome has an insidious, rather than a sudden, onset, it is not clear to what extent memory deficits for events prior to diagnosis reflect the retrograde disruption of existing long-term memories or the gradually worsening anterograde blockage of the formation of new ones. Squire (1982a) has suggested that Korsakoff patients have cognitive difficulties that equally impede the recall of all past experiences and that their particular difficulty in recalling events occurring in the months and years preceding their hospitalization reflects the progressive development of anterograde amnesia.

Does Medial Diencephalic Damage Cause the Amnesia Observed in Korsakoff Patients?

Because the brain damage associated with Korsakoff's syndrome is so diffuse, it has not been easy to identify the portion of it that is specifically responsible for the amnesia. The first hypothesis, which was based on several small postmortem studies, was that damage to the **mammillary bodies** of the hypothalamus was responsible for the memory deficits of Korsakoff patients. However, a large-scale postmortem study by Victor, Adams, and Collins (1971) subsequently revealed several severe cases of Korsakoff's amnesia with no mammillary body damage, but none was found that did not have damage to another medial diencephalic structure: the **mediodorsal nuclei** of the thalamus. Independent support for the mediodorsal-nucleus-damage interpretation of Korsakoff amnesia comes from the observation that otherwise healthy patients with relatively localized **infarcts** (areas of cell death produced by ischemia) in the area of the mediodorsal nuclei often suffer from amnesia (e.g., Graff-Radford, Damasio, Yamada, Eslinger, & Damasio, 1985; von Cramon, Hebel, & Schuri, 1985; Winocur, Oxbury, Roberts, Agnetti, & Davis, 1984). However, amnesia can occur in Korsakoff patients in the absence of mediodorsal nuclei damage (Brion & Mikol, 1978). It is unlikely that the memory deficits of Korsakoff patients are attributable to the degeneration of any single structure (see Butters & Stuss, 1989).

The Cases of N.A. and B.J.

With respect to the study of amnesia, N.A. has been to the diencephalon as H.M. has been to the medial temporal lobes. After a year of junior college, N.A. joined the air force and served as a radar technician until his accident in December of 1960. On that fateful day,

> N.A., was assembling a model airplane in his barracks room. His roommate had removed a miniature fencing foil from the wall and was making thrusts behind N.A.'s chair. N.A. turned suddenly and was stabbed through the right nostril. The foil penetrated the *cribriform plate* [the thin bone around the base of the brain], taking an upward course to the left into the forebrain. (Squire, 1987, p. 177)

> The examiners . . . noted that at first he seemed to be unable to recall any significant personal, national or international events for the two years

preceding the accident, but this extensive retrograde amnesia appeared to shrink. . . . Two-and-a-half years after the accident, the retrograde amnesia was said to involve a span of perhaps two weeks immediately preceding the injury, but the exact extent of this retrograde loss was (and remains) impossible to determine. . . .

During . . . convalescence (for the first six to eight months after the accident), the patient's recall of day-to-day events was described as extremely poor, but "occasionally some items sprang forth uncontrollably; he suddenly recalled something he seemed to have no business recalling." His physicians thus gained the impression that his memory was patchy: he appeared to have difficulty in calling up at will many things that at other times emerged spontaneously. . . .

Since his injury, he has been unable to return to any gainful employment, although his memory has continued to improve, albeit slowly. (Teuber, Milner, & Vaughan, 1968, pp. 268–269)

N.A. received a CAT scan test (see Chapter 5) in the late 1970s (Squire & Moore, 1979). The scan revealed a lesion in the left mediodorsal nucleus of the thalamus, the nucleus implicated in the amnesia of Korsakoff patients. Damage to other neural structures along the path of the foil was not visible.

The recently reported case of B.J. (Dusoir, Kapur, Byrnes, McKinstry, & Hoare, 1990) puts the case of N.A. in perspective. The case of B.J. is almost identical to that of N.A., except that it involves the left nostril rather than the right, a snooker cue rather than a fencing foil, and the mammillary bodies rather than the mediodorsal nuclei.

The Contribution of Prefrontal Damage to Korsakoff Amnesia

In addition to their medial thalamic lesions, Korsakoff patients commonly have diffuse damage to the prefrontal cortex (Jacobson & Lishman, 1990). Investigators have used two strategies to determine how this prefrontal damage contributes to the amnesia of Korsakoff patients. They have compared the memorial deficits of Korsakoff patients with those of patients with prefrontal damage, and they have compared the memorial deficits of Korsakoff patients with those of N.A.

Two features of Korsakoff amnesia seem to result from prefrontal damage: failure to release from proactive interference and amnesia for temporal order. **Proactive interference** refers to the interfering effects of performing one task on the performance of a subsequent one. For example, subjects exhibit a gradual decline in their ability to learn and recall successive lists of words of the same category, for example, lists of animal names, due to the accumulating proactive interference from learning preceding lists. However, when a list of words from a different category, for example, a list of vegetables, is inserted in the series, normal subjects and N.A. display an improvement in their ability to recall these novel items (Squire, 1982). Such a release from proactive interference does not occur in Korsakoff patients (Cermak, Uhly, & Reale, 1980) or in patients with localized prefrontal damage (Moscovitch, 1982). This suggests that the inability of Korsakoff's patients to release from proactive interference is associated with their diffuse prefrontal damage.

Another memory deficit that is common in Korsakoff patients and in patients with prefrontal lobe damage (Milner, 1974), but has not been observed in N.A., is a deficit in *memory for temporal sequence* (see Squire, Nadel, & Slater, 1981). In one study (Squire, 1982b), N.A., a group of Korsakoff patients, and a group of control subjects received a test of memory for temporal order that had previously been shown to be sensitive to prefrontal damage. The subjects read 12 unrelated sentences, and then waited 3 minutes and read another 12. Later, their ability to recognize the sentences and to recall whether they had appeared in the first or second list was assessed. Like the Korsakoff patients, N.A. had difficulty recognizing the sentences, but unlike the Korsakoff patients, N.A. had no more difficulty than did the control subjects in specifying whether those sentences that he recognized were from the first or second list. In another study that employed the same test, H.M. was able to "guess" which of two test items he had seen more recently, even though he could not recall seeing them before (Sagar, Gabrieli, Sullivan, & Corkin, 1990).

The Amnesia of Alzheimer's Disease

You learned about Alzheimer's disease in Chapter 6, but let me refresh your memory. Alzheimer's disease is the most common cause of *dementia* (general intellectual deterioration) in old people; close to 5% of all people over 65 suffer from the disorder. It is a terminal disorder. Autopsy reveals that the brains of Alzheimer's patients contain **neurofibrils** (thread-like structures in the neural cytoplasm) and **amyloid plaques** (tangles of degenerating neurons interspersed with an abnormal protein, called *amyloid*). In addition, there is extensive neuronal degeneration, particularly in the cortex, hippocampus, and basal forebrain.

One of the first signs of Alzheimer's disease is a deterioration of memory. An individual in the early stages of Alzheimer's disease begins to have more than the usual difficulty remembering recently learned information, such as names, appointments, and phone numbers. In its advanced stages, Alzheimer's disease is characterized by severe intellectual deterioration of all kinds, including an almost total loss of memory. At this stage, the patient is totally confused, requires constant supervision, and may fail to remember even the most basic information, such as the face of a son or daughter.

There is a massive reduction in cholinergic activity in the brains of Alzheimer's patients; there is less acetylcholine, less *choline acetyltransferase* (the enzyme that stimulates the synthesis of acetylcholine), and less *acetylcholinesterase* (the enzyme that breaks down acetylcholine in the synapses)—(see Coyle, Price, & DeLong, 1983; Marchbanks, 1982). However, there is little reduction in the density of cholinergic receptors (see Bartus, Dean, Beer, & Lippa, 1982), which suggests that the degenerative changes occur to the cholinergic neurons, rather than to the postsynaptic neurons on which they terminate. Many of the cholinergic axons that terminate in the neocortex and hippocampus originate in cell bodies that are located in the basal forebrain just in front of the hypothalamus: for example, in the *nucleus basalis of Meynert,* the *diagonal band of Broca,* and the *medial septal nucleus.* Alzheimer's disease is virtually always associated with massive cell loss in these nuclei. Whitehouse, Price, Struble, Clark, Coyle, and DeLong (1982) found that there were 79% fewer neurons in the nucleus basalis of Meynert of deceased Alzheimer's victims than in the brains of deceased age-matched control patients.

Although cholinergic neurons are not the only ones attacked by Alzheimer's disease (see Coyle, 1987), efforts have been made to treat Alzheimer's disease with cholinergic agonists, such as *choline,* the precursor of acetylcholine—in the same way that L-DOPA, the precursor of dopamine, has been used to treat Parkinson's disease (see Chapter 6). Unfortunately, choline and other cholinergic agonists have not been able to forestall the inexorable progression of Alzheimer's disease (Fibiger, 1991).

The discovery of the degeneration of cholinergic neurons in Alzheimer's disease led to the hypothesis that acetylcholine is involved in memory. This hypothesis was supported by the finding that cholinergic antagonists disrupt memory. For example, the drug *scopolamine,* which blocks cholinergic receptors of the *muscarinic* subtype (see Chapter 4), has been shown to disrupt the recent memory of healthy subjects (Drachman & Leavitt, 1974; Sitaram, Weingartner, & Gillin, 1978). There have also been some reports that cholinergic agonists are **nootropics** (memory-improving agents; pronounced no oh TROPE iks). However, despite some promising results in laboratory animals (e.g., Meck, Smith, & Williams, 1989), claims of drug-induced memory enhancement are best viewed with caution at the present time (see Thal, 1989).

Another approach to the study of cholinergic systems and memory has been to assess the effects of bilateral lesions to the basal forebrain on the behavior of experimental animals. Fibiger, Murray, and Phillips (1983) made such lesions in rats and then assessed their ability to learn a 16-arm radial maze (see Chapter 5). Each day the same 8 arms of the maze were baited with food, while the other 8 arms always remained empty. The control rats, readily learned to visit only the 8 food-baited arms without visiting an arm twice on the same day. In contrast, the rats with lesions solved only part of the problem; they readily learned to visit only the 8 food-baited arms, but they often visited an arm more than once on the same day. This suggests that cholinergic circuits might be involved in **working memory** (temporary memory necessary for the successful performance of tasks on which one is currently working), but not **reference memory** (memory for the general principles and skills that are required to perform a task). However, Dunnett, Everitt, and Robbins (1991) have recommended caution in interpreting the effect of chemical and electrolytic basal forebrain lesions because their damage is not restricted to cholinergic neurons (see Wenk, Markowska, & Olton, 1989).

14.4

The Amnesia after Closed-Head Injury

Blows to the head that do not penetrate the skull (i.e., *closed-head injuries*) are the most common causes of amnesia (see Levin, 1989). Amnesia so produced is referred to as **posttraumatic amnesia (PTA).**

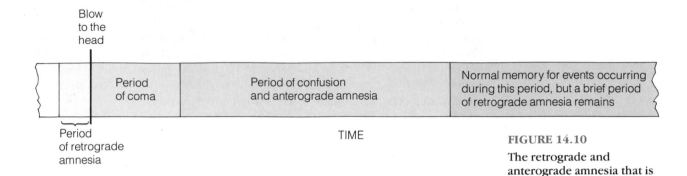

FIGURE 14.10

The retrograde and anterograde amnesia that is produced by a closed-head injury.

Following a blow to the head of sufficient intensity to produce amnesia, there is a period of coma, which usually lasts a few seconds or minutes, but can in more extreme cases last for weeks. Once the victim regains consciousness, he or she is often confused. For example, an individual who has had the circumstances of his or her accident explained to him or her often asks for the same information a few seconds later.

Victims of a closed-head injury are not usually referred to a neuropsychologist for testing until several days after the blow to the head, if they are referred at all. At this point, the confusion has usually subsided, unless the blow was particularly severe. Testing usually reveals that the patient has a permanent retrograde amnesia for the events that led up to the accident and a permanent anterograde amnesia for the events that followed it. The anterograde memory deficits that follow a closed-head injury are often quite puzzling to the friends and relatives who talk to the patient soon after the accident. The patient may seem perfectly lucid at the time, but later she or he often has no recollection of the conversation.

Figure 14.10 summarizes the effects of closed-head injury on memory. It illustrates that the duration of the period of anterograde amnesia is typically longer than the coma, which is usually longer than the period of permanent retrograde amnesia. More severe blows to the head tend to produce longer comas, longer periods of anterograde amnesia, and longer periods of retrograde amnesia (Levin, Papanicolaou, & Eisenberg, 1984). Not illustrated in Figure 14.10 are islands of memory, which are a poorly understood feature of many cases of amnesia. **Islands of memory** are memories for isolated events that occurred during periods that have otherwise been forgotten.

Electroconvulsive Shock and Gradients of Retrograde Amnesia

Electroconvulsive shock (ECS) has amnesic effects similar to those produced by a blow to the head. The advantage of ECS over accidental closed-head injury in the study of posttraumatic amnesia is that ECS is a scheduled and precisely administered treatment.

In the 1950s and 1960s, ECS seemed to provide the ideal method for testing the theory that memory consolidation reflects the transfer of memory from short-term storage by reverberatory neural activity to long-term structural storage (Hebb, 1949). The idea was that the ECS would erase from storage any memories that had not already been converted to structural synaptic changes, but that it would leave the structural changes unaffected. In other words, it was assumed that the duration of the period of retrograde amnesia prior to an **electroconvulsive shock** would provide a means of estimating the amount of time that it takes for memory consolidation. For example, if a subject remembered events that occurred 5 minutes before an ECS, but had some difficulty remembering those that occurred 4 minutes before, it would suggest that consolidation takes between 4 and 5 minutes.

In one such study (Pinel, 1969), thirsty rats were placed for 10 minutes on each of 5 consecutive days in a test box that contained a small niche. By the fifth of these habituation sessions, most rats explored the niche only 1 or 2 times per session. On the sixth day, there was a water spout in the niche, and each rat was allowed to drink for 15 seconds after it discovered the spout. This was the learning trial. Then 10 seconds, 1 minute, 10 minutes, 1 hour, or 3 hours later each rat received a single ECS. The electrodes were attached to the control subjects, but these rats received no ECS. The next day the retention of all subjects was assessed by recording how many times each explored the niche when the water spout was no longer present. The no-ECS control rats explored the empty niche an average of 10 times during the 10-minute test session, thus indicating that they remembered their discovery of water the previous day. As indicated in Figure 14.11, the rats that had received ECS 1 hour or 3 hours after the learning trial also explored the niche about 10 times. In contrast, the rats that received the ECS 10 seconds, 1 minute, or 10 minutes after the learning trial explored the empty niche significantly less on the test day. This suggested that the consolidation of the memory of the learning trial took between 10 minutes and 1 hour.

Numerous variations of this experiment were conducted in the 1950s and 1960s, with different learning tasks, different species, and different numbers and intensities of ECSs. Initially, there was some consistency in the findings; most seemed to suggest a rather brief consolidation time of a few minutes or less (e.g., Chorover & Schiller, 1965). But then things became complicated. It was reasonable to think of the neural activity resulting from an experience reverberating through the brain for a few seconds or even a few minutes, but reports of ECS gradients of retrograde amnesia covering hours, days, and even weeks began to appear (e.g., Squire & Spanis, 1984). Whatever the ECS gradients were measuring, it did not seem to be the automatic transfer of a memory from short-term reverberatory activity to long-term structural change. It was a good idea to try to use ECS to estimate consolidation times, but things just didn't work out. Long gradients of ECS-produced retrograde amnesia suggested that the resistance of memories to disruption by ECS continues to increase for a very long time after learning, if not indefinitely.

The long-term progressive increase in the resistance of memories to disruption has been demonstrated by studies of the retrograde amnesia of patients following electroconvulsive therapy. For example, Squire and his colleagues (e.g., Squire & Cohen, 1979; Squire, Slater, & Chace, 1975) measured the memory of a sample of patients for television shows that had played for only one season in different years prior to their electroconvulsive therapy. They tested each subject twice on different forms of the test, once before they received a series of five ECSs and once 1 hour after. The difference between the before and after scores served as an objective estimate of memory loss for the events of each year. Figure 14.12 illustrates that five ECSs disrupted the retention of television shows that played in the 3 years prior to treatment, but not before.

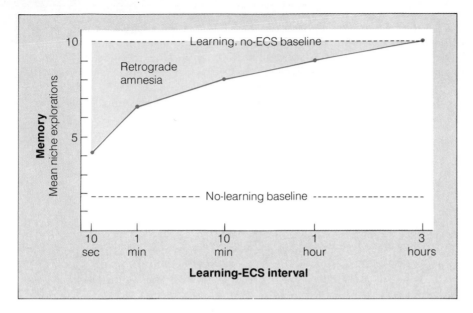

FIGURE 14.11

Retention of one-trial appetitive learning by no-ECS control rats and by groups of rats that received ECS at various intervals after the learning trial. (Adapted from Pinel, 1969.)

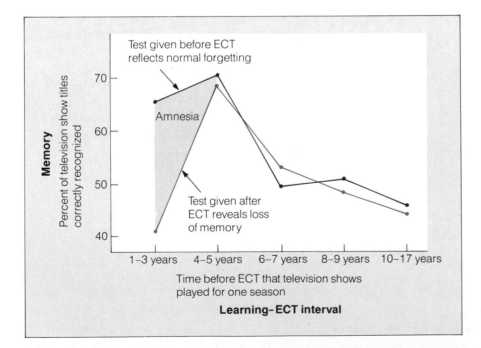

FIGURE 14.12

A series of five ECSs produced retrograde amnesia for television shows that played for only one season between 1 and 3 years before the ECSs. They did not produce amnesia for one-season shows that had played prior to that. (Adapted from Squire et al., 1975.)

SELF TEST

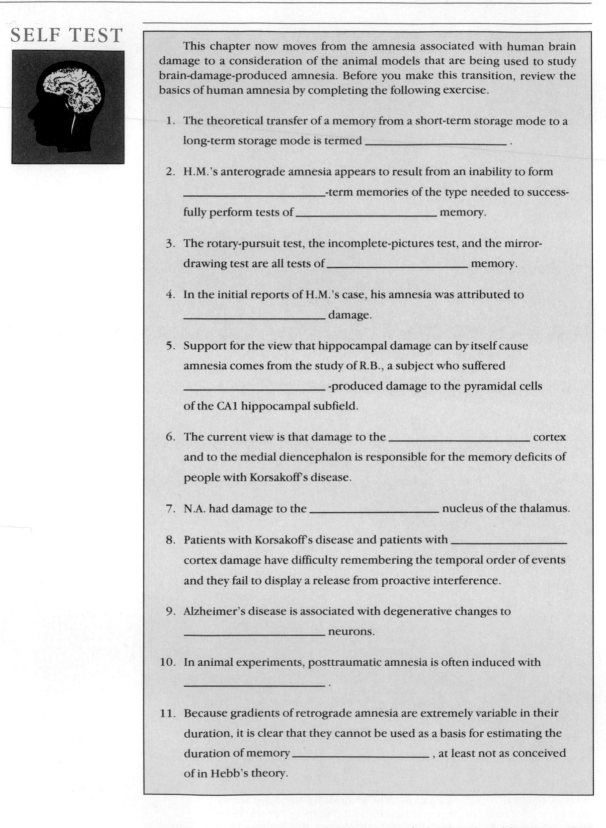

This chapter now moves from the amnesia associated with human brain damage to a consideration of the animal models that are being used to study brain-damage-produced amnesia. Before you make this transition, review the basics of human amnesia by completing the following exercise.

1. The theoretical transfer of a memory from a short-term storage mode to a long-term storage mode is termed _____ .

2. H.M.'s anterograde amnesia appears to result from an inability to form _____-term memories of the type needed to successfully perform tests of _____ memory.

3. The rotary-pursuit test, the incomplete-pictures test, and the mirror-drawing test are all tests of _____ memory.

4. In the initial reports of H.M.'s case, his amnesia was attributed to _____ damage.

5. Support for the view that hippocampal damage can by itself cause amnesia comes from the study of R.B., a subject who suffered _____ -produced damage to the pyramidal cells of the CA1 hippocampal subfield.

6. The current view is that damage to the _____ cortex and to the medial diencephalon is responsible for the memory deficits of people with Korsakoff's disease.

7. N.A. had damage to the _____ nucleus of the thalamus.

8. Patients with Korsakoff's disease and patients with _____ cortex damage have difficulty remembering the temporal order of events and they fail to display a release from proactive interference.

9. Alzheimer's disease is associated with degenerative changes to _____ neurons.

10. In animal experiments, posttraumatic amnesia is often induced with _____ .

11. Because gradients of retrograde amnesia are extremely variable in their duration, it is clear that they cannot be used as a basis for estimating the duration of memory _____ , at least not as conceived of in Hebb's theory.

The following are the answers to the preceding questions: (1) consolidation, (2) long, explicit, (3) implicit, (4) hippocampal, (5) ischemia, (6) prefrontal, (7) mediodorsal, (8) prefrontal, (9) cholinergic, (10) electroconvulsive shock, and (11) consolidation.

Animal Models of Brain-Damage-Produced Amnesia

As you have just learned, the investigation of the memory deficits of brain-damaged patients has contributed much to our understanding of the neural bases of memory and amnesia. As informative as the study of amnesic patients has proven to be, it has major limitations. Many important questions about the neural bases of memory and amnesia require controlled multisubject experiments for their resolution. For example, in order to determine the effects of damage to various brain structures on memory, it is necessary to make discrete lesions in different structures in the brains of groups of subjects, and to control what and when the subjects learn and how and when their retention is tested. Because such experiments are clearly not feasible in human subjects, there has been considerable effort to develop useful animal models of brain-damage-produced amnesia to complement the study of human cases.

One particularly useful animal model of human amnesia has been developed in the macaque monkey. Before I describe it, I want to emphasize the obvious: Macaque monkeys are not humans; the results of their study must be applied to humans with caution. This point was made by Mishkin and Appenzeller (1987).

> Our route to understanding human memory is an indirect one, with unavoidable drawbacks. The macaque brain is about one-fourth the size of the brain of the chimpanzee, the nearest relative of human beings, and the chimpanzee brain in turn is only about one-fourth the size of the human brain. With the increase in size has come greater complexity. The structures we study in the macaque all have counterparts in the human brain, but their functions may well have diverged in the course of evolution. The unique human capacity for language, in particular, and the cerebral specializations it has brought set limits to the comparative approach. Yet basic neural systems are likely to be common to monkeys and human beings . . . (p. 80).

For these reasons, it is clear that the study of animal models of amnesia (see Ridley & Baker, 1991) can never by itself provide unequivocal answers to questions about human amnesia. The power of animal models lies in their convergence with human case studies. Because the animal-model and human case-study approaches each compensate for shortcomings of the other, together they can provide convincing answers to questions that neither can answer satisfactorily by itself.

The task that has been used most successfully to assess memorial deficits in the monkey model of amnesia is the **nonrecurring-items delayed nonmatching-to-sample task.** A monkey with a brain lesion is presented with a distinctive object (the *sample*), under which it finds a simian delicacy such as banana pellet. Then, after a delay, the monkey is presented with two test objects: the original sample and an unfamiliar object. To perform correctly on this test, the monkey must remember the sample and select the unfamiliar object to obtain the food concealed beneath it. New objects (i.e., nonrecurring items) are used on each trial. The performance of a correct trial is illustrated in Figure 14.13. When the delay between the presentation of the sample object is a few minutes or less, normal monkeys trained on the nonrecurring-items delayed nonmatching-to-sample task perform almost perfectly.

FIGURE 14.13

The correct performance of a nonrecurring-items delayed nonmatching-to-sample trial. (Adapted from Mishkin & Appenzeller, 1987.)

The monkey moves the sample object to obtain food from the well beneath it.

A screen is lowered in front of the monkey during the delay period.

The monkey is confronted with the sample object and an unfamiliar object.

The monkey must remember the sample object and select the unfamiliar object to obtain the food beneath it.

Does the performance of brain-damaged monkeys on the nonrecurring-items delayed nonmatching-to-sample task model the memory deficits of human amnesics? The performance of monkeys with bilateral medialtemporal lobectomies suggests that it does. Their performance is near normal at brief delays (i.e., a few seconds), but it falls off to near-chance levels at longer delays (see Figure 14.14). Moreover, their performance is extremely susceptible to the disruptive effects of distraction (see Zola-Morgan & Squire, 1984; Squire & Zola-Morgan, 1985).

The fact that humans can perform the monkey version of the nonrecurring-items delayed nonmatching-to-sample task created an interesting opportunity for validating the monkey model. In recent studies (Aggleton, Nicol, Huston, & Fairbairn, 1988; Squire, Zola-Morgan, & Chen, 1988), human amnesics have been tested on the monkey nonrecurring-items delayed nonmatching-to-sample task and on a few of the other tasks that are currently being used to assess memory deficits in brain-damaged monkeys (e.g., object-

reward association, concurrent discrimination, and object discrimination) —
in case you were wondering, the rewards were coins rather than banana pellets. The performance of amnesic humans mirrored the performance of amnesic monkeys in almost all respects.

There were many unsuccessful efforts to model human brain-damage-
produced amnesia in laboratory animals before the development of the non-
recurring-items-delayed-nonmatching-to-sample-task model. Why did more
conventional animal learning-and-memory tasks (e.g., operant conditioning,
Pavlovian conditioning, avoidance conditioning) prove unsuccessful? In retrospect, the answer is obvious. Most animal learning-and-memory tasks do
not tap the cognitive processes that are disrupted in human brain-damage-
produced amnesia. They are tests of implicit memory, the very type of memory tests on which human amnesics display no deficits. This point was recently made in a study by Zola-Morgan and Squire (1984). They tested the
performance of monkeys on two tests of implicit memory: the **lifesaver
motor-skill task,** in which monkeys learn to obtain a lifesaver-shaped candy
by quickly threading it along a metal rod and around a bend (see Figure
14.15), and the **barrier motor-skill task,** in which monkeys learn to obtain a
fragile bread stick by manipulating it through a system of barriers. Monkeys
with large medial-temporal-lobe lesions learned and retained these two tasks
as well as did control monkeys.

Medial-Temporal-Lobe Amnesia: Testing Neuroanatomical Hypotheses in Monkeys and Rats

Scoville and Milner (1957) originally attributed medial-temporal-lobe amnesia to hippocampal damage; two alternative hypotheses were proposed in the
1970s. Mishkin (1978) hypothesized that combined hippocampal and amygdalar damage is necessary for full-blown medial-temporal-lobe amnesia,

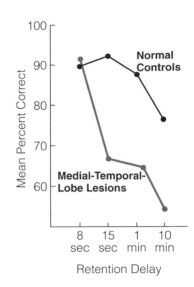

FIGURE 14.14

The deficits of monkeys with
large bilateral medial-
temporal-lobe lesions on the
nonrecurring-items delayed
nonmatching-to-sample task.
These deficits parallel the
memory deficits of human
medial-temporal-lobe
amnesics. (Adapted from
Squire and Zola-Morgan,
1991.)

FIGURE 14.15

A monkey performing the
lifesaver motor-skill task.
(Adapted from Zola-Morgan,
1984.)

and Horel (1978) hypothesized that damage to the temporal stem is the critical factor—the temporal stem carries information from temporal cortex past the hippocampus and amygdala to other parts of the brain, including the prefrontal cortex and medial thalamus.

The nonrecurring-items delayed nonmatching-to-sample model opened up these three hypotheses to experimental investigation. Early studies suggested that bilateral hippocampal damage can produce medial-temporal-lobe amnesia (e.g., Mahut, Moss, Zola-Morgan, 1981). However, there was considerable debate over the effect of amygdalar damage. The results of some experiments suggested that amygdalar lesions exacerbated the deficits produced by hippocampal lesions (e.g., Mishkin, 1978; Squire & Zola-Morgan, 1985); the results of other experiments suggested that they did not (e.g., Mahut, Moss, Zola-Morgan, 1981). The temporal-stem hypothesis seemed to be ruled out by an early report (Zola-Morgan, Squire, & Mishkin, 1982) that the nonrecurring-items delayed nonmatching-to-sample of monkeys was not disrupted by bilateral transection of the temporal stem. Recent studies of the monkey model have challenged these early conclusions, and they have led to yet another neuroanatomical hypothesis of medial-temporal-lobe amnesia (see Murray, 1991; Squire & Zola-Morgan, 1991).

In the early studies of the monkey model, hippocampal and amygdalar lesions were usually made by *aspiration* (see Chapter 5). Consequently, overlying cortical tissue and white matter were removed to expose the hippocampus and amygdala to the surgeon's pipette. Figure 14.16 illustrates the location of the hippocampus and amygdala and the areas of overlying medial-temporal cortex that are routinely damaged during hippocampal and amygdalar aspiration: the *perirhinal cortex,* the *periamygdaloid cortex,* the *entorhinal cortex,* and the *parahippocampal cortex.*

It is now clear that bilateral lesions to medial-temporal cortex of monkeys produce large deficits in nonrecurring-items delayed nonmatching-to-sample (Meunier, Murray, Bachevalier, & Mishkin, 1990; Zola-Morgan, Squire, Amaral, & Suzuki, 1989), even when there is no subcortical damage. In contrast, hippocampal lesions that do not damage overlying cortex produce only mild

FIGURE 14.16

A ventral view of the monkey brain. The subcortical location of the hippocampus and amygdala are indicated by diagonal lines. The four areas of overlying cortex are shown in color: perirhinal cortex (blue), periamygdaloid cortex (yellow), entorhinal cortex (pink), and para-hippocampal (green).

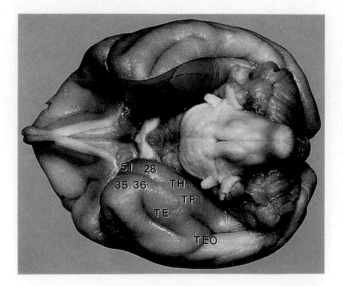

deficits in nonrecurring-items delayed nonmatching-to-sample (Clower, Alvarez-Royo, Zola-Morgan, & Squire, 1991), and lesions of the amygdala that do not damage overlying cortex produce few, if any, deficits (Murray, 1991; Zola-Morgan, Squire, & Amaral, 1989). The early conclusion that temporal-stem damage does not contribute to medial-temporal-lobe amnesia has also been challenged. The transections that were performed in the influential early study (Zola-Morgan et al., 1982) were incomplete. Complete bilateral transections of the monkey temporal stem produce profound deficits in non-recurring-items delayed nonmatching-to-sample (Cirillo, Horel, & George, 1989).

The results of research on the nonrecurring-items delayed nonmatching-to-sample model suggest that the following three temporal-lobe structures are involved in memory (see Murray, 1992; Squire & Zola-Morgan, 1991): (1) medial-temporal cortex, which includes the entorhinal, perirhinal, and perihippocampal cortices; (2) the hippocampus; and (3) the temporal stem and other interconnecting fibers. This conclusion is schematically illustrated in Figure 14.17. Consistent with this emerging view of medial-temporal-lobe amnesia is the recent report that the entorhinal cortex is the most heavily damaged cortex in cases of Alzheimer's disease (Van Hoesen, Hyman, & Damasio, 1991).

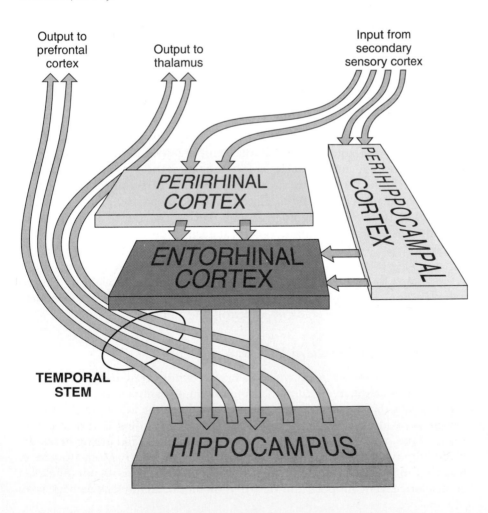

FIGURE 14.17

A schematic diagram of the structures of the medial-temporal lobes that are thought to play major roles in memory.

The rat model of medial-temporal-lobe amnesia   Three years ago, when I was writing the first edition of this chapter, it occurred to me that a rat model of medial-temporal-lobe amnesia that was based on the nonrecurring-items delayed nonmatching-to-sample task would be extremely useful. It would facilitate the conduct of large-scale parametric studies of brain-damage-produced amnesia, which are difficult in monkeys for economic and ethical reasons, and it would make it possible to compare the performance of three species—humans, monkeys, and rats—on the same memory task. Dave Mumby and I—mainly Dave Mumby—subsequently designed the apparatus and nonrecurring-items delayed nonmatching-to-sample paradigm that is depicted in Figure 14.18 (Mumby, Pinel, & Wood, 1989). This apparatus is now widely referred to as the **Mumby box.**

Can rats perform a task as complex as nonrecurring-items delayed nonmatching-to-sample? Yes they can (see Aggleton, 1985; Rothblat & Hayes, 1987); in fact, rats perform almost as well as monkeys at delays up to 1 minute (Mumby, Pinel, & Wood, 1989)—see Figure 14.19. Moreover, the effects of bilateral medial-temporal-lobe lesions on the nonrecurring-items delayed nonmatching-to-sample of rats are proving to be similar to those reported for monkeys. In one experiment (Mumby, Wood, & Pinel, 1992), hippocampal lesions, amygdalar lesions, or combined lesions of the amygdala and hippocampus produced only slight deficits if the lesions did not extend significantly into surrounding white matter and medial-temporal cortex. In contrast, hippocampal lesions that inadvertently extended into the surrounding white matter and into the perirhinal and entorhinal cortices produced profound deficits.

Medial-Temporal-Lobe Lesions and Retrograde Amnesia in Monkeys

Do monkeys with large, bilateral medial-temporal-lobe lesions display gradients of retrograde amnesia? The answer seems to be "yes" (Salmon, Zola-Morgan, & Squire, 1987). In a recent experiment (Zola-Morgan, & Squire, 1990), monkeys were trained to discriminate between 100 pairs of objects; they had to learn which member of each pair was correct. They learned to discriminate between 20 pairs of objects at each of the following five intervals before surgery: 16, 12, 8, 4, and 2 weeks. Removal of the hippocampus and the overlying white matter and cortex produced a greater impairment for discriminations learned 2 and 4 weeks prior to surgery than for those learned sooner. Thus, in monkeys, as in humans, large bilateral lesions of the medial-temporal lobes produce gradients of retrograde amnesia.

Diencephalic Amnesia in Monkeys and Rats

Aggleton and Mishkin (1983) were the first to demonstrate that performance of the nonrecurring-items delayed nonmatching-to-sample task is sensitive to diencephalic damage in monkeys. They found that large lesions to the medial thalamus produce severe deficits. The subsequent finding that discrete lesions of the mediodorsal nuclei produce deficits in nonrecurring-items delayed nonmatching-to-sample performance in monkeys (Zola-Morgan & Squire, 1985) in monkeys, but that mammillary body lesions do not (Aggleton & Mishkin, 1983), supports the view that mediodorsal nucleus damage is an

The sample object is placed over one food cup at one end. An object identical to the sample object and a novel object are placed over the two food cups at the other end.

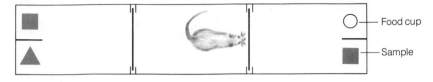

When the sliding door is raised exposing the sample, a trained food-deprived rat runs down to it and pushes it aside. Then a piece of food is deposited by a food-delivery mechanism into the exposed food cup.

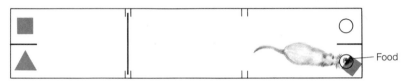

The sample object is immediately removed by the experimenter, and the rat remains in the same end of the Mumby box until the prescribed delay period is over (e.g., for 1 minute).

Then, the other sliding door is raised to expose the two objects at the other end. Trained rats, remembering their previous encounter with the sample, run to the novel object, push it aside, and food is delivered to the exposed food cup. The sliding door at the other end is lowered behind the rat.

The rat then runs to the center of the Mumby box, and the sliding door is closed behind it. Then new objects are arranged for the next trial. One advantage of the Mumby-box paradigm is that the rats do not have to be handled either during or between trials.

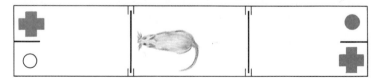

FIGURE 14.18

The Mumby box and the rat nonrecurring-items delayed nonmatching-to-sample paradigm.

important factor in Korsakoff amnesia. Additional support for this conclusion was provided by the recent report that bilateral mediodorsal nucleus lesions disrupt nonrecurring-items delayed nonmatching-to-sample in rats (Mumby & Pinel, 1990).

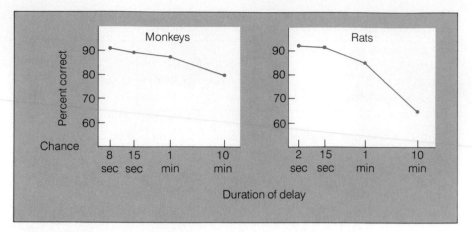

FIGURE 14.19

A comparison of the performance of rats (Mumby, Pinel, & Wood, 1989) and the performance of monkeys (Zola-Morgan, Squire, & Mishkin, 1982) on the nonrecurring-items delayed nonmatching-to-sample task.

Memory Deficits in Monkeys with Prefrontal Cortex Damage

Because the prefrontal cortex contains no primary sensory or motor areas, it has long been assumed to be involved in complex cognitive functions, and studies of human clinical cases with prefrontal damage have borne this out. For example, you may recall from earlier in this chapter that Korsakoff patients and other patients with prefrontal damage often have difficulty remembering the temporal order of events. Monkeys with prefrontal lesions seem to have a similar problem. Although monkeys with prefrontal lesions have no deficits on the nonrecurring-item delayed nonmatching-to-sample task (Bachevalier & Mishkin, 1986; Kowalska, Bachevalier, & Mishkin, 1984), they have difficulty performing the **recurring-items delayed matching-to-sample task** (Mishkin & Manning, 1978). In this task, the same two items are presented on each trial, and the monkeys must select the one that matches the sample. Because the same two items are presented on each trial, the monkeys must remember which one of the two they have seen most recently and choose it.

Monkeys with prefrontal lesions also have difficulty performing the **delayed-alternation task** (Mishkin, 1957). In this task, the position of the reward alternates between the two test objects from trial to trial. Thus, in order to receive a pellet, the monkey must remember where the pellet was on the preceding trial and select the other object.

The prefrontal cortex is not a homogeneous area of the brain; it comprises many structurally distinct areas of neocortex that have their own unique patterns of connection with other parts of the brain (see Petrides, 1989). It is not surprising then that different areas of prefrontal cortex seem to play different roles in memory. This point was made in a recent monkey experiment that involved a task called the **self-ordered task.** The self-ordered task was designed to be sensitive to a memory deficit that is displayed by many human patients with prefrontal damage. They have difficulty performing the various components of a multiple-component task in proper sequence; for example, they may pick up the phone to call for a pizza before they have looked up the phone number or decided which kind of pizza they want. In the monkey self-ordered task, a monkey is presented with three containers, each of which contains a reward. On the first day, the monkey is permitted to open one container to obtain the enclosed reward. The next day the same three boxes are presented in a different arrangement, and the monkey must select one of the other two containers to obtain one of the two remaining rewards. The daily trials continue until the monkey has managed to obtain all three rewards. Petrides (1988) assessed the effects of two prefrontal lesions on the performance of this task. One group of monkeys received lesions to midlateral prefrontal cortex; another received lesions to adjacent dorsolateral prefrontal cortex (see Figure 14.20). Lesions to the midlateral prefrontal cortex disrupted the performance of the self-ordered task; lesions to the dorsolateral prefrontal cortex did not.

In the self-ordered task, a monkey is presented with three containers, each of which contains a reward. The monkey is allowed to open one container, and the next day it is offered three again, and it must select one of the remaining two to obtain one of the two remaining rewards. Daily trials continue until the monkey obtains all three rewards.

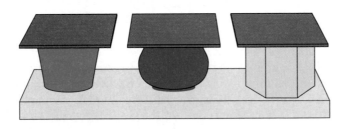

Monkeys with bilateral excisions of midlateral prefrontal cortex are severely impaired on this task; monkeys with bilateral excisions of adjacent dorsolateral prefrontal cortex are not.

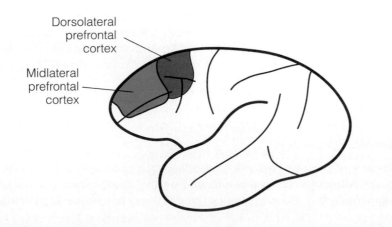

Dorsolateral prefrontal cortex

Midlateral prefrontal cortex

FIGURE 14.20

Lesions of the midlateral prefrontal cortex disrupted the ability of monkeys to perform the self-ordered task; lesions of the adjacent dorsolateral prefrontal cortex did not. (Adapted from Petrides, 1989.)

14.6

Current Theoretical Issues in the Study of Memory and Amnesia

To bring the data already reviewed in this chapter into sharper focus, the remainder of the chapter dwells on five central theoretical issues: (1) Where are memories stored? (2) Are there different systems for explicit and implicit memory? (3) Does amnesia result from a defect in encoding, storage, or retrieval? (4) Are the amnesias associated with medial-temporal-lobe and medial diencephalic damage distinct from one another? and (5) What does the hippocampus do?

Where Are Memories Stored?

Lashley's ground-breaking research focused attention on the question of whether memories are stored diffusely throughout the brain or localized at particular sites. It now seems that the answer lies somewhere between these two extremes. Memory storage appears to be diffuse in the sense that no single center exists for the storage of all memories and in the sense that several parts of the brain appear to participate in the storage of the memory for any single experience, but it appears to be localized in the sense that there are specific areas of the brain that seem to be specialized for memory storage.

The current consensus (see Mishkin & Appenzeller, 1987; Squire & Zola-Morgan, 1991) is that memories of particular events are likely stored in the very sensory areas of the cortex that are involved in their initial analysis. The strongest support for this view comes from the study of the memorial functions of inferotemporal cortex. **Inferotemporal cortex,** you may recall from Chapter 8, is a site of complex visual processing. Mishkin (1982) found that monkeys that were trained on the nonrecurring-items delayed nonmatching-to-sample task had difficulty relearning the task after bilateral inferotemporal cortex lesions. After 1,500 trials, they did manage to improve their performance from 50% to 85% correct when the delay was only 10 seconds, thus indicating that they could perceive the difference between the test objects and learn the principle of the task; however, they could not perform the task at intervals greater than 1 minute.

Analogous lines of evidence have been used to implicate other areas of sensory cortex in memory storage. For example, evidence suggests that **posterior parietal cortex** stores information about spatial location (Ungerleider & Mishkin, 1982), that **secondary somatosensory cortex** stores tactile pattern information (Mishkin, 1979), and that **secondary auditory cortex** stores auditory information (Colombo, D'Amato, Rodman, & Gross, 1990).

Are There Different Systems for Explicit and Implicit Memory?

The memory of amnesic patients has traditionally been assessed by tests that require the conscious retrieval of information about past events (i.e., by *recall* or *recognition tests*). However, since the discovery that amnesic patients can display savings on certain memory tests in the absence of conscious recall or recognition, there has been a growing interest in such tests (Schacter, 1987; Verfaellie, Bauer, & Bowers, 1991).

On what kinds of tests do amnesic patients display savings in the absence of recall or recognition; that is, on what kinds of tests do they display implicit memory? H.M. was found to have implicit memory for various sensory-motor tasks, and subsequent research revealed that many amnesic patients retain sensory-motor skills without consciously remembering the training sessions that produced them. Since these early observations, amnesic patients have demonstrated implicit memory on three additional kinds of tests: *perceptual learning, classical conditioning,* and *priming.* In a study of perceptual learning, amnesic patients retained the ability to read the mirror images of words over a 3-month retention interval, although they often failed to recall the training sessions (Cohen & Squire, 1980). In a study of classical conditioning (Weiskrantz & Warrington, 1979), two amnesic patients retained a conditioned eyeblink response for 24 hours, despite the fact that just minutes after their training was completed, they had no conscious recollection of it. Most of the recent research on implicit memory in amnesic subjects has employed a task called **repetition priming.** A list of words is presented, and then later, the subjects are presented with fragments of the words that were in the list (e.g., _SS_SS_ _). Then they are asked to complete the fragments with the first words that come to mind. Despite the fact that they display no recall or recognition for the words on the list, they are often able to correctly complete the word fragments (e.g., ASSASSIN).

The current consensus is that implicit and explicit tests of memory tap different systems of memory storage (Tulving & Schacter, 1990). Supporting this view are two kinds of evidence. First, a number of studies have shown that certain experimental manipulations can influence performance on implicit tests of memory without influencing performance on explicit tests and vice versa (see Graf & Schacter, 1987; Haist, Musen, & Squire, 1991; Schacter, Tharan, Cooper, & Rubens, 1991). Second, some amnesic subjects whose performance on explicit tests of memory is pitiful perform as well as normals on tests of implicit memory (Graf, Squire, & Mandler, 1984).

Several theories have been proposed to explain why many amnesics do not have deficits on implicit tests of memory; the most influential is that of Squire and his colleagues (e.g., Squire, 1987). They contend that there are two memory storage systems in the brain, one for **declarative memories** and one for what they call **procedural memories,** and that it is only the system for storing declarative memories that is disturbed in most amnesics. Squire describes these two systems this way:

> Declarative memory is explicit and accessible to conscious awareness, and it includes the facts, episodes, lists, and routes of everyday life. It can be declared, that is, brought to mind verbally as a proposition or nonverbally as an image. It includes both **episodic memory** (specific time-and-place events) as well as **semantic memory** (facts and general information gathered in the course of specific experiences). Declarative memory depends on the integrity of the neural systems damaged in amnesia as well as on the particular neural systems that store the information being learned.
>
> In contrast, procedural memory is implicit, and it is accessible only through performance, by engaging in the skills or operations in which the

knowledge is embedded. . . . In priming, preexisting representations are activated, and the information that is acquired is implicit and has other characteristics of procedural knowledge. (Squire, 1986, p. 1614)

Does Amnesia Reflect a Deficit in Encoding, Storage, or Retrieval?

Like the storage of information in a computer, the storage of information in memory is commonly considered to comprise three separate stages: (1) the information is encoded and entered, (2) it is stored, and (3) it is retrieved (see Jacoby, 1984). Amnesia could result from a malfunction at any one of these three stages, or at any combination of them.

Because retrograde amnesia is by definition amnesia for events that precede the amnesia-producing brain disturbance, it cannot be the result of an encoding problem. There are two patterns of retrograde amnesia, one that is commonly attributed to a disruption of storage and one that is commonly attributed to a disruption of retrieval. The temporally graded form of retrograde amnesia—that is, the form of retrograde amnesia that preferentially disturbs recent memories and leaves more remote memories undisturbed—is commonly assumed to reflect a disturbance in the consolidation of memories during storage. As you have already learned, consolidation was at one time thought to be a relatively brief postencoding process that translates labile short-term memories into more stable long-term memories; however, the fact that some gradients of retrograde amnesia extend back for years (see Squire, Haist, & Shimamura, 1989) suggests that consolidation is a very long-term process.

Retrograde amnesia that is not temporally graded is usually thought to reflect a deficiency in retrieval. Amnesics who have difficulty in recalling remote as well as recent events are assumed to have difficulty engaging in the complex cognitive activities involved in searching memory and retrieving the required piece of information. Memory retrieval is a very complex process, which involves much more than simply calling up stored representations of previous events. We usually think of our own memories as being accurate representations of real events, but they are not; they are complex *reconstructions.* Numerous experiments have shown that we remember only a few details of any event, and from these we reconstruct our memory of the event by filling in the gaps with best guesses of what was likely to have happened given the circumstances. The remembered details and best guesses meld inseparably to form the memory.

The fact that most of our memories are best guesses rather than accurate representations complicates the interpretation of eyewitness testimony. Consider the results of the following classic experiment of Loftus and Palmer, 1974.

Students watched a film of a traffic accident. One group was asked, "About how fast were the cars going when they hit each other?" Another group was asked, "About how fast were the cars going when they smashed into each other?" The "hit" group estimated 34 miles an hour; the "smashed into" group estimated 41 miles an hour. When asked whether they remembered seeing broken glass—actually, the film showed no broken glass—only 14 percent of the hit group remembered broken glass, but 32 percent of the "smashed into" group remembered broken glass. (Kalat, 1985, p. 218)

Most efforts to characterize anterograde amnesia have focused on the anterograde amnesia of Korsakoff patients. Although the situation is far from clear, there is support for the view that the anterograde amnesia of Korsakoff patients reflects a general cognitive deficit that affects encoding as well as retrieval. The theory is that the tendency of Korsakoff patients to rigidly focus on superficial aspects of their environment and to adhere to particular lines of thought makes it difficult for them at the time of encoding to establish the rich network of associations that facilitates subsequent retrieval. The same superficiality and rigidity makes it difficult for them at the time of retrieval to scan and evaluate various associations to reactivate and reconstruct the memory (e.g., Jacoby, 1982; Winocur, Kinsbourne, & Moscovitch, 1981).

Are the Amnesias Associated with Medial-Temporal-Lobe Damage and Medial Diencephalic Damage Distinct from One Another?

There are two different views of the neural basis of amnesia. One is that all cases of amnesia are qualitatively the same. According to this view, differences between different cases of amnesia are either simply a matter of degree, or they result from damage to parts of the brain that are not directly involved in the amnesia. The other view is that damage to different parts of the memory system produce qualitatively different forms of amnesia. The debate over whether amnesia is best viewed as a unitary disorder or as a group of different disorders has focused on the differences between medial-temporal-lobe amnesia and medial diencephalic amnesia.

Although early analyses emphasized the similarity of medial-temporal-lobe amnesia and medial diencephalic amnesia, recent studies suggest that they are fundamentally different. One current hypothesis is that medial-temporal-lobe amnesia is a storage disorder and is thus associated with rapid forgetting, whereas medial diencephalic amnesia is an encoding and retrieval disorder and is thus associated with a normal rate of forgetting. Two attempts to confirm this hypothesis used the same procedure. In both experiments, an effort was made to insure that all groups began with equivalent memory by allowing amnesic patients more time than the normal subjects to learn the test material—it is impossible to compare forgetting rates if retention is unequal to begin with. One of the experiments compared normal humans, H.M., and a sample of Korsakoff patients (Huppert & Piercy, 1978, 1979); the other compared normal monkeys, monkeys with combined hippocampus and amygdala lesions, and monkeys with mediodorsal nucleus lesions (Zola-Morgan & Squire, 1982). The results of both studies suggest that medial-temporal-lobe damage accelerates forgetting and that medial diencephalic damage does not. When the diencephalic amnesics were given enough time to learn the test material, their forgetting curve was not substantially different from that of normal control subjects.

What Does the Hippocampus Do?

H.M.'s case focused the attention of biopsychologists on the hippocampus. It has stayed there ever since; the hippocampus has been and continues to be, one of the most intensely studied brain structures (see Barnes, 1988).

One important clue to the function of the hippocampus comes from studies in which the extracellular activity of single neurons has been recorded in freely moving animals—most commonly in freely moving rats. Some hippocampal neurons become active only when an animal is in a particular part of the test apparatus; these neurons have been termed **place cells** (O'Keefe & Dostrovsky, 1971). The memorial function of these place cells was demonstrated by O'Keefe and Speakman.

O'Keefe and Speakman (1987) recorded the extracellular activity of individual hippocampal neurons while rats performed an *elevated four-arm maze task.* On each learning trial, a food reward was available at the end of the same arm, and the rats quickly learned to go directly to the reward after being placed on one of the other arms of the maze. Because all arms were identical and a black curtain surrounded the apparatus, the rats had to learn to orient themselves in relation to cue objects that were pinned to the curtains. To insure that the rats were orienting in relation to the cue objects, the maze and all of the cue objects were rotated together between each trial (e.g., 90° to the right) so that the goal area always maintained its relation to the cue objects. O'Keefe and Speakman found that many of the neurons from which they recorded had well-defined *place fields* (i.e., they fired only when the rat was in a particular part of the maze) and that the place fields were determined by the position of the cue objects. Thus, if all the cue objects were rotated 90° to the right, the place field moved 90° to the right. The most important result of O'Keefe and Speakman's experiment emerged during a test in which rats that had learned the task were tested in the absence of the external cue objects. First, they enclosed the rat in various arms of the maze to identify the neurons' place fields; then, they allowed the rat to choose a goal arm. Remarkably, in the absence of the spatial cues, the location of the place fields of hippocampal neurons indicated where the rats "thought" they were. If, on the learning trials, the place field of the neuron was 90° to the left of the goal arm; on the test, the rat selected the goal arm that was 90° to the right of the neuron's place field. This result is illustrated in Figure 14.21.

On the basis of research on the place fields of hippocampal neurons, O'Keefe and Nadel (1978) proposed the **cognitive-mapping theory** of hippocampal function. They suggest that the hippocampus participates in the storage of information about an animal's position with respect to important landmarks in its environment. Strongly supporting the cognitive-mapping theory is the finding that hippocampal lesions disrupt the performance of tasks that have a substantial spatial component (e.g., Rasmussen, Barnes, & McNaughton, 1989; Sherry & Vaccarino, 1989)—tasks such as the *Morris water maze* and *radial-arm maze* (see Chapter 5). Foster, Castro, and McNaughton (1989) found that hippocampal place cells do not fire when subjects are first restrained and then placed in the cells' place field; this suggests that the hippocampus stores spatial information that is used to guide an animal's movement through its environment.

The cognitive-mapping theory does not imply that the spatial mapping is the only function of the hippocampus (see Eichenbaum & Wiener, 1989; Olton, Wible, Pang, & Sakurai, 1989). Recently, Sutherland and Rudy (1989) proposed that the hippocampus and associated structures are specialized for the acquisition, storage, and retrieval of what they term *configural associations,* associations between simple stimulus-stimulus or stimulus-response associations and particular contexts, which may or may not be spatial.

Rats learned to run the goal arm of an elevated 4-arm maze. The maze was enclosed by a black curtain, and six objects (illustrated schematically in blue) provided the only spacial cues. Many hippocampal neurons were found to have place fields. Illustrated in red is the place field of one neuron; its place field was halfway down the arm opposite the goal arm.

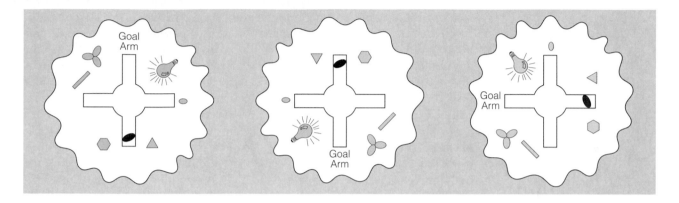

During the test, no spacial cues were present. The neuron was found to have a place field half way down one arm.

When the rat was given an opportunity to choose the goal arm, it chose the arm opposite to the arm that contained the neuron's place field.

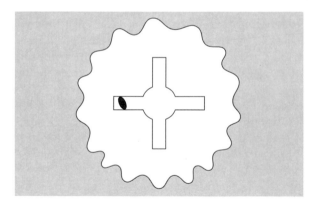

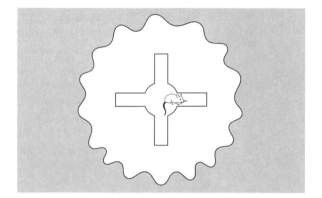

These results support O'Keefe and Nadel's theory that one function of the hippocampus is the retention of an internal cognitive map. (Adapted from O'Keefe and Speakman, 1987.)

FIGURE 14.21

An illustration of the experiment of O'Keefe and Speakman (1987). Some hippocampal units (place cells) were active only when the rat was in a particular part of the elevated 4-arm maze. When there were no external position cues, the activity of these units fired in relation to where the rat "thought" it was, as indicated by the goal arm that it selected.

14.7

Conclusion: The Ironic Case of R.M.

This chapter began with the case of H.M. Next was a discussion of Korsakoff's syndrome and of the memory deficits that characterize it. The hypothesized role of cholinergic dysfunction in the amnesia of Alzheimer's disease was described next, followed by an explanation of how gradients of retrograde amnesia have been used to estimate the time course of consolidation. Then, you learned how the development of the nonrecurring-items delayed nonmatching-to-sample model of amnesia in monkeys and rats has provided a means of investigating brain-damage-produced amnesia in controlled experiments. Finally, five current theoretical issues were discussed.

In the introduction, I said that this chapter would end with the ironic case of R.M., and so it shall. The case of R.M. differs in two ways from the other cases that have already been described in this chapter: first, the case has not been previously reported, and second, R.M. is himself a biopsychologist.

R.M. fell on his head while skiing, and when he regained consciousness, he was suffering from both retrograde and anterograde amnesia. For several hours, he could recall little of his previous life: he could not remember if he was married, where he lived, or where he worked. Also, many of the things that happened to him in the hours after his accident were forgotten as soon as his attention was diverted from them. His was a classic case of posttraumatic amnesia. Like H.M., he was trapped in the present with only a cloudy past and seemingly no future. The irony of the situation was that during these few hours, when R.M. could recall few of the events of his own life, his thoughts repeatedly drifted to one person—a person whom he remembered hearing about somewhere in his muddled past. Through the haze he remembered H.M., his fellow prisoner of the present, and he wondered if the same fate lay in store for him.

R.M. is now fully recovered and looks back on what he can recall of his experience with relief and bemusement, and with a certain feeling of empathy for H.M. Unlike H.M., R.M. received a reprieve, but his experience left him with a better appreciation for the situation of those, like H.M., who are serving life sentences. For the amusement of the jargon-lovers among you, I have coined a term for R.M.'s experience: *hypermetaamnesia,* the loss of memory of everything except H.M.

R.M. recently phoned me. He was disappointed that even his own students had not managed to guess R.M.'s identity from my description in the first edition of this text, and he suggested that I provide a more obvious clue than just his initials in the second edition. Here it is. His name is Ralph Mistlberger; his research on circadian rhythms was cited in Chapter 12.

Food for Thought

1. The study of the anatomy of memory has come a long way since H.M.'s misfortune. What kind of research on this topic do you think will prove to be most important in the next decade?

2. What are the advantages and shortcomings of animal models of amnesia?

3. Using examples from your own experience, compare implicit and explicit memory.

KEY TERMS

To help you study the material in this chapter, all of the key terms—those that have appeared in bold type—are listed and briefly defined here.

Amyloid plaques. Tangles of degenerating neural fibers and amyloid protein found in the brains of patients with Alzheimer's disease.

Anterograde amnesia. Loss of memory for events occurring after the amnesia-inducing event.

Barrier motor-skill task. A task in which monkeys learn to obtain a fragile bread stick by manipulating it around a system of barriers.

Bilateral medial-temporal lobectomy. The removal of the medical portions of both temporal lobes, including the amygdalas and hippocampuses; H.M.'s operation.

Block-tapping memory-span test. A nonverbal equivalent of the digit-span test.

CA1 subfield. An area of the hippocampus; R.B.'s ischemic brain damage was restricted to the pyramidal cell layer of this area.

Cognitive-mapping theory. The theory that one function of the hippocampus is to store memories of spatial location.

Consolidation. The hypothetical process by which a memory is transferred from a short-term mode of storage to a long-term mode of storage.

Declarative memory. Memory for which there is conscious awareness; a memory that car be declared (i.e., stated).

Delayed-alternation task. The subject must choose between the same two items on each trial, and the correct choice is the item that was wrong on the previous trial.

Digit span. The standard measure of verbal short-term memory.

Digit span +1 test. Each time the subject correctly repeats a sequence of digits, the next test item is the same sequence with an additional digit added to the end of it.

Electroconvulsive shock (ECS). A massive electric shock to the head that induces a convulsion.

Engram. The hypothetical change in the brain responsible for the storage of a memory.

Episodic memory. Memory for specific events.

Explicit memory. Memories that result from the deliberate effort to remember; memory expressed on tests of recall or recognition.

Global amnesia. Amnesia for information in all sensory modalities.

Implicit memory. Memory that results in improved performance without conscious recall or recognition.

Incomplete-pictures test. A test of memory involving the improved ability to identify fragmented figures that have been previously observed.

Infarct. Area of cell death produced by an interruption of blood supply.

Inferotemporal cortex. A site of complex visual processing.

Ischemia. Shortage in blood supply to an area that results in the death of cells.

Islands of memory. Memories for isolated events that occurred during periods that have otherwise been totally forgotten.

Korsakoff's syndrome. A memory disorder that develops in individuals who chronically consume alcohol; the memory deficits appear to result from a combination of diencephalic and prefrontal damage.

Lifesaver motor-skill task. A task in which monkeys learn to obtain a lifesaver-shaped piece of candy by threading it along a metal rod and around a bend.

Lobectomy. An operation in which a lobe, or a major part of one, is removed from the brain.

Lobotomy. An operation in which a lobe, or a major part of one, is separated from the brain by a large cut, but is not removed.

Mammillary bodies. A pair of hypothalamic nuclei; damage to these nuclei was originally thought to produce the memory deficits associated with Korsakoff's syndrome.

Matching-to-sample test. A sample stimulus is momentarily presented, followed by a delay, and then the subject must select the sample stimulus from a group of test stimuli.

Mediodorsal nuclei. Damage to these thalamic nuclei is thought to be responsible for some of the memory deficits associated with Korsakoff's syndrome.

Mirror-drawing test. A test in which the subject traces a star while watching her or his hand in a mirror.

Mumby-box. An apparatus designed to test nonrecurring-items delayed nonmatching-to-sample in rats.

Neurofibrils. Thread-like structures in the neural cytoplasm of patients with Alzheimer's disease.

Nonrecurring-items delayed nonmatching-to-sample task. A task in which the subject is presented with an unfamiliar sample object and then, after a delay, is presented with a choice between the same object and another unfamiliar object; the correct choice is the nonsample object.

Nootropics. Memory-improving agents; choline has been hypothesized to be a nootropic.

Place cells. Hippocampal neurons that have place fields, that is, hippocampal neurons that fire rapidly only when the subject is in a particular place in its environment.

Posterior parietal cortex. An area of cortex thought to store information about spatial location.

Posttraumatic amnesia (PTA). Amnesia produced by closed-head injuries, which typically includes both retrograde and anterograde memory deficits.

Principle of equipotentiality.   The idea that all parts of the neocortex play an equal role in the storage of memories for complex tasks.

Principle of mass action.   The idea that memories for complex tasks are stored diffusely throughout the neocortex.

Proactive interference.   The interfering effects of performing one task on performance of a subsequent one.

Procedural memory.   Memory that is revealed by improved performance without conscious recall; also referred to as implicit memory.

Pyramidal cell layer.   A major layer of cell bodies in the hippocampus.

Recurring-items delayed matching-to-sample task.   A sample object that the subject has seen on each previous trial is presented, then after a delay it and the other object seen on previous trials is presented; the subject must choose the sample; monkeys with prefrontal lesions have difficulty performing this task.

Reference memory.   Memory for the general principles and skills that are required to perform a task.

Repetition priming.   A test of implicit memory in which a list of words is presented; later, fragments of the original words are presented and the subject is asked to complete the fragments.

Retrograde amnesia.   Backward-acting memory deficit; loss of memory for information learned before the amnesia-inducing event.

Rotary pursuit test.   A test in which the subject tries to keep the end of a stylus in contact with a target rotating on a turntable.

Secondary auditory cortex.   An area of sensory cortex that is thought to store auditory memories.

Secondary somatosensory cortex.   An area of cortex that is thought to store tactile memories.

Self-ordered task.   A task in which a monkey is allowed to open one of a set of three containers on each trial; in order to obtain a reward on each trial, the monkey must remember which of the containers it has emptied on previous trials; the task is complete when all three rewards have been obtained.

Semantic memory.   Memory for facts and general information gathered in the course of specific experiences.

Temporal stem.   A fiber bundle lying just above the hippocampus; damage to the temporal stem has been hypothesized to be responsible for medial-temporal-lobe amnesia.

Working memory.   Temporary memory necessary for the successful completion of tasks on which one is currently working.

ADDITIONAL READING

The following five sources provide excellent readable reviews of much of the material in this chapter.

Barnes, C. A. (1988). Spatial learning and memory processes: The search for their neurobiological mechanisms in the rat. *Trends in Neuroscience, 11,* 163–169.

Mishkin, M., & Appenzeller, T. (1987). The anatomy of memory. *Scientific American, 256,* 80–89.

Squire, L. R. (1987). *Memory and the brain.* New York: Oxford University Press.

Squire, L. R., & Zola-Morgan, S. (1991). The medial temporal lobe memory system. *Science, 253,* 1380–1386.

Sutherland, R. J., & Rudy, J. W. (1989). Configural association theory: The role of the hippocampal formation in learning, memory, and amnesia. *Psychobiology, 17,* 129–144.

15

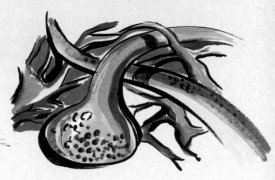

Neuroplasticity: Development, Learning, and Recovery from Brain Damage

15.1	Neural Development
15.2	The Neural Bases of Learning in Simple Systems
15.3	Neural Degeneration, Regeneration, and Reorganization
15.4	Neurotransplantation in the Central Nervous System

Most of us tend to think of the nervous system as a three-dimensional array of neural elements "wired" together in a massive network of circuits. The sheer magnitude and complexity of this wiring-diagram concept of the nervous system is staggering, but it sells the nervous system short by failing to capture one of its most important features. The nervous system is not a static network of interconnected elements as is implied by the wiring-diagram model. It is a plastic, living organ, which grows and changes continuously in response to the interaction between its genetic programs and its environment. These neuroplastic processes are the subject of this chapter.

This chapter has four sections, each of which deals with a different aspect of neuroplasticity. Section 15.1 is about neural development; it describes how the billions of specialized neurons that compose the nervous system are created, travel to their appropriate locations, and establish appropriate synaptic contacts. Section 15.2 describes current efforts to identify the neuroplastic mechanisms of learning. Section 15.3 deals with the responses of the nervous system to damage; it discusses neural degeneration, regeneration, and reorganization. And finally, Section 15.4 describes recent developments in the exciting field of neurotransplantation research.

The Simple-Systems Approach

This chapter features the **simple-systems approach** to the study of the neural basis of behavior. In this chapter, you will encounter numerous studies that at first appear to be strange fodder for students of biopsychology: studies of fish, chicks, frogs, salamanders, and snails. Why have researchers who are interested in neuroplasticity dedicated their lives to the study of such an odd assortment of creatures? The answer in one word is "simplicity." There is a great advantage in studying neural plasticity and behavior in neural circuits that are complex enough to mediate behavioral change, but simple enough to be analyzed neuron by neuron.

15.1

Neural Development

In the beginning there is a *zygote,* a single cell formed by the amalgamation of an ovum and a sperm. The zygote divides to form two daughter cells (Why aren't they ever called son cells?). These two divide to form four, these four divide to form eight, and so on . . . until a mature organism is produced. Of course, there must be more to it than this; if there were not, each of us would have ended up like a bowl of rice pudding—an amorphous mass of homogeneous cells. To save us from this fate, three things other than cell multiplication must happen. First, each cell must *differentiate;* some must become muscle cells, some must become multipolar neurons, some must become glial cells, and so on. Second, each cell must make its way to an appropriate site and align itself with the cells around it to form an organ. Third, each cell must establish appropriate functional relations with other cells. Section 15.1 describes how neurons accomplish these three things.

Three weeks after conception, the tissue that is destined to develop into the human nervous system becomes recognizable as the **neural plate,** a small patch of ectodermal tissue (*ectoderm* is the outermost layer of cells) on the dorsal surface of the developing embryo. As illustrated in Figure 15.1, the neural plate folds to form the *neural groove,* and the lips of the neural groove then fuse to form the **neural tube.** The inside of the neural tube eventually

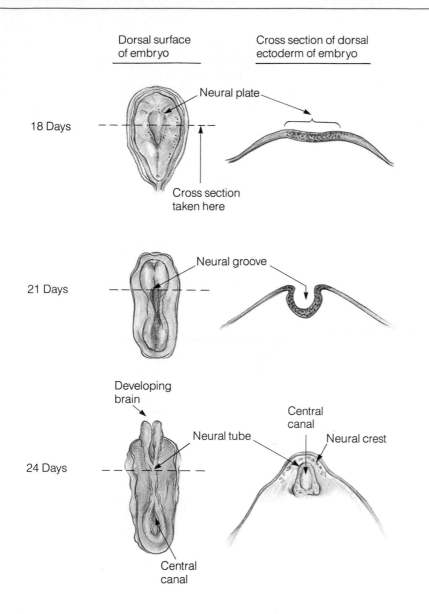

Dorsal surface of embryo

Cross section of dorsal ectoderm of embryo

18 Days

Neural plate

Cross section taken here

21 Days

Neural groove

24 Days

Developing brain

Neural tube

Central canal

Neural crest

Central canal

FIGURE 15.1

How the neural plate develops into the neural tube during the third and fourth weeks of human embryologic development. (Adapted from Cowan, 1979.)

becomes the *spinal canal* and *ventricles*. By 40 days of age, three swellings are clearly visible at the anterior end of the neural tube; these ultimately develop into the *forebrain, midbrain,* and *hindbrain* (see Figure 3.18).

The development of the brain and the rest of the nervous system occurs in five phases: (1) induction of the neural plate, (2) neural proliferation, (3) migration and aggregation, (4) axon growth and the formation of synapses, and (5) neuron death and synapse rearrangement. These five phases are discussed in the following five subsections.

Induction of the Neural Plate

Prior to the development of the neural plate, the cells of the dorsal ectoderm are **totipotential;** that is, each has the potential to develop into any type of body cell. With the development of the neural plate, they lose their totipotency; neural-plate cells develop into nervous-system tissue even if they are transplanted to a different part of the embryo.

The neural plate seems to develop under the direction of chemical signals from the underlying **mesoderm layer** (see Guthrie, 1991). Tissue taken from the dorsal mesoderm of one embryo and implanted beneath the ventral ectoderm of another, induces the development of an extra neural plate on the ventral surface of the host. One of the most fanciful demonstrations of **induction** is one that may require the abandonment of the expression, "as scarce as hen's teeth." Believe it or not, Kollar and Fisher (1980) induced teeth to grow from the ectodermal cells of chick embryos by implanting beneath them a tiny piece of mouse-embryo mesoderm taken from under the portion of the ectoderm that would normally have developed into the mouse's mouth.

Neural Proliferation

Once the lips of the invaginated neural plate have fused to create the neural tube, the cells of the tube begin to *proliferate* (increase greatly in number). Proliferation does not occur simultaneously or equally in all parts of the tube. In each species, the cells in different parts of the neural tube proliferate in a characteristic sequence that is responsible for the pattern of swelling and folding that gives each brain its species-characteristic shape. Most cell division in the neural tube occurs in a layer called the **ventricular zone,** which is adjacent to the *ventricle* (the fluid-filled center of the tube).

Migration and Aggregation

Migration   Once cells have been created in the ventricular zone of the neural tube, they must migrate to an appropriate location. During the period of **migration,** a temporary network of glial cells, called **radial glial cells** (see Figure 15.2), is present in the developing neural tube. Migrating neurons appear to move along these radial glial cells to their destinations (see Hatten, 1990; Sanes, 1989). Most migrate to a progressively thickening layer of cells called the *intermediate zone* (see Figure 15.2). After the intermediate zone is well established, some of the migrating cells form a layer between the ventricular and intermediate zones. The cells that migrate to this so-called *subventricular zone* are destined to become either glial cells or interneurons. In the forebrain, new cells begin to migrate through these layers to establish a layer of cells called the *cortical plate,* which eventually develops into the layers of the cerebral cortex. Because the cells of the deepest of the six layers of neocortex arrive at their destination first, the cells of progressively higher layers must migrate through them; this is referred to as the **inside-out pattern of cortical development.** When the migration of cells away from the ventricular zone is complete, the cells remaining there develop into *ependymal cells,* which form the lining of the ventricles of the brain and central canal of the spinal cord.

The **neural crest** is a structure that is situated just dorsal to, and to both sides of, the neural tube (see Figure 15.1). It is formed from cells that break off from the neural tube. Neural crest cells develop into the neurons and glia of the peripheral nervous system, and thus many of them must migrate over

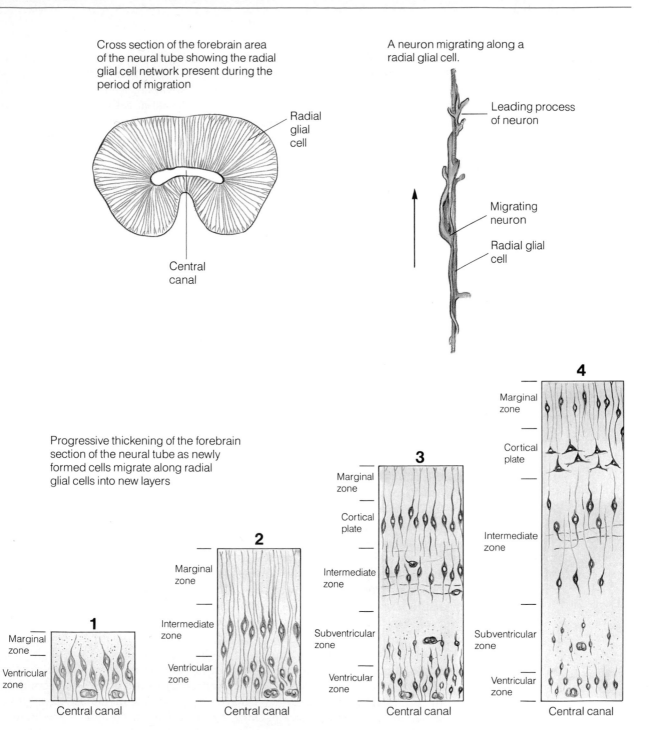

Cross section of the forebrain area of the neural tube showing the radial glial cell network present during the period of migration

Radial glial cell

Central canal

A neuron migrating along a radial glial cell.

Leading process of neuron

Migrating neuron

Radial glial cell

Progressive thickening of the forebrain section of the neural tube as newly formed cells migrate along radial glial cells into new layers

1

Marginal zone

Ventricular zone

Central canal

2

Marginal zone

Intermediate zone

Ventricular zone

Central canal

3

Marginal zone

Cortical plate

Intermediate zone

Subventricular zone

Ventricular zone

Central canal

4

Marginal zone

Cortical plate

Intermediate zone

Subventricular zone

Ventricular zone

Central canal

FIGURE 15.2

New cells are created by cell division in the ventricular zone of the developing neural tube; then they migrate out of the ventricular zone to create new layers of cells. Shown here is the expansion of the forebrain area of the tube.

great distances. It appears to be the media through which they travel, rather than information contained within the cells themselves, that directs them to their destination. The **differential adhesion hypothesis** is that neural crest cells migrate through tissue by following pathways to which they tend to adhere. In support of this hypothesis is the finding that cells transplanted from one part of the neural crest to another adopt the route characteristic of their new location.

Aggregation   Once developing neurons have migrated to the area in which they will function in the adult nervous system, they must align themselves in precise relation to the other cells that have migrated to the same area to form the structures of the nervous system. This process is called **aggregation.** Aggregation is thought to be mediated by **neural cell adhesion molecules (NCAMs),** which are located on the surface of the neurons. Neural cell adhesion molecules have the ability to recognize other neurons of the same type and adhere to them in specific orientations (Rutishauser, Acheson, Hall, Mann, & Sunshine, 1988).

Axon Growth and the Formation of Synapses

Once neurons have migrated to their appropriate position, axons and dendrites begin to grow from them. Intuitively, one would expect that these neural projections would be established in a very precise, species-characteristic manner; it is hard to imagine how the nervous system could work if its parts were not wired up according to a prescribed plan. In fact, accurate patterns of axonal growth have been demonstrated in a variety of systems: for example, the point-to-point projections of retinal ganglion cells onto the surface of the *optic tectum* in lower vertebrates and the specific patterns of outgrowth of motor neurons to various muscles in chicks.

At each growing tip of an axon or dendrite is an amoeba-like structure called a **growth cone** (Letourneau, Kater, & Macagno, 1991), which extends and retracts finger-like cytoplasmic extensions called *filopodia* (see Figure 15.3)—as if groping for the correct route. Three hypotheses have been proposed to explain how growth cones find their way to their appropriate destination (see Dodd & Jessell, 1988): the *chemoaffinity hypothesis,* the *blueprint hypothesis,* and the *topograhic-gradient hypothesis.*

Chemoaffinity hypothesis   In 1943, Sperry conducted an enlightening series of experiments. In one of them, he cut the optic nerves of frogs, rotated their eyeballs 180°, and waited for the **retinal ganglion cells,** which compose the optic nerve, to *regenerate* (regrow)—frogs, unlike mammals, have retinal ganglion cells that regenerate. Once regeneration was complete, Sperry used a convenient behavioral test to assess the frogs' visual capacities—see Figure 15.4. When he dangled a lure behind the frogs, they struck forward, thus indicating that their visual world, like their eyes, had been rotated 180°. Frogs whose eyes had been rotated, but whose optic nerves had not been cut, responded in exactly the same way. This was strong evidence that each retinal neuron had grown back to the same part of the **optic tectum** on which it had originally synapsed. A subsequent neuronanatomical tracing study confirmed this conclusion (Attardi & Sperry, 1963).

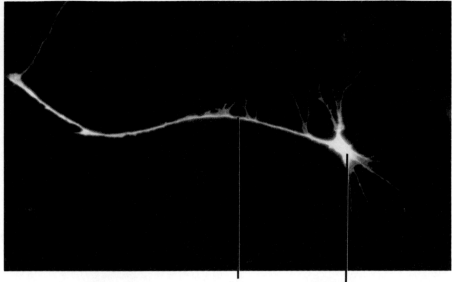

Axon   Growth cone

FIGURE 15.3

A growth cone. Photograph courtesy of Andrew Bulloch, University of Calgary

Sperry's classic studies of regeneration in the optic nerve were the basis of his **chemoaffinity hypothesis** of axonal development (Sperry, 1963). He hypothesized that each postsynaptic surface in the nervous system bears a specific chemical label, and that each growing axon is attracted by the label of its postsynaptic target during neural development and regeneration. The chemoaffinity hypothesis receives general support from the discovery of several chemicals that have the capacity to attract growing axons. The most well known of these is **nerve growth factor (NGF),** which has the ability to attract the growing axons of sympathetic nervous system neurons. Levi-Montalcini (1952, 1975) discovered that injections of nerve growth factor into the brains of neonatal rats caused the axons of sympathetic neurons to grow into the spinal cord (which they normally never do) and from there into the brain.

The strongest evidence in support of the chemoaffinity hypothesis comes from *in vitro studies* (studies conducted outside the living body, in tissue cultures). Even in a tissue culture, where normal spatial cues are totally lacking, axons can grow out from one developing structure and make appropriate connections with another (Hefner, Lumsden, & O'Leary, 1990; Yamamoto, Kurotani, & Toyami, 1989).

The chemoaffinity hypothesis accounts for many aspects of axon growth (see Tessier-Lavigne & Placzek, 1991), but it cannot explain why targets transplanted to novel positions sometimes become incorrectly innervated. For example, when Whitelaw and Hollyday (1983) implanted an extra thigh segment in the legs of developing chick embryos so that the sequence was thigh, thigh, calf, foot instead of the normal thigh, calf, foot, the second thigh segment became innervated by axons that normally would have innervated the calf. Also, the chemoaffinity hypothesis has difficulty explaining how some axons manage to follow exactly the same circuitous route to their target in every member of a species. For example, the axons of distinctive neurons in developing insect (e.g., Bastiani, Doe, Gelfand, & Goodman, 1985) and fish nervous systems (Kuwada, 1986) have been shown to grow to their targets by highly stereotyped indirect routes.

FIGURE 15.4

Sperry's classic study of eye rotation and regeneration.

When an insect is dangled in front of a normal frog, the frog strikes at it accurately with its tongue.

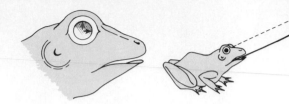

When the eye is rotated 180° without cutting the optic nerve, the frog misdirects its strikes by 180°.

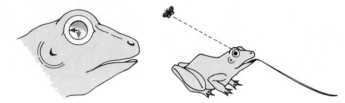

When the optic nerve is cut and the eye rotated by 180°, at first the frog is blind, but once the optic nerve has regenerated the frog misdirects its strikes by 180°.

This suggests that the cut axons of the optic nerve grew back out to their original synaptic targets in the optic tectum.

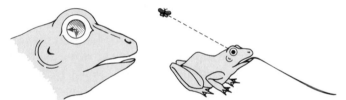

Optic tectum

Axons of optic nerve

Retina

Normal connections

Optic nerve cut and eye rotated 180°

Optic neurons grow back to their original targets, thus the frog sees things located 180° from their actual position

Blueprint hypothesis   The inability of the chemoaffinity hypothesis to account for certain aspects of axon development led to the proposal of the **blueprint hypothesis** (Singer, Nordlander, & Egar, 1979). According to the blueprint hypothesis, the undeveloped nervous system contains specific chemical and/or mechanical trails that growing axons follow to their destinations. **Pioneer growth cones,** the first growth cones to travel from one particular structure to another in a developing nervous system, are presumed to follow the correct trail by interacting with the cells along the route. Then, subsequent growth cones seem to just follow the routes blazed by the pioneers (see McConnell, Ghosh, & Shatz, 1989). The tendency of growing axons to grow along the same path established by preceding axons is called **fasciculation.** When pioneer axons in the fish spinal cord were destroyed with a laser, subsequent axons did not reach their usual destinations (Klose & Bentley, 1989; Kuwada, 1986).

Although the blueprint hypothesis can account for some aspects of axon growth, it cannot account for the ability of some developing axons to reach their correct destinations in tissue culture. Nor can it account for the ability of some developing axons to reach their correct destination *in vivo* (in the living organism) when their starting points have been shifted. For example, when Lance-Jones and Landmesser (1980) cut a small portion of the spinal cord from a chick embryo, inverted it, and implanted it back into the same embryo, the axons grew out to their original target muscles despite the fact that they started from a new location (see Figure 15.5).

Topographic-gradient hypothesis Much of the axonal growth in complex nervous systems involves growth from one topographic array of neurons to another. The neurons on one array project to another, maintaining the same topographic relation that they had on the first; for example, the topographic map of the retina (see Figure 15.6) is maintained on the optic tectum. It was initially believed that the integrity of such topographical relations was maintained by point-to-point chemoaffinity. Although this rigid mechanism may prevail in invertebrates and in some simple vertebrate systems, research on the vertebrate visual system has led to the less restrictive **topographic-gradient hypothesis** (Easter, Purves, Rakic, & Spitzer, 1985). According to this hypothesis, axons that have grown out from one sheet of cell bodies (e.g., the retina) to another (e.g., the optic tectum) arrange their synaptic terminals according to the relative position of their cell bodies on the original sheet (e.g., the retina), as defined by two intersecting right-angle gradients (e.g., an up-down gradient and a left-right gradient).

Three kinds of studies support the topographic-gradient hypothesis. In the first (e.g., Gaze & Sharma, 1970; Yoon, 1971), the optic nerves of mature frogs were cut and their pattern of regeneration was assessed after parts of either the retina or the optic tectum had been destroyed. In both cases, axons did not grow out to their original points of connection as predicted by the chemoaffinity or blueprint hypotheses; they grew out to fill the available space in an orderly fashion. Axons from the remaining portion of a lesioned retina spread out in an orderly fashion to fill all of the available space on an intact tectum. Conversely, axons from an intact retina growing to a lesioned tectum "squeezed in" so that the retina was completely mapped on the remaining portion of the tectum. These results are illustrated schematically in Figure 15.6.

In the second kind of study supporting the topographic-gradient hypothesis, the connectivity between the retina and optic tectum was determined at different stages of development. It was found that the synaptic connections between eyes and tectums are established long before either reaches full size.

FIGURE 15.5

An illustration of the study of Lance-Jones and Landmesser (1980). A section of spinal cord was cut from a chick embryo, inverted, and reimplanted. The motor neuron axons grew out to their original target muscles, despite the inversion. (Adapted from Hopkins & Brown, 1984.)

The pathways normally followed by the motor neuron axons growing out from the spinal cord of a chick embryo to two target muscles.

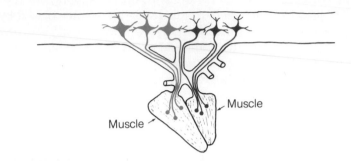

Before the motor neuron axons grew to their target muscles, Lance-Jones and Landmesser cut out a section from a developing chick spinal cord and reversed it.

Although the cell bodies of the motor neurons were now in an abnormal position, they grew out to their appropriate muscle.

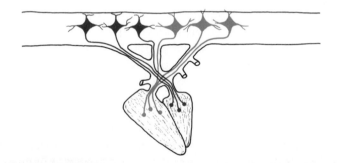

As both the eyes and the optic tectums grow at different rates, the initial synaptic connections shift to other tectal neurons so that the retina is always faithfully mapped onto the tectum, regardless of their relative size (Gaze, Keating, Ostberg, & Chung, 1979; Reh & Constantine-Paton, 1984).

The third kind of support for the topographic-gradient hypothesis comes from the studies of Jacobson (1968). When he rotated the eyes of frog embryos 180° at an early stage in their development, the axons grew out from the eye to the tectum in the normal pattern (i.e., not rotated by 180°). However, if the eyes were rotated 180° just a few hours later, the eventual projections of the retina were reversed in both their front-back and top-bottom dimensions (see Figure 15.7). The key result occurred in frog embryos whose eyes were rotated 180° at an intervening stage. The eventual retinal projections of these frogs were normal in the up-down dimension, but inverted in

Axons normally grow out from the frog retina to fill up the available space on the optic tectum in an orderly fashion. This was initially taken as evidence for the idea that there was accurate point-to-point growth (i.e., for the chemoaffinity theory).

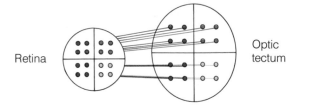

However, the following two observations challenge the point-to-point (i.e. chemoaffinity) interpretation.

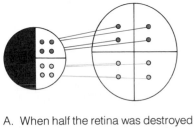

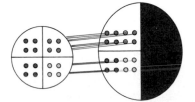

A. When half the retina was destroyed and the optic nerve cut, the remaining retinal ganglion cells regenerated their axonal projections systematically over the entire tectum.

B. When half the optic tectum was destroyed and the optic nerve cut, the axons of the retinal ganglion cells grew back out in an orderly fashion to the remaining tectum.

FIGURE 15.6

The regeneration of the optic nerve of the frog after portions of either the retina or the optic tectum had been destroyed.

the front-back dimension (see Figure 15.7). Thus, the growth of frog retinal projections appears to be guided by two intersecting gradients that are established at different stages of development.

Axon growth and the synapse formation: Current status Over half a century of research on the miraculous ability of developing axons to grow to their correct targets has led to the conclusion that no single mechanism can account for all instances. The main guiding force appears to be the growth cones' attraction to specific chemical signals that are released by their targets, but there are well-documented instances in which the growth cones follow specific routes through the extracellular matrix. The ability of growing axons to establish topographic gradients seems to require a spatially graded signal from the target structure (see Baier & Bonhoeffer, 1992) and a gradient-related mechanism of axon-axon interaction (see Udin & Fawcett, 1988).

Neuron Death and Synapse Rearrangement

Neural development operates on the principle of survival of the fittest: More neurons and synapses are produced than are required, they compete for limited resources, and only the fittest survive. Accordingly, a *period of neuron death* is a major part of the development of most neural systems (Oppenheim, 1991; Williams & Herrup, 1988). Three findings suggest that neurons

The results of Jacobson suggest that the retinal ganglion cell axons grow to targets on the optic tectum that are defined by positions on two intersecting gradients (up-down and back-front). Control frogs did not have their eyes rotated 180°, whereas experimental frogs had their eyes rotated 180° at one of three different stages of development.

Control frogs display a normal pattern of axon growth from the retina to the optic tectum.

RETINA

MAP OF PROJECTIONS ONTO OPTIC TECTUM

Early rotation of eye by 180° does not affect the pattern of projections to the retina; the retinal ganglion cells grow to the destinations that are normal for their new position.

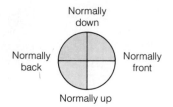

Late rotation of the eye by 180° reverses the projections in both the up-down and back-front dimensions; by this stage the destination of each axon appears to have been determined and each grows to its prescribed destination despite the rotation.

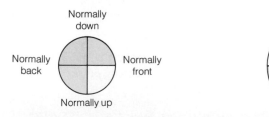

Rotation of the eye by 180° at an intermediate stage reverses the projections in the front-back dimension but not in the up-down dimension.

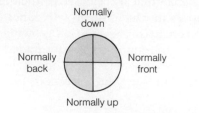

FIGURE 15.7

A schematic representation of the effects of eye rotation on the growth of the axons from the eye to the optic tectum at different stages of the frog's development. These results suggest that the retinal projections are guided by two gradients that are established at different stages of development.

die because of their failure to compete successfully for some life-preserving factor that is supplied by their targets. First, the implantation of extra target sites decreases neuron death. For example, Hollyday and Hamburger (1976) grafted an extra limb on one side of a chick embryo, and fewer motor neurons on that side died. Second, destroying some of the neurons growing into an area before the period of cell death increases the survival rate of the remaining neurons (e.g., Pilar, Landmesser, & Burstein, 1980). And third, increasing the number of axons that initially innervate a target decreases the proportion that survive.

During the period of cell death, neurons that have established incorrect connections are particularly likely to die. As they die, the space that they vacate on the postsynaptic membranes of other cells is filled by the sprouting axon terminals of surviving neurons. Thus, the consequence of cell death is a massive rearrangement of synapses, which increases the overall accuracy of neural transmission. In addition, the period of neuron death and synapse rearrangement typically focuses the output of each neuron on a smaller number of cells (Lamb, 1984)—see Figure 15.8.

Synapse rearrangement and experience   Synapse rearrangement is influenced by the activity of the developing nervous system (see Kalil, 1989). The main governing principle appears to be, "Use it, or lose it." Synapses that are inactive do not survive. For example, the primary visual cortices of animals

A diffuse pattern of synaptic contact is characteristic of early stages of development.

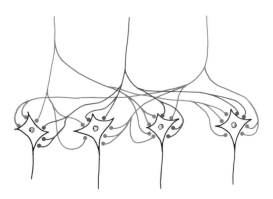

A more focused pattern of synaptic contact is present after synapse rearrangement.

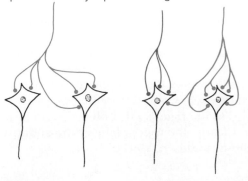

FIGURE 15.8

During neuron death and synapse rearrangement, the synaptic contacts of each axon become focused on a small number of cells.

reared in the dark have been found to have fewer synapses (e.g., Cragg, 1975) and fewer dendritic spines (e.g., Valverde, 1971), and dark-reared animals have deficits in depth (e.g., Walk & Walters, 1973) and pattern (e.g., Tees, 1968; Tees & Cartwright, 1972) perception as adults. Also, the cortices of rats that have been reared by themselves in barren cages have been found to be thinner (Bennett, Diamond, Krech, & Rosenzweig, 1964), with less dendritic development (Greenough & Volkmar, 1973), and with fewer synapses per neuron (Turner & Greenough, 1983) than the cortices of rats that have been reared in enriched group cages.

The effect of neural activity on synapse rearrangement was recently demonstrated in an experiment on motor neurons and muscle cells—in neonates, each muscle cell is innervated by several motor neurons, and then all but one are eliminated during the course of development. Lo and Poo (1991) developed an *in vitro* preparation in which one developing muscle cell was innervated by two developing motor neurons. Applying 50 to 100 pulses of electrical stimulation to one of them caused a rapid degradation in the synaptic contacts of the other. This finding confirms that active synapses take precedence over inactive synapses, and it shows that presynaptic neurons compete with one another for synaptic contacts on postsynaptic cells.

The competitive nature of synapse rearrangement is further illustrated by the fact that the disruptive effects of early deprivation of one eye on the development of the visual circuits associated with that eye are often greater if the other eye is not also deprived. For example, if one eye is deprived of input early in life, there is a marked reduction in the number of cortical neurons that can be activated by stimulation of that eye and an increase in the number of cortical neurons that can be activated by stimulation of the nondeprived eye. These effects of *monocular deprivation* result from changes in the pattern of synaptic input into layer IV of the primary visual cortex. In newborn cats and monkeys, the input into layer IV from the left and right eyes is intermingled, and then during the course of normal development, it becomes segregated into alternating equal stripes of ocular dominance (see Figure 7.22). Hubel, Wiesel, and LeVay (1977) have shown that early monocular deprivation decreases the width of the stripes of input from the deprived eye and increases the width of the stripes of input from the nondeprived eye.

Some of the most spectacular illustrations of the effects of neural activity on synapse rearrangement come from lines of research that involve the interaction between the topographic maps of the auditory and visual systems. I will describe two of them. First, Roe, Pallas, Hahm, and Sur (1990) caused the developing axons of ferret *retinal ganglion cells* to synapse in the *medial geniculate nuclei* of the auditory system by lesioning their normal thalamic destinations, the *lateral geniculate nuclei*. Remarkably, once the ferrets matured, their auditory cortex neurons responded like visual cortex neurons to various visual stimuli, and their auditory cortices were laid out *retinotopically*. Second, Knudsen and Brainard (1991) raised barn owls with vision-displacing prisms over their eyes. This led to a corresponding change in the auditory spatial map in the *tectum*. For example, an owl that was raised wearing prisms that shifted its visual world 23° to the right had an auditory map that was also shifted 23° to the right, so that objects were heard to be where they were seen to be. Clearly, the topography of the auditory tectal map is influenced by visual input (Knudsen, 1991).

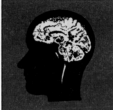

In order to provide yourself with an overview of neural development before proceeding to Section 15.2, fill in the blanks in the following chronological list of the major stages in the development of the nervous system:

1. Induction of the neural _____ .

2. Formation of the neural tube.

3. Neural _____ .

4. Neural _____ .

5. Neural aggregation.

6. Growth of _____ .

7. Formation of _____ .

8. Neuron _____ and synapse _____ .

The Neural Bases of Learning in Simple Systems

So far, this chapter has focused on the plasticity of developing nervous systems. Now the emphasis changes to the plasticity of adult nervous systems. This section discusses how sensory experience can change nervous system function—in other words, it focuses on the neural bases of *learning*.

This section describes two influential lines of research, both of which feature the simple systems approach. The first part of the section focuses on the neural basis of learning in *Aplysia,* a simple marine invertebrate; the second part focuses on *long-term potentiation,* a learning-related phenomenon of the mammalian brain.

Has it occurred to you that the study of learning and the study of memory are inseparable? The study of learning focuses on the changes in the brain that are *induced* by various experiences, whereas the study of memory focuses on how these changes are *maintained* and *expressed.* Learning is impossible without memory, and memory is impossible without learning.

The following are the answers to the preceding questions: (1) plate, (3) proliferation, (4) migration, (6) neural processes (axons and dendrites), (7) synapses, and (8) death; rearrangement.

Nonassociative and Associative Learning in the Gill-Withdrawal Reflex Circuit of Aplysia

The *Aplysia* is a simple marine snail that spends its life oozing along the ocean floor eating seaweed and avoiding predation by tasting as bad as it looks (see Figure 15.9). The Aplysia *siphon* is a small fleshy spout that is used to expel seawater and waste. When the siphon is touched, it and the adjoining gill are reflexively drawn up under its protective *mantle.* This response to touch is the Aplysia *gill-withdrawal reflex.* The neural circuit that mediates the gill-withdrawal reflex is relatively simple. There are 24 sensory neurons in the skin of the siphon that synapse on 6 motor neurons that are responsible for retracting the siphon and gill. The sensory neurons also activate interneurons that in turn synapse on the motor neurons. This circuit is illustrated schematically in Figure 15.10.

Nonassociative learning in Aplysia   Nonassociative learning is a change in behavior that results from the repeated experience of a single stimulus or of two or more different stimuli that are not spatially or temporally related. The two most commonly studied forms of nonassociative learning are *habituation* and *sensitization.*

Habituation is the progressive decrease in the strength of the behavioral reaction to a stimulus that occurs when that stimulus is repeatedly presented. For example, if the Aplysia siphon is touched repeatedly at relatively brief intervals (e.g., once every 30 seconds), the gill-withdrawal reflex becomes less and less vigorous. Habituation of the Aplysia gill-withdrawal reflex lasts 2 or 3 hours following a single 10-stimulus habituation session; several such sessions can produce habituation that lasts for weeks (Carew, Pinsker, & Kandel, 1972).

What is the neural mechanism of habituation of the Aplysia gill-withdrawal reflex? The first clue came from the discovery (Castellucci, Pinsker, Kupfermann, & Kandel, 1970) that habituation is associated with a decline in the number of action potentials that are elicited in the gill motor neurons by each touch. Because the responsiveness of the motor neurons to the neurotransmitter released by the sensory neurons did not decline during habituation (Castellucci & Kandel, 1974), it was concluded that the progressive decline in the number of motor neuron action potentials that are elicited by each siphon touch during the course of habituation results from a progressive decline in

FIGURE 15.9
An Aplysia.

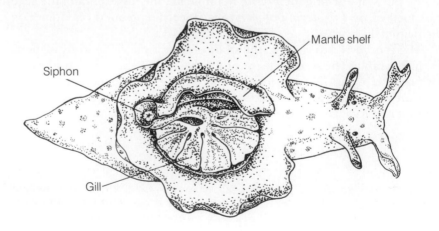

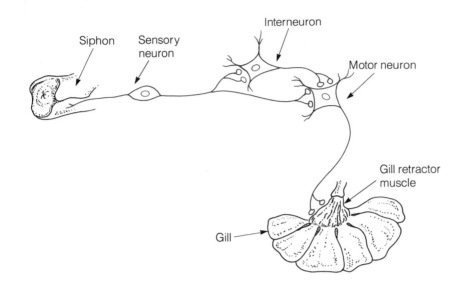

FIGURE 15.10
A schematic illustration of the neural circuit that mediates the Aplysia gill-withdrawal reflex.

the amount of neurotransmitter that is released from the sensory neurons onto the postsynaptic membranes of the motor neurons.

What causes the siphon sensory neurons to release progressively less neurotransmitter in response to each successive touch of the siphon during the course of habituation? There are two possibilities. One is that less neurotransmitter is released from the siphon sensory neurons during the course of habituation because progressively fewer action potentials are elicited in them by each successive touch; the other is that there is a decline in the amount of neurotransmitter that is released in response to each action potential. The discovery that the number of siphon-sensory-neuron action potentials does not decline during the course of habituation (Castellucci & Kandel, 1974) supported the latter alternative.

Once it became clear that the habituation of the Aplysia gill-withdrawal reflex results from a decrease in the amount of neurotransmitter that is released from siphon sensory neurons in response to each of their own action potentials, researchers began the search for the mechanism of this decrease. The search focused on *calcium ion influx* because it is the influx of calcium ions into the terminal buttons that permits synaptic vesicles to fuse with the presynaptic membrane and release their contents into the synapse. It was soon established that the decrease in siphon-sensory-neuron neurotransmitter release during habituation of the gill-withdrawal reflex results from a decrease in the number of calcium ions entering the terminal buttons of the siphon sensory neurons in response to each of their own action potentials (Klein & Kandel, 1978; Klein, Shapiro, & Kandel, 1980).

The following theory of habituation of the Aplysia gill-withdrawal reflex has emerged from this line of research (see Figure 15.11). With repeated elicitation of the gill-withdrawal reflex, each siphon stimulation continues to fully activate the sensory neurons, sending the same full barrage of action potentials down their axons. However, because fewer calcium ions enter the synaptic terminals in response to each successive barrage of action potentials, less and less neurotransmitter is released from the sensory neurons into the synapses, fewer and fewer action potentials are elicited in the motor neurons,

MECHANISM OF HABITUATION

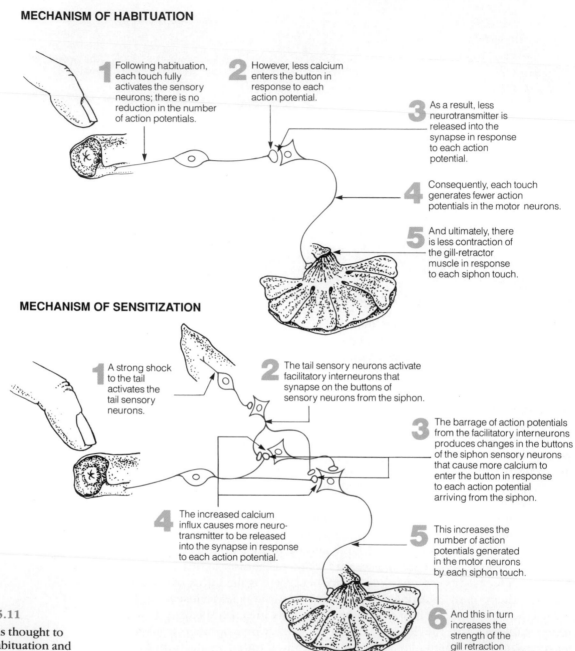

MECHANISM OF SENSITIZATION

FIGURE 15.11

Mechanisms thought to underlie habituation and sensitization of the Aplysia gill-withdrawal reflex.

and the contraction of the gill muscle in response to each siphon stimulation grows weaker and weaker (see Hawkins, 1983; Kandel, 1985; Quinn, 1984).

Sensitization is the general increase in an animal's responsiveness to stimuli that occurs following a noxious stimulus. For example, the gill-withdrawal reflex that is elicited by touching an Aplysia's siphon is increased in intensity for several minutes following the administration of a single severe shock to its tail (Carew, Castelluci, & Kandel, 1971). The sensitization of the Aplysia gill-withdrawal reflex can last for weeks following a series of tail shocks administered over several days (Pinsker, Hening, Carew, & Kandel, 1973). In contrast to the mechanism of habituation, sensitization has been shown to result from an increase in the amount of neurotransmitter that is released by the siphon sensory neurons in response to their own action potentials (Castellucci & Kandel, 1976).

How does tail shock cause the siphon sensory neurons to increase their release of neurotransmitter onto the gill motor neurons? By **presynaptic facilitation.** Sensory fibers from the Aplysia tail synapse on facilitatory *serotonergic* interneurons that in turn synapse on the buttons of siphon sensory neurons (see Mercer, Emptage, & Carew, 1991). It is via these interneurons that the tail shock changes the siphon sensory neuron buttons so that each action potential arriving there from the siphon results in a greater influx of calcium ions and a greater release of serotonin onto the motor neurons (Figure 15.11).

Bailey and Chen (1983, 1988) showed that long-term habituation and sensitization can induce structural changes in the synaptic terminals of the siphon sensory neurons. They labeled the siphon sensory neurons of three groups of Aplysia with *horseradish peroxidase* and examined their synaptic terminals by electron microscopy. Relative to the sensory neurons of control Aplysia, those of the habituated subjects had fewer active zones of transmitter release, smaller active zones, and fewer synaptic vesicles. In contrast, the sensory neurons of the sensitized Aplysia had more active zones, larger active zones, and more synaptic vesicles than did the controls. Because such structural changes cannot occur rapidly enough to account for short-term retention of sensitization and habituation, they are presumed to mediate long-term storage. By repeatedly applying *serotonin,* Glanzman, Kandel, and Schacter (1990) induced increases in the size and number of synaptic contacts in Aplysia sensory neurons that were grown in culture.

Associative learning in Aplysia   Aplysia are capable of several different kinds of associative learning (Carew & Sahley, 1986); however, it is the **Pavlovian conditioning** of the gill-withdrawal reflex that is best understood. In Pavlovian conditioning, the subject learns an association between a *conditional stimulus* and an *unconditional stimulus* (see Chapter 5). If a light touch of the siphon (the conditional stimulus) is paired with a strong shock to the tail (the unconditional stimulus) every few minutes for several trials, the light touch by itself begins to elicit a robust gill-withdrawal response similar to that induced by the tail shock. The associative nature of this effect is shown by the fact that the increase in the intensity of the reflex is not nearly so great if the two stimuli are presented in an unpaired fashion (Carew, Walters, & Kandel, 1981)—unpaired presentations produce sensitization, but no conditioning. The conditional response is typically retained for several days after 20 or so conditioning trials.

The Aplysia gill-withdrawal reflex has also been shown to be capable of **discriminated Pavlovian conditioning** (Carew, Hawkins, & Kandel, 1983). In the discriminated version of the paradigm (see Figure 15.12), two conditional stimuli are administered, mild stimulation to the mantle and mild stimulation to the siphon, each of which elicits a weak gill-withdrawal response.

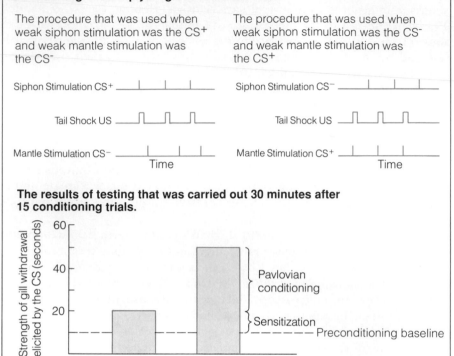

FIGURE 15.12

The discriminated Pavlovian conditioning of the Aplysia gill-withdrawal reflex. (Adapted from Carew, Hawkins, & Kandel, 1983.)

During training, one of these stimuli (called the CS^+) is always paired with the unconditional stimulus, a severe tail shock, and the other conditional stimulus (called the CS^-) is not. At the end of training, the CS^+ elicits a strong withdrawal reaction, whereas the CS^- elicits a weak reaction (the initial reaction plus the nonassociative effects of the tail shock). Optimal conditioning occurs when the CS^+ precedes the unconditional stimulus by 0.5 second, and it doesn't occur at all when the CS^+ follows the unconditional stimulus.

Pavlovian conditioning of the gill-withdrawal reflex can be thought of as a special case of sensitization. In effect, it is a demonstration that tail shock has the greatest sensitizing effect on reflexes that are active during the shock. This relation between sensitization and Pavlovian conditioning is reflected in the model that has been proposed to explain it (see Figure 15.13). Like sensitization, Pavlovian conditioning of the gill-withdrawal reflex is assumed to be mediated by the action of tail-shock-activated interneurons on the sensory neurons that normally activate the reflex. However, unlike sensitization, Pavlovian conditioning depends on the temporal relation between the activation of the interneuron by tail shock and the sensory neuron by the CS^+. The greatest increase in the release of neurotransmitter from the CS^+ sensory neurons is produced following trials in which they are in the act of firing at the time when input reaches their presynaptic terminals from the tail-shock activated interneurons. Accordingly, the synaptic facilitation that mediates associative learning has been termed **activity-dependent enhancement** (see Buonomano & Byrne, 1990; Small, Kandel, & Hawkins, 1989).

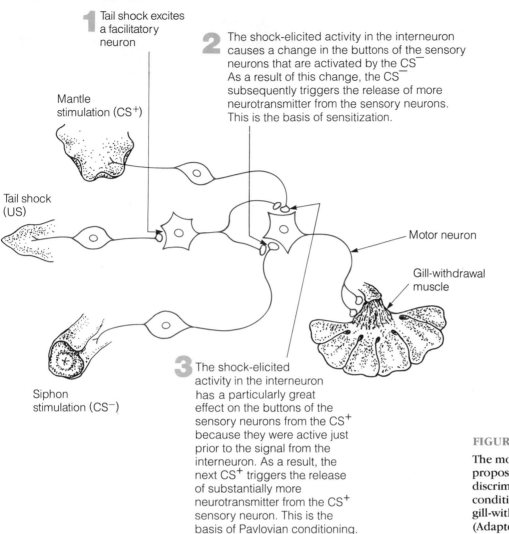

1 Tail shock excites a facilitatory neuron

Mantle stimulation (CS⁺)

2 The shock-elicited activity in the interneuron causes a change in the buttons of the sensory neurons that are activated by the CS⁻ As a result of this change, the CS⁻ subsequently triggers the release of more neurotransmitter from the sensory neurons. This is the basis of sensitization.

Tail shock (US)

Siphon stimulation (CS⁻)

Motor neuron

Gill-withdrawal muscle

3 The shock-elicited activity in the interneuron has a particularly great effect on the buttons of the sensory neurons from the CS⁺ because they were active just prior to the signal from the interneuron. As a result, the next CS⁺ triggers the release of substantially more neurotransmitter from the CS⁺ sensory neuron. This is the basis of Pavlovian conditioning.

FIGURE 15.13

The model that has been proposed to explain discriminated Pavlovian conditioning of the gill-withdrawal reflex. (Adapted from Kandel, 1985.)

Long-Term Potentiation in the Mammalian Hippocampus

Not all attempts to identify the cellular mechanisms of learning and memory have focused on learning in simple organisms. A slightly different strategy has been to study neuroplastic phenomena in simple circuits that are components of complex nervous systems. Long-term potentiation is the most widely studied neuroplastic phenomenon of the mammalian nervous system.

Long-term potentiation (LTP) is the enduring facilitation of synaptic transmission that occurs following activation of a synapse by intense high-frequency stimulation of the presynaptic neuron (Bliss & Gardner-Medwin, 1973; Bliss & Lømø, 1973). Long-term potentiation has been demonstrated in several neural structures, but it has been most frequently studied at three synapses in the hippocampus: (1) the synapse of *perforant path* axons from the *entorhinal cortex* on the *granule cells of the dentate gyrus,* (2) the synapse of dentate granule cell axons on the *pyramidal cells of the CA3 field,* and (3) the synapse of the CA3 pyramidal cell axons on the *pyramidal cells of the CA1*

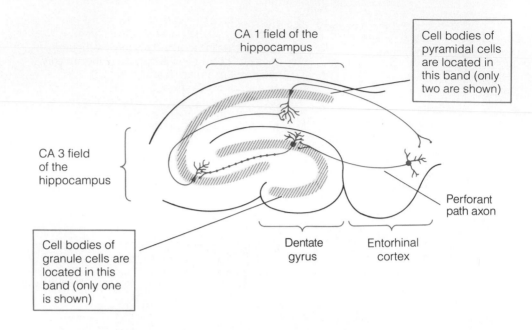

FIGURE 15.14

A slice of hippocampal tissue that illustrates the three synapses at which LTP is most commonly studied: (1) the dentate granule-cell synapse, (2) the CA3 pyramidal-cell synapse, and (3) the CA1 pyramidal-cell synapse. *CA* stands for *cornu ammonis,* another name for hippocampus.

field—see Figure 15.14. Long-term potentiation is studied in freely moving animals (most commonly in rats and rabbits), in anesthetized animals, or in **hippocampal-slice preparations** (i.e., in slices of hippocampal tissue that have been cut from a living brain and maintained alive for many hours in a saline bath). See Figure 15.15 for an illustration of a conventional LTP experiment.

The reason why long-term potentiation is one of the most widely studied neuroscientific phenomena goes back to 1949 and D.O. Hebb. Hebb argued that the facilitation of synaptic transmission is the fundamental mechanism of learning and memory. He believed that each experience triggers a unique pattern of neural activity, which reverberates through cerebral circuits. He further believed that this reverberating activity causes structural changes in the synapses of the activated circuits. These synaptic changes, according to Hebb, store the information of the initial experience and are thus the physiological mechanism of learning and memory.

Interest in LTP as a putative mechanism of learning and memory was initially stimulated by the discovery that it is long lasting, the primary prerequisite of any putative mechanism of long-term memory storage. LTP can last for hours after a single stimulation, or weeks after multiple stimulations (Racine & deJonge, 1988; Racine, Milgram, & Hafner, 1983). Additional support for the idea that LTP is the neural mechanism of learning and memory has come from several other sources (see Brown, Chapman, Kairiss, & Keenan, 1988): (1) LTP can be elicited by low levels of stimulation that mimic normal neural activity; (2) LTP effects are most prominent in structures, such as the hippocampus, that have been implicated in learning and memory; (3) behavioral

A. Experimental set-up

Extracellular multiple-unit
recording electrode in
granule cell layer

Stimulation
electrode
in perforant
path

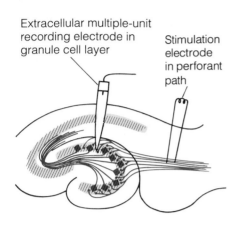

B. The response to a single
pulse of stimulation at the
beginning of the experiment

Stimulation

FIGURE 15.15

Long-term potentiation at the
dentate granule-cell synapse
following stimulation of the
perforant path.

C. The potentiated responses that were
elicited by a single pulse of stimulation
at various intervals after 10 seconds of
intense high-frequency stimulation

1 Hour   2 Days   4 Days

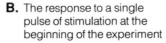

Stimulation

conditioning can produce LTP-like changes in the hippocampus (e.g., Iriki, Pavlides, Keller, & Asanuma, 1989); (4) many drugs that influence learning and memory have parallel effects on LTP; (e.g., Brown, Chapman, Kairiss, & Keenan, 1988; Skelton, Scarth, Wilkie, Miller, & Phillips, 1987); and (5) the induction of maximal LTP blocks the learning of a Morris water maze until the LTP has subsided (Castro, Silbert, McNaughton, & Barnes, 1989). These parallels and relations do not prove that LTP is the neural mechanism of learning and memory; however, they suggest that the study of LTP may lead to important insights into such a mechanism.

LTP: Two key discoveries Of the many findings that have implicated LTP in learning and memory, two have been of particular theoretical significance. The first was the discovery that LTP is amenable to associative conditioning. Kelso and Brown (1986) implanted four electrodes in a hippocampal slice preparation: three stimulation electrodes in fibers projecting into the CA1 area and one recording electrode in the CA1 area itself. Next, stimulation intensities at each stimulation electrode were set so that stimulation through two of them (termed W_1 and W_2) was not strong enough to induce LTP, whereas stimulation through the third (S) was strong enough to induce LTP. As illustrated in Figure 15.16, Kelso and Brown found that after pairing stimulation through one of the "weak electrodes" (conditional stimulus) with stimulation through the "strong electrode" (unconditional stimulus) five times, stimulation through the same weak electrode, but not through the other weak electrode, elicited a potentiated multiple-unit response.

The second key finding to implicate LTP in learning and memory was the discovery that LTP is just the kind of synaptic facilitation that Hebb (1949)

Position of stimulation and recording electrodes in the CA1 field of a
hippocampal slice in Kelso and Brown's experiment.

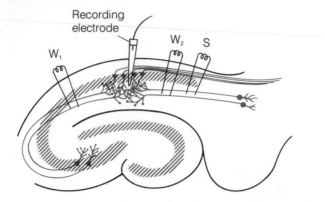

W₁   First weak-stimulation
     electrode

W₂   Second weak-
     stimulation electrode

S   Strong-stimulation
     electrode

When stimulation through one of the weak-stimulation electrodes was
followed by stimulation through the strong-stimulation electrode for
several trials, stimulation through that weak electrode (CS+)
but not the other (CS−) elicited a potentiated response.

A. After W₁ served as the CS+ and W₂ as the CS−, W₁ elicited a
    potentiated response

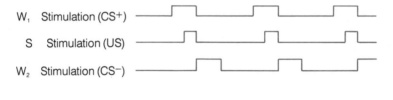

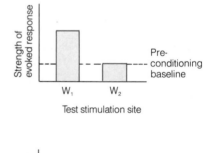

B. After W₂ served as the CS+ and W₁ as the CS−, W₂ elicited a
    potentiated response

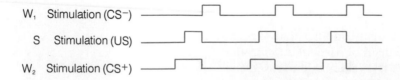

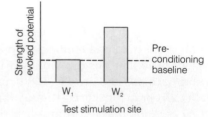

FIGURE 15.16

The experiment of Kelso and
Brown (1986): associative
conditioning of long-term
potentiation.

originally argued is the basis of learning and memory. The following statement has become known as *Hebb's postulate for learning:*

> When an axon of cell A is near enough to excite cell B and repeatedly or
> persistently takes part in firing it, some growth process or metabolic change
> takes place in one or both cells such that A's efficiency, as one of the cells
> firing B, is increased. (p. 62)

Hebb's point was that in order to account for associative learning and memory, synaptic facilitation must result from an interaction of simultaneous presynaptic and postsynaptic activity.

Several experiments (e.g., Kelso, Ganong, & Brown, 1986; Sastry, Goh, & Auyeung, 1986) have confirmed the Hebbian nature of hippocampal LTP. LTP does not occur when the presynaptic cell fires in the absence of postsynaptic cell firing, and it does not occur when the postsynaptic cell fires in the absence of presynaptic activity. It occurs only when the presynaptic and postsynaptic cells are simultaneously activated by the *tetanic stimulation* (intense high-frequency stimulation). The *co-occurrence* of activity in presynaptic and postsynaptic cells is now recognized as the primary factor in all forms of associative neural plasticity.

Mechanisms of LTP   The Hebbian nature of LTP results from the properties of the **NMDA receptor.** The NMDA receptor is one of the receptors for **glutamate,** the main excitatory neurotransmitter of the hippocampus. The NMDA receptor is so named because it, but not other glutamate receptors, is activated by *N-methyl-D-aspartate* (NMDA), an analogue of glutamate.

The critical event in the *induction* of LTP is an influx of *calcium ions* into the postsynaptic neuron. In order for calcium ions to flow into the postsynaptic neuron, two things must happen at the same time: glutamate must bind to glutamate receptors and the postsynaptic neuron must be sufficiently depolarized. When these two conditions are met, the calcium channels that are associated with the glutamate receptors open, and the resulting influx of calcium ions triggers a sequence of enzymatic events in the postsynaptic neuron. Preventing either the binding of glutamate to the NMDA receptor or the simultaneous depolarization of the postsynaptic neuron prevents the induction of LTP (e.g., Collingridge & Bliss, 1987; Cotman, Monaghan, & Ganong, 1988). Microfluorometric techniques for visualizing the influx of calcium ions into active neurons have recently been developed (Tank, Sugimori, Connor & Llinás, 1988)–see Figure 15.17.

One of the major debates about LTP has been whether it is a presynaptic or postsynaptic phenomenon: Does the facilitation of synaptic transmission result from changes in the presynaptic neuron, or does it result from changes

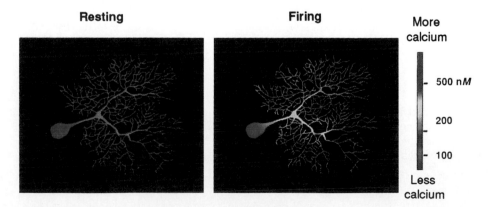

FIGURE 15.17

A recently developed microfluorometric technique permits the influx of calcium into neurons to be visualized. (Adapted from Tank, Sugimori, Connor, & Llinás, 1988.)

INTRODUCTION

Tetanic stimulation of the presynaptic neuron triggers the release of glutamate.

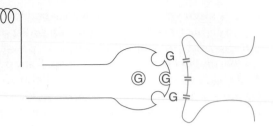

Enough glutamate binds to NMDA receptors to fire the postsynaptic neuron.

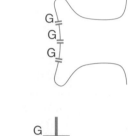

The co-occurrence of glutamate binding and depolarization opens the calcium channels that are associated with the NMDA receptors, and calcium ions enter the postsynaptic neuron.

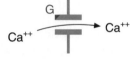

The influx of calcium ions causes the release of a retrograde messenger, perhaps nitric oxide, into the synapse by the postsynaptic neuron, and this induces long-term changes in the presynaptic neuron.

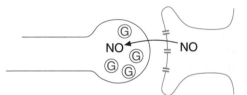

MAINTENANCE

Long-term changes in the presynaptic neuron increase its tendency to release glutamate into synapses between neurons that were co-active during the tetanic stimulation.

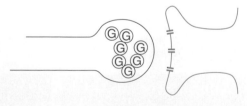

EXPRESSION

When the presynaptic neuron is stimulated, it releases more glutamate at the synapses between neurons that were co-active during the tetanic stimulation. As a result, the postsynaptic response is potentiated.

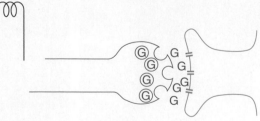

FIGURE 15.18

The mechanisms that are currently thought to underlie the induction, maintenance, and expression of long-term potentiation.

in the postsynaptic neuron? Although this issue is far from settled, the answer seems to be, "both." As you have just learned, the *induction* of LTP depends on postsynaptic mechanisms, but recent evidence suggests that the *maintenance* and *expression* of LTP may be presynaptic (see Siegelbaum & Kandel, 1991). Recent studies suggest that synaptic transmission is facilitated following intense high-frequency stimulation because more glutamate is released from the presynaptic neuron (Bashir, Alford, Davies, Randall, & Collingridge, 1991; Bekkers & Stevens, 1990; Tsien & Malinow, 1991).

If the induction of LTP is postsynaptic and the maintenance and expression is presynaptic, some kind of LTP-related signal must be transmitted from the postsynaptic neuron to the presynaptic neuron following induction. One candidate for this retrograde messenger is *nitric oxide.* Schuman and Madison (1991) recently showed that blocking the synthesis of nitric oxide in the postsynaptic neuron or blocking its passage between neurons prevents the expression of LTP.

The nature of the LTP-related changes in the presynaptic neuron that maintain its increased release of glutamate are not well understood—indeed, there is no general agreement that postsynaptic changes are not also involved. However, the research of Chang and Greenough (1984) has suggested one interesting possibility; they found that hippocampal LTP is associated with an increase in the number of hippocampal synapses.

Figure 15.18 summarizes the mechanisms that are currently believed to be associated with induction, maintenance, and expression of LTP. To put Figure 15.18 and the preceding discussion in perspective, it is important to be aware that the mechanisms of LTP are not the same at every synapse and that most of the research on the mechanisms of LTP has focused on hippocampal CA1 pyramidal-cell synapses and hippocampal granule-cell synapses (see Lynch & Baudry, 1991; Madison, Malenka, & Nicholl, 1991; Zalutsky & Nicholl, 1990).

15.3

Neural Degeneration, Regeneration, and Reorganization

The third section of this chapter is about three responses of the nervous system to damage: *degeneration, regeneration,* and *reorganization.*

Neural Degeneration

After a multipolar neuron has been **axotomized** (i.e., after its axon has been severed), two kinds of neural degeneration (i.e., neural deterioration) occur: degeneration of the **distal segment,** the segment between the cut and the synaptic terminals, and degeneration of the **proximal segment,** the segment between the cut and the cell body. Degeneration of the distal segment is called **anterograde degeneration,** and degeneration of the proximal segment is called **retrograde degeneration** (see Figure 15.19).

Anterograde degeneration occurs quickly following axotomy because the cut separates the distal segment of the axon from the cell body, which is the

FIGURE 15.19

Neuronal and transneuronal
degeneration following
axotomy.

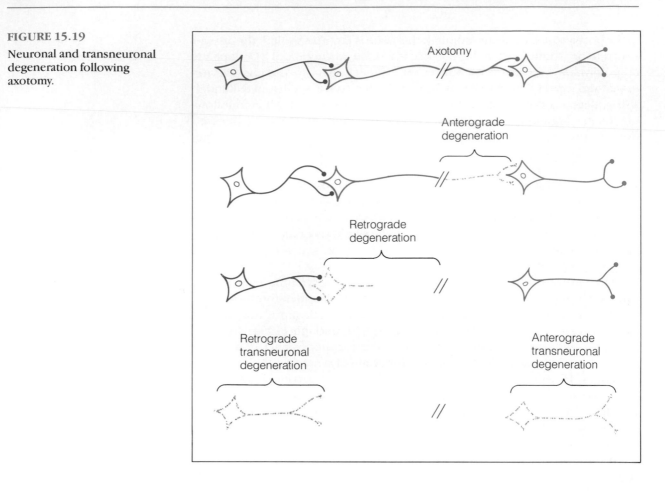

metabolic center of the neuron. The entire distal segment becomes badly
swollen within a few hours, and by the fifth day it has broken into fragments.
The course of retrograde degeneration is different; it progresses gradually
back from the cut. The first retrograde reaction to the cut is the degeneration
of the axon back from the cut to the first *node of Ranvier* or to the first point
at which a major *collateral branch* leaves the axon. Within 2 or 3 days, major
changes in the cell body become apparent. These cell body changes are of
one of two types: degenerative or regenerative. Early degenerative changes in
the cell body of an axotomized neuron (e.g., a decrease in the size) suggest
that it will ultimately die. Early regenerative changes (e.g., an increase in size)
indicate that the cell body is involved in a massive synthesis of the proteins
that are needed to replace the degenerated portions of the axon. But regeneration does not guarantee the long-term survival of the neuron. If a regenerating axon does not manage to make synaptic contact with an appropriate
target, it eventually dies.

Following CNS damage, **astrologia** (see Chapter 3), proliferate and absorb the debris. This reaction is termed **phagocytosis,** and astroglia are thus
referred to as **phagocytes.** In the PNS, degenerating neurons are partially absorbed by **Schwann cells,** the cells that compose the myelin sheaths of peripheral axons.

Transneuronal degeneration Degeneration is not limited to the damaged neurons. In some cases, the neurons on which damaged neurons synapse degenerate (**anterograde transneuronal degeneration**), and in some cases, the neurons that synapse on damaged neurons degenerate (**retrograde transneuronal degeneration**). Figure 15.19 is a schematic illustration of the various kinds of neuronal and **transneuronal degeneration.**

Neural Regeneration

Neural regeneration (i.e., regrowth of damaged neurons) does not proceed as successfully in mammals and other higher vertebrates as it does in most invertebrates and lower vertebrates. For some reason, the capacity for accurate axon growth, which is possessed by higher vertebrates during their original development, is lost once they reach maturity. Regeneration is virtually nonexistent in the central nervous systems of adult mammals, and regeneration in their peripheral nervous systems is at best a hit-or-miss affair (see Fawcett & Keynes, 1990).

Regrowth from the proximal stump of a damaged mammalian peripheral nerve begins a day or two after the damage. If the original Schwann-cell myelin sheaths remain intact, the regenerating axons grow through them to their original targets at a rate of a few millimeters per day. However, if the nerve is completely severed and the cut ends become separated, the regrowth is not nearly so accurate because regenerating axon tips often grow into incorrect sheaths and are guided by them to incorrect destinations. This is why it often requires great effort for victims of peripheral nerve damage to relearn to use affected limbs.

If the cut ends of a mammalian peripheral nerve become widely separated, or if a lengthy section of the nerve is damaged, there may be no meaningful regeneration at all. Regenerating axon tips that do not encounter the Schwann-cell sheaths of the distal portion usually grow in a tangled mass around the proximal stump and ultimately die. In contrast, the regenerating axons of lower vertebrates usually reach their original targets even when they do not grow into remnant Schwann-cell sheaths. The accuracy of regeneration in lower vertebrates is like a carrot dangling in front of the noses of the women and men of medical neuroscience. If the factors that promote accurate regeneration in lower vertebrates can be identified and applied to humans, it might prove possible to promote recovery from brain damage. (In writing this paragraph, I discovered a tongue-twister: "Schwann-cell sheaths." Try repeating it quickly.)

Healthy axons sometimes respond to the degeneration of adjacent axons by developing collateral sprouts that grow to the synaptic sites that have been abandoned by the degenerating axons (e.g., Cotman, Nieto-Sampedro, & Harris, 1981; Tsukahara, 1981). **Collateral sprouting** is illustrated in Figure 15.20. Notice that collateral sprouts may originate from the axon terminals or from a node of Ranvier.

Collateral sprouting appears to be stimulated by some factor that is released from denervated tissue. It can be induced in motor neuron axons merely by rendering the target muscle inactive (e.g., Brown & Ironton, 1977), and conversely, the collateral sprouting that normally occurs in motor neuron axons following damage to adjacent axons can be blocked by electrically stimulating the target muscle (Ironton, Brown, & Holland, 1978).

FIGURE 15.20

Collateral sprouting after neuron damage.

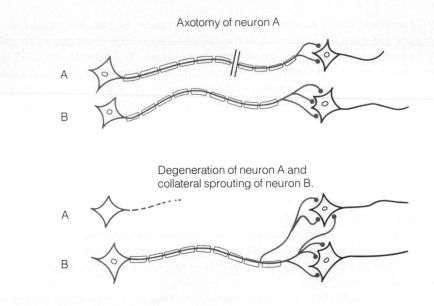

Neural reorganization after brain damage   Plasticity is often assumed to be a characteristic of developing nervous systems, rather than of nervous systems in general. The plasticity of adult mammalian nervous systems is often thought to be limited to the minor functional changes necessary for learning, and even these are thought to decline with age—most people believe that "you can't teach an old dog new tricks." However, it is now clear that the adult mammalian nervous system is extremely plastic; it retains the ability to undergo massive reorganization. Most studies of neural reorganization have focused on the reorganization of sensory and motor systems in response to damage (see Kaas, 1991). Sensory and motor systems are ideally suited to the study of neural reorganization because of their topographic layout.

Sensory systems   In sensory systems, neural reorganization in response to brain damage has been studied in two ways: (1) by disrupting the input to sensory cortex or (2) by damaging sensory cortex itself. The first approach is illustrated by two recent studies, one on the somatosensory system and one on the visual system. Pons et al. (1991) mapped the somatosensory cortex of monkeys whose contralateral arm sensory neurons had been cut years earlier. They found that the area of the somatosensory cortex that had previously received input from the *deafferented* arm, now responded to touches of the face—the somatotopic face representation had systematically expanded into the previous arm area. Kaas et al. (1990) conducted a similar study of visual-cortex reorganization. They assessed the effect of depriving a small area of cat visual cortex of input by making a small lesion in one retina and removing the other. Their results were similar to those of Pons et al.; several months after the retinal lesions, cortical neurons that originally had receptive fields in the lesioned area of the retina had acquired new receptive fields in the area of the retina around the lesion.

Damaging sensory cortex produces a different kind of reorganization. Jenkins and Merzenich (1987) removed the small area of monkey somatosensory cortex that responded to a touch of the central area of the palm of the contralateral hand. Several weeks later, they found neurons adjacent to the lesion that responded to the light touch of the disconnected palm area. However, the number of neurons that responded was small, and larger lesions did not produce a similar reorganization.

Motor system Similar reorganization of neural circuits has been observed following damage to the motor system. Sanes, Suner, and Donoghue (1990) sectioned the motor neurons of rats that controlled the muscles of their *vibrissae* (i.e., whiskers). A few weeks later, stimulation of the area of motor cortex that had previously elicited vibrissae movement, now activated other muscles of the face. This result is illustrated in Figure 15.21.

Mechanisms of neural reorganization Two kinds of mechanisms have been proposed to account for the reorganization of neural circuits after nervous system damage: (1) a change in the strength of existing connections and (2) the establishment of new connections by collateral sprouting. Indirect support for the first alternative comes from the observation that reorganizational effects are often observed within a day or two of the damage—too soon to be attributable to sprouting. On the other hand, the magnitude of

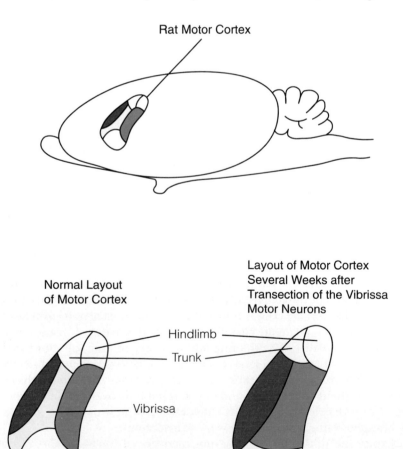

Rat Motor Cortex

Normal Layout of Motor Cortex

Layout of Motor Cortex Several Weeks after Transection of the Vibrissa Motor Neurons

Hindlimb

Trunk

Vibrissa

Mouth and Neck

FIGURE 15.21

Reorganization of the rat motor cortex several weeks following transection of the motor neurons of the vibrissae. The motor cortex was mapped by brain stimulation several weeks after transection. (Adapted from Sanes, Suner, & Donoghue, 1990.)

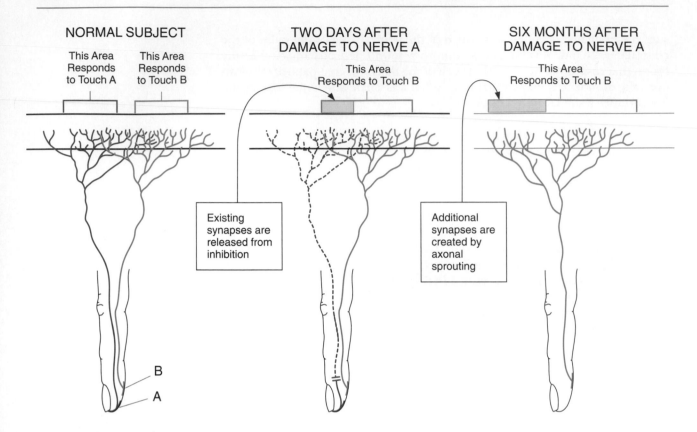

FIGURE 15.22

A two-stage model of neural reorganization: (1) strengthening of existing connections and (2) sprouting.

many of the long-term reorganizational effects seems to be too great to be attributable solely to changes in existing connections. Accordingly, it seems that both mechanisms may play a role in neural reorganization following damage to some areas—Figure 15.22 illustrates these two mechanisms.

Recovery of function   The role of neural reorganization in recovery of function is controversial (Finger, LeVere, Almli, & Stein, 1988). Many researchers who study neural reorganization believe that it contributes substantially to recovery from brain damage, but so far, all of the evidence for this view is indirect. In fact, there is very little that is known with absolute certainty about recovery from brain damage. This is not because of the lack of interest from researchers; helping the hundreds of thousands of patients who suffer brain damage each year is one of the top priorities of neuroscience. The problem is that brain damage elicits a variety of adaptive responses, several of which are easily confused with bona fide recovery of function. For example, any improvement in the week or two after damage could reflect a decline in diffuse postinjury swelling rather than recovery from the defects that were produced by the damage itself; and any gradual improvement in the months or years after damage could reflect the learning of new cognitive and behavioral strategies rather than the recovery of lost abilities.

Despite the difficulties in studying recovery of function, three general conclusions have emerged from its investigation (Kolb & Whishaw, 1990). One is that bona fide recovery of function is much less common and less complete than most people believe. Think of patient H.M. from the last chapter;

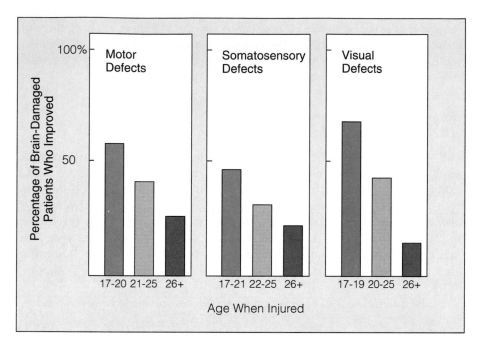

FIGURE 15.23

Percentage of patients showing improvement following brain injury.
Teuber (1975) assessed brain-damaged soldiers within a week of their
injury and again 20 years later. (Adapted from Teuber, 1975.)

his memory has not improved one bit in over 40 years. A second is that small
lesions are more likely than large lesions to be associated with recovery. And
a third is that the likelihood of recovery is greater in young patients than in
old patients—see Figure 15.23. The fact that neural reorganization is also
greater when lesions are small (Jenkins & Merzenich, 1987) and subjects are
young (Gall, McWilliams, & Lynch, 1980) provides indirect support for the
working hypothesis that neural reorganization is a major contributor to recovery
from brain damage.

15.4

Neurotransplantation in the Central Nervous System

I was introduced to the concept of brain transplantation at an early age. Perhaps
you were introduced to it in the same way—by television cartoons. A
common scenario in these cartoons is one in which a mad scientist places a
wired helmet on the head of one animal subject and another wired helmet on
the head of another animal of a different species. Then he throws a massive
switch. There are some sparks, a puff of smoke, and voilà, the brains of the
two subjects are switched. This is good for a few laughs, but the highlight of
the cartoon comes when the scientist accidentally gets one of the helmets on
his own head, and his brain ends up in the body of a chicken, and vice versa. It

is ironic that this childhood fantasy is now one of the most exciting lines of research in neuroscience. Real-life neurotransplantations are not performed by the simple pull of a switch, and they involve only portions of the nervous system, but they are no less amazing.

The Modern Era of Research on CNS Neurotransplantation

In 1971, the modern era of neurotransplantation began with a study that provided conclusive evidence of the survival of transplanted neural tissue in the brain of a host. First, radioactively labeled *thymidine* was injected into the brains of 7-day-old donor rats, and it was incorporated into the DNA of their neurons. Then, slabs of labeled cerebellum were removed from the donor rats and transplanted in the cerebellums of host rats of the same age. Two weeks later, autoradiographs of slides taken from the host cerebellum indicated that many of the transplanted neurons had survived (Das & Altman, 1971).

Subsequent research has proven that rejection of conspecific CNS transplants is rare, particularly if the tissue is taken from neonatal donors (Das, Hallas, & Das, 1980) and/or implanted in neonatal hosts (Hallas, Oblinger, & Das, 1980). The optimal sites for neurotransplants are those that are highly vascularized and have sufficient growth space (Brundin & Björklund, 1987; Fine, 1986). A piece of tissue can be implanted in some existing cavity such as the wall of a ventricle, it can be implanted in a cavity that has been surgically created, or it can be broken up into individual cells and injected into the host brain.

Does transplanted embryonic brain tissue develop as it would have had it been left in the donor, or is its development determined more by its site of implantation in the host? The experimental evidence leans toward the first alternative. In one series of studies, embryonic precursors of visual cortex (Jaeger & Lund, 1981) or retina (McLoon & Lund, 1980) were transplanted into the *superior colliculi* (optic tectums) of neonatal rats, and the result was the development of normal appearing cortical and retinal tissue, respectively.

Do neural fibers grow from the host's nervous system into a neural implant, and is the pattern of projections normal? The answer to the first question is "Yes," and the answer to the second is, "It depends." If the implant is placed in the host at the same site that it occupied in the donor, it seems to become innervated in a reasonably normal pattern. For example, superior colliculus tissue implanted in rats at a site created in the superior colliculus became innervated by axons from both the retina and visual cortex (Lund & Harvey, 1981). In contrast, visual cortex tissue implanted in the superior colliculus became innervated by fibers from several structures that do not normally innervate either the visual cortex or the superior colliculus (e.g., Jaeger & Lund, 1981).

Studies of the establishment of connections in the other direction, that is, from the implant to surrounding tissue, seem to tell a similar story: An implant will develop a reasonably normal pattern of projections if it is implanted at its usual site. For example, when embryonic retinal precursors were implanted in neonatal rats in structures such as the cortex or cerebellum, which do not normally receive retinal inputs, the implants survived, but no fibers grew to other structures. However, when retinal implants were positioned next to the superior colliculus, a structure to which it normally projects, a reasonably normal pattern of axonal projections from the implant developed (McLoon & Lund, 1980). Furthermore, more projections grew from the retinal transplant if the eye contralateral to the implant was first removed, thus reducing competition for synaptic sites. Similarly, a *locus coeruleus* tissue (pronounced LOW-kus se-RULE-ee-us) transplanted into the hippocampus of adult rats established its normal pattern of projections into the hippocampus only if the host's own locus coeruleus had first been lesioned (Björkland, Segal, & Stenevi, 1979).

Raisman, Morris, and Zhou (1987) took advantage of the highly regular arrangement of cell bodies and connections in the hippocampus to study the ability of tiny hippocampal transplants to establish normal connections. Figure 15.24 is a photograph of a slice taken through a granule cell implant that was first labeled with *horseradish peroxidase* (see Chapter 3). Notice how precisely the axons grew out to their normal targets.

CNS neurotransplantation research has focused on three related objectives: (1) to understand the mechanisms by which CNS neurotransplants interact with the host tissue (e.g., Lund, Radel, & Coffey, 1991), (2) to use CNS

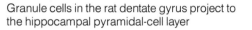

Granule cells in the rat dentate gyrus project to the hippocampal pyramidal-cell layer

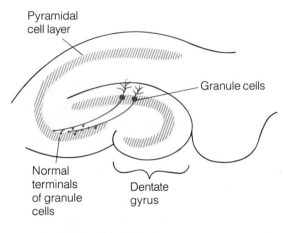

Pyramidal cell layer

Granule cells

Normal terminals of granule cells

Dentate gyrus

FIGURE 15.24

The axonal termination of embryonic rat granule cells labeled with horseradish peroxidase and implanted in an adult hippocampus.

Granule cells were removed from a rat embryo, labelled with horseradish peroxidase, and implanted in the hippocampus of an adult rat whose natural granule-cell projections had been destroyed. Notice that axons from the implant grew out to their normal target.

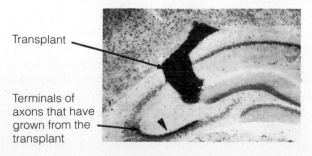

Transplant

Terminals of axons that have grown from the transplant

neurotransplantation as a tool for the study of brain function (e.g., Ralph & Lehman, 1991), and (3) to develop CNS neurotransplantation procedures for the treatment of brain damage (e.g., Lindvall, 1991). It is the third objective that is the focus of the remainder of this chapter.

Efforts to develop neurotransplantation treatments for CNS disorders have adopted two different strategies. One strategy has been to transplant tissue to stimulate the function of the patient's own tissue—for example, by stimulating or directing regeneration. The other has been to transplant tissue that becomes integrated into the recipient's own CNS and replaces damaged cells. In the following two sections, each of these two approaches is considered in turn.

Promotion of Regeneration with CNS Transplants

Efforts to promote regeneration in the mammalian CNS have focused on the question of why PNS neurons regenerate and CNS neurons do not (see Freed, Medinaceli, & Wyatt, 1985). One simple hypothesis is that CNS and PNS neurons are intrinsically different and that CNS neurons do not have the capacity to regenerate. Evidence against this hypothesis has come from studies in which CNS neurons implanted in the PNS have regenerated, and PNS neurons implanted in the CNS have not. Furthermore, peripheral sensory neurons regenerate normally until they reach the spinal cord, at which point their regeneration comes to a halt. These findings suggest that CNS neurons can regenerate, but that there is something about the environment of the CNS that impedes regeneration. What could that something be? The first possibility to be considered was that fibrous astroglia scar tissue, which forms in the CNS but not in the PNS, prevents CNS regeneration. However, the removal of scar tissue from CNS lesions does not increase regeneration.

Regeneration does not occur in the mammalian CNS because **oligodendroglia** do not provide the same stimulation and guidance that are provided by their PNS counterparts, the Schwann cells. *Schwann-cell sheaths* stimulate regeneration by releasing *nerve growth factor,* and they provide paths along which regenerating axons can grow (see Carbonetto, 1991). Not only do oligodendroglia not support regeneration, but they appear to actively block it (see Fawcett, 1991)—an extract of oligodendroglia myelin inhibits neural regeneration in tissue culture (Schwab, 1990).

Two kinds of implants have been used to increase CNS regeneration. It is too early to speculate on the degree to which they will be able to promote recovery in human patients. One approach has been to implant, near the lesion, cloned tumor cells that release an antibody against the regeneration-inhibiting ingredient of CNS myelin (Schnell & Schwab, 1990). The other approach, which has been developed by Aguayo and his colleagues, has been to transplant Schwann-cell sheaths to stimulate and direct CNS regeneration.

David and Aguayo (1981) dissected 35-millimeter segments of peripheral nerve from donor rats and grafted one end of each segment to the brain stem and the other to the spinal cord of host rats. Both the brain stem and spinal cord were damaged at the grafting sites. Several months later, histological examination revealed that axons from cell bodies at both ends of the graft had grown into the graft, along it, and out the other end back into the CNS. However, once the growing axon tips reentered the CNS, they stopped growing. Bray, Vidal-Sanz, and Aguayo (1987) employed a similar procedure for pro-

The optic nerve of a rat was cut, and a segment of peripheral nerve excised from another rat was grafted to the proximal stump. The other end of the graft was brought outside the body and tied off. Two months later the axons of many retinal ganglion cells had regenerated into the graft.

In some rats, the other end of the graft was implanted in the superior colliculus. Subsequent injections of horseradish peroxidase into the eye revealed that the axons of many retinal ganglion cells had grown through the graft and into the superior colliculus.

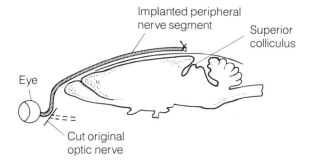

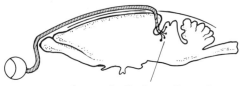

Axons of retinal ganglion cells that have grown through the graft.

FIGURE 15.25

Illustration of the transplantation study of Bray, Vidal-Sanz, and Aguayo (1987).

moting neural regeneration in the brain (see Figure 15.25). First, they cut the optic nerves of several rats and grafted a 4-centimeter length of peripheral nerve to each of the proximal stumps. The other end of the transplant was brought outside the skull and tied off. Two months later, the tied-off end of the transplant was untied. In half the cases, the untied end was injected with horseradish peroxidase, which revealed that axons from approximately 12,000 retinal ganglion cells had regenerated into the transplant. In the other half of the cases, the untied end of the transplant was grafted to one of the superior colliculi. Two months later, histological examination indicated that many retinal ganglion cells had regenerated through the Schwann-cell bridge into the superior colliculus. After regeneration, superior-colliculus neurons responded to light shone in the subjects' eyes (Keirstead et al., 1989).

The Transplantation of Neural Replacement Parts in the Brain

The second experimental approach to the treatment of brain damage by transplantation has been to replace damaged tissue with similar healthy tissue. This approach has been used on several fronts, but the most progress has been made in applying it to the treatment of Parkinson's disease (see Yurek & Sladeck, 1990). You may recall from Chapter 6 that the symptoms of Parkinson's disease (e.g., rigidity, tremor at rest, and lack of spontaneous movement) result from the degeneration of a population of dopamine-releasing neurons that projects from the *substantia nigra* to the *striatum* via the *nigrostriatal bundle*.

The first demonstration that transplanted neural tissue can improve the behavior of a brain-damaged mammal came from a study of *6-hydroxy-dopamine* lesions (Perlow, Freed, Hoffer, Seiger, Olson, & Wyatt, 1979). First, 6-hydroxydopamine was injected into one substantia nigra. The resulting unilateral destruction of dopaminergic neurons caused the rats to circle toward the side of the lesion each time they walked. Dopamine-releasing substantia nigra precursor cells obtained from rat embryos were then implanted in the ventricular wall next to the lesion. These implants reduced the circling behavior of the lesioned rats even though only a few axons from the implant grew into the striatum. In a similar study (Björklund & Stenevi, 1979), substantia nigra precursor cells were implanted in a prepared cavity adjacent to the striatum. Numerous axons from the implant grew into the striatum, and the degree of innervation in various rats was related to the degree of their behavioral improvement. The behavioral improvement following nigral implants in rats with unilateral 6-hydroxydopamine lesions lasted for at least 6 months (Freed, Perlow, Karoum, Seiger, Olson, Hoffer, & Wyatt, 1980), but the circling could be fully reinstated by surgical removal of the graft (Björkland, Dunnett, Stenevi, Lewis, & Iversen, 1980).

Bilateral transplantation of fetal substantia nigra cells has also proven successful in alleviating the parkinsonian symptoms induced in monkeys by intramuscular injections of MPTP (Sladek, Redmond, Collier, Haber, Elsworth, Deutch, & Roth, 1987). (You may remember from Chapter 6 that MPTP was discovered in 1982 when a group of young drug addicts developed Parkinson's disease after they self-administered a synthetic opiate that had been incorrectly manufactured and contained the MPTP toxin.) Fetal substantia nigra transplants survived in the MPTP-treated monkeys; they innervated adjacent striatal tissue; they released dopamine; and most importantly, they alleviated the severe poverty of movement, tremor, and rigidity produced by the MPTP. The fact that the degree of improvement observed in each monkey was related to the degree to which dopaminergic axons from the graft invaded the striatum suggested that the innervation of the striatum by the implant was the critical factor in their recovery.

Recently, Parkinson's patients have been treated with unilateral implants into the striatum of fetal substantia nigra dopamine cells. The results have been promising (see Lindvall et al., 1990). The implants survive and release dopamine, and the patients improve. The patients become more active, and their rigidity declines, particularly on the side contralateral to the transplant. Despite these promising early results, it is unlikely that human fetal implants will ever be widely used in the treatment of Parkinson's disease because of the ethical barriers against the acquisition of donor tissue from human fetuses.

A transplant procedure with fewer ethical constraints involves the transplantation of a portion of the patient's own *adrenal medulla,* which is a good source of dopamine, next to the striatum. Despite the fact that the beneficial effects of adrenal medulla **autotransplants** were found to be both modest and temporary in rats with 6-hydroxydopamine lesions (e.g., Strömberg, Herrera-Marschitz, Ungerstedt, Ebendal, & Olson, 1985), this procedure was subsequently tried on people with Parkinson's disease. Some clinical investigators claim that this method has little or no therapeutic benefit (Backlund, Granberg, Hamberger, Sedvall, Seiger, & Olson, 1985), whereas others have heralded it as a major breakthrough in the treatment of Parkinson's disease (Madrazo, Drucker-Colín, Díaz, Martínez-Mata, Torres, & Becerril, 1987). Despite the controversy, this operation is currently being performed at dozens of hospitals around the world.

In some ways, a paradox exists in neural grafting in the dopaminergic system. The cautious conclusion reached following an analysis of current data would be to postpone further human clinical studies until the experimental work can catch up with, explain, and provide more rational approaches and methods for clinical application. For better or for worse, however, clinical reports continue to stimulate and aggravate the basic science. (Gage, Kang, & Fisher, 1991, p. 417.)

Conclusion

In this chapter you have learned about various aspects of neuroplasticity. You have learned about the changes in the nervous system that occur during development (Section 15.1); about the changes in simple neural circuits that may be the basis of learning (Section 15.2); and about neural regeneration, degeneration, and reorganization (Section 15.3). Section 15.4 began with the image of a cartoon scientist running about clucking like a chicken, and the chapter ends on a similar, but less frivolous, note. It ends with the incredible experiment of Balaban, Teillet, and LeDouarin (1988), who removed the segment of the neural tube of a chicken fetus that would have normally developed into the mesencephalon and diencephalon, and in its place implanted tissue from the corresponding area of a Japanese quail neural tube. A few days after the five chicks in this condition hatched, Balaban and his colleagues performed a spectrographic analysis of their crowing sounds. All five of the chicks made abnormal crowing sounds, and three of them made sounds unmistakably like those of a Japanese quail. Transplantation of other segments of the neural tube did not have this effect. With this experiment, the cross-species transfer of behavior by neuronal transplantation has left the realm of childhood fantasy. The possibilities of this procedure boggle the imagination.

After the furor died down, the rooster moved to New York and became a regular on the talkshow circuit. Dr. Tees quit his job and wandered out West, where he was arrested for making lewd comments to chickens.

Food for Thought

1. Neurotransplants are now being used in the treatment of Parkinson's disease. Can you think of some other potential applications of this procedure?

2. Do you think it will ever be possible to transplant memories? How might such an experiment be conducted?

3. How has this chapter changed your concept of the brain?

KEY TERMS

To help you study the material in this chapter, all of the key terms—those that have appeared in bold type—are listed and briefly defined here.

Activity-dependent enhancement.   Enhancement of a neuron's synaptic activity that depends on the neuron being active during the activity of the enhancing presynaptic neuron; activity-dependent enhancement is thought to be the mechanism of associative learning.

Aggregation.   The alignment of cells during development to form the various organs of the body.

Anterograde degeneration.   The degeneration of the distal segment of a cut axon.

Anterograde transneuronal degeneration.   The degeneration of a neuron caused by damage to neurons that synapse on it.

Astroglia.   Specialized glial cells that absorb debris at sites of neuronal damage in the CNS.

Autotransplantation.   Transplanting a body part to a different location in the same body.

Axotomy.   Severing an axon or bundle of axons.

Blueprint hypothesis.   The hypothesis that developing axons grow to their correct targets by following chemical or mechanical trails.

Chemoaffinity hypothesis.   The hypothesis that each postsynaptic surface in the nervous system bears a specific chemical label to which particular axons are attracted during development.

Collateral sprouting.   When processes grow out of the axons of healthy cells to synapse on sites abandoned by adjacent degenerating axons.

Differential adhesion hypothesis.   The hypothesis that neural crest cells migrate through tissue by following pathways to which they tend to adhere.

Discriminated Pavlovian conditioning.   A conditional stimulus that has been paired with the unconditional stimulus elicits a conditional response, but a conditional stimulus that has not been paired with the unconditional stimulus does not.

Distal segment.   The segment of a cut axon from the cut to the axon terminals.

Fasciculation.   The tendency of growing axons to follow the route of preceding axons.

Glutamate.   The main excitatory neurotransmitter of the hippocampus, and perhaps the brain.

Growth cone.   The structure at the growing tip of an axon or dendrite, which is thought to guide its growth.

Habituation.   The decrease in the strength of the behavioral reaction to a repeatedly presented stimulus.

Hippocampal-slice preparation.   A slice of hippocampal tissue that is kept alive in a saline bath so that the activity of its neurons can be studied.

Induction.   When a cell's environment influences its course of development; the mesoderm seems to induce changes in adjacent neural-plate cells.

Inside-out pattern of cortical development.   The deepest layers of the cortex are formed first; thus, cells migrating to the outer layers must pass through the deepest layers.

Long-term potentiation (LTP).   After a few seconds of intense high-frequency electrical stimulation to presynaptic fibers, the response of the postsynaptic neurons to low-intensity stimulation of the presynaptic fibers is increased; LTP can last for many days.

Mesoderm layer.   The cell layer beneath the ectoderm in the developing fetus.

Migration.   The movement of cells from their site of creation in the ventricular zone of the neural tube to their ultimate location in the mature nervous system.

Nerve growth factor (NGF).   A chemical that has the ability to attract the growing axons of the sympathetic nervous system.

Neural cell adhesion molecules (NCAMs).   The molecules on the surface of the neural cells that are thought to mediate aggregation.

Neural crest.   The structure formed above and to the sides of the neural tube, which develops into the peripheral nervous system.

Neural plate. A small patch of embryonic ectodermal tissue from which the neural groove, the neural tube, and ultimately the mature nervous system develops.

Neural tube. The tube formed in the embryo when the edges of the neural groove fuse; the neural tube develops into the central nervous system.

N-methyl-D-aspartate (NMDA) receptor. A glutamate receptor subtype that is thought to play a critical role in LTP.

Nonassociative learning. A change in behavior that results from the repeated experience of a single stimulus or of two or more stimuli that are not temporally or spatially related.

Oligodendroglia. Glial cells that myelinate CNS neurons.

Optic tectum. In lower vertebrates, the main destination of visual neurons—rather than the visual cortex.

Pavlovian conditioning. A procedure in which a conditional stimulus comes to elicit a conditional response as the result of its being paired with an unconditional stimulus.

Phagocytes. Cells, such as astroglia, that absorb dead or foreign material.

Phagocytosis. The act of absorbing cellular debris.

Pioneer growth cones. The first growth cones to grow into a particular area of the developing nervous system.

Presynaptic facilitation. The cellular mechanism thought to underlie sensitization and Pavlovian conditioning.

Proximal segment. The segment of a cut axon between the cut and the cell body.

Radial glial cells. Glial cells found in the neural tube only during the period of neural migration; they form a matrix along which developing neurons migrate.

Retinal ganglion cells. The cells that compose the optic nerve.

Retrograde degeneration. Degeneration of the proximal segment.

Retrograde transneuronal degeneration. When a neuron degenerates as the result of damage to neurons on which it synapses.

Schwann cells. The cells that compose the myelin sheaths of peripheral nervous system axons.

Sensitization. The increase in an animal's responsiveness to stimuli following a noxious stimulus.

Simple-systems approach. Attempting to find the neural basis of complex processes such as learning and memory by studying them in simple neural systems.

Topographic-gradient hypothesis. The hypothesis that neuronal growth is guided by relative position on intersecting gradients, rather than by a point-to-point coding of neural connections.

Totipotential. Capable of developing into any type of body cell if transplanted to the appropriate site of the developing embryo.

Transneuronal degeneration. Degeneration of a neuron that is caused by damage to other neurons in the same neural circuit.

Ventricular zone. The zone adjacent to the ventricle in the developing neural tube.

ADDITIONAL READING

The following review articles provide up-to-date introductions to the study of neuroplasticity.

Hatten, M. E. (1990). Riding the glial monorail: A common mechanism for glial-guided neuronal migration in different regions of the developing mammalian brain. *Trends in Neurosciences, 13,* 179–184.

Kalil, R. E. (1989). Synapse formation in the developing brain. *Scientific American, 261,* 76–85.

Lindvall, O. (1991). Prospects of transplantation in human neurodegenerative diseases. *Trends in Neurosciences, 14,* 376–384.

Tessier-Lavigne, M. & Paczek, M. (1991). Target attraction: Are developing axons guided by chemotropism? *Trends in Neurosciences, 14,* 303–310.

Sur, M., Pallas, S. L., & Roe A. W. (1990). Cross-modal plasticity in cortical development: Differentiation and specification of sensory neocortex. *Trends in Neurosciences, 13,* 227–233.

16

Lateralization, Language, and the Split Brain

With the exception of a few midline orifices, we have two of almost everything—one on the left and one on the right. Even the brain, which most people view as the unitary indivisible basis of self, reflects this general principle of bilateral duplication. In its upper reaches, the brain comprises two structures, the left and right cerebral hemispheres, which are completely separate except for the **cerebral commissures,** which connect them. The fundamental duality of the human forebrain and the location of the cerebral commissures is illustrated in Figure 16.1.

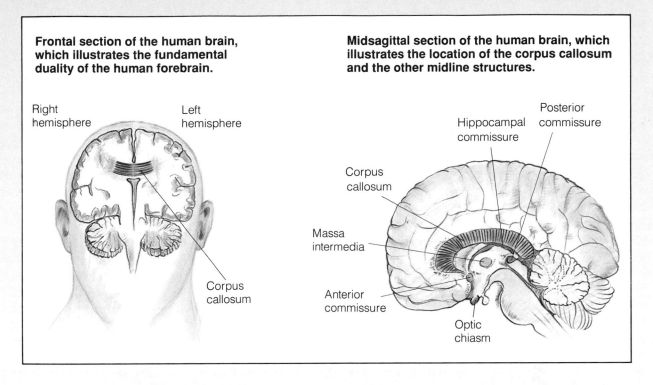

Frontal section of the human brain, which illustrates the fundamental duality of the human forebrain.

Right hemisphere

Left hemisphere

Corpus callosum

Midsagittal section of the human brain, which illustrates the location of the corpus callosum and the other midline structures.

Posterior commissure

Hippocampal commissure

Corpus callosum

Massa intermedia

Anterior commissure

Optic chiasm

FIGURE 16.1

The cerebral commissures and the hemispheres of the human brain. (Adapted from Sperry, 1964.)

The first section of this chapter, Section 16.1, is about the discovery that the two hemispheres, although comparable in general appearance, differ markedly in function—a topic commonly referred to as **lateralization of function.** The different abilities of the two hemispheres are most evident in patients in whom the cerebral commissures have been severed so that the two hemispheres function independently. The study of these **commissurot-omized (split-brain)** patients is the subject of Section 16.2. Section 16.3 focuses on language, the most lateralized of all human cognitive functions, and in particular on the localization of language circuits in the cortex of the left hemisphere.

This chapter challenges the concept that you have of yourself as a unitary being; it shows that your two hemispheres have different abilities and are capable of functioning independently. I hope that you both enjoy it.

16.1

Lateralization of Function

In 1836, Marc Dax, an unknown country doctor, presented a short report at a medical society meeting in Montpellier, France. It was his first and only scientific presentation. Dax was struck by the fact that, of the 40 or so brain-damaged patients with speech problems whom he had seen during his career, not a single case had damage restricted to the right hemisphere. His report aroused little interest, and Dax died the following year unaware that he had anticipated one of today's most important areas of neuropsychological research: the study of lateralization of function.

Aphasia and Unilateral Brain Damage

One reason why Dax's paper had little impact was that his contemporaries believed that the brain acted as a whole and that specific functions could not be attributed to particular parts of it. This view began to change 25 years later, when Paul Broca reported his *postmortem examination* of two *aphasic* patients—**aphasia** refers to brain-damage-produced deficits in the ability to produce or comprehend language. Both patients had a left-hemisphere lesion that centered on an area in the frontal cortex just in front of what we now know to be the "face area" of *primary motor cortex* (see Chapter 9). Broca at first did not realize that there was a relation between aphasia and the side of the brain damage; he had not heard of Dax's paper. However, by 1864 Broca had performed postmortem examinations on seven more aphasic patients, and he was struck by the fact that, like his first two cases, they all had damage to the *inferior prefrontal cortex* of the left hemisphere—which by then had become known as **Broca's area** (see Figure 16.2).

In the early 1900s, another example of lateralization of function was uncovered. Liepmann discovered that **apraxia,** like aphasia, is almost always associated with left-hemisphere damage, despite the fact that its symptoms are

FIGURE 16.2

The location of Broca's area in the inferior left prefrontal cortex.

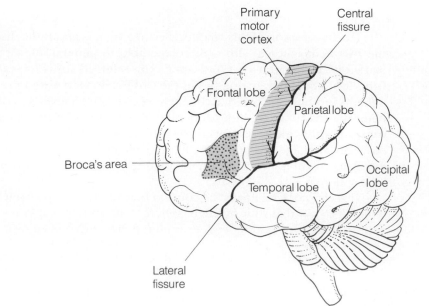

bilateral (involving both sides of the body). Apraxic patients have difficulty performing movements when asked to perform them out of context (see Chapter 9), even though they often have no difficulty performing the same responses when they are not thinking about what they are doing.

The combined impact of the evidence that the left hemisphere plays a special role in both language and voluntary movement led to the concept of *cerebral dominance.* According to this view, one hemisphere—usually the left—assumes the dominant role in the control of all complex behavioral and cognitive processes and the other plays only a minor role. Consequently, the left hemisphere was dubbed the **dominant hemisphere,** and the right hemisphere was referred to as the **minor hemisphere.**

Speech Laterality and Handedness

Two early large-scale lesion studies clarified the relation between aphasia and handedness. One study was of military personnel who suffered brain damage in World War II (Russell & Espir, 1961), and the other was of neurological patients who underwent unilateral excisions for the treatment of neurological disorders (Penfield & Roberts, 1959). In both studies, approximately 60% of right-handers (**dextrals**) with left-hemisphere lesions and 2% of those with right-hemisphere lesions were diagnosed as aphasic, and the comparable figures for left-handers (**sinestrals**) were about 30% and 24%, respectively. These results suggest that the left hemisphere is dominant for language-related abilities in almost all right-handers and in the majority of left-handers (see Annett, 1978; Benson, 1985). In effect, sinestrals are more variable than dextrals with respect to language lateralization (see Hellige, 1990; Joanette, 1989).

The Sodium Amytal Test

The **sodium amytal test** is a test of language lateralization that is often given to patients prior to neurosurgery. The neurosurgeon uses the results of the test to plan the surgery—every effort is made to avoid damaging areas of the cortex that are likely to be involved in language. The sodium amytal test involves the injection of a small amount of sodium amytal into the *carotid artery* on one side of the neck, which anesthetizes the hemisphere on that side for a few minutes, thus allowing the capacities of the other hemisphere to be assessed. During the test, the patient is asked to recite well-known series (i.e., letters of the alphabet, days of the week, months of the year, etc.) and to name pictures of common objects. Then an injection is administered to the other side, and the test is repeated. When the anesthetized hemisphere is the one dominant for speech, the subject is rendered completely mute for a minute or two, and once the ability to talk returns, errors of serial order and naming are common. In contrast, when the minor hemisphere is anesthetized, *mutism* often does not occur at all, and errors are few.

Sodium-amytal-test results have confirmed the relation between handedness and language lateralization that emerged from early lesion studies. For example, Milner (1974) found that almost all right-handed patients were left-hemisphere dominant for speech (92%), that most left-handed and ambidextrous patients without early left-hemisphere damage were left-hemisphere dominant for speech (69%), and that early left-hemisphere damage greatly decreased left-hemisphere dominance in left-handed and ambidextrous patients (30%). In interpreting these results, it is important to remember that sodium amytal tests are administered to only those people who are experiencing brain dysfunction, that early brain damage can cause the lateralization of speech to shift, and that many more people are left-hemisphere dominant to start with. Considered together, these points suggest that Milner's findings likely underestimate the proportion of left-hemisphere dominant individuals among healthy members of the general population.

The Dichotic Listening Test

The main shortcoming of unilateral-lesion and sodium-amytal studies of speech lateralization is that they are studies of brain-damaged patients. Accordingly, Kimura's (1961) demonstration that the dichotic listening test can be used to measure the lateralization of language in healthy subjects ranks as a particularly important contribution. In the standard **dichotic listening test,** three pairs of spoken digits are presented through earphones; the digits of each pair are presented simultaneously, one to each ear. For example, a subject might hear the sequence 3, 9, 2 through one ear and at the same time 1, 6, 4 through the other. The subject is then asked to report all of the digits that she or he heard. Kimura found that most people report more of the digits presented to the right ear than to the left ear. On the basis of these observations, Kimura hypothesized that the right-ear superiority of most people for the recall of spoken digits on the dichotic listening test was attributable to the fact that most people are left-hemisphere dominant for language. She argued that, although the sounds from each ear are projected to both hemispheres, the contralateral connections are stronger and take precedence when two different sounds are simultaneously competing for access to the same cortical auditory centers. In support of her hypothesis, she found that 13 patients who were shown by the sodium amytal test to be right-hemisphere dominant for language all performed better with the left ear than the right.

In a subsequent study, Kimura (1964) compared the performance of 20 right-handers on the standard, digit version of the dichotic listening test with their performance on a version of the test involving the dichotic presentation of melodies. In the melody version of the test, Kimura simultaneously played two different melodies—one to each ear—and then she asked the subjects to identify the two that they had just heard from four that were subsequently played individually to both ears. Because Milner (1962) had shown that right temporal lobe lesions are more likely to disrupt music discriminations than are left temporal lobe lesions, Kimura hypothesized that there would be a left ear superiority for melodic stimuli on the dichotic listening test. This proved to be the case.

Other Tests of Language Laterality in Healthy Subjects

Since the development of the dichotic listening test, several other tests of laterality appropriate for healthy subjects have been developed. One such test is based on a comparison of the ability of subjects to identify words presented in their left or right visual fields. The subject fixates on the center of a screen, and then a word is flashed on the screen for less than 0.1 second (see Figure

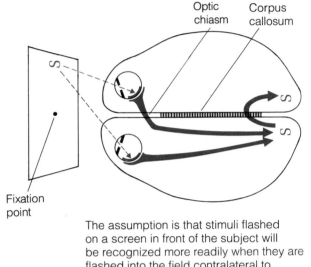

Visual input to one visual field goes directly to the contralateral hemisphere, and from there it reaches the ipsilateral hemisphere via the corpus callosum.

Optic chiasm

Corpus callosum

Fixation point

The assumption is that stimuli flashed on a screen in front of the subject will be recognized more readily when they are flashed into the field contralateral to the hemisphere specialized for perceiving them. For most subjects, language-related material is identified more readily when it is presented in the right visual field than when it is presented in the left.

FIGURE 16.3

One method of studying lateralization of language abilities. (Adapted from Springer & Deutsch, 1981.)

16.3); this is just long enough to allow some of the subjects to recognize the word, but not long enough for eye movements to be initiated. The words are often presented vertically to control for the fact that English-speaking subjects have a tendency to scan from left to right. The usual finding of such tests is a slight tendency for words presented in the right visual field to be recognized more readily than those presented in the left. This right-field advantage is attributed to the fact that information in the right visual field is transmitted directly to the left hemisphere, which is the dominant language hemisphere in most subjects. Supporting this interpretation is the fact that there is no corresponding right-field advantage for the identification of nonlanguage material (e.g., faces).

Another method of studying language lateralization is to assess the asymmetry of motor movements that accompany speech. Because fine motor movements are under contralateral control, it is assumed that their prevalence on one side of the body during speech indicates lateralization of speech on the other side. For example, Kimura (1973) reported that the gestures of the hands that accompany speech tend to be made with the hand contralateral to the dominant hemisphere for speech as determined by the dichotic listening test. Such movements rarely accompany nonverbal oral activities such as humming. It has also been reported that right-handed subjects tend to make larger movements with the right side of their mouths than with the left (e.g., Graves, Goodglass, & Landis, 1982). Wolf and Goodale (1987) and Wylie and Goodale (1988) reported that the same movement asymmetry occurred during complex nonverbal mouth movements, thus leading them to conclude that the left hemisphere is specialized for the control of all complex motor movements, of which speech movements are but one example (see Kimura & Archibald, 1974).

Sex Differences in Lateralization of Function

Interest in the possibility that the brains of females and males differ in their degree of lateralization was stimulated by a series of papers by McGlone (e.g., 1977, 1980). She proposed, on the basis of her studies with victims of unilateral strokes, that the brains of males are more lateralized than those of females. Key in supporting this hypothesis were two observations: that left-hemisphere lesions are much more likely to produce language-related deficits in males than in females, and that males are three times more likely to become aphasic after unilateral brain injury than are females. McGlone's hypothesis has led to the suggestion that a gender difference in lateralization might be the basis for the slight tendency for females to perform better on verbal tasks and males to perform better on visuospatial tasks.

McGlone's hypothesis has been challenged (see Kolb & Whishaw, 1990). For example, Inglis and Lawson (1982) found that left-hemisphere lesions were just as likely to disrupt the performance of language-related tests in females as in males, and Hier and Kaplan (1980) and De Renzi (1980) found the incidence of aphasia to be only slightly greater (about 12% greater) in males than in females. Kimura (1987) has argued that left-hemisphere lesions may be more likely to produce aphasia in males than in females in some patient populations because of sex differences in the location of the language areas— not because of sex differences in language laterality. She suggested that females are more likely than males to have their speech programming circuits localized in an area of the left frontal lobe that is rarely influenced by stroke.

16.2

Studying Lateralization of Function in Split-Brain Patients

In the early 1950s, the corpus callosum constituted a paradox of major proportions. Its size (an estimated 200 million axons) and its central position (right between the two cerebral hemispheres) implied that it performed an extremely important function, yet research in the 1930s and 1940s seemed to suggest that it did nothing at all. The corpus callosum had been cut in monkeys and in several other laboratory species, but the animals seemed no different after the surgery than they had been before. Similarly, human patients who were born without a corpus callosum seemed perfectly normal. In the early 1950s, Roger Sperry and his colleagues were attracted by this paradox.

> As recently as 1951 the psychologist Karl S. Lashley, director of the Yerkes Laboratories of Primate Biology, was still offering his own jocular surmise that the corpus callosum's purpose "must be mainly mechanical . . . i.e., to keep the hemispheres from sagging." The curious capacity of the brain to carry on undisturbed after the destruction of what is by far its largest central fiber system came to be cited rather widely in support of some of the more mystical views in brain theory.

Intrigued by the problem of the great cerebral commissure and the theoretical implications of this problem, my colleagues and I began an intensive investigation of the matter . . . (Sperry, 1964, p. 42)

The Groundbreaking Experiment of Myers and Sperry

The answer to the puzzle of the corpus callosum was provided in 1953 by an experiment on cats by Myers and Sperry. It made two astounding theoretical points. First, it showed that one function of the corpus callosum is to transfer learned information from one hemisphere to the other. Second, it showed that when the corpus callosum was cut, each hemisphere could function independently—amazingly, each split-brain cat appeared to have two brains. If you find the thought of a cat with two brains provocative, you will almost certainly be bowled over by similar observations in split-brain humans. But I am getting ahead of myself. Let's first consider the research on cats.

In their experiment, Myers and Sperry trained cats to perform a simple visual discrimination. On each trial, each cat was confronted by two panels, one with a circle on it and one with a square on it. The relative positions of the circle and square (right or left) were varied randomly from trial to trial, and the cats had to learn which symbol to press in order to get a food reward. Myers and Sperry correctly surmised that the key to split-brain research was to develop procedures for teaching and testing one hemisphere at a time. Figure 16.4 illustrates the method that they used to isolate visual-discrimination

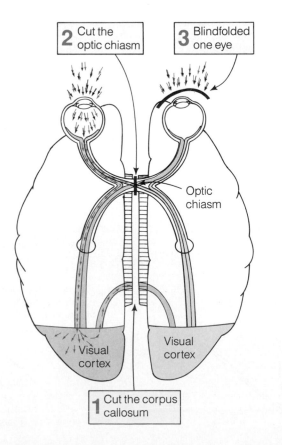

FIGURE 16.4

To restrict visual information to one hemisphere of cats, Myers and Sperry (1) cut the corpus callosum, (2) cut the optic chiasm, and (3) blindfolded one eye.

learning in one hemisphere of their cats. There are two routes by which visual information can cross from one eye to the contralateral hemisphere: via the corpus callosum or via the optic chiasm. Accordingly, Myers and Sperry *transected* (cut completely through) both the optic chiasm and the corpus callosum of each cat in their key experimental group; then they put a patch on one eye in order to restrict all incoming visual information to the hemisphere on the same side as the uncovered eye.

The results of Myers and Sperry's experiment are illustrated in Figure 16.5. In the first phase of the study, the cats in the key experimental group (i.e., the cats with both their optic chiasm and corpus callosum transected) learned the simple discrimination with a patch on one eye as rapidly as unlesioned control cats, despite the fact that cutting the optic chiasm produced a **scotoma** (an area of blindness; see Chapter 7) in the medial half of each retina. This suggested that one hemisphere working alone can learn simple tasks as rapidly as two hemispheres working together. Even more surprising were the results of the second phase of the experiment, during which the

FIGURE 16.5

Schematic illustration of the results of Myers and Sperry's (1953) split-brain experiment.

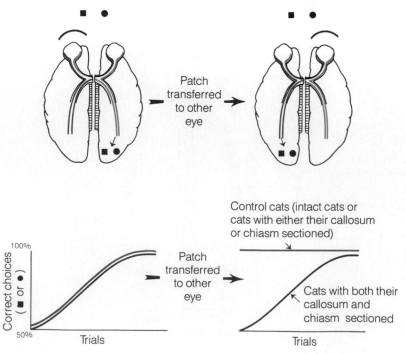

PHASE 1

Cats with both their corpus callosum and their optic chiasm sectioned and one eye blindfolded learned the discrimination as rapidly as control cats

PHASE 2

When the patch was transfered to the other eye, the performance of the cats with both their callosums and chiasms sectioned fell to chance, and they had to relearn the descrimination.

Patch transferred to other eye

Control cats (intact cats or cats with either their callosum or chiasm sectioned)

Patch transferred to other eye

Cats with both their callosum and chiasm sectioned

Correct choices (■ or ●)

Trials

Trials

patch was transferred to the other eye. The transfer of the patch had no effect on the performance of intact control cats or of control cats with only their optic chiasms or their corpus callosums transected; these subjects continued to perform the task with close to 100% accuracy. In contrast, transferring the eye patch had a devastating effect on the performance of the experimental cats. In effect, it blindfolded the hemisphere that had originally learned the task and tested the knowledge of the other hemisphere, which had been blindfolded during initial training. When the patch was transferred, the performance of the experimental cats dropped immediately to baseline (50% correct), and then they relearned the task with no *savings* whatsoever, as if they had never seen it before. Myers and Sperry concluded that each cat brain has the capacity to act as two separate brains and that the function of the corpus callosum is to transmit information between them.

Myers and Sperry's startling conclusions about the fundamental duality of the brain and the information-transfer function of the corpus callosum have been confirmed in a variety of species with a variety of test procedures. For example, *split-brain* monkeys cannot perform tasks requiring fine tactual discriminations (e.g., rough versus smooth) or fine motor responses (e.g., unlocking a puzzle) with one hand if they have learned them with the other—provided that they are not allowed to watch their hands, which allows the information to enter both hemispheres. There is no transfer of fine tactual and motor information in split-brain monkeys because the somatosensory and motor fibers involved in fine sensory and motor discriminations with the right hand all project from or to the left hemisphere, and those from the left hand all project from or to the right hemisphere (see Chapters 8 and 9).

Commissurotomy in Human Epileptics

In the first half of this century, when the normal function of the corpus callosum was still a mystery, it was known that epileptic discharges often spread from one hemisphere to the other through the corpus callosum. This fact, and the fact that cutting the corpus callosum has no obvious effect on performance outside of contrived laboratory testing situations, led two neurosurgeons, Vogel and Bogen, to initiate a program of **commissurotomy** for the treatment of severe intractable cases of epilepsy. The rationale underlying their treatment—which entailed transecting the corpus callosum as well as the *anterior commissure,* and the *hippocampal commissure*—was that the severity of the patient's convulsions might be reduced if the discharges could be limited to the hemisphere of their origin. However, the therapeutic benefits of commissurotomy were even greater than anticipated. Despite the fact that commissurotomy is performed in only the most severe cases, many commissurotomized patients do not experience another major convulsion.

The evaluation of the split-brain patient's neuropsychological status was placed in the capable hands of Sperry and his associate Gazzaniga. First, they developed a battery of tests that was based on the same methodological strategy that had proven so informative in studies of laboratory animals; that is, they developed procedures for delivering information to one hemisphere while keeping it out of the other. They could not use the same visual discrimination procedure that had been used in studies of split-brain laboratory animals (i.e., cutting the optic chiasm and blindfolding one eye) because cutting the optic chiasm produces partial blindness. Instead, they employed the testing procedure that is illustrated in Figure 16.6. Each patient was asked to *fixate* on the center of a display screen; then, visual stimuli were flashed onto the left or right side of the screen for only 0.1 second. The 0.1-second exposure time was long enough for the subjects to perceive the stimuli, but short enough to preclude the confounding effects of eye movement. Accordingly, all stimuli that were presented in the left visual field were transmitted to the right visual cortex, and all stimuli that were presented in the right visual field were transmitted to the left visual cortex (see Figure 16.7). Fine tactual and motor tasks were performed by the hands under a ledge so that the nonperforming hemisphere could not monitor their performance via the visual system (see Figure 16.6).

The results of the tests on split-brain patients confirmed the research with split-brain laboratory animals in one major respect, but not in another. Like split-brain laboratory animals, the human split-brain patients seem to have two independent brains, each with its own stream of consciousness, abilities, memories, and emotions (e.g., Gazzaniga, 1967; Gazzaniga & Sperry, 1967; Sperry, 1964). But unlike the brains of the split-brain laboratory animals, the brains of the split-brain patients are far from equal in their ability to perform certain tasks. Most notably, the left hemisphere is capable of speech, whereas the right hemisphere is not—all of the patients in the initial series of tests were right-handed.

Before I recount some of the key results of the tests on split-brain humans, let me give you some advice. Some students become confused by the results of these tests because their tendency to think of the human brain as a single unitary organ is deeply engrained. If you become confused, think of each split-brain patient as two separate subjects: Mr. or Ms. Right Hemisphere, who understands a few simple instructions but cannot speak, who receives sensory information from the left visual field and left hand, and who controls the fine motor responses of the left hand; and Mr. or Ms. Left Hemisphere, who is verbally adept, who receives sensory information from the

FIGURE 16.6

The testing arrangement that is used to evaluate the neuropsychological status of split-brain patients.

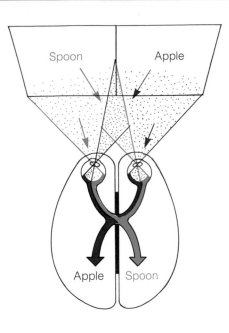

FIGURE 16.7

The paths of input to the visual cortex in Sperry's tests of split-brain patients.

right visual field and right hand, and who controls the fine motor responses of the right hand. In everyday life, the behavior of split-brain subjects is reasonably normal because their two brains go through life together and acquire much of the same information; however, in the neuropsychological laboratory, major discrepancies in what the two hemispheres learn can be created. As you are about to learn, this has some interesting consequences.

Evidence That the Hemispheres of Split-Brain Patients Function Independently

If a picture of a spoon is flashed in the right visual field of a split-brain patient, the left hemisphere can do one of two things to indicate that it has received and stored the information. Because it is the hemisphere that speaks, the left hemisphere can simply tell the experimenter that it saw a picture of a spoon. Or, the patient can reach under the ledge with his or her right hand, feel the test objects that are there, and pick out the spoon. Similarly, if the spoon is presented to the left hemisphere by placing it in the patient's right hand, the left hemisphere can indicate to the experimenter that it was a spoon either by saying so or by putting the spoon down and picking out another spoon with the right hand from the test objects under the ledge. If, however, the nonspeaking, right hemisphere is asked to indicate the identity of an object that has been presented to left hemisphere, it cannot do so. Although objects that have been presented to the left hemisphere can be accurately identified with the right hand, performance is no better than chance with the left hand.

When test objects are presented to the right hemisphere either visually (in the left visual field) or tactually (in the left hand), the pattern of responses is entirely different. If the patient is asked to name an object flashed in the left visual field, he or she is likely to claim that nothing appeared on the screen. (Remember that it is the left hemisphere who is talking and the right hemisphere who has seen the stimulus.) If the patient is asked to name an object placed in the left hand, he or she is usually aware that something is there (presumably because of the crude tactual information carried by ipsilateral somatosensory fibers; see Chapter 8), but is unable to say what it is. Amazingly, all the while the patient is claiming (i.e., all the while that the left hemisphere is claiming) that he or she cannot identify a test object presented in the left visual field or left hand, the left hand (i.e., the right hemisphere) can identify the correct object. Imagine how confused the patient (the left hemisphere) must become when in trial after trial, the left hand can feel an object and then fetch another just like it from a collection of test items under the ledge, while the left hemisphere is vehemently claiming that it does not know the identity of the test object.

Cross-Cuing

Although the two hemispheres of a split-brain subject have no means of direct neural communication, they sometimes communicate with each other indirectly by a method called **cross-cuing.** An example of cross-cuing occurred during a series of tests designed to determine whether the left hemisphere could respond to colors presented in the left visual field. To test this possibility, a red or a green stimulus was presented in the left visual field, and the subject was asked to verbally report the color: red or green. At first the patient performed at a chance level on this task (i.e, 50% correct), but after several trials performance improved appreciably, thus suggesting that the color information was somehow being transferred over neural pathways from the right hemisphere to the left. However, this proved not to be the case.

> We soon caught on to the strategy the patient used. If a red light was flashed and the patient by chance guessed red, he would stick with that answer. If the flashed light was red, and the patient by chance guessed green, he would frown, shake his head and then say, "Oh no, I meant red." What was happening was that the right hemisphere saw the red light and heard the left hemisphere make the guess "green." Knowing that the answer was wrong, the right hemisphere precipitated a frown and a shake of the head, which in turn cued in the left hemisphere to the fact that the answer was wrong and that it had better correct itself! . . . The realization that the neurological patient has various strategies at his command emphasizes how difficult it is to obtain a clear neurological description of a human being with brain damage (Gazzaniga, 1967, p. 27).

Learning Two Things at Once

In most of the classes that I teach, there is a student who fits the following stereotype. He sits—or rather sprawls—near the back of the class, and despite good grades, he tries to create the impression that he is above it all by making sarcastic comments. I am sure that you recognize him—and it is almost always a him. Recently, such a student inadvertently triggered an interesting discussion in one of my classes. His comment went something like this: "If getting my brain cut in two could create two separate brains, perhaps I should get it done so that I could study for two different exams at the same time."

The question that was raised by this comment is a good one. If the two hemispheres of a split-brain patient are capable of total independence, then they should be able to learn two different things at the same time. Can they? Remarkably, they can. For example, in one test two different visual stimuli appeared simultaneously on the test screen—let's say a pencil in the left visual field and an apple in the right visual field. Then the subject was asked to simultaneously reach into two bags—one with each hand—and grasp in each hand the object that was on the screen. After grasping the objects, but before withdrawing them, the subject was asked to tell the experimenter what was in the two hands, and the subject (the left hemisphere) replied "two apples." Much to the bewilderment of the verbal left hemisphere, when the hands were withdrawn, there was an apple in the right hand and a pencil in the left. The two hemispheres of the split-brain subject had learned two different things at exactly the same time.

In another test in which two visual stimuli were presented simultaneously—again let's say a pencil to the left visual field and an apple to the right—the subjects were asked to pick up the presented object from an assortment of objects, which were on the table in full view. As the right hand reached out to pick up the apple under the direction of the left hemisphere, the right hemisphere saw what was happening and thought that an error was being made (remember that the right hemisphere saw a pencil). As a result, in a few cases, the left hand shot out, grabbed the right hand away from the apple, and redirected it to the pencil. This response is called the **helping-hand phenomenon.**

Yet another example of simultaneous learning in the two hemispheres involves the phenomenon of **visual completion.** As you may recall from Chapter 8, subjects with scotomas (i.e., areas of blindness in their visual fields) are often unaware of them because their brains have the capacity to fill them in (i.e., to complete them) by using information from the surrounding areas of the visual field. In a sense, each hemisphere of a split-brain patient is a subject with a scotoma covering her or his entire ipsilateral visual field. The ability of each hemisphere of a split-brain subject to simultaneously and independently engage in completion has been demonstrated in studies using the **chimeric figures test**—named after *Chimera,* a mythical monster composed of the combined parts of different animals. Levy, Trevarthen, and Sperry (1972) flashed photographs composed of the fused half faces of two different people onto the center of a screen in front of their split-brain subjects. The subjects were then asked to describe what they saw or to point to what they saw from a series of normal photographs. Amazingly, each subject (i.e., each left hemisphere) reported seeing a complete, bilaterally symmetrical face, even when asked such leading questions as, "Did you notice anything peculiar about what you just saw?" When the subjects were asked to describe what they saw, they usually described a completed version of the half that had been presented to the right visual field (left hemisphere). In contrast, when the subjects were asked to point out the correct face from a series of possibilities, they usually pointed to the completed version of the half that had been presented to the left visual field (right hemisphere), regardless of which hand was used for pointing. Pointing is a crude motor response, and thus it can be controlled by the contralateral or ipsilateral hemisphere. Clearly, each hemisphere of a split-brain patient is capable of visual completion, and each can see a different face in exactly the same place at exactly the same time.

Comparing the Abilities of the
Left and Right Hemispheres of Split-Brain Subjects

Once it was firmly established that the two hemispheres of each split-brain patient can function independently, it became clear that the study of split-brain patients provided a unique opportunity to compare the abilities of left and right hemispheres. However, early studies of the lateralization of function in split-brain patients were limited by the fact that visual stimuli requiring more than 0.1 second to perceive could not be studied using the conventional method for restricting visual input to one hemisphere. This methodological barrier was eliminated by Zaidel in 1975. Zaidel developed a lens that limits visual input to one hemisphere of split-brain patients while they scan complex visual material such as pages of a book. As illustrated in Figure 16.8, the **Z lens,** as it has been termed (after Zaidel), is a contact lens that is opaque on one side. Because it moves with the eye, it permits visual input to enter only one hemisphere, irrespective of eye movement. Zaidel used the Z lens to compare the ability of the left and right hemispheres of split-brain patients to perform various tests.

The usefulness of the Z-lens is not restricted to purely visual tests. For example, here is how it has been used to compare the ability of the left and right hemispheres to comprehend speech. Because each ear projects to both hemispheres, it is not possible to present spoken words to only one hemisphere. Thus, to assess the ability of a hemisphere to comprehend spoken words or sentences, Zaidel presented them to both ears, and then he asked the subject to pick the correct answer or to perform the correct response under the direction of visual input to only that hemisphere. For example, to test the ability of the right hemisphere to understand the oral commands of the *token test* (see Chapter 5), the subjects were given an oral instruction (such as, "put the green square under the red circle"), and then the right hemisphere's ability to comprehend the direction was tested by allowing only the right hemisphere to observe the colored tokens while the task was being completed.

Z-lens studies of split-brain patients have shown that the right hemisphere is not devoid of language ability (see Zaidel, 1983, 1987). Although the

FIGURE 16.8

The Z-lens system, which was developed by Zaidel to study functional asymmetry in split-brain patients. (Adapted from Springer & Deutsch, 1981.)

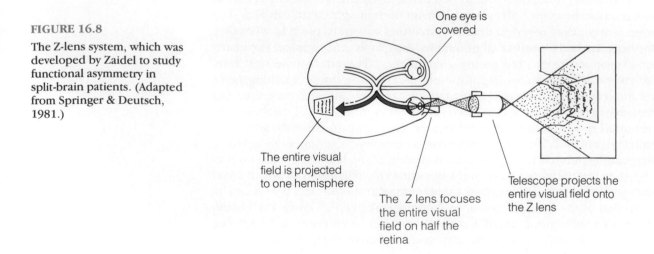

right hemisphere cannot speak, it can understand many spoken or written words, particularly concrete words. In contrast, its comprehension of sentences is restricted to short phrases and simple syntactic constructions; it has particular difficulty understanding sentences whose construction places a load on memory—the average verbal memory span of disconnected right hemispheres is only three items; the average for intact subjects and disconnected left hemispheres is seven. Although it is impossible to characterize the language comprehension abilities of the right hemisphere in any simple way, the performance of the right hemisphere on various tests of language comprehension is often comparable to that of a normal child between 3 and 6 years old. For any given sentence, comprehension by the right hemisphere is poorer when it is read than when it is heard.

The old concept of left-hemisphere dominance (the idea that the left hemisphere dominates the right in all important activities) was put to rest by the discovery that the right hemisphere is superior to the left at many tasks that involve spatial ability. For example, Levy (1969) placed a three-dimensional block of a particular shape in either the right hand or the left hand of her split-brain subjects, and then after they had thoroughly *palpated* it (tactually investigated it), she asked them to point to the two-dimensional test stimulus that best represented what the three-dimensional block would look like if it were made of cardboard and unfolded. Not only did she find a striking superiority of the right hemisphere on this task, but she also discovered that the two hemispheres seemed to go about the task in entirely different ways. The performance of the left hand and right hemisphere was rapid and silent, whereas the performance of the right hand and left hemisphere was hesitant and often accompanied by a running verbal commentary that was difficult for the subjects to inhibit. Levy concluded that the left hemisphere thinks in a verbal, analytic mode and that thinking in the right hemisphere is direct, perceptual, and synthetic. The superiority of the right hemisphere of split-brain patients at spatial and pattern tasks is consistent with the finding that *contralateral neglect* and *constructional apraxia* (see Chapter 9) are associated with right-hemisphere damage.

When the concept of left-hemisphere dominance was widely accepted, the right hemisphere was often portrayed as bereft of emotion and incapable of self-awareness, two higher cognitive functions that were assumed to be the sole purview of the dominant hemisphere. Both of these presumptions have been proved false. Sperry, Zaidel, and Zaidel (1979) used the Z lens to assess the reaction of the right hemispheres of split-brain patients to various emotion-charged images: photographs of themselves; of relatives; of pets; and of political, historical, and religious figures and emblems. The right hemispheres could readily pick out pictures of themselves, thus indicating that they had a concept of self. Moreover, their emotional reactions to various stimuli were entirely appropriate—in fact, the right hemisphere may be even better than the left at processing emotional stimuli (Bowers, Bauer, Coslett, & Heilman, 1985).

Unexpectedly, the emotional reactions of the right hemispheres of the split-brain patients of Sperry et al. were often reflected in their speech, as well as in their postures, expressions, and gestures. This indicated that emotional information was somehow being passed between the right and left hemispheres of the split-brain subjects. The ability of emotional reactions, but not visual information, to be passed from the right hemisphere to the left hemisphere created a bizarre situation. A subject's left hemisphere often reacted with the appropriate emotional verbal response to an image that had been presented to the right hemisphere, even though it could not say what the image was. In several instances, the experimenter had to stop the right hemisphere from communicating the identity of the image to the left hemisphere by writing with the left hand on the back of the right hand. Consider the following paraphrased exchange.

The patient's right hemisphere was presented with an array of nine photos, and he was asked if one was familiar. He pointed to the photo of his aunt.

Experimenter: Is this a neutral, a thumbs-up, or a thumbs-down person?

Patient: With a smile, he made a thumbs-up sign and said, "This is a happy person."

Experimenter: "Do you know him personally?"

Patient: "Oh, it's not a him; it's a her."

Experimenter: "Is she an entertainment personality or an historical figure?"

Patient: "No, just . . ."

Experimenter: "Someone you know personally?"

Patient: He traced something with his left index finger on the back of his right hand, and then he exclaimed, "My aunt, my aunt Edie."

Experimenter: "How do you know?"

Patient: "By the E on the back of my hand."

(Paraphrased from Sperry, Zaidel, & Zaidel, 1979, pp. 161–162.)

Two Theories of Cerebral Asymmetry

Several theories have been proposed to explain why cerebral asymmetry evolved. The two most prominent theories of lateralization of function are based on the premise that there are advantages for areas of the brain that perform similar functions to be located in the same hemisphere. One of these theories (see Levy, 1969; Sperry, 1974, 1985) is that there are two basic modes of thinking, an *analytic mode* and a *synthetic mode,* and that the neural circuitry required for each is intrinsically different. As a result, those functions that benefit from the analytic and synthetic modes of treatment have become segregated during the course of evolution, the analytic mechanisms in the left hemisphere and the synthetic mechanisms in the right.

In the words of Harris (1978),

The left hemisphere operates in a more logical, analytical, computer-like fashion, analyzing stimulus information input sequentially, abstracting out the relevant details to which it attaches verbal labels; the right hemisphere is primarily a synthesizer, more concerned with the overall stimulus configuration, and organizes and processes information in terms of gestalts or wholes (p. 463).

The major problem with this theory is its vagueness. Because the degree to which a particular task requires analytic or synthetic processing is never clear, it has been impossible to subject the synthetic-analytic theory of cerebral lateralization to critical tests.

Kimura (1979) proposed a *sensorimotor theory of cerebral lateralization.* She suggested that, although speech is the most well-known and highly lateralized ability of the human left hemisphere, the left hemisphere is not specialized for the control of speech per se but for the control of fine motor movements, of which speech is only one, albeit particularly notable, example. Kimura offered two major lines of evidence in support of her theory. First, lesions of the left hemisphere often disrupt voluntary oral movements, even when they are unrelated to speech. And second, the degree of disruption of voluntary nonspeech facial movements produced by left-hemisphere lesions is positively correlated with the degree of aphasia that they produce. Kimura believes that verbal communication evolved from a stage of communication that was primarily gestural with a few vocal components to one that is primarily vocal with a few gestural components.

Although the *analytic-synthetic theory of cerebral lateralization* has become the darling of "pop science," experimental support for the sensorimotor theory is steadily accumulating. For example, Kimura and Watson (1989) assessed the speech and motor abilities of 479 right-handed patients with unilateral brain lesions. Lesions in the left frontal lobe produced deficits in the patients' abilities to make individual speech sounds and individual facial movements, whereas lesions in the left temporal or parietal lobes produced deficits in the patients' abilities to make sequences of speech sounds and sequences of facial movements. In addition, Wolff, Michel, Ovrut, and Drake (1990) found that subjects with reading disabilities had difficulty performing a bimanual timing motor task; they had difficulty tapping the index finger of one hand with every beat of a metronome while they tapped the index finger of the other hand with every other beat. This finding suggests that reading deficits, like speech deficits, may be a manifestation of a general sensorimotor deficit (see Wolff, Michel, & Ovrut, 1990). The sensorimotor theory of language lateralization explains why speech has become lateralized in the left hemisphere: Because that is where sensorimotor abilities had become lateralized. But, why did sensorimotor abilities become lateralized in the first place, and why in the left hemisphere (see Michel & Harkins, 1987)?

Questions about the evolution of motor and language laterality have generated interest in the laterality of nonhuman species (see Glick, 1985). Hand (paw) preferences have been reported in several species. For example, Westergaard (1991) recently reported that most *capuchin* and *macaque* monkeys display a consistent preference for one hand over the other in the manufacture of the tools that they use to probe for termites—slightly more monkeys preferred the left hand. The documentation of hand preference in nonhuman species refutes the hypothesis that hand preference evolved in early *hominids* in response to their manufacture and use of tools. There is also some evidence that the control of communicative vocalizations (see Owren, 1990; Pepperberg, 1990; Seyfarth, Cheney, and Marler, 1980) is lateralized in some nonhuman species. For example, the songs of some avian species are predominantly under left-hemisphere control (Nottebohm & Nottebohm, 1976) and the left hemispheres of macaque monkeys play the dominant role in the discrimination of macaque vocalizations (Hefner & Hefner, 1984).

Lateralization of Function and Split-Brains: Fact or Fiction?

Recently, one of us received a phone call from a well-known Hollywood actress who related an argument with a friend concerning left-hemisphere-right-hemisphere differences. She had read that left-right brain differences are real, pervasive, and the subject of intense scientific studies. Her companion said they were pseudoscientific, popularized stuff, the fad of the decade. Who was right? (Zaidel, 1985, p. 307).

In a sense, both were. On one hand, there is no question that the study of the lateralization of function is one of the most important and productive lines of research in neuropsychology. It has led to the development of a successful treatment for epilepsy; it has facilitated the diagnosis and treatment of brain damage; and it has changed the way that we think about ourselves. On the other hand, the broad dissemination and popular appeal of this research has led to major distortions and abuses. Slight hemispheric differences have been transformed by the popular press into clear-cut, all-or-none dichotomies that have been used to account for everything from baseball batting averages to socioeconomic class.

16.3

The Cortical Localization of Language

So far, this chapter has focused on the functional asymmetry of the brain, with an emphasis on the lateralization of language-related functions. At this point, it shifts course, from language lateralization to language localization. In contrast to *language lateralization,* which refers to the relative control of language-related functions by the left and right hemispheres, *language localization* refers to the location within the hemispheres of the circuits that participate in language-related activities.

My treatment of language localization is orthodox in one respect and unorthodox in another. Like most introductions to language localization, the following discussion revolves around the **Wernicke-Geschwind model,** which has dominated the teaching of the neuropsychology of language localization for 25 years. However, unlike the usual introductions to language localization, the ensuing coverage does not suggest that the Wernicke-Geschwind model provides an adequate explanation. In fact, you will learn that the Wernicke-Geschwind model is consistent with few of the findings of the research that it has stimulated.

You may be wondering now why I have organized this section of the chapter around the Wernicke-Geschwind model if it is, as I have just pointed out, inconsistent with most of the relevant data. The reason is that the Wernicke-Geschwind model, despite its inaccuracy, has been the primary stimulus for most of the research and debate about the cortical localization of language. Because most of the research that is described in this section was conducted and interpreted within the context of the Wernicke-Geschwind model, the model provides you with a means of integrating, evaluating, and remembering most of what you are about to read. Reading about the localization of language without a basic understanding of the Wernicke-Geschwind model would be like watching a game of chess without knowing the rules—not a very fulfilling experience.

Historic Antecedents of the Wernicke-Geschwind Model

The history of the localization of language and the history of the lateralization of function began at the same point, with Broca's assertion that a small area in the inferior portion of the left prefrontal cortex (subsequently called **Broca's area**) is the center for speech production. Broca hypothesized that programs of articulation are stored within this area and that speech is produced when these programs activate the adjacent portion of the precentral gyrus, which controls the muscles of the face and oral cavity. According to this theory, damage restricted to Broca's area should disrupt speech production without producing deficits in language comprehension.

The next major chapter in the story of the cerebral localization of language began in 1874, when Wernicke (pronounced VER ni key) claimed to have identified, on the basis of 10 clinical cases, a second cortical language center, which later became known as **Wernicke's area.** He contended that the area in the left temporal lobe just posterior to the primary auditory cortex (see Chapter 8) is the center for language comprehension (see Figure 16.9). In Wernicke's experience, lesions to Broca's area produce a syndrome of aphasia—termed **Broca's aphasia**—that is primarily **expressive,** characterized by speech that retains its meaningfulness, but is slow, labored, disjointed, and poorly articulated. In contrast, he claimed that the deficits produced by lesions of Wernicke's area are primarily **receptive.** According to Wernicke, people with damage to Wernicke's area have difficulty understanding language, and their speech is meaningless. However, despite its lack of meaning, it has the superficial structure, rhythm, and intonation of proper speech—it is referred to as **word salad.**

Wernicke reasoned that damage to the pathway connecting Broca's area and Wernicke's area should produce a third type of aphasia, one that he called **conduction aphasia.** He argued that comprehension and spontaneous speech would be intact in patients with damage to this pathway, but that there would be a difficulty in repeating words that were heard. The major pathway connecting Wernicke's and Broca's areas was subsequently identified and termed the left **arcuate fasciculus** (see Figure 16.9).

The following are examples of the kinds of speech that are presumed to be associated with localized damage to Broca's and Wernicke's areas, respectively (Geschwind, 1979).

> **Broca's Aphasia:** A patient asked about a dental appointment said hesitantly and indistinctly: "Yes . . . Monday . . . Dad and Dick . . . Wednesday nine o'clock . . . 10 o'clock . . . doctors . . . and . . . teeth."
>
> **Wernicke's Aphasia:** A patient who was asked to describe a picture that showed two boys stealing cookies behind a woman's back reported: "Mother is away here working her work to get her better, but when she's looking the two boys looking in the other part. She's working another time." (p. 181)

Another cortical area that seems to be involved in language comprehension was identified by Dejerine in 1892 on the basis of his postmortem examination of one patient. The patient suffered from **alexia** and **agraphia;** he could not read or write, respectively, although his visual and motor abilities were otherwise normal. The case was particularly informative because the

FIGURE 16.9

Components of the
Wernicke-Geschwind model.

The Seven Components of the Wernicke-Geschwind Model

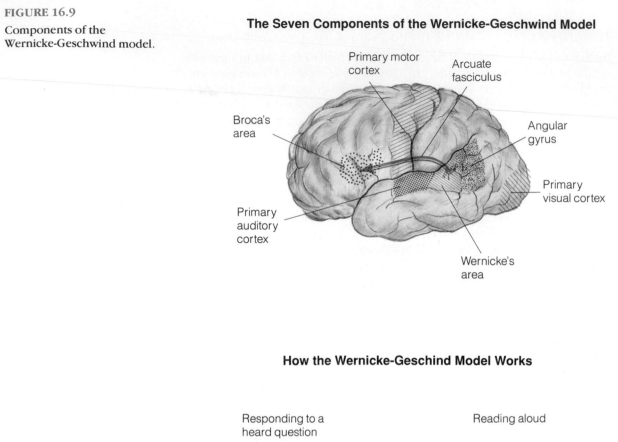

FIGURE 16.9

Components of the
Wernicke-Geschwind model.

How the Wernicke-Geschind Model Works

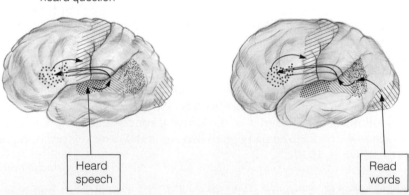

alexia and agraphia were uncharacteristically pure; they occurred in the absence of major deficits in the production or comprehension of speech. Dejerine's postmortem examination revealed damage in the pathways connecting the visual cortex to the left **angular gyrus** (see Figure 16.9), an area of left temporal and parietal cortex just posterior to Wernicke's area. Dejerine concluded that the left angular gyrus is responsible for comprehending language-related visual information, which is received directly from the adjacent left visual cortex and indirectly from the right visual cortex via the corpus callosum.

During the era of Broca, Wernicke, and Dejerine, there were many influential scientists who opposed their attempts to localize various language-related abilities to specific neocortical areas (e.g., Head, Freud, Marie). In fact, the advocates of a more holistic approach to brain function gradually gained the upper hand, and interest in the localization of language waned. However, in 1965, Geschwind revived the old localizationist ideas of Broca, Wernicke, and Dejerine and melded them into a powerful theory that emphasized that damage to the language areas of the left hemisphere or to the connections between them was the major cause of aphasia and other language-related disorders. This *Wernicke-Geschwind model,* as it became known, spurred a resurgence of interest in the neuropsychology of language.

The Wernicke-Geschwind Model

The seven components of the Wernicke-Geschwind model are illustrated in Figure 16.9: primary visual cortex, angular gyrus, primary auditory cortex, Wernicke's area, the arcuate fasciculus, Broca's area, and the primary motor cortex—all in the left hemisphere. The following two examples illustrate how this model is presumed to function. First, when you are having a conversation, the auditory signals triggered by the speech of the other person are received by your primary auditory cortex and conducted to Wernicke's area, where they are comprehended. If a response is in order, Wernicke's area generates the neural representation of the thought underlying the reply, and it is transmitted to Broca's area via the arcuate fasciculus. In Broca's area, this signal activates the appropriate program of articulation that drives the appropriate orofacial neurons of the primary motor cortex and ultimately your muscles of articulation. Second, when you are reading aloud, the signal received by your primary visual cortex is transmitted to the angular gyrus, which translates the visual form of the word into its auditory code and transmits it to Wernicke's area for comprehension. Wernicke's area then triggers the appropriate responses in the arcuate fasciculus, Broca's area, and motor cortex, respectively, to elicit the appropriate speech sound.

The Wernicke-Geschwind model is a **serial model;** it involves a chain of responses that are triggered in linear sequence, like a single line of falling dominoes. **Parallel models** involve two or more routes of activity (see Chapter 9).

SELF TEST

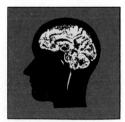

Before proceeding to an evaluation of the Wernicke-Geschwind model, complete the following exercise to confirm that you understand its fundamentals. According to the Wernicke-Geschwind model:

1. The _____ gyrus translates the visual form of a read word into meaningful auditory code,

2. The _____ cortex controls the muscles of articulation,

3. The _____ cortex receives the written word,

4. _____ area is the center for language comprehension,

(Test continues on the following page.)

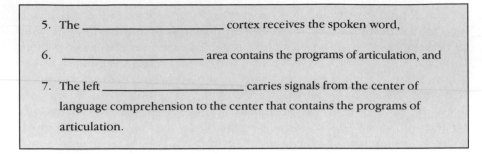

5. The _____ cortex receives the spoken word,

6. _____ area contains the programs of articulation, and

7. The left _____ carries signals from the center of language comprehension to the center that contains the programs of articulation.

Evaluation of the Wernicke-Geschwind Model

You should have digested the preceding description of the Wernicke-Geschwind model with some degree of skepticism—unless you are reading this text from back to front. By this point in the text, you will almost certainly recognize that any model of a complex cognitive process that involves a few highly localized neocortical centers joined in a linear fashion by a few arrows is sure to have major shortcomings. You have learned in almost every chapter that the brain—and especially the neocortex—is not divided into neat little compartments whose functions conform to vague concepts such as language comprehension, speech motor programs, and conversion of written language to auditory language.

The evidence offered by advocates of the Wernicke-Geschwind model is composed almost entirely of selected case studies of patients with strokes, tumors, and penetrating brain injuries. Damage in such cases is almost always diffuse, and it inevitably encroaches on underlying myelinated fiber systems that are coursing through the lesion site to other areas of the brain. Clearly, such case studies are a questionable basis for deriving a strictly localizationist theory (cf. Bogen & Bogen, 1976). For example, illustrated in Figure 16.10 is the diffuse cortical damage of one of the original two cases on which Broca based his claim that a discrete area of frontal cortex (i.e., Broca's area) controls speech programming.

The ultimate test of a theory's validity is the degree to which its predictions are consistent with the empirical evidence. The remainder of the chapter reviews several lines of research that have tested predictions of the Wernicke-Geschwind model. But first, two confusing points concerning the use of the terms "Broca's aphasia" and "Wernicke's aphasia" must be clarified. The first is that Broca's and Wernicke's aphasia probably do not exist in their pure forms as defined by Wernicke and Geschwind—or if they do, they are extremely rare. Broca's and Wernicke's aphasia are predictions of the Wernicke-Geschwind model, rather than descriptions of the dysfunctions commonly experienced by aphasic patients. Almost all aphasic patients have a complex mixture of both expressive and receptive symptoms (Benson, 1985), and even in those few reported cases that appear to closely comply with the specific deficits predicted by the model, one has to wonder whether other

Correct answers to the questions on the preceding page: (1) angular, (2) primary motor, (3) primary visual, (4) Wernicke's, (5) primary auditory, (6) Broca's, and (7) arcuate fasciculus.

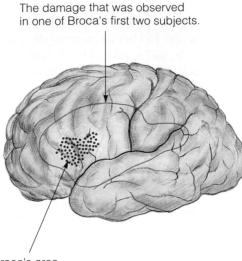

The damage that was observed in one of Broca's first two subjects.

Broca's area

FIGURE 16.10
Extent of the brain damage in one of Broca's two original patients. (Adapted from Mohr, 1976.)

deficits may have been revealed by more extensive testing. Accordingly, the terms of Broca's and Wernicke's aphasia are generally used to designate aphasic disorders that are primarily—not completely—expressive or receptive, respectively. The second confusing point about the terms "Broca's aphasia" and "Wernicke's aphasia" is that they do not—as their names imply—necessarily result from damage to Broca's and Wernicke's areas. This is another prediction of the model, not a description of the evidence.

The Effects of Brain Damage on Language-Related Abilities

Surgical removal of cortical tissue In view of the fact that the Wernicke-Geschwind model grew out of the study of patients with cortical damage, it is appropriate to begin evaluating it by assessing its ability to predict the language-related deficits produced by damage to various parts of the cortex. The study of patients in whom discrete areas of cortex have been surgically removed has proven particularly informative in this regard because the location and extent of their lesions can be derived from the surgeon's report. The study of patients in whom the Wernicke-Geschwind language areas have been surgically removed has not confirmed the predictions of the model by any stretch of the imagination. For example, lesions that destroy all of Broca's area, but little surrounding tissue, typically have no lasting effects on language-related abilities (Penfield & Roberts, 1959; Rasmussen & Milner, 1975; Zangwill, 1975). There is often some aphasia after such a discrete lesion, but its temporal course suggests that it results from postsurgical *edema* (swelling) in the surrounding neural tissue, rather than from the *excision* (cutting out) of Broca's area per se. The patient typically has no speech problems immediately after Broca's area has been excised; speech deficits develop several hours later and then gradually subside in the ensuing weeks. Similarly, permanent speech difficulties are not produced by discrete surgical lesions to the arcuate fasciculus, and permanent alexia and agraphia are not produced by surgical lesions restricted to the cortex of the angular gyrus (Rasmussen & Milner, 1975). The consequences of the surgical removal of Wernicke's area are less well documented; surgeons have been hesitant to remove it in light of Wernicke's dire predictions. Nevertheless, in some cases, a good portion of Wernicke's area has been removed without lasting language-related deficits (e.g., Ojemann, 1979; Penfield & Roberts, 1959). Figure 16.11 summarizes the language-related effects of six cortical excisions performed by Penfield and Roberts (1959).

Figure 16.11

There is often little permanent disruption of language-related abilities after surgical excision of the classic Wernicke-Geschwind language areas. (Adapted from Penfield & Roberts, 1959.)

Case J.M. No speech difficulties for 2 days after his surgery, but by Day 3 he was almost totally aphasic; 18 days after his operation he had no difficulty in spontaneous speech, naming, or reading, but his spelling and writing were poor.

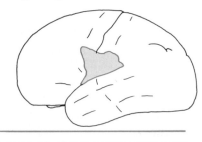

Case P.R. He had no immediate speech difficulties; 2 days after his operation, he had some language-related problems but they cleared up.

Case D.H. This operation was done in two stages; following completion of the second stage, no speech-related problems were reported.

Case A.D. He had no language-related problems after his operation, except for a slight deficit in silent reading and writing.

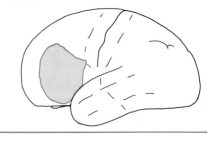

Case J.C. There were no immediate speech problems; 18 hours after his operation he became completely aphasic, but 21 days after surgery, only a mild aphasia remained.

Case H.N. After his operation, he had a slight difficulty in spontaneous speech, but 4 days later he was unable to speak; 23 days after surgery, there were minor deficits in spontaneous speech, naming and reading aloud, and a marked difficulty in oral calculation.

Supporters of the Wernicke-Geschwind model argue that, despite the precision of surgical excision, negative evidence obtained from the study of the effects of brain surgery should be discounted because the brain pathology that warranted the surgery may have reorganized the control of language by the brain.

Accidental or disease-related brain damage Hécaen and Angelergues (1964) rated the articulation, fluency, comprehension, naming ability, ability to repeat spoken sentences, reading, and writing of 214 right-handed patients with small, medium, or large accidental of disease-related lesions to the left hemisphere. The extent and location of the damage in each case was estimated by either postmortem histological examination or visual inspection during subsequent surgery. Hécaen and Angelergues found that small lesions to Broca's area seldom produced lasting language deficits and that those restricted to Wernicke's area sometimes did not. Medium-sized lesions did produce some deficits, but in contrast to the predictions of the Wernicke-Geschwind model, problems of articulation were just as likely to occur following medium-sized parietal or temporal lesions as they were following comparable lesions in the vicinity of Broca's area. All other symptoms that were produced by medium-sized lesions were more likely to appear following parietal or temporal lesions than following frontal damage. The only observation from this study that is consistent with the Wernicke-Geschwind model came from the analysis of the effects of large lesions (i.e., those involving three lobes). Large lesions of the anterior brain were more likely to be associated with articulation problems than were large lesions of the posterior brain. It is noteworthy that not one of the 214 subjects displayed specific syndromes of expressive (Broca's aphasia) or receptive (Wernicke's aphasia) aphasia. The effects of lesions to the frontal, temporal, parietal, or occipital lobes, or to the area of the central fissure are summarized in Figure 16.12.

CAT and MRI scans of neuropsychological patients with language-related problems Since the development of *computerized axial tomography* (CAT) and *magnetic resonance imaging* (MRI), it has been possible to visualize the brain damage of living aphasic patients (see Damasio, 1989). In the CAT studies by Mazzocchi and Vignolo (1979) and Naeser, Hayward, Laughlin, and Zatz (1981), none of the aphasic patients had damage restricted to Broca's and Wernicke's areas, and all had extensive damage to subcortical white matter. However, both studies confirmed that large anterior

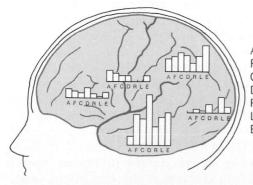

A: Articulatory disturbances.
F: Difficulties in the fluency of speech.
C: Disturbances of verbal comprehension.
D: Disturbances of naming.
R: Disturbances of repetition.
L: Disturbances in reading.
E: Disturbances of writing.

FIGURE 16.12

The effects of medium-sized lesions to various cortical areas on language-related abilities. (Adapted from Hécaen & Angelergues, 1964.)

lesions of the left hemisphere were more likely to produce deficits in language expression than were large posterior lesions, and that large posterior lesions were more likely to produce deficits in language comprehension than were large anterior lesions. In both studies, **global aphasia,** an almost total elimination of all language-related abilities, was associated with very large left-hemisphere lesions that involved both the anterior and posterior cortex and substantial portions of subcortical white matter. The findings of these CAT studies have been confirmed by Damasio's (1989) MRI studies. In addition, Damasio discovered a few aphasic patients whose damage was restricted to the *mesial frontal lobes* (to the supplementary motor area and the anterior cingulate cortex).

CAT and MRI studies have confirmed previous claims that aphasia can result from damage to subcortical structures (see Alexander, 1989). Aphasia can occur following damage restricted to the left subcortical white matter, the left basal ganglia, or the left thalamus (e.g., Naeser et al., 1982).

Cortical Stimulation and the Localization of Language

The first large-scale brain-stimulation studies of humans were conducted by Penfield and his colleagues in the 1940s at the Montreal Neurological Institute (see Feindel, 1986). One purpose of the studies was to map the language areas of each patient's brain so that tissue involved in language could be avoided during the surgery. The mapping was done by assessing the responses of conscious patients under local anesthetic to stimulation applied to various points on the cortical surface. The description of the effects of stimulation were dictated to a stenographer—this was before the days of tape recorders—and then a tiny numbered card was dropped on the stimulation site for subsequent photography. Figure 16.13 illustrates the responses to stimulation of a 37-year-old, right-handed patient. He had started to have seizures about 3 months after receiving a blow to the head, and at the time of his operation in 1948, he had been suffering from seizures for 6 years, despite efforts to control them with medication. In considering his responses, remember that the cortex just posterior to the central fissure is *primary somatosensory cortex* (see Chapter 8), and that the cortex just anterior to the central fissure is *primary motor cortex* (see Chapter 9).

Such early clinical observations suggested that it might be possible to determine the cortical organization of the control of speech by systematically assessing the nature of the speech disturbances produced by stimulation to various parts of the cortex. Because mild brain stimulation is a much more local event than a brain lesion, Penfield and Roberts (1959) thought that the procedure might provide strong support for the Wernicke-Geschwind model. But it did not. Illustrated in Figure 16.14 is the wide distribution of sites in the left hemisphere at which stimulation produced either a complete cessation of speech or various speech disturbances (distortion of speech, confusion of numbers while counting, inability to name with retained ability to speak, misnaming). Right-hemisphere stimulation almost never disrupted speech.

Ojemann and his colleagues (see Ojemann, 1983) assessed naming, reading of simple sentences, short-term verbal memory, ability to mimic orofacial movements, and the ability to recognize **phonemes** (individual speech sounds) during cortical stimulation. In contrast to the predictions of the

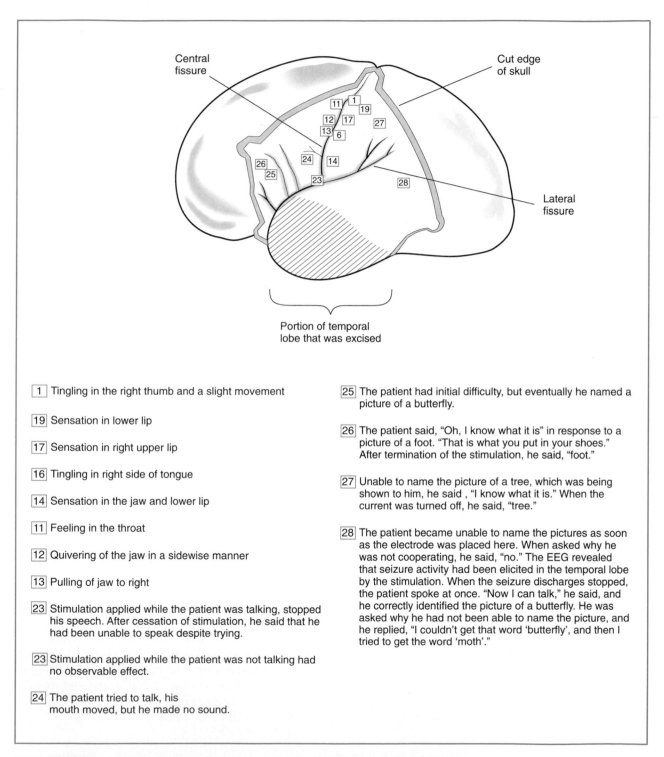

FIGURE 16.13

The responses of the left hemisphere of a 37-year-old epileptic to electrical stimulation. The numbered cards were placed on the brain during surgery to mark the sites where brain stimulation had been applied. (Adapted from Penfield & Roberts, 1959.)

The following text appears within the figure:

1 Tingling in the right thumb and a slight movement

19 Sensation in lower lip

17 Sensation in right upper lip

16 Tingling in right side of tongue

14 Sensation in the jaw and lower lip

11 Feeling in the throat

12 Quivering of the jaw in a sidewise manner

13 Pulling of jaw to right

23 Stimulation applied while the patient was talking, stopped his speech. After cessation of stimulation, he said that he had been unable to speak despite trying.

23 Stimulation applied while the patient was not talking had no observable effect.

24 The patient tried to talk, his mouth moved, but he made no sound.

25 The patient had initial difficulty, but eventually he named a picture of a butterfly.

26 The patient said, "Oh, I know what it is" in response to a picture of a foot. "That is what you put in your shoes." After termination of the stimulation, he said, "foot."

27 Unable to name the picture of a tree, which was being shown to him, he said , "I know what it is." When the current was turned off, he said, "tree."

28 The patient became unable to name the pictures as soon as the electrode was placed here. When asked why he was not cooperating, he said, "no." The EEG revealed that seizure activity had been elicited in the temporal lobe by the stimulation. When the seizure discharges stopped, the patient spoke at once. "Now I can talk," he said, and he correctly identified the picture of a butterfly. He was asked why he had not been able to name the picture, and he replied, "I couldn't get that word 'butterfly', and then I tried to get the word 'moth'."

FIGURE 16.14

Distribution of left
hemisphere sites where
stimulation either disrupted
speech or eliminated it
completely. (Adapted from
Penfield & Roberts, 1959.)

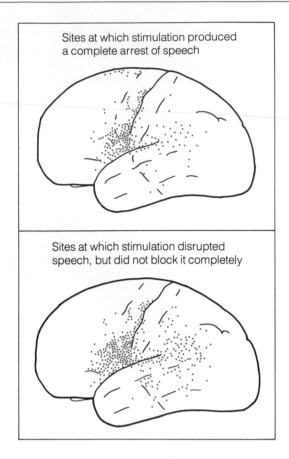

Wernicke-Geschwind model, they found that the areas of the cortex at which
stimulation could disrupt language extended far beyond the boundaries of
the Wernicke-Geschwind language areas; they found that all of the language
abilities that they assessed were represented at both anterior and posterior
sites; and they found that there was considerable difference in the organization of these language abilities in different subjects. Because the disruptive
effects of stimulation at a particular site were frequently quite specific (disrupting only a single test), Ojemann (1983) suggested that the language cortex might be organized like a mosaic, with those discrete columns of tissue
performing a particular function being widely distributed throughout the language area of the cortex. In contrast Mateer and Cameron (1989) concluded
on the basis of their brain-stimulation studies that the function of the frontal
and temporal cortex around the lateral fissure is primarily *phonological* (pertaining to the perception and the production of speech sounds) and that the
functions of the other language areas are primarily *grammatical* (pertaining
to the structure of language) and *semantic* (pertaining to meaning).

Language Laterality
and Neuroanatomical Asymmetry

There are numerous structural differences between the left and right hemispheres of human brains (see Kolb & Whishaw, 1990). Although the first reports of *neuroanatomical asymmetries* were published in the 1800s (see von

Bonin, 1962), they were largely ignored until Geschwind and Levitsky (1968) reported that the left **planum temporale** is larger than the right planum temporale in 65% of human brains. This stimulated great interest, because the planum temporale is considered to be part of Wernicke's area. It is tucked in the lateral fissure just behind **Heschl's gyrus,** which is the site of primary auditory cortex—see Figure 16.15. To compensate for the smaller planum temporale on the right, the right temporal lobe sometimes has two Heschl's gyri. The finding that the left hemispheres of fetal brains (Wada, Clarke, & Hamm, 1975) often have larger planum temporales suggests that the left temporal lobe may be structurally specialized for language-related activities even before the development of speech. The **frontal operculum** (the location of Broca's area in the left hemisphere) also tends to be larger on the left than the right (Falzi, Perrone, & Vignolo, 1982). It should be emphasized, however, that there is no evidence that people with asymmetric brains are more likely to have highly lateralized language functions—although about 95% of the population are left-hemisphere dominant for speech, only about 65% have a larger left planum temporale.

Cognitive Neuroscience: Reading Aloud with the Right Hemisphere

Cognitive neuroscience is an approach to the study of the neural basis of cognitive processes that has focused on the study of brain-damaged subjects. The basic research strategy of cognitive neuroscientists is to identify clusters of specific cognitive functions that tend to be disturbed or spared as a group in brain-damaged patients and to infer from these clusters the nature of the neural systems that underlie various cognitive processes (see Kosslyn, 1988; Posner, Petersen, Fox, & Raichle, 1988).

Since the emergence of cognitive neuroscience in the 1960s, it has focused on the analysis of the cognitive processes that are involved in reading aloud (see Coltheart, 1985; Marin, Schwartz, & Saffran, 1979). Most models

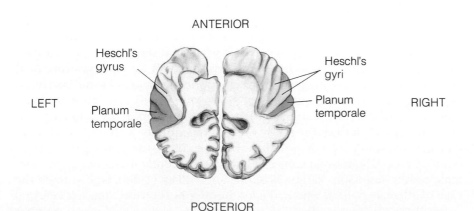

FIGURE 16.15

The location of the planum temporale and Heschl's gyrus. The planum temporale is often bigger in the left hemisphere, and there are often two Heschl's gyri in the right hemisphere. (Adapted from Geschwind, 1972.)

of reading aloud that have emerged from these studies are based on the hypothesis that there are two different systems for reading aloud: one called a **lexical procedure,** which is based on stored information that we have acquired about specific written words in our vocabulary, and another called a **nonlexical procedure,** which is based on the general rules of pronunciation and allows us to pronounce unfamiliar words, or nonwords such as "spleemer" and "twiple." The lexical-nonlexical model of reading aloud is a **dual-route model,** a model of a cognitive process that is based on the premise that the process is mediated by two different pathways of neural activity.

Evidence in support of the *lexical-nonlexical dual-route model* comes from cases of **dyslexia** (a pathological difficulty in reading) in which either the lexical or nonlexical procedure is impaired while the other is not. On one hand there have been reports (e.g., Coltheart, Masterson, Byng, Prior, & Riddoch, 1983; Shallice & Warrington, 1980) of **surface dyslexia,** a reading disorder in which the nonlexical procedure remains largely intact, but there is a great difficulty in pronouncing words whose pronunciation does not follow normal rules (e.g., yacht, sew). For example, M.P., a woman who was hit by a motor vehicle at the age of 59, subsequently lost her ability to read exceptional words, while her ability to read regular words and nonwords remained normal. Moreover, most of the incorrect responses that she made while reading exceptional words involved the misapplication of common rules of English pronunciation: "have," "lose," "own," and "steak" were pronounced as if they rhymed with "cave," "hose," "down," and "beak."

On the other hand, there have been reports (e.g., Patterson, 1982; Shallice & Warrington, 1980) of **deep dyslexia,** a reading disorder in which the nonlexical procedure is severely disrupted while the lexical procedure is not. Patients with deep dyslexia have great difficulty in following the rules of pronunciation to translate the written word into the spoken word. Instead, they try to react to it by using various lexical strategies such as responding to the overall look of the word, the meaning of the word, or the derivation of the word. This leads to a characteristic pattern of errors. A patient with deep dyslexia might say "quill" for "quail" (responding to the overall look of the word), "hen" for "chicken" (responding to the meaning of the word), or "wise" for "wisdom" (responding to the derivation of the word). He or she would have more difficulty pronouncing abstract words than concrete words.

Coltheart (1980) has argued that both the left and right hemispheres participate in reading aloud, but in different ways: that the left hemisphere performs **phonological analysis** (sound-related analysis) and **grammatical analysis,** whereas the right hemisphere performs a **graphemic analysis,** (analysis of the overall appearance of the written word) and extracts certain kinds of **semantic** (meaning-related) information. Support for Coltheart's hypothesis has come from the study of dyslexic patients with unilateral brain damage and from the analysis of the reading errors made by the left and right hemispheres of split-brain subjects. However, recently it was put to the ultimate test by Patterson, Vargha-Khadem, and Polkey (1989), who studied the case of a female patient who had a left **hemispherectomy** (her left cerebral hemisphere was removed) at the age of 14. The reading performance of her right hemisphere on various reading tests was poor, but, in support of Coltheart's hypothesis, she had a pattern of retained and impaired reading skills that was strikingly similar to that of adult deep dyslexics and to the right hemispheres of split-brain patients.

Before we leave the topic of dyslexia, I must keep a promise. I promised one of my students that I would tell you about a case of dyslexia that he brought to my attention. He told me about a woman who is a dyslexic, an agnostic, and an insomniac—she stays awake every night wondering if there really is a doG.

PET Scans During Language-Related Activities

The application of modern PET-scan techniques (see Chapter 5) is in the process of revolutionizing the study of the cerebral localization of language (see Damasio, 1989). In one particularly noteworthy line of studies, Petersen and his colleagues (e.g., Petersen, Fox, Mintun, Posner, & Raichle, 1989; Petersen, Fox, Posner, Mintun, & Raichle, 1988; Petersen, Fox, Snyder, & Raichle, 1990) are using PET to measure the amount of blood flow to various parts of the brain during various language-related activities—there are increases in blood flow to parts of the brain that are particularly active.

The PET-scan technique of Petersen and his colleagues features three important innovations (see Raichle, 1987). First, rather than injecting a radioactive gas, they inject radioactive water. The advantage of water over the gas is that it quickly passes from the bloodstream, thus making it possible for several tests to be given to each subject, one every 10 minutes. Second, injections of the radioactive water are made intravenously, rather than into the *carotid artery.* This allows the material to be dispersed equally to both hemispheres so that they can be studied simultaneously. Third, Petersen and his colleagues use a computer program to subtract the changes in blood flow during one activity from those observed during another. The utility of this subtraction procedure will become apparent as I describe their experiments.

The blood flow of each subject was measured under two sets of conditions: visual and auditory. Both sets comprised four conditions of progressively increasing complexity. In the four visual conditions, the subjects were asked to do the following: (1) to fixate on (i.e., to stare at) a crosshair on a display screen, (2) to fixate on the crosshair while printed nouns were being presented, (3) to fixate on the crosshair while repeating aloud the printed nouns, and (4) to fixate on the crosshair while saying an appropriate verb to go with the printed noun (e.g., cake:eat, radio:listen). The four auditory conditions were identical to the four visual conditions except that tape-recorded nouns were played to the subjects while they stared at the crosshair.

Three levels of subtraction were performed on the images recorded during these two sets of tests. The activity during the fixation-only condition was subtracted from that during the passive-noun condition to get a measure of the activation produced by passively observing or hearing the nouns. The activity during the passive-noun condition was subtracted from that during the saying-noun condition to get a measure of the activation produced by saying the noun. And the activity during the saying-noun condition was subtracted from that during the verb-association condition to get a measure of the activation produced by the cognitive processes involved in forming the association. The results of these three subtractions in both the visual and auditory conditions are summarized in Figure 16.16.

It is apparent in Figure 16.16 that the mere presentation of printed nouns produced activation in the secondary visual cortex (see Chapter 8) which was not present when the subjects just stared at the crosshair, and auditory noun

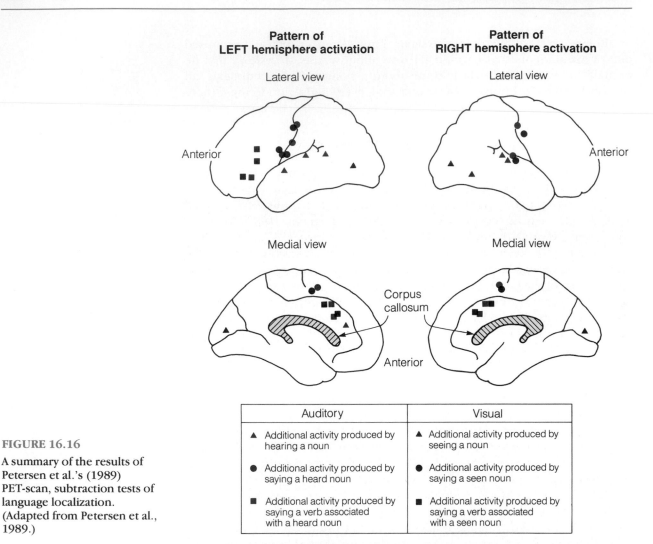

**Pattern of
RIGHT hemisphere activation**

Lateral view

Lateral view

Anterior

Anterior

Medial view

Medial view

Corpus
callosum

Anterior

Auditory	Visual
▲ Additional activity produced by hearing a noun	▲ Additional activity produced by seeing a noun
● Additional activity produced by saying a heard noun	● Additional activity produced by saying a seen noun
■ Additional activity produced by saying a verb associated with a heard noun	■ Additional activity produced by saying a verb associated with a seen noun

FIGURE 16.16

A summary of the results of Petersen et al.'s (1989) PET-scan, subtraction tests of language localization. (Adapted from Petersen et al., 1989.)

presentation produced bilateral activity in both the primary and secondary auditory cortex, which was not present when they stared at the crosshair in silence. Regardless of whether the nouns were presented in printed or auditory form, repeating them aloud activated the same general cortical areas that were not activated in the passive-word conditions; activation occurred along the central fissures of both hemispheres and along the lateral fissure of the right hemisphere. Similarly, regardless of whether the words were presented in a printed or auditory form, the verb-association condition added activity in the prefrontal cortex of the left hemisphere just in front of Broca's area and in the medial cortex just above the front portion of the corpus callosum. The computer-generated images of these same subtracted patterns of cortical activation (averaged over all of the subjects) are presented in Figure 16.17.

What type of model do these impressive results support? Certainly not the Wernicke-Geschwind model. There was no evidence of activation in either Wernicke's area or in the angular gyrus during the visual tests, and the semantic processing of verb association appeared to occur in frontal and medial cortex rather than in Wernicke's area. Moreover, none of the activity in the right

**Patterns of Activity
Identified by the
*Three Auditory Subtractions***

**Patterns of Activity
Identified by the
*Three Visual Subtractions***

Additional activity produced by
hearing a noun:

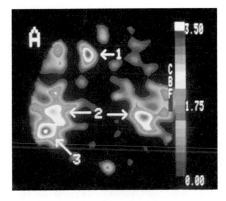

Additional activity produced by
seeing a noun:

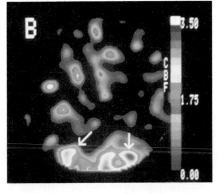

Additional activity produced by
saying a heard noun:

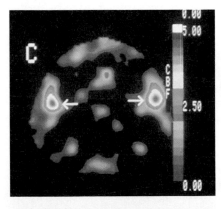

Additional activity produced by
saying a seen noun:

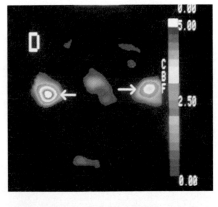

Additional activity produced by
saying a verb associated with a
heard noun:

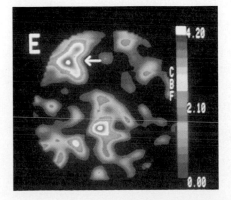

Additional activity produced by
saying a verb associated with a
seen noun:

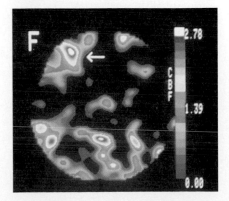

FIGURE 16.17

PET-scan computer printouts of the subtracted patterns of blood flow from the experiment of Petersen et al. (1989). Each printout represents a horizontal section of the brain averaged over all of the subjects in that condition. Anterior is toward the top of the page; posterior is toward the bottom. The right hemisphere is on your right; the left hemisphere is on your left. As indicated by the adjacent scales, the highest levels of activity are indicated by yellow, orange, red, and white (the very highest). (Courtesy of Steve Petersen.)

hemisphere and in the midline areas of both hemispheres was predicted by the Wernicke-Geschwind model. On a more general level, these results challenge any serial model of language. When subjects were repeating words, input seemed to move directly from the respective secondary sensory areas to the output areas of the central fissure. When the task involved semantic processing (verb association), the signals seemed to follow an alternative route from secondary sensory areas, to frontal cortex, to the central fissure motor areas.

Conclusion

Chapter 16 is the story of two theories: one largely right and one largely wrong, but both extremely important. On the one hand, Sperry's theory of brain duality and asymmetry has withstood the empirical challenge of the research that it has generated. Study after study has confirmed and extended its basic tenets: that the two hemispheres of the human brain can function independently and that they possess different capacities that are normally integrated by the cerebral commissures. On the other hand, the empirical evidence has not been so kind to the strict localizationist theories of language organization proposed by Broca, Wernicke, and Geschwind. Lesion, brain-stimulation, and brain-scan studies have all failed to confirm its specific predictions.

The juxtaposition of these two theories illustrates a frequently misunderstood point: Theories are important because they are useful, and to be useful they do not have to be right. Both Sperry's theory of the dual brain and the Wernicke-Geschwind model of language localization have dominated their respective fields for over a quarter of a century. The strengths of the Wernicke-Geschwind model lie in its clarity and testability. Because it is clear, scientists and students alike have found it to be a useful vehicle for organizing their thinking about the localization of language. And because it is so eminently testable, its predictions have stimulated and guided much of the research in the field. Considering that it is only the first step toward the solution of an extremely difficult problem, it is not at all surprising that it has proven to be flawed, but it is the mass of research that it has generated that is the ultimate testimonial to its worth.

Food for Thought

1. Design an experiment to show that it is possible for a human split-brain student to study for an English exam and a geometry exam at the same time by using the Z lens.

2. The decision to perform commissurotomies on epileptic patients turned out to be a good one; the decision to perform prefrontal lobotomies on mental patients (see Chapter 1) did not. Was this just the luck of the draw? Discuss.

KEY TERMS

To help you study the material in this chapter, all of the key terms—those that have appeared in bold type—are listed and briefly defined here.

Agraphia. A specific inability to write, one that does not result from general visual or motor deficits.

Alexia. A specific inability to read, one that does not result from general visual or motor deficits.

Angular gyrus. A gyrus of the posterior cortex at the boundary between the temporal and parietal lobes; the angular gyrus of the left hemisphere is thought to play a role in reading.

Aphasia. Any brain-damage-produced disturbance in the ability to use or comprehend language.

Apraxia. A condition in which patients have great difficulty performing movements with either side of the body when asked to do so out of context, even though they have no trouble performing the same responses when they are not thinking about what they are doing.

Arcuate fasciculus. The major neural pathway between Wernicke's area and Broca's area.

Broca's aphasia. A disorder of speech production with no deficits in language comprehension; it is doubtful if such cases exist in the strict sense of the term; all cases of aphasia involve both expressive and receptive deficits.

Broca's area. The area of the inferior prefrontal cortex of the left hemisphere hypothesized by Broca to be involved in speech production.

Cerebral commissures. Tracts that connect the left and right cerebral hemispheres; the corpus callosum is the largest cerebral commissure.

Chimeric figures test. A test of visual completion in split-brain subjects that uses pictures composed by left and right halves of two different faces.

Cognitive neuroscience. An approach to the study of the neural basis of cognitive processes; cognitive neuropsychologists infer the nature of the neural systems underlying cognitive processes by identifying the clusters of specific cognitive functions that tend to be disturbed together in brain-damaged subjects.

Commissurotomy. Severing the cerebral commissures.

Conduction aphasia. Aphasia that was hypothesized to result from damage to the neural pathway between Wernicke's area and Broca's area; however, surgical transection of this pathway produces no permanent aphasia.

Cross-cuing. Nonneural communication between hemispheres separated by commissurotomy.

Deep dyslexia. A reading disorder in which the nonlexical procedure is severely disrupted while the lexical procedure is not.

Dextrals. Right-handers.

Dichotic listening test. Two sequences of three spoken digits are presented simultaneously to each ear, and the subject is asked to report all of the digits that he or she heard; a test of language lateralization.

Dominant hemisphere. A term used in the past to refer to the left hemisphere; it is based on the incorrect assumption that the left hemisphere is dominant in all complex activities.

Dual-route models. Models of a cognitive process that are based on the premise that the process is mediated by two different pathways of neural activity.

Dyslexia. A specific pathological difficulty in reading; in contrast, *alexia* refers to the total inability to read.

Expressive. Referring to the generation of speech (i.e., writing or talking).

Frontal operculum. The neuroanatomical designation for the area of prefrontal cortex that in the left hemisphere roughly corresponds to Broca's area.

Global aphasia. Almost total elimination of all language-related abilities.

Grammatical analysis. Analysis in terms of the rules of sentence structure of a language.

Graphemic analysis. Analysis of the overall appearance of the written word.

Helping-hand phenomenon. When one hand of a split-brain patient redirects the other hand.

Hemispherectomy. The removal of one cerebral hemisphere.

Heschl's gyrus. A temporal-lobe gyrus that is the site of primary auditory cortex.

Lateralization of function. When the two hemispheres of the brain differ in their functions.

Lexical procedure. A procedure for reading aloud that is based on stored information that we have acquired about the pronunciation of specific written words.

Minor hemisphere. A term used in the past to refer to the right hemisphere; it is based on the incorrect assumption that the left hemisphere is dominant in all complex activities.

Nonlexical procedure. A procedure for reading aloud that is based on the general rules of pronunciation of a language.

Parallel models. Models involving two or more routes of activity (e.g., the dual-route model).

Phonemes. Individual speech sounds.

Phonological analysis. Sound-related analysis.

Planum temporale. An area of the temporal lobe, which in the left hemisphere roughly corresponds to Wernicke's area.

Receptive.   Referring to the comprehension of speech.

Scotoma.   An area of blindness in the visual field.

Semantic analysis.   Meaning-related analysis.

Serial model.   A model that involves a chain of responses that are triggered in linear sequence; a single-route model.

Sinestrals.   Left-handers.

Sodium amytal test.   A test of speech lateralization administered to some patients before neurosurgery; each hemisphere is anesthetized with sodium amytal so that the speech abilities of the other hemisphere can be assessed.

Split-brain patients.   Commissurotomized patients.

Surface dyslexia.   A deficit in lexical reading out loud that is not accompanied by deficits in nonlexical reading.

Visual completion.   When the brain completes or fills in a scotoma.

Wernicke's area.   An area of the left temporal cortex hypothesized by Wernicke to be the center of language comprehension.

Wernicke-Geschwind model.   A serial model of language localization.

Word salad.   Speech that has the overall sound and flow of fluid speech, but is totally incomprehensible.

Z lens.   A contact lens that is opaque on one side and thus allows visual input to enter only one hemisphere of a split-brain subject, irrespective of eye movement; developed by, and named after, Zaidel.

ADDITIONAL READING

Two collections of papers written by prominent researchers provide excellent coverage of key issues in cerebral lateralization and the localization of language.

Bensen, D. F., & Zaidel, E. (Eds.). (1985). *The dual brain: Hemispheric specializations in humans.* New York: Guilford Press.

Boller, F. & Grafman, J. (Eds.). (1989). *Handbook of Neuropsychology: Language, Aphasia, and Related Disorders, Vol. 2, Section 3.* New York: Elsevier.

Handbook of neuropsychology: Language, aphasia and related disorders, Vol. 2.

17

The Biopsychology of Emotions and Mental Illness

Conscious experience is saturated with emotion. The emotional impact of major life events (e.g., falling in love, losing a friend, moving to a new city, being in a car accident) can be overwhelming, and even relatively minor experiences can trigger strong emotional reactions. Think of how you felt the last time that you misplaced your keys, met somebody whom you really liked, "aced" an exam, bought a bouquet of flowers, argued with a friend, or had a good laugh. Notice how just thinking about past events can rekindle some of the original emotional experience. Biopsychological research on emotions is the subject of this chapter.

Emotional extremes are a prominent feature of many psychological disorders. That is why the initial focus of this chapter, on the physiological and behavioral correlates of normal emotional experience, gradually shifts as the chapter progresses to emotion-related clinical issues.

Everyday language is laced with terms that refer to emotional states: happiness, guilt, love, ecstacy, hate, depression, admiration, and anxiety—to name just a few. There are over 400 of them in the English language. Most people have a reasonably good sense of what these words mean; however, because of the subjective nature of emotional experience, it has proven extremely difficult to define emotions objectively (see Feyereisen, 1989). Despite this difficulty, the study of emotions has been one of the major success stories of biopsychological research. It is no accident that I have reserved this topic for the final chapter.

Section 17.1 provides a brief overview of some of the key early events in the study of the biopsychology of emotions. Sections 17.2 and 17.3 discuss the two most widely studied correlates of emotional experience: autonomic nervous system activity and facial expression, respectively. Then, Section 17.4 reviews the effects of brain damage on human emotion; Section 17.5 deals with stress; and Section 17.6 discusses two of the most widely studied behavioral expressions of emotion, aggression and defense, and their relation to anxiety disorders. Finally, in Section 17.7, the focus shifts exclusively to clinical issues, to schizophrenia and to the affective disorders.

17.1

Biopsychology of Emotions: Early Progress

Section 17.1 sets the stage for the remainder of the chapter by describing some of the key early events and concepts in the study of the biopsychology of emotions.

The Expression of Emotions in Humans and Other Animals

The first major event in the study of the biopsychology of emotions was the publication in 1872 of Darwin's book, *The Expression of Emotions in Man and Animals*. In it, Darwin argued, largely on the basis of anecdotal evidence, that particular emotional responses, such as facial expressions, tend to accompany the same emotional states in humans of all races and cultures—even in humans who have been blind from birth. Darwin believed that expressions of human emotion, like other human behaviors, are products of evolution; thus, he tried to understand them by comparing them with similar behaviors in other species. From such comparisons, Darwin developed a theory of the evolution of emotional expression that was composed of three main ideas:

(1) that expressions of emotion evolve from behaviors that signal what an animal is likely to do next; (2) that if such behaviors benefit the animal that displays them, they will evolve in ways that enhance their communicative function and their original function may be lost; and (3) that opposite messages are often signaled by opposite movements and postures, *the principle of antithesis.*

Consider how Darwin's theory accounts for the evolution of *threat displays.* Originally, facing one's enemies, rising up, and exposing one's weapons were just the early components of animal combat. But once the enemies began to recognize these behaviors as signals of impending aggression, a survival advantage accrued to those attackers that could communicate their aggression most effectively and intimidate their victims without actually fighting. As a result, elaborate threat displays evolved and actual combat declined. To be most effective, signals of aggression and submission must be clearly distinguishable; thus they tended to evolve in opposite directions. For example, gulls signal aggression by pointing their beaks at one another and submission by pointing their beaks away from one another, and primates signal aggression by staring and submission by averting their gaze. Figure 17.1 is a reproduction of the actual woodcuts that Darwin used in his 1872 book to illustrate this principle of antithesis.

The James-Lange Theory of Emotions

The first physiological theory of emotions was proposed independently by James and by Lange in 1884; it became known as the **James-Lange theory.** According to the James-Lange theory, emotion-inducing sensory stimuli are received and interpreted by the cortex. The cortex then triggers changes in

Aggression   **Submission**

FIGURE 17.1

The two woodcuts from Darwin's 1872 book, *The Expression of Emotions in Man and Animals,* which he used to illustrate the principle of antithesis. The aggressive posture features ears forward, back up, hair up, and tail up; the submissive posture features ears back, back down, hair down, and tail down.

the visceral organs via the *autonomic nervous system* and in the skeletal muscles via the *somatic nervous system.* The main point of the James-Lange theory was that the experience of the emotion is produced by the brain's perception of the body's reactions, particularly those produced by the autonomic nervous system. In effect, what the James-Lange theory did was to reverse the usual way of thinking about the causal relation between the experience of emotion and its expression, James and Lange argued that the autonomic activity and behavior that are triggered by the emotional event produce the feeling of emotion, not vice versa.

> Our natural way of thinking . . . is that the mental perception of some fact excites the mental affection called the emotion, and that this latter state of mind gives rise to the bodily expression. My theory, on the contrary, is that *the bodily changes follow directly the perception of the exciting fact, and that our feeling of the same changes as they occur IS the emotion.* Common sense says, we lose our fortune, are sorry, and weep; we meet a bear, are frightened, and run; we are insulted by a rival, are angry, and strike. The hypothesis here to be defended says that this order of sequence is incorrect . . . and that the more rational statement is that we feel sorry because we cry, angry because we strike, afraid because we tremble, and not that we cry, strike, or tremble, because we are sorry, angry, or fearful. . . . Without the bodily states following on the perception, the latter would be purely cognitive in form, pale, colorless, destitute of emotional warmth. We might then see the bear, and judge it best to run, receive the insult, and deem it right to strike, but we should not actually feel afraid or angry. (James, 1890)

The James-Lange theory was proposed prior to the emergence of psychology as science. It was thus based largely on introspective and anecdotal evidence—which is the way that things were done in psychology in those days. Subsequent empirical tests of the theory have been mixed. Patients with spinal damage report that feedback from the body is not a major factor in emotion; they report that their emotions are as strong as ever despite the lack of feedback from their viscera (Lowe & Carroll, 1985). However, there is considerable evidence—some of which you will soon encounter—that the body's responses to emotional stimuli do contribute to emotional experience.

The Cannon-Bard Theory of Emotions

In the early 1900s, Cannon proposed a theory of emotions, which was subsequently extended and promoted by Bard; it became known as the **Cannon-Bard theory.** According to the Cannon-Bard theory, emotional stimuli have two separate effects: They excite the feeling of emotion in the cortex and the expression of emotion in the autonomic and somatic nervous systems. In contrast to the James-Lange theory, the Cannon-Bard theory views emotional experience and emotional expression as parallel processes that have no direct causal relation.

Figure 17.2 illustrates four ways of thinking about the relation between emotional experience and emotional expression: (1) the common sense way, (2) the James-Lange way, (3) the Cannon-Bard way, and (4) the right way—the way that has emerged from decades of research on emotion. Today's researchers appreciate that each of the three responses to emotional stimuli—the perception of the emotional stimulus, the experience of the emotion, and the expression of the emotion—influences the other two.

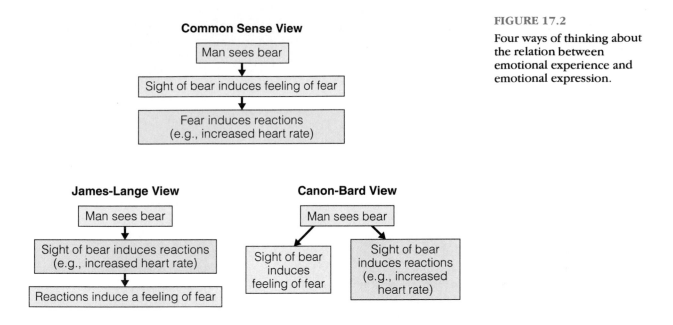

FIGURE 17.2

Four ways of thinking about the relation between emotional experience and emotional expression.

Sham Rage

In the late 1920s, Bard (1929) made a remarkable observation. **Decorticate** cats, cats whose cortex had been completely removed, responded to the slightest provocation with an aggressive response. After a light touch, for example, the cats would arch their backs, erect their hair, growl, hiss, and expose their teeth. These aggressive responses were abnormal in two respects: they were extremely severe, and they were not directed at particular targets. Bard referred to the exaggerated, poorly directed aggressive responses of decorticate animals as **sham rage.**

Bard found that sham rage could be elicited in cats whose cerebral hemispheres had been removed, right down to the level of the hypothalamus. However, cats that were **decerebrate,** that is, cats that had their entire cerebral hemispheres removed, including the hypothalamus, did not display sham rage. On the basis of this observation, Bard concluded that the hypothalamus and adjoining structures are critical for the expression of aggressive responses, and that the function of the cortex is to inhibit and direct them.

Support for the view that the hypothalamus plays an important role in emotional expression came from early electrical stimulation studies. Studies published in the 1940s, 50s, and 60s showed that a variety of aggressive responses could be elicited in laboratory animals by stimulation of particular sites in the hypothalamus. For example, hypothalamic stimulation can induce a rat to attack and kill a mouse that it had previously been ignoring.

The Limbic System

In 1937, Papez (pronounced Payps) proposed that emotional expression is controlled by several interconnected neural structures that became known as the **limbic system.** The limbic system is a collection of nuclei and tracts that borders on the thalamus, which is in the core of the brain—*limbic* means *border.* Figure 17.3 illustrates the location of the limbic system and some of its key structures: the amygdala, hippocampus, septum, fornix, olfactory bulb, mammillary body, and cingulate cortex (see Macchi, 1989).

Papez believed that emotional states were expressed through the action of the limbic structures on the hypothalamus and that they were experienced through the action of the limbic structures on the cortex. The notion of an ancient, deep part of the brain that unconsciously controls emotion appealed to a discipline that was, at the time, awash in a sea of Freudian dogma.

The Kluver-Bucy Syndrome

In 1939, Kluver and Bucy observed a striking pattern of behavior in monkeys that had had their anterior temporal lobes removed. This syndrome, which is commonly referred to as the **Kluver-Bucy syndrome,** includes the following behaviors: (1) indiscriminate consumption of almost anything that is edible, (2) increased sexual activity, (3) sexual activity directed at inappropriate objects, (4) a tendency to repeatedly investigate familiar objects, (5) a tendency

FIGURE 17.3

The location of the limbic system in the core of the brain. Also see Figure 3.26.

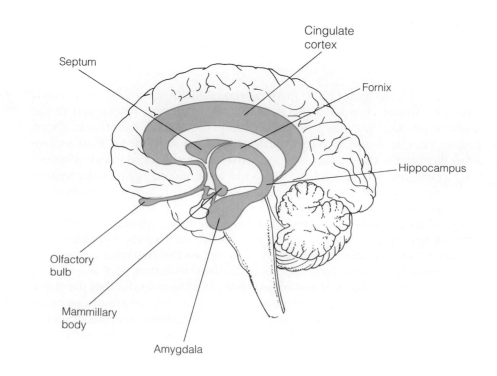

to investigate objects with the mouth, and (6) tameness and lack of fear. Monkeys that could not be handled before surgery were transformed by the lesions into tame subjects that showed no fear whatsoever—even in response to snakes or threat stares from humans.

The Kluver-Bucy syndrome has been observed in several species. The following is a description of the Kluver-Bucy syndrome in a human patient with a brain infection.

As regards his visual functions, the patient seemed unable to recognize a wide variety of common objects. He examined each object placed before him as though seeing it for the first time, explored it repetitively and seemed unaware of its significance. . . . He exhibited a flat affect, and, although originally restless, ultimately became remarkably placid. He appeared indifferent to people or situations. He spent much time gazing at the television, but never learned to turn it on; when the set was off, he tended to watch reflections of others in the room on the glass screen. On occasion he became facetious, smiling inappropriately and mimicking the gestures and actions of others. Once initiating an imitative series, he would perseverate copying all movements made by another for extended periods of time. . . . He engaged in oral exploration of all objects within his grasp, appearing unable to gain information via tactile or visual means alone. All objects that he could lift were placed in his mouth and sucked or chewed. . . . Hyperbulimia [excessive, insatiable appetite] was prominent; he ingested virtually everything within reach, including the plastic wrapper from bread, cleaning pastes, ink, dog food, and feces.

The patient's sexual behavior was a particular source of concern while in hospital. Although vigorously heterosexual prior to his illness, he was observed in hospital to make advances toward other male patients by stroking their legs and inviting fellatio by gesture; at times he attempted to kiss them. Although on a sexually mixed floor during a proportion of his recovery, he never made advances toward women, and, in fact, his apparent reversal of sexual polarity prompted his fiance to sever their relationship (Marlowe, Mancall, & Thomas, 1975, pp. 55–56).

In monkeys, the Kluver-Bucy syndrome appears to result from damage to the amygdala and to adjacent temporal cortex. It is curious that patient H.M. (see Chapter 14) shows none of the Kluver-Bucy symptoms.

17.2

Emotions and the Autonomic Nervous System

The James-Lange and Cannon-Bard theories were based on different conceptions of the role of the autonomic nervous system (ANS) in emotion. The James-Lange theory was built on the premise that different emotional stimuli induce different patterns of ANS activity, and that the perception of these different patterns of ANS activity produce different emotional experiences. In contrast, Cannon and Bard believed that the ANS responds in the same way to all emotional stimuli. According to the Cannon-Bard theory, all emotional stimuli activate the sympathetic branch of the ANS, and this general sympathetic activation prepares the organism for action—for fight or flight. The changes that are produced by sympathetic activation include increased heart rate and blood pressure, pupil dilation, increased flow of blood to the muscles, increased respiration, and increased release of epinephrine and norepinephrine from the adrenal medulla.

Despite the lack of direct evidence, the Cannon-Bard idea that the ANS responds indiscriminately to all emotional stimuli gained wide acceptance in the early part of this century. Lending indirect support to this view was the discovery that *norepinephrine* is the neurotransmitter at all synapses between the sympathetic branch of the ANS and the organs of the body, and that *acetylcholine* is the neurotransmitter at all synapses between the parasympathetic branch and the same organs. The shotgun nature of sympathetic activation was thought to be reinforced by the **adrenal medullas;** once activated by the sympathetic nervous system, the adrenal medullas release norepinephrine into the bloodstream, which presumably augments the general sympathetic activation of other organs.

The belief that all emotional stimuli produce the same general pattern of sympathetic activation influenced how biopsychologists tended to study the ANS correlates of emotion (see Schacter & Singer, 1962). There seemed to be no need to study more than a single emotion because all emotions were assumed to be associated with the same ANS changes, and there seemed to be no need to monitor more than a single index of ANS activity because all measures were assumed to change in unison. Accordingly, the belief that all emotional stimuli produce the same general pattern of ANS activation proved to be a self-fulfilling prophecy—any experiment that involves only a single emotion and a single index of ANS activation cannot possibly refute it.

In 1955, Ax published the results of a provocative experiment that renewed interest in the possibility that different patterns of ANS activity are associated with different emotions. He measured various aspects of electrodermal, electromyographic, cardiovascular, and respiratory activity during the induction of both fear and anger in the same subjects. Volunteer subjects were told that they were participating in a study of hypertension, and they were asked to lie quietly on a couch while the measures were being taken. While the electrodes were being attached, it was casually mentioned that the regular technician, who usually operated the polygraph in the adjacent room, was sick and that a man who had recently been fired for incompetence and arrogance was filling in for him. After a few minutes, during which baseline measures were recorded, one of the two conditions of the experiment was administered; half were tested first in the "anger condition" and then in the "fear condition," while the other subjects received the two treatments in the opposite order. In the "anger condition," the technician, who was in reality an actor, entered the test room and spent 5 minutes checking the wiring. During this period, the technician jostled the subject, he criticized the attending nurse, and he blamed the subject for creating an equipment malfunction. In the fear condition, a continuous mild shock was administered to the finger of the subject with no word of warning or explanation, and its intensity was gradually increased until the subject complained. When the subject did complain, the experimenter expressed surprise and, unbeknownst to the subject, pressed a button that caused sparks to jump. Ax analyzed 14 different psychophysiological measures and found that the changes in 7 of them were significantly different in the two conditions.

As influential as Ax's experiment has proven to be, it would not be permitted today; the deceptive and extreme methods that Ax used to generate emotions in his subjects would not receive ethical clearance. Instead, recent experiments on emotions and ANS activity have employed either the *directed-facial-action method* or the *relived-emotion method.* In the **directed-facial-action method,** subjects are instructed to make the facial expressions that are characteristic of various emotions while their ANS activity is being recorded; in the **relived-emotion method,** subjects are instructed to think about previous emotional experiences while their ANS activity is being recorded. Both kinds of experiments have revealed reliable differences in the patterns of ANS activity that are associated with different emotions (see Levenson, 1992). For example, anger, fear, and sadness are associated with an acceleration of heart rate, whereas disgust is associated with either no change or deceleration.

On the basis of existing evidence, it seems most reasonable to take an intermediate position on the issue of ANS emotional specificity. On one hand, the Cannon-Bard view that the ANS responds in the same way to all emotional stimuli is clearly incorrect; several differences have been well documented. On the other hand, there is insufficient evidence to make a strong case for the James-Lange view that each emotion is characterized by a different pattern of ANS activity.

Psychophysiological Methods of Lie Detection

Lie detection or **polygraphy** involves monitoring various autonomic nervous system indices of emotion during interrogation and using them to infer the veracity of the subject's responses. Polygraph tests administered by skilled examiners can be useful additions to normal interrogation procedures, but they are far from infallible (Iacono & Patrick, 1987). The main problem involved in evaluating the effectiveness of any particular polygraphic technique is that it is rarely possible in real-life situations to determine whether a polygrapher's verdict is correct. Because of this difficulty, many studies of lie detection have employed the **mock-crime procedure;** volunteer subjects participate in a mock crime and are then subjected to a polygraph test by an examiner who is unaware of their "guilt" or innocence. The interrogation method used by many polygraphers in laboratory and real-life situations is the **control-question technique.** The physiological response to the target question (Did you steal that purse?) is compared to the responses to a variety of control questions whose answers are known (What is your name? Have you ever been in jail before?). The average success rate in various mock-crime studies using this control-question technique is about 80 percent.

There are two problems with the mock-crime, control-question studies. One is that, unlike real suspects, the subjects are under no particular threat. In real life, the question, "Did you steal that purse?" is likely to elicit an emotional reaction from all suspects, regardless of their guilt or innocence, making it much more difficult to detect deception. The lie detector does not detect lies; it detects arousal. Lykken (1959) developed the **guilty-knowledge technique** to circumvent this problem. In order to use this technique, the *polygrapher* must have a piece of information concerning the crime that would be known to the subject only if he or she were guilty. The polygrapher, rather than attempting to catch the suspect in a lie, simply assesses his or her reaction to a list of actual and contrived details of the crime. Innocent parties, because they have no knowledge of the crime, will react to all such items in the same way; the guilty will react differentially. For example, in one of Lykken's (1959) experiments, "guilty" subjects waited until the occupant of an office went to the washroom. Then they entered her office, stole her purse from her desk, removed the money, and hid the purse in a locker. The critical part of the interrogation went something like this. "We know where the thief hid the purse. Where do you think that we found it? In the washroom? . . . In a locker? . . . Hanging on a coat rack? . . . " Even though electrodermal activity was the only measure used in this study, 44 of 50 mock criminals were correctly identified, and none of the 48 "innocent" parties was judged guilty. Patrick (1987) found that a group of psychopathic prison inmates were no better than control subjects at deceiving a professional polygrapher.

17.3

Emotions and Facial Expression

As you have already learned, Darwin believed that people in all parts of the world inherit the tendency to make similar facial expressions when experiencing the same emotions—for example, he believed that a smile signals happiness in all cultures. In contrast, most of Darwin's contemporaries believed that facial expressions are learned and are culturally variable. This remained the dominant point of view until Ekman and his colleagues began to publish the results of a series of influential studies of facial expression in the late 1960s (see Ekman, 1992).

Ekman and Friesen (1975) began by analyzing hundreds of films and photographs of people experiencing various emotions. From these, they compiled an atlas of the facial expressions that are normally associated with different emotions. They concluded that six emotions are primary: anger, fear, happiness, surprise, sadness, and disgust. Facial expressions that correspond to these six emotions are presented in Figure 17.4; can you match each expression with its corresponding emotion? Ekman and Friesen further concluded that all genuine facial expressions of emotions are mixtures of these six primaries—for example, see Figure 17.5.

The actual facial expressions that were published in Ekman and Friesen's atlas were not photographs of people experiencing various emotions. They were photographs of models who were instructed to contract specific facial muscles. For example, to produce the facial expression for surprise, models were instructed to pull their brows upward so as to wrinkle their forehead, to open their eyes wide so as to reveal white above the iris, to slacken the muscles around their mouth, and to drop their jaw.

Ekman, Sorenson, and Friesen (1969) and Izard (1971) showed people in 12 different cultures a collection of photographs that depicted the six primary facial expressions. The people in all 12 cultures were able to accurately identify the emotion that corresponded to each expression. This suggested that Darwin was right about the universality of human expression; however, some critics argued that the concordance of facial expressions in the 12 cultures could have resulted from exposure to tourists, movies, television shows, and magazines. Ekman and Friesen (1971) countered by showing that the members of an isolated New Guinea tribe could correctly match the photographs

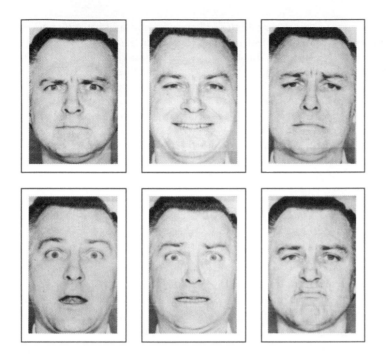

FIGURE 17.4

Examples of the six different facial expressions that were considered to be primary by Ekman and Friesen (1975): anger, fear, happiness, surprise, sadness, and disgust. Can you identify which facial expression corresponds to which emotion?

of Western facial expressions with their corresponding emotions, and conversely, that Western subjects could correctly match photographs of New Guinean facial expressions with their corresponding emotions.

Facial Expression and Deception

Because we can exert voluntary control over our facial muscles, it is possible, to some degree, to inhibit true facial expressions and to substitute false ones. Ekman and Friesen (1969) hypothesized that minor cultural differences in the facial expression of emotions may result from differences in how various cultures try to control their emotions in social situations. Friesen (1972) tested this hypothesis by studying the facial expressions that were generated in Japanese and American subjects by unpleasant film clips. When they thought that they were alone, there were no differences in the facial expressions of the Japanese and the American subjects. However, when an authority figure was present, the Japanese, more than the Americans, tried to mask their negative expressions with the semblance of a smile.

There are many reasons why one would choose to alter one's facial expression. Some of these reasons are positive (e.g., putting on a false smile to reassure a worried friend); some are negative (e.g., putting on a false smile to disguise a lie). In either case, it is difficult to fool an expert. There are two ways of distinguishing true expressions from false ones (Ekman, 1985). First, *microexpressions* of the real emotion often "break through" the false one. These microexpressions last only about .05 second, but with practice they can be detected without the aid of slow-motion photography. Second, there are often subtle differences between genuine emotions and false emotions, which can be detected by skilled observers. The most widely studied of these differences was first described by the French anatomist, Duchenne in 1862.

FIGURE 17.5

The kind of expression that you might see on the face of a person who is visiting a sick friend. It is a combination of sadness in the upper half of the face and happiness in the lower half.

Duchenne said that the smile of enjoyment could be distinguished from deliberately produced smiles by considering two facial muscles: *zygomaticus major,* which pulls the lip corners up obliquely, and *orbicularis oculi,* which orbits the eye, pulling the skin from the cheeks and forehead toward the eyeball. According to Duchenne, "The first *[zygomaticus major]* obeys the will but the second *[orbicularis oculi]* is only put in play by sweet emotions of the soul; the . . . fake joy, the deceitful laugh, cannot provoke the contraction of this latter muscle . . . " (p. 126). The *orbicularis oculi* "does not obey the will; it is only brought into play by a true feeling. . . . Its inertia in smiling, unmasks a false friend." (p. 72) (Ekman, 1992, p. 36)

Ekman named the legitimate smile, which involves contraction of the *orbicularis oculi,* the **Duchenne smile.**

Feedback of Facial Expression

Is there any truth to the old idea that putting on a happy face can make you feel better? Recent research suggests that there is (see Adelmann & Zajonc, 1989). The hypothesis that our facial expressions influence our emotional experience is called the **facial feedback hypothesis.**

Most tests of the facial feedback hypothesis have taken the same general form. Subjects are instructed to make the combination of facial muscle contractions that correspond to a particular emotion— they are not told which emotion or the purpose of the experiment. For example, they might receive the following instruction: "Pull your eyebrows down and together; raise your upper eyelids and tighten your lower eyelids; narrow your lips and press them together." Try this pose yourself; try to hold it for 30 seconds. What does it make you feel like? If it makes you feel slightly angry, you have just experienced the finding that has been reported in several experiments. Making the facial expression that corresponds to a particular emotion tends to make us feel that emotion. For example, Rutledge and Hupka (1985) had subjects assume happy, angry, or neutral faces as they viewed a series of emotion-charged and neutral slides. The subjects reported feeling slightly more happy and less angry when they were making happy faces—and slightly less happy and more angry when they were making angry faces. The results of Rutledge and Hupka (1985) are illustrated in Figure 17.6.

Unobservable Facial Expression and Emotion

Not all emotions are accompanied by obvious changes in facial expression— as any good poker player will tell you. A more sensitive measure of the activity of facial muscles can be obtained by *facial electromyography* (EMG). Facial EMG activity is a more sensitive indicator of the activity of facial muscles than is overt facial expression because slight changes in the motor-neuron input to a muscle can occur in the absence of observable changes in the muscles' contraction.

Are changes in the EMG activity of facial muscles related to emotional state, even when there are no observable changes in facial expression? The results of several studies suggest that they are (see Tassinary & Cacioppo, 1992). For example, Cacioppo, Petty, Losch, and Kim (1986) showed subjects slides of natural scenes that were moderately pleasant or moderately unpleas-

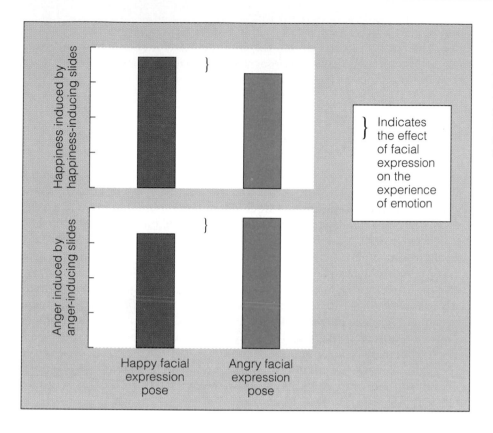

FIGURE 17.6
The results of Rutledge and Hupka (1985). The subjects reported feeling more happy and less angry when they viewed emotion-charged and neutral slides while making a happy face, and less happy and more angry while making an angry face.

ant while they recorded the EMG activity of several facial muscles. The subjects viewed each slide for 5 seconds, and then they were asked to rate how much they liked the scene. Despite the fact that facial expressions were seldom evoked, the EMG activity of several muscles during the 5-second viewing time was related to how much the subjects subsequently reported that they liked the slide. For example, the two facial muscles that you previously encountered in the discussion of the *Duchenne smile,* the *orbicularis oculi* and the *zygomaticus major,* tended to be more active during the presentation of slides that were judged to be pleasant. In a similar study (Cacioppo, Bush, & Tassinary, in press), similar results were obtained even when subjects were asked to conceal their facial reaction.

17.4

Lateralization and Localization of Human Emotions

Neuropsychological research on human emotions has addressed two kinds of questions, one about *lateralization* and one about *localization:* (1) Does one hemisphere participate more than the other in emotion-related processes, and if so, which one? (2) Which particular areas of cortex participate in emotion-related processes? In this section of the chapter, research on the lateralization and localization of human emotion is discussed in two subsections. The first subsection deals with the experience and expression of emotion, and the second deals with the recognition of emotional signals that are received from other people.

The Effects of Brain Damage on the Experience and Expression of Human Emotion

According to the pop-science industry, emotion resides in the right hemisphere. This claim bears little relation to the evidence (see Kolb & Whishaw, 1990; Pizzamiglio, Caltagirone, & Zoccaoloti, 1989).

The first systematic study of the lateralization of emotion was published by Gainotti in 1972. Gainotti compared the emotional impact of left-hemisphere and right-hemisphere strokes. He found that both left-hemisphere and right-hemisphere lesions had emotional effects, but that the effects were different. Extreme fearfulness and depression were observed in 62% of the patients with left-hemisphere lesions and in only 10% of the patients with right-hemisphere lesions. In contrast, 38% of the patients with right-hemisphere lesions and only 11% of the patients with left-hemisphere lesions were indifferent to their disorder. Although Gainotti's results are consistent with the experience of many clinical neuropsychologists (see Goldstein, 1939), efforts to confirm them using the *sodium amytal test* have been inconsistent (see Kolb & Milner, 1981; Rossi & Rosandini, 1967).

A few studies of patients with unilateral brain damage have indicated a right-hemisphere dominance for emotion. The following are two of them. First, Tucker and his colleagues (see Tucker, 1981) found that right-hemisphere lesions interfered with the ability of patients to communicate emotion by tone of voice. When asked to read passages with happiness, anger, or sadness, the tone of patients with right-hemisphere lesions was flat in comparison to the tone of patients with left-hemisphere lesions—the lack of emotional tone in one's speech is called **aprosodia.** Second, Caltagirone and his colleagues (see Caltagirone et al., 1989) found the heart rate and skin conductance changes induced by emotion-charged film clips to be less in right-hemisphere-damaged patients than in left-hemisphere-damaged patients. However, there are many studies of patients with unilateral brain lesions that have found no evidence of lateralization of emotional experience or expression. Studies by Kolb and his colleagues suggest that this inconsistency may be largely attributable to two factors: the location of the lesions within the hemispheres and the particular measure of emotion. Kolb and his colleagues (see Kolb & Milner, 1981; Kolb & Taylor, 1981) compared the effects of left or right frontal, parietal, and temporal lesions on the frequency of spontaneous talking and the number of facial expressions during a routine neuropsychological test session. The results are illustrated in Figure 17.7. There was no evidence for lateralization of facial expression, but there was evidence for localization; both left-hemisphere and right-hemisphere frontal-lobe lesions significantly reduced the number of facial expressions relative to temporal and parietal lesions. In contrast, Kolb and his colleagues found evidence for both lateralization and localization of talking frequency. Patients with left frontal lesions talked less than patients with temporal or parietal lesions, and patients with right frontal lesions talked more.

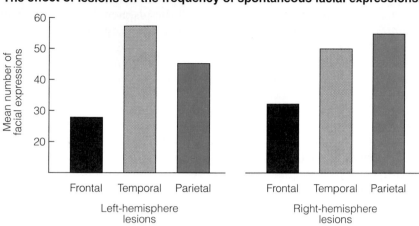

The effect of lesions on the frequency of spontaneous facial expressions.

FIGURE 17.7

The results of Kolb and Milner (1981); the effects of left or right frontal, temporal, or parietal lesions on the frequency of spontaneous talking and facial expressions during a neuropsychological examination. (Adapted from Kolb & Whishaw, 1990.)

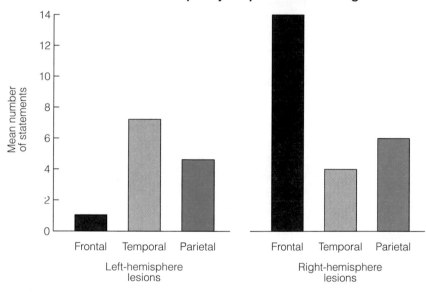

The effect of lesions on the frequency of spontaneous talking.

The Effects of Brain Damage on the Recognition of Human Emotion

The ability to recognize the emotional states of others is one of the most important human perceptual abilities—it is difficult to imagine how anybody could prosper without being able to recognize whether others are angry or pleased. Most of the neuropsychological research on recognizing emotion has focused on facial expression, but there have been several studies of recognizing **prosody** (i.e., tone of voice).

Evidence of a right-hemisphere superiority for the perception of facial expression is strong (see Etcoff, 1989). Groups of patients with right-hemisphere lesions are typically deficient in recognizing both facial expression and facial identity in comparison to patients with left-hemisphere lesions. However, there are many individual subjects with right-hemisphere lesions who cannot recognize facial expression but have no difficulty recognizing facial identity (e.g., Etcoff, 1984). Kolb and Taylor (1988) studied the localization of the recognition of facial expression by asking neurosurgical patients to match photographs of faces on the basis of expression. As illustrated in Figure 17.8, patients with right-hemisphere excisions were generally poorer at this task than patients with left-hemisphere excisions; however, patients with left-frontal excisions also displayed statistically significant deficits. This result suggests that although the right hemisphere may be generally dominant for processing facial expression, the left hemisphere may also play a role—perhaps by assigning verbal tags to various expressions.

Two kinds of evidence support the view that the right hemisphere is superior to the left in the recognition of emotional **prosody** (tone of voice). First, right-hemisphere lesions disrupt various prosody-recognition tasks more than do left-hemisphere lesions (e.g., Bowers et al., 1987). Second, in most normal subjects, the left ear (i.e., right hemisphere) is dominant over the right ear (i.e., left hemisphere) in recognizing emotional prosody in the *dichotic listening task* (see Chapter 16). For example, Ley and Bryden (1982) played spoken sentences simultaneously to each ear, one spoken in an emotional tone and one not. The subjects were instructed to attend to a particular ear and then to indicate the content and prosody of that sentence. Almost every subject displayed a left-ear advantage for identifying emotional tone and a right-ear advantage for identifying content.

FIGURE 17.8

The ability of control subjects and patients with cortical excisions to match photographs of faces on the basis of expression. (Adapted from Kolb and Whishaw, 1990.)

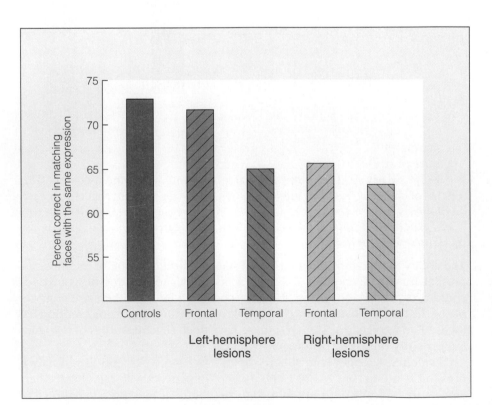

Conclusion

It is a mistake to think of emotion as a single global faculty that resides in the right hemisphere. True, many studies have demonstrated a right-hemisphere superiority for the expression of emotion and the recognition of emotional stimuli, but the dominance of the right hemisphere is far from total. The degree of dominance in brain-damage studies depends on the particular measure of emotion and on the localization of the damage within each hemisphere. The frontal and temporal lobes appear to play particularly important roles in the expression and recognition of emotion.

17.5

Stress and Health

The body responds to brief periods of threat in ways that facilitate adaptive reactions to it, that is, in ways that reduce it. For example, brief periods of threat are associated with **fear** of the threatening stimulus and elevated levels of sympathetic nervous system activity. However, if the threat persists, it can be associated with subjective and physiological responses that are largely maladaptive. The subjective emotional state that is associated with chronic threat is termed **anxiety;** the physiological response to chronic threat is termed **stress.**

The concept of stress was developed by Hans Selye (pronounced SELL yay) in the 1950s. Selye observed that different forms of chronic insult to the body (e.g., excessive heat, excessive cold, injury, disease) produce a similar physiological reaction, which he termed the **general adaptation syndrome.** Symptoms of the general adaptation syndrome include enlarged *adrenal glands, gastric ulcers,* and a shrunken *thymus gland.*

Selye attributed the general adaptation syndrome to the activation of the *anterior-pituitary adrenal-cortex system.* Stressors stimulate the release of *adrenocorticotropic hormone* from the *anterior pituitary,* which in turn triggers the release of *glucocorticords* from the **adrenal cortex. Glucocorticoids** (e.g., *cortisol)* are *steroid* hormones that promote mobilization of energy resources, combat inflammation, and facilitate healing. The level of circulating glucocorticords is the most commonly employed physiological measure of stress.

Selye's early studies of the general adaptation syndrome focused on the effects of chronic *physical stressors;* however, he discovered that chronic *psychological stressors* had the same effect. For example, moving a male rat from its home cage to one with the odors of strange males, or exposing a monkey to a light that had previously been associated with painful electric shock was enough to produce large increases in circulating glucocorticoids. In humans, similar increases are often associated with the death of a friend, losing one's job, divorce, or changing one's residence (see Burns, 1990).

Selye's ideas about the stress response have been expanded. Although modern researchers acknowledge that increased adrenocortical activity is an important physiological consequence of exposure to stressors, they do not believe that it is the only important physiological stress response (see Dunn, 1989; Sachar, 1980). For example, Selye largely ignored the existing research on the relation between stress and sympathetic nervous system activation;

FIGURE 17.9

The physiological stress response: Selye's original one-system view and today's two-system view.

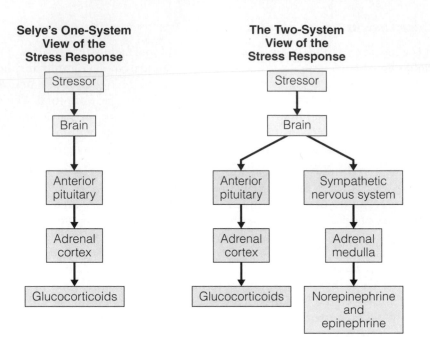

stressors also increase the release of *epinephrine* and *norepinephrine* from the adrenal medulla. Figure 17.9 illustrates Selye's one-system view of the stress response and today's two-system view, which is itself an oversimplification.

Stress and Psychosomatic Disorders: Gastric Ulcers

Psychosomatic disorders are organic (physical) illnesses that are caused by experiential (psychological) factors. In the not too distant past, psychosomatic disorders befuddled attending physicians; patients who suffered from them were often assumed to be "mentally ill" and were referred to a psychiatrist for analysis. Research on stress has done much to bring psychosomatic disorders to the attention of the medical profession; it has clarified the mechanisms underlying some of the more common psychosomatic disorders; and it has led to the development of effective modes of treatment and prevention. Research on gastric ulcers is a case in point.

Gastric ulcers are lesions to the lining of the stomach and duodenum. The fact that they are particularly prevalent in people who have been exposed to chronic stress suggests that they can be psychosomatic. This hypothesis has been confirmed by experiments in which exposure to psychological stressors has produced gastric ulcers in laboratory animals (e.g., Weiss, 1971).

Two factors appear to contribute to the formation of gastric ulcers. One is the excessive release of hydrochloric acid and other digestive juices that often follows periods of stress—stress is associated with sympathetic activation, which inhibits gastric secretion, but after a period of stress, there is often a parasympathetic rebound that increases gastric secretion (see Desiderato, MacKinnon, & Hissom, 1974). The second factor that can contribute to the formation of gastric ulcers is the shunting of blood away from the stomach to the skeletal muscles by the sympathetic nervous system—the mucus membrane that protects the stomach lining from its own hydrochloric acid requires a continuous flow of blood to function effectively.

Henke (1988) induced gastric ulcers in rats by placing them in a restraint tube (a tube that is too small for them to move around) for just 4 hours. He found that ulcer formation was associated with a particular pattern of activity in the amygdala and that ulcers could be induced by 2 hours of amygdalar stimulation. Because previous studies had shown that electrical stimulation of the amygdala decreases gastric blood flow, Henke suggested that this was the mechanism by which amygdalar activity induces gastric ulcers.

The response of humans to stressors is variable—more variable than the responses of other animals. The stress responses of humans can be reduced by a variety of psychological coping strategies. For example, in one study (Katz, 1970), many of the women who were awaiting surgery for possible breast cancer coped with the stress in a variety of ways (e.g., denial, prayer, intellectualization). Women who adopted these coping strategies displayed little emotional distress and their corticosteroid levels were low; in contrast, women who did not adopt such strategies were extremely anxious and had elevated corticosteroid levels.

Psychoneuroimmunology: Stress and the Immune System

Microorganisms of every description revel in the warm, damp, nutritive climate of your body. Your **immune system** keeps your body from being overwhelmed by these omnipresent invaders; it identifies infectious organisms and destroys them.

The most important cells of the immune system are the **leucocytes,** which are commonly referred to as *white blood cells.* Leucocytes combat foreign microorganisms in two fundamentally different ways. Some leucocytes respond generally to dead tissue and to certain microorganisms by **phagocytosis,** that is, by consuming them. Other leucocytes respond specifically to combat particular invaders—these leucocytes are called **lymphocytes.**

Lymphocytes destroy foreign microorganisms by reacting to their antigens. **Antigens** are proteins on the surface of foreign organisms that are different from the proteins of the body. When one class of lymphocytes, the **B cells,** encounter an antigen, they begin to manufacture **antibodies,** which are proteins that bind specifically to antigens, in much the same way that specific neurotransmitters bind to specific receptors. Once antibodies bind to the surface of an invading microorganism, it is deactivated and tagged for destruction by phagocytes. The antibody response to a particular antigen is more rapid and effective in individuals who have been previously exposed to it; this is why *inoculation* is an effective treatment against some diseases. The *antigen-antibody response* is illustrated in Figure 17.10.

T cells are another class of lymphocytes. T cells, like other leucocytes, are created in *bone marrow* and are released in an immature form. T cells mature in the *thymus gland,* which is why they are called T cells, whereas other leucocytes mature in the *spleen* and *lymphatic system.* T cells do not produce antibodies, but they do have antibody-like molecules with which they bind to antigens. Some types of T cells kill microorganisms directly; others stimulate

FIGURE 17.10

The antigen-antibody response.

B cells encounter microorganisms and manufacture antibodies to their antigens.

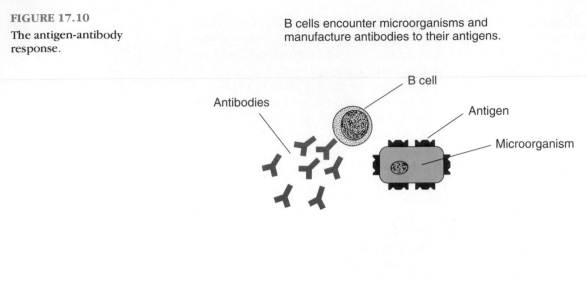

The antibodies bind to the antigens; this deactivates the microorganisms and tags them for phagocytosis.

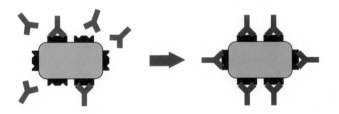

their destruction by phagocytes. B cells are more effective against bacteria and viruses in the body fluids; T cells are more effective against bacteria and viruses that have entered body cells, and against fungi and protozoans. It is the T cells that react to transplanted tissue.

You might be wondering right now what antigens and antibodies have to do with psychology. The idea that a person's emotional state can influence his or her resistance to infectious disease is an old one; however, it is only recently that advances in the study of immunology have made it possible to put this idea to the test. The early studies of the relations between emotions and the immune response were so exciting that an entire new area of biopsychological research rapidly coalesced in the late 1970s (see Ader, 1981). This area of research is **psychoneuroimmunology,** the study of the effects of psychological factors on the immune response and the mediation of these effects by the neuroendocrine system. Much of the research in this area has focused on the adverse effects of stress on immune function.

Psychoneuroimmunological research on stress has focused on three different questions: (1) Can stress disrupt immune function? (2) Is stress associated with an increased susceptibility to disease? (3) What is the mechanism by which stress influences immune function? These three questions are dealt with, in turn, in the following three subsections.

Can stress disrupt immune function? The results of numerous studies suggest that it can. For example, Sklar and Anisman (1981) injected two groups of mice with the virus that is responsible for the common cold. Then, they exposed the mice in one of the groups to a stressful shock-avoidance training procedure. These mice developed more severe cold symptoms than did unstressed control mice.

Several studies have documented the effects of stress on the immune systems of human subjects (see O'Leary, 1990). These studies are of two types: those that have assessed the effects of *acute stress* (relatively brief periods of stress) and those that have assessed the effects of *chronic stress* (relatively long periods of stress). For example, Glaser, Kiecolt-Glaser, and their colleagues demonstrated a variety of changes in the immune system during the acute stress associated with writing examinations (e.g., Glaser et al., 1987) and during the chronic stress associated with caring for a relative with Alzheimer's disease (Kiecolt-Glaser et al., 1987).

Is stress associated with an increased susceptibility to disease? In other words, are stress-related changes in immune function large enough to be of clinical significance? The results of several studies suggest that people are more susceptible to infection during times of stress. For example, in a study by Glaser et al. (1987), students reported that they were more likely to contract respiratory infections during examination periods. However, the results of such studies have been more suggestive than conclusive. Stressed subjects may report more illness during times of stress merely because they expect to be more ill or because the experience of illness during times of stress is more unpleasant (see Watson & Pennebaker, 1989). Moreover, even if stressed people were proven to be more susceptible to illness, the increased susceptibility might not be a direct consequence of the stress; it could be an indirect consequence of stress-related changes in behavior, such as changes in diet, drug use, and sleep patterns.

What is the mechanism by which stress influences immune function? As you have already learned, two interacting physiological systems are activated by stressors: (1) the sympathetic adrenal-medulla system and (2) the anterior-pituitary adrenal-cortex system. Both of these systems can influence immunologic activity in a variety of ways (see Antoni, 1987). For example, the release of norepinephrine and epinephrine from the sympathetic adrenal-medulla system can increase the levels of circulating lymphocytes, and the release of corticosteroids from the anterior-pituitary adrenal-cortex system can reduce the levels of circulating lymphocytes. In fact, stress can influence immunologic function by so many different mechanisms that it has been extremely difficult to sort things out. Most hormones and neurotransmitters are responsive to stress; most can influence immunologic activity; and most bind to receptors on the surfaces of lymphocytes.

17.6

Aggression, Defense, and Anxiety

The study of aggressive and defensive behaviors has a long history—biopsychologists have been particularly interested in these behaviors because of the important role that they play in evolution and because of their relation to emotional states such as anger, fear, and anxiety. I am not going to describe this history here. Instead, I am going to move directly to today, to one particularly productive approach to the study of aggressive and defensive behaviors: the ethoexperimental approach (see Blanchard, Brain, Blanchard, & Parmigiani, 1989). The **ethoexperimental approach** has two defining characteristics: (1) it involves studying behaviors in laboratory environments that have been constructed to mimic features of the subjects' natural environment, and (2) it involves studying these behaviors by carefully analyzing videotaped behavioral sequences, rather than by focusing on one or two measures of behavior, such as the number of lever presses or the latency to respond.

You have already encountered in this text one example of how the ethoexperimental approach has clarified an early confusion about aggressive and defensive behaviors (see Chapter 5). When two rats receive multiple electric shocks through the floor of a small chamber, they rear up on their hind legs and direct boxing movements with their forepaws at the other rat. This phenomenon has been termed **shock-elicited aggression** and has been widely studied by researchers interested in aggression. However, the ethoexperimental research of Blanchard and Blanchard (see 1988) suggests that this is defensive behavior, not aggressive behavior. When a small male stranger is placed in an established mixed-sex colony, it is attacked by the colony's **alpha male** (dominant male in the colony), and the following interaction occurs.

The attack of an experienced **alpha male** on a stranger in his colony is very stereotyped and usually quite intense. The alpha approaches the stranger and sniffs at its perianal area. . . . If the intruder is an adult male, the alpha's sniff leads to piloerection. . . .

Shortly after piloerecting, the alpha male usually bites the intruder, and the intruder runs away. The alpha chases after it, and after one or two additional bites, the intruder stops running and turns to face its attacker. It rears up on its hind legs, using its forelimbs to push off the alpha. . . . However, rather than standing nose to nose with the **"boxing"** intruder, the attacking rat abruptly moves to a lateral orientation, with the long axis of its body perpendicular to the front of the defending rat. . . . It moves sideways toward the intruder, crowding and sometimes pushing it off balance. If the defending rat stands solid against this **"lateral attack"** movement, the alpha may make a quick lunge forward and around the defender's body to bite at its back. In response to such a lunge, the defender usually pivots on its hindfeet, in the same direction as the attacker is moving, continuing its frontal orientation to the attacker. If the defending rat moves quickly enough, no bite will be made.

However, after a number of instances of the lateral attack, and especially if the attacker has succeeded in biting the intruder, the stranger rat may roll backward slowly from the boxing position, to lie on its back. The attacker then takes up a position on top of the supine animal, digging with its forepaws at the intruder's sides. If the attacker can turn the other animal over, or expose some portion of its back . . . it bites. In response to these efforts, the defender usually moves in the direction of the attacker's head, rolling slightly on its back to continue to orient its ventrum [front] toward the alpha, and continuing to push off with both forelimbs and hindlimbs. Although all four legs and abdomen of the defending rat are exposed, the attacker does not bite them. This sequence of bites, flight, chasing, boxing, lateral attack, lying on the back, and standing on top is repeated . . . until the stranger rat is removed. (Blanchard & Blanchard, 1984, pp. 8–9)

From the study of such interactions, it is clear that shock-elicited aggression is really shock-elicited defense.

A study of cat play behavior by Pellis and his colleagues provides another excellent example of ethoexperimental research on defense and aggression (Pellis, O'Brien, Pellis, Teitelbaum, Wolgin, & Kennedy, 1988). Pellis et al. studied videotaped behavioral interactions between cats and mice. They found that different cats reacted to the mice in different ways; some were efficient killers, some reacted defensively, and some "played" with the mice. Their ethoexperimental analyses of these behavioral patterns made two important points. First, they showed that, in contrast to common belief, cats do not play with their prey; those cats who appeared to be playing with the mice were simply vacillating between attack and defense. Second, each cat's interactions with mice (or with balls of string, for that matter) can be understood by locating them on a linear scale with total aggressiveness at one end, total defensiveness at the other, and various proportions of the two in between. Pellis and his colleagues validated this scale by showing that an injection of an antianxiety drug moved cats along the scale toward more efficient killing. Cats that avoided mice before the injection played with them after the injection; those that played with them before the injection killed them after the injection; and those that killed them before the injection killed them more quickly after the injection.

Types of Aggressive and Defensive Behavior

Defensive and aggressive behaviors can be divided into eight different categories on the basis of three different criteria: (1) their *topography* (their form), (2) the situations that elicit them, and (3) their apparent function.

1. *Predatory aggression* refers to the stalking and killing of members of other species for the purposes of eating them. Rats kill prey, such as mice and frogs, by delivering bites to the back of the neck.

2. *Social aggression* is unprovoked aggression that is directed at a conspecific for the purpose of establishing, altering, or maintaining a social hierarchy. In rats, and many other mammals, social aggression occurs only among males that are living in mixed-sex groups. Social aggression is characterized by piloerection, lateral attack, and bites directed at the defender's back (see Blanchard & Blanchard, 1990a).

[1]From "Affect and aggression: An animal model applied to human behavior" by D.C. Blanchard and R.J. Blanchard in *Advances in the Study of Aggression, Volume 1,* 1984, edited by D.C. Blanchard and R.J. Blanchard. San Diego: Academic Press. Copyright 1984 by Academic Press. Reprinted by permission.

3.   *Defensive attack* refers to attacks that are delivered by animals, when they are cornered by threatening conspecifics or members of other species. In rats, these are lunging, shrieking, biting attacks that are typically directed at the face of the attacker. Defensive attacks are common in wild rats, but they rarely occur in laboratory rats (see Blanchard & Blanchard, 1990c).

4.   *Freezing and flight* are responses that animals use to avoid attack. Animals often freeze (i.e., remain totally immobile) as a threatening animal approaches. In some environments, freezing helps animals avoid detection; it also prepares them for action. For example, if a human approaches a freezing wild rat, the rat will explode into flight as soon as the human penetrates its safety zone or makes a sudden movement. If the human chases and corners it, the rat will turn to face its pursuer and freeze once again. Continued approach or a sudden movement from the pursuer usually elicits a defensive attack.

5.   *Protecting target sites* is the function of many defensive behaviors. For example, rats that are the targets of social aggression behave in specific ways to defend their backs, which are the targets of the attack; they face their attacker, they rear up, and they fend off their attacker with their forepaws. If the attacker makes a move to the defender's right, the defender pivots in a clockwise fashion to keep the attacker's head away from its back.

6.   *Defensive coping behaviors* are an important component of the defensive repertoires of many species; these are complex, flexible behaviors that are designed to reduce contact with dangerous organisms or objects. **Defensive burying** is one of the most common coping behaviors of rats (see Chapter 5); rats use the defensive burying response (i.e., spraying sand or dirt ahead with their forepaws) to bury dangerous objects in their environment, to drive off predators, and to construct barriers (see Pinel & Wilkie, 1983).

7.   *Defensive information gathering* refers to behaviors that are performed by animals in order to obtain specific information that helps them defend themselves more effectively. The function of some information gathering is **risk assessment;** for example, rats that have been chased by a cat into their burrow do not emerge until they have spent considerable time at the entrance scanning the surrounding environment (see Blanchard, Blanchard, & Rodgers, 1991). The function of other defensive information gathering is the collection of information about the identity of dangerous objects. For example, rats that have received a single shock from a novel object in their test chamber return to the object and investigate it in a cautious *stretched-approach posture* (Pinel & Mana, 1989). This period of postshock investigation helps them recognize the object if they encounter it again (Pinel, Mana, & Wilkie, 1986).

8.   *Maternal defensiveness* refers to the constellation of hyperdefensive behaviors by which mothers protect their young. A major component of maternal defensiveness in rats is an increase in the tendency of nursing mothers to attack conspecific or nonconspecific intruders that approach the nest site. Because the behavior sequence that is directed by nursing mothers at conspecifics that approach the nest looks like male social aggression, it is often called **maternal aggression,** despite its defensive function. In addition to maternal aggression, rat mothers display a variety of defensive coping behaviors that

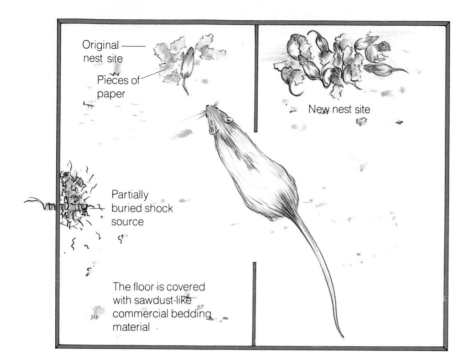

FIGURE 17.11

A rat mother that was shocked by a wire-wrapped dowel inserted into her nest chamber carried her pups to the safety of an adjoining chamber, buried the shock source, dismantled the original nest, and built a new nest in the adjoining chamber from material salvaged from the original nest. Here she is fetching her last pup to transport it to the new nest. (Adapted from Pinel & Mana, 1989.)

protect their pups from risk. For example, if a dangerous object is placed near the nest site, rat mothers bury the object and move both their pups and their nest to a safer location (Pinel & Mana, 1989). See Figure 17.11.

The Concept of Target Sites

It may have already occurred to you from the preceding descriptions that many of the complex aggressive-defensive interactions between conspecifics boil down to one simple principle. The social aggressor is trying to attack a particular site on the defender's body—in the case of rats, trying to deliver bites to the back near the tail—and the defender is trying to protect those sites. Conversely, the aggressor is trying to protect its face, the likely target of defensive attacks.

The emergence of the **target-site concept** illustrates what etho-experimental analysis is all about. Ethoexperimentalists do not study the details of behavioral sequences to accumulate libraries full of behavioral minutiae; they do so to extract simple explanatory principles. The research of Pellis and his colleagues on play fighting (see Pellis, 1989) is a good example of this point. When you watch two young rats fighting, what you see is a blur. By viewing play-fighting sequences in slow motion, Pellis learned that several particular sequences of interaction recur. By studying these complex sequences, Pellis discovered a simple explanation for them: Each rat changes its body position to increase its chances of delivering a bite to the back of the neck of the opponent, while at the same time protecting the back of its own neck. As rats mature, there are complex changes in their fighting sequences. Pellis's research suggests that these changes occur because there is a shift in the target site from the back of the neck to the back near the base of the tail. In my discussions with Pellis, he has repeatedly stressed how difficult it is to identify such simple principles from the analysis of complex behavioral sequences, but how easy it is to understand the sequences once the principles have been identified.

Mechanisms of Aggression and Defense

Figure 17.12 is a schematic horizontal cross section of the six brain structures that have been most frequently implicated in the modulation of defensive and aggressive behaviors. These six structures are (1) the lateral septum, (2) the raphé nuclei, (3) the medial accumbens, (4) the medial hypothalamus, (5) the

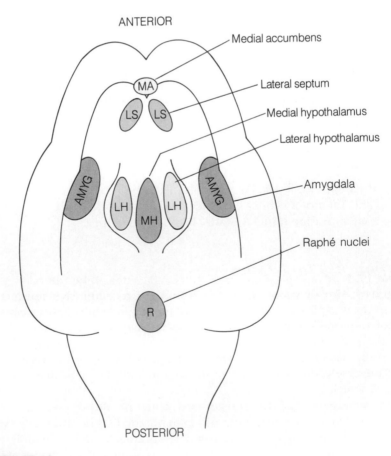

FIGURE 17.12

A schematic horizontal cross section of six of the areas of the rat brain that influence defensive attack, predatory aggression, and social aggression.

lateral hypothalamus, and (6) the amygdala (see Albert & Walsh, 1984). Most of the research that has assessed the functions of these six structures has focused on defensive attack, predatory aggression, and social aggression.

Large bilateral lesions to the six brain structures that are illustrated in Figure 17.12 have different effects, but they always affect defensive attack and predatory aggression in similar ways. Lesions of the lateral septum, medial accumbens, medial hypothalamus, or raphé nuclei increase both defensive attack (e.g., Brady & Nauta, 1955; Malsbury, Kow, & Pfaff, 1977) and predatory aggression (e.g., Albert, Walsh, Siemens, & Louie, 1986; Marques, Malsbury, & Daood, 1979; Penot, Vergnes, Mack, & Kempf, 1978) in most laboratory species, whereas lesions of the lateral hypothalamus and the amygdala commonly decrease both (e.g., Shipley & Kolb, 1977; Woods, 1956). However, despite the fact that large bilateral lesions of the aforementioned six structures have the same general effects on both defensive and predatory aggression, there is reason to believe that these two kinds of aggression are independently regulated. In a key series of studies, Albert and Wong (1978a, 1978b) assessed the effects of small temporary lesions produced by microinjections of a local anesthetic to various parts of the septum and medial hypothalamus. They found that many of the lesions had selective effects; some lesions affected predatory aggression without affecting defensive attack, whereas others affected defensive attack without affecting predatory aggression. Thus, in the rat at least, it seems that the neural substrates of defensive attack and predatory aggression are intertwined but separate.

The pattern of lesion effects on social aggression is quite different from the pattern of lesion effects on defensive attack and predatory aggression. Rather than producing increases, lesions of the lateral septum, medial accumbens, medial hypothalamus, and raphé nuclei usually decrease social aggression in male animals (e.g., Albert, Dyson, & Walsh, 1987; Blanchard, Blanchard, & Takahashi, 1977). The effects of brain lesions on defensive attack, predatory aggression, and social aggression are summarized in Table 17.1.

Unlike defensive attack and predatory aggression, in many species social aggression is displayed almost exclusively by males and is dependent on the

Table 17.1 The Typical Effects of Bilateral Lesions of the Lateral Septum, Medial Accumbens, Medial Hypothalamus, Raphé Nucleus, Amygdala, and Lateral Hypothalamus on Defensive Attack, Predatory Aggression, and Social Aggression (Based on Albert & Walsh, 1984).

	Effect on Defensive Attack	*Effect on Predatory Aggression*	*Effect on Social Aggression*
Lateral Septum	+	+	–
Medial Accumbens	+	+	–
Medial Hypothalamus	+	+	–
Raphé Nuclei	+	+	–
Amygdala	–	–	–
Lateral Hypothalamus	–	–	–

gonadal hormone *testosterone*. Following castration, alpha males lose their dominant position in their colony to other males (e.g., Albert, Walsh, Gorzalka, Siemens, & Louie, 1986; Debold & Miczek, 1984), but soon regain it if they are given testosterone replacement injections.

Albert, Jonik, and Walsh (1992) have recently argued that maternal aggression is most appropriately viewed as a type of social aggression, although social aggression is commonly assumed to be restricted to males. Albert et al. marshalled three lines of evidence to support their view. First, they pointed out that the topography of rat maternal aggression and rat social aggression is the same—most notably, both include piloerection and lateral attack. Second, they pointed out that both social aggression and maternal aggression are *hormone dependent*—social aggression depends on testosterone and maternal aggression seems to depend on a combination of testosterone and estradiol. Third, they pointed out that social aggression is reliably elicited in females that have been injected with testosterone and estradiol by the very situations that elicit it in males—by exposure to intruders or by competition for food. Albert et al. propose that both social aggression and maternal aggression should be referred to as **hormone-dependent aggression.**

Human Aggression, the Amygdala, and Psychosurgery

Simple solutions to complex problems should always be treated with skepticism; they are appealing, but they rarely work. A case in point is the idea that **psychosurgery** (the destruction of a part of the brain for the purpose of changing behavior) provides an effective solution to the problem of human violence. The advocates of this view (e.g., Mark & Ervin, 1970) argue that violent people have excessive activity in the structures of the brain that produce violent behavior and that their violence should be controlled by destroying these structures. The amygdala is the most commonly advocated target of such psychosurgery.

Advocates of *amygdalectomy* for the "treatment" of human aggression commonly support their recommendation with two lines of evidence, both of which are seriously flawed. First, they point out that bilateral amygdalectomy has been shown to significantly reduce the aggression of laboratory animals. This is true, but not particularly relevant. True, amygdalectomy often reduces the average level of aggressive behavior in a group of experimental animals, but there are many individual animals that show no decrease—too many to warrant using amygdalectomy to treat human aggression. Another problem with this line of evidence is that it focuses on one kind of test at the exclusion of others. The advocates of human amygdalectomy commonly cite the observation that amygdalectomized laboratory animals are easier to handle, but they rarely acknowledge studies in which free-ranging animals have been captured, amygdalectomized, and returned to their natural habitat. In such a study by Kling (1972), amygdalectomized monkeys were found to be incapable of responding appropriately to a variety of social signals. This did have the effect of reducing their aggressive behavior in some situations, but it had other important consequences as well. Frequently, when approached by other monkeys in a nonthreatening way, amygdalectomized monkeys fled or cowered. Conversely, they would sometimes fail to respond submissively when approached by a dominant troop member, and they would take a severe beating as a result. The consequence of this social ineptitude was isolation from the troop and death from starvation or predation—hardly a strong basis for adopting amygdalectomy as a form of therapy for human aggression.

A second line of evidence that is offered in support of the use of amygdalectomy to treat human aggression is based on the claim that *temporal-lobe epilepsy* (see Chapter 6) is associated with aggressive behavior—the amygdala is a temporal-lobe structure. However, several studies have failed to observe any relation between temporal-lobe epilepsy and aggression. Pinel, Treit, and Rovner (1972) attempted to circumvent the problems involved in studying aggression in human temporal-lobe epileptics by using the *kindled seizure animal model* (see Chapter 6). Kindled epileptic foci were established in rats in one of two temporal-lobe structures—the amygdala or the hippocampus—or in the caudate nucleus by briefly (for 1 second) stimulating the target site about 15 times per week for 8 weeks. At first there was no response to the stimulations, but by the end of the 8 weeks, each stimulation elicited a generalized clonic convulsion in each rat. As indicated in Figure 17.13, only the groups kindled in one of the two temporal-lobe structures displayed statistically significant increases in defensive aggression. However, despite the high degree of control provided by the kindling model, the effects of temporal-lobe foci on aggressive behavior were variable. The high mean defensive aggression scores displayed by the temporal-lobe groups reflected the fact that a few of the 20 subjects in each of these two groups became extremely aggressive; most remained unchanged. This pattern of results may explain why attempts to document the existence of hyperaggressiveness in human epileptics have yielded such inconsistent results. The take-home message is clear: Amygdalectomy for the treatment of human aggression cannot be justified on the basis of existing evidence.

Testosterone and Aggression

The fact that social aggression in many species occurs more commonly among males than among females is usually explained with reference to the organizational and activational effects of testosterone (e.g., Edwards, 1969). The brief period of testosterone release that occurs around birth in genetic males is thought to organize their nervous systems along masculine lines and hence to create the potential for male patterns of aggressive behavior to be activated by the high testosterone levels that are present in genetic males after puberty. The strongest support for this view comes from the observation that male and female mice castrated at birth display high levels of intraspecific fighting in response to testosterone injections in adulthood only if they receive organizing testosterone injections as neonates. The most striking demonstration of the activational role of testosterone in adult male social aggression is the sudden decrease in intermale fighting that is observed following castration in various species of rodents and *ungulates* (animals with hooves).

Attempts to demonstrate organizational and activational effects of testosterone on the aggressive behavior of humans and other primates have been inconsistent (Meyer-Bahlburg, 1981). This inconsistency is often taken as evidence that testosterone plays a less prominent role in organizing and activating the aggressive behavior of male primates (Dixson, 1980; Meyer-Bahlburg, 1981) than it does in other species. Alternatively, the inconsistency of findings

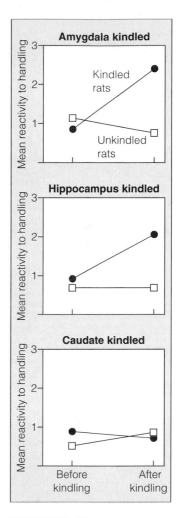

FIGURE 17.13

Reactivity to handling of rats kindled in the caudate, the amygdala, or the hippocampus. Only rats with epileptic foci in the two temporal-lobe structures (the amygdala or hippocampus) were hyperreactive. (Adapted from Pinel et al., 1977.)

in humans may in part reflect differences in the type of aggression under investigation rather than differences between species. Most studies of the effects of testosterone on the aggressive behavior of humans have focused on forms of aggression quite different from the intermale fighting that has been shown to be influenced by testosterone in rodents and ungulates. Measures of aggression used in the studies of human aggression include the frequency of violent crimes, the scores on paper-and-pencil tests of aggression, and the aggressiveness of athletic play.

Several studies have found that criminals who have been jailed for violent crimes tend to have slightly higher testosterone levels than criminals who have been jailed for nonviolent crimes. However, this weak correlation does not necessarily mean that high testosterone levels cause violent behavior; it could reflect the fact that repeated aggressive encounters produce increases in testosterone (see Archer, 1991).

Ethoexperimental Models of Anxiety

Fear and anxiety are related emotional states. *Fear* is normally triggered by the presence of a particular threat in the environment; it is normally adaptive because it motivates defense against the threat. In contrast, anxiety is a feeling of fear that persists after the threat has passed. When anxiety disrupts normal functioning, it is referred to as an **anxiety disorder.** Major categories of anxiety disorders include *panic attacks, phobias,* and *generalized anxiety.* In panic attacks and phobias, normal functioning is disrupted because nonthreatening objects or situations induce extreme fear. In generalized anxiety, normal functioning is disrupted because the fear is chronic and not associated with any particular threat—generalized anxiety is often referred to as *free-floating anxiety.* All anxiety disorders are associated with autonomic symptoms: for example, *tachycardia* (rapid heart beat), *hypertension* (high blood pressure), nausea, and difficulty breathing. Anxiety disorders are the most prevalent of all psychiatric disorders. Anxiety disorders are usually treated with drugs such as *chlordiazepoxide* (Librium) and *diazepam* (Valium), which belong to the class of drugs called **benzodiazepines.** Benzodiazepines are the most widely prescribed psychoactive drugs. Despite the fact that they produce sedative side effects and adverse withdrawal reactions (e.g., rebound anxiety, tremor, and nausea), approximately 10% of North Americans are currently taking them.

Anxiety is believed to result from a decrease in GABAergic transmission. The main evidence for this theory is that benzodiazepines bind to sites on GABA receptors; in so doing, they increase the effect that GABA molecules have when they bind to the same receptors. The major challenge to this theory of anxiety comes from the recent introduction of the *anxiolytic* (anti-anxiety) drug, **buspirone** into clinical practice. Buspirone is not a benzodiazepine, and it does not bind to GABA receptors; yet, it is just as effective in the treatment of anxiety as the benzodiazepines. Moreover, it does not produce sedation or withdrawal effects. Buspirone is an agonist at one *serotonin* receptor subtype.

Animal models (see Chapter 6) of anxiety have played an important role in the study of anxiety and in the assessment of the anxiolytic potential of new drugs (see Green, 1991; Treit, 1985). These models typically involve animal defensive behaviors, the implicit assumption being that defensive behavior is motivated by fear and that fear and anxiety are similar states. Various animal models of anxiety share another feature; they have all been validated by showing that they are responsive to benzodiazepines. A case in point is the **elevated-plus-maze** test of anxiety for rats, one of the most widely used animal models of anxiety. The elevated-plus-maze is a four-armed cross-shaped maze that is raised approximately 50 cm from the floor; two arms have sides and two arms have no sides. The measure of fearfulness (i.e., anxiety) is the proportion of time that rats spend in the enclosed arms, rather than venturing out onto the exposed arms. Pellow, Chopin, File, and Briley (1985) validated this test by showing that benzodiazepines, but not antidepressants or tranquilizers, significantly increase the time that rats spend on the exposed arms.

There is a potential problem with basing the validation of animal models of anxiety entirely on their responsiveness to benzodiazepines. This problem stems from the fact that many cases of anxiety do not respond well to benzodiazepine therapy. Accordingly, existing animal models of anxiety may in fact be models of only benzodiazepine-sensitive anxiety, and these models may not be sensitive to anxiolytic drugs that act by a different (i.e., a non-GABAergic) mechanism. The reality of this problem became apparent when existing animal models were used to assess the effectiveness of buspirone. Most so-called animal models of anxiety proved to be insensitive to the effects of buspirone. For example, the effect of buspirone on the performance of rats in the elevated-plus-maze suggests that it is *anxiogenic* (anxiety-producing); rats injected with buspirone spend less than the usual amount of time on the exposed arms. The differences between the effects of benzodiazepines and buspirone on various animal models of anxiety may ultimately prove to be informative, once they have been fully characterized (see Green, 1991).

Blanchard, Blanchard, and Rodgers (1991) have suggested that *risk-assessment behavior* is a particularly good model of generalized anxiety. In Blanchard and Blanchard's experiments (see 1989), brief exposure to a cat causes rats to flee into their burrows and freeze for an hour or two. As they gradually become active, they begin to engage in a variety of risk-assessment behaviors (e.g., scanning their enclosure from the mouth of their burrow and exploring the enclosure in a cautious-stretched posture). After several hours, risk-assessment behaviors cease and normal patterns of behavior ensue.

Blanchard et al. believe that risk assessment is a particularly good generalized model of anxiety because, like generalized anxiety, risk-assessment behavior occurs in the absence of the fear-inducing stimulus and is characterized by hypervigilance. As Blanchard et al. predicted, benzodiazepines were found to have a major effect on risk-assessment behaviors (Blanchard, Blanchard, Tom, & Rodgers, 1990) and relatively little effect on other defensive behaviors (Blanchard & Blanchard, 1990b). Benzodiazepines sometimes increased risk assessment, and sometimes they decreased it. If the rats were freezing when they received their injection, they began to engage in risk assessment, whereas if the rats were engaging in risk assessment when they received their injection, they began to behave normally. This pattern of results is consistent with the view that freezing in the absence of threat is a sign of extreme anxiety, whereas risk assessment is a sign of intermediate levels of anxiety. As I write this, Blanchard and Blanchard have not yet reported the effects of buspirone on risk assessment, but I am sure that these data will soon be forthcoming.

17.7

Biopsychology of Schizophrenia and Affective Disorders

The most serious mental disorders (i.e., those that require hospitalization or some comparable form of care) are called **psychoses;** those that are less severe (e.g., anxiety disorders) are called **neuroses.** The remainder of this chapter focuses on two major classes of psychoses: schizophrenia and the affective disorders.

The term *mental disorders* is a poor one because it is based on the premise that there are two kinds of disorders: organic (physiological) and mental (psychological). If you find yourself falling into the seductive embrace of this kind of misguided thinking, take a cold shower, and read the following quotation—10 times.

> Biopsychologists have rejected conventional physiological-or-psychological and nature-or-nurture dichotomies in favor of a more enlightened alternative. Now, they—and I hope you—view all behavior and the psychological processes that underlie it as products of patterns of neural activity, which are shaped by the interaction among genes, experience, and the current situation.

Do you recognize this quotation? It is from Chapter 2 of this text.

SCHIZOPHRENIA

By general consensus (see the *Diagnostic and Statistical Manual of Mental Disorders-IIIR* of the American Psychiatric Association, *DSM-IIIR),* individuals with one or more of the following symptoms are classified as schizophrenic:

bizarre delusions   delusions of being controlled (e.g., thought broadcasting, thought insertion); delusions of persecution (e.g., "My mother is trying to poison me" or "The communists are following me"); delusions of grandeur (e.g., "The Pope wants to meet me," or "Michael Jordan admires my sneakers").

blunted affect   failure to react with an appropriate level of emotionality to positive or negative events.

hallucinations   usually voices telling the patient what to do, commenting negatively on her or his behavior, or talking to one another.

incoherent thought   illogical thinking, peculiar associations between ideas, belief in supernatural forces.

odd behavior   such as **catatonia** (long periods with no movement), marked impairment of personal hygiene, or talking in rhymes.

About 1% of the population is clearly schizophrenic, and about another 2 or 3% display schizophrenic symptoms that are of insufficient severity or frequency to make the diagnosis unambiguous (Snyder, 1986). Many schizophrenics display long periods of relative normality between periods of active psychosis. The incidence of schizophrenia is the same in all racial and social classes and in all parts of the world, despite wide variations in political, social, and economic climate (Strömgren, 1987).

The Genetics of Schizophrenia

In the first half of this century, the cloak of mysticism began to be removed from mental illness by a series of studies that clearly established that schizophrenia has a genetic basis. First, it was discovered that schizophrenia runs in families. Although only about 1% of the population is diagnosed as schizophrenic, the probability of schizophrenia occurring in the close biological relatives of a schizophrenic (i.e., parents, children, or siblings) was found to be between 5 and 15%. Because these percentages were found to be about the same in children who had been adopted into healthy families as babies (e.g., Kendler & Gruenberg, 1984; Rosenthal, Wender, Kety, Welner, & Schulsinger, 1980), it was concluded that the tendency for schizophrenia to run in families was largely genetic.

Further evidence of schizophrenia's genetic basis has come from numerous studies reporting higher concordance rates for schizophrenia in *monozygotic* (identical) twins than in dizygotic (fraternal) twins (e.g., Kallman, 1946). You may recall from Chapter 2 that monozygotic twins are those with identical genes, and dizygotic twins are no more genetically related than any two *siblings* (brothers and sisters). If a schizophrenic is a monozygotic twin, the probability of his or her twin also being schizophrenic is about 45%, whereas if the schizophrenic is a dizygotic twin, the probability falls to the usual sibling baseline of between 5 and 15% (see Holzman & Matthysse, 1990). The 45% concordance rate for schizophrenia in monozygotic twins makes two important points. First, it proves that schizophrenia has a genetic basis; an individual with the same genes as a schizophrenic is 45 times more likely to become a schizophrenic than a person with no schizophrenic relatives (45% versus 1%). Second, it proves that genetics is not the entire story—if it were, the concordance rate would be 100 percent. Although it is clear that environmental factors contribute to the development of schizophrenia, it is not at all clear what these environmental factors are. Hypotheses that prenatal, natal, or childhood trauma can influence the development of schizophrenia have yet to receive strong support. The fact that *linkage studies* (see Chapter 2) have not been successful in locating a schizophrenia gene on a particular chromosome (see Risch, 1990) suggests that schizophrenia is influenced by genes on more than one chromosome.

Evidence of schizophrenia's genetic basis has done much to counteract the tendency to think of mental illness as supernatural. It is difficult to imagine how genes, which exert their effects by controlling protein and peptide synthesis, could lead to a disorder that is not itself fundamentally biochemical.

The Discovery of the First Two Antischizophrenic Drugs

The first major breakthrough in the study of the biochemistry of schizophrenia was the accidental discovery in the early 1950s of the first antischizophrenic drug, **chlorpromazine.** Chlorpromazine was first developed by a French drug company as an antihistamine. In 1950, a French surgeon noticed that chlorpromazine given prior to surgery to counteract swelling had a calming effect on his patients, and he suggested that it might be useful for calming difficult-to-manage psychotic patients. This suggestion proved to be incorrect, but the clinical trials that were triggered by it led to an important chance discovery: Exposure to high levels of chlorpromazine for 2 weeks or more produced a specific alleviation of the schizophrenic symptoms of some patients. Agitated schizophrenic patients were calmed by chlorpromazine, but catatonic or emotionally blunt schizophrenics were activated. Don't get the idea that the chlorpromazine cured schizophrenia. It didn't. But in many cases, it reduced the severity of schizophrenic symptoms enough to allow institutionalized patients to be discharged.

An important feature of the antischizophrenic effect of chlorpromazine — the importance of which will become more apparent in the following paragraphs — is that it is frequently associated with motor effects like those of Parkinson's disease. At about the same time that the chlorpromazine regimen begins to take effect on the schizophrenic symptoms (e.g., in 2 or 3 weeks), it often begins to elicit mild tremors, muscular rigidity, and a general decrease in voluntary movement.

In the early 1950s, at the same time that the early research on chlorpromazine was going on, an American psychiatrist became interested in reports that an extract of the snakeroot plant had long been used in India for the treatment of mental illness. He gave **reserpine,** the active ingredient of the snakeroot plant, to his schizophrenic patients and confirmed its antischizophrenic action. Although the chemical structure of reserpine is unlike that of chlorpromazine, its antischizophrenic effect is similar to that of chlorpromazine in two important respects: it is not manifested until the patient has been medicated for 2 or 3 weeks, and it is typically associated with parkinsonian side effects. This suggested that chlorpromazine and reserpine were acting through the same mechanism, one that was related to Parkinson's disease. Reserpine is no longer used in the treatment of schizophrenia because it produces a precipitous decline in blood pressure at antischizophrenic doses.

The Dopamine Theory of Schizophrenia

Paradoxically, the next major breakthrough in the study of schizophrenia came from research on Parkinson's disease. In 1960, it was reported that the normally dopamine-rich *striatums* of persons dying of Parkinson's disease had little dopamine (Ehringer & Hornykiewicz, 1960). This finding suggested that a disruption of dopaminergic transmission might produce Parkinson's disease, and because of the relation between Parkinson's symptoms and antischizophrenic effects, it suggested that antischizophrenic drug effects might be produced in the same way. Thus, the *dopamine theory of schizophrenia* was born—the theory that schizophrenia is caused by an excess of activity at dopaminergic synapses, and conversely that antischizophrenic drugs exert their effects by decreasing dopaminergic activity.

Lending instant support to the dopamine theory of schizophrenia were two already well-established facts. First, the antischizophrenic drug reserpine was known to be a dopamine *antagonist*—it depletes the brain of dopamine and other monoamines. Second, drugs, such as amphetamine, cocaine, methylphenidate, and L-DOPA, which trigger schizophrenic episodes in normal subjects (see Chapter 12), were known to be dopamine *agonists*—they increase the activity of dopamine and other monoamines by increasing their release, by blocking their reuptake, or both.

Dopamine Receptors and Antischizophrenic Drugs

In 1963, Carlsson and Lindqvist attempted to test the dopamine theory of schizophrenia in rats by assessing the effects of chlorpromazine on dopamine and its metabolites, the chemicals that are created when a substance is metabolized (broken down). They expected to find that chlorpromazine, like reserpine, depletes the brain of dopamine, but they didn't. The levels of both norepinephrine and dopamine were unchanged by chlorpromazine, and the levels of the metabolites of both norepinephrine and dopamine were increased. These findings, at first sight, appeared to be inconsistent with the dopamine theory of schizophrenia, but Carlsson and Lindqvist interpreted them in the following manner. They concluded that both chlorpromazine and reserpine produce antischizophrenic effects by antagonizing transmission at dopamine synapses, but that they do it in different ways—reserpine by depleting the brain of dopamine and chlorpromazine by binding to dopamine receptors. They argued that chlorpromazine is a **false transmitter** at dopamine synapses; that is, that it binds to dopamine receptors without activating them, and in so doing, keeps dopamine from activating them. They further postulated that the lack of activity at the postsynaptic dopamine receptor sent a feedback signal to the presynaptic cell to increase its release of dopamine and that the excess dopamine released into the synapse was quickly metabolized. This explained why the dopamine levels stayed about the same and why the levels of its metabolites increased. Carlsson and Lindqvist's findings and their interpretation of them are illustrated in Figure 17.14.

In the mid-1970s, Snyder and his colleagues (Creese, Burt, & Snyder, 1976; Snyder, 1976) assessed the degree to which various antischizophrenic drugs bind to dopamine receptors. First, they added radioactively labeled dopamine to samples of dopamine-receptor-rich neural membrane obtained

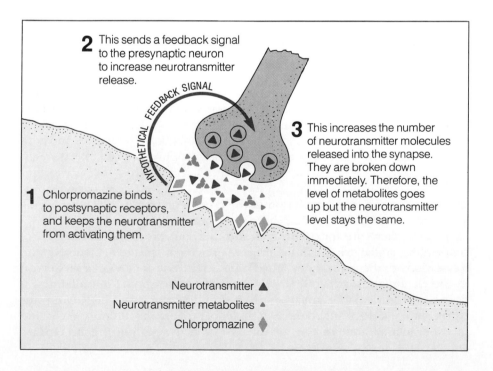

FIGURE 17.14

The effects of chlorpromazine on the levels of dopamine and its metabolites, and an interpretation of these effects.

from the striatums of calves' brains. Then, they "washed" away the unbound dopamine molecules from the samples and measured the amount of radioactivity left in them. The amount of remaining radioactivity in each sample provided a measure of the number of dopamine receptors in it. Next, Snyder and his colleagues estimated the degree to which various drugs bind to these dopamine receptors by measuring each drugs' ability to block the binding of radioactive dopamine. The rationale for their method was that drugs with a high affinity for dopamine receptors would leave fewer sites available for the dopamine. In general, they found that chlorpromazine and the other effective antischizophrenic drugs that had been developed by that time had a high affinity for dopamine receptors, whereas ineffective antischizophrenic drugs had a low affinity. There was, however, one embarrassing exception: the antischizophrenic drug **haloperidol.** Although haloperidol is an extremely potent antischizophrenic drug, it bound to relatively few dopamine receptors. As you might imagine, Snyder and his colleagues, who are strong advocates of the dopamine theory of schizophrenia, were not exactly overjoyed with this haloperidol finding; however, subsequent research resolved the inconsistency.

The answer to the haloperidol puzzle lay in the discovery that dopamine binds to two different kinds of receptor subtypes, called D_1 and D_2 receptors. It turned out that chlorpromazine and the other antischizophrenic drugs in the same chemical class (the **phenothiazines)** all bind effectively to both D_1 and D_2 receptors, whereas haloperidol and the other antischizophrenic drugs in its chemical class (the **butyrophenones)** all bind with great potency to D_2 receptors, but not to D_1 receptors. This key finding suggested an important revision in the dopamine theory of schizophrenia. The fact that potent antischizophrenic drugs such as haloperidol selectively bound to only D_2 receptors suggested that schizophrenia is caused by hyperactivity specifically at D_2 receptors, rather than at dopamine receptors in general. Snyder and his colleagues (see Snyder, 1978) subsequently confirmed their D_2 receptor modification of the dopamine theory by assessing the degree to which the **neuroleptics** (antischizophrenic drugs) that were in current use bound to D_2 receptors. As illustrated in Figure 17.15, they found that the degree to which the neuroleptics bound to D_2 receptors accurately predicted their effectiveness in suppressing schizophrenic symptoms. For example, they found that the butyrophenone *spiroperidol* had the greatest affinity for D_2 receptors and the most potent antischizophrenic effect.

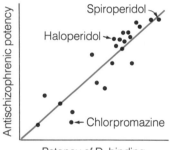

FIGURE 17.15

The positive correlation between the ability of various neuroleptics to bind to D_2 receptors and their clinical potency. (Adapted from Snyder, 1978).

Current Research on the Dopamine Theory of Schizophrenia

The major events in the evolution of the dopamine theory of schizophrenia are summarized in Table 17.2. But this evolution is not over yet—not by a long shot. There are four thorny questions about the dopamine theory of schizophrenia that are still in the process of being resolved. (1) One of them has to do with the neuroleptic, **clozapine.** Clozapine is particularly effective in the treatment of schizophrenia, yet unlike conventional neuroleptics, it does not produce parkinsonian side effects; it does not have a high affinity for D_2 receptors; it does not counteract the effects of amphetamine and cocaine in experimental animals (see Chapter 6); and it does not induce **tardive**

Table 17.2 The Key Events That Led to the Development and Refinement of the Dopamine Theory of Schizophrenia

Early 1950s	The antischizophrenic effects of both chlorpromazine and reserpine were observed to be related to parkinsonian side effects.
Late 1950s	The brains of recently deceased Parkinson's patients were found to have little dopamine.
Early 1960s	It was hypothesized that schizophrenia is caused by excessive activity at dopaminergic synapses.
1960s and 70s	Various dopamine agonists were shown to induce schizophrenic symptoms.
Mid 1960s	It was discovered that chlorpromazine and other clinically effective neuroleptics are false transmitters at dopamine synapses.
Mid 1970s	The dopamine-receptor binding of phenothiazines, but not of butyrophenones, was found to be roughly correlated with their antischizophrenic potency.
Late 1970s	The binding of antischizophrenic drugs to D_2 receptors was found to be highly correlated with their antischizophrenic potency.
Currently	The D_2-receptor modification of the dopamine theory is the dominant theory of schizophrenia; schizophrenia is thought to be produced by excessive activity at D_2 receptors.
Future	The recent discovery of D_3 receptors is likely to lead to major revisions of the dopamine theory.

dyskinesia, an incurable motor disorder that develops in some patients who have been maintained on conventional neuroleptics for many years (see Kane et al., 1988; Meltzer et al., 1990; Owen et al., 1989). Because clozapine produces a dangerous reduction of *leucocytes* in a small percentage of patients, it is prescribed for only those schizophrenics who have not responded to conventional neuroleptics and whose leucocyte count remains at normal levels throughout therapy. The following are the three other remaining questions about the dopamine theory of schizophrenia: (2) Where in the brain are the dopamine receptors that are involved in schizophrenia? (3) Why do antischizophrenic drugs help some schizophrenics and not others? (4) And why does it usually take weeks for the antischizophrenic effects of the neuroleptic drugs to be manifested when they block transmission at dopamine synapses almost immediately?

Tentative answers to these four questions are currently emerging. (1) An explanation of the antischizophrenic action of clozapine is emerging from the recent discovery of a third dopamine receptor subtype: the D_3 receptor (Sokoloff et al., 1990). Conventional neuroleptics have a higher affinity for D_2 receptors than for D_3 receptors, whereas clozapine binds equally to both. This has led to the suggestion that perhaps D_3 receptors mediate antischizophrenic drug effects (see Stevens, 1991). (2) The D_3 hypothesis suggests that the dopamine receptors that are involved in schizophrenia are located in the *limbic system*—in contrast to D_2 receptors, which are mainly in motor structures,

D_3 receptors are mainly in limbic structures. (3) It has been suggested that some schizophrenics are helped more than others by antischizophrenic drugs because there are two kinds of schizophrenia (Carpenter, Heinrichs, & Alphs, 1985): one characterized by **positive schizophrenic symptoms,** such as incoherence, hallucinations, and delusions, which are assumed to be caused by increased neural activity, and one characterized by **negative schizophrenic symptoms,** such as blunt affect, catatonia, and poverty of speech, which are assumed to be caused by decreased neural activity. It has been suggested that dopamine hyperactivity produces the positive symptoms and that the negative symptoms are associated with structural abnormalities (Roberts, 1990; Suddath et al., 1990). Accordingly, the schizophrenics with a predominance of positive symptoms benefit most from dopamine blockers. (4) It has been argued that the long delay in therapeutic effects following the onset of neuroleptic drug treatment indicates that the dopamine receptor blockade is not the specific mechanism by which schizophrenic symptoms are alleviated. It appears that the blockade of dopamine receptors triggers some slow-developing compensatory change in the brain that is the key mediator of the therapeutic effect.

AFFECTIVE DISORDERS

All of us have experienced depression. Depression is a normal reaction to grievous loss—the loss of a loved one, the loss of self-esteem, the loss of important personal possessions, or the loss of health. However, there are people whose tendency toward depression is out of all proportion. These people repeatedly fall into the depths of despair, often for no apparent reason, and their depression can be so extreme that it is almost impossible for them to meet the essential requirements of their daily lives—to keep a job, to maintain social contacts, or even to maintain an acceptable level of personal hygiene. It is these people who are said to be suffering from the psychiatric disorder of **depression.**

Many people who suffer from periods of recurring depression also experience periods of mania. **Mania** is at the other end of the scale of mood. During periods of mild mania, people are talkative, energetic, impulsive, positive, and very confident. In this state, they can be effective at certain jobs, and they can be great fun to be with. But when their mania becomes full-blown, it is quite a different story. The florid manic often awakens in a state of unbridled enthusiasm, with an outflow of incessant chatter that careens nonstop from topic to topic. The world is in the palm of her or his hand. No task is too difficult. No goal is unattainable. This confidence and grandiosity, coupled with high energy, distractibility, and a leap-before-you-look impulsiveness, result in a continual series of disasters. Mania leaves behind it a trail of unfinished projects, unpaid bills, and broken relationships.

Not all depressive patients experience periods of mania. The 60% that do not are said to suffer from **unipolar affective disorder;** the 40% that do are said to suffer from **bipolar affective disorder.** Although there is considerable variability, the periods of depression usually predominate in bipolar affective disorder; most periods of mania last a few days to a few weeks, whereas periods of depression often last for months. About 5% of men and 8% of women suffer from affective disorders. About 10% of these commit suicide.

The Genetics of Affective Disorders

Like schizophrenia, affective disorders have been shown to run in families. About 25% of patients with unipolar affective disorder and 50% of those with bipolar affective disorder have parents with either unipolar or bipolar affective disorder. Twin studies and studies of adoptees have shown that this tendency for affective disorders to run in families is in part attributable to genetic factors. Twin studies of bipolar affective disorder suggest a concordance rate of about 70% for identical twins and 20% for fraternal twins, whether they are reared together or apart (Winokur, 1978). The concordance rates for unipolar affective disorder are lower. Biological relatives of adoptees with bipolar affective disorder are six times more likely to commit suicide than are their adoptive relatives (Kety, 1979).

The Discovery of Antidepressant Drugs: The Monoamine Oxidase Inhibitors

Iproniazid, the first antidepressant drug, was originally developed for the treatment of tuberculosis, and as such it proved to be a dismal flop. However, interest in the antidepressant potential of iproniazid was kindled by the observation that iproniazid left patients with tuberculosis less depressed about their disorder, although otherwise unimproved. As a result, iproniazid was tested on a mixed group of psychiatric patients and was found to be effective against depression. It was first marketed as an antidepressant in 1957.

Iproniazid is a monoamine agonist; it increases activity at monoamine synapses by inhibiting the activity of *monoamine oxidase* (MAO), the enzyme that breaks down monoamine neurotransmitters in the cytoplasm of the neuron. Iproniazid and the other **MAO inhibitors** have several side effects; the most dangerous is known as the **cheese effect.** Foods such as cheese, wine, and pickles contain an amine called *tyramine,* which is a potent elevator of blood pressure. Normally, these foods have little effect on blood pressure because tyramine is rapidly *metabolized* (broken down) in the liver by MAO. Because people who take MAO inhibitors have difficulty metabolizing tyramine, they run the risk of strokes caused by great surges in blood pressure if they consume tyramine-rich foods.

The Tricyclic Antidepressants

The **tricyclic antidepressants** are so named because of their antidepressant action and because their chemical structures all include a three-ring chain. **Imipramine,** the first tricyclic antidepressant, was initially thought to be an antischizophrenic drug. However, when its effects on a mixed sample of psychiatric patients were assessed, its antidepressant effects were immediately obvious. After several confirmations of this discovery, imipramine was marketed as an alternative to the MAO-inhibitor antidepressants.

Despite the fact that they belong to different drug classes, iproniazid (MAO inhibitor) and imipramine (tricyclic antidepressant) have similar effects on behavior. Both drugs produce a mild degree of sedation and a general alleviation of depressive symptoms, which is typically not apparent until 2 or 3 weeks after the beginning of drug therapy.

The Monoamine Hypothesis of Depression

Because the behavioral effects of the tricyclic antidepressants are similar to those of the MAO inhibitors, it was thought that the tricyclics might also act on monoamine oxidase. When this turned out not to be the case, it was assumed that tricyclics must increase the release of monoamine neurotransmitters in some other way. But this did not prove to be the case either. How then do the tricyclics exert their antidepressant effect?

In the late 1950s, it was known that acetylcholinesterase terminates the action of acetylcholine in the synapse, and it was assumed that all neurotransmitters had a similar deactivation mechanism. However, over the ensuing years, each of the monoamine and amino acid neurotransmitters was shown to be deactivated, not by enzymatic degradation, but by reuptake into the presynaptic neuron. The discovery that reuptake is the primary mechanism of deactivation in monoaminergic neurons suggested that tricyclic antidepressants might function as monoamine agonists by blocking monoamine reuptake. Subsequent experiments have confirmed this hypothesis. All effective tricyclic antidepressants have been found to inhibit the reuptake of both *serotonin* and *norepinephrine*. Many tricyclic antidepressants also inhibit the reuptake of dopamine, but because some of the more effective tricyclic antidepressants have no effect at all on dopamine reuptake, it has been generally assumed that depression is not a disorder of the dopamine system. Thus was born the *monoamine theory of depression*—the theory that depression is caused by underactivity at noradrenergic and serotonergic synapses and that antidepressant drugs act by increasing noradrenergic and serotonergic effects. Consistent with this theory is the observation that many patients taking the monoamine antagonist reserpine for high blood pressure became deeply depressed and the finding that the cerebrospinal fluid of some severely depressed patients has high levels of serotonin metabolites (Åsberg, Träskman, & Thorén, 1976).

Challenges to the Monoamine Theory of Depression

Although there is considerable evidence linking serotonergic and noradrenergic effects with depression, there are a number of serious challenges still faced by the theory. The following are three of them. First, the ability of particular tricyclic antidepressants to block serotonin and norepinephrine reuptake is not highly correlated with their ability to alleviate depression. Second, although both the MAO inhibitors and the tricyclic antidepressants agonize serotonergic and noradrenergic transmission almost immediately, therapeutic effects are usually not seen for at least 2 or 3 weeks. The answer to this problem may lie in a phenomenon called *down regulation*. In rats, it has been shown that the high levels of serotonin and norepinephrine produced by antidepressant drugs gradually lead to a reduction in the number of some noradrenergic and serotonergic receptor subtypes. Because the time course of this down regulation in rats is similar to the time course of the development of antidepressant effects in humans, it has been suggested that down regulation might be the mechanism of antidepressant drug action. The third challenge faced by the monoaminergic theory of depression is its inability to account for the remarkable therapeutic effects of lithium.

Lithium: The Wonder Metal

The discovery of the ability of **lithium,** a simple metallic ion, to block mania is yet another important pharmacological breakthrough that was made by accident. An Australian psychiatrist, John Cade, in attempting to test his theory that the urine of manic patients contains a chemical that causes mania, mixed uric acid with lithium to form a soluble injectable salt. He injected it into a group of guinea pigs, and as a control for the effects of the lithium, he injected lithium salt into another group. Instead of inducing mania, the uric acid solution seemed to calm the guinea pigs. Because the effect of the lithium control injections was as great as the uric-acid-plus-lithium injections, Cade concluded that lithium, not uric acid, was the calming agent. He then set out to confirm this conclusion in human patients. In retrospect, Cade's conclusion was incredibly foolish. We know now that at the doses used by Cade, lithium salts produce extreme nausea. To Cade's untrained eye, his subjects' inactivity may have looked like calmness, but they weren't calm; they were ill. Be that as it may, flushed with what he thought was the success of his guinea pig experiments, Cade tried the lithium on a group of 10 manic patients, and it proved remarkably effective.

Cade reported lithium's ability to alleviate mania in 1949, but there was little reaction to his report. It was not replicated until 1954 (Schou, Juel-Nielsen, Stromberg, & Voldby, 1954), and lithium was not marketed for the treatment of mania until the mid-1960s. One reason for the relatively slow reaction to Cade's report was that Cade was not a respected scientist; another was that few drug companies were interested in spending millions of dollars to study the therapeutic potential of a simple metallic ion, which could not be protected by a patent.

The therapeutic potential of lithium was not fully appreciated until the late 1960s, when two large-scale studies (Angst, Weis, Grof, Baastrup, & Schou, 1970; Baastrup & Schou, 1967) found that lithium is also effective against depression. Today, lithium is the treatment of choice for bipolar affective disorder.

The fact that both depression and mania are alleviated by lithium suggests that they are symptoms of the same underlying neurochemical defect. Although lithium has been shown to influence norepinephrine and serotonin in a variety of ways (Gerbino, Oleshansky, & Gershon, 1978), none has yet been directly linked to its therapeutic action.

Conclusion

In this chapter, you have encountered a number of different biological approaches to the study of emotion. The chapter began by introducing several fundamental concepts (Section 17.1) and discussing two of the most widely studied correlates of emotional experience: autonomic nervous system activity (Section 17.2) and facial expression (Section 17.3). Then, the chapter gradually began to shift its focus to clinical issues, with discussions of brain damage and emotion (Section 17.4); stress (Section 17.5); aggression, defense, and anxiety (Section 17.6); and finally the biopsychology of schizophrenia and affective disorders (Section 17.7).

It is fitting for me to be writing the last few words of a chapter on emotion at a time that is such an emotional one. You and I have taken a long journey together, and like the end of all long journeys, good or bad, the end of this one is suffused with emotion. I feel relieved to be achieving the goal that I set out to achieve six long years ago, and I am also excited by the knowledge that now many students will be able to share my efforts with me.

It is a peculiar journey that you and I have shared. We have experienced much together, but our mutual experiences transcend space and time. Right now, I am looking out over the Pacific Ocean as the red-winged black birds trill at my backyard feeder. It is 7:00 A.M. on Easter Sunday, 1992. Where and when are you?

Food for Thought

1. With practice, you could become an expert in the production and recognition of facial expression. How could you earn a living with these skills?
2. Does the concept of target sites have any relevance to human aggression, defense, and play fighting?
3. Blunder often plays an important role in scientific inquiry. Discuss this with respect to the development of drugs for the treatment of schizophrenia and affective disorders.

KEY TERMS

Adrenal cortex. The cortex of the adrenal gland; both adrenal cortices release glucocorticoids in response to stressors.

Adrenal medulla. The core of the adrenal glands; both adrenal medullas release epinephrine and norepinephrine in response to stressors.

Alpha male. The dominant male of a colony.

Antibodies. Proteins that bind specifically to antigens; antibodies deactivate invading microorganisms and tag them for phagocytosis.

Antigens. Proteins on the surface of foreign microorganisms that are different from the proteins of the body; specific antigens trigger the production of specific antibodies that bind to them.

Anxiety. The subjective emotional state that is associated with chronic threat.

Anxiety disorder. A feeling of anxiety that is so extreme and so pervasive that it disrupts normal functioning; panic attacks, phobias, and generalized anxiety are anxiety disorders.

Aprosodia. The lack of emotional tone in one's speech.

B cells. One class of lymphocytes; when they encounter an antigen, they begin to manufacture antibodies against it.

Benzodiazepines. The major class of anxiolytic drugs; for example, chlordiazepoxide (Librium) and diazepam (Valium).

Bipolar affective disorder. A depressive condition in which the patient experiences periods of mania.

Boxing. A defensive movement that rats use to defend themselves from lateral attack; they rear up and fend the attacker off with pushing movements of their forepaws.

Buspirone. An effective nonbenzodiazepine anxiolytic drug; unlike benzodiazepine anxiolytics, it does not bind to GABA receptors, it does not produce sedation or withdrawal effects, and it does not produce anxiolytic effects in many animal models.

Butyrophenones. One common class of antischizophrenic drugs (e.g., haloperidol); they bind primarily to D_2 receptors.

Cannon-Bard theory. The theory that emotional experience and emotional expression are parallel processes that have no direct causal relation.

Cheese effect. Refers to large surges in blood pressure that occur when individuals taking MAO inhibitors consume tyramine-rich foods.

Chlorpromazine. One of the first antischizophrenic drugs; a false transmitter at dopamine receptors.

Clozapine. A drug that is particularly effective in the treatment of schizophrenia but does not produce parkinsonian side effects and tardive dyskinesia, which are side effects of conventional neuroleptics.

Control-question technique. A lie-detection technique in which the polygrapher compares the responses to target questions (Did you steal the purse?) with the responses to control questions (What is your name?).

Decerebrate. Lacking cerebral hemispheres.

Decorticate. Lacking a cortex.

Defensive burying. A defensive coping behavior that is commonly used by rats; they spray material at threatening animals (e.g., snakes) and dangerous objects (e.g., traps) with their forepaws.

Depression. A normal reaction to grievous loss; when it is excessive and disruptive and is not accompanied by periods of mania, it is referred to as *unipolar affective disorder*.

Directed-facial-action method. A method of studying physiological correlates of emotion; subjects are instructed to make various facial expressions while their physiological activity is being recorded.

Duchenne smile. A genuine smile, which includes contraction of the *orbicularis oculi* muscles.

Elevated-plus-maze. A four-armed cross-shaped elevated maze with two enclosed arms and two exposed arms; rats that have been injected with a benzodiazepine anxiolytic spend more time than usual on the exposed arms.

Ethoexperimental approach. The study of behavior in seminatural laboratory environments by the careful analysis of videotaped sequences of behavior.

Facial feedback hypothesis. The hypothesis that our facial expressions can influence how we feel.

False transmitter. A chemical that binds to a synaptic receptor without activating it, and in so doing it blocks the action of the normal receptor; chlorpromazine is a false transmitter at dopamine receptors.

Fear. The emotion that is normally elicited by the presence or expectation of threatening stimuli; fear usually motivates adaptive reactions to the threatening stimuli.

Gastric ulcers. Lesions to the lining of the stomach and duodenum; gastric ulcers are a common symptom of stress.

General adaptation syndrome. The pattern of physiological responses (e.g., glucocorticoid release) that is produced by exposure to physical and psychological stressors.

Glucocorticoids. Steroid hormones that are released from the adrenal cortex in response to stressors; they promote mobilization of energy resources, combat inflammation, and facilitate healing.

Guilty-knowledge technique. A polygraphic technique in which the polygrapher records ANS responses to control and crime-related information known only to the criminal.

Haloperidol. An effective antischizophrenic drug; a butyrophenone.

Hormone-dependent aggression. Aggression that is dependent on hormones; social and maternal aggression.

Imipramine. The first tricyclic antidepressant drug.

Immune system. The system that identifies infectious microorganisms and destroys them.

Iproniazid. The first antidepressant drug.

James-Lange theory. The theory that the experience of a particular emotion results from the brain's perception of the pattern of ANS activation.

Kluver-Bucy syndrome. A pattern of complex behavioral changes (e.g., tameness and hypersexuality) that is induced in several species by bilateral damage to the anterior temporal lobes.

Lateral attack. The posture of rat social aggression; the attacking rat moves sideways toward the defender so that it is in a position to lunge around the defender and deliver a bite to its back.

Leucocytes. The most important cells in the immune system, commonly referred to as *white blood cells*.

Limbic system. A collection of interconnected nuclei and tracts that borders on the thalamus; limbic structures (e.g., the amygdala) are thought to play a role in emotion.

Lithium. A metallic ion used in the treatment of mania and depression.

Lymphocytes. A class of leucocytes; lymphocytes destroy invading microorganisms by reacting to their antigens.

Mania. A mental disorder in which the patient is impulsive, over-confident, highly energetic, and distractable. .

MAO inhibitors. Drugs that increase the level of monoamine neurotransmitters by inhibiting the action of monoamine oxidase.

Maternal aggression. Behavior that nursing mothers direct at intruders; it looks like social aggression, but its function is to defend the young.

Mock-crime procedure. A method of studying the effectiveness of polygraphy; some of the subjects participate in a mock crime and then try to mislead a polygrapher.

Negative schizophrenic symptoms. Schizophrenic symptoms such as blunt affect, catatonia, and poverty of speech.

Neuroleptics. Drugs that suppress schizophrenic symptoms.

Neuroses. Psychological disorders that do not require hospitalization or some comparable form of care; for example, anxiety disorders.

Phagocytosis. Destroying dead tissue and invading microorganisms by consuming them; some leucocytes are phagocytes.

Phenothiazines. One common class of antischizophrenic drugs (e.g., chlorpromazine); they bind effectively to both D_1 and D_2 receptors.

Polygraphy. A method of lie detection that is based on recording ANS activity (e.g., heart rate, skin conductance, respiration) during questioning.

Positive schizophrenic symptoms. Schizophrenic symptoms such as incoherence, hallucinations, and delusions.

Prosody. Tone of voice.

Psychoneuroimmunology. A field of biopsychology that focuses on the study of the effects of psychological factors on the immune system and the mediation of these effects by the neuroendocrine system.

Psychoses. The most serious psychological disorders, which require hospitalization or some comparable form of care; for example, schizophrenia and affective disorders.

Psychosomatic disorders. Organic (physical) disorders that are caused by experiential (psychological) factors.

Psychosurgery. The destruction of part of the brain for the purpose of changing behavior.

Relived-emotion method. A method of studying physiological correlates of emotion; subjects are asked to think of past emotional experiences while their physiological activity is being recorded.

Reserpine. The active ingredient of the snakeroot plant; it has antischizophrenic effects and is a monoamine antagonist.

Risk assessment. A form of defensive information-gathering behavior; for example, rats that have been frightened by a cat scan the surrounding environment before they emerge from their burrows.

Sham rage. The exaggerated, poorly directed aggressive responses of decorticate animals.

Shock-elicited aggression. When two rats receive multiple electric shocks through the floor of a small chamber, they rear up on their hind legs and direct boxing movements with their forepaws at one another; such behavior is, in fact, defensive.

Stress. The physiological response to chronic physical or psychological threat.

T cells. A class of lymphocytes that mature in the thymus; they do not form antibodies, but they have antibody-like molecules that bind to antigens.

Tardive dyskinesia. An incurable motor disorder that develops in patients who have been maintained on conventional neuroleptics for many years.

Target-site concept. The idea that many of the complex sequences of attack and defense that are displayed by various animals can be reduced to the fact that they are trying to attack a specific site on the other animal's body to protect a specific site on their own, or both.

Tricyclic antidepressants. Drugs with an antidepressant action and a three-ring structure.

Unipolar affective disorder. A depressive disorder in which the patient does not experience periods of mania.

ADDITIONAL READING

The following four references provide excellent, up-to-date reviews of the autonomic nervous system and emotion, facial expression and emotion, stress and human immune function, and ethoexperimental animal models of anxiety, respectively.

Levenson, R. W. (1992). Autonomic nervous system differences among emotions. *Psychological Science, 3,* 23–27.

Ekman, P. (1992). Facial expressions of emotion: New findings, new questions. *Psychological Science, 3,* 34–38.

O'Leary, A. (1990). Stress, emotion, and human immune function. *Psychological Bulletin, 108,* 363–382.

Blanchard, D. C., Blanchard, R. J., & Rodgers, R. J. (1991). Risk assessment and animal models of anxiety. *Animal Models in Psychopharmacology: Advances in Pharmacological Sciences.* Basel: Birkhauser Verlag.

EPILOGUE

Biopsychology is a fascinating discipline. I have tried to let you see this for yourself by peeling away its complexities and serving up the fundamentals with big helpings of clear writing, good humor, and personal implication. If you liked my approach, let your instructor know, so that it can benefit future students.

Like good friends, we have shared good times and bad. We have shared the fun and wonder of Rhonda the dextrous cashier, the Nads basketball team, people who rarely sleep, the MAMAWAWA, split brains, Freddie the Finn, and neurotransplantation. And together we have been touched by the personal tragedies of Alzheimer's disease, MPTP poisoning, the lost mariner, H.M., and the man who mistook his wife for a hat. Thank you for allowing me to share *Biopsychology* with you. I wish you good fortune.

If you have any comments, questions, or suggestions, please write to me (Department of Psychology, University of British Columbia, Vancouver, B.C., Canada V6T IZ4)—or better yet, if you are ever on the U.B.C. campus, stop by for a visit.

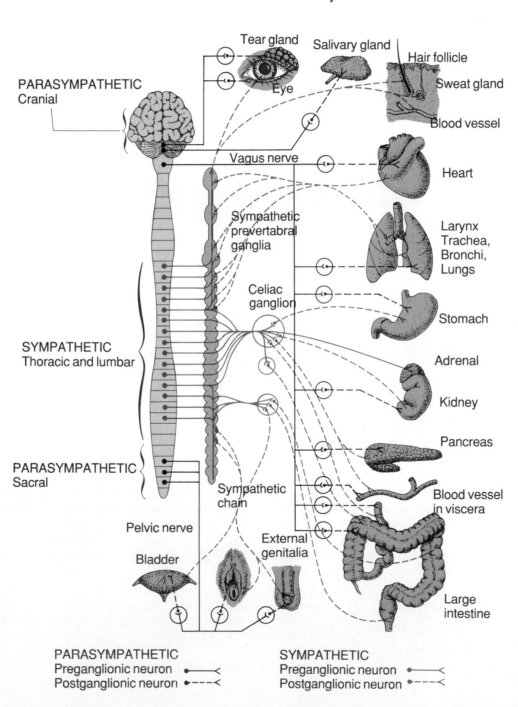

Tear gland

Salivary gland

Hair follicle

PARASYMPATHETIC
Cranial

Eye

Sweat gland

Blood vessel

Vagus nerve

Heart

Sympathetic
prevertabral
ganglia

Larynx
Trachea,
Bronchi,
Lungs

Celiac
ganglion

Stomach

SYMPATHETIC
Thoracic and lumbar

Adrenal

Kidney

Pancreas

PARASYMPATHETIC
Sacral

Blood vessel
in viscera

Sympathetic
chain

Pelvic nerve

External
genitalia

Bladder

Large
intestine

PARASYMPATHETIC
Preganglionic neuron
Postganglionic neuron

SYMPATHETIC
Preganglionic neuron
Postganglionic neuron

617

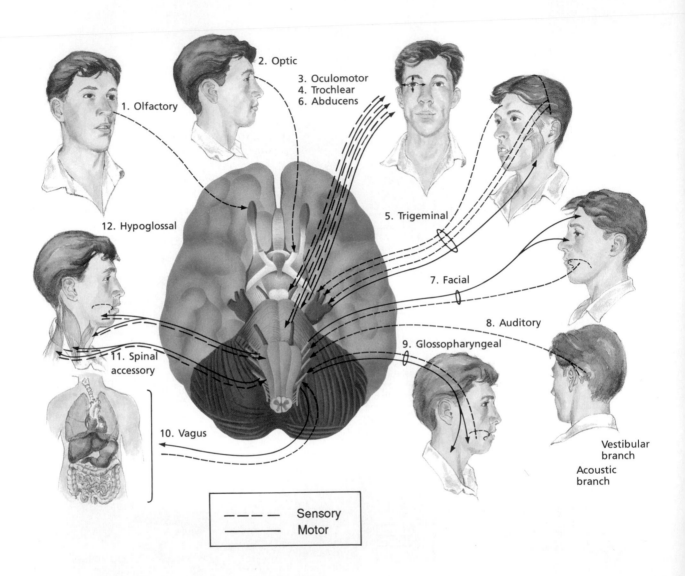

1. Olfactory
2. Optic
3. Oculomotor
4. Trochlear
6. Abducens
5. Trigeminal
7. Facial
8. Auditory
9. Glossopharyngeal
10. Vagus
11. Spinal accessory
12. Hypoglossal

Vestibular branch
Acoustic branch

- - - - Sensory
———— Motor

Functions of the Cranial Nerves

Number	Name	General Function	Specific Functions
1	Olfactory	Sensory	Smell
2	Optic	Sensory	Vision
3	Oculomotor	Motor Sensory	Eye movement and pupillary constriction Sensory signals from certain eye muscles
4	Trochlear	Motor Sensory	Eye movement Sensory signals from certain eye muscles
5	Trigeminal	Sensory Motor	Facial sensations Chewing
6	Abducens	Motor Sensory	Eye movement Sensory signals from certain eye muscles
7	Facial	Sensory Motor	Taste from anterior two-thirds of tongue Facial expression, secretion of tears, salivation, cranial blood vessel dilation
8	Auditory-Vestibular	Sensory	Audition; sensory signals from the organs of balance in the inner ear
9	Glossopharyngeal	Sensory Motor	Taste from posterior third of the tongue Salivation, swallowing
10	Vagus	Sensory Motor	Sensations from abdominal and thoracic organs Control over abdominal and thoracic organs and muscles of the throat
11	Spinal Accessory	Motor Sensory	Movement of neck, shoulders, and head Sensory signals from muscles of the neck
12	Hypoglossal	Motor Sensory	Tongue movements Sensory signals from tongue muscles

Nuclei of the Thalmus

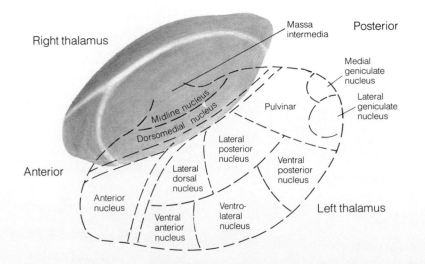

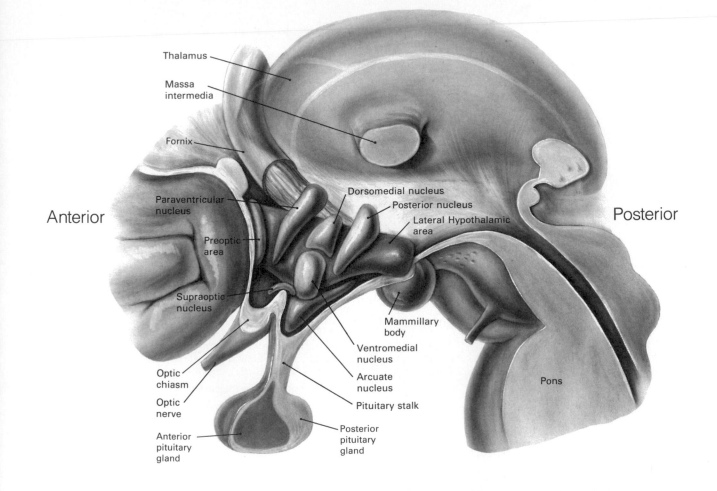

Thalamus

Massa intermedia

Fornix

Paraventricular nucleus

Preoptic area

Supraoptic nucleus

Anterior

Optic chiasm

Optic nerve

Anterior pituitary gland

Dorsomedial nucleus

Posterior nucleus

Lateral Hypothalamic area

Posterior

Mammillary body

Ventromedial nucleus

Arcuate nucleus

Pituitary stalk

Posterior pituitary gland

Pons

APPENDIX VI
Some of the Peptides That Have Been Found in Mammalian Neurons

Pituitary Peptides

Corticotropin

Growth hormone

Lipotropin

α-Melanocyte stimulating
hormone

Oxytocin

Prolactin

Vasopressin

Hypothalamic Peptides

Luteinizing hormone-releasing
hormone

Somatostatin

Thyrotropin-releasing hormone

Gut Peptides

Cholecystokinin

Gastrin

Motilin

Pancreatic polypeptide

Secretin

Substance P

Vasoactive intestinal
polypeptide

Opioid Peptides

Dynorphin

β-Endorphin

Met Enkephalin

Leu Enkephalin

Miscellaneous Peptides

Angiotensin

Bombesin

Bradykinin

Carnosine

Glucagon

Insulin

Neuropeptide Y

Neurotensin

Proctolin

APPENDIX VII
Phases of the Human Menstrual Cycle

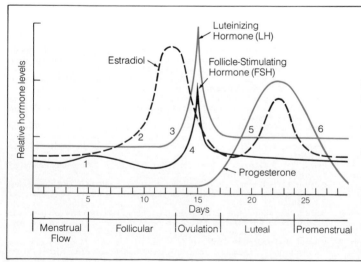

Phases of the human menstrual cycle

1. In response to an increase in FSH, small spheres of cells called ovarian follicles begin to grow around individual egg cells (ova).

2. The follicles begin to release estrogens such as estradiol.

3. The estrogens stimulate the hypothalamus to increase the release of LH and FSH from the anterior pituitary.

4. In response to the LH surge, one of the follicles ruptures and releases its ovum.

5. The ruptured follicle under the influence of LH develops into a corpus luteum (yellow body) and begins to release progesterone, which prepares the lining of the uterus for the implantation of a fertilized ovum.

6. Meanwhile, the ovum is moved into the fallopian tube by the rowing action of ciliated cells. If the ovum is not fertilized, progesterone and estradiol levels fall and the walls of the uterus are sloughed off as menstrual flow and the cycle begins once again.

References

Abramson, H. A. (1974). Editorial: Respiratory disorders and marijuana use. *Journal of Asthma Research, 11,* 97.

Acker, W., Ron, M. A., Lishman, W. A., & Shaw, G. K. (1984). A multivariate analysis of psychological, clinical and CT scanning measures in detoxified chronic alcoholics. *British Journal of Addiction, 79,* 293–301.

Adair, E. R., Casby, J. U., & Stolivijk, J. A. J. (1970). Behavioral temperature regulation in the squirrel monkey: Changes induced by shifts in hypothalamic temperature. *Journal of Comparative and Physiological Psychology, 72,* 17–27.

Adamec, R. (1990). In J. A. Wada, (Ed.), *Kindling 4* (pp. 329–341). New York: Plenum Press.

Adelmann, P. K., & Zajonc, R. B. (1989). Facial efference and the experience of emotion. *Annual Review of Psychology, 40,* 249–280.

Ader, R. (Ed.). (1981). *Psychoneuroimmunology.* New York: Academic Press.

Adkins-Regan, E. (1988). Sex hormones and sexual orientation in animals. *Psychobiology, 16,* 335–347.

Adolph, E. F. (1947). Urges to eat and drink in rats. *American Journal of Physiology, 151,* 110–125.

Aggleton, J. P. (1985). One-trial object recognition by rats. *Quarterly Journal of Experimental Psychology, 37b,* 279–294.

Aggleton, J. P., & Mishkin, M. (1983). Visual recognition impairment following medial thalamic lesions in monkeys. *Neuropsychologia, 21,* 189–197.

Aggleton, J. P., Nicol, R. M., Huston, A. E., & Fairbairn, A. F. (1988). The performance of amnesic subjects on tests of experimental amnesia in animals: Delayed matching-to-sample and concurrent learning. *Neuropsychologia, 26,* 265–272.

Aguayo, A. J. (1987). Regeneration of axons from the injured central nervous system of adult mammals. In G. Adelman (Ed.), *Encyclopedia of Neuroscience* (pp. 1040–1043). Boston: Birkhäuser.

Ahlskog, J. E., Randall, P. K., & Hoebel, B. G. (1975). Hypothalamic hyperphagia: Dissociation from hyperphagia following destruction of noradrenergic neurons. *Science, 190,* 399–401.

Akabas, M. H., Dodd, J., & Al-Awqati, Q. (1988). A bitter substance induces a rise in intracellular calcium in a subpopulation of rat taste cell. *Science, 242,* 1047–1049.

Åkerstedt, T., & Gillberg, M. (1981). The circadian variation of experimentally displaced sleep. *Sleep, 4,* 159–169.

Albert, D. J., Dyson, E. M., & Walsh, M. L. (1987). Competitive behavior: Intact male rats but not hyperdefensive males with medial hypothalamic lesions share water with females. *Physiology & Behavior, 41,* 549–553.

Albert, D. J., Jonik, R. H., & Walsh, M. L. (1992). Hormone-dependent aggression in male and female rats: experiential, hormonal, and neural foundations. *Neuroscience and Biobehavioral Reviews, 16,* 1–16.

Albert, D. J., Petrovic, D. M., Jonik, R. H., & Walsh, M. L. (1991). Enhanced defensiveness and increased food motivation each contribute to aggression and success in food competition by rats with medial hypothalamic lesions. *Physiology & Behavior, 49,* 13–19.

Albert, D. J., & Walsh, M. L. (1984). Neural systems and the inhibitory modulation of agonistic behavior: A comparison of mammalian species. *Neuroscience & Biobehavioral Reviews, 8,* 5–24.

Albert, D. J., Walsh, M. L., Gorzalka, B. B., Siemens, Y., & Louie, H. (1986). Testosterone removal in rats results in a decrease in social aggression and a loss of social dominance. *Physiology & Behavior, 36,* 401–407.

Albert, D. J., Walsh, M. L., Siemens, Y., & Louie, H. (1986). Spontaneous mouse killing rats: Gentling and food deprivation result in killing behavior almost identical to that of rats with medial hypothalamic lesions. *Physiology & Behavior, 36,* 1197–1199.

Albert, D. J., & Wong, R. C. K. (1978). Hyperactivity, muricide, and intraspecific aggression in the rat produced by infusion of local anesthetic into the lateral septum or surrounding areas. *Journal of Comparative and Physiological Psychology, 92,* 1062–1073.

Albert, D. J., & Wong, R. C. K. (1978). Interanimal aggression and hyperreactivity following hypothalamic infusion of local anesthetic in the rat. *Physiology & Behavior, 20,* 755–761.

Alexander, M. P. (1989). Clinical-anatomical correlations of aphasia following predominantly subcortical lesions. In H. Goodglas (Ed.), *Handbook of neuropsychology, II, part 2.* New York: Elsevier.

Allegretta, M., Nicklas, J. A., Sriram, S., & Albertini, R. J. (1990). T cells responsive to myelin basic protein in patients with multiple sclerosis. *Science, 247,* 718–720.

Allen, L. S., Hines, M., Shryne, J. E., & Gorski, R. A. (1989). Two sexually dimorphic cell groups in the human brain. *Journal of Neuroscience, 9,* 497–506.

Alpers, B. J. (1937). Relation of the hypothalamus to disorders of personality. *Archives of Neurology, 38,* 291–303.

Alvarez-Buylla, A., Kirn, J. R., & Nottebohm, F. (1990). Birth of projection neurons in adult avian brain may be related to perceptual or motor learning. *Science, 249,* 1444–1445.

Amoore, J. E., Johnston, J. W., & Rubin, M. (1964). The stereochemical theory of odor. *Scientific American, 210,* 42–49.

Anand, B. K., & Brobeck, J. R. (1951). Localization of a "feeding center" in the hypothalamus of the rat. *Proceedings of the Society for Experimental Biology and Medicine, 77,* 323–324.

Anch, A. M., Browman, C. P., Mitler, M. M., & Walsh, J. K. (1988). *Sleep: A scientific perspective.* Englewood Cliffs, NJ: Prentice Hall.

Anderson, R. H., Fleming, D. E., Rhees, R. W., & Kinghorn, E. (1986). Relationships between sexual activity, plasma testosterone, and the volume of the sexually dimorphic nucleus of the preoptic area in prenatally stressed and non-stressed rats. *Brain Research, 370,* 1–10.

Andreassi, J. L. (1980). *Psychophysiology: Human behavior and physiological response.* New York: Oxford University Press.

Andreassi, J. L. (1989). *Psychophysiology: Human behavior and physiological response.* Hillsdale, NJ: Erlbaum.

Angrist, B., Rotrosen, J., & Gershon, S. (1980). Responses to apomorphine, amphetamine, and neuroleptics in schizophrenic subjects. *Psychopharmacology, 72,* 17–19.

Angst, J., Weis, P., Grof, P., Baastrup, P. G., & Schou, M. (1970). Lithium prophylaxis in recurrent affective disorders. *British Journal of Psychiatry, 116,* 604–614.

Annett, J. (1985). Motor learning: A review. In H. Heuer, U. Kleinbeck, & K. H. Schmidt (Eds.), *Motor behavior: Programming, control, and acquisition* (pp. 188–212). Berlin: Springer-Verlag.

Annett, M. (1978). Genetic and nongenetic influences on handedness. *Behavior Genetics, 8,* 227–249.

Antoni, M. H. (1987). Neuroendocrine influences in psychoimmunology and neoplasia: A review. *Psychology and Health, 1, 3–24.

Applebury, M. L. (1991). Molecular determinants of visual pigment function. *Current Opinion in Neurobiology, 1,* 263–269.

Arbour, K. W., & Wilkie, D. M. (1988). Rodents' (*Rattus, Mesocricetus,* and *Meriones*) use of learned caloric information in diet source. *Journal of Comparative Psychology, 102,* 177–181.

Archer, J. (1991). The influence of testosterone on human aggression. *British Journal of Psychology, 82,* 1–28.

Asberg, M., Träskman, L., & Thorén, P. (1976). 5-HIAA in the cerebrospinal fluid: A biochemical suicide predictor? *Archives of General Psychiatry, 33,* 1193–1197.

Aserinsky, E., & Kleitman, N. (1953). Regularly occurring periods of eye motility and concomitant phenomena, during sleep. *Science, 118,* 273–274.

Attardi, D. G., & Sperry, R. W. (1963). Preferential selection of central pathways by regenerating optic fibers. *Experimental Neurology, 7,* 46–64.

Auerbach, S. H., Allard, T., Naeser, M., Alexander, M. P., & Albert, M. L. (1982). Pure word deafness. Analysis of a case with bilateral lesions and a defect at the prephonemic level. *Brain, 105,* 271–300.

Ax, A. F. (1955). The physiological differentiation between fear and anger in humans. *Psychosomatic Medicine, 15,* 433–442.

Baastrup, P. C., & Schou, M. (1967). Lithium as a prophylactic agent. *Archives of General Psychiatry, 16,* 162–172.

Babor, T. F., Mendelson, J. H., Greenberg, I., & Kuehnle, J. C. (1975). Marijuana consumption and tolerance to physiological and subjective effects. *Archives of General Psychiatry, 32,* 1548–1552.

Bachevalier, J., & Mishkin, M. (1986). Visual recognition impairment follows ventromedial but not dorsolateral prefrontal lesions in monkeys. *Behavioral Brain Research, 20,* 249–261.

Backlund, E. O., Granberg, P. O., Hamberger, B., Sedvall, G., Seiger, A., & Olson, L. (1985). Transplantation of adrenal medullary tissue to striatum in Parkinsonism. In A. Björklund & U. Stenevi (Eds.), *Neuronal grafting in the mammalian CNS* (pp. 551–556). Berlin: Elsevier.

Baier, H., & Bonhoeffer, F. (1992). Axon guidance by gradients of a target-derived component. *Science, 255,* 472–475.

Bailey, C. H., & Chen, M. C. (1983). Morphological basis of long-term habituation and sensitization in *Aplysia. Science, 220,* 91–93.

Bailey, C. H., & Chen, M. C. (1988). Long-term memory in *Aplysia* modulates the total number of varicosities of single identified sensory neurons. *Proceedings of the National Academy of Sciences (USA), 85,* 2373–2377.

Bailey, M. J., & Pillard, R. C. (1991). A genetic study of male sexual orientation. *Archives of General Psychiatry, 48,* 1089–1096.

Baizer, J. S., Ungerleider, L. G., & Desimone, R. (1991). Organization of visual inputs to the inferior temporal and posterior parietal cortex in Macaques. *The Journal of Neuroscience, 11,* 168–190.

Baker, B. J., & Booth, D. A. (1989). Preference conditioning by concurrent diets with delayed proportional reinforcement. *Physiology & Behavior, 46,* 585–590.

Baker, R. R. (1982). *Migration: Paths through time and space.* New York: Holmes & Meier.

Baker, T. B., & Tiffany, S. T. (1985). Morphine tolerance as habituation. *Psychological Review, 92,* 78–108.

Balaban, E., Teillet, M. A., & Le Douarin, N. (1988). Application of the quail-chick chimera system to the study of brain development and behavior. *Science, 241,* 1339–1342.

Ballard, P. A., Tetrud, J. W., & Langston, J. W. (1985). Permanent human parkinsonism due to 1-methyl-4-phenyl-1,2,3,6-tetrahydropyridine (MPTP): Seven cases. *Neurology, 35,* 949–956.

Bancroft, J., Danders, D., Davidson, D., & Warner, P. (1983). Mood, sexuality, hormones and the menstrual cycle: III. Sexuality and the role of androgens. *Psychosomatic Medicine, 45,* 509–516.

Bard P. (1929). The central representation of the sympathetic system. *Archives of Neurology and Psychiatry, 22,* 230–246.

Barnes, C. A. (1988). Spatial learning and memory processes: The search for their neurobiological mechanisms in the rat. *Trends in Neurosciences, 11,* 163–169.

Bartus, R. T., Dean, R. L., Beer, B., & Lippa, A. S. (1982). The cholinergic hypothesis of geriatric memory dysfunction. *Science, 217,* 408–417.

Basbaum, A. I., Clanton, C. H., & Fields, H. L. (1976). Opiate and stimulus-produced analgesia: Functional anatomy of a medullospinal pathway. *Proceedings of the National Academy of Sciences (USA), 73,* 4685–4688.

Basbaum, A. I., & Fields, H. L. (1978). Endogenous pain control mechanisms: Review and hypothesis. *Annals of Neurology, 4,* 451–462.

Bashir, Z. I., Alford, S., Davies, S. N., Randall, A. D., & Collingridge, G. L. (1991). Long-term potentiation of NMDA receptor-mediated synaptic transmission in the hippocampus. *Nature, 349,* 156–158.

Baskin, D. G., Woods, S. C., West, D. B., van Houten, M., Posner, B. I., Dorsa, D. M., & Porte, D., Jr. (1983). Immunocytochemical detection of insulin in rat hypothalamus and its possible uptake from cerebrospinal fluid. *Endocrinology, 113,* 1818–1825.

Bastiani, M. J., Doe, C. Q., Helfand, S. L., & Goodman, C. S. (1985). Neuronal specificity and growth cone guidance in grasshopper and *Drosophilia* embryos. *Trends in Neurosciences, 8,* 257–266.

Baum, M. J., Erskine, M. S., Kornberg, E., & Weaver, C. E. (1990). Prenatal and neonatal testosterone exposure interact to affect differentiation of sexual behavior and partner preference in female ferrets. *Behavioral Neuroscience, 104,* 183–198.

Bayer, S. A., & Altman, J. (1991). *Neocortical development.* New York: Raven Press.

Bazett, H. C., McGlone, B., Williams, R. G., & Lufkin, H. M. (1932). Sensation: I. Depth, distribution, and probable identification in the prepuce of sensory end-organs concerned in sensations of temperature and touch: Thermometric conductivity. *Archives of Neurology and Psychiatry, 27,* 489–517.

Bedard, M., & Weingarten, H. P. (1989). Postabsorptive glucose decreases excitatory effects of taste on ingestion. *The American Physiological Society,* 1142–1147.

Beecher, H. K. (1959). *Measurement of subjective responses: Quantitative effects of drugs.* New York: Oxford University Press.

Bekkers, J. M., & Stevens, C. F. (1990). Presynaptic mechanism for long-term potentiation in the hippocampus. *Nature, 346,* 724–729.

Bell, D. S. (1973). The experimental reproduction of amphetamine psychosis. *Archives of General Psychiatry, 29,* 35–40.

Bennett, E. L., Diamond, M. C., Krech, D., & Rosenzweig, M. R. (1964). Chemical and anatomical plasticity of brain. *Science, 146,* 610–619.

Benowitz, L. I., Bear, D. M., Mesulam, M.-M., Rosenthal, R., Zaidel, E., & Sperry, R. W. (1983). Nonverbal sensitivity following lateralized cerebral injury. *Cortex, 19,* 5–12.

Benson, D. F. (1985). Aphasia. In K. M. Heilman & E. Valenstein (Eds.), *Clinical neuropsychology* (pp. 17–47). New York: Oxford University Press.

Benson, D. F., & Zaidel, E. (Eds.). (1985). *The dual brain: Hemispheric specialization in humans.* London: The Guilford Press.

Benton, A. (1985). Visuoperceptual, visuospatial, and visuoconstructive disorders. In K. M. Heilman & E. Valenstein (Eds.), *Clinical neuropsychology* (pp. 151–185). New York: Oxford University Press.

Berger, R. J., & Oswald, I. (1962). Effects of sleep deprivation on behaviour, subsequent sleep, and dreaming. *Journal of Mental Science, 106,* 457–465.

Berkley, M., & Stebbins, W. (Eds.). (1990). *Comparative Perception, Vol. II: Communication.* New York: Wiley & Sons.

Berlucchi, G., Maffei, L., Moruzzi, G., & Strata, P. (1964). EEG and behavioral effects elicited by cooling of medulla and pons. In A. Mosso, V. Aducco, & G. Moruzzi (Eds.), *Archives Italiennes de biologie, 102,* (pp. 373–392). Pisa: Universita Degli Studi.

Bernstein, I. L., & Webster, M. M. (1980). Learned taste aversion in humans. *Physiology & Behavior, 25,* 363–366.

Berridge, K. C., & Valenstein, E. S. (1991). What psychological process mediates feeding evoked by electrical stimulation of the lateral hypothalamus? *Behavioral Neuroscience, 105,* 3–14.

Berridge, V., & Edwards, G. (1981). *Opium and the people: Opiate use in nineteenth-century England.* New York: St. Martin's Press.

Bielajew, C., & Shizgal, P. (1986). Evidence implicating descending fibers in self-stimulation of the medial forebrain bundle. *Journal of Neuroscience, 6,* 919–929.

Bishop, M. P., Elder, S. T., & Heath, R. G. (1963). Intracranial self-stimulation in man. *Science, 140,* 394–396.

Bishop, P. O., & Pettigrew, J. D. (1986). Neural mechanisms of binocular vision. *Vision Research, 26,* 1587–1600.

Björklund, A., Dunnett, S. B., Stenevi, U., Lewis, M. E., & Iversen, S. D. (1980). Reinnervation of the denervated striatum by substantia nigra transplants: Functional consequences as revealed by pharmacological and sensorimotor testing. *Brain Research, 199,* 307–333.

Björklund, A., & Lindvall, O. (1986). Catecholaminergic brainstem regulatory systems. In V. B. Mountcastle, F. E. Bloom, & S. R. Geiger (Eds.), *Handbook of physiology: The nervous system* (Vol. 4, pp. 155–236). Bethesda, MD: American Physiological Society.

Björklund, A., Segal, M., & Stenevi, U. (1979). Functional reinnervation of rat hippocampus by locus coeruleus implants. *Brain Research, 170,* 409–426.

Björklund, A., & Stenevi, U. (1979). Reconstruction of the nigrostriatal dopamine pathway by intracerebral nigral transplants. *Brain Research, 177,* 555–560.

Blackmore, S. (1991). Lucid dreaming: Awake in your sleep? *Skeptical Inquirer, 15,* 362–370.

Blackshear, P. J. (1979). Implantable drug-delivery systems. *Scientific American, 241,* 66–73.

Blaha, C. D., Coury, A., Fibiger, H. C., & Phillips, A. G. (1990). Effects of neurotensin on dopamine release and metabolism in the rat striatum and nucleus accumbens: Cross-validation using in vivo voltammetry and microdialysis. *Neuroscience, 34,* 669–705.

Blaha, C. D., & Jung, M. E. (1991). Electrochemical evaluation of stearate-modified graphite paste electrodes: Selective detection of dopamine is maintained after exposure to brain tissue. *Journal of Electroanalytical Chemistry, 310,* 317–334.

Blanchard, D. C., & Blanchard, R. J. (1984). Affect and aggression: An animal model applied to human behavior. In D. C. Blanchard & R. J. Blanchard (Eds.), *Advances in the study of aggression* (pp. 1–62). Orlando, FL: Academic Press.

Blanchard, D. C., & Blanchard, R. J. (1988). Ethoexperimental approaches to the biology of emotion. *Annual Review of Psychology, 39,* 43–68.

Blanchard, D. C., & Blanchard, R. J. (1990a). Behavioral correlates of chronic dominance-subordination relationships of male rats in a seminatural situation. *Neuroscience and Biobehavioral Reviews, 14,* 455–462.

Blanchard, D. C., & Blanchard, R. J. (1990b). Effects of ethanol, benzodiazepines and serotonin compounds on ethopharmacological models of anxiety. In N. McNaughton & G. Andrews (Eds.), *Anxiety,* (pp. 188–199). Dunedin: University of Otago Press.

Blanchard R. J., & Blanchard, D. C. (1990c). Anti-predator defense as models of animal fear and anxiety. In P. F. Brain, S. Parmigiani, R. J. Blanchard, and D. Mainardi (Eds.), *Fear and defense* (pp. 89–108). New York: Harwood Academic Publishers.

Blanchard, D. C., Blanchard R. J., & Rodgers, R. J. (1991). Risk assessment and animal models of anxiety. *Animal Models in Psychopharmacology: Advances in Pharmacological Sciences.* Basel: Birkhauser Verlag.

Blanchard, D. C., Blanchard, R. J., Tom, P., & Rodgers, R. J. (1990). Diazepam changes risk assessment in an anxiety/defense test battery. *Psychopharmacology, 101,* 511–518.

Blanchard, R. J., & Blanchard, D. C. (1989). Anti-predator defensive behaviors in a visible burrow system. *Journal of Comparative Psychology, 103,* 70–82.

Blanchard, R. J., Blanchard, D. C., & Takahashi, L. K. (1977). Reflexive fighting in the albino rat: Aggressive or defensive behavior. *Aggressive Behavior, 3,* 145–155.

Blanchard, R. J., Brain, P. F., Blanchard, D. C., & Parmigiani, S. (Eds.). (1989). *Ethoexperimental approaches to the study of behavior.* Dordrecht: Kluwer Academic Publishers.

Blass, E. M., & Epstein, A. N. (1971). A lateral preoptic osmosensitive zone for thirst in the rat. *Journal of Comparative and Physiological Psychology, 76,* 378–394.

Blass, E. M., & Hall, W. G. (1976). Drinking termination: Interactions between hydrational, orogastric and behavioral controls in rats. *Psychological Review, 183,* 356–374.

Blaustein, J. D., King, J. C., Toft, D .O., & Turcotte, J. (1988). Immunocytochemical localization of estrogen-induced progestin receptors in guinea pig brain. *Brain Research, 474,* 1–15.

Bliss, T. V. P., & Gardner-Medwin, A. R. (1973). Long-lasting potentiation of synaptic transmission in the dentate area of the unanaesthetized rabbit following stimulation of the perforant path. *Journal of Physiology, 232,* 357–374.

Bliss, T. V. P., & Lømø, T. (1973). Long-lasting potentiation of synaptic transmission in the dentate area of the anaesthetized rabbit following stimulation of the perforant path. *Journal of Physiology (London), 232,* 331–356.

Blizard, D. A. (1981). The Maudsley reactive and nonreactive strains: A North American perspective. *Behavior Genetics, 11,* 469–489.

Bloch, G. J., & Gorski, R. A. (1988). Cytoarchitectonic analysis of the SDN-POA of the intact and gonadectomized rat. *Journal of Comparative Neurology, 275,* 604–612.

Block, M. L., & Fisher, A. E. (1970). Anticholinergic central blockade of salt-aroused and deprivation-induced thirst. *Physiological Behavior, 5,* 525–527.

Bogen, J. G., & Bogen, G. M. (1976). Wernicke's region—Where is it? *Annals of the New York Academy of Science, 280,* 834–843.

Boller, F., & Grafman, J. (Eds.). (1989). *Handbook of neuropsychology: Language, Aphasia, and related disorders, Vol. 2, Section 3.* New York: Elsevier.

Bolles, R. C. (1980). Some functionalistic thought about regulation. In F. M. Toates & T. R. Halliday (Eds.), *Analysis of motivational processes* (pp. 63–75). London: Academic Press.

Booth, D. A. (1981). The physiology of appetite. *British Medical Bulletin, 37,* 135–140.

Booth, D. A. (1985). Food-conditioned eating preferences and aversions with interoceptive elements: Conditioned appetites and satieties. *Annals of the New York Academy of Sciences, 443,* 22–41.

Booth, D. A., Fuller, J., & Lewis, V. (1981). Human control of body weight: Cognitive or physiological? Some energy-related perceptions and misperceptions. In L. A. Cioffi (Ed.), *The body weight regulatory system: Normal and disturbed systems* (pp. 305–314). New York: Raven Press.

Booth, J. E. (1977). Sexual behaviour of male rats injected with the anti-oestrogen MER-25 during infancy. *Physiology & Behavior, 19,* 35–39.

Borbély, A. A. (1980). The sleep process: Circadian and homeostatic aspects. *Advances in Physiological Sciences, 18,* 85–91.

Borbély, A. A. (1983). Pharmacological approaches to sleep regulation. In A. R. Mayes (Ed.), *Sleep mechanisms and functions in humans and animals* (pp. 232–261). Wokingham, England: Van Nostrand Reinhold.

Borbély, A. A. (1984). Sleep regulation: Outline of a model and its implications for depression. In A. Borbély & J. L. Valatx (Eds.), *Sleep mechanisms* (pp. 272–284). Berlin: Springer-Verlag.

Borbély, A. A., Baumann, F., Brandeis, D., Strauch, I., & Lehmann, D. (1981). Sleep deprivation: Effect on sleep stages and EEG power density in man. *Electroencephalography and Clinical Neurophysiology, 51,* 483–493.

Bouchard, T. J. (Jr.), Lykken, D. T., McGue, M., Segal, N. L., & Tellegen, A. (1990). Sources of human psychological differences: The Minnesota study of twins reared apart. *Science, 250,* 223–228.

Bowers, D., Bauer, R. M., Coslett, H. B., & Heilman, K. M. (1985). Processing of face by patients with unilateral hemisphere lesions. I. Dissociations between judgements of facial affect and facial identity. *Brain Cognition, 4,* 258–272.

Bowers, D., Coslett, H. B., Bauer, K. M., Speedie, L. J., & Heilman, K. M. (1987). Comprehension of emotional prosody following unilateral hemispheric lesions: Processing defect versus distraction defect. *Neuropsychologia, 25,* 317–328.

Boyd, E. S., & Gardiner, L. C. (1962). Positive and negative reinforcement from intracranial stimulation of teleost. *Science, 136,* 648–649.

Bozarth, M. A. (1987). Ventral tegmental reward system. In J. Engel & L. Oreland (Eds.), *Brain reward systems and abuse* (pp. 1–17). New York: Raven Press.

Bozarth, M. A., & Wise R. A. (1981). Heroin reward is dependent on a dopaminergic substrate. *Life Sciences,* 29, 1881–1886.

Bozarth, M. A, & Wise, R. A. (1982). Localization of the reward-relevant opiate receptors. In L. S. Harris (Ed.), *Problems of drug dependence, 1981* (pp. 158–164). Washington, D.C.: National Institute on Drug Abuse.

Brady, J. V., & Nauta, W. J. H. (1955). Subcortical mechanisms in emotional behavior: The duration of affective change following septal and habenular lesions in the albino rat. *Journal of Comparative and Physiological Psychology, 48,* 412–420.

Bray, G. M., Vidal-Sanz, M., & Aguayo, A. J. (1987). Regeneration of axons from the central nervous system of adult rats. In F. J. Seil, E. Herbert, & B. M. Carlson (Eds.), *Progress in brain research* (Vol. 71, pp. 373–378). New York: Elsevier.

Brecher, E. M. (1972). *Licit and illicit drugs.* Boston: Little, Brown & Co.

Bremer, F. (1936). Nouvelles recherches sur le mécanisme du sommeil. *Comptes Rendus de la Société de Biologie, 122,* 460–464.

Bremer, F. (1937). L'activité cérébrale au cours du sommeil et de la narcose. Contribution à l'étude du mécanisme du sommeil. *Bulletin de l'Académie Royale de Belgique, 4,* 68–86.

Bremer, J. (1959). *Asexualization.* New York: Macmillan Publishing Co.

Brewster, J. M. (1986). Prevalence of alcohol and other drug problems among physicians. *Journal of the American Medical Association, 255,* 1913–1920.

Brill, N. Q., & Christie, R. L. (1974). Marihuana use and psychosocial adaptation. *Archives of General Psychiatry, 31,* 713–719.

Brime, J. I., Lopez-Sela, P., Bernado, R., Costales, M., Diaz, F., Marin, B., & Vijande, M. (1991). Psychological aspects of insulin-induced thirst. *Physiology & Behavior, 49,* 153–154.

Brinkman, C. (1984). Supplementary motor area of the monkey's cerebral cortex: Short- and long-term deficits after unilateral ablation and the effects of subsequent callosal section. *Journal of Neuroscience, 4,* 918–929.

Brinkman, C., & Porter, R. (1983). Supplementary motor area and premotor area of monkey cerebral cortex: Functional organization and activities of single neurons during performance of a learned movement. In J. E. Desmedt (Ed..), *Motor control mechanisms in health and disease* (pp. 393–420). New York: Raven Press.

Brion, S., & Mikol, J. (1978). Atteinte du noyau lateral dorsal du thalamus et syndrome de Korsakoff alcoolique. *Journal of Neurological Science, 38,* 249–261.

Britt, M. D., & Wise, R. A. (1983). Ventral tegmental site of opiate reward: antagonism by a hydrophilic opiate receptor blocker. *Brain Research, 258,* 105–108.

Brobeck, J. R. (1955). Neural regulation of food intake. *Annals of the New York Academy of Sciences, 63,* 44–55.

Brooks, P. L., Frost, B. J., Mason, J. L., & Gibson, D. M. (1986). Continuing evaluation of the Queen's University tactile vocoder: II Identification of open set sentences and tracking narrative. *Journal of Rehabilitation Research and Development, 23,* 129–138.

Brooks, V. B. (1986). *The neural basis of motor control.* New York: Oxford.

Brou, P., Sciascia, T. R., Linden, L., & Lettvin, J. Y. (1986). The colors of things. *Scientific American, 255,* 84–91.

Brown, M. C., & Ironton, R. (1977). Motor neurone sprouting induced by prolonged tetrodotoxin block of nerve action potentials. *Nature, 265,* 459–461.

Brown, T. H., Chapman, P. F., Kairiss, E. W., & Keenan, C. L. (1988). Long-term synaptic potentiation. *Science, 242,* 724–728.

Brundin, P., & Björklund, A. (1987). Survival, growth and function of dopaminergic neurons grafted to the brain. In F. J. Seil, E. Herbert, & B. M. Carlson (Eds.), *Progress in brain research* (Vol. 71, pp. 293–307). New York: Elsevier.

Brundin, P., & Björklund, A. (1987). Survival, growth and function of dopaminergic neurons grafted to the brain. In F. J. Seil, E. Herbert, & B. M. Carlson (Eds.), *Progress in brain research, 71* (pp. 293–307).

Brunner, D. P., Kijk, D.-J., Tobler, I., & Borbély, A. A. (1990). Effect of partial sleep deprivation on sleep stages and EEG power spectra: Evidence for non-REM and REM sleep homeostasis. *Electroencephalography and Clinical Neurophysiology, 75,* 492–499.

Brush, F. R., Froehlich, J. C., & Baron, S. (1979). Genetic selection for avoidance behavior in the rat. *Behavior Genetics, 9,* 309–316.

Bryne, J. H. (1987). Cellular analysis of associative learning. *Physiological Reviews, 67,* 329–437.

Buggy, J., Fisher, A. E., Hoffman, W. E., Johnson, A. K., & Phillips, M. I. (1975). Ventricular obstruction: Effect on drinking induced by intracranial injection of angiotensin. *Science, 190,* 72–74.

Buonomano, D. V., & Byrne, J. H. (1990). Long-term synaptic changes produced by a cellular analog of classical conditioning in aplysia. *Science, 249,* 420–423.

Burns, R. S., Chiueh, C. C., Markey, S. P., Ebert, M. H., Jacobowitz, D. M., & Kopin, I. J. (1983). A primate model of Parkinsonism: Selective destruction of dopaminergic neurons in the pars compacta of the substantia nigra by N-methyl-4-phenyl-1,2,3,6-tetrahydropyridine. *Proceedings of the National Academy of Sciences (USA), 80,* 4546–4550.

Burns, S. L. (1990). *How to survive unbearable stress.* Huntington Beach, CA: I-MED Press.

Bushnell, M. C., Goldberg, M. E., & Robinson, D. L. (1981). Behavioral enhancement of visual responses in monkey cerebral cortex: I. Modulation in posterior cortex related to selective visual attention. *Journal of Neurophysiology, 46,* 755–772.

Butters N., & Stuss, D. T. (1989). Diencephalic amnesia. In F. Boller & J. Grafman (Eds.), *Handbook of neuropsychology, 3* (pp. 107–148). New York: Elsevier.

Byrne, J. H. (1974). *Mrs. Byrne's dictionary of unusual, obscure, and preposterous words.* Secaucus, NJ: Citadel Press.

Cabanac, M. (1971). Physiological role of pleasure. *Science, 173,* 1103–1107.

Cabanac, M. (1990). Taste: The maximization of multidimensional pleasure. In E. D. Capaldi & T. L. Powley (Eds.), *Taste, experience, & feeding* (pp. 28–42). Washington, DC: American Psychological Association.

Cacioppo, J. T., Bush, L. K., & Tassinary, L. G. (in press). Microexpressive facial actions as a function of affective stimuli: Replication and extension. *Personality and Social Psychology Bulletin.*

Cacioppo, J. T., Petty, R. E., Losch, M., & Kim, H. S. (1986). Electromyographic activity over facial muscle regions can differentiate the valence and intensity of emotional reactions. *Journal of Personality and Social Psychology, 50,* 260–268.

Cade, J. F. J. (1949). Lithium salts in treatment of psychotic excitement. *Medical Journal of Australia, 2,* 349–352.

Caggiula, A. R. (1970). Analysis of the copulation-reward properties of posterior hypothalamic stimulation in male rats. *Journal of Comparative and Physiological Psychology, 70,* 399–412.

Cain, D. P. (1986). The transfer phenomenon in kindling. In J. A. Wada, (Ed.), *Kindling 3* (pp. 231–245). New York: Raven Press.

Calne, S., Schoenberg, B., Martin, W., Uitti, J., Spencer, P., & Calne, D. B. (1987). Familial Parkinson's disease: Possible role of environmental factors. *Canadian Journal of Neurological Sciences, 14,* 303–305.

Caltagirone, C., Zoccolotti, P., Originale, G., Daniele, A., & Mammucari, A. (1989). Autonomic reactivity and facial expression of emotion in brain damaged patients. In G. Gainotti and C. C. Caltagirone (Eds.), *Emotion and dual brain.* New York: Springer Verlag.

Camhi, J. M. (1984). *Neuroethology: Nerve cells and the behavior of animals.* Sunderland, MA: Sinauer Associates, Inc.

Campfield, L. A., Brandon, P., & Smith, F. J. (1985). On-line continuous measurement of blood glucose and meal pattern in free-feeding rats: The role of glucose in meal initiation. *Brain Research Bulletin, 14,* 605–616.

Canady, R. A., Kroodsma, D. E., & Nottebohm, F. (1984). Population differences in complexity of a learned skill are correlated with the brain space involved. *Proceedings of the National Academy of Sciences, U.S.A., 81,* 6232–6234.

Cannon, W. B., & Washburn, A. L. (1912). An explanation of hunger. *American Journal of Physiology, 29,* 441–454.

Capaldi, E. D., & Powley, R. L. (Eds.), (1990). *Taste, experience, and feeding.* Washington, DC: American Psychological Association.

Carbonetto, S. (1991). Facilitatory and inhibitory effects of glial cells and extracellular matrix in axonal regeneration. *Current Opinion in Neurobiology, 1,* 407–413.

Carew, T. J., Castellucci, V. F., & Kandel, E. R. (1971). Analysis of dishabituation and sensitization of the gill-withdrawal reflex in *Aplysia. International Journal of Neuroscience, 2,* 79–98.

Carew, T. J., Hawkins, R. D., & Kandel, E. R. (1983). Differential classical conditioning of a defensive withdrawal reflex in *Aplysia californica. Science, 219,* 397–400.

Carew, T. J., Pinsker, H. M., & Kandel, E. R. (1972). Long-term habituation of a defensive withdrawal reflex in *Aplysia. Science, 175,* 451–454.

Carew, T. J., & Sahley, C. L. (1986). Invertebrate learning and memory: From behavior to molecules. *Annual Review of Neuroscience, 9,* 435–487.

Carew, T. J., Walters, E. T., & Kandel, E. R. (1981). Associative learning in *Aplysia:* Cellular correlates supporting a conditioned fear hypothesis. *Science, 211,* 501–503.

Carey, D. P., Goodale, M. A., & Sprowl, E. G. (1990). Blindsight in rodents: The use of a 'high-level' distance cue in gerbils with lesions of primary visual cortex. *Behavioural Brain Research, 38,* 283–289.

Carlson, A. J. (1912). Contributions to the physiology of the stomach: II. The relation between the contractions of the empty stomach and the sensation of hunger. *American Journal of Physiology, 31,* 175–192.

Carlson, N. R. (1991). *Physiology of behavior* (4th ed.). Boston, MA: Allyn and Bacon.

Carlsson, A., & Linqvist, M. (1963). Effect of chlorpromazine or haloperidol on formation of 3-methoxytyramine and normetanephrine in mouse brains. *Acta Pharmacologica et Toxicologica, 20,* 140–144.

Carlton, P. L., & Wolgin, D. L. (1971). Contingent tolerance to the anorexinergic effects of amphetamine. *Physiology & Behavior, 7,* 221–225.

Carpenter, W. T., Heinrichs, D. W., & Alphs, L. D. (1985). Treatment of negative symptoms. *Schizophrenia Bulletin, 11,* 440–452.

Carr, G. D., Fibiger, H. C, & Phillips, A. G. (1989). Conditioned place preference as a measure of drug reward. In J. M. Liebman & S. J. Cooper (Eds.), *The neuropharmacological basis of reward* (pp. 264–319). Oxford: Clarendon Press.

Carroll, D. (1984). *Biofeedback in practice.* New York: Longman Group.

Castellucci, V., & Kandel, E. R. (1974). A quantal analysis of the synaptic depression underlying habituation of the gill-withdrawal reflex in *Aplysia. Proceedings of the National Academy of Sciences (USA), 71,* 5004–5008.

Castellucci, V., & Kandel, E. R. (1976). Presynaptic sensitization as a mechanism for behavioral sensitization in *Aplysia. Science, 194,* 1176–1178.

Castellucci, V., Pinsker, H., Kupfermann, I., & Kandel, E. R. (1970). Neuronal mechanisms of habituation and dishabituation of the gill-withdrawal reflex in *Aplysia. Science, 167,* 1745–1748.

Castro, C. A., Silbert, L. H., McNaughton, B. L., & Barnes, C. A. (1989). Recovery of spatial learning deficits after decay of electrically induced synaptic enhancement in the hippocampus. *Nature, 342,* 545–548.

Cermak, L. S., Uhly, B., & Reale, L. (1980). Encoding specificity in the alcoholic Korsakoff patient. *Brain and Language, 11,* 119–127.

Chan-Ling, T., & Stone, J. (1991). Factors determining the morphology and distribution of astrocytes in the cat retina: A 'contact-spacing' model of astrocyte interaction. *The Journal of Comparative Neurology, 303,* 387–399.

Chang, F. L., Greenough, W. T. (1984). Transient and enduring morphological correlates of synaptic activity and efficacy change in the rat hippocampal slice. *Brain Research, 309*, 35–46.

Chen, C. S. (1968). A study of the alcohol-tolerance effect and an introduction of a new behavioral technique. *Psychopharmacology, 12*, 433–440.

Cheney, P. D. (1985). Role of cerebral cortex in voluntary movements. *Physical Therapy, 65*, 624–635.

Choi, D. W., & Rothman, S. M. (1990). The role of glutamate neurotoxicity in hypoxicischemic neuronal death. *Annual Review of Neuroscience, 13*, 171–182.

Chorover, S. L., & Schiller, P. H. (1965). Short-term retrograde amnesia in rats. *Journal of Comparative and Physiological Psychology, 59*, 73–78.

Cirillo, R. A., Horel, J. A., & George, P. J. (1989). Lesions of the anterior temporal stem and the performance of delayed match-to-sample and visual discriminations in monkeys. *Behavioural Brain Research, 34*, 55–69.

Clower, R., Alvarez-Royo, P., Zola-Morgan, P., & Squire, L. R. (1991). Recognition memory impairment in monkeys with selective hippocampal lesions. *Society for Neuroscience Abstracts, 17*, 338.

Cohen, D. B. (1979). *Sleep and dreaming: Origins, nature and functions.* Oxford: Pergamon Press.

Cohen, H., & Squire, L. R. (1980). Preserved learning and retention of pattern-analysing skill in amnesia: Dissociation of knowing how and knowing that. *Science, 210*, 207–210.

Cohen, S., & Stillman, R. C. (Eds.) (1976). *The therapeutic potential of marihuana.* New York: Plenum Medical Book Company.

Coindet, J., Chouvet, G., & Mouret, J. (1975). Effects of lesions of the suprachiasmatic nuclei on paradoxical sleep and slow wave sleep circadian rhythms in the rat. *Neuroscience Letters, 1*, 243–247.

Coleman, R. M. (1986). *Wide awake at 3:00 A.M.* New York: W. H. Freeman.

Collier, G. H. (1980). An ecological analysis of motivation. In F. M. Toates & T. R. Halliday (Eds.), *Analysis of motivational processes* (pp. 125–151). London: Academic Press.

Collingridge, G. L., & Bliss, T. V. P. (1987). NMDA receptors—Their role in long-term potentiation. *Trends in Neurosciences, 10*, 288–293.

Colombo, M., D'Amato, M. R., Rodman, H. R., & Gross, C. G. (1990). Auditory association cortex lesions impair auditory short-term memory in monkeys. *Science, 247*, 336–338.

Coltheart, M. (1980). Deep dyslexia: A right hemisphere hypothesis. In M. Coltheart, K. Patterson, and J. C. Marshall (Eds.) *Deep Dyslexia*, (pp. 326–380). London: Routledge.

Coltheart, M. (1985). Cognitive neuropsychology and the study of reading. In M. I. Posner & O. S. M. Marin (Eds.), *Attention and performance: Vol. 11* (pp. 3–37). Hillsdale, NJ: Erlbaum.

Coltheart, M., Masterson, J., Byng, S., Prior, M., & Riddoch, J. (1983). Surface dyslexia. *Quarterly Journal of Experimental Psychology, 35A*, 469–496.

Conover, K. L., Collins, S. M., & Weingarten, H. P. (1989). Gastric emptying changes are neither necessary nor sufficient for CCK-induced satiety. *American Journal of Physiology, 256*, 56–62.

Coons, E. E., Levak, M., & Miller, N. E. (1965). Lateral hypothalamus: Learning of food-seeking response motivated by electrical stimulation. *Science, 150*, 1320–1321.

Cooper, K. E., Cranston, W. I., & Honour, A. J. (1967). Observations on the site and mode of action of pyrogens in the rabbit brain. *Journal of Physiology, 191*, 325–337.

Cooper, R. M., & Zubek, J. P. (1958). Effects of enriched and restricted early environments on the learning ability of bright and dull rats. *Canadian Journal of Psychology, 12*, 159–164.

Cooper, S. J., & Dourish, C. T. (1990). Multiple cholecystokinin (CCK) receptors and CCK-monoamine interactions are instrumental in the control of feeding. *Physiology & Behavior, 48*, 849–857.

Corbett, D., & Wise, R. A. (1980). Intracranial self-stimulation in relation to the ascending dopaminergic systems of the midbrain: A moveable electrode mapping study. *Brain Research, 185*, 1–15.

Corbetta, M., Marzi, C. A., Tassinari, G., & Aglioti, S. (1990). Effectiveness of different task paradigms in revealing blindsight. *Brain, 113*, 603–616.

Corbetta, M., Miezin, F. M., Dobmeyer, S., Shulman, G. L., & Petersen, S. E. (1990). Attentional modulation of neural processing of shape, color, and velocity in humans. *Science, 248*, 1556–1559.

Corcoran, M. E., McCaughran, J. A., Jr., & Wada, J. A. (1973). Acute anti-epileptic effects of Δ⁹-Tetrahydrocannabinol in rats with kindled seizures. *Experimental Neurology, 40*, 471–483.

Coren, S., & Ward, L. M. (1989). *Sensation and perception* (3rd ed.). New York: Harcourt Brace Jovanovich.

Corkin, S. (1968). Acquisition of motor skill after bilateral medial temporal-lobe excision. *Neuropsychologia, 6*, 255–265.

Corkin, S., Milner, B., & Rasmussen, T. (1970). Somatosensory thresholds. *Archives of Neurology, 23*, 41–59.

Corsi, P. I. (1991). *The enchanted loom: Chapters in the history of neuroscience.* New York: Oxford.

Corwin, J. T., & Warchol, M. E. (1991). Auditory hair cells. *Annual Review of Neuroscience, 14*, 301–333.

Costall, B., & Naylor, R. J. (1977). Mesolimbic and extrapyramidal sites for the mediation of stereotyped behaviour patterns and hyperactivity by amphetamine and apomorphine in the rat. In E. H. Ellinwood, Jr. & M. M. Kilbey (Eds.), *Cocaine and other stimulants* (pp. 47–76). New York: Plenum Press.

Costanzo, R. M., & Becker, D. P. (1986). Smell and taste disorders in head injury and neurosurgery patients. In H. Meiselman & R. S. Rivlin (Eds.), *Clinical measurement of taste and smell* (pp. 565–578). New York: Macmillan Publishing Co.

Cotman, C. W., Monoghan, D. T., & Ganong, A. H. (1988). Excitatory amino acid neurotransmission: NMDA receptors and Hebb-type synaptic plasticity. *Annual Review of Neuroscience, 11*, 61–80.

Cotman, C. W., Nieto-Sampedro, M., & Harris, E. W. (1981). Synapse replacement in the nervous system of adult vertebrates. *Physiological Reviews, 61*, 684–784.

Cowan, W. M. (1979). The development of the brain. *Scientific American, 241*, 113–133.

Cowey, A., & Stoerig, P. (1991). The neurobiology of blindsight. *Trends in Neurosciences, 14*, 140–145.

Coyle, J. T. (1987). Alzheimer's disease. In G. Adelman (Ed.), *Encyclopedia of neuroscience* (pp. 29–31). Boston: Birkhäuser.

Coyle, J. T., Price, D. L., & DeLong, M. R. (1983). Alzheimer's disease: A disorder of cortical cholinergic innervation. *Science, 219*, 1184–1190.

Crabbe, J. C., Kosubud, A., Young, E. R., Tam, B. R., & McSwigan, J. D. (1985). Bidirectional selection for susceptibility to ethanol withdrawal seizures in *Mus musculus. Behavior Genetics, 15*, 521–536.

Cragg, B. G. (1975). The development of synapses in kitten visual cortex during visual deprivation. *Experimental Neurology, 46*, 445–451.

Craig, J. C. (1977). Vibrotactile pattern perception: Extraordinary observers. *Science, 196*, 450–452.

Creese, I., Burt, D. R., & Snyder, S. H. (1976). Dopamine receptor binding predicts clinical and pharmacological potencies of antischizophrenic drugs. *Science, 192*, 481–483.

Crews, D. (1988). The problem with gender. *Psychobiology, 16*, 321–334.

Crow, T. J. (1972). A map of the rat mesencephalon for electrical self-stimulation. *Brain Research, 36*, 265–273.

Crowell, C. R., Hinson, R. E., & Siegel, S. (1981). The role of conditional drug responses in tolerance to the hypothermic effects of ethanol. *Psychopharmacology, 73*, 51–54.

Cumming, G. D. (1978). Eye movements and visual perception. In E. C. Carterette & M. P. Friedman (Eds.), *Handbook of perception* (Vol. 9, pp. 221–255). New York: Academic Press.

Currier, R. D., & Eldridge, R. (1982). Possible risk factors in multiple sclerosis as found in a national twin study. *Archives of Neurology, 39*, 140–144.

Czeisler, C. A., Kronauer, R. E., Allan, J. S., Duffy, J. F., Jewett, M. E., Brown, E. N., & Ronda, J. M. (1989). Bright light induction of strong (Type O) resetting of the human circadian pacemaker. *Science, 244*, 1328–1333.

Daan, S., & Lewy, A. J. (1984). Scheduled exposure to daylight: A potential strategy to reduce "jet lag" following transmeridian flight. *Psychopharmacology Bulletin, 20*, 566–568.

Daly, M., & Wilson, M. (1983). *Sex, Evolution, and Behavior.* Boston, MA: Allard Grant Press.

Damasio, A. R. (1985). Prosopagnosia. *Trends in Neurosciences, 8*, 132–135.

Damasio, A. R. (1990). Category-related recognition defects as a clue to the neural substrates of knowledge. *Trends in Neurosciences, 13*, 95–98.

Damasio, A. R., Damasio, H., & Van Hoesen, G. W. (1982). Prosopagnosia: Anatomic basis and behavioral mechanisms. *Neurology, 32*, 331–341.

Damasio, A. R., Tranel, D., & Damasio, H. (1990). Face agnosia and the neural substrates of memory. *Annual Review of Neuroscience, 13*, 89–109.

Damasio, H. (1989). Neuroimaging contributions to the understanding of aphasia. In F. Boller & J. Grafman (Eds.), *Handbook of neuropsychology, Vol. 2* (pp. 3–46). New York: Elsevier.

Dartnall, H. J. A., Bowmaker, J. K., & Mollon, J. D. (1983). Microspectrophotometry of human photoreceptors. In J. D. Mollon & L. T. Sharpe (Eds.), *Colour vision: Physiology and psychophysics* (pp. 69–80). New York: Academic Press.

Darwin, C. (1872). *The expression of emotions in man and animals.* New York: Philosophical Library.

Das, G. D., & Altman, J. (1971). Transplanted precursors of nerve cells: Their fate in the cerebellums of young rats. *Science, 173*, 637–638.

Das, G. D., Hallas, B. H., & Das, K. G. (1980). Transplantation of brain tissue in the brain of rat: I. Growth characteristics of neocortical transplants from embryos of different ages. *American Journal of Anatomy, 158*, 135–145.

David, S., & Aguayo, A. J. (1981). Axonal elongation into peripheral nervous system "bridges" after central nervous system injury in adult rats. *Science, 214*, 931–933.

Davidson, J. M. (1980). Hormones and sexual behavior in the male. In D. T. Krieger and J. C. Hughes (Eds.), *Neuroendocrinology* (pp. 232–238). Sunderland, MA: Sinauer Associates.

Davidson, J. M., Kwan, M., & Greenleaf, W. J. (1982). Hormonal replacement and sexuality in men. *Clinics in Endocrinology and Metabolism, 11*, 599–623.

Davis, H. P., Rosenzweig, M. R., Becker, L. A., & Sather, K. J. (1988). Biological psychology's relationships to psychology and neuroscience. *American Psychologist, 43*, 359–371.

DeBold, J. F., & Miczek, K. A. (1984). Aggression persists after ovariectomy in female rats. *Hormones and Behavior, 18*, 177–190.

De Camilli, P., & Jahn, R. (1990). Pathways to regulated exocytosis in neurons. *Annual Review of Physiology, 52*, 625–645.

de Castro, J. M. (1981). Feeding patterns and their control mechanisms. *Behavioral and Brain Sciences, 4*, 581.

DeFries, J. C., Gervais, M. C., & Thomas, E. A. (1978). Response to 30 generations of selection for open-field activity in laboratory mice. *Behavior Genetics, 8*, 3–13.

De Jonge, F. H., Louwerse, A. L., Ooms, M. P., Evers, P., Endert, E., & van de Poll, N. E. (1989). Lesions of the SDN-POA inhibit sexual behavior of male Wistar rats. *Brain Research Bulletin, 23*, 483–492.

de Kruif, P. (1945). *The male hormone.* New York: Harcourt, Brace and Co.

DeLong, M., & Strick, P. L. (1974). Motor functions of the basal ganglia: Single unit activity during movement. In F. O. Schmidt and F. G. Worden (Eds.), *The neurosciences: The third study program* (pp. 319–326). Cambridge, MA: MIT Press.

Demellweek, C., & Goudie, A. J. (1983). An analysis of behavioural mechanisms involved in the acquisition of amphetamine anorectic tolerance. *Psychopharmacology, 79*, 58–66.

Dement, W. C. (1960). The effect of dream deprivation. *Science, 131,* 1705–1707.

Dement, W. C. (1978). *Some must watch while some must sleep.* New York: W. W. Norton.

Dement, W. C., & Kleitman, N. (1957). The relation of eye movement during sleep to dream activity: An objective method for the study of dreaming. *Journal of Experimental Psychology, 53,* 339–553.

Dement, W. C., Milter, M., & Henriksen, S. (1972). Sleep changes during chronic administration of parachorophenylalanine. *Revue Canadianne de Biologie, 31,* 239–246.

Dement, W. C., & Wolpert, E. A. (1958). The relation of eye movements, body motility and external stimuli to dream content. *Journal of Experimental Psychology, 55,* 543–553.

Dennerstein, L., & Burrows, G. D. (1982). Hormone replacement therapy and sexuality in women. *Clinics in Endocrinology and Metabolism, 11,* 661–679.

De Renzi, E. (1980). The influence of sex and age on the incidence and type of aphasia. *Cortex, 16,* 627–630.

De Renzi, E. (1982). *Disorders of space exploration and cognition.* New York: Wiley.

Desiderato, O., MacKinnon, J. R., & Hissom, H. (1974). Development of gastric ulcers in rats following stress termination. *Journal of Comparative and Physiological Psychology, 87,* 208–214.

Desimone, R., & Ungerleider, L. G. (1989). Neural mechanisms of visual processing in monkeys. In F. Boller, and J. Grafman (Eds.), *Handbook of neuropsychology Vol. 2,* (pp. 267–299). New York: Elsevier.

Detke, M. J., Brandon, S. E., Weingarten, H. P., Rodin, J., & Wagner, A. R. (1989). Modulation of behavioral and insulin responses by contextual stimuli paired with food. *Physiology & Behavior, 45,* 845–851.

Deutsch, J. A., Young, W. G., & Kalogeris, T. J. (1978). The stomach signals satiety. *Science, 21,* 165–167.

DeValois, R. L., & DeValois, K. K. (1988). *Spatial Vision.* New York: Oxford University Press.

DeVoogd, T. J. (1991). Endocrine modulation of the development and adult function of the avian song system. *Psychoneuroendocrinology, Vol. 16,* 41–66.

Dewsbury, D. A. (1967). A quantitative description of the behavior of rats during copulation. *Behavior, 29,* 154–178.

Dewsbury, D. A. (1990). *Contemporary issues in comparative psychology.* Sunderland, Massachusetts: Sinauer.

Dewsbury, D. A. (1991). Psychobiology. *American Psychologist, 46,* 198–205.

Diamond, J. (1982). Modelling and competition in the nervous system: Clues from sensory innervation of skin. *Current Topics in Developmental Biology, 17,* 147–205.

Diamond, J. (1986). I want a girl just like the girl . . . *Discover, 7,* 65–68.

Dicker, S. E., & Nunn, J. (1957). The role of antidiuretic hormone during water deprivation in rats. *Journal of Physiology, 136,* 235–248.

Dixson, A. F. (1980). Androgens and aggressive behavior. *Aggressive Behavior, 6,* 37–67.

Dobelle, W. H., Mladejovsky, M. G., & Girvin, J. P. (1974). Artificial vision for the blind: Electrical stimulation of visual cortex offers hope for a functional prosthesis. *Science, 183,* 440–444.

Dodd, J., & Jessell, T. M. (1988). Axon guidance and the patterning of neuronal projections in vertebrates. *Science, 242,* 692–699.

Dooling, R. J., & Hulse, S. H. (Eds.), (1989). *The Comparative Psychology of Audition. Perceiving Complex Sounds.* Hillsdale, NJ: Erlbaum.

Dornan, W. A., Malsbury, C. W., & Penney, R. B. (1987). Facilitation of lordosis by injection of substance P into the midbrain central gray. *Neuroendocrinology, 45,* 498–506.

Doty, R. L. (1986). Gender and endocrine-related influences on human olfactory perception. In H. Meiselman & R. S. Rivlin (Eds.), *Clinical measurement of taste and smell* (pp. 377–413). New York: Macmillan Publishing Co.

Doty, R. L., Ford, M., Preti, G., & Huggins, G. R. (1975). Changes in the intensity and pleasantness of human vaginal odors during the menstrual cycle. *Science, 190,* 1316–1318.

Doty, R. L., Green, P. A., Ram, C., & Yankell, S. L. (1982). Communication of gender from human breath odors: Relationship to perceived intensity and pleasantness. *Hormones and Behavior, 16,* 13–22.

Doty, R. L., Snyder, P. J., Huggins, G. R., & Lowry, L. D. (1981). Endocrine, cardiovascular, and psychological correlates of olfactory sensitivity changes during the human menstrual cycle. *Journal of Comparative and Physiological Psychology, 95,* 45–60.

Dourish, C. T., Rycroft, W., & Iversen, S. D. (1989). Postponement of satiety by blockade of brain cholecystokinin (CCK-B) receptors. *Science, 245,* 1509–1511.

Dowling, J. E. (1979). Information processing by local circuits: The vertebrate retina as a model system. In F. O. Schmitt & F. G. Worden (Eds.), *The neurosciences fourth study program* (pp. 163–181). Cambridge, MA: MIT Press.

Drachman, D. A., & Arbit, J. (1966). Memory and the hippocampal complex. *Archives of Neurology, 15,* 52–61.

Drachman, D. A., & Leavitt, J. (1974). Human memory and the cholinergic receptor. *Archives of Neurology, 30,* 113–121.

Dunant, Y., & Israël, M. (1985). The release of acetylcholine. *Scientific American, 252,* 58–66.

Dunn, A. J. (1989). Neurochemistry of stress. In G. Adelman (Ed.), *Encyclopedia of neuroscience, Vol. II,* (pp. 1146–1150) Boston: Birkhäuser.

Dunnett, S. B., Everitt, B. J., & Robbins, T. W. (1991). The basal forebrain-cortical cholinergic system: interpreting the functional consequences of excitotoxic lesions. *Trends in Neurosciences, 14,* 494–501.

Dusoir, H., Kapur, N., Byrnes, D. P., McKinstry, S., & Hoare, R. D. (1990). The role of diencephalic pathology in human memory disorder. *Brain, 113,* 1695–1706.

Duvoisin, R. C., Heikkila, R. E., Nicklas, W. J., & Hess, A. (1986). Dopaminergic neurotoxicity of MPTP in the mouse: A murine model of parkinsonism. In S. Fahn, C. D. Marsden, P. Jenner, & P. Teychenne (Eds.), *Recent developments in Parkinson's disease* (pp. 147–154). New York: Raven Press.

Dykes, R. W. (1983). Parallel processing of somatosensory information: A theory. *Brain Research Reviews, 6,* 47–115.

Easter, S. S., Jr., Purves, D., Rakic, P., & Spitzer, N. C. (1985). The changing view of neural specificity. *Science, 230,* 507–511.

Edwards, D. A. (1969). Early androgen stimulation and aggressive behavior in male and female mice. *Physiology & Behavior, 4,* 333–338.

Ehrhardt, A. A., Epstein, R., & Money, M. (1968). Fetal androgens and female gender identity in the early-treated androgenital syndrome. *Johns Hopkins Medical Journal, 122,* 160–167.

Ehrhardt, A. A., & Meyer-Bahlberg, H. F. L. (1981). Effects of prenatal sex hormones on gender-related behavior. *Science, 211,* 1312–1317.

Ehrhardt, A. A., Meyer-Bahlberg, H. F. L., Rosen, L. R., Feldman, J. F., Veridiano, N. P., Zimmerman, I., & McEwen, B. S. (1985). Sexual orientation after prenatal exposure to exogenous estrogen. *Archives of Sexual Behavior, 14,* 57–77.

Ehringer, H., & Hornykiewicz, O. (1960). Verteilung von Noradrenalin und Dopamin (3-Hydroxytyramin) im gehirn des Menschen und ihr Verhalten bei Erkrankungen des Extrapyramidalen Systems. *Klinische Wochenschrift, 38,* 1236–1239.

Eichenbaum, H., & Wiener, S. I. (1989). Is place the (only) functional correlate? *Psychobiology, 17,* 217–220.

Eidelberg, E. (1987). Flexion reflexes. In G. Adelman (Ed.), *Encyclopedia of neuroscience, I,* (pp. 431–432). Boston, MA: Birkhauser.

Eikelboom, R., & Stewart, J. (1982). Conditioning of drug-induced physiological responses. *Psychological Review, 89,* 507–528.

Ekman, P. (1985). *Telling lies.* New York: Norton.

Ekman, P. (1992). Facial expressions of emotion: New findings, new questions. *Psychological Science, 3,* 34–38.

Ekman, P., & Friesen, W. V. (1969). The repertoire of nonverbal behavior: Categories, origins, usage, and coding. *Semiotica, 1,* 49–98.

Ekman, P., & Friesen, W. V. (1971). Constants across cultures in the face and emotion. *Journal of Personality and Social Psychology, 17,* 124–129.

Ekman, P., & Friesen, W. V. (1975). *Unmasking the face: A guide to recognizing emotions from facial clues.* Englewood Cliffs, NJ: Prentice-Hall.

Ekman, P., Sorenson, E. R., & Friesen, W. V. (1969). Pan-cultural elements in facial displays of emotions. *Science, 164,* 86–88.

Ellis, L., & Ames, M. A. (1987). Neurohormonal functioning and sexual orientation: A theory of homosexuality-heterosexuality. *Psychological Bulletin, 101,* 233–258.

Epstein, A. N. (1982). The physiology of thirst. In D. W. Pfaff (Ed.), *The physiological mechanisms of motivation* (pp. 165–214). New York: Springer-Verlag.

Epstein, A. N. (1987). Drinking behavior. In G. Adelman (Ed.), *Encyclopedia of neuroscience* (pp. 340–342). Boston: Birkhäuser.

Epstein, A. N., Spector, D., Samman, A., & Goldblum, C. (1964). Exaggerated prandial drinking in the rat without salivary glands. *Nature, 201,* 1342–1343.

Epstein, A. N., & Teitelbuam, P. (1962). Regulation of food intake in the absence of taste, smell, and other oropharyngeal sensations. *Journal of Comparative and Physiological Psychology, 55,* 753–759.

Esch, F. S., Keim, P. S., Beattie, E. C., Blacher, R. W., Culwell, A. R., Oltersdorf, T., McClure, D., & Ward, P. J. (1990). Cleavage of amyloid peptide during constitutive processing of its precursor. *Science, 248,* 1122–1124.

Etcoff, N. L. (1984). Selective attention to facial identity and facial emotion. *Neuropsychologia, 22,* 281–295.

Etcoff, N. L. (1989). Asymmetries in recognition of emotion. In F. Boller and J. Grafman (Eds.), *Handbook of neuropsychology, 3,* (pp. 363–402).

Everitt, B. J., & Herbert, J. (1972). Hormonal correlates of sexual behavior in subhuman primates. *Danish Medical Bulletin, 19,* 246–258.

Everitt, B. J., Herbert, J., & Hamer, J. D. (1971). Sexual receptivity of bilaterally adrenalectomized female rhesus monkeys. *Physiology & Behavior, 8,* 409–415.

Everitt, B. J., & Stacey, P. (1987). Studies of instrumental behavior with sexual reinforcement in male rats (Rattus norvegicus): II Effects of preoptic area lesions, castration, and testosterone. *Journal of Comparative Psychology, 101,* 407–419.

Evarts, E. V. (1981). Functional studies of the motor cortex. In F. O. Schmitt, F. G. Worden, G. Adelman, & S. G. Dennis (Eds.), *The organization of the cerebral cortex* (pp. 263–283). Cambridge, MA: MIT Press.

Fadem, B. H., & Barfield, R. J. (1981). Neonatal hormonal influences on the development of proceptive and receptive feminine sexual behavior in rats. *Hormones and Behavior, 15,* 282–288.

Faden, A. I., Demediuk, P., Panter, S. S., & Vink, R. (1989). The role of excitatory amino acids and NMDA receptors in traumatic brain injury. *Science, 244,* 798–800.

Falk, J. L. (1964). Production of polydipsia in normal rats by an intermittent food schedule. *Science, 133,* 195–196.

Falzi, G., Perrone, P., & Vignolo, L. A. (1982). Right-left asymmetry in anterior speech region. *Archives of Neurology, 39,* 239–240.

Faris, P. L., & Olney, J. W. (1985). Suppression of food intake in rats by microinjection of cholecystokinin (CCK) to the paraventricular nucleus (PVN). *Society for Neuroscience Abstracts, 2,* 39.

Faust, I. M., Johnson, P. R., & Hirsch, J. (1977). Adipose tissue regeneration following lipectomy. *Science, 197,* 391–393.

Fawcett, J. W. (1991). Bridging the gaps. *Current Opinion in Neurobiology, 1,* 55–56.

Fawcett, J. W., & Keynes, R. J. (1990). Peripheral nerve regeneration. *Annual Review of Neuroscience, 13,* 43–60.

Feder, H. H. (1981). Perinatal hormones and their role in the development of sexually dimorphic behaviors. In N. T. Adler (Ed.), *Neuroendocrinology of reproduction: Physiology and behavior* (pp. 127–157). New York: Plenum Press.

Feder, H. H. (1984). Hormones and sexual behavior. *Annual Review of Psychology, 35,* 165–200.

Feindel, W. (1986). Electrical stimulation of the brain during surgery for epilepsy—historical highlights. In G. P. Varkey (Ed.), *Anesthetic considerations for craniotomy in awake patients* (pp. 75–87). Boston: Little, Brown and Company.

Feldman, S. M., & Waller, H. J. (1962). Disassociation of electrocortical activation and behavioral arousal. *Nature, 196,* 1320–1322.

Fentress, J. C. (1973). Development of grooming in mice with amputated forelimbs. *Science, 179,* 704–705.

Fentress, J. C., & McLeod, P. J. (1986). Motor patterns in development. In E. M. Blass (Ed.), *Handbook of behavioral neurobiology, Volume 8, Developmental psychobiology and developmental neurobiology* (pp. 35–97.) New York: Plenum Press.

Feyereisen, P. (1989). Theories of emotions and neuropsychological research. In F. Boller and J. Grafman (Eds.), *Handbook of neuropsychology,* 3, (pp. 271–282). New York: Elsevier.

Fibiger, H. C. (1991). Cholinergic mechanisms in learning, memory and dementia: A review of recent evidence. *Trends in Neurosciences, 14,* 20–223.

Fibiger, H. C., LePiane, F. G., Jakubovic, A., & Phillips, A. G. (1987). The role of dopamine in intracranial self-stimulation of the ventral tegmental area. *Journal of Neuroscience, 7,* 3888–3896.

Fibiger, H. C., Murray, C. L., & Phillips, A. G. (1983). Lesions of the nucleus basalis magnocellularis impair long-term memory in rats. *Society for Neuroscience Abstracts, 9,* 332.

Fields, H. L., & Basbaum, A. I. (1984). Endogenous pain control mechanisms. In P. D. Wall & R. Melzack (Eds.), *Textbook of pain* (pp. 142–152). Edinburgh: Churchill Livingstone.

Fillion, T. J., & Blass, E. M. (1986). Infantile experience with suckling odors determines adult sexual behavior in male rats. *Science, 231,* 729–731.

Fine, A. (1986). Transplantation in the central nervous system. *Scientific American, 255,* 52–58.

Finger, S., Le Vere, T. E., Almli, C. R., & Stein, D. G. (1988). *Brain injury and recovery: Theoretical and controversial issues.* New York: Plenum.

Fitzsimons, J. T. (1961). Drinking by rats depleted of body fluid without increase in osmotic pressure. *Journal of Physiology, 159,* 297–309.

Fitzsimons, J. T., Epstein, A. N., & Johnson, A. K. (1978). Peptide antagonists of the renin-angiotensin system in the characterisation of receptors for angiotensin-induced drinking. *Brain Research, 153,* 319–331.

Fitzsimons, J. T. (1972). Thirst. *Physiological Reviews, 52,* 468–561.

Fitzsimons, J. T., & LeMagnen, J. (1969). Eating as a regulatory control of drinking in the rat. *Journal of Comparative and Physiological Psychology, 67,* 273–283.

Fitzsimons, J. T., & Simons, B. J. (1969). The effect on drinking in the rat of intravenous infusion of angiotensin, given alone or in combination with other stimuli of thirst. *Journal of Physiology, 203,* 45–57.

Foster, T. C., Castro, C. A., & McNaughton, B. L. (1989). Spatial selectivity of rat hippocampal neurons: Dependence on preparedness for movement. *Science, 244,* 1580–1582.

Freed, W. J., de Medinaceli, L., & Wyatt, R. J. (1985). Promoting functional plasticity in the damaged nervous system. *Science, 227,* 1544–1552.

Freed, W. J., Perlow, M. J., Karoum, F., Seiger, A., Olson, L., Hoffer, B. J., & Wyatt, R. J. (1979). Restoration of dopaminergic function by grafting of fetal rat substantia nigra to the caudate nucleus: Long-term behavioral, biochemical, and histochemical studies. *Annals of Neurology, 8,* 510–519.

Freeman, W. J. (1991). The physiology of perception. *Scientific American, 264,* 78–85.

Friedman, J., Globus, G., Huntley, A., Mullaney, D., Naitoh, P., & Johnson, L. (1977). Performance and mood during and after gradual sleep reduction. *Psychophysiology, 14,* 245–250.

Friedman, M. I. (1981). Metabolic elements of eating behavior. *Behavioral and Brain Sciences, 4,* 583–584.

Friedman, M. I., & Stricker, E. M. (1976). The physiological psychology of hunger: A physiological perspective. *Psychological Review, 83,* 409–431.

Friesen, W. V. (1972). Cultural differences in facial expression in a social situation: An experimental test of the concept of display rules. *Unpublished doctoral dissertation,* University of California, San Francisco.

Fritsch, G., & Hitzig, E. (1870). Über die elektrische Erregbarkeit des Grosshirns. *Archiv für Anatomie Physiologie und Wissenschaftliche Medicin, 37,* 300–332. In G. von Bonin (Trans.), (1960). *Some papers on the cerebral cortex* (pp. 73–96). Springfield, IL: Charles C. Thomas.

Furedy, J. J. (1983). Operational, analogical and genuine definitions of psychophysiology. *International Journal of Psychophysiology, 1,* 13–19.

Gackenbach, J., & LaBerge, S. (Eds.). (1988). *Conscious mind, sleeping brain.* New York: Plenum.

Gage, F. H., Kang, U. J., & Fisher, L. J. (1991). Intracerebral grafting in the dopaminergic system: Issues and controversy. *Current Opinion in Neurobiology, 1,* 414–419.

Gainotti, G. (1972). Emotional behavior and hemispheric side of the lesion. *Cortex, 8,* 41–55.

Galef, B. G. (1989). Laboratory studies of naturally-occurring feeding behaviors: Pitfalls, progress and problems in ethoexperimental analysis. In R. J. Blanchard, P. F. Brain, D. C. Blanchard, & S. Parmigiani (Eds.), *Ethoexperimental approaches to the study of behavior* (pp. 51–77). Dordrecht, The Netherlands: Kluwer Academic Publishers.

Galef, B. G., Jr., Attenborough, K. S., & Whiskin, E. E. (1990). Responses of observer rats (*rattus norvegicus*) to complex, diet-related signals emitted by demonstrator rats. *Journal of Comparative Psychology, 104,* 11–19.

Galef, B. G., & Sherry, D. F. (1973). Mother's milk: A medium for transmission of cues reflecting the flavor of mother's diet. *Journal of Comparative and Physiological Psychology, 83,* 374–378.

Gall, C., McWilliams, R., & Lynch, G. (1980). Accelerated rates of synaptogenesis by "sprouting" afferents in the immature hippocampal formation. *Journal of Comparative Neurology, 193,* 1047–1061.

Gallistel, C. R., Gomita, Y., Yadin, E., & Campbell, K. A. (1985). Forebrain origins and terminations of the medial forebrain bundle metabolically activated by rewarding stimulation or by reward-blocking doses of pimozide. *Journal of Neuroscience, 5,* 1246–1261.

Gallup, G. G. (Jr.) (1983). Toward a comparative psychology of mind. In R. L. Mellgren (Ed.), *Animal cognition and behavior* (pp. 473–505). New York: North-Holland Publishing.

Garcia, J., & Koelling, R. A. (1966). Relation of cue to consequence in avoidance learning. *Psychonomic Science, 4,* 123–124.

Garrigues, A-M., & Cazala, P. (1983). Central catecholamine metabolism and hypothalamic self-stimulation behaviour in two inbred strains of mice. *Brain Research, 265,* 265–271.

Garrow, J. S. (1974). *Energy balance and obesity in man.* (pp. 210–217). New York: Elsevier Publishing Company.

Gawin, F. H. (1991). Cocaine addiction: Psychology and neurophysiology. *Science, 251,* 1580–1586.

Gaze, R. M., Keating, M. J., Ostberg, A., & Chung, S. H. (1979). The relationship between retinal and tectal growth in larval *Xenopus:* Implications for the development of the retino-tectal projection. *Journal of Embryology and Experimental Morphology, 53,* 103–143.

Gaze, R. M., & Sharma, S. C. (1970). Axial differences in the reinnervation of the goldfish optic tectum by regenerating optic nerve fibres. *Experimental Brain Research, 10,* 171–181.

Gazzaniga, M. S. (1967). The split brain in man. *Scientific American, 217,* 24–29.

Gazzaniga, M. S., & Sperry, R. W. (1967). Language after section of the cerebral commissure. *Brain, 90,* 131–148.

Geiselman, P. J. (1987). Carbohydrates do not always produce satiety: An explanation of the appetite- and hunger-stimulating effects of hexoses. *Progress in Psychobiology and Physiological Psychology, 12,* 1–46.

Georgopoulos, A. P. (1991). Higher order motor control. *Annual Review of Neuroscience, 14,* 361–377.

Gerbino, L., Oleshansky, M., & Gershon, S. (1978). Clinical use and mode of action of lithium. In M. A. Lipton, A. DiMascio, & K. F. Killam (Eds.), *Psychopharmacology: A generation of progress* (pp. 1261–1275). New York: Raven Press.

Geschwind, N. (1972). Language and the brain. *Scientific American, 226,* 76–83.

Geschwind, N. (1979). Specializations of the human brain. *Scientific American, 241,* 180–199.

Geschwind, N., & Levitsky, W. (1968). Human brain: Left-right asymmetries in temporal speech region. *Science, 161,* 186–187.

Ghez, C. (1985). Voluntary movement. In E. R. Kandel & J. H. Schwartz (Eds.), *Principles of neuroscience* (pp. 487–501). New York: Elsevier.

Gibbs, J., Maddison, S. P., & Rolls, E. T. (1981). Satiety role of the small intestine examined in sham-feeding rhesus monkeys. *Journal of Comparative and Physiological Psychology, 95,* 1003–1015.

Gibbs, J., Young, R. C., & Smith, G. P. (1973). Cholecystokinin decreases food intake in rats. *Journal of Comparative and Physiological Psychology, 84,* 488–495.

Gilbert, C. D. (1977). Laminar differences in receptive field properties of cells in cat primary visual cortex. *Journal of Physiology, 268,* 391–421.

Gilliam, T. C., Gusella, J. F., & Lehrach, H. (1987). Molecular genetic strategies to investigate Huntington's disease. *Advances in Neurology, 48,* 17–29.

Gilman, A. (1937). The relation between blood osmotic pressure, fluid distribution and voluntary water intake. *American Journal of Physiology, 120,* 323–328.

Glanzman, D. L., Kandel, E. R., & Schacher, S. (1990). Target-dependent structural changes accompanying long-term synaptic facilitation in *Aplysia* neurons. *Science, 249,* 799–802.

Glaser, R., Rice, J., Sheridan, J., Fertel, R., Stout, J., Speicher, C., Pinsky, D., Koture, M., Post, A., Beck, M., & Kiecolt-Glaser, J. K. (1987). Stress-related immune suppression: Health implications. *Brain, Behavior & Immunity, 1,* 7–20.

Glick, S. D. (Ed.). (1985). *Cerebral lateralization in nonhuman species.* New York: Academic Press.

Glickman, S. E., & Schiff, B. B. (1967). A biological theory of reinforcement. *Psychological Review, 74,* 81–109.

Goate, A., Chartier-Harlin, M-C., Mullan, M., Brown, J., Crawford, F., Fidani, L., Giuffra, L., Haynes, A., Irving, N., James, L., Mant, R., Newton, P., Rooke, K., Roques, P., Talbot, C., Pericak-Vance, M., Roses, A., Williamson, R., Rossor, M., Wen, M., & Hardy, J. (1991). Segregation of a missense mutation in the amyloid precursor protein gene with familial Alzheimer's disease. *Nature, 349,* 704–706.

Goddard, G. V., McIntyre, D. C., & Leech, C. K. (1969). A permanent change in brain function resulting from daily electrical stimulation. *Experimental Neurology, 25,* 295–330.

Goeders, N. E., Dworkin, S. I., & Smith, J. E. (1986). Neuropharmacological assessment of cocaine self-administration into the medial prefrontal cortex. *Pharmacology Biochemistry & Behavior, 24,* 1429–1440.

Goeders, N. E., Lane, J. D., & Smith, J. E. (1984). Self-administration of methionine enkephalin into the nucleus accumbens. *Pharmacology Biochemistry & Behavior, 20,* 451–455.

Gold, R. M. (1973). Hypothalamic obesity: The myth of the ventromedial nucleus. *Science, 182,* 488–490.

Gold, R. M., Jones, A. P., Sawchenko, P. E., & Kapatos, G. (1977). Paraventricular area: Critical focus of a longitudinal neurocircuitry mediating food intake. *Physiology & Behavior, 18,* 1111–1119.

Goldberg, M. E., & Bushnell, M. C. (1981). Behavioral enhancement of visual responses in monkey cerebral cortex: II. Modulation in frontal eye fields specifically related to saccades. *Journal of Neurophysiology, 46,* 773–787.

Goldman, B. (1984). *Death in the locker room: Steroids and sports.* South Bend, IN: Icarus Press.

Goldman-Rakic, P. S., & Selemon, L. D. (1990). New frontiers in basal ganglia re-search. *Trends in Neurosciences, 13,* 241–244.

Goldstein, A., & Kalant, H. (1990). Drug policy: Striking the right balance. *Science, 249,* 1513–1521.

Goldstein, G. W., & Betz, A. L. (1986). The blood-brain barrier. *Scientific American, 255,* 74–83.

Goldstein, K. (1939). *The Organism: A holistic approach to biology, derived from pathological data in man.* New York: American Book.

Gollin, E. S. (1960). Developmental studies of visual recognition of incomplete objects. *Perceptual Motor Skills, 11,* 289–298.

Gollnick, P. D., & Hodgson, D. R. (1986). The identification of fiber types in skeletal muscle: A continual dilemma. *Exercise and Sport Sciences Reviews, 14,* 81–104.

Goodale, M. A. (1983). Neural mechanisms of visual orientation in rodents: Targets versus places. In A. Hein & M. Jeannerod (Eds.), *Spatially oriented behavior* (pp. 36–61). New York: Springer-Verlag.

Goodenough, D. R., Shapiro, A., Holden, M., & Steinschriber, L. (1959). A comparison of "dreamers" and "nondreamers": Eye movements, electroencephalograms, and the recall of dreams. *Journal of Abnormal and Social Psychology, 59,* 295–303.

Goodglass, H., & Kaplan, E. (1979). Assessment of cognitive deficit in the brain-injured patient. In M. S. Gazzaniga (Ed.), *Handbook of behavioral neurobiology: Vol. 2. Neuropsychology* (pp. 3–22). New York: Plenum Press.

Goodlett, C. R., Marcussen, B. L., & West, J. R. (1990). A single day of alcohol exposure during the brain growth spurt induces brain weight restriction and cerebellar Purkinje cell loss. *Alcohol, 7,* 107–114.

Gorski, R. A. (1971). Gonadal hormones and the perinatal development of neuroendocrine function. In L. Martini & W. F. Ganong (Eds.), *Frontiers in neuroendocrinology* (pp. 237–290). New York: Oxford University Press.

Gorski, R. A. (1980). Sexual differentiation in the brain. In D. T. Krieger & J. C. Hughes (Eds.), *Neuroendocrinology* (pp. 215–222). Sunderland, MA: Sinauer.

Gorski, R. A. (1985). The 13th J. A. Stevenson Memorial Lecture: Sexual differentiation of the brain: Possible mechanisms and implications. *Canadian Journal of Physiology and Pharmacology, 63,* 577–594.

Gorski, R. A., Gordom, J. H., Shryne, J. E., & Southam, A. M. (1978). Evidence for a morphological sex difference within the medial preoptic area of the rat brain. *Brain Research, 148,* 333–346.

Gottlieb, D. I. (1988). GABAergic neurons. *Scientific American, 258,* 82–89.

Gottlieb, G. (1983). The psychobiological approach to developmental issues. In P. H. Mussen (Ed.), *Handbook of child psychology: Vol. 2. Infancy and developmental psychobiology* (pp. 1–26). New York: Wiley.

Gould, S. J. (1980). *The Panda's thumb: More reflections in natural history.* W. W. Norton: New York.

Gould, S. J. (1991). Bully for Brontosaurus: Reflections in natural history. W. W. Norton: New York.

Goy, R. W. (1970). Experimental control of psychosexuality. *Philosophical Transactions of the Royal Society of London, (B), 259,* 149–162.

Goy, R. W. (1978). Development of play and mounting behaviour in female rhesus virilized prenatally with esters of testosterone or dihydrotestosterone. In D. J. Chivers & J. Herbert (Eds.), *Recent advances in primatology* (pp. 449–462). London: Academic Press.

Goy, R. W., & McEwen, B. S. (1980). *Sexual differentiation of the brain.* Cambridge, MA: MIT Press.

Grady, K. L., Phoenix, C. H., & Young, W. C (1965). Role of the developing rat testis in differentiation of the neural tissues mediating mating behavior. *Journal of Comparative and Physiological Psychology, 59,* 176–182.

Graf, M. V., & Kastin, A. J. (1984). Delta-sleep-inducing peptide (DSIP): A review. *Neuroscience and Biobehavioral Review, 8,* 83–93.

Graf, P., & Schacter, D. J. (1987). Selective effects of interference on implicit and explicit memory for new associations. *Journal of Experimental Psychology: Learning, Memory, and Cognition, 13,* 45–53.

Graf, P., Squire, L. R., & Mandler, G. (1984). The information that amnesic patients do not forget. *Journal of Experimental Psychology, Learning, Memory, and Cognition, 10,* 164–178.

Graff-Radford, N., Damasio, H., Yamada, T., Eslinger, P. J., & Damasio, A. R. (1985). Nonhaemorrhagic thalamic infarction. *Brain, 108,* 485–516.

Grant, P. R. (1991). Natural selection and Darwin's finches. *Scientific American, 265,* 82–87.

Graves, R., Goodglass, H., & Landis, T. (1982). Mouth asymmetry during spontaneous speech. *Neuropsychologia, 20,* 371–381.

Gray, T. S., & Morley, J. E. (1986). Minireview: Neuropeptide Y: Anatomical distribution and possible function in mammalian nervous system. *Life Sciences, 38,* 389–401.

Green, S. (1991). Benzodiazepines, putative anxiolytics and animal models of anxiety. *Trends in Neurosciences, 14,* 101–103.

Greenough, W. T., & Volkmar, F. R. (1973). Pattern of dendritic branching in occipital cortex of rats reared in complex environments. *Experimental Neurology, 40,* 491–504.

Grillner, S. (1985). Neurobiological bases of rhythmic motor acts in vertebrates. *Science, 228,* 143–149.

Grinspoon, L. (1971). *Marihuana reconsidered.* Cambridge, MA: Harvard University Press.

Groos, G. (1983). Regulation of the circadian sleep-wake cycle. *Sleep 1982, 6th European Congress on Sleep Research* (Zurich, 1982) (pp. 19–29). Basel: Karger.

Groos, G. (1984). The physiological organization of the circadian sleep-wake cycle. In A. Borbély & J. L. Valatx (Eds.), *Sleep mechanisms* (pp. 241–257). Berlin: Springer-Verlag.

Groos, G., & Hendricks, J. (1982). Circadian rhythms in electrical discharge of rat suprachiasmatic neurones recorded in vitro. *Neuroscience Letters, 34,* 283–288.

Gross, C. G., Desimone, R., Albright, T. D., & Schwarz, E. L. (1985). Inferior temporal cortex and pattern recognition. In C. Chagas, R. Gattass, & C. Gross (Eds.), *Pattern recognition mechanisms* (pp. 179–201). Berlin: Springer-Verlag.

Grossman, S. P. (1967). *A textbook of physiological psychology.* New York: John Wiley & Sons, Inc.

Grossman, S. P. (1990). *Thirst and sodium appetite: Physiological basis.* New York: Academic Press, Inc./Harcourt Brace Jovanovich.

Grudin, J. T. (1983). Error patterns in skilled and novice transcription typing. In W. E. Cooper (Ed.), *Cognitive aspects of skilled typewriting* (pp. 121–144). New York: Springer.

Grunt, J. A., & Young, W. C. (1952). Differential reactivity of individuals and the response of the male guinea pig to testosterone propionate. *Endocrinology, 51,* 237–248.

Gunne, L. M., Ånggård, E., & Jönsson, L. E. (1972). Clinical trials with amphetamine-blocking drugs. *Psychiatria, Neurologia, Neurochirurgia, 75,* 225–226.

Guthrie, S. (1991). Horizontal and vertical pathways in neural induction. *Trends in Neurosciences, 14,* 123–126.

Guyton, A. C. (1987). *Human physiology and mechanisms of disease* (4th ed.) Philadelphia, PA: W. B. Saunders.

Haber, S., Barchas, P. R., & Barchas, J. D. (1981). A primate analogue of amphetamine-induced behavior in humans. *Biological Psychiatry, 16,* 181–195.

Haist, F., Musen, G., & Squire, L. R. (1991). Intact priming of words and nonwords in amnesia. *Psychobiology, 19,* 275–285.

Hallas, B. H., Oblinger, M. M., & Das, G. (1980). Heterotopic neural transplants in the cerebellum of the rat: Their afferents. *Brain Research, 196,* 2442–2446.

Halmi, K. A., Ackerman, S., Gibbs, J., & Smith, G. (1987). Basic biological overview of eating disorders. In H. Y. Meltzer (Ed.), *Psychopharmacology: The third generation of progress* (pp. 1255-1266). New York: Raven Press.

Hammond, P. H., Merton, P. A., & Sutton, G. G. (1956). Nervous gradation of muscular contraction. *British Medical Bulletin, 12,* 214–218.

Han, P. J., Feng, L. Y., & Kuo, P. T. (1972). Insulin sensitivity of pair-fed, hyperlipemic, hyperinsulinemic, obese hypothalamic rats. *American Journal of Physiology, 222,* 1206–1209.

Hannah, J., & Hansen, B. C. (1990). Food intake and meal patterns in rhesus monkeys: Significance of chronic hyperinsulinemia. *Physiology & Behavior, 48,* 519–522.

Harris, G. W. (1955). *Neural control of the pituitary gland.* London: Edward Arnold (Pub.) Ltd.

Harris, G. W., & Jacobsohn, D. (1952). Functional grafts of the anterior pituitary gland. *Proceedings of the Royal Society of London (B), 139,* 1951–1952.

Harris, G. W., & Levine, S. (1965). Sexual differentiation of the brain and its experimental control. *Journal of Physiology, 181,* 379–400.

Harris, L. J. (1978). Sex differences in spatial ability: Possible environmental, genetic, and neurological factors. In M. Kinsbourne (Ed.), *Asymmetrical function of the brain* (p. 463). Cambridge: Cambridge University Press.

Harris, L. J., Clay, J., Hargreaves, F. J., & Ward, A. (1933). Appetite and choice of diet: The ability of the vitamin B deficient rat to discriminate between diets containing and lacking the vitamin. *Proceedings of the Royal Society of London, (B), 113,* 161–190.

Hartmann, E. (1980). Effects of psychotropic drugs on sleep: The catecholamines and sleep. In M. A. Lipton, A. DiMascio, & K. F. Killam (Eds.), *Psychopharmacology: A generation of progress* (pp. 711–728). New York: Raven Press.

Hartmann, E. L. (1973). *The functions of sleep.* Westford, MA: Murray Printing Company.

Harvey, P. H., & Krebs, J.R. (1990). Comparing brains. *Science, 249,* 140–145.

Haseltine, F. P., & Ohno, S. (1981). Mechanisms of gonadal differentiation. *Science, 211,* 1272–1277.

Hasselmo, M. E., Rolls, E. T., Baylis, G. C., & Nalwa, V. (1989). Object-centered encoding by face-selective neurons in the cortex in the superior temporal sulcus of the monkey. *Experimental Brain Research, 75,* 417–429.

Hatten, M. E. (1990). Riding the glial monorail: A common mechanism for glial-guided neuronal migration in different regions of the developing mammalian brain. *Trends in Neurosciences, 13,* 179–184.

Haupt, H. A., & Revere, G. D. (1984). Anabolic steroids: A review of the literature. *American Journal of Sports Medicine, 12,* 469–484.

Hawkins, R. D. (1983). Cellular neurophysiological studies of learning. In J. A. Deutsch (Ed.), *The physiological basis of memory* (pp. 71–120). New York: Academic Press.

Hearne, K. (1978). Lucid Dreams. London: Hamish Hamilton.

Hearne, K. (1978). Lucid dreams: An electrophysiological and psychological study. Unpublished Ph.D. thesis, University of Hull, Hull, England.

Hebb, D. O. (1949). *The organization of behavior.* New York: John Wiley & Sons, Inc.

Hécaen, H., & Angelergues, R. (1964). Localization of symptoms in aphasia. In A. V. S. de Reuck & M. O'Connor (Eds.), *CIBA foundation symposium on the disorders of language* (pp. 222–256). London: Churchill Press.

Heffner, H. E., & Heffner, R. S. (1984). Temporal lobe lesions and perception of species-specific vocalizations by macaques. *Science, 226,* 75–76.

Heffner, H. E., & Heffner, R. S. (1988). Effect of bilateral auditory cortex lesions in monkeys on sound localization. *Abstracts of the Eleventh Midwinter Meeting of the Association for Research in Otolaryngology, 85.*

Heffner, H. E., & Heffner, R. S. (1989). Effect of restricted cortical lesions on absolute thresholds and aphasia-like deficits in Japanese macaques. *Behavioral Neuroscience, 103,* 158–169.

Heffner, H. E., & Heffner, R. S. (1990). Role of primate auditory cortex in hearing. In M. Berkley and W. Stebbins (Eds.), *Comparative perception, Vol. II: Communication.* New York: Wiley & Sons.

Heffner, H. E., & Masterton, R. B. (1990). Sound localization in mammals: Brainstem mechanisms. In M. Berkley and W. Stebbins (Eds.), *Comparative perception, Vol. I: Discrimination.* New York: Wiley & Sons.

Hefner, C. D., Lumsden, A. G. S., & O'Leary, D. D. M. (1990). Target control of collateral extension and directional axon growth in the mammalian brain. *Science, 247,* 217–220.

Heilman, K. M., & Watson, R. T. (1977). The neglect syndrome—A unilateral defect of the orienting response. In S. Harnad, R. W. Doty, L. Goldstein, J. Jaynes, & G. Krauhamer (Eds.), *Lateralization in the nervous system* (pp. 285–302). New York: Academic Press.

Heilman, K. M., Watson, R. T., & Valenstein, E. (1985). Neglect and related disorders. In K. M. Heilman & E. Valenstein (Eds.), *Clinical neuropsychology* (pp. 243–293). New York: Oxford University Press.

Hellige, J. B. (1990). Hemispheric asymmetry. *Annual Review of Psychology, 41,* 55–80.

Helmholtz, H. L. F. (1852). *On the sensation of tone* (2nd Eng. ed.). New York: Dover (1954).

Hendrickson, A. E., Wagoner, N., & Cowan, W. M. (1972). Autoradiographic and electron microscopic study of retinohypothalamic connections. *Zeitschrift für Zellforschung und Mikroskopische Anatomie, 125,* 1–26.

Henke, P. G. (1988). Electrophysiological activity in the central nucleus of the amygdala: Emotionality and stress ulcers in rats. *Behavioral Neuroscience, 102,* 77–83.

Hetherington, A. W., & Ranson, S. W. (1940). Hypothalamic lesions and adiposity in the rat. *Anatomical Record, 78,* 149–172.

Heuser, J. E. (1977). Synaptic vesicle exocytosis revealed in quick-frozen frog neuromuscular junctions treated with 4-aminopyridine and given a single electrical shock. In W. M. Cowan & F. A. Ferrendelli (Eds.), *Society for neuroscience symposia: Approaches to the cell biology of neurons* (Vol. 11, pp. 215–239). Bethesda, MD: Society for Neuroscience.

Hier, D. B., & Kaplan, J. (1980). Are sex differences in cerebral organization clinically significant? *Behavioral and Brain Sciences, 3,* 238–239.

Hillyard, S. A., & Kutas, M. (1983). Electrophysiology of cognitive processing. *Annual Review of Psychology, 34,* 33–61.

Hinde, R. A. (1983). Ethology and child development. In P. H. Mussen (Ed.), *Handbook of child psychology: Vol. 2. Infancy and developmental psychobiology* (pp. 27–93). New York: Wiley.

Hirst, W., Spelke, E. S., Reaves, C. C., Canarack, G., & Neisser, U. (1980). Dividing attention without alteration or automaticity. *Journal of Experimental Psychology: General, 109,* 98–117.

Hobson, J. A. (1989). *Sleep.* New York: Scientific American Library.

Hodgkin, A. L., & Keynes, R. D. (1955). Active transport of cations in giant axons from *Sepia* and *Loligo. Journal of Physiology, 128,* 28–60.

Hoebel, B. G., Monaco, A. P., Hernandez, L., Aulisi, E. F., Stanley, B. G., & Lenard, L. (1983). Self-injection of amphetamine directly into the brain. *Psychopharmacology, 81,* 158–163.

Hoebel, B. G., & Teitelbaum, P. (1961). Hypothalamic control of feeding and self-stimulation. *Science, 135,* 375–377.

Hofer, M. A. (1981). *The Roots of Human Behavior: An Introduction to the Psychobiology of Early Development.* San Francisco, CA: W. H. Freeman & Co..

Hofman, M. A., & Swaab, D. F. (1989). The sexually dimorphic nucleus of the preoptic area in the human brain: A comparative morphometric study. *Journal of Anatomy, 164,* 55–72.

Hollyday, M., & Hamburger, V. (1976). Reduction of the naturally occurring motor neuron loss by enlargement of the periphery. *Journal of Comparative Neurology, 170,* 311–320.

Holm, H., Hustvedt, B. E., & Løvø, A. (1973). Protein metabolism in rats with ventromedial hypothalamic lesions. *Metabolism, 22,* 1377–1387.

Holman, G. L. (1968). Intragastric reinforcement effect. *Journal of Comparative and Physiological Psychology, 69,* 432–441.

Holtzman, P. S., & Matthyse, S. (1990). The genetics of schizophrenia: A review. *American Psychological Society, 1,* 279–286.

Holzman, P. S., Solomon, C. M., Levin, S., & Waternaux, C. S. (1984). Pursuit eye movement dysfunctions in schizophrenia. *Archives of General Psychiatry, 41,* 136–139.

Hopkins, W. G., & Brown, M. C. (1984). *Development of nerve cells and their connections.* Cambridge: Cambridge University Press.

Horel, J. A. (1978). The neuroanatomy of amnesia: A critique of the hippocampal memory hypothesis. *Brain, 101,* 403–445.

Horne, J. A. (1976). Recovery sleep following different visual conditions during total sleep deprivation in man. *Biological Psychology, 4,* 107–118.

Horne, J. A. (1983). Mammalian sleep function with particular reference to man. In A. R. Mayes (Ed.), *Sleep mechanisms and functions in humans and animals* (pp. 262–312). Wokingham, England: Van Nostrand Reinhold.

Howlett, A. C., Bidaut-Russell, M., Devane, W. A., Melvin, L. S., Johnson, M. R., & Herkenham, M. (1990). The cannabinoid receptor: Biochemical, anatomical and behavioral characterization. *Trends in Neurosciences, 13,* 420–423.

Hoyle, G. (1984). The scope of neuroethology. *Behavioral and Brain Sciences, 7,* 367–412.

Hubel, D. H. (1982). Exploration of the primary visual cortex. *Nature, 299,* 515–524.

Hubel, D. H., & Wiesel, T. N. (1979). Brain mechanisms of vision. *Scientific American, 249,* 150–162.

Hubel, D. H., Wiesel, T. N., & LeVay, S. (1977). Plasticity of ocular dominance columns in the monkey striate cortex. *Philosophical Transactions of the Royal Society of London, 278,* 377–409.

Hubel, D. H., Wiesel, T. N., & Stryker, M. P. (1977). Orientation columns in macaque monkey visual cortex demonstrated by the 2-deoxyglucose autoradiographic technique. *Nature, 269,* 328–330.

Hughes, J., Smith, T. W., Kosterlitz, H. W, Fothergill, L. A., Morgan, B. A., & Morris, H.

R. (1975). Identification of two related pentapeptides from the brain with potent opiate agonist activity. *Nature, 258,* 577–581.

Hume, K. I., & Mills, J. N. (1977). Rhythms of REM and slowwave sleep in subjects living on abnormal time schedules. *Waking and Sleeping, 1,* 291–296.

Humphrey, D. R. (1979). On the cortical control of visually directed reaching: Contributions by nonprecentral motor areas. In R. E. Talbot & D. R. Humphrey (Eds.), *Posture and movement* (pp. 51–112). New York: Raven Press.

Huppert, F. A., & Piercy, M. (1978). Dissociation between learning and remembering in organic amnesia. *Nature, 275,* 317–318.

Huppert, F. A., & Piercy, M. (1979). Normal and abnormal forgetting in organic amnesia: Effect of locus of lesion. *Cortex, 15,* 385–390.

Hurlbert, A. (1991). Deciphering the colour code. *Nature, 349,* 191–193.

Hustvedt, B. E., & Løvø, A. (1972). Correlation between hyperinsulinemia and hyperphagia in rats with ventromedial hypothalamic lesions. *Acta Physiologica Scandinavica, 84,* 29–33.

Iacono, W. G. (1985). Psychophysiologic markers in psychopathology: A review. *Canadian Psychology, 26,* 96–111.

Iacono, W. G., & Koenig, W. G. R. (1983). Features that distinguish the smooth-pursuit eye-tracking performance of schizophrenic, affective-disorder, and normal individuals. *Journal of Abnormal Psychology, 92,* 29–41.

Iacono, W. G., & Patrick, C. J. (1987). What psychologists should know about lie detection. In I. B. Weiner & A. K. Hess (Eds.), *Handbook of forensic psychology* (pp. 460–489). New York: John Wiley & Sons.

Ibuka, N., Inouye, S. I., & Kawamura, H. (1977). Analysis of sleep-wakefulness rhythms in male rats after suprachiasmatic nucleus lesions and ocular enucleation. *Brain Research, 122,* 33–47.

Ichikawa, S., & Fujii, Y. (1982). Effect of prenatal androgen treatment on maternal behavior in the female rat. *Hormones and Behavior, 16,* 224–233.

Inglis, J., & Lawson, J. S. (1982). A meta-analysis of sex-differences in the effects of unilateral brain damage on intelligence test results. *Canadian Journal of Psychology, 36,* 670–683.

Inouye, S. I., & Kawamura, H. (1982). Characteristics of a circadian pacemaker in the suprachiasmatic nucleus. *Journal of Comparative Psychology, 146,* 153–160.

Iriki, A., Pavlides, C., Keller, A., & Asanuma, H. (1989). Long-term potentiation in the motor cortex. *Science, 245,* 1385–1387.

Ironton, R., Brown, M. C., & Holland, R. L. (1978). Stimuli to intramuscular nerve growth. *Brain Research, 156,* 351–354.

Iversen, L. L. (1987). Neurotransmitters. In G. Adelman (Ed.), *Encyclopedia of neuroscience* (pp. 856–858). Boston: Birkhäuser.

Iversen, S. D., & Koob, G. F. (1977). Behavioral implications of dopaminergic neurons in the mesolimbic system. In E. Costa & G. L. Gessa (Eds.), *Nonstriatal dopaminergic neurons: Advances in biochemical psychopharmacology* (pp. 209–214). New York: Raven.

Izard, C. E. (1971). *The face of emotion.* New York: Appleton-Century-Crofts.

Jacobs, W., Blackburn, J. R., Buttrick, M., Harpur, T. J., Kennedy, D., Mana, M. J., MacDonald, M. A., McPherson, L. M., Paul, D., & Pfaus, J. G. (1988). Observations. *Psychobiology, 16,* 3–9.

Jacobson, M. (1968). Development of neuronal specificity in retinal ganglion cells of *Xenopus. Developmental Biology, 17,* 202–218.

Jacobson, R. R., & Lishman, W. A. (1990). Cortical and diencephalic lesions in Korsakoff's syndrome: A clinical and CT scan study. *Psychological Medicine, 20,* 63–75.

Jacoby, L. L. (1982). Knowing and remembering: Some parallels in the behavior of Korsakoff patients and normals. In L. S. Cermack (Ed.), *Human memory and amnesia.* Hillsdale, NJ: Erlbaum.

Jacoby, L. L. (1984). Incidental versus intentional retrieval: Remembering and awareness as separate issues. In L. R. Squire & N. Butters (Eds.), *Neuropsychology of memory* (pp. 145–156). New York: Guilford Press.

Jaeger, C. B., & Lund, R. D. (1981). Transplantation of embryonic occipital cortex to the brain of newborn rats: A Golgi study of mature and developing transplants. *Journal of Comparative Neurology, 200,* 213–230.

James, W. (1890; reprinted 1950). *The principles of psychology.* New York: Dover.

Janosky, D. S., Huey, L., & Storms, L. (1977). Psychologic test responses and methylphenidate. In E. H. Ellinwood, Jr. & M. M. Kilbey (Eds.), *Cocaine and other stimulants* (pp. 675–688). New York: Plenum Press.

Jarvik, M. E. (1990). The drug dilemma: Manipulating the demand. *Science, 250,* 387–392.

Jenkins, W. M., & Merzenich, M. M. (1987). Reorganization of neocortical representations after brain injury: A neurophysiological model of the bases of recovery from stroke. *Progressive Brain Research, 71,* 249–266.

Jensen, T. S., & Rasmussen, P. (1989). Phantom pain and related phenomena after amputation. In P. D. Wall and R. Melzack (Eds.), *Textbook of pain* (pp. 508–521). New York: Churchill & Livingstone.

Jewett, D. L., & Williston, J. S. (1971). Auditory-evoked far fields averaged from the scalp of humans. *Brain, 94,* 681–696.

Jilge, B. (1991). Restricted feeding: A nonphotic zeitgeber in the rabbit. *Physiology & Behavior, 51,* 157–166.

Joanette, Y. (1989). Aphasia in left-handers and crossed aphasia. In F. Boller and J. Grafman (Eds.), *Handbook of neuropsychology, Vol. 2* (pp. 176–183). New York: Elsevier.

Johnston, T. D. (1987). The persistence of dichotomies in the study of behavioral development. *Developmental Review, 7,* 149–182.

Jones, H. S., & Oswald, I. (1966). Two cases of healthy insomnia. *Electroencephalography and Clinical Neurophysiology, 24,* 378–380.

Jones, H. W., & Park, I. J. (1971). A classification of special problems in sex differentiation. In D. Bergsma (Ed.) *The clinical delineation of birth defects. Part X: The endocrine system* (pp. 113–121). Baltimore: The Williams and Wilkins Company.

Jones, R. T. (1987). Tobacco dependence. In H. Y. Meltzer (Ed.), *Psychopharmacology: The third generation of progress* (pp. 1589–1596). New York: Raven Press.

Jost, A. (1972). A new look at the mechanisms controlling sex differentiation in mammals. *Johns Hopkins Medical Journal, 130,* 38–53.

Jouvet, M. (1972). The role of monoamines and acetylcholine-containing neurons in the regulation of the sleep-waking cycle. *Ergebnisse der Physiologie, 64,* 166–307.

Jouvet, M., & Renault, J. (1966). Insomnie persistante après lésions des noyaux du raphé chez le chat. *Comptes Rendus de la Société de Biologie (Paris), 160,* 1461–1465.

Julesz, B. (1986). Stereoscopic vision. *Vision Research, 26,* 1601–1612.

Julien, R. M. (1981). *A primer of drug action.* San Francisco: W. H. Freeman.

Jung, L. J., & Scheller, R. H. (1991). Peptide processing and targeting in the neuronal secretory pathway. *Science, 251,* 1330–1335.

Kaas, J. H. (1991). Plasticity of sensory and motor maps in adult mammals. *Annual Review of Neuroscience, 14,* 137–167.

Kaas, J. H., & Garraghty, P. E. (1991). Hierarchical, parallel, and serial arrangements of sensory cortical areas: Connection patterns and functional aspects. *Current Opinion in Neurobiology, 1,* 248–251.

Kaas, J. H., Krubtzer, L. A., Chino, Y. M., Langston, A. L., Polley, E. H., & Blair, N. (1990). Reorganization of retinotopic cortical maps in adult mammals after lesions of the retina. *Science, 248,* 229–231.

Kaas, J. H., Nelson, R. J., Sur, M., & Merzenich, M. M. (1981). Organization of somatosensory cortex in primates. In F. O. Schmitt, F. G. Worden, G. Adelman, & S. G. Dennis (Eds.), *The organization of the cerebral cortex* (pp. 237–261). Cambridge, MA: MIT Press.

Kalat, J. W. (1985). *Introduction to psychology.* Belmont, CA: Wadsworth Publishing Company.

Kalil, R. E. (1989). Synapse formation in the developing brain. *Scientific American, 261,* 76–85.

Kallman, F. J. (1946). The genetic theory of schizophrenia: An analysis of 691 schizophrenic twin index families. *American Journal of Psychiatry, 103,* 309–322.

Kandel, E. R. (1985). Cellular mechanisms of learning and the biological basis of individuality. In E. R. Kandel & J. H. Schwartz (Eds.), *Principles of neural science* (pp. 816–833). New York: Elsevier.

Kandel, E. R., & Schwartz, J. H., (Eds.). (1991). *Principles of neural science,* (2nd ed.) New York: Elsevier.

Kandel, E. R., & Siegelbaum, S. (1985). In E. R. Kandel and J. H. Schwartz (Eds.), *Principles of neural science* (2nd ed.) (pp. 89–107). New York: Elsevier.

Kane, J., Honigfield, G., Singer, J., & Melzer, H. (1988). Clozapine for the treatment-resistant schizophrenic. *Archives of General Psychiatry, 45,* 789–796.

Karacan, I., Goodenough, D. R., Shapiro, A., & Starker, S. (1966). Erection cycle during sleep in relation to dream anxiety. *Archives of General Psychiatry, 15,* 183–189.

Karacan, I., Williams, R. L., Finley, W. W., & Hursch, C. J. (1970). The effects of naps on nocturnal sleep: Influence on the need for stage-1 REM and stage-4 sleep. *Biological Psychiatry, 2,* 391–399.

Karadžić, V. T. (1973). Physiological changes resulting from total sleep deprivation. *1st European Congress on Sleep Research* (Basal, 1972), (pp. 165–174). Basel: Karger.

Karsch, F. J. (1987). Central actions of ovarian steroids in the feedback regulation of pulsatile secretion of luteinizing hormone. *Annual Review of Physiology, 49,* 365–382.

Katz, J. L., Ackman, P., Rothwax, Y., Sachar, E. J., Weiner, H., Hellman, L., & Gallagher, T. F. (1970). Psychoendocrine aspects of cancer of the breast. *Psychosomatic Medicine, 32,* 1–8.

Kavanagh, G. L., & Kelly, J. B. (1987). Contribution of auditory cortex to sound localization by the ferret (*Mustela putorius*). *Journal of Neurophysiology, 57,* 1746–1765.

Kavanagh, G. L., & Kelly, J. B. (1988). Hearing in the ferret (*Mustela putorius*): Effects of primary auditory cortical lesions on thresholds for pure tone detection. *Journal of Neurophysiology, 60,* 879–888.

Keesey, R. E., & Powley, T. L. (1975). Hypothalamic regulation of body weight. *American Scientist, 63,* 558–635.

Keesey, R. E., & Powley, T. L. (1986). The regulation of body weight. *Annual Review of Psychology, 37,* 109–133.

Keirstead, S. A., Rasminsky, M., Fukuda, Y., Carter, D. A., Aguayo, A. J., & Vidal-Sanz, M. (1989). Electrophysiologic responses in hamster superior colliculus evoked by regenerating retinal axons. *Science, 246,* 255–257.

Kelly, J. B. (1980). Effects of auditory cortical lesions on sound localization by the rat. *Journal of Neurophysiology, 44,* 1161–1174.

Kelsey, J. E., Carlezon, W. A., Jr., & Falls, W. A. (1989). Lesions of the nucleus accumbens in rats reduce opiate reward but do not alter context-specific opiate tolerance. *Behavioral Neuroscience, 103,* 1327–1334.

Kelso, S. R., & Brown, T. H. (1986). Differential conditioning of associative synaptic enhancements in hippocampal brain slices. *Science, 232,* 85–87.

Kelso, S. R., Ganong, A. H., & Brown, T. H. (1986). Hebbian synapses in hippocampus. *Proceedings of the National Academy of Sciences U.S.A., 83,* 5326–5330.

Kendler, K. S., & Gruenberg, A. M. (1984). An independent analysis of the Danish adoption study of schizophrenia: VI. The relationship between psychiatric disorders as defined by DSM-III in the relatives and adoptees. *Archives of General Psychiatry, 41,* 555–564.

Kendrick, K. M., & Baldwin, B. A. (1987). Cells in temporal cortex in conscious sheep can respond preferentially to the sight of faces. *Science, 236,* 448–450.

Kennedy, G. C. (1953). The role of depot fat in the hypothalamic control of food intake in the rat. *Proceedings of the Royal Society of London, 140,* 578–592.

Kephalas, T. A., Kiburis, J., Michael, C. M., Miras, C. J., & Papadakis, D. P. (1976). Some aspects of cannabis smoke chemistry. In G. G. Nahas (Ed.), *Marihuana:*

Chemistry, biochemistry, and cellular effects (pp. 39–49). New York: Springer-Verlag.

Kety, S. S. (1979). Disorders of the human brain. *Scientific American, 241,* 202–214.

Keynes, R. D. (1958). The nerve impulse and the squid. *Scientific American, 199,* 83–90.

Keynes, R. D. (1979). Ion channels in the nerve-cell membrane. *Scientific American, 240,* 126–135.

Kiecolt-Glaser, J. K., Glaser, R., Shuttleworth, E. C., Dyer, C. S., Ogrocki, P., & Speicher, C. E. (1987). Chronic stress and immunity in family caregivers of Alzheimer's disease victims. *Psychosomatic Medicine, 49,* 523–535.

Kimble, G. A. (1989). Psychology from the standpoint of a generalist. *American Psychologist, 44,* 491–499.

Kimelberg, H. K., & Norenberg, M. D. (1989). Astrocytes. *Scientific American, 260,* 66–76.

Kimura, D. (1961). Some effects of temporal-lobe damage on auditory perception. *Canadian Journal of Psychology, 15,* 156–165.

Kimura, D. (1964). Left-right differences in the perception of melodies. *Quarterly Journal of Experimental Psychology, 16,* 355–358.

Kimura, D. (1973). The asymmetry of the human brain. *Scientific American, 228,* 70–78.

Kimura, D. (1977). Acquisition of a motor skill after left-hemisphere damage. *Brain, 100,* 527–542.

Kimura, D. (1979). Neuromotor mechanisms in the evolution of human communication. In H. E. Steklis & M. J. Raleigh (Eds.), *Neurobiology of social communication in primates* (pp. 197–219). New York: Academic Press.

Kimura, D. (1987). Sex differences, human brain organization. In G. Adelman (Ed.), *Encyclopedia of neuroscience, Vol. II.* Boston: Birkhäuser.

Kimura, D., & Archibald, Y. (1974). Motor functions of the left hemisphere. *Brain, 97,* 337–350.

Kimura, D., & Watson, N. (1989). The relation between oral movement control and speech. *Brain and Language, 37,* 565–690.

King, A. J., & Moore, D. R. (1991). Plasticity of auditory maps in the brain. *Trends in Neurosciences, 14,* 31–37.

King, H. E. (1961). Psychological effects of excitation in the limbic system. In D. E. Sheer (Ed.), *Electrical stimulation of the brain* (pp. 477–486). Austin, TX: University of Texas Press.

King, M. B., & Hoebel, B. G. (1968). Killing elicited by brain stimulation in rats. *Communications in Behavioral Biology, Part A, 2,* 173–177.

Klawans, H. L. (1990). *Newton's madness: Further tales of clinical neurology.* New York: Harper & Row.

Klein, M., & Kandel, E. R. (1978). Presynaptic modulation of voltage-dependent Ca^{2+} current: Mechanism for behavioral sensitization in *Aplysia californica. Proceedings of the National Academy of Sciences (USA), 75,* 3512–3516.

Klein, M., Shapiro, E., & Kandel, E. R. (1980). Synaptic plasticity and the modulation of the Ca^{2+} current. *Journal of Experimental Biology, 89,* 117–157.

Kleitman, N. (1963). *Sleep and wakefulness.* Revised and enlarged edition. Chicago: University of Chicago.

Kling, A. (1972). Effects of amygdalectomy on social-affective behavior in non-human primates. In B. E. Eleftherlou (Ed.), *The neurobiology of the amygdala* (pp. 536–551). New York: Plenum Press.

Klose, M., & Bentley, D. (1989). Transient pioneer neurons are essential for formation of an embryonic peripheral nerve. *Science, 245,* 982–984.

Kluver, H., & Bucy, P. C. (1939). Preliminary analysis of the temporal lobes in monkeys. *Archives of Neurology and Psychiatry, 42,* 979–1000.

Knight, D. E., von Grafenstein, H., & Athayde, C. M. (1989). Calcium-dependent and calcium-independent exocytosis. *Trends in Neurosciences, 12,* 451–458.

Knoth, R. L., & Mair, R. G. (1991). Response latency and accuracy on a pretrained nonmatching-to-sample task in rats recovered from pyrithiamine-induced thiamine deficiency. *Behavioral Neuroscience, 105,* 375–385.

Knudsen, E. I. (1981). The hearing of the barn owl. *Scientific American, 245,* 113–125.

Knudsen, E. I. (1991). Dynamic space codes in the superior colliculus. *Current Opinion in Neurobiology, 1,* 628–632.

Knudsen, E. I., & Brainard, M. S. (1991). Visual instruction of the neural map of auditory space in the developing optic tectum. *Science, 253,* 85–87.

Kolb, B. (1989). Brain development, plasticity, and behavior. *American Psychologist, 44,* 1202–1212.

Kolb, B., & Milner, B. (1981). Performance of complex arm and facial movements after focal brain lesions. *Neuropsychologia, 19,* 491–503.

Kolb, B., & Taylor, L. (1981). Affective behavior in patients with localized cortical excisions: Role of lesion site and side. *Science, 214,* 89–91.

Kolb, B., & Taylor, L. (1988). Facial expression and the neocortex. *Society for Neuroscience Abstracts, 14,* 1934.

Kolb, B., & Tees, R. C. (Eds.). (1990). *The cerebral cortex of the rat.* Cambridge, MA: MIT Press.

Kolb, B., & Whishaw, I. Q. (1990). *Fundamentals of human neuropsychology* (3rd ed.). New York: Freeman.

Kollar, E. J., & Fisher, C. (1980). Tooth induction in chick epithelium: Expression of quiescent genes for enamel synthesis. *Science, 207,* 993–995.

Kolodny, R. C., Masters, W. H., Kolodner, R. M., & Toro, G. (1974). Depression of plasma testosterone levels after chronic intensive marihuana use. *New England Journal of Medicine, 290,* 872–874.

Koob, G. F., & Bloom, F. E. (1988). Cellular and molecular mechanisms of drug dependence. *Science, 242,* 715–723.

Koob, G. F., Pettit, H. O., Ettenberg, A., & Bloom, F. E. (1984). Effects of opiate antagonists and their quaternary derivatives on heroin self-administration in the rat. *Journal of Pharmacology of Experimental Therapeutics, 229,* 481–487.

Koob, G. F., Vaccarino, F., Amalric, M., & Bloom, F. E. (1987). Positive reinforcement properties of drugs: Search for neural substrates. In J. Engel & L. Oreland (Eds.), *Brain reward systems and abuse* (pp. 35–50). New York: Raven Press.

Koolhaas, J. M., Schuurman, T., & Wierpkema, P. R. (1980). The organization of intraspecific agonistic behaviour in the rat. *Progress in Neurobiology, 15,* 247–268.

Koopmans, H. S. (1981). The role of the gastrointestinal tract in the satiation of hunger. In L. A. Cioffi, W. B. T. James, & T. B. Van Italie (Eds.), *The body weight regulatory system: Normal and disturbed mechanisms* (pp. 45–55). New York: Raven Press.

Kornetsky, C. (1977). Animal models: Promises and problems. In I. Hanin & E. Usdin (Eds.), *Animal models of psychiatry and neurology* (pp. 1–7). Oxford: Pergamon Press.

Kosambi, D. D. (1967). Living prehistory in India. *Scientific American, 216,* 105–114.

Kosslyn, S. M. (1988). Aspects of a cognitive neuroscience of mental imagery. *Science, 240,* 1621–1626.

Kowalaska, D. M., Bachevelier, J., & Mishkin, M. (1984). Inferior prefrontal cortex and recognition memory. *Society for Neuroscience Abstracts, 10,* 385.

Kowler, E. (Ed.). (1990). *Eye movements and their role in visual and cognitive processes.* New York: Elsevier.

Kraly, F. S., & Gibbs, J. (1980). Vagotomy fails to block the satiating effect of food in the stomach. *Physiology & Behavior, 24,* 1007–1010.

Kraly, F. S., & Smith, G. P. (1978). Combined pregastric and gastric stimulation by foods is sufficient for normal meal size. *Physiology & Behavior, 21,* 405–408.

Krieger, D. T., & Hughes, J. C. (1980). *Neuroendocrinology.* Sunderland, MA: Sinauer.

Kuffler, S. W. (1953). Discharge patterns and functional organization of mammalian retina. *Journal of Neurophysiology, 16,* 37–68.

Kuffler, S. W., Nicholls, J. G., & Martin, A. R. (1984). *From neuron to brain: A cellular approach to the function of the nervous system.* Sunderland, MA: Sinauer Associates, Inc.

Kuhar, M. J., Ritz, M. C., & Boja, J. W. (1991). The dopamine hypothesis of the reinforcing properties of cocaine. *Trends in Neurosciences, 14,* 299–302.

Kuwada, J. Y. (1986). Cell recognition by neuronal growth cones in a simple vertebrate embryo. *Science, 233,* 740–746. @REFS-MS = LaBerge, S. (1985). *Lucid dreaming.* Los Angeles: Tarcher.

LaBerge, S., Greenleaf, W., & Kedzierski, B. (1983). Physiological responses to dreamed sexual activity during lucid REM sleep. *Psychophysiology, 20,* 454–455.

Laguzzi, R., & Adrien, J. (1980). Effets des antagonistes de la serotonine sur le cycle veille-sommeil au rat. *Journal de Physiologie et Pathalogie, 76,* 20A.

Lamb, A. H. (1984). Motoneuron death in the embryo. *Critical Reviews in Clinical Neurobiology, 1,* 141–173.

Lance-Jones, C., & Landmesser, L. (1980). Motoneuron projection patterns in the chick hind limb following early partial spinal cord reversals. *Journal of Physiology, 302,* 559–580.

Land, E. H. (1977). The retinex theory of color vision. *Scientific American, 237,* 108–128.

Langston, J. W. (1985). MPTP and Parkinson's disease. *Trends in Neuroscience, 8,* 79–83.

Langston, J. W. (1986). MPTP-induced parkinsonism: How good a model is it? In S. Fahn, C. P. Marsden, P. Jenner, & P. Teychenne (Eds.), *Recent developments in Parkinson's disease* (pp. 119–126). New York: Raven Press.

Langston, J. W., Forno, L. S., Robert, C. S., & Irwin, I. (1984). Selective nigral toxicity after systemic administration of 1-methyl-4-phenyl-1,2,3,6-tetrahydropyridine (MPTP) in the squirrel monkey. *Brain Research, 292,* 390–394.

Lashley, K. S. (1941). Patterns of cerebral integration indicated by the scotomas of migraine. *Archives of Neurology and Psychiatry, 46,* 331–339.

Latimer, D., & Goldberg, J. (1981). *Flowers in the blood.* New York: Franklin Watts.

Lavie, P., Pratt, H., Scharf, B., Peled, R., & Brown, J. (1984). Localized pontine lesion: Nearly total absence of REM sleep. *Neurology, 34,* 1118–1120.

Lawrence, D. G., & Kuypers, H. G. J. M. (1968). The functional organization of the motor system in the monkey: I. The effects of bilateral pyramidal lesions. *Brain, 91,* 1–14.

Lawrence, D. G., & Kuypers, H. G. J. M. (1968). The functional organization of the motor system in the monkey: II. The effects of lesions of the descending brain-stem pathways. *Brain, 91,* 15–36.

Lê, A. D., Poulos, C. X., & Cappell, H. (1979). Conditioned tolerance to the hypothermic effects of ethyl alcohol. *Science, 206,* 1109–1110.

Leech, C. K., & McIntyre, D. C. (1976). Kindling rates in inbred mice: An analog to learning? *Behavioral Biology, 16,* 439–452.

Leibowitz, S. F., Hammer, N. J., & Chang, K. (1981). Hypothalamic paraventricular nucleus lesions produce overeating and obesity in the rat. *Physiology & Behavior, 27,* 1031–1040.

Leiner, H. C., Leiner, A. L., & Dow, R. S. (1989). Reappraising the cerebellum: What does the hindbrain contribute to the forebrain? *Behavioral Neuroscience, 103,* 998–1008.

LeMagnen, J. (1981). The metabolic basis of dual periodicity of feeding in rats. *Behavioral and Brain Sciences, 4,* 561–607.

Lemberger, L., & Rowe, H. (1975). Clinical pharmacology of nabilone, a cannabinol derivative. *Clinical Pharmacology and Therapeutics, 18,* 720–726.

Lennox, W. G. (1960). *Epilepsy and related disorders.* Boston: Little, Brown and Co.

Lester, G. L. L., & Gorzalka, B. B. (1988). Effect of novel and familiar mating partners on the duration of sexual receptivity in the female hamster. *Behavioral and Neural Biology, 49,* 398–405.

Letourneau, P. C., Kater, S. B., & Macagno, E. R. (Eds.). (1991). *The nerve growth cone.* New York: Raven Press.

LeVay, S. (1991). A difference in hypothalamic structure between heterosexual and homosexual men. *Science, 253,* 1034–1037.

LeVay, S., Hubel, D. H., & Wiesel, T. N. (1975). The pattern of ocular dominance columns in Macaque visual cortex revealed by a reduced silver stain. *Journal of Comparative Neurology, 159,* 559–576.

Levenson, R. W. (1992). Autonomic nervous system differences among emotions. *Psychological Science, 3,* 23–27.

Levi-Montalcini, R. (1952). Effects of mouse motor transplantation on the nervous system. *Annals of the New York Academy of Science, 55,* 330–344.

Levi-Montalcini, R. (1975). NGF: An uncharted route. In F. G. Worden, J. P. Swazey, & G. Adelman (Eds.), *The neurosciences: Paths of discovery* (pp. 245–265). Cambridge, MA: MIT Press.

Levin, H. S. (1989). Memory deficit after closed-head injury. *Journal of Clinical and Experimental Neuropsychology, 12,* 129–153.

Levin, H. S., Papanicolaou, A., & Eisenberg, H. M. (1984). Observations on amnesia after non-missile head injury. In L. R. Squire & N. Butters (Eds.), *Neuropsychology of memory* (pp. 247–257). New York: Guilford Press.

Levine, D. G. (1974). "Needle freaks": Compulsive self-injection by drug users. *American Journal of Psychiatry, 131,* 297–301.

Levy, E., Carman, M. D., Fernandez-Madrid, I. J., Power, M. D., Lieberburg, I., van Duinen, S. G., Bots, G.Th. A. M., Luyendijk, W., & Frangione, B. (1990). Mutation of the Alzheimer's disease amyloid gene in hereditary cerebral hemorrhage, Dutch type. *Science, 248,* 1124–1126.

Levy, J. (1969). Possible basis for the evolution of lateral specialization of the human brain. *Nature, 224,* 614–615.

Levy, J., Trevarthen, C., & Sperry, R. W. (1972). Perception of bilateral chimeric figures following hemispheric deconnection. *Brain, 95,* 61–78.

Ley, R. G., & Bryden, M. P. (1982). A dissociation of right and left hemispheric effects for recognizing emotional tone and verbal content. *Brain Cognition, 1,* 3–9.

Liebling, D. S., Eisner, J. D., Gibbs, J., & Smith, G. P. (1975). Intestinal satiety in rats. *Journal of Comparative and Physiological Psychology, 89,* 955–965.

Linden, W., & Estrin, R. (1988). Computerized cardiovascular monitoring: Method and data. *Psychophysiology, 25,* 227–234.

Lindsey, D. B., Bowden, J., & Magoun, H. W. (1949). Effect upon the EEG of acute injury to the brain stem activating system. *Electroencephalography and Clinical Neurophysiology, 1,* 475–486.

Lindvall, O. (1991). Prospects of transplantation in human neurodegenerative diseases. *Trends in Neurosciences, 14,* 376–384.

Lindvall, O., Brundin, P., Widner, H., Rehncrona, S., Gustavi, B., Frackowiak, R., Leenders, K. L., Sawle, G., Rothwell, J. C., Marsden, C. D., & Björklund, A. (1990). Grafts of fetal dopamine neurons survive and improve motor function in Parkinson's disease. *Science, 247,* 374–577.

Lishman, W. A. (1990). Alcohol and the brain. *British Journal of Psychiatry, 156,* 635–644.

Livingstone, M. S., & Hubel, D. H. (1984). Anatomy of physiology of a color system in the primate visual cortex. *Journal of Neuroscience, 4,* 309–356.

Livingstone, M. S., & Hubel, D. S. (1988). Segregation of form, color, movement, and depth: Anatomy, physiology, and perception. *Science, 240,* 740–749.

Llinás, R. R. (1982). Calcium in synaptic transmission. *Scientific American, 247,* 56–65.

Lo, Y-J. & Poo, M-M. (1991). Activity-dependent synaptic competition *in vitro:* Heterosynaptic suppression of developing synapses. *Science, 254,* 1019–1022.

Loeb, G. E. (1990). Cochlear prosthetics. *Annual Review of Neuroscience, 13,* 357–371.

Loftus, E. F., & Palmer, J. C. (1974). Reconstruction of automobile destruction: An example of the interaction between language and memory. *Journal of Verbal Learning and Verbal Behavior, 13,* 585–589.

Loomis, A. L., Harvey, E. N., & Hobart, G. (1936). Electrical potentials of the human brain. *Journal of Experimental Psychology, 19,* 249–279.

LoPiccolo, M. A. (1977). Behavioral and neuronal effects of EEG synchronizing stimuli in the cat. *Unpublished doctoral dissertation.* McMaster University, Hamilton.

Lowe, J., & Carroll, D. (1985). The effects of spinal injury on the intensity of emotional experience. *British Journal of Clinical Psychology, 24,* 135–136.

Lucas F., & Sclafani, A. (1989). Flavor preferences conditioned by intragastric fat infusions in rats. *Physiology & Behavior, 46,* 403–412.

Ludwig, A. M., & Wikler, A. (1974). "Craving" and relapse to drink. *Quarterly Journal of Studies on Alcohol, 35,* 108–130.

Lund, R. D., & Harvey, A. R. (1981). Transplantation of tectal tissue in rats: I. Organization and transplants and pattern of distribution of host afferents within them. *Journal of Comparative Neurology, 201,* 191–209.

Lund, R. D., Radel, J. D., & Coffey, P. J. (1991). The impact of intracerebral retinal transplants on types of behavior exhibited by host rats. *Trends in Neurosciences, 14,* 358–361.

Luria, A. R. (1972). *The history of a brain wound. The man with a shattered world.* Cambridge, MA: Harvard University Press.

Lydic, R., McCarley, R. W., & Hobson, J. A. (1983). The time-course of dorsal raphé discharge, PGO waves, and muscle tone averaged across multiple sleep cycles. *Brain Research, 274,* 365–370.

Lykken, D. T. (1959). The GSR in the detection of guilt. *Journal of Applied Psychology, 43,* 385–388.

Lynch, C. B. (1981). Genetic correlation between two types of nesting in Mus musculus: Direct and indirect selection. *Behavior Genetics, 11,* 267–272.

Lynch, G. & Baudry, M. (1991). Reevaluating the constraints on hypotheses regarding LTP expression. *Hippocampus, 1,* 9–14.

Macchi, G. (1989). Anatomical substrate of emotional reactions. In F. Boller and J. Grafman (Eds.), *Handbook of neuropsychology, Vol. 3,* (pp. 283–304). New York: Elsevier.

MacLusky, N. J., & Naftolin, F. (1981). Sexual differentiation of the central nervous system. *Science, 211,* 1294–1302.

MacNichol, E. F., Jr. (1964). Three-pigment color vision. *Scientific American, 211,* 48–67.

Maddison, S., Wood, R. J., Rolls, E. T., Rolls, B. J., & Gibbs, J. (1980). Drinking in the rhesus monkey: Peripheral factors. *Journal of Physiology, 272,* 365–374.

Madison, D. V., Malenka, R. C., & Nicoll, R. A. (1991). Mechanisms underlying long-term potentiation of synaptic transmission. *Annual Review of Neuroscience, 14,* 379–97.

Madrazo, I., Drucken-Colín, R., Díaz, V., Martínez-Mata, J., Torres, C., & Becerril, J. J. (1987). Open microsurgical autograft of adrenal medulla to the right caudate nucleus in two patients with intractable Parkinson's disease. *New England Journal of Medicine, 316,* 831–834.

Magni, F., Moruzzi, G., Rossi, G. F., & Zanchetti, A. (1957). EEG arousal following inactivation of the lower brain stem by selective injection of barbiturate into the vertebral circulation. *Archives Italiennes de Biologie, 95,* 33–46.

Mahut, H., Moss, M., & Zola-Morgan, S. (1981). Retention deficits after combined amygdalo-hippocampal and selective hippocampal resections in the monkey. *Neuropsychologia, 19,* 201–225.

Mair, R. G., Knoth, R. L., Rabchenuk, S. A., & Langlais, P. J. (1991). Impairment of olfactory, auditory, and spatial serial reversal learning in rats recovered from pyrithiamine-induced thiamine deficiency. *Behavioral Neuroscience, 105,* 360–374.

Mair, R. G., Otto, T. A., Knoth, R. L., & Langlais, P. J. (1991). Analysis of aversively conditioned learning and memory in rats recovered from pyrithiamine-induced thiamine deficiency. *Behavioral Neuroscience, 105,* 351–359.

Malmo, R. B., & Malmo, H. P. (1979). Responses of lateral preoptic neurons in the rat to hypertonic sucrose and NaCl. *Electroencephalography and Clinical Neurophysiology, 46,* 401–408.

Malsbury, C. W. (1971). Facilitation of male rat copulatory behavior by electrical stimulation of the medial preoptic area. *Physiology & Behavior, 7,* 797–805.

Malsbury, C. W., Kow, L. M., & Pfaff, D. W. (1977). Effects of medial hypothalamic lesions on the lordosis response and other behaviors in female golden hamsters. *Physiology & Behavior, 19,* 223–237.

Malsbury, C. W., & Pfaff, D. W. (1974). Neural and hormonal determinants of mating behavior in adult male rats. A review. In L. V. DiCara (Ed.), *Limbic and autonomic nervous system research* (pp. 85–136). New York: Plenum Press.

Mana, M. J., Kim, C. K., Pinel, J. P. J., & Jones, C. H. (1991). Contingent tolerance to the anticonvulsant effects of carbamazepine, diazepam, and sodium valproate in kindled rats. *Pharmacology Biochemistry & Behavior, 41,* 121–126.

Mansfield, J. G., & Cunningham, C. L. (1980). Conditioning and extinction of tolerance to the hypothermic effects of ethanol in rats. *Journal of Comparative and Physiological Psychology, 94,* 962–969.

Marchbanks, R. M. (1982). Biochemistry of Alzheimer's dementia. *Journal of Neurochemistry, 39,* 9–15.

Marin, O. S. M., Schwartz, M. F., & Saffran, E. M. (1979). Origins and distribution of language. In M. I. Gazzaniga (Ed.), *Handbook of behavioral neurobiology: Vol. 2. Neuropsychology* (pp. 179–213). New York: Plenum Press.

Mark, V. H., & Ervin, F. R. (1970). *Violence and the brain.* New York: Harper & Row, Publ.

Mark, V. H., Ervin, F. R., & Yakolev, P. I. (1962). The treatment of pain by stereotaxic methods. *1st International Symposium on Stereoencephalotomy (Philadelphia, 1961), Confina Neurologica, 22,* 238–245.

Marks, W. B., Dobelle, W. H., & MacNichol, E. F. (1964). Visual pigments of single primate cones. *Science, 143,* 1181–1183.

Marler, P. (1970a). Birdsong and speech development: Could there be parallels? *American Scientist, 58,* 669–673.

Marler, P. (1970b). A comparative approach to vocal learning: Song development in white-crowned sparrows. *Journal of Comparative and Physiological Psychology Monograph, 71,* 1–25.

Marler, P. (1991). Song learning behavior: The interface with neuroethology. *Trends in Neurosciences, 14,* 199–206.

Marler, P., & Tamura, M. (1962). Song "dialects" in three populations of white-crowned sparrows. *The Condor, 64,* 368–377.

Marlowe, W. B., Mancall, E. L., & Thomas, J. J. (1975). Complete Kluver-Bucy syndrome in man. *Cortex, 11,* 53–59.

Marques, D. M., Malsbury, C. W., & Daood, J. (1979). Hypothalamic knife cuts dissociate maternal behaviors, sexual receptivity, and estrous cyclicity in female hamsters. *Physiology & Behavior, 23,* 347–355.

Marshall, F. H. A. (1937). On the changeover in the oestrous cycle in animals after transference across the equator, with further observations on the incidence of the breeding seasons and the factors controlling sexual periodicity. *Proceedings of the Royal Society of London, (B), 122,* 413–428.

Marshall, N. B., Barnett, R. J., & Mayer, J. (1955). Hypothalamic lesions in gold thioglucose injected mice. *Proceedings of the Society for Experimental Biology and Medicine, 90,* 240–244.

Marslen-Wilson, W. D., & Teuber, H. L. (1975). Memory for remote events in anterograde amnesia: Recognition of public figures from newsphotographs. *Neuropsychologia, 13,* 353–364.

Martin, B. J. (1986). Sleep deprivation and exercise. In K. B. Pandolf (Ed.), *Exercise and Sport Sciences Reviews* (pp. 213–229). New York: Macmillan Pub. Co.

Martin, J. B. (1987). Molecular genetics: Applications to the clinical neurosciences. *Science, 238,* 765–772.

Martin, J. H. (1985). Receptor physiology and submodality coding in the somatic sensory system. In E. R. Kandel & J. H. Schwartz (Eds.), *Principles of neuroscience* (pp. 287–300). New York: Elsevier.

Martin, R. L., Roberts, W. V., & Clayton, P. J. (1980). Psychiatric status after a one-year prospective follow-up. *JAMA, 244,* 350–353.

Mateer, C. A., & Cameron, P. A. (1989). Electrophysiological correlates of language: Stimulation mapping and evoked potential studies. In F. Boller and J. Grafman (Eds.) *Handbook of neuropsychology, Vol. 2* (pp. 91–116). New York: Elsevier.

Matsuda, L. A., Lolait, S. J., Brownstein, M. J., Young, A. C., & Bonner, T. I. (1990). Structure of a cannabinoid receptor and functional expression of the cloned DNA. *Nature, 346,* 561–564.

Matteoli, M., & De Camilli, P. (1991). Molecular mechanisms in neurotransmitter release. *Current Opinion in Neurobiology, 1,* 91–97.

Matthews, P. B. C. (1991). The human stretch reflex and the motor cortex. *Trends in Neurosciences, 3,* 87–91.

Mattson, S. N., Barron, S., & Riley, E. P. (1988). The behavioral effects of prenatal alcohol exposure. In K. Kuriyama, A. Takada, & H. Ishii (Eds.), *Biomedical and social aspects of alcohol and alcoholism* (pp. 851–853). Tokyo: Elsevier.

Mayer, D. J., & Liebeskind, J. C. (1974). Pain reduction by focal electrical stimulation of the brain: An anatomical and behavioral analysis. *Brain Research, 68,* 79–93.

Mayer, J. (1955). Regulation of energy intake and the body weight: The glucostatic theory and the lipostatic hypothesis. *Proceedings of the New York Academy of Sciences, 63,* 15–43.

Mayer, J., & Marshall, N. B. (1956). Specificity of gold thioglucose for ventromedial hypothalamic lesions and hyperphagia. *Nature, 178,* 1399–1400.

Mazzocchi, F., & Vignolo, L. A. (1979). Localisation of lesions in aphasia: Clinical-CT scan correlations in stroke patients. *Cortex, 15,* 627–654.

McAuliffe, W. E., Feldman, B., Friedman, R., Launer, E., Magnuson, E., Mahoney, C., Santangelo, S., Ward, W., & Weiss, R. (1986). Explaining relapse to opiate addiction following successful completion of treatment. In F. M. Tims & C. G. Leukefield (Eds.), *Relapse and recovery in drug abuse: National Institute on Drug Abuse Research Monograph Series* (Vol. 72, pp. 136–156). Rockville, MD.

McBurney, D. H. (1986). Taste, smell, and flavor terminology: Taking the confusion out of fusion. In H. Meiselman & R. S. Rivlin (Eds.), *Clinical measurements of taste and smell* (pp. 117–125). New York: Macmillan Publishing Co.

McCann, T. S. (1981). Aggression and sexual activity of male southern elephant seals, *Mirounga leonina. Journal of Zoology, 195,* 295–310.

McClearn, G. E. (1976). Experimental behavioral genetics. In D. Bartrop (Ed.), *Aspects of genetics in paediatrics* (pp. 31–39). London: Fellowship of Postdoctorate Medicine.

McClintock, M. K. (1971). Menstruation synchrony and suppression. *Nature, 229,* 244–245.

McClintock, M. K. (1984). Group mating in the domestic rat as a context for sexual selection: Consequences for the analysis of sexual behavior and neuroendocrine responses. In J. S. Rosenblatt, C. Beer, M. C. Busnel, & P. C. Slater (Eds.), *Advances in the study of behavior, (Vol. 14,* pp. 2–50). New York: Academic Press, Inc.

McConnell, S. K., Ghosh, A., & Shatz, C. J. (1989). Subplate neurons pioneer the first axon pathway from the cerebral cortex. *Science, 245,* 978–982.

McDonald, W. I. (1984). Multiple sclerosis: Epidemiology and HLA associations. *Annals of the New York Academy of Sciences, 436,* 109–117.

McEwen, B. S. (1983). Gonadal steroid influences on brain development and sexual differentiation. In R. O. Greep (Ed.), *Reproductive physiology IV.* Baltimore, MD: University Park Press.

McEwen, B. S. (1987). Sexual differentiation. In G. Adelman (Ed.), *Encyclopedia of neuroscience, Vol. II* (pp. 1086–1088). Boston, MA: Birkhäuser.

McEwen, B. S., Davis, P. G., Parsons, B., & Pfaff, D. W. (1979). The brain as a target for steroid hormone action. *Annual Reviews in Neuroscience, 2,* 65–112.

McEwen, B. S., Lieburburg, I., Chaptal, C., & Krey, L. C. (1977). Aromatization: Important for sexual differentiation of the neonatal rat brain. *Hormones and Behavior, 9,* 249–263.

McFarland, H. F., Greenstein, J., McFarlin, D. E., Eldridge, R., Xu, X. H., & Krebs, H. (1984). Family and twin studies in multiple sclerosis. *Annals of the New York Academy of Sciences, 436,* 118–124.

McGinty, D. J., & Sterman, M. B. (1968). Sleep suppression after basal forebrain lesions in the cat. *Science, 160,* 1253–1255.

McGlone, J. (1977). Sex differences in the cerebral organization of verbal functions in patients with unilateral brain lesions. *Brain, 100,* 775–793.

McGlone, J. (1980). Sex differences in human brain asymmetry: A critical survey. *Behavioral and Brain Sciences, 3,* 215–263.

McHugh, P. R., & Moran, T. H. (1985). The stomach: A conception of its dynamic role in satiety. In J. M. Sprague & A. N. Epstein (Eds.), *Progress in psychobiology and physiological psychology, 11,* 197–232.

McKim, W. A. (1986). *Drugs and behavior: An introduction to behavioral pharmacology.* Englewood Cliffs, NJ: Prentice-Hall.

McLoon, S. C., & Lund, R. D. (1980). Identification of cells in retinal transplants which project to host visual centers: A horseradish peroxidase study in rats. *Brain Research, 197,* 491–495.

Meadows, J. C. (1974). The anatomical basis of prosopagnosia. *Journal of Neurology, Neurosurgery, and Psychiatry, 37,* 489–501.

Meaney, M. J., & Stewart, J. (1981). Neonatal androgens influence the social play of prepubescent rats. *Hormones and Behavior, 15,* 197–213.

Meck, W. H., Smith, R. A., & Williams, C. L. (1989). Organizational changes in cholinergic activity and enhanced visuospatial memory as a function of choline administered prenatally or postnatally or both. *Behavioral Neuroscience, 103,* 1234–1241.

Meddis, R. (1977). *The sleep instinct.* London: Routledge & Kegan Paul.

Mellgren, R. L. (1983). *Animal Cognition and Behavior.* New York: North-Holland Publishing.

Mello, N. K., & Mendelson, J. H. (1972). Drinking patterns during work-contingent and noncontingent alcohol acquisition. *Psychosomatic Medicine, 34,* 139–165.

Mello, N. K., Mendelson, M. P., Bree, M. P., & Lukas, S. E. (1989). Buprenorphine suppresses cocaine self-administration by rhesus monkeys. *Science, 245,* 859–862.

Meltzer, H. Y. (Ed.). (1987). *Psychopharmacology: The third generation of progress.* New York: Raven Press.

Meltzer, L. D. et al. (1990). Clinical efficacy of clozapine in the treatment of schizophrenia. *Clinical Neuropharmacology, 13, supplement 2,* 259–260.

Melzack, R. (1990). Phantom limbs and the concept of a neuromatrix. *Trends in Neurosciences, 13,* 88–92.

632

Melzack, R., & Wall, P. D. (1965). Pain mechanisms: A new theory. *Science, 150,* 971–979.

Melzack, R., & Wall, P. D. (1982). *The challenge of pain.* Harmondsworth, England: Penguin Books.

Mendelson, J. H. (1987). Marijuana. In H. Y. Meltzer (Ed.), *Psychopharmacology: The third generation of progress* (pp. 1565–1571). New York: Raven Press.

Mendelson, J. H., Kuehnle, J. C., Greenberg, I., & Mello, N. K. (1976). The effects of marihuana use on human operant behavior: Individual data. In M. C. Braude and S. Szara (Eds.), *The Pharmacology of Marihuana* (pp. 643–653). New York: Raven Press.

Mendelson, S. D., & Gorzalka, B. B. (1987). An improved chamber for the observation and analysis of the sexual behavior of the female rat. *Physiology & Behavior, 39,* 67–71.

Mercer, A. R., Emptage, N. J., & Carew, T. J. (1991). Pharmacological dissociation of modulatory effects of serotonin in *Aplysia* sensory neurons. *Science, 254,* 1811–1813.

Merzenich, M. M., & Kaas, J. H. (1980). Principles of organization of sensory-perceptual systems in mammals. In J. M. Sprague & A. N. Epstein (Eds.), *Progress in psychobiology and physiological psychology, 9,* 1–42.

Merzenich, M. M., Knight, P. L., & Roth, G. L. (1975). Representation of cochlea within primary auditory cortex in the cat. *Journal of Neurophysiology, 61,* 231–249.

Meunier, M., Murray, E. A., Bachevalier, J., & Mishkin, M. (1990). Effects of perirhinal cortical lesions on visual recognition memory in rhesus monkeys. *Society for Neuroscience Abstracts, 17,* 337.

Meyer-Bahlburg, H. F. L. (1981). Androgens and human aggression. In P. F. Brain & D. Benton (Eds.), *The biology of aggression* (pp. 263–290). Alpen ann den Rijn: Sijthoff & Noordhoff.

Michel, G. F., & Harkins, D. A. (1987). Ontogenetic consideration in the phylogenetic history and adaptive significance of the bias in human handedness. *Behavioral and Brain Sciences, 10,* 283–284.

Michelson, H. B., & Wong, R. K. S. (1991). Excitatory synaptic responses mediated by GABA receptors in the hippocampus. *Science, 253,* 1420–1423.

Miller, N. E. (1957). Experiments on motivation: Studies combining psychological, physiological, and pharmacological techniques. *Science, 126,* 1271–1278.

Miller, N. E. (1960). Motivational effects of brain stimulation and drugs. *Federation Proceedings, 19,* 846–854.

Miller, N. E., Bailey, C. J., & Stevenson, J. A. F. (1950). Decreased "hunger" but increased food intake resulting from hypothalamic lesions. *Science, 112,* 256–259.

Miller, R. L., & Baum, J. (1987). Naloxone inhibits mating and conditioned place preference for an estrous female in male rats soon after castration. *Pharmacology Biochemistry & Behavior, 26,* 781–789.

Miller, T. M., & Heuser, J. E. (1984). Endocytosis of synaptic vesicle membrane at the frog neuromuscular junction. *The Journal of Cell Biology, 98,* 685–698.

Milner, B. (1962). Laterality effects in audition. In V. B. Mountcastle, (Ed.), *Interhemispheric relations and cerebral dominance.* (pp. 177–195). Baltimore, MD: The Johns Hopkins Press.

Milner, B. (1965). Memory disturbances after bilateral hippocampal lesions. In P. Milner & S. Glickman (Eds.), *Cognitive processes and the brain* (pp. 104–105). Princeton, NJ: D. Van Nostrand Co. Inc.

Milner, B. (1971). Interhemispheric differences in the localization of psychological processes in man. *British Medical Bulletin, 27,* 272–277.

Milner, B. (1974). Hemispheric specialization: Scope and limits. In F. O. Schmitt & F. G. Worden (Eds.), *The neurosciences: Third study program* (pp. 75–89). Cambridge, MA: MIT Press.

Milner, B., Corkin, S., & Teuber, H. L. (1968). Further analysis of the hippocampal amnesic syndrome: 14-year follow-up study of H.M. *Neuropsychologia, 6,* 317–338.

Milner, P. M., & White, N. M. (1987). What is physiological psychology? *Psychobiology, 15,* 2–6.

Mishkin, M. (1957). Effects of small frontal lesions on delayed alternation in monkeys. *Journal of Neurophysiology, 20,* 615–622.

Mishkin, M. (1978). Memory in monkeys severely impaired by combined but not by separate removal of amygdala and hippocampus. *Nature, 273,* 297–298.

Mishkin, M. (1979). Analogous neural models for tactual and visual learning. *Neuropsychologia, 17,* 139–151.

Mishkin, M. (1982). A memory system in the monkey. *Philosophical Transactions of the Royal Society of London [Biol.], 298,* 85–95.

Mishkin, M., & Appenzeller, T. (1987). The anatomy of memory. *Scientific American, 256,* 80–89.

Mishkin, M., & Manning, F. J. (1978). Nonspatial memory after selective prefrontal lesions in monkeys. *Brain Research, 143,* 313–323.

Mistlberger, R., Bergmann, B., & Rechtschaffen, A. (1987). Period-amplitude analysis of rat electroencephalogram: Effects of sleep deprivation and exercise. *Sleep, 10,* 508–522.

Mistlberger, R. E. (1990). Circadian pitfalls in experimental designs employing food restriction. *Psychobiology, 18,* 23–29.

Mistlberger, R. E. (1991). Scheduled daily exercise of feeding alters the phase of photic entrainment in Syrian hamsters. *Physiology & Behavior, 50,* 1257–1260.

Mlinar, E. J., & Goodale, M. A. (1984). Cortical and tectal controls of visual orientation in the gerbil: Evidence for parallel channels. *Experimental Brain Research, 55,* 33–48.

Mohr, J. P. (1976). Broca's area and Broca's aphasia. In H. Whitaker & H. A. Whitaker (Eds.), *Studies in neurolinguistics: Volume 1* (pp. 201–235). New York: Academic Press.

Moll, L., & Kuypers, H. G. J. M. (1977). Premotor cortical ablations in monkeys: Contralateral changes in visually guided reaching behavior. *Science, 198,* 318–319.

Money, J. (1975). Ablatio penis: Normal male infant sex-reassigned as a girl. *Archives of Sexual Behavior, 4,* 65–186.

Money, J. (1987). Sin, sickness, or status? Homosexual gender identity and psychoneuroendocrinology. *American Psychologist, 42,* 384–399.

Money, J., & Ehrhardt, A. A. (1972). *Man & woman, boy & girl.* Baltimore: Johns Hopkins University Press.

Monnier, M., Dudler, L., Gaechter, R., Maier, P. F., Tobler, H. J., & Schoenenberger, G. A. (1975). The delta sleep inducing peptide (DSIP): Comparative properties of the original and synthetic nonapeptide. *Experientia, 33,* 548–552.

Moonen, C. T. W., van Zijl, P. C. M., Frank, J. A., Le Bihan, D., & Becker, E. D. (1990). Functional magnetic resonance imaging in medicine and physiology. *Science, 250,* 53–61.

Moore, R. Y. (1982). The suprachiasmatic nucleus and the organization of a circadian system. *Trends in Neurosciences, 5,* 404–407.

Moore, R. Y., & Eichler, V. B. (1972). Loss of a circadian adrenal corticosterone rhythm following suprachiasmatic lesions in the rat. *Brain Research, 42,* 201–206.

Moore, R. Y., & Lenn, N. J. (1972). A retinohypothalamic projection in the rat. *Journal of Comparative Neurology, 146,* 1–14.

Mora, F., Rolls, E. T., & Burton, M. J. (1976). Modulation during learning to the responses of neurons in the lateral hypothalamus to the sight of food. *Experimental Neurobiology, 53,* 508–519.

Moran, J., & Desimone, R. (1985). Selective attention gates visual processing in the extrastriate cortex. *Science, 229,* 782–784.

Morgan, T. H., Sturtevant, A. H., Muller, H. J., & Bridges, C. B. (1915). *The mechanism of Mendelian heredity.* New York: Henry Holt.

Mori, N., & Wada, J. A. (1990). Does electrical and excitatory amino acid kindling share a common neurobiological mechanism? In J. A. Wada, (Ed.), *Kindling 4* (pp. 209–222). New York: Plenum Press.

Morris, N. M., Udry, J. R., Khan-Dawood, F., & Dawood, M. Y. (1987). Marital sex frequency and midcycle female testosterone. *Archives of Sexual Behavior, 16,* 27–37.

Morris, R. G. M. (1981). Spatial localization does not require the presence of local cues. *Learning and Motivation, 12,* 239–260.

Moruzzi, G., & Magoun, H. W. (1949). Brain stem reticular formation and activation of the EEG. *Electroencephalography and Clinical Neurophysiology, 1,* 455–473.

Moscovitch, M. (1982). Multiple dissociations of function in amnesia. In L. S. Cermak (Ed.), *Human memory and amnesia* (pp. 337–370). Hillsdale, NJ: Erlbaum.

Moskowitz, H., Hulbert, S., & McGlothin, W. H. (1976). Marihuana: Effects on simulated driving performance. *Accident Analysis and Prevention, 8,* 45–50.

Motter, B. C., & Mountcastle, V. B. (1981). The functional properties of the light-sensitive neurons of the posterior parietal cortex studied in waking monkeys: Foveal sparing and opponent vector organization. *Journal of Neuroscience, 1,* 3–26.

Mouret, J., Bobillier, P., & Jouvet, M. (1968). Insomnia following parachlorophenylalanin in the rat. *European Journal of Pharmacology, 5,* 17–22.

Mrosovsky, N. (1988). Phase response curves for social entrainment. *Journal of Comparative Physiology, 162,* 35–46.

Mrosovsky, N., & Salmon, P. A. (1987). A behavioral method for accelerating re-entrainment of rhythms to new light-dark cycles. *Nature, 330,* 372–373.

Mucha, R. F., Van der Kooy, D., O'Shaughnessy, M., & Bucenieks, P. (1982). Drug reinforcement studied by the use of place conditioning in rat. *Brain Research, 243,* 91–105.

Mullaney, D. J., Johnson, L. C., Naitoh, P., Friedman, J. K., & Globus, G. G. (1977). Sleep during and after gradual sleep reduction. *Psychophysiology, 14,* 237–244.

Mumby, D. G., & Pinel, J. P. J. (1990). A rat model of medial-diencephalic amnesia: Nonrecurring items delayed nonmatching-to-sample. *Society for Neuroscience Abstracts, 16,* 606.

Mumby, D. G., Pinel, J. P. J., & Wood, E. R. (1989). Nonrecurring items delayed nonmatching-to-sample in rats: A new paradigm for testing nonspatial working memory. *Psychobiology, 18,* 321–326.

Mumby, D. G., Wood, E. R., & Pinel, J. P. J. (1992). Object-recognition memory is only mildly impaired in rats with lesions of the hippocampus and amygdala. *Psychobiology, 20,* 18–27.

Murphy, M. R., & Schneider, G. E. (1970). Olfactory bulb removal eliminates mating behavior in the male golden hamster. *Science, 157,* 302–304.

Murray, E. A. (1992). Medial temporal lobe structures contributing to recognition memory: The amygdaloid complex versus the rhinal cortex. In J. Aggleton (Ed.), *The amygdala: Neurobiological aspects of emotion, memory, and mental dysfunction,* (pp. 453–470). New York: Wiley & Sons.

Musto, D. F. (1991). Opium, cocaine and marijuana in American history. *Scientific American, 265,* 40–47.

Myers, R. E., & Sperry, R. W. (1953). Interocular transfer of a visual form discrimination habit in cats after section of the optic chiasma and corpus callosum. *American Association of Anatomists: Abstracts of Papers from Platform,* p. 351.

Näätänen, R. (1990). The role of attention in auditory information processing as revealed by event-related potentials and other brain measures of cognitive function. *Behavioural and Brain Sciences, 13,* 201–288.

Nadelman, E. A. (1989). Drug prohibition in the United States: Costs, consequences, and alternatives. *Science, 245,* 939–947.

Naeser, M., Alexander M. P., Helm-Estabrooks, N., Levine, H. L., Laughlin, S. A., & Geschwind, N. (1982). Aphasia with predominantly subcortical lesion sites. *Archives of Neurolinguistics, 39,* 2–14.

Naeser, M. A., Hayward, R. W., Laughlin, S. A., & Zatz, L. M. (1981). Quantitative CT scan studies in aphasia. *Brain and Language, 12,* 140–164.

Nathans, J. (1989). The genes for color vision. *Scientific American, 260,* 42–49.

National Commission on Marijuana and Drug Abuse (1972). R. P. Schafer, Chairman. *Marijuana: A signal of misunderstanding.* New York: New American Library.

Netter, F. H. (1962). *The CIBA collection of medical illustrations: Vol. 1. The nervous system.* New York: CIBA.

Newman, E. A., & Hartline, P. H. (1982). The infrared "vision" of snakes. *Scientific American, 246,* 116–127.

Nicholaidis, S., & Rowland, N. (1975). Regulatory drinking in rats with permanent access to a bitter fluid source. *Physiology & Behavior, 14,* 819–824.

Nicholaidis, S., & Rowland, N. (1977). Intravenous self-feeding: Long-term regulation of energy balance in rats. *Science, 195,* 589–591.

Nordeen, E. J., & Nordeen, K. W. (1990). Neurogenesis and sensitive periods in avian song learning. *Trends in Neurosciences, 13,* 31–36.

Nottebohm, F. (1991). Reassessing the mechanisms and origins of vocal learning in birds. *Trends in Neurosciences, 14,* 206–211.

Nottebohm, F., Kasparian, S., & Pandazis, C. (1981). Brain space for a learned task. *Brain Research, 213,* 99–109.

Nottebohm, F., & Nottebohm, M. (1976). Left hypoglossal dominance in the control of canary and white-crowned sparrow song. *Journal of Comparative Physiology, 108A,* 227–240.

Novin, D. (1964). The effects of insulin on water intake in the rat. In M. J. Wayner (Ed.), *Proceedings of the 1st international symposium in the regulation of body water* (pp. 177–184). Oxford: Pergamon Press.

Nyhan, W. L. (1987). Phenylalanine and mental retardation (PKU). In G. Adelman (Ed.), *Encyclopedia of Neuroscience Vol. II* (pp.940–942). Boston: Birkhäuser.

Oakley, B. (1986). Basic taste physiology. In H. Meiselman & R. S. Rivlin (Eds.), *Clinical measurement of taste and smell* (pp. 5–18). New York: Macmillan Publishing Co.

O'Brien, C. P., Chaddock, B., Woody, G., & Greenstein, R. (1974). Systematic extinction of addictionassociated rituals using narcotic antagonists. *Psychosomatic Medicine, 36,* 458.

O'Brien, C. P., Ternes, J. W., Grabowski, J., & Ehrman, R. (1981). Classically conditioned phenomena in human opiate addiction. *National Institute for Drug Research Monograph Series, 37,* 107–115.

O'Brien, D. F. (1982). The chemistry of vision. *Science, 218,* 961–966.

O'Callaghan, M. A. J., & Carroll, D. (1982). *Psychosurgery: A scientific analysis.* Ridgewood, NJ: George A. Bogdaen & Son, Inc.

Ohzawa, I., DeAngelis, G. C., & Freeman, R. D. (1990). Stereoscopic depth discrimination in the visual cortex: Neurons ideally suited as disparity detectors. *Science, 249,* 1037–1040.

Ojeda, S. R., Kalra, P. S., & McCann, S. M. (1975). Further studies on the maturation of the estrogen negative feedback on gonadotropin release in the female rat. *Neuroendocrinology, 18,* 242–255.

Ojemann, G. A. (1979). Individual variability in cortical localization of language. *Journal of Neurosurgery, 50,* 164–169.

Ojemann, G. A. (1983). Brain organization for language from the perspective of electrical stimulation mapping. *Behavioral and Brain Sciences, 2,* 189–230.

O'Keefe, J., Dostrovsky, J. (1971). The hippocampus as a spatial map. Preliminary evidence from unit activity in the freely-moving rat. *Brain Research, 34,* 171–175.

O'Keefe, J., & Nadel, L. (1978). *The hippocampus as a cognitive map.* Oxford: Clarendon Press.

O'Keefe, J., & Speakman, A. (1987). Single unit activity in the rat hippocampus during a spatial memory task. *Experimental Brain Research, 68,* 1–27.

Olds, J., & Milner, P. (1954). Positive reinforcement produced by electrical stimulation of septal area and other regions of rat brain. *Journal of Comparative and Physiological Psychology, 47,* 419–427.

Olds, M. E., & Olds, J. (1963). Approach-avoidance analysis of rat diencephalon. *Journal of Comparative Neurology, 120,* 259–295.

O'Leary, A. (1990). Stress, emotion, and human immune function. *Psychological Bulletin, 108,* 363–382.

Oliveras, J-L., & Besson, J-M. (1988). Stimulation-produced analgesia in animals: Behavioural investigations. *Progress in Brain Research, 77,* 141–157.

Oliveras, J-L., Besson, J-M., Guilbaud, G., & Liebeskind, J. C. (1974). Behavioral and electrophysiological evidence of pain inhibition from midbrain stimulation in the cat. *Experimental Brain Research, 20,* 32–44.

Olton, D. S., & Samuelson, R. J. (1976). Remembrance of places: Spatial memory in rats. *Journal of Experimental Psychology: Animal Behavior Processes, 2,* 97–116.

Olton, D. S., Wible, C. G., Pang, K., & Sakurai, Y. (1989). Hippocampal cells have mnemonic correlates as well as spatial ones. *Psychobiology, 17,* 228–229.

Oppenheim, R. W. (1991). Cell death during development of the nervous system. *Annual Review of Neuroscience, 14,* 453–501.

Owen, R. R., Beake, B. J., Marby, D., Dessain, E. C., & Cole, J. (1989). Response to clozapine in chronic psychotic patients. *Psychopharmacology Bulletin, 25,* 253–257.

Owren, M. J. (1990). Acoustic classification of alarm calls by vervet monkeys (*Cercopithecus aethiops*) and humans (*Homo sapiens*): II. Synthetic calls. *Journal of Comparative Psychology, 104,* 29–40.

Paletta, M. S., & Wagner, A. R. (1986). Development of context specific tolerance to morphine: Support for a dual-process interpretation. *Behavioral Neuroscience, 100,* 611–623.

Panksepp, J. (1975). Metabolic hormones and regulation of feeding: A reply to Woods, Decke, and Vaselli. *Psychological Review, 82,* 158–164.

Panksepp, J., & Trowill, J. A. (1967). Intraoral self-injection: II. The simulation of self-stimulation phenomena with a conventional reward. *Psychonomic Science, 9,* 407–408.

Papez, J. W. (1937). A proposed mechanism of emotion. *Archives of Neurology and Psychiatry, 38,* 725–743.

Parker, G. H. (1919). *The elementary nervous system.* Philadelphia: J. B. Lippincott.

Parkinson Study Group (1989). Effect of Deprenyl on the progression of disability in early Parkinson's disease. *New England Journal of Medicine, 321,* 1364–1371.

Paton, J. A., O'Loughlin, B., & Nottebohm, F. (1985). Cells born in adult canary forebrain are local interneurons. *Journal of Neuroscience, 5,* 3088–3093.

Patrick, C. J. (1987). *The validity of lie detection with criminal psychopaths.* Unpublished doctoral dissertation, University of British Columbia, Vancouver.

Patterson, K., Vargha-Khadem, F., & Polkey, C. E. (1989). Reading with one hemisphere. *Brain, 112,* 39–63.

Patterson, K. E. (1982). The relation between reading and phonological coding: Further neuropsychological observations. In A. W. Ellis (Ed.), *Normality and pathology in cognition functions* (pp. 77–111). London: Academic Press.

Pavlov, I. P. (1927). *Conditioned reflexes: An investigation of the physiological activity of the cerebral cortex.* New York: Dover Publishing Inc.

Peck, J. W., & Blass, E. M. (1975). Localization of thirst and antidiuretic osmoreceptors by intracranial injections in rats. *American Journal of Physiology, 228,* 1501–1509.

Peck, J. W., & Novin, D. (1971). Evidence that osmoreceptors mediating drinking in rabbits are in the lateral preoptic area. *Journal of Comparative and Physiological Psychology, 74,* 134–147.

Pellis, S. M. (1989). Fighting: The problem of selecting appropriate behavior patterns. In R. J. Blanchard, P. F. Brain, D. C. Blanchard, and S. Parmigiani (Eds.), *Ethoexperimental approaches to the study of behavior.* Dordrecht: Kluwer Academic Publishers.

Pellis, S. M., O'Brien, D. P., Pellis, V. C., Teitelbaum, P., Wolgin, D. L., & Kennedy, S. (1988). Escalation of feline predation along a gradient from avoidance through "play" to killing. *Behavioral Neuroscience, 102,* 760–777.

Pellow, S., Chopin, P., File, S. E., & Briley, M. (1985). Validation of open:closed arm entries in an elevated plus-maze as a measure of anxiety in the rat. *Journal of Neuroscience Methods, 14,* 149–167.

Penfield, W., & Boldrey, E. (1937). Somatic motor and sensory representations in cerebral cortex of man as studied by electrical stimulation. *Brain, 60,* 389–443.

Penfield, W., & Rasmussen, T. (1950). *The cerebral cortex of man: A clinical study of the localization of function.* New York: Macmillan Pub. Co.

Penfield, W., & Roberts, L. (1959). *Speech and brain mechanisms* (pp. 133–191). Princeton, NJ: Princeton University Press.

Penot, C., Vergnes, M., Mack, G., & Kempf, E. (1978). Interspecific aggression and reactivity in the rat: Compared effects of electrolytic raphé lesions and intraventricular 5,7 DHT administration. *Biology of Behavior, 3,* 71–85.

Pepperberg, I. M. (1990). Cognition in an African gray parrot (*Psittacus erithacus*): Further evidence for comprehension of categories and labels. *Journal of Comparative Psychology, 104,* 41–52.

Percival, J. E., Horne, J. A, & Tilley, A. J. (1983). Effects of sleep deprivation on tests of higher cerebral functioning. *Sleep 1982. 6th European Congress on Sleep Research* (Zurich, 1982). (pp. 390–391). Basel: Karger.

Perlow, M. J., Freed, W. J., Hoffer, B. J., Seiger, A., Olson, L., & Wyatt, R. J. (1979). Brain grafts reduce motor abnormalities produced by destruction of nigrostriatal dopamine system. *Science, 204,* 643–647.

Peterhans, E., & von der Heydt, R. (1991). Subjective contours—bridging the gap between psychophysics and physiology. *Trends in Neurosciences, 14,* 112–119.

Petersen, S. E., Fox, P. T., Mintun, M. A., Posner, M. I., & Raichle, M. E. (1989). Studies of the processing of single words using averaged positron emission tomographic measurements of cerebral blood flow change. *Journal of Cognitive Neuroscience,* Vol. 1, pp. 153–170.

Petersen, S. E., Fox, P. T., Posner, M. I., Mintun, M., & Raichle, M. E. (1988). Positron emission tomographic studies of the cortical anatomy of single-word processing. *Nature, 331,* 585–589.

Petersen, S. E., Fox, P. T., Snyder, A. Z., & Raichle, M. E. (1990). Activation of extrastriate and frontal cortical areas by visual words and word-like stimuli. *Science, 249,* 1041–1044.

Petrides, M. (1988). Performance on a non-spatial self-ordered task after selective lesions of the primate frontal cortex. *Society for Neuroscience Abstracts, 14,* 2.

Petrides, M. (1989). Frontal lobes and memory. In F. Boller and J. Grafman (Eds.) *Handbook of neuropsychology, Vol. III,* (pp. 75–90). New York: Elsevier.

Petrides, M., & Iversen, S. D. (1979). Restricted posterior parietal lesions in the rhesus monkey and performance on visuospatial tasks. *Brain Research, 161,* 63–77.

Petrinovitch, L. (1988). The role of social factors in white-crowned sparrow song development. In T. R. Zentall and B. G. Galef (Jr.) (Eds.), *Social learning, psychological and biological perspectives* (pp. 255–278). Hillsdale, NJ: Lawrence Erlbaum Associates.

Pfaff, D., & Modianos, D. (1985). Neural mechanisms of female reproductive behavior. In N. Adler, D. Pfaff, and R. W. Goy (Eds.), *Handbook of behavioral neurobiology, Vol. 7,* Reproduction (pp. 423–493). New York: Plenum Press.

Pfaus, J. G., & Pinel, J. P. J. (1989). Alcohol inhibits and disinhibits sexual behavior in the male rat. *Psychobiology, 17,* 195–201.

Pfeiffer, C. A. (1936). Sexual differences of the hypophyses and their determination by the gonads. *American Journal of Anatomy, 58,* 195–225.

Phelps, M. E., & Mazziotta, J. C. (1985). Positron emission tomography: Human brain function and biochemistry. *Science, 288,* 782–799.

Phillips, A. G., & Fibiger, H. C. (1989). Neuroanatomical bases of intracranial self-stimulation: Untangling the Gordian knot. In J. M. Leibman & S. J. Cooper (Eds.), *The neuropharmacological basis of reward* (pp. 66–105). Oxford: Clarendon Press.

Phillips, A. G., & LePiane, F. G. (1980). Reinforcing effects of morphine microinjection into the ventral tegmental area. *Pharmacology Biochemistry & Behavior, 12,* 965–968.

Phillips, A. G., Spyraki, C., & Fibiger, H. C. (1982). Conditioned place preference with amphetamine and opiates as reward stimuli: Attenuation by haloperidol. In B. G. Hoebel & D. Novin (Eds.), *The neural basis of feeding and reward* (pp. 455–464). Brunswick, MN: Haer Institute.

Phillips, D. P. (1989). Neurobiology relevant to some central auditory processing disorders. *Journal of Speech-Language Pathology and Audiology (Human Communication Canada), 13,* 17–34.

Phillips, M. I., & Felix, D. (1976). Specific angiotensin II receptive neurons in the cat subfornical organ. *Brain Research, 109,* 531–540.

Phoenix, C. H., Goy, R. W., Gerall, A. A., & Young, W. C. (1959). Organizing action of prenatally administered testosterone proprionate on the tissues mediating mating behavior in the female guinea pig. *Endocrinology, 65,* 369–382.

Piercy, M., Hécaen, H., & Ajuriaguerra, J. de (1962). Constructional apraxia associated with unilateral cerebral lesions—left and right sided cases compared. In V. B. Mountcastle (Ed.), *Interhemispheric relations and cerebral dominance* (pp. 225–242). Baltimore, MD: The Johns Hopkins Press.

Pilar, G., Landmesser, L., & Burstein, L. (1980). Competition for survival among developing ciliary ganglion cells. *Journal of Neurophysiology, 43,* 233–254.

Pinel, J. P. J. (1969). A short gradient of ECS-produced amnesia in a one-trial appetitive learning situation. *Journal of Comparative and Physiological Psychology, 68,* 650–655.

Pinel, J. P. J. (1981). Spontaneous kindled motor seizures in rats. In J. A. Wada (Ed.), *Kindling 2* (pp. 179–192). New York: Raven Press.

Pinel, J. P. J., & Huang, E. (1976). Effects of periodic withdrawal on ethanol and saccharin selection in rats. *Physiology & Behavior, 16,* 693–698.

Pinel, J. P. J., Kim, C. K., & Mana, M. J. (1990). Contingent tolerance to the anticonvulsant effects of drugs on kindled convulsions. In J. A. Wada, (Ed.) *Kindling 4* (pp. 283–297). New York: Plenum Press.

Pinel, J. P. J., & Mana, M. J. (1989). Adaptive interactions of rats with dangerous inanimate objects: Support for a cognitive theory of defensive behavior. In R. J. Blanchard, P. F. Brain, D. C. Blanchard, & S. Parmigiani (Eds.), *Ethoexperimental approaches to the study of behavior* (pp. 137–150). Dordrecht, The Netherlands: Kluwer Academic Publishers.

Pinel, J. P. J., Mana, M. J., & Kim, C. K., (1989). Effect-dependent tolerance to ethanol's anticonvulsant effect on kindled seizures. In R. J. Porter, R. H. Mattson, J. A. Cramer, & I. Diamond (Eds.), *Alcohol and seizures: Basic mechanisms and clinical implications* (pp. 115–125). Philadelphia: F. A. Davis.

Pinel, J. P. J., Mana, K. J., & Wilkie, D. M. (1986). Postshock learning and conditioned defensive burying. *Animal Learning and Behavior, 14,* 301–304.

Pinel, J. P. J., & Mucha, R. F. (1980). Increased susceptibility to kindled seizures following brief exposure to alcohol. In K. Erikson, J. D. Sinclair, & K. Kiianma (Eds.), *Animal models in alcohol research* (pp. 413–418). New York: Academic Press.

Pinel, J. P. J., Pfaus, J. G., & Christensen, B. K. (1991). Contingent tolerance to the disruptive effects of alcohol on the copulatory behavior of male rats. *Pharmacology Biochemistry & Behavior, 41,* 133–137.

Pinel, J. P. J., & Rovner, L. I. (1977). Saccharin elation effect. *Bulletin of the Psychonomic Society, 9,* 275–278.

Pinel, J. P. J., & Treit, D. (1978). Burying as a defensive response in rats. *Journal of Comparative and Physiological Psychology, 92,* 708–712.

Pinel, J. P. J., Treit, D., & Rovner, L. I. (1972). Temporal lobe aggression in rats. *Science, 197,* 1088–1089.

Pinel, J. P. J., & Wilkie, D. M. (1983). Conditioned defensive burying: A biological and cognitive approach to avoidance learning. In R. L. Mellgren (Ed.), *Animal Cognition and Behavior* (pp. 285–318). Amsterdam: North-Holland.

Pinsker, H. M., Hening, W. A., Carew, T. J., & Kandel, E. R. (1973). Long-term sensitization of a defensive withdrawal reflex in *Aplysia. Science, 182,* 1039–1042.

Pizzamiglio, L., Caltagirone, C., & Zoccaoloti, P. (1989). Facial expression of emotion. In F. Boller and J. Grafman (Eds.), *Handbook of neuropsychology, 3,* (pp. 383–402). New York: Elsevier.

Plapinger, L., McEwen, B. S., & Clemens, L. E. (1973). Ontogeny of estradiol-binding sites in rat brain. II. characteristics of a neonatal binding macromolecule. *Endocrinology, 93,* 1129–1139.

Plomin, R. (1990a). The role of inheritance in behavior. *Science, 248,* 183–188.

Plomin, R. (1990b). *Nature and nurture: An introduction to human behavioral genetics.* Pacific Grove, CA: Brooks/Cole.

Pohl, W. (1973). Dissociation of spatial discrimination deficits following frontal and parietal lesions in monkeys. *Comparative and Physiological Psychology, 82,* 227–239.

Polivy, J., & Herman, C. P. (1985). Dieting and binging: A causal analysis. *American Psychologist, 40,* 193–201.

Pons, T. P., Garraghty, P. E., Friedman, D. P., & Mishkin, M. (1987). Physiological evidence for serial processing in somatosensory cortex. *Science, 237,* 417–420.

Pons, T. P., Garraghty, P. E., Ommaya, A. K., Kaas, J. H., Taub, E., & Mishkin, M. (1991). Massive cortical reorganization after sensory deafferentation in adult macaques. *Science, 252,* 1857–1860.

Pope, H. G., & Katz, D. L. (1987). Bodybuilder's psychosis. *Lancet, 1(8537),* 863.

Poppelreuter, W. (1917). *Die psychischen Schädigungen durch Kopfschuss im Kriege 1914–1916: die Störungen der niederen und höheren Sehleistungen durch Verletzungen des Okzipitalhirns.* Leipzig: Voss.

Porrino, L. J. (1987). Cerebral metabolic changes associated with activation of reward systems. In J. Engel & L. Oreland (Eds.), *Brain reward systems and abuse* (pp. 51–60). New York: Raven Press.

Porrino, L. J., Esposito, R. U., Seeger, T. F., Crane, A. M., Pert, A., & Sokoloff, L. (1984). Metabolic mapping of the brain during rewarding self-stimulation. *Science, 224,* 306–309.

Porte, D., Jr., & Woods, S. C. (1981). Regulation of food intake and body weight by insulin. *Diabetologia, 20,* 274–280.

Posner, M. I., Petersen, S. E., Fox, P. T., & Raichle, M. E. (1988). Localization of cognitive operations in the human brain. *Science, 240,* 1627–1631.

Post, R. M., Weiss, S. R. B., Clark, M., Nakajima, T., & Pert, A. (1990). Amygdala versus local anesthetic kindling: Differential anatomy, pharmacology, and clinical implications. In J. A. Wada (Ed.), *Kindling 4* (pp. 357–369). New York: Plenum Press.

Poulos, C. X., & Cappell, H. (1991). Homeostatic theory of drug tolerance: A general model of physiological adaptation. *Psychological Review, 98,* 390–408.

Poulos, C. X., & Hinson, R. E. (1984). A homeostatic model of Pavlovian conditioning: Tolerance to scopolamine-induced adipsia. *Journal of Experimental Psychology: Animal Behavioral Processes, 10,* 75–89.

Powers, J. B., Newman, S. W., & Bergondy, M. L. (1987). MPOA and BNST lesions in male Syrian hamsters: Differential effects on copulatory and chemoinvestigatory behaviors. *Behavioral Brain Research, 23,* 181–195.

Powley, T. L., Opsahl, C. A., Cox, J. E., & Weingarten, H. P. (1980). The role of the hypothalamus in energy homeostasis. In P. J. Morgane & J. Panksepp (Eds.), *Handbook of the Hypothalamus—3A: Behavioral studies of the hypothalamus* (pp. 211–298). New York: Marcel Dekker Inc.

Pritchard, R. M. (1961). Stabilized images on the retina. *Scientific American, 204,* 72–78.

Pugh, E. N., & Lamb, T. D. (1990). Cyclic GMP and calcium: The internal messengers of excitation and adaptation in vertebrate photoreceptors. *Vision Research, 30,* 1923–1948.

Pujol, J. F., Buguet, A., Froment, J. L., Jones, B., & Jouvet, M. (1971). The central metabolism of serotonin in the cat during insomnia: A neurophysiological and biochemical study after administration of P-chlorophenylalanine or destruction of the raphé system. *Brain Research, 29,* 195–212.

Qualtrochi, J. J., Mamelak, A. N., Madison, R. D., Macklis, J. D., & Hobson, J. A. (1989). Mapping neuronal inputs to REM sleep induction sites with carbachol-fluorescent microspheres. *Science, 245,* 984–986.

Quinn, W. G. (1984). Work in invertebrates in the mechanisms underlying learning. In P. Marler & H. S. Terrace (Eds.), *The biology of learning* (pp. 197–246). Berlin: Springer-Verlag.

Racine, R. J. (1972). Modification of seizure activity by electrical stimulation: II. Motor seizure. *Electroencephalography and Clinical Neurophysiology, 32,* 281–294.

Racine, R. J. (1978). Kindling: The first decade. *Neurosurgery, 3,* 234–252.

Racine, R. J., & Burnham, W. M. (1984). The kindling model. In P. A. Schwartzkroin & H. Wheal (Eds.), *Electrophysiology of epilepsy* (pp. 153–171). London: Academic Press.

Racine, R. J., Burnham, W. M., Gartner, J. G., & Levitan, D. (1973). Rates of motor seizure development in rats subjected to electrical brain stimulation: Strain and interstimulation interval effects. *Electroencephalography and Clinical Neurophysiology, 35,* 553–556.

Racine, R. J., & deJonge, M. (1988). Short-term and long-term potentiation in projection pathways and local circuits. In P. W. Landfield & S. A. Deadwyler (Eds.), *Long-term potentiation: From biophysics to behavior* (p. 167). New York: Liss.

Racine, R. J., Livingston, K., & Joaquin, A. (1975). Effects of procaine hydrochloride, diazepam, and diphenylhydantoin on seizure development in cortical and subcortical structures in rats. *Electroencephalography and Clinical Neurophysiology, 38,* 355–365.

Racine, R. J., Milgram, N. W., & Hafner, S. (1983). Long-term potentiation phenomena in the rat limbic forebrain. *Brain Research, 260,* 217–233.

Rafal, R., Smith, J., Krantz, J., Cohen, A., & Brennan, C. (1990). Extrageniculate vision in hemianopic humans: Saccade inhibition by signals in the blind field. *Science, 250,* 118–121.

Raichle, M. E. (1987). Circulatory and metabolic correlates of brain function in normal humans. In J. B. Brookhart & V. B. Mountcastle (Eds.), *Handbook of physiology: The nervous system V* (pp. 643–674). Bethesda, MD: American Physiological Society.

Raisman, G., & Field, P. M. (1971). Sexual dimorphism in the neuropil of the preoptic area of the rat and its dependence on neonatal androgens. *Brain Research, 54,* 1–29.

Raisman, G., Morris, R. J., & Zhou, C. F. (1987). Specificity in the reinnervation of adult hippocampus by embryonic hippocampal transplants. In F. J. Seil, E. Herbert, & B. M. Carlson (Eds.), *Progress in Brain Research* (Vol. 71, pp. 325–333). New York: Elsevier.

Ralph, M. R., Foster, T. G., Davis, F. C., & Menaker, M. (1990). Transplanted suprachiasmatic nucleus determines circadian period. *Science, 247,* 975–978.

Ralph, M. R., & Lehman, M. N. (1991). Transplantation: A new tool in the analysis of the mammalian hypothalamic circadian pacemaker. *Trends in Neurosciences, 14,* 362–365.

Ramsay, D. J., Rolls, B. J., & Wood, R. J. (1977). Body fluid changes which influence drinking in the water deprived rat. *Journal of Physiology, 266,* 453–469.

Rasmussen, M., Barnes, C. A., & McNaughton, B. L. (1989). A systematic test of cognitive mapping, working-memory, and temporal discontiguity theories of hippocampal function. *Psychobiology, 17,* 335–348.

Rasmussen, T., & Milner, B. (1975). Excision of Broca's area without persistent aphasia. In K. J. Zulch, O. Creutzfeldt, & G. C. Galbraith (Eds.), *Cerebral localization* (pp. 258–263). New York: Springer-Verlag.

Ratliff, F. (1972). Contour and contrast. *Scientific American, 226,* 90–101.

Reame, N., Sauder, S. E., Kelch, R. P., & Marshall, J. C. (1984). Pulsatile gonadotropin secretion during the human menstrual cycle: Evidence for altered frequency of gonadotropin releasing hormone secretion. *Journal of Clinical Endocrinology and Metabolism, 59,* 328.

Rebec, G. V., & Bashore, T. R. (1984). Critical issues in assessing the behavioral effects of amphetamine. *Neuroscience and Biobehavioral Reviews, 8,* 153–158.

Rechtschaffen, A., Gilliland, M. A., Bergmann, B. M., & Winter, J. B. (1983). Physiological correlates of prolonged sleep deprivation in rats. *Science, 221,* 182–184.

Rechtschaffen, A., & Kales, A. (1968). *A manual of standardized terminology, techniques and scoring systems for sleep stages of human subjects.* Washington, DC: U. S. Government Printing Office.

Rechtschaffen, A., Wolpert, E. A., Dement, W. C., Mitchell, S. A., & Fisher, C. (1963). Nocturnal sleep of narcoleptics. *Electroencephalography and Clinical Neurophysiology, 15,* 599–609.

Reh, T. A., & Constantine-Paton, M. (1984). Retinal ganglion cell terminals change their projection sites during larval development of *Rana pipiens. Journal of Neuroscience, 4,* 442–457.

Revusky, S. H., & Garcia, J. (1970). Learned associations over long delays. In G. H. Bower & J. T. Spence (Eds.), *The psychology of learning and motivation* (Vol. 4, pp. 1–85). New York: Academic Press.

Reynolds, D. V. (1969). Surgery in the rat during electrical analgesia induced by focal brain stimulation. *Science, 164,* 444–445.

Richter, C. P. (1967). Sleep and activity: Their relation to the 24-hour clock. *Proceedings of the Association for Research on Nervous and Mental Disorders, 45,* 8–27.

Richter, C. P. (1971). Inborn nature of the rat's 24-hour clock. *Journal of Comparative and Physiological Psychology, 75,* 1–14.

Ridley, R. M., & Baker, H. F. (1991). A critical evaluation of monkey models of amnesia and dementia. *Brain Research Reviews, 16,* 15–37.

Ridley, R. M., & Ettlinger, G. (1975). Visual discrimination performance in the monkey: The activity of single cells in infero-temporal cortex. *Brain Research, 55,* 179–182.

Rindi, G. (1989). Alcohol and thiamine of the brain. *Alcohol & Alcoholism, 24,* 493–495.

Risch, N. (1990). Genetic linkage and complex diseases with special reference to psychiatric disorders. *Genetic Epidemiology, 7,* 3–16.

Risner, M. E., & Jones, B. E. (1980). Intravenous self-administration of cocaine and norcocaine by dogs. *Psychopharmacology, 71,* 83–89.

Roberts, D. C. S., Corcoran, M. E., & Fibiger, H. C. (1977). On the role of ascending catecholaminergic systems in intravenous self-administration of cocaine. *Pharmacology Biochemistry & Behavior, 6,* 615–620.

Roberts, D. C. S., & Koob, G. F. (1982). Disruption of cocaine self-administration following 6-hydroxydopamine lesions of the ventral tegmental area in rats. *Pharmacology Biochemistry & Behavior, 17,* 901–904.

Roberts, D. C. S., Koob, G. F., Klonoff, P., & Fibiger, H. C. (1980). Extinction and recovery of cocaine self-administration following 6-hydroxydopamine lesions of the nucleus accumbens. *Pharmacology Biochemistry & Behavior, 12,* 781–787.

Roberts, D. C. S., & Zito, K. A. (1987). Interpretation of lesion effects on stimulant self-administration. In M. A. Bozarth (Ed.), *Methods of assessing the reinforcing properties of abused drugs* (pp. 87–103). New York: Springer-Verlag.

Roberts, G. W. (1990). Schizophrenia: The cellular biology of a functional psychosis. *Trends in Neurosciences, 13,* 207–211.

Robinson, B. W. (1964). Forebrain alimentary responses: Some organizational principles. In M. J. Wayner (Ed.), *Thirst: Proceedings of the First International Symposium in Thirst in the Regulation of Body Water* (pp. 411–427). New York: Macmillan.

Robinson, T. E. (1991). Persistent sensitizing effects of drugs on brain dopamine systems and behavior: Implications for addiction and relapse. In J. Barchas and S. Korenman (Eds.), *The biological basis of substance abuse and its therapy.* New York: Oxford University Press.

Robinson, T. E., & Justice, J. B., Jr. (Eds.). (1991). *Microdialysis in the Neurosciences. Vol. 7, Techniques in the neural and behavioral sciences.* Elsevier: Amsterdam.

Robitaille, R., Adler, E. M., & Charlton, M. P. (1990). Strategic location of calcium channels at transmitter release sites at frog neuromuscular synapses. *Neuron, 5,* 773–779.

Roe, A. W., Pallas, S. L., Hahm, J-O., & Sur, M. (1990). A map of visual space induced in primary auditory cortex. *Science, 250,* 818–820.

Rogers, P. J., & Blundell, J. E. (1980). Investigation of food selection and meal parameters during the development of dietary induced obesity. *Appetite, 1,* 85–88.

Roitblat, H. L., Bever, T. G., & Terrace, H. S. (Eds.). (1984). *Animal Cognition.* Hillsdale, NJ: Laurence Erlbaum.

Roland, P. E., & Larsen, B. (1976). Focal increase of cerebral blood flow during stereognostic testing in man. *Archives of Neurology, 33,* 551–558.

Roland, P. E., Larsen, B., Lassen, N. A., & Skinhøj, E. (1980). Supplementary motor area and other cortical areas in organization of voluntary movements in man. *Journal of Neurophysiology, 43,* 118–136.

Roland, P. E., Skinhøj, E., Lassen, N. A., & Larsen, B. (1980). *Journal of Neurophysiology, 43,* 137–150.

Rolls, B. J. (1986). Sensory-specific satiety. *Nutrition Reviews, 44,* 93–101.

Rolls, B. J. (1990). The role of sensory-specific satiety in food intake and food selection. In E. D. Capaldi and T. L. Powley (Eds.), *Taste, experience, & feeding* (pp. 28–42). Washington, DC: American Psychological Association.

Rolls, B. J., & Rolls, E. T. (1982). *Thirst.* Cambridge: Cambridge University Press.

Rolls, B. J., Rolls, E. T., Rowe, E. A., & Sweeney, K. (1981). Sensory specific satiety in man. *Physiology & Behavior, 27,* 137–142.

Rolls, B. J., Wood, R. J., & Rolls, R. M. (1980). Thirst: The initiation, maintenance, and termination of drinking. In J. M. Sprague and A. N. Epstein (Eds.). *Progress in psychology and physiological psychology.* New York: Academic Press.

Rolls, B. J., Wood, R., Rolls, E. T., Lind, H., Lind, R., & Ledingham, J. G. (1980). Thirst following water deprivation in humans. *American Journal of Physiology, 239,* 476–482.

Rolls, B. J., Wood, R. J., & Stevens, R. M. (1978). Effects of palatability on body fluid homeostasis. *Physiology & Behavior, 20,* 15–19.

Rolls, E. T. (1981). Central nervous mechanisms related to feeding and appetite. *British Medical Bulletin, 37,* 131–134.

Rolls, E. T. (1985). Neuronal activity in relation to the recognition of stimuli in the primate. In C. Chagas, R. Gattass, & C. Gross (Eds.), *Pattern recognition mechanisms* (pp. 203–213). Berlin: Springer-Verlag.

Rolls, E. T., & Rolls, B. J. (1982). Brain mechanisms involved in feeding. In L. M. Barker (Ed.), *The psychobiology of human food selection* (pp. 33–65). Westport, CT: AVI Pub. Co.

Rolls, E. T., Sanghera, M. K., & Roper-Hall, A. (1979). The latency of activation of neurons in the lateral hypothalamus and substantia innominata during feeding in the monkey. *Brain Research, 164,* 121–135.

Rosenthal, D., Wender, P. H., Kety, S. S., Welner, J., & Schulsinger, F. (1980). The adopted-away offspring of schizophrenics. *American Journal of Psychiatry, 128,* 87–91.

Rossi, G. F., & Rosandini, G. (1967). Experimental analysis of cerebral dominance in man. In C. H. Millikan and F. L. Darley, (Eds.), *Brain mechanisms underlying speech and language.* New York: Grune & Stratton.

Rothblat, L. A., & Hayes, L. L. (1987). Short-term object recognition memory in the rat: Nonmatching with trial-unique junk stimuli. *Behavioral Neuroscience, 101,* 587–590.

Rothwell, J. C., Traub, M. M., Day, B. L., Obeso, J. A., Thomas, P. K., & Marsden, C. D. (1982). Manual motor performance in a deafferented man. *Brain, 105,* 515–542.

Rothwell, N. J., & Stock, M. J. (1979). A role for brown adipose tissue in diet-induced thermogenesis. *Nature, 281,* 31–35.

Rothwell, N. J., & Stock, M. J. (1982). Energy expenditure derived from measurements of oxygen consumption and energy balance in hyperphagic, 'cafeteria'-fed rats. *Journal of Physiology, 324,* 59–60.

Routtenberg, A., & Malsbury, C. (1969). Brainstem pathways of reward. *Journal of Comparative and Physiological Psychology, 68,* 22–30.

Rovasio, R. A., Delouvée, A., Yamada, K. M., Timpl, R., & Thiery, J. P. (1983). Neural crest cell migration: Requirements for exogenous fibronectin and high cell density. *Journal of Cell Biology, 96,* 462–473.

Rowland, N. (1981a). Feeding behaviour: Caused by, or just correlated with, physiology? *Behavioral and Brain Sciences, 4,* 589–590.

Rowland, N. (1981b). Glucoregulatory feeding on cats. *Physiology & Behavior, 26,* 901–903.

Rowland, N. E. (1990). Sodium appetite. In E. D. Capaldi and T. L. Powley (Eds.), *Taste, experience, and feeding* (pp. 94–104). Washington, DC: American Psychological Association.

Rowland, N. E. (1990). On the waterfront: Predictive and reactive regulatory descriptions of thirst and sodium appetite. *Physiology & Behavior, 48,* 899–903.

Rowland, N., & Nicolaidis, S. (1976). Metering of fluid intake and determinants of ad libitum drinking in rats. *American Journal of Physiology, 231,* 1–8.

Rozin, P. (1988). Social learning about food by humans. In T. R. Zentall, & B. G. Galef, Jr. (Eds.), *Social learning: Psychological and biological perspectives* (pp. 165–187). Hillsdale, NJ: Lawrence Erlbaum Associates.

Rubin, B. S., & Barfield, R. J. (1983). Induction of estrous behavior in ovariectomized rats by sequential replacement of estrogen and progesterone to the ventromedial hypothalamus. *Neuroendocrinology, 37,* 218–224.

Rudomin, P. (1990). Presynaptic inhibition of muscle spindle and tendon organ afferents in the mammalian spinal cord. *Trends in Neurosciences, 13,* 499–505.

Rummelhart, D. E., & Norman, D. A. (1982). Simulating a skilled typist: A study of skilled cognitive motor performance. *Cognitive Science, 6,* 1–36.

Rusak, B. (1979). Neural mechanisms for entrainment and generation of mammalian circadian rhythms. *Proceedings of the Federation of American Societies for Experimental Biology, 38,* 2589–2595.

Rusak, B., & Bina, K. G. (1990). Neurotransmitters in the mammalian circadian system. *Annual Review of Neuroscience, 13,* 387–401.

Rusak, B., & Groos, G. (1982). Suprachiasmatic stimulation phase shifts rodent circadian rhythms. *Science, 215,* 1407–1409.

Rusak, B., Mistlberger, R. E., Losier, B., & Jones, C. H. (1988). Daily hoarding opportunity entrains the pacemaker for hamster activity rhythms. *Journal of Comparative Physiology, 164,* 165–171.

Rusak, B., Robertson, H. A., Wisden, W., & Hunt, S. P. (1990). Light pulses that shift rhythms induce gene expression in the suprachiasmatic nucleus. *Science, 248,* 1237–1240.

Rusak, B., & Zucker, I. (1979). Neural regulation of circadian rhythms. *Psychological Reviews, 59,* 449–526.

Rushton, W. A. H. (1962). Visual pigments in man. *Scientific American, 207,* 120–132.

Russek, M. (1975). Current hypotheses in the control of feeding behaviour. In G. J. Mogenson & F. R. Calaresu (Eds.), *Neural integration of physiological mechanisms and behavior* (pp. 128–147). Toronto: University of Toronto Press.

Russek, M. (1981). Current status of the hepatostatic theory of food intake control. *Appetite, 2,* 137–143.

Russell, W. R., & Espir, M. I. E. (1961). *Traumatic aphasia—a study of aphasia in war wounds of the brain.* London: Oxford University Press.

Rutishauser, U., Acheson, A., Hall, A. K., Mann, D. M., & Sunshine, J. (1988). The neural cell adhesion molecule (NCAM) as a regulator of cell-cell interactions. *Science, 240,* 53–57.

Rutledge, L. L., & Hupka, R. B. (1985). The facial feedback hypothesis: Methodological concerns and new supporting evidence. *Motivation and Emotion, 9,* 219–240.

Sachar, E. J. (1980). Hormonal changes in stress and mental illness. In D. T. Krieger & J. C. Hughes (Eds.), *Neuroendocrinology.* Sunderland, MA: Sinauer & Associates.

Sacks, O. (1985). *The man who mistook his wife for a hat and other clinical tales.* New York: Summit Books.

Sagar, H. J., Gabrieli, J. D. E., Sullivan, E. V., & Corkin, S. (1990). Recency and frequency discrimination in the amnesic patient H. M. *Brain, 113,* 581–602.

Sager, R. (1989). Tumor suppressor genes: The puzzle and the promise. *Science, 246,* 1406–1412.

Salmon, D. P., Zola-Morgan, S., & Squire, R. L. (1987). Retrograde amnesia following combined hippocampus-amygdala lesions in monkeys. *Psychobiology, 15,* 37–47.

Sanders, D., & Bancroft, J. (1982). Hormones and the sexuality of women—the menstrual cycle. *Clinics in Endocrinology and Metabolism, 11,* 639–659.

Sanes, J. N., Suner, S., & Donoghue, J. P. (1990). Dynamic organization of primary motor cortex output to target muscles in adult rats. I. Long-term patterns of reorganization following motor or mixed peripheral nerve lesions. *Experimental Brain Research, 79,* 479–491.

Sanes, J. R. (1989). Extracellular matrix molecules that influence neural development. *Annual Review of Neuroscience, 12,* 491–516.

Sastry, B. R., Goh, J. W., & Auyeung, A. (1986). Associative induction of posttetanic and long-term potentiation in CA1 neurons of rat hippocampus. *Science, 232,* 988–990.

Sawchenko, P. E., Eng, R., Gold, R. M., & Simson, E. L. (1977). *Effects of selective subdiaphragmatic vagotomies on knife cut induced hypothalamic hyperphagia.* Paper presented at the Sixth International Conference on the Physiology of Food and Fluid Intake, Paris, France.

Scarr, S., & Kidd, K. K. (1983). Developmental behavior genetics. In P. H. Mussen (Ed.), *Handbook of child psychology: Vol. 2. Infancy and developmental psychobiology* (pp. 345–434). New York: Wiley.

Schacter, D. L. (1987). Implicit memory: History and current status. *Journal of Experimental Psychology: Learning, Memory and Cognition, 13,* 501–518.

Schacter, D. L., Tharan, M., Cooper, L. A., & Rubens, A. B. (1991). Preserved priming of novel objects in patients with memory disorders. *Journal of Cognitive Neuroscience, 3,* 117–130.

Schacter, S., & Singer, J. E. (1962). Cognitive, social, and physiological determinants of emotional state. *Psychological Review, 69,* 379–399.

Schallert, T., Whishaw, I. Q., & Flannigan, K. P. (1977). Gastric pathology and feeding deficits induced by hypothalamic damage in rats: Effects of lesion type, size, and placement. *Journal of Comparative and Physiological Psychology, 91* (3), 598–610.

Schally, A. V. (1978). Aspects of hypothalamic regulation of the pituitary gland. *Science, 202,* 18–28.

Schally, A. V., Kastin, A. J., & Arimura, A. (1971). Hypothalamic follicle-stimulating hormone (FSH) and luteinizing hormone (LH)-regulating hormone: Structure, physiology, and clinical studies. *Fertility and Sterility, 22,* 703–721.

Schatzman, M., Worsley, A., & Fenwich, P. (1988). Correspondence during lucid dreams between dreamed and actual events. In J. Gackenbach and S. LaBerge (Eds.), *Conscious mind, sleeping brain* (pp. 67–103). New York: Plenum.

Schelling, T. C. (1992). Addictive drugs: The cigarette experience. *Science, 255,* 430–433.

Schenck, C. H., Bundlie, S. R., Ettinger, M. G., & Mahowald, M. W. (1986). Chronic behavioral disorders of human REM sleep: A new category of parasomnia. *Sleep, 9,* 293–308.

Scherschlicht, R. (1983). Pharmacological profile of delta sleep-inducing peptide (DSIP) and a phosphorylated analogue, (Ser-PO$_4$) DSIP. *Sleep 1982, 6th European Congress for Sleep Research, Zurich, 1982* (pp. 109–111). Basel, Karger.

Scherschlicht, R., & Marias, J. (1983). Effects of oral and intravenous midazolam, trizolam and flunitrazepam on the sleep-wakefulness cycle of rabbits. *British Journal of Clinical Pharmacology, 16* (Supplement 1), 29S–35S.

Schieber, M. H. (1990). How might the motor cortex individuate movements? *Trends in Neurosciences, 13,* 440–445.

Schiller, P. H. (1986). The central visual system. *Vision Research, 26,* 1351–1386.

Schleidt, M., Hold, B., & Attili, G. (1981). A cross-cultural study on the attitude towards personal odors. *Journal of Chemical Ecology, 7,* 19–31.

Schlundt, D. G., & Johnson, W. G. (1990). *Eating disorders: Assessment and treatment.* Boston, MA: Allyn and Bacon.

Schnapf, J. L., & Baylor, D. A. (1987). How photoreceptor cells respond to light. *Scientific American, 256,* 40–47.

Schneider, G. E. (1969). Brain mechanisms for localization and discrimination are dissociated by tectal and cortical lesions. *Science, 163,* 895–902.

Schneider, L. H., Cooper, S. J., & Halmi, K. A. (1989). *The psychology of human eating disorders: Preclinical and clinical perspectives.* New York: New York Academy of Sciences.

Schneider-Helmert, D. (1985). Clinical evaluation of DSIP. In A. Wauquier, J. M. Gaillard, J. M. Monti, & M. Radulovacki (Eds.), *Sleep: Neurotransmitters and neuromodulators* (pp. 279–289). New York: Raven Press.

Schnell, L., & Schwab, M. E. (1990). Axonal regeneration in the rat spinal cord produced by an antibody against myelin-associated neurite growth inhibitors. *Nature, 343,* 269–272.

Schoenenberger, G. A., & Graf, M. V. (1985). Effects of DSIP and DSIP-P on different biorhythmic parameters. In A. Wauquier, J. M. Gaillard, J. M. Monti, & M. Radulovacki (Eds.), *Sleep: Neurotransmitters and neuromodulators* (pp. 265–277). New York: Raven Press.

Schoenlein, R. W., Peteanu, L. A., Mathies, R. A., & Shank, C. V. (1991). The first step in vision: Femtosecond isomerization of rhodopsin. *Science, 254,* 412–421.

Schou, M., Juel-Neilsen, N., Stromberg, E., & Voldby, H. (1954). The treatment of manic psychoses by the administration of lithium salts. *Journal of Neurology, Neurosurgery and Psychiatry, 17,* 250–260.

Schuman, E. M., & Madison, D. V. (1991). A requirement for the intercellular messenger nitric oxide in long-term potentiation. *Science, 254,* 1503–1506.

Schwab, M. E. (1990). Myelin-associated inhibitors of neurite growth and regeneration in the CNS. *Trends in Neurosciences, 13,* 452–456.

Schwartz, J. H. (1980). The transport of substances in nerve cells. *Scientific American, 242,* 152–171.

Schwartz, J. H. (1987). Molecular aspects of postsynaptic receptors. In E. R. Kandel & J. H. Schwartz (Eds.), *Principles of neural science* (pp. 159–168). New York: Elsevier.

Schwartz, W. J., & Gainer, H. (1977). Suprachiasmatic nucleus: Use of 14-C-labelled deoxyglucose uptake as a functional marker. *Science, 197,* 1089–1091.

Sclafani, A. (1981). Correlation and causation in the study of feeding behavior. *Behavioral and Brain Sciences, 4,* 590–591.

Sclafani, A. (1990). Nutritionally based learned flavor preferences in rats. In E. D. Capaldi and T. L. Powley (Eds.), *Taste, experience, and feeding* (pp. 139–156). Washington, D.C: American Psychological Association.

Scott, J. W. (1986). The olfactory bulb and central pathways. *Experientia, 42,* 223–231.

Scott, T. R. (1990). The effect of physiological need on taste. In E. D. Capaldi & T. L. Powley (Eds.), *Taste, experience, and feeding* (pp. 45–61). Washington, DC: The American Psychological Association.

Scott, T. R., & Giza, B. K. (1990). Coding channels in the taste system of the rat. *Science, 249,* 1585–1587.

Scoville, W. B., & Milner, B. (1957). Loss of recent memory after bilateral hippocampal lesions. *Journal of Neurology, Neurosurgery and Psychiatry, 20,* 11–21.

Searle, L. V. (1949). The organization of hereditary maze-brightness and maze-dullness. *Genetic Psychology Monographs, 39,* 279–325.

Seitz, R. J., Roland, P. E., Bohm, C., Greitz, T., & Stone-Elanders, S. (1990). Motor learning in man: A positron emission tomographic study. *NeuroReport, 1,* 17–20.

Selmanoff, M. K., Brodkin, L. D., Weiner, R. I., & Siiteri, P. K. (1977). Aromatization and 5-alpha-reduction of androgens in discrete hypothalamic and limbic regions of the male and female rat. *Endocrinology, 108,* 841–848.

Seyfarth, R. M., Cheney, D. L., & Marler, P. (1980). Monkey responses to three different alarm calls: Evidence of predator classification and semantic communication. *Science, 210,* 801–803.

Shallice, T., & Warrington, E. K. (1980). Single and multiple component central dyslexic syndromes. In M. Coltheart, K. E. Patterson, & J. C. Marshall (Eds.), *Deep dyslexia* (pp. 119–145). London: Routledge & Kegan Paul.

Shapiro, B. H., Levine, D. C., & Adler, N. T. (1980). The testicular feminized rat: A naturally occurring model of androgen independent brain masculinization. *Science, 209,* 418–420.

Sherman, S. M. (1985). Functional organization of the W-, X-, and Y-cell pathways in the cat: A review and hypothesis. In J. M. Sprague & A. N. Epstein (Eds.), *Progress in psychobiology and physiological psychology* (Vol. 11, pp. 233–314). New York: Academic Press.

Sherry, D. F., & Vaccarino, A. L. (1989). Hippocampus and memory for food caches in black-capped chickadees. *Behavioral Neuroscience, 103,* 308–318.

Sherwin, B. B. (1985). Changes in sexual behavior as a function of plasma sex steroid levels in post- menopausal women. *Maturitas, 7,* 225–233.

Sherwin, B. B. (1988). A comparative analysis of the role of androgen in human male and female sexual behavior: Behavioral specificity, critical thresholds, and sensitivity. *Psychobiology, 16,* 416–425.

Sherwin, B. B., Gelfand, M. M., & Brender, W. (1985). Androgen enhances sexual motivation in females: A prospective cross-over study of sex steroid administration in the surgical menopause. *Psychosomatic Medicine, 47,* 339–351.

Shettleworth, S. J. (1983). Memory in food-hoarding birds. *Scientific American, 248,* 102–110.

Shipley, J. E., & Kolb, B. (1977). Neural correlates of species-typical behavior in the Syrian golden hamster. *Journal of Comparative and Physiological Psychology, 91,* 1056–1073.

Shizgal, P., & Murray, B. (1989). Neuronal basis of intracranial self-stimulation. In J. M. Liebman & S. J. Cooper (Eds.), *The neuropharmacological basis of reward* (pp. 106–163). Oxford: Clarendon Press.

Shouse, M. N., King, A., Langer, J., Vreeken, T., King, K., & Richkind, M. (1990). The ontogeny of feline temporal lobe epilepsy: Kindling a spontaneous seizure disorder in kittens. *Brain Research, 525,* 215–224.

Shuttlesworth, D., Neill, D., & Ellen, F. (1984). Current issues: The place of physiological psychology in neuroscience. *Physiological Psychology, 12,* 3–7.

Sidman, M., Stoddard, L. T., & Mohr, J. P. (1968). Some additional quantitative observations of immediate memory in a patient with bilateral hippocampal lesions. *Neuropsychologia, 6,* 245–254.

Siegel, J. M. (1983). A behavioral approach to the ananlysis of reticular formation unit activity. In T. E. Robinson (Ed.), *Behavioral approaches to brain research* (pp. 94–116). New York: Oxford University Press.

Siegel, J. M., Nienhuis, R., Fahringer, H. M., Paul, R., Shiromani, P., Dement, W. C., Mignot, E., & Chui, C. (1991). Neuronal activity in narcolepsy: Identification of cataplexy-related cells in the medial medulla. *Science, 252,* 1315–1318.

Siegel, S. (1978). Tolerance to the hyperthermic effect of morphine in the rat is a learned response. *Journal of Comparative and Physiological Psychology, 92,* 1137–1149.

Siegel, S. (1983). Classical conditioning, drug tolerance, and drug dependence. In Y. Israel, F. B. Graser, H. Kalant, W. Popham, W. Schmidt, & R. G. Smart (Eds.), *Research advances in alcohol and drug problems.* (Vol. 7, pp. 207–246). New York: Plenum.

Siegel, S., Hinson, R. E., Krank, M. D., & McCully, J. (1982). Heroin "overdose" death: Contribution of drug-associated environmental cues. *Science, 216,* 436–437.

Siegelbaum, S. A., & Kandel, E. R. (1991). Learning-related synaptic plasticity: LTP and LTD. *Current Opinion in Neurobiology, 1,* 113–120.

Simpson, J. B., Epstein, A. N., & Camardo, J. S. (1978). Localization of receptors for the dipsogenic action of angiotensin II in the subfornical organ of rat. *Journal of Comparative and Physiological Psychology, 92,* 581–608.

Simpson, J. B., & Routtenberg, A. (1974). Subfornical organ: Acetylcholine application elicits drinking. *Brain Research, 79,* 179–184.

Sinclair, D. (1981). *Mechanisms of cutaneous sensation.* New York: Oxford University Press.

Sinclair, J. D. (1972). The alcohol-deprivation effect: Influence of various factors. *Quarterly Journal of Studies on Alcohol, 33,* 769–782.

Singer, J. (1968). Hypothalamic control of male and female sexual behavior. *Journal of Comparative and Physiological Psychology, 66,* 738–742.

Singer, M., Nordlander, R. H., & Egar, M. (1979). Axonal guidance during embryogenesis and regeneration in the spinal cord of the newt: The blueprint hypothesis of neuronal pathway patterning. *Journal of Comparative Neurology, 185*, 1–22.

Sitaram, N., Moore, A. M., & Gillin, J. C. (1978). Experimental acceleration and slowing of REM sleep ultradian rhythm by cholinergic agonist and antagonist. *Nature, 274*, 490–492.

Sitaram, N., Weingartner, H., & Gillin, J. C. (1978). Human serial learning: Enhancement with acetylcholine and choline and impairment with scopolamine. *Science, 201*, 271–276.

Skelton, R. W., Scarth, A. S., Wilkie, D. M., Miller, J. J., & Phillips, A. G. (1987). Long-term increases in dentate granule cell responsivity accompany operant conditioning. *Journal of Neuroscience, 7*, 3081–3087.

Sklar, L. S., & Anisman, H. (1981). Stress and cancer. *Psychological Bulletin, 89*, 369–406.

Sladek, J. R., Jr., Redmond, D. E., Jr., Collier, T. J., Haber, S. N., Elsworth, J. D., Deutch, A. Y., & Roth, R. H. (1987). Transplantation of fetal dopamine neurons in primate brain reverses MPTP induced parkinsonism. In F. J. Seil, E. Herbert, & B. M. Carlson (Eds.), *Progress in brain research* (Vol. 71, pp. 309–323). New York: Elsevier.

Slaunwhite, W. R., III, Goldman, J. K., & Bernardis, L. L. (1972). Sequential changes in glucose metabolism by adipose tissue and liver of rats after destruction of the ventromedial hypothalamic nuclei: Effect of three dietary regimes. *Metabolism, 21*, 619–631.

Small, S. A., Kandel, E. R., & Hawkins, R. D. (1989). Activity-dependent enhancement of presynaptic inhibition in *Aplysia* sensory neurons. *Science, 243*, 1603–1606.

Snyder, S. H. (1976). The dopamine hypothesis of schizophrenia: Focus on the dopamine receptor. *American Journal of Psychiatry, 133*, 197–202.

Snyder, S. H. (1978). Neuroleptic drugs and neurotransmitter receptors. *Journal of Clinical and Experimental Psychiatry, 133*, 21–31.

Snyder, S. H. (1985). The molecular basis of communication between cells. *Scientific American, 253*, 132–141.

Snyder, S. H. (1986). *Drugs and the brain.* New York: Scientific American Books.

Sochurek, H., & Miller, P. (1987). Medicine's new vision. *National Geographic, 171*, 2–41.

Sokoloff, P., Giros, B., Martres, M. P., Bouthenet, M. L., & Schwartz, J. C. (1990). Molecular cloning and characterization of a novel dopamine receptor (D3) as a target for neuroleptics. *Nature, 347*, 146–151.

Spector, R., & Johanson, C. E. (1989). The mammalian choroid plexus. *Scientific American, 261*, 68–74.

Sperry, R. W. (1943). Effect of 180 degrees rotation of the retinal field on visuomotor coordination. *Journal of Experimental Zoology, 92*, 263–279.

Sperry, R. W. (1963). Chemoaffinity in the orderly growth of nerve fiber patterns and connections. *Proceedings of the National Academy of Sciences (USA), 50*, 703–710.

Sperry, R. W. (1964). The great cerebral commissure. *Scientific American, 210*, 42–52.

Sperry, R. W. (1974). Lateral specialization in the surgically separated hemispheres. In F. O. Schmitt & F. G. Worden (Eds.), *The neurosciences: Third study program* (pp. 5–19). Cambridge, MA: MIT Press.

Sperry, R. W. (1985). Consciousness, personal identity, and the divided brain. In D. F. Benson & E. Zaidel (Eds.), *The dual brain: Hemispheric specialization in humans* (pp. 11–26). New York: Guilford Press.

Sperry, R. W., Zaidel, E., & Zaidel, D. (1979). Self recognition and social awareness in the deconnected minor hemisphere. *Neuropsychologia, 17*, 153–166.

Spillman, L., & Werner, J. S. (1990). *Visual perception: The neurophysiological foundations.* New York: Academic Press.

Spitzer, H., Desimone, R., & Moran, J. (1988). Increased attention enhances both behavioral and neuronal performance. *Science, 240*, 338–340.

Spreen, O., Benton, A. L., & Fincham, R. W. (1965). Auditory agnosia without aphasia. *Archives of Neurology, 13*, 84–92.

Springer, S. P., & Deutsch, G. (1981). *Left brain, right brain.* San Francisco: W. H. Freeman and Company.

Squire, L. R. (1982a). The neuropsychology of human memory. *Annual Review of Neuroscience, 5*, 241–273.

Squire, L. R. (1982b). Comparisons between forms of amnesia: Some deficits are unique to Korsakoff's syndrome. *Journal of Experimental Psychology: Learning, Memory, and Cognition, 8*, 560–571.

Squire, L. R. (1986). Mechanisms of memory. *Science, 232*, 1612–1619.

Squire, L. R. (1987). *Memory and brain* (p. 139). New York: Oxford University Press.

Squire, L. R. & Cohen, N. (1979). Memory and amnesia: Resistance to disruption develops for years after learning. *Behavioral and Neural Biology, 25*, 115–125.

Squire, L. R., & Moore, R. Y. (1979). Dorsal thalamic lesion in a noted case of human memory dysfunction. *Annals of Neurology, 6*, 503–506.

Squire, L. R., Haist, F., & Shimamura, A. P. (1989). The neurology of memory: Quantitative assessment of retrograde amnesia in two groups of amnesic patients. *The Journal of Neuroscience, 9*, 828–839.

Squire, L. R., Nadel, L., & Slater, P. C. (1981). Anterograde amnesia and memory for temporal order. *Neuropsychologia, 19*, 441–445.

Squire, L. R., Slater, P. C., & Chace, P. M. (1975). Retrograde amnesia: Temporal gradient in very long term memory following electroconvulsive therapy. *Science, 187*, 77–79.

Squire, L. R., & Spanis, C. W. (1984). Long gradient of retrograde amnesia in mice: Continuity with the findings in humans. *Behavioral Neuroscience, 98*, 345–348.

Squire, L. R., & Zola-Morgan, S. (1985). The neuropsychology of memory: New links between humans and experimental animals. *Annals of the New York Academy of Sciences, 444*, 137–149.

Squire, L. R., Zola-Morgan, S., & Chen, K. (1988). Human amnesia and animal models of amnesia: Performance of amnesic patients on tests designed for the monkey. *Behavioral Neuroscience, 102*, 210–221.

Squire, L. R., & Zola-Morgan, S. (1991). The medial temporal lobe memory system. *Science, 253*, 1380–1386.

Stellar, E. (1954). The physiology of motivation. *Psychological Review, 61*, 5–22.

Stellar, J. R. (1990). Investigating the neural circuitry of brain stimulation reward. *Progress in psychobiology and physiology, 14*, 235–294.

Stephan, F. K., & Nunez, A. A. (1977). Elimination of circadian rhythms in drinking, activity, sleep, and temperature by isolation of the suprachiasmatic nucleus. *Behavioral Biology, 20*, 1–16.

Stephan, F. K., & Zucker, I. (1972). Circadian rhythms in drinking behaviour and locomotor activity of rats are eliminated by hypothalamic lesions. *Proceedings of the National Academy of Science (USA), 60*, 1583–1586.

Steriade, M., & Hobson, J. A. (1976). Neuronal activity during the sleep-waking cycle. *Progress in Neurobiology, 6*, 155–376.

Sterman, M. B., & Clemente, C. D. (1962). Forebrain inhibitory mechanisms: Cortical synchronization induced by basal forebrain stimulation. *Experimental Neurology, 6*, 91–102.

Sterman, M. B., & Clemente, C. D. (1962). Forebrain inhibitory mechanisms: Sleep patterns induced by basal forebrain stimulation in the behaving cat. *Experimental Neurology, 6*, 103–117.

Sternbach, L. H. (1983). The benzodiazepine story. *Journal of Psychoactive Drugs, 15*, 15–17.

Stevens, C. F. (1991). New recruit to the magnificent seven. *Current Biology, 1*, 20–22.

Stewart, J., de Wit, H., & Eikelboom, R. (1984). Role of unconditioned and conditioned drug effects in the self-administration of opiates and stimulants. *Psychological Review, 91*, 251–268.

Stewart, J., & Eikelboom, R. (1987). Conditioned drug effects. In L. L. Iversen, S. D. Iversen, & S. H. Snyder (Eds.), *Handbook of psychopharmacology: Volume 19. New directions in behavioral pharmacology* (pp. 1–57). New York: Plenum Press.

Strömberg, I., Herrara-Marschitz, M., Ungerstedt, U., Ebendal, T., & Olson, L. (1985). Chronic implants of chromaffin tissue into the dopamine-denervated striatum. Effects of NGF on graft survival, fiber growth and rotational behavior. *Experimental Brain Research, 60*, 335–349.

Strick, P. L., & Preston, J. B. (1983). Input-output organization of the primate motor cortex. In J. E. Desmedt (Ed.), *Motor control mechanisms in health and disease* (pp. 321–327). New York: Raven Press.

Stricker, E. M. (1973). Thirst, sodium appetite, and complementary physiological contributions to the regulation of intravascular fluid volume. In A. N. Epstein, H. R. Kissileff, & E. Stellar (Eds.), *The neuropsychology of thirst: New findings and advances in concepts* (pp. 73–98). Washington, D. C.: Winston.

Stricker, E. M. (1981). Factors in the control of food intake. *Behavioral and Brain Sciences, 4*, 591–592.

Stricker, E. M., Rowland, N., Saller, C. F., & Friedman, M. I. (1977). Homeostasis during hypoglycemia: Central control of adrenal secretion and peripheral control of feeding. *Science, 196*, 79–81.

Stripling, J. S., & Ellinwood, E. H., Jr. (1976). Cocaine: Physiological and behavioral effects of acute and chronic administrations. In S. J. Mule (Ed.), *Cocaine: Chemical, biological, clinical, social and treatment aspects.* Cleveland, OH: CRC Press.

Strömgren, E. (1987). Schizophrenia. In G. Adelman (Ed.), *Encyclopedia of neuroscience* (pp. 1072–1074). Boston: Birkhauser.

Strubbe, J. H., & Steffens, A. B. (1977). Blood glucose levels in portal and peripheral circulation and their relation to food intake in the rat. *Physiology & Behavior, 19*, 303–307.

Suddath, R. L., Christison, G. W., Torrey, E. F., Casanova, M. F., & Weinberger, D. R. (1990). Anatomical abnormalities in the brains of monozygotic twins discordant for schizophrenia. *The New England Journal of Medicine, 322*, 789–794.

Summers, W. K., Majovski, L. V., Marsh, G. M., Tachiki, K., & Kling, A. (1986). Oral tetrahydroaminoacridine in long-term treatment of senile dementia, Alzheimer type. *The New England Journal of Medicine, 315*, 1241–1245.

Sur, M., Pallas, S. L., & Roe, A.W. (1990). Cross-modal plasticity in cortical development: Differentiation and specification of sensory neocortex. *Trends in Neurosciences, 13*, 227–233.

Sutherland, R. J., & Dyck, R. H. (1984). Place navigation by rats in a swimming pool. *Canadian Journal of Psychology, 38*, 322–347.

Sutherland, R. J., & Rudy, J. W. (1989). Configurational association theory: The role of the hippocampal formation in learning, memory, and amnesia. *Psychobiology, 17*, 129–144.

Sutton, S., & Ruchkin, D. S. (1984). The late positive complex: Advances and new problems. In R. Karrer, J. Cohen, and P. Teuting (Eds.), *Brain and information: Event-related potentials (pp. 1–23).* In Annals of the New York Academy of Sciences, Vol. 425. New York: New York Academy of Sciences.

Sutton, S., Teuting, P., Zubin, J., & John, E. R. (1967). Information delivery and the sensory evoked potentials. *Science, 155*, 1436–1439.

Svaetichin, G. (1956). Spectral response curves from single cones. *Acta Physiologica Scandinavica, 39*, 17–46.

Swaab, D. F., & Fliers, E. (1985). A sexually dimorphic nucleus in the human brain. *Science, 188*, 1112–1115.

Swanson, L. W., & Sharpe, L. G. (1973). Centrally induced drinking: Comparison of angiotensin II- and carbachol-sensitive sites in rats. *American Journal of Physiology, 225*, 566–573.

Sweet, W. H. (1982). Cerebral localization of pain. In R. A. Thompson & J. R. Green (Eds.), *New perspectives in cerebral localization* (pp. 205–242). New York: Raven Press.

Szmukler, G. I., Eisler, I., Gillies, C., & Hayward, M. E. (1985). The implications of anorexia nervosa in a ballet school. *Journal of Psychiatric Research, 19*, 177–181.

Takahashi, J. S. (1991). Circadian rhythms: From gene expression to behavior. *Current Opinion in Neurobiology, 1,* 556–561.

Talbot, J. D., Marrett, S., Evans, A. C., Meyer, E., Bushnell, M. C., & Duncan, G. H. (1991). Multiple representations of pain in human cerebral cortex. *Science, 251,* 1355–1358.

Tanaka, A. (1972). A progressive change of behavioral and electroencephalographic response to daily amygdaloid stimulations in rabbits. *Fukuoka Acta Medica, 63,* 152–163.

Tanji, J., & Kurata, K. (1983). Functional organization of the supplementary motor area. In J. E. Desmedt (Ed.), *Motor control mechanisms in health and disease* (pp. 421–431), New York: Raven Press.

Tank, D. W., Sugimori, M., Connor, J. A., & Llinas, R. R. (1988). Spatially resolved calcium dynamics of mammalian Purkinje cells in cerebellar slice. *Science 242,* 773–777.

Tassinary, L. G., & Cacioppo, J. T. (1992). Unobservable facial actions and emotion. *Psychological Science, 3,* 28–33.

Taub, E. (1976). Movement in nonhuman primates deprived of somatosensory feedback. *Exercise and Sport Sciences Reviews, 4,* 335–374.

Taylor, J. R., Elsworth, J. D., Roth, J. R., Sladek, J. R., Jr., & Redmond, D. E., Jr., (1990). Cognitive and motor deficits in the acquisition of an object retrieval/detour task in MPTP-treated monkeys. *Brain, 113,* 617–637.

Taylor, R. (1991). A lot of "excitement" about neurodegeneration. *Science, 252,* 1380–1381.

Tees, R. C. (1968). Effect of early visual restriction on later visual intensity discrimination in rats. *Journal of Comparative and Physiological Psychology, 66,* 224–227.

Tees, R. C., & Cartwright, J. (1972). Sensory preconditioning in rats following early visual deprivation. *Journal of Comparative and Physiological Psychology, 81,* 12–20.

Teitelbaum, P. (1957). Random and food-directed activity in hyperphagic and normal rats. *Journal of Comparative and Physiological Psychology, 50,* 486–490.

Teitelbaum, P. (1961). Disturbances in feeding and drinking behavior after hypothalamic lesions. In M. R. Jones (Ed.), *Nebraska Symposium on Motivation* (pp. 39–69). Lincoln, NB: University of Nebraska Press.

Teitelbaum, P., & Campbell, B. A. (1958). Ingestion patterns in hyperphagic and normal rats. *Journal of Comparative and Physiological Psychology, 51,* 135–141.

Teitelbaum, P., & Epstein, A. N. (1962). The lateral hypothalamic syndrome: Recovery of feeding and drinking after lateral hypothalamic lesions. *Psychological Review, 69,* 74–90.

Terman, G. W., Shavit, Y., Lewis, J. W., Cannon, J. T., & Liebeskind, J. C. (1984). Intrinsic mechanisms of pain inhibition: Activation by stress. *Science, 226,* 1270–1277.

Tessier-Lavigne, M., & Placzek, M. (1991). Target attraction: Are developing axons guided by chemotropism? *Trends in Neurosciences, 14,* 303–310.

Teuber, H.-L. (1975). Recovery of function after brain injury in man. In *Outcome of severe damage to the nervous system, Ciba Foundation Symposium 34.* Amsterdam: Elsevier North-Holland.

Teuber, H.-L., Battersby, W. S., & Bender, M. B. (1960). *Visual field defects after penetrating missile wounds of the brain.* Cambridge, MA: Harvard University Press.

Teuber, H.-L., Milner, B., & Vaughan, H. G., Jr. (1968). Persistent anterograde amnesia after stab wound of the basal brain. *Neuropsychologia, 6,* 267–282.

Teyler, T. J. (1986). Electrophysiology of memory. In J. L. Martinez, Jr., & R. P. Kesner (Eds.), *Learning and memory: A biological view* (pp. 237–265). Orlando, FL: Academic Press.

Thal, L. J. (1989). Pharmacological treatment of memory disorders. In F. Boller and J. Grafman, (Eds.), *Handbook of neuropsychology, Vol. 3.,* (pp. 247–267). New York: Elsevier.

Thorn, B. E., Applegate, L., & Johnson, S. W. (1989). Ability of periaqueductal gray subdivisions and adjacent loci to elicit analgesia and ability of naloxone to reverse analgesia. *Behavioral Neuroscience, 103,* 1335–1339.

Thureson-Klein, A. K., & Klein, R. L. (1990). Exocytosis from neuronal large dense-cored vesicles. *International Review of Cytology, 121,* 67–126.

Tilles, D., Goldenheim, P., Johnson, D. C., Mendelson, J. H., Mello, N. K., & Hales, C. A. (1986). Marijuana smoking as cause of reduction in single-breath carbon monoxide diffusing capacity. *American Journal of Medicine, 80,* 601–606.

Tinbergen, N., & Perdeck, A. C. (1950). On the stimulus situation releasing the begging response in the newly hatched herring gull chick (*Larus argentatus argentatus* Pont). *Behavior, 3,* 1–39.

Tinklenberg, J. R. (1974). Marijuana and human aggression. In L. L. Miller (Ed.), *Marijuana, effects on human behavior* (pp. 339–358). New York: Academic Press.

Toates, F. M. (1981). The control of ingestive behaviour by internal and external stimuli—A theoretical review. *Appetite, 2,* 35–50.

Toates, F. M., & Halliday, T. R. (Eds.). (1980). *Analysis of motivated processes.* New York: Academic Press.

Tranel, D., & Damasio, A. R. (1985). Knowledge without awareness: An autonomic index of facial recognition by prosopagnosics. *Science, 228,* 1453–1454.

Trayhurn, P., & James, W. P. T. (1981). Thermogenesis: Dietary and non-shivering aspects. In L. A. Cioffi, W. P. T. James, & T. B. Vanitalie (Eds.), *The body weight regulatory system: Normal and disturbed mechanisms* (pp. 97–105). New York: Raven Press.

Traynor, A. E., Schlapfer, W. T., & Barondes, S. J. (1980). Stimulation is necessary for the development of tolerance to a neural effect of ethanol. *Journal of Neurobiology, 11,* 633–637.

Treit, D. (1985). Animal models for the study of anti-anxiety agents: A review. *Neuroscience and Biobehavioral Reviews, 9,* 203–222.

Treit, D. (1987). RO 15-1788, CGS 8216, picrotoxin, pentylenetetrazol: Do they antagonize anxiolytic drug effects through an anxiogenic action? *Brain Research Bulletin, 19,* 401–405.

Trulson, M. E., & Jacobs, B. L. (1979). Raphe unit activity in freely moving cats: Correlation with level of behavioral arousal. *Brain Research, 163,* 135–150.

Tryon, R. C. (1934). Individual differences. In Moss, F. A. (Ed.), *Comparative Psychology* (pp. 409–448). New York: Prentice-Hall Inc.

Tsien, R. W. & Malinow, R. (1991). Long-term potentiation: Presynaptic activation of Ca^{2+}—dependent protein knases. *Cold Spring Harbor Symposium on Quantitative Biology.*

Tsukahara, N. (1981). Sprouting and the neuronal basis of learning. *Trends in Neurosciences, 4,* 234–240.

Tuck, R. R., Brew, B. J., Britton, A. M., & Loewy, J. (1984). Alcohol and brain damage. *British Journal of Addiction, 79,* 251–259.

Tucker, D. M. (1981). Lateral brain function, emotion, and conceptualization. *Psychological Bulletin, 89,* 19–46.

Tulving, E., & Schacter, D. L. (1990). Priming and human memory systems. *Science, 247,* 301–306.

Turkenburg, J. L., Swaab, D. F., Endert, E., Louwerse, A. L., & van de Poll, N. E. (1988). Effects of lesions of the sexually dimorphic nucleus on sexual behavior of testosterone-treated female Wistar rats. *Brain Research Bulletin, 329,* 195–203.

Turner, A. M., & Greenough, W. T. (1983). Synapses per neuron and synaptic dimensions in occipital cortex of rats reared in complex, social, or isolation housing. *Acta Stereologica, Vol. 2, Suppl. 1,* 239–244.

Udin, S., & Fawcett, J. W. (1988). Formation of topographic maps. *Annual Review of Neuroscience, 11,* 289–327.

Uhl, R., Wagner, R., & Ryba, N. (1990). Watching G proteins at work. *Trends in Neurosciences, 13,* 64–70.

Ulrich, R. E. (1991). Animal rights, animal wrongs and the question of balance. *Psychological Science, 2,* 197–201.

Ungerleider, L. G., Mishkin, M. (1982). Two cortical visual systems. In D. J. Ingle, M. A. Goodale, & R. J. W. Mansfield (Eds.), *Analysis of visual behavior* (pp. 549–586). Cambridge, MA: MIT Press.

Vaccarino, F. J., Pettit, H. O., Bloom, F. E., & Koob, G. F. (1985). Effects of intracerebroventricular administration of methylnaloxone chloride on heroin self-administration in the rat. *Pharmacology Biochemistry & Behavior, 23,* 495–498.

Valenstein, E. S. (1973). *Brain control.* New York: John Wiley and Sons.

Valenstein, E. S. (1980). *The psychosurgery debate: Scientific, legal, and ethical perspectives.* San Francisco: W. H. Freeman and Co.

Valenstein, E. S. (1986). *Great and desperate cures: The rise and decline of psychosurgery and other radical treatments for mental illness.* New York: Basic Books.

Valenstein, E. S., & Campbell, J. F. (1966). Medial forebrain bundle-lateral hypothalamic area and reinforcing brain stimulation. *American Journal of Physiology, 210,* 270–274.

Vallee, R. B., & Bloom, G. S. (1991). Mechanisms of fast and slow axonal transport. *Annual Review of Neuroscience, 14,* 59–92.

Valverde, F. (1971). Rate and extent of recovery from dark rearing in the visual cortex of the mouse. *Brain Research, 33,* 1–11.

Van Broeckhoven, C., Haan, J., Bakker, E., Hardy, J. A., Van Hul, W., Wehner, A., Vegter-Van der Vlis, M., & Roos, R. A. C. (1990). Amyloid β protein precursor gene and hereditary cerebral hemorrhage with amyloidosis (Dutch). *Science, 248,* 1120–1112.

Van Buren, J. M., Ajmone-Marsan, C., Mutsuga, N., & Sadowsky, D. (1975). Surgery of temporal lobe epilepsy. In D. P. Purpura, J. K. Penry, & R. D. Walter (Eds.), *Advances in neurology: Volume 8. Neurosurgical management of the epilepsies* (pp. 155–196). New York: Raven Press.

Van der Kooy, D. (1987). Place conditioning: A simple and effective method for assessing the motivational properties of drugs. In M. A. Bozarth (Ed.), *Methods of assessing the reinforcing properties of abused drugs* (pp. 229–240). New York: Springer-Verlag.

Vanderwolf, C. H. (1988). Cerebral activity and behavior: Control by central cholinergic and serotonergic systems. *International Review of Neurobiology, 30,* 225–340.

Vanderwolf, C. H., & Robinson, T. E. (1981). Reticulo-cortical activity and behavior: A critique of the arousal theory and a new synthesis. *Behavioral and Brain Sciences, 4,* 459–514.

Van Hoesen, G. W., Hyman, B. T., & Damasio, A. R. (1991). Entorhinal cortex pathology in Alzheimer's disease. *Hippocampus, 1,* 1–8.

Vaughan, H. G., Jr., & Arezzo, J. C. (1988). The neural basis of event-related potentials. In T. W. Picton (Ed.), *Human event-related potentials: Handbook of electroencephalography and clinical neurophysiology, Vol. III.* Amsterdam: Elsevier.

Verfaellie, M., Bauer, R. M., & Bowers, D. (1991). Autonomic and behavioral evidence of "implicit" memory in amnesia. *Brain and Cognition, 15,* 10–25.

Vertes, R. P. (1983). Brainstem control of the events of REM sleep. *Progress in Neurobiology, 22,* 241–288.

Vessie, P. R. (1932). On the transmission of Huntington's Chorea for 300 years—the Bures family group. *The Journal of Nervous and Mental Disease, 76,* 553–573.

Victor, M., Adams, R. D., & Collins, G. H. (1971). *The Wernicke syndrome* (p. 22). Philadelphia: F. A. Davis.

von Bonin, G. (1962). Anatomical asymmetries of the cerebral hemispheres. In V. B. Mountcastle, (Ed.), *Interhemispheric relations and cerebral dominance* (pp. 1–6). Baltimore, MD: The Johns Hopkins Press.

von Cramon, D. Y., Hebel, N., & Schuri, U. (1985). A contribution to the anatomical basis of thalamic amnesia. *Brain, 108,* 993–1008.

Wada, J. A. (1949). A new method for the determination of the side of cerebral speech dominance. *Igaku to Seibutsugaku, 14,* 221–222.

Wada, J. A. (1990a). Erosion of kindled epileptogenesis and kindling-induced long-term seizure suppressive effect in primates. In J. A. Wada, (Ed.), *Kindling 4* (pp. 382–394) New York: Plenum Press.

Wada, J. A. (Ed.). (1990b). *Kindling 4.* Plenum Press: New York.

Wada, J. A., Clarke, R., & Hamm, A. (1975). Cerebral hemispheric asymmetry in humans. *Archives of Neurology, 32,* 239–246.

Wada, J. A., & Sato, M. (1974). Generalized convulsive seizures induced by daily electrical stimulation of the amygdala in cats: Correlative electrographic and behavioral features. *Neurology, 24,* 565–574.

Wada, J. A., Sato, M., & Corcoran, M. E. (1974). Persistent seizure susceptibility and recurrent spontaneous seizures in kindled cats. *Epilepsia, 15,* 465–478.

Wald, G. (1964). The receptors of human color vision. *Science, 145,* 1007–1016.

Wald, G. (1968). The molecular basis of visual excitation. *Nature, 219,* 800–807.

Walk, R. D., & Walters, C. P. (1973). Effect of visual deprivation on depth discrimination of hooded rats. *Journal of Comparative and Physiological Psychology, 85,* 559–563.

Watson, D., & Pennebaker, J. W. (1989). Health complaints, stress, and distress: Exploring the central role of negative affectivity. *Psychological Review, 96,* 234–254.

Watson, J. B. (1930). *Behaviorism.* New York: W. W. Norton.

Wauquier, A., Ashton, D., & Melis, W. (1979). Behavioral analysis of amygdaloid kindling in beagle dogs and the effects of clonazepam, diazepam, phenobarbital, diphenylhydantoin, and flunarizine on seizure manifestion. *Experimental Neurology, 64,* 579–586.

Webb, W. B. (1968). *Sleep: An experimental approach.* New York: Macmillan Company.

Webb, W. B. (1973). Selective and partial deprivation of sleep. In W. P. Koella & P. Levin (Eds.), *Sleep: Physiology, biochemistry, psychology, pharmacology, clinical implications* (pp. 176–204). Basel: Karger.

Webb, W. B., & Agnew, H. W. (1967). Sleep cycling within the twenty-four hour period. *Journal of Experimental Psychology, 74,* 167–169.

Webb, W. B., & Agnew, H. W. (1970). Sleep stage characteristics of long and short sleepers. *Science, 163,* 146–147.

Webb, W. B., & Agnew, H. W. (1974). The effects of a chronic limitation of sleep length. *Psychophysiology, 11,* 265–274.

Webb, W. B., & Agnew, H. W. (1975). The effects on subsequent sleep of an acute restriction of sleep length. *Psychophysiology, 12,* 367–370.

Wechsler, D. (1981). *Wechsler adult intelligence scale—revised.* New York: The Psychological Corporation.

Weingarten, H. P. (1983). Conditioned cues elicit feeding in sated rats: A role for learning in meal initiation. *Science, 220,* 431–433.

Weingarten, H. P. (1984). Meal initiation controlled by learned cues: Basic behavioral properties. *Appetite, 5,* 147–158.

Weingarten, H. P. (1990). Learning, homeostasis, and the control of feeding behavior. In E. D. Capaldi and T. L. Powley (Eds.), *Taste, experience, and feeding* (pp. 14–27). Washington, DC: American Psychological Association.

Weingarten, H. P., Chang, P. K., & Jarvie, K. R. (1983). Reactivity of normal and VMH-lesion rats to quinine-adulterated foods: Negative evidence for negative finickiness. *Behavioral Neuroscience, 97,* 221–233.

Weingarten, H. P., & Kulikovsky, O. T. (1989). Taste-to-postingestive consequence conditioning: Is the rise in sham feeding with repeated experience a learning phenomenon? *Physiology & Behavior, 45,* 471–476.

Weinrich, M., & Wise, S. P. (1982). The premotor cortex of the monkey. *Journal of Neuroscience, 2,* 1329–1345.

Weisinger, R. S. (1975). Conditioned and pseudoconditioned thirst and sodium appetite. In G. Peters, J. T. Fitzsimons, & L. Peters-Haefeli (Eds.), *Control Mechanisms of Drinking* (pp. 149–154). New York: Springer-Verlag.

Weiskrantz, L., & Warrington, E. K. (1979). Conditioning in amnesic patients. *Neuropsychologia, 17,* 187–194.

Weiskrantz, L., Warrington, E. K., Sanders, M. D., & Marshall, J. (1974). Visual capacity in the hemianopic field following a restricted occipital ablation. *Brain, 97,* 709–728.

Weiss, J. H., Hartley, D. M., Koh, J., & Choi, D. W. (1990). The calcium channel blocker nifedipine attenuates slow excitatory amino acid neurotoxicity. *Science, 247,* 1474–1477.

Weiss, J. M. (1971). Effects of coping behavior in different warning signal conditions on stress pathology in rats. *Journal of Comparative and Physiological Psychology, 77,* 1–13.

Weller, A., Smith, G. P., & Gibbs, J. (1990). Endogenous cholecystokinin reduces feeding in young rats. *Science, 247,* 1589–1590.

Wenger, J. R., Tiffany, T. M., Bombardier, C., Nicholls, K., & Woods, S. C. (1981). Ethanol tolerance in the rat is learned. *Science, 213,* 575–577.

Wenk, G. L., Markowska, A. L., & Olton, D. S. (1989). Basal forebrain lesions and memory: Alterations in neurotensin, not acetylcholine, may cause amnesia. *Behavioral Neuroscience, 103,* 765–769.

Westergaard, G. C. (1991). Hand preference in the use and manufacture of tools by Tufted capuchin (*Cebus apella*) and Lion-tailed Macaque (*Macaca silenus*) monkeys. *Journal of Comparative Psychology, 105,* 172–176.

Westerink, B. H. C., & Justice, J. B., Jr. (1991). Microdialysis compared with other in vivo release models. In T. E. Robinson and J. B. Justice, Jr. (Eds.), *Microdialysis in the neurosciences. Vol. 7, Techniques in the neural and behavioral sciences* (pp. 23–43). Amsterdam: Elsevier.

Wever, R. A. (1979). *The circadian system of man.* Andechs: Max-Planck-Institut fur Verhaltensphysiologie.

Wexler, N. S., Rose, E. A., & Housman, D. E. (1991). Molecular approaches to hereditary diseases of the nervous system: Huntington's disease as a paradigm. *Annual Review of Neuroscience, 14,* 503–529.

Whalen, R. E., & Rezek, D. L. (1974). Inhibition of lordosis in female rats by subcutaneous implants of testosterone, androstenedione or dihydrotestosterone in infancy. *Hormones and Behavior, 5,* 125–128.

Whishaw, I. Q., Kolb, B., & Sutherland, R. J. (1983). The analysis of behavior in the laboratory rat. In T. E. Robinson (Ed.), *Behavioral approaches to brain research* (pp. 141–211). New York: Oxford University Press.

White, N., Sklar, L., & Amit, Z. (1977). The reinforcing action of morphine and its paradoxical side effect. *Psychopharmacology, 52,* 63–66.

Whitehouse, P. J., Price, D. L., Stuble, R. G., Clark, A. W., Coyle, J. T., & DeLong, M. R. (1982). Alzheimer's disease and senile dementia: Loss of neurons in the basal forebrain. *Science, 215,* 1237–1239.

Whitelaw, V., & Hollyday, M. (1983). Position-dependent motor innervation of the chick hindlimb following serial and parallel duplications of limb segments. *Journal of Neuroscience, 3,* 1216–1225.

Whittaker, D. G., & Cummings, R. W. (1990). Foveating saccades. *Vision Research, 30,* 1363–1366.

Wickelgren, W. A. (1968). Sparing of short-term memory in an amnesic patient: Implications for strength theory of memory. *Neuropsychologia, 6,* 235–244.

Wikler, A. (1980). *Opioid dependence: Mechanisms and treatment.* New York: Plenum Press.

Wilhelm, P. (1983). *The Nobel prize.* London: Springwood Books.

Wilkinson, R. T. (1965). Sleep deprivation. In O. G. Edholm & A. L. Bacharach (Eds.), *The physiology of human survival* (pp. 399–430). London: Academic Press.

Williams, R. W., & Herrup, K. (1988). The control of neuron number. *Annual Review of Neuroscience, 11,* 423–453.

Willing, A. E., Walls, E. K., & Koopmans, H. S. (1990). Insulin infusion stimulates daily food intake and body weight gain in diabetic rats. *Physiology & Behavior, 48,* 893–898.

Wilson, J. D., George, F. W., & Griffin, J. E. (1981). The hormonal control of sexual development. *Science, 211,* 1278–1284.

Wilson, J. D., & Griffin, J. E. (1980). The use and misuse of androgens. *Progress in Endocrinology and Metabolism, 29,* 1278–1295.

Winokur, G. (1978). Mania and depression: Family studies and genetics in relation to treatment. In M. A. Lipton, A. DiMascio, & K. F. Killam (Eds.), *Psychopharmacology: A generation of progress* (pp. 1213–1221). New York: Raven Press.

Winocur, G., Kinsbourne, M., & Moscovitch, M. (1981). The effects of cuing on release from proactive interference in Korsakoff amnesia patients. *Journal of Experimental Psychology: Human Learning and Memory, 1,* 56–65.

Winocur, G., Oxbury, S., Roberts, R., Agnetti, V., & Davis, C. (1984). Amnesia in patients with bilateral lesions to the thalamus. *Neuropsychologia, 22,* 123–143.

Wirtshafter, D., & Davis, J. D. (1977). Set points, settling points, and the control of body weight. *Physiology & Behavior, 19,* 75–78.

Wise, R. A. (1987). The role of reward pathways in the development of drug dependence. *Pharmac. Ther., 35,* 227–263.

Wise, R. A., & Bozarth, M. A. (1987). A psychomotor stimulant theory of addiction. *Psychological Review, 94,* 469–492.

Wise, R. A., & Rompre, P.-P. (1989). Brain dopamine and reward. *Annual Review of Psychology, 40,* 191–225.

Witelson, S. F. (1991). Neural Sexual mosaicism: Sexual differentiation of the human temporo-parietal region for functional asymmetry. *Psychoneuroendocrinology, 16,* 133–153.

Wodak, A., Richmond, R., & Wilson, A. (1990). Thiamin fortification and alcohol. *The Medical Journal of Australia, 152,* 97–99.

Wolf, M. E., & Goodale, M. A. (1987). Oral asymmetries during verbal and non-verbal movements of the mouth. *Neuropsychologia, 25,* 375–396.

Wolf, S., & Wolff, H. G. (1947). *Human gastric function* (2nd ed.), London: Oxford University Press.

Wolff, P. H., Michel, G. F., & Ovrut, M. (1990). The timing of syllable repetitions in developmental dyslexia. *Journal of Speech and Hearing Research, 33,* 281–289.

Wolff, P. H., Michel, G. F., Ovrut, M., & Drake, C. (1990). Rate and timing precision of motor coordination in developmental dyslexia. *Developmental Psychology, 26,* 349–359.

Woo, S. L. C., Lidsky, A., Chandra, T., Stackhouse, R., Gottler, F., & Robson, K. J. H. (1983). Prenatal diagnosis and carrier detection of classical phenylketonuria by cloning and characterization of human phenylalanine hydroxylase gene. *Clinical Research, 31,* 479A.

Wood, R. J., Rolls, B. J., & Ramsay, D. J. (1977). Drinking following intracarotid infusions of hypertonic solutions in dogs. *American Journal of Physiology, 1,* R88–R91.

Woods, J. W. (1956). "Taming" of the wild Norway rat by rhinencephalic lesions. *Science, 178,* 869.

Woods, S. C. (1991). The eating paradox: How we tolerate food. *Psychological Review, 98,* 488–505.

Woods, S. C., & Gibbs, J. (1989). The regulation of food intake by peptides. The psychobiology of human eating disorders: Preclinical and clinical perspectives. *Annals of the New York Academy of Sciences, 75,* 236–242.

Woods, S. C., Lotter, E. C., McKay, L. D., & Porte, D., Jr. (1979). Chronic intraceroventricular infusion of insulin reduces food intake and body weight of baboons. *Nature, 282,* 503–505.

Woods, S. C., & Porte, D., Jr. (1977). Relationship between plasma and cerebrospinal fluid insulin levels of dogs. *American Journal of Physiology, 233,* E331–E334.

Woods, S. C., Taborsky, G. J., & Porte, D., Jr. (1986). Central nervous system control of nutrient homeostasis. In V. B. Mountcastle & F. E. Bloom (Eds.), *Handbook of physiology: The nervous system IV: Intrinsic regulatory systems of the brain* (pp. 365–411). Bethesda, MD: American Physiological Society.

Woolsey, C. N. (1960). Organization of cortical auditory system: A review and a synthesis. In G. L. Rasmussen & W. F. Windle (Eds.), *Neural mechanisms of the auditory and vestibular systems* (pp. 165–180). Springfield, IL: Charles C Thomas.

Wurtman, R. J. (1985). Alzheimer's disease. *Scientific American, 252,* 62–74.

Wylie, D. R., & Goodale, M. A. (1988). Left-sided oral asymmetries in spontaneous but not posed smiles. *Neuropsychologia, 26,* 823–832.

Yadin, E., Guarini, V., & Gallistel, C. R. (1983). Unilaterally activated systems in rats self-stimulating at sites in the medial forebrain bundle, medial prefrontal cortex, or locus coeruleus. *Brain Research, 266,* 39–50.

Yamamoto, N., Kurotani, T., & Toyama, K. (1989). Neural connections between the lateral geniculate nucleus and visual cortex in vitro. *Science, 245,* 192–194.

Yamamoto, T., Yuyama, N., & Kawamura, Y. (1981). Central processing of taste perception. In Y. Katsuki, R. Norgren, and M. Sato (Eds.), *Brain Mechanisms of Sensation* (pp. 197–208). New York: John Wiley & Sons.

Yaqub, B. A., Gascon, G. G., Al-Nosha, M., & Whittaker, H. (1988). Pure word deafness (acquired verbal auditory agnosia) in an Arabic speaking patient. *Brain, III,* 457–466.

Yau, K-W. (1991). Calcium and light adaptation in retinal photoreceptors. *Current Opinion in Neurobiology, 1,* 252–257.

Yau, K-W., & Baylor, D. A. (1989). Cyclic GMP-activated conductance of retinal photoreceptor cells. *Annual Review of Neuroscience, 12,* 289–327.

Yeung, J. C., & Rudy, T. A. (1978). Sites of antinociceptive action of systemically injected morphine: Involvement of supraspinal loci as revealed by intracerebroventricular injection of naloxone. *Journal of Pharmacology and Experimental Therapeutics, 215,* 626–632.

Yokel, R. A. (1987). Intravenous self-administration: Response rates, the effects of pharmacological challenges, and drug preference. In M. A. Bozarth (Ed.), *Methods of assessing the reinforcing properties of abused drugs* (pp. 1–33). New York: Springer-Verlag.

Yoon, M. (1971). Reorganization of retinotectal projection following surgical operations on the optic tectum in goldfish. *Experimental Neurology, 33,* 395–411.

Young T., (1802). The Bakerian Lecture: On the theory of light and colours. *Philosophical Transactions of the Royal Society of London,* 12–48.

Yurek, D. M., & Sladek, J. R., Jr. (1990). Dopamine cell replacement: Parkinson's disease. *Annual Review of Neuroscience, 13,* 415–440.

Zaidel, E. (1975). A technique for presenting lateralized visual input with prolonged exposure. *Vision Research, 15,* 283–289.

Zaidel, E. (1983). Disconnection syndrome as a model for laterality effects in the normal brain. In J. B. Hellige (Ed.), *Cerebral hemisphere asymmetry: Method, theory, and application* (pp. 95–151). New York: Praeger Press.

Zaidel, E. (1985). Introduction. In F. D. Benson & E. Zaidel (Eds.), *The dual brain: Hemispheric specialization in humans* (pp. 47–63). London: The Guilford Press.

Zaidel, E. (1987). Language in the disconnected right hemisphere. In G. Adelman (Ed.), *Encyclopedia of Neuroscience* (pp. 563–564). Cambridge, MA: Birkhäuser.

Zalutsky, R. A., & Nicoll, R. A. (1990). Comparison of two forms of long-term potentiation in single hippocampal neurons. *Science, 248,* 1619–1624.

Zangwill, O. L. (1975). Excision of Broca's area without persistent aphasia. In K. J. Zulch, O. Creutzfeldt, & G. C. Galbraith (Eds.), *Cerebral localization* (pp. 258–263). New York: Springer-Verlag.

Zatz, M., & Herkenham, M. A. (1981). Intraventricular carbachol mimics the phase-shifting effect of light on the circadian rhythm of wheel-running activity. *Brain Research, 212,* 234–238.

Zeki, S., Watson, J. D.G., Lueck, C. J., Friston, K. J., Kennard, C., & Frackowiak, R. S. J. (1991). A direct demonstration of functional specialization in human visual cortex. *The Journal of Neuroscience, 11,* 641–649.

Zelman, D. C., Tiffany, S. T., & Baker, T. B. (1985). Influence of stress on morphine induced pyrexia: Relevance to a pavlovian model of tolerance development. *Behavioral Neuroscience, 99,* 122–144.

Zimitat, C., Kril, J., Harper, C. G., & Nixon, P. F. (1990). Progression of neurological disease in thiamin-deficient rats is enhanced by ethanol. *Alcohol, 7,* 493–501.

Zivin, J. A., & Choi, D. W. (1991). Stroke therapy. *Scientific American, 265,* 56–63.

Zola-Morgan, S., & Squire, L. R. (1982). Two forms of amnesia in monkeys: Rapid forgetting after medial temporal lesions but not diencephalic lesions. *Society for Neuroscience Abstracts, 8,* 24.

Zola-Morgan, S., & Squire, L. R. (1984). Preserved learning in monkeys with medial temporal lesions: Sparing of motor and cognitive skills. *Journal of Neuroscience, 4,* 1072–1085.

Zola-Morgan, S., & Squire L. R. (1985). Medial temporal lesions in monkeys impair memory on a variety of tasks sensitive to human amnesia. *Behavioral Neuroscience, 99,* 22–34.

Zola-Morgan, S. M., & Squire, L. R. (1990). The primate hippocampal formation: Evidence for a time-limited role in memory storage. *Science, 250,* 288–290.

Zola-Morgan, S., Squire, L. R., & Amaral, D. G. (1986). Human amnesia and the medial temporal region: Enduring memory impairment following a bilateral lesion limited to field CA1 of the hippocampus. *Journal of Neuroscience, 6,* 2950–2967.

Zola-Morgan, S. M., Squire, L. R., Amaral, D. G., & Suzuki, W. A. (1989). Lesions of perirhinal and parahippocampal cortex that spare the amygdala and hippocampal formation produce severe memory impairment. *The Journal of Neuroscience, 9,* 4355–4370.

Zola-Morgan, S., Squire, L. R., & Mishkin, M. (1982). The neuroanatomy of amnesia: Amygdala-hippocampus versus temporal stem. *Science, 218,* 1337–1339.

Zusho, H. (1983). Posttraumatic anosmia. *Archives of ontolaryngology, 4,* 252–256.

Name Index

644

Subject Index

656